lonely planet



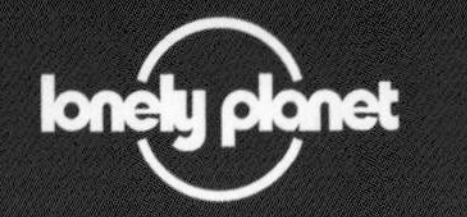

# Cuba

Brendan Sainsbury

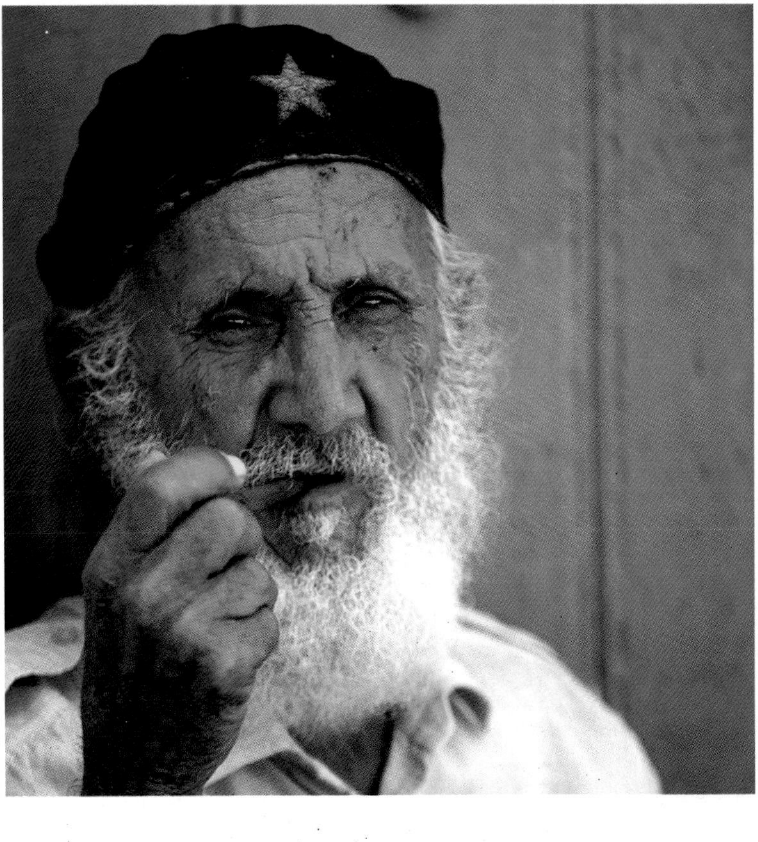

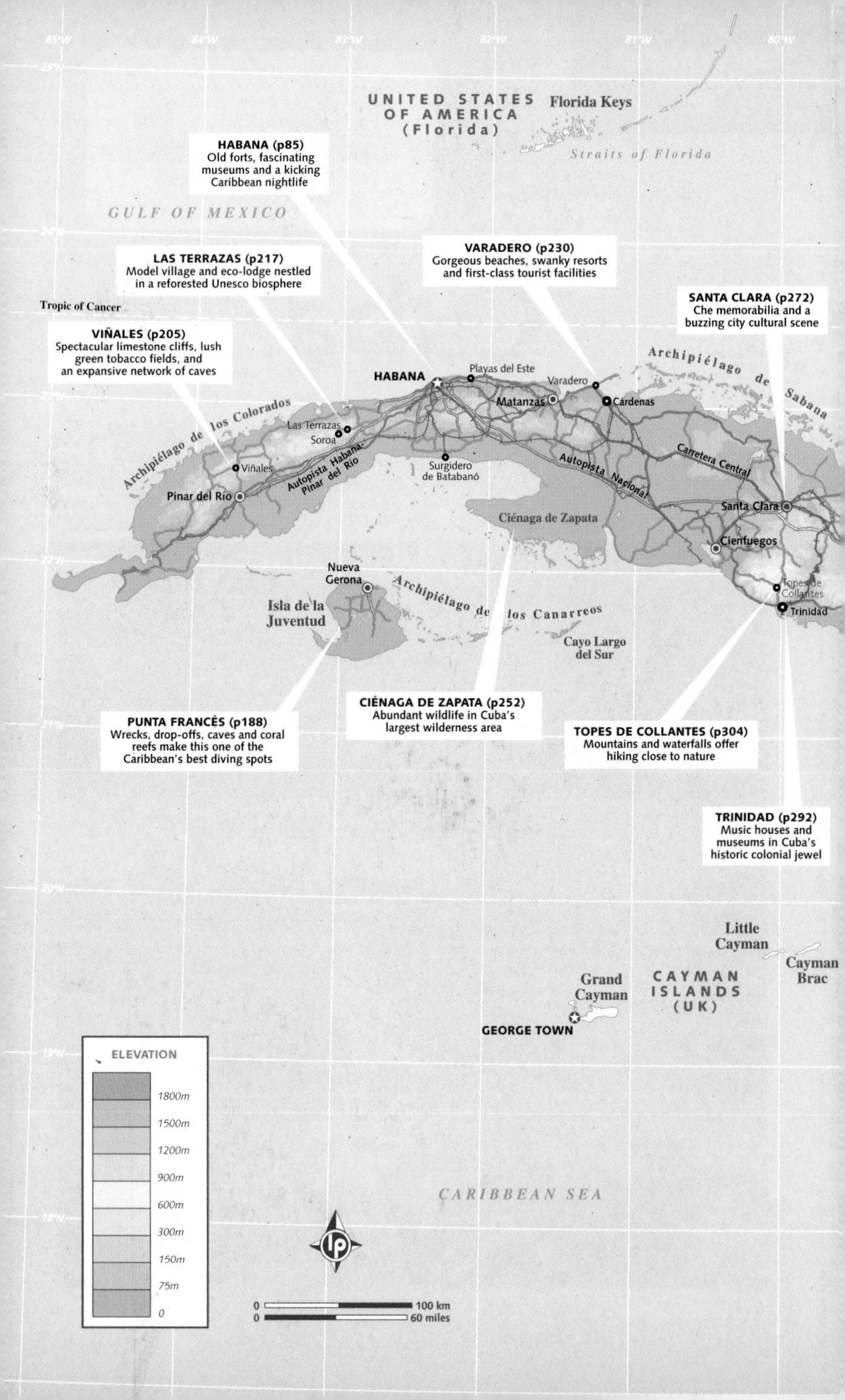

85°W 84°W 83°W 82°W 81°W 80°W

25°N 24°N 23°N 22°N 21°N 20°N 19°N 18°N

UNITED STATES OF AMERICA (Florida)

Florida Keys

Straits of Florida

GULF OF MEXICO

Tropic of Cancer

**HABANA (p85)**
Old forts, fascinating museums and a kicking Caribbean nightlife

**LAS TERRAZAS (p217)**
Model village and eco-lodge nestled in a reforested Unesco biosphere

**VARADERO (p230)**
Gorgeous beaches, swanky resorts and first-class tourist facilities

**SANTA CLARA (p272)**
Che memorabilia and a buzzing city cultural scene

**VIÑALES (p205)**
Spectacular limestone cliffs, lush green tobacco fields, and an expansive network of caves

HABANA
Playas del Este
Varadero
Matanzas
Cárdenas
Archipiélago de Sabana
Archipiélago de los Colorados
Las Terrazas
Soroa
Viñales
Pinar del Río
Autopista Habana-Pinar del Río
Surgidero de Batabanó
Autopista Nacional
Carretera Central
Santa Clara
Ciénaga de Zapata
Cienfuegos
Nueva Gerona
Isla de la Juventud
Archipiélago de los Canarreos
Topes de Collantes
Trinidad
Cayo Largo del Sur

**PUNTA FRANCÉS (p188)**
Wrecks, drop-offs, caves and coral reefs make this one of the Caribbean's best diving spots

**CIÉNAGA DE ZAPATA (p252)**
Abundant wildlife in Cuba's largest wilderness area

**TOPES DE COLLANTES (p304)**
Mountains and waterfalls offer hiking close to nature

**TRINIDAD (p292)**
Music houses and museums in Cuba's historic colonial jewel

Little Cayman
Cayman Brac
Grand Cayman
CAYMAN ISLANDS (UK)
GEORGE TOWN

ELEVATION
1800m
1500m
1200m
900m
600m
300m
150m
75m
0

CARIBBEAN SEA

0 100 km
0 60 miles

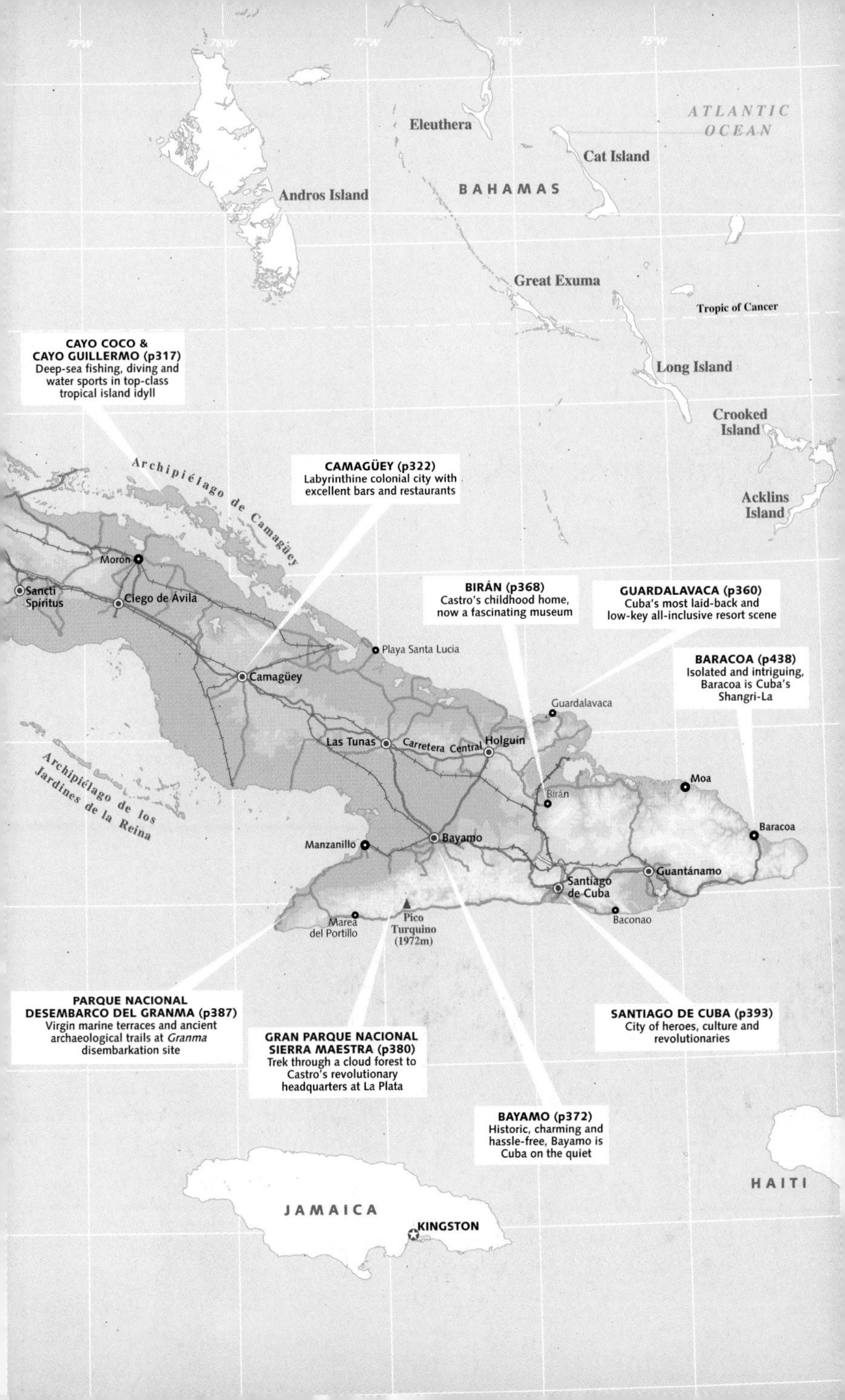

**CAYO COCO & CAYO GUILLERMO (p317)**
Deep-sea fishing, diving and water sports in top-class tropical island idyll

**CAMAGÜEY (p322)**
Labyrinthine colonial city with excellent bars and restaurants

**BIRÁN (p368)**
Castro's childhood home, now a fascinating museum

**GUARDALAVACA (p360)**
Cuba's most laid-back and low-key all-inclusive resort scene

**BARACOA (p438)**
Isolated and intriguing, Baracoa is Cuba's Shangri-La

**PARQUE NACIONAL DESEMBARCO DEL GRANMA (p387)**
Virgin marine terraces and ancient archaeological trails at *Granma* disembarkation site

**GRAN PARQUE NACIONAL SIERRA MAESTRA (p380)**
Trek through a cloud forest to Castro's revolutionary headquarters at La Plata

**SANTIAGO DE CUBA (p393)**
City of heroes, culture and revolutionaries

**BAYAMO (p372)**
Historic, charming and hassle-free, Bayamo is Cuba on the quiet

79°W
78°W
77°W
76°W
75°W
ATLANTIC OCEAN
Eleuthera
Cat Island
Andros Island
BAHAMAS
Great Exuma
Tropic of Cancer
Long Island
Crooked Island
Acklins Island
Archipiélago de Camagüey
Morón
Sancti Spíritus
Ciego de Ávila
Playa Santa Lucia
Camagüey
Guardalavaca
Las Tunas
Carretera Central
Holguín
Moa
Birán
Archipiélago de los Jardines de la Reina
Baracoa
Bayamo
Manzanillo
Guantánamo
Santiago de Cuba
Marea del Portillo
Pico Turquino (1972m)
Baconao
JAMAICA
KINGSTON
HAITI

# Destination Cuba

Welcome to Cuba; land of trade embargoes and clapped-out old cars, free health care and a light-hearted libidinous energy that can turn skeptics into pleasure-seekers and pleasure-seekers into salsa dancers.

Nearly 50 years after a cigar-puffing Fidel Castro first rolled triumphantly into Habana, Cuba remains famous for its failed politics, questionable human rights record, and a transport system stuck incongruously in the 1950s.

But beneath the austere veneer a bright light beckons. Amid the warm azure waters of the rippling Caribbean, blind fate has thrown up one of the most brazen, colorful, contradictory, shocking and schizophrenic societies the world has ever seen.

It nearly didn't happen like this. In fact, it nearly didn't happen at all. Yet somehow through the midst of war, revolution, invasion, colonialism, neocolonialism and crippling economic meltdown, this most adaptable of countries has survived – and continues to survive – warts and all. Cuba the anachronism, Cuba the muse, Cuba the longest-standing socialist state in the western hemisphere; an island of unique historical heritage floating like a time-warped *Titanic* amid a sea of encroaching globalization.

For first-time travelers a visit can be a challenging and eye-opening experience. Defying standard classification, Cuba is a complex and idiosyncratic society with a thousand different layers. To explore it you'll need at least two weeks; to dig deeper, a couple of months; to understand it – a lifetime. Go with an open mind and come back with a head full of unanswered questions. Never straightforward, but always fascinating, Cuba requires faith, hope, understanding, and an innate ability to branch out and discover things on your own. Visit soon, while the legacy is still intact.

OPPOSITE: VERONICA GARBUTT

ALFREDO MAIQUEZ

# Rhythm & Color

CHRISTOPHER P BAKER

Take in a cabaret show at the world-famous Tropicana Nightclub (p152), La Habana

Catch some *trovadores* (p68) on the streets of La Habana

OLIVIER CIRENDI

OLIVIER CIRENDINI

Enjoy an authentic Cuban cigar (p110) with Grandma, La Habana

Get up close and personal on a tobacco farm (p201), Pinar del Río Province

CHRISTINE OSBORNE

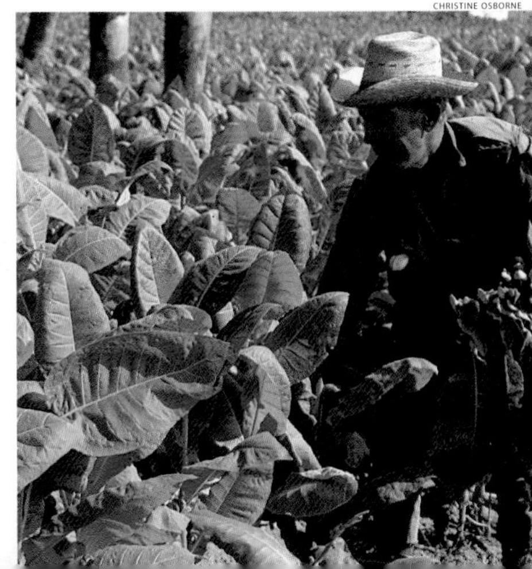

## OTHER HIGHLIGHTS

- Baseball (p57) might be the national sport, but *dominó* and chess (p57) are the national passions.
- Indulge in a glass of Havana Club rum (p77) or the tasty aroma of a homegrown Cohiba cigar (p462).
- Cuba marches to its own beat, and music (p66), dancing and movement are integral parts of culture and society.

# Cityscapes

CHRISTOPHER P BAKER

Submit to the charms of Plaza Mayor (p293) in World Heritage–listed Trinidad

Admire the varied styles of Cuban architecture (p62), Santa Clara

RICHARD I'ANS

CHRISTOPHER P BAKER

Stroll along the sea-swept Malecón (p110), La Habana

Join the locals for a coffee, Habana Vieja (p93)

ALFREDO MAIQUEZ

## OTHER HIGHLIGHTS

- Aside from its well-documented Che memorabilia, Santa Clara (p272) is also one of Cuba's most understated cultural centers.
- Santiago de Cuba (p393) has made an unparalled contribution to the world of art, music, poetry and literature.

# On History's Trail

RICHARD I'ANSON

See eye to eye with a colorful Che Guevara (p275), Matanzas

CHRISTOPHER P BAKER

Pause at the monument to one of the martyrs of the attack at Cuartel Moncada (p402), Santiago de Cuba

Follow the lead of General Antonio Maceo (p402), Santiago de Cuba

RICK GERHARTER

RHONDA GUTENBERG

Stand before giants: the Memorial José Martí (p105), Plaza de la Revolucíon, La Habana

MARTIN LLADÓ

Visit a relic from times past – the Slave Watchtower at Manaca Iznaga (p303), Sancti Spíritus Province

## OTHER HIGHLIGHTS

- Don't miss the imposing façade of the Museo de la Revolucíon (p102), or the equally magnificent Capitolio Nacional (p99), La Habana.
- There are colonial treasures in time-warped Trinidad (p292), and dusty historical secrets await in Sancti Spíritus (p287), Camagüey (p322) and Cienfuegos (p258).
- For quieter corners hit the hassle-free streets of Bayamo (p372) and Holguín (p348).

Experience life (p53) in Socialist Cuba, Parque Maceo, La Habana

TOM SMALLMAN

# Liquid Dreams

Escape from the city for a day at the beach, Santa María del Mar, Playas del Este (p164), La Habana

RHONDA GUTENBERG

Find a windswept corner for yourself in upmarket Cayo Largo del Sur (p189), Isla de la Juventud

ALFREDO MAIQ

SIMON FOALE

Savour the excellent diving at María la Gorda (p203), Pinar del Río Province, or laze languidly on the beach

Try your luck fishing (p452), Cuban style

PETER PTSCHELINZEW

## OTHER HIGHLIGHTS

- Track the Iréné Dupont legend to Varadero (p230) for cocktail talk and mojitos at the magical Mansión Xanadu (p239).
- Go deep-sea fishing with the ghost of Ernest Hemingway off exotic Cayo Guillermo (p320).
- For a taste of isolation, seek out Playa Maguana opposite the Villa Maguana (p446) or head off to desolate Cayo Sabinal (p334).

# Wild Adventures

ALFREDO MAIQUEZ

Visit the birthplace of cigars in the tobacco heartland of Cuba, Pinar del Río Province (p192)

RICK GERHARTER

Take a tour to the Valle del Yumurí (p236), Matanzas Province for spectacular views

Head off into the Big Blue, María la Gorda (p203), Pinar del Río Province

SIMON FOALE

ALFREDO MAIQUEZ

Catch the morning mist over the Valle de Viñales (p204), Pinar del Río Province

JERRY ALEXANDER

Visit verdant Cuban countryside in Pinar del Río Province (p192)

*Overleaf:*
Take the plunge in La Habana (p85)
CAROLE MARTIN

## OTHER HIGHLIGHTS

- Cuba has some of the Caribbean's most pristine coral reefs and top of the pile is translucent Cayo Francés (p283).
- Join an organized ascent on Pico Turquino (p427), Cuba's tallest mountain, or tackle the more diminutive Gran Piedra (p419).
- Take a slippery stroll down to the gushing torrents of Salto del Caburni (p304) or El Rocio (p306) in the Escambray Mountains.

Sample some of the best diving (p451) in the Caribbean, Pinar del Río Province

SIMON FOALE

# Contents

# Regional Map Contents

# The Authors

## BRENDAN SAINSBURY

Brendan is a British freelance writer based in British Columbia, Canada. In between penning offbeat travel stories for the likes of *Africa Geographic*, he has hitchhiked across Mozambique, taught English in Thailand, dug latrines in Angola, and worked as an adventure travel guide in Spain and Morocco.

Brendan first 'discovered' Cuba in 1997 after throwing in a career running health and fitness clubs in central London. Fascinated by the country's exotic mix of melodious *trova* (poetic singing/songwriting) and bombastic Che Guevara iconology, he returned again in 2002 to lead a succession of cultural and cycling trips countrywide. He's been coming back ever since.

### My Favorite Trip

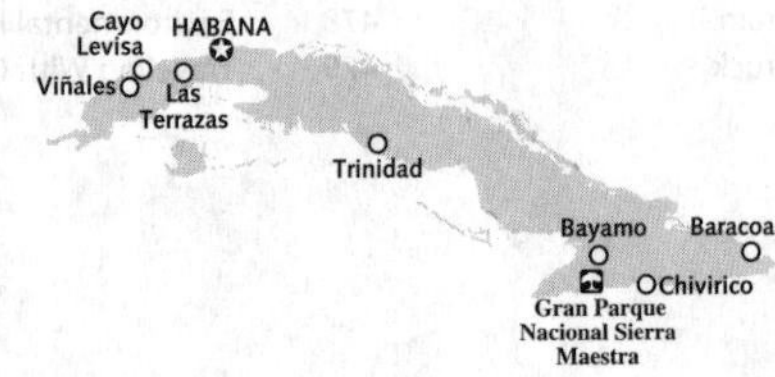


When planning a trip I linger in Habana (p85) before heading west, to the village of Viñales (p205) via a zigzag route that takes me past the mellow eco-village of Las Terrazas (p217) and the unkempt beaches of Cayo Levisa (p213). Next I track backwards to the Oriente, with a pit stop in Trinidad (p292), bedding down after two long days on the road in easygoing Bayamo (p372).

Arriving in the exotic east I continue my wanderings in Gran Parque Nacional Sierra Maestra (p380) re-emerging one lengthy trek later in Las Cuevas for a long-awaited glimpse of the azure Caribbean.

Overnighting in Chivirico (p426) I borrow a bicycle, sling it aboard a truck and disembark in hot, dry Cajababo. I take the last 55km into Baracoa (p438) across the precipitous La Farola on two wheels, arriving hot, knackered and ready to drop. It's a sort of homecoming.

## CONTRIBUTING AUTHOR

**David Goldberg, MD** wrote the Health chapter. David completed his training in internal medicine and infectious diseases at Columbia-Presbyterian Medical Center in New York City, where he has also served as voluntary faculty. At present, he is an infectious diseases specialist in Scarsdale, New York, and the editor-in-chief of the website MDTravelHealth.com.

### LONELY PLANET AUTHORS

Why is our travel information the best in the world? It's simple: our authors are independent, dedicated travellers. They don't research using just the Internet or phone, and they don't take freebies in exchange for positive coverage. They travel widely, to all the popular spots and off the beaten track. They personally visit thousands of hotels, restaurants, cafés, bars, galleries, palaces, museums and more – and they take pride in getting all the details right, and telling it how it is. For more, see the authors section on www.lonelyplanet.com.

# Getting Started

Cuba is a unique country with many distinct characteristics. Travel here not only requires a passport, money and a good sturdy rucksack; but it also requires flexibility, creativity, good humor, patience and a healthy sense of adventure. Speaking Spanish, though not a prerequisite, is undoubtedly a huge advantage, and will allow you to travel further and dig deeper than the average tourist.

Linguistic dexterity aside, Cuba remains an easy country to travel in and there are few barriers stopping you from wandering around pretty much how and as you choose. The infamous Resolution 10 ruling passed by the Cuban National Assembly in 2005 has led some sources to claim that Cubans have been discouraged from interacting with foreigners and prohibited from receiving 'tips' in the line of duty. In truth, the facts are rather less dramatic. Resolution 10 is actually aimed more at tourist officials and Cuban diplomats traveling overseas on business where (in the eyes of the Cuban government) they are prime fodder for bribery, corruption and running up unnecessary expense accounts. Back on the home front, the hard-working waiters and the towel-folding room maids of the vibrant tourist sector are as ingratiating and chatty as they have always been, and a small gratuity or 'tip' will go a long way in supplementing their relatively meager salaries.

Recent legislation by the American government has further tightened the rules governing travel of US citizens to Cuba. For more information on legal travel to the island check out the Center for Cuban Studies' website on www.cubaupdate.org. For additional advice see p469.

## WHEN TO GO

See Climate Charts p453 for more information.

The best time to go to Cuba is between December and April, after the lashing rains of the hurricane season and before the hot and sticky discomfort of the scorching summer months. The downside is that during this period – the high season or *temporada alta* as it is called in Cuba –

### DON'T LEAVE HOME WITHOUT...

You'll quickly find that basic commodities such as toothpaste, toilet paper and soap are widely available in Cuba. However, condoms, aspirin, dental floss, sunscreen, insect repellant, contact-lens solution, moisturizing lotion and reading material in any language besides Spanish definitely aren't.

Clothing-wise come prepared. Aside from the ubiquitous Che Guevara T-shirts fashionable beach wear is overpriced or low quality. You might also want to bring your own snorkel gear. A flashlight will be handy during blackouts. An alarm clock for predawn bus departures, a universal plug for sinks and tubs and a little washing powder are all useful. People staying in campismos will need a sheet as linen isn't always provided.

Aside from a scant supply of biscuits/cookies and soggy sandwiches, take-out fare is hard to find. Gatorade powder, granola and protein bars, nuts, dried fruit, peanut butter and trail mix provide energy and a break from the vicious pizza/ice-cream/fried-chicken cycle of appetizers. See Staying Fed (p76) for more food advice.

Money-wise, your best bet is to bring cash, preferably in Canadian dollars, euros or pound sterling (avoid US dollars as the cost of changing them into Cuban Convertibles is a lot higher). A credit card will provide a good emergency back-up and traveler's checks from non-American banks are usually acceptable. Unfortunately few, if any, foreign debit cards will work in Cuban ATMs.

accommodation prices are hiked up by about 20% (see p448). You'll also find the country a little more crowded at this time, particularly in the resort areas although, off the beaten track, it is unlikely that you will ever have trouble in finding a room in a casa particular.

Weather aside, Cuba has few other hurdles for visitors. Culture vultures should keep a close eye on the annual arts calendar (p457) for festivals and events; baseball fans will certainly not want to miss the postseason, which runs from April to May; and political junkies may want to catch important days in the socialist calendar, particularly *Día de los Trabajadores* (May Day; May 1) and Day of the National Rebellion (July 26).

## COSTS & MONEY

For seasoned budget travelers Cuba can be a bit of a financial shock. There's no network of dirt-cheap backpacker hostels here and not a lot of bargaining potential. In fact, compared with say Guatemala or Peru, you could feel yourself staring at a veritable financial conundrum with little or no room to maneuver. Furthermore there is a tendency in Cuba to herd all foreign visitors around in one state-controlled tourist sector. Follow this well-trodden path of organized excursions and prepackaged cultural 'experiences' at your peril. The costs will soon add up.

With a little guile and a certain amount of resilience, however, it needn't all be overpriced hotel rooms and wallet-whacking credit-card bills. Underneath the surface (and contrary to what a lot of tour reps will tell you) Cuba has a whole guidebook's worth of cheaper alternatives. On

### PUTTING THE GUIDEBOOK DOWN

Here at Lonely Planet we like to say that 'the greatest adventure of all is to fly by the seat of your pants' and for several decades successive editions of our guidebooks have been enthusiastically promoting this independent travel culture.

Rather than give you a written itinerary and lead you protectively through the obstacles, we prefer to inspire and suggest, prompt and propose – but never to hand hold.

In Cuba there are countless opportunities to cross the unofficial line that exists between the all-inclusive tourist resorts and the island of revolutionary myth. Throughout the course of this book we will try to offer you a whole range of possibilities about how this border can best be breached. Often the information we put forward will be deliberately vague. Indeed, at times, we will actively encourage you to put the guidebook down for a day or three and venture off intrepidly on your own. Adventurers should bear in mind the following:

- Cuba is a large country of approximately 11.3 million people and far too complex to squeeze into a modestly sized book. Rather than treat this guide as 'gospel', think of it more as a starting point. Get inventive, fill in the gaps, change the itineraries, rework the reviews and don't forget to write in and tell us what we missed.
- Buses break down, hotels close, restaurants change chefs and old revolutionaries eventually die. A guidebook is a stencil; it tells you what's *supposed* to happen. What *actually* happens is often very different – and largely up to you.
- There are no timetables for Santería rituals, cockfights, spontaneous rumba sessions, gorgeous sunsets or anything involving a Cuban train journey. Keep your ear to the ground, follow the crowds and don't be afraid to experiment with something new.
- Cuba's best tour agencies are its casas particulares. There are thousands of these congenial private houses scattered across the country and each and every one has the potential to be a fact-packed Lonely Planet guidebook in its own right.

the hotel front, the vibrant casa particular scene can cut accommodation costs by more than half, while do-it-yourself grocery purchasing and an ability to muck in with the resourceful locals on trucks, buses, trains and bicycles can give you access to a whole new world of interesting food and transport opportunities.

For those more interested in service and comfort, prices are equally variable, from CUC$50 per person at Varadero's cheapest all-inclusive to CUC$200 per person at a swanky Playa Esmeralda resort. If you're interested in getting away to the beach, prearranged air and hotel packages from Canada and Europe can be absurdly affordable (less than US$500 for a week in Varadero from Toronto) and seasoned Cuba travelers often take these deals because it works out cheaper than just the airfare alone. Most resorts and hotels offer big discounts for children under 12 years of age; it's worth asking. Children also travel half-price on Víazul buses, and many museums and attractions offer a 50% discount for kids. See the Transport chapter for further information on travel agencies (p469) who can arrange travel and tours to Cuba.

As with most islands, Cuba struggles with food supply and prices reflect this – especially if you crave something imported like canned corn or nuts. Paladares and casas particulares usually offer good value, with monstrous meal portions (no rationing here), including a pork chop, rice and beans, salad and French fries, costing around CUC$8. Add a couple of beers, dessert and a tip and you're looking at CUC$12 (or more). Drinking is considerably more affordable than eating, with a strong mojito costing CUC$2 (in a non-Hemingway-esque bar) and a fresh juice or beer CUC$1.

For tourists to Cuba, there are many transport options and as many prices to go with them. From Habana to Santiago de Cuba for example, a trip of 861km, you will pay around CUC$114 to fly one-way with Cubana, from CUC$50 to CUC$62 to take the train and from CUC$41 to CUC$52 to do the journey on the bus. Rental cars start at CUC$35 a day for a small Fiat to CUC$220 a day for a convertible Audi, though a more average price is something in the region of CUC$65 for a weekly rental of a Toyota Yaris.

There is, of course, the double economy, whereby Convertibles and Cuban pesos circulate simultaneously. In theory, tourists are only supposed to use Convertibles but, in practice, there is nothing to stop you walking into a *cadeca* (change booth) and swapping your Convertibles into *moneda nacional* (pesos). With an exchange rate of 24 pesos per Convertible, there are fantastic saving opportunities with pesos if you're willing to sacrifice a little (or a lot!) in quality, service and/or comfort. For example, a pizza in a fast-food joint costs CUC$1, but street pizzas cost seven pesos (less than CUC$0.25). Pesos are also useful for urban transport and some cultural activities (such as movies), but almost everything else is sold to foreigners only in Convertibles: the symphony or theater, interprovincial transport and taxis are but a few examples where Cubans will pay in pesos, but you won't.

Before you become indignant about the marked price differential, remember that the double economy cuts both ways: while Cubans may sometimes pay less for the same services as foreigners they also have to stand in line, frequent ration shops and stay in the kind of fly-blown substandard hotels that most foreigners wouldn't poke a stick at. Furthermore, Cubans (who earn between 190 and 325 pesos, or CUC$8 and CUC$13, a month) have to survive in an entirely different economy from affluent outsiders; a financial minefield where access to valuable

**HOW MUCH?**

Room in a casa particular CUC$15-30

Museum entrance CUC$1-5

Taxi CUC$2-4

Bike rental per day CUC$3-5

Internet use per hour CUC$6

See also Lonely Planet index, inside front cover.

Convertibles is a daily crapshoot between tips, personal guile and who you know.

Cuban-Americans traveling legally to Cuba in order to visit relatives are currently restricted to spending the equivalent of US$50 a day. This was reduced from US$167 a day by the Bush administration in June 2004. There are also new limits on how much money Cuban-Americans can send back to the island from the US.

## TRAVEL LITERATURE

Zoë Bran's *Enduring Cuba* (2002), an illuminating and beautifully written book, conveys the daily shortages, slowdowns and *lucha* (struggle) of the Cuban reality with a keen eye for detail. Isadora Tatlin's *Cuba Diaries* (2002) takes an equally eye-opening look at a similarly thought-provoking and contradictory subject.

Even better on the travelogue scene is *Trading with the Enemy: A Yankee Travels through Castro's Cuba* (1992), by Tom Miller, a rich feast of Cuban lore gleaned during eight months of perceptive travel in Cuba. It may be the best travel book about Cuba ever written. Miller also collected the 38 pieces in *Travelers' Tales Cuba: True Stories* (2001), a medley of views, experiences and takes on the island.

Reminiscent of the uncompromising, in-your-face style of Irvine Welsh or Charles Bukowski, Pedro Juan Gutierrez's *Dirty Havana Trilogy* (2000), is a fascinating, if sometimes disturbing insider look at life in Habana during the dark days of the *período especial* (special period). Carlos Eire's *Waiting for Snow in Havana* (2003), meanwhile, is a nostalgic account of boyhood during the tumultuous days of the Cuban Revolution.

### CUBA ON THE CHEAP

Accommodation and transport are two areas where foreigners almost always have to pay in Convertibles and the bill can add up, fast. Food is another budget parasite. Here are some budget-friendly ideas:

- Families traveling together are pulling from the same financial pool; owners of private rooms recognize this and will often offer a discount to travelers with children. This can occur in hotels too.
- In private rooms, try negotiating a discount for multiple nights or by agreeing not to use the air-con.
- Never arrive anywhere with a *jinetero* (male hustler) in tow. This universally hikes the room price up by CUC$5 a night.
- The cheapest accommodation is in campismo cabins, which are often payable by the person, not the unit: good for solo travelers or those with a bike or car.
- Astro buses are cheaper than Víazul coaches, and trucks are cheaper than both. Stoics might want to try arranging a *botella* (free or cheap lift) with the *amarillos* (yellow jackets; workers who match potential passengers with empty cars). Use this method and you'll save bundles.
- Learn the public transport mechanism, rent a bicycle or take to the streets and walk.
- Food sold in pesos – bread at the Empresa Cubana del Pan, fruits and vegetables at agropecuarios (agricultural markets) or full meals from someone's living-room window such as pizza or *cajitas* (take-out meals in small boxes) – is very kind on the wallet.
- Cooking at 'home' is cheap and fun. Hit the market and host a dinner party.
- Brush up on some Spanish: nothing jacks up a price or keeps it inflated more effectively than an inability to communicate.

**TOP TENS**

## Places to find the 'real' Cuba

Endless line-ups, dirty washrooms, the ever-present *jineteros*, crowded buses, awful food – the search for the 'real' Cuba can sometimes be a little hard on the nerves. And then suddenly, like a blinding light, you find it…

- Weekend street party – La Fiesta de Cubanía (p376), Bayamo
- Riding the rails Cuban style – the Hershey train (p173), Habana Province
- Any given Sunday – baseball (p356) in Holguín
- Hanging out with the locals – Puerto Padre (p345)
- Beach alternative – Guanabo (p164), Playas del Este
- Campismo culture – La Sierrita (p381), Granma
- Rodeo fever – Feria Ganado (p343), Las Tunas
- Market shopping – Agropecuario del Rio (p326), Camagüey
- Art talk – Uneac cultural center (p356), Holguín
- Choosing a casa – Nueva Gerona (p184), Isla de la Juventud

## Beaches

From five-star deluxe to no-star nirvana, Cuba's beaches – all 300 of them – are some of the best places on the island to kick off your shoes, lock up your worries and spend a day or two relaxing in quiet contemplation. The following hints should provide enough inspiration to send you running for your bucket and spade:

- Playa Ancón (p301), Sancti Spíritus
- Varadero (p230), Matanzas
- Playa Santa Lucía (p335), Camagüey
- Playa Maguana (p446), Baracoa
- Cayo Levisa (p213), Pinar del Río
- Playa Pilar (p320), Ciego de Ávila
- Playa Guardalavaca (p360), Holguín
- Playa Boca Ciega (p168), Playas del Este, Habana
- Playa Sevilla(p426), Chivirico, Santiago de Cuba
- Playa de los Pinos (p334), Cayo Sabinal, Camagüey

## Cycle Routes

Cuba is one of the best countries in the world for bike enthusiasts and, with an estimated 500,000 cyclists in Habana alone, you won't be short of company. To get off the beaten track and discover the corners of the island that most tour excursions fail to penetrate, test your metal on a few of the following:

- Marea del Portillo to Chivirico – the seaside rollercoaster
- Cajababo to Baracoa – tackle the white-knuckle bends and switchbacks of La Farola, the famous 'lighthouse' road
- Valle de Viñales – meander meditatively among the mogotes
- Bartomlomé Maso to Santo Domingo – the guerrilla killer, Cuba's toughest road ascent is not for the faint-hearted
- Guardalavaca to Banes – scenic undulations from all-inclusive resort to all-Cuban town
- Baracoa to Maguana Beach – the rutted road to paradise
- Camilo Cienfuegos to the Valle de Yumurí – Habana to Matanzas, via the back door
- Morón to San José del Lago – wake up where the cock crows and fall asleep in a sumptuous spa
- Bayamo to El Saltón – time-warped villages and bucolic *bohíos* (thatched huts) in the Sierra Maestra's rural foothills
- Trinidad to Playa Ancón – from mountains to sea in one fell swoop

In the literary field, classics include Hemingway's Nobel Prize–winning *Old Man and the Sea* (1952), and his less-heralded, but equally compelling *Islands in the Stream* (1970). Graham Greene captures the prerevolutionary essence of Habana in *Our Man in Havana* (1958) while Elmore Leonard documents the events surrounding the explosion of the battleship USS *Maine* and the Cuban-Spanish-American War with thrill-a-minute panache in *Cuba Libre* (2000).

Biographies of Che Guevara abound, although there's no contest when it comes to size, quality and enduring literary legacy. Jon Lee Anderson's *Che Guevara: a Revolutionary Life* (1997) is one of the most groundbreaking biographies ever written and during the research for the book Mr Anderson initiated the process by which Guevara's remains were found and dug up in Bolivia before being returned to Cuba in 1997. Unauthorized biographies of Castro are equally authoritative: try Volker Skierka's *Fidel Castro: a Biography* (2000).

## INTERNET RESOURCES

**AfroCuba Web** (www.afrocubaweb.com) Everything imaginable on Cuban culture, with worldwide concert listings, dance and drum workshops, seminars and encounters in Cuba.

**BBC** (www.bbc.co.uk) One of the best sites for up-to-date Cuba news stories, BBC Cuba correspondent Stephen Gibbs uncovers some classic journalistic gems. Type Cuba into the search engine on main page to reveal what's on offer.

**Boomers Abroad** (www.boomersabroad.com) Choose the Cuba icon on the main page for links galore on everything from caving to Che Guevara.

**Cubacasas.net** (www.cubacasas.net) Informative and regularly updated Canadian website with information on casas particulares and much more besides. Versions in English and French.

**Granma Internacional** (www.granma.cu) Official newspaper of the Cuban Communist Party; news from Cuba in five languages.

**LonelyPlanet.com** (www.lonelyplanet.com) Summaries on traveling to Cuba, the Thorn Tree bulletin board, travel news and links to useful travel resources elsewhere on the Web.

# Itineraries

## CLASSIC ROUTES

### HABANA **Two Weeks to One Month**

Mandatory museums include the Cuban collection of the **Museo Nacional de Bellas Artes** (p102) in Centro Habana; the **Museo de la Revolución** (p102) also in Centro Habana; the **Museo Fortificaciones y Armas** (p162) to the north of Bahía de La Habana; the inspiring (despite so much taxidermy) **Museo Hemingway** (p160); and the fascinating **Museo de Fundación de Naturaleza y El Hombre** (p148) in Miramar.

After museum fatigue sets in, head to the azure waters and white sands of **Playas del Este** (p164), trot around verdant **Parque Lenin** (p154) on horseback or re-energize with some flower power at the **Jardín Botánico Nacional** (p154) in the Parque Lenin area.

When the moon goes up, Habana gets down. Music lovers will enjoy **Jazz Club La Zorra y El Cuervo** (p133) in Vedado; the **Teatro Amadeo Roldán** (p137), seat of the national symphony in Vedado; the **Casa de la Trova** (p133) in Centro Habana; or just hanging out on the **Malecón** (p110) in Habana Vieja. For salsa, it's the **Casa de la Música** in Centro Habana (p135) or Miramar (p152); there are discos or check out the legendary rumbas hosted in **Callejón de Hamel** (p115) in Vedado. Of course, fabulousness happens nightly at the world-famous **Tropicana Nightclub** (p152) in Mariano.

You'll find all manner of transport options in Habana; see Getting Around (p153).

**Habana isn't just a city; it's a chameleon, a conundrum, a cultural extravaganza. To see all the main sights in a week is like trying to squeeze the complete works of Shakespeare into just one act. For a brief initiation stick aside a fortnight; to delve deeper count on a month.**

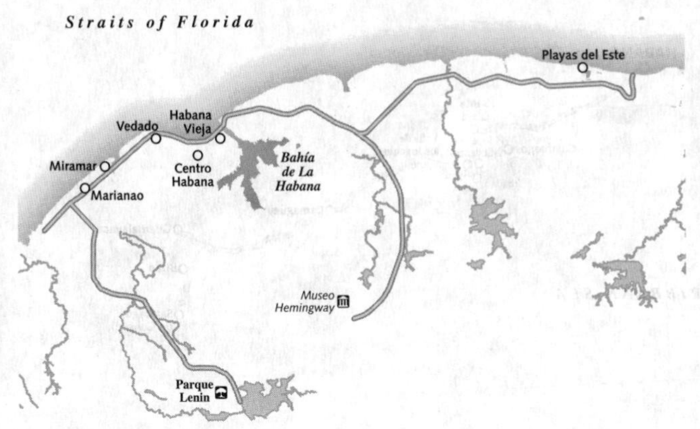

## THE WHISTLE STOP

**Two Weeks to Two Months**

After ogling the incredible architecture of **Habana** (p93), head to **Santa Clara** (p272) and the venerable **Monumento Ernesto Che Guevara** (p274), with its superb mausoleum. Press southwest to charming **Cienfuegos** (p258) next, with its large, placid bay and its noble neoclassical buildings, before working your way slowly down the coast to **Trinidad** (p292). A Unesco World Heritage site, you can easily spend a week in this colonial town hiking in **Topes de Collantes** (p304) and horseback riding in **Valle de los Ingenios** (p303) or lazing at **Playa Ancón** (p301). Smiling is infectious in the labyrinthine streets of **Camagüey** (p322), where a bustling new bar scene will mean you get lost without even realizing it. **Guardalavaca** (p360) is one of the finest resort areas with terrific diving, paragliding and a smattering of local native history. Welcome to **Holguín Province** (p347), with its friendly capital and Fidel's childhood home in **Birán** (p368). Leave time for **Santiago de Cuba** (p393) and its many attractions including **El Cobre** (p424), **La Gran Piedra** (p419), the **Castillo de San Pedro del Morro** (p404), the **Cuartel Moncada** (p402) and of course, the kicking nighttime **music scene** (p412).

Most international flights take you into Habana or Santiago de Cuba, but you can easily start this adventure in **Varadero** (p230) or **Holguín** (p348), other popular entry points.

**With two weeks and a car you can see a lot of Cuba, but using public transport can give you a good (sometimes better!) taste too. With two months, you can travel the breadth in depth.**

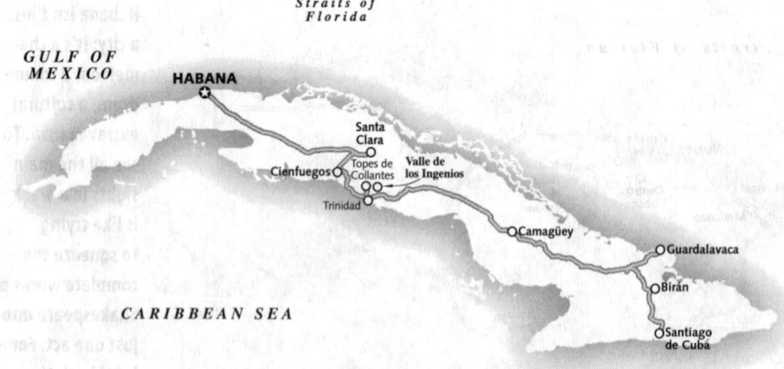

# ROADS LESS TRAVELED

## CUBA THROUGH THE BACK DOOR One Month

Boycott Habana and head east to the beaches of **Playas del Este** (p164), where private houses and picturesque sunsets abound, or leapfrog straight to **Santa Cruz del Norte** (p173), a worthwhile base camp situated within hiking distance of the golden sands of Playa Jibacoa. Switch west next along the beautiful (and deserted) northern coast route to **Puerto Esperanza** (p212) for a few days of turning off, tuning in and dropping out before pressing on to **Sandino** (p204) within striking distance of María la Gorda. The Bahía de Cochinos (Bay of Pigs) area is awash with decent casas, none better than those found on shimmering **Playa Larga** (p253) and you can easily work your way along the coast from here to **Rancho Luna** (p267) and **La Boca** (p304) where assorted private houses offer up an ideal antidote to the tourist hotels of Cienfuegos and Trinidad. The long road east presents ample opportunities to avoid the city hustlers in Ciego de Ávila and Camagüey. Check out unsung **Florida** (p332), with its archetypal sugar mills or bustling **Guáimaro** (p333), with its groundbreaking constitutional history. Turn left in **Las Tunas** (p339) and detour to the remote northern beach 'resort' of **Playa Las Bocas** (p346), where you'll see no one, but a handful of ingratiating casa particular owners. Homing in on Holguín Province, check out the pretty town of **Banes** (p365) as a launching pad for Guardalavaca before making one last fling down to Santiago de Cuba, where peace and tranquility await you in sleepy **Siboney** (p417).

**These little-known towns and villages have two things in common: a handful of legal casas particulares and a dearth of regular visitors. If you don't mind roughing it on local transport, conversing in barely intelligible Spanish or reading your Lonely Planet by torchlight, read on.**

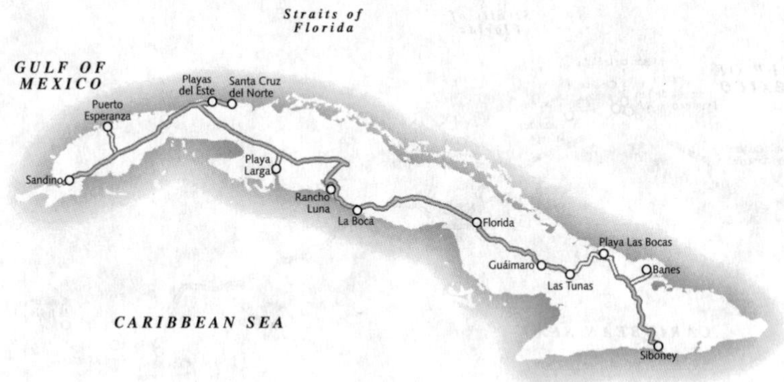

## THE MUSICAL TOUR

**Two Weeks to One Month**

**Cuban music is famous the world over, but to break free of the *Buena Vista Social Club* ditties that have become the staple diet in Cuban restaurants you have to wander off the beaten track. This compact itinerary details some of Cuba's eclectic music venues.**

Ease in gently at Habana's **Iglesia de San Francisco de Asís** (p97), where refined classical music echoes eerily through the cloisters of a converted 18th-century church. Next shimmy a couple of blocks west to **Mesón de la Flota** (p119), where rasping vocals and furious flamenco invites listeners to discover the elusive spirit of what aficionados call *duende* (a term used in flamenco to describe the ultimate climax to the music). For something more authentically Cuban, visit Habana's **Casa de la Música** (p135) in El Centro, or forge your way west to venerable Viñales, home of the *Guajira* (a type of flamenco) and location of the spanking new **Centro Cultural Polo Montañez** (p208). In unsung Matanzas, live rumba performances reverberate in **Plaza de la Vigía** (p224) while, an hour or two further on, in Santa Clara's **Club Mejunje** (p278) loose rhythms and heavy bass mix in one of Cuba's most vibrant and underrated cultural institutions. Trinidad has *trova* (traditional poetic singing) and *son* (Cuba's popular music) and a lot more besides in **Palanque de los Congos Reales** (p300), while the long journey east to Santiago's spit and sawdust **Casa de las Tradiciones** (p413) is a musical homecoming, akin to sailing down the Mississippi to New Orleans. With the hangover starting to bite, tie in Haitian drums and voodoo rhythms in Guantánamo's **Tumba Francesa Pompadour** (p435) before heading over the Sierra Puril Mountains for the grand finale: a frenetic all-out Cuban knees-up at the amiable **Casa de la Trova** (p443) in Baracoa.

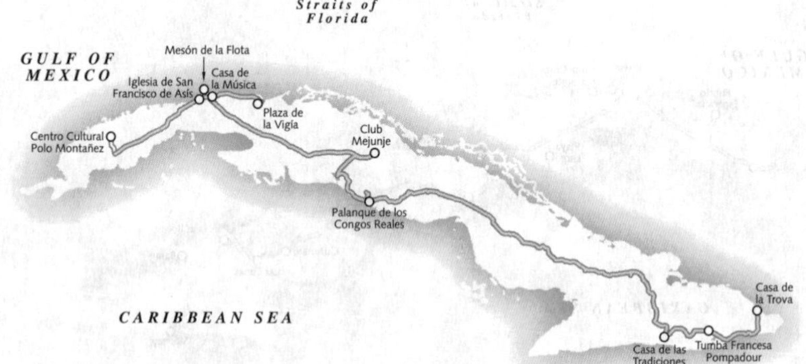

# TAILORED TRIPS

## PILGRIMAGE **Two Weeks to One Month**

No one can fill the shoes of Che, Camilo or Fidel, but you *can* follow in their footsteps, visiting pivotal sites in the Cuban Revolution. This itinerary follows a loose chronological order (see Map pp42–3).

In Santiago de Cuba visit the **Granjita Siboney** (p418) and **Cuartel Moncada** (p402) before heading to **Playa las Coloradas** (p387), where the rebels alit from the yacht *Granma.* Diehards might head to **El Uvero** (p426), site of the first major rebel victory. Summit **Pico Turquino** (p427) and come out the other side at **Comandancia de la Plata** (p382). Head to **Yaguajay** (p307) in Sancti Spíritus, where Camilo Cienfuegos led one of the last battles, or visit the virgin sands of **Cayo Santa María** (p283) – even wannabe rebels need a holiday – before pushing on to **Santa Clara** (p272), where Che led the decisive victory. Don't miss **Habana** (p85), where that victory was declared. As well as having historical significance, **Playa Girón** (p254) and the **Bahía de Cochinos** (p255) have terrific beaches and snorkeling. Last stop: **Isla de la Juventud** (p180), where Fidel was incarcerated after Moncada.

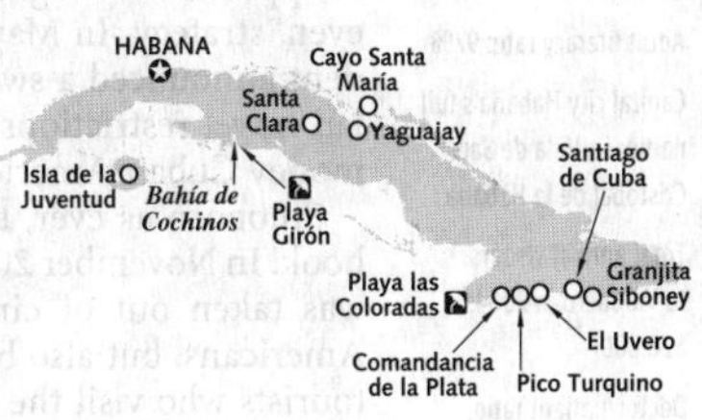


Rebels with a cause should note that public transport on Santiago de Cuba's coast is tricky and there are no buses out to Cayo Santa María. Access to Isla de la Juventud is by boat or plane. See Transport (p473) for more.

## BIRD-WATCHING CUBA **Two to Three Weeks**

With your binoculars polished, sally forth into the verdant **Valle de Viñales** (p204), where, with a bit of patience and the help of the locals, you can catch glimpses of Cuban Bullfinches or chirpy Cuban Peewees. The **Península de Guanahacabibes** (p202) has virgin beaches and dense flora that attracts everything from tody flycatchers to migratory ruby-throated hummingbirds. Don't overlook the **Sierra del Rosario Reserve** (p217) where it's possible to spot up to 50% of Cuba's endemic birds, including the often elusive carpinteros. The **Gran Parque Natural Montemar** (p252) is a huge protected area encompassing Cuba's largest wetland. Wait around for a few hours (or days) and you might see *zunzuns* – the world's smallest bird. In **Topes de Collantes** (p304) keep an eye out for the bright red, white and blueTocororo (Cuba's national bird), then venture into **Cayo Romano** (p334) to get a look at some of the island's more than 30,000 flamingos. **La Hacienda la Belén Reserve** (p332) near Camagüey promises glimpses of Cuban Parakeets, Giant Kingbirds and Antillean Palm Swifts. While the journey might appear long and the hiking arduous, no Cuban birding adventure is complete without a visit to the almost-virgin **Parque Nacional Alejandro de Humboldt** (p446) for viewings of Cuban Amazon parrots, hook-billed kites and – unlikely but not impossible – ivory-billed woodpeckers last spotted here in the early 1980s.

# Snapshot

In a country not given to prophesying about the future, the question of 'what happens after Fidel?' is often greeted with a dismissive shrug. But with Castro fast approaching his ninth decade, the issue of adaptation and transition in a socialist state that has been locked in a pre-1960s time warp for nearly 50 years can no longer be brushed underneath the carpet.

Omnipresent and expectant on the sidelines, the bellicose Bush administration has not been shy in adding its two-penny's worth to the debate. In 2003 US President George W Bush set up the Commission for Assistance to a Free Cuba under the then-Secretary of State Colin Powell to prepare for – in Bush's words – 'the happy day when Castro's regime is no more.'

True to form, the Commission didn't take long to muster up a 500-page defamatory document. Tightening the noose on the already embargo-strapped Castro regime had long been Bush the younger's 'get mad, get even' strategy. In May 2004, using the report as a pretext, the US president announced a sweeping set of new proposals that included draconian travel restrictions and stringent financial limitations on how much money Cuban-Americans could send to their families in Cuba.

Stubborn as ever, the pugnacious Fidel responded with a killer right hook. In November 2004 the US dollar – legal tender in Cuba since 1993 – was taken out of circulation, a measure that not only hurt Cuban-Americans, but also burnt a hole in the pockets of the two million–plus tourists who visit the island on an annual basis.

Caught up in the middle of all this diplomatic posturing are the long-suffering Cubans, a proud populace (p53), long bored by the crippling embargo (p47), and frustrated in equal measure by their government's tendency to give with one hand while taking away with the other.

Life today in Cuba is a complex dichotomy of economic hardship versus guarded optimism about the future. Despite growing trade ties with India and China, and notwithstanding a so-called 'new left tide' in Latin American politics spearheaded by Hugo Chavez in Venezuela and Evo Morales in Bolivia, the effects of the hated *bloqueo* (US embargo) are still felt widely across Cuban society. Even more disturbing are the 100 or more so-called dissidents who continue to languish in Cuban jails for daring to speak out against their government (p49).

But while there's grumbling on the streets of Habana, the spark of insurrection is still a long way from fruition. Loathed though US observers would be to admit it, nationalism remains a potent force in Cuba and the likelihood of Castro's imminent political demise remains about as likely as George 'Dubya' going for a golfing vacation in Varadero. Flaws and all he will always be the island's great liberator, its George Washington, the only person in 500 years who made his people feel inherently Cuban.

In cultural terms, the *período especial* (special period; p49) has had a heavy cost. Few first-time visitors to Cuba will fail to spot the haranguing hustlers who stalk tourists on the streets of Vedado, or the ridiculously over-qualified doctor who's given up his medical degree to earn tips from waiting tables. Exposed to capitalism via tourism, Che Guevara's 'New Man' is looking decidedly old hat these days and, among younger Cubans, the cultural zeitgeist is gradually changing. Proud as they are of their groundbreaking revolution and respectful as they may be of a government that sends 2000 doctors for earthquake relief in Kashmir, the desire for change is powerful. It's not so much a case of 'if' but 'when.'

**FAST FACTS**

Population: 11.3 million

Area: 110,860 sq km

GNP: US$33.92 billion

Life expectancy: 75 (men); 79 (women)

Adult literacy rate: 97%

Capital city Habana's full name: La Villa de San Cristóbal de la Habana

Total annual visitors to Varadero in 2004: 826,000

Doctor/patient ratio: 1/170

First Cuban heart transplant performed: 1985

# History

Embellished by breathless feats of revolutionary derring-do, and plagued routinely by meddling armies of uninvited foreign invaders, Cuban history has achieved a level of importance way out of proportion to its size. Indeed, with its strategic position slap-bang in the middle of the Caribbean and its geographic closeness to its venerable (or not-so-venerable) US neighbor to the north, the historical annals of the Cuban archipelago often read more like the script of an action-packed Hollywood movie production than a dull end-of-year school exam paper. Read on.

## PRE-COLUMBIAN HISTORY

According to exhaustive carbon dating, Cuba has been inhabited by humans for over 4000 years. The first known civilization to settle on the island were the Guanahatabeys, a primitive Stone Age people who lived in caves around Viñales in Pinar del Río Province and eked out a meager existence as hunter-gatherers. At some point over the ensuing 2000 years the Guanahatabeys were gradually displaced by the arrival of a new preceramic culture known as the Siboneys, a significantly more developed group of fishermen and small-scale farmers who settled down comparatively peacefully on the archipelago's sheltered southern coast.

For the most comprehensive all-round news about Cuba today click on the Havana Journal (www.havanajournal.com; in five different languages).

The island's third and most important pre-Columbian civilization, the Taínos, first started arriving in Cuba around AD 1100 in a series of waves, concluding a migration process that had begun in the Orinoco River delta in South America several centuries earlier. Taíno culture was far more developed and sophisticated than its two archaic predecessors, with the adults practicing a form of cranial transformation by flattening the soft skulls of their young children (flat foreheads were thought to be a sign of great beauty). Related to the Greater Antilles Arawaks, the new natives were skillful farmers, weavers and boatbuilders and their complex society boasted an organized system of participatory government that was overseen by series of local *caciques* or chiefs. Taínos are thought to be responsible for pioneering approximately 60% of the crops still grown in Cuba today and they were the first of the world's pre-Columbian cultures to nurture the delicate tobacco plant into a form that could easily be processed for smoking.

Despite never reaching the heights of the Aztec civilization in Mexico or the Inca civilization in South America, Cuba's Taíno culture has left its indelible mark on the island today. Cuba's traditional *guajiros* (a Taíno word meaning 'one of us,' and used to describe people from the country) still industriously work the land for a living, and evidence of native Indian ancestry in modern Cuban bloodlines remains surprisingly intact in the villages of eastern Guantánamo. Furthermore, in keeping with their tobacco-addicted predecessors, a whole generation of Cuban cigar aficionados continues to obsessively smoke *cohibas* (cigars) for their aroma and taste. To get a sniff of this all-pervading national passion you can visit cigar factories in Habana (p110) or Santa Clara (p274).

**TIMELINE**

| AD 1100 | 1492 |
|---|---|
| Taíno people start arriving in Cuba | Christopher Columbus discovers Cuba and names it Juana |

## FROM COLONY TO REPUBLIC

When Columbus neared Cuba on October 27, 1492, he described it as 'the most beautiful land human eyes had ever seen,' naming it Juana in honor of a Spanish heiress. But deluded in his search for the kingdom of the Great Khan, and finding little gold in Cuba's lush and heavily forested interior, Columbus quickly abandoned the territory in favor of Hispaniola (modern-day Haiti and the Dominican Republic).

The colonization of Cuba didn't begin until nearly 20 years later in 1511 when Diego Velázquez de Cuéllar led a flotilla of four ships and 400 men from Hispaniola destined to conquer the island for the Spanish Crown. Docking near present-day Baracoa, the conquistadors promptly set about establishing seven pioneering settlements throughout their new colony, namely at Baracoa, Bayamo, Trinidad, Sancti Spíritus, Puerto Príncipe (Camagüey), Habana, and Santiago de Cuba. Watching nervously from the safety of their *bohíos* (thatched huts), a scattered population of Taíno Indians looked on with a mixture of fascination and fear.

In the United States there are 815 motor vehicles per 1000 people; in Cuba there are just 23.

Despite Velázquez's attempts to protect the local Indians from the gross excesses of the Spanish swordsmen, things quickly got out of hand and the invaders soon found that they had a full-scale rebellion on their hands. Leader of the embittered and short-lived insurgency was the feisty Hatuey, an influential Taíno *cacique* and archetype of the Cuban resistance, who was eventually captured and burned at the stake, inquisition style, for daring to challenge the iron fist of Spanish rule.

With the resistance decapitated, the Spaniards sordidly set about emptying Cuba of its relatively meager gold and mineral reserves using the beleaguered natives as forced labor. As slavery was nominally banned under a papal edict, the Spanish got around the various legal loopholes by introducing a ruthless *encomienda* system, whereby thousands of hapless natives were rounded up and forced to work for Spanish landowners on the pretext that they were receiving free 'lessons' in Christianity. The brutal system lasted 20 years before the 'Apostle of the Indians,' Fray Bartolomé de Las Casas, appealed to the Spanish Crown for more humane treatment, and in 1542 the *encomiendas* were abolished. Catastrophically, for the unfortunate Taínos, the call came too late. Those who had not already been worked to death in the gold mines quickly succumbed to fatal European diseases such as smallpox and by 1550 only about 5000 scattered survivors remained.

Another great up-to-date news source is the BBC website. Click on www.bbc.co.uk and type Cuba into the search engine for a long list of recent news stories.

### A Taste for Sugar

In 1522, with the local natives perishing fast, the first slaves arrived in Cuba from Africa via Hispaniola. While certainly no saints in the business of slave trafficking, the Spanish colonizers were marginally less repressive in the treatment of their African brethren than the ruthless plantation owners further north, and this, in part, has left its mark on the island's latter-day culture and music. Cuba's African slaves were kept together in tribal groups, enabling them to retain certain elements of their indigenous culture and, in contrast to their counterparts in Haiti or the United States, they retained various legal rights: to own property, get married and even buy their own freedom.

**1508**

Sebastián de Ocampo circumnavigates Cuba, proving it's an island and not part of Asia as Columbus thought

**1511**

Diego Velázquez de Cuéllar lands at Baracoa; Cuba's first rebel Hatuey is burned at the stake

Put to work on cattle ranches, tobacco plantations and the fledgling sugar mills that had already started to spring up around the countryside, the slaves were integral to the slow and gradual growth of the Cuban economy over the ensuing 100 years from subsistence colony to grand commercial enterprise. But it wasn't all one-way traffic.

From the mid-16th century to the mid-18th century, Cuba became the nexus point for a vicious power struggle between wealthy Spanish traders on the one hand and pirates flying the Jolly Roger on the other. The bountiful booty of New World gold and silver shored up in Cuban harbors was too hard for the corsairs to resist. Santiago de Cuba was plundered in 1554 and Habana was attacked a year later leading the embattled Spaniards to construct an impressive line of fortifications around the island's most vulnerable harbors. It made little difference. By the 1660s a new generation of marauding pirates led by the wily Welsh governor of Jamaica, Henry Morgan, revealed further holes in Spain's weak naval defenses and, with Spanish power in Europe constantly under threat, the healthy economic future of the Cuban colony looked to be seriously in doubt.

*Espejo de Paciencia* (Mirror of Patience) written by Balboa in 1608 is considered to be the oldest Cuban literary work.

In 1762 Spain joined in the Seven Years' War on the side of France against the British. For Cuba it quickly turned out to be a fatal omen. Unperturbed by their new Spanish foes and sensing an opportunity to disrupt trade in Spain's economically lucrative Caribbean empire, 20,000 British troops homed in on Habana, landing in the small village of Cojímar on June 6 and attacking and capturing the seemingly impregnable castle of El Morro from the rear. Worn down and under siege the Spanish reluctantly surrendered Habana two months later, leaving the British to become the city's (and Cuba's) rather unlikely new overlords.

The British occupation turned out to be brief but incisive. Bivouacking themselves inside Habana's formidable city walls for 11 months, the enterprising English flung open the doors to free trade and sparked a new rush of foreign imports into the colony in the form of manufacturing parts and consumer goods. Not surprisingly, it was the sugar industry that benefited most from this economic deregulation and in the years that followed the British handover (they swapped Habana for Florida at the Treaty of Paris in 1763) the production of sugarcane boomed like never before.

Cuba's railway system first became operational in 1837. Colonizing power Spain didn't get a railway system until 11 years later.

The industry got a further stimulus in the 1790s when a bloody slave rebellion on the neighboring island of Haiti led 30,000 French planters to flee west and seek asylum in Cuba. Well-skilled in the intricacies of sugar and coffee production, the new immigrants quickly mastered the island's difficult terrain and built a series of pioneering coffee *cafétales* (estates) in the mountainous regions of Pinar del Río and the Sierra Maestra. The influx of Gallic culture also permeated Cuban music, furniture, architecture and manners, particularly in the intrinsically 'French' cities of Cienfuegos, Santiago de Cuba and Guantánamo. See the boxed text, p267 for further details.

By the 1820s, Cuba was the world's largest sugar producer and the freshly inaugurated United States – hooked on sugar and spice and all things nice – was its most prestigious market. Indeed, so important was Cuban sugar to the American palate that a growing movement inside

**1522**

First slaves arrive in Cuba from Africa

**1607**

Habana declared capital of Cuba

In 1824 priest Félix Varela published an independent newspaper called *El Habanero* in Philadelphia. It was considered to be the first Cuban revolutionary publication.

the US started petitioning the government for annexation of the island during the 19th century. In 1808 Thomas Jefferson became the first of four US presidents to offer to buy Cuba from its increasingly beleaguered Spanish owners and in 1845 President Polk upped the ante further when he slapped down a massive US$100 million bid for the jewel of the Caribbean.

For better or for worse, Spain refused to sell, preferring instead to import more slaves and bank more pesetas. By 1840 there were 400,000 slaves incarcerated on the island, the bulk of them of West African origin.

On the political front the sugar boom went some way in forestalling the formation of a coherent independence movement in Cuba before 1820. Curiously, Cuba played little part in the sweeping liberation of South America spearheaded by Simón Bolívar in the 1820s, preferring instead to stay loyal to the Spanish Crown – along with Puerto Rico, Guam and the Philippines. Nonetheless, the rumblings of discontent wouldn't be long in coming.

## The War for Independence

For the most comprehensive book on Cuban history in English check out Hugh Thomas' *Cuba: The Pursuit of Freedom*. It may be 35 years old but it's still a classic.

Fed up with Spain's reactionary policies and enviously eyeing Lincoln's new American dream to the north, *criollo* (Spaniards born in the Americas) landowners around Bayamo began plotting rebellion in the late 1860s. The spark was auspiciously lit on October 10, 1868, when Carlos Manuel de Céspedes, a budding poet, lawyer and sugar plantation owner, launched an uprising from his Demajagua sugar mill near Manzanillo in the Oriente (see p384). Calling for the abolition of slavery, and freeing his own slaves in an act of solidarity, Céspedes proclaimed the famous *Grito de Yara*, a cry of liberty for an independent Cuba, encouraging other disillusioned separatists to join him. For the colonial administrators in Habana such a bold and audacious bid to wrest control from their incompetent and slippery grasp was an act tantamount to treason. The furious Spanish reacted accordingly.

Fortuitously, for the loosely organized rebels, the cagey Céspedes had done his military homework. Within weeks of the historic *Grito de Yara* the diminutive lawyer turned general had raised an army of over 1500 men and marched defiantly on Bayamo, taking the city in a matter of days. But initial successes soon turned to lengthy deadlock. A tactical decision not to invade western Cuba along with an alliance between *peninsulares* (Spaniards born in Spain but living in Cuba) and the Spanish soon put Céspedes on the back foot. Temporary help arrived in the shape of mulato general Antonio Maceo, a tough and uncompromising Santiagüero nicknamed the 'Bronze Titan' for his ability to defy death on countless occasions, and the equally formidable Dominican Máximo Gómez, but, despite economic disruption and the periodic destruction of the sugar crop, the rebels lacked a dynamic political leader capable of uniting them behind a singular ideological cause.

With the loss of Céspedes in battle in 1874, the war dragged on for another four years, reducing the Cuban economy to tatters and leaving an astronomical 200,000 Cubans and 80,000 Spanish dead. Finally in February 1878 a lackluster pact was signed at El Zanjón between the uncom-

**1728**
University of Habana founded

**1762**
Spain joins France in the Seven Years' War; Habana is surrendered to the British

promising Spanish and the militarily exhausted separatists, a rambling and largely worthless agreement that solved nothing and acceded little to the rebel cause. Maceo, disgusted and disillusioned, made his feelings known in the antidotal 'Protest of Baraguá' but after an abortive attempt to restart the war briefly in 1879, both he and Gómez disappeared into a prolonged exile.

The 1880s brought an end to slavery, a boom in railway construction and Cuba's worst economic crisis for over a century. With the price of sugar falling on the world market, the island's old landowning oligarchy was forced to sell out to a newer and slicker competitor – the United States. By the end of the 19th century US trade with Cuba was larger than US trade with the rest of Latin America combined and Cuba was America's third-largest trading partner after Britain and Germany. The island's sweet-tasting mono-crop economy – a thorn in its side since time immemorial – was translating into a US monopoly and some wealthy Cuban landowners were readvocating the old annexation argument.

Chess is big in Cuba and one of its most famous exponents was Carlos Manuel de Céspedes. When he was killed in combat in 1874 Céspedes was found to have a chess set among the personal possessions he was carrying.

## Spanish-Cuban-American War

Cometh the hour, cometh the man: José Martí, poet, patriot, visionary and intellectual had grown rapidly into a patriotic figure of Bolívarian proportions in the years following his ignominious exile in 1870, not just in Cuba, but in the whole of Latin America. After his arrest at the age of 16 during the First War of Independence for a minor indiscretion, Martí had spent 20 years formulating his revolutionary ideas abroad in places as diverse as Guatemala, Mexico and the US. Although impressed by American business savvy and industriousness, he was equally repelled by the country's all-consuming materialism, and was determined to present a workable Cuban alternative.

Dedicating himself passionately to the cause of the resistance, Martí wrote, spoke, petitioned and organized tirelessly for independence for well over a decade and by 1892 had enough momentum to coax Maceo and Gómez out of exile under the umbrella of the Partido Revolucionario Cubano (PRC). At last, Cuba had found its Bolívar.

Predicting that the time was right for another revolution, Martí and his compatriots set sail for Cuba in April 1895 landing near Baracoa two months after PRC-sponsored insurrections had tied down Spanish forces in Habana. Raising an army of 40,000 men the rebels promptly regrouped and headed west engaging the Spanish for the first time on May 19 in a place called Dos Ríos. It was on this bullet-strafed and strangely anonymous battlefield that Martí, conspicuous on his white horse and dressed in his trademark black dinner suit, was shot and killed as he charged suicidally toward the Spanish lines. Had he lived he would certainly have become Cuba's first president; instead, he became a hero and a martyr whose life and legacy would inspire generations of Cubans in the years to come.

A 1976 book entitled *How the Battleship Maine was Destroyed* concluded that the explosion of the *Maine* in Habana Harbor in 1898 was caused by the spontaneous combustion of coal in the ship's bunker.

Conscious of mistakes made during the First War of Independence, Gómez and Maceo stormed west in a scorched earth policy that left everything from the Oriente to Matanzas up in flames. Early victories quickly led to a sustained offensive and by January 1896 Maceo had broken through to Pinar del Río, while Gómez was tying down Spanish forces

**1790**
Mass importation of African slaves

**1808**
Thomas Jefferson offers to buy Cuba from the Spanish

## JOSÉ MARTÍ

For millions of Cubans worldwide José Martí is a heroic and emblematic figure; a potent unifying symbol in a nation fractiously divided by economy, ideology and 90 miles of shark-infested ocean. In Florida they have named a TV station after him. In Habana, Castro touts his name with an almost religious reverence. Throughout Cuba there is barely a town or village that hasn't got at least one street, square or statue named proudly in his honor. The fact that Martí, who died prematurely at the age of 42 leading a suicidal cavalry charge headlong toward the Spanish lines, spent less that one-third of his life residing in his beloved motherland is largely academic.

Born in Habana in 1853 to Spanish parents, Martí grew up fast, publishing his first newspaper *La Patria Libre* at the age of 16. But his provocative writings, flushed with the fervent prose and lyrical poetry that would one day make him famous, soon landed him in trouble. Tried and convicted in 1870 for penning a letter denouncing a friend who had attended a pro-Spanish rally during the First War of Independence, he was charged with treason and sentenced to six months of hard labor in a Habana stone quarry. Later that year, thanks to the influence of his father, the still-teenage Martí was moved to the Isla de Pinos and in 1871 he was exiled to Spain.

Slightly built with a well-waxed Dali-esque moustache and trademark black business suit, Martí cut a rather unlikely hero-to-be in his formative years. Graduating with a degree in law from Saragossa University in 1874 he relocated to Mexico City where he tentatively began a career in journalism.

For the next seven years Martí was constantly on the move, living successively in Guatemala, Spain, France, Venezuela and Cuba, from where he was exiled for a second time in 1879 for his conspiratorial activities and anticolonial statements.

Gravitating toward the US, the wandering writer based himself in the Big Apple for 14 years with his wife and son, devoting his time to poetry, prose, politics and journalism. He was the New York correspondent for two Latin American newspapers, *La Nación* in Buenos Aires and

near Habana. The Spaniards responded with an equally ruthless general named Valeriano Weyler, who built countrywide north–south fortifications to restrict the rebels' movements. Aiming to break the under ground resistance, *guajiros* (country people) were forced into camps in a process called *reconcentración,* and anyone supporting the rebellion became liable for execution. The brutal tactics started to show results and on December 7, 1896 the *Mambíses* (19th-century rebels fighting Spain) suffered a major military blow to their confidence when Antonio Maceo was killed south of Habana trying to break out to the east.

A 1975 book entitled *How the Battleship Maine was Destroyed* concluded that the explosion of the *Maine* in Habana Harbor in 1998 was caused by the spontaneous combustion of coal in the ship's bunker.

By this time Cuba was a mess: thousands were dead, the country was in flames and William Randolph Hearst and the tub-thumping US tabloid press were leading a hysterical war campaign characterized by sensationalized, often inaccurate reports about Spanish atrocities.

Preparing perhaps for the worst, the US battleship *Maine* was sent to Habana in January 1898, on the pretext of 'protecting US citizens.' Fatefully its eponymous task never saw fruition. On February 15, 1898 the *Maine* exploded out of the blue in Habana Harbor, killing 266 US sailors. The Spanish claimed it was an accident, the Americans blamed the Spanish, and some Cubans accused the US, saying it provided a convenient pretext for intervention. The real cause may remain one of history's great mysteries, as the hulk of the ship was scuttled in deep waters in 1911.

**1850**

The Cuban flag is raised for the first time, by Narciso López in Cárdenas

**1868**

Céspedes launches an uprising and proclaims the *Grito de Yara*, a cry for liberty, starting the war for independence.

*La Opinión Nacional* in Caracas, and was later appointed New York consul for the countries of Uruguay, Paraguay and Argentina.

Always adamant to avoid cultural assimilation in the American melting pot, Martí nurtured a deep-rooted mistrust for the US system of government borne out of insider experience and a canny sense of political calculation. He argued vociferously for Cuban independence, and claimed consistently that the Americans were no better than the Spanish in their neocolonial ambitions. 'I have lived inside the monster and know its entrails,' he once stated portentously.

Never one to rest on his rhetoric, Martí left for Florida in 1892 to set up the Cuban Revolutionary Party, the grassroots political movement that spearheaded the 1895–98 War of Independence against the Spanish.

Landing in Cuba in April 1895 at the remote beach of La Playita in Guantánamo Province, Martí's personal war effort lasted precisely 38 days. Destined to be more of a theorist than a man of action, he was cut down at a skirmish at Dos Ríos on May 19, one of the war's first casualties and an instantly recognizable martyr.

Though never ostensibly a socialist during his lifetime, Martí propounded the values of liberty, equality and democracy as central to his fledgling manifesto for an independent Cuba. Unflinching in his hatred of racism and imperialism, he believed in the power of reason, extending friendship to those Spaniards who supported Cuban independence, but war against those who didn't.

The spirit of José Martí is still very much alive in Cuba today. Indeed, it is difficult to imagine the country – with its distinct culture and enviable health and education systems – functioning without him. Artistically speaking the scope of Martí the writer was, and still is, mind-boggling. From his eloquent political theorizing, to his populist *Verso Sencillos* and his best-selling children's magazine *La Edad de Oro* he was a cultural icon without equal in Latin America. It is with little wonder that Cubans today refer to him quite simply as 'El Maestro.'

After the *Maine* debacle, the US scrambled to take control. They offered Spain US$300 million for Cuba and when this deal was rejected, demanded a full withdrawal. The long-awaited US-Spanish showdown that had been simmering imperceptibly beneath the surface for decades had finally ended in war.

The only important land battle of the conflict was on July 1, when the US Army attacked Spanish positions on San Juan Hill (p403) just east of Santiago de Cuba. Despite vastly inferior numbers and limited, antiquated weaponry, the under-siege Spanish held out bravely for over 24 hours before future US president Theodore Roosevelt broke the deadlock by leading a celebrated cavalry charge of the 'Rough Riders' up San Juan Hill. It was the beginning of the end, as far the Spaniards were concerned and an unconditional surrender was offered to the Americans on July 17, 1898.

On December 12, 1898 a peace treaty ending the Spanish-Cuban-American War was signed in Paris by the Spanish and the Americans. Despite three years of blood, sweat and sacrifice, no Cuban representatives were invited. After a century of trying to buy Cuba from the Spanish, the US – wary of raised voices among shortchanged Cuban nationalists – decided to appease the situation temporarily by offering the island a form of quasi-independence that would dampen internal discontent while keeping any future Cuban governments on a tight leash. In November

**1886**
Slavery officially abolished

**1898–1902**
US military government controls Cuba

1900, US Governor of Cuba, General Leonard Wood, convened a meeting of elected Cuban delegates who drew up a constitution similar to that of the US. The then-Connecticut Senator Orville Platt attached a rider to the US Army Appropriations Bill of 1901 giving the US the right to intervene militarily in Cuba whenever they saw fit. This was approved by President McKinley, and the Cubans were given the choice of accepting what became known as the Platt Amendment, or remaining under a US military occupation indefinitely. The US also used its significant leverage to secure a naval base in Guantánamo Bay in order to protect its strategic interests in the Panama Canal region.

## BETWEEN REPUBLIC & REVOLUTION

Trotsky assassin, Ramón Mercader was welcomed to Cuba by Fidel Castro on his release from a Mexican prison in 1960. Splitting his time between the Soviet Union and the Caribbean country he died in Habana in 1978.

On May 20, 1902 Cuba became an independent republic. Hopelessly unprepared for the system of US-style democracy that its northern neighbors optimistically had in mind, the country quickly descended into five decades of on-off chaos headed up by a succession of weak, corrupt governments that called upon US military aid anytime there was the merest sniff of trouble. Intervening three times militarily in the ensuing years (see the boxed text, opposite) the US walked a narrow tightrope between benevolent ally and exasperated foreign meddler. There were, however, some coordinated successes, most notably the eradication of yellow fever using the hypotheses of Cuban doctor Carlos Finlay, and the transformation of the ravaged Cuban economy from postwar wreck into nascent sugar giant.

The postwar economic growth was nothing short of astounding. By the 1920s US companies owned two-thirds of Cuba's farmland and most of its mineral resources. The sugar industry was booming and, with the US gripped by prohibition from 1919 to 1933, the Mafia moved into Habana and gangsters such as Al Capone began to set up a lucrative tourist sector based on drinking, gambling and prostitution. When commodity prices collapsed following the Great Depression, Cuba, like most other Western countries, was plunged into chaos and president-turned-dictator Gerardo Machado y Morales (1925–33) went on a terror campaign to root out detractors. Hoist by his own petard, Machado was toppled during a spontaneous general strike in August 1933 that left a seemingly innocuous army sergeant named Fulgencio Batista (who took no part in Machado's overthrow) to step into the power vacuum.

Batista was a wily and shrewd negotiator who presided over Cuba's best and worst attempts to establish an embryonic democracy in the '40s and '50s. From 1934 onwards he served as the army's chief of staff and in 1940 in a relatively free and fair election he was duly elected president. Given an official mandate, Batista began to enact a wide variety of social reforms and set about drafting Cuba's most liberal and democratic constitution to date. But neither the liberal honeymoon nor Batista's good humor were to last. Stepping down in 1944 the former army sergeant handed over power to the politically inept President Ramón Grau San Martín, and corruption and inefficiency soon reigned like never before.

Aware of his underlying popularity and sensing an easy opportunity to line his pockets with one last big paycheck, Batista cut a deal with the American Mafia in Daytona Beach, Florida, and positioned himself for a

**1903**
US takes Guantánamo naval base

**1925**
Cuban Communist Party founded by Julio Antonio Mella

### A HISTORY OF US INTERVENTION

In 1823 US Secretary of State John Quincy Adams, mastermind of the audacious Monroe Doctrine – an idea which boldly asserted that the whole of the Western hemisphere fell under US influence – declared that Cuba, like a ripe apple, should gravitate naturally toward the US if cut off from Spain. For the Americans, the proclamation seemed to set some kind of unofficial precedent. Over the ensuing 175 years, US involvement in Cuba has gone from overt to covert to underhand.

- Throughout the 19th century four US presidents – namely, Jefferson, Polk, Pierce and Buchanan – tried unsuccessfully to buy Cuba from Spain.
- After independence in 1902 the US intervened militarily on the island on three separate occasions; in 1906 to restore order after an armed rebellion, in 1912 after a short-lived black uprising and again in 1917 after a general strike.
- A summit of the American Mafia convened in Habana's Hotel Nacional in 1946 turned Cuba into a playground for the rich and famous and Habana into a disreputable city of sin. The Mafia influence ultimately led to the return of US-backed General Batista in an illegal coup in March 1952.
- In April 1961 a CIA-backed invasion of the Bay of Pigs was stamped out by the Cuban army inside 72 hours.
- Operation Mongoose, also known as the Cuban Project, was a covert plan initiated by the Kennedy administration in 1961 to 'help Cuba overthrow the communist regime' and, by definition, covertly aid and abet the elimination of its leader Fidel Castro. In the hope of spreading discontent among the Cuban population the project hatched nearly 30 plots between 1961 and 1965. Abortive schemes included the destruction of the sugar crop, the mining of Cuban harbors, and the sprinkling of Castro's shoes with thallium salts: a tactic that was supposed to make his hair and beard fall out, thus making him look ridiculous.
- Successive postrevolutionary laws such as the 1992 Cuban Democracy Act and the 1996 Helms-Burton law have increasingly tightened the screws on a 45-year US trade embargo.

comeback. On March 10, 1952, three months before scheduled elections that he looked like losing, Batista staged a second military coup. Wildly condemned by opposition politicians inside Cuba but foolishly recognized by the US government two weeks later, Batista quickly let it be known that his second incarnation wasn't going to be quite as enlightened as his first.

## THE CUBAN REVOLUTION

After Batista's second coup, a revolutionary circle formed in Habana around the charismatic figure of Fidel Castro, a qualified lawyer and gifted orator who had been due to stand in the cancelled 1952 elections. Supported by his younger brother Raúl and aided intellectually by his trusty lieutenant Abel Santamaría (later tortured to death by Batista's thugs), Castro saw no alternative to the use of force in ridding Cuba of its detestable dictator. Low on numbers but adamant to make a political statement, Castro led 119 rebels in an attack on the strategically important Moncada army barracks in Santiago de Cuba on July 26, 1953 (see p402). The audacious and poorly planned assault failed dramatically when the rebel's driver (who was from Habana) took the wrong turning in Santiago's badly signposted streets and the alarm was raised.

**1934**
Platt Amendment abrogated, but Guantánamo US naval base lease extended for 99 years

**1952**
Batista military coup

Fooled, flailing and hopelessly outnumbered, 64 of the Moncada conspirators were rounded up by Batista's army and brutally tortured and executed. Castro and a handful of others managed to escape into the nearby mountains, where they were found a few days later by a sympathetic army lieutenant named Sarría, who had been given instructions to kill them. 'Don't shoot, you can't kill ideas!' Sarría is alleged to have shouted on finding Castro and his exhausted colleagues. By taking him to jail instead of doing away with him, Sarría – a foresighted and highly principled man – ruined his military career, but saved Fidel's life. (One of Fidel's first acts after the revolution triumphed was to release Sarría from the prison where Batista had incarcerated him and give him a commission in the revolutionary army.) Castro's capture soon became national news, and he was put on trial in the full glare of the media spotlight. A lawyer by profession, the loquacious Fidel defended himself in court writing an eloquent and masterfully executed speech that he later transcribed into a comprehensive political manifesto entitled *History Will Absolve Me.* Basking in his newfound legitimacy and backed by a growing sense of restlessness with the old regime in the country at large, Castro was sentenced to 15 years imprisonment on Isla de Pinos (a former name for Isla de la Juventud). Cuba was well on the way to gaining a new national hero.

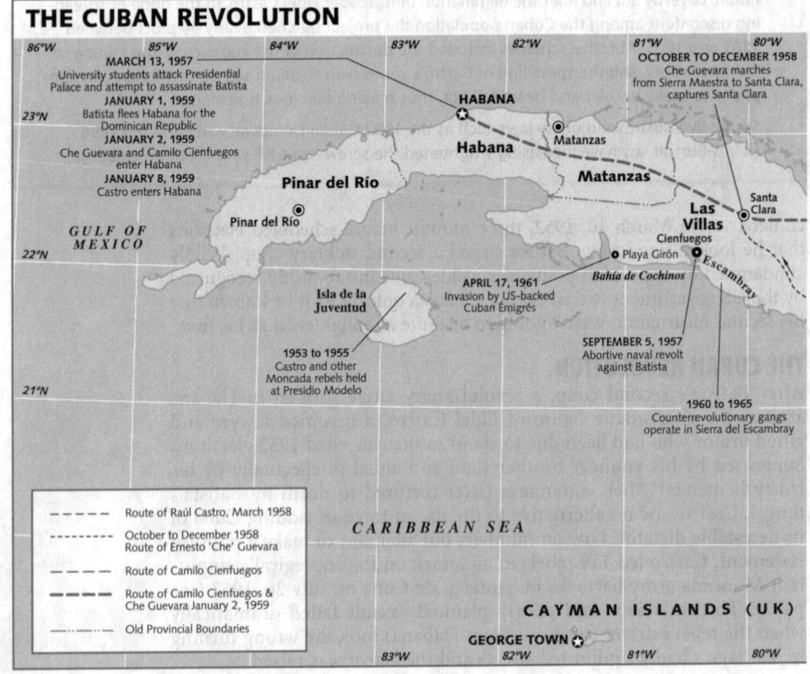
THE CUBAN REVOLUTION
86°W
85°W
84°W
83°W
82°W
81°W
80°W
23°N
22°N
21°N
MARCH 13, 1957
University students attack Presidential Palace and attempt to assassinate Batista
JANUARY 1, 1959
Batista flees Habana for the Dominican Republic
JANUARY 2, 1959
Che Guevara and Camilo Cienfuegos enter Habana
JANUARY 8, 1959
Castro enters Habana
OCTOBER TO DECEMBER 1958
Che Guevara marches from Sierra Maestra to Santa Clara, captures Santa Clara
HABANA
Habana
Matanzas
Matanzas
Pinar del Río
Pinar del Río
Las Villas
Santa Clara
Cienfuegos
Playa Girón
Bahía de Cochinos
Escambray
GULF OF MEXICO
APRIL 17, 1961
Invasion by US-backed Cuban Emigrés
Isla de la Juventud
1953 to 1955
Castro and other Moncada rebels held at Presidio Modelo
SEPTEMBER 5, 1957
Abortive naval revolt against Batista
1960 to 1965
Counterrevolutionary gangs operate in Sierra del Escambray
Route of Raúl Castro, March 1958
October to December 1958 Route of Ernesto 'Che' Guevara
Route of Camilo Cienfuegos
Route of Camilo Cienfuegos & Che Guevara January 2, 1959
Old Provincial Boundaries
CARIBBEAN SEA
CAYMAN ISLANDS (UK)
GEORGE TOWN
83°W
82°W
81°W
80°W

**1953**
Castro leads band of rebels in an attack on Moncada army barracks

**1956**
Ernesto 'Che' Guevara joins Fidel and his compatriots in Mexico

In February 1955, Batista won the presidency in what were widely considered to be fraudulent elections and, in an attempt to curry favor with growing internal opposition, agreed to an amnesty for all political prisoners, including Castro. Realizing that Batista's real intention was to assassinate him once out of jail, Castro fled to Mexico leaving Baptist schoolteacher Frank País in charge of a fledgling underground resistance campaign the vengeful Moncada veterans had christened the 26th of July Movement (M-26-7).

Cocooned in Mexico, Fidel and his compatriots plotted and planned afresh, drawing in key new figures such as Camilo Cienfuegos and the Argentine doctor Ernesto 'Che' Guevara, both of whom added strength and panache to the nascent army of disaffected rebel soldiers. On the run from the Mexican police and adamant to arrive in Cuba in time for an uprising Frank País had planned for late November 1956 in Santiago de Cuba, Castro and 81 companions set sail for the island on November 25 in an old and overcrowded leisure yacht named *Granma*. After seven dire days at sea they arrived at Playa Las Coloradas near Niquero in Oriente (p386) on December 2 two days late, and after a catastrophic landing – 'it wasn't a disembarkation; it was a shipwreck' a wry Guevara later commented – they were spotted and routed by Batista's soldiers in a sugarcane field at Alegría de Pío three days later.

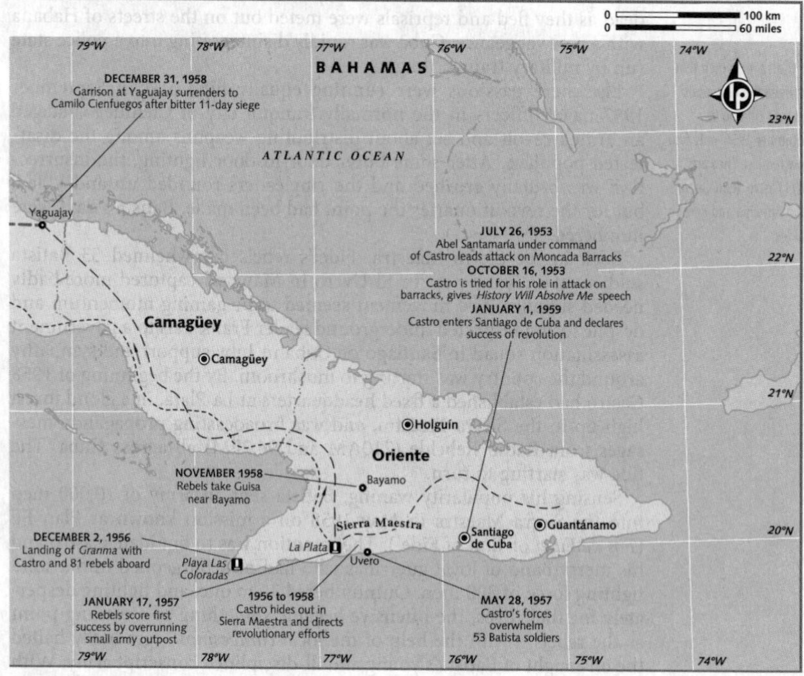


**1959**

Castro gives a triumphal speech at the successful conclusion of the Revolution

**1960**

Cuba nationalizes US assets

Of the 82 rebels soldiers who had left Mexico, only 12 managed to escape. Splitting into three tiny groups the survivors wandered around hopelessly for days half-starved, wounded and assuming that the rest of their compatriots had been killed in the initial skirmish. 'At one point I was Commander in Chief of myself and two other people,' commented Fidel sagely years later. However, with the help of the local peasantry, the dozen or so hapless soldiers finally managed to reassemble two weeks later in Cinco Palmas, a clearing in the shadows of the Sierra Maestra Mountains where a half-delirious Fidel gave a rousing and premature victory speech. 'We will win this war,' he proclaimed confidently, 'We are just beginning the fight!'

Che Guevara – whose father's family name was Guevara Lynch – can trace his Celtic roots back to a Patrick Lynch, born in Galway in Ireland in 1715, who emigrated to Buenos Aires via Bilbao in 1749.

The comeback began on January 17, 1957, when the guerrillas scored an important victory by sacking a small army outpost on the south coast called La Plata (p426). This was followed in February by a devastating propaganda coup when Fidel persuaded *New York Times* journalist Herbert Matthews to come up into the Sierra Maestra to interview him. The resulting article made Castro internationally famous and gained him much sympathy among liberal Americans. Suffice to say, by this point, he wasn't the only anti-Batista agitator. On March 13, 1957 university students led by José Antonio Echeverría attacked the Presidential Palace in Habana (now the Museo de la Revolución; see p102) in an unsuccessful attempt to assassinate Batista. Thirty-two of the 35 attackers were shot dead as they fled and reprisals were meted out on the streets of Habana with a new vengeance. Cuba was rapidly disintegrating into a police state run by military trained thugs.

Of the 12 or so men that survived the disastrous *Granma* landing in December 1956, only four now remain. They are Fidel Castro, Raúl Castro, Juan Almeida and Ramiro Valdés.

Elsewhere passions were running equally high and in September 1957 naval officers in the normally tranquil city of Cienfuegos staged an armed revolt and set about distributing weapons among the disaffected populace. After some bitter door-to-door fighting, the insurrection was brutally crushed and the ringleaders rounded up and killed, but for the revolutionaries the point had been made. Batista's days were numbered.

Back in the Sierra Maestra, Fidel's rebels overwhelmed 53 Batista soldiers at an army post in El Uvero in May and captured more badly needed supplies. The movement seemed to be gaining momentum and despite losing respected underground leader Frank País to a government assassination squad in Santiago de Cuba in July, support and sympathy around the country was starting to mushroom. By the beginning of 1958 Castro had established a fixed headquarters at La Plata, in a cloud forest high up in the Sierra Maestra, and was broadcasting propaganda messages from Radio Rebelde (710AM and 96.7FM) all across Cuba. The tide was starting to turn.

Sensing his popularity waning, Batista sent an army of 10,000 men into the Sierra Maestra in May 1958 on a mission known as Plan FF (*Fin de Fidel* or End of Fidel). The intention was to liquidate Castro and his merry band of loyal guerrillas who had now burgeoned into a solid fighting force of 300 men. Outnumbered 30 to one, and fighting desperately for their lives, the offensive became something of a turning point as the rebels – with the help of the local *campesinos* – gradually halted the onslaught of Batista's young and ill-disciplined conscript army. With

**1961**
Bay of Pigs invasion; US declares a full trade embargo

**1962**
Cuban missile crisis

the Americans increasingly embarrassed by the no-holds-barred terror tactics of their onetime Cuban ally, Castro sensed an opportunity to turn defensive into offensive and signed the groundbreaking Caracas Pact with eight leading opposition groups calling on the US to stop all aid to Batista. Che Guevara and Camilo Cienfuegos were promptly dispatched off to the Escambray Mountains to open up new fronts in the west and by December, with Cienfuegos holding down troops in Yaguajay (the garrison finally surrendered after an 11-day siege) and Guevara closing in on Santa Clara, the end was in sight. It was left to Che Guevara to seal the final victory, employing classic guerrilla tactics to derail an armored train in Santa Clara and split the country's battered communications system in two. By New Year's Eve 1958, the game was up: a sense of jubilation filled the country, and Che and Camilo were on their way to Habana unopposed.

On January 2, 1959, the Cuban government announced that 50% to 60% of all casino profits would be directed to welfare programs.

In the small hours Batista fled by private plane to the Dominican Republic, taking US$40 million in embezzled government funds with him. Materializing in Santiago de Cuba on January 1 meanwhile, Fidel made a rousing victory speech from the town hall in Parque Céspedes before jumping into a jeep and traveling across the breadth of the country to Habana in a Caesar-like cavalcade. The triumph of the revolution was complete. Or was it?

## CONSOLIDATING POWER

On January 5, 1959, the Cuban presidency was assumed by Manuel Urrutia, a judge who had defended the M-26-7 prisoners during the 1953 Moncada trials, though the leadership and real power remained unquestionably with Fidel. Riding on the crest of a popular wave the self-styled *Líder Máximo* began to mete out revolutionary justice with an iron fist and within a matter of weeks hundreds of Batista's supporters and military henchmen had been rounded up and executed inside the walls of La Cabaña fort. Already suspicious of Castro's supposed communist leanings, the US viewed these openly antagonistic developments with a growing sense of alarm and when Fidel visited Richard Nixon in the White House on a state visit in April 1959 the vicepresident gave him a decidedly cool and terse reception.

Among over a thousand laws and acts passed by revolutionary government in its first year were rent and electricity cost reductions, the abolition of racial discrimination and the much-lauded First Agrarian Reform Act. This landmark piece of legislation nationalized all rural estates over 400 hectares (without compensation), and infuriated Cuba's largest landholders, the bulk of whom were American. Establishing the embryonic Instituto Nacional de Reforma Agraria (Agrarian Reform Institute; INRA) as an umbrella organization, the government slowly began to piece together the rural apparatus that would later prove decisive in promoting its ambitious literacy and community doctor programs.

Meanwhile back on the political scene, entities with vested interests in Cuba were growing increasingly bellicose. Perturbed by Castro's intransigent individual style and increasingly alarmed by his gradual and none-too-subtle shift to the left, dissidents started voting with their feet. Between 1959 and 1962 approximately 250,000 judges, lawyers, managers

**1967**
Ernesto 'Che' Guevara executed in Bolivia

**1972**
Cuba joins Comecon (Council for Mutual Economic Assistance) trading bloc

and technicians left Cuba, primarily for the United States and throughout the top professions Cuba began to experience an economically debilitating brain drain. Fidel, meanwhile, hit back at the counter-revolutionaries with stringent press restrictions and the threat of arrest and incarceration for anyone caught being outwardly critical of the new regime.

La Rosa Blanca (the White Rose), the first anti-Castro movement to take hold in the US, was formed in January 1959 by Dr Rafael Díaz-Balart, Fidel's former brother-in-law.

Crisis begot crisis, and in June 1960 Texaco, Standard Oil and Shell refineries in Cuba buckled under US pressure and refused to refine Soviet petroleum. Sensing an opportunity to score diplomatic points over his embittered American rivals, Castro dutifully nationalized the oil companies. President Eisenhower was left with little choice: he cut 700,000 tons from the Cuban sugar quota in an attempt to get even. Rather worryingly for Cold War relations, the measure played right into the hands of the Soviet Union. Already buttered up by a 1959 visit from Che Guevara, the USSR stepped out of the shadows the following day and promised to buy the Cuban sugar at the same preferential rates. The tit-for-tat war that would come to characterize Cuban-Soviet-US relations for the next 30 years had well and truly begun.

The diplomatic crisis heated up again in August when Cuba nationalized US-owned telephone and electricity companies and 36 sugar mills, including US$800 million in US assets. Outraged, the American government forced through an Organization of American States (OAS) resolution condemning 'extra-continental' (Soviet) intervention in the Western hemisphere while Cuba responded by establishing diplomatic relations with communist China and edging ever closer to its new Soviet ally, via a hastily signed arms deal.

By October 1960, 382 major Cuban-owned firms, the majority of its banks and the whole rental housing market had been nationalized and both the US and Castro were starting to prepare for the military showdown that by this point seemed inevitable. Turning the screw ever tighter, the US imposed a partial trade embargo on the island as Che Guevara (now Minister of Industry) nationalized all remaining US businesses. In the space of just three short years Fidel had gone from the darling of the American liberals to US public enemy number one. The stage was set.

## COLD WAR DEEP FREEZE

The brick finally hit the window in early 1961 when Castro ordered US embassy reductions in Habana. Barely able to conceal their fury, the Americans broke off diplomatic relations with Cuba, banned US citizens from traveling to the island and abolished the remaining Cuban sugar quota. At the same time the government, in collusion with the CIA, began to initiate a covert program of action against the Castro regime that included invasion plans, assassination plots and blatant acts of sabotage. Much of this aid was filtered through to counter-revolutionary gangs who – borrowing a tactic from Fidel – had set up in the Escambray Mountains in an attempt to initiate a guerrilla war against the new government. At the center of subterfuge lay the infamous Bay of Pigs invasion (see boxed text, p255), a poorly conceived military plot that honed 1400 disaffected Cuban exiles into a workable fighting force in the jungles of Guatemala. Deemed sufficiently armed and ready to fight, the émigrés sailed on April 14, 1961 with a US navy escort from Puerto

**1976**
Terrorist group bombs Cuban jet, killing all 73 aboard

**1977**
US establishes Interests Section in Habana; Cuba opens one in Washington DC

Cabeza in Nicaragua, to the southern coast of Cuba. But military glory wasn't forthcoming. Landing at Playa Girón and Playa Larga three days later, the US-backed expeditionary forces took a conclusive drubbing, in part because President Kennedy canceled US air cover during the landings, a decision which has been the subject of much revisionist analysis (and possibly cost him his life?).

Rocked and embarrassed by what had been a grave and politically costly military defeat, the Americans declared a full trade embargo on Cuba in June 1961, and in January 1962 the US used diplomatic pressure to expel the island from the OAS (Organization of American States). To the dismay of the Americans, their closest neighbors, Mexico and Canada, refused to bow to US pressure to sever diplomatic relations with Cuba completely, thus throwing the country a valuable lifeline which – in the case of Canada – still exists to this day. Spinning inexorably into the Soviet sphere of influence, Castro began to cement closer relations with Khrushchev and upped the ante even further in April 1962 when, exploiting American weakness after the Bay of Pigs fiasco, he agreed to effect the installation of Soviet-made medium-range missiles on the island.

Castro has admirers everywhere. In 2005 even ex-US secretary of state Colin Powell conceded in congressional testimony that 'he's done some good things for his people.'

The Americans were furious and, anxious not to lose any more face on the international scene, the Kennedy administration decided to act quickly and decisively. On October 22, 1962, President Kennedy ordered the US Navy to detain Cuba-bound Soviet ships and search for missiles, provoking the Cuban Missile Crisis, which brought the world closer to the nuclear brink than it has ever been before or since. Six days later, only after receiving a secret assurance from Kennedy that Cuba would not be invaded, Khrushchev ordered the missiles dismantled. Castro, who was not consulted nor informed of the decision until it was a done deal, was livid and reputedly smashed a mirror in his anger. More bad luck was on the way.

## BUILDING SOCIALISM WORLDWIDE

The learning curve was steep in the revolution's first decade. The economy continued to languish in the doldrums despite massive injections of Soviet aid and production was marked by all of the normal inconsistencies, shortages and quality issues that characterize uncompetitive socialist markets. As National Bank president and later Minister of Industry, Che Guevara advocated centralization and moral, rather than material, incentives for workers. But despite his own tireless efforts to lead by example and sponsor voluntary work weekends, all attempts to create the 'New Man,' ultimately proved to be unsustainable.

Similarly the effort to produce a 10-million-ton sugar harvest in 1970 was equally misguided and almost led to economic catastrophe, as the country ditched everything in pursuit of one all-encompassing obsession.

Adamant to learn from its mistakes, the Cuban government elected to diversify and mechanize after 1970, ushering in a decade of steadier growth and relative economic prosperity. As power was de-centralized and a small market economy permitted to flourish, people's livelihoods gradually began to improve and, for the first time in decades, Cubans started to live more comfortably, due in no small part to burgeoning

**1991**
Soviet Union collapses; future of Cuba enters uncertain waters

**1993**
US dollar legalized

trade with the Soviet bloc, which increased from 65% of the total in the early 1970s to 87% in 1988.

With the home front starting to reawaken from a deep slumber, Castro turned his attention towards the international stage and his vision for Cuba as leader of a Third World coalition in global affairs. The idea was nothing new. Covertly, Cuba had been sponsoring guerrilla activity in South America and Africa since the early 1960s, and in 1965 Che Guevara had spent nine largely fruitless months in the Republic of Congo trying to ignite a popular uprising among a fractious band of antigovernment rebels. Quickly abandoning his plans in frustration, Guevara resurfaced a year later in Bolivia where he launched another equally fruitless campaign aimed at inspiring the Bolivian peasantry to rise up against their oppressive militaristic government. Unfortunately the Cuban model didn't translate well to the Bolivian reality and Bolivian troops, with heavy US support, captured Guevara on October 8, 1967. Shot the next day by a nervous alcohol-plied executioner he went down in history much as Martí had done before him – a martyr.

Longevity runs in the family. All of Fidel Castro's six siblings are still alive, from Angela, three years his senior, to Agostina, 11 years his junior.

In an interesting footnote to the story, Guevara's remains, which lay in an unmarked grave beneath a Bolivian airfield for nearly 30 years, were rediscovered in 1997 and returned to Cuba amid much ceremony. They now rest in a mausoleum adjacent to the Plaza de la Revolución in Che's adopted Cuban city of Santa Clara (p274).

Cuba's involvement in the Angolan war was a heavy and costly adven ture. Initially invited to send troops to Luanda by Angolan leader Agostinho Neto in November 1975, the Cubans quickly became bogged down in a long and complex bush war that pitted tribe against tribe and Marxist MPLA (Movimento Popular de Libertação de Angola) government against South Africa's reactionary apartheid regime. Famous for their tenacity in battle and oft-lauded for their bravery under fire, the Cubans slugged it out for over 10 years alongside poorly trained MPLA forces and heavy-duty Soviet weaponry. But, despite a conclusive military defeat over the apartheid regime in 1988, the price of the Angolan escapade was inexorably high – for many, too high. Barely mentioned in Cuban history books, the Angolan war conscripted over 300,000 Cubans between 1975 and 1991 and left 14,000 of them dead. And the end result was negligible. The war in Angola dragged on until 2002 killing an estimated 1.5 million Angolans and leaving the country a mess.

In 1999 American President Bill Clinton granted GlaxoSmithKline permission to develop a Cuban Meningitis B vaccine.

In 1976 a third Cuban constitution was drawn up and approved by referendum; Fidel Castro replaced Osvaldo Dorticós as president.

## CRISIS AS THE WALL FALLS

After almost 25 years of a top-down Soviet-style economy, it was obvious that quality was suffering and ambitious production quotas were becoming increasingly unrealistic. In 1986 Castro initiated the 'rectification of errors' campaign, a process that aimed to reduce malfunctioning bureaucracy and allow more local-level decision making to wrest control. Just as the process was reaping some rewards the Eastern bloc collapsed in the dramatic events that followed the fall of the Berlin Wall in Europe. As trade and credits amounting to US$5 billion vanished almost overnight from the Cuban balance sheet, Castro – adamant to avoid the fate of East

| 1995 | 1996 |
|---|---|
| Direct foreign investment approved; tourism becomes main money earner | Brothers to the Rescue planes shot down by Cuban jets |

German leader Erich Honecker and Romanian president Ceausescu – declared a five-year *período especial* (special period; Cuba's new economic reality post 1991) austerity program that sent living standards plummeting and instituted a system of rationing that would make the sacrifices of wartime Europe almost pale in comparison. Any Cuban over the age of 25 can furnish you with painful horror stories from this era, including tales of fried grapefruit skins, microjet rice and pigs being reared in the bathroom.

Sniffing the blood of a dying communist animal, the US tightened the noose in 1992 with the harsh Torricelli Act, which forbade foreign subsidiaries of US companies from trading with Cuba and prohibited ships

**HUMAN RIGHTS IN CUBA**

Called to task by the UN and regularly berated by the powers that be in Washington, Cuba's human rights record has always been a political hot potato.

The party got off to a bad start in January 1959 when the revolutionary government – under the auspices of Che Guevara – rounded up Batista's top henchmen and summarily executed them inside Habana's La Cabaña fort with barely a lawyer in sight. Within a matter of months the Cuban press had been silenced, and worried onlookers inside the Eisenhower administration were vociferously crying 'foul.'

After lengthy spats of back-and-forth recrimination in the years since, little appears to have changed. To Western observers the continued denial of free speech and basic civil liberties in socialist Cuba is a measure that reeks of repression. To make matters worse, Amnesty International is currently calling on the Cuban authorities to release 100 or more 'prisoners of conscience' who dared to speak out against the government before two draconian crackdowns in March 2003 and July 2005 (the Cubans claim the dissidents were being funded by the US Special Interests Office). It has also – interestingly – called for an end to the US trade embargo which it claims has long had a detrimental effect on human rights on the island.

The argument, as ever, is complex. To compare Cuba to the Stalinist Soviet Union, or former US-backed dictatorships such as Rios Montt's Guatemala, is something of a conundrum, even for the regime's worst critics. There are no middle-of-the-night 'disappearances' in Cuba and no institutionalized torture of the kind perpetuated by former Mafia puppet President Batista.

Rather, to understand Cuba's attitude to human rights it is important to try to view the issue in a relative context. Firstly socialist ideology tends to emphasize duties over individual liberties and basic needs such as free health, education and housing over the right to own four SUVs. Secondly, after 45 years of sabotage, espionage and badly hatched assassination plots by an aggressive and more powerful US neighbor, Cuba has been forced to cultivate a tight-knit fortress mentality in order to ward off its enemies and keep an easily heckled populace in check.

None of this, of course, can obscure the hard facts: in Cuba, to speak out against the government is a serious and heavily punishable crime that – if it doesn't first land you in jail – will undoubtedly lead to job stagnation, petty harassment and social ostracism. To add insult to injury, in April 2005 Cuba announced that it would not cooperate in any way with a mandate for a UN envoy to investigate human rights abuses on the island. The announcement followed a couple of years after the Cuban government had handed out the death sentence to a group of hijackers who had apprehended a boat and attempted to sail it to Florida.

This issue can be given a sharper focus by looking across the barbed wire into Guantánamo naval base where, with heavy irony and under the watchful eye of a largely powerless international community, the United States has perpetuated a good few human rights abuses of its own.

**1997**

Lonely Planet's virgin *Cuba* edition hits the streets

**1998**

Pope John Paul II visits Cuba

that had called at Cuban ports from docking at US ports for six months. Ninety percent of the trade banned by this law consisted of food, medicine and medical equipment, which led the American Association for World Health to conclude that the US embargo has caused a significant rise in suffering – even deaths – in Cuba.

In August 1993, with the country slipping rapidly into an economic coma and Habana on the verge of riot, the US dollar was legalized, allowing Cubans to hold and spend foreign currency and open US dollar bank accounts. Spearheaded by the unlikely figure of Raúl Castro, other liberal reforms followed including limited private enterprise, self-employment, the opening of farmers' markets and the expansion of the almost non-existent tourist sector into a mainstay of the new burgeoning economy.

In November 2005 the UN Assembly voted 182-4 to urge the United States to end its 44-year-old trade embargo against Cuba. Voting with the US against the resolution were Israel, Palau and the Marshall Islands.

But the recovery was not without its problems. Class differences reemerged as people with US dollars began to gain access to goods and services not available in pesos, while touts and prostitutes known as *jineteros/as* took up residence in tourist areas where they preyed upon rich foreigners whose designer clothes and comfortable capitalist lifestyles they longed to emulate.

Although some of the worst shortages have been alleviated thanks to the reinvestment of tourist revenue into public services, the *período especial* has left a nasty scar. Much to the popular chagrin, the government also started to go back on some of its earlier liberalization measures in an attempt to reestablish an updated brand of old socialist orthodoxy.

Following the 1994 Balsero crisis (p247) and a handful of further shots in the ongoing diplomatic war that had been plaguing US-Cuban relations for decades, the US pulled the embargo a notch tighter in 1996 by signing the Helms-Burton Bill into law. Widely condemned by the international community, and energetically leapt upon by Castro as a devastating propaganda tool, the bill allows US investors to take legal action in the American courts against foreign companies utilizing their confiscated property in Cuba. It also prevents any US president from lifting the embargo until a transitional government is in place in Habana.

## INTO THE NEW MILLENNIUM

Cuba entered the new millennium in the throes of the Elián González drama, a tragic family crisis that was to become an allegory for the all-pervading senselessness of the ongoing Cuban-American immigration showdown.

Failing to learn the lessons of its predecessors (nine of whom had tried and failed to 'get rid of Castro), the Bush administration came out all guns blazing in November 2000, following the victory-clinching Florida vote recount; a state in which conservative Cuban exiles have always punched way above their weight.

Promising to crack down on Cuba's purported human rights' abuses, George W Bush's rhetoric turned venomous after September 11, when the president began mentioning the Castro regime in the same breath as North Korea and Iraq. Subsequently US policy was rolled back to resemble the worst of the Cold War years with rigid travel restrictions, economically damaging financial constraints and a hawkish no-compromise political rhetoric.

**1998**

Five Cubans are arrested by US authorities on questionable spy charges; they remain in prison

**2002**

First US Food & Agribusiness Exhibition held in Habana

Rather than score much-needed capital out of Bush's belligerence, Castro elected to shoot himself in the foot by proceeding to arrest scores of so-called dissidents who had – allegedly – been sponsored by US Special Interests Office chief James Cason to spread social unrest across the island. Whether or not this was true, the trials and hefty prison sentences meted out to more than 100 of these 'antes' gained little sympathy from horrified human rights groups worldwide, as Castro's heavy-handed crackdown was condemned by everyone from Amnesty International to the Vatican.

Things turned uglier in April 2003 when three hijackings by Cubans seeking transport to the US presaged a possible migratory crisis (Cuban officials uncovered more than 20 other hijacking plans in the works). Armed with guns, knives and, in one case, grenades, two planes and a ferry were hijacked in a series of separate dramatic events that had news, gossip and speculation flying. One plane made it to the US, but the ferry and second plane didn't. Three of the hijackers apprehended in Cuba were tried, sentenced to death and executed, triggering another avalanche of international criticism from intellectuals, human rights advocates, politicians and religious leaders.

In 2005 *Human Rights Watch* condemned the travel restrictions imposed by both Cuba and the US, saying: 'Both countries are sacrificing people's freedom of movement to promote dead-end policies.'

While ostensibly things have improved immeasurably in Cuba since the dark days of the *período especial*, the economic meltdown has left its bloody mark. By dangling the carrot of capitalism in front of the Cuban populace in the form of all-inclusive tourism, limited private enterprise and the legalization of US dollar (1993 to 2004), the psychology of Cuba's 'New Man' has been irrevocably damaged.

But it's not all bad news. On the international scene Cuba has successfully managed to wrest itself free from its once near-fatal addiction to sugar cane and has branched out confidently into other areas. Spearheading a mini-economic revival are a clutch of new industries such as tourism, nickel mining (although the first two have led to an element of environmental damage) and the island's internationally famous medical sector. Indeed, the latter service has played a large part in fostering a strong new economic and political alliance with Cuba's new friends in Venezuela and, in exchange for the Cuban doctors and teachers needed to enact vital social reforms, Venezuelan president Hugo Chavez has furnished Cuba with millions of dollars worth of petroleum from his country's abundant oil wells. It doesn't end there. Thanks to a recent medical exchange program known as Misión Milagros (see p449) this cooperation has been extended to a number of other countries throughout the region and evidence of a new left tide in Latin America politics, which may one day challenge the hegemony of the United State in the region, is growing.

Cuba began its Third World medical assistance by sending 56 doctors to Algeria. It now has ongoing medical programs with 58 Third World countries.

But what of the future? For decades Fidel's chosen heir has been his younger brother, head of the armed forces, Raúl, a lifelong communist and fellow survivor of the ill-fated *Granma* expedition and subsequent war in the mountains.

Patient and little more forgiving than his volatile older sibling, the younger Castro – insiders claim – is a cagey and diplomatic negotiator who does not share his brother's pathological hatred of the United States; a factor that could play an important part in reopening dialogue with Cuba's hostile neighbors to the north.

**2002**

Half of Cuba's sugar refineries are closed, signaling the end of an era

**2003**

George W Bush tightens travel noose for US citizens traveling to Cuba

But, negotiation skills aside, it is unlikely that Raúl, who lacks both the charisma and popular support of the Machiavellian Fidel, could rule alone. What is more likely is some kind of collective government propped up by other key figures such as Vice President Carlos Lage, the economic guru responsible for dragging Cuba's battered economy through the darkest days of the *período especial*.

In 2001 Maine became the first US state to pass a resolution calling for a complete end to the trade and travel ban against Cuba.

Concern over how Cuban exiles living in Florida will react to Castro's death is well-founded. Bitterness over the Cuban government's requisition of millions of dollars worth of private property in the early 1960s is still palpable in Miami and the 1996 Helms-Burton Act, which gives American citizens the right to sue for confiscated property through the US courts, has exacerbated the problem.

For a peaceful transition of power, restraint by governments on both sides is key, coupled with the understanding that many of Cuba's postrevolutionary advances – healthcare and education to name but two – are certainly worth preserving. As to whether this is possible: only time will tell.

**2004**
US dollar taken out of circulation

**2006**
Castro celebrates his 80th birthday

# The Culture

## THE NATIONAL PSYCHE

Funny, gracious, generous, tactile and slow to anger, the Cuban people are the Irish of the Americas; a small nation with a big personality, and plenty of rum-fueled backs-to-the-wall boisterousness to go with it. Take the time to get to know them on their own turf and you're halfway to understanding what this most confounding and contradictory of Caribbean countries is all about.

Survivors by nature and necessity, Cubans have long displayed an almost inexhaustible ability to bend the rules and 'work things out' when it matters. In a country where everything is illegal, anything becomes possible and from the backstreets of Baracoa to the hedonistic heights of Habana nobody's shy about 'giving it a go.'

The two most over-used verbs in the national phrasebook are *conseguir* (to get, manage) and *resolver* (to resolve, work out) and Cubans are experts at doing both. Their intuitive ability to bend the rules and make something out of nothing is borne out of economic necessity. In a small nation bucking modern sociopolitical realities, where monthly salaries top out at around the equivalent of US$20, survival can often mean getting innovative as a means of supplementing personal income. Cruise the crumbling streets of Habana Centro and you'll see people *conseguir*-ing and *resolver*-ing wherever you go. There's the barber giving straight razor shaves on his patio, or the lady selling fresh eggs door to door. Other schemes may be ill-gotten or garnered through trickery, like the *compañera* (female revolutionary) who siphons cooking oil from her day job to sell on the side. Old Cuba hands know one of the most popular ways to make extra cash is working with (or over) tourists.

In Cuba, hard currency (ie Convertible pesos) rules, primarily because it is the only way of procuring the modest luxuries that make living in this austere socialist republic vaguely bearable. Paradoxically, the post-1993 double economy has reinvigorated the class system the revolution worked so hard to neutralize and it's no longer rare to see Cubans with access to Convertibles touting designer clothing while others hassle tourists mercilessly for spare change. This stark re-emergence of 'haves' and 'have nots' is among the most ticklish issues facing Cuba today.

Other social traits absorbed since the revolution are more altruistic and less divisive. In Cuba sharing is second nature and helping out your

### RESPONSIBLE TRAVEL

- If you're staying in a resort, venture outside for a day in order to gain an insight into how real Cubans live, work and play.
- You're in a rationing state. Make allowances for shortages, slow service, unavailability of goods and higher levels of state bureaucracy.
- While Cuban law has many grey areas, try to avoid offers that are blatantly illegal (an unauthorized paladar, more than two people per room in a casa particular). Such actions are more likely to get your Cuban hosts into trouble than yourself.
- Go open-minded and leave any preconceptions you may have about Castro, Che and communism at home. Try to see through the haranguing of the street hustlers in order to find the proud, open, welcoming and fascinatingly paradoxical country that lies underneath.

*compañero* with a lift, a square meal or a few Convertibles when they're in trouble is considered a national duty. Check the way that strangers interact in queues or at transport intersections and log how your casa particular owner always refers you onto someone else, often on the other side of the country.

In such an egalitarian system the notion of fairness is often sacred and although the image of Che's 'New Man' might be looking a little worn around the edges these days, the social cohesion that characterized the lean years of the *período especial* (special period; Cuba's economic reality post 1991) still remains loosely intact. One of the most common arguments you'll see in a Cuban street is over queue-jumping – a fracas that won't just involve the one or two people directly involved, but half the town.

Life in Cuba is open and interactive. Come 10pm the whole population will be sitting outside on their rocking chairs shooting the breeze over dominos, cigars, cheap rum or the omnipresent TV sets. Home life is important here and often three generations of the same family can be found living together under one roof. Such binding ties make the complex question of the embargo all the more painful. One of the saddest effects of the US-Cuban deep freeze is the broken families. Precipitated by prejudicial immigration policies on Washington's part and downright intransigence on Fidel's, many Cubans have left home in search of brighter horizons and almost everyone has a long-lost sister, cousin, twin or aunt making it good (or not so good) overseas.

For the best up-to-date Cuban cultural news in English click onto www.cubanow.net for an informative and easy-to-read exposé on everything and everyone connected with Cuban culture from Frank Sinatra to Graham Greene.

But it's not all bad news. In April 2005, riding high on the back of a closer trade relations with Venezuela and China, Fidel Castro announced plans to double the minimum wage from 100 pesos a month (CUC$4) to 225 pesos (CUC$9). While the increase might sound laughable by any Western standard, the move stood to directly benefit 1.6 million Cuban workers including farmhands and plumbers.

## LIFESTYLE

Cuban socialism dances to its own drummer. Though housing is free, shortages mean three or even four generations might live under the same roof, which gets tight in a two-bedroom apartment. This also cramps budding love lives and Cubans will tell you it's the reason the country has one of the world's highest divorce rates. Gays and lesbians, who do not have the option of getting married and living with the family, are in a particularly difficult spot vis-à-vis their private affairs. On the flip side, a full house means there's almost always someone to babysit, take care of you when you're sick or do the shopping while you're at work.

Cuban women have been liberated in the sense that they have access to education and training of whatever sort they desire. In fact, women make up 66.4% of the professional and technical workforce. But, like everywhere, a glass ceiling still exists in some fields (eg politics) and the home is still largely the woman's responsibility, which translates to a 'double work day' – women go to work and then come home, to work. Thanks to specific governmental policies, such as one year guaranteed maternity leave and free day care, it's easier being a mother *and* a career woman in Cuba. Children are an integral part of life and kids are everywhere – the theater, church, restaurants and rock concerts. It's refreshing that Cubans don't drastically alter their lives once they become parents.

That women are turning to hustling to make some extra cash or attain baubles is disturbing. While some *jineteras* (a woman who attaches herself to male foreigners for monetary or material gain) are straight-up hookers, others are just getting friendly with foreigners for the perks they provide: a ride in a car, a night out in a fancy disco or a new pair of jeans. Some are after more, others nothing at all. It's a complicated state of affairs and can be especially confusing for male travelers who get swept up in it.

Most homes don't have a phone or computer, infinitesimally few have Internet access and disposable income is an oxymoron. All of this has a huge effect on lifestyle. What makes Cuba different from somewhere like Bolivia or Appalachia though, is the government's heavy subsidies of every facet of life, especially culture. Consider the fact that in Habana there are some 200 movie theaters and a ticket costs two pesos (US$0.08), or that a front-row seat at the Gran Teatro de la Habana costs 10 pesos (US$0.40), rap concerts cost two pesos and a patch of cement bench at the ballpark is one peso (US$0.04). Now if only there was the transport to get there. Still, with a set of dominoes or a guitar, a bottle of rum and a group of friends, who needs baseball or the ballet?

## ECONOMY

Nearly destroyed during the economic meltdown that followed the collapse of the Soviet Union in the early 1990s, the Cuban economy has defied all logic by its continued survival. Given new life with a three-pronged recovery plan in 1993 that included the legalization of the US dollar (retracted in 2004), the limited opening up of the private sector and the frenzied promotion of the tourist industry in resort areas such as Varadero and Cayo Coco, net advances have been slow but steady with much of the benefits yet to filter down to the average person on the street in Habana or Santiago. Throwing off its heavy reliance on old staples such as sugar and tobacco Cuba's recent economic development has spun inexorably toward Latin America in the shape of new trade agreements such as the 2004 ALBA (Bolivarian Alternative of the Americas) accords that have exchanged Cuban medical know-how for Venezuelan oil. Other modern economic mainstays include nickel mining (Cuba is the world's third largest producer) and pharmaceuticals.

The US spends US$4176 per person annually on health care. In embargo-strapped Cuba the government coughs up $186 per head to finance their citizens. Yet the overall health indices (life expectancy, infant mortality rates) in both countries are almost the same.

## POPULATION

The slave trade and the triumph of the Cuban revolution are two of the most important factors in Cuba's population mix. From Santería traditions to popular slang, Afro-Cuban culture is an integral part of the national identity. According to the 2002 official census Cuba's racial breakdown is 51% mulatto, 37% white, 11% black and 1% Chinese. Aside from the obvious Spanish legacy, many of the so-called 'white' population are the descendants of French immigrants who arrived on the island in various waves during the early part of the 19th century. Indeed, the cities of Guantánamo, Cienfuegos and Santiago were all either pioneered or heavily influenced by French émigrés and much of Cuba's coffee and sugar industry owes its development to French entrepreneurship.

The black diaspora is also made up of an eclectic mix of different elements. Numerous Haitians and Jamaicans came to Cuba to work in the sugar fields in the 1920s and they brought many of their customs and traditions with them. Their descendants can be found in Guantánamo and Santiago in the Oriente or places such as Venezuela in Ciego de Ávila Province where Haitian voodoo liturgies are still practiced. Another important immigrant town is Baraguá in Ciego de Ávila, which is famous for its English-speaking West Indian community who still celebrate their annual 'freedom day' each August with a game of cricket.

**THE RATION CARD**

The *libreta* (ration card) was created in 1962 to provide a basic social safety net for the population and to limit price gouging on basic goods via the black market. During the relatively affluent '70s and '80s, with Soviet subsidized products pouring into Cuba, it seemed that the card might be on the way out, but the economic crisis of the '90s has ensured its survival.

The basic 30-product monthly food basket allotted to every Cuban includes 2.7kg of rice, 1.5kg of refined sugar and 1kg of brown sugar, 0.25kg of beans, a measly amount of coffee, 2kg of salt, 0.25kg of cooking oil and 1.5kg of pasta. Everyone receives one toilet roll a day, plus soap and toothpaste. Chicken, hot dogs, fish and vegetables are distributed pending availability. Another 29 products are distributed irregularly on a per family basis, including cornmeal, food paste, crackers and tinned tomatoes. Children up to the age of one get two bottles of fresh or condensed milk monthly, plus soy yogurt every other day. Children to the age of seven get an allotment of powdered milk. Pensioners, pregnant women and those with certain chronic diseases or special diets (eg for high cholesterol) also receive special rations.

Rationed goods are sold at bodegas (government stores), at subsidized peso prices that haven't changed for years. The same items sold freely without ration cards at farmers markets cost 20 times more. Bodegas often sell items *libre* (outside the ration card), meaning anyone, including foreigners, can buy those products. Maintaining the ration system is a serious drain on state finances, but without it many Cubans would suffer real hardship in a society where the circulation of two unequal currencies has created tangible class differences. As it is, the monthly ration is only a supplement that must somehow be topped up elsewhere.

The invitation to partake in free education up to university level had Cubans pouring into the cities from the countryside after the revolution, so that today the urban population is a top-heavy 75%. In efforts to stem or reverse this trend the government offered land incentives to urbanites during the *período especial* to encourage resettling in rural areas, and since May 1998 Cubans have needed official permission to relocate to Habana.

There are no official class breakdowns in Cuba although class divisions based on income have begun to rear their ugly head since the beginning of the *período especial*. More refreshingly, Cuba is one of the few countries in the world where the notion of doffing your cap to someone of higher social stature is virtually nonexistent.

## SPORT

Considered a right of the masses, professional sport was abolished by the government after the revolution. Performance-wise it was the best thing the new administration could have done. Since 1959 Cuba's Olympic medal haul has rocketed into the stratosphere. The crowning moment came in 1992 when Cuba – a country of 11 million people who languish 172nd on the world's 'rich list', in between Mongolia and the Central African Republic – brought home 14 gold medals and finished fifth on the overall medals table. It's a testament to Cuba's high sporting standards that their 11th place finish in Athens in 2004 was considered something of a national failure.

Characteristically the sporting obsession starts at the top. Fidel Castro is widely renowned for his baseball hitting prowess, but what is less known is his personal commitment to the establishment a widely-accessible national sporting curriculum at all levels. In 1961 the National Institute of Sport, Physical Education and Recreation (Inder) founded a system of sport for the masses that eradicated discrimination and integrated children from a young age. By offering paid leisure-time to workers and dropping entrance fees to major sports events the organization caused participation in popular sports to multiply tenfold by the 1970s and the knock-on effect to performance was tangible.

Cuban *pelota* (baseball) is legendary and the country is riveted during the October to March regular season, turning rabid for the play-offs in April. You'll see passions running high in the main square of provincial capitals, where fans debate minute details of the game with lots of finger-wagging in what is known as a *peña deportiva* (fan club) or *esquina caliente* (hot corner). These are among the most opinionated venues in Cuba and the *esquina* in Habana's Parque Central (p101) is highly entertaining, especially in the postseason when funereal wreaths and offerings to *orishas* (Santería deities) appear for eliminated teams and those still contending. Sometimes a Cuban player is lured to the US, like José Ariel Contreras, who pitched for Pinar, but now earns millions playing for the Chicago White Sox (he formerly played for the Yankees). Most players, however, shun the big money bait and the opportunity to play in baseball's greatest stadiums, opting instead to continue earning the equivalent of US$13 per month – decisions that make their athletic achievements all the more admirable.

Cuba won the first ever Olympic baseball tournament held in Barcelona in 1992 thumping the US in the semifinals and Taiwan in the final.

Cuba is also a giant in amateur boxing, as indicated by champions Teófilo Stevenson, who brought home Olympic gold in 1972, 1976 and 1980, and Félix Savón, another triple medal winner, most recently in 2000. Every sizable town has an arena called a *sala polivalente,* where big boxing events take place, while training and smaller matches happen at gyms, many of which train Olympic athletes. Travelers interested in sparring lessons or seeing a match should drop in at a gym (see individual regional chapters for information). For boxing shows, ask around at the local *sala polivalente* or keep an eye out for posters advertising upcoming bouts. As with all sporting events in Cuba, entrance to professional-standard (though technically amateur) shows is cheap and relatively hassle-free.

Basketball, volleyball (the national women's team won gold at the 2000 Sydney Olympic Games) and, to a lesser extent, football are all popular in Cuba, but *dominó* (always referred to in the singular) and chess, both considered sports, are national passions. Self-taught José Raúl Capablanca, touted as the greatest ever natural chess player, became World Chess Champion in 1921 and you'll see chess matches on the street and read about the masters in the sports pages. *Dominó* is everywhere and you'll see quartets of old men and young bucks slugging back shots of rum and slamming down their tiles in every Cuban neighborhood. In March 2003 Habana hosted the first annual Campeonato Mundial de Dominó (World Domino Championship), with 10 countries and thousands of players participating. The finals were held in Ciudad Deportiva, where Cuba won it all. Cockfighting, while technically illegal, is still practiced widely in Cuba (see p210) with clandestine shows attracting a large number of mainly male spectators who come to gamble away their hard-earned pesos.

*My Footsteps in Baraguá* (1996) is an English-speaking documentary made by Cuban director Gloria Rolando about Cuba's extensive West-Indian population from Jamaica and Barbados, who have resettled in the Ciego de Ávila town of Baraguá.

## MULTICULTURALISM

Despite the fact that institutionalized racism was abolished by law after the revolution, Cuba is still facing up to the difficult challenges of establishing lasting racial equality in a widely cosmopolitan and multicultural society. While there are no ghettos or gangs in Cuba's larger cities, a quick tally of the roaming *jineteros/as* in Vedado and Habana Vieja will reveal a far higher proportion of black participants. On the other side of the coin, over 90% of Cuban exiles are of white descent and of the victorious rebel army that took control of the government in 1959 only a handful (Juan Almeida being the most obvious example) were of mixed heritage.

## MEDIA

In a country replete with writers, scribes and poets, Cuba's media is without doubt one of the revolution's greatest failures. The only daily national newspaper – a dour eight-paged tabloid called *Granma* – is an insipid dose of politics, politics and yet more politics, all of which pours forth from the all-pervading, all-encompassing propaganda ministries of the Cuban Communist Party.

The silencing of the press was one of Castro's first political acts on taking power in 1959. Challenged with the crime of speaking out against the revolution, nearly all of Cuba's once independent newspapers were either closed down or taken over by the state by the summer of 1960. Many freelance operators faced a similar fate. In 1965 Guillermo Cabrera Infante, one of Cuba's most respected writers left for an ignominious exile in London after serving as a cultural attaché in Brussels while, three years later, Castro's former journalistic guru, Carlos Franqui – the man who had been responsible for the establishment of rebel newspaper *Revolución* in the Sierra Maestra – earned his own place on the black list for daring to speak out in opposition to the Soviet invasion of Czechoslovakia.

Of the 110 journalists imprisoned throughout the world in 2005, 23 were incarcerated in Cuba.

Although art, music and culture are actively encouraged in Cuban society, writers of all genres are set strict limits. Budding conformists, such as national poet, Nicolas Guillén, enjoy prestige, patronage and a certain amount of artistic freedom, while dissidents – Franqui, Infante and Herberto Padilla to name but three – face oppression, incarceration and the knowledge that their hard-won literary reputation will be quickly airbrushed out of Cuban history.

Despite some relaxation of press restrictions since the heavy-handed days of the 1970s and '80s, Cuban journalists must still operate inside strict press laws that prohibit the use of antigovernment propaganda and ban the seemingly innocuous act of 'insulting officials in public', a crime that carries a three year jail term.

Other limitations include the prohibition of private ownership of the electronic media and a law that prohibits foreign news agencies from hiring local journalists without first going through official government channels.

Most foreign observers, both in and outside of Cuba, agree that the Cuban media situation is an unmitigated disaster. Furthermore, in 2005 the New York–based Committee to Protect Journalists revealed that Cuba was one of the world's leading jailers of journalists.

## RELIGION

Religion is among the most misunderstood, misrepresented (by Castro's critics) and complex aspects of Cuban culture. Before the revolution 85% of Cubans were nominal Roman Catholics, though only 10% attended church regularly. Protestants made up most of the rest of the church-going public, though a smattering of Jews and Muslims have always practiced in Cuba and still do. When the revolution triumphed, 140 Catholic priests were expelled for reactionary political activities and another 400 left voluntarily, while the majority of Protestants, who represented society's poorer sector, had less to lose and stayed.

When the government declared itself Marxist-Leninist and therefore atheist, life for *creyentes* (literally 'believers') took on new difficulties. Though church services were never banned and freedom of religion never revoked, Christians were sent to Unidades Militares de Ayuda a la Producción (UMAPs; Military Production Aid Units), where it was hoped hard labor might reform their religious ways; homosexuals and vagrants

## CUBAN RELIGIONS OF AFRICAN ORIGIN

The complex religious rites of Regla de Ocha, or Santería as it is more widely known, offer a fascinating glimpse into the ancient traditions that permeate modern Cuba's ancient African soul.

The practice first took root in the 17th and 18th centuries when thousands of Yoruba slaves transported from West Africa brought with them a system of animistic beliefs that they hid beneath a Catholic veneer. Keeping tribes together in order to pit one group against another, the Spanish – who summarily baptized their new brethren on arrival – unwittingly allowed the practice of African religions to persist and prosper. Their survival depended on the convergence of ancient Yoruba beliefs with those of traditional Catholicism into a practice that came to be known as Santería (a derisive term invented by the Spanish).

By the 18th century, tribes such as the Arará, the Lucumí and the Congo were allowed to organize themselves into *cabildos* (associations). These *cabildos* provided entertainment, involving dance and music, on feast days for Catholic saints. Meanwhile, away from the spotlight, the slaves had begun to practice a crude form of their own religious worship, replacing each Catholic saint with an equivalent Yoruba *orisha* (a Santería deity).

Among the most important *orishas* is the androgynous creator god Obatalá, who is always dressed in white and associated with Christ or Nuestra Señora de la Merced. Obatalá's wife, Odudúa, goddess of the underworld, is replicated in a similar way by the image of the Virgin. Obatalá's son, Elegguá (St Anthony), is the god of destiny. Yemayá, the goddess of the ocean and mother of all *orishas,* is identified by the color blue and associated with Nuestra Señora de Regla. Changó, the Yoruba god of fire and war, lives in the tops of the royal palm trees and controls the lightning; his color is red and he's associated with Santa Bárbara. His son Aggayú Solá, god of land and protector of travelers, is associated with San Cristóbal (St Christopher). Ochún, wife of Changó and companion of Yemayá, is the goddess of love and the rivers, and is associated with Cuba's patron saint, the Virgin de la Caridad del Cobre (whose color is yellow). Ogún is associated with John the Baptist. Babalú Ayé (St Lazarus) is the *orisha* of disease.

It's likely there are more followers of the Afro-Cuban religions than practicing Roman Catholics in contemporary Cuba and although Regla de Ocha is by far the largest group it is by no means the only strand. *Orishas* in Santería, differ significantly from Catholic saints in the sense that they are fallible. The concepts of original sin and a final judgment are unknown. Instead, ancestral spirits are worshipped.

The rites of Santería are controlled by a male priest called a *babalawo,* of whom there are estimated to be 4000 in Cuba. The *babalawos* are often consulted for advice, to cure sicknesses or to grant protection, and offerings are placed before a small shrine in his home. Other rituals involve ecstatic dance, singing chants and animal sacrifice. The blood of animals such as chickens, doves and goats is offered to the *orishas* along with fruit and herbs at elaborate ceremonies as the *babalawo* sprays rum onto the altar from his mouth.

Cubans are surprisingly open about Santería, and travelers are welcome to inspect household shrines and attend ceremonies. Many hotels stage special Santería shows for visitors, but to uncover the real essence of Regla de Ocha you'll have to scratch a little deeper underneath the surface. Get talking at your casa particular, hang around the urban hotbeds (Guanabacoa in Habana, or Matanzas) or take to the streets and follow the sound of the drums. Don't forget to take a gift for the *orishas.*

were also sent to the fields to work. This was a short-lived experiment, however. More trying for believers were the hard-line Soviet days of the '70s and '80s when they were prohibited from joining the communist party and few, if any, believers held political posts. Certain university careers, notably in the humanities, were off-limits as well.

Things have changed dramatically since then, particularly in 1992 when the constitution was revised, removing all references to the Cuban state as Marxist-Leninist and recapturing the laical nature of the Cuban government. This led to an aperture in civil and political society for religious adherents and leaders and other reforms; for example, believers are now eligible for party membership. Since Cuban Catholicism gained the papal seal of approval with Pope John Paul II's visit in 1998, church attendance has surged and posters welcoming him are still displayed with pride. It's worth noting that churches have a strong youth presence. There are currently 400,000 Catholics regularly attending mass and 300,000 Protestants from 54 denominations. More evangelical denominations such as the Seventh Day Adventists and Pentecostals are rapidly growing in popularity.

The religious beliefs of Africans brought to Cuba as slaves were originally layered over Catholic iconography and doctrines, eventually forming new belief systems; see the boxed text p59. Santería is the most widespread of these and is an integrated part of daily life here; you'll see initiates dressed in white everywhere you go and many homes have altars tucked into the corners. Santería has served as a cultural ambassador of sorts, with new museums and dance and drum performances becoming standard itinerary fare. Some take exception to this 'folkloricization' of the sacred – dressing all in white has now become fashionable whether you're initiated or not, for example – and curious tourists may be taken to consultations with *babalawos* (priests) more interested in your money than your dilemmas.

## ARTS

In contrast to other communist countries, Cuba's reputation as a powerhouse of art and culture is nothing short of staggering. Each provincial town, no matter how small, has a Casa de Cultura that stages everything from traditional salsa music to innovative comedy nights and, on top of this, countless other theaters, organizations and institutions bring highbrow art to the masses completely free of charge.

In 1930 Spanish poet Federico Garcia Lorca escaped corrupt New York for harmonious Habana. Appearing as a guest university speaker he later described his three month stay in Cuba as 'the time of his life.'

The quality of what's on offer is equally amazing. The Cubans seem to have made a habit out of taking almost any artistic genre and replicating it perfectly. You'll pick up first-class Flamenco, ballet, classical music and Shakespearean theater here in the most mundane of places, not to mention Lorca plays, alternative cinema and illuminating deconstructions of novels by the likes of Márquez and Carpentier.

Several governmental organizations countrywide oversee the work of writers and artists, including the revered Casa de las Américas, the Unión de Escritores y Artistas de Cuba (Uneac; National Union of Cuban Writers and Artists) and its junior counterpart, Asociacíon Hermanos Saíz.

For information on Cuban music, check out the Music chapter (p66).

### Literature

In a country strewn with icons like rice at a wedding, José Martí (1853–95) is the master. Visionary, patriot and rebel, he was also a literary giant whose collected plays, essays and poetry fill 30 volumes. Exiled for his writings before he was 20, Martí lived most of his life outside Cuba, primarily in the US. His last book of poetry, *Versos Sencillos* (Simple Verses), is, as the title proclaims, full of simple verses and is arguably one of his best. Though written more than a century ago, the essays collected in *Nuestra America* (Our America) and *Los Estados Unidos* (The United States) are remarkably forward-thinking, providing a basis for Latin American self-determination in the face of US hegemony. For more on Martí's role as Cuban independence leader, see the History chapter (p38).

Like Martí, mulatto Nicolás Guillén (1902–89) is considered one of Cuba's world-class poets. Ahead of his time, he was one of the first mainstream champions of Afro-Cuban culture, writing rhythmic poems such as *Sóngoro Cosongo* (1931). A Communist who believed in social and racial equality, Guillén lived in exile during Batista's regime, writing *Elegía a Jesús Menéndez* (1951) and *La Paloma de Vuelo Popular* (*Elegías;* 1958). Some of his most famous poems are available in the English collection entitled *New Love Poetry: Elegy* (University of Toronto). He returned after the revolution and cofounded the Unión Nacional de Escritores y Artistas Cubanas (Uneac). Guillén was Cuba's national poet until his death.

Cubans are crazy for poetry, so don't be surprised when someone starts reeling off verses by Dulce María Loynaz (1902–97), recipient of Spain's coveted Miguel de Cervantes award; Eliseo Diego (1920–94), the poet's poet, whose words give wings to the human spirit; or singer-songwriter Silvio Rodríguez, who is a good guitar player, but a great poet (see p176).

In literature, as in poetry, the Cuban bibliography is awe inspiring. Novelist Alejo Carpentier (1904–80) was another exiled writer, returning after the revolution to write *El Recurso del Método* (Resource of Method) and *Concierto Barroco,* both published in 1974. The latter is considered his masterpiece. Habana fans will want to check out his *Ciudad de las Columnas* (The City of Columns; 1970), which juxtaposes B&W photographs of the city's architectural details with insightful prose.

Hollywood actor Andy Garcia – star of *The Untouchables, The Godfather III* and *Ocean's Eleven* – was born Andrés Arturo Garcia in Habana in 1956, but moved to Miami with his family at the age of five.

*Paradiso* by José Lezama Lima (1910–76) was a 'scandalous novel' when it appeared in 1966 because of its erotic (homosexual) scenes. Now it's considered a classic. Lezama was a poet and essayist who cofounded the influential magazine *Orígenes* in 1944.

Notable writers who left Cuba after the revolution include playwright Reinaldo Arenas, whose autobiography *Before Night Falls* (1943–90) was made into a critically acclaimed drama for the silver screen; and Guillermo Cabrera Infante (b 1929), whose *Tres Tristes Tigres* (Three Trapped Tigers; 1967) describes cultural decadence during the Batista era. Of course, Cuba's most famous foreign writer-in-residence was Ernest Hemingway, who wrote *For Whom the Bell Tolls* in the Ambos Mundos Hotel in Habana (p118).

### Cinema & Television

The film industry is run by the Instituto Cubano del Arte e Industria Cinematográficos, better known as Icaic, and it has been creating quality films since its founding in 1959. You can't talk about Icaic and not Alfredo Guevara, the institute's longtime director. Guevara is recognized, along with several influential filmmakers including Tomás Gutiérrez Alea (aka Titón, 1928–96), as the spinal column of Cuban cinema. Themes that aren't generally explored in other parts of Cuban society (bureaucratic paranoia, homosexuality and misogyny for starters) are given full airtime in Cuban movies and this quasi-autonomous, critical space carved out by Icaic is almost one-of-a-kind; *nueva trova* (philosophical folk/guitar music) commentary comes close, but few songs are as explicit as the film *Fresa y Chocolate* (Strawberry and Chocolate) for example.

Cuba's macro-cultural approach has fueled other mediums, including animation and video, genres that cinema snobs might sniff at but which are full-blown industries here. Movies, shorts, videos and animation from all over the hemisphere can be seen at the annual Festival Internacional del Nuevo Cine Latinoamericano in Habana (p457), which is like Cannes without the ass kissing. To say that Cubans are cinema buffs is an understatement: the crush of a crowd shattered the glass doors of a movie theater during the 2001 festival and an adoring mob nearly rioted trying to get into Steven Spielberg's *Minority Report* premier in 2002. If you're headed for a flick, queue early.

*Viva Cuba* (2005), written and directed by Juan Carlos Cremata Malberti, is Cuba's most recent internationally-profiled cinematic offering. Billed as part Romeo-and-Juliet romance and part quirky coming-of-age road movie, it tells the story of two children from vastly different Cuban backgrounds who travel across the length of the country in order to find a lost relative. Mixing humor with pathos the movie, which is ostensibly about the emigration issue, covers a multitude of different aspects of Cuban life and is, in the words of its director Cremata 'the story of everything that is happening in Cuba today.'

Cuban TV is special (not least of all because the most unattractive people you're likely to see in Cuba are on it). There are only three national channels, no commercials and charming touches (eg the nightly programming announcement closes with the advisory: 'consume only what is necessary'). Educational programming dominates, with Universidad Para Todos offering full university-level courses in everything from astronomy to film editing and Canal Educativo broadcasting primary and secondary classes. The news is a predictable litany of good things Cuba has done (eg big tobacco harvest, sending doctors to Africa) and bad things the US is up to (eg mucking around in the Middle East, big corporations buying influence). *Mesa Redonda* (Round Table) is a nightly program where several people sharing the same opinion sit around discussing a topic of national or global import. *Telenovelas* (soap operas) are a national obsession and things often grind to a halt when the *telenovela* starts.

In 1983 Cuban exiles in Miami blocked the filming of the Brian de Palma movie *Scarface* in their home city after writer Oliver Stone refused to yield to their demands to include scenes of anti-Castro activity in the script.

## Architecture

Stylistically-speaking, Cuba is a smorgasbord of different architectural genres with influences ranging from Spanish Moorish to French neoclassical to decorative colonial-baroque. Emerging relatively unscathed from the turmoil of three separate revolutionary wars, well-preserved cities such as Camagüey, Santiago and the capital Habana have survived into the 21st century with the bulk of their original colonial features remarkably intact. The preservation has been aided further by the nomination of Trinidad, Cienfuegos and Habana Vieja as Unesco World Heritage sites.

Some of Cuba's oldest and most engaging architectural creations can be seen in the network of Spanish fortresses erected around the country during the 16th and 17th centuries to deter attacks from pirates and corsairs on the island's coastal cities. Notable examples include Habana's Castillo de la Real Fuerza (p96), the second oldest fort in the Americas; the labyrinthine Castillo de San Pedro del Morro (p404), in Santiago, designed by Italian military architect Giovanni Bautista Antonelli; and the massive Cabaña (p161) overlooking Habana Bay, the largest fort in the Americas.

Cuban townscapes in the 17th and 18th centuries were dominated by ecclesial architecture, reflected initially in the noble cloisters of Habana's Convento de Santa Clara (p98) built in 1632, and culminating a century or so later in the magnificent Catedral de San Cristóbal (p93), considered by many as the country's most outstanding baroque monument. Some of the best architecture from this period can be viewed in Habana Vieja whose peculiar layout around *four* main squares – each with its own specific social or religious function – set it apart from other Spanish colonial capitals.

With a booming economy and cash raked in from a series of record-breaking sugarcane harvests, plantation-owners in the small town of Trinidad had money to burn at the start of the 19th century. Ideally positioned to the south of the verdant Valle de los Ingenios and heavily influenced by haute couture furnishings of Italy, France and Georgian England, the city's enterprising sugar merchants ploughed their vast industrial profits into a revitalized new city full of exquisite homes and businesses that juxtaposed popular baroque and neoclassical styles with vernacular Cuban features such as wooden *rejas* (grilles), high ceilings, and tiny *postigos* (doors). Isolated on the southern coast and protected by law as part of a Unesco World Heritage site, the unique and beautiful streets of 19th-century Trinidad remain one of Latin America's most intact colonial cities.

By the mid-19th century sturdy neoclassical buildings were the norm among the country's native bourgeoisie in cities such as Cienfuegos and Matanzas with bold symmetrical lines, grandiose frontages and rows of imposing columns replacing the decorative baroque flourishes of the early colonial period. The style reached its high water mark in an impressive trio of glittering theaters: the Caridad in Santa Clara (p276), the Sauto in Matanzas (p228) and the Terry Tomás in Cienfuegos (p259). In the 1920s and '30s a neoclassical revival delivered a brand new clutch of towering giants onto the Habana skyline, including the Washington-influenced Capitolio (p99), the monumental Hotel Nacional (p104) and the Athenian Universidad de la Habana (p104).

Eclecticism was the leading style in the new republican era post-1902, with a combination of regurgitated genres such as neo-Gothic, neo-baroque, neo-renaissance and neo-Moorish giving rise to a hotchpotch of groundbreaking buildings that were as eye-catching as they were outrageous. For a wild tour of Cuban eclecticism check out the Museo de Ciencias Naturales Sandalio de Noda in Pinar del Río (p196), the Presidential Palace (now the Museo de la Revolución) in Habana (p102) or the Byzantium-meets-Arabic Palacio de Valle in Cienfuegos (p259).

Fidel and Hemingway met only once at a 1960 fishing tournament organized by Hemingway in Habana. Not surprisingly, the combative Castro won first prize.

Bridging the gap between eclecticism and modernism was art deco, a lavish architectural style epitomized in structures such as New York's Chrysler building, but best manifested in Cuba in Habana's opulent Bacardí building (p113) or some of the religious iconology exhibited in the Necrópolis Cristóbal Colón (p108).

Modernism arrived in Habana in the 1950s with a rapid surge of prerevolutionary skyscrapers that eliminated decorative flourishes and merged 'function' rather harmoniously with 'form.' Visitors can pursue this rich architectural legacy in the cubic Hotel Habana Libre (p104) or the skyline-hogging Focsa building (p104), an edifice that was constructed – legend has it – without the use of a single crane.

## Painting & Sculpture

Painting and sculpture is alive and well in Cuba, despite more than four decades of asphyxiating on-off censorship. From the archaic cave paintings of Cueva Punta del Este on Isla de la Juventud to the vibrant poster art of 1960s Habana, a colorful and broad-ranging artistic pastiche has been painstakingly conserved through arts schools, government sponsorship and an eclectic mix of cross-cultural influences that include everything from Diego Rivera–style murals to European avant-gardism.

Engaging and visceral, modern Cuban art combines lurid Afro–Latin American colors with the harsh reality of a 47-year-old revolution. For visiting foreign art lovers it's a unique and intoxicating brew. Forced into a corner by the constrictions of the culture-redefining Cuban Revolution, budding artists have invariably found that, by co-opting with (as opposed to confronting) the socialist regime, opportunities for academic training and artistic encouragement are almost unlimited. Encased in such a volatile creative climate the concept of graphic art in Cuba – well-established in its own right before the revolution – has flourished exponentially.

Serigraphy was first employed on the island at the beginning of the 20th century, but this distinctive style of silk-screen printing didn't gather ground until the 1940s when, in connection with film and political posters, it enjoyed a wide distribution. The genre exploded after the 1959 revolution when bodies such as Icaic and the propagandist Editora Política were enthusiastically sponsored by the Castro government to create thousands of informative posters designed to rally the Cuban population behind the huge tasks of building a 'New Society.' Eschewing standard Soviet realism, Cuban poster artists mixed inherent Latin American influences with the eye-catching imagery of 1960s pop culture to create a brand new subgenre of their own. This innovative form of poster art can best be viewed at the Taller de Serigrafia Rene Portocarrero in Habana Vieja (p139).

The 1964 Cuban/Soviet film *Soy Cuba* (I am Cuba) has recently been resurrected as an erstwhile movie classic by a clutch of contemporary directors such as Martin Scorcese for its highly innovative tracking shots and poetic plot.

Internationally-speaking, art in Cuba is dominated by the prolific figure of Wilfredo Lam, a painter, sculptor and ceramicist of mixed Chinese, African and Spanish ancestry. Born in Sagua Grande, Villa Clara Province in 1902, Lam studied art and law in Habana before departing for Madrid in 1923 to pursue his artistic ambitions in the fertile fields of post-WWI Europe. Displaced by the Spanish Civil War in 1937 he gravitated toward France where he became friends with Pablo Picasso and swapped ideas with the pioneering surrealist André Breton. Having absorbed various cubist and surrealist influences, Lam returned to Cuba in 1941 where he produced his own seminal masterpiece *La Jungla* (the Jungle), considered by critics to be one of the Third World's most representative paintings.

Post-Lam Cuba's unique artistic heritage has survived and prospered in Habana's Centro Wilfredo Lam (p93) and the Instituto Superior de Arte (p148) in outlying Cubanacán. The capital is also blessed with a splendid national art museum, the sprawling Museo Nacional de Bellas Artes (p102) housed in two separate buildings. Outside of Habana further inspiration can be found in scattered artistic communities in the cities of Santiago, Camagüey and Baracoa. Diehards can also uncover notable artistic work hiding beneath the surface in other less heralded cultural outposts such as Las Tunas (known locally as the 'city of sculptures').

## Theater & Dance

Cuban ballet is synonymous with prima ballerina Alicia Alonso. After her pointe days she cofounded the Ballet Nacional de Cuba and her choreography is still in heavy rotation – classic stuff such as *Don Quixote* and *Giselle*, with few surprises. The International Ballet Festival (p457) takes Habana by storm every other year, when you can see a *Swan Lake* matinee and an evening performance of *Carmen* – a ballet junkie's dream. The Ballet de Camagüey also features talented dancers, with a riskier, less formal, repertory.

Modern dance, mixing ballet, folklore and sensualized choreography, is the purview of DanzAbierta, Así Somos (founded by US-born Lorna Burdsall in 1981) and Danza Teatro Retazos. The latter is directed by Ecuadorian spitfire Isabel Bustos, who also organizes the Encuentro

Internacional de Danza en Paisajes Urbanos, an event that sees national and international dance companies take over the streets of Habana Vieja. Danza Contemporánea de Cuba (also cofounded by Burdsall) blends ballet with Cuban rhythms and themes that some purists find too commercial. Still, the dancing is exceptional and the company has fresh choreography, costuming and storytelling ideas. The flexible Lizt Alfonso company has been repeatedly turning heads lately with their unique blend of Cuban, African and Spanish rhythms and moves. Look for their work called *Elementos*.

In response to the 2005 Kashmir earthquake, Cuba sent 2260 health workers to Pakistan, 1400 of them doctors, where they have attended to more than 200,000 patients.

The repertory of the Conjunto Folklórico Nacional de Cuba (founded in 1962) is a veritable history of Cuban popular dance, and the palpitating rainbow of traditional Afro-Cuban dances they perform often has Teatro Mella audiences on their feet. You can rumba along with them every Saturday at Habana's El Gran Palenque (p133). La Colmenita is Cuba's respected National Children's Theater Company whose cast of seven- to 15-year-olds interprets classics such as Shakespeare's *A Midsummer Night's Dream*.

Of course, Cuba also means salsa. Kids here pair off as soon as they can walk and once the basic steps and turns are rote they move on to *la rueda* (the wheel), where two concentric circles move in opposite directions – boys on the outside, girls on the inside – with each pair taking a twirl together before the wheel turns and they're dancing with someone new. It's as hard as it looks, and you might want to look into some classes when you arrive (see p454).

# Music

'In Cuba the music flows like a river,' wrote Ry Cooder in his sleeve notes to the seminal *Buena Vista Social Club* CD, 'It takes care of you and rebuilds you from the inside out.'

Rich, vibrant, layered and soulful, Cuban music has long acted as a standard bearer for the sounds and rhythms emanating out of Latin America. From the down-at-heel docks of Matanzas to the bucolic local villages of the Sierra Maestra, everything from *son*, salsa, rumba, mambo, *chachachá, charanga* and *danzón* owe at least a part of their existence to the magical musical dynamism that was first ignited here.

Aside from the obvious Spanish and African roots, Cuban music has intermittently called upon a number of other important influences in the process of its embryonic development. Mixed into an already exotic melting pot are genres from France, the United States, Haiti and Jamaica. Conversely Cuban music has also played a key role in developing various melodic styles and movements in other parts of the world. In Spain they called this process *ida y vuelta* (return music) and it is most clearly evident in a style of Nuevo flamenco called *Guajira*. Elsewhere the 'Cuban effect' can be traced back to forms as diverse as New Orleans jazz, New York salsa and West African Afrobeat.

Hello, Goodbye. In January 2000 Paul McCartney became the only member of The Beatles to visit Cuba when he stopped over for four hours in Santiago de Cuba during the course of a vacation in the Caicos Islands. Popping into the Casa de la Trova he enjoyed a brief set of traditional music before heading for lunch in the nearby Restaurante El Morro.

## FOLKLORIC ROOTS

*Son,* Cuba's instantly recognizable signature music, first emerged from the mountains of the Oriente region in the second half of the 19th century; though the earliest known testimonies go back as far as 1570. Famously described by Cuban ethnologist Fernando Ortiz as 'a love affair between the African drum and the Spanish guitar,' the roots of this eclectic and intricately fused rural music lie in two distinct subgenres: rumba and *danzón.*

While drumming in the North American colonies was ostensibly prohibited, the Spanish were slightly less mean-spirited in the treatment of their African brethren. As a result Cuban slaves were able to preserve and pass on many of their musical traditions via influential Santería *cabildos,* religious brotherhoods that re-enacted ancient African percussive music on simple *batá* drums or *chequeré* rattles. Performed at annual festivals or on special Catholic saint's days, this rhythmic yet highly textured dance music was offered up as a form of religious worship to the *orishas* (deities).

Over time the ritualistic drumming of Santería evolved into a more complex genre known as rumba. Rumba first metamorphosed in the dock areas of Habana and Matanzas during the 1890s when slaves, exposed to itinerant foreign influences, began to knock out rhythmic patterns on old cargo boxes in their spare time. Vocals were added, dances emerged, and pretty soon the music had grown into a collective form of social expression for all black Afro-Cubans.

Rumba music today has three basic forms: *guaguancó* (an overtly sexual dance), *yambú* (a slow couple's dance) and *columbia* (a fast aggressive male dance often involving fire torches and machetes).

On the other side of the musical equation sat *danzón,* a type of refined European dance closely associated with the French contredanse or the English 'country dance' of the 19th century. Pioneered by innovative Matanzas band leader Miguel Failde in the 1880s, the Cuban *danzón* quickly developed its own peculiar syncopated rhythm borrowing heavily from Haitian slave influences and, later on, adding such improbable extras as conga drums and vocalists. By the early 20th century Cuban *danzóns* had evolved from a stately ballroom dance played by an *orchestra típica* into a more jazzed up free-for-all known alternatively as *charanga, danzonete* or *danzón-chá*.

Welded together, rumba and *danzón* provided the musical backbone that ultimately paved the way for *son*, a distinctive blend of anticipated African rhythms and melodic rustic guitars over which a singer would improvise from a traditional 10-line Spanish poem known as a *décima*.

In its pure form, *son* was played by a sextet consisting of guitar, *tres* (guitar with three sets of double strings), double bass, bongo and two singers who played maracas and *claves* (sticks that tap out the beat). Arising from the precipitous mountains of Cuba's influential east, the genre's earliest exponents were the legendary Trio Oriental, who stabilized the sextet format in 1912 when they were reborn as the Sexteto Habanero. Another early *sonero* was singer Miguel Matamoros, whose self-penned *son* classics such as *Son de la Loma* and *Lagrimas Negras* are de rigueur among Cuba's ubiquitous musical entertainers, even today.

By the 1930s the sexteto had become a septeto with the addition of a trumpet and exciting new musicians such as blind *tres* player Arsenio Rodríguez – a songwriter who Harry Belafonte once called the 'father of salsa' – were paving the way for mambo and *chachachá*.

Cuban mambo king Benny Moré's great-great-grandfather was the king of a tribe in the Congo who was captured by slave traders and sold to a Cuban plantation owner.

## EL BÁRBARO DEL RITMO

In the '40s and '50s the *son* bands grew from seven pieces to eight and beyond until they became big bands boasting full horn and percussion sections that played rumba, *chachachá* and mambo. The reigning mambo king was Benny Moré, who, with his velvety voice and rocking 21-piece all-black band, was known as *El Bárbaro del Ritmo* (The Barbarian of Rhythm).

Born in Santa Isabel de las Lajas, Cienfuegos Province in 1919, the eldest of 18 children, Moré quickly became the nexus point for almost every new Cuban sound in production and was largely responsible for placing Cuban music on the international map. Proficient in *son*, mambo, bolero, *guaracha, afro* and *guaguancó* he toured Mexico, Venezuela, Haiti and the US throughout the 1950s and his 40-piece Banda Gigante even performed at Hollywood's Academy Awards ceremony. Few Cubans deny him his place in musical folklore. 'He was a showman and he was the greatest of them all,' said Compay Segundo of Moré years later, 'No one else came near.'

## SALSA & JAZZ

Salsa emerged from the fertile Latin New York scene of the '60s and '70s when jazz, *son* and rumba blended to create a new brassier sound. Self-styled queen of salsa Celia Cruz was a leading exponent in the US while Cuba's most famous salsa outfit was (and still is) Los Van Van, formed by Juan Formell in 1969. Still performing regularly throughout the island, Los Van Van won top honors in 2000 when they memorably took home a Grammy for their classic album, *Llego Van Van*.

Jazz, considered the music of the enemy in the revolution's most dogmatic days, has always seeped into Cuban sounds. Jesus 'Chucho' Valdes' band Irakere, formed in 1973, broke the Cuban music scene wide open with its heavy Afro-Cuban drumming laced with jazz and *son*. Jazz also mixed with rap and deep salsa grooves in a new style called *timba*, championed by NG La Banda, which formed in 1988. Other musicians associated with the Cuban jazz set include pianist Gonzalo Rubalcaba, Isaac Delgado and Adalberto Álvarez y Su Son.

## LOS TROVADORES

Initially *trovadores* (traditional singers/songwriters) were like old-fashioned traveling minstrels, itinerant songsmiths who plied their musical trade across the island in the early part of the 20th century, moving from village to village and city to city with the carefree spirit of perennial gypsies. Armed with simple acoustic guitars and furnished with a seemingly limitless repertoire of soft lilting rural ballads, early Cuban *trovadores* included Sindo Garay, Nico Saquito and Joseíto Fernández, the man responsible for composing all-time Cuban blockbuster, *Guantanamera.* As the style developed into the 1960s, new advocates such as Carlos Puebla from Bayamo gave the genre a grittier and more political edge penning classic songs such as *Hasta Siempre Comandante,* his romantic if slightly sycophantic ode to Che Guevara.

*Nueva trova* was very much a product of the revolution and paralleled – though rarely copied – folk music in the US and the emerging *nueva canción* scene that was taking shape in Chile and Argentina. Stylistically the music also paid indirect homage to the rich tradition of French *chansons* that had been imported into Cuba via Haiti in the 19th century. Political in nature, yet melodic in tone, *nueva trova* first burst forth from the Oriental towns of Manzanillo and Bayamo in the early 1970s before being driven outwards and upwards by such illustrious names as Silvio Rodríguez and native Bayameso Pablo Milanés. Highly influential

### TROVA: CUBA'S MUSIC HOUSES

In March 1968 – hot on the heels of The Beatles' *Sgt Pepper's Lonely Heart's Club Band* and Dylan's *Highway 61 Revisited* – the Castro administration opened up Cuba's first Casa de la Trova in the eastern city of Santiago de Cuba. Founded on the philosophy of 'if you can sing or play an instrument, show us what you can do,' these legendary impromptu musical houses quickly became a national phenomenon, spreading in a matter of months to other provincial towns such as Camagüey, Guantánamo and Trinidad.

Aside from offering first-class musical entertainment, *trova* (traditional poetic singing) houses were created with two distinct aims. Firstly, to keep alive Cuba's unique cultural heritage and secondly, to pass its skills and showmanship onto future generations.

In the decades since the 1960s, despite challenges from other embryonic musical genres such as *reggaeton* (Cuban hip-hop), the houses have grown and prospered.

Indeed, in cities such as Santiago de Cuba, a *trova* gig is still considered to be the ultimate artistic accolade, with old stalwarts – such as Buena Vista Social Club luminary Eliades Ochoa – regularly hosting shows, for an entry fee of as little as CUC$2.

For the Cubans, the venues have multiple attractions. At liberty to drink, talk, date and debate inside the smoky dancehalls and atmospheric colonial courtyards that characterize these timeless music houses, cash-pinched locals can salsa energetically into the small hours, temporarily oblivious to the difficulties and hardships that have become a way of life since the onset of the *período especial* (special period).

Culturally speaking, different casas showcase different music depending on the region. In cosmopolitan Santiago de Cuba, *son* is the signature tune while 100km to the east, in provincial Guantánamo, a more rhythmic genre called *chagúi* is king. Head west toward Pinar del Río, however, and you're back in the land of the *Guajira.*

Since the early 1990s Casas de la Trova have welcomed tourists and foreigners in increasing numbers. For the most popular venues check out the individual city sections.

**HIP-HOP NATION**

Born in the ugly concrete housing projects of Alamar, Habana, Cuban hip-hop, rather like its US counterpart, has gritty and impoverished roots.

First beamed across the nation in the early 1980s when American rap was picked up on homemade rooftop antennae from Miami-based radio stations, the new musical genre quickly gained ground among a population of urban blacks culturally redefining themselves during the inquietude of the *período especial*. By the 1990s groups like Public Enemy and NWA were de rigueur on the streets of Alamar and in 1995 there was enough hip-hop to throw a festival.

Tempered by Latin influences and censored by the parameters of strict revolutionary thought, *reggaeton* has taken on a distinctive flavor all of its own. Instrumentally the music uses *batás* (conical two-headed drums), congos and electric bass, while lyrically the songs tackle important national issues such as sex tourism and the difficulties of the stagnant Cuban economy.

Today there are upwards of 800 hip-hop groups in Cuba and the Cuban Rap Festival (held every August) is entering its second decade. The event even has a sponsor, the fledgling Cuban Rap Agency, a government body formed in 2002 to give official sanction to the country's burgeoning alternative music scene.

throughout the Spanish-speaking world during the '60s and '70s, *nueva trova* was often an inspirational source of protest music for the impoverished and downtrodden populations of Latin America, many of whom looked to Cuba for spiritual leadership in an era of corrupt dictatorships and US cultural hegemony. This reciprocated solidarity is echoed in many of Rodríguez's internationally lauded classics such as *Canción Urgente para Nicaragua* (in support of the Sandinistas), *La Maza* (in support of Salvador Allende in Chile) and *Canción para mi Soldado* (in support of Cuban soldiers in Angola).

## MODERN CURRENTS

The contemporary Cuban music scene is an interesting mix of enduring traditions, modern sounds, old hands and new blood. With low production costs, solid urban themes and lots of US-inspired crossover styles, hip-hop and rap are taking the younger generation by storm. Groups like Obsession, 100% Original, Freehole Negro (co-fronted by a woman) and Anónimo Consejo perform regularly and everyone comes out for the Cuban Rap Festival held in the Habana suburb of Alamar every August (see boxed text, above).

It's hard to categorize Interactivo, a collaboration of young, talented musicians led by pianist Robertico Carcassés. Part funk, jazz and rock, and very 'in the groove,' this band jams to the rafters; a guaranteed good time. Interactivo's bassist is Yusa, a young black woman whose eponymous debut album made it clear she's one of the most innovative musicians on the Cuban scene today.

Meanwhile, back at base camp, US guitar virtuoso Ry Cooder inadvertently breathed new life into Cuban *son* music 10 years ago with his remarkable *Buena Vista Social Club* CD. Linking together half a dozen or so long-retired musical sages from the '40s and '50s, including 90-year-old Compay Segundo, (writer of Cuba's second-most played song *Chan Chan*) and the pianist Rúben González (ranked by Cooder as the greatest piano player he had ever heard), the unprepossessing American producer sat back in the studio and let his ragged clutch of old-age pensioners work their erstwhile magic. Over two million albums later and European and North American audiences are still enraptured by the sounds.

In 2001 Welsh group the Manic Street Preachers became the first Western rock band to play live in Cuba. After the concert, which took place in Habana's Karl Marx theater, Castro commented that he considered their music to be 'louder than war.'

# Environment

## THE LAND

Measuring 1250km from east to west and from between 31km and 193km north to south, Cuba is the Caribbean's largest island with a total land area of 110,860 sq km. Shaped like an alligator and situated just south of the Tropic of Cancer the country is actually an archipelago made up of 4195 smaller islets and coral reefs, though the bulk of the territory is concentrated on the expansive Isla Grande and its 2200-sq-km smaller cousin, La Isla de la Juventud.

Formed by a volatile mixture of volcanic activity, plate tectonics and erosion, the landscape of Cuba is a lush and varied concoction of caves, mountains, plains, mogotes and strange flat-topped hills. The highest point, Pico Turquino (1972m) is situated in the east among the lofty triangular peaks of the Sierra Maestra while further west, in the no less majestic Escambray Mountains, ruffled hilltops and gushing waterfalls straddle the borders of Cienfuegos, Villa Clara and Sancti Spíritus Provinces. Rising like purple shadows in the far west, the 175km-long Cordillera de Guanguanico, is a more diminutive range that includes the protected Sierra del Rosario reserve and the distinctive pincushion hills of the Viñales Valley.

The hottest ever temperature recorded in Cuba was 38.6°C (101.5°F) at Guantánamo on August 7, 1969.

Lapped by the warm turquoise waters of the Caribbean Sea in the south and the foamy, white chop of the Atlantic Ocean in the north, Cuba's 5746km of coastline shelters more than 300 natural beaches and features one of the largest tracts of coral reef in the world. Home to more than 900 reported species of fish and more than 410 varieties of sponge and coral, the country's unspoiled coastline is a marine wonderland that entices tourists from all over the globe.

The 7200m-deep Cayman Trench between Cuba and Jamaica forms the boundary of the North American and Caribbean plates. Tectonic movements have tilted the island over time, creating uplifted limestone cliffs along parts of the north coast and low mangrove swamps on the south. Over millions of years, Cuba's limestone bedrock has been eroded by underground rivers, creating interesting geological features including the 'haystack' hills of Viñales and more than 20,000 caves countrywide.

As a sprawling archipelago, Cuba boasts thousands of islands and keys (most uninhabited) in four major offshore groups: the Archipiélago de los Colorados, off northern Pinar del Río; the Archipiélago de Sabana-Camagüey (or Jardines del Rey), off northern Villa Clara and Ciego de Ávila; the Archipiélago de los Jardines de la Reina, off southern Ciego de Ávila; and the Archipiélago de los Canarreos, around Isla de la Juventud. Most visitors will experience one or more of these island idylls, as the majority of resorts, scuba diving and virgin beaches are found in these regions.

Being a narrow island, never measuring more than 200km north to south, means Cuba's capacity for large lakes and rivers is severely limited (preventing hydroelectricity). Cuba's longest river, the 343km-long Río Cauto, that flows from the Sierra Maestra in a rough loop north of Bayamo, is only navigable by small boats for 80km. To compensate, 632 *embalses* (reservoirs) or *presas* (dams), larger than 5km altogether, have been created for irrigation and water supply; these supplement the almost unlimited groundwater held in Cuba's limestone bedrock.

Lying in the Caribbean's main hurricane region, Cuba has been hit by some blinders in recent years including the two devastating 2005 storms: Dennis and Wilma.

Dennis, an unseasonable early arrival, ripped across the island's southern coast on July 7 from Santiago de Cuba to Cienfuegos causing US$1.4 billion of damage, destroying 120,000 homes and claiming 16 lives. Wilma, meanwhile, unleashed its full fury on Habana on October 22 causing extensive flooding to already dilapidated buildings along the famous Malecón seawall. Although more than 700,000 people were evacuated in anticipation of Wilma's arrival, Cuban rescue services still had to bale out hundreds of stranded householders using special amphibious vehicles.

## WILDLIFE

### Animals

While it isn't exactly the Serengeti, Cuba has its fair share of indigenous fauna and animal lovers won't be disappointed. Birds are probably the biggest draw card (see p31) and Cuba boasts more than 350 different varieties, 70 of which are indigenous. Head to the mangroves of Ciénaga de Zapata near the Bahía de Cochinos (Bay of Pigs) or the Península de Guanahacabibes in Pinar del Río for the best sightings of the blink-and-you'll-miss-it *zunzuncito* (bee hummingbird), the world's smallest bird and, at 6.5cm, not much longer than a toothpick. These areas are also home to the *tocororo* (Cuban trogon), Cuba's national bird, which sports the red, white and blue colors of the Cuban flag. Other popular bird species include flamingos (by the thousand), *cartacubas* (a type of Cuban bird), herons, spoonbills, parakeets and rarely-spotted Cuban Pygmy Owls.

Cuba's worst ever hurricane occurred on November 9, 1932 off the southern coast of Camagüey Province. It caused a 6m high tidal wave and left more than 3000 people dead.

Land mammals have been hunted almost to extinction with the largest indigenous survivor the friendly *jutía* (tree rat), a 4kg edible rodent that scavenges on isolated keys living in relevant harmony with armies of inquisitive iguanas. Other odd species include the *mariposa de cristal* (Cuban clearwing butterfly), one of only two clear-winged butterflies in the world; the rare *manjuarí* (Cuban alligator gar), an odd, ancient fish considered a living fossil; and the *polimita*, a unique land snail distinguished by its festive yellow, red and brown bands.

Reptiles are well represented in Cuba. Aside from crocodiles, iguanas and lizards, there are 15 species of snake, none of which are poisonous. Cuba's largest snake is the *majá*, a constrictor related to the anaconda that grows up to 4m long; it's nocturnal and doesn't usually mess with humans.

Cuba's marine life makes up for what it lacks in land fauna. The manatee, the world's only herbivorous aquatic mammal, is found in the Bahía de Taco and the Península de Zapata, and whale sharks frequent the María la Gorda area at Cuba's eastern tip from August to November. Four turtle species (leatherback, loggerhead, green and hawksbill) are found in Cuban waters and they nest annually in isolated keys or on the protected western beaches of the Guanahacabibes Peninsula.

#### ENDANGERED SPECIES

Due to habitat loss and persistent hunting by humans many of Cuba's animals and birds are listed as endangered species. These include the Cuban crocodile, a fearsome reptile that has the smallest habitat of any crocodile, existing only in the Zapata swamps and in the Lanier swamps on Isla de la Juventud. Other vulnerable species include the *jutía*, which was hunted mercilessly during the *período especial* (special period; Cuba's new economic reality post 1991) when hungry Cubans tracked them for their meat (they still do – in fact it is considered something of a delicacy); the Tree Boa, a native snake that lives in rapidly diminishing woodland areas; and the elusive *carpintero real* (royal carpenter woodpecker), spotted after a 40-year gap in the Parque Nacional Alejandro de Humboldt near Baracoa in the late 1980s, but not seen since.

The seriously endangered West Indian manatee, while protected from illegal hunting, continues to suffer from a variety of manmade threats, most notably from contact with boat propellers, suffocation caused by fishing nets and poisoning from residues pumped into rivers from sugar factories.

Cuba is home to both the world's smallest toad, the *ranita de Cuba* (Cuban tree toad; 1cm), and the world's smallest bird, the *zunzuncito* (bee hummingbird; 6.5cm).

Cuba has an ambiguous attitude toward the hunting of turtles. Hawksbill turtles are protected under the law, though a clause allows for up to 500 of them to be captured per year in certain areas (Camagüey and Isla de la Juventud). Travelers will occasionally encounter *tortuga* (turtle) on the menu in places such as Baracoa. You are advised not to partake as these turtles may have been caught illegally.

## Plants

Cuba is synonymous with the palm tree and through songs, symbols, landscapes and legends the two are inextricably linked. The national tree is the *palma real* (royal palm), and it's central to the country's coat of arms and the Cristal beer logo. It's believed there are 20 million royal palms in Cuba and locals will tell you that wherever you stand on the island you'll always be within sight of one of them. Marching single file by the roadside or clumped on a hill, these majestic trees reach up to 40m tall and are easily identified by their lithesome trunk and green stalk at the top. There are also *cocotero* (coconut palms); *palma barrigona* (big belly palms), with their characteristic bulge; and the extremely rare *palma corcho* (cork palm). The latter is a link with the Cretaceous period (between 65 and 135 million years ago) and is cherished as a living fossil. You can see examples of it on the grounds of the Museo de Ciencias Naturales Sandalio de Noda (p196) and La Ermita (p207), both in Pinar del Río Province. All told, there are 90 palm tree types in Cuba.

Cuban tobacco and cigar exports net approximately CUC$200 million annually, but every year 6000 Cubans die from smoking-related illnesses.

Other important trees include mangroves, in particular the spiderlike mangroves that protect the Cuban shoreline from erosion and provide an important habitat for small fish and birds. Mangroves account for 26% of Cuban forests and cover almost 5% of the island's coast; Cuba ranks ninth in the world in terms of mangrove density, and the most extensive swamps are situated in the Ciénaga de Zapata.

The largest native pine forests grow on Isla de la Juventud (the former Isle of Pines), in western Pinar del Río, in eastern Holguín (or more specifically the Sierra Cristal Mountains) and in central Guantánamo. These forests are especially susceptible to fire damage, and pine reforestation has been a particular headache for the island's environmentalists.

Rain forests exist at higher altitudes – between approximately 500m and 1500m – in the Escambray, Sierra Maestra and Macizo de Sagua-Baracoa Mountains. Original rain forest species include ebony and mahogany, but today most reforestation is in eucalyptus, which is graceful and fragrant, but invasive.

Dotted liberally across the island, ferns, cacti and orchids contribute hundreds of species, many endemic, to Cuba's rich cornucopia of plant life. For the best concentrations check out the botanical gardens in Santiago de Cuba (p421) for ferns and cacti and Pinar del Río (p215) for

### UNESCO WORLD HERITAGE & BIOSPHERE RESERVE SITES

There are currently six Unesco Biosphere Reserves in Cuba and eight World Heritage sites. The most recent addition was the city of Cienfuegos, whose splendidly preserved neoclassical core was deservedly added to the list in July 2005.

The biosphere reserves are: the Reserva Sierra del Rosario (25,000 hectares; declared in 1984) and the Reserva Península de Guanahacabibes (101,500 hectares; 1987), both in Pinar del Río; Ciénaga de Zapata (628,171 hectares; 2001) in Matanzas; Buenavista (313,500 hectares; 2000) in parts of Villa Clara, Sancti Spíritus and Ciego de Ávila; Parque Baconao (84,600 hectares; 1987) in Santiago de Cuba; and the Reserva Cuchillas de Toa (127,500 hectares; 1987) in Guantánamo. Standards, services and administration of these reserves vary greatly. For example, the Península de Guanahacabibes is carefully protected, while Parque Baconao has small communities and many tourist installations within its boundaries.

Cuba boasts eight World Heritage sites: Habana Vieja, the historical core of Habana (declared in 1982); Trinidad and adjacent Valle de los Ingenios (1988) in Sancti Spíritus; Castillo de San Pedro del Morro (1997) and the First Coffee Plantations in the Southeast of Cuba (2000), both in Santiago de Cuba; Desembarco del Granma (1999) in Granma; Valle de Viñales (1999) in Pinar del Río; Alejandro de Humboldt (2001) in Guantánamo; and the Urban Historic Centre of Cienfuegos (2005) in Cienfuegos Province.

orchids. Most orchids bloom from November to January, and one of the best places to see them is in the Sierra del Rosario reserve. The national flower is the graceful *mariposa* (butterfly jasmine); you'll know it by its white floppy petals and strong perfume.

Medicinal plants are widespread in Cuba due largely to a chronic shortage of prescription medicines (banned under the US embargo). Pharmacies are well stocked with effective tinctures such as aloe (for cough and congestion) and a bee by-product called *propólio,* used for everything from stomach amoebas to respiratory infections. On the home front, every Cuban patio has a pot of *orégano de la tierra* (Cuban oregano) growing and if you start getting a cold you'll be whipped up a wonder elixir made from the fat, flat leaves mixed with lime juice, honey and hot water.

## NATIONAL PARKS

In 1978 Cuba established the National Committee for the Protection and Conservation of Natural Resources and the Environment (Comarna). Attempting to reverse 400 years of deforestation and habitat destruction the body set about designating green belts and initiated ambitious reforestation campaigns. It is estimated that at the time of Columbus' arrival in 1492, 95% of Cuba was covered in virgin forest. By 1959 this area had been reduced to just 16%. The implementation of large-scale tree planting and the organization of large tracts of land into protected parks has seen this figure creep back up to 20%, but there is still a lot of work to be done.

In 1991 Cuba began its pioneering 'Urban Agricultural Program', a scheme whereby large tracts of urban wasteland are put to productive use to grow food organically for purely domestic consumption.

As of 2006, there were six national parks in Cuba: Parque Nacional Península de Guanahacabibes, Parque Nacional Viñales (both Pinar del Río); the Gran Parque Natural Montemar (Matanzas); Gran Parque Nacional Sierra Maestra and Parque Nacional Desembarco del Granma (Granma and Santiago de Cuba Provinces); and Parque Nacional Alejandro de Humboldt (Guantánamo). Of these Desembarco del Granma and Parque Humboldt are also both Unesco World Heritage sites.

In Cuba the state protects national monuments and areas of outstanding natural beauty for the benefit of the population. Law 239 passed in

1959 proposed the creation of nine national parks and declared a desire to promote tourism. By the 1990s the plan had finally reached fruition. These days national conservation policies are directed by Comarna which acts as a coordinating body, overseeing 15 ministries and ensuring that current national and international environmental legislation is being carried out efficiently and effectively. This includes adherence to various international treaties such as the World Heritage Convention and the Unesco Man and Biosphere program.

## ENVIRONMENTAL ISSUES

Cuba's greatest environmental problems are aggravated by an economy struggling to survive. As the country pins its hopes on tourism to save the financial day, a schizophrenic environmental policy has evolved, cutting right to the heart of the dilemma: how can a developing nation provide for its people *and* maintain high (or at least minimal) ecological standards?

One disaster in this struggle, most experts agree, was the 2km-long stone *pedraplén* (causeway) constructed to link offshore Cayo Sabinal

**PROTECTED AREAS**

| Park | Features | Activities | Best Time to Visit | Page |
|---|---|---|---|---|
| Parque Nacional Península de Guanahacabibes | mangrove/beach: whale sharks, marine turtles, rare birds | scuba diving, remote, hiking, birding | Jun-Oct for nesting turtles, few visitors | p202 |
| Parque Nacional Viñales | verdant valley: caves, pincushion hills, tobacco fields, visitors center | spelunking, hiking, horseback riding, rock climbing | year-round | p209 |
| Gran Parque Natural Montemar | wetland: mangroves, 190 bird species, manatees, crocodile breeding, Taíno village replica | birding, boat tours, fishing | Nov-Apr | p252 |
| Gran Parque Nacional Sierra Maestra | mountains: Cuban Revolution headquarters, cloud forest, high peaks, views, museum | trekking, camping | Oct-May dry season | p380 & p426 |
| Parque Nacional Desembarco del Granma | forests/beach: rain forest, reef, trails, *Granma* replica,cacti, lighthouse, caves, petroglyphs | hiking, spelunking, swimming, fishing | Sep-Jun | p387 |
| Parque Nacional Alejandro de Humboldt | mangroves/forest: well-protected bayside setting, on-site specialists, visitors center, manatees, trails | boat tours, birding, hiking | year-round | p446 |

with mainland Camagüey. This massive project involved piling boulders in the sea and laying a road on top, which interrupted water currents and caused irreparable damage to bird and marine habitats. Other longer causeways were built connecting Los Jardines del Rey to Ciego de Ávila (27km long; p317) and Cayo Santa María to Villa Clara (a 48km-long monster; p283). The full extent of the ecological damage wreaked by these causeways won't be known for another decade at least.

Building new roads and airports, package tourism that shuttles large groups of people into sensitive habitats and the frenzied construction of giant resorts on virgin beaches exacerbates the clash between human activity and environmental protection. The grossly shrunken extents of the Reserva Ecológica Varahicacos in Varadero due to encroaching resorts is just one example. Dolphins rounded up as entertainers has rankled activists as well. Overfishing (including turtles and lobster for tourist consumption), agricultural runoff, industrial pollution and inadequate sewage treatment have contributed to the decay of coral reefs, and diseases such as yellow band, black band and nuisance algae have begun to appear.

As soon as you arrive in Habana or Santiago de Cuba you'll realize that air pollution is a problem. Airborne particles, old cars belching black smoke and by-products from burning garbage are some of the culprits. Cement factories, sugar refineries and other heavy industry take their toll. The nickel mines engulfing Moa serve as stark examples of industrial concerns taking precedence: this is some of the prettiest landscape in Cuba, made a barren wasteland of lunar proportions.

The Cuban government planted more than three billion trees in a reforestation program known as Plan Manatí. Though half of those trees perished, another reforestation program aims to recover a million hectares with new trees by 2015.

On the bright side is the enthusiasm the government has shown for reforestation and protecting natural areas – there are several projects on the drawing board – and its willingness to confront mistakes from the past. Habana Harbor, once Latin America's most polluted, has been undergoing a massive clean-up project, as has the Río Almendares, which cuts through the heart of the city. Both programs are beginning to show positive results. Sulfur emissions from oil wells near Varadero have been reduced and environmental regulations for developments are now enforced by the Ministry of Science, Technology and the Environment. Fishing regulations, as local fisherman will tell you, have become increasingly strict. Striking the balance between Cuba's immediate needs and the future of its environment is one of the revolution's increasingly pressing challenges.

# Food & Drink

Let's face it, you don't come to Cuba for the food. But while Cuban cuisine is often portrayed as bad, boring or both, the truth is Cuban cooks are extraordinarily creative, and home cooking, whether in someone's home or paladar (privately owned restaurant), is plentiful and delicious – and grease-laden: anyone with high cholesterol might consider vacationing elsewhere.

Resort food is a different story. If you're headed to an all-inclusive, there will be tomatoes in August and cheese year-round. Eating options shrink astronomically as soon as you venture outside the home, paladar or resort and you'll probably find yourself going hungry at least once during your travels. To avoid this fate, see below.

## STAPLES & SPECIALTIES

Known as *comida criolla* (Creole food), Cuban meals always feature *congrí* (rice flecked with black beans), fried plantains (green bananas) and salad. In the Oriente it's called *moros y cristianos* (literally 'Moors and Christians') or *congrí oriental* if the beans are red. Salad is a euphemism for 'whatever raw thing is available,' mostly tomato or cucumber slices and/or shredded cabbage.

Protein means pork and you'll become well acquainted with *lomo ahumado* (aromatic smoked loin), *chuletas* (thin juicy filet) and fricassee with peppers and onions. *Filete Uruguayo* is a breaded, deep-fried cutlet stuffed with ham and cheese.

**STAYING FED**

In Cuba, someone who is always eating is called a *jamaliche* or *camelón* but, unless you're staying at an all-inclusive resort, there's going to be hours, days – even whole weeks – when you're going to wish you'd stuffed a jar of peanut butter into your rucksack. Here's some advice to keep all you *jamaliches* out there fed:

- Always carry Cuban pesos (which can be easily changed in Cadeca banks). Pesos are good for ice cream, peanuts, egg sandwiches, fruit shakes, bread, fruits, vegetables and above all peso pizza.
- Keep a spare plastic bag (a rarity in Cuba) and fill it up at bakeries and fruit markets.
- Keep an eye out for 24-hour peso stalls which usually congregate around hospitals.
- If you are fortunate enough to stumble upon an as-much-as-you-can-eat buffet, wrap up your leftovers in a napkin and smuggle it out for later.
- Cyclists, exercise freaks or any other type of *jamaliche* should come prepared with power bars, nuts, dried fruit and other lightweight, high-protein snacks.
- Be willing to eat fried food, including unidentifiable tidbits sold on the street.
- Stock up on cookies and biscuits whenever you see a grocery store.
- Look for good yogurt in gas stations and caféterías (especially the El Rápido chain).
- Rent a room with kitchen privileges, then hit the *agropecuario* (vegetable market) and have a dinner party.
- Become a Cuban and never waste *anything*.
- Don't forget the peanut butter!

It will seem like Cuban chickens are born already fried and any *pescado* (fish) has made for distant waters. Though you'll come across *pargo* (red snapper) occasionally, you're more likely to see lobster or shrimp *ajillo* (sautéed in oil and garlic) or *enchilado* (in tomato sauce). *Ostiones* (small oysters served with tomato sauce and lime juice) are also popular. Cow production is controlled by the Cuban government so beef products such as steak are sold only in state-run restaurants. Fast-food places sell tasty hamburgers, though there's probably more ham than burger in there.

*Yuca* (cassava) and *calabaza* (pumpkinlike squash) are served with an insanely addictive sauce called *mojo* made from oil, garlic and bitter orange. Green beans, beets and avocados (June to August) are likely to cross your lips too. However, you're likely to see more vegetables at the market than on your plate.

Very few restaurants do breakfast (though pastries are sold at chains like Pain de Paris and Doña Neli), so if this is an important meal for you, stock up at a hotel buffet or arrange for your casa particular to provide it. Most casas do huge, hearty breakfasts of eggs, toast, fresh juice, coffee and piles of fruit for CUC$2 to CUC$3.

Cuba is famous for its mojitos and, if you can't stand another mound of rice and beans, why not opt for a liquid supper of these smooth cocktails made from rum, mint, sugar, seltzer and fresh lime juice?

The Cuban sandwich is a classic Cuban export that you're more likely to find in Miami than Habana. It's a grilled combination of sliced roast pork, Serrano ham and thinly cut swiss cheese garnished with pickles and yellow mustard.

## Desserts

At last count there were 14 brands of *helado* (ice cream) and Cubans are aficionados (eg Alondra's strawberry tastes fake, while Nevada's hazelnut is creamy). Coppelia's ice cream is legendary, ridiculously cheap tubs of other brands (440g for CUC$1) can be procured almost everywhere, and even the machine-dispensed peso stuff ain't half bad. Walk down any Cuban street at any time of the day or night and you'll see somebody coming to grips with a huge tub of Nestlés or enjoying a fast-melting cornet. See the boxed text Making Cents of Coppelia (p131).

*Flan* is baked custard with a caramel glaze served in individual portions. Cubans also make pumpkin and coconut flan of Spanish origin. Huge sickly sweet cakes are wheeled out at the smallest excuse – and usually transported around the town on a wobbling bicycle first. Habana and a couple of the larger cities also have some good patisseries. The standard (and only) dessert in all cheap restaurants and Islazul hotels is the incongruous *mermalada con queso* (tinned jam with a slice of stale cheese). It's as vile as it sounds!

During the worst of the *período especial* (1990–95), every adult Cuban lost between 2.25kg and 4.5kg due to food shortages.

# DRINKS

## Alcoholic Drinks

In Cuba it's all about the *ron* (rum). Minty mojitos, Cuba *libres* (rum and Coke), daiquirís, *Cubanitos* (rum and tomato juice), straight up or on the rocks, it's served all ways. Havana Club is Cuba's most famous brand, with Silver Dry (the cheapest) and three-year-old Carta Blanca used for mixed drinks, while five-year-old Carta de Oro and seven-year-old Añejo are best enjoyed in a highball. Cuba's finest rum is Matusalem Añejo Superior, brewed in Santiago de Cuba since 1872. Other top brands include Varadero, Caribbean Club and Caney (made at the old Bacardí factory in Santiago de Cuba, though the name Bacardí is anathema as the exiled family decided to sue the Cuban government under US embargo laws). Sharing your bottle is all you need to know about Cuban party etiquette.

Cuba's star ingredient is lobster and no one is better qualified to talk about it than Gilberto Smith Duquesne, chairman of the Cuban Culinary Association. Check out his classic book *El Rey Langosta* with 60 fabulous recipes.

The drink made from fermented cane is called *aguardiente* (fire water) and a few shots will knock you on your ass. In bodegas (stores distributing ration-card products) it's sold as *ron a granel* for 20 pesos (equivalent to US$0.77 per 1500ml) – bring an empty bottle. Local nicknames for this hooch include 'drop her drawers' and 'train spark.' Popular bottled brands are Santero and El Niño. Cubans also make fruit wines from mango, pineapple or raisins. Big city stores usually carry a limited selection of Spanish, Chilean and Cuban wines. Top beer brands include Mayabe (3.8% alcohol) and Hatuey (5.4%). These are like microbreweries though, and you'll spend most of your time drinking super light Cristal (4.9%) or Bucanero (5.4%). Imported beers include Lagarto, Bavaria and Heineken.

Cuban cooking boring? Look out for the book *Three Guys from Miami Cook Cuban* by Glenn M Lindgren, Raúl Musibay and Jorge Castillo and you'll soon discover otherwise.

### Nonalcoholic Drinks

Cuban coffee *(cafécito* or *café cubano)* is strong, black and super sweet. Unless you say otherwise it will come served in a small cup with sugar already added. A morning treat is a big cup of *café con leche* (a mixture of strong coffee and hot milk) or *leche con chocolate* (sickly sweet hot chocolate). *Café americano* is diluted Cuban coffee and only worth mentioning so you can avoid it. There isn't much of a tea *(té)* culture in Cuba, but you can always get a pot of hot water at hotels or restaurants. Tea bags are sold in stores that sell items in Convertibles.

Any place serving mojitos can whip up a refreshing *limonada* (limeade). Pure *jugo* (fruit juice), *refresco* (instant powdered drink) and *batidos* (fruit milkshakes) are sold in street stalls for a few pesos. Note that they are made with water and/or ice, so if you have a sensitive stomach you might take a pass.

*Guarapo* is a popular sugarcane juice (see p363). *Prú* is a special nonalcoholic brew from the Oriente made from spices, fermented *yuca* (cassava) and secret ingredients *prú*-meisters won't divulge.

Tap water quality is variable and many Cubans have gory amoebic tales, including giardia. To be safe you can drink *agua natural* (bottled water), but that gets expensive over longer trips. You can also boil it (the local method) or buy bottled chlorine drops called Gotica. Available in most stores that sell products in Convertibles for CUC$1.25, one drop makes 3L of drinkable water; this works well in the provinces, but in Habana it's better to boil or buy bottled water. Don't touch the water in Santiago, even to brush your teeth. It's famously dirty – and brown!

Cuban paladares are only supposed to serve 12 covers at any one time. They are also barred from serving lobster and beef, both of which are considered to be government monopolies.

## CELEBRATIONS

New Year's Eve, birthdays, family reunions: whatever the reason, big events are celebrated with *lechón asado* (roast pork). As much about the process and camaraderie as the food, a pig roast is a communal effort where the jokes fly, the rum flows and dancing or *dominó* somehow figures in. Once the pig is killed, cleaned and seasoned, it's slowly pit-roasted over a charcoal fire. Traditional sides include *yuca con mojo, congrí* and salad. Stall after stall peddles freshly carved *lechón asado,* sliced down the middle and splayed on platters, during Holguín's Carnaval (see p354), and many families celebrate Christmas Eve *(Noche Buena)* with this local favorite.

## WHERE TO EAT & DRINK

### State-Run Restaurants

Restaurant opening hours are generally 11am to 11pm daily although staff sometimes drift off for lunch unannounced, or will be too busy engaged in a stocktake to serve you right away. Government or state-run restaurants are either in pesos or Convertibles. Peso restaurants are notorious for handing you a nine-page menu (in Spanish), when the only thing available is fried chicken. Obviously you're supposed to pick up this information via telepathy because you'll sit for half an hour or more before learning this while the waitress falls asleep, wakes up, takes a phone call, files her nails wipes the bar with a dirty cloth and fall asleep again. But it's not all pain and stomachache. Some peso restaurants are quite good; all are absurdly cheap and they're often your only option off the tourist circuit, so don't discount them altogether (Doña Yulla is a nationwide chain to look out for). Sometimes workers in peso restaurants either won't show you the menu in an effort to overcharge you, or they will charge Convertibles at a one-to-one ratio – making the food ridiculously overpriced. Verify *before* you order that you're looking at peso prices (meals will be in the 15- to 25-peso range). Some peso restaurants have one menu in Convertibles at a reasonable rate and another in pesos.

*Moros y cristianos* (Moors and Christians) is a typical Cuban meal of white rice cooked with black beans. *Congrí oriental* is rice with red beans sometimes mixed in with crispy pork slices.

Restaurants that sell food in Convertibles are generally more reliable, but this isn't capitalism: just because you're paying more doesn't necessarily mean better service. In fact, after a week or two roaming the streets of Cuba's untouristed provincial towns in search of a decent meal you'll quickly realize that Cuban restaurants are the Achilles heel of the socialist revolution. Food is often limp and unappetizing and discourses with bored and disinterested waiters worthy of something out of a Monty Python sketch ('we can't do you a cheese sandwich, but we can do you a cheese and ham sandwich'). There are a few highlights in an otherwise dull field. The Palmares group runs a wide variety of excellent restaurants countrywide from a small shabby hut on Maguana beach, Baracoa to the *New York Times*–lauded El Aljibe in Miramar, Habana. Another safe, if uninspiring certainty is El Rápido, the Cuban version of McDonald's, which offers a generic menu of microwave pizzas, hot dogs, sandwiches and – sometimes – excellent yogurt. Cuba would do well to open more La Vicarias, where the service is uniformly good, the prices fair and the food palatable. Habana is, of course, a different ballpark, with many state-run restaurants in the Old Town and Miramar of excellent quality. All state-run restaurant employees earn the standard CUC$8 to CUC$13 a month, so tips are highly appreciated (see p80).

Nitza Villapol, Cuban cook and TV personality, carried on rustling up resourceful recipes throughout the darkest days of the *período especial*. Indeed, legend has it that her show was once canceled after she tried to present an innovative new menu alternative called 'black bean dessert.'

### Paladares

The Cuban dining scene brightened considerably with the advent of paladares (private restaurants) in 1995. Legally, paladares can only have 12 seats and cannot serve beef, lobster or shrimp. In practice, however, paladares routinely offer forbidden foods and have doors leading from the kitchen to back rooms or patios where they can accommodate far more than 12 diners.

Because these restaurants are in private residences (and the owners pay a stiff monthly tax for the privilege), each atmosphere is different, from romantic garden dining to windowless rooms with the air-con set to 'polar cap.' Some paladares have written menus, while others don't; some take pesos, but most want Convertibles. If there's a menu, check how much beer costs, and if it's over CUC$10 (Convertibles and pesos use the same symbol!) you can assume the menu is in pesos, which always works out cheaper. In monetary terms, a filling meal costs anywhere between CUC$4 and CUC$12. Always check prices beforehand, as some paladares are rip-offs. If a paladar doesn't have a written menu with prices listed, it's a negative sign. Many paladares have two or three menus all listing the same dishes but with different prices, depending on how much they think you might be willing to pay (often directly related to your Spanish abilities) and whether a commission must be paid to the *jinetero* who led you there. These touts will add a few Convertibles to every meal.

A number of paladares are listed in this book, but beware – the situation is changing fast and many places close down when owners emigrate or can't pay their taxes. Furthermore, the government has become increasingly strict with inspections and licencing, making it more difficult than ever to maintain a paladar. Some large cities such as Cienfuegos have only one or two legal paladares. Of course, there's always someone willing to cook meals clandestinely (ie nontax paying), but this can incur heavy fines, so discretion is advised.

To allow readers to quickly distinguish between private and state-run restaurants, all privately operated eateries are listed as paladares. Whenever this book refers to a 'restaurant,' it means it's a government-operated place.

When cooked 'Habana style,' mincemeat should be well-seasoned with garlic, laurel, onion, paprika, tomato, oregano, pepper, olives and raisins, and arranged with a fried egg on top.

## Quick Eats

Like all private industry, *cafeterías* (street stalls) are government regulated so – although they might look a bit grungy – hygiene isn't usually a problem. Cuban street pizza, with its pungent cheese and occasional glob of tomato, is surprisingly good and became the new national dish during the *período especial*. Good standards on the street dining scene include *batidos*, *asado* (roasted) or breaded pork cutlet sandwiches, fruit cocktail and ice cream. There's also a whole category of *pan con…* (bread with…) – whatever can be put inside bread, from tortilla (tasty eggs) to *pasta* (an icky mayonnaise substance).

Keep an eye out for stalls and windows with *comida criolla* signs. These places sell *cajitas* (literally 'little boxes'): full meals of salad, baked vegetables, *congrí* and pork cutlets that are sold in little take-away boxes with a cardboard spoon cutout on the lid for CUC$1.

All street food is sold in pesos. For more information see the boxed text (p76).

# VEGETARIANS & VEGANS

In a land of rationing and food shortages, strict vegetarians (ie no lard, no meat bullion, no fish) will have a hard time. Cubans don't really understand vegetarianism and, when they do (or when they *say* they do),

### TIPPING & RESERVATIONS

Remembering to tip is important in Cuba. In a country where the doctors work as waiters and the waiters double up as musicians serenading mojito-sipping tourists as they tuck tentatively into *moros y cristianos* (rice and beans), a couple of Convertibles left in the bread basket at the end of the meal can effectively make or break a person's week. It is important to bear in mind that most of these people earn their salaries in *moneda nacional* (pesos), which works out to the equivalent of US$10 to US$25 a month. Access to hard currency is necessary to make up the shortfall. However mediocre your food, a Convertible or two isn't just a show of appreciation; it's a vital contribution to the local economy.

In Cuba, a 10% tip is usually sufficient, with CUC$1 being the appropriate minimum in a restaurant that accepts Convertibles. Tipping in peso restaurants is not compulsory, but is greatly appreciated. Leaving 10 pesos or CUC$0.50 in Convertible peso change is a generous tip.

Unless you're in a large group or want to eat at one of the chic, trendy paladares (eg La Guarida in Habana), there's no need for a reservation.

it can be summarized rather adroitly in one key word: omelette – or, at a stretch, scrambled eggs. The other problem is preparation. Even if your omelette has no meat in it, don't assume that it has been prepared in a manner that is in any way sympathetic to vegetarian requirements. Indeed, Cubans often interpret vegetarianism as 'no meat chunks in the soup.' The solution: pick out the offending items out just before serving. Thankfully change is on the horizon. The opening of a handful of new vegetarian restaurants in Habana (see p128) has coincided with a nationwide educational campaign about the health benefits of a vegetarian diet. Furthermore, cooks in casas particulares who may already have had experience cooking meatless dishes for other travelers are usually more than happy to accommodate vegetarians; just ask.

Vegans have little choice but to cook for themselves. Many people rent rooms with kitchen privileges or entire self-sufficient apartments; this book makes a conscious effort to provide information about cooking options in casas particulares. Other options for serious vegans and/or vegetarians:

**Agropecuarios** Vegetable markets; also sell rice, beans, fruit (for a list of Habana's best markets, see p130).
**Organopónicos** Organic vegetable markets.
**Proteina vegetal** Dried soy protein (sold in bodegas).
**Spirulina** Spirulina powder (an aquatic plant offering high protein and vitamins).
**Yogurt de soya** Soy yogurt (sold in bodegas; regular yogurt is sold in stores that sell goods in Convertibles).

In Cuba the taste of the orangey-red *mamey* fruit is loved by almost everybody. So much so, that the word *mamey* has entered the Cuban vocabulary as an oft-used superlative. To describe a woman as *'mamey'* is to pay her the ultimate compliment.

## EAT YOUR WORDS

Managing a menu in Spanish, making special requests or maneuvering a meal in pesos – your eating options will expand if you can speak the language. For pronunciation guidelines see p486.

### Useful Phrases

**Is there food?**
*¿Hay comida?* ai ko·*mee*·da
**What kind of food is there?**
*¿Qué comida hay?* ke ko·*mee*·da ai
**Table for ..., please.**
*Una mesa para ..., por favor.* *oo*·na *me*·sa *pa*·ra ... por fa·*vor*
**Can I see the menu please?**
*¿Puedo ver la carta, por favor?* *pwe*·do ver la *kar*·ta, por fa·*vor*
**This menu is in pesos, right?**
*¿Esta carta está en moneda nacional, verdad?* esta *kar*·ta es·*ta* en mo·*ne*·da na·syo·*nal* ver·*da*
**Do you have a menu in English?**
*¿Tienen una carta en inglés?* *tye*·nen oon·a *kar*·ta en een·*gles*
**What is today's special?**
*¿Cuál es el plato del día?* kwal es el *pla*·to del *dee*·a
**I'll try what she's/he's having.**
*Probaré lo que ella/él está comiendo.* pro·*ba*·ray lo ke *e*·lya/el es·*ta* ko·*myen*·do
**I'd like the set lunch.**
*Quisiera el almuerzo, por favor.* kee·*sye*·ra el al·*mwer*·so, por fa·*vor*
**What's in that dish?**
*¿De qué es ese plato?* de ke es *es*·e *pla*·to
**Thank you, that was delicious.**
*Muchas gracias, estaba buenísimo.* *moo*·chas *gra*·syas es·*ta*·ba bwe·*nee*·see·mo
**The bill, please.**
*La cuenta, por favor.* la *kwen*·ta por fa·*vor*

**I'm a vegetarian.**
*Soy vegetariano/a.* soy ve·khe·ta·*rya*·no/a
**Do you have any vegetarian dishes?**
*¿Tienen algún plato vegetariano?* *tye*·nen al·*goon pla*·to ve·khe·ta·*rya*·no
**I'm allergic to ...**
*Tengo alergía a ...* *ten*·go a·lair·*jee*·ya a

## Menu Decoder

| | | |
|---|---|---|
| *ajiaco* | a·*khya*·ko | a 'kitchen sink' stew that has potatoes, squash, *malanga*,(root vegetable similar to taro); plantains, corn, meat, tomato paste, spices, old beer, lemon juice and whatever else is around |
| *arroz con pollo* | a·*ros* kon *po*·lyo | rice and bits of chicken mixed together |
| *bocadito* | bo·ka·*dee*·to | sandwich on round bread |
| *café cortado* | ka·*fe* kor·*ta*·do | espresso with a shot of milk |
| *cajita* | ka·*khee*·ta | take-out meal that comes in a small box |
| *caldosa* | kal·*do*·sa | similar to *ajiaco*; literally 'stew' |
| *chicharitas/ mariquitas* | chee·cha·*ree*·tas/ ma·ree·*kee*·tas | plantain (green banana) chips; sometimes made from potatoes or *malanga* |
| *chicharrones* | chee·cha·*ro*·nes | fried pork rinds |
| *crema de queso* | *kre*·ma de *ke*·so | heavy cheese soup that has as much flour as cheese; variations include *crema Aurora* and *crema Virginia* |
| *entremes* | en·tre·*mes* | finger food or appetizer, usually with ham and cheese slices and green olives; sometimes quite large servings |
| *filete Canciller* | fi·*le*·te kan·*see*·lyer | breaded fish stuffed with ham and cheese |
| *filete Monte Toro* | fi·*le*·te *mon*·te *to*·ro | delicately breaded fish filet, fried and stuffed with cheese |
| *filete Uruguayo* | fi·*le*·te oo·ro·*gwai*·yo | fried, breaded pork cutlet stuffed with ham and cheese |
| *Gordon Bleu* | *gor*·don bloo | chicken stuffed with ham and cheese; charming anthropomorphism of cordon bleu |
| *guarnición* | gwar·nee·*syon* | side dish |
| *hígado a la italiana* | *ee*·ga·do a la ee·tal·*ya*·na | liver sautéed in tomato sauce, with peppers and onions |
| *lomo ahumado* | *lo*·mo a·oo·*ma*·do | smoked pork loin |
| *potaje* | po·*ta*·khe | subtly spiced black beans with pork bones or chunks, served in its own soupy juices |
| *ropa vieja* | *ro*·pa *vye*·kha | traditional Cuban dish of mounds of shredded beef livened with tomatoes and onions; only available in state-run restaurants |
| *servicio incluído* | ser·*vee*·syo een·kloo·*ee*·do | tip included |
| *table 1, 2* etc | *ta*·ble *oo*·no dos etc | different meal *offers* (distinguished by the numbers) that include a main dish, salad, side and dessert, usually with smaller portions |
| *tamal en cazuela* | ta·*mal* en ka·*swe*·la | ground fresh corn, boiled with meat and spices and served in a pot; called *tamales* when wrapped in corn husks |
| *tostones* | tos·*to*·nes | fried plantain patties |

| | | |
|---|---|---|
| *vegetales Macedonias* | ve·khe·*ta*·les ma·se·*don*·yas | a mix of carrots and green beans boiled to death or canned |
| *vianda* | vee-*an*-dah | any root vegetable (potato, yuca, *malanga*, plantain etc). This appears on many menus as *vianda frita*. |

## Food Glossary

### FRUTAS (FRUITS)

| | | |
|---|---|---|
| *fruta bomba* | *froo*·ta *bom*·ba | papaya |
| *guayaba* | gwa·*ya*·ba | guava |
| *mamey* | ma·*me* | brown-skinned fruit with orange flesh |
| *melón* | me·*lon* | watermelon |
| *naranja (agria)* | na·*ran*·kha (a·*gree*·a) | orange (bitter) |
| *piña* | *pee*·nya | pineapple |
| *plátano fruta* | *pla*·ta·no froo·ta | banana |
| *toronja* | *to*·*ron*·*kha* | grapefruit |
| *zapote* | sa·*po*·te | brown-skinned fruit with orange flesh |

### VERDURAS (VEGETABLES)

| | | |
|---|---|---|
| *berenjena* | be·*ren*·kha | eggplant |
| *boniato* | bo·*nya*·to | sweet potato |
| *calabaza* | ka·la·*ba*·sa | squash |
| *champiñon* | cham·*pee*·nyon | mushroom |
| *espinaca* | es·pee·*na*·ka | spinach |
| *maíz* | mai·*ees* | corn |
| *malanga* | ma·*lan*·ga | root vegetable similar to taro |
| *papa* | *pa*·pa | potato |
| *plátano verde* | *pla*·ta·no *ver*·de | green plantain (savory) |
| *plátano maduro* | *pla*·ta·no ma·*doo*·ro | green plantain (sweet) |

### ENSALADA (SALAD)

| | | |
|---|---|---|
| *aguacate* | a·gwa·*ka*·te | avocado |
| *aliño* | a·*lee*·nyo | oil and vinegar dressing/carafes |
| *berro* | *be*·ro | watercress |
| *col* | kol | cabbage |
| *ensalada de estación* | en·sa·*la*·da de es·ta·*syon* | seasonal salad |
| *ensalada mixta* | en·sa·*la*·da *meeks*·ta | mixed salad; usually tomatoes, cucumbers and cabbage/ lettuce |
| *habichuela* | a·bee·*chwe*·la | green beans |
| *lechuga* | le·*choo*·ga | lettuce |
| *pepino* | pe·*pee*·no | cucumber |
| *remolacha* | re·mo·*la*·cha | beets |
| *zanahoria* | sa·na·*o*·rya | carrot |

### CARNE (MEAT)

| | | |
|---|---|---|
| *cerdo* | *ser*·do | pork |
| *chorizo* | cho·*ree*·so | sausage |
| *jamón* | kha·*mon* | ham |
| *lechón asado* | le·*chon* a·*sa*·do | roast pork |
| *picadillo* | pee·ka·*dee*·lyo | ground beef |
| *pollo frito* | *po*·lyo *free*·to | fried chicken |
| *puerco* | *pwer*·ko | pork |

### PESCADO & MARISCOS (FISH & SHELLFISH)

| | | |
|---|---|---|
| *calamar* | ka·*la*·mar | squid |
| *camarones* | ka·ma·*ro*·nes | shrimp |
| *cangrejo* | kan·*gre*·kho | crab |
| *langosta* | lan·*gos*·ta | lobster |
| *mariscos* | ma·*rees*·kos | shellfish |
| *ostiones* | os·*tyo*·nes | oysters |
| *pargo* | *par*·go | red snapper |

### POSTRES (DESSERTS)

| | | |
|---|---|---|
| *arroz con leche* | a·*ros* kon *le*·che | rice and milk pudding |
| *flan* | flan | baked custard with caramel glaze |
| *helado (en pote)* | e·*la*·do (en po·te) | ice cream (cup) |
| *jimagua* | khee·*ma*·gwa | two scoops of ice cream |
| *lolita* | lo·*lee*·ta | flan à la mode |
| *natilla* | na·*tee*·lya | sinful custard made almost entirely of egg yolks |
| *pudín* | poo·*deen* | bread pudding |
| *tres gracias* | tres *gra*·syas | three scoops of ice cream |

### SNACKS & STREET FOOD

| | | |
|---|---|---|
| *maní en grano* | ma·*nee* en *gra*·no | peanut brittle |
| *maní molido* | ma·*nee* mo·*lee*·do | peanut paste (similar to peanut butter) |
| *pan con tortilla* | pan kon tor·*tee*·lya | bread with egg |
| *pasta/croqueta* | pas·ta/kro·*ke*·ta | mayonnaise/fritter |
| *tortica* | tor·*tee*·ka | butter cookie (often made with lard) |

### TÉCNICAS (COOKING TECHNIQUES)

| | | |
|---|---|---|
| *a la plancha* | a la *plan*·cha | cooked in a skillet |
| *asado* | a·*sa*·do | roasted |
| *empanizado* | em·pa·nee·*sa*·do | breaded |
| *parrillada/grille* | pa·ree·*lya*·da/*gree*·lye | on the grill |
| *sofrito* | so·*free*·to | Cuban seasoning made by sautéing onions, garlic and sweet peppers |

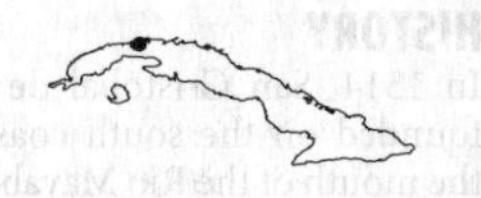

# La Habana

There is nowhere in the world like Habana. From the crumbling apartment buildings of Centro Habana to the grandiose colonial edifices of the Habana Vieja (Old Habana), the Caribbean's largest and most vivacious city bewitches and beguiles, confounds and frustrates. Federico Lorca eulogized it; Hemingway made it his permanent home; British novelist Graham Greene fell unashamedly for its dark and seedy nocturnal habitats. They weren't the only converts. Over a period of five centuries Habana has seduced everyone from buccaneering Caribbean pirates, to foreign tourists in Che Guevara T-shirts.

The essence of the city's unique atmosphere is hard to pin down. Habana works its magic slowly, gradually crawling underneath your skin with an indefatigable combination of music, passion, serendipity and soul. But Habana's greatest attraction is its gritty authenticity. This is no touched-up tourist complex or hastily made-over museum piece. The ration shops here are *real* ration shops and the Jurassic Pontiacs that ply the traffic-choked streets around Parque de la Fraternidad aren't lovingly restored collector's items – they're an economic necessity.

The opportunities to lose yourself in the melee are endless. For architectural buffs there's the baroque Gran Teatro or the art-deco Edificio Bacardí building. For music fiends there's rumba and salsa, *trova* (poetic singing/songwriting) and *son* (Cuba's popular music). Even hardcore Cuba cynics will have trouble resisting the sensuous pleasures of vibrant Vedado, or the sun-streaked colonnades of the Malecón at dusk.

## HIGHLIGHTS

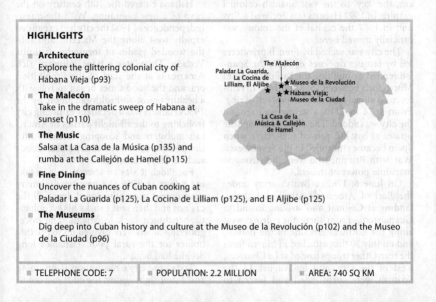

- **Architecture**
  Explore the glittering colonial city of Habana Vieja (p93)
- **The Malecón**
  Take in the dramatic sweep of Habana at sunset (p110)
- **The Music**
  Salsa at La Casa de la Música (p135) and rumba at the Callejón de Hamel (p115)
- **Fine Dining**
  Uncover the nuances of Cuban cooking at Paladar La Guarida (p125), La Cocina de Lilliam (p125), and El Aljibe (p125)
- **The Museums**
  Dig deep into Cuban history and culture at the Museo de la Revolución (p102) and the Museo de la Ciudad (p96)

The Malecón
Paladar La Guarida, La Cocina de Lilliam, El Aljibe
Museo de la Revolución
Habana Vieja; Museo de la Ciudad
La Casa de la Música & Callejón de Hamel

- TELEPHONE CODE: 7
- POPULATION: 2.2 MILLION
- AREA: 740 SQ KM

## HISTORY

In 1514, San Cristóbal de la Habana was founded on the south coast of Cuba near the mouth of the Río Mayabeque by Spanish conquistador Pánfilo de Narváez. Named after a famous Taíno Indian chief the city was moved twice during its first five years due to mosquito infestations and wasn't finally established on its present site until 17 December 1519. According to local legend, the first Mass was said beneath a ceiba tree in present day Plaza de Armas.

Habana is the most westerly and isolated of Diego Velázquez's original villas and life was hard in the early days. Things didn't get any better in 1538 when French corsairs and local slaves razed the city to the ground.

It took the Spanish conquest of Mexico and Peru to swing the pendulum in Habana's favor. The town's strategic location, at the mouth of the Gulf of Mexico made it a perfect nexus point for the annual treasure fleets to regroup in the sheltered harbor before heading east. Thus endowed, its ascension was quick and decisive and in 1556 Habana replaced Santiago de Cuba as seat of the Spanish captains general. The first combined flota sailed to Spain from here in 1564, and for the next 200 years Habana was the most important port in the Americas, the 'key' to the vast Spanish colonial empire. In 1592 Habana was declared a city, and in 1607 the capital of the colony was officially moved here.

The city was sacked by French privateers led by Jacques de Sores in 1555; the Spanish replied by building the La Punta and El Morro forts between 1558 and 1630 to reinforce an already formidable protective ring. From 1674 to 1740, a strong wall around the city was added. These defenses kept the pirates at bay but proved ineffective when Spain became embroiled in the Seven Years' War with Britain, who were the strongest maritime power of the era.

On June 6, 1762, a British army under the Earl of Albemarle attacked Habana, landing at Cojímar and striking inland to Guanabacoa. From there they drove west along the northeastern side of the harbor, and on July 30 they attacked El Morro from the rear. Other troops landed at La Chorrera, west of the city, and by August 13 the Spanish were surrounded and forced to surrender. The British held Habana for 11 months. (The same war cost France almost all its colonies in North America, including Québec and Louisiana – a major paradigm shift.)

When the Spanish regained the city a year later in exchange for Florida, they began a crash building program to upgrade the city's defenses in order to avoid another debilitating siege. A new fortress, La Cabaña, was built along the ridge from which the British had shelled El Morro, and by the time the work was finished in 1766, Habana had become the most heavily fortified city in the New World, the 'bulwark of the Indies.'

The British occupation resulted in Spain opening Habana to freer trade. In 1765 the city was granted the right to trade with seven Spanish cities instead of only Cádiz, and beginning in 1818 Habana was allowed to ship its sugar, rum, tobacco and coffee directly to any part of the world. The 19th century was an era of steady progress: first came the railway in 1837, followed by public gas lighting (1848), the telegraph (1851), an urban transport system (1862), telephones (1888) and electric lighting (1890). By 1902 the city, which had been physically untouched by the devastating wars of independence, boasted a quarter of a million inhabitants.

Habana entered the 20th century on the cusp of a new beginning. With the quasi-independence of 1902 the city had expanded rapidly west along the Malecón and into the wooded glades of formerly off-limits Vedado. There was a large influx of rich Americans at the start of the Prohibition era, and the good times began to roll with a healthy or not-so-healthy abandon; by the 1950s Habana was a decadent gambling city frolicking to the all-night parties of American mobsters and scooping fortunes into the pockets of various disreputable hoods such as Meyer Lansky.

For Fidel, it was an aberration. On taking power in 1959 the new revolutionary government promptly closed down all the casinos and then sent Lansky his sycophantic henchmen back to Miami. The once-glittering hotels were divided up to provide homes for the rural poor. Habana's long decline had begun.

Today the city's restoration is on-going and a stoic fight against the odds in a country where shortages are part of everyday life and money for raw materials is scarce. Since 1982, City Historian Eusebio Leal has been piecing Old Habana back together street by street and square by square with the aid of Unesco and a variety of foreign investors. Slowly but surely, the old starlet is starting to rediscover her former greatness.

## ORIENTATION

Surrounded by Habana Province, the City of Habana is divided into 15 municipalities (see Map p87).

Habana Vieja, sometimes referred to as the 'Old Town,' sits on the western side of the harbor in an area once bounded by 17th-century city walls that ran along present Av de Bélgica and Av de las Misiones. In 1863 these walls were demolished and the city spilled west into Centro Habana, bisected by busy San Rafael (the dividing line between the two is still fuzzy). West of Calzada de Infante lies Vedado, the 20th-century hotel and entertainment district that developed after independence in 1902. Near Plaza de la Revolución and between Vedado and Nuevo Vedado, a huge government complex was erected in the 1950s. West of the Río Almendares are Miramar, Marianao and Playa, Habana's most fashionable residential suburbs prior to the 1959 revolution.

Between 1955 and 1958, a 733m-long tunnel was drilled between Habana Vieja and Habana del Este under the harbor mouth, and since 1959 a flurry of ugly high-rise housing blocks have been thrown up in Habana del Este, Cojímar (a former fishing village), and Alamar, northeast of the harbor. South of Habana del Este's endless blocks of flats are the prettier colonial towns of Guanabacoa, San Francisco de Paula and Santa María del Rosario. On the eastern side of the harbor are Regla and Casablanca.

Totally off the beaten track for most tourists are Habana's working-class areas south of Centro Habana including Cerro, Diez de Octubre and San Miguel del Padrón. Further south still is industrial Boyeros, with the golf course, zoo and international airport, and Arroyo Naranjo with Parque Lenin.

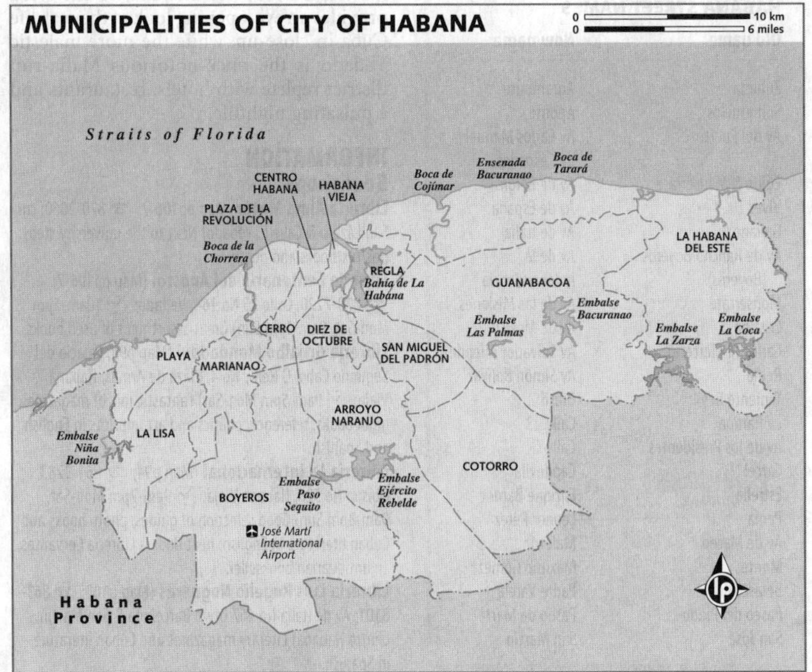

Visitors spend the bulk of their time in Habana Vieja, Centro Habana and Vedado. Important streets here include: Obispo, a pedestrian mall cutting through the center of Habana Vieja; Paseo de Martí (aka Paseo del Prado or just 'Prado'), an elegant 19th-century promenade in Centro Habana; Av de Italia (aka Galiano), Centro Habana's main shopping street for Cubans; Malecón, Habana's broad coastal boulevard; and Calle 23 (aka La Rampa), the heart of Vedado's commercial district.

Confusingly, many main avenues around Habana have two names in everyday use – a new name that appears on street signs and in this book, and an old name overwhelmingly preferred by locals. See the boxed text to sort it all out (below).

### Maps

Your best guide to the old city is *La Habana Vieja Guía Turística,* published by the Instituto Cubano de Geodesia y Cartografía (GeoCuba). It contains 35 maps of the old town, along with 222 pages of references and helpful descriptions in Spanish, English, French and German. It is available at some hotel shops.

GeoCuba also publishes *Ciudad de la Habana Mapa Turístico,* which covers all 15 municipalities in detail, including good scale street maps of the central city and Playas del Este. The fold-out *Guía de Carreteras,* with countrywide and Habana city maps, is very useful if you'll also be exploring other provinces. Highway signs around Habana are poor to nonexistent, and these maps are almost essential for drivers. **Infotur** (Map p94; ☎ 33 33 33; Obispo btwn Bernaza & Villegas) can provide you with a selection of good city maps.

#### HABANA STREET NAMES

| Old name | New name |
|---|---|
| Zulueta | Agramonte |
| Someruelos | Aponte |
| Av del Puerto | Av Carlos Manuel de Céspedes |
| Egido & Monserrate | Av de Bélgica |
| Vives | Av de España |
| Galiano | Av de Italia |
| Av de Rancho Boyeros (Boyeros) | Av de la Independencia |
| Monserrate | Av de las Misiones |
| Cristina | Av de México |
| Carlos III (Tercera) | Av Salvador Allende |
| Reina | Av Simón Bolívar |
| Teniente Rey | Brasil |
| La Rampa | Calle 23 |
| Av de los Presidentes | Calle G |
| Cárcel | Capdevila |
| Estrella | Enrique Barnet |
| Paula | Leonor Pérez |
| Av de Maceo | Malecón |
| Monte | Máximo Gómez |
| Belascoaín | Padre Varela |
| Paseo del Prado | Paseo de Martí |
| San José | San Martín |

# DOWNTOWN HABANA

For simplicity's sake downtown Habana can be split into three main component parts: Habana Vieja, Centro Habana and Vedado, which between them contain the bulk of the tourist sights. Centrally-located Habana Vieja is the city's atmospheric historical masterpiece; Centro Habana, to the west, provides an eye-opening look at the real-life Cuba in close-up, while the more majestic Vedado is the once-notorious Mafia-run district replete with hotels, restaurants and a pulsating nightlife.

## INFORMATION

### Bookshops

**Librería Alma Mater** (Map pp106-7; ☎ 870-2060; cnr San Lázaro & Calle L, Vedado) Next to the university steps. Has textbooks and poetry.

**Librería Centenario del Apóstol** (Map pp106-7; ☎ 870-7220; Calle 25 No 164, Vedado; 🕒 10am-5pm Mon-Sat, 9am-1pm Sun) Great assortment of used books.

**Librería Grijalbo Mondadovi** (Map p94; Palacio del Segundo Cabo, O'Reilly No 4, Plaza de Armas, Habana Vieja; 🕒 9am-5pm Mon-Sat) Fantastic mix of magazines, guidebooks, reference, politics and art imprints in English and Spanish.

**Librería La Internacional** (Map p94; ☎ 861-3283; Obispo No 526, Habana Vieja; 🕒 9am-7pm Mon-Sat, 9am-3pm Sun) Good selection of guides, photo books and Cuban literature in English; next door is Librería Cervantes, an antiquarian bookseller.

**Librería Luis Rogelio Nogueras** (Map p100; ☎ 863-8101; Av de Italia No 467 btwn Barcelona & San Martín, Centro Habana) Literary magazines and Cuban literature in Spanish.

**Librería Rayuela** (Map pp106-7; ☎ 55 27 06; Casa de las Américas, cnr Calles 3 & G, Vedado; 🕒 9am-4:30pm Mon-Fri) Terrific for contemporary literature, compact discs; some guidebooks.

**Moderna Poesía** (Map p94; ☎ 861-6640; Obispo 525, Habana Vieja; 🕒 10am-8pm) Perhaps Habana's best spot for Spanish-language books.

**Plaza de Armas Secondhand Book Market** (Map p94; cnr Obispo & Tacón, Habana Vieja) Old, new and rare books; some in English.

## Cultural Centers

**Alliance Française** (Map pp106-7; ☎ 33 33 70; Calle G No 407 btwn Calles 17 & 19, Vedado) Free French films Monday (11am), Wednesday (3pm) and Friday (5pm); good place to meet Cubans (including children for French travelers with kids) interested in French culture.

**Casa de las Américas** (Map pp106-7; ☎ 55 27 06/07; cnr Calles 3 & G, Vedado) Powerhouse of Cuban and Latin American culture, with conferences, exhibitions, a gallery, book launches and concerts. The casa's annual literary award is one of the Spanish-speaking world's most prestigious. Pick up a schedule of weekly events in the library. Hosts an international seminar on Afro-Cuban culture every August.

**Casa de la Cultura** Centro Habana (Map pp106-7; ☎ 878-4727; Av Salvador Allende No 720); Habana Vieja (Map p94; ☎ 863-4860; Aguiar No 509); Vedado (Map pp106-7; ☎ 831-2023; Calzada No 909) High-quality concerts and festivals.

**Fundación Alejo Carpentier** (Map p94; Empedrado No 215, Habana Vieja; 🕒 8am-4pm Mon-Fri) Near the Plaza de la Catedral. Check for cultural events at this baroque former palace of the Condessa de la Reunión (1820s) where Carpentier set his famous novel *El Siglo de las Luces (Explosion in a Cathedral)*.

**Instituto Cubano de Amistad con los Pueblos** (ICAP; Map pp106-7; ☎ 55 23 95; Paseo No 406 btwn Calles 17 & 19, Vedado; 🕒 11am-11pm) Rocking cultural and musical events in elegant mansion (1926); restaurant, bar and cigar shop also here.

**Union Nacional de Escritores y Artistas de Cuba** (Uneac; Map pp106-7; ☎ 832-4551; cnr Calles 17 & H, Vedado) The pulse-beat of the Cuban arts scene, this place is the first point of call for anyone with more than a passing interest in poetry, literature, art and music.

## Emergency

**Ambulance** (☎ 40 50 93/4)

**Asistur** (Map p100; ☎ 33 85 27, 33 89 20; asisten@asisten.get.cma.net; Casa del Científico, Paseo de Martí No 212, Centro Habana; 🕒 8:30am-5:30pm Mon-Fri, 8am-2pm Sat) Someone on staff should speak English; the alarm center here is open 24 hours.

**Poison Control** (☎ 260-1230, 260-8751)

### GETTING IN FROM THE AIRPORT

Habana airport is notoriously inaccessible by public transport. For first-time visitors a taxi is your best bet. Shop around at the arrivals terminal and you should get something in the vicinity of CUC$20.

Old stalwarts or those in the know might want to wait around for the sporadic terminal connector bus (a red, white and blue vehicle with 'conexión' displayed on the front) which for CUC$1 will drop you in nearby Av Boyeros where a cheaper yellow or white Lada taxi will take you into the centre for CUC$10 to CUC$15.

## Internet Access

**Biblioteca Nacional de Ciencias y Técnica** (Map p100; Capitolio Nacional, cnr Paseo de Martí & Brasil, Centro Habana; 🕒 8:15am-5pm Mon-Fri) Enter through stairs on left of main entrance.

**Cibercafé Capitolio** (Map p100; ☎ 862-0485; cnr Paseo de Martí & Brasil; per hr CUC$5; 🕒 8am-8pm) Inside main entrance.

**Cibercorreos** (Map p94; Obispo No 457 btwn Villegas & Aguacate; 🕒 8am-6pm; per hr CUC$4.50)

**Etecsa** Centro (Map p100; Aguilar No 565; 🕒 8am-9:30pm); Habana Vieja (Map p94; Habana 406) You can't miss this magnificent building.

**Hotel Business Centers** Hotel Habana Libre (Map pp106-7; Calle L btwn Calles 23 & 25); Hotel Inglaterra (Map p100; Paseo de Martí No 416); Hotel Nacional (Map pp106-7; cnr Calles O & 21, Vedado); Hotel NH Parque Central (Map p100; Neptuno cnr Paseo de Martí & Zulueta, Centro Habana) Usually a couple Convertibles more expensive, but reliable and shorter wait times.

## Laundry

**Lavandería Alaska** (Map p94; ☎ 863-0463; Villegas No 256; 🕒 6am-5pm Mon-Sat) Laundromat charging CUC$3 a load to wash and dry.

## Libraries

Foreign students with a Carnet (or letter from their academic institution) can get library cards. Each library requires its own card; show up with two passport photos. The following are open to the public, except for the Casa de las Américas' closed stacks, which require a card.

**Biblioteca José A Echevarría** (Map pp106-7; ☎ 832-6380; Casa de las Américas, Av de Presidentes No 210) Best art, architecture and general culture collection; books can't leave library.

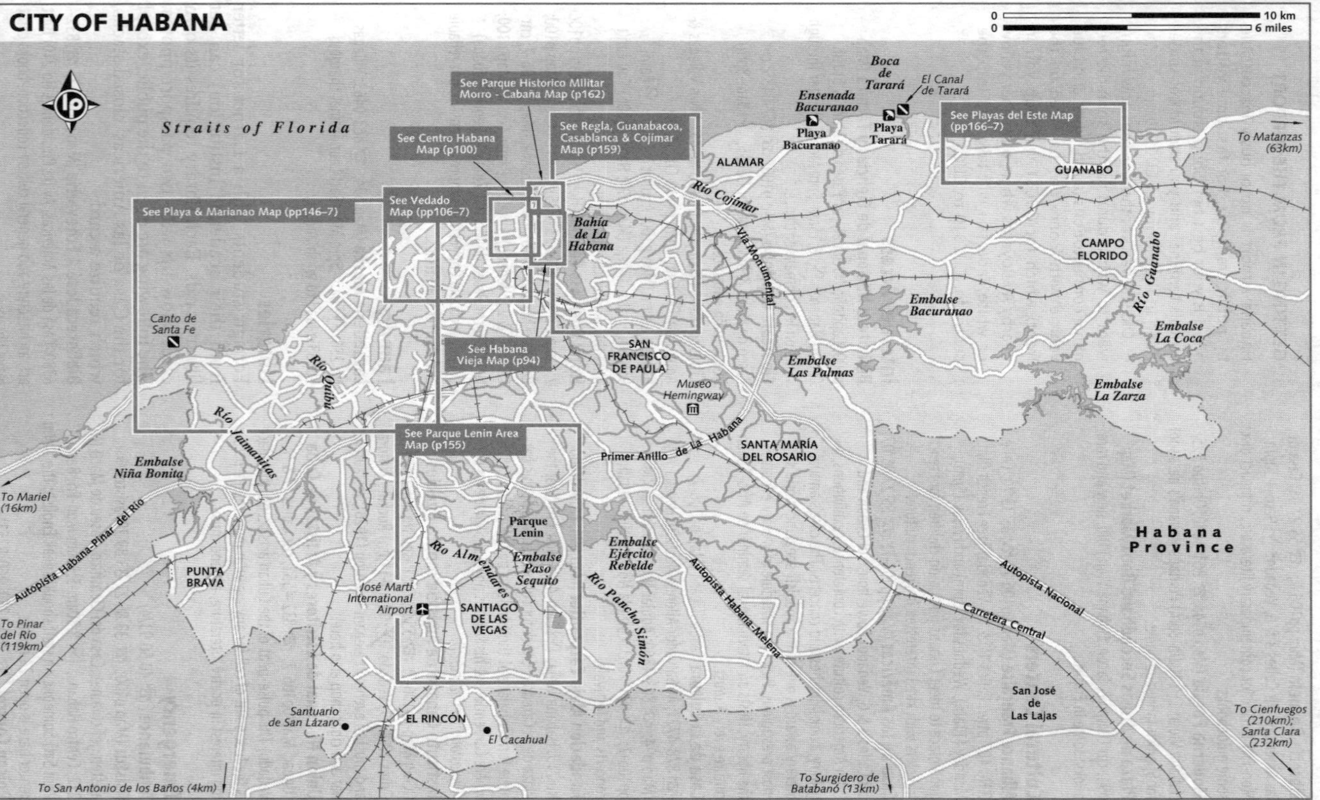
CITY OF HABANA
0 10 km
0 6 miles
Straits of Florida
See Parque Historico Militar Morro - Cabaña Map (p162)
See Centro Habana Map (p100)
See Regla, Guanabacoa, Casablanca & Cojímar Map (p159)
See Playas del Este Map (pp166–7)
See Vedado Map (pp106–7)
See Playa & Marianao Map (pp146–7)
See Habana Vieja Map (p94)
See Parque Lenin Area Map (p155)
Boca de Tarará
El Canal de Tarará
Ensenada Bacuranao
Playa Bacuranao
Playa Tarará
ALAMAR
GUANABO
To Matanzas (63km)
Río Cojímar
Vía Monumental
Bahía de La Habana
CAMPO FLORIDO
Río Guanabo
Embalse Bacuranao
Embalse La Coca
Embalse La Zarza
Embalse Las Palmas
Canto de Santa Fe
SAN FRANCISCO DE PAULA
Museo Hemingway
Río Quibú
Río Jaimanitas
Primer Anillo de La Habana
SANTA MARÍA DEL ROSARIO
Embalse Niña Bonita
To Mariel (16km)
Autopista Habana-Pinar del Río
Parque Lenin
Río Almendares
Embalse Paso Sequito
Embalse Ejército Rebelde
Río Pancho Simón
Autopista Habana-Melena
Autopista Nacional
Carretera Central
Habana Province
PUNTA BRAVA
José Martí International Airport
SANTIAGO DE LAS VEGAS
To Pinar del Río (119km)
San José de Las Lajas
Santuario de San Lázaro
EL RINCÓN
El Cacahual
To Cienfuegos (210km); Santa Clara (232km)
To San Antonio de los Baños (4km)
To Surgidero de Batabanó (13km)

**Biblioteca Nacional José Martí** (Map pp106-7; ☎ 55 54 42; Av de la Independencia, Plaza de la Revolución; 🕑 8am-5:45pm Mon-Sat) Habana's biggest library. Book and magazine launches are often held here.

**Biblioteca Rubén M Villena** (Map p94; ☎ 862-9038; cnr Obispo & Baratillo, Habana Vieja; 🕑 8am-9pm Mon-Sat, 9am-4pm Sat) Nice reading rooms and garden.

## Media

Cuba has a fantastic radio culture, where you'll hear everything from salsa to Supertramp, plus live sports broadcasts and soap operas. Radio is also the best source for listings on concerts, plays, movies and dances.

**Radio Ciudad de la Habana** (820AM & 94.9 FM) Cuban tunes by day, foreign pop at night; great '70s flashback at 8pm on Thursday and Friday.

**Radio Metropolitana** (910AM & 98.3 FM) Jazz and traditional boleros (music in 3/4 time); excellent Sunday afternoon rock show.

**Radio Musical Nacional** (590AM & 99.1FM) Classical.

**Radio Progreso** (640AM & 90.3 FM) Soap operas and humor.

**Radio Rebelde** (640AM, 710AM & 96.7 FM) News, interviews, good mixed music, plus baseball games.

**Radio Reloj** (950AM & 101.5 FM) News, plus the time every minute of every day.

**Radio Taíno** (1290AM & 93.3 FM) National tourism station with music, listings and interviews in Spanish and English. Nightly broadcasts (5pm to 7pm) list what's happening around town.

## Medical Services

Many of Cuba's specialist hospitals offering services to foreigners are based in Habana; see the site www.cubanacan.cu for details. Also consult the Playa & Marianao section of this chapter (p145) for listings of pharmacies and hospitals serving the diplomatic community.

**Centro Oftalmológico Camilo Cienfuegos** (Map pp106-7; cnr Calle L No 151 & Calle 13, Vedado) Head straight here with eye problems; also has an excellent pharmacy.

**Drogería Johnson** (Map p94; ☎ 862-6870; Obispo No 260, Habana Vieja; 🕑 24hr) Old-fashioned pharmacy in pesos.

**Farmacia Homopática** (Map pp106-7; cnr Calles 23 & M, Vedado; 🕑 8am-8pm Mon-Fri, 8am-4pm Sat)

**Farmacia: Hotel Habana Libre** (Map pp106-7; ☎ 55 45 93; Calle L btwn Calles 23 & 25, Vedado) Products sold in Convertibles.

**Farmacia Taquechel** (Map p94; ☎ 862-9286; Obispo No 155, Habana Vieja; 🕑 9am-6pm) Next to the Hotel Ambos Mundos. Cuban wonder drugs such as anticholesterol medication PPG sold in pesos here.

**Hospital Nacional Hermanos Ameijeiras** (Map pp106-7; ☎ 877-6053; fax 33 50 36; San Lázaro No 701, Centro Habana) Special hard-currency services; general consultations (CUC$25), hospitalization (CUC$75 per night) and cosmetic surgery. Enter via the lower level below the parking lot off Padre Varela (ask for 'CEDA' in Section N).

## Money

**Banco de Crédito y Comercio** Vedado (Map pp106-7; ☎ 33 76 33; cnr Línea & Paseo) Vedado (Map pp106-7; ☎ 870-2684; Airline Bldg, Calle 23); Vedado (Map pp106-7; ☎ 879-2074; Av Independencia No 101) The last – in post office between Terminal de Ómnibus and Plaza de la Revolución – is most convenient to immigration for visa extension stamps. Expect lines.

**Banco Financiero Internacional** Habana Vieja (Map p94; ☎ 860-9369; cnr Oficios & Brasil); Vedado (Map pp106-7; ☎ 55 44 29; Hotel Habana Libre, Calle L btwn Calles 23 & 25)

**Banco Metropolitano** Centro Habana (Map p100; cnr Av de Italia & San Martin); Vedado (Map pp106-7; ☎ 55 33 16/7; cnr Línea & Calle M, Vedado)

**Cadeca** Centro Habana (Map p100; cnr Neptuno & Agramonte; 🕑 9am-noon, 1-7pm Mon-Sat); Habana Vieja (Map p94; cnr Oficios & Lamparilla; 🕑 8am-7pm Mon-Sat, 8am-1pm Sun); Vedado (Map pp106-7; Calle 23 btwn K & L; 🕑 7am-2:30pm, 3:30-10pm); Vedado (Map pp106-7; mercado agropecuario, Calle 19 btwn Calles A & B; 🕑 7am-6pm Mon-Sat, 8am-1pm Sun); Vedado (Map pp106-7; cnr Malecón & Calle D) Cadeca gives cash advances and changes traveler's checks at 3.5% commission Monday to Friday (4% weekends).

**Cambio** (Map p94; Obispo No 257, Habana Vieja; 🕑 8am-10pm) The best opening hours in town.

## Post

**DHL** Vedado (Map pp106-7; ☎ 832-2112; Calzada No 818 btwn Calles 2 & 4; 🕑 8am-5pm Mon-Fri); Vedado (Map pp106-7; ☎ 55 00 04; Hotel Nacional, cnr Calles O & 21).

**Post offices** Centro Habana (Map p100; Gran Teatro, cnr San Martín & Paseo de Martí); Habana Vieja (Map p94; Plaza de San Francisco de Asís, Oficios No 102); Habana Vieja (Map p94; Unidad de Filatelia, Obispo No 518; 🕑 9am-7pm); Vedado (Map pp106-7; cnr Línea & Paseo; 🕑 8am-8pm Mon-Sat); Vedado (Map pp106-7; cnr Calles 23 & C; 🕑 8am-6pm Mon-Fri, 8am-noon Sat); Vedado (Map pp106-7; Av de la Independencia btwn Plaza de la Revolución & Terminal de Ómnibus; 🕑 stamp sales 24hr) This last has many services including photo developing, a bank and Cadeca. The Museo Postal Cubano (☎ 870-5581; admission CUC$1; open 10am to 5pm Saturday and Sunday) here has a philatelic shop. The post office at Obispo, Habana Vieja also has stamps for collectors.

## Telephone

**Etecsa** Centro Habana (Map p100; Aguilar No 565; 8am-9:30pm); Habana Vieja (Map p94; cnr Habana 406 & Obispo) There's also a Museo de las Telecomunicaciones (open 9am to 6pm Tuesday to Saturday) here.

## Toilets

Not over-endowed with clean available public washrooms, your best bet is to slip subtly into an upscale hotel. The following are all fairly relaxed about toilet security.

**Hotel Ambos Mundos** (Map p94; Obispo No 153) Tip the attendant.

**Hotel Habana Libre** (Map pp106-7; Calle L btwn Calles 23 & 25) Upstairs and by the elevators.

**Hotel Nacional** (Map pp106-7; Calle L btwn Calles 23 & 25) Right in the lobby and left past the elevators.

**Hotel Sevilla** (Map p100;Trocadero No 55 btwn Paseo de Martí & Agramonte) Turn right inside the lobby.

## Tourist Information

**Buró de Convenciones de Cuba** (Map pp106-7; ☎ 66 20 15; Calle M btwn Calles 17 & 19, Vedado; 8am-5pm Mon-Fri, 8am-noon Sat) Conferences, special events and festival information available here.

**Infotur** Airport (Map p155; ☎ 66 61 01; Terminal 3 Aeropuerto Internacional José Martí; 24hr); Expocuba (Map p155; ☎ 66 43 96; Carretera de Rocio Km 3.5); Habana Vieja (Map p94; ☎ 33 33 33; Obispo btwn Bernaza & Villegas); Habana Vieja (Map p94; ☎ 63 68 84; cnr Obispo & San Ignacio; 10am-1pm, 2-7pm) Books excursions, sells maps and phonecards, transport schedules.

## Travel Agencies

Many of the following agencies also have offices in the international arrivals lounge of Terminal 3.

**Cubamar** (Map pp106-7; ☎ 831-3151; www.cubamarviajes.cu; cnr Calle 3 & Malecón, Vedado; 8:30am-5pm Mon-Sat) Travel agency for Campismo Popular cabins countrywide. Also rents mobile homes.

**Cubanacán** Vedado (Map pp106-7; ☎ 873-2686; Hotel Nacional, cnr Calles O & 21; 8am-7pm); Vedado (Map pp106-7; Calle 23 btwn Calles N & O) Very helpful; head here if you want to arrange fishing or diving at Marina Hemingway; also in Hotel NH Parque Central, Hotel Inglaterra and Habana Libre.

**Cubatur** (Map pp106-7; ☎ 33 31 70/1; cnr Calles 23 & M, Vedado; 8am-8pm) Below Hotel Habana Libre. This agency pulls a lot of weight and finds rooms where others can't, which goes a long way toward explaining its slacker attitude.

**Havanatur** (Map pp106-7; ☎ 830- 8227; Galerías de Paseo, cnr Calle 1 & Paseo, Vedado)

**San Cristóbal Agencia de Viajes** (Map p94; ☎ 861-9171/2; www.sancristobaltravel.com; Oficios No 110 btwn Lamparilla & Amargura, Habana Vieja; 8:30am-5:30pm Mon-Fri, 8:30am-2pm Sat, 9am-noon Sun) Habaguanex agency operates Habana Vieja's classic hotels; income helps finance restoration.

### HABANA IN...

#### Two Days

Splash out on an early breakfast in the elegant **Hotel Sevilla** (p119), with bird's-eye views over the city from the famous 9th-floor restaurant. The **Museo de la Revolución** (p102) will take up most of the morning but clear your head afterwards with a revitalizing stroll through **Habana Vieja** (opposite) taking in the four archetypal 16th-century plazas. Take lunch in **El Patio** (p126) and spend the afternoon in the **Museo Nacional de Bella Artes** (p102). Grab dinner and a flamenco show in the **Mesón de la Flota** (p119) in Mercaderes afterwards.

Head west on day two through Centro stopping off at the **Callejón de Hamel** (p115) en route. Grab an ice cream in the **Coppelia** (p130) and a mojito in the **Hotel Nacional** (p104) and stroll back along the **Malecón** (p110) at sunset toward El Prado. Taxi it to La Cabaña for the 9pm **cañonazo ceremony** (p115) and get back in time for a late dinner in **La Dominica** (p125).

#### Four Days

Follow the two-day itinerary, with day three split between the **Plaza de la Revolución** (p105), and the **Real Fábrica de Tabacos Partagás** (p99). Buy a copy of *Cartelera* and check out the nighttime activities at **Uneac** (p89) or the **Casa de la Música** (p135) before hitting the Miramar **paladar** (p151) scene for delicious dinner. On day four, pack up your beach bag and head out to the **Playas del Este** (p164) for the day.

**Sol y Son** (Map pp106-7; ☎ 33 32 71; fax 33 51 50; Calle 23 No 64; 8:30am-7pm Mon-Fri, 8:30am-noon Sat) Sells Cubana flights.

## DANGERS & ANNOYANCES

Habana is an ostensibly safe city, and violent crime is rare. A heavy police presence on the streets and stiff prison sentences for crimes such as robbery and assault have acted as a major deterrent to potential thieves and kept the dirty tentacles of organized crime firmly at bay.

That is not to say that incidents do not occur. Indeed petty crime against tourists is on the rise in Habana, with bag snatching by youths mounted on bicycles a particular worry.

Keep your money belt on you at all times making sure that you wear it concealed – and tightly secured – around your waist.

In hotels always use a safety deposit box (if there is one) and never leave money/passports/credit cards lying around during the day. Theft from hotel rooms was particularly rife in Habana at the time of writing, with the temptation of earning three times your monthly salary in one fell swoop often too hard to resist.

In bars and restaurants it is wise to always check your change. Purposeful overcharging, especially when someone is mildly inebriated, is tediously common.

Visitors from the well-ordered countries of Europe or litigation-obsessed North America should be subconsciously aware of crumbling sidewalks, manholes with no covers, over-enthusiastic drivers, veering cyclists, carelessly lobbed front door keys (in Centro Habana) and badly-pitched baseballs (almost everywhere). Waves cascading over the Malecón sea-wall might look romantic, but the resulting slime-fest has been known to throw Lonely Planet–wielding tourists flying unceremoniously onto their asses.

For more popular scams see the boxed text, p114.

## SIGHTS & ACTIVITIES

### Habana Vieja

Colonial Habana is packed full with museums, art galleries, churches, restaurants and drinking houses; way too much to see in a day or three, though most of the sights can be visited on foot. For a whistle-stop introduction to the best parts of the city, check out the suggested walking tours (p111) or stick closely to the four main squares of Armas, Vieja, San Francisco and Catedral.

#### PLAZA DE LA CATEDRAL

Dominated by two unequal towers, the **Catedral de San Cristóbal de la Habana** (cnr San Ignacio & Empedrado; before noon) was described by novelist Alejo Carpentier as 'music set in stone.' Its striking baroque facade (à la Italian architect Francesco Borromini) creates unrivaled ambience, especially at night when live music mingles with laughter in the wide open plaza. The Jesuits began construction of the church in 1748, and work continued despite their expulsion in 1767. When the building was finished in 1787 the diocese of Habana was created. A year later the city became a bishop's seat, elevating the church to a cathedral – one of the oldest in the Americas. Perhaps the best time to visit is during Mass, celebrated Sunday at 10:30am; smaller services happen in the adjacent chapel Monday to Friday at 8pm.

While circumnavigating the plaza, be sure to visit the **Centro Wilfredo Lam** (☎ 862-2611; cnr San Ignacio & Empedrado; admission CUC$3; 10am-5pm Mon-Sat) next to the cathedral, which displays the works of one of Cuba's leading modern painters and hosts shows by local and international artists. A Cuban of Chinese and African ancestry, Lam was strongly influenced by Pablo Picasso, whom he met in 1936. Many other noble buildings face the Plaza de la Catedral, including the 1760 **Palacio de los Marqueses de Aguas Claras** (San Ignacio No 54), now drawing crowds as Restaurante El Patio. The outdoor tables make a nice spot for a break.

Across the square are the 18th-century **Casa de Lombillo** and the **Palacio del Marqués de Arcos** (1746), today a Telecorreo Internacional office. During the mid-19th century this palace served as Habana's main post office and the stone mask ornamental mailbox built into the wall is still in use.

The **Museo de Arte Colonial** (☎ 862-6440; San Ignacio No 61; unguided/guided CUC$2/3, plus camera CUC$2; 9am-6:30pm), on the southern side of the plaza, displays colonial furniture and decorative arts in the **Palacio de los Condes de Casa Bayona** (1720), the oldest house on the square. One of the funkiest sights around here (aside from the folkloric mulattas

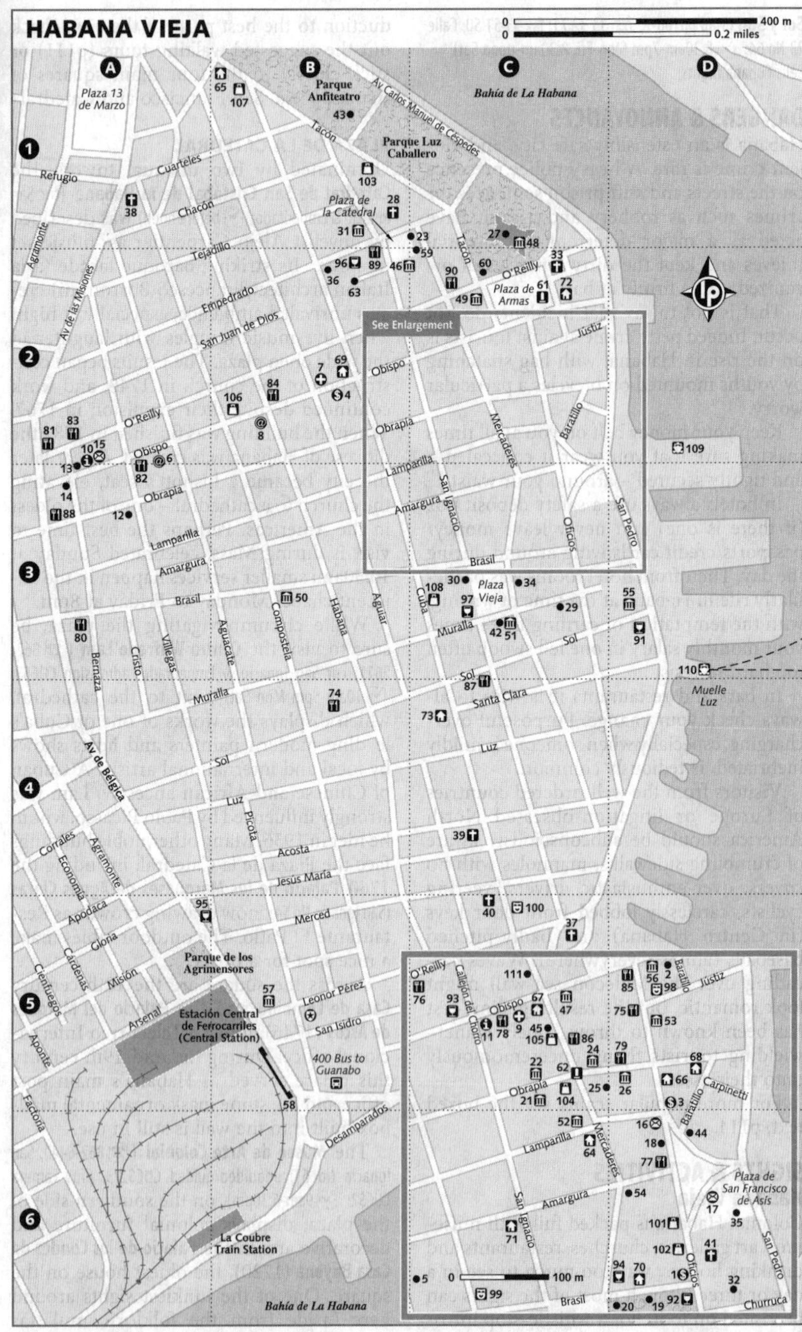
HABANA VIEJA
0 400 m
0 0.2 miles
Bahía de La Habana
Plaza 13 de Marzo
Parque Anfiteatro
Parque Luz Caballero
Plaza de la Catedral
Plaza de Armas
See Enlargement
Plaza Vieja
Muelle Luz
Parque de los Agrimensores
Estación Central de Ferrocarriles (Central Station)
400 Bus to Guanabo
La Coubre Train Station
Plaza de San Francisco de Asís
Av Carlos Manuel de Céspedes
Tacón
Refugio
Cuarteles
Chacón
Tejadillo
Empedrado
San Juan de Dios
O'Reilly
Obispo
Obrapía
Lamparilla
Amargura
Brasil
Muralla
Sol
Santa Clara
Luz
Acosta
Jesús María
Merced
Leonor Pérez
San Isidro
Desamparados
Arsenal
Misión
Gloria
Apodaca
Corrales
Economía
Agramonte
Cárdenas
Cienfuegos
Aponte
Factoría
Av de las Misiones
Av de Bélgica
Bernaza
Cristo
Villegas
Aguacate
Compostela
Habana
Picota
Aguiar
Cuba
Mercaderes
San Ignacio
Oficios
San Pedro
Baratillo
Justiz
Callejón del Chorro
Carpinetti
Churruca
0 100 m

**INFORMATION**

Banco Financiero Internacional....1 D6
Biblioteca Rubén M Villena..........2 D5
Cadeca.......................................3 D5
Cambio.......................................4 B2
Casa de la Cultura de La Habana Vieja.......................................5 C6
Cibercorreos...............................6 A2
Drogería Johnson.......................7 B2
Etecsa........................................8 B2
Farmacia Taquechel....................9 C5
Infotur.......................................10 A2
Infotur.......................................11 C5
Lavandería Alaska.....................12 A3
Librería Cervantes..................(see 13)
Librería Grijalbo Mondadovi..........................(see 60)
Librería La Internacional...........13 A3
Moderna Poesía.........................14 A3
Post Office................................15 A2
Post Office................................16 D6
Post Office................................17 D6
San Cristóbal Agencia de Viajes.......................................18 D6

**SIGHTS & ACTIVITIES**

Aquarivm...................................19 D6
Cámara Oscura..........................20 D6
Casa de África...........................21 C5
Casa de la Obra Pía...................22 C5
Casa de Lombillo.......................23 C1
Casa de México Benito Juárez......................................24 C5
Casa del Albanico......................25 C5
Casa Oswaldo Guayasamín............................26 D5
Castillo de la Real Fuerza...........27 C1
Catedral de San Cristóbal de la Habana.....................................28 B1
Centro Cultural Pablo de la Torriente Brau..........................29 C3
Centro de Desarollo de los Artes Visuales.........................30 C3
Centro Wilfredo Lam..................31 B1
Coche Mambí.............................32 D6
Diago Galería de Arte..............(see 42)
El Templete................................33 C2
Fototeca de Cuba.......................34 C3
Fuente de los Leones..................35 D6
Fundación Alejo Carpentier........36 B2
Iglesia de San Francisco de Paula.......................................37 C5
Iglesia del Santo Angel Custodio...................................38 A1
Iglesia Parroquial del Espíritu Santo.......................................39 C4
Iglesia y Convento de Nuestra Señora de la Merced.............40 C5
Iglesia y Convento de Santa Clara.................................(see 73)
Iglesia y Monasterio de San Francisco de Asís.....................41 D6
Instituto Cubano del Libro......(see 60)
La Casona Centro de Art............42 C3
La Maestranza...........................43 B1
Lonja del Comercio....................44 D6
Maqueta de la Habana Vieja.......45 C5
Museo de Arte Colonial (Palacio de los Condes de Casa Bayona).......46 B2
Museo de Arte del Lejano Oriente....................................47 C5
Museo de la Cerámica Artística Cubana.....................................48 C1
Museo de la Ciudad (Palacio de los Capitanes Generales).....49 C2
Museo de la Farmacia Habanera...................................50 B3
Museo de Naipes........................51 C3
Museo de Simón Bolívar............52 C6
Museo de Tabaco...................(see 105)
Museo del Automóvil..................53 D5
Museo del Chocolate..................54 D6
Museo del Ron (Fundación Havana Club)............................55 D3
Museo Nacional de Historia Natural....................................56 D5
Museo-Casa Natal de José Martí.......................................57 B5
Old City Wall.............................58 B5
Palacio de los Capitanes Generales..............................(see 49)
Palacio de los Condes de Casa Bayona...............................(see 46)
Palacio de los Condes de Santovenia...........................(see 72)
Palacio de los Marqueses de Aguas Claras........................(see 89)
Palacio del Marqués de Arcos.......................................59 C2
Palacio del Segundo Cabo (Instituto Cubano del Libro)......................60 C2
Sala Galería Raúl Martínez......(see 60)
Statue of Carlos Manuel de Céspedes.................................61 C2
Statue of Simón Bolívar.............62 C5
Taller Experimental de Gráfica.....................................63 B2

**SLEEPING**

Hostal Condes de Villanueva......64 C6
Hostal San Miguel......................65 B1
Hostal Valencia..........................66 D5
Hotel Ambos Mundos.................67 C5
Hotel El Comendador.................68 D5
Hotel Florida..............................69 B2
Hotel Los Frailes........................70 D6
Hotel Raquel..............................71 C6
Hotel Santa Isabel......................72 C2
Residencia Académica Convento de Santa Clara.........................73 C4

**EATING**

Agropecuario Sol........................74 B4
Al Medina...................................75 D5
Bar-Restaurant La Luz............(see 78)
Café de O'Reilly..........................76 C5
Café del Oriente.........................77 D6
Café Santo Domingo...................78 C5
Cafe Wilfredo Lam.................(see 31)
Cafetería Torre La Vega..............79 D5
El Mecurio...........................(see 44)
Hanoi.........................................80 A3
Harris Brothers...........................81 A2
Heladería Obispo........................82 A3
La Julia.......................................83 A2
La Lluvia de Oro.........................84 B2
La Mina......................................85 D5
La Torre de Marfil.......................86 C5
Paladar La Mulata del Sabor.......87 C4
Restaurante El Castillo de Farnés........................................88 A3
Restaurante El Patio....................89 B2
Restaurante La Dominica............90 C2
Restaurante La Paella............(see 66)
Restaurante Mirador de la Bahía...................................(see 56)

**DRINKING**

Bar Dos Hermanos......................91 D3
Bar La Marina.............................92 D6
Café París...................................93 C5
Café Taberna..............................94 D6
El Baturro...................................95 A5
La Bodeguita del Medio..............96 B2
Taberna de la Muralla.................97 C3

**ENTERTAINMENT**

Casa de la Comedia....................98 D5
Casa de la Cultura de La Habana Vieja...........................99 C6
Gimnasio de Boxeo Rafael Trejo......................................100 C5

**SHOPPING**

Casa de Carmen Montilla.........101 D6
Estudio Galería Los Oficios.....102 D6
Feria de la Artesanía................103 B1
Fundación Havana Club Shop...................................(see 55)
Habana 1791............................104 C5
La Casa del Habano..................105 C5
Longina Música........................106 B2
Palacio de la Artesanía.............107 B1
Taller de Serigrafía René Portocarrero...........................108 C3

**TRANSPORT**

Cruise Ship Terminal................109 D2
Ferries to Regla & Casablanca...............................110 D3
Horse Carriages.......................111 C5

posing for pictures) is the **Taller Experimental de Gráfica** (☎ 862-0979; tgrafica@cubarte.cult.cu; Callejón del Chorro No 6; admission free; 🕑 10am-4pm Mon-Fri) up the alley from the southwestern corner of Plaza de la Catedral. You will see reams of original prints freshly inked and hanging to dry; you can buy what you like. This workshop accepts serious students interested in mastering the art of engraving (see Courses, p114).

## PLAZA DE ARMAS

This lovely plaza and book bazaar was the seat of authority and power in Cuba for

400 years. A square has existed on this site since 1582, although the present Plaza de Armas dates only from 1792. In the center of the park surrounded by stately royal palms is a marble **statue of Carlos Manuel de Céspedes** (1955), the man who set Cuba on the road to independence in 1868. Live music floats about, while the breeze flutters over from the Malecón – it's a nice spot to chill out.

With lots of stained glass and gigantic chandeliers, the baroque **Palacio de los Capitanes Generales**, on the western side of the Plaza de Armas, is one of Cuba's most majestic buildings. Construction began on the site of the old parochial church in 1776, and from 1791 until 1898 this was the residence of the Spanish governor. From 1899 until 1902, the US military governors were based here, after which the building became the presidential palace. In 1920 the president moved to the building now housing the Museo de la Revolución in Centro Habana and this palace became the city hall. The municipal authorities moved out in 1967 and since 1968 it has been home to the **Museo de la Ciudad** (☎ 861-6130; Calle Tacón No 1; unguided/guided CUC$3/4, plus camera CUC$2; 🕑 9am-6pm). Peacocks strut about the courtyard, there's a spooky crypt and an even more eerie Jesus. The marble bathtubs are marvelous. The guided tour gets you behind the velvet ropes and up close with the lush collection. Come early to beat the tour-bus crowd.

The **Palacio del Segundo Cabo** (O'Reilly No 4; admission CUC$1), the former headquarters of the Spanish vice-governor at the northwestern corner of the plaza, is another baroque beauty, built in 1772. Later it became the Supreme Court, and today it houses the **Instituto Cubano del Libro**. It's worth glimpsing into the arcaded inner courtyard and visiting the very good (with air-con) bookshop here. Pop-art fans should take a look in the **Sala Galería Raúl Martínez** (🕑 9am-6pm Mon-Sat).

On the northeastern side of the Plaza de Armas is the oldest extant colonial fortress in the Americas, the **Castillo de la Real Fuerza**, built between 1558 and 1577 on the site of an earlier fort destroyed by French privateers in 1555. The west tower is crowned by the famous bronze weather vane called **La Giraldilla**, cast in Habana in 1632 by Jerónimo Martínez Pinzón and popularly believed to be Doña Inés de Bobadilla, the wife of explorer Hernando de Soto. The original Giraldilla is in the Museo de la Ciudad and the figure also appears on the Havana Club rum label. The Spanish governor resided in the castle for 200 years until they finally got around to constructing a palace of their own across the square. La Fuerza now shelters the **Museo de la Cerámica Artística Cubana** (☎ 861-6130; admission CUC$2; 🕑 9am-6pm) downstairs. Worth a look, this museum displays works by some of Cuba's leading contemporary artists. Upstairs affords a great view of the harbor entrance.

In 1519 the Villa de San Cristóbal de la Habana was founded on the spot marked by **El Templete** (admission CUC$2; 🕑 8:30am-6pm) a neoclassical Doric chapel erected on the eastern side of the Plaza de Armas in 1828. The first Mass was held below a ceiba tree similar to the one presently in front of the building, and inside the chapel are three paintings of the event by the French painter Jean Baptiste Vermay. Adjacent to El Templete is the late-18th-century **Palacio de los Condes de Santovenia**, today the five-star, 27-room Hotel Santa Isabel. Nearby is the **Museo Nacional de Historia Natural** (☎ 863-9361; Obispo No 61; admission CUC$3; 🕑 9:30am-7pm Tue-Sun), which contains examples of Cuba's flora and fauna. The restaurant-bar upstairs has fabulous vistas across the bay.

Perhaps one of Habana's most amusing sights is the small and vaguely surreal **Museo del Automóvil** (Oficios No 13; admission CUC$1; 🕑 9am-7pm), stuffed full with ancient Thunderbirds and Pontiacs and Ford Model Ts, at least half of which appear to be in better shape that the asthmatic automobiles in the streets outside. They've even got the car that Che Guevara once drove (very badly apparently) after he was installed as a member of the revolutionary government as head of the National Bank.

### ALONG MERCADERES & OBRAPÍA

This stretch is packed with quirky little places such as the **Museo de Arte del Lejano Oriente** (☎ 863-9740; Mercaderes No 111; 🕑 10am-6pm Tue-Sat, 9am-1pm Sun), with Far Eastern art, and the **Museo de Tabaco** (☎ 861-5795; Mercaderes No 120; 🕑 10am-5pm Mon-Sat), where you can gawp at various indigenous pipes and idols. The **Maqueta de la Habana Vieja** (Mercaderes No 114;

unguided/guided CUC$1/2; 9am-6pm) is a 1:500 scale model of Habana Vieja complete with an authentic soundtrack meant to replicate a day in the life of the city. It's incredibly detailed and provides an excellent way of geographically acquainting yourself with what the central historical district has to offer. Go here first. You might glimpse a young woman celebrating her *quinciñera* (Cuban rite of passage for girls turning 15) at **Casa de la Obra Pía** (Obrapía No 158; admission CUC$1, plus camera CUC$2; 9am-4:30pm Tue-Sat, 9:30am-12:30pm Sun) around the corner. This typical Habana aristocratic residence was originally built in the first half of the 17th century and rebuilt in 1780 soon after the British occupation. Decorative flourishes cover the exterior facade, and between the two inner courtyards is a wonderfully refreshing room. Across the street is the **Casa de África** (☎ 861-5798; Obrapía No 157) housing artifacts from Fidel Castro's 1977 African tour, plus sacred objects relating to Santería, formerly in the collection of ethnographer Fernando Ortíz.

On the corner of Mercaderes and Obrapía is a bronze **statue** of Latin America liberator Simón Bolívar, to whom a **museum** (☎ 861-3988; Mercaderes No 160; donations accepted; 9am-5pm Tue-Sun) is dedicated nearby. The **Casa de México Benito Juárez** (☎ 861-8166; Obrapía No 116; admission CUC$1; 10:15am-5:45pm Tue-Sat, 9am-1pm Sun) exhibits Mexican folk art in an 18th-century palace; there's a specialized library here for all things *mexicana*. Just east is the **Casa Oswaldo Guayasamín** (☎ 861-3843; Obrapía No 111; donations accepted; 9am-2:30pm Tue-Sun), the old studio, now a museum, of the great Ecuadorian painter. (Fidel sat for Guayasamín; to see the portrait, visit the Fundación Naturaleza y El Hombre, p148.) Openings and exhibits of Cuban and international art are held here.

### PLAZA DE SAN FRANCISCO DE ASÍS

Another of Habana Vieja's picturesque plazas, **Plaza de San Francisco de Asís** is a dockside beauty dominated by the domed **Lonja del Comercio**, a former commodities market erected in 1909 and restored in 1996 to provide office space for foreign companies with joint ventures in Cuba. Enter the building to admire its central dome. Across from 'La Lonja' is the white marble **Fuente de los Leones** (Fountain of Lions) carved by the Italian sculptor Giuseppe Gaginni in 1836. The southern side of the square is taken up by the impressive **Iglesia y Monasterio de San Francisco de Asís**. Originally constructed in 1608 and rebuilt in the baroque style from 1719 to 1738, San Francisco de Asís was taken over by the Spanish state in 1841 as part of a political move against the powerful religious orders of the day, when it ceased to be a church. Today the church itself is a **concert hall** ( starting 5pm or 6pm) hosting classical, chamber and choral music and a **museum** (☎ 862-3467; admission CUC$1, plus camera CUC$2; 9am-5:30pm) in the two large cloisters. Price of admission allows access to the tallest church tower in Habana; money well spent.

### MUSEO DEL RON

Even for teetotalers, the intriguing **Museo del Ron** (☎ 861-8051; San Pedro No 262; admission incl guide CUC$5; ☎ 9am-5pm Mon-Fri, 10am-4pm Sat & Sun) in the Fundación Havana Club is worth a turn. The interesting bilingual guided tour shows rum-making antiquities (check out the funky terra-cotta flask), plus explains the entire brewing process, from cane cutting to quaffing amber Añejo Reserva in the museum's tasting room. The scale model of the Central La Esperanza, with working train, is especially cool. The dancing lessons here are said to be excellent (see Courses, p114).

### PLAZA VIEJA

Certainly one of Habana Vieja's most dazzling public spaces, **Plaza Vieja**, dating from the 16th century, is surrounded by several sites not to be missed. It was an open-air marketplace until 1835, and hideous underground parking lot during the Batista regime; since the mid-1990s there has been a concerted effort to restore this plaza to its former grandeur. On the northwestern corner is Habana's **cámara oscura** (admission CUC$1; 9am-5pm Tue-Sat, 9am-1pm Sun), providing live, 360-degree views of the city from atop a 35m-tall tower. Sheets flap in the breeze, old cars amble by and the docent does an admirable job explaining Habana's architectural highlights in Spanish and English. In the arcade adjacent is **Fototeca de Cuba** (☎ 862-2530; Mercaderes No 307; admission free; 10am-5pm Tue-Fri, 9am-noon Sat), a photo gallery with intriguing exhibits by local and international artists.

On the southern side of the plaza is the quirky **Museo de Naipes** (Muralla No 101; admission CUC$1; 9am-6pm Tue-Sun), with a collection of every playing card imaginable. Rock stars, rum drinks, round cards – they've got 2000 of them here. Next door is **La Casona Centro de Arte** (861-8544; Muralla No 107; 10am-5pm Mon-Fri, 10am-2pm Sat), with great solo and group shows by up-and-coming Cuban artists such as Abel Barroso. Also here is **Diago Galería de Arte** (863-4703). On the western side of the park is yet another gallery in another gorgeous colonial building at the **Centro de Desarollo de los Artes Visuales** (862-2611; San Ignacio No 352; admission free; 10am-5pm Tue-Sat); here you'll find good contemporary Cuban art.

Around the corner, the **Centro Cultural Pablo de la Torriente Brau** (861-6251; www.centropablo.cult.cu; Muralla No 63; admission free; 9am-5:30pm Tue-Sat) hosts a variety of expositions of substance, including poetry readings and a live acoustic music series called 'Guitarra Limpia.' Its Salón de Arte Digital is renowned for its groundbreaking digital art.

Sidetrack up Brasil and you'll stumble upon the **Museo de la Farmacia Habanera** (cnr Brasil & Compostela; admission free) founded in 1886 by Catalan José Sarrá and once considered the second most important pharmacy in the world. The museum got the Habaguanex makeover in 2004 and, aside from the elegant mock-up of an old drugstore with some interesting historical explanations; it still acts as a working shop for Cubans.

### CHURCHES

South of Plaza Vieja are a string of stunning and important churches. The 1638–43 **Iglesia y Convento de Santa Clara** (866-9327; Cuba No 610; admission CUC$2; 9am-4pm Mon-Fri) stopped being a convent in 1920. Later this complex was the Ministry of Public Works, and today the Habana Vieja restoration team is based there. You can visit the large cloister and nuns' cemetery or even spend the night (with reservations far in advance, see p117). Habana's oldest surviving church (built in 1640, and rebuilt in 1674) is the **Iglesia Parroquial del Espíritu Santo** (862-3140; Acosta 161; 8am-noon, 3-6pm), with many burials in the crypt. Built in 1755 the **Iglesia y Convento de Nuestra Señora de la Merced** (Cuba No 806; 8am-noon & 3-5:30pm) was reconstructed in the 19th century. Beautiful gilded altars, frescoed vaults and a number of old paintings create a sacrosanct mood; there's a quiet cloister adjacent.

The **Iglesia de San Francisco de Paula** (41 50 37; cnr Leonor Pérez & Desamparados) is one of Haba-

### RESTORING OLD HABANA

Stuffed with architectural jewels from every era, Habana Vieja offers visitors one of the finest collections of urban edifices in the Americas. At a conservative estimate, Habana Vieja alone contains more than 900 buildings of historical importance with myriad examples of illustrious architecture ranging from intricate baroque to glitzy art deco.

Since 1982, when Unesco added Habana Vieja to its World Heritage list, a massive regeneration project has been rolled out under the auspices of longstanding city historian, Eusebio Leal.

Acting in tandem with a government-run company Habaguanex, Leal's restoration is being mapped out in stages with priority being given to buildings that once revamped will generate enough tourist Convertibles to finance further renovation schemes.

At any one time Habaguanex' combined operations employ more than 10,000 people and generate up to the equivalent of US$160 million a year in profits. Of this cash approximately 45% is reinvested into new projects, 30% is earmarked for social programs, while the remaining 25% is channeled into state reserves for deserving schemes elsewhere in the city.

But remodeled buildings are only half the story. 'We have decided in favor of a living historic centre,' master plan architect Patricia Rodríguez is on record as saying.

Unique among projects of this type, Leal's makeover also includes major social and cultural benefits for Habana Vieja's long-suffering population of 70,000 people, 45% of whom still live in houses deemed unfit for human habitation.

Among the social projects sponsored by the institution in the last few years are a maternity home, 10 refurbished schools and a rehabilitation center for children with diseases of the central nervous system.

na's most attractive churches. Fully restored in 2000, this church is all that remains of the San Francisco de Paula women's hospital from the mid-1700s. Lit up at night for concerts (most notably by the medieval ensemble Ars Longa) the stained glass, heavy cupola and baroque facade are utterly romantic and inviting.

#### MUSEO-CASA NATAL DE JOSÉ MARTÍ

If you visit only one *casa natal* (birth house) in Cuba, make it **Museo-Casa Natal de José Martí** (☎ 861-3778; Leonor Pérez No 314; admission CUC$1, plus camera CUC$2; 🕑 9am-5pm Tue-Sat), the birthplace of José Martí. The apostle of Cuban independence was born in this humble dwelling on January 28, 1853, and the museum displays letters, manuscripts, photos, books and other mementos of his life. Nearby, to the west across Av de Bélgica, is the longest remaining stretch of the **old city wall** (building began in 1674). A bronze map shows the outline of the original layout. To the west is Habana's huge Estación Central de Férrocarriles where *La Junta,* the steam locomotive that inaugurated the line to Matanzas in 1843, is on display.

### Centro Habana

#### CAPITOLIO NACIONAL

Washington, DC and Habana have more in common than you may think, evidenced by the dominating marble-covered **Capitolio Nacional** (☎ 863-7861; admission unguided/guided CUC$3/4; 🕑 9am-8pm), which is similar to the US Capitol Building, but richer in detail. This is one of Habana's divine architectural highlights. To enter, climb the monumental stairway on the eastern side of the building. The tour is highly recommended.

Initiated by the US-backed dictator Gerardo Machado in 1929, the Capitolio took 5000 workers three years, two months and 20 days to build at a cost of the equivalent of US$17 million. It was the seat of the Cuban Congress until 1959 and now houses the Cuban Academy of Sciences and the National Library of Science and Technology. Entering the great domed hall through huge bronze doors (notice the important events in Cuban history they depict) imbues just how monumental this building is.

Across what seems like kilometers of intricately laid portico marble is the 49-metric-ton, 17m statue of the republic (a woman, don't you know?), the third-largest indoor bronze statue in the world; only the Buddha in Nava, Japan, and the Lincoln Memorial in Washington, DC, are bigger. Directly below the Capitolio's 62m-high dome, a 24-carat diamond replica is set in the floor. Highway distances between Habana and all sites in Cuba are calculated from this point. Visitors are also shown the mahogany-covered library and the former chambers of the Senate and Deputies. It's an extraordinary edifice and you can spend a whole afternoon gawking at the architectural details, taking coffee at the lovely balcony café (see p129).

Behind the Capitolio is the **Real Fábrica de Tabacos Partagás** (☎ 862-0086; Industria No 520 btwn Barcelona & Dragones; 🕑 tours every 15 min btwn 9:30-11am & 12:30-3pm); for tours of this and other Habana cigar factories, see the boxed text, p110.

#### PARQUE LA FRATERNIDAD

The **Fuente de la India** (the traffic island at Dragones near Máximo Gómez, east of the park) is a white Carrara marble fountain carved by Giuseppe Gaginni in 1837. Honoring heritage old and new, the sculpture is an indigenous girl seated above four dolphins, a famous symbol of Habana. She's embracing the city's coat of arms.

Just east of the sculpture across Paseo de Martí is the **Asociación Cultural Yoruba de Cuba** (☎ 863-5953; Paseo de Martí No 615; admission CUC$6; 🕑 9am-4pm Mon-Sat). The museum here provides a worthwhile overview of the Santería religion, the saints and their powers. There are free *tambores* (Santería drum ceremonies) here alternate Fridays at 4:30pm (when you can check out the museum for free), and you can arrange consultations as well. Note that there's a church dress code for the *tambores* (no shorts or tank tops).

Across the street is leafy **Parque de la Fraternidad**, originally a Spanish military parade ground. The first park was laid out here in 1892 to commemorate the fourth centenary of the Spanish arrival in the Americas, and in 1928 the park was remodeled in honor of the Pan-American Conference hosted in Habana that year. The grand ceiba tree dominating the park was planted in a mixture of soil from all the countries of the Americas, and busts of prominent Latin and North Americans were set up in the vicinity

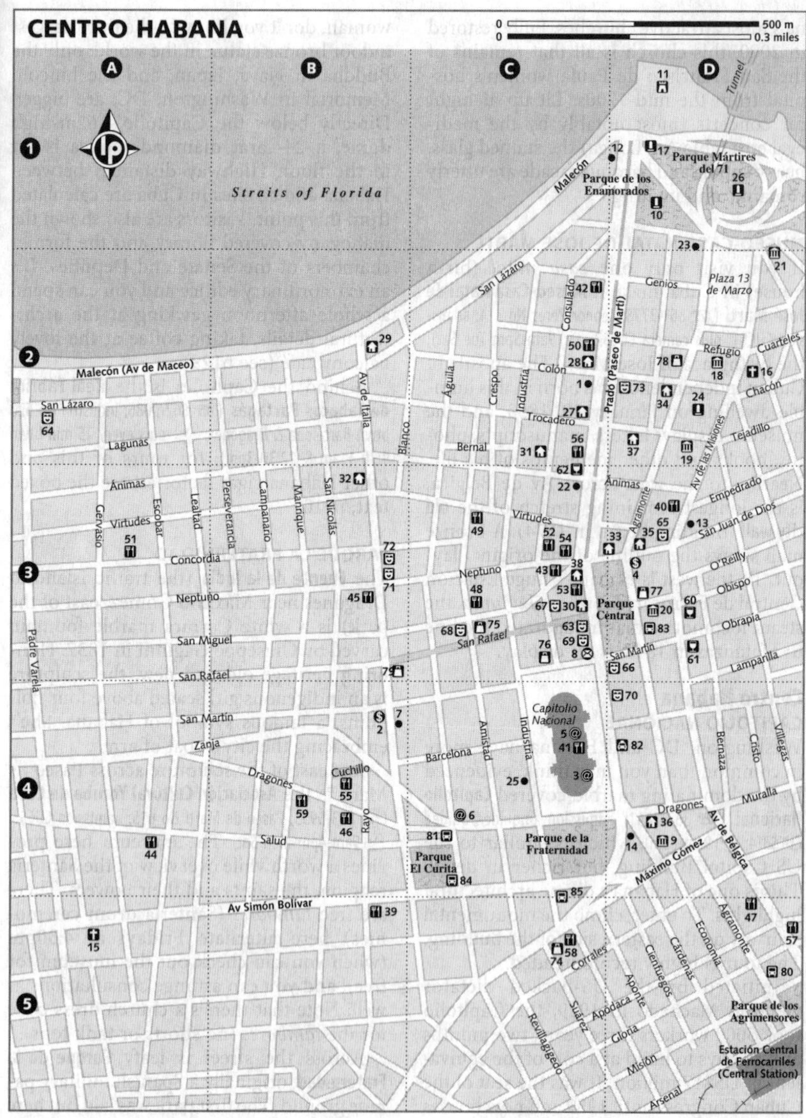


(including Abe Lincoln, a hero in Cuba). Today this area is the terminus of numerous city bus routes, and you'll see rows of lovingly restored American cars sparkling in the morning sunlight. Cubans dub this antiquated parking lot 'Jurassic Park.'

A little out on a limb, but well worth the walk, is the **Iglesia del Sagrado Corazón de Jesus** (Av Simon Bolivar btwn Gervasio & Padre Varela), an inspiring marble creation with a distinctive white steeple, where you can enjoy a few precious minutes of quiet and cool contemplation away from the craziness of the street. This church is rightly famous for its magnificent stained-glass windows and the light that penetrates through the eaves first

**INFORMATION**

Asistur ... 1 C2
Banco Metropolitano ... 2 B4
Biblioteca Nacional de Ciencias y Técnica ... 3 C4
Cadeca ... 4 D3
Cibercafe Capitolio ... 5 C4
Etecsa ... 6 C4
Librería Luis Rogelio Nogueras ... 7 B4
Post Office ... 8 C3

**SIGHTS & ACTIVITIES**

Asociación Cultural Yoruba de Cuba ... 9 D4
Cárcel ... 10 D1
Castillo de San Salvador de la Punta ... 11 D1
Centro Gallego ... (see 69)
Centro Hispano Americano de Cultura ... 12 D1
Edificio Bacardí ... 13 D3
Fuente de la India ... 14 D4
Iglesia del Sagrado Corazón de Jesus ... 15 A5
Iglesia del Santo Angel Custodio ... 16 D2
Memorial a los Estudiantes de Medicina ... 17 D1
Museo de la Revolución ... 18 D2
Museo Nacional de Bellas Artes (Colección de Arte Cubano) ... 19 D2
Museo Nacional de Bellas Artes (Colección de Arte Universal) ... 20 D3
Museo Nacional de la Música ... 21 D2
Palacio de los Matrimonios ... 22 C3
Palacio Velasco (Spanish Embassy) ... 23 D1
Pavillón Granma ... 24 D2
Real Fábrica de Tabacos Partagás ... 25 C4
Statue of General Máximo Gómez ... 26 D1

**SLEEPING**

Casa del Científico ... 27 C2
Hotel Caribbean ... 28 C2
Hotel Deauville ... 29 B2
Hotel Inglaterra ... 30 C3
Hotel Lido ... 31 C2
Hotel Lincoln ... 32 B3
Hotel NH Parque Central ... 33 D3
Hotel Park View ... 34 D2
Hotel Plaza ... 35 D3
Hotel Saratoga ... 36 D4
Hotel Sevilla ... 37 D2
Hotel Telégrafo ... 38 C3

**EATING**

Almacenes Ultra ... 39 B5
Asociación Canaria de Cuba ... 40 D3
Cafe La Logia ... 41 C4
Centro Andaluz ... 42 C2
Feria Los Fornos ... 43 C3
Flor de Lotu ... 44 A4
La Época ... 45 B3
Los Dos Dragones ... 46 B4
Mercado Agropecuario Egido ... 47 D5
Paladar Amistad de Lanzarote ... 48 C3
Paladar Bellamar ... 49 C3
Paladar Doña Blanquita ... 50 C2
Paladar La Guarida ... 51 A3
Paladar Las Delicias de Consulado ... 52 C3
Pastelería Francesa ... 53 C3
Prado y Neptuno ... 54 C3
Restaurant Tien-Tan ... 55 B4
Restaurante Oasis ... 56 C2
Restaurante Puerto de Sagua ... 57 D5
Supermercado Isla de Cuba ... 58 C5
Tres Chinitos ... 59 B4

**DRINKING**

El Floridita ... 60 D3
La Zaragozana ... (see 60)
Monserrate Bar ... 61 D3
Restaurante Prado 264 ... 62 C3

**ENTERTAINMENT**

Cabaret Nacional ... 63 C3
Casa de la Trova ... 64 A2
Cine Actualidades ... 65 D3
Cine Payret ... 66 D3
Cinecito ... 67 C3
Discoteca Ribera Azul ... (see 29)
El Palermo ... 68 C3
Gran Teatro de La Habana ... 69 C3
Kid Chocolate ... 70 D4
La Casa de la Música Centro Habana ... 71 B3
Teatro América ... 72 B3
Teatro Fausto ... 73 D2

**SHOPPING**

Area de Vendedores por Cuenta Propia ... 74 C5
El Bulevar ... 75 C3
Galería La Acacia ... 76 C3
Galería Orígenes ... (see 69)
La Manzana de Gómez ... 77 D3
Real Fábrica de Tabacos La Corona ... 78 D2
Variadades Galiano ... 79 B3

**TRANSPORT**

Blue Buses & Colectivos to Guanabo ... 80 D5
CicloBus ... 81 C4
Colectivo ... 82 D4
El Orbe ... (see 77)
M-1 bus stop ... 83 D3
M-2 stop ... 84 C4
M-7 stop ... 85 C4

thing in the morning (when the church is deserted) gives the place an almost ethereal quality.

## GRAN TEATRO & AROUND

On the northern side of the Capitolio is the ornate neo-baroque **Centro Gallego** (Paseo de Martí No 458) erected as a Galician social club between 1907 and 1914. The Centro was built around the existing Teatro Tacón, which opened in 1838 with five masked Carnaval dances. This connection is the basis of claims by the present 2000-seat **Gran Teatro de La Habana** (☎ 861-3077; guided tours CUC$2; 🕑 9am-6pm) that it's the oldest operating theater in the Western Hemisphere. Never mind the date details, this is an outrageously beautiful building inside and out. You can catch the National Ballet of Cuba and the State Opera in the Sala García Lorca here (see p136).

Just across the San Rafael pedestrian mall is **Hotel Inglaterra**, one of Habana's finest grand hotels. José Martí made a speech advocating independence at a banquet here in 1879, and much later US journalists covering the so-called Spanish-American War stayed at this hotel. Bar La Sevillana just inside the Inglaterra is a nice place for a break, as is the hotel's sidewalk terrace. **San Rafael**, a riot of ice-cream stalls, vintage clothing shops, plumbing supplies and more, is a fun detour where everything is sold in pesos.

Diminutive **Parque Central** across from the Inglaterra, was expanded to its present size after the city walls were knocked down in the late 19th century, and the marble **statue of José Martí** (1905) surrounded by 28 palm trees was the first statue of the poet to be erected in Cuba. Nowadays, this park is the turf of baseball fans who linger, seemingly 24 hours a day, around the famous *esquina caliente* (literally, 'hot corner'; a place where baseball fans gather to discuss the game), debating in the most animated fashion about statistics, play-off predictions and the chances of US defector Liván Hernández coming home for Christmas.

### MUSEO NACIONAL DE BELLAS ARTES

Cuba's newly renovated Fine Arts Museum has a collection so extensive it needs two buildings to house it all.

The **Colección de Arte Universal** (☎ 863-9484; www.museonacional.cult.cu; cnr Agramonte & San Rafael; admission CUC$5, children under 14 free; ⏲ 10am-6pm Tue-Sat, 10am-2pm Sun) features European and Latin American paintings and ancient Greek and Roman artifacts. It's a beautiful eclectic building (1886), though the permanent collection itself can't compare to others in larger cities. Good temporary exhibits do pass through, however.

Then there's the **Colección de Arte Cubano** (☎ 861-3858; Trocadero btwn Agramonte & Av de las Misiones; admission CUC$5; ⏲ 10am-6pm Tue-Sat, 10am-2pm Sun). If you visit one fine art museum in Cuba, make it this world-class facility and set aside an entire afternoon. Split into three floors (all handicap accessible), the museum houses a sculpture garden, café and good museum shop on the ground floor. The 2nd floor is contemporary and modern art (look especially for works by Kcho, Raúl Martínez, Portocarrero and, of course, Wilfredo Lam), while the 3rd floor collects everything from the 16th century up to 1951. There's also a terrific art reference library here and a concert hall with varied events, including children's activities most weekends.

### MUSEO DE LA REVOLUCIÓN

You can't miss the imposing **Pavillón Granma** facing the Colección de Arte Cubano. Since 1976, this has been the home to the 18m 'yacht' *Granma* that ushered Fidel Castro and 81 others from Tuxpán, Mexico, into Cuba and world history in 1956. It is encased in glass and heavily guarded 24 hours a day, presumably to stop anyone breaking in and making off for Florida in it. Other vehicles associated with the armed struggle surround the outdoor pavilion, which is accessible from the museum proper.

The **Museo de la Revolución** (☎ 862-4093; Refugio No 1; admission unguided/guided CUC$4/6, cameras extra; ⏲ 10am-5pm) is housed in the former Palacio Presidencial (1913–20), a signature of the Habana skyline. Tiffany of New York decorated the interior and you can gawap at the opulent decor as you wander around the museum's interesting array of exhibits. This palace was the site of an unsuccessful assassination attempt against Fulgencio Batista in March 1957 (see History, p44). The exhibits inside provide a exhaustive documentary and photographic account of the Cuban Revolution (from the guns shot to the bread sacks), and it's a must for anyone with a taste for history – allow yourself plenty of time. Labels are in English and Spanish and one English-speaking guide is available, which can really make the difference here. Start on the top floor and work down if you want to move in chronological order. In front of the building is an SAU-100 tank, used by Fidel Castro during the 1961 Battle of the Bay of Pigs, and a fragment of the former city wall.

### PRADO (PASEO DE MARTÍ)

Technically it's called Paseo de Martí, but Cubans know and love it as **Prado** (to avoid confusion addresses always list it as Paseo de Martí). Construction of this stately boulevard began outside the city walls in 1770, and the work was completed in the mid-1830s during the term of Captain-General Miguel Tacón, who ruled from 1834 to 1838. He also constructed the original Parque Central. The figures of lions along the promenade were added in 1928. You'll see happy couples arriving to tie the knot in 1950s convertibles at the neo-Renaissance **Palacio de los Matrimonios** (Paseo de Martí No 302). For more sights along here, see the walking tour (p112).

### ESCUELA NACIONAL DE BALLET

The **Escuela Nacional de Ballet** (cnr Paseo de Martí & Trocadero), Alicia Alonso's famous ballet school, is in an appropriately grand building on Prado and you can sometimes spot the well-honed physiques of the dedicated dancers rushing inside for a rehearsal.

### EDIFICO BACARDÍ

Finished in 1929 the magnificent Edificio Bacardí is a triumph of art-deco architecture with a whole host of lavish finishings that somehow manage to blend the kitsch with the cool. Hemmed in by other buildings it's hard to get a full kaleidoscopic view of the structure from street level though the opulent bell-tower can be glimpsed from all over Habana. There's a bar in the lobby and for a few Convertibles you can travel up to the tower for a bird's-eye view.

#### IGLESIA DEL SANTO ANGEL CUSTODIO

This small but important **church** (☎ 861-0469; Compostela No 2; 9am-noon & 3-6pm Tue, Thu & Fri, 3-6pm Wed, Mass 7:15am Tue, Wed & Fri, 6pm Thu, Sat & Sun) was rebuilt in neo-Gothic style in 1871. Not only were both Felix Varela and José Martí baptized here (in 1788 and 1853 respectively), but Cirilo Villaverde also set the main scene of his novel *Cecilia Valdés* in this church. Don't miss the statue Cristo Yacente, (literally 'Christ lying down') titillating in his lacy net covering. You can hear the 1869 organ ringing out here during Mass.

#### MUSEO NACIONAL DE LA MÚSICA

Musicians especially will dig this **museum** (☎ 863-0052; Capdevila No 1; admission CUC$2, cameras extra; 10am-5:45pm), with its extensive collection of Cuban and international instruments. Exhibited in the eclectic residence (1905) of a wealthy Habana merchant, the stringed room is particularly impressive. The museum shop sells recordings of Cuban music, and concerts take place in the music room a couple of nights a week (check the schedule at the museum entrance for events). Guides (in Spanish) are available for CUC$1 extra.

There are two important monuments just across hectic Av de los Estudiantes from here. A surviving section of the colonial **Cárcel** (1838) where many Cuban patriots, including José Martí, were imprisoned is in **Parque de los Enamorados** (Lover's Park, which sees few for lack of shade). Beyond that is the **Memorial a los Estudiantes de Medicina**, a fragment of wall encased in marble where eight Cuban medical students chosen at random were shot by the Spanish in 1871 as a reprisal for allegedly desecrating the tomb of a Spanish journalist (in fact, they didn't do it). That beautiful art nouveau building behind, flying the Spanish flag, is the old **Palacio Velasco** (1912), now the Spanish embassy, but on the skids with the Cuban government since they agreed to restrictive embargo-type legislation at the behest of the US in 2003.

Across the street is the picturesque **Castillo de San Salvador de la Punta**, designed by the Italian military engineer Giovanni Bautista Antonelli and built between 1589 and 1600. During the colonial era, a chain was stretched 250m to the castle of El Morro every night to close the harbor mouth to shipping. The castle's **museum** (admission CUC$5; 10am-6pm Wed-Sun) was renovated in 2002 and displays artifacts from sunken Spanish treasure fleets, a collection of model ships and information on the slave trade.

That monumental **statue** of a strapping man on a huge bronze horse is the memorial to Dominican General Máximo Gómez, number one in command during the wars of independence.

## Vedado

Today Vedado is finally the suburb it was designed to be – a place to sleep, dine and go dancing – but really, the bulk of sites are in Habana Vieja and Centro Habana. The very name Vedado means 'forest reserve'; during the colonial era, felling trees was forbidden here and that's why it's so green. Habana's US community established itself in this area after 1898, and within a few decades Vedado was thick with high-rises, restaurants, nightclubs and other businesses.

Vedado boomed during the Batista era, and the East Coast Mafia of the US had a hand in it all. The Hotel Capri was a favorite haunt of Mafia bigwigs such as Lucky Luciano, Meyer Lansky, and American actor Gerge Raft; the same mob that was behind the Las Vegas–style Hotel Riviera. The cheap sex, liquor and gambling were big attractions for US tourists, and Batista's thugs made sure everything ran smoothly. The party ended in January 1959 when Fidel Castro and his *barbudas* (literally 'bearded ones,' the name given to Castro's rebel army) arrived from the Sierra Maestra and set up headquarters on the 22nd floor of the 25-story Havana Hilton, now called the Hotel Habana Libre (a permanent photo exhibit on the 2nd floor documents the transition).

Beatles fans will want to make a special trip to **Parque Lennon** (Calles 15 & 17 btwn Calles 6 & 8) where a hyper-realistic bronze of John lounges on a bench. Every December 8 there are vigils and music jams here remembering his murder. The statue was unveiled in December 2000 by Fidel Castro on the 20th anniversary of Lennon's death. Culturally speaking, it was one of the Cuban leaders more remarkable policy u-turns. The Beatles' music was banned in Cuba in the 1960s for being too 'decadent.' But following Lennon's strong social activism and opposition to US involvement in the Vietnam war he quickly became a hero among Cuban music fans and Castro has recently re-branded him as a 'revolutionary.' Tempting bait for would-be souvenir hunters, the bronze reincarnation of Lennon has suffered the ignominy of having his glasses stolen on a number of occasions and a guard has now been employed to keep a regular watch.

#### HOTEL NACIONAL

The neocolonial-style **Hotel Nacional** (☎ 873-3564; cnr Calles O & 21) was built in 1930. In August 1933 the US-backed dictator Gerardo Machado was overthrown during a popular uprising, and a month later army sergeant Fulgencio Batista seized power. Two months later, some 300 army officers displaced by Batista's coup sought refuge in the newly opened Hotel Nacional, where the US ambassador Sumner Wells was staying. Aware that the reins of power had changed hands, Ambassador Wells found urgent business elsewhere and Batista's troops attacked the officers, many of whom were shot after surrendering. The Nacional's tiled lobby, oversized chairs and aristocratic air capture the atmosphere of a bygone era and it's a nice place for a coffee or cocktail. Stroll straight through the lobby to the gardens behind the hotel. Several huge naval guns set up by the Spanish during the late 19th century still point out to sea from this clifftop park where benches overlook the Malecón. If you're not down with crowds, this is a good perch for those frequent mass marches to the US Interests Section. The most recent demonstration revolved around the case of Luís Posada Carriles, a man suspected of bombing a Cubana Airlines flight in 1976 that killed 73 people. After the US refused to extradite American resident Carriles for trial in Venezuela (where he is alleged to have hatched the plot) in 2005, the Cuban government organized mass demos outside the US Interests Office and raised 73 huge black flags; one for each person that was killed in the crash. The Nacional is also headquarters for the Festival Internacional del Nuevo Cine Latinoamericano (p457).

#### HOTEL HABANA LIBRE

Formerly the Havana Hotel it was commandeered by triumphant revolutionaries in 1959 and promptly renamed the **Habana Libre** (☎ 55 47 04; Calle L btwn Calles 23 & 25); the art here, starting with the 670-sq-meter Venetian-tile mural by Amelia Peláez splashed across the front of the building, is worth a look. Upstairs is Alfredo Sosa Bravo's *Carro de la Revolución* made from 525 ceramic pieces, plus a rotating painting exhibit. The shopping arcade has a good liquor store and there are some great 1959 B&W photos of the all-conquering *barbudas* lolling around with their guns in the hotel's lobby.

#### EDIFICIO FOCSA

Unmissable on the Habana skyline the modernist Focsa building was built in 1954–56 in a record 28 months using pioneering computer technology. In 1999 was listed as one of the seven modern engineering wonders of Cuba. With 39 floors housing 373 apartments it was, on its completion in June 1956, the second largest concrete structure of its type in the world; constructed in its entirety without the use of cranes. Falling on hard times in the early '90s, the upper floors of the Focsa became nests for vultures and in 2000 an elevator cable snapped killing one person. Sparkling once more after a recent restoration project, this skyline-dominating Habana giant nowadays contains refurbished apartments and – in the shape of top-floor restaurant La Torre (p128) – one of the city's most celebrated eating establishments.

#### UNIVERSIDAD DE LA HABANA

Every great city deserves a great university and the **Universidad de La Habana** (cnr Neptuno & San Lázaro) is just that (it even hosted anti-war protests when the US invaded Iraq in

2003). Before climbing the monumental stairs toward alma mater, head downhill to check out the **Monumento a Julio Antonio Mella** (cnr Neptuno & San Lázaro), a monument to the student leader who founded the first Cuban Communist Party in 1925. In 1929 the dictator Machado had Mella assassinated in Mexico City. More interesting than the monument, however, are the black and white **Mella portraits** permanently mounted in the wall in the little park across San Lázaro.

The university was founded by Dominican monks in 1728 and secularized in 1842. The present neoclassical complex dates from the second quarter of the 20th century, and today some 30,000 students (2000 of them foreigners), taught by 1700 professors, take courses in the social sciences and humanities, natural sciences, mathematics and economics.

Go up the stairway and through the monumental gateway into Plaza Ignacio Agramonte, the university's central square. In front of you is the **biblioteca** (library) and to your left the **Edificio Felipe Poey**, with two **museums** (admission CUC$1; 9am-noon & 1-4pm Mon-Fri). Downstairs, the **Museo de Historia Natural** is the oldest museum in Cuba, founded in 1874 by the Royal Academy of Medical, Physical and Natural Sciences. Many of the stuffed specimens of Cuban flora and fauna here date from the 19th century. Upstairs is the **Museo Antropológico Montané**, established in 1903, with a rich collection of pre-Columbian Indian artifacts. The most important objects are the wooden 10th-century Ídolo del Tobaco, discovered in Guantánamo Province, and the stone Ídolo de Bayamo, but the mummies are also cool. Keep this building on your left, and the next building on your left is the **Anfiteatro Enrique José Varona**; films are screened here during the Festival Internacional del Nuevo Cine Latinamericano.

Go down through the park on the north side of the Edificio Felipe Poey and exit the university compound via a small gate to reach the **Museo Napoleónico** (☎ 79 14 60; San Miguel No 1159; unguided/guided CUC$3/6; 10am-5:30pm Mon-Sat), containing 7000 objects associated with Napoleon Bonaparte, including his 1821 death mask. The 10,000-seat **Estadio Universitario Juan Abrahantes**, where students play soccer and baseball, is just up the hill from this museum.

#### MUSEUMS

Two museums further afield in Vedado that are worthwhile if you're in the neighborhood are the **Museo de Artes Decorativas** (☎ 830-9848; Calle 17 No 502 btwn Calles D & E; admission CUC$2; 11am-7pm Tue-Sat), with its fancy rococo, oriental and art-deco baubles and the **Museo de Danza** (☎ 831-2198; Línea No 365; admission CUC$2; 11am-6:30pm Tue-Sat), which collects objects from Cuba's rich dance history, including some personal effects of Alicia Alonso.

#### PARQUE ALMENDARES

Running along the banks of the city's Río Almendares, below the bridge on Calle 23, is this wonderful oasis of green and fresh air in the heart of chaotic Habana. The park was restored in 2003 and they did a beautiful job: benches now line the river promenade, plants grow profusely and there are many facilities here, including an antiquated **miniature golf course**, the **Anfiteatro Parque Almendares** (see Entertainment, p134) and a **playground**. There are several good places to eat. Take a 20-minute stroll through old-growth trees in the **Bosque de la Habana** and you'll feel transported (take a friend though: this is a very isolated spot and is considered unsafe by locals).

### Plaza de la Revolución Area

#### PLAZA DE LA REVOLUCIÓN

Those tingles you feel may be the emotion of being in Cuba's most important public space or maybe it's just the oppressive heat (for which the square is famous). Predating the 1959 triumph, the **Plaza de la Revolución** was once called Plaza de la República. Although this gigantic square has come to symbolize the Cuban Revolution due to the huge political rallies held here in the '60s, most buildings date from the Batista era. On important occasions Castro and others (including the Pope) have addressed up to 1.2-million Cubans and supporters from the podium in front of the star-shaped, 142m-high **Memorial José Martí** (☎ 59 23 47; admission CUC$5; 9:30am-5pm Mon-Sat). Head here on May 1 or July 26 at 7am if you want to experience it yourself (most hotels offer excursions). The 17m marble Martí statue

## VEDADO

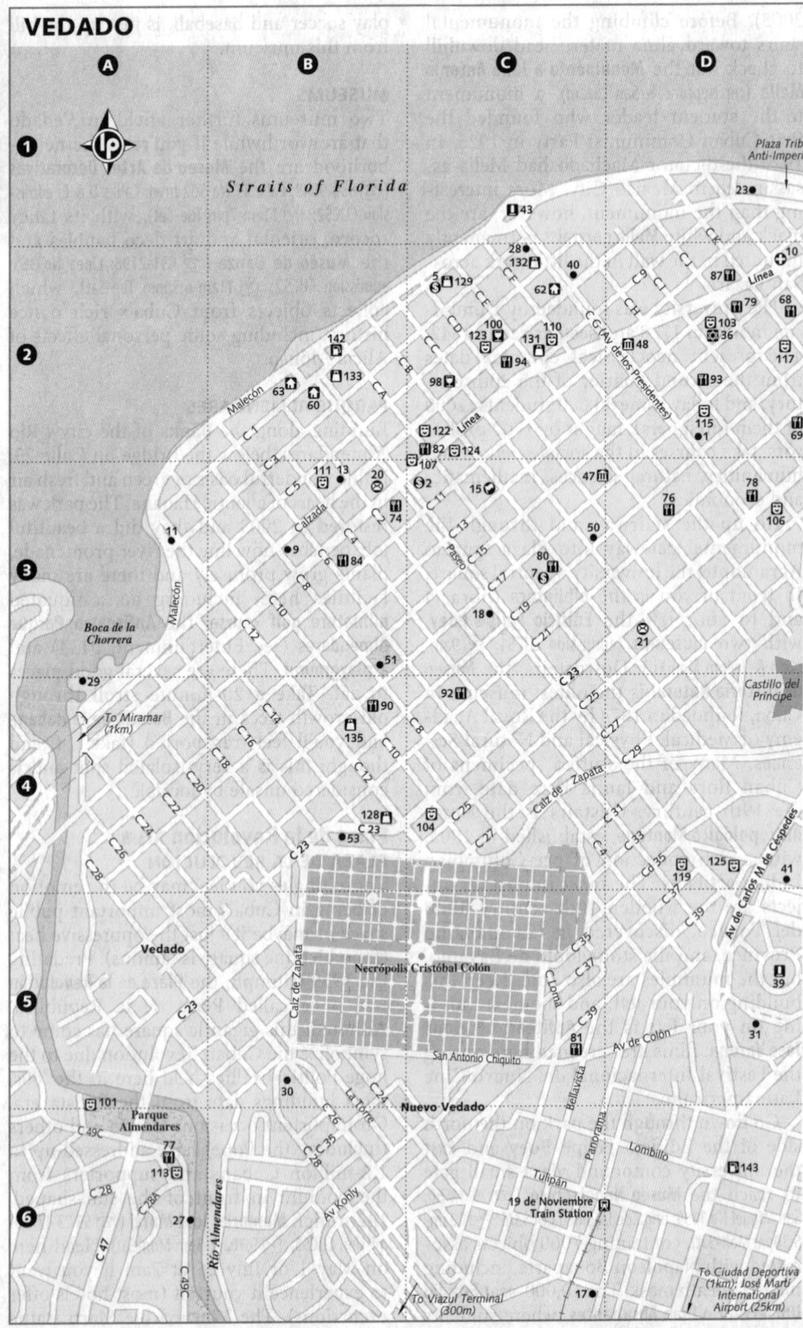
Straits of Florida
Malecón
Línea
Calzada
Paseo
C G (Av de los Presidentes)
Boca de la Chorrera
To Miramar (1km)
Castillo del Príncipe
Plaza Trib Anti-Imperi
Calz de Zapata
Av de Carlos M de Céspedes
Necrópolis Cristóbal Colón
Vedado
Nuevo Vedado
C Loma
Bellavista
Panorama
San Antonio Chiquito
Av de Colón
Lombillo
Tulipán
19 de Noviembre Train Station
La Torre
Av Kohly
Parque Almendares
Río Almendares
To Viazul Terminal (300m)
To Ciudad Deportiva (1km); José Martí International Airport (25km)

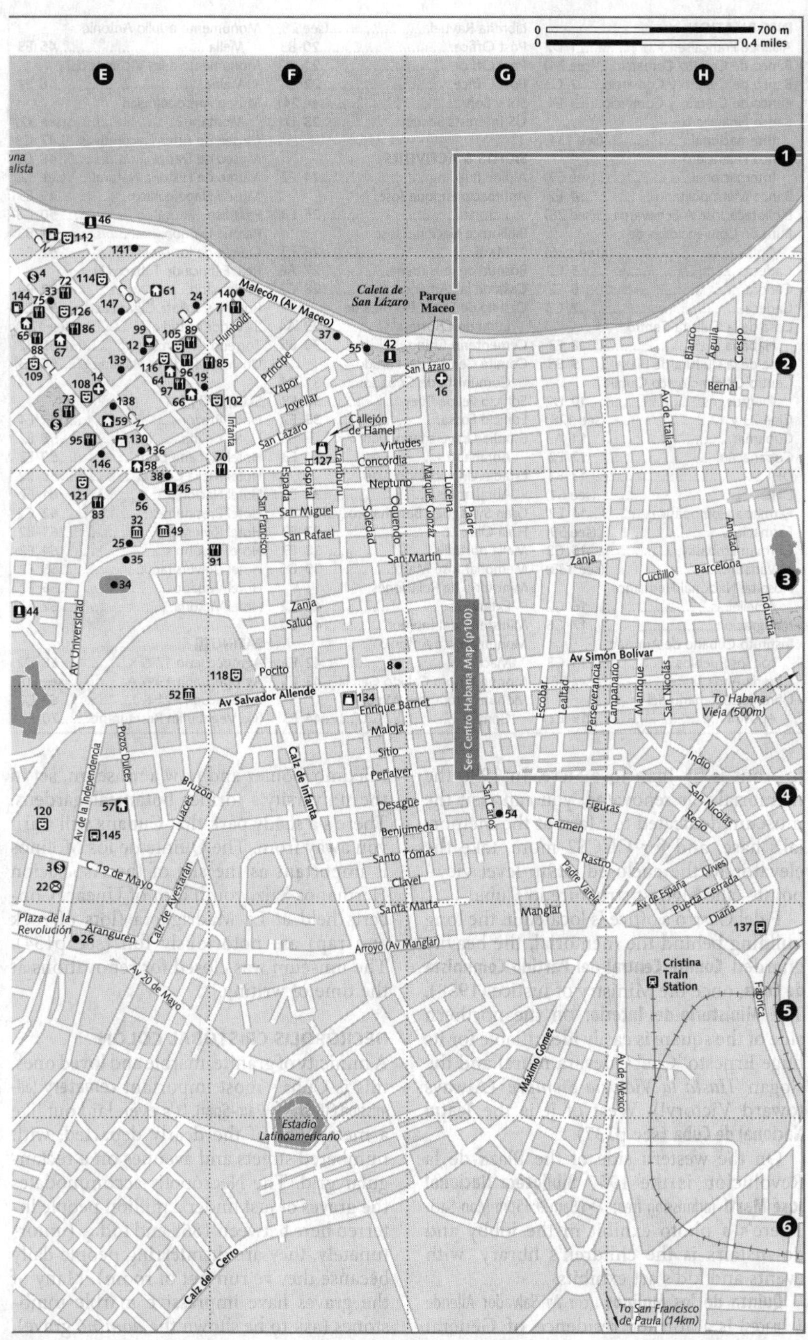

Caleta de San Lázaro
Parque Maceo
Malecón (Av Maceo)
Callejón de Hamel
Av Simón Bolívar
Av Salvador Allende
Calz de Infanta
Av Universidad
Av de la Independencia
C 19 de Mayo
Plaza de la Revolución
Aranguren
Calz de Avestarán
Av 20 de Mayo
Estadio Latinoamericano
Calz del Cerro
Máximo Gómez
Av de México
Cristina Train Station
Arroyo (Av Manglar)
See Centro Habana Map (p100)
To Habana Vieja (500m)
To San Francisco de Paula (14km)
Av de Italia
Av de España (Vives)
Puerta Cerrada
Padre Varela
San Lázaro
Zanja
Industria
Fabrica
700 m
0.4 miles

**INFORMATION**
Alliance Française........................1 D2
Banco de Crédito Comercio....(see 24)
Banco de Crédito y Comercio......2 C3
Banco de Crédito y Comércio.....3 E4
Banco Financiero Internacional....................(see 134)
Banco Financiero Internacional......................(see 59)
Banco Metropolitano..................4 E2
Biblioteca José A Echevarría....(see 28)
Buró de Convenciones de Cuba................................(see 126)
Cadeca....................................5 C2
Cadeca....................................6 E2
Cadeca....................................7 C3
Casa de la Cultura Centro Habana..................................8 F3
Casa de la Cultura de Plaza.........9 B3
Centro Oftalmológico Camilo Cienfuegos..........................10 D2
Cine 23 y 12........................(see 128)
Cubamar.................................11 A3
Cubanacán..............................12 E2
DHL........................................13 B3
DHL......................................(see 61)
Farmacia Homopática................14 E2
Farmacia................................(see 59)
German Embassy......................15 C3
Havanatur............................(see 133)
Hospital Nacional Hermanos Ameijeiras..........................16 G2
Inmigración............................17 C6
Instituto Cubano de Amistad con los Pueblos......................18 C3
Librería Alma Mater................(see 56)
Librería Centenario del Apóstol................................19 E2
Libreria Rayuela.....................(see 28)
Post Office...............................20 B3
Post Office...............................21 D3
Post Office...............................22 E4
Sol y Son..............................(see 24)
US Interests Section.................23 D1

**SIGHTS & ACTIVITIES**
Airline Building.........................24 E2
Anfiteatro Enrique José Varona...................................25 E3
Biblioteca Nacional José Martí.....................................26 E5
Bosque de la Habana................27 A6
Casa de las Américas................28 C2
Castillo de Santa Dorotea de Luna de Chorrera'.................29 A4
Cementerio Chino.....................30 B5
Comité Central del Partido Comunista de Cuba.............31 D5
Edificio Felipe Poey...................32 E3
Edificio Focsa...........................33 E2
Estadio Universitario Juan Abrahantes...........................34 E3
Estadio Universitario Juan Abrahantes...........................35 E3
Gran Synagoga Bet Shalom......36 D2
Holá Ola...................................37 F2
Mella portraits..........................38 E3
Memorial José Martí..................39 D5
Ministerio de Relaciones Exteriores..............................40 C2
Ministerio del Interior...............41 D4
Monumento a Antonio Maceo.....................................42 F2
Monumento a Calixto García....43 C1
Monumento a José Miguel Gómez...................................44 E3
Monumento a Julio Antonio Mella.....................................45 E3
Monumento a las Víctimas del Maine.....................................46 E1
Museo Antropológico Montané..........................(see 32)
Museo de Artes Decorativas.....47 C3
Museo de Danza......................48 D2
Museo de Historia Natural......(see 32)
Museo Napoleónico..................49 E3
Paradiso...................................50 C3
Parque Lennon.........................51 B3
Quinta de los Molinos...............52 E4
Real Fábrica de Tabacos H Upmann..................................53 B4
Romeo y Julieta Cigar Factory..54 G4
Salvador's Studio.................(see 127)
Torreón de San Lázaro..............55 F2
Universidad de La Habana........56 E3

**SLEEPING**
Hotel Bruzón............................57 E4
Hotel Colina.............................58 E2
Hotel Habana Libre...................59 E2
Hotel Meliá Cohiba...................60 B2
Hotel Nacional.........................61 E2
Hotel Presidente.......................62 C2
Hotel Riviera............................63 B2
Hotel St John's.........................64 E2
Hotel Universitario....................65 E2
Hotel Vedado...........................66 E2
Hotel Victoria...........................67 E2

**EATING**
Agropecuario 17 & K.................68 D2
Agropecuario 19 & A.............(see 80)
Agropecuario 21 & J.................69 D2
Biki Vegetarian Restaurant........70 F2

in front is by Juan José Sicre. In 1996 the memorial was renovated; you can visit the museum dedicated to Martí at the memorial's base, and for CUC$2 more, take the elevator to the enclosed 129m-level viewpoint – the highest structure in Cuba.

Fidel Castro's office is located in the long building behind the memorial, the heavily guarded **Comité Central del Partido Comunista de Cuba**, once the Ministry of Justice (1958). The **Ministerio del Interior** on the northern side of the square is easily identifiable for its huge Ernesto 'Che' Guevara mural and the slogan *'Hasta la Victoria Siempre'* (Always toward Victory!). West of it is the **Teatro Nacional de Cuba** (see p137).

On the western side of the Plaza de la Revolución is the 1957 **Biblioteca Nacional José Martí** (admission free; 8am-9:45pm Mon-Sat). There's a photo exhibit in the lobby and downstairs is the children's library, with events and kid's art exhibits.

**Quinta de los Molinos** (cnr Av Salvador Allende & Luaces) is a former residence of General Máximo Gómez and now a museum, set in the university's former botanical gardens. There's a shady park that Cubans will warn you away from. The Quinta de los Molinos is important as the site of the Asociación Hermanos Saíz, youth arm of Uneac. Concerts held at La Madriguera (lots of rock and rap) are notoriously fun (see p134). The museum was closed for renovations at the time of writing.

### NECRÓPOLIS CRISTÓBAL COLÓN

A minicity of granite, marble and loved ones, this is Cuba's most important **cemetery** (admission CUC$1; 7am-5pm). It's even laid out like a metropolis of the dearly departed, with numbered streets and avenues on a rectangular grid. The Necrópolis accommodates the graves of just under a million people interred here between 1868 and today (unfortunately, they are disinterring people daily because they've run out of room). Many of the graves have impressive marble tombstones (ask to be shown the *dominó* grave),

Bim Bom 71 F2
CafeTV 72 E2
Coppelia 73 E2
Decameron 74 B3
El Conejito 75 E2
El Gringo Viejo 76 D3
El Lugar 77 A6
G-Café 78 D3
La Torre (see 33)
Le Chansonnier 79 D2
Mercado Agropecuario 80 C3
Mesón de la Chorrera (see 29)
Organoponico Plaza 81 C5
Pain de París 82 C2
Pain de Paris (see 19)
Paladar Aries 83 E3
Paladar El Helecho 84 B3
Paladar El Hurón Azul 85 F2
Paladar Escorpión (see 75)
Paladar Los Amigos 86 E2
Paladar Monopoly 87 D2
Paladar Nerei 88 E2
Palmares Centro 89 E2
Pan.com 90 B4
Peso pizza 91 F3
Peso Stalls 92 C4
Peso Stalls 93 D2
Restaurant Vegetariano Carmelo 94 C2
Restaurante Bulerías 95 E2
Restaurante Wakamba 96 E2
Supermercado Meridiano (see 133)
Trattoría Maraka's 97 E2

**DRINKING**
Bar-Club Imágenes 98 C2
Centro de Prensa Internacional 99 E2
Opus Bar 100 C2

**ENTERTAINMENT**
Anfiteatro Parque Almendares 101 A5
Cabaret Las Vegas 102 F2
Cabaret Parisién (see 61)
Cabaret Turquino (see 59)
Cafe Cantante (see 125)
Café Teatro Brecht 103 D2
Cine Charles Chaplin 104 C4
Cine La Rampa 105 E2
Cine Riviera 106 D3
Cine Trianón 107 C3
Cine Yara 108 E2
Club La Red 109 E2
Club Tropical 110 C2
Conjunto Folklórico Nacional de Cuba 111 B3
Discoteca Amanecer 112 E1
El Chevere 113 A6
El Gato Tuerto 114 E2
El Gran Palenque (see 111)
El Hurón Azul 115 D2
Habana Café (see 60)
Jazz Cafe (see 133)
Jazz Club La Zorra y El Cuervo 116 E2
Karachi Club 117 D2
La Colmenita (see 125)
La Madriguera 118 F3
Patio de María 119 D4
Piano Bar Delirio Habanero (see 125)
Pico Blanco (see 64)
Sala Polivalente Ramón Fonst 120 E4
Sala Teatro El Sótano 121 E3
Sala Teatro Hubert de Blanck 122 C2
Teatro Amadeo Roldán 123 C2
Teatro Mella 124 C2
Teatro Nacional de Cuba 125 D4
Teatro Nacional de Guiñol 126 E2
Uneac (see 115)

**SHOPPING**
ARTex (see 108)
Callejón de Hamel 127 F2
Centro de Arte 23 y 12 128 B4
Feria de la Artesanía 129 C2
Galería Ciudades del Mundo 130 E2
Galería Habana 131 C2
Galería Haydee Santamaría 132 C2
Galerías de Paseo 133 B2
Photo Service (see 133)
Photo Service (see 99)
Plaza Carlos III 134 F4
Registro Nacional de Bienes Culturales 135 B4

**TRANSPORT**
Aerocaribbean (see 24)
Aerotaxi 136 E2
Bus 400 to Guanabo 137 H5
Cubana Airlines (see 24)
Cubatur 138 E2
Havanautos 139 E2
Micar 140 F2
Micar (see 133)
Rex Rent a Car 141 E1
Servi-Cupet Gas Station 142 B2
Servi-Cupet Gas Station 143 D6
Servi-Cupet Petrol Station 144 E2
Terminal de Ómnibus 145 E4
Transtur 146 E2
Transtur 147 E2

making this the largest sculpture park in the country. Silvio Rodríguez filmed his latest video *Cita con Angeles* among all the cherubs here. A guidebook with a detailed map (CUC$5) is for sale at the entrance.

After entering the neo-Romanesque **northern gateway** (1870), there's the tomb of independence leader **General Máximo Gómez** (1905) on the right (look for the bronze face in a circular medallion). Further along past the first circle, and also on the right, are the **monument to the firefighters** (1890); the **Familia Falla Bonet mausoleum** (of artistic interest); and the **Capilla Central** (1886) in the center of the cemetery. Just northeast of this chapel is the tomb of **Señora Amelia Goyri** (cnr Calles 1 & F), better known as *La Milagrosa* (the miraculous one) who died while giving birth on May 3, 1901. The marble figure of a woman with a large cross and a baby in her arms is easy to find, due to the many flowers piled on the tomb and the local devotees in attendance. For many years after her death, her heartbroken husband visited the grave several times a day. He always knocked with one of four iron rings on the burial vault and walked away backwards so he could see her for as long as possible. When the bodies were exhumed some years later Amelia's body was uncorrupted (a sign of sanctity in the Catholic faith) and the baby, who had been buried at its mother's feet, was – allegedly – found in her arms. As a result *La Milagrosa* became the focus of a huge spiritual cult in Cuba and thousands of people come here annually with gifts in the hope of fulfilling dreams or solving problems. In keeping with tradition, pilgrims knock with the iron ring on the vault and walk away backwards when they leave.

Also worth seeking out is the tomb of Orthodox Party leader **Eduardo Chibás** (Calle 8 btwn Calles E & F). During the 1940s and early '50s Chibás was a relentless crusader against political corruption, and as a personal protest he committed suicide during a radio broadcast in 1951. At his burial ceremony a

### CIGAR FACTORY TOURS

There are two factories presently allowing tours in Habana, and the programs are roughly the same. Visitors check out the ground floor where the leaves are unbundled and sorted before proceeding to the upper floors to watch the tobacco get rolled, pressed, adorned with a band, and boxed. Remember, these are factories where people toil (sometimes for 12 hours a day or more) for around 200 pesos a month, and some visitors find they smack of a human zoo. Still, if you have even a passing interest in tobacco, Cuban work environments or economies of scale, you'll enjoy one of the CUC$10, 45-minute tours held Monday to Friday at the following factories:

**Real Fábrica de Tabacos Partagás** (Map p100; ☎ 862-0086; Industria No 520 btwn Barcelona & Dragones; ⌚ tours every 15 min btwn 9:30am-11am & 12:30-3pm) The tobacco shop (open 9am to 5pm Monday to Saturday) and smoking lounge are bonuses here. This is one of Habana's oldest cigar factories (1845).

**Real Fábrica de Tabacos H Upmann** (Map pp106-7; ☎ 862-0081; Calle 23 btwn Calles 16 & 14; ⌚ tours 9:30am-2:30pm Mon-Fri) Founded in 1844 and housed in an impressive neoclassical building, Romeo y Julieta, Montecristo and Cohibas are rolled here.

At the time of writing the **Romeo y Julieta** (Map pp106-7; Padre Varela No 852) and the **Real Fábrica de Tabacos La Corona** (Map p100; Calle Agramonte No 106 btwn Colón & Refugio) factories were closed to the public, though the shop and smoking rooms were still open.

young Orthodox activist named Fidel Castro jumped atop Chibás' grave and made a fiery speech denouncing the old establishment – the political debut of the most influential Cuban of the 20th century.

A bronze **plaque** (cnr Calles 14 & 23), one block from the cemetery entrance, marks the spot where Fidel proclaimed the socialist nature of the Cuban Revolution on April 16, 1961, at a funeral service for those killed during a counter-revolutionary raid on a Habana air base the previous day.

For something completely different, exit the west gate of the cemetery and walk south for three blocks to the **Cementerio Chino** (cnr Av 26 & Zapata; ⌚ 6am-6pm).

## Along the Malecón

Habana has become synonymous with the Malecón, its 8km seawall. Constructed during the American administration in 1901, it snakes along the coast from the Castillo de la Punta in Habana Vieja to Castillo de Santa Dorotea de Luna de Chorrera, another castle at the mouth of the Río Almendares. Here two one-way tunnels dive under the river, and the main thoroughfare continues through Miramar as Av 5, eventually becoming the Autopista (freeway) to Mariel. In the rougher months, waves splash high over the wall, soaking cars and strollers alike. Half-eaten by the salt spray, the pastiche of architectural gems, restored or collapsing, backing the Malecón is enchanting. A new project erecting old-fashioned-style street lamps makes it even more attractive at night, when lovers paste themselves to the wall, wandering *trovadores* sing for tips, and there's always a bottle of rum being passed your way. Hustlers here can be fierce: tell them directly and unequivocally that you're hanging out on your own, and they'll soon go away. The Malecón was severely lashed by Hurricane Wilma in October 2005. Huge waves rose to 3m above the Morro lighthouse, chunks were taken out of the battered sea wall, and more than 250 people had to be evacuated by amphibious vehicles.

The 24-story **Hospital Nacional Hermanos Ameijeiras** (1980), the highest building in Centro Habana (but not in Habana – that would be the Focsa), dominates this area. Some of the clinics specialize in treating foreigners (see Medical Services, p91). Opposite the hospital is the **Monumento a Antonio Maceo** (1916), the mulatto general who cut a blazing trail across the entire length of Cuba during the First War of Independence. The nearby 18th-century **Torreón de San Lázaro** was built as a watchtower by the Spanish.

West beyond Hotel Nacional is a stretch of the Malecón known as Av Washington because the old US Embassy was here. In the center of the boulevard is the **Monumento a las Víctimas del Maine** (1926), which had an American eagle on top until the 1959 revolution. The current inscription on the side of the monument alludes to the theory that US agents deliberately blew up their own ship to create a pretext for declaring war on Spain: '*A las víctimas de el* Maine *que fueron sacrificados por la voracidad imperialista en su afán de apoderarse de la Isla de Cuba*' (To the victims of the *Maine* who were sacrificed by voracious imperialism in its desire to gain control of the island of Cuba). The modern seven-story building with high security fencing at the western end of this open space is the **US Interests Office** first set up by the Carter administration in the late 1970s. Surrounded by hysterical graffiti that links Bush to all kinds of monsters including Hitler, the building is the site of some of the worst tit-for-tat finger wagging on the island. Facing the office front is the Plaza Tribuna Anti-Imperialista, built during the Elián González affair to host major in-your-face protests (earning it the local nickname *protestódromo*). Concerts, protests and marches – some one million strong – are still held here.

Built in 1959 another impressive memorial is the **Monumento a Calixto García** (cnr Malecón & Calle G) to the valiant Cuban general who US military leaders in Santiago de Cuba prevented from attending the Spanish surrender in 1898. Twenty-four bronze plaques around the equestrian statue provide a history of García's 30-year struggle for Cuban independence. On Calle G just behind the monument is the **Casa de las Américas** (☎ 55 27 06; Calle G btwn Calles 3 & 5; admission CUC$2; 🕑 10am-4:40pm Tue-Sat, 9am-1pm Sun), a major cultural institution set up by Moncada survivor Haydee Santamaría in 1959 sponsoring literary and artistic seminars, concerts and exhibitions. Inside there's an art gallery and a bookshop.

Many busts and statues line Calle G (Av de los Presidentes). In the middle of the avenue is a former monument to Cuba's first president – and ex-friend of José Martí – Tomás Estrada Palma, who is now considered a US puppet. His statue was toppled and all that remains of the monument are his shoes. On the other side of Calle G is the neo-baroque **Ministerio de Relaciones Exteriores**.

A large **feria de la artesanía** (craft fair) with handicrafts and used books is at the corner of Malecón and Calle D.

Cuba has three synagogues servicing a Jewish population of approximately 1:500. The main community center and library is at the **Gran Synagoga Bet Shalom** (Calle I btwn 13 & 15) where the friendly staff would be happy to tell interested visitors about the fascinating history of the Jews in Cuba.

## HABANA VIEJA WALKING TOUR

It's unlikely you'll get to both the Habana Vieja and Centro Habana walking tours in a day, unless you hop some transport halfway through. You can connect with a horse carriage (CUC$10 per hour) on Mercaderes just off Obispo, a coco-taxi anywhere around Plaza de San Francisco de Asís (horse carriages hang out here too) or a bici-taxi near the Estacíon Central de Férrocarriles (Central Station).

Plaza de la Catedral is a moveable feast and you can espy most of what's going on from the lush **Restaurante El Patio** (**1**; p126), before heading into the **Catedral de San Cristóbal de la Habana** (**2**; p93). Track southwest next, past the resident fortune teller and the brightly clad ladies in polka-dot dresses (who'll plant a kiss on your cheek for a ludicrous tip), and pop into the alleyway on the right housing the **Taller Experimental de Gráfica** (**3**; p114). Here, in what must be Habana's funkiest art gallery, Pink Floyd meets Jackson Pollack

**WALK FACTS**

**Start** Restaurante El Patio
**Finish** Taberna de la Muralla
**Distance** 1.3km
**Duration** Three hours

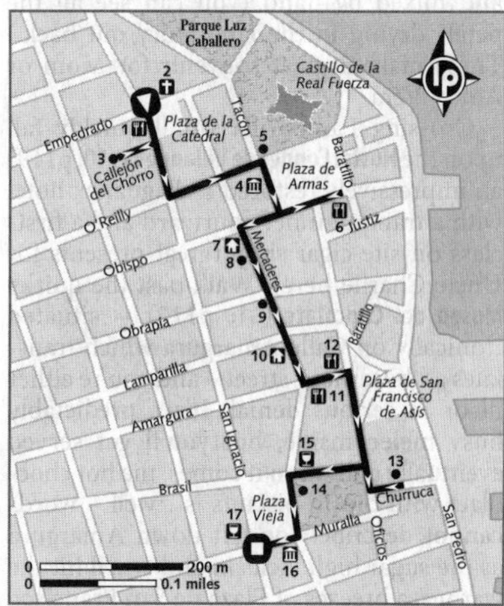

meets Wilfredo Lam with a bit of Picasso thrown in for good measure. Use your excellent map-reading skills to deliver you in front of the gargantuan **Museo de la Ciudad** (**4**; p96) on the western side of Plaza de Armas before the crowds arrive. If they've already beaten you to it, take a break outside in the breezy plaza, a bibliophile's Nirvana, with an outdoor book fair, if it's Wednesday, or if it's not pop into one of Habana's top bookshops in the **Palacio del Segundo Cabo** (**5**; p96). You might skip the stuffed animals at the Museo Nacional de Historia Natural and head straight to the 5th-floor terrace bar at **Restaurante Mirador de la Bahía** (**6**; p125), where the burgers are good and the views even better.

Breaking out of the plaza head south on Obispo past some of Habana's oldest surviving houses to the corner of Mercaderes. The lurid pink pastel building on the left is the **Hotel Ambos Mundos** (**7**; p118), where Ernest Hemingway stayed off and on during the 1930s. You can visit room 511 (admission CUC$2; open 9am to 5pm Monday to Saturday) where he started writing *For Whom the Bell Tolls* or enjoy a few romantic tunes from the resident pianist in the lobby downstairs. A few doors south on Mercaderes is the **Maqueta de la Habana Vieja** (**8**; p96), a darling scale model of everyone's favorite Unesco World Heritage site. Continuing straight to the intersection with Obrapia at the next corner, drop into **Habana 1791** (**9**; p139) where floral fragrances are made and mixed by hand (you can see all the petals drying in the laboratory out back.) These make a great souvenir for Mom or Aunty Vera.

Crossing Lamparilla you'll quickly fall upon the **Hostal Condes de Villanueva** (**10**; p119) an impressively restored Habaguanex hotel with a tranquil inner courtyard and a first-class on-site cigar shop (great presents for Uncle Charlie here). Walk past the quirky **Museo del Chocolate** (**11**; p115) – situated ironically on Calle Amargura which translates as 'bitterness' street – and you're either ill or in serious denial. It's a predictably busy melee inside, but you'll get served eventually and when it comes, the hot chocolate with dip-in biscuits is...well – words cannot describe! Jog left down Amargura as the sugar high kicks in and you'll hit the warm sea breezes of Plaza de San Francisco de Asís. The western side of the plaza hosts several art galleries (see p139), some with little gardens out back if you need a break. Or splurge with a cappuccino at **Café del Oriente** (**12**; p126).

Train lovers will want to detour half a block south on Oficios and turn left on Churruca to check out the **Coche Mambí** (**13**; admission free; 9am-2pm Tue-Sat), a 1900 train car built in the US and brought to Cuba in 1912. Put into service as the 'Presidential Car,' it's a palace on wheels, with a formal dining room, louvered wooden windows and, back in its heyday, fans cooling the car with dry ice.

Otherwise, turn right at the corner of Oficios and Brasil and you're headed toward Plaza Vieja. This plaza is captivating: you'll get some of the city's best views from atop the tower housing the **cámara oscura** (**14**; p97) on the northeastern corner. Peek quickly into **Café Taberna** (**15**; p132), a temple to the late Beny Moré and other assorted mambo kings before nosing through the card collection at **Museo de Naipes** (**16**; p98), on the square's southeastern corner. Finish the tour with a glass of Habana's best beer brewed on the premises at **Taberna de la Muralla** (**17**; p132). There's an outdoor grill here too if you're feeling peckish.

If you want to say goodbye to tourist-brochure Habana Vieja and hello to the real world, continue west on Muralla for one block and then south on Cuba. Here ceilings fall without warning and power outages, water shortages and garbage-strewn streets are the norm. This is one of the roughest parts of the city, so be on your toes. Everyone will see at a glance that you're a tourist, but try not to look like an easy mark. If in doubt, head back toward the Plaza de Armas. Avoid these areas after dark. If you want to check out some churches and link up with the Centro Habana Walking Tour, continue six blocks south on Cuba and then go left on Leonor Pérez for five blocks.

## CENTRO HABANA WALKING TOUR

While this route might not look far on paper, you will need to put aside at least four hours for this culture-packed walking tour. Out here on the cusp of the Habana Vieja and Centro Habana there are too many captivating distractions – too many

**WALK FACTS**

**Start** Museo de la Revolución
**Finish** Museo Casa-Natal de José Martí
**Distance** 2.5km
**Duration** Four hours

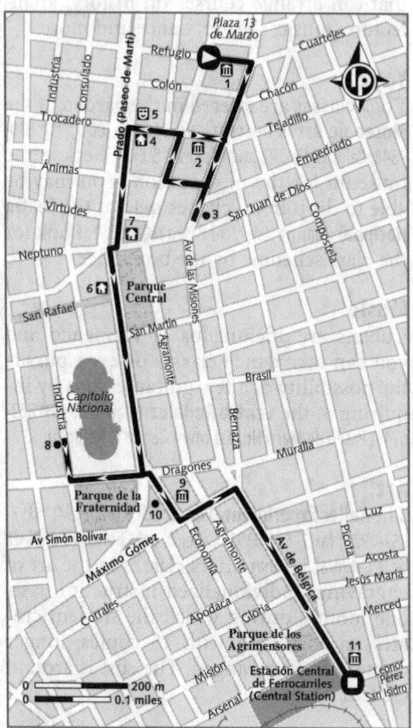


intriguing side streets to wander down – to set aside only a brief time period. Kick off in the heart of matters, at the **Museo de la Revolución** (**1**; p102) and **Museo Nacional de Bellas Artes** (**2**; p102). Both deserve two hours minimum so, unless you've brought a sleeping bag, toss a coin and take your pick – history or art? Head south a block and a half next to the **Edificio Bacardí** (**3**; p102), one of Habana's most striking buildings – garnished with granite, Capellanía limestone, and multicolored bricks – and considered by many to be one of the best examples of art-deco architecture in the world.

Retrace your steps for a few meters and head left on Ánimas, right onto Agramonte and then left into Trocadero. Glittering before you is the sumptuous **Hotel Sevilla** (**4**; p119) where Enrico Caruso stayed in 1920 and where the Mary Pickford cocktail was first concocted (rum, pineapple juice and grenadine). Built in 1908 the Prado end of the lobby has a wall of interesting historic photos. A few steps more and you're on the Prado, that leafy urban glade where tykes skate by and sinuous youths from the **Escuela Nacional de Ballet** (**5**; p102) nurse sore muscles.

The hustlers can be fierce along here, so you'll want to make your way south at some point to Parque Central to admire the José Martí statue (first among thousands!) and catch the latest baseball gossip at the *esquina caliente*. A 360-degree turn reveals the baroque Gran Teatro, the royal blue Hotel Telégrafo and a sneak preview of the Capitolio. Ignore these for the moment and consider lunch or a drink, either curbside at the stately **Hotel Inglaterra** (**6**; p121) or on the exquisite rooftop bar at the **Hotel NH Parque Central** (**7**; p121). The latter is strictly five-star stuff, so slackers beware.

If you want to get off the tourist track, head up Neptuno, alongside the Hotel Telégrafo. Within a block you'll be into the bombed-out shell of Centro Habana. Calle Consulado's a baseball diamond during the day with tomorrow's Liván Hernándezes sprinting to make it past first base; watch out for the holes here, and the rotting garbage and the house keys that sometimes get flung out of top floor windows.

If you get out unscathed home in on the Capitolio Nacional, Habana's Washington wannabe built by Yanqui sycophant President Gerardo Machado y Morales in 1929. Photographers might want to stroll across the road to the famous Jurassic opposite where long-suffering colectivo taxi drivers rest their asthmatic Buicks and Olsmobiles in between fares. Keep walking south on Prado and turn right on Dragones just at the edge of the Capitolio for an informative cigar tour at the **Real Fábrica de Tabacos Partagás** (**8**; p99) or continue straight past the **Fuente de la India** (**9**; p99) sculpture at the crazy roundabout (cross carefully here) to the **Asociación Cultural Yoruba de Cuba** (**10**; p99) with their fascinating well-laid-out museum.

Jog left on Máximo Gómez for two blocks and then turn right onto chaotic Av de Bélgica and into the 'real' Habana, where peso cafeterias and one of the city's biggest markets provide cheap eating opportunities.

If you don't feel like walking the five long blocks south to the **Museo-Casa Natal de José Martí (11**; p99), flag down a bici-taxi here.

## COURSES

Aside from Spanish-language courses (see the boxed text, opposite), Habana offers a wide number of learning activities for aspiring students.

### Dance

The easiest way to take a dance class is at the **Museo del Ron** (Map p94; ☎ 861-8051; San Pedro No 262) which offers on-the-spot lessons Monday to Friday at 9am, for CUC$10 for the first two hours; it always gets good reports. Another option is the **Teatro América** (Map p100; ☎ 862-5416; Av de Italia No 253 btwn Concordia & Neptuno, Centro Habana) next to the Casa de la Música which can fix you up with both a class and a partner for CUC$8 per hour under the eye of Artistic Director Jorge Samá.

The **Conjunto Folklórico Nacional** (Map pp106-7; ☎ 7-830-3060; Calle 4 No 103 btwn Calzada & Calle 5, Vedado) teaches highly recommended classes in *son*, salsa, rumba, mambo and more. Classes start on the first Monday in January and July, and cost in the vicinity of CUC$400 to CUC$500, for a 15-day course. An admission test places students in classes of four different levels.

### Culture

**Centro Hispano Americano de Cultura** (Map p100; ☎ 860-6282; Malecón No 17 btwn Prado & Capdevila; 🕑 9am-5pm Tue-Sat, 9am-1pm Sun) has all kinds of facilities including a library, cinema, Internet café and concert venue. Pick up their excellent monthly brochure and ask about the literature courses. Another place worth approaching is **Paradiso** (Map pp106-7; ☎ 832-9538; fax 33 39 21; Calle 19 No 560, Vedado) a cultural agency that can arrange courses on history, architecture, music, theater, dance and more.

### Yoga

Yoga classes are offered in the garden of the **Museo de Artes Decorativas** (Map pp106-7; ☎ 830-9848; Calle 17 No 502 btwn Calles D & E). Check at the museum for the next session. You may be able to drop in on classes held at the **Teatro Nacional** (Map pp106-7; cnr Paseo & Calle 39). Look for the class schedule by the box office.

### Music

Cubans are aficionados of Flamenco and you can take dance classes or even pursue the possibility of a few guitar lessons by inquiring at the **Centro Andaluz** (Map p100; ☎ 863-6745; Paseo de Martí No 104 btwn Genios & Refugio).

### Art

The **Taller Experimental de Gráfica** (Map p94; ☎ 7-862-0979; fax 7-824-0391; Callejón del Chorro No 6; Plaza de la Catedral, Habana) offers classes in the art of engraving. Individualized instruction lasts one month, during which the student creates an engraving with 15 copies; longer classes can be arranged. The cost is around CUC$250.

#### SCAMS

Well documented *jinetero* (tout) problem aside, Habana is a remarkably safe city – particularly when compared with other Latin American capitals. Stroll through the atmospheric backstreets of Centro Habana or Habana Vieja of an evening and your biggest worry is likely to be a badly pitched baseball or a flailing line of household washing.

But innocents beware. Scams do exist, particularly in the more touristy areas where well-practiced hustlers lurk outside the big hotels waiting to prey on unsuspecting foreign visitors.

One popular trick is for young men in the street to offer to change foreign currency into Cuban Convertibles at very favorable rates. Accept this at your peril. The money that you will be given is *moneda nacional* or Cuban pesos, visually similar to Convertibles, but worth approximately one-twenty-fifth of the value when you take them into a shop.

A second scam is the illicit sale of cheap cigars usually perpetuated by hissing street salesmen around Centro Habana and Habana Vieja. It is best to politely ignore these characters. Any bartering is not worth the bother. Cigars sold on the street are almost always sub-standard – something akin to substituting an expensive French wine with cheap white vinegar. Instead, buy your cigars direct from the factory or visit one of the numerous Casas del Habana that are scattered throughout the city.

**TALK CUBAN ASERE**

For aspiring language students, uncovering the nuances of Cuban Spanish is rather like learning English from a Glaswegian. There's plenty of lewd and colorful language, but it doesn't always correspond to the phrasebook. Here's a list of some of the more accessible institutions that offer Spanish study in Habana:

- The first port of call for foreign language students is **Universidad de la Habana** (Map pp106-7; Edificio Varona, 2nd fl, Calle J No 556) which offers Spanish courses 12 months a year, beginning on the first Monday of each month. Costs start at CUC$100 for 20 hours (one week), including textbooks, and cover all levels from beginners to advanced. You must first sit a placement test to determine your level. Aspiring candidates can sign up in person at the university or reserve beforehand via e-mail or phone (☎ 832-4245; 831-3751; dpg@uh.cu). You can also check out the UniversiTUR website (www.universitur.com).
- Other places to check out Spanish courses include **Uneac** (Map pp106-7; ☎ 832-4551; cnr Calles 17 & H, Vedado) and **Paradiso** (Map pp106-7; ☎ 832-9538; Calle 19 No 560).
- Private lessons can be arranged by asking around locally – try your casa particular.

## HABANA FOR CHILDREN

Cubans love kids, and families traveling together will have special experiences not available to other travelers. Staying in casas particulares is especially recommended as it provides the opportunity for cross-cultural family exchanges. Vagaries of the Cuban reality will demand patience and creativity by parents (particularly when it comes to food) but there is no lack of fun things to do here including the big aquarium in Playa (see Acuario Nacional, p148), plus the freshwater **Aquarivm** (Map p94; ☎ 863-9493; Calle Brasil No 9 btwn Mercaderes & Oficios, Habana Vieja; 🕒 9am-5.30pm Tue-Sun); the fantastic **playground** right on the Malecón (at Tacón), replete with rides; **horseback riding** in Parque Lenin; and water slides and bumper cars at **Complejo Recreo** in Marina Hemingway. Head to the **beach** at Playas del Este to sail, kayak and swim. For inflatable castles try **La Maestranza** (Map p94; Carlos Manuel de Céspedes, Habana Vieja; admission CUC$1; under 4s only).

Culturally, there are slews of things specifically for kids including **La Colmenita** children's theater (p137); and **Cinecito** (p137), with all-kids' movies all the time and kids concerts, films and activities every Saturday (3pm) and Sunday (11am) at the Museo Nacional de Bellas Artes, Colección de Arte Cubano (p102).

All the **ice-cream parlors** are a delight for children and playing a round of **miniature golf** in Parque Almendares (p134) or seaside at **Holá Ola** (Map pp106-7; Malecón btwn Principe & Valor; minigolf CUC$2; 🕒 11am-sunset) is fun for everyone. Even the transport here is kid friendly: hop in an old Chevy, grab a coco-taxi or hire a bici-taxi and discover Habana.

## QUIRKY HABANA

Since 1990 local painter Salvador González Escalona has converted **Callejón de Hamel**, between Aramburu and Hospital, off San Lázaro, into an open-air art center with zany murals, sculpture and found-object art. Visit Salvador's **studio** (Map pp106-7; ☎ 878-1661; Callejón de Hamel No 1054; 🕒 10am-6pm) to view (and perhaps purchase) his work. The studio also organizes free cultural activities along the Callejón de Hamel such as the **Sunday rumba** at 11am (beware, this is *jinetero* city), **children's theater** (🕒 10am 3rd Sat of the month), and **street theater** (🕒 7pm, 4th Thu of the month).

The nightly **cañonazo ceremony** at the Fortaleza de la Cabaña, where young actors decked out in 18th-century military regalia shoot off cannons in keeping with a 400-year-old Habana tradition (see p162) is a popular excursion frequented by vast crowds.

**Taller Experimental de Gráfica** (Map p94; ☎ 862-0979; tgrafica@cubarte.cult.cu; Callejón del Chorro No 6; 🕒 10am-4pm Mon-Fri) is an active workshop off Plaza de la Catedral selling engravings and prints that you can watch being made on the premises (CUC$15 to CUC$800).

Chocolate addicts beware: Habana Vieja's **Museo del Chocolate** (Map p94; cnr Calle Amargura & Mercaderes; 🕒 9am-8pm) is a lethal

**GET INVOLVED**

There are a number of bodies offering volunteer work in Cuba though it is always best to organize things in your home country first. Just turning up in Habana and volunteering can be difficult, if not impossible. Take a look at the following websites (for more on volunteering, see p466):

**Canada World Youth** (☎ 514 931-3526; www.cwy-jcm.org) Head office in Montreal, Canada.
**Canada-Cuba Farmer to Farmer Project** (www.farmertofarmer.ca) Vancouver-based sustainable agriculture organization.
**Cuban Solidarity Campaign** (☎ 020 7263 6452; www.cuba-solidarity.org) Head office in London, UK.
**National Network on Cuba** (www.cubasolidarity.com) US-based solidarity group.
**Witness for Peace** (WFP; ☎ 202-588-1471; www.witnessforpeace.org) Looking for Spanish-speakers with a two-year commitment.
**Pastors for Peace** (PFP; ☎ 212-926-5757; www.ifconews.org) Collects donations across the US to take to Cuba.

dose of chocolate, truffles, and yet more chocolate (and it's all made on the premises too). Situated rather amusingly on the corner of Calle Amargura (Bitterness St), this venerable sweet-toothed establishment is actually more a café than a museum, with a small cluster of marble tables set among an interesting assortment of chocolate paraphernalia. Not surprisingly everything on the rather delicious menu contains one all-pervading ingredient: have it hot, cold, white, dark, rich, or smooth, the stuff is divine, whichever way you choose.

## TOURS

Most general agencies offer the same tours, with some exceptions noted below. The regular tour diet includes a four-hour city tour (CUC$15), a specialized Hemingway tour (from CUC$20), a *cañonazo* ceremony (shooting of the cannons at the Fortaleza de la Cabaña; without/with dinner CUC$15/25), a Varadero day trip (from CUC$35), and, of course, excursions to Tropicana Nightclub (starting at CUC$65). Other options include tours to Boca de Guamá crocodile farm (CUC$48), Playas del Este (CUC$20, includes lunch), Viñales (CUC$44), Cayo Largo del Sur (CUC$137) and a Trinidad–Cienfuegos overnight (CUC$129). Children usually pay a fraction of the price of adults and solo travelers get socked with a CUC$15 supplement. Note that if the minimum number of people don't sign up, the trip will be cancelled. Any of the following agencies (most of which also have offices in Playa/Miramar) can arrange these tours and more:

**Cubatur** (Map pp106-7; ☎ 33 31 70/1; cnr Calles 23 & M, Vedado; ⏲ 8am-8pm) Below the Hotel Habana Libre.
**Havanatur** (Map pp106-7; ☎ 33 46 51; www.havanatur.cu; Galerías de Paseo, cnr Calle 1 & Paseo, Vedado)
**Infotur** Airport (Map p155; ☎ 66 61 01; Terminal 3 Aeropuerto Internacional José Martí; ⏲ 24hr); Habana Vieja (Map p94; ☎ 63 68 84; cnr Obispo & San Ignacio; ⏲ 10am-1pm & 2-7pm); Habana Vieja (Map p94; ☎ 33 33 33; Obispo btwn Bernaza & Villegas)
**Paradiso** (Map pp106-7; ☎ 832-9538; fax 33 39 21; Calle 19 No 560, Vedado) Tours with art emphasis in several languages and departing from many cities. Check out Martí's Habana or special concert tours.
**San Cristóbal Agencia de Viajes** (Map p94; ☎ 861-9171/2; Oficios No 110 btwn Lamparilla & Amargura, Habana Vieja; ⏲ 8:30am-5:30pm Mon-Fri, 8:30am-2pm Sat, 9am-noon Sun) Offers an Habana archaeological tour (CUC$8) and a Buena Vista Social Club tour (CUC$15) with 'band members' of the famous group.

## FESTIVALS & EVENTS

The major cultural events in Habana include: FolkCuba in mid-January of odd-numbered years; Festival Internacional del Libro in the last week of January; PerCuba (Festival Internacional de Percusión) every mid-April; Cubadisco and the Festival Internacional de Guitarra every May; and the Ernest Hemingway Dialog each May in odd-numbered years; the Festival Internacional de Boleros de Oro in June; Festival de Rap Cubana Hip Hop in August; the Festival de Teatro de la Habana odd-numbered years in September; the Festival de Música Contemporanea (Festival of Contemporary Music) every October; the Internacional de Ballet Festival in October in even-numbered years; the annual Marabana Marathon in November; the Festival de Raíces Africanas Wemilere (Wemilere African Roots Festival) in Guanabacao in late November; the Bienial de la Habana in November in odd-numbered years; the Festival Internacional de Jazz in December of even-numbered years; and the Festival Internacional del Nuevo Cine Latinamericano every December.

For advance information about all special events in Cuba, visit AfroCuba web at www.afrocubaweb.com/festivals.htm.

## SLEEPING

Private rooms are readily available throughout the city. You'll pay anywhere from CUC$20 to CUC$35 per room, with those in Vedado usually better quality and more expensive than those in Centro Habana; however, Vedado is also more suburban, and some people find it too far removed from the action. Don't allow a room tout to lead you around; their commission will add CUC$5 per night to the cost.

Some of Habana hotels are historic monuments in their own right. Worth a look, even if you're not booking a room, are the Hotel Sevilla, the Nacional, the Habana Libre, the Saratoga, the Raquel, the Hostal Condes de Villanueva and Hotel Florida.

### Habana Vieja

#### BUDGET

**Residencia Académica Convento de Santa Clara** (☎ 866-9327; Cuba No 610 btwn Luz & Sol; r per person CUC$25) The Old Town's only real budget option (bar the plentiful private rooms) is an old nunnery that has been partially converted to take in travelers. Wedged inconspicuously into Habana Vieja's tightly packed grid, this convent-turned-hostel offers peace and tranquility in the center of the city at a very reasonable price. What's more, it's a tourist site in its own right. Book ahead.

#### MIDRANGE

**Hostal Valencia** (Habaguanex; ☎ 867-1037; Oficios No 53; s/d incl breakfast low season CUC$62/100, high season CUC$72/120) The Valencia is a veritable Spanish posada (inn) with hanging vines, huge doorways (and rooms) and its own renowned paella restaurant. You half-expect Don Quixote and Sancho Panza to come wandering down the stairway. Slap bang in the middle of the historical core and with a price that makes it one of the cheapest offerings in the current Habaguanex stable, this

#### CASAS PARTICULARES – HABANA VIEJA

**Casa de Pepe & Rafaela** (☎ 862-9877; San Ignacio No 454 btwn Sol & Santa Clara; r CUC$30) One of Habana's best: antiques and Moorish tiles throughout, three rooms each with balconies and gorgeous new baths, excellent location. The son also rents in charming colonial house at San Ignacio No 656 (CUC$25).

**Eliberto Barrios Suárez** (☎ 863-3782; eliberto62@webcorreosdecuba.cu; San Juan Díos No 112 apt 3A btwn Aguacate & Compostela; apt CUC$30) Nice two-bedroom duplex apartment with kitchen.

**Jesús & María** (☎ 861-1378; jesusmaria2003@yahoo.com; Aguacate No 518 btwn Sol & Muralla; r CUC$25) Rents three rooms, try for one upstairs; inviting inner patio.

**Juan & Margarita** (☎ 867-9592; Obispo No 522 apt 8 btwn Bernaza & Villegas; apt CUC$60) Two-bedroom apartment, super central, flexible and friendly hosts. Juan speaks excellent English and has a lot of local knowledge.

**Luis Fornaris & Mirtha García** (☎ 860-0650; mfornaris@empresch.get.tur.cu; Compostela No 119; r CUC$25) Basic room sleeps three, warmly reader recommended.

**Migdalia Carraballe** (☎ /fax 861-7352; Santa Clara No 164 btwn Cuba & San Ignacio; r CUC$25-35) Rents three rooms, two with balconies overlooking Santa Clara convent.

**Noemi Moreno** (☎ 862-3809; Cuba No 611 apt 2 btwn Luz & Santa Clara; r CUC$25) Simple, clean room in great location behind convent; also rent in apartment one.

**Pablo Rodríguez** (☎ 861-2111; pablo@sercomar.telemar.cu; Compostela No 532 btwn Brasil & Muralla; r CUC$30) Old colonial with original frescos. Rents two rooms with bath, fan and fridge.

**Ramón & Maritza** (☎ 862-3303; Calle Luz No 115 btwn San Ignacio & Inquisidor; r CUC$25) Two big interconnecting rooms in colonial house; friendly.

hostel is an excellent old-world choice with good service and plenty of atmosphere.

**Hotel El Comendador** (Habaguanex; ☎ 867-1037; cnr Obrapía & Baratillo; ) Situated next door to the Valencia, the El Comendador has the same prices.

### TOP END

**Hotel los Frailes** ( ☎ 862-9383; Calle Brasil btwn Oficios & Mercaderes; s/d incl breakfast CUC$72/120; ) This engaging 22-room hotel just off Plaza Vieja sports a tranquil inner courtyard where staff bustle to and fro dressed up as monks. Stained-glass windows and rough-hewn furniture add an extra monastical feel. Upstairs, away from the frivolities, comfortable rooms are distinguished by good art, tasteful furniture and bright modern fittings. The four rooms with balconies are best. An added perk is the resident woodwind quartet in the lobby; the musicians are so good that they regularly lure in bevies of passing tour groups.

**Hostal San Miguel** (Habaguanex; ☎ 862-7656; Calle Cuba No 52; s/d CUC$90/150; P ) Positioned close to Habana harbor with tremendous views out across the water to La Cabaña fort, the elegant San Miguel was once owned by Cuban newspaper director Antonio San Miguely Segalá, whose periodical *La Lucha* played an important role in the First War of Independence. Characterized by its high ceilings, Carrara marble floors and a plethora of old faded prerevolution-era photos, the San Miguel's 10 rooms retain a rather fetching old-world feel that blends in nicely with the building's neoclassical belle-époque decor; it's a pleasant Old Town retreat.

**Hotel Florida** (Habaguanex; ☎ 862-4127; Obispo No 252; s/d incl breakfast CUC$90/150; P ) An architectural extravaganza, the Florida is a three-story jewel built in the purest colonial style, with arches and pillars clustered around a central courtyard loaded with atmosphere. Constructed in 1836, Habaguanex has restored the building with loving attention to detail; the nicely furnished rooms retaining their original high ceilings and luxurious furnishings. Complemented with an elegant café and an amiable bar-nightspot (open from 8pm) anyone with even a passing interest in Cuba's architectural heritage will want to check this one out.

**Hotel Ambos Mundos** (Habaguanex; ☎ 860-9529; Obispo No 153; s/d low season CUC$80/130, high season CUC$90/150; ) Hemingway's Habana hideout and the place where he is said to have penned his seminal guerrilla classic *For Whom the Bell Tolls* (Castro's bedtime reading during the war in the mountains), the pastel pink Ambos Mundos is a Habana institution and a obligatory pit stop for anyone on a world tour of 'Hemingway-once-fell-over-here' bars. Small sometimes windowless rooms suggest overpricing but the lobby bar is classic enough (follow the romantic piano melody) and drinks on the rooftop restaurant one of the city's finest treats.

**Hotel Raquel** (Habaguanex; ☎ 860-8280; cnr Calle Amargura & San Ignacio; s/d CUC$115/200; ) You'll get a neck ache checking out the astounding stained-glass ceilings and authoritative Italian marble pillars here. One of Habaguanex' gorgeously-restored colonial diamonds, the Raquel offers travelers the best of both worlds with a gym, sauna, plush rooms and classy restaurant along with one of the most eye-catching and illustrious front lobbies in any hotel anywhere. Arrive and be seduced.

**Hotel Santa Isabel** (Habaguanex; ☎ 860-8201; Baratillo No 9; s/d incl breakfast CUC$190/240; P ) Originally the Palacio de los Condes de Santovenia, this weighty colonial colossus on the eastern side of Plaza de Armas is loaded with architectural details, soft lighting, amenable staff and perks such as views, terraces and tubs in every room. The spacious suites are especially nice, with large balconies overlooking the plaza. Jimmy Carter is one of many famous guests who stayed here.

## Centro Habana

### BUDGET

**Casa del Científico** ( ☎ 862-1607/8, Paseo de Martí No 212; s/d with shared bath CUC$25/31, with private bath CUC$45/55; ) This is a very welcome budget option slap bang in the middle of the central district which means it fills up fast. The Casa del Gentifico is an elegant old building with grand stairways, marble columns, courtyards, and terraces overlooking the Prado, making this a nice and atmospheric introduction to Habana. A nice thick coating of dust adds extra authenticity. Nevertheless, services abound

**THE AUTHOR'S CHOICE**

**Hostal Condes de Villanueva** (Habanaguanex; Map p94; ☎ 862-9293; Mercaderes No 202, Habana Vieja; s/d low season CUC$67/98, high season CUC$93/150; ) If you are going to splash out on one night of luxury in Habana, you'd do well to check out this highly-lauded colonial gem. Restored under the watchful eye of city historian Eusebio Leal a few years back, the Hostal Condes de Villanueva has converted a grandiose city mansion into an intimate and thoughtfully-decorated hotel with nine bedrooms spread spaciously around an attractive inner courtyard (complete with resident peacock). Opening onto the cobbled streets below, the upstairs suites contain stained-glass windows, chandeliers, arty sculptures, huge baths and – best of all – a fully-workable whirlpool bathtub. After a few weeks in the Cuban outback, it could be just what the doctor ordered.

**Hotel Sevilla** (Gran Caribe; Map p100; ☎ 860-8560; Trocadero No 55 btwn Paseo de Martí & Agramonte; s/d incl breakfast CUC$150/210; ) Al Capone once hired out the whole 6th floor, Graham Greene used it as a setting for his novel *Our Man in Havana,* and the Mafia requisitioned it as operations centre for their prerevolutionary North American drugs racket. Refurbished by the French Sofitel group in 2002 the Hotel Sevilla now sparkles like the colonial jewel of old with large spacious rooms, comfortable beds and a rather surreally-located ground floor swimming pool (bathers are overlooked by a crumbling city tenement complete with lines of drying washing). The hotel's high point (in more ways than one) has to be the superb 9th-floor restaurant where you can enjoy breakfast overlooking the muggy and mildewed streets of Habana Vieja. A solitary violinist serenades early morning breakfasters with a wonderfully melancholic rendition of *As Time Goes By*.

**Meson de la Flota** (Habanaguanex; Map p94; ☎ 863-3838; Mercaderes No 257 btwn Amargura & Brasil, Habana Vieja; s/d CUC$45/65; ) Habana Vieja's smallest and most reasonably priced period hotel is an old Spanish tavern decked out with maritime motifs and located within spitting distance of gracious Plaza Vieja. Five individually crafted rooms contain all of the modern comforts and amenities while downstairs a busy restaurant serves up delicious tapas (check out the garbanzos with chorizo) and scrumptiously-prepared *platos principales* (main courses). For music lovers the real draw, however, is the nightly Flamenco tablaos, the quality of which could rival anything in Andalusia. Sit back and soak up the *duende* (spirit).

here (Internet, restaurants, bars, dancing) and it serves as a sort of social center for the neighborhood and traveler traffic (though the guard at the door tempers any hard-core mingling). The rooms are rather ordinary but adequate.

**Hotel Lido** (Islazul; ☎ 867-1102; Consulado No 210 btwn Ánimas & Trocadero; s/d low season CUC$21/31, high season CUC$28/38) A travelers' institution, the lackluster Lido probably boasts a higher concentration of Lonely Planet readers than any other hotel in Cuba. The secret lies in a strangely unexotic mix of location, price, and friendly, no-nonsense service offered up by the staff at reception. If you don't mind cold showers, lumpy beds, and a breakfast that will leave you searching hungrily for an early lunch, this could be a worthwhile Habana base.

**Hotel Lincoln** (Islazul; ☎ 33 82 09; Av de Italia btwn Virtudes & Ánimas; s/d low season CUC$30/40, high season CUC$39/46; ) A venerable nine-story giant on busy Calle Ánimas, the Hotel Lincoln was the second-tallest building in Habana when it was built in 1926. These days it offers 135 air-con rooms with bath and TV in an atmosphere that is more 1950s than 2000s. Notoriety hit this hotel in 1958 when Castro's M-26-7 (July 26 Movement) kidnapped five-time motor-racing world champion Carlos Fangio from the downstairs lobby on the eve of the Cuban Grand Prix in a propaganda coup. Apparently they planned to kidnap Stirling Moss as well until they found out that the British driver was still on his honeymoon (real gents those Cubans!). Fangio was released a few days later unharmed, speaking highly of his polite captors. As a political protest, the exercise had clearly worked. In the dusty lobby you can see a picture of Fangio meeting a beaming Fidel Castro 20 years later, old grudges apparently forgotten.

**Hotel Caribbean** (Islazul; ☎ 860-8233; Paseo de Martí No 164 btwn Colón & Refugio; s/d low season CUC$33/48, high season CUC$36/54; ) The last and undoubtedly the worst of Islazul's trio of centrally located downtown hotels, the Caribbean gives a new meaning to the term 'rough-around-the-edges.' Don't be fooled by the shiny lobby and adjacent bar; the upper floors hide infinitely more moth-eaten secrets.

## MIDRANGE

**Hotel Park View** (Habaguanex; Calle Colón No 101; s/d CUC$50/80) Park View's reputation as the poor man's 'Sevilla' isn't entirely justified. Its location alone (within baseball-pitching distance of the Museo de la Revolución) is enough to recommend this mint-green city charmer as a viable option. Chuck in clean rooms, modern furnishings and a small but perfectly-poised 7th-floor restaurant

### CASAS PARTICULARES – CENTRO HABANA

**Alejandro Osés** (☎ 863-7359; Malecón No 163 1st fl; r CUC$25) Three rooms, sea views very popular, English spoken.

**Amada Pérez Güelmes & Antonio Clavero** (☎ 862-3924; Lealtad No 262 Altos btwn Neptuno & Concordia; r CUC$25) Four rooms available in pleasant colonial house.

**Carlos Luis Valerrama Moré** (☎ 867-9842; Neptuno No 404 2nd fl btwn San Nicolás & Manrique; r CUC$25) Big space with living/dining room and balcony.

**Casa Marta** (☎ 863-3078; bienvenidoalcorazon@yahoo.com; Manrique No 362; r CUC$30) Three rooms around inner patio; chance to meet other travelers.

**Dulce Hostal – Dulce María González** (☎ 863-2506; Amistad No 220 btwn Neptuno & San Miguel; r CUC$20) Beautiful colonial house, tile floors, soaring ceilings, quiet, friendly hostess.

**Elicio Fernández** (☎ 861-7447; Aguila No 314 apt 405 btwn Neptune & Concordia; r CUC$25) Breezy rooms with lots of natural light. Fan and shared bath. Doorman and elevator. Rooftop views.

**Esther Cardoso** (☎ 862-0401; esthercv2551@cubarte.cult.cu; Aguila No 367 btwn Neptuno 7 San Miguel; r CUC$25) Artist's palace; this place is like an oasis in the desert with tasteful decor, funky posters, spick-and-span baths and spectacular roof terrace. Book early.

**José Ricardo** (☎ 861-6413; Neptuno No 560 1st fl btwn Lealtad & Escobar; CUC$25) Nice hosts with good local knowledge. Meals available.

**Juan Carlos** (☎ 863-6301, 861-8003; Crespo No 107 btwn Colón & Trocadero; r CUC$15-20) Big, spotless house. Cheapest room has shared bath and fan. Natural light throughout. Value.

**Julio & Elsa Roque** (☎ 861-8027; julioroq@yahoo.com; Consulado No 162, apt 2, btwn Colón & Trocadero; r CUC$15-25) Rents two rooms with different amenities. Cheapest has shared bath, fan only and cold water. Both Julio – who is a pediatrician – and Elsa are super-helpful and a mine of information. English spoken.

**La Casona Colonial – Jorge Díaz** (☎ 870-0489; cubarooms2000@yahoo.com; Gervasio No 209 btwn Concordia & Virtudes; r CUC$25) Several rooms around nice courtyard, one has three beds, shared bath; good for longer stays.

**Martha Obregón** (☎ 870-2095; marthaobregon@yahoo.com; Gervasio No 308 Altos btwn Neptuno & San Miguel; r CUC$20-25) Nice home, little balconies have small street views. Popular, often full.

**Niurka O Rey** (☎ 863-0278; Aguila No 206 btwn Animas & Virtudes; r CUC$20-25) Sparkling blue house with slightly less sparkling but adequate interior. One room with bath and parking close by.

**Paraiso 'Vista al Mar' – Tamara Valdés** (☎ 861-8112; Malecón No 51 14th fl, btwn Carcel & Genios; r CUC$30) If it's a view you're after and you don't mind traveling up 14 floors in an antiquated lift, check out this spacious option right on the Malecón.

**Rufino Añel Martín & Pilar Rodríguez Santos** (☎ 862-4149; Neptuno No 556 btwn Lealtad & Escobar; r CUC$25) Lively, edgy area. Can cook and do laundry; helpful hosts.

**Sandra Elso Aguilera** (☎ 861-2944, 70 75 16; Consulado No 304 apt 3E btwn Neptuno & Virtudes; r CUC$25) Friendly.

**Triny Vital** (☎ 867-9132; Calle Aguila No 118 Bajos btwn Colón & Trocadero; apt CUC$50) Two-bedroom independent apartment with kitchen sleeps four to five.

**Victoria Rivero Nuñez** (☎ 863-7750; Consulado No 304 apt 2D btwn Neptuno & Virtudes; r CUC$30) Spacious. Eighteen others renting in this building.

and you've got yourself a veritable bargain. Other bonuses include cable TV, a small downstairs bar and tiny balconies (in street-facing rooms).

**Hotel Deauville** (Hotetur; ☎ 33 88 13; cnr Av de Italia No 1 & Malecón; s/d/tr CUC$61/88/99; P) The Deauville is housed in a kitschy seafront high-rise that sharp-eyed Habana-watchers will recognize from picturesque Malecón-at-sunset postcards. But while the location might be postcard perfect, the facilities inside this former Mafia gambling den don't quite match up to the stellar views. Currently reborn in peach and red, Deauville's handy facilities, decent car rental and reasonable restaurant are ever popular with the midpriced tour-circuit crowd; plus it's great for an early morning Malecón stroll.

### TOP END

**Hotel Inglaterra** (Gran Caribe; ☎ 860-8595; www.grancaribe.cu; Paseo de Martí No 416; s/d/tr CUC$84/120/168; P) It's José Martí's one-time Habana hotel of choice and it's still playing on the fact – which says something about the current state of affairs. The Inglaterra is a better place to hang-out than actually to stay in, with its exquisite Moorish lobby and crusty colonial interior easily outshining the lackluster and often viewless rooms. The rooftop bar's a popular watering hole and the downstairs foyer is a hive of bustling activity where there's always music blaring. Beware of the streets outside which are full of over-zealous hustlers waiting to pounce.

**Hotel Plaza** (Gran Caribe; ☎ 860-8592; www.grancaribe.cu; Agramonte No 267; s/d CUC$84/120;) Not a bad hotel, but it suffers because of the rather illustrious company on its doorstep (NH Parque Central & Telégrafo). Still, the lobby's nice even if the rooms ain't so spiffy, with a pleasant café and three decent Internet terminals. Popular on the package-tour circuit, the piano bar makes another good diversion and the adjoining Las Portales restaurant serves pizza for less than CUC$5 (unusual in a four-star hotel).

**Hotel Telégrafo** (Habaguanex; ☎ 861-1010, 861-4741; Paseo de Martí No 408; s/d from CUC$90/150; P) Offered as a new addition to the Habaguanex chain when it first opened its doors in 2001, this hotel juxtaposes old style architectural features (the original building hails from 1888) with futuristic design flourishes that include silver sofas, a huge winding central staircase, and an awesome tile mosaic emblazoned on the wall of the downstairs café. The rooms are equally spiffy.

**Hotel Saratoga** (Habaguanex; Paseo de Martí No 603; s/d CUC$150/190; P) In a city with a dearth of budget hotel options another five-star outfit was probably the last thing we needed. Still, the restored Saratoga is big and beautiful, with huge baths, modern funky furnishings, mosaic tiles and panoramic views over the Capitolio. Built originally as a hotel in the 1930s the Saratoga Mark I was requisitioned by the Castro government in 1959 and converted into homes for Habana's urban poor. Mark II reopened in November 2005, back to its luxurious best. There's a swimming pool on the roof and the rooms are positively opulent. It's worth a peep even if you're not staying there.

**Hotel NH Parque Central** (NH Hotels; Map100; ☎ 860-6627; www.nh-hotels.com; Neptuno btwn Agramonte & Paseo de Martí; s/d CUC$185/215; P) Facility-wise the NH Parque Central is Habana's luxury giant and the luscious ground-floor lobby is the ultimate place to relax after a day spent trudging the uneven cobbles of Old Habana (great coffee). Blessed with a rooftop pool, international-standard rooms and a sharp and breezy business center open to all-comers, the only real let-down in this oasis of urban peace is the cool, almost aloof attitude of the overly-efficient staff who seem to have had every last element of their Cuban-ness sucked out of them.

## Vedado

### BUDGET

**Hotel Bruzón** (Islazul; ☎ 877-5684; Bruzón No 217 btwn Pozos Dulces & Av de la Independencia; s/d CUC$22/28;) The price comes with a price: tired and worn facilities and an ugly and highly inconvenient location. The one and only reason to stay at this hotel is for its proximity to the (Astro) bus station. Bleary-eyed arrivals on the 6:30am guagua (bus) from Santiago might appreciate its lumpy beds.

**Hotel Universitario** (☎ 33 34 03; cnr Calle 17 & Calle L; s/d CUC$25/34) This friendly place opposite the Servi-Cupet gas station has a good location. It's basic, but you won't find another hotel in central Vedado for this price.

### MIDRANGE

**Hotel Colina** (Gran Caribe; ☎ 33 40 71; cnr Calles L & 27; s/d low season CUC$40/50, high season CUC$44/54; ) Well-worn rooms, bored staff and sparse facilities; the Colina often gets a bad press. But with its central location opposite the university and its slightly cheaper prices compared with other midrange options, budget travelers will find a good base here. An added bonus: it isn't normally full.

**Hotel St John's** (Gran Caribe; ☎ 33 37 40; Calle O No 216 btwn Calles 23 & 25; s/d incl breakfast low season CUC$50/67, high season CUC$56/80; ) The rooftop pool is small and the staff unresponsive, but the beds are good, the baths clean and western-facing rooms have killer Malecón views. Vibrant Vedado awaits outside your window. Use the safe deposit box when you hit the town and check out the 14th-floor Pico Blanco nightclub (p134).

**Hotel Vedado** (Gran Caribe; ☎ 832-2806; Calle O No 244 btwn Calles 23 & 25; s/d low season CUC$50/67, high season CUC$56/80; ) St John's versus

### CASAS PARTICULARES – VEDADO

**Angela Muñiz Rubio** (☎ 879-6851; San Miguel No 1116 btwn Mazón & Basarrate; r CUC$25) Rents rooms near Museo Napoleónico, two with private bath.

**Armando Gutiérrez** (☎/fax 832-1876; Calle 21 No 62 apt 7 btwn M & N; r CUC$25-30) Nice room with balcony and fridge. Friendly; English spoken; elevator.

**Basilia Pérez Castro** (☎ 832-3953; bpcdt@hotmail.com; Calle 25 No 361 apt 7 Bajos btwn K & L; r CUC$25) Two rooms with independent entrances, fridge, phone, TV. Mellow, good value.

**Beatriz & Julio** (☎ 832-5778; Calle 25 No 367 btwn K & L; r CUC$25-30; ) Close to university and central hotels. Separate entrance.

**Casa de Jannett** (☎ 831-7367; Calle F No 610 btwn 25 & 27; r CUC$25) Colonial house, close to university.

**Casa Teresita** (☎ 832-0777; Calle 21 No 4 apt 54 btwn O & N; r CUC$25) Clean room, doting hostesses. Good for bikes.

**Conchita García** (☎ 832-6187; conchitagarcia21@hotmail.com; Calle 21 No 4 apt 74 btwn N & O; r CUC$30-35) Well-kept apartment with two rooms, TV, nice terrace. Numerous others in this building.

**Doris Jorge** (☎ 32 50 29; Calle 21 No 15, Apt 9, btwn N & O; r CUC$25) Penthouse with views. Rooms are huge and hostess amiable. Ascend in elevator to 6th floor.

**Eddy Gutiérrez Bouza** (☎ 832-5207; Calle 21 No 408 btwn F & G; r CUC$30; P ) Huge colonial house with fantastic host. Eddy is an excellent source of information about Habana.

**Guillermina & Roberto Abreu** (☎ 833-6401; Paseo No 126 apt 13A btwn 5 & Calzada; r CUC$25) Two spacious rooms with views. Elevator here.

**Iraida Carpio** (☎ 832-4084; Calle 19 No 376 fl 10A btwn G & H; r CUC$25) Take antiquated elevator. A splendid view.

**Julio Padilla Martín** (☎ 832-5709; juliop_martin@hotmail.com; Calle K No 210 apt 7B btwn Línea & 15; r CUC$30-35) Good for groups. English spoken.

**Manuel Martínez** (☎ 832-6713; Calle 21 No 4 apt 22 btwn N & O; r CUC$30-35) There are 10 to 12 casas in this magnificent art-deco building constructed in 1945 opposite the Hotel Nacional. This one overlooks the hotel gardens; it's a classic view.

**Maribel y Luis Garcé** (☎ 832-1619; Calle 19 No 356 upstairs btwn G & H; r CUC$25) Nice young couple rent smallish room, little balcony.

**Marta Vitorte** (☎ 885- 7792; martavitorte@hotmail.com; Calle G No 301 apt 14 btwn 13 & 15; r CUC$35-40) Two rooms in deluxe apartment with phenomenal views, great beds, wraparound terrace. English spoken.

**Melba Piñeda Bermudez** (☎ 832-5929; lienafp@yahoo.com; Calle 11 No 802 btwn Calles 2 & 4; r CUC$25-30) Sweet room with nice furnishings and private terrace in beautiful colonial home. Quiet street. Helpful owners.

**Natalia Rodes** (☎ 832-8909; Calle 19 No 376 fl 11B btwn G & H; r CUC$25) Shared bath, nice bed, expansive views.

**Nelsy Alemán Machado** (☎ 832-8467; Calle 25 No 361 apt 1 btwn K & L; r CUC$25) Independent, laid-back place. Fridge.

**Pilar Palma** (☎ 831-8918; Calle O No 202 apt 9 btwn 23 & 25; r CUC$25) Prime La Rampa location; friendly.

**MARRIED TO THE MOB**

'We invented Havana and we can goddamn well move it someplace else if [Batista] can't control it' boasted Mafia boss Meyer Lansky in the Sydney Pollack–directed movie *Havana*.

Brazen and hyperbolic, Lansky's comments carry a certain amount of historical weight. Cuba's on-off marriage with the American Mafia first took root in the 1920s when Prohibition in the US sent pleasure-seeking Americans flocking south to line up their rum cocktails in the bars and hotels of sensuous Habana. Al Capone was an early adherent, financing an illegal molasses-supplying racket for illicit Cuban rum factories; though the real deal – high-stakes gambling – didn't take off until after World War II.

Lansky and notorious Mafia Don, Salvatore 'Lucky' Luciano were the main second-phase instigators. In December 1946, the two corpulent mobsters coordinated the largest ever get together of North American mafia hoods in Habana's Hotel Nacional under the cover of a Frank Sinatra concert. Hatching a plan to open up the Cuban capital to narcotics, pornography and large-scale gambling houses, the duo enlisted the clandestine support of opportunist ex-President Fulgencio Batista.

The plan reached fruition in March 1952 when a Batista coup toppled the regime of Carlos Prío Socarrás and enacted laws that gave organized crime a free rein in Cuba's corrupt capital. Over the next eight years Habana became a gambling and vice mecca to rival Las Vegas, a veritable den of iniquity where – in the words of Graham Greene – 'anything was possible.'

Grossly underestimating the popular force of Fidel Castro, the Mob was largely taken by surprise when the scruffily-attired *barbudas* rolled into Habana in January 1959 with their puritanical socialist ideals taped to their rifles. Greeting them gruffly at the door of the Hotel Capri, famous Hollywood actor and Mafia henchman George Raft is said to have furiously slammed the door in their faces. Fatefully, such bold acts of arrogance weren't to last. With the casinos closed down and the high spending tourists packed off across the water to Florida, Lansky and the rest of his cash-embezzling cronies were summarily kicked out of Cuba in June 1959, after which they beat a hasty retreat back to the US with their tail between their legs. The era of loose morals and decadent high-rolling gambling was over as quickly as it had begun.

Vedado is a toss-up. Stakeout the lobbies of both (they're virtually next door to each other) and see which staff seem *less* stroppy. The hotel itself is reasonable enough, with swimming pool, small gym and nightly cabaret show, but at this price you're better off treating yourself to a night in the Old Town.

**Hotel Victoria** (Gran Caribe; ☎ 33 35 10; fax 33 31 09; Calle 19 No 101; s/d incl breakfast low season CUC$55/70, high season CUC$65/90; P ⌘ 💻 🏊) This intimate five-story hotel off the main strip has only 31 rooms and is a good Vedado option if you want more personable service than the Nacional or Habana Libre offer. Rooms are tight, but well-equipped with fridge, safe and minibar. Built in the roaring '20s, it has buckets of style.

**TOP END**

**Hotel Riviera** (Gran Caribe; ☎ 33 40 51; www.grancaribe.cu; cnr Paseo & Malecón; s/d incl breakfast low season CUC$74/105, high season CUC$91/130; ⌘ 💻) Built by US Mafia boss Meyer Lansky in 1957, this hotel oozes character – all the spacious lobby lacks is a lounge lizard in a sharkskin suit. Some of the 354 rooms have terrific sea views and balconies; two have been laid out for disabled guests. The big pool catches sea breezes and the Copa Room here hosts top bands nightly. There are lots of facilities (bank, shops, tourism desks etc), making this a decent choice, especially if you want to be by the water and not pay through the nose. The location means lots of walking, guaguas (local buses) or taxis.

**Hotel Presidente** (Gran Caribe; ☎ 55 18 01; www.grancaribe.cu; cnr Calzada & Calle G; s/d CUC$90/140; P ⌘ 💻 🏊) Fully restored in 2000, this 160-room hotel wouldn't be out of place on a street just off Times Square in New York. Built the same year as the Victoria (1928), the Presidente is similar but larger, with gruffer staff. Unless you're a walker or are comfortable working Habana's transport system, the location can be awkward.

**Hotel Meliá Cohiba** (Sol Meliá; ☎ 33 36 36; fax 33 45 55; Paseo btwn Calles 1 & 3; r low season CUC$180, high season CUC$225; P ✤ 💻 ♿) Professional with a capital P, Meliá hits the spot with know ledgeable, consistent staff and modern, well-polished facilities in this oceanside concrete giant. After a few weeks in go-slow mode you'll be impressed by the responsiveness of the service here, although the building itself is architecturally ugly and the ambience inside more international than Cuban. For workaholics there are rooms especially kitted out for business travelers and 59 units have Jacuzzis. There's also a shopping arcade and the Habana Café here.

**Hotel Nacional** (Gran Caribe; ☎ 55 00 04; cnr Calles 0 & 23; s/d/tr CUC$120/170/238; P ✤ 💻 ♿) The cream of the crop in Cuban hotels and flagship of the government-run Gran Caribe chain; the neoclassical Hotel Nacional is as much a city monument as it is an international accommodation option. Even if you haven't got the money to stay here, chances are you'll end up sipping at least one icy mojito in its exquisite oceanside bar. Steeped in history and furnished with rooms that enthusiastically advertise the details of illustrious occupants past (emblazoned on plaques in the corridors), this towering Habana landmark sports two swimming pools, a sweeping manicured lawn, a couple of lavish restaurants, and its own top-class nighttime cabaret show (the Parisièn). While the rooms might lack the fancy gadgets of deluxe Varadero, the ostentatious communal areas and the erstwhile ghosts of Winston Churchill, Frank Sinatra, Lucky Luciano and Errol Flynn that hover like invisible statues around the luxurious lobby, all add up to a fascinating and unforgettable experience.

**Hotel Habana Libre** (Gran Caribe; ☎ 55 47 04; www.solmeliacuba.com; Calle L btwn Calles 23 & 25; d/ste incl breakfast CUC$200/300; P ✤ 💻 ♿) Habana's biggest and brassiest hotel opened in March 1958 on the eve of Batista's last waltz. Once part of the Hilton chain, it was commandeered by Castro's rebels in January 1959 who put their boots over all the plush furnishings and turned it into a temporary headquarters (Castro effectively ran the country from a suite on the 24th floor). Now efficiently managed by Spain's Tryp Hotels all 574 rooms in this modernist giant are kitted out to international standard with small balconies and up-to-date fittings that still somehow feel old. The tour desks in the lobby are helpful for out-of-town excursions and the weekend music shows often showcase notable artists such as Buena Vista star Eliades Ochoa. Nonguests can use the pool (admission with food-and-drink purchase of at least CUC$15; open 8am to 6:30pm).

## EATING

### Habana Vieja

#### PALADARES

Most of Habana's best paladares are in Miramar or Vedado leaving Habana Vieja, with its plethora of enticingly restored state-run restaurants, with no more than a few metaphoric crumbs. Not that this has stopped an undercover army off-duty waiters/*jineteros* creeping around with the word *langosta* (lobster) planted on their lips. The following two paladares are worth a second glance.

**La Julia** (☎ 862-7438; O'Reilly No 506A btwn Bernaza & Villegas; meals under CUC$10; 🕑 noon-midnight) The pick of the Habana Vieja litter by consensus, this is *comida criolla* (traditional Cuban food) in a friendly, familial setting.

**Paladar La Mulata del Sabor** (☎ 867-5984; Sol No 153; btwn Cuba & San Ignacio; meals CUC$10; 🕑 noon-midnight) Just off Plaza Vieja, this place is OK if you've been overdosing on the historic Habaguanex restaurant scene and want a little more intimacy.

#### RESTAURANTS

**Cafetería Torre La Vega** (Obrapía No 114a btwn Mercaderes & Oficios; 🕑 9am-9pm) This friendly, reliable place is hard to beat with it's outdoor tables and large bowls of spaghetti for just over CUC$1. Try some of the crispy, handmade chips with your cold beer. Next door is a phenomenal batido (fruit shake) and juice joint.

**La Lluvia de Oro** (☎ 862-9870; Obispo No 316; meals under CUC$3; 🕑 24hr) An seedily atmospheric restaurant and bar with overhead ceiling fans stirring up the cigar smoke and loud trumpet blasts emanating from a live Cuban septet that rarely seem to leave the stage. This is a good place for a pizza and beer or mojito and sandwich. It's also a popular traveler hang-out, which also means there's plenty of business-touting *jineteras* (women who attach themselves to foreigners for material or monetary gain) on hand.

**Restaurante Mirador de la Bahía** (Obispo No 61; noon-midnight). On the 5th floor above the Museo Nacional de Historia Natural, this place has great views – when it's open (you'll know if it's not because the security guard will shoo you away). Dine on cheeseburgers and pizza for less than CUC$6 while gazing over the bay at El Cristo. Has live music and dancing during lunch and dinner hours.

**Al Medina** (867-1041; Oficios No 12 btwn Obrapía & Obispo; noon-midnight) This is Habana's top Middle Eastern place, where you can dine on lamb (CUC$9) or chicken (CUC$5) with a spicy twist. It's especially recommended for its voluminous veggie platter that comes with hummus, tabbouleh, dolma, pilaf and felafel. Budget eaters will dig the cheaper specials at the cafeteria just inside on the left (kebab, rice, salad and drink). There's live music in the courtyard.

**Restaurante La Paella** (867-1037; Hostal Valencia, cnr Oficios & Obrapía; noon-11pm) Known for its paella or fish (CUC$10) this place has a nice inner decor and is attached to the Hostal Valencia. Food is middling to good when they don't run out of vegetables.

**Hanoi** (867-1029; cnr Brasil & Bernaza; noon-11pm) The name might be demonstrating solidarity with formerly 'communist' Vietnam, but the food certainly isn't. Straight-up Creole cuisine with a couple of fried rice dishes thrown in for good measure characterize this Old Town favorite which mixes Cuban clientele with a liberal smattering of budget travelers with their noses in the Lonely Planet. Live music to dine by.

**La Mina** (862-0216; cnr Obispo & Oficios; 24hr) An institution with side-by-side patio restaurants with a classic Plaza de Armas location. Stick to the chicken or pork (CUC$7 to CUC$8) if you're peaked, but this place is better for mojitos, coffee and people watching.

**Restaurante La Dominica** (860-2918; O'Reilly No 108; noon-midnight) Widely considered to be Habana's finest Italian restaurant, this elegantly restored dining establishment on O'Reilly offers everything from spaghetti and pizza (CUC$5 to CUC$7) to shrimp and lobster (CUC$10 to CUC$18). Service is efficient if a little sterile, and the food tastes authentically Mediterranean, though the chefs are sometimes a little overzealous

## THE AUTHOR'S CHOICE

If you're looking for a memorable dining experience in Habana, the following restaurants are recommended:

**La Cocina de Lilliam** (Map pp146-7; 209-6514; Calle 48 No 1311 btwn 13 & 15, Miramar; noon-midnight) Slick service, secluded ambience and freshly-cooked food to die for, La Cocina de Lilliam has all the ingredients of a prize-winning restaurant par excellence. In the circumstances it's no small wonder that Jimmy Carter made a pit stop here during his landmark 2002 visit (for the record he had *ropa vieja,* or shredded beef). Set in an illustrious villa in Miramar and surrounded by a garden of trickling fountains and lush tropical plants, diners can tuck into such Cuban rarities as chicken mousse and tuna bruschetta in an atmosphere more European than Caribbean. Not a cheese and ham sandwich in sight!

**El Aljibe** (Map pp146-7; 204-1583/4; Av 7 btwn Calles 24 & 26, Miramar; noon-midnight). On paper a humble Palmares restaurant, but in reality a rip-roaring culinary extravaganza, El Aljibe has been delighting both Cuban and foreign diplomatic taste buds for years. The furor surrounds the gastronomic mysteries of just one dish, the obligatory *pollo asado* (roast pork) which is served up with as-much-as-you-can-eat helpings of white rice, black beans, fried plantain, French fries and salad. The accompanying bitter orange sauce is said to be a state secret.

**Paladar La Guarida** (Map p100; 863-7315; Calle Concordia No 418 btwn Gervasio & Escobar; noon-3pm & 7pm-midnight) Located on the top floor of a spectacularly dilapidated Habana tenement, La Guarida's lofty reputation rests on its movie-location setting (*Fresa y Chocolate* was filmed in this building), and a clutch of swashbuckling newspaper reviews (including the *New York Times* and the *Guardian*). The food, as might be expected, is up there with Habana's best, shoehorning its captivating blend of Cuban 'Nueva Cocina' into dishes such as sea bass in a coconut reduction, and chicken with honey and lemon sauce. Reservations required.

with the olive oil. Professional house bands will serenade you with music that occasionally departs from the obligatory Buena Vista staples.

**Restaurante El Castillo de Farnés** (☎ 867-1030; Av de Bélgica No 361; seafood CUC$7-20; ⏰ noon-midnight) This is a good pre- or post-theater place but don't make a special trip. The bar alongside with sidewalk tables is a good spot to cool your heels awhile.

**La Torre de Marfil** (☎ 867-1038; Mercaderes No 111 btwn Obispo & Obrapía; ⏰ noon-10pm Mon-Thu, noon-midnight Fri-Sun) Often touted as one of Habana's best Chinese restaurants, the atmosphere and decor in this minimalist Old Town classic are certainly authentic. The chop suey and chow mein plates – when they arrive – are huge and the vegetables unusually fresh and crisp. After the noise and music of other Habana restaurants this place feels quieter and more discreet.

**Restaurante El Patio** (☎ 867-1034/5; San Ignacio No 54; meals CUC$15-20; ⏰ noon-midnight) Possibly one of the most romantic settings on planet earth when the hustlers stay away, the mint stalks in your mojito are pressed to perfection and the band break spontaneously into your favorite tune. This place – in the Plaza de la Catedral – must be experienced at night al fresco when the atmosphere is almost other-worldly.

**Café del Oriente** (☎ 860-6686; Oficios 112; appetizers CUC$8-12, mains CUC$20-27; ⏰ noon-11pm) Habana suddenly becomes 'posh' when you walk through the door at this choice establishment on breezy Plaza de San Francisco de Asís. Smoked salmon, caviar (yes, caviar!), goose liver pate, lobster thermidor, steak au poivre, cheese plate, and a glass of port. Plus service in a tux, no less. There's just one small problem: the price. But what the hell?

## Centro Habana

### PALADARES

**Paladar Bellamar** (Virtudes No 169 near Amistad; dishes from CUC$6; ⏰ noon-10pm) A good standby. The amiable family here offers classic chicken, pork and fish dishes. The walls are decorated with graffiti in the style of the famous Bodeguita del Medio, Hemingway's Habana Vieja drinking haunt.

**Paladar Amistad de Lanzarote** (☎ 863-6172; Amistad No 211 btwn Neptuno & San Miguel; meals CUC$6-8; ⏰ noon-midnight) The portions are large and English is spoken.

**Paladar Doña Blanquita** (no phone; Paseo de Martí No 158 btwn Colón & Refugio; meals CUC$7-9; ⏰ noon-10pm) The balcony overlooking Prado here is a romantic, if bustling, spot for classic Cuban cuisine (lots of pork, rice and beans). The service is friendly and the food reliable. Enter through the narrow, unmarked doorway and go upstairs.

**Paladar Las Delicias de Consulado** (☎ 863-7722; Consulado No 309 btwn Neptuno & Virtudes; meals from CUC$8; ⏰ noon-midnight) This place in the scrappy Consulado corridor has a small upstairs terrace for dining. Dishes are the usual pork-and-bean fare. It also rents rooms.

### RESTAURANTS

**Restaurante Oasis** (Centro Cultural Cubano Árabe, Paseo de Martí No 256; ⏰ 2pm-3am) The Arab-inspired menu here is reasonable and there is also a floor show on Saturday at 9pm. A shop at the entrance sells bread. The disco is a *jineteras*-fest.

**Los Dos Dragones** (☎ 862-0909; Dragones No 311; ⏰ noon-10:30pm) Away from the Cuchillo madness, this is Chinatown's most reliable restaurant, serving up tremendous portions of shrimp in red sauce and chicken with bamboo shoots and mushrooms. It does a booming business in oyster cocktails.

**Tres Chinitos** (☎ 863-3388; Dragones No 355 btwn San Nicolás & Manrique; ⏰ noon-midnight) A Chinese restaurant that specializes in (good) Italian fare; this, after all, is Cuba. Tres Chinitos is famous for its pizzas (CUC$4), salads and long snaking line-ups. Hit Chinatown and find out what it's all about.

**Flor de Loto** (Salud No 313 btwn Gervasio & Escobar; dishes CUC$4-8; ⏰ noon-midnight) Chinatown's newest addition is this place specializing in grilled lobster and interesting dishes such as fish with almond sauce. The portions are tremendous – try a mountain of fried rice – and the kitchen opens into the dining room, giving you a sneak peak.

**Restaurante Tien-Tan** (☎ 861-5478; Cuchillo No 17 btwn Rayo & San Nicolás; ⏰ 11am-11pm) Of the cookie-cutter Chinese places on the Cuchillo, this is the best hands down. There're 130 dishes to choose from and you can eat several for under CUC$10 (payable in pesos or Convertibles). It does an especially good wonton soup. Expect a 20% service charge to be added to your bill.

**Prado y Neptuno** (cnr Paseo de Martí & Neptuno; dishes CUC$6-9; ⏰ noon-5pm & 6:30pm-11:30pm) Dark lighting and tinted windows lure you into this trusty pizza and pasta joint; one of central Habana's better Italian restaurants.

Some of the street stalls selling *cajitas* (take-out meals) in Chinatown's Cuchillo are better than the actual restaurants.

Also recommended:

**Feria Los Fornos** (Neptuno btwn Paseo de Martí & Consulado; 24hr) Try the grilled meats (CUC$2 to CUC$6) in this open courtyard if you're not rushed for time.

**Restaurante Puerto de Sagua** (☎ 867-1026; Av de Bélgica No 603; noon-midnight) Nautical-themed place with super-friendly staff serving fish dishes starting at CUC$5 and shrimp at CUC$8.

## Vedado

### PALADARES

Better than Centro and Vieja, but not in the same bracket as Miramar, Vedado has it coming and going with the paladar selection. These are some of the tried and true favorites; you're encouraged to find your own.

**Paladar El Helecho** (☎ 831-3552; Calle 6 No 203 btwn Línea & Calle 11; dishes around CUC$5; noon-10:30pm) Tucked along a leafy side street in western Vedado, this romantic little place is a longtime favorite. The nice atmosphere is complemented by decent prices (around the CUC$5 mark) and good portions. The food is remarkably good. Try the chicken soup which a Cuban friend called 'the best I've had outside my own kitchen': high praise.

**El Gringo Viejo** (☎ 831-1946; Calle 21 No 454 btwn Calles E & F; noon-11pm) Locals and visitors alike swear by this place for the speedy service, a fine wine list and big portions of more adventurous plates such as smoked salmon with olives and gouda or crabmeat in red sauce (both around CUC$8).

**Paladar Nerei** (cnr Calles 19 & L; noon-midnight Mon-Fri, 6pm-midnight Sat & Sun) Where else can you get roast pig on a spit served al fresco right in the middle of the city? Nowhere but here, according to the owners. Nerei is a good central dining option in old eclectic villa with indoor and outdoor seating. Family-run.

**Paladar Aries** (☎ 831-9668; Ave Universidad No 456, bajos, btwn J & K; noon-midnight) Traditional Cuban fare mixed with what are generously referred to as 'international dishes,' this nicely decked out family-run place with occasional wandering *trovadores* (traditional singer/songwriters) is conveniently located behind the university.

**Paladar El Hurón Azul** (☎ 879-1691; Humboldt No 153; dishes CUC$7-12; noon-midnight Tue-Sun) You'll eat well here; it's a solid central Vedado paladar with windowless but tasteful dining rooms. Meals start with a nice fruit plate, but save room for the scrumptious mains (try the snapper in red and green sauce or the 'La Guajira' house special). You may have to wait for a table here; there's a 10% service charge.

**Decameron** (☎ 832-2444; Línea No 753 btwn Paseo & Calle 2; meals CUC$10-12; noon-midnight) Nothing mediocre will ever pass your lips at this intimate Italian restaurant, so order from the varied menu with abandon. Veggie pizza, lasagna Bolognese, a sinful calabaza soup, steak au poivre: it's all good. There's a decent wine selection and vegetarians will find heavenly options.

**Le Chansonnier** (☎ 832-1576; Calle J No 257 btwn Calles 13 & 15; mains CUC$10-12; 12:30pm-12:30am) You'll sup in your own elegant dining room in this Vedado mansion-turned-paladar specializing in French flavors. Rabbit in red-wine sauce, chicken smothered in mushrooms, and gigantic salads for herbivores are some of the offers in this gay-friendly establishment. Save room for dessert.

Also recommended:

**Paladar Escorpión** (Calle 17 No 105 btwn Calles L & M; meals CUC$6-7; noon-2am) Next to El Conejito Bar.

**Paladar Los Amigos** (out back, Calle M No 253; noon-midnight) Handy location beside the Focsa building.

**Paladar Monopoly** (☎ 832-2471; Calle K No 154 btwn Línea & Calle 11; noon-1am) Museum-quality dining digs; unsignposted, ask a neighbor if in doubt.

### RESTAURANTS

**Cafe TV** (☎ 33 44 99; cnr Calles N & 19; 10am-9pm) This bar-restaurant in the bowels of the Focsa Building has real breakfast: eggs, toast, juice etc, with nothing over CUC$1. The lunch and dinner menu is varied and cheap and at night there's live music. Televisión Cubana is around the corner, hence the name and theme.

**Pan.com** (☎ 53 50 40; cnr Calles 17 & 10; 10am-2am) Cuba's answer to Subway, this place does big, fresh sandwiches (turkey with cheese on a baguette for example), bacon and egg breakfast and veggie burgers heavy on the fixings. The milkshakes (real milk, creamy ice cream) are incredible. Nothing is over CUC$5. There's an even better branch in Miramar.

**El Lugar** (☎ 204-5162; cnr Calles 49C & 28A; 🕑 noon-midnight) Even more reason to come to Parque Almendares, this restaurant just across the road from the river below the bridge is fantastic value. For under CUC$5 you get a juicy pork filet, a whole heap of *congrí* (rice flecked with black beans), salad, *tostones* (fried plantain patties), ice cream and coffee. Add a Convertible or two for *ropa vieja* or fish. There's a talented trio playing nights. The pizza place attached is good too.

**Trattoría Maraka's** (☎ 33 37 40, ext143; Calle 0 No 260 btwn Calles 23 & 25; 🕑 10am-11pm) Real olive oil, parmesan and mozzarella cheese, plus a wood oven, mean this pizza is among the city's best. Also on offer are Greek salads, tortellini with red sauce, spinach-stuffed cannelloni – the menu is long and quality, with few items over CUC$8.

**El Conejito** (☎ 832-4671; Calle M No 206; 🕑 noon-midnight) The odd, Tudor-type brick building on the corner is the 'little rabbit' and that's the house specialty. There are many other items on the menu, all done equally reliably. There's a lively bar scene here too.

**Mesón de la Chorrera** (☎ 33 45 04; cnr Malecón & Calle 20; 🕑 10am-2am) In the Castillo de Santa Dorotea de Luna de Chorrera (1643).

**Restaurante 1830** (☎ 55 30 90; Malecón No 1252; 🕑 noon-10pm) One of Habana's most elegant restaurants is this old stalwart (though one reader called it 'terrible'). After the kitchen closes at 10pm there's live music and salsa dancing in the garden behind the restaurant (don't come on a windy night).

**La Torre** (☎ 55 30 89; Edificio Focsa, Calle 17 & M) One of Habana's tallest and most talked about restaurants is perched high above downtown Vedado atop the skyline-hogging Focsa building. A colossus of both modernist architecture and French/Cuban haute cuisine, this lofty fine-dining extravaganza combines sweeping city views with a progressive French-inspired menu that serves everything from artichokes to foie gras to tart almandine. The prices at CUC$30 a pop (and the rest!) are as distinctly un-Cuban as the ingredients, but

## MEAT'S NOT FOR ME

Cubans like their meat and who can blame them. Not only is the cuisine traditionally carnivorous, but after the leanest years of the *período especial* (special period; Cuba's new economic reality post 1991), people are anxious to consume as much protein as possible – just in case. It's surprising then, that a new chain of vegetarian restaurants, plus TV cooking shows advocating healthy (and often meatless) eating habits have been such a big hit. They certainly are with foreigners and even if you're not a vegetarian, the restaurants listed below provide great and welcomed variety to the same old pork/chicken/rice/bean scenario.

**Biki Vegetarian Restaurant** (Map pp106-7; cnr Infanta & San Lázaro, Centro Habana-Vedado border; 🕑 noon-10pm, closed Mon) This place near the university has dozens of selections daily, laid out cafeteria style; grab a tray and pick from several fresh juices and salads (four to six pesos), veggie paella, fried rice or stuffed peppers (10 to 15 pesos), root vegetables (six pesos) and desserts such as rice pudding. Be aware that the staff at this restaurant and the branch on Calzada have developed the nasty habit of charging foreigners indiscriminate Convertible prices. This is a peso restaurant; don't let them bully you into paying Convertibles.

**Restaurant Vegetariano Carmelo** (Map pp106-7; Calzada btwn Calles D & E; 🕑 noon-midnight, closed Mon) This place has the same menu as Biki, but a much nicer locale opposite the Teatro Amadeo Roldán, with patio dining and a full bar. Once again be careful with the over-charging. One tip is to refuse the table service they try to push upon you and just proceed cafeteria style.

**Restaurante El Bambú** (Map p155; Jardín Botánico; 🕑 noon-5pm, closed Mon) This is the first and finest in Habana vegetarian dining and has led the way in education efforts as to the benefits of a meatless diet. The all-you-can-eat lunch buffet is served al fresco deep in the botanical gardens, with the natural setting paralleling the wholesome tastiness of the food. For CUC$15 you can gorge on soups and salads, root vegetables, tamales and eggplant caviar. Herbs grown on the premises figure prominently in the dishes. Juices, desserts and coffee are on offer too. Coupled with a visit to the garden, it makes an excellent side trip.

with this level of service, it's probably worth it.

Also recommended:

**Restaurante Bulerías** (☎ 832-3823; Calle L No 414 btwn Calles 23 & 25; 🕑 11am-10pm) Don't venture into the basement here, but eat at the sidewalk tables.

**Restaurante Wakamba** (☎ 878-4526; Calle O btwn Calles 23 & 25; 🕑 24hr) Forty years and still going, this bar/counter place serving light meals hosts many late-night characters.

**Palmares Centro** (cnr Calles 23 & P) Cheap, cheerful and central on La Rampa.

## Spanish Clubs

Several Spanish clubs that are open to the public have excellent, inexpensive restaurants. Most are in pesos (but can also accept Convertibles), which makes them an attractive option if you're 'going Dutch' with Cuban friends or colleagues.

**Asociación Canaria de Cuba** (Map p100; ☎ 862-5284; Av de las Misiones No 258 btwn Neptuno & Ánimas; 🕑 noon-8:30pm) Go to the 2nd-floor dining room of this club across from the Edificio Bacardí and you'll be treated to a varied menu featuring shrimp or lobster, fish and several chicken dishes. The atmosphere is fluorescent lights and plastic flowers in the dining room, but the foyer is grand.

**Centro Andaluz** (Map p100; ☎ 863-6745; Paseo de Martí No 104 btwn Genios & Refugio; 🕑 6-11pm Tue-Sun) For a CUC$10 plus price-tag, you might splash out and try the house paella for two, or pinch some pennies and go for the fish or pork filet for under CUC$5. Regardless, try the house cocktail *'locura flamenca.'* You can see flamenco dancing here starting at 9pm Tuesday to Sunday.

## Cafés

**Café Santo Domingo** (Map p94; Obispo No 159 btwn San Ignacio & Mercaderes; 🕑 9am-9pm) Tucked away upstairs above the excellent pastry/bread shop this laid-back café is cheap and tasty. Check out the ice-cream shakes, huge *sandwich especial* or smuggle up some of the cakes from downstairs to enjoy over a steaming cup of *café con leche* (coffee with warm milk).

**Bar-Restaurant La Luz** (Map p94; 🕑 24hr) Next door to Café Santo Domingo with a resident *jinetero* normally calling you in, this place offers one-peso shots of strong coffee.

**Pastelería Francesa** (Map p100; Parque Central No 411) Great location in among the five-star hotels, this place sells delicious pastries, sturdy sandwiches and OK coffee. The swarming *jineteras* spoil the French flavor a little and the service is slow, but for the sheer convenience it can't be beaten.

**El Mercurio** (Map p94; ☎ 860-6188; Lonja del Comercio; 🕑 24hr) On Plaza de San Francisco de Asís, this is an elegant café-restaurant ('for businessmen and travelers') with fresh salads and sandwiches.

**Cafe La Logia** (Map p100; ☎ 861-5657; Capitolio; 🕑 9am-7pm) With tropical atmosphere to spare, this breezy terrace café provides excellent views of all the classic cars and general action going on below the Capitolio. Hole up here and nosh on a good veggie or meat sandwich or sip a cappuccino or mojito.

**Pain de Paris** (Vedado Map pp106-7; Calle 25 No 164 btwn Infanta & O; 🕑 8am-midnight; Vedado Map pp106-7; Línea btwn Paseo & Calle A; 🕑 24hr) This chain serves reliable cappuccino, croissants (with ham and cheese if you like), napoleons and other pastries. A box of treats from here is nice to share if you're invited to a Cuban home for dinner.

**Café de O'Reilly** (Map p94; O'Reilly No 203 btwn Cuba & San Ignacio; 🕑 11am-3am) Upstairs at O'Reilly is a Habana classic for both nighttime rum shots and late-morning hair of the dog.

**Cafe Wilfredo Lam** (Map p94; San Ignacio No 22; 🕑 10am-5pm Mon-Sat) At the center of the same name, this is an arty nook for a drink. Next to the cathedral.

**G-Café** (Map pp106-7; Calle 23 btwn Av de los Presidentes & Calle H) The ultimate student hangout with arty wall drawings and a modernist mural behind the bar. An airy front patio has lots of greenery and there are more than 400 books and magazines to read, lend and sell. Along with deftly concocted mojitos this place hosts *trova*, jazz and poetry auditions.

## Ice-Cream Parlors

Habana has some fabulous ice cream, available both in Convertibles and pesos – just the ticket on a hot day. *Paleticas* are popsicles (usually chocolate covered), while *bocaditos* are big, delicious ice-cream sandwiches (often handmade). For more ice-cream vocab, see the Food & Drink chapter (p84). Ice-cream cones are sold on the street for three pesos. Otherwise you can try these parlors:

**Bim Bom** (Map pp106-7; ☎ 879-2892; cnr Calles 23 & Infanta, Vedado) Phenomenally creamy stuff in flavors like coffee, condensed milk (sounds gross, tastes great) and rum raisins; in Convertibles.
**Coppelia** (Map pp106-7; ☎ 832-6184; cnr Calles 23 & L, Vedado) The original. See the boxed text, opposite.
**Heladería Obispo** (Map p94; Obispo No 58) New peso parlor in the heart of Habana Vieja; often has fruit flavors (pineapple, strawberry etc).

## Take-out

There are some great peso places sprinkled about. Some of the most outstanding **peso pizza** (Map pp106–7) is at San Rafael just off Infanta (look for the line). They make the pizza on the roof, so you have to shout up your order (there's a menu posted) and then it comes down via a rope/basket rig. This may be the only peso place offering 'pizza Hawaiiana' (ham and pineapple). In Vedado try around Calles H and 17 where there are clusters of **peso stalls** (Map pp106–7) and Calle 21 between Calles 4 and 6 (Map pp106–7); this area is close to the hospital, so there's great variety and long hours.

*Cajitas* can save your night: these complete take-out meals in cardboard boxes usually cost about CUC$1. Some boxes have cut-out spoons on the lid, but most don't, so you'll have to supply your own fork (or use part of the box itself as a shovel). You can usually buy *cajitas* at agropecuarios (vegetable markets); otherwise, private cafeteria and *merendero* (snack seller) windows sell them. Chinatown is known for its *cajitas.*

## Self-Catering

### HABANA VIEJA

**Café Santo Domingo** (Map p94; Obispo No 159 btwn San Ignacio & Mercaderes; 9am-9pm) Some of the best bread and pastries can be procured at this place, downstairs underneath the café.

The local farmers market is called **Agropecuario Sol** (see below).

### CENTRO HABANA

**Harris Brothers** (Map p94; O'Reilly No 526; 9am-9pm Mon-Sat) The best-stocked store in the entire area. It's just off Parque Central, with a large liquor selection (including wine),

### HABANA'S BEST AGROPECUARIOS

Agropecuarios are free enterprise markets (legalized in 1994) where farmers sell their surplus produce to private consumers (after selling a set quota to the state); they are not to be confused with *organopónicos* which are urban vegetable gardens run by local community groups that sell organic produce from small kiosks on-site (see the boxed text, p158).

Agros are not only good for buying raw, fresh foods; they are also handy for getting pesos (every large market has a Cadeca), *cajitas,* fresh meat, bread, cut flowers and other natural products such as herbs, honey, spices, beeswax candles etc. Every market also has a *'protección de consumidor'* section with a scale where they'll weigh what you've purchased. Go here if you think you've been ripped off (a merchant caught three times cheating is booted from the market). Most markets are closed Monday. Here are some of Habana's biggest:

**Agropecuario Sol** (Map p94; Calle Sol btwn Habana & Compostela, Habana Vieja) Compact, well-stocked market; decent variety.
**Calle 17 & K** (Map pp106-7; cnr Calles 17 & K, Vedado) Another 'capped' market with cheap prices, but limited selection.
**Calle 19 & A** (Map pp106-7; Calle 19 btwn Calles A & B, Vedado) Habana's 'gourmet' market with cauliflower, fresh herbs and rarer produce during shoulder seasons; prices reflect the selection.
**Calle 21 & J** (Map pp106-7; cnr Calles 21 & J, Vedado) Good selection, including potted plants; watch for overcharging.
**Mercado Agropecuario Egido** (Map p100; Av de Bélgica btwn Corrales & Apodaca, Centro Habana) Gigantic market: the action is over by 2pm.
**Organopónico Plaza** (Map pp106-7; cnr Av de Colón & Bellavista, Plaza) One of Habana's biggest organic farms with a retail market.
**Plaza de Marianao** (Map pp146-7; cnr Av 51 & Calle 124, Marianao) Friendly local market with produce downstairs and flowers and plants upstairs. Head east up Av 51 for amazingly varied peso shopping.
**Tulipán** (Map pp106-7; Av Tulipán, Plaza) This is a huge, 'capped' market, with prices set by the government; so it's cheap.

**MAKING CENTS OF COPPELIA**

Until you've gone slack jawed watching a young woman with a model's body wolf down nine scoops of ice cream followed by a cake à la mode with childish delight, you haven't eaten at Coppelia. Truly a cultural phenomenon without equal, waiting a near eternity to enter the weirdly futuristic but retro halls of this Habana ice-cream institution is an essential part of getting to know Cuba (and the Cubans). Loitering around the perimeter, strategically-positioned security guards try to usher foreigners toward the Coppelia's sterile Convertible café but, with a little persistence and a few persuasive words in Spanish, there's no reason why you can't join one of the long and seemingly disorganized queues on the periphery. Ah…the queues. Hard though it may be to believe, there's a system to the peso part which many foreigners don't observe or get. Here's how it works.

There are several entrances to Coppelia, each with their own menu, line and dining area. Die-hards cruise the different entrances to see what's on each menu. What the menu says and what's actually on offer once you're inside is another story, but more often than not you'll encounter *fresa y chocolate* (strawberry and chocolate), coconut, banana and orange-pineapple, so it's not just vanilla (though Coppelia's vanilla is luscious). Shout out *Quien es último?* (Who is last?), as you approach the line and remember to log the face of whoever is in front of you. Sections are seated all at once, so some 20 people are let in en masse and are shown to their section. A server comes around, tells you what's available, takes your order and brings back the goods. They come around afterward to collect your money. Rainy days are classically slow here, so you might minimize wait times by showing up then. The language of ice-cream love is complex here. Suffice to say, a movie at Cine Yara across the street, followed by a *jimagua* (two scoops of ice cream) at Coppelia is the classic Habana date.

cheeses, bread, olives and other picnic goodies.

**Supermercado Isla de Cuba** (Map p100; cnr Máximo Gómez & Factoría; ⌚ 10am-6pm Mon-Sat, 9am-1pm Sun) On the southern side of Parque de la Fraternidad, with yogurt, cereals, pasta etc. You have to check your bag outside, to the right of the entrance.

**Almacenes Ultra** (Map p100; Av Simón Bolívar No 109; ⌚ 9am-6pm Mon-Sat, 9am-1pm Sun) A decent supermarket in Centro Habana, at the corner of Rayo, near Av de Italia.

**La Época** (Map p100; cnr Av de Italia & Neptuno; ⌚ 9am-9pm Mon-Sat, 9am-noon Sun) A hard-currency department store with a supermarket in the basement. Check your bags outside before entering this epic Habana emporium.

For fresh produce hit the free enterprise **Mercado Agropecuario Egido** (Map p100; Av de Bélgica btwn Corales & Apodaca).

### VEDADO

**Supermercado Meridiano** (Map pp106-7; Galerías de Paseo, cnr Calle 1 & Paseo; ⌚ 10am-5pm Mon-Fri, 10am-2pm Sun) Across the street from the Hotel Meliá Cohiba, this supermarket has a good wine and liquor selection, lots of yogurt, cheese and chips. The bread is overpriced.

## DRINKING

### Habana Vieja

**La Bodeguita del Medio** (☎ 33 88 57; Empedrado No 207; ⌚ 11am-midnight) La Bodeguita was made famous thanks to the rum-swilling exploits of Ernest Hemingway (who by association instantly sends the prices soaring), and a visit to Habana's most celebrated bar has become de rigueur for literary sycophants and Walt Whitman wannabes. Notables including Salvador Allende, Fidel Castro, Nicolás Guillén, Harry Belafonte and Nat King Cole have all left their autographs on La Bodeguita's wall. These days the clientele is less luminous, with package tourists bussed in from Varadero delighting in the bottled (some say canned) bohemian atmosphere and the CUC$4 mojitos (which though good have lost their Hemingway-esque shine). The menu specialty is *comida criolla* or 'the full monty' Cuban style.

**Cafe París** (Obispo No 202; ⌚ 24hr) Jump into the mix by grabbing one of the rough hewn tables at this Habana Vieja standby, known for its live music and gregarious atmosphere. On good nights, the rum flows, talented musicians jam and spontaneous dancing and singing erupt from the crowd. Filling slices of pizza (CUC$0.50) are sold at a take-out window on the side of the building.

**Bar La Marina** (cnr Oficios & Brasil; ⏰ 10am-11pm) The courtyard is an inviting glen in which to take a break after visiting the Monasterio de San Francisco de Asís. A Cuban combo plays in the afternoons. The popcorn is very good (when the machine is working).

**Bar Dos Hermanos** (☎ 861-3436; San Pedro No 304; ⏰ 24hr) On the corner of Sol near Muelle Luz. A wonderful old wooden dive, this was a favorite Habana hang-out of Spanish poet Federico García Lorca during his three months in Cuba in 1930. Pub snacks such as oyster cocktails, hamburgers and chicken go well with the drinks. The salty atmosphere adds to the flavor, but this is a rather seedy area late at night.

**Fundación Havana Club** (cnr Sol & Malecón; ⏰ 9am-midnight) For something more upscale, try the bar inside this place, where it's all rum all the time, plus live music.

**Café Taberna** (☎ 861-1637; cnr Calle Brasil & Mercaderes) Founded in 1772 and still glowing after a recent 21st-century makeover, this drinking and eating establishment is a great place to prop up the (impressive) bar and sink a few cocktails before dinner. The music – which gets swinging around 8pm – doffs its cap, more often than not, to one-time resident mambo king Benny Moré. Skip the food.

**Taberna de la Muralla** (☎ 866-4453; cnr San Ignacio & Muralla; ⏰ 11am-midnight) Habana's best (and only) homebrew pub is situated on a quiet corner of Plaza Vieja. Set up by an Austrian company a couple of years back, this unique no-nonsense drinking establishment sells smooth cold homemade beer at sturdy wooden benches set up outside on the cobbles or indoors in a couple of atmospheric beer halls. Get a group together and they'll serve the amber nectar in a tall plastic tube which you draw out of a tap at the bottom. There's also an outside grill here where you can order good helpings of chorizos, fish and kebabs.

For bars with views, try the Restaurante Mirador de la Bahía on the southern side of the Plaza de Armas, above the Museo Nacional de Historia Nacional, or one of the 24-hour Cristal kiosks along the Malecón (at the end of O'Reilly for instance).

If you need to kill time before a train departure, try **El Baturro** (cnr Av de Bélgica & Merced; ⏰ 11am-11pm) If you ever need to kill time before a train departure, try El Baturro, a Spanish bistro with a long wooden bar and an all-male – aggressively so – drinking clientele.

**La Zaragozana** (☎ 867-1040; Av de Bélgica btwn Obispo & Obrapía; ⏰ noon-midnight) Established in 1830 this is Habana's oldest restaurant but a long way from being its best. Skip the food, but drop in for a drink, and music from 9pm.

## Centro Habana

**El Floridita** (☎ 867-1300; Obispo No 557; ⏰ 11am-midnight) Hemingway was a bar-hopper and name maker and this place, like La Bodeguita del Medio, cashes in on the literary legend. A bartender named Constante Ribalaigua assured El Floridita's place in drinking history when he used shaved ice to make frozen daiquiris here in the 1920s. A decade later Hemingway arrived and the Papa Hemingway Special (rum with grapefruit juice, lemon juice and crushed ice) was created in his honor. His record (legend has it) was 13 doubles in one sitting. Any attempt to equal it at the current prices (CUC$6 a single shot) will cost you a small fortune – and a huge hangover.

Rather than rubbing sunburned elbows with the tour-bus crowd in El Floridita, drop in next door to the **Monserrate Bar** (☎ 860-9751; Obrapía No 410) Rather than rubbing sunburned elbows with the tour-bus crowd in El Floridita, drop in next door to the Monserrate Bar, where you can enjoy the same drink for a third of the price quoted by the red-coated waiters in Hemingway's habitual hang-out. Skip the cheap (for a reason) food. Across the street, Restaurante El Castillo de Farnés has good value, light food and an infinitely more airy atmosphere.

**Restaurante Prado 264** (Paseo de Martí No 264; btwn Animas & Trocadero; ⏰ noon-10:30pm) Has a long wooden bar in the back. Don't eat here if they ask you to pay Convertibles for peso food.

## Vedado

**Opus Bar** (cnr Calzada & Calle D; ⏰ 3pm-3am) Above Teatro Amadeo Roldán. With individual candle-lit tables, overstuffed chairs and Sly and the Family Stone on the airways, this is Habana's (good) approximation of a lounge. The wall of windows make it a great sunset spot and performances in the theater downstairs are broadcast via closed-circuit TV; a good alternative if that hot concert is sold out.

**Bar-Club Imágenes** (☎ 33 36 06; Calzada No 602; drink minimum CUC$5; 9pm-5am) This upscale piano bar attracts something of an older crowd with its regular diet of boleros and *trova*, but sometimes there are surprise concerts by big name musicians; check the schedule posted outside. Meals are available (and affordable).

For a more intellectual scene, check out the bar/café in the basement of the **Centro de Prensa Internacional** (cnr Calles 23 & 0; 9am-7pm), where journalists and writers talk shop over coffee, whiskey and wine.

## ENTERTAINMENT

One Saturday a month, the Plaza de la Catedral is closed off for a spectacular **Noche Plaza** (night plaza) with 100 of Cuba's finest singers, dancers and other entertainers performing on a stage directly in front of the cathedral. The staff at Restaurante El Patio should know the date of the next extravaganza.

### Folk & Traditional Music

**Casa de la Cultura de La Habana Vieja** (Map p94; ☎ 863-4860; Aguiar No 509 btwn Amargura & Brasil; admission adult/child 5 pesos/free; 9pm) Habana Vieja's active casa usually has something on like Afro-Cuban dancing or folk singing nightly. The program varies every week (and it could be canceled if it's raining). The staff can arrange Cuban dancing lessons. They sometimes charge foreigners CUC$5 instead of five pesos, which might be worth it depending on the event.

**Casa de la Trova** (Map p100; ☎ 879-3373; San Lázaro No 661; admission free; 7pm-late Tue-Sun) Surprisingly one of Cuba's most lackluster *trova* houses, if it's open at all. You're better off following the live sounds around the nocturnal nooks of Habana Vieja.

**El Hurón Azul** (Map pp106-7; ☎ 832-4551; cnr Calles 17 & H, Vedado) Uneac is the nerve center of official art and intellectual life in Cuba, and this is its social club. Intellectuals associated with Uneac are usually in attendance and you might even hobnob with hip Minister of Culture Abel Prieto (you'll know him by his mullet). Wednesday is the Afro-Cuban Peña del Ambia (CUC$5), Saturday it's authentic Cuban boleros (CUC$1; open 10pm to 2am) and alternate Thursdays there's jazz and *trova* (CUC$1; open 5pm). It doesn't get much better than this.

**El Gato Tuerto** (Map pp106-7; ☎ 66 22 24; Calle O No 14 btwn Calles 17 & 19, Vedado; drink minimum CUC$5; dusk-dawn) Once the headquarters of Habana's alternative artistic and sexual scene, this chic bar with live music still packs in the folks from the old days, although now they're a little softer around the middle. It's amazing to behold on a crowded weekend night as scores of 40-somethings belt out boleros word-for-word with the band, shouting requests and cramming the dance floor.

**Conjunto Folklórico Nacional de Cuba** (Map pp106-7; Calle 4 No 103 btwn Calzada & Calle 5, Vedado; admission CUC$5; 3pm Sat) Founded in 1962, this high energy ensemble specializes in Afro-Cuban dancing (all of the drummers are Santería priests). See them perform, and dance along during the regular Sábado de Rumba at El Gran Palenque. This group also performs at Teatro Mella. A major festival called FolkCuba unfolds here biannually during the second half of January.

The other space to experience rumba includes the wild Callejón de Hamel (see p115) where you'll need to look out for the *jineteros*.

### Jazz

**Jazz Club La Zorra y El Cuervo** (Map pp106-7; ☎ 66 24 02; cnr Calles 23 & O, Vedado; admission CUC$5-10; 10pm) The house band is good, and its freestyle jazz is a nice change from salsa. Thursday is blues night and this place hosts great late-night jams during the International Jazz Fest; check out the cool photos by local photographer Leslie Sinclair (and cast member of Lonely Planet's *Six Degrees Havana*).

**Jazz Cafe** (Map pp106-7; ☎ 55 33 02; top fl, Galerías de Paseo, cnr Calles 1 & Paseo; drink minimum CUC$10; noon-late) This upscale joint overlooking the Malecón is like a jazz supper club, with tables and a decent menu (come here for cocktails at sunset). At night, the club swings into action with jazz, *timba* (Cuban popular music) and occasionally, straight up salsa. Pity the dance floor is just a strip between the tables.

## Rock, Reggae & Rap

**Patio de María** (Map pp106-7; Calle 37 No 262 btwn Paseo & Calle 2; admission 5 pesos) This legendary club near the Teatro Nacional de Cuba is run by the equally legendary María Gattorno. A great old-school venue with indoor and outdoor space, it's packed to the rafters with head-banging Habaneros. Check the *cartelera* (cultural calendar or schedule) posted at the door or head to Parque de los Rockeros (corner of Calles 23 and G) to find out what's happening. This unpretentious counterculture venue has received considerable media coverage in Cuba and abroad, partly due to Gattorno's AIDS- and drug-prevention educational work. It was undergoing a restoration, but should be open again soon.

**La Madriguera** (Map pp106-7; ☎ 879-8175; cnr Salvador Allende & Luaces, Quinta los Molinos; admission 5-10 pesos) Connected with the Asociación's Hermanos Saíz, Uneac's youth arm, rock, rap and reggae concerts occur at this venue in Quinta los Molinos (enter via Calzada de Infanta). A local scene, this is a good place to meet young Cuban artists and musicians.

**Anfiteatro Parque Almendares** (Map pp106-7; cnr Calle 23 & Río Almendares; admission 2 pesos) This riverside amphitheater hosts regular musical events and special concerts by the likes of Frank Delgado and Interactivo. It's an intimate place to catch some terrific music. Regular *peñas* (musical performances) include reggae (8pm Friday) and rap (8pm Saturday). You can also catch a rap matinee (4pm Saturday) at Cafe Cantante (right) and the rock cover band Los Kents (4pm Sunday).

## Dance Clubs

In Cuba, a dance club usually means DJs and recorded music, with a dance floor taking priority over seating (your basic disco), while a nightclub features live music and table seating. Female travelers should be prepared for lots of attention in Habana's discos, whether they're traveling solo or not. Cuban dance styles involve lots of touching, grinding and frisson in general and if you're in the mix, it's assumed you're game. Set your boundaries early.

### CENTRO HABANA

**El Palermo** (☎ 861-9745; cnr San Miguel & Amistad; admission CUC$2; 🕑 from 11pm Thu-Sun) Your casa hostess will likely warn you away from this local disco. It's very much in the 'hood, with a heavy rap scene. Fun, but *fuerte* (intense).

**Discoteca Ribera Azul** (☎ 833-8813; cnr Av de Italia & Malecón; per couple CUC$5; 🕑 closed Tue) More tame than El Palermo, this place is downstairs from the lobby of the Hotel Deauville.

### VEDADO

**Cabaret Las Vegas** (☎ 870-7939; Infanta No 104 btwn Calles 25 & 27; admission CUC$5; 🕑 10pm-4am) Mostly a local scene; head here to cut loose with Cubans. There's recorded music followed by a show at midnight. The patio overlooking the street is a nice place for a beer.

**El Chevere** (Parque Almendares, cnr Calles 49A & 28A; admission CUC$6-10; 🕑 from 10pm) One of Habana's most popular discos, this al fresco place in a lush park setting hosts a good mix of locals and tourists.

**Pico Blanco** (☎ 833-4187; Calle O btwn Calles 23 & 25; admission CUC$5; 🕑 9pm) This disco on the 14th floor of the Hotel St John's ('the cathedral of *filin*' say fans of this soupy music) can be hit or miss. Some nights it's karaoke and cheesy boleros, another night it's jamming with some rather famous Cuban musicians. Check the schedule posted in the hotel window. The rooftop bar here has terrific views.

**Cafe Cantante** (☎ 879-0710; cnr Paseo & Calle 39; admission CUC$10; 🕑 9pm-5am Tue-Sat) Below the Teatro Nacional de Cuba (side entrance), is this disco with live salsa music and dancing. The music is good and it's a popular place, despite being in a low-ceilinged basement. The crowd is usually a decent mix, though a certain type of tourist and the local women they favor are very much in evidence. No shorts, T-shirts, hats, photos or under 18s allowed.

Vedado has a few mixed peso-Convertible discos that are great fun (especially if your budget has blown out) including **Club La Red** (☎ 832-5415; cnr Calles 19 & L; admission CUC$3-5) and **Karachi Club** (☎ 832-3485; cnr Calles 17 & K; admission CUC$3-5; 🕑 10pm-5am). As with all clubs, late night Friday and Saturday are best.

To the west are **Discoteca Amanecer** (☎ 832-9075; Calle 15 No 12 btwn Calles N & O; admission CUC$3-5; 🕑 10pm-4am) and **Club Tropical** (☎ 832-7361; cnr Línea & Calle F; 🕑 9pm-2am).

## Nightclubs

**Piano Bar Delirio Habanero** (Map pp106-7; ☎ 873-5713; cnr Paseo & Calle 39; admission CUC$5; 🕑 from 6pm Tue-Sun) This plush lounge upstairs in the Teatro Nacional hosts everything from young *trovadores* to aging *salseros* (salsa singers) and when it gets hot, it rocks to the rafters. The deep red couches abut a wall of glass overlooking the Plaza de la Revolución and it's stunning at night with the Martí Memorial alluringly backlit.

**Habana Café** (Map pp106-7; ☎ 33 36 36; Hotel Meliá Cohiba, Paseo btwn Calles 1 & 3; minimum at bar/table, plus cover CUC$5/10; 🕑 from 9:30pm) If you prefer to see big salsa acts such as Pupi y Su Son Son or NG La Banda in a controlled, upscale setting, come here. (Otherwise, cut way loose at Salón Rosado Benny Moré, p153.) The layout at Habana Café is cabaret style, with tables and chairs surrounding a stage and dance floor; American 1950s memorabilia, including old cars, motorcycles and gas pumps, constitute the decoration. You can eat here too.

**La Casa de la Música Centro Habana** (Map p100; ☎ 878-4727; Av de Italia btwn Concordia & Neptuno; admission CUC$5-10) Imagine seeing U2 live for CUC$5. One of the understated successes of the Cuban Revolution is that you can see top performers play classy music for next to nothing. The Centro Casa is a little edgier than its Miramar counterpart (some have complained it's too edgy), with big salsa bands and the odd 'name' act thrown in for good measure.

## Cabarets

**Cabaret Nacional** (Map p100; ☎ 863-2361; San Rafael No 208; per couple CUC$10; 🕑 9pm-2am) Come to this cabaret alongside the Gran Teatro de La Habana, for a mix of show (as captivating as it is camp) and dancing. The show kicks off at 11:30pm, followed by steamy dancing. Thursday to Sunday is best; there's also a matinee (admission CUC$5; 3pm till 8pm) here. The Nacional maintains a couples-only and minimum-dress policy: definitely no shorts or T-shirts.

### WHAT'S HAPPENING?!

Plays, concerts, book launches, ballets, poetry readings, rap *peñas* – there's always something happening in Habana. The problem is finding out when and where. Here are some tips to get plugged in to what's on.

- 'Hurón Azul' – This is a select schedule of the week's biggest cultural events broadcast every Thursday night at 10:25pm on Cubavisión (Channel 6).
- *Cartelera de la Habana* – Broader listings (in Spanish) of things happening all over town, published biweekly by the Ministry of Culture. This is one of your best resources; sold at newspaper kiosks (20 centavos). Look for it alternate Thursdays.
- *Cartelera* – Bilingual English-Spanish for the tourist population (www.cartelera.com; Calle 15 No 602) comes out every Thursday, but it lists what they think you want to see. Still, good for non-Spanish speakers. Look for it in big hotels.
- *Juventud Rebelde* – The daily newspaper has decent cultural listings.
- Posters – Concert flyers usually appear around La Rampa, from Calle L up to 'Rocker's Park' at Calle de los Presidentes (also known as Calle G).
- Radio – Radio stations are constantly promoting upcoming cultural events; tune to Radio Taíno (93.3 FM) or Radio Habana (94.9FM).
- Web – Check out www.cubarte.cult.cu and www.afrocubaweb.com for concerts, dance and fine art listings.
- Word of Mouth – There's nothing better. Because the state publishes *Cartelera* and produces 'Hurón Azul,' you have no chance of learning of anything underground. Also, you'll learn about spontaneous/spur-of-the-moment happenings by talking to people.
- Pounding the pavement – Cubans know it's hard to get the word out, so every cinema posts the week's showings at every other city cinema (called the Icaic Cartelera) and theaters post a schedule at their box office. If all else fails, make the rounds to see what's happening.

**Cabaret Turquino** (Map pp106-7; cnr Calles 23 & L; admission CUC$15; opens 10pm) Some of Cuba's biggest bands play here (including Los Van Van) and superstar parties (to close the film or jazz festival, for instance) sometimes happen here too. It's a spectacular place on the 25th floor of the Hotel Habana Libre, with unsurpassable views.

**Cabaret Parisién** (Map pp106-7; ☎ 33 35 64; cnr Calles 21 & O; admission CUC$35; 9pm) If you want to experience Cuban cabaret but aren't quite up for the Tropicana, this room at the western end of the Hotel Nacional lobby is a good choice. You get all the feathers and fun, plus it becomes a disco after midnight and if there are any VIPs in town, they'll be here.

## Theater

Ballet, opera and theater performance are mostly at 8:30pm Monday to Saturday, with a matinee at 5pm Sunday.

### HABANA VIEJA

The **Casa de la Comedia** (cnr Calle Jústiz & Baratillo) sometimes presents live theater in Spanish.

### CENTRO HABANA

**Gran Teatro de La Habana** (La Sala García Lorca; ☎ 861-3077; cnr Paseo de Martí & San Rafael; per per-

### THE SEX TRADE

'The one thing Castro can't ration is sex' Cuban commentators have been prone to quip and one look around the bars and clubs of nocturnal Habana, where impossibly attractive Cuban prostitutes stroll arm in arm with ageing 'sugar-daddies' from Torino or Dusseldorf, is enough to prove them correct.

It's ironic that in a state where rationing is a given and empty supermarket shelves are a wearisome part of everyday life that there never seems to be any shortage of young, pretty señoritas 'available' for carnal relationships. Indeed, while technically illegal, prostitution in Cuba – which was equally rampant during the Batista era – is the one of the few capitalist enterprises that the socialist government has so far failed to stamp out.

Economically speaking the situation is understandable. Contact with foreign men gives Cuban woman access to interchangeable currency and the opportunity of bagging double a doctor's monthly salary in a week. There's even the not-so-remote possibility of spontaneous nuptials and the promise of a new and better life overseas.

For the planeloads of over-sexed foreign males who fly in weekly to find out that they've been suddenly reborn as Brad Pitt, the attractions are equally libidinous. Indeed, Cuba's growing reputation as an exotic mix of sun, sand, socialism and…sex, with no strings attached, has given rise to an whole new (unofficial) sex industry based on the well-tested economic laws of supply and demand.

Not surprisingly the 'rules of engagement' have a number of peculiarly Cuban characteristics. Unlike other financially disadvantaged countries in the developing world, Cuban prostitutes – or *jineteras* as they are popularly known – are not part of any highly organized network of pimps. Furthermore, Cuba is not a society where sex is sold to fuel a drug habit, or procure the next square meal. On the contrary, many of these illicit rendezvous' are innocuous and open-ended couplings perpetuated by young girls looking for friendship, blind opportunity, or a free pass into some of Habana's best nightclubs.

Despite the island's generally lax attitude to sexual promiscuity, clampdowns in the sex trade can and do occur. The all-inclusive resort areas are particularly prone to police attention. In 1996 the authorities rounded up legions of prostitutes in Varadero and placed a barring order on the resort's paladares and casas particulares. As a result, the town lost an element of its essential Cuban character and tourism in the resort noticeably blipped.

Unfortunately the problems associated with the sex trade have also served to reinforce Cuba's rather unpleasant system of tourist 'apartheid.' Nearly all of the island's tourist-class hotels bar access to *all* Cuban guests to their rooms on the pretext that some of them might be *jineteras*. But while the tight laws that govern these institutions might have temporarily nipped the problem of outright prostitution in the bud, they have done little to foster the long-term betterment of Cuban-tourist relations.

son CUC$10; box office 9am-6pm Mon-Sat, until 3pm Sun) This magnificent theater is closely associated with its most famous resident: the acclaimed Ballet Nacional de Cuba and its founder Alicia Alonso. The National Opera performs here occasionally. You'll often hear this theater referred to as the Sala García Lorca, which is the grandest of several concert halls here (the others are the Sala Alejo Carpentier and Sala Ernesto Lecuono, where art films are sometimes shown). You can count on some type of live musical event every Friday, Saturday and Sunday (check the notices posted outside the theater).

**Teatro Fausto** (☎ 863-1173; Paseo de Martí No 201) Presents lighter fare. The humorous programs on Friday and Saturday at 8:30pm and on Sunday at 5pm are great fun. See the schedule posted outside.

**Teatro América** (☎ 862-5695; Av de Italia No 253 btwn Concordia & Neptuno) This theater made its name with big variety shows by talents like Roberto Carcassés, and you still might catch his jazzy act here, but it also hosts blowout rumba, rap and drum concerts too (tickets are sold on the day of the performance). You can also have dance lessons here (p114).

### VEDADO

**Teatro Nacional de Cuba** (☎ 879-6011; cnr Paseo & Calle 39; per person CUC$10; box office 9am-5pm & before performances) This modern theater on the Plaza de la Revolución hosts landmark concerts, foreign theater troupes, La Colmenita children's company and the Ballet Nacional de Cuba. The main hall is the Sala Avellaneda and hosts big events, while the smaller Sala Covarrubias along the back side puts on a more daring program like the recent Cuban adaptation of Eve Ensler's *Vagina Monologues*. The 9th floor is a rehearsal and performance space where the newest, most experimental stuff happens like Teatro El Puente. The ticket office is at the far end of a separate single-story building beside the main theater.

**Teatro Mella** (☎ 833-8696; Línea No 657 btwn Calles A & B) This cozy theater hosts all manner of dance, music and theater performances. The Festival Internacional de Ballet happens here and the Conjunto Folklórico Nacional calls this theater home. Travelers with kids will enjoy the children's show Sunday at 11am.

**Sala Teatro Hubert de Blanck** (☎ 833-5962; Calzada No 657 btwn Calles A & B) This theater is named for the founder of Habana's first conservatory of music (1885). The Teatro Estudio based here is Cuba's leading theater company. You can usually see plays in Spanish here Saturday at 8:30pm and Sunday at 7pm. Tickets are sold just prior to the performance.

**Teatro Nacional de Guiñol** (☎ 832-6262; Calle M btwn Calles 17 & 19) Has quality puppet shows and children's theater.

If you understand Spanish, it's well worth attending some of the cutting-edge contemporary theater that's a staple of Grupo Teatro Rita Montaner in the **Sala Teatro El Sótano** (☎ 832-0833; Calle K No 514 btwn Calles 25 & 27; 5-8:30pm Fri & Sat, 3-5pm Sun), not far from the Habana Libre. Performances are Friday and Saturday at 8:30pm, Sunday at 5pm. Also check **Café Teatro Brecht** (cnr Calles 13 & I), where varied performances take place. Tickets go on sale one hour before the performance.

## Classical Music

**Teatro Amadeo Roldán** (Map pp106-7; ☎ 832-4522; cnr Calzada & Calle D; per person CUC$10) This lovely modern theater is the seat of the Orquesta Sinfónica Nacional, which plays in the 886-seat Sala Amadeo Roldán (concerts on Sundays at 11am in season). Try to catch a program conducted by master Leo Brouwer. Major concerts (eg Síntesis, Egberto Gismonti, Aldo Pérez-Gavilán) also go down here. Soloists and small groups play in the 276-seat Sala Caturla. Built in 1922, this magnificent building was destroyed by an arsonist in 1977 and only reopened in 1999 after a careful restoration.

Classical and chamber music concerts also happen nearly nightly at the **Iglesia de San Francisco de Asís** (Map p94; Plaza de San Francisco de Asís) and the **Iglesia de San Francisco de Paula** (Map p94).

## Cinemas

There are about 200 cinemas in Habana. Most have several screenings daily and every theater posts the *Cartelera Icaic*, which lists show times for the entire city. Tickets are usually two pesos; queue early. Hundreds of movies are screened throughout Habana during the Festival Internacional del Nuevo Cine Latinoamericano. Schedules are published daily in the *Diario del Festival*, available in the morning at big theaters and the Hotel Nacional. We've whittled the theater list down to these select few:

**Acapulco** (Map pp106-7; ☎ 833-9573; cnr Avs 26 & 35, Nuevo Vedado) Concerts and special events happen here too.

**Cine 23 y 12** (Map pp106-7; ☎ 833-6906; cnr Calles 23 & 12)

**Cine Actualidades** (Map p100; ☎ 861-5193; Av de Bélgica No 262) Behind the Hotel Plaza.

**Cine Charles Chaplin** (Map pp106-7; ☎ 831-1101; Calle 23 No 1157 btwn Calles 10 & 12) Previews and special screenings and events happen at Icaic's theater; don't miss the poster gallery of great Cuban classic films here.

**Cine La Rampa** (Map pp106-7; ☎ 878-6146; Calle 23 No 111) Catch film festivals here (DeNiro, French films etc).

**Cine Payret** (Map p100; ☎ 863-3163; Paseo de Martí No 505) Opposite the Capitolio, this is Centro Habana's largest and most luxurious cinema, erected in 1878.

**Cine Riviera** (Map pp106-7; ☎ 830-9648; Calle 23 No 507) Big pop, rock and sometimes rap concerts happen here.

**Cine Trianón** (Map pp106-7; ☎ 830-9648; Línea No 706) Movies or live theater.

**Cine Yara** (Map pp106-7; ☎ 832-9430; cnr Calles 23 & L) One big screen and two video *'salas'* (cinemas) here at Habana's most famous cinema (with the best popcorn).

**Cinecito** (Map p100; ☎ 863-8051; San Rafael No 68) Films for kids behind the Hotel Inglaterra.

## Gay & Lesbian Habana

While there aren't any specific gay venues as yet, Habana's burgeoning gay scene is relatively open and there are plenty of cruising opportunities in Vedado. While the night is still young, most of the action takes place on the Malecón where up to 200 people congregate expectantly on the sea wall in front of the Hotel Nacional to shoot the breeze and find out about what's happening later on. Another smaller meeting point is outside Cine Yara on the corner of Calles 23 and L and in the streets and spaces surrounding the Coppelia.

Head to any of these spots on a Friday and Saturday night to find out about the private fiestas – spontaneous parties that are mostly gay, with a healthy dose of fag hags, bisexuals and friends thrown in. Habana's scene is renowned for its talented drag shows, although you'll rarely see transvestites flaunting it in public. A popular venue for bigger shindigs is Parque Lenin, a little removed from the center, but reputedly an excellent night out. There'll be plenty of people willing to pool in a taxi. As with other foreign-Cuban couplings, non-Cubans will often be expected to pick up the bill for drinks, taxis, etc when escorting Cuban partners to these places.

## Sport

**Estadio Latinoamericano** (Map pp106-7; ☎ 870-6526; Zequiera No 312) From October to April (and into May if Habana's Industriales 'Los Azules' make it into the playoffs), baseball games happen at this 58,000-seat stadium in Cerro, just south of Centro Habana. Entry costs three pesos (but they like to charge foreigners CUC$1). The Metropolitanos also play here, but they are to the Industriales what the Mets are to the Yankees. Games are 7:30pm Tuesday, Wednesday and Thursday, 1:30pm Saturday and Sunday. Unfortunately, getting here by public transport is difficult. The benches are cement – painful after nine innings.

**Ciudad Deportiva** (Map pp106-7; ☎ 54 50 00; cnr Av de la Independencia & Vía Blanca; admission 5 pesos) 'Sport City' is Cuba's premier sports training center and big basketball, volleyball, boxing and track contests happen at the coliseum here. The M-2 camello (metrobus) from Av Bolívar in Centro Habana stops across the street.

**Sala Polivalente Ramón Fonst** (Map pp106-7; ☎ 881-4196; Av de la Independencia; 1 peso) Raucous basketball and volleyball games are held at this stadium opposite the main bus station.

For boxing, try **Kid Chocolate** (Map p100; ☎ 861-1546; Paseo de Martí), directly opposite the Capitolio, which usually hosts matches on Fridays at 7pm or **Gimnasio de Boxeo Rafael Trejo** (Map p94; ☎ 862-0266; Calle Cuba No 815 btwn Merced & Leonor Pérez, Habana Vieja). Here you can see matches on Friday at 7pm (CUC$1) or drop by any day after 4pm to watch training. Travelers (including women) interested in boxing can find a trainer here.

Before you forget to pack your running shoes, let it be known that, with its oceanside Malecón, Habana boasts one of the world's nicest municipal jogging routes. Keep your eyes out for holes in the pavement, splashing waves, *jineteros* and old men with fishing lines.

# SHOPPING

## Art Galleries

The art scene in Habana is cutting edge and ever-changing and collectors, browsers and admirers will find many galleries in which to while away hours. Remember that you'll need official receipts or export permits to take artwork home with you (see the boxed text, p140). For gallery events, look for the free *Arte en La Habana,* a triquarterly listings flyer (the San Cristóbal agency on Plaza San Francisco de Asís usually has them) or visit www.galeriascubanas.com.

### HABANA VIEJA

**Casa de Carmen Montilla** (☎ 33 87 68; Oficios No 164; ⏲ 10:30am-5:30pm Tue-Sat, 9am-1pm Sun) This gallery features a huge ceramic mural by Sosa Bravo in the pretty rear courtyard.

**Estudio Galería Los Oficios** (☎ 863-0497; Oficios No 166; ⏲ 10am-5:30pm Mon-Sat) Pop in to this gallery to see the large, hectic, but intriguing canvasses by Nelson Domínguez, whose workshop is upstairs.

**Taller de Serigrafía René Portocarrero** (☎ 862-3276; Cuba No 513 btwn Brasil & Muralla; ⏲ 9am-4pm Mon-Fri) Paintings and prints by young Cuban artists are exhibited and sold here (from CUC$30 to CUC$150). You can also see the artists at work.

### CENTRO HABANA

**Galería Orígenes** (☎ 863-6690; Paseo de Martí No 458; ⏲ 9am-6pm) Paintings and sculptures are exhibited and sold at this gallery inside the Gran Teatro de La Habana, opposite Parque Central.

**Galería La Acacia** (☎ 861-3533; San Martín No 114 btwn Industria & Consulado; ⏲ 10am-3:30pm Mon-Fri, 10am-1pm Sat) This important gallery behind the Gran Teatro de La Habana has paintings by leading artists like Zaida del Rio, plus antiques. Export permits are arranged.

### VEDADO

**Galería Ciudades del Mundo** (☎ 832-3175; Calle 25 No 307; ⏲ 8:30am-5pm Mon-Fri) Interesting expositions on Habana and other cities of the world are put up here.

**Galería Habana** (☎ 832-7101; Línea No 460 btwn Calles E & F; ⏲ 10am-5pm Mon-Sat) This wonderful space in the heart of Vedado shows contemporary Cuban art in big, bright galleries. Come here to see what's new and different from artists such as Aimée García.

**Galería Haydee Santamaría** (Calle G), next to the Casa de las Américas, was being renovated at the time of writing. If it's still closed have a look at the gallery inside the **Casa de las Américas** (cnr Calles 3 & G; admission CUC$2; ⏲ 10am-4:30pm Tue-Sat, 9am-1pm Sun) which has fine exhibits featuring art from all over Latin America.

Other galleries worth a peek in Vedado are the **Centro de Arte 23 y 12** (cnr Calles 12 & 23; ⏲ 10am-5pm Tue-Sat) for contemporary Cuban art and the gallery at **Uneac** (cnr Calles 17 & H).

## Shops & Markets

### HABANA VIEJA

**Palacio de la Artesanía** (Cuba No 64; ⏲ 9am-7pm) For one-stop shopping for souvenirs, cigars, crafts, musical instruments, CDs, clothing and jewelry at fixed prices, join the gaggle of tour-bus escapees here. This building is the former Palacio de Pedroso, erected by Habana Major Mateo Pedroso in 1780. In the mid-19th century it was Habana's high court and later its police headquarters.

**Habana 1791** (Mercaderes No 156 btwn Obrapia & Lamparilla) A one-off store that specializes in old-fashioned perfumes concocted from aromatic flowers and plant oils. Nicely-presented gifts start at around CUC$5.

**Fería de la Artesanía** (Tacón btwn Tejadillo & Chacón; ⏲ Wed-Sat) Paintings, *guayaberas* (men's shirts), woodwork, leather items, Che everything, jewelry and more can be haggled over at this open-air handicraft market. If you buy paintings, make sure you arrange an export license (see the boxed text, p140) or risk losing your loot at customs upon leaving Cuba (if they're deemed 'national treasures' they'll be confiscated). Smaller artwork can easily be tucked safely in luggage.

**Longina Música** (☎ 862-8371; Obispo No 360 btwn Habana & Compostela; ⏲ 10am-7pm Mon-Sat, 10am-1pm Sun) This place on the pedestrian mall has a good selection of CDs, plus musical instruments such as bongos, guitars, maracas, guiros and *tumbadoras* (conga drum). Shop around and you'll probably find cheaper instruments.

You can also check out the **Fundación Havana Club shop** (San Pedro No 262; ⏲ 9am-9pm).

### CENTRO HABANA

**El Bulevar** (San Rafael btwn Paseo de Martí & Av de Italia) This is a pedestrian mall and peso bazaar full of snacks and surprises.

**EXPORTING ARTWORK**

When buying art at an official outlet always ask for an official receipt to show Cuban customs, especially if the object won't fit in your suitcase. To discourage private trading, officials often confiscate undocumented artwork at the airport. If you've purchased a work of art at state-run galleries and have the receipts, you shouldn't have a problem, but it's always better to have a certificate to export artwork (and you'll definitely need one if you purchase directly from the artist).

Certificates to export artwork are issued by the **Registro Nacional de Bienes Culturales** (Map pp106-7; Calle 17 No 1009 btwn Calles 10 & 12, Vedado; 9am-noon Mon-Fri). To obtain an export certificate you must bring the objects here for inspection; fill in a form; queue for two hours; pay a fee of between CUC$10 to CUC$30, which covers from one to five pieces of artwork; and return 24 hours later to pick up the certificate. Do not leave this bit of business until your last day. Some artists will offer to obtain the permit for you upon payment of a deposit. However, the only way to be sure that your paintings won't be confiscated at the airport is to obtain the permit yourself in person.

**Variadades Galiano** (cnr San Rafael & Av de Italia; 10am-6pm Mon-Sat, 9am-noon Sun) Exiting El Bulevar onto Av de Italia, you come to an equally important shopping strip for Cubans containing giant department stores including Variadades Galiano. This former Woolworth's has a great lunch and ice-cream counter and a wide selection of interesting stuff such as old records and those mesh tank tops you see everyone wearing.

**La Manzana de Gómez** (cnr Agramonte & San Rafael) This faded but elegant European-style covered shopping arcade built in 1910 is full of stores. La Exposición, in a downstairs corner, sells reproductions of the works of famous Cuban painters. Opposite the Plaza hotel is El Orbe bike rentals.

**Area de Vendedores por Cuenta Propia** (Máximo Gómez No 259; 9am-5pm Mon-Sat) This is a permanent flea market where you can pick up Santería beads, old books, leather belts and so on.

## VEDADO

**ARTex** (cnr Calles 23 & L; 10am-11pm Mon-Sat, 10am-2pm Sun) This shop opposite the Hotel Habana Libre has a good selection of CDs, cassettes, books, crafts and postcards.

**Fería de la Artesanía** (Malecón btwn Calles D & E; from 10:30am, closed Wed) This artisan market has much of the same as its Habana Vieja counterpart with some key differences: the side facing Calle D is all handmade shoes and sandals, there's a whole section of numismatic interest, with old stamps, coins, bills and other ephemera and there are many more kitschy paintings for sale. It's also a better set-up allowing for easier browsing.

**Cine Yara** (☎ 832-9430; cnr Calles 23 & L) A fabulous selection of old movie posters, antique postcards, T-shirts and, of course, all the greatest Cuban films on videotape are sold at this shop inside the theater.

**Galerías de Paseo** (cnr Calle 1 & Paseo; 9am-6pm Mon-Sat, 9am-1pm Sun) This shopping mall across from the Hotel Meliá Cohiba is the most upscale east of the Río Almendares, with Adidas, Chanel, and even a car dealership. There is also a Bim Bom ice-cream parlor too.

**Plaza Carlos III** (Av Salvador Allende btwn Arbol Seco & Retiro; 10am-6pm Mon-Sat) After Plaza de las Américas in Varadero, this is probably Cuba's flashiest shopping mall – and there's barely a foreigner in sight. Step in on a Saturday and see the double economy working at a feverish pitch.

**Photo Service** (Vedado ☎ 33 50 31; Centro de Prensa Internacional, cnr Calles 23 & O; 8:30am-midnight; Vedado ☎ 55 39 74; Galerías de Paseo, cnr Calle 1 & Paseo; 9am-6pm) Two-hour film developing, photocopies, passport photos (CUC$2 for four).

# GETTING THERE & AWAY

## Air

Take a number at the **Cubana Airlines** (Map pp106-7; ☎ 33 49 49; Calle 23 No 64; 8:30am-4pm Mon-Fri, 8:30am-noon Sat) bustling head office at the Malecón end of the Airline Building, where you can buy international or domestic tickets. If it's packed, book Cubana flights for the same price a few doors down at the helpful **Sol y Son Travel Agency** (Map pp106-

7; ☎ 33 02 93/4; fax 33 51 50; Calle 23 No 64 btwn Calle P & Infanta; ⏲ 8:30am-6pm Mon-Fri, 8:30am-noon Sat).

Other airlines with domestic services:

**Aerocaribbean** (Map pp106-7; ☎ 33 36 21; fax 33 38 71; Airline Building, Calle 23 No 64)

**Aerotaxi** (Map pp106-7; ☎ 53 53 48; fax 33 40 64; cnr Calles 27 & M, Vedado) Private charters only.

## Boat

Buses connecting with the hydrofoil service to Isla de la Juventud leave at 9am from the **Terminal de Ómnibus** (Map pp106-7; ☎ 878-1841; cnr Av de la Independencia & Calle 19 de Mayo), near the Plaza de la Revolución, but often they're late. You'll be told to arrive at least an hour before the bus when you buy your ticket and it's best to take heed of this advice. Bus tickets are sold at the kiosk marked 'NCC' between gate Nos 9 and 10 in the middle of the departures hall (CUC$2) though you're advised to buy a bus/boat ticket combined for CUC$13 rather than waiting until you get to Surgidero de Batabanó. Bring your passport.

## Bus

Astro buses to all corners of Cuba depart from the **Terminal de Ómnibus** (Map pp106-7; ☎ 870-9401; cnr Av de la Independencia & Calle 19 de Mayo) near the Plaza de la Revolución. Tickets sold in Cuban Convertibles are readily available at the office marked **Venta de Boletines** (☎ 870-3397; ⏲ 24hr), down the hall to the right of the main entrance. Two seats on each bus are available for sales in Convertibles, and you can usually get one on any Astro bus the same day. The staff will take you right to your bus and help you board (no pushing in line). For departure information see below. Astro buses have no website and no printed schedule and times and prices are subject to change. On the upside, the company took possession of a whole new fleet of spanking new Chinese buses in December 2005 so conditions have improved.

**Víazul** (☎ 881-1413, 881-5652; www.viazul.com; cnr Calle 26 & Zoológico, Nuevo Vedado) covers most destinations of interest to travelers, in deluxe, air-conditioned coaches. You can

### BUS TIMETABLE

#### Astro

| Destination | Cost (one way) | Distance | Duration (hr) | Departure time |
|---|---|---|---|---|
| Cienfuegos | CUC$17 | 254km | 5 | 6:15am, noon, 4:15pm, 7:30pm, 9:15pm |
| Pinar del Río | CUC$8 | 162km | 4 | 8am, 12:30pm, 5pm, 8:20pm |
| Santa Clara | CUC$15 | 276km | 5 | 2:30am, 7:40pm |
| Santiago de Cuba | CUC$42 | 861km | 15 | 12:15pm, 7:20pm |
| Trinidad | CUC$17 | 335km | 7½ | 5:45am |
| Varadero | CUC$8 | 140km | 3 | 4:35am |

#### Víazul

| Destination | Cost (one way) | Distance | Duration (hr) | Departure time |
|---|---|---|---|---|
| Cienfuegos | CUC$20 | 254km | 5 | 8:15am, 1pm |
| Holquín | CUC$44 | 743km | 10½ | 8:30pm |
| Pinar del Río | CUC$11 | 162km | 4 | 9am, 2pm |
| Playas del Este | CUC$4 | 20km | ½ | 8:40am, 2:20pm |
| Santiago de Cuba | CUC$51 | 861km | 16 | 9:30am, 3pm, 10pm |
| Trinidad | CUC$25 | 335km | 6 | 8:15am, 1pm |
| Varadero | CUC$10 | 140km | 3 | 8am, 12pm, 2pm, 6pm |
| Viñales | CUC$12 | 189km | 3¼ | 9am |

board at the inconveniently located terminal 3km southwest of Plaza de la Revolución, or at the Terminal de Ómnibus. Here tickets for Víazul services are sold immediately prior to the departure in the Venta de Boletines office. You can get full schedules on the website or at **Infotur** (Map p100; Obispo btwn Bernaza & Villegas), which also sells tickets requiring you to board at its originating station in Nuevo Vedado.

Habana-bound, you can get off the Víazul bus from Varadero/Matanzas in Centro Habana right after the tunnel, but if you arrive from most other points you'll be let out at the Nuevo Vedado terminal. From here city bus 27 will take you to Vedado or Centro Habana (ask). Otherwise, if your bus stops at the Terminal de Ómnibus on Av de la Independencia, jump off there. The M-2 camello stops in front of the terminal along with many other buses en route to Parque Fraternidad in Centro Habana. The local buses won't accommodate backpacks. See the boxed text, p141, for departure information.

The bus to Santiago de Cuba (CUC$51, 16 hours 10 minutes) also stops at Santa Clara (CUC$18, three hours 40 minutes), Sancti Spíritus (CUC$23, five hours 40 minutes), Ciego de Ávila (CUC$27, seven hours), Camagüey (CUC$33, eight hours 50 minutes), Las Tunas (CUC$39, 11 hours 25 minutes), Holguín (CUC$44, 12 hours 40 minutes) and Bayamo (CUC$44, 14 hours).

Any of the tour buses parked near the Palacio de la Artesanía (Cuba No 64) near the cathedral, will happily take you to Varadero in the afternoon for CUC$10 to CUC$20 per person. Just ask the driver.

Buses to points in the Habana Province leave from Apodaca No 53, off Agramonte, near the main railway station. They go to Güines, Jaruco, Madruga, Nueva Paz, San José, San Nicolás and Santa Cruz del Norte, but expect large crowds and come early to get a peso ticket.

### Taxi

Small Lada taxis, operated by Cubataxi, park on Calle 19 de Mayo beside the Terminal de Ómnibus. They charge approximately CUC$44 to Varadero, CUC$54 to Pinar del Río, CUC$75 to Santa Clara, CUC$85 to Cienfuegos, CUC$100 to Trinidad. Up to four people can go for that price. It's worth considering in a pinch and is perfectly legal.

### Train

Trains to most parts of Cuba depart from **Estación Central de Ferrocarriles** (Map p100; ☎ 862-4971, 861-8540; cnr Av de Bélgica & Arsenal), on the southwestern side of Habana Vieja. Foreigners must buy tickets in Convertibles at La Coubre station (☎ 862-1006; cnr Av del Puerto & Desamparados; 9am-3pm Mon-Fri). If it's closed, try the Lista de Espera office adjacent which sells tickets for trains leaving immediately. Kids under 12 travel half-price. Rail services include:

| Destination | Cost (one way) | Distance | Frequency |
|---|---|---|---|
| Bayamo | CUC$26 | 744km | 3 weekly |
| Camagüey | CUC$19/32 | 534km | daily |
| Ciego de Ávila | CUC$16/22 | 435km | 3 daily |
| Cienfuegos | CUC$11 | 254km | 3 weekly |
| Holguín | CUC$27 | 743km | 1 daily |
| Las Tunas | CUC$23 | 652km | 2 daily |
| Manzanillo | CUC$28 | 775km | 3 weekly |
| Matanzas | CUC$4 | 105km | 8 daily |
| Morón | CUC$24 | 446km | 3 weekly |
| Pinar del Río | CUC$6.50 | 162km | daily |
| Sancti Spíritus | CUC$13.50 | 354km | 1 daily |
| Santa Clara | CUC$14/17 | 276km | 4 daily |
| Santiago de Cuba | CUC$30/50/62 | 861km | 2-3 daily |

The above information is only a rough approximation of what should happen; services are routinely delayed or canceled. Always double-check scheduling and from which terminal your train will leave.

For information about the electric train from Casablanca to Matanzas, see p163. Suburban trains and local services to points within the Habana Province are discussed under Getting Around, following.

## GETTING AROUND

### To/From the Airport

Aeropuerto Internacional José Martí is at Rancho Boyeros, 25km southwest of Habana via Av de la Independencia. There are several terminals here. Terminal No 1, on the southeastern side of the runway, handles only domestic Cubana flights. Three kilometers away, via Av de la Independencia, is the dreaded Terminal No 2, which receives

Corsair flights and charters from Miami. All other international flights use Terminal No 3, a modern facility at Wajay, 2.5km west of Terminal No 2. Charter flights on Aerocaribbean, Aerogaviota, Aerotaxi etc, to Cayo Largo del Sur and elsewhere use the Caribbean Terminal (also known as Terminal No 5), at the northwestern end of the runway, 2.5km west of Terminal No 3. (Terminal No 4 hasn't been built yet.) Check carefully which terminal you'll be using.

**Víazul** (☎ 881-5652; www.víazul.com; cnr Calle 26 & Zoológico, Nuevo Vedado) has a very sporadic service to the airport at around 6pm-ish (CUC$3) from their Nuevo Vedado terminal and the Hotel Plaza on Parque to Terminal 3. Don't rely on it and certainly don't turn up without checking first.

### To/From the Bus Terminal

The crowded M-2 Metro Bus from Santiago de las Vegas stops outside the Terminal de Ómnibus and runs directly to Parque de la Fraternidad near the Capitolio. In the other direction ask someone where to get out, as the southbound M-2 stops across the Plaza de la Revolución, out of sight of the bus station.

### Bici-taxi

Two-seater bici-taxis will take you anywhere around Centro Habana for CUC$1/2 for a short/long trip, after bargaining. It's a lot more than a Cuban would pay, but cheaper and more fun than a tourist taxi. Laws prohibit bici-taxis from taking tourists and they may wish to go via a roundabout route through the back streets to avoid police controls – a cheap tour! If they get stopped, it's their problem, not yours.

### Bicycle & Moped

After years in the two-wheeled wilderness, travelers now have the opportunity to hire decent bikes from a new outlet called **El Orbe** (Map p94; ☎ 860-2617; cnr Monserrate & Ignacio Agramonte; 9:30am-4:40pm Mon-Sat) in the La Manzana de Gómez shopping center in Habana Vieja. This excellent shop rents out class bikes (many are Raleighs) imported from Canada with 21 gears and shimano brakes. They also have a supply of helmets and bike locks, as well as an on-site mechanic who'll fix up your bike for free.

Prices are as follows: one hour (CUC$2), one day (CUC$12), two to seven days (CUC$8 a day), seven days (CUC$60), 10 days (CUC$75).

### Boat

Passenger **ferries** (Map p94; ☎ 867-3726) shuttle across the harbor to Regla and Casablanca, leaving every 10 or 15 minutes from Muelle Luz, corner of San Pedro and Santa Clara, on the southeast side of Habana Vieja. The fare is a flat 10 centavos. Since the ferries were hijacked to Florida in 1994 (and later returned) and again in 2003 (the hijackers never made it outside Cuban waters), security has been tightened. Expect bag searches and screening.

### Car

There are lots of car rental offices in Habana, so if you're told there are no cars or there isn't one in your price range just try another office or agency. All agencies have offices at Terminal 3 at Aeropuerto Internacional José Martí. Here's a quick in-town list:

**Cubacar** (☎ 33 22 77) Desks at the following hotels: Meliá Cohiba, Meliá Habana, NH Parque Central, Habana Libre, Comodoro and Bello Caribe.

**Havanautos** Vedado (Map pp106-7; ☎ 33 34 84; cnr Calles 23 & M); Playa (Map pp146-7; ☎ 204-3203; cnr Av 5 & Calle 112) Desks at the Habana Libre, Nacional, Riviera, Sevilla, Complejo Neptuno-Tritón and Deauville hotels.

**Micar** Vedado (Map pp106-7; ☎ 24 24 44; Galerías de Paseo, cnr Calle 1 & Paseo; 24hr); Vedado (Map pp106-7; cnr Calle 23 & Infanta) Micar has one or two super cheapie cars (CUC$35 per day); but gets complaints about car quality (often knock-offs from other agencies) and customer service. Go in person and size them up.

**Rex Rent a Car** (Map pp106-7; ☎ 33 77 88; cnr Línea & Malecón) Fancy cars.

**Transtur** Vedado (Map pp106-7; ☎ 33 40 38; cnr Calles 21 & N); Vedado (Map pp106-7; ☎ 55 32 52; Calle 25 btwn Calles K & L) Desks at the Ambos Mundos, Copacabana, Deauville, Inglaterra, Nacional, Neptuno-Tritón, Panamericano, Plaza, Riviera and Sevilla hotels. Transtur and Havanautos offices in Habana tend not to have the cheaper models you can find in other cities.

**Vía Rent a Car** (☎ 204-3606; cnr Avs 47 & 36, Kohly)

Servi-Cupet gas stations are in Vedado at Calles L and 17; Malecón and Calle 15; Malecón and Paseo, near the Riviera and Meliá Cohiba hotels; and on Av de la Independencia (northbound lane) south of Plaza de la Revolución. All are open 24 hours a day.

Guarded parking is available for approximately CUC$1 all over Habana including in front of the Hotel Sevilla, in front of the Hotel Inglaterra and Hotel Nacional.

## Colectivos

All those beautiful hulks parked in front of the Capitolio are 'colectivos' – collective taxis that hold six or more people and run on fixed routes. They're not supposed to take tourists, but many will, typically asking CUC$2 for the Centro Habana–Vedado run; a trip that costs Cubans 10 pesos.

## Public Transport

### BUS

Habana's local bus service is either improving slightly or going straight to hell, depending on who you ask. Regular city buses are called guaguas (pronounced 'WA was'), while the much larger Metro Buses are camellos (camels) for their two humps. Within the city the fare is a flat 20 centavos in a camello, and 40 centavos in a regular bus, which you must toss into a box near the driver or pay to a conductor who's also by necessity an excellent contortionist. Unfortunately, no bus-route map is available.

There are *colas* (lines) at most *paradas* (bus stops) even though it may not appear so at first glance. To mark your place ask for *el último* (the last in line), and when the bus arrives get behind that person. This excellent, efficient system is (mostly) rigorously followed, with *cola*-breakers taken to task by their compatriots.

Since 1995 the public-transport crisis in Habana has been eased by the introduction of Metro Buses: huge 300-plus passenger buses hauled by trucks. Color-coded, they all have the prefix M before their number:

**M-1** Alamar–Vedado via Parque de la Fraternidad (pink)
**M-2** Parque de la Fraternidad–Santiago de las Vegas (blue)
**M-3** Alamar–Ciudad Deportiva (orange)
**M-4** Parque de la Fraternidad–San Agustín via Marianao (green)
**M-5** Vedado-San Agustín (red)
**M-6** Calvario–Vedado (cnr 21 & L; beige)
**M-7** Parque de la Fraternidad–Alberro via Cotorro (red– they ran out of colors)

As you can see, many of the Metro Buses leave from Parque de la Fraternidad on the southern side of the Capitolio in Centro Habana. At the originating places of these buses there will be two lines, one for *sentados* (people who want a seat) and another for *parados* (those willing to stand). The second line moves faster and is best if you're only going a short distance and have no luggage. There is sometimes a third line for *embarazadas* (pregnant women).

The camello is known as the 'Saturday night movie' because it contains sex, violence and adult language (the warning that precedes the weekend movie on Cuban TV). It can be intimidating at first. Expect to be crushed by the crowd.

### TRAIN

**Cristina Station** (Map pp106-7; ☎ 878-4971; cnr Av de México & Arroyo, Cuatro Caminos) lies south of Centro Habana and about a kilometer southwest of the train station. It handles local trains within the city limits. Trains to Batabanó leave twice a day (2½ hours), and four trains a day go to Wajay (one hour). In July and August only, there's a train from here to Guanabo three times a day except Monday (1½ hours). There are also daily trains to Artemisa and Güines. Cristina was the first train station built in Habana, and it's worth checking out if you're spending some time in Habana and want to get around cheaply.

**19 de Noviembre Train Station** (Map pp106-7; ☎ 881-4431; Tulipán, Nuevo Vedado) has trains to a couple of points in the Habana Province, including six to San Antonio de los Baños (one hour). There's railcar service to ExpoCuba (40 minutes) at 9:30am Wednesday to Sunday.

## Taxi

Metered tourist taxis are readily available at all of the upscale hotels, with the air-con Nissan taxis charging higher tariffs than the nonair-con Ladas. The cheapest official taxis are operated by **Panataxi** (☎ 55 55 55), costing CUC$1 flagfall, then CUC$0.50 a kilometer. Tourist taxis charge CUC$1 a kilometer and can be ordered from **Havanautos Taxi** (☎ 32 32 32), **Turistaxi** (☎ 33 66 66) and **Transgaviota** (☎ 33 97 80). **Taxi OK** (☎ 204-0000) is based in Miramar. Drivers of the tourist taxis are government employees who work for a peso salary.

The cheapest taxis are the older yellow-and-black Ladas, which are state-owned but rented out to private operators. They won't wish to use their meters, as these are set at an unrealistically low rate, but you can bargain over the fare. They're not supposed to pick up passengers within 100m of a tourist hotel.

Private pirate taxis with yellow license plates are a bit cheaper, but you must agree on the fare before getting into the car, and carry exact change. There are usually classic-car taxis parked in front of the Inglaterra.

# OUTER HABANA

Splaying out on three sides from the downtown district, Habana's suburbs are full of quirky and easy-to-reach sights and activities that can make interesting day and half-day trips from the city center. Playa boasts a decent aquarium, top-class conference facilities and Cuba's best restaurants; Guanabacoa and Regla are famous for their Afro-Cuban religious culture, and the bayside forts of La Cabaña and El Morro exhibit some of the island's most impressive military architecture.

## PLAYA & MARIANAO

The municipality of Playa, west of Vedado across the Río Almendares, is a paradoxical mix of prestigious residential streets and tough proletarian housing schemes.

Gracious Miramar is a leafy neighborhood of broad avenues and weeping laurel trees where the traffic moves more sedately and diplomat's wives – clad in sun-visors and Lycra leggings – go for gentle afternoon jogs along Av Quinta (Fifth Avenue). Many of Habana's foreign embassies are housed here in old prerevolution mansions, and business travelers and conference attendees flock in from around the globe to make use of some of Cuba's grandest and most luxurious facilities. If you're interested primarily in sightseeing and entertainment, commuting to Vedado or Habana Vieja is a nuisance and an expense. However, some of the best salsa clubs, discos and restaurants are out this way and the casas particulares are positively luxurious.

Cubanacán plays host to many of Habana's business or scientific fairs and conventions, and it is also where several specialized medical institutes are situated. Despite the austerity of the *período especial*, vast resources have been plowed into biotechnological and pharmaceutical research institutes in this area. Yachties, anglers and scuba divers will find themselves using the Marina Hemingway at Playa's west end. Marianao is world famous for the Tropicana Nightclub, but locally it's known as a tough, in parts rough, neighborhood with a powerful Santería community and a long history of social commitment.

### Information

#### INTERNET ACCESS

**Hotel Business Centers** (Hotel Meliá Habana; Av 3 btwn Calles 76 & 80) Meliá Habana charges CUC$7 per half-hour for Internet access.

#### MEDIA

The best **newsstand** in Habana is in the parking lot of **Supermercado 70** (cnr Av 3 & Calle 70; 9am-6pm Mon-Sat). You can usually get *Time*, *Newsweek*, the *Economist*, and *Rolling Stone* here.

#### MEDICAL SERVICES

**Clínica Central Cira García** (☎ 204-2811; fax 24 16 33; Calle 18A No 4101, Playa) Emergency, dental and medical consultations for foreigners (consultations CUC$25 to CUC$35).

**Farmacia Internacional** (☎ 204-9385; Hotel El Comodoro, cnr Av 3 & Calle 84)

**Pharmacy** (☎ 204-2880; Calle 18A No 4104, Playa; 24hr) In Clínica Central Cira García; one of the city's best, along with the pharmacy across the street on the corner of Calle 20 and Av 41 (open 9am to 8:45pm).

#### MONEY

**Banco Financiero Internacional** Miramar (☎ 203-9762; Sierra Maestra Bldg, cnr Av 1 & Calle 0); Playa (☎ 267-5500; cnr Av 5 & Calle 92)

**Cadeca** Miramar (Av 5A btwn Calles 40 & 42; 9am-5pm Mon-Sat, 9am-noon Sun); Playa (cnr Av 3 & Calle 70)

#### POST

**DHL** (☎ 204-1578; cnr Av 1 & Calle 26, Miramar; 8am-8pm)

**Post office** (Calle 42 No 112 btwn Avs 1 & 3, Miramar; 8am-11:30am, 2-6pm Mon-Fri, 8am-11:30am Sat)

#### TOURIST INFORMATION

**Infotur** (☎ 24 70 36; cnr Av 5 & Calle 112, Playa; 8:30am-5pm Mon-Sat, 8:30am-noon Sun)

# PLAYA & MARIANAO

A B C D

1 2 3 4 5 6

**INFORMATION**

- Austrian Embassy 1 H1
- Banco Financiero Internacional 2 E4
- Banco Financiero Internacional (see 37)
- Belgian Embassy 3 F3
- British Embassy 4 G2
- Cadeca 5 G2
- Cadeca (see 69)
- Canadian Embassy 6 G2
- Clínica Central Cira García 7 H2
- Cubanacán 8 F3
- Cubanacán Naútica 9 B4
- DHL 10 G2
- Farmacia Internacional (see 43)
- French Embassy 11 G2
- Gaviota 12 H3
- Havanatur (see 37)
- Hotel Business Centers (see 45)
- Infotur 13 E4
- Italian Embassy 14 F3
- Japanese Embassy 15 F3
- Mexico Embassy 16 H2
- Netherlands Embassy 17 H2
- Pharmacy 18 H2
- Pharmacy (see 7)
- Post Office 19 F2
- Russian Embassy 20 F3
- Swedish Embassy 21 G2
- Swiss Embassy 22 G2

**SIGHTS & ACTIVITIES**

- Acuario Nacional 23 F3
- Centro de Ingenería Genética y Biotecnología 24 E6
- Centro Internacional de Restuaración Neurológica (CIREN) 25 E5
- Centro Nacional de Investigaciones Científicas (CENIC) 26 E5
- Complejo Recreo 27 A5
- Fundación Naturaleza y El Hombre 28 F3
- Iglesia Jesús de Miramar 29 F3
- Instituto Superior de Arte (ISA) 30 E4
- La Aguja Marlin Diving Center 31 B4
- La Maqueta de La Habana 32 G2
- Museo de la Alfabetización 33 G5
- Museo del Aire 34 D6
- Pabexpo 35 D5
- Palacio de las Convenciones 36 E5
- Sierra Maestra Building 37 H1

**SLEEPING**

- Aparthotel Montehabana 38 F3
- Hostal Costa Sol 39 F3
- Hotel Bello Caribe 40 E6
- Hotel Chateau Miramar 41 F3
- Hotel El Bosque 42 H2
- Hotel El Comodoro 43 E3
- Hotel El Viejo y El Mar 44 B4
- Hotel Meliá Habana 45 F3
- Hotel Mirazul 46 G2
- Occidental Miramar 47 F3
- Panorama Hotel Havana 48 F3
- Residencia Universitaria Ispjae 49 G2

**EATING**

- Cafetería de 3 y 62 50 F3
- Don Cangrejo 51 G2
- Dos Gardenias 52 G2
- El Aljibe 53 G2
- El Buganvil 54 D5
- El Elegante 55 H3
- El Rancho Palco 56 E5
- El Tocororo 57 G2
- La Cecilia 58 E4
- La Esperanza 59 G2
- La Ferminia 60 D5
- La Flora 61 G4
- La Paila 62 H5
- Paladar Calle 10 63 G2
- Paladar La Fontana 64 F3
- Paladar Los Cactus de 33 65 H3
- Paladar Mi Jardín 66 F3
- Pan com 67 G2
- Pizza Nova 68 B5
- Supermercado 70 69 F3
- Supermercado Universo 70 B4

**ENTERTAINMENT**

- Casa de la Música 71 H2
- Circo Trompoloco 72 E4
- Estadio Pedro Marrero 73 H3
- Havana Club Disco 74 E3
- Río Club 75 H1
- Salón Rosado Benny Moré (El Tropical) 76 H3
- Teatro Karl Marx 77 G1
- Tropicana Nightclub 78 G4

**SHOPPING**

- Casa del Habano 79 G2
- Egrem Tienda de Música 80 G2
- La Maison 81 H2
- Photo Club 82 E3

**TRANSPORT**

- Buses P1 and 100 83 F3
- Cubacar 84 B4
- Cubacar 85 F3
- Havanautos 86 E4
- Havanautos (see 37)
- Servi-Cupet Gas Station 87 G4
- Servi-Cupet Gas Station 88 E4
- Servi-Cupet Gas Station 89 E4
- Vía Rent A Car 90 H2

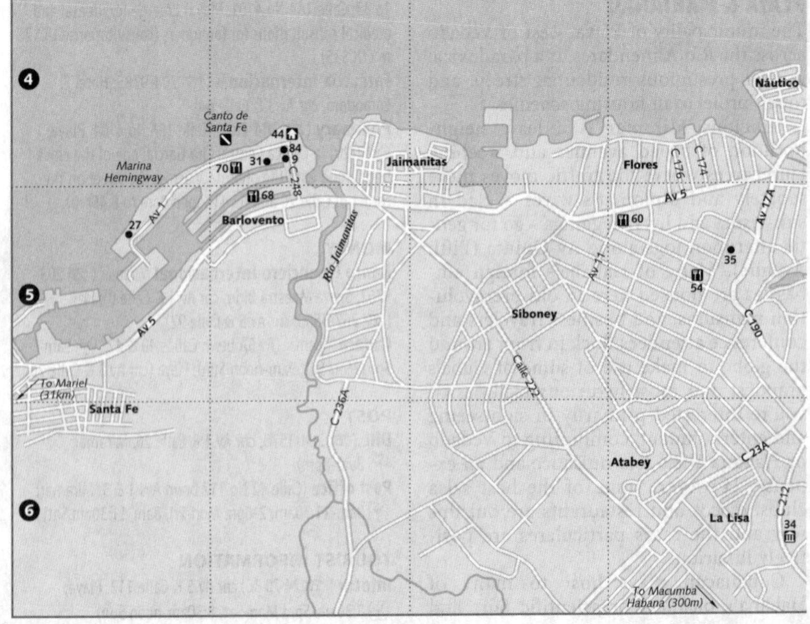

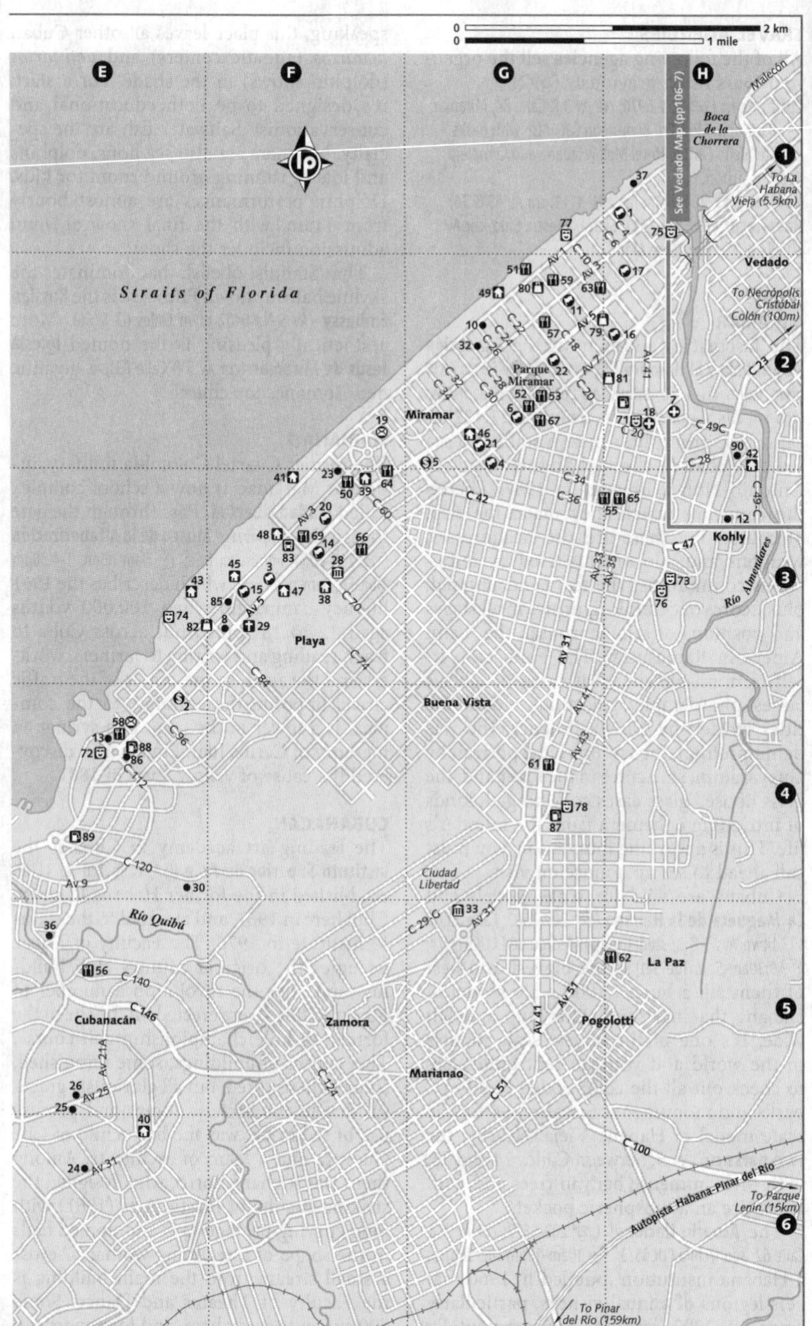
0 2 km
0 1 mile
Straits of Florida
See Vedado Map (pp106–7)
Boca de la Chorrera
Malecón
To La Habana Vieja (5.5km)
Vedado
To Necrópolis Cristóbal Colón (100m)
Miramar
Parque Miramar
Kohly
Río Almendares
Playa
Buena Vista
Ciudad Libertad
Río Quibú
La Paz
Pogolotti
Cubanacán
Zamora
Marianao
Autopista Habana-Pinar del Río
To Parque Lenin (15km)
To Pinar del Río (159km)

### TRAVEL AGENCIES

All of the following agencies sell the organized tours listed previously (p92).

**Cubanacán** (☎ 204-6970; cnr Av 3 & Calle 84, Miramar; 8am-5pm Mon-Fri, 8am-noon Sat) Also with desks at Hotel Bello Caribe, Hotel Meliá Habana and Complejo Neptuno-Tritón.

**Gaviota** (☎ 204-4411; fax 204-4111; cnr Av 49 & 36)

**Havanatur** (☎ 204-7541; Sierra Maestra Bldg, cnr Av 1 & Calle 0; 9am-6pm Mon-Sat)

## Sights

### MIRAMAR

The fascinating museum at the **Fundación Naturaleza y El Hombre** (☎ 204-0438; Av 5B No 6611 btwn Calles 66 & 70; admission CUC$3; 10am-4pm Mon-Fri) displays artifacts from the 17,422km canoe trip from the Amazon source to sea led by Cuban intellectual and nature-lover Antonio Nuñez Jiménez in 1987. There's the canoe in which they made the trip, of course, but there are also headdresses, weapons and adornments used by indigenous communities the team encountered, plus, scores of ceramic figurines in all stages and positions of sexual arousal; the 'Latin American Kamasutra.' The Fundación itself is mind-blowing, with one of Cuba's largest photography collections, plus all the titles written by Nuñez Jiménez, (he was damn prolific), the famous Fidel portrait by Guayasamín, stalactites in the foyer and 'the glass house,' glass cases collecting all kinds of intriguing ephemera from the founder's life. This is a working foundation; you must call ahead to set up a museum visit.

Cubans are wild for scale models and **La Maqueta de la Habana** (☎ 202-7303; Calle 28 No 113 btwn Avs 1 & 3; student/unguided/guided CUC$1/3/4; 9:30am-5pm Tue-Sat) is the biggest and best of them all: a huge 1:1000 scale model of Habana that measures 22m long and 8m wide. It's one of the largest scale models in the world and you can rent binoculars to check out all the color-coded buildings, parks and monuments. See also p96 for the scale model of Habana Vieja. Nearby, the two **parks** on Av 5, between Calles 24 and 26, with their immense banyan trees and dark lanes, are an atmospheric pocket.

The **Acuario Nacional** (☎ 202-5872; cnr Av 3 & Calle 62; adult/child CUC$5/3; 10am-10pm Tue-Sun) is a Habana institution founded in 1960 that gets legions of annual visitors, particularly since its 2002 revamp. Environmentally speaking, this place leaves all other Cuban *acuarios* (aquatic centers) and *definarios* (dolphin shows) in the shade. For a start, it's designed to be both educational and conservationist. Saltwater fish are the specialty, but there are also sea lions, dolphins and lots of running-around room for kids. Dolphin performances are almost hourly from 11am, with the final show at 9pm; admission includes the show.

That Stalinist obelisk that dominates the skyline halfway down Fifth Ave is the **Russian Embassy** (Av 5 No 6402 btwn Calles 62 & 66). More aesthetically pleasing is the domed **Iglesia Jesús de Miramar** (cnr Av 5 & Calle 82), a gigantic neo-Romanesque church.

### MARIANAO

The former Cuartel Colombia military airfield at Marianao is now a school complex called **Ciudad Libertad**. Pass through the gate to visit the inspiring **Museo de la Alfabetización** (☎ 260-8054; admission free; 8am-noon, 1-4:30pm Mon-Fri, 8am-noon Sat), which describes the 1961 literacy campaign, when 100,000 youths aged 12 to 18 spread out across Cuba to teach reading and writing to farmers, workers and the aged. In the center of the traffic circle, opposite the entrance to the complex, is a tower in the form of a syringe in memory of Carlos Juan Finlay, who discovered the cause of yellow fever in 1881.

### CUBANACÁN

The leading art academy in Cuba is the **Instituto Superior de Arte** (ISA; Calle 120 No 1110), established in the former Habana Country Club here in 1961, and elevated to the status of institute in 1976. The Faculty of Music occupies the original country-club building, and after the revolution a number of other facilities were erected on the site of the former 18-hole championship golf course. This cluster of buildings, some unfinished, some half-restored, but all gloriously graceful due to the arches, domes and profuse use of red brick, was the brainchild of Che Guevara and a team of architects. Among them was Richard Porro, who designed the striking Faculty of Plastic Arts (1961) with long curving passageways and domed halls in the shape of a reclining woman. Across a small stream from the main building is the Faculty of Theater and Dance. Some 800 students study here, and foreigners can too (see p114). It is accessible only from the northwest.

Also known as the Habana Convention Center, the **Palacio de las Convenciones** (☎ 20 60 11; Calle 146 btwn Avs 11 & 13) is one of Cuba's most dramatic modern buildings. Built for the Non-aligned Conference in 1979, the four interconnecting halls contain a state-of-the-art auditorium with 2101 seats and 11 smaller halls. The 589-member National Assembly meets here twice a year and the complex hosts more than 50,000 conference attendees annually. Not far from here is **Pabexpo** (☎ 54 91 11; cnr Av 17 & Calle 180), just two blocks off Av 5. Opened in 1987, Pabexpo's 20,000 sq meters of exhibition space in four interconnecting pavilions is filled with about 15 business or scientific shows a year. Cubadisco (Cuba's Grammys) are held here each May.

Many of Cuba's cutting-edge scientific and medical facilities are out here including: **Centro de Ingenería Genética y Biotecnología** (☎ 271-6022; cnr Av 31 & Calle 190), the focus of Cuba's genetic engineering and biotechnology research; the **Centro Nacional de Investigaciones Científicas** (Cenic; ☎ 208-2546; cnr Av 25 & Calle 158), where the anticholesterol wonder drug Ateromixol, or PPG, was created; and the **Centro Internacional de Restuaración Neurológica** (Ciren; ☎ 271-6844; cnr Av 25 & Calle 158), where Cuba has developed breakthrough neurological treatments. All these installations are heavily guarded, so unless you're a patient, don't even think about visiting.

**Museo del Aire** (☎ 271-0632; Calle 212 btwn Avs 29 & 31, La Coronela; unguided/guided CUC$2/3, plus camera CUC$2; 🕑 9am-4pm Tue-Sun) has 22 planes and helicopters on display, most of them ex-military aircraft. Don't miss Che Guevara's personal Cessna 310, or the space suit used by Cuba's first cosmonaut.

## Activities

There are many water activities available at Marina Hemingway in Barlovento, 20km west of central Habana. Deep-sea fishing can be arranged at **Cubanacán Naútica** (☎ 204-6848; cnr Av 5 & Calle 248) from CUC$150 for four anglers for four hours depending on the boat. Included are a captain, sailor, open bar and tackle. Marlin season is June to October. Scuba packages for CUC$35 per dive and tours of Habana's littoral can also be arranged. Hotel tour desks should also be able to arrange these things.

**La Aguja Marlin Diving Center** (☎ 204-5088; cnr Av 5ta & 248, Santa Fe), between Cubanacán Naútica and the shopping center, offers scuba diving for CUC$30 per dive, plus CUC$5 for gear. It has one morning and one afternoon departure. A diving excursion to Varadero or Playa Girón can also be arranged. Reader reviews have been favorable.

## Sleeping

### MIRAMAR

**Hostal Costa Sol** (☎ 202-8269; Calle 60 No 307, Miramar; s/d CUC$25/36) Operated by the Ministerio de Educación Superior, this is an intimate place with only 11 rooms, but is far from everything. The restaurant is cheap and decent if you happen to be out this way.

**Residencia Universitaria Ispjae** (☎ 203-6633; cnr Av 1 & Calle 22; s/d CUC$27/44) Miramar's rock-bottom place is hard to pick out on the rocky shoreline just west of Teatro Karl Marx. There are eight basic rooms with baths that are usually booked up by foreigners studying with UniversiTUR (☎ 203-5370); call the hotel before rolling up.

**Hotel Mirazul** (☎ 204-0088/45; Av 5 No 3603 btwn Calles 36 & 40; s/d CUC$45/50; ❄) An elegant old mansion operated as a hotel by the Ministerio de Educación Superior. The eight air-con rooms with baths and TVs are all different, so look first. There's a restaurant-bar. It's excellent value compared with the larger tourist hotels found here, but not always available; call ahead.

**Hotel El Bosque** (Gaviota; ☎ 204-9232; Calle 28A btwn 49A & 49B; s/d CUC$45/60; ❄ 💻) A rank outsider, El Bosque is often overlooked by less savvy travelers who prefer to flock toward Miramar's ever popular strip of four- and five-star piles. Their loss is somebody else's gain. This clean, friendly and gentile hotel lies on the banks of the Río Almendares – Habana's green lungs – and is a good (and rare) midrange choice in this neck of the woods. Rooms are small but functional, there's 24-hour Internet, and out back a pleasant terrace overlooks the wooded slopes of the nearby river.

**Aparthotel Montehabana** (Gaviota; ☎ 206-9595; Calle 70 btwn Av 5A & 7; s/d/tr CUC$50/70/100; 🅿 ❄ 💻) This brand new Gaviota giant opened in December 2005 and consists of

101 one-room apartments with living room and fully-equipped kitchen. If you're not up to cooking the restaurant does a CUC$8 breakfast and a CUC$15 dinner buffet. Facilities are shiny and new and from the outside you could mistake this three-star establishment for a full-blown five-star.

**Hotel El Comodoro** (Cubanacán; ☎ 204-5551; cnr Av 3 & Calle 84; s/d low season CUC$65/90, high season CUC$80/110; P) Right on the coast, about 15km west of Habana Vieja, this complex is a maze of shops, restaurants and accommodation, both old and new. The 134 rooms in the main four-story building date from before the revolution; another 10 rooms in a two-story cabana block facing the ocean cost the same. You're better off paying about 10% more for one of the Bungalows Alborada or Pleamar, which are fairly new. The hotel's small, sandy beach is protected from the waves by a large iron seawall, and the Comodoro is a good choice for anyone looking for real resort atmosphere within a taxi ride of the city.

**Hotel Chateau Miramar** (Cubanacán; ☎ 24 19 51/2/3; Av 1 btwn Calles 60 & 70; s/d CUC$90/120; P) Marketed as a 'boutique hotel' and considering neighboring properties, this hotel, with only five floors and 50 rooms, does have a more intimate feel. But 'chateau' and 'boutique' are a bit of a stretch. Still, professionals will appreciate the free cell phone, computer connection and direct international phone service that come with rooms.

> **CASAS PARTICULARES – PLAYA & MIRAMAR**
>
> **Marta Rodríguez** (☎ 203-8596; Calle 42 No 914; r CUC$40; P) Rents two outfitted rooms with TV/VCR, stereo and fridge.
>
> **Mayda Bellón Trueba** (☎ 203-4490; Av 33 No 3404 btwn Calles 34 & 36, Playa; r CUC$30) Opposite Los Cactus de 33. Palatial, private. English spoken. Nine houses renting on this tranquil block, allowing big groups to arrange casa accommodation together.
>
> **Rina & Geraldo** (☎ 202-4112; Av 3A No 8610 btwn 86 & 88, Miramar; r CUC$25-30) Two clean rooms, one with sun terrace. Flexible hosts.
>
> **Suites Olimpia Jorge Pérez** (☎ /fax 202-4126; Calle 96 No 535 btwn Avs 5F & 7, Miramar; r CUC$30-35; P) Fridge. Private.

**Panorama Hotel Havana** (Gaviota; ☎ 204-0100; cnr Av 3 & Calle 70; s/d CUC$95/120; P) One of Miramar's newest hotels, which opened in spring 2003, is an architectural oddity with hectares of glass and a huge ostentatious lobby that stands as a kind of cathedral to bad taste. Still, the 317 rooms are spacious and comfortable enough and a rooftop bar-restaurant offers great views all the way over to Vedado. Suites have terraces and whirlpools and the fantastic pool is right on the ocean. Kids under 12 stay for half price.

**Occidental Miramar** (Gaviota; ☎ 204-3584; fax 204-3583; cnr Av 5 & Calle 74; s/d CUC$100/130; P) Formerly the Novotel, this 427 room giant was recently taken over by Gaviota and has benefited as a result. Professional staff, great business facilities, and high standards of service throughout are par for the course here. A regular shuttle bus whizzes guests into Central Habana.

**Hotel Meliá Habana** (Cubanacán; ☎ 204-8500; Av 3 btwn Calles 76 & 80; r CUC$225; P) The pros choice; what the Meliá lacks in old-world charm it makes up for in razor-sharp professionalism. While some of Habana's flagship hotels suffer from a standard staple of annoying 'Cubanisms' (bored staff, iffy food, shoddy workmanship) this place, on the rocky shores of breezy Playa, rarely misses a beat. Don't be put off by the dull-grey facade, the facilities inside are beautiful, including a vine-draped lobby and a succession of nicely laid out swimming pools. A great business center and tremendous food seal the deal.

### CUBANACÁN

**Hotel Bello Caribe** (Cubanacán; ☎ 33 05 67; cnr Av 31 & Calle 158; s/d low season CUC$45/64, high season CUC$55/78; P) A couple of kilometers south of Hotel Palco, next to the huge Centro de Ingeniería Genética y Biotecnología. The 120 rooms are generally used by foreigners undergoing treatment at the nearby medical facilities. Though this place is inconveniently located, we've received favorable letters about the facilities and services; there is a good buffet and salad bar.

### MARINA HEMINGWAY

**Hotel El Viejo y El Mar** (Cubanacán; ☎ 204-6336; fax 204-6823) Lured by the Hemingway connection (the name is taken from Papa's Nobel

Prize-winning book: *The Old Man and the Sea*) El Viejo has disappointed many an unassuming punter. Even more so at the moment as it's closed to the general public for Misión Milagros (p449); call ahead to check current status.

## Eating

Playa is paladar heaven and contains some of the best places to eat in Cuba. Food, ambience and culinary creativity are never in short supply in this neck of the woods and could have you seriously retracting all of those oft-told jokes about tomato-less pizzas and soggy cheese and ham sandwiches. Get out there and enjoy it while you can.

### PLAYA & MARIANAO

**La Flora** (☎ 209-5889; cnr Av 41 & Calle 68, Playa) Unique in Habana, catch a colectivo on Calle 23 in Vedado to visit this bakery selling whole wheat bread *(¡sí señor!)*, brownies, éclairs, cinnamon-raisin buns and other sweet treats – in Convertibles of course. It claims to be 24 hours.

**La Paila** (☎ 267-1771; Ave 51A No 8827 btwn Calles 88B & 88C, Marianao; noon-midnight) If this place wasn't so off the beaten track, it would be in Habana's Top Five; and it's cheap too. With just a few tables ensconced in a lush garden replete with soft-lit lanterns, this is the most romantic paladar no one knows about. And the food is infallible. They do a great *bistec Uruguayo* (steak) or try one of the famous pizzas – both less than CUC$5. The menu is in pesos, but they take Convertibles.

**El Elegante** (☎ 203-8215; Av 33 No 3410 btwn 34 & 36, Playa) Humble El Elegante is good value, and it's open 'whenever you want it to be.'

**Paladar Los Cactus de 33** (☎ 203-5139; Av 33 No 3405 btwn Calles 34 & 36, Playa; noon-midnight) Reviewed in international lifestyle magazines and used as a setting for TV specials, this place has impeccable service, elegant surroundings, well-prepared food and (in a Cuban context) outrageous prices. A full pork meal with all the sides is pushing CUC$20, the house special chicken breast with mushrooms, olives and cheese even more.

### MIRAMAR

**Pan.com** (☎ 204-4232; cnr Av 7 & Calle 26; 10am-midnight) You can't help but love this place with its hearty sandwiches, fantastic burgers and ice-cream milkshakes to die for. Seating is in a shaded outdoor patio and service is surprisingly warm and efficient; the ultimate Habana comfort-food haven.

**Dos Gardenias** (☎ 204-2353; cnr Av 7 & Calle 28; noon-midnight) You can choose from grill, Chinese and pasta restaurants in this complex; also a bolero hot spot.

**Paladar Mi Jardín** (☎ 203-4627; Calle 66 No 517; noon-midnight) It's the rare Cuban menu that offers chicken mole or tacos and quesadillas, which makes this Mexican place a keeper. Dining beneath the vine-covered trellis in the garden is recommended, as is the house special fish Veracruz.

**Paladar Calle 10** (☎ 205-3970; Calle 10 No 314 btwn Avs 3 & 5; noon-3pm & 6-11pm) Hidden in a back garden, the specialty here is outstandingly delicious barbecue: the lamb skewers marinated in oregano (CUC$8ish) just might be the tastiest meat to pass your lips in Cuba, while the exotic red snapper stuffed with seafood and flambéed with rum is out of this world. The kitchen is wide open so you can watch and learn. Italian, French and English spoken. Reservations recommended.

**Paladar La Fontana** (☎ 202-8337; Calle 3A No 305) Habana discovers the barbecue or, more to the point, the full-on charcoal grill. Huge portions of meat and fish are served up in this amiable villa-cum-paladar, so go easy on the starters which include crab mixed with eggplant, quails eggs and fried chick peas. La Fontana specializes in just about everything you'll never see elsewhere in Cuba from lasagna to huge steaks. Big shot reviews from *Cigar Aficionado* and the *Chicago Tribune* testify the burgeoning legend.

**La Esperanza** (☎ 202-4361; Calle 16 No 105 btwn Avs 1 & 3; 6:30-11pm, closed Thu) This lovely home on a Miramar side street is worth a special trip. The well-prepared and well-presented food is served by wonderfully friendly staff in antique outfitted dining rooms or a leafy backyard. Reservations are advised, but not to worry if you have to wait; the couches, coffee-table books and a glass of fine wine will keep you occupied.

**Don Cangrejo** (☎ 204-4169; Av 1 No 1606 btwn Calles 16 & 18; noon-midnight) Right on the water, this seafood restaurant (fish CUC$8 to CUC$12 or lobster CUC$20 to CUC$25) scores high points for atmosphere (love the buccaneer waitstaff!). There's a pool table and pool, an inexpensive pizza and grill menu and one of Habana's classic signs out front.

**El Tocororo** (☎ 202-4530; Calle 18 No 302; meals CUC$12-35; ⏰ noon-midnight) Considered one of Habana's finest restaurants, be prepared to open your billfold at this place. Fried fish, lobster tail or a live lobster plucked from the tank is just the beginning. Everything, even the bread and rice, is à la carte, and 10% is added on top. The candlelit tables and garden are plusses, but don't believe the hype.

**Supermercado 70** (cnr Av 3 & Calle 70; ⏰ 9am-6pm Mon-Sat, 9am-1pm Sun) Still known as the 'Diplomercado' from the days when you had to show a foreign passport to be able to shop here, this place is gigantic. One of the best in Habana with lots of selection.

If you're staying in one of the pricey hotels and want a cheaper place to eat than what the hotels offer, there's the **Cafetería de 3 y 62** (☎ 204-0369; cnr Av 3 & Calle 62; ⏰ 8am-11pm), on the eastern side of the Russian Embassy. There is also a row of simple restaurant kiosks facing Supermercado 70.

### CUBANACÁN

**El Buganvil** (☎ 271-4791; Calle 190 No 1501 btwn Calles 15 & 17, Siboney; ⏰ noon-midnight) Another solid paladar with a pleasant outdoor plant and thatch setting, this place has sterling service and good *comida criolla*. The house specialty is *loma ahumado* (smoked pork loin; CUC$4), but if you get a group of six together, they'll smoke a whole pig for you.

**La Cecilia** (☎ 204-1562; Av 5 No 11010 btwn Calles 110 & 112; ⏰ noon-midnight) All-time Habana classic, this classy place is up there with the Aljibe in terms of food quality (check out the *ropa vieja*), but trumps all comers with its big band music that blasts out on weekend nights inside its large but atmospheric courtyard.

**El Rancho Palco** (cnr Av 19 & Calle 140; ⏰ noon-11pm) An upscale place, in a forest near the Palacio de las Convenciones. Steaks, seafood and Cuban cooking are served under a thatched roof.

**La Ferminia** (☎ 33 67 86; Av 5 No 18207) Habana gets swanky. Dine in the mansion or out in the garden patio at this fine restaurant – it doesn't matter. The point is the food. A wonderful mixed grill, pulled straight from the fire onto your plate, or a thick filet mignon will set you back more than CUC$20, but it will be money well spent.

At Marina Hemingway is the terrific **Pizza Nova** (cnr Av 5ta & 248), serving pies on the water and the well-stocked Supermercado Universo.

## Entertainment

### MIRAMAR

**Teatro Karl Marx** (☎ 203-0801, 209-1991; cnr Av 1 & Calle 10) The very biggest events happen here, such as the closing galas for the jazz and film fests (with Harry Belafonte and Roman Polanski in the house) and rare concerts by *trovador* Carlos Varela. Get tickets for row 20 or closer because the acoustics crumple if you're back under the balcony.

**Casa de la Música** (☎ 202-6147; Calle 20 No 3308; admission CUC$5-20; ⏰ 10pm Tue-Sat) One of Habana's premier venues, you're good time is almost guaranteed at this casa run by recording company Egrem. Renowned jazz pianists Chuchu Valdés, NG la Banda, Los Van Van, Aldaberto Alvarez y Su Son: all the platinum players gig here. If you can only make it out one night for live music, this is the place.

**Havana Club Disco** (☎ 202-7712; cnr Av 1 & Calle 86; admission CUC$10; ⏰ 10pm-3am Mon-Sat) This tremendous video disco behind the Hotel Comodoro is probably more trouble than it's worth: no posted prices, lots of *jineteras* and their over-50 benefactors and itty-bitty drinks in plastic cups.

**Río Club** (☎ 209-3389; Calle A No 314 btwn Avs 3 & 3A; ⏰ 10pm) This disco claims to offer *el sonida más duro de la ciudad* (the hardest sound in town). The location is reflected in the scene, which is a good mix of locals and tourists, but pricey for what it is.

### MARIANAO

**Tropicana Nightclub** (☎ 267-1871; Calle 72 No 4504; ⏰ show at 10pm) Cuba's most famous nightclub. Since the Tropicana opened in 1939, famous artists such as Benny Moré, Nat King Cole and Maurice Chevalier have appeared here. More than 200 dancers perform during Tropicana's 1950s-style cabaret show 'Paradise Under the Stars,' a spectacle not soon forgotten. The doors open at 8:30pm. Admission including one drink is from CUC$65 per person, depending on the table. Tropicana bookings can be made through any hotel tour desk, with hotel transfers included. The Tropicana box office opens 10am to 4pm daily, and although booking in person is no cheaper, you'll be able to choose your own table (important as we've received several complaints about switched tables and botched reservations). When bookings are light, bar seats might be available (CUC$25), but these can't be reserved in advance. Just turn up at 8:30pm and ask.

Order a bottle of rum and your mixers straight away to avoid fighting for your server's attention during the show. The dress code here requires that men wear long pants and shoes (important to remember if you arrive by tour bus straight from a day of sightseeing). An after-hours club called Arcos de Cristal is on the same premises as the Tropicana, and it has a show that starts after the one at the Tropicana finishes.

**Salón Rosado Benny Moré** (El Tropical; ☎ 206-1281; cnr Av 41 & 46, Playa; admission 10 pesos-CUC$10; ⌚ 9pm-late) For something completely different, check out the very *caliente* (hot) action at this outdoor venue. This place (aka El Tropical) packs in hot, sexy Cuban youths dancing madly to Los Van Van, Pupi y Su Son Son or Habana Abierta. It's a fierce scene and female travelers should expect aggressive come-ons. Friday to Sunday is best. Some travelers pay pesos, others Convertibles – more of that Cuban randomness for you.

**The Circo Trompoloco** (cnr Av 5ta & 112; admission CUC$10) Habana's permanent circus with shows at 7pm Thursday to Sunday plus a weekend matinee.

**Estadio Pedro Marrero** (cnr Av 41 & Calle 46) You can see soccer matches on weekends at 3pm at this 15,000-seat stadium.

#### LA LISA

**Macumba Habana** (☎ 33 05 68/9; cnr Calle 222 & Av 37; admission CUC$10-20; ⌚ 10pm) This residential neighborhood southwest of Cubanacán holds Macumba Habana, one of Habana's biggest venues for live salsa. The outdoor setting is refreshing and the sets long, so you'll get a lot of dancing in. You can also dine at La Giradilla in the same complex. Great place to catch jazz-salsa combos. Hotels and Infotur (p145 ) sell excursions here, but you're better off getting here yourself (a Convertible taxi should cost around CUC$8 to CUC$10).

### Shopping

**La Casa del Habano** (cnr Av 5 & Calle 16; ⌚ 10am-6pm Mon-Sat, 10am-1pm Sun) Smokers and souvenir seekers will like La Casa, arguably Habana's top cigar store. There's a comfy smoking lounge and a decent restaurant here as well.

**La Maison** (Calle 16 No 701, Miramar) The Cuban fashion fascination is in high gear at this place, with a large boutique selling designer clothing, shoes, handbags, jewelry, cosmetics and souvenirs.

**Photo Club** (☎ 204-1969; cnr Av 3 & Calle 84, Playa) Develops prints, sells batteries and film.

For CDs head to **Egrem Tienda de Música** (Calle 18 No 103; ⌚ 9am-6pm Mon-Sat), which has a great selection, or visit the **Casa de la Música** (cnr Av 35 & Calle 20; ⌚ 10am-10pm).

### Getting There & Away

To get to Playa from Habana, take bus 264 from Desamparados, between Picota and Compostela, near the old city wall southeast of the Estacíon Central de Férrocarriles (Central Station). Otherwise try bus 132 or 232 from Dragones and Industria beside the Capitolio. From Vedado to Playa you can catch the P1 from in front of Coppelia on Calle 23 or the P4 along Línea, just before Paseo toward Calle A. For Marianao, take bus 34 from Dragones and Industria or the M-4 camello from Parque Fraternidad (a long, slow ride).

To reach the Marina Hemingway, take bus 9 or 420 from near the tunnel under the Río Almendares in Miramar.

### Getting Around

There are two **Havanautos** (Miramar ☎ 203-9104; 3rd fl Sierra Maestra Bldg, cnr Av 1 & Calle 0; Playa ☎ 204-3203; cnr Av 5ta & 112).

**Cubacar** (☎ 204-1707) has an office across the street from Hotel El Viejo y El Mar at the Marina Hemingway, plus at the Chateau Miramar, the Bello Caribe and the Meliá Habana.

**Via Rent-a-Car** (☎ 24 34 29) has an office opposite the Hotel El Bosque in Kohly district of Miramar.

There are Servi-Cupet gas stations at Av 31, between Calles 18 and 20, in Miramar; on the corner of Calle 72 and Av 41 in Marianao (near the Tropicana); and on the traffic circle at Av 5 and Calle 112 in Cubanacán. Oro Negro is at Av 5 and Calle 120, Cubanacán. All are open 24 hours.

## PARQUE LENIN AREA

Parque Lenin, off the Calzada de Bejucal in Arroyo Naranjo, 20km south of central Habana, is the city's largest recreational area. Constructed between 1969 and 1972, this is one of the few developments in Habana from that era. These 670 hectares of green parkland and beautiful old trees surround an artificial lake, the Embalse Paso Sequito, just west of the much larger Embalse Ejército Rebelde.

Although the park itself is attractive enough, the mish-mash of available facilities inside has fallen on hard times since the onset of the *período especial*. Taxi drivers will wax nostalgic about when 'Lenin' was an idyllic weekend getaway for scores of pleasure-seeking Habana families, though these days the place retains more of a neglected and surreal air. Fortunately help is on the way. New management is currently in the throes of a major renovation project to bring the park back to its former glory. Expect some of this information to have changed by the time you read it.

### Sights

The main things to see are south of the lake, including the **Galería de Arte Amelia Peláez** (admission CUC$1). Up the hill there's a dramatic white marble **monument to Lenin** (1984) by the Soviet sculptor LE Kerbel, and west along the lake is an overgrown **amphitheater** and an **aquarium** (admission CUC$2; 10am-5pm Tue-Sun, closed Mon) with freshwater fish and crocodiles. The 1985 bronze **monument to Celia Sánchez** (now deceased), a longtime associate of Fidel Castro who was instrumental in having Parque Lenin built, is rather hidden beyond the aquarium. A **ceramics workshop** is nearby.

Most of these attractions are open 9am to 5pm Tuesday to Sunday, and admission to the park itself is free. You can rent a **rowboat** on the Embalse Paso Sequito from a dock behind the **Rodeo Nacional**. A 9km **narrow-gauge railway** with four stops operates inside the park from 10am to 3pm Wednesday to Sunday.

A visit to Parque Lenin can be combined with a trip to **ExpoCuba**, (☎ 66 42 92; admission CUC$1; 9am-5pm Wed-Sun) at Calabazar on the Carretera del Rocío in Arroyo Naranjo, 3km south of Las Ruinas restaurant. Opened in 1989, this large permanent exhibition showcases Cuba's economic and scientific achievements in 25 pavilions based on themes such as sugar, farming, apiculture, animal science, fishing, construction, food, geology, sports and defense. Cubans visiting ExpoCuba flock to the amusement park at the center of the complex, bypassing the rather dry propaganda displays. **Don Cuba** (☎ 57 82 87), a revolving restaurant is atop a tower. The Feria Internacional de La Habana, Cuba's largest trade fair, is held at ExpoCuba the first week of November. Parking is available at Gate E, at the south end of the complex (CUC$1).

Across the highway from ExpoCuba is the 600-hectare **Jardín Botánico Nacional** (☎ 54 93 65; admission CUC$1; 8:30am-4:30pm Wed-Sun). The **Pabellones de Exposición** (1987), near the entry gate, is a series of greenhouses with cactuses and tropicals, while 2km beyond is the tranquil **Japanese Garden** (1992). Nearby is the celebrated **Restaurante El Bambú**, where a vegetarian buffet is CUC$14 (see the boxed text, p128). The tractor train ride around the park departs four times a day and costs CUC$3, gardens admission included. Parking costs CUC$2.

The extensive **Parque Zoológico Nacional** (☎ 44 76 13; adult/child CUC$3/2; 9am-3:30pm Wed-Sun) off Calzada de Bejucal, on Av Zoo-Lenin in Boyeros, is 2km west of the Parque Lenin riding school. Worlds apart from the inner-city zoo at Av 26 near the Víazul terminal in Nuevo Vedado, with its stagnant crocodile ponds and jail cells for cages, this is more of a zoo/safari park where rhinos, hippos and other imported fauna have free reign. A trolley bus tours the grounds all day (included in admission). The caged animals (big cats, primates etc) are more akin to Latin American zoo-style.

### Activities

In the northwestern corner of Parque Lenin, behind Motel La Herradura, is the **Club Hípico Iberoamericano** (☎ 44 10 58; 9am-5pm). Horseback riding through the park on a steed rented from the club costs CUC$12 an hour, but horses rented from boys at the nearby amusement park (currently undergoing major renovations) or at the entrance to Parque Lenin proper (you'll be besieged) costs CUC$3 per hour, guide included. Keep an eye out for undernourished or maltreated horses.

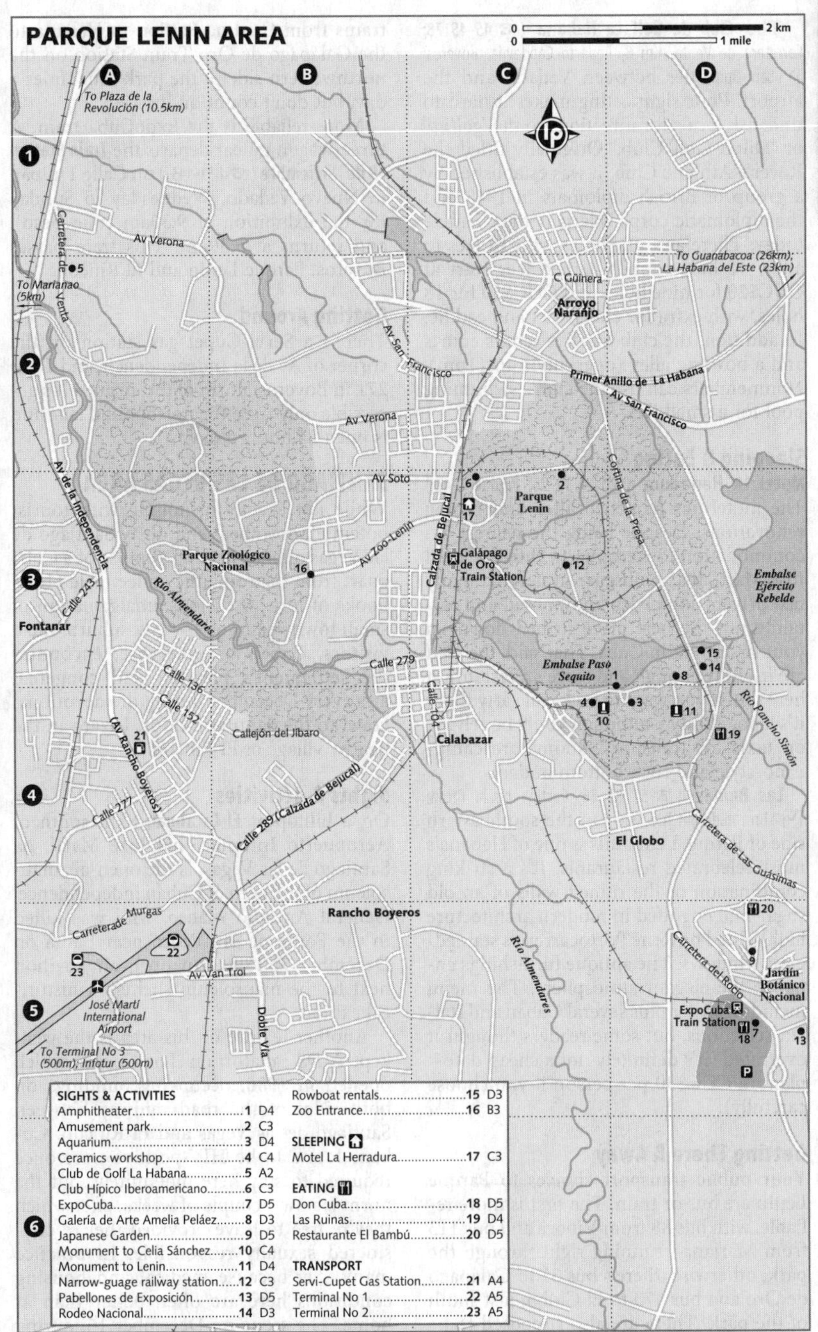
PARQUE LENIN AREA
0 2 km
0 1 mile
To Plaza de la Revolución (10.5km)
To Marianao (5km)
To Guanabacoa (26km); La Habana del Este (23km)
To Terminal No 3 (500m); Infotur (500m)
Carretera de Venta
Av Verona
C Güinera
Arroyo Naranjo
Av San Francisco
Primer Anillo de La Habana
Av Soto
Parque Lenin
Cortina de la Presa
Av de la Independencia
Parque Zoológico Nacional
Av Zoo-Lenin
Calzada de Bejucal
Galápago de Oro Train Station
Embalse Ejército Rebelde
Calle 243
Fontanar
Río Almendares
Calle 279
Embalse Paso Sequito
Calle 136
Calle 152
Callejón del Jíbaro
Calle 104
Calabazar
Río Pancho Simón
(Av Rancho Boyeros)
Calle 277
Calle 289 (Calzada de Bejucal)
El Globo
Carretera de Las Guásimas
Carreterade Murgas
Rancho Boyeros
Av Van Trol
José Martí International Airport
Doble Vía
Carretera del Rocío
Jardín Botánico Nacional
ExpoCuba Train Station
SIGHTS & ACTIVITIES
Amphitheater 1 D4
Amusement park 2 C3
Aquarium 3 D4
Ceramics workshop 4 C4
Club de Golf La Habana 5 A2
Club Hípico Iberoamericano 6 C3
ExpoCuba 7 D5
Galería de Arte Amelia Peláez 8 D3
Japanese Garden 9 D5
Monument to Celia Sánchez 10 C4
Monument to Lenin 11 D4
Narrow-guage railway station 12 C3
Pabellones de Exposición 13 D5
Rodeo Nacional 14 D3
Rowboat rentals 15 D3
Zoo Entrance 16 B3
SLEEPING
Motel La Herradura 17 C3
EATING
Don Cuba 18 D5
Las Ruinas 19 D4
Restaurante El Bambú 20 D5
TRANSPORT
Servi-Cupet Gas Station 21 A4
Terminal No 1 22 A5
Terminal No 2 23 A5

The **Club de Golf La Habana** (☎ 45 45 78; Carretera de Venta, Km 8, Reparto Capdevila, Boyeros; 🕑 8am-8pm) lies between Vedado and the airport. Poor signposting makes it hard to find: ask locals for directions to the '*golfito*' or 'Dilpo Golf Club.' Originally titled the Rover's Athletic Club, it was established by a group of British diplomats in 1948 and the diplomatic corps is largely the clientele today. There are nine holes with 18 tees to allow 18-hole rounds. Green fees start at CUC$20 for nine holes and CUC$30 for 18 holes, with extra for clubs, cart and caddie. In addition, the club has five tennis courts and a bowling alley (open noon to 11pm). Nonmembers can use the club's swimming pool for a small fee.

### Sleeping & Eating

**Motel La Herradura** (☎ 44 30 26; Parque Lenin) The motel has reopened after undergoing renovations. Despite being the nearest accommodation to Aeropuerto Internacional José Martí, it's an obscure motel that many taxi drivers don't even know about and certainly not the best place to bed down on your first night in Cuba. That said, the staff are friendly enough and there's a restaurant here too. If you want to make an early flight it's a possibility – although you'll be relying on taxis for transport. Rooms are campismo-style and rock-bottom budget.

**Las Ruinas** (☎ 57 82 86; Cortina de la Presa; 🕑 11am-midnight Tue-Sun) On the southeastern side of Parque Lenin this is one of Habana's most celebrated restaurants. It's a striking combination of the ruined walls of an old sugar mill engulfed in modern architecture highlighted by René Portocarrero's stained-glass windows. The antique furnishings enhance the elegant atmosphere. The menu includes lobster plus several Cuban and Italian selections, but some readers thought it overrated (it's definitely not a cheap date – plan on CUC$30 per person if you choose carefully).

### Getting There & Away

Your public transport choices to Parque Lenin are bus or train. The first is more reliable, with bus 88 from Víbora and bus 113 from Marianao running right through the park; otherwise, there's bus 31 to Galápago de Oro and bus 473 to El Globo, just south of the park. There are also supposed to be trains from Cristina Station in Habana to the Galápago de Oro Train Station on the northwestern side of the park four times a day, but don't count on it.

More reliable is the ExpoCuba train. A three-wagon railcar departs the **Train Station 19 de Noviembre** (☎ 881-4431) on Calle Tulipán in Nuevo Vedado, Wednesday to Sunday for the exhibition at 9:30am (one peso), and returns at 5:30pm. This train passes Boyeros, Parque Lenin and El Rincón.

### Getting Around

There's a Servi-Cupet gas station on the corner of Av de la Independencia and Calle 271 in Boyeros, north of the airport. It's accessible only from the northbound lane and is open 24 hours a day.

## SANTIAGO DE LAS VEGAS AREA

While not exactly brimming with tourist potential, downbeat and dusty Santiago de las Vegas offers a fleeting glimpse of a Cuba apart from the romantic coffee table photo books of lore. A curious amalgamation of small town versus sleepy city suburb, most visitors, Cuban or otherwise, encounter the settlement's pleasant and congenial airs every December during the devotional crawl to the Santuario de an Lázaro in the nearby village of El Rincón.

### Sights & Activities

On a hilltop at **El Cacahual**, 8km south of Aeropuerto Internacional José Martí via Santiago de las Vegas, is the open-air mausoleum of the hero of Cuban independence, General Antonio Maceo, who was killed in the Battle of San Pedro near Bauta on December 7, 1896. An open-air pavilion next to the mausoleum shelters a historical exhibit.

Another feature of this area is the well-kept AIDS sanatorium 'Los Cocos,' which opened in 1986, occupying buildings on both sides of the road midway between Santiago de las Vegas and El Rincón. Cubans found to be HIV-positive were once required to stay here indefinitely, but the norm is now a couple of weeks, after which they're free to leave provided they're considered sexually responsible. In practice many stay because medical and housing conditions here are often better than at home. The scene on December 16, during the Procession of San Lázaro, with many patients pressed against the fence flirting and conversing on living with HIV with passersby is what the Cuban character is all about, as it's socializing, questioning, joking and educating all in one.

### Getting There & Away

To get here, take the M-2 Metro Bus from Parque de la Fraternidad in Habana to Santiago de las Vegas. Bus 476 between Santiago de las Vegas and La Ceiba passes both the AIDS sanatorium and the sanctuary. On December 16, trains run all night from Train Station 19 de Noviembre, on Calle Tulipán in Nuevo Vedado (one peso).

## REGLA

**pop 42,390**

The old town of Regla, just across the harbor from Habana Vieja, is an industrial port town known as a center of Afro-Cuban religions, including the all-male secret society Abakúa. Several *babalawos* (Santería priests) reside in Regla, and it's not hard to find one if you're in need of advice (in Spanish). Long before the triumph of the 1959 revolution, Regla was known as the Sierra Chiquita (Little Sierra, after the Sierra Maestra) for its revolutionary traditions. This working-class neighborhood is also notable for a large thermoelectric power plant and shipyard. Regla is almost free of tourist trappings, and makes a nice afternoon out of the city; the skyline views from this side of the harbor offer perspective. There are lots of little peso food items for sale along Martí, a good vegetable market and lots of local street scenes.

### Sights & Activities

Beyond a huge ceiba tree on Santuario, in front of you as you get off the ferry, is the **Iglesia de Nuestra Señora de Regla** (☎ 97 62 88; 🕑 7:30am-6pm) with La Santísima Virgen de Regla on the main altar. This black Madonna is associated with Yemayá, the *orisha* (deity) of the ocean and patron of sailors (always represented in blue). Legend claims this image was carved by St Augustine 'The African' in the 5th century, and that in the year AD 453 a disciple brought the statue to Spain to safeguard it from barbarians. The small vessel in which the image was traveling survived a storm in the Strait of Gibraltar, so the figure was recognized as the patron of sailors. These days, rafters attempting to reach the US also evoke the protection of the Black Virgin.

In the early 17th century a hut was built at Regla to shelter a copy of the image, and when this was destroyed during a hurricane, a new Virgen de Regla was brought from Spain in 1664. In 1714 Nuestra Señora de Regla was proclaimed patron of Bahía de La Habana. A pilgrimage is celebrated here on September 7, when the image is taken out for a **procession** through the streets. **Mass** is said at 8am Tuesday, Wednesday, Friday, Saturday and Sunday, and on Sunday a second Mass is said at 5pm. There is no better (public) place to see the layering and transference between Catholic beliefs and African traditions than in this church. A branch of the Museo Municipal de Regla is next door.

To visit a *babalawo* is not impossible if you've got a bit of time and are willing to do a bit of do-it-yourself hunting around. You'll probably be presented with protective beads and/or prescriptions for treatment. A donation left on the altar in the living room is expected (CUC$5). One

> **THE PROCESSION OF SAN LÁZARO**
>
> There can be few pilgrimages more powerful or disturbing than the devotional crawl to the Santuario de San Lázaro in Santiago de las Vegas that takes place each December 16 on the outskirts of Habana. Every year up to 50,000 Cubans descend en masse on the venerated shrine of Lazarus – a Christian saint known for his ministrations to lepers and the poor – some on bloodied knees; others dragging themselves prostrate across the asphalt or walking barefoot for kilometers through the night to exorcise evil spirits and pay off debts for miracles granted.
>
> Along the long and winding route offerings of flowers, candles and coins are made to the impoverished figure of San Lázaro, a figure paralleled in Afro-Cuban Santería by the *orisha* (deity) Babalú Ayé, the god of sick ness. By the time the church's bells chime at midnight in an atmosphere heavy with cigar fumes, idolatry and heartfelt petition, the distinction is barely necessary.

famous Regla *babalawo* is **Eberardo Marero** (Ñico López No 60 btwn Coyola & Camilo Cienfuegos), and others live nearby.

The main outpost of the **Museo Municipal de Regla** (☎ 97 69 89; Martí No 158; admission CUC$2; 9am-5pm Mon-Sat, 9am-1pm Sun) is a couple of blocks straight up the main street from the ferry. It records the history of Regla and its Afro-Cuban religions, and there's an interesting, small exhibit on Remigio Herrero, first *babalawo* of Regla, as well as a bizarre statue of Napoleon with his nose missing. An **Observatorio Astronómico** was established in the museum building in 1921. Price of admission includes both museum outposts and the Colina Lenin exhibit.

From the museum head straight (south) on Martí past **Parque Guaicanamar**, and turn left on Albuquerque and right on 24 de Febrero, the road to Guanabacoa. About 1.5km from the ferry you'll see a high metal stairway that gives access to **Colina Lenin**. In 1924 Antonio Bosch, the socialist mayor of Regla, created a monument to Lenin's death, one of the first of its kind outside the USSR. Above the monolithic image of Lenin is an olive tree planted by Bosch surrounded by seven lithe figures; unlike many other Soviet-inspired monuments you'll find in Cuba, this one imbues hope. Maybe it's the fine harbor views from here. A small exhibition on the history of Colina Lenin is in a pavilion on the back side of the hill (it's often closed).

## Getting There & Away

Regla is easily accessible on the regular passenger ferry that departs every 10 minutes (10 centavos) from Muelle Luz, San Pedro and Santa Clara, in Habana Vieja. Bicycles are readily accepted via a separate line that boards first. Bus 29 runs to Guanabacoa from Parque Maceo between the ferry terminal and the Museo Municipal de Regla, but the boat is much more fun.

# GUANABACOA

**pop 106,374**

In the 1540s the Spanish conquerors concentrated the few surviving indigenous people at Guanabacoa, 5km east of central Habana. A town was founded here in 1607, and this later became a center of the slave trade. In 1762 the British occupied

### URBAN AGRICULTURE

In 1991 with the Soviet Union consigned forever to the garbage can of history, Cuba waved goodbye to over 1.3 million tons of chemical fertilizers. Almost overnight an agricultural sector based on oil-derived pesticides and intensive modern farming techniques slipped into a life-threatening coma.

In a desperate bid to offset countrywide food shortages on a massive scale the Cuban government initiated the so-called Urban Agricultural Program, a pioneering scheme of drastic austerity measures that sponsored new organic farming techniques and outlawed the use of chemical pesticides for good.

In Habana where the problem of food security was particularly acute, the authorities aimed to reduce transport, refrigeration and storage costs by moving agricultural production closer to the city. In a flurry of land reclamation schemes garbage dumps, ornamental gardens, railway sidings and private balconies were hastily requisitioned by community groups and converted into *organipónicos* (urban vegetable gardens).

Varying in size from a few square meters to 3 hectares these pioneering vegetable gardens – farmed by a mixture of individuals, families and local community groups – helped to foster the implementation of such eco-friendly practices as nutrient recycling, soil and water management, and land-use planning.

For environmentalists, the scheme was a triumph in green thinking and ecological innovation. As well as providing up to 30% of Cuba's daily food requirements through the provision of fresh, homegrown produce, urban agriculture has also served to empower fragmented communities, renew local solidarity and clear up urban eyesores with vivid splashes of greenery.

Today the program returns an annual yield of 3.7 million tons from a land base of approximately 45,000 hectares. The project has also had a marked social impact creating 320,000 new jobs countrywide.

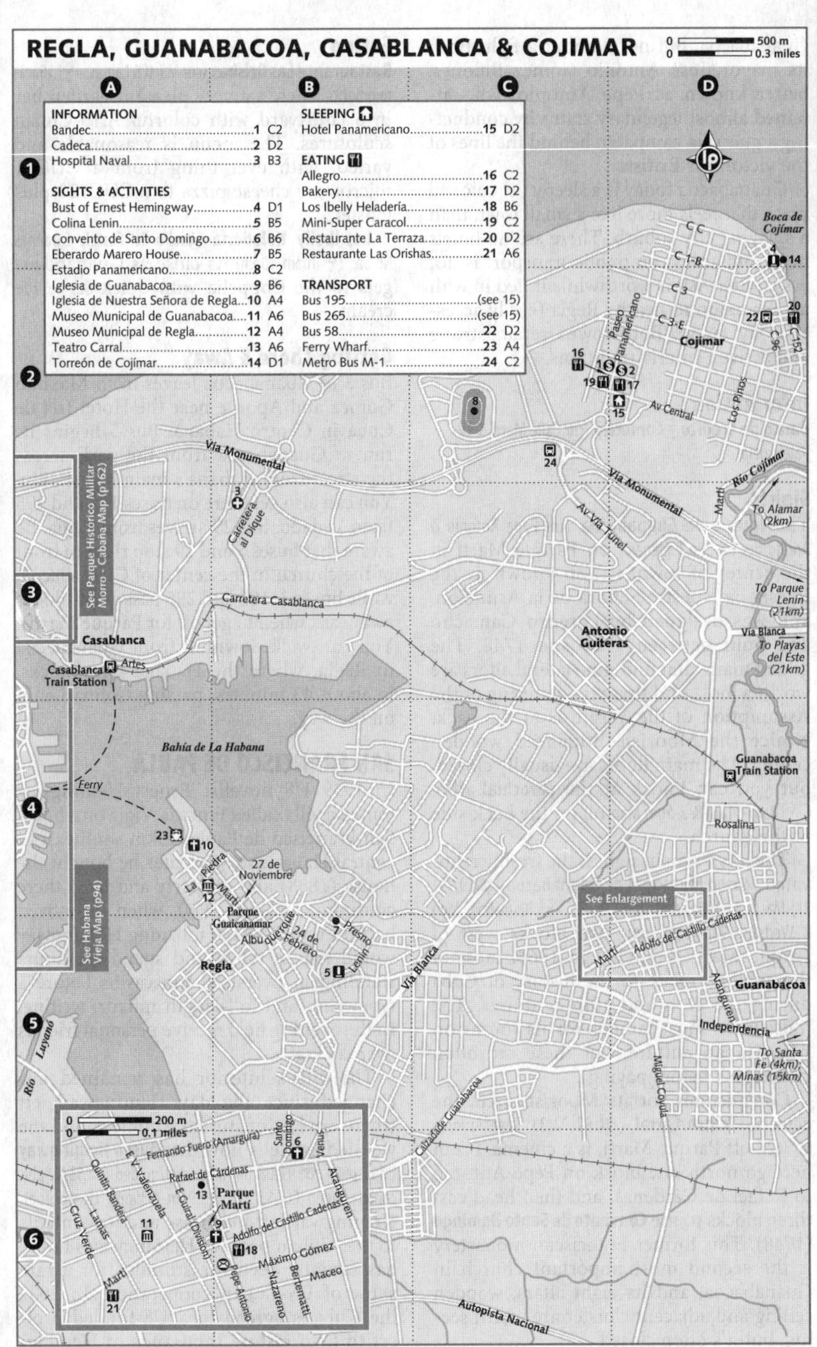
REGLA, GUANABACOA, CASABLANCA & COJIMAR
0 500 m
0 0.3 miles
INFORMATION
Bandec 1 C2
Cadeca 2 D2
Hospital Naval 3 B3
SIGHTS & ACTIVITIES
Bust of Ernest Hemingway 4 D1
Colina Lenin 5 B5
Convento de Santo Domingo 6 B6
Eberardo Marero House 7 B5
Estadio Panamericano 8 C2
Iglesia de Guanabacoa 9 B6
Iglesia de Nuestra Señora de Regla 10 A4
Museo Municipal de Guanabacoa 11 A6
Museo Municipal de Regla 12 A4
Teatro Carral 13 A6
Torreón de Cojímar 14 D1
SLEEPING
Hotel Panamericano 15 D2
EATING
Allegro 16 C2
Bakery 17 D2
Los Ibelly Heladería 18 B6
Mini-Super Caracol 19 C2
Restaurante La Terraza 20 D2
Restaurante Las Orishas 21 A6
TRANSPORT
Bus 195 (see 15)
Bus 265 (see 15)
Bus 58 22 D2
Ferry Wharf 23 A4
Metro Bus M-1 24 C2
Boca de Cojímar
Cojímar
Paseo Panamericano
Av Central
Los Pinos
Vía Monumental
Carretera al Dique
Río Cojímar
To Alamar (2km)
Av Vía Tunel
To Parque Lenin (21km)
Vía Blanca
To Playas del Este (21km)
Carretera Casablanca
Casablanca
Casablanca Train Station
Artes
Antonio Guiteras
See Parque Histórico Militar Morro - Cabaña Map (p162)
Bahía de La Habana
Ferry
Guanabacoa Train Station
Rosalina
27 de Noviembre
La Piedra
Martí
Parque Guaicanamar
Albuquerque
24 de Febrero
Presno
Lenin
Regla
See Habana Vieja Map (p94)
See Enlargement
Adolfo del Castillo Cadenas
Guanabacoa
Aranguren
Independencia
To Santa Fe (4km); Minas (15km)
Miguel Coyula
Río Luyanó
Calzada de Guanabacoa
Autopista Nacional
0 200 m
0 0.1 miles
Fernando Fuero (Amargura)
Santo Domingo
Venus
Quintín Bandera
E V Valenzuela
Rafael de Cárdenas
E Guiral (División)
Parque Martí
Lamas
Cruz Verde
Máximo Gómez
Pepe Antonio
Nazareno
Bertemattí
Maceo

Guanabacoa, but not without a fight from its mayor, José Antonio Gómez Bulones, better known as Pepe Antonio, who attained almost legendary status by conducting a guerrilla campaign behind the lines of the victorious British.

Guanabacoa today is a sleepy yet colorful place that feels more like a small town than a splaying city suburb. There are no hotels here, and access on public transport is not easy, but a visit is worthwhile if tied in with an excursion to nearby Regla (easily accessible by ferry). Both towns retain strong and active Santería traditions.

## Information

**Banco de Crédito y Comercio** (cnr Calle Martí & EV Valenzuela)

## Sights

The **Iglesia de Guanabacoa** (cnr Pepe Antonio & Adolfo del Castillo Cadenas), on Parque Martí in the center of town, is also known as the Iglesia de Nuestra Señora de la Asunción, and was designed by Lorenzo Camacho and built between 1721 and 1748. The gilded main altar and nine lateral altars are worth a look, and there is a painting of the Assumption of the Virgin is at the back. Notice the Moorish-influenced wooden ceiling. The main doors are usually closed, but you can knock at the **parochial office** (🕑 8am-11am & 2-5pm Mon-Fri) on the back side of the church.

The town's main sight is the freshly renovated **Museo Municipal de Guanabacoa** (☎ 97 91 17; Martí No 108; admission CUC$2; 🕑 10am-6pm Mon & Wed-Sat, 9am-1pm Sun), two blocks west of Parque Martí. Founded in 1964, most of the exhibits relate to the history of Cuba during the 18th and 19th centuries. The museum is most famous for its rooms on Afro-Cuban culture, but these are often closed (ask before paying).

Conspicuous for its Moorish arch, the eclectic **Teatro Carral** (☎ 97 92 33; Pepe Antonio No 362), off Parque Martí, is a cinema. From here go north one block on Pepe Antonio to Rafael de Cárdenas, and then head east three blocks to the **Convento de Santo Domingo** (1748). This former Franciscan monastery is the second most important church in Guanabacoa, and its eight altars, wooden ceiling and adjacent cloister are worth seeing, but it's often closed.

## Eating

**Restaurante Las Orishas** (cnr Martí & Lamas; 🕑 10am-midnight) There's a very pleasant garden bar in a courtyard with colorful Afro-Cuban sculptures. The menu is reasonable and varied, with everything from a CUC$1 microwave cheese pizza to a CUC$20-plus lobster.

**Los Ibelly Heladería** (Adolfo del Castillo Cárdenas No 5a; 🕑 10am-10pm) As close as Guanabocoa gets to the Coppelia with quick-serve ice cream.

## Getting There & Away

Bus 3 to Guanabacoa leaves from Máximo Gómez and Aponte near the Hotel Isla de Cuba in Centro Habana. Bus 5 begins its run to Guanabacoa from the park across the street from Habana's main bus station. You can also get there on buses 195 and 295 from Vedado. Bus 29 arrives from Regla. Be aware that buses 5 and 29 stop right in front of the church in the center of Guanabacoa, while buses 3, 195 and 295 pass a few blocks away (ask when to get off for Parque Martí). You can walk downhill from Guanabacoa to Regla, where the Habana ferry docks, in about 45 minutes, passing Colina Lenin on the way.

# SAN FRANCISCO DE PAULA

In 1939 US novelist Ernest Hemingway rented a villa called Finca la Vigía on a hill at San Francisco de Paula, 15km southeast of central Habana. A year later he bought the house (1888) and property and lived there continuously until 1960, when he moved back to the US. Each morning Hemingway would rise at dawn and spend six hours standing in oversized moccasins before a typewriter and full-length mirror, writing. In the evening he'd receive personal friends over cocktails.

The villa's interior has remained unchanged since the day Hemingway left (there are lots of stuffed trophies), and the wooded estate is now the **Museo Hemingway** (Map p90; ☎ 91 08 09; unguided/guided CUC$3/4, plus camera/video CUC$5/25; 🕑 9am-4:30pm, closed Tue). Hemingway left his house and its contents to the 'Cuban people.' Hemingway's house has recently been the stimulus for a rare show of US-Cuban cooperation. In 2002 the Cubans agreed to a US-funded project to help restore thousands of Hemingway artifacts from Finca La Vigía and in May 2006 11,000 documents relating to Hemingway's work were sent to the JFK Presidential library in America for digitalization. To prevent the pilfering of objects, visitors are not allowed inside the house, but there are enough open doors and windows to allow a proper glimpse into Papa's universe. There are books everywhere (including beside the toilet), a large Victrola and record collection and an astounding number of knickknacks. Don't come when it's raining as the house itself will be closed. A stroll through the garden is worthwhile to see the surprisingly sentimental dog cemetery, Hemingway's fishing boat *El Pilar* and the pool where actress Ava Gardner once swam naked. You can chill out on a chaise lounge below whispering palms and bamboo here.

At the time of writing most of the house was closed for major renovations. Check the current situation in your Habana hotel or tourist agency before setting out.

To reach San Francisco de Paula, take Metro Bus M-7 (Cotorro) from Industria, between Dragones and Av Simón Bolívar, on Parque de la Fraternidad, in Centro Habana. You'll go eight stops to San Miguel del Padrón.

## SANTA MARÍA DEL ROSARIO

**☎ 6820**

Santa María del Rosario, 19km southeast of central Habana, is an old colonial town founded in 1732. Unlike most other towns from that period it has not become engulfed in modern suburbs, but stands alone in the countryside. The charms of this area were recognized by one of Cuba's greatest living painters, Manuel Mendive, who selected it for his personal residence. You can also see the countryside of this area in Tomás Gutiérrez Alea's metaphorical critique of slavery in his movie *La Última Cena.*

The **Iglesia de Nuestra Señora del Rosario** (🕒 5:30-7:30pm) also called the Catedral de los Campos de Cuba, on Santa María del Rosario's old town square, was built in 1720 by the Conde de Casa Bayona near the Quiebra Hacha Sugar Mill, of which nothing remains today. Inside are a gilded mahogany altar and a painting by Veronese.

On a rear wall of the **Casa de la Cultura**, opposite the church, is a great mural by Manuel Mendive depicting the legends of this region.

From Habana take the Metro Bus M-7 to Cotorro and then bus 97, which runs from Guanabacoa to town.

## PARQUE HISTÓRICO MILITAR MORRO-CABAÑA

The sweeping views of Habana from the other side of the bay are lovely and a trip to the two old forts of the **Parque Histórico Militar Morro-Cabaña** is worthwhile. It gets very hot around midday with the sun pounding down; beat the heat with a drink at one of the shoreline bars or restaurants or come at sunset – sensational. All the Habana travel agencies offer tours here; the **cañonazo ceremony** (p115) is especially popular (without/with dinner CUC$15/25).

The **Castillo de los Tres Santos Reyes Magnos del Morro** (El Morro; per person incl museum entrance CUC$4) was erected between 1589 and 1630 on an abrupt limestone headland to protect the entrance to the harbor. In 1762 the British captured El Morro by attacking from the landward side and digging a tunnel under the walls. The castle's gallant Spanish commander, Don Luís de Velasco, was killed in the battle, and the British buried him with full military honors. In 1845 a lighthouse was added to the castle, the first in Cuba. Since 1986 the castle has hosted a **maritime museum** (☎ 863-7941; guide CUC$1, plus camera CUC$2; 🕒 8am-8pm). To climb to the top of the lighthouse is an additional CUC$2.

The **Fortaleza de San Carlos de la Cabaña** (La Cabaña; ☎ 862-0617; admission day CUC$4, night CUC$6, guide CUC$1; 🕒 8am-11pm) was built between 1763 and 1774 to deny the long ridge overlooking Habana to attackers. It's one of the largest colonial fortresses in the Americas, replete with grassy moats, ancient chapel, cobblestone streets and shops inside. It cost so much to build, Carlos III of Spain supposedly tried to spy it through a telescope, convinced it must be visible from Madrid. During the 19th century, Cuban patriots faced firing squads in the **Foso de los Laureles** outside La Cabaña's southeastern wall. Dictators Machado and Batista used the fortress as a military prison, and immediately after the revolution, Che Guevara set up his headquarters there. Be sure to visit the creative Habana skyline **mirador** (lookout) on the other side of the **Museo de Comandancia**

**del Che** here. Later it served as a military academy.

Visitors are welcome to see the collection of armaments at the **Museo Fortificaciones y Armas**. Nightly at 9pm a cannon is fired on the harbor side of La Cabaña by a squad attired in 19th-century uniforms, a hold-over from Spanish times when such a shot signaled that the city gates were closing. The **cañonazo** begins at 8:30pm and is included in the regular admission price (as is the concert following by Moncada, a locally famous geriatric rock band). A smaller cannon, with equally overdressed young men, is shot off daily at 3pm.

Surprisingly, almost no tourists visit the more interesting La Cabaña, while El Morro is usually jammed (tour buses unload their masses at El Morro but never have time for La Cabaña). Around mid-morning it's especially chaotic at El Morro, as the tour buses from Varadero stop there on their way to Habana, so you'll need to plan accordingly. The annual Feria Internacional del Libro is held at El Morro each January.

## Eating

**Paladar Doña Carmela** (☎ 863-6048; Calle B No 10; ⏲ evenings only) A private eating option that offers quality chicken and pork in a very pleasant al fresco setting (when it's open). Makes a good dinner before or after the *cañonazo,* but check ahead as opening times are sporadic.

Parts of the fortresses have been converted into good restaurants and atmospheric bars. The **Restaurante Los Doce Apóstoles** (☎ 863-8295; ⏲ noon-11pm) below El Morro, so named for the battery of 12 cannons atop its ramparts, serves *comida criolla.* It's a better-than-average government-run kitchen, and the prices are fair. **Bar El Polvorín** (☎ 860-9990; ⏲ 10am-4am) just beyond Los Doce Apóstoles, offers drinks and light snacks on a patio overlooking the bay. There's zero shade, but it's perfect for those famous Habana sunsets.

Back below La Cabaña, just beyond the Dársena de los Franceses, is another battery of huge 18th-century cannons. The upscale but approachable **Restaurante La Divina Pastora** (☎ 860-8341; ⏲ noon-11pm) behind the guns, offers well-prepared seafood, including lobster and fish. You can also just sit and soak in the views with an icy Cristal and some crisp *tostones*.

### Getting There & Away

Cyclists can get to the fortresses from Habana with the specially designed Ciclo-Bus leaving from Dragones and Águila on Parque El Curita (Map p100). This seatless bus is accessible via small ramps that lead to the doors. Cyclists are obliged to use it to get to La Habana del Este as riding a bicycle through the tunnel is prohibited. If you don't have a bicycle, you can walk to the head of the line and get on the first bus (ask the person selling bus tickets). Get off at the first stop after the tunnel; it's only a 10-minute walk back to either fortress. You can also get there on the pink M-1 Metro Bus, (get off at the first stop after the tunnel), but make sure you're near an exit as very few other people get out there. Otherwise, a metered tourist taxi from Habana Vieja should cost around CUC$3.

An interesting way to return to Habana is via the Casablanca ferry. From the entrance to La Cabaña, go down into the moat and follow it around to a gate just below the huge Christ statue.

Parking costs CUC$1 at the fortresses.

## CASABLANCA

Casablanca, just across the harbor from Habana Vieja, is best known for its towering white marble **Estatua de Cristo**, created in 1958 by J Madera. As you disembark the harbor ferry, keep going straight up the stairway in front of you. Follow the road on the left to the impressive, but discordant, statue – an easy 10-minute walk. There's a splendid view of Habana from the statue (a popular nighttime hang-out spot), and a 24-hour snack bar at its base. You can reach the fortress of La Cabaña from this side via a red gate at the switchback in the road on your way up to the statue. Behind the statue is the **Observatorio Nacional** (closed to tourists).

The **Hospital Naval** (☎ 62 68 25), off the Vía Monumental in La Habana del Este, northeast of Casablanca, has a recompression chamber accessible 24 hours a day.

Passenger ferries to Casablanca depart Muelle Luz, San Pedro and Santa Clara, in Habana Vieja, about every 15 minutes (10 centavos). Bicycles are welcome.

The **Casablanca train station** (☎ 862-4888), next to the ferry wharf, is the western terminus of the only electric railway in Cuba. In 1917 the Hershey Chocolate Company of the US state of Pennsylvania built this line to Matanzas, and trains still depart for Matanzas five times a day (currently at 4:46am, 8:35am, 12:48pm, 4:38pm and 8:46pm). The 8:35am service is an 'express.' You'll travel via Guanabo (CUC$0.80, 25km), Hershey (CUC$1.45, 46km), Jibacoa (CUC$1.65, 54km), and Canasí (CUC$1.95, 65km) to Matanzas (CUC$2.80, 90km). The train usually leaves Casablanca on time but often arrives an hour late. No one on a tight schedule should use this train. Apparently bicycles aren't allowed on this train, but try anyway. It's a scenic four- to five-hour trip, and tickets are easily obtainable at the station (except on weekends and holidays when it could be crowded).

## COJÍMAR AREA

Situated ten kilometers east of Habana is the little port town of Cojímar, famous for harboring Ernest Hemingway's fishing boat *El Pilar* in the 1940s and '50s. This picturesque, if slightly run-down, harbor community served as the prototype for the fishing village in Hemingway's novel *The Old Man and the Sea*, which won him the Nobel Prize for Literature in 1954. Cojímar native and fishing sage Gregorio Fuentes (recently deceased) inspired Hemingway's 'Old Man.' It was founded in 17th century at the mouth of the Río Cojímar; in 1762 an invading British army landed here; and in 1994, thousands of 'rafters' split from the sheltered but rocky bay, lured to Florida by US radio broadcasts and promises of political asylum.

If you're not a Hemingway devotee or particularly enamored of nondescript seaside villages, there's little reason to visit here.

### Information

**Bandec** (🕑 8:30am-3pm Mon-Fri, 8:30-11am Sat), which is just down the Paseo Panamericano, changes traveler's checks and gives cash advances. For Cuban pesos there's **Cadeca** (cnr Paseo Panamericano & 5D), just down the side street, across the avenue from Bandec.

### Sights

The huge 55,000-seat **Estadio Panamericano**, on the Vía Monumental between Habana and Cojímar, was built for the 1991 Pan-American Games and is already looking suitably dilapidated. There are also tennis courts, Olympic-sized swimming pools and other sporting facilities nearby.

Overlooking the harbor is the **Torreón de Cojímar**, an old Spanish fort (1649) presently occupied by the Cuban coast guard. Next to this tower and framed by a neoclassical archway is a gilded **bust of Ernest Hemingway** erected by the residents of Cojímar in 1962.

Ernest Hemingway's old captain, Gregorio Fuentes, lived in the green-and-white house at Calle 98 No 209, at the corner of 3D, five blocks up the hill from Restaurante La Terraza.

East across the river from Cojímar is Alamar, a large housing estate of prefabricated apartment blocks built by *micro brigadas* (small armies of workers responsible for building much of the post-revolutionary housing) beginning in 1971. Eye-catching architectural form trails way behind function in Cuban public housing, but it beats living on the streets.

### Sleeping

**Hotel Panamericano** (Av Central; ☎ 95 10 00/10; s/d incl breakfast low season CUC$45/59, high season CUC$54/71; P) At the entrance to Cojímar, 2km from the Hemingway bust, this four-story hotel was built in 1991 (though you could be forgiven for thinking it was 1961) to house athletes attending the 11th Pan-American Games. Inconveniently-located and a little rough around the edges, the establishment was housing Misión Milagros patients as of early 2006. Call ahead to check the status.

### Eating

**Restaurante La Terraza** (☎ 93 92 32; Calle 152 No 161; noon-11pm) Specializes in seafood such as stuffed squid (CUC$7) and paella (CUC$7 to CUC$15). The terrace dining room overlooking the bay is pleasant. More atmospheric, however, is the old bar out front (open 10:30am to 11pm) where a mojito is just CUC$1.75. Check out the classic wooden refrigerators and don't miss the B&W photos of Hemingway in the terrace dining room.

Just down from the Hotel Panamericano is a **bakery** (8am-8pm). Across the Paseo Panamericano is a grocery store, the **Mini-Super Caracol** (9am-8pm) and a clean and reasonably-priced Italian restaurant **Allegro** (noon-11pm) with lasagna, risotto, spaghetti and pizza all for CUC$4.

### Getting There & Away

Bus 58 from Av de la Independencia and Bruzón, near Habana's main bus station, reaches Cojímar. In Centro Habana, get this bus at Paseo de Martí No 59, near the Malecón. You can catch it back to Habana from Calle 92 in Cojímar, though it's sometimes full and won't stop.

Alternatively, catch the Metro Bus M-1 (Alamar) at the corner of Calles G and 27 in Vedado, or at Paseo de Martí No 563 opposite the Capitolio in Centro Habana, and get out at the third stop after the tunnel. Cross the highway to the Hotel Panamericano, from which it's around 2km downhill through the village to the Hemingway bust. Buses 195 and 265 from Habana also service the Hotel Panamericano.

## PLAYAS DEL ESTE

Habana's pine-fringed Riviera, Playas del Este, begins at Bacuranao, 18km east of central Habana, and continues to the east through Tarará, El Mégano, Santa María del Mar and Boca Ciega to the town of Guanabo, 27km from the capital. This is where all of Habana comes to lounge on soft white sands and bathe in aquamarine waters. About a dozen large resorts are scattered along this 9km stretch of beach, with the largest concentration at Santa María del Mar (Santa María). For a more affordable and local experience here, you can rent a private room in Guanabo (where most Cubans stay) or a little beach house in Boca Ciega. The latter is great for families, as are the spacious houses at Villa Marina Tarará.

The hotel area of Santa María is now heavily patrolled by uniformed security guards to keep prostitution in check, and the prostitutes withdrawn to the western end of El Mégano and Guanabo. If you come to Santa María with Cuban friends, expect the police to ask for their identification. If everything isn't in order, it's trouble. The heavy security presence makes this area safe and hassle-free, but it also eliminates much of the local color, and at times Santa María can be like a graveyard. You'll find Cuban families on the beach at Guanabo, Cuban holidaymakers at Boca Ciega, foreign tourists and their friends at Santa María, and men and women in search of each other at the western end of El Mégano. A very pretty part of Santa María is accessible from the parking area on Calle 13.

Cheap tour packages to Santa María are readily available in Canada and Europe, and the resorts provide a base from which you can visit Habana while enjoying a relaxing seaside holiday. Alternatively, these beaches provide an easy and effortless escape from Habana should you need feel the need for it. Access is simple: the Vía Blanca runs right along the back side of the seaside strip, and there are buses between Habana and Guanabo. However, those interested mostly in museums and historical sites would do better to stay in Habana itself.

Approximately 13,500 radiation-affected children and 2500 adults from Ukraine have received medical treatment at a sanatorium at Tarará since February 1989.

## Information

### MEDICAL SERVICES

**Clínica Internacional Habana del Este** (☎ 204-9385; Av de las Terrazas, Santa María) West of Calle 9. Open 24 hours and doctors can make hotel visits. There's also a well-stocked pharmacy on-site.

**Farmacia** (cnr Av 5 & Calle 466)

### MONEY

**Banco Popular de Ahorro** (☎ 96 22 69; Av 5 No 47810 btwn Calles 478 & 480, Guanabo; 🕑 8:30am-5:30pm Mon-Fri) Changes traveler's checks.

**Cadeca** Guanabo (Av 5 No 47614 btwn 476 & 478; 🕑 8am-6pm); Santa María (Edificio Los Corales, Av de las Terrazas btwn Calles 10 & 11)

### POST

**Post office** Guanabo (Av 5 btwn Calles 490 & 492; 🕑 8am-6pm Mon-Sat); Santa María (Edificio Los Corales, Av de las Terrazas btwn Calles 10 & 11; 🕑 7:30am-6:30pm)

### TELEPHONE

**Etecsa** (Edificio Los Corales, Av de las Terrazas btwn Calles 10 & 11)

### TOURIST INFORMATION

**Infotur** Guanabo (☎ 96 68 68; Av 5 btwn Calles 468 & 470); Santa María (☎ 96 11 11; Edificio Los Corales, Av Las Terrazas btwn Calles 10 & 11)

### TRAVEL AGENCIES

Cubatur and Havanatur both have desks at Hotel Tropicoco, between Avs del Sur and de las Terrazas in Santa María. Their main business is booking bus tours, though they might be willing to help with hotel reservations in other cities.

## Activities

Yacht charters, deep-sea fishing and scuba diving are offered by **Cubanacán Naútica Tarará** (☎ 96 15 08/9; VHF channels 16 & 77; cnr Av 8 & Calle 17, Tarará), 22km east of Habana. Ask about this at your hotel tour desk.

There are a number of **Club Nautica** points spaced along the beaches aside from **Club Megano** at the westernmost end of the Playas. The most central is outside Club Atlántico in the middle of Playa Santa María del Mar. Here you can rent pedal boats (CUC$6 per hour; four to six people), banana boats (CUC$5 for five minutes; maximum five people), one- and two-person kayaks (CUC$2/4 per hour), snorkel gear (CUC$4) and catamarans (CUC$12 per hour; maximum four people plus lifeguard). A paddle around the coast exploring the mangrove-choked canals is a pleasure.

Beach toys such as sailboards, water bikes and badminton gear may also be available; ask. Many people rent similar equipment all along the beach to Guanabo, but check any water vessels and gear carefully as we've received complaints about faulty equipment. Consider leaving a deposit instead of prepaying in full, should anything go awry.

## Sleeping

### GUANABO

**Hotel Gran Vía** (Islazul; ☎ 96 22 71; cnr Av 5 & Calle 462; s/d CUC$19/22; P ❄ 🍽) A good budget choice, but because there are only 10 rooms, it's quite difficult to get in. Not all are the same, so if you can look at a few, go for it. The hotel restaurant has a dirt-cheap menu, and a pleasant open-terrace bar is next to the hotel.

**Villa Playa Hermosa** (Islazul; ☎ 96 27 74; Av 5D btwn Calles 472 & 474; s/d low season CUC$18/25, high season CUC$20/29; P ❄ 🍽) This villa has 47

rooms in small single-story bungalows with shared bath and TV. It's a popular spot with vacationing Cubans, so expect music, dancing and drinking to all hours; the beach is nearby.

### PLAYA SANTA MARÍA DEL MAR

Some of the places listed here offer 'all-inclusive' rates that include meals, drinks, accommodation, water toys and (sometimes) bicycles.

**Aparthotel Atlántico** (Islazul; ☎ 97 14 94; Av de las Terrazas btwn Calles 11 & 12; 1/2/3-bedroom apt low season CUC$36/42/60, high season CUC$42/60/80; P) This hotel is just across the street from Club Atlántico. Families make up most of the clientele here. There are 60 apartments with cooking facilities in this four-story development. The two-bedroom units sleep four people and the three-bedrooms accommodate six, so it's great for a group. Ask specifically if your unit will have a fridge, as not all of them do. This is a decent-value choice that is just 100m from the beach.

**Aparthotel Las Terrazas** (Islazul; ☎ 97 13 44; Av del Sur btwn Calles 9 & 10; 1/2/3-bedroom apt low season CUC$36/54/63, high season CUC$50/75/88; P) A bit more upscale than Aparthotel Atlántico, the 154 apartments here have cooking facilities, fridges and TVs. The split-level pool is kind of cool and it's only 100m from the beach. The disco, apart from the hotel, is a popular night spot.

**Hotel Tropicoco** (Cubanacán; ☎ 97 13 71; btwn Av del Sur & Av de las Terrazas; s/d all-inclusive low season CUC$45/75, high season CUC$60/80; ) Picked up by Cubanacán from the now-defunct Horizontes chain, there's still a bit of work to be done to knock this big blue monster into shape. The food pretty much stinks, the pool is indoors and the disco has shut. The main benefit is the price: cheap, and the location: you could hit a (big) home-run onto the beach from here.

**Hotel Blau Club Arenal** (☎ 97 15 20; s/d all-inclusive low season CUC$70/100, high season CUC$95/150; P) Playas del Este's most stylish option, this modern hotel is on the Laguna Itabo, between Boca Ciega and Santa María del Mar. It has 166 rooms set around a translucent pool. Ground-floor rooms have patios but suites are much larger and cost

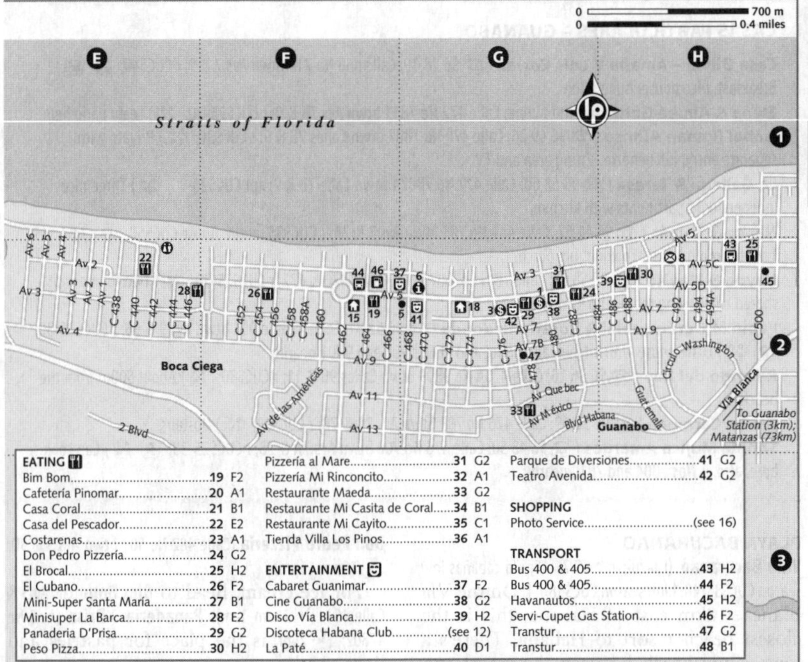


about 20% more. The beach is just 150m away via a wooden footbridge suspended over the lagoon (which you can explore by rowboat). If you want a peaceful setting that feels pleasantly secluded, this is your bag.

**Club Atlántico** (Gran Caribe; ☎ 97 10 85; fax 96 15 32; cnr Av de las Terrazas & Calle 11; s/d all-inclusive CUC$105/150; P) Right on the beach, the Atlántico – after the Blau – comes a close second in Playas del Este's high quality bracket. The 92 rooms are well equipped with fridge, satellite TV and little balconies. There are tennis courts, a swimming pool and cabaret. This stretch of beach also has a Club Náutica point renting boats, etc right next to the hotel.

### PLAYA EL MÉGANO

**Villa Los Pinos** (Gran Caribe; ☎ 97 13 61; fax 97 15 24; Av de las Terrazas No 21 btwn Calles 5 & 7; 2-bedroom house low/high season CUC$120/160) A terrific option if you're after private accommodation with style. The collection of houses here have kitchens, TVs and a personal feel (these were holiday getaways before the Cuban Revolution); the majority also have swimming pools, making them a great option for families when price isn't important. Three- (CUC$170/210) and four-bedroom (CUC$220/250) houses are also available.

### PLAYA TARARÁ

**Villa Marina Tarará** (Cubanacán; ☎ 97-1616/17; 1-/2-bedroom houses low season CUC$35/60, high season CUC$40/65) Reached through the Campamento de Pioneros José Martí off the Vía Blanca, 22km east of Habana. The entrance is poorly marked, so be alert. You have to show your passport and receive a pass before you can enter. This is truly a gated community and the well-maintained quiet streets are almost eerie in their order. They have houses with up to seven bedrooms, and the beach is small but nice here so it makes a good family or group getaway. The cheapest houses are far from the beach. Scuba diving, deep-sea fishing, and yachting are readily available at the marina, and there's a disco, swimming pool and gym.

**CASAS PARTICULARES – GUANABO**

**Casa Olivia – Amada V Lois Correa** (☎ 96 28 19; Calle 468 No 714 btwn Avs 7 & 9; r CUC$40; ) Breakfast, nice house, huge salon.

**Elena & Aimeé González** (no phone; Calle 472 No 7B11 btwn Avs 7B & 9; r CUC$25-30; ) Leafy patio here.

**Isabel Roman Alonso** (☎ 96 49 26; Calle 470 No 7B07 btwn Calles 7B & 9; r CUC$30; ) Private with separate entry, kitchenette, sitting area and TV.

**La Gallega & Teresa** (☎ 96 68 60; Calle 472 No 7B07A btwn Calle 7B & 9; apt CUC$25-30; ) Three nice independent apartments with kitchen.

**Nancy & Tomás** (☎ 96 41 57; Calle 444 No 701 btwn Avs 7 & 7A; r CUC$35, entire house CUC$50; P ) Two-bedroom house; cooking; big porch.

**Neyda & Mayito** (☎ 96 58 62; Calle 7B No 47007 btwn Calles 470 & 472; r CUC$25-30; ) Two rooms with shared bath, living room, and kitchen.

**Pablo M Durán Jubiel & Rosario Redonda** (☎ 96 52 81; Calle 476 No 905 btwn Avs 9 & 9B; r CUC$25-30; P ) Little house with kitchen and patio, also at Nos 906 and 9B01 nearby.

**Rolando del Rey** (☎ 96 36 16; Calle 470A No 9B09 btwn Calles 9B & 11; r CUC$30; ) About 500m from the beach.

**Teresa Carmona** (☎ 96 30 69; Calle 476 No 703 btwn Avs 7A & 7B; r CUC$30; ) Upstairs.

**Sonnia Mujica Amargós** (☎ 96 48 50; Calle 476 No 706 btwn Avs 7A & 7B; r CUC$25-30; P ) Can cook here, also at Nos 7B04 and 7B10 nearby.

#### PLAYA BACURANAO

**Villa Bacuranao** (Islazul; ☎ 65 76 45; s/d cabañas low season CUC$33/40, high season CUC$38/44) On the Vía Blanca, 18km east of Habana, this is the closest beach resort to Habana. There's a long sandy beach between the resort and mouth of the Río Bacuranao, across which is the old Torreón de Bacuranao (inside the compound of the Military Academy and inaccessible). The beach here isn't as nice as its more easterly counterparts, but the price is nice.

## Eating

#### GUANABO

**El Brocal** (☎ 96 28 92; cnr Av 5 & Calle 500; noon-11pm) Want a nice surprise? Then check out this place, which serves up tacos (CUC$1.50 to CUC$3), quesadillas and a big combo of shrimp cocktail, fish, rice, salad and dessert (CUC$7.50) in a little ranch house. There are porch tables here.

**Restaurante Maeda** (Av Quebec; noon-midnight) Near Calle 476. Guanabo's paladar scene is going strong with this restaurant hidden away on the hill.

Pizza for CUC$1.50 and up per slice is available at **Pizzería al Mare** (cnr Av 5 & Calle 482; 24hr), although the peso stuff served out of the charcoal-stained shack, **Peso pizza** (cnr 5ta Av & Calle 488), a few blocks to the east is just as good. Spend a little more and you'll be treated to real wood-brick oven slices at **Don Pedro Pizzería** (Calle 482 No 503 btwn Avs 5 & 5D; 11am-11pm).

For ice cream, head to **Bim Bom** (cnr Av 5 & Calle 464; 11am-1am). **Panaderia D'Prisa** (Av 5 No 47802; 24hr) is the place for pastries and light snacks.

Just when you thought you'd had enough pizza, here's **Casa Coral** (Av 5 btwn Calles 10 & 11): clean, modern, cheap – and close to the beach!

#### PLAYA BOCA CIEGA

**El Cubano** (Av 5 btwn Calles 456 & 458; 11am-midnight) A spick and span place with a full wine-rack (French and Californian), checkered tablecloths and a good version of chicken Cordon Bleu.

**Casa del Pescador** (cnr Av 5 & Calle 442; noon-10:45pm) A good medium-priced seafood restaurant for those who like to dine in style.

#### PLAYA SANTA MARÍA DEL MAR

**Restaurante Mi Cayito** (☎ 97 13 39; 10am-6pm) On a tiny island in the Laguna Itabo, this serves lobster, shrimp and grilled fish in an open-air locale. Nice ambience and cheap pork fillets. There's a live show here every Saturday and Sunday at 3pm, which you can enjoy for the price of a drink.

**Restaurante Mi Casita de Coral** (cnr Av del Sur & Calle 8; 10am-11pm) A good seafood restaurant with reasonable prices; more upscale than most here.

**Costarenas** (Av de las Terrazas; 10am-midnight) Conveniently situated across from Hotel Tropicoco, this is another fine choice. Costarenas specializes in seafood dishes like paella and a mixed grill with lobster, shrimp and fish. The upstairs terrace is a good place to catch a beer and breeze. Fishermen sell their catch nearby for CUC$1 per pound; terrific if you've got cooking facilities.

Among the many small grocery stores here are **Minisuper La Barca** (cnr Av 5 & Calle 446; 9:15am-6:45pm Mon-Sat; 9:15am-2:45pm Sun); **Mini-Super Santa María** (cnr Av de las Terrazas & Calle 7; 9am-6:45pm), located opposite Hotel Tropicoco; and **Tienda Villa Los Pinos** (Av del Sur btwn 5 & 7; 9am-6:45pm).

#### PLAYA EL MÉGANO

**Cafetería Pinomar** (cnr Av del Sur & Calle 7; 24hr) This is the least expensive place to eat in this part of Playas del Este. Hamburgers, chicken, hot dogs and beer are served on its outdoor terrace and inside.

**Pizzería Mi Rinconcito** (cnr Av de las Terrazas & Calle 4; noon-9:45pm) Near Villa Los Pinos, it has pizza (CUC$2 to CUC$3), cannelloni, lasagna, salads and spaghetti (CUC$2 to CUC$3.50). A Dutch traveler said this was the best pizza she had in Cuba (thin crust and lots of fresh toppings).

### Entertainment

#### GUANABO

**Disco Vía Blanca** (cnr Av 5 & Calle 486; males/couples CUC$1/3; 9pm-2:30am) Below Hotel Vía Blanca, this disco bar is best on weekends and all summer.

**Cabaret Guanimar** (96 29 47; cnr Av 5 & Calle 468; per couple CUC$10; 9pm-3am Tue-Sat) An outdoor club with a show at 11pm; if you want to be in the front rows, it's CUC$16 for a couple.

A children's park and playground, the **Parque de Diversiones** (Av 5 btwn Calles 468 & 470) will get the kids laughing, as will the **children's matinees** (3pm Sat & Sun) at **Teatro Avenida** (96 29 44; Av 5 No 47612 btwn Calles 476 & 478).

For a movie try **Cine Guanabo** (96 24 40; Calle 480; films at 5:30pm except Wed) off Av 5.

#### PLAYA SANTA MARÍA DEL MAR

**Discoteca Habana Club** (97 13 44; Av de las Terrazas btwn Calles 9 & 10; admission CUC$5; 10pm-3am) Located at the Aparthotel Las Terrazas this club attracts a good mix of both locals and tourists.

Playas del Este's gay scene revolves around a beach bar called **La Paté** (Calle 1ra), near Restaurante Mi Cayito, at the east end of Santa María del Mar. You might also check all the way west on Playa El Mégano for cruising opportunities.

#### THE PHOTO THAT LAUNCHED A THOUSAND T-SHIRTS

Immortalized in a 1960 photograph taken at a funeral service for the victims of *La Coubre,* a French freighter that had been blown up in Habana harbor (reputedly by the CIA), Alberto Korda's timeless image of Che Guevara – expression defiant and eyes gazing wistfully into the future – needs little introduction. By turns it has been touted as the most famous photograph in the world and a defining symbol of the 20th century.

But, classic as it may be, Korda's extraordinary portrait of the dashing *guerrillero* inspired little interest at the time. More valuable to the international newspapers of the day were shots of Jean Paul Sârtre and Simone de Beauvoir that the photographer had captured on the same Kodak Plus-X reel. In fact, it wasn't until after Che's death more than seven years later that Italian book publisher Giangiacomo Feltrinelli – having procured a cropped version of the print from a third party (some claim from Sârtre himself) – re-worked the image into poster format in order to publicize the Italian release of Che's Bolivian diaries.

In the years that followed a high contrast bust print of the photo made by Irish artist John Fitzpatrick in 1968 was hijacked by everyone from Andy Warhol to rock band *Rage Against the Machine*. It has been decorating the walls of innumerable student bedrooms ever since.

In an ironic twist to the story, Korda, a lifelong socialist and Che supporter, consistently refused to bank a cent for his photographic efforts, although he did once successfully sue Smirnoff vodka for using the image illicitly in an advertisement. Donating his US$50,000 settlement to the Cuban healthcare system he commented rather nobly, 'If Che were alive, he would have done the same.'

## Shopping

**Photo Service** (Hotel Tropicoco btwn Avs del Sur & de las Terrazas) This place will satisfy most of your film and camera needs.

## Getting There & Away

### BUS & TAXI

Private blue buses (five pesos) from Gloria and Agramonte, near Habana's Estacíon Central de Férrocarriles (Central Station), will bring you to Guanabo, though they don't pass through Santa María del Mar.

Bus 400 to Guanabo leaves every hour or so from Taya Piedra, a park two blocks east of Cristina Station in Habana. Going the other way, it stops all along Av 5, but it's best to catch it as far east as possible. Bus 405 runs between Guanabacoa and Guanabo.

A tourist taxi from Playas del Este to Habana will cost around CUC$20.

### TRAIN

One of the best ways to get to Guanabo is on the Hershey Train which leaves five times a day from either Casablanca train station in Habana or from Matanzas. The train will drop you at Guanabo station (little more than a hut in a field) approximately 2km from the far east end of Guanabo. It's a pleasant walk along a quiet road to the beaches.

## Getting Around

A large guarded parking area is off Calle 7, between Av de las Terrazas and Av del Sur, near Hotel Tropicoco (CUC$1 a day from 8am to 7pm). Several other paid parking areas are along Playa Santa María del Mar.

**Havanautos** (☎ 96 38 45; Calle 500 btwn Avs 5C & D, Guanabo) has an office at Hotel Tropicoco and next door to the Servi-Cupet.

**Transtur** (Guanabo cnr Calle 478 & Av 9A; Santa María del Mar ☎ 97 15 35; Av de las Terrazas) has its main office between Aparthotel Atlántico and Aparthotel Las Terrazas in Santa María del Mar. It also has desks at the Hotel Tropicoco and the Blau Arenal resorts, and another office in Guanabo, next to Hotel Gran Vía, across the street from the Servi-Cupet on Av 5.

Both **Servi-Cupet** (24hr; Guanabo ☎ 96 38 58; cnr Av 5 & Calle 464; west of Bacuranao Vía Blanca) gas stations have snack bars. The gas station west of Bacuranao is opposite the military academy.

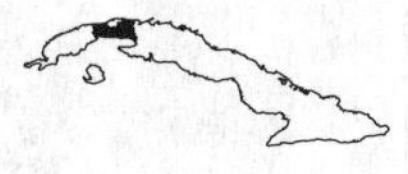

# Habana Province

Patchwork fields, palm-dotted villages and a craggy coastline of brush-covered cliffs: the first and last view most visitors get of Habana Province is from a Boeing 747 as it descends into José Martí International Airport. Though neither as geographically spectacular as Viñales nor as picture-postcard perfect as Trinidad, the flat and agriculturally rich landscape that splays like a broken wheel out from the City of Habana has its own individual charm.

The best way to get to know the area is by hopping onto an antiquated Hershey train as it plies its way east from Habana to Matanzas via Santa Cruz del Norte, Jibacoa Pueblo, Arcos de Canasí and just about every house, hut, horse and hillock in between. Stop off in Camilo Cienfuegos and poke around the rusting hulk of an abandoned sugar mill, or disembark at dusty Jibacoa Pueblo where, 5km to the north, one of Cuba's most low-key and underrated beach resorts beckons invitingly.

Tempting visitors in the extreme east is Ranchón Gaviota, a picturesque country lodge where you can pitch off on bikes, boats or horses into the scenic Valle de Yumurí. Further west, in the former tobacco growing town of San Antonio de los Baños, birthplace of Cuban singer/songwriter Silvio Rodríguez, culture vultures can chase *trova* (traditional poetic singing/songwriting) music through the sunbaked streets, or stop off to chuckle ruefully at the sartorial exhibits on display at the quirky Museo del Humor. A tempting finale awaits in Bejucal at the annual Charangas, a popular feast where two rival dancing ensembles – *La Espina de Oro* (The Golden Thorn) and *La Ceiba de Plata* (The Silver Ceiba Tree) – compete for popularity in an orgy of laughing, dancing, singing and music. Habana Province – boring? Are you kidding?



**HIGHLIGHTS**

- **Garden Escape**
  Enjoy a lazy lunch at the Jardines de Hershey (p174)
- **R and R**
  Rediscover rural life in the Valle de Yumurí at bucolic Ranchón Gaviota (p174)
- **Train Trek**
  Escape the tourist trails on the historic Hershey Electric Railway (p173)
- **Humor House**
  Have a laugh at the Museo del Humor (p177) in San Antonio de los Baños
- **Beach Escape**
  Lie low on unspoiled Playa Jibacoa (p173)

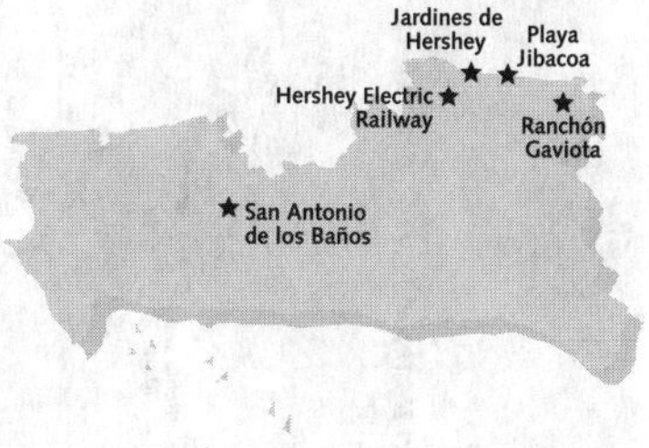

- TELEPHONE CODE: VARIES
- POPULATION: 711,590
- AREA: 5731 SQ KM

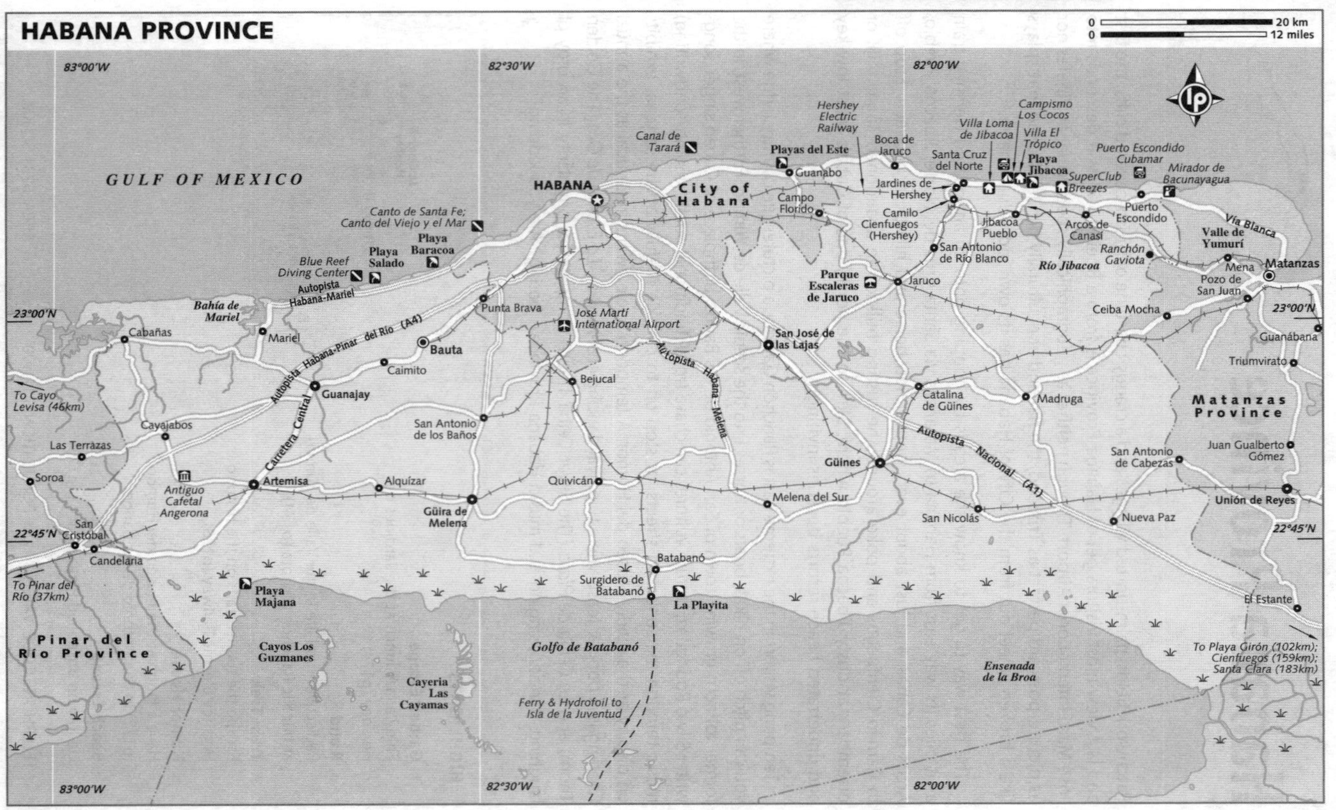
HABANA PROVINCE
0 20 km
0 12 miles
GULF OF MEXICO
HABANA
City of Habana
Matanzas Province
Pinar del Río Province
Golfo de Batabanó
Ensenada de la Broa
Bahía de Mariel
Cayeria Las Cayamas
Cayos Los Guzmanes
83°00'W
82°30'W
82°00'W
23°00'N
22°45'N
To Cayo Levisa (46km)
To Pinar del Río (37km)
To Playa Girón (102km); Cienfuegos (159km); Santa Clara (183km)
Ferry & Hydrofoil to Isla de la Juventud
Cabañas
Mariel
Soroa
Las Terrazas
Cayajabos
San Cristóbal
Candelaria
Antiguo Cafetal Angerona
Artemisa
Guanajay
Caimito
Bauta
Punta Brava
Alquízar
Güira de Melena
San Antonio de los Baños
Quivicán
Bejucal
José Martí International Airport
Surgidero de Batabanó
Batabanó
La Playita
Playa Majana
Blue Reef Diving Center
Playa Salado
Playa Baracoa
Canto de Santa Fe; Canto del Viejo y el Mar
Canal de Tarará
Autopista Habana-Mariel
Autopista Habana-Pinar del Río (A4)
Carretera Central
Autopista Habana - Melena
Autopista Nacional (A1)
San José de las Lajas
Melena del Sur
Güines
San Nicolás
Nueva Paz
Catalina de Güines
Madruga
Jaruco
Parque Escaleras de Jaruco
Playas del Este
Guanabo
Campo Florido
Hershey Electric Railway
Boca de Jaruco
Jardines de Hershey
Camilo Cienfuegos (Hershey)
Santa Cruz del Norte
San Antonio de Río Blanco
Jibacoa Pueblo
Villa Loma de Jibacoa
Villa El Trópico
Campismo Los Cocos
Playa Jibacoa
SuperClub Breezes
Arcos de Canasí
Río Jibacoa
Puerto Escondido
Puerto Escondido Cubamar
Ranchón Gaviota
Mirador de Bacunayagua
Ceiba Mocha
Valle de Yumurí
Vía Blanca
Mena
Pozo de San Juan
Matanzas
Guanábana
Triumvirato
San Antonio de Cabezas
Juan Gualberto Gómez
Unión de Reyes
El Estante

## PLAYA JIBACOA AREA

☎ 692

Little beaches, clusters of campismos and good offshore snorkeling make Playa Jibacoa, 60km east of Habana and 50km west of Varadero, the preferred getaway for Cubans of ordinary means. It doesn't have the white sand (or high price tag) of Playas del Este or Varadero, but the lofty limestone terrace overlooking the coast provides terrific views and hiking. Travelers with children will find interesting things to do in the surrounding area and the popularity of the region with Cuban families means fast friends are made wherever you go. The Vía Blanca, with beguiling sea and oil derrick vistas from Habana to Matanzas, runs along this coast; just inland are picturesque farming communities linked by the Hershey Electric Railway. Although Playa Jibacoa is a good pit stop between Habana and Matanzas, getting there will be difficult without your own transport (or catching rides Cuban-style). This area is changing fast and there are already two deluxe resorts at Arroyo Bermejo at the east end of the beach.

### Sights

Above the Vía Blanca on the border of Habana and Matanzas Provinces is the **Mirador de Bacunayagua**, a lookout over Cuba's longest (313m) and highest (100m) bridge. This is one of the best views in Cuba, with densely wooded valley chasms backed by blue waves. Aside from the stupendous vista, the building contains a restaurant, pool table and bar serving a selection of cold beers and freshly squeezed juice. Most tour buses between Varadero and Habana stop here and few motorists can resist the temptation.

West of here is **Santa Cruz del Norte**, a relatively quiet and unassuming town despite the presence of a famous rum factory. The plant in question is the Ronera Santa Cruz, producer of Havana Club rum and is one of the largest plants of its kind in Cuba.

Havana Club, founded in 1878 by the Arrechabala family of Cárdenas, opened its first distillery at Santa Cruz del Norte in 1919, and in 1973 a new factory was erected with the capacity to produce 30 million liters of rum a year. Unfortunately, for whatever reason (industrial espionage?), tourist visits are prohibited. A thermoelectric power station burning oil extracted from the coastal wells near Boca de Jaruco is just to the west. These and other oilfields west of Santa Cruz del Norte have been heavily exploited in recent years.

Five kilometers south of Santa Cruz del Norte is one of Cuba's largest sugar mills, the **Central Camilo Cienfuegos**, formerly owned by the US-based Hershey Chocolate Company. The headquarters of the Casablanca–Matanzas electric railway (**Hershey Electric Railway**), built by Hershey in 1917, is here. Five daily trains between Habana (Casablanca train station) and Matanzas cross nearby; there are also three trains from Hershey (as Camilo Cienfuegos is commonly called) to Santa Cruz del Norte and six from Hershey to Jaruco.

**THE SUGAR MILLING PROCESS**

In the mid-18th century, sugar replaced tobacco as Cuba's main crop. During the sugarcane harvest *(zafra)*, from January to May, the country's sugar mills are working 24/7 cutting, chipping, shredding and crushing the cane. Like almost everything in Cuba, the process wastes nothing: the leaves are fed to animals, the fibers (or *bagasse*) are used as fuel to make cardboard, and a centrifuge spins off molasses used to make rum or animal feed.

It's a labor-intensive business. The harvested cane must be brought to the mill within two days of being cut, or it ferments – hence all those overloaded, double-hitch trailers hauling the stuff along the Carretera Central. Once at the *central* (sugar mill), the cane is crushed between huge rollers that squeeze out the juice. Milk of lime is added to the juice, and the mixture is fed into a clarifier and heated. Evaporators remove excess water from the purified juice and sugar crystals begin to form in a vacuum pan after further boiling under pressure. Once the molasses is spun off, hot air dries the raw sugar crystals that are now ready for export or refining into white sugar. In Cuba, white sugar is somewhat of a luxury, with brown or raw sugar being what is usually dispensed on the ration card.

 

## Activities

The **Jardines de Hershey** (☎ 20 26 85) is a tract of land formerly owned by the famous American chocolate tycoon, Milton Hershey who ran the nearby sugar mill. It's pretty wild these days, with attractive paths, plenty of green foliage and a beautiful river, and this essentially is part of its charm. There are a couple of thatched roof restaurants on site and an all-pervading sense of peace and tranquility. It's a lovely spot for lunch and a stroll. The gardens are situated approximately 1km north of Camilo Cienfuegos railway station on the Hershey train line. Alternatively, if you're staying in Playa Jibacoa, it's approximately 4km south of Santa Cruz del Norte. The road is quiet and it makes a nice hike if you're up to it.

**Puerto Escondido Cubamar** (☎ 866-2524; Carretera Panamericana km 80) has a smallish water sports center at Puerto Escondido, 1.5km off the Vía Blanca, 7km east of Arcos de Canasí. It offers scuba diving at the usual prices of CUC$30 per dive and two-hour snorkeling trips for CUC$10 (four-person minimum), both including gear. Deep-sea fishing is also available.

Take any signposted side road heading toward the coast and you'll end up at one of the 10 national campismos (national network of 82 camping installations, not all of which rent to foreigners) that dot the landscape here. They all have their attractions and for an entry fee of CUC$1, you can explore at will. There is good snorkeling from the beach facing Campismo Los Cocos and heading westward along the coast you'll find unpopulated pockets where you can don a mask or relax under a palm.

You'll need your own wheels to get to **Ranchón Gaviota** (☎ 61 47 02 admission incl meal CUC$8; 9am-6pm), 12km inland from Puerto Escondido; it's a pretty drive through verdant countryside sprinkled with palms and sugarcane toward the Valle del Yumurí. This hilltop ranch overlooking a reservoir offers horseback riding, kayaking, cycling and a massive feast of *ajiaco* (meat stew), roasted pork, *congrí* (rice with beans), salad, dessert and coffee. To get here take the inland road for 2km to Arcos de Canasí, turn left at the fork for another 10km to the sign for Ranchón Gaviota.

## Sleeping & Eating

**Campismo Los Cocos** (Cubamar; ☎ 29 52 31/32; s/d/t CUC$19/30/41; P) The newest of Cubamar's stable of rural retreats, this is a modern hotel-standard collection of self-contained bungalows arranged around a swimming pool and set flush onto the beach. There is a number of facilities here including a small library, a medical post, an à la carte restaurant, a games room and plenty of walks and trails that disappear off into the surrounding hills. The campismo is also a fully equipped camper van site. You can book ahead with Cubamar (see p448) or just turn up. The only downside is the blaring poolside music that seems to keep the Cuban clientele entertained day and night.

**Villa Loma de Jibacoa** (Islazul; ☎ 8-5316; s/d CUC$29/38; P) This hotel stands on a hill overlooking a small beach near the mouth of the Río Jibacoa, just off the Vía Blanca. The perfect place for a family or group beach vacation, it is actually 13 individual houses of one to four rooms each sharing a TV, fridge and bath. As each one is different, you should look at a few before deciding – not always possible at this popular, heavily booked place.

**Villa El Trópico** (Gran Caribe; ☎ 8-4203; s/d CUC$70/100; P) A little to the east of Campismo Los Cocos is this all-inclusive resort that recently reopened and is marketed mainly to Canadians on all-inclusive deals.

**SuperClub Breezes** (☎ 8-5122; s/d low season CUC$151/242, high season CUC$223/356) Just east of El Trópico this is a nicely laid-out all-inclusive that kisses a choice stretch of sandy beach. Rooms are in attractive two-story bungalows and the place has a low-key and tranquil air that trumps most of what Playas del Este has to offer. Children under 16 are not accepted here. SuperClub has a reputation for good food, entertainment and activities. Coming from Matanzas, the turnoff is 13km west of the Bacunayagua Bridge – you can't miss it.

Eating is a grim prospect over this way unless you're in a hotel. There's a couple of dodgy bars around selling microwave pizza. Striking up a friendly conversation with the locals pulling in their fishing nets and arranging a meal is the best way to go.

**Caracol Tienda** (9am-4:30pm Mon-Fri, 9am-6:30pm Sat & Sun). Located on the inland side of the road just before the turnoff to Villa Loma de Jibacoa, it offers a small range of groceries.

### Entertainment

**Discoteca Jibacoa** (9pm-4am Tue-Sun) This is a local disco between Campismo Los Cocos and Villa Loma de Jibacoa. Great place to catch the locals shakin' their hips J-Lo style (well almost).

### Getting There & Away

The most interesting way to get to Playa Jibacoa is on the Hershey Electric Railway from Casablanca train station in Habana to Jibacoa Pueblo. There's no bus to the beach from there and traffic is sporadic, so you'll probably end up walking the 5km to Villa Loma de Jibacoa. The electric train also stops at Arcos de Canasí, but that's still 6km from El Abra and it's not as nice a walking road (though the hitchhiking might be easier).

Another option is to take crowded bus 669 from outside **Estación La Coubre** (Desamparados), just south of Habana's Estación Central, to Santa Cruz del Norte. Unfortunately, this bus only operates three times a day and you'd still have to hitchhike or take a taxi 9km further east to Villa Loma de Jibacoa (for information on the risks associated with hitching see p477). Your best bet is probably to go to the Habana bus station and take any bus headed for Matanzas along the Vía Blanca. Talk to the driver to arrange a drop-off at Playa Jibacoa, just across a long bridge from Villa Loma de Jibacoa.

## JARUCO

☎ 64 / pop 20,400

Jaruco, halfway between Habana and Matanzas but inland, is a good day trip for travelers with transport who value the journey over the destination. The **Parque Escaleras de Jaruco**, 6km west of Jaruco village, features interesting forests, caves, rock formations and limestone cliffs, but the picturesque countryside on unmarked roads along the way to Jaruco is what recommends this trip. It's a scenic 32km drive southeast from Guanabo via Campo Florido, and you can make it a loop by returning through Santa Cruz del Norte, 18km northeast of Jaruco via Central Camilo Cienfuegos. This is a good moped or bicycle adventure from Playas del Este or Jibacoa.

## SURGIDERO DE BATABANÓ

☎ 62 / pop 22,587

The small town of Batabanó, 51km south of central Habana, has few attractions for visitors except, perhaps, its **Museo Municipal** (Calle 64 No 7502; 9am-5pm Tue-Sun, closed Mon). The real reason to come here is to board a boat for La Isla de la Juventud (known locally as La Isla). Fidel Castro and the other Moncada prisoners disembarked here on May 15, 1955, after Fulgencio Batista granted them amnesty.

Surgidero de Batabanó receives mixed reviews from visitors. Some find charm in its rundown collection of ramshackle wooden houses and covered porches. Others feel the atmosphere is a little heavy and complain about hassle from *jineteros*. If you're stuck here there's a selection of little eateries selling fried fish and a small beach, **La Playita** (Little Beach) situated 2km east of the dock. Realistically, though, Surgidero de Batabanó is a transit stop and not a place to visit in its own right.

### Sleeping & Eating

This is no place to get stranded overnight. If desperation strikes try the old four-story **Hotel Dos Hermanos** (☎ 8-8975; Calle 68 No 315) in Surgidero de Batabanó, a huge 29-room peso hotel looming near the port and train station. Expect no water unless it rains, in which case you'll get some through the ceiling.

**END OF A SWEET ERA**

In 2000 Cuba shut over half its 156 sugar mills in recognition of the industry's inefficiencies, signifying a shift away from the sugar dependency that had typified the country for over a century. One of the biggest casualties was the huge Central Camilo Cienfuegos mill in Habana Province built by the American entrepreneur Hershey in the early 20th century.

Out-of-work mill workers were given the opportunity to attend university or technical college. Though many took advantage, sugar towns throughout the country once reliant on the mill are struggling to adjust to their new, less sweet reality.

Better situated are the 20 small prefabricated cabanas with baths on the beach at La Playita, 2km east by road from the ferry terminal (or less on foot via the beach). How foreigners are received at these places and how much they're charged varies. Ask around for a private room; delicious fresh fish meals will find you.

## Getting There & Away

The train station is just down the street from the Hotel Dos Hermanos and less than 1km from the ferry terminal. Trains from the Estación Cristina in Habana (2½ hours) should arrive/depart here twice a day, but they're often canceled.

The *kometa* (hydrofoil) from Surgidero de Batabanó to Isla de la Juventud is supposed to leave daily at 1pm (CUC$11, two hours). In addition, a normal ferry (CUC$7, five hours) leaves intermittently – supposedly on Wednesday, Friday and Sunday at 7:30pm, but don't bank on it. It is strongly advisable to buy your bus/boat combo ticket in Habana (p140) rather than turning up and doing it here. More often than not tickets are sold out to bus passengers. Call the **Agencia de Pasajes** (☎ 8-5355) in Surgidero de Batabanó for hydrofoil or ferry reservations. For information on direct bus connections from Habana, see p141.

Vehicles are shipped by barge daily and load at 1pm (CUC$20 each way). One passenger per vehicle is allowed on the cargo barge. It's time-consuming and not always guaranteed to work. For information on the car barge, call the **Empresa Naviera** (☎ 8-4455).

There's a **Servi-Cupet** (Calle 64 No 7110 btwn Calles 71 & 73) gasoline station in the center of Batabanó town. The next Servi-Cupet station to the east is in Güines.

# SAN ANTONIO DE LOS BAÑOS

**☎ 650 / pop 37,059**

San Antonio de los Baños, 35km southwest of central Habana, is famous for the Escuela Internacional de Cine y TV. Founded with generous donations from supporters of Cuban culture like Gabriel García Márquez, the world-class facilities at this film school include an Olympic-sized pool for practicing underwater shooting techniques. Despite being the hometown of musical giant Silvio Rodríguez (see below), friendly San Antonio de los Baños (founded in 1775) doesn't warrant a special trip, but the riverside Hotel Las Yagrumas is a nice escape from Habana's kinetic pace. The surrounding countryside is more citrus and tobacco than anything else; the region makes some of Cuba's finest Partidos cigars.

### SILVIO RODRÍGUEZ

One of the undisputed giants of Cuban 'Nueva Trova' music, Silvio Rodríguez, was born in the small tobacco-growing town of San Antonio de los Baños in 1946 into a household replete with melodic boleros. With his father an ardent socialist and his grandfather a onetime associate of José Martí, it was perhaps inevitable that Silvio would one day grow up to compose the soundtrack to Cuba's burgeoning social revolution almost single-handed. It was Silvio's mother, an enthusiastic amateur singer who probably had the biggest influence on his musical awakening.

From the poignant melodies of *Ojalá* (an intimate love song), to the strident chords of *La Maza* (a lament about the fall of Salvador Allende's socialist government in Chile), to the poetic restraints of 1992 *El Necio* (Rodríguez's satire on the US 'occupation' of Guantánamo naval base), Silvio's lyrics – rather like those of his American counterpart Bob Dylan – have never been far from the pulse of popular consciousness.

Labeled in turn as a poet, visionary, dreamer and genius, Silvio remains an icon of idealism in Latin America despite his relative lack of fame in North America and Europe. 'I am quite an optimist,' he is once reported to have said, 'At the time (of the revolution), it seemed to me that song could truly change the world.'

Now approaching 60, Silvio, despite wider international fame, continues to reside in Cuba where he remains true to the values of the revolution. Intermittent live performances have included recent shows in Argentina, Puerto Rico and Venezuela. In July 2004 Silvio performed live in Habana's Plaza de la Revolución backed by a symphony orchestra with a be-suited Fidel Castro in attendance.

The post office is at the corner of Calles 41 and 64. Photo Service is across the street.

### Sights & Activities

San Antonio de los Baños has several attractive squares, like the one with the old church at the corner of Calles 66 and 41. Nearby is the **Museo Municipal** (☎ 2539; Calle 66 No 4113 btwn Calles 41 & 43; admission CUC$1; 10am-6pm Tue-Sat, 9am-noon Sun).

Unique in Cuba is the collection of cartoons, caricatures and other ha-ha objects at the **Museo del Humor** (Cnr Calle 60 & Av 45; admission CUC$2; 10am-6pm Tue-Sat, 9am-1pm Sun). Among the drawings exhibited in this colonial house are saucy and satirical cartoons that capture the best of Cuban humor. If you like to laugh, head here in April for the **International Humor Festival**; winning entries remain on display for several weeks following.

The work of local artists is displayed at the **Galería Provincial Aduardo Abela** (☎ 4224; Calle 58 No 3708 btwn Calles 37 & 39; admission free; 1-5pm Mon-Fri).

A footbridge across the river next to La Quintica restaurant leads to a couple of **hiking trails**. Enjoy a drink in the bar, before sallying forth on a DIY adventure around the leafy banks.

### Sleeping & Eating

Av 41 is the main shopping strip, and there are numerous places to snack on peso treats along this street.

**Hotel Las Yagrumas** (Islazul; ☎ 38 44 60/61/62; s/d CUC$30/40; P) Situated 3km north of San Antonio de los Baños, it overlooks the picturesque, but polluted Río Ariguanabo. Each of the 120 damp rooms has a balcony or terrace. Take a room facing the river for maximum peace and quiet. All meals are (surprisingly decent) buffets. You can poke along the river in a rowboat, take a 6km river exploration in a motorboat or rent a bicycle for a zoom into town. There's table tennis, a gigantic pool and hilarious karaoke. Families will love this place.

### Entertainment

**Taberna del Tío Cabrera** (Calle 56 No 3910 btwn Calles 39 & 41; 2-5pm Mon-Fri, 2pm-1am Sat & Sun) This is an attractive garden nightclub where you can unwind with a cocktail in the courtyard.

**La Quintica** (Tues-Sun) A local peso restaurant, you'll find it just past the baseball stadium alongside the river 2km north of town. There's live music Friday and Saturday nights (closed Monday).

### Getting There & Away

There are supposedly four trains a day to Habana's Estación 19 de Noviembre (sometimes known as Tulipán; one peso) from the train station at the corner of Calles 53 & 54 on the south side of town. The other option is to take a 30-peso car from the **Intermunicipal Terminal** (El Lido, Av 41) in Marianao.

## BEJUCAL

☎ 66 / pop 20,442

This teeny town right on the edge of Habana Province is recommended for one reason: the **Charangas de Bejucal** that takes over every December 24. A cross between Carnaval and the more famous Parrandas in Remedios, this festival – dating from the 1800s – sends 10,000 people into the streets laughing, dancing and singing among outrageously large, dazzling floats and countless brass bands. Things heat up at midnight in the central plaza. Trains shuttle between here and Habana's Estación Cristina day and night on December 24.

## ARTEMISA

☎ 63 / pop 60,477

Artemisa is a bustling sugar town 60km southwest of Habana. If you're passing this way, it's worth a quick stopover – at least for a little pizza. Beside the Carretera Central between Artemisa and Guanajay is a restored section of the Trocha Mariel-Majana, a defensive wall erected by the Spanish during the Wars of Independence.

Revolution buffs may want to peel off the Carretera Central to visit the **Mausoleo a las Mártires de Artemisa** (☎ 3-3276; Av 28 de Enero; admission CUC$1; 9am-6pm Tue-Sun). Of the 119 revolutionaries who accompanied Fidel Castro in the 1953 assault on the Moncada Barracks, 28 were from Artemisa or this region. Fourteen of the men presently buried below the cube-shaped bronze mausoleum died in the actual assault or were killed soon after by Batista's troops. The other Moncada

**IF YOU HAVE A FEW MORE DAYS**

To catch a quick and easily accessible glimpse of Cuba behind the socialist mask there's no better method of transportation than the Habana to Matanzas Hershey train. Running five times a day from Casablanca train station on the eastern side of Habana Bay, electric trains ply their lazy route west to east from Habana to Matanzas, stopping every 10 minutes or so at all kinds of eccentrically-named places. Timetables are erratic and interrupted by such spontaneous calamities as 'cow on the line' or 'train shut for cleaning', but the countryside is verdant and the party on board typically Cuban. If you're up for a bit of do-it-yourself adventure you can wander off at one of a dozen or more rural stations, including the following:

**Central Camilo Cienfuegos** – stroll around the ruins of the old Hershey sugar mill or wander a kilometer or so to the north for lunch in the rural ambience of the Jardines de Hershey.

**Guanabo** – Habana's rustic eastern beach resort with plenty of welcoming casas particulares. A 2km stroll from the Guanabo station.

**Jibacoa** – from the station it's a pleasant 5km walk to beautiful Playa Jibacoa and the brand new campismo of Los Cocos.

veterans buried here died later in the Sierra Maestra. Guides are available.

The **Antiguo Cafetal Angerona**, 17km west of Artemisa on the road to Cayajabos and the Autopista Habana–Pinar del Río (A4), has been preserved as a museum. Angerona was erected between 1813 and 1820 by Cornelio Sauchay, who had 450 slaves tending 750,000 coffee plants. Behind the ruined mansion lie the slave barracks and an old watchtower, from which the slaves' comings and goings were monitored. The estate is mentioned in novels by Cirilo Villaverde and Alejo Carpentier, and James A Michener devotes several pages to it in *Six Days in Havana*.

A **pizza joint** (cnr Calles 31 & 54) serves up seriously good peso pizza, a block west of Artemisa's bus station. Try a *batido* (fruit milkshake).

The **Artemisa Train Station** (Av Héroes del Moncada) is four blocks east of the bus station. Only two trains a day pass through Artemisa, one around noon to Habana and another at midnight to Pinar del Río.

The bus station is on the Carretera Central in the center of town.

## MARIEL

☎ 63 / pop 31,922

Mariel, 45km west of Habana, is known mostly for the 125,000 Cubans who left here for Florida in April 1980. Once you see it, you'll want to flee too. Founded in 1762, Mariel is a major industrial town and port with the largest cement factory in Cuba, a huge thermoelectric power plant, military airfield and shipyards. There's also a new duty-free industrial zone adding to the action. It sits on the Bahía de Mariel at Cuba's narrowest point, just 31km north of the Caribbean at Playa Majana.

After Moa in Holguín Province, Mariel is Cuba's most heavily polluted town. The filthy cement factory at Mariel (once belonging to American cement producer Lone Star) is now run by the Mexican cement giant Cemex as a joint venture with the Cuban government.

The local **Museo Histórico** (☎ 9-2954; Calle 132 No 6926) is opposite the church at the entrance to town. A huge castlelike mansion, now a naval academy, stands on a hilltop overlooking Mariel.

Twenty-two kilometers east of Mariel on the Autopista is **Playa Salado**, a popular beach that swarms with locals in summer, but is largely deserted at other times. The shoreline is rocky instead of sandy, but the water is mostly clean. A few kilometers east of Playa Salado is the more developed **Playa Baracoa**. Come here for the local party atmosphere rather than the surf and sand (crowded, dark and limited). Imagine *West Side Story* meets West Palm Beach, with swarthy men and their beautiful dates hanging about big old American cars drinking beer while fishermen throw lines from the rocky shore. There are two *parrilladas* (barbecue restaurants) and the more upscale El Yunque in a big thatched hut. Alternatively, you can nosh on the best *chicharitas* (plantain chips) in Cuba (five pesos a box). It's a nice sunset spot.

# Isla de la Juventud (Special Municipality)

Siguanea, Juan El Evangelista, Parrot Island, Isla de Pinos – Isla de la Juventud has had more incarnations than Fidel Castro has had policy u-turns. A veritable no-man's-land compared with the more popular tourist haunts on the Cuban 'mainland', La Isla – as locals affectionately call it – is an engaging blend of sleepy Cuban backwater and untamed ecological wilderness.

The island's most celebrated attraction is its underwater coral formations and scuba divers flock here for what are considered to be the most impressive collections of drop-offs, wrecks, caves and marine life in the Caribbean. But, for those more at home on dry land, there's plenty of quieter corners in which to slow down, put your feet up, and get to know the locals.

Nueva Gerona is the best place to start, the island's cheerful capital, an architectural hotchpotch of old and new that feels as if it fell asleep in 1945 and woke up 60 years later. Other curiosities include the indigenous cave paintings in Cueva Punta del Este, a turtle breeding center on the isolated south coast and the botanical gardens of La Jungla de Jones.

The island has served as a prison, with such infamous dissidents as Fidel Castro and José Martí banished here. Cuba's alternative Alcatraz can be viewed in a cluster of grotesque circular buildings known collectively as Presidio Modelo. Situated 114km to the east, brilliant Cayo Largo del Sur is Cuba's most 'exclusive' all-inclusive resort. In dramatic contrast to the humdrum pace and underlying Cuban character of La Isla, the atmosphere here is plush, foreign and ruthlessly professional, though the beaches are pristine and the cluster of high-ranking hotels as good as you'll find anywhere.

**HIGHLIGHTS**

- **Getting There**
  Cross the Golfo de Batabanó in a speedy hydrofoil or lumbering on the ferry (p186)
- **Jail Break**
  Explore the eerily empty Presidio Modelo (p187), where Fidel Castro and other Moncada Barracks rebels were imprisoned
- **Indigenous Art**
  Admire the 'Sistine Chapel' of primitive cave paintings in Cueva de Punta del Este (p189)
- **Going Deep**
  Wrecks, walls, coral gardens and caves; Punta Francés (p188) is *the* best place to dive in Cuba
- **Beach Comb**
  Relax on the white, soft sands of Playa Sirena (p189) on Cayo Largo del Sur



| TELEPHONE CODE: 46 | POPULATION: 80,625 | AREA: 2398 SQ KM |
|---|---|---|

### History

The first settlers on La Isla (a common abbreviation of Isla de la Juventud) were the Siboney Indians, a preceramic civilization who arrived on the island more than 1000 years ago via the Lesser Antilles and settled down as hunters and fishermen on the coasts. Naming their new-found homeland Siguanea they made tools from conches and other shells and left a fascinating set of cave paintings in Cueva Punta del Este (p189).

By the time Columbus arrived on these shores in June 1494, the Siboney had long departed (either dying out or returning to the mainland) and the intrepid navigator promptly renamed the island Juan El Evangelista, claiming it for the Spanish crown. But, knotted with mangroves and surrounded by a circle of shallow reefs, the Spanish did little to develop their new possession.

Instead La Isla became a hideout for pirates, including Francis Drake, John Hawkins, Thomas Baskerville and Henry Morgan. They called it Parrot Island, and their exploits are said to have inspired Robert Louis Stevenson's idea for the novel *Treasure Island*.

In December 1830 the Colonia Reina Amalia (now Nueva Gerona) was founded, and throughout the 19th century the island served as a place of imposed exile for independence advocates and rebels, including José Martí. Twentieth-century dictators Gerardo Machado and Fulgencio Batista followed this Spanish example by sending political prisoners – Fidel Castro included – to the island which had by then reincarnated for a fourth time as Isla de Pinos (Isle of Pines).

Aside from its Spanish heritage, La Isla also has a marked English influence. During the late 19th century, some fishing families from the British colony of the Cayman Islands established a settlement called Jacksonville (now Cocodrilo) on the southwest tip of Isla de Pinos; you'll still occasionally meet people who can converse fluently in English. Additionally, just prior to Cuban independence in 1902, the infamous Platt Amendment included a proviso that placed Isla de Pinos outside the boundaries of the 'mainland' part of the archipelago. Some 300 US colonists established themselves here soon after, and only in March 1925 did the US recognize the island as an integral part of Cuba.

The Americans stayed and thrived making good business from the island's first (but not the last) citrus plantations and building an efficient infrastructure of banks, hotels and public buildings. During World War II, the Presidio Modelo was used by the US to inter Axis prisoners and by the 1950s La Isla had become a favored vacation spot for rich Americans who flew in daily from Miami. The decadent party – which by this point included the age-old staples of gambling and prostitution – ended rather abruptly in 1959 with the ascendancy of Fidel Castro.

Before the revolution Isla de Pinos was sparsely populated. In the 1960s and 1970s, however, tens of thousands of young people volunteered to study here at specially built 'secondary schools' in the countryside, which now dot the plains in the northern part of the island. Students at these schools worked the fields in shifts, creating the vast citrus plantations that can still be seen today. In 1978 their role in developing the island was officially recognized when the name was changed for the fifth time to Isla de la Juventud (Isle of Youth). Numerous young people from Africa have also studied here, and foreign students still come to the island today, though in smaller numbers.

# ISLA DE LA JUVENTUD

One of the most welcoming places you will come across in Cuba, Isla de la Juventud is a world apart from anywhere else on the archipelago. The laid-back pace and opportunities for getting (way) off the beaten track here will appeal to both escape artists and adventure types alike. While the hotel scene is a little thin on the ground, the social opportunities are good and the ingratiating casas particulares dotted around the capital Nueva Gerona are run by the kind of generous people who open both their homes and hearts to guests. The island's southern half, with its preserved ecosystems and rich natural wildlife, is a largely undiscovered wilderness while the southwestern part of the island around Punta Francés is known for its magnificent scuba diving.

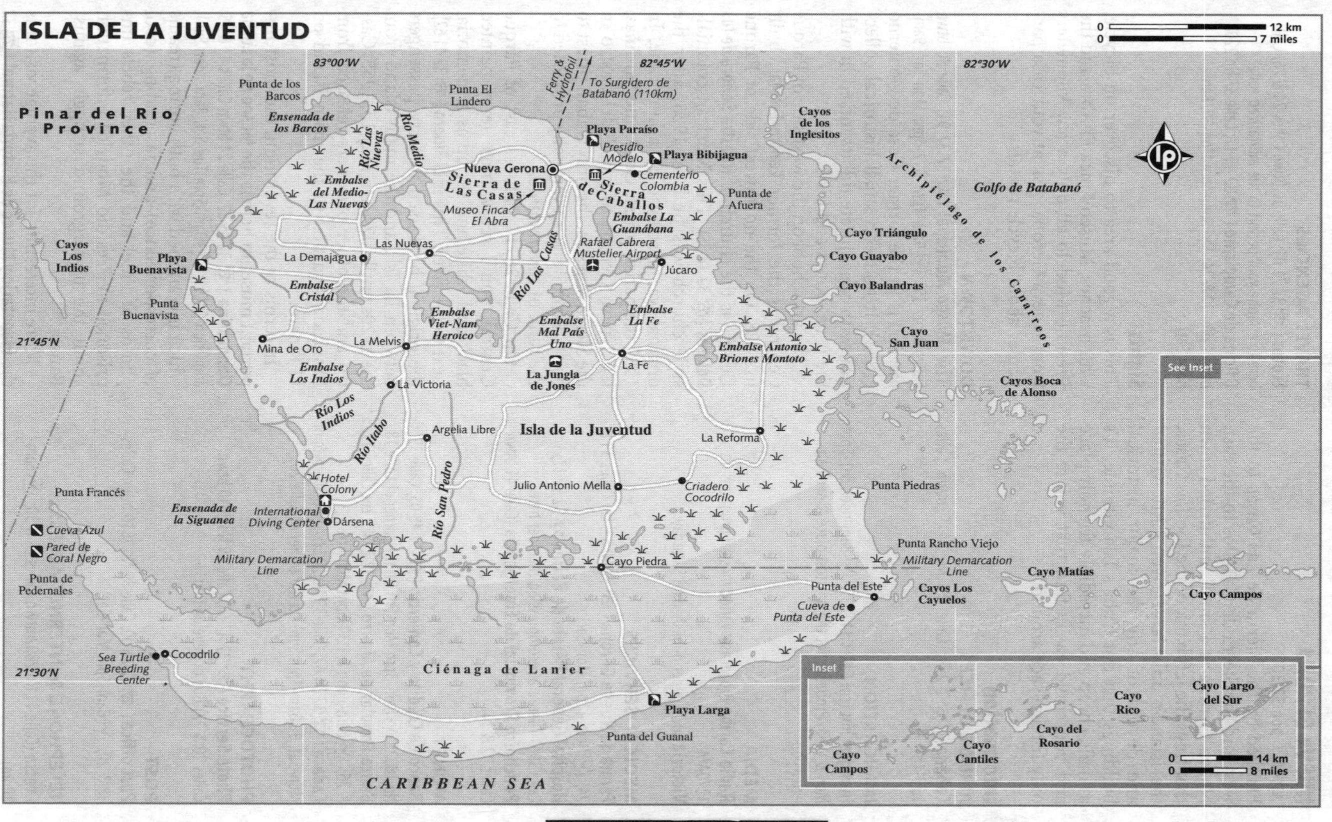
ISLA DE LA JUVENTUD
0 12 km
0 7 miles
83°00'W
82°45'W
82°30'W
21°45'N
21°30'N
Pinar del Río Province
Punta de los Barcos
Ensenada de los Barcos
Punta El Lindero
Río Medio
Río Las Nuevas
Ferry & Hydrofoil
To Surgidero de Batabanó (110km)
Playa Paraíso
Presidio Modelo
Playa Bibijagua
Nueva Gerona
Cementerio Colombia
Sierra de Las Casas
Sierra de Caballos
Embalse del Medio-Las Nuevas
Museo Finca El Abra
Punta de Afuera
Embalse La Guanábana
Rafael Cabrera Mustelier Airport
Cayos de los Inglesitos
Archipiélago de los Canarreos
Golfo de Batabanó
Cayo Triángulo
Cayo Guayabo
Cayo Balandras
Cayo San Juan
Cayos Boca de Alonso
Cayos Los Indios
Playa Buenavista
Punta Buenavista
La Demajagua
Las Nuevas
Júcaro
Río Las Casas
Embalse Cristal
Embalse Viet-Nam Heroico
Embalse Mal País Uno
Embalse La Fe
Embalse Antonio Briones Montoto
Mina de Oro
La Melvis
La Fe
Embalse Los Indios
La Victoria
La Jungla de Jones
Río Los Indios
Río Itabo
Argelia Libre
Isla de la Juventud
La Reforma
Hotel Colony
Río San Pedro
Julio Antonio Mella
Criadero Cocodrilo
Punta Piedras
Punta Francés
Ensenada de la Siguanea
International Diving Center
Dársena
Cueva Azul
Pared de Coral Negro
Military Demarcation Line
Cayo Piedra
Punta Rancho Viejo
Military Demarcation Line
Cayo Matías
Punta de Pedernales
Punta del Este
Cayos Los Cayuelos
Cayo Campos
Cueva de Punta del Este
See Inset
Sea Turtle Breeding Center
Cocodrilo
Ciénaga de Lanier
Playa Larga
Punta del Guanal
CARIBBEAN SEA
Inset
Cayo Largo del Sur
Cayo Rico
Cayo del Rosario
Cayo Cantiles
Cayo Campos
0 14 km
0 8 miles

## NUEVA GERONA

☎ 46 / pop 37,300

Flanked by the Sierra de Las Casas to the west and the Sierra de Caballos to the east, Nueva Gerona is a small, unhurried town that hugs the left bank of the Río Las Casas, the island's only large river. Little-visited and devoid of any the major historical buildings that dot Cuba's Isla Grande, it's a small, cheap and incredibly friendly place and you could easily find that you're the only foreign face around.

### Information

#### AIRLINE OFFICES

**Cubana** (☎ 2-253; Calle 39 No 1415 btwn Calles 16 & 18)

#### IMMIGRATION

**Inmigración** (cnr Calles 34 & 35; 8am-noon & 1-5pm Mon & Wed) Probably not the greatest place to seek an extension.

#### MEDIA

**Radio Caribe** Broadcasts varied musical programs on 1270AM.
**Victoria** Local paper published on Saturday.

#### MEDICAL SERVICES

**Farmacia Nueva Gerona** (☎ 32 60 84; cnr Calles 39 & 24; 8am-11pm Mon-Sat)
**Hospital General Héroes de Baire** (☎ 32 30 12; Calle 39A) There's a recompression chamber here.
**Policlínico Provincial de Emergencia** (Calle 41 btwn Calles 32 & 34)

#### MONEY

**Banco de Crédito y Comercio** (☎ 32 48 05; Calle 39 No 1802; 8am-3pm Mon-Fri) On the corner of Calle 18.
**Banco Popular de Ahorro** (☎ 32 27 42; cnr Calles 39 & 26; 8am-noon & 1:30-5pm Mon-Fri)
**Cadeca** (☎ 32 34 62; Calle 39 No 2022; 8:30am-6pm Mon-Sat, 8:30am-1pm Sun) On the corner of Calle 20.

#### PHOTOGRAPHY

**Photo Service** (☎ 32 47 66; Calle 39 No 2010 btwn Calles 20 & 22) Buy or develop film.

#### POST

**Post office** (☎ 32 26 00; Calle 39 No 1810 btwn Calles 18 & 20; 8am-6pm Mon-Sat)

#### TELEPHONE & INTERNET ACCESS

**Etecsa** (Calle 41 No 2802 btwn Calles 28 & 30; 6am-10pm)

#### TRAVEL AGENCIES

**Ecotur** (☎ 32 71 01; Calle 39 btwn Calles 24 & 26) Call here to arrange your permit to the militarized zone.
**Oficina de Campismo** (☎ 32 45 17; Calle 37 No 2208 btwn Calles 22 & 24; 8am-4pm Mon-Fri, 8am-noon Sat)

### Sights

This is a good area to discover on bicycle, with beaches, Museo Finca El Abra and the Presidio Modelo all only a few kilometers from Nueva Gerona. Ask at your casa particular about bicycle rentals.

#### DOWNTOWN

The **Museo Municipal** (☎ 32 37 91; Calle 30 btwn Calles 37 & 39; 9am-1pm & 2-6pm Mon-Sat, 9am-noon Sun) is in the former Casa de Gobierno (1853). It houses a small historical collection with a few pirate tidbits mixed in with the usual bones and birds.

The art school on the west side of Parque Central is the former **Centro Escolar**, built in 1928. On the northwest side of Parque Central is the church of **Nuestra Señora de los Dolores** (☎ 32 18 35). This Mexican colonial-style church was built in 1926, after the original was destroyed by a hurricane. In 1957 the parish priest, Guillermo Sardiñas, left Nueva Gerona to join Fidel Castro in the Sierra Maestra, the only Cuban priest to do so. Sardiñas was eventually promoted to the rank of *comandante*.

On Calle 28, two blocks east of Parque Central, you'll see a huge ferry painted black and white and set up as a memorial next to the river. This is **El Pinero** (☎ 32 41 62), the original boat used to ferry passengers between La Isla and the main island from the 1920s until 1974. On May 15, 1955, Castro and the other prisoners released from Moncada returned to the main island on El Pinero.

In terms of the revolution, the most important museum here is the **Museo de la Lucha Clandestina** (☎ 32 45 82; Calle 24 btwn Calles 43 & 45; admission CUC$1; 9am-5pm Tue-Sat, 8am-noon Sun), which is crammed with both boring (reams of correspondence) and fascinating (cool photos of Fidel and the other rebels imprisoned in Presidio Modelo) information about the underground struggle against Batista.

More interesting for the average visitor is the **Planetario y Museo de Historia Natural** (☎ 32

31 43; cnr Calles 41 & 52; admission CUC$2; 🕑 8am-5pm Tue-Sat, 9am-noon Sun), showcasing the natural history, geology and archaeology of the island. There's a replica of the Cueva Punta del Este cave paintings here if you can't make it out there (see p189). You might gain access to the planetarium (and use of the telescope therein) by talking to the guard.

### MUSEO FINCA EL ABRA

This **museum** (Carretera Siguanea Km 2; 🕑 9am-5pm Tue-Sun) is 3km southwest of Nueva Gerona, off the road to La Demajagua (the continuation of Calle 41). Coming from Motel El Rancho El Tesoro, go southwest a few hundred meters on a dirt road to another highway. Turn right and cross a bridge over the Río Las Casas. At the next junction, turn right again, and you'll soon come to a sign indicating the access road to Finca El Abra.

The teenage José Martí arrived at Finca El Abra on October 17, 1870, to spend nine weeks of exile on this farm, prior to his deportation to Spain. Legend has it that the shackles he wore here were forged into a ring by his mother, which Martí wore to his death. The old hacienda is directly below the Sierra de Las Casas and it's worth coming as much for the surroundings as for the museum. Cuban oaks and eucalyptus trees line the access road, and a huge ceiba tree stands next to the museum. A

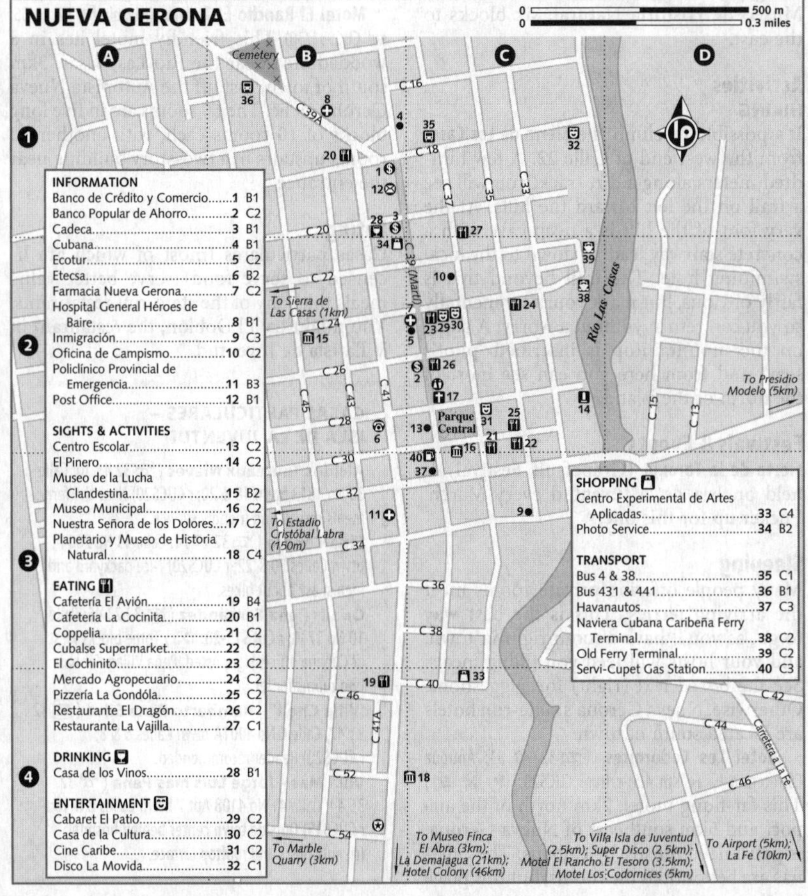

sundial (1868) is outside the museum. The adjacent house is still occupied by Omar Sarda, whose ancestor Giuseppe Girondella hosted Martí here.

To loop back to town, look for the dirt road just before the museum. This road leads north to the island's former **marble quarry**, which is clearly visible in the distance. The quarry is moderately interesting (if you dig big holes in the ground), but the real attraction is the climb up the hill, from where there are lovely views. After descending, continue north between a garbage dump and several rows of pig pens (not very attractive, but any loop has got to be better than backtracking, right?) to Calle 54 on the right. This street will bring you into town via the Planetario y Museo de Historia Natural, six blocks to the east.



## Activities

### HIKING

It's possible to climb the **Sierra de Las Casas** from the west end of Calle 22. A few hundred meters along a dirt track, you will see a trail on the left toward the hills. At the very foot of the hill is a deep cave with a concrete stairway leading down to the local swimming hole. The trail beyond this is fairly obvious, but mark your way mentally so you can return without a worry. A stone on the mountaintop is inscribed 'pilot's seat', and from here you can see most of the north of the island.

## Festivals & Events

**Fiesta de la Toronja** (Grapefruit Festival) is held on Isla de la Juventud every March. Pucker up for this one.

## Sleeping

Many people offering private rooms meet the arriving ferries. This is the best way to go, as you'll have a room right in town, and your hosts will feed you filling meals. See the boxed text (right) for suggestions. Otherwise, Nueva Gerona's state-run hotels are located south of town.

**Motel Los Codornices** (☎ 32 49 81; Antigua Carretera a La Fe Km 4.5; r from CUC$20; P ) This far-flung motel, 2km north of the airport and 5km southeast of Nueva Gerona, is patronized mostly by Cubans. The cabanas are better than the rooms, but this place is so far removed it's an 'only if desperate' option.

**Villa Isla de Juventud** (Islazul; ☎ 32 32 90; Autopista Nueva Gerona-La Fe Km 1; s/d incl breakfast CUC$29/33; P ) Situated about 5km from the airport and 2.5km from Nueva Gerona, this is the best accommodation option and has friendly staff to boot. There are 20 rooms with fridges in two-story, four-unit blocks. Framed by the island's twin marble mountains, Villa Isla de Juventud has a surprising amount of atmosphere. The Villa's reputation is enhanced by a suspension bridge behind the hotel that crosses the Río Las Casas. It's not a bad spot, especially around sunset, but make sure you're well lathered with insect repellent.

**Motel El Rancho El Tesoro** (Islazul; ☎ 32 30 35; s/d CUC$31/36) This friendly motel lies in a wooded area near the Río Las Casas, 3km south of town, just off the Autopista Nueva Gerona La Fe. The 60 rooms are in five long blocks of 10 rooms each, with another 10 rooms upstairs in a two-story building near the entrance.

## Eating

Casas particulares (most of which are licensed to serve food) serve better value meals than any of the state-run restaurants. You might try El Doblón, the restaurant in Villa Isla de Juventud.

### CASAS PARTICULARES – ISLA DE LA JUVENTUD

**Alcides Taureaux Nieves** (☎ 32 43 10; Calle 35 No 1813 btwn 18 & 20; r CUC$20) Near the ferry; meals served and friendly service.

**Elda Cepero** (☎ 32 27 74; Calle 43 No 2004 btwn Calles 20 & 22; r CUC$20) Nice backyard and meals; ask about bikes.

**Odalis Peña Fernández** (☎ 32 23 45; Calle 10 No 3710; r CUC$15-20; ) Three blocks west of Cubana office, signposted 'Peña Village' it has two rooms for let.

**'Villa Choli' – Ramberto Pena Silva** (☎ 32 31 47; Calle C No 4001A btwn Calles 6 & 8; r CUC$20) Reader recommended.

**Villa Mas - Jorge Luis Mas Peña** (☎ 32 35 44; Calle 41 No 4108 Apt 7 btwn Calles 8 & 10; r CUC$15) Outside town center behind hospital; friendly hosts and rooftop terrace.

#### RESTAURANTS

**El Cochinito** (☎ 32 28 09; cnr Calles 39 & 24; noon-11pm, closed Wed) Get your pork steaks, yucca, rice and beans here and eat al fresco out the back.

**Restaurante El Dragón** (☎ 32 44 79; cnr Calles 39 & 26; meals CUC$3; noon-10pm, closed Wed) Specializes in Chinese food, but there's little selection and it's not recommended for vegetarians. There's sometimes live music after 8pm and there's always a big gong to beat if the inspiration hits.

**Pizzería La Góndola** (cnr Calles 30 & 35; noon-10pm) Offering a break from the pork-chicken-*congrí* (rice flecked with beans) cycle, the pizza here is on par with other Cuban pizza places.

**Restaurante La Vajilla** (☎ 32 46 92; Calle 37 btwn Calles 20 & 22; mains CUC$4; noon-9pm, closed Thu) For cheap *comida criolla* (Creole food) try this large hangarlike building that becomes a disco at night. Main plates cost around CUC$4.

**Cafetería La Cocinita** (☎ 32 46 40; Calles 18 & 41; 24hr) This is a good place for peso sandwiches and juice or more substantial meals in the nicer sit-down section in the back.

**Cafetería El Avión** (☎ 32 29 70; cnr Calles 41 & 40; 10am-7pm) Another peso place. The adjacent snack counter is open 24 hours.

**Coppelia** (☎ 32 22 25; Calle 37 btwn Calles 30 & 32; noon-10pm Tue-Sun) You wouldn't be in Cuba if there wasn't a Coppelia. Head here to sate that ice-cream craving.

#### GROCERIES

**Mercado agropecuario** (cnr Calles 24 & 35) Try this large market for fresh vegetables and meat.

**Cubalse Supermarket** (Calle 35 btwn Calles 30 & 32; 9:30am-6pm Mon-Sat) Sells groceries and sundries.

### Drinking

**Casa de los Vinos** (cnr Calles 20 & 41; 1-10pm Mon-Wed, 1pm-midnight Fri-Sun, closed Thu) A nice local drinking hole with 'ahoy matey!' nautical decor. Aside from ham sandwiches, you can get wine made from grapefruit, grapes and melon by the glass.

### Entertainment

Evening events are often held at the **Casa de la Cultura** (☎ 32 35 91; cnr Calles 37 & 24). Also ask about the famous local *sucu-sucu* (a variation of *son*, Cuba's popular music) group led by Mongo Rives, which sometimes plays at the Casa de la Cultura in **La Fe** (☎ 39 74 68; cnr Calles 7 & 8).

#### DANCE CLUBS

**Disco La Movida** (Calle 18; from 11pm) For a little atmospheric booty shaking, join the throngs of locals dancing in an open-air locale hidden among the trees near the river.

**Cabaret El Patio** (☎ 32 23 46; Calle 24 btwn Calles 37 & 39; per couple CUC$3; 10pm-2am Thu-Sun) Next door to the Casa de la Cultura, this venue has an entertaining floorshow at 11pm. Show up early to get in; official policy is couples only.

**Restaurante El Dragón** (cnr Calles 39 & 26; from 10pm Tue & Wed, 8pm Thu-Sun) This restaurant has disco dancing in the rear courtyard.

**Super Disco** (admission CUC$1; from 10pm Thu-Sun) You've got to love a place with a name like this. The locals do: this club next to Villa Isla de la Juventud is always packed.

**Restaurante La Vajilla** (☎ 32 46 92; Calle 37 btwn Calles 20 & 22; noon-9pm, closed Thu) Less popular but worth a mention in Nueva Gerona's small-town nightlife is this place which offers a disco in a hangarlike building at night.

#### CINEMAS

**Cine Caribe** (☎ 32 24 16; cnr Calles 37 & 28) For a film or video, check out this cinema on Parque Central.

#### SPORT

**Estadio Cristóbal Labra** (☎ 32 10 44; cnr Calles 32 & 53) Nueva Gerona's baseball stadium, Estadio Cristóbal Labra, is six blocks west of the Policlínico Provincial de Emergencia. From October to April, the local team usually plays here at 1:35pm daily except Monday and Friday, though not every week. Ask at your local casa particular for details of upcoming games.

### Shopping

Calle 39, also known as Calle Martí, is a pleasant pedestrian mall interspersed with small parks.

**Centro Experimental de Artes Aplicadas** (Calle 40 btwn 39 & 37; 8am-4pm Mon-Fri, 8am-noon Sat) This center, near the planetarium, makes and sells artistic ceramics.

## Getting There & Away

### AIR

The easiest way to get to the Isla is to fly and when you weigh up cost over hassle you might think it's worth the money. Rafael Cabrera Mustelier Airport (airport code GER) is 5km southeast of Nueva Gerona. Cubana flies here from Habana three times a day for CUC$34.50 one-way. There are no international flights. Aerotaxi offers charter flights (you have to buy all the seats on the plane) and you could arrange passage in Habana if you have about CUC$500 to blow. For contact details see p474.

There's no regular air or sea connection from Isla de la Juventud to Cayo Largo del Sur. It is, however possible to charter an 11-passenger Aerotaxi biplane for a day trip at CUC$470, including waiting time. Otherwise, you must return to Habana to go to Cayo Largo del Sur.

### BOAT

Getting to La Isla by boat isn't the piece of cake it ought to be. Tickets for the Soviet-made Kometa hydrofoils (known locally simply as the *kometa*) or the infinitely slower Mexican ferries that ply the route between Surgidero de Batabanó and Nueva Gerona are sold at the **NCC kiosk** (☎ 878-1841; 🕑 7am-noon) in the main bus station in Habana, where you can pay for both your bus transfer and ferry reservation in one shot (CUC$13). Due to recent popularity it is wise to make a reservation in person one or two days in advance at the NCC kiosk though, oddly, return tickets off the island are not available here or anywhere else in Habana. In terms of getting back you'll have to chance your arm in Nueva Gerona where you can purchase a return ticket on arrival. If you're on a tight schedule save yourself the hassle and take a plane.

It's advisable not to show up independently in Batabanó with the intention of buying a ferry ticket direct from the dock. Although technically doable, a number of travelers have come unstuck here, being told, more often than not, that the tickets have been sold out days in advance through the NCC kiosk in Habana. Furthermore, bedding down for the night in Batabanó is not a particularly inspiring experience.

The return leg is equally problematic. Procure your ticket as early as possible in Nueva Gerona's **Naviera Cubana Caribeña (NCC) ferry terminal** (☎ 32 49 77, 32 44 15; cnr Calles 31 & 24), beside the Río Las Casas. The *kometa* leaves for Surgidero de Batabanó daily at 9am (CUC$11), but you'd be wise to get there at least two hours beforehand to tackle the infamous queues.

Before reserving tickets, ask if there's a bus connection from Surgidero de Batabanó to Habana, as a number of northbound catamaran departures have no connection at all. A connecting bus should cost CUC$2 and you will need to make a reservation as you buy your boat ticket. If you find yourself stranded, large passenger trucks with rows of benches often meet the ferries at Surgidero de Batabanó, charging 10 pesos per person to go to the Habana bus station. It ain't comfy, but it'll get you there.

True to form, there are no printed schedules for the boat or ferry crossings to and from La Isla. Theoretically the *kometas* are supposed to leave Nueva Gerona at 9am and dock in Batabanó at noon, returning back to the island at 1pm. But don't take anything as a given until you have booked your ticket. Isla boat crossings, rather like Cuban trains, have an annoying tendency of being late, breaking down or getting cancelled altogether.

Traveling in either direction you'll need to show your passport. See Surgidero de Batabanó (p176) and Habana City (p141) for more.

## Getting Around

### TO/FROM THE AIRPORT

From the airport, look for the bus marked 'Servicio Aereo', which will take you into town for one peso. To get to the airport, catch this bus in front of **Cine Caribe** (cnr Calles 28 & 37). A taxi to town will cost about CUC$5, or CUC$30 to the Hotel Colony.

### BUS

Bus 431 to La Fe (35 centavos, 26km) and 441 to the Hotel Colony (two pesos; La Fe: 17km; Hotel Colony: 45km) leave from a stop opposite the cemetery on Calle 39A, just northwest of the hospital.

Bus 38 leaves from the corner of Calles 18 and 37 departing for Chacón (Presidio Modelo), Playa Paraíso and Playa Bibijagua at 7:30am Monday to Saturday. It makes four additional trips throughout the day.

Bus 4 also leaves from this stop, but it only goes as far as Chacón.

### CAR

**Havanautos** (☎ 32 44 32; cnr Calles 32 & 39; 🕑 7am-7pm) rents cars, and can arrange transport into the military zone.

The Servi-Cupet gasoline station is at the corner of Calles 30 and 39 in the center of town.

### HORSE CARTS

Horse *coches* (carts) often park next to the Cubalse Supermarket on Calle 35. You can easily rent one at CUC$10 per day for excursions to the Presidio Modelo, Museo Finca El Abra, Playa Bibijagua and other nearby destinations.

## EAST OF NUEVA GERONA

The island's most impressive but depressing sight is the **Presidio Modelo** at Reparto Chacón, 5km east of Nueva Gerona. Built between 1926 and 1931, during the repressive regime of Gerardo Machado, the prison's four five-story, yellow circular blocks were modeled after those of a notorious penitentiary in Joliet, Illinois, and could hold 5000 prisoners at a time. During WWII, assorted enemy nationals who happened to find themselves in Cuba (including 350 Japanese, 50 Germans and 25 Italians) were interned in the two rectangular blocks at the north end of the complex.

The Presidio's most famous inmates, however, were Fidel Castro and the other Moncada rebels who were imprisoned here from October 1953 to May 1955. They were held separately from the other prisoners, in the hospital building at the south end of the complex. After heckling Batista during a February 1954 prison visit, Castro was thrown into solitary confinement. In 1967, the prison was closed and the section where Castro stayed was converted into a **museum** (☎ 32 51 12; admission CUC$2; 🕑 8am-4pm Tue-Sat, 8am-noon Sun). Admission includes a tour, but cameras/videos are CUC$3/25 extra. Bring exact change. Admission to the circular blocks is free.

**Cementerio Colombia**, with the graves of Americans who lived and died on the island during the 1920s and 1930s, is about 7km east of Nueva Gerona and 2km east of Presidio Modelo. Bus 38 passes here.

**Cabañas Playa Paraíso** (☎ 32 52 46), on a beach 2km north of Chacón (about 6km northeast of Nueva Gerona), usually doesn't rent rooms to foreigners, but the **bar & restaurant** (🕑 noon-8pm) are open to all. Playa Paraíso itself is no paradise, but more a dirty brown beach. Still, it's in a scenic spot, with a high hill behind and a small island offshore. The wharf here was originally used to unload prisoners for the Presidio Modelo. If you're driving around this way there's a better beach called Playa Bibijagua 4km to the east of Chacón. Here there are pine trees, a peso restaurant and plenty of low-key Cuban ambience. Nondrivers can catch bus 38 from Nueva Gerona.

## SOUTH OF NUEVA GERONA

### Sights & Activities

The main reason to come here is for the diving at Punta Francés (see the boxed text, p188), but there are a couple of other interesting diversions for those who have time.

#### FIDEL IN PRISON

Beaten but not defeated after the abortive attack on Moncada Barracks, Fidel was banished to the Isla de Pinos in October 1953 to lick his wounds and plot afresh. Incarcerated in the barren Presidio Modelo along with 25 fellow conspirators prisoner number RN3859, as Castro was officially known, shared a cell with his brother Raúl who he kept awake day and night with hours of incessant ranting.

Not surprisingly there was plenty to talk about. Taking advantage of their privileged status as political prisoners, the Castro brothers lost no time in setting up an in-house revolutionary academy that schooled fellow inmates in the intricacies of economic theory and guerilla warfare.

Meanwhile, back in his cell, Fidel passed the long daylight hours transforming his epic *History Will Absolve Me* speech into an authoritative political manifesto. Scribbling down the text from memory the document was smuggled out of his cell in matchboxes whereupon a few thousand copies were run off and circulated by supporters around the country.

**INTO THE BLUE**

Protected from sea currents off the Gulf of Mexico and blessed with a remarkable diversity of coral and marine life, Isla de la Juventud offers some of the best diving possibilities in the Caribbean. They're 56 buoyed dive sites here including everything from caves and passages, to vertical walls and coral hillocks. Wreck diving is also possible further east where the remains of 70 ships have been found in an area known as **Bajo de Zambo**.

Center of operations for the diving crowd is the **International Diving Center** (☎ 39 82 82/84) run from the Marina Siguanea a few kilometers south of Hotel Colony. The establishment has a modern on-site recompression chamber along with the services of a dive doctor, and it is from here that you can organize trips out to the National Maritime Park at **Punta Francés**.

Boat transfers to Punta Francés take about an hour and deliver you to gorgeous stretch of white-sand beach (complete with rustic restaurant) from which most of the main dive sites are easily accessible. The cream of the crop are **Cueva Azul** (advanced) and **Pared de Coral Negro** (intermediate) where you'll see abundant numbers of fish including tarpon, barracuda, groupers, snooks and angelfish – along with the odd sea turtle.

Diving costs start at CUC$30. Nondivers can get to the beach for CUC$8 where there's a lunch buffet at a rustic restaurant for CUC$12.



Situated 6km west of Santa Fe in the direction of El Colony, **La Jungla de Jones** (☎ 39 62 46; admission CUC$3; 🕐 24hr) is a rich and verdant botanical garden containing more than 80 varieties of tree. Bisected by a network of shaded trails and punctuated by a cornucopia of cacti, bamboo and mangoes, this expansive and recently restored garden once belonged to two American botanists, Helen and Harris Jones, who set up the establishment in 1902 with the intention of studying plants and trees from around the world. The highlight of La Jungla is the aptly named Bamboo Cathedral, an enclosed space surrounded by huge clumps of craning bamboo that only a few strands of sunlight manage to penetrate.

**Criadero Cocodrilo** (admission CUC$3; 🕐 7am-5pm) has played an important part in crocodile conservation in Cuba over the last few years and the results are interesting to see. Harboring more than 500 crocodiles of all shapes and sizes, the *criadero* (hatchery) acts as a breeding center, similar to the one in Guamá in Matanzas (p250), although the setting here is infinitely wilder. Taken care of until they are seven years old, the center releases groups of crocs back into the wild when they reach a length of about 1m. To get to the criadero turn left 12km south of La Fe just past Julio Antonio Mella.

## Sleeping & Eating

**Hotel Colony** (Gran Caribe; ☎ 39 81 81; fax 39 84 28; s/d incl breakfast, low season CUC$38/64, high season CUC$56/84) This hotel on the Ensenada de la Siguanea, 46km southwest of Nueva Gerona, originated in 1958 as part of the Hilton chain but was confiscated by the revolutionary government before it got off the ground. Today the main building's a bit run down but the newer bungalows are in good shape; clean, bright and airy. You might save a few cents by taking a package which includes three meals and scuba diving. The water off the hotel's white-sand beach is shallow, with sea urchins littering the bottom. Take care if you decide to swim. A better (and safer?) bet is the Colony's pleasant pool. A long wharf (with a bar perfect for sunset mojitos) stretches out over the bay, but snorkeling in the immediate vicinity of the hotel is mediocre. The diving, however, is to die for. A Havanautos car-rental office is at the hotel.

## Getting There & Away

Transport is tough on La Isla and bus schedules make even the rest of Cuba seem efficient. Try bus 441 from Nueva Gerona. Otherwise, your best bet to get to the hotel is by taxi (approximately CUC$30 from the airport) or hire car (see p187).

# THE SOUTHERN MILITARY ZONE

The entire area south of Cayo Piedra is a military zone and to enter you must first procure a one-day pass (CUC$12) from the **Ecotur office** (☎ 32 71 01) in Nueva Gerona. The company will provide you with a Spanish/English/German/French/Italian-speaking guide, but it is up to you to find your own 4WD transport for within the zone itself. This can be organized with Havanautos in Nueva Gerona (p187). Traveling in the military zone is not possible without a guide or an official pass so don't arrive at the Cayo Piedra checkpoint without either. As the whole excursion can wind up rather expensive it's an idea to split the transport costs with other travelers. Good places to fish around for other people are Hotel Colony and the Villa Isla de la Juventud. Both of these places also have tourist information offices that can give you more up-to-date advice on the region.

### Cueva de Punta del Este

The Cueva de Punta del Este, a national monument 59km southeast of Nueva Gerona, has been called the 'Sistine Chapel' of Caribbean Indian art. Long before the Spanish conquest (experts estimate around AD 800), Indians painted some 235 pictographs on the walls and ceiling of the cave. The largest has 28 concentric circles of red and black, and the paintings have been interpreted as a solar calendar. Discovered in 1910, they're considered the most important of their kind in the Caribbean. Smaller, similar paintings can be seen in the Cueva de Ambrosio in Varadero (p234). The long, shadeless white beach nearby is another draw (for you and the mosquitoes – bring insect repellent).

### Crocodrilo

Cocodrilo, 50km southwest of Cayo Piedra, is a friendly village of 750 residents, still untouched by tourism. Through the lush vegetation beside the potholed road one catches glimpses of cattle, birds, lizards and bee hives. The rocky coastline, with its natural inlets and small, white sandy beaches lapped by crystal-blue water, is magnificent. One kilometer west of this tiny settlement is the **Sea Turtle Breeding Center** (admission CUC$1; 8am-6pm) where visitors can view rows of green-stained glass tanks that teem with turtles of all sizes. While not quite as captivating as watching the creatures nesting in the wild, the breeding center does an excellent job in conserving one of Cuba's rarest and most endangered species.

# CAYO LARGO DEL SUR

☎ 45

Cayo Largo del Sur's 26km of glittering white sands, teeming coral reefs, and chain of fabulous all-inclusive resorts add up to a tropical paradise par excellence. What Cayo Largo del Sur is not, is Cuba. Here, women sunbathe topless, you can throw your toilet paper into the toilet rather than the bin, and an inordinate number of people speak a language (or several) other than Spanish. If you're looking for fun in the sun, spectacular scuba diving and all the creature comforts upmarket resorts are famous for, then you'll love this little tropical idyll. Packages from Habana are relatively affordable if you just want to jump over for a couple of days. In winter especially, the weather tends to be warmer and more stable than at resorts along Cuba's north coast.

Cayo Largo del Sur is the second largest (38 sq km) and easternmost island of the Archipiélago de los Canarreos. It lies between the Golfo de Batabanó and the Caribbean Sea, 177km southeast of Habana, 114km east of Isla de la Juventud, 80km south of the Península de Zapata and 300km due north of Grand Cayman Island. Though 26km long, this sandy coral key is never more than a couple of kilometers wide. Due to the island's isolation, there's a profusion of turtles, iguanas and bird life including cranes, *zunzuncitos* (bee hummingbirds) and flamingos.

## Information

The **Cubatur** (☎ 34 80 18) and Transtur offices, **bank** (☎ 34 82 25) and medical clinic are all at Hotel Isla del Sur (p191), and the telephone center is across the street. Euros are accepted at all the tourist installations here.

Due to dangerous currents, swimming is occasionally forbidden. This will be indicated by red flags on the beach, and care should be taken with waves, which can suddenly throw snorkelers into the reef. Mosquitoes can be a nuisance here, too, so bring repellent.

## Sights & Activities

Cayo Largo del Sur's finest beach is the broad westward-facing **Playa Sirena**, where 2km of powdery white sand is well protected from the waves and wind. Tourists

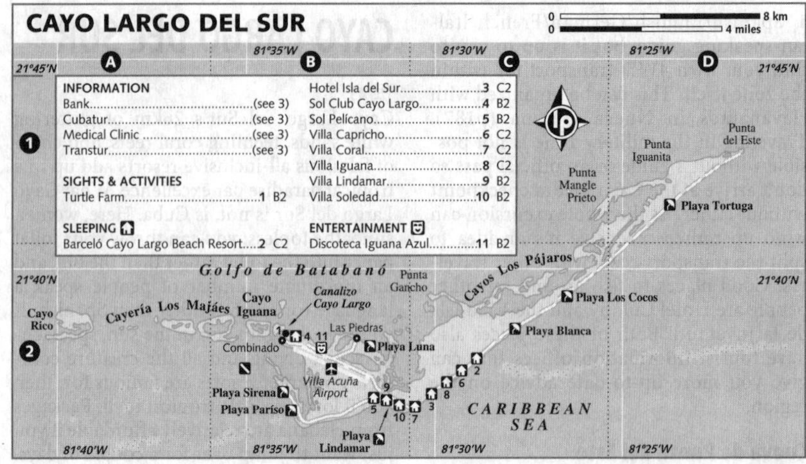


on day trips from Habana and Varadero are often brought here. Various nautical activities are available, including scuba diving and certification courses with Puertosol. A dive shop and restaurant are at Playa Sirena. All of Cayo Largo del Sur's hotels offer day excursions to Playa Sirena for around CUC$25, or you can walk there in less than two hours from Sol Pelícano via **Playa Paraíso**, a nudist beach (several stretches of sand on this island are clothing optional).

The island's other big day-trip destinations are **Cayo del Rosario** and **Cayo Rico** between Cayo Largo del Sur and Isla de la Juventud. Boat excursions to these beaches from the hotels cost around CUC$35 per person. **Cayo Iguana**, off the northwest tip of Cayo Largo del Sur, is home to hundreds of friendly iguanas; unfortunately, many perished in Hurricane Michelle – the worst tropical storm to hit Cuba in 50 years – in 2001 though the population now seems to have recovered. Equally stoic is the tourist population that despite mass evacuations and extensive hotel damage after the hurricane remains similarly unfazed by the challenges of nature.

You can rent a bicycle and head east to **Playa Los Cocos**, where there's good snorkeling, or continue further northeast to **Playa Tortuga**, where sea turtles lay their eggs in the sand. A **turtle farm** *(granja de las tortugas)* is at Combinado, on the northwest end of the island beyond the airstrip.

Sporting activities available on the island include snorkeling, scuba diving, windsurfing, sailing, kayaking, tennis, horseback riding, cycling and volleyball. The best selections of these are at the Sol Pelícano and Isla del Sur hotels.

There's also deep-sea fishing from powerboats for marlin, dorado, snapper and bonito. Two international fishing tournaments are held here in September.

## Sleeping & Eating

All of Cayo Largo del Sur's hotels face the 4km beach on the south side of the island. It's said that these white sands are unique in that they aren't heated up by the sun's rays. This permits barefoot (and bare-bottomed – Cayo Largo is known for its naturism) traffic along the shore and kind of compensates for the lack of shade.

This resort island is unique in Cuba in that you buy an all-inclusive package with Gran Caribe or Sol Meliá and your color-coded bracelet allows you to use whatever facilities belong to that chain. At the time of writing, Sol Meliá owned Sol Club Cayo Largo, and Sol Pelícano; while Gran Caribe Club had Villas Coral, Soledad, Lindamar, Hotel Isla del Sur, Iguana, Barceló and Capricho. Virtually everyone arrives on prepaid package tours, with transport, accommodation and meals included. Rack rates for the Gran Caribe properties are single/double CUC$103/147 all-inclusive, or upwards of CUC$160 per person for the Sol Meliá properties. Check at Cubatur in Habana for better deals.

**Barceló Cayo Largo Beach Resort** (☎ 24 80 80; P) The 306-room Barceló is Cayo Largo's newest resort and is set apart from the other hotels on an expansive stretch of Playa Blanca. Rather drab architecture is augmented by a smorgasbord of different dining options and an impressive array of energetic sporting activities. Good testimonies abound.

**Sol Pelícano** (☎ 34 82 60; www.solpelicano.solmeliacuba.com; P) This Spanish-style resort on Playa Lindamar, 5km southeast of the airport, has 203 rooms in a series of three-story buildings and two-story duplex cabanas built in 1995. This is the island's largest resort and facilities include a nightclub. A small bridge links the complex to the beach.

**Sol Club Cayo Largo** (☎ 34 82 60; www.solmeliacuba.com; P) Sol Meliá's other property is the five-star Sol Club Cayo Largo on the northwestern nub of the island. The beach out here is fantastic and every room comes with a terrace or balcony. To date, it's Cayo Largo's most exclusive resort (but watch for Meliá's Linda Arena, still under construction at the time of writing).

**Villa Coral** (El Pueblito; ☎ 34 81 11; fax 34 81 60; P) Also known as El Pueblito, this villa consists of 10 two-story buildings outfitted to look like colonial villas (eg faux terra-cotta roofs, wooden balconies) arranged around a swimming pool. There are 60 rooms here.

**Villa Soledad** (☎ 34 81 11; fax 34 81 60; P) This adjacent cluster of single-story, plainer bungalows has another 43 rooms (but no restaurant – you have to go to one of the neighboring hotels held by Gran Caribe).

**Villa Lindamar** (☎ 34 81 11; fax 34 81 60; P) These 63 thatched bungalows are the only four-star rooms in this chain – love the hammocks. The Piazzoletta Italian Restaurant on the premises offers pizza and more.

**Hotel Isla del Sur** (☎ 34 81 11; fax 34 81 60; P) This hotel has 59 rooms with minifridges in a long, two-story building. Built in 1981 on the point between Playa Lindamar and Playa Blanca, this was the first hotel on Cayo Largo del Sur. All meals here are served buffet style, and there's poolside entertainment nightly. A small shopping arcade is opposite the hotel, and guests at Villa Coral and Villa Iguana must come here for sporting activities such as horseback riding, tennis, deep-sea fishing and scuba diving. Bicycle rentals are available and there's a Transtur and Cubatur desk here.

**Villa Iguana** (☎ 34 81 11) This accommodation option has 114 rooms with fridges in 10 two-story blocks. The swimming pool (also used for scuba instruction) sits in the center of the resort and the beach is just 200m away down a flight of steps. Buffet-style meals are served in the Gavilán restaurant.

**Villa Capricho** (☎ 34 81 11; P) Just east of Villa Iguana, this place has 62 pleasant, individual wooden cabins, each with a porch and hammock. Windsurfing, kayaking and sailing are possible off its beach, and its Restaurante Blue Marlin specializes in paella and seafood.

## Entertainment

After 11pm, there's a minibus service between the hotels and the Discoteca Iguana Azul, near the airport.

## Getting There & Away

Several charter flights arrive directly from Canada weekly, and Cubana has weekly flights from Montreal and Milan.

For pop-by visitors, daily flights from Habana to Cayo Largo del Sur with Cubana cost CUC$80 one way. But getting around once you arrive on the island can prove to be problematic. An easier option is to take an organized day trip from Habana or Varadero to Cayo Largo del Sur for in the vicinity of CUC$137, including airport transfers, return flights and a sumptuous barbecue lunch. All the Habana agencies offer this (see p92).

# Pinar del Río Province

Rust-red soil, well-tended fields of tobacco, Chevrolets and Buicks rattling along rutted roads: the images of bucolic Pinar del Río Province are Cuban to the core. Situated on the island's western extremity and within easy reach of the capital Habana, the 'Garden of Cuba', as picturesque Pinar is often called, has been attracting visitors for decades. Most come to sample the plethora of astounding natural attractions that have made the region internationally famous. Others prefer to linger, rum glass in hand, on the sun-dappled beaches of Cayo Jutías and Cayo Levisa.

Transcended by the hilly Sierra del Rosario reserve in the east and the more isolated Península de Guanahacabibes in the west, Pinar del Río is the only province in Cuba to boast two Unesco biospheres. Nestled somewhere in between lies the majestic Valle de Viñales, a geological anomaly with its complicated cave systems and craggy limestone mogotes that lures everyone from birders to rock climbers.

Southwest of the provincial capital, the Autopista gives way to the misty fields of the San Luis region; the world's finest tobacco-growing area, and a landscape punctuated by lone straw-hatted *guajiros* (farmers) laboring industriously under the hot, tropical sun. Continue driving for a few hours more and the road finally runs out in María la Gorda, one of Pinar's best beaches and the 'operations center' for an enthusiastic fraternity of international scuba divers who revel in its sheltered waters and dazzling underwater coral formations.

## HIGHLIGHTS

- **Sunrise over Tobacco Country**
  Hike up to Hotel Los Jazmines and watch the early morning mist lift off the Valle de Viñales (p207)
- **Underwater Odyssey**
  Experience scuba diving at translucent Playa María la Gorda (p203)
- **Splendid Isolation**
  Stop and smell the roses on idyllic Cayo Levisa (p213)
- **Hot Water Hedonism**
  Soak up medicinal mineral waters in San Diego de los Baños (p214)
- **Eco-village**
  Enjoy the artistic ambience of model village, Las Terrazas (p217)

Cayo Levisa
Las Terrazas
Valle de Viñales
San Diego de los Baños
Playa María la Gorda

- TELEPHONE CODE: VARIES
- POPULATION: 739,473
- AREA: 10,924 SQ KM

## HISTORY

Western Cuba's pre-Columbian history is synonymous with the Guanahatabeys, a group of nomadic Indians who lived in caves and procured most of their livelihood from the sea. Less advanced than the other indigenous natives who lived on the island, the Guanahatabeys were a peaceful and passive race whose culture had developed, more or less independently of the Taíno and Siboney cultures further east. Extinct by the time the Spanish arrived in 1492, little firsthand documentation remains on how the archaic Guanahatabey society was structured and organized although some archeological sites have been found on the Guanahacabibes Peninsula.

Post-Columbus the conquistadors left rugged Pinar del Río largely to its own devices, and the area developed lackadaisically only after Canary Islanders started arriving in the late 1500s. It was originally called Nueva Filipina (New Philippines), but the region was renamed Pinar del Río in 1778, supposedly for the pine forests crowded along the Río Guamá. Tobacco plantations and cattle ranches quickly sprang up in the rich soil and open grazing land that typifies Pinar and the fastidious farmers who made a living from the delicate and well-tended crops were colloquially christened *guajiros,* a native word that means – literally – 'one of us.' By the mid-1800s, Europeans were hooked on the fragrant weed and the region flourished. Sea routes opened up and the railway was extended to facilitate the shipping of the perishable product.

These days, tobacco, along with tourism, keep Pinar del Río both profitable and popular. Quiet and laid-back compared with the car-crazy capital 160km or so to the east, the relaxed Pinareños – despite the countless *guajiro* jokes – are some of the friendliest, most ingratiating people you'll meet on the island.

# PINAR DEL RÍO AREA

## PINAR DEL RÍO

☎ 82 / pop 148,295

Pinar del Río, 162km southwest of Habana via the Autopista, is a bustling Cuban town of rusty bicycles and beaten up old American cars that has developed a rather unsavory reputation for its aggressive *jineteros* (touts). You'll get used to saying *'no me moleste, por favor'* (don't bother me please) quite a lot here.

Situated right in the center of Cuba's prime tobacco-growing area and characterized by a surprisingly well-maintained collection of pastel-colored, neoclassical buildings, the town lacks the tourist facilities of nearby Viñales and is often overlooked by independent travelers, who use it as a springboard for the more accessible natural attractions of the villages further north.

Founded in 1774 by a Spanish army captain, Pinar del Río was one of the last provincial capitals on the island to take root. Neglected by successive central governments who preferred sugarcane to tobacco,

### GUAJIRO NATURAL

In a country where disparaging nicknames are part of the national culture, the label *guajiro* has a peculiarly rural connotation. Used interchangeably to mean farmer, hillbilly, simpleton or bumpkin, this much maligned regional stereotype has its spiritual home in Pinar del Río Province where cigar-chewing tobacco farmers are characterized by a level of generosity that verges on the gullible.

Polo Montañez, a humble and much-loved musician who rose to national and international fame as a singer in the early 2000s, did much to de-stigmatize the traditional *guajiro* stereotype. Resident of a small agrarian community in Pinar del Río Province, he worked by day as a lumberjack and by night as a self-taught guitarist and singer in a luxury tourist hotel in the model settlement of Las Terrazas. Fame came late. In fact, Polo's first commercial success, the aptly named *Guajiro Natural,* didn't hit the big-time until 2001 by which time the singer had attained the ripe old age of 46. Tragically the honeymoon wasn't to last. In November 2002, while returning by car from Habana to his home in Pinar, Polo was involved in a fatal collision with a truck trailer. He died a week later of severe head injuries. A new *guajiro* legend had been created.

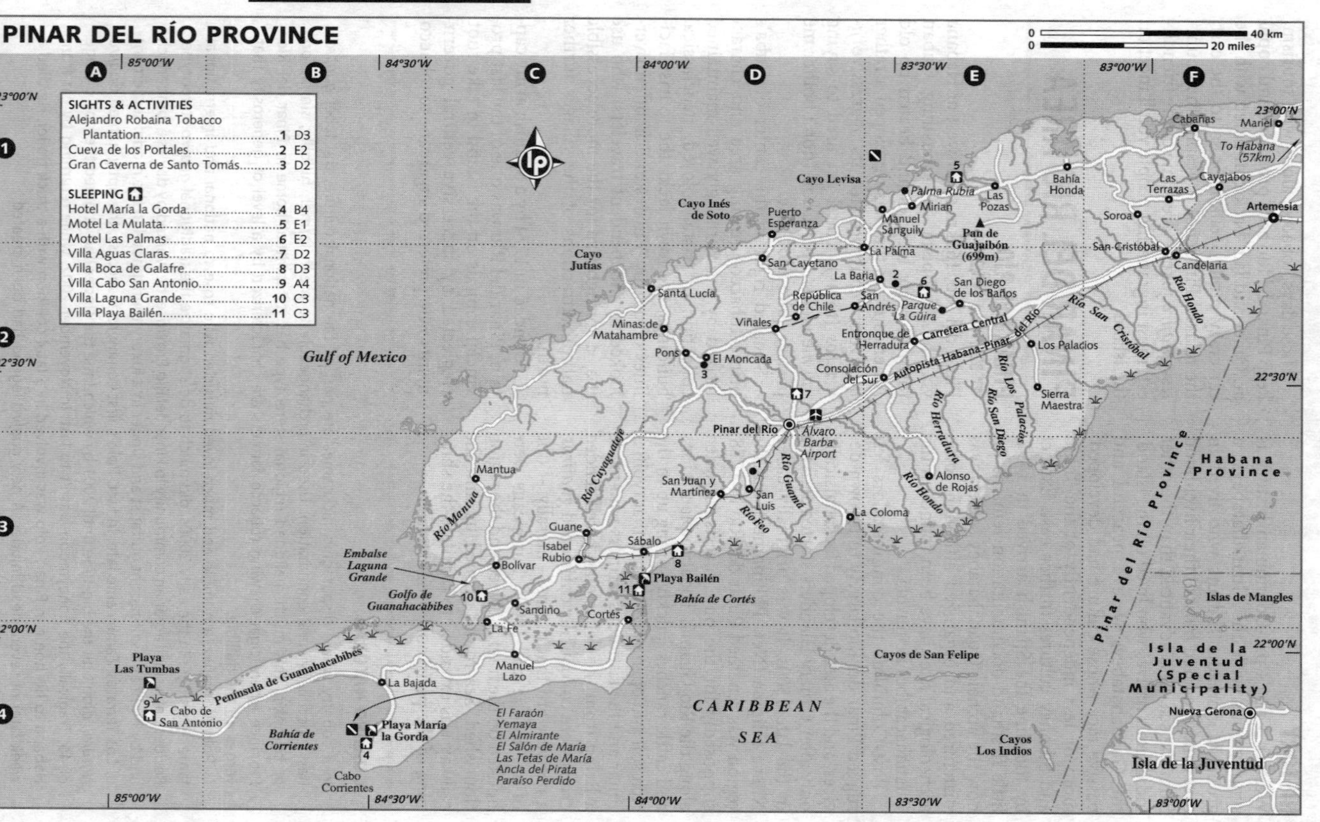

PINAR DEL RÍO PROVINCE
SIGHTS & ACTIVITIES
Alejandro Robaina Tobacco Plantation 1 D3
Cueva de los Portales 2 E2
Gran Caverna de Santo Tomás 3 D2
SLEEPING
Hotel María la Gorda 4 B4
Motel La Mulata 5 E1
Motel Las Palmas 6 E2
Villa Aguas Claras 7 D2
Villa Boca de Galafre 8 D3
Villa Cabo San Antonio 9 A4
Villa Laguna Grande 10 C3
Villa Playa Bailén 11 C3
Gulf of Mexico
CARIBBEAN SEA
Habana Province
Pinar del Río Province
Isla de la Juventud (Special Municipality)
Isla de la Juventud
Nueva Gerona
Islas de Mangles
Cayos de San Felipe
Cayos Los Indios
Cayo Levisa
Cayo Inés de Soto
Cayo Jutías
Pinar del Río
Álvaro Barba Airport
Viñales
Artemesia
Mariel
Cabañas
To Habana (57km)
Las Terrazas
Cayajabos
Soroa
San Cristóbal
Candelaria
Bahía Honda
Las Pozas
Palma Rubia
Mirian
Manuel Sanguily
Pan de Guajaibón (699m)
La Palma
La Baría
San Diego de los Baños
Parque La Güira
San Andrés
República de Chile
Puerto Esperanza
San Cayetano
Santa Lucía
Minas de Matahambre
Pons
El Moncada
Entronque de Herradura
Carretera Central
Autopista Habana-Pinar del Río
Consolación del Sur
Los Palacios
Sierra Maestra
Río Hondo
Río San Cristóbal
Río Los Palacios
Río San Diego
Río Herradura
Río Guamá
Río Feo
Río Cuyaguateje
Río Mantua
Alonso de Rojas
La Coloma
San Juan y Martínez
San Luis
Mantua
Guane
Isabel Rubio
Sábalo
Playa Bailén
Bahía de Cortés
Bolívar
Embalse Laguna Grande
Golfo de Guanahacabibes
Sandino
La Fe
Cortés
Manuel Lazo
La Bajada
Península de Guanahacabibes
Playa Las Tumbas
Cabo de San Antonio
Bahía de Corrientes
Playa María la Gorda
Cabo Corrientes
El Faraón
Yemaya
El Almirante
El Salón de María
Las Tetas de María
Ancla del Pirata
Paraíso Perdido
23°00'N
22°30'N
22°00'N
85°00'W
84°30'W
84°00'W
83°30'W
83°00'W
0 40 km
0 20 miles

the city developed into an urban backwater and became the butt of countless jokes about easily-to-fool *guajiros* who were popularly portrayed as simple-minded rural hicks. In 1896 General Antonio Maceo brought the Second War of Independence to Pinar del Río in an ambitious attempt to split the island in two and the town finally got its wake-up call.

Following the 1959 revolution Pinar del Río's economic fortunes improved exponentially; this was facilitated further by the building of the Autopista Nacional from Habana and the development of tourism in the 1980s.

## Orientation

The main street in Pinar del Río is called Martí and there are also many facilities on Máximo Gómez and Antonio Maceo, which run parallel to Martí just to the south. An important cross street is Isabel Rubio, which becomes the Carretera Central north of the city toward Habana and on the road to San Juan y Martínez to the southwest.

To avoid going the wrong way when you're looking for addresses, it's important to know that the street numbering begins at two base streets: Gerardo Medina divides the numbering of east–west streets while Martí marks the division between the north–south streets.

## Information

### BOOKSTORES

**Havanatur** (☎ 77 84 94; cnr Martí & Colón; 🕒 8am-noon & 1:30-6pm Mon-Fri, 8am-noon & 1-4pm Sat) Best selection of maps, books in English and office supplies.

#### PINAR DEL RÍO STREET NAMES

Locals stick to the old street names; this chart should help:

| Old name | New name |
|---|---|
| Recreo | Isabel Rubio |
| Caubada | Commandante Pinares |
| Calzada de la Coloma | Rafael Ferro |
| Vélez Caviedes | Gerardo Medina |
| Rosario | Ormani Arenado |
| San Juan | Rafael Morales |
| Virtudes | Ceferino Fernández |

### INTERNET ACCESS

**Etecsa Telepunto** (cnr Gerardo Medina & Juan Gómez; per hr CUC$6; 🕒 24hr)

### LEFT LUGGAGE

Downstairs at the bus station you can talk your way into leaving your bag(s) at the luggage storage window for CUC$1.

### MEDIA

*Guerrillero* is published on Friday. Radio Guamá airs on 1080AM or 90.2FM.

### MEDICAL SERVICES

**Farmacia Martí** (Martí Este No 50; 🕒 8am-11pm)

**Hospital Provincial León Cuervo Rubio** (☎ 75 44 43; Carretera Central) Two kilometers north of town.

### MONEY

**Banco Financiero Internacional** (☎ 77 81 53; Gerardo Medina Norte No 46) Opposite Casa de la Música.

**Bandec** (☎ 75 26 07; Martí Este No 32; 🕒 8:30am-noon & 1:30-3:30pm Mon-Fri) There's another branch on Martí No 53.

**Cadeca** (☎ 77 83 57; Martí No 46; 🕒 8:30am-5:30pm Mon-Sat)

### POST

**Post office** (Martí Este No 49; 🕒 8am-8pm Mon-Sat)

### TELEPHONE

**Etecsa** (cnr Gerardo Medina & Juan Gómez; 🕒 24hr)

### TRAVEL AGENCIES

**Campismo Popular** (☎ 75 26 77; Isabel Rubio Norte No 20A; 🕒 8am-noon & 1-5pm Mon-Fri, 8am-noon Sat) Near Adela Azcuy.

**Cubatur** (☎ 77 84 05; Ormani Arenado btwn Martí & Máximo Gómez; 🕒 8am-noon & 1-5pm Mon-Fri, 8am-noon Sat)

**Havanatur** (☎ 77 84 94; cnr Martí & Colón; 🕒 8am-noon & 1:30-6pm Mon-Fri, 8am-noon & 1-4pm Sat)

**Islazul** (☎ 75 56 62; Martí Oeste No 127A)

## Dangers & Annoyances

For a relatively untouristed city Pinar del Río has its fair share of unsolicited touts or *jineteros* (p397). When you're strolling along Martí young men will try their hardest to attach themselves to you as a paid guide or to lead you to a private room or paladar. You may also be pursued by youths on bicycles as you arrive in town by car, or accosted when you stop at the first traffic light after the Autopista. If the light is

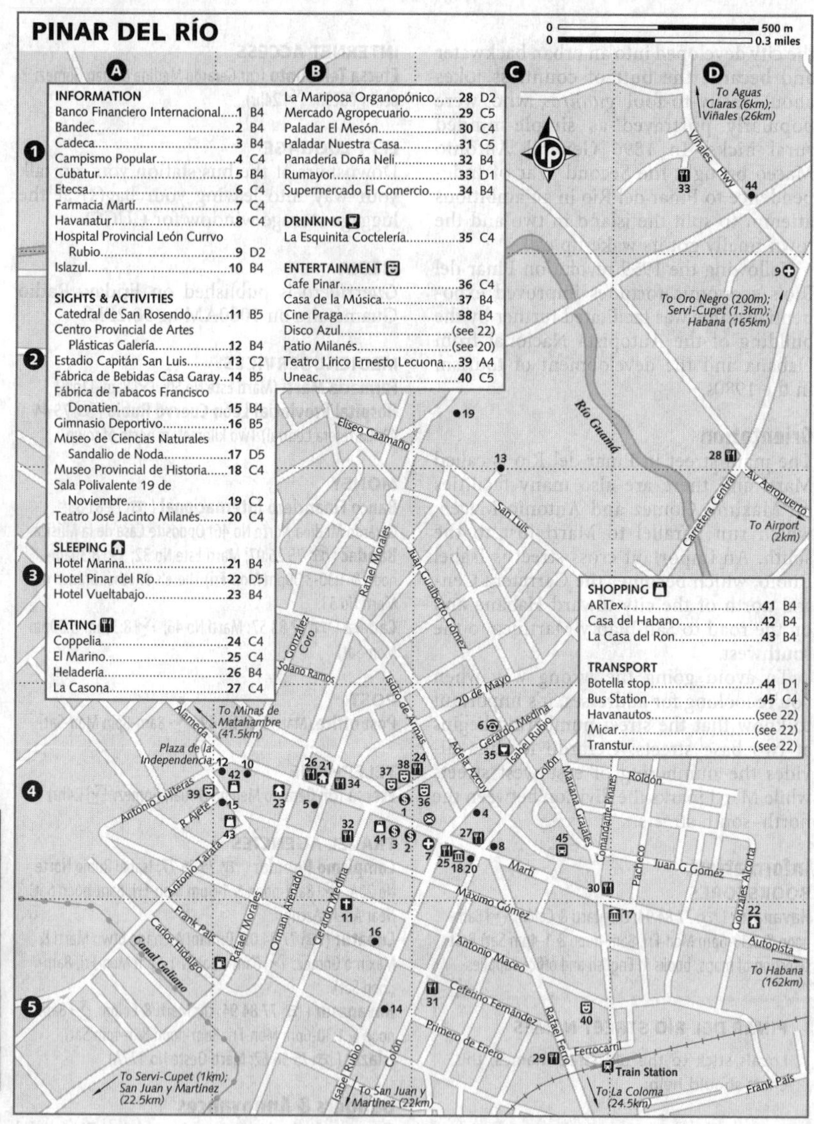


green, they'll swerve dangerously in front of you to try to get you to stop. Keep your windows closed and ignore them if they point to one of your tires, pretending it's flat.

## Sights

The most interesting sight is the **Museo de Ciencias Naturales Sandalio de Noda** (☎ 77 94 83; Martí Este No 202; admission CUC$1, plus camera CUC$1; 🕒 9am-6pm Mon-Sat, 9am-1pm Sun). In a wild, neo-Gothic-meets-Moorish mansion built by local doctor and world traveler Francisco Guasch, this museum (called Palacio de Guasch by locals) has everything from a concrete T-Rex to a stuffed baby giraffe. Come for the flowering garden, architectural details and friendly specialist staff.

Nearby is the **Museo Provincial de Historia** (☎ 75 43 00; Martí Este No 58 btwn Colón & Isabel Rubio; admission CUC$1; 8:30am-6:30pm Mon-Fri, 9am-1pm Sat), collecting the history of the province from pre-Columbian times to the present. Look for the Enrique Jorrín ephemera – Jorrín was the creator of the *chachachá* (cha-cha).

Four blocks south is the **Fábrica de Bebidas Casa Garay** (Isabel Rubio Sur No 189 btwn Ceferino Fernández & Frank País; admission CUC$1; 9am-3:30pm Mon-Fri, 9am-12:30pm Sat). Erected in 1892, this factory uses a secret recipe to distill sweet and dry versions of the famous Guayabita del Pinar guava brandy. Factory tours are offered in Spanish, English and French, topped off by a taste of the brew in the sampling room. There's a shop adjacent.

You can observe people busily rolling cigars at the **Fábrica de Tabacos Francisco Donatien** (Maceo Oeste No 157; admission CUC$5; 9am-noon & 1-4pm Mon-Fri). Until 1961 this building was a jail, but now it's tobacco central on the tourist circuit. Unless you're really interested, it's not worth the admission price, as the guides are untrained and the workers want extra money for photos. The factory in Santa Clara's a better bet. Check out its cigar store, however. The top brand produced here is called Vegueros.

On Plaza de la Independencia near Alameda and around the corner from the cigar factory is the **Centro Provincial de Artes Plásticas Galería** (Antonio Guiteras; admission free; 8am-9pm Mon-Sat), which presents good local art. The **Taller Provincial del Grabado**, a large engraving workshop welcoming visitors, is adjacent.

The wooden, 500-seat **Teatro José Jacinto Milanés** (cnr Martí & Colón) is a gorgeous venue from 1845; too bad it has been undergoing restoration since 1991.

Pinar del Río's understated **Catedral de San Rosendo** (Maceo Este No 3) dates from 1883 and its pastel yellow exterior gleams with a recent coat of paint. As with most Cuban churches the building is often closed. Slip inside for a peek during the Sunday morning service.

## Activities

Gym freaks might want to check out the **Gimnasio Deportivo** (Ceferino Fernández No 43 btwn Isabel Rubio & Gerardo Medina) where, with some fumbling Spanish and a bit of deft sign language, you can talk your way into tai chi, weightlifting or somersaulting over a horsebox. Alternatively there's the **Sala Polivalente 19 de Noviembre** (Rafael Morales) for boxing, volleyball and basketball.

From October to April, exciting baseball games happen at the **Estadio Capitán San Luis** (☎ 75 38 95; 1 peso), on the north side of town. Pinar del Río is one of the country's best teams. Pop by in the evening to see the players going through a training session.

## Festivals & Events

**Carnaval** in early July features a procession of *carrozas* (carriages) through the streets with couples dancing between the floats. It's a big drunken, dance party.

## Sleeping

### IN TOWN

**Hotel Marina** (☎ 75 25 58; Martí Oeste No 56 btwn Rafael Morales & Ormani Arenado; r CUC$16) A rock bottom peso place that will probably take you if you pay in Convertibles. Facilities are basic and the reception more than a tad fly-blown.

**Hotel Pinar del Río** (Islazul; ☎ 50 70 74; cnr Gonzales Alcorta & Autopista; s/d low season CUC$24/34, high CUC$29/38; P) Situated at the eastern end of town, where tourists are supposed to stay (and many do), the 136 rooms have bright spots such as refrigerators and radios, but the bad lighting and dizzying

> **LOS AMARILLOS**
>
> Motor tentatively out of any Cuban town and, more often than not, you'll pass a large group of patient hitchhikers standing clustered around an authoritative-looking figure dressed in yellow. These are the ubiquitous *amarillos* or traffic organizers whose job it is to stand at preorganized pick-up points and place ride-seekers into queues via an old-fashioned numbering system.
>
> In Cuba hitchhiking – or *hacer botella* as it is known locally – is an essential part of the countrywide transport network and the practice of catching a lift via the *amarillos* is legally enforced (for information on the risks associated with hitching see p477). All cars with blue (government-owned) license plates are obliged to stop and take on passengers if they have room.

decor cast a shadow. The disco is popular with the locals who can afford it.

**Hotel Vueltabajo** (Islazul; ☎ 75 53 63; cnr Martí & Rafael Morales; s/d low season CUC$42/55, high CUC$48/65; ) A rare newcomer in Cuba's stable of midrange hotels is this fabulous hotel, a lovingly restored colonial building with high ceilings, striped window awnings and various other decorative flourishes. The large rooms are a little under-furnished, but they're clean and spacious, and old-fashioned shutters give out onto the street. Downstairs there's a bar/restaurant; a reasonable breakfast is included in the price.

For a capital city, Pinar del Río has few private rooms. See the boxed text, below for recommendations.

#### OUTSIDE TOWN

**Villa Aguas Claras** (Cubamar; ☎ 77 84 27; s/d low season incl breakfast CUC$19/30, high CUC$21/34; P ) The plushest of all Cuba's 85-plus campismos, Villa Aguas Claras is 8km north of town on the Viñales Hwy and has facilities more akin to a midrange hotel. The 50 bungalows with hot showers sleep two (10 have air-con). The rooms are adequate, the landscaping lush and the staff congenial, making this a better overall choice than Hotel Pinar del Río. The Villa Aguas Claras also offers horseback riding and day trips. Insect repellent is essential here. Aguas Claras is accessible from Pinar del Río by bus 7 six times a day.

## Eating

#### PALADARES

**Paladar El Mesón** (Martí Este No 205; noon-10pm Mon-Sat) This long-standing paladar opposite the Museo de Ciencias Naturales serves chicken, pork and fish in a pleasant colonial atmosphere. Main plates start at CUC$4.50 with side dishes extra; the service is efficient and friendly.

**Paladar Nuestra Casa** (☎ 77 51 43; Colón Sur No 161 btwn Ceferino Fernández & Primero de Enero) Another good, private eatery a bit out of the center, this serves fish all ways including *filete Canciller* (fish stuffed with ham and cheese).

#### RESTAURANTS

**Coppelia** (Gerardo Medina Norte No 33; noon-midnight Tue-Sun) You'll require line-waiting skills, but the two peso a scoop ice cream (when there *is* ice cream) is dreamy.

**Heladería** (Martí cnr Rafael Morales; 9am-9pm) Even dreamier is this clean and friendly place where you can get a substantial *tres gracias* (three scoops) for the price of a teaspoon's worth of Haagen Daas.

**El Marino** (Martí Este No 52; 6:30-9pm Mon-Tue & Thu-Fri, 8pm-midnight Sat) On the corner of Isabel Rubio, El Marino specializes in seafood and does a decent fish filet for CUC$4.50.

**La Casona** (☎ 77 82 63; cnr Martí & Colón; 11am-11pm) Further down the street, this colonial-style restaurant has steak, chicken and pasta. Atmosphere hovers around zero at

### CASAS PARTICULARES – PINAR DEL RÍO

**Anna Maria García & Salvador Reyes** (☎ 77 31 46; Alameda No 24 Bajos btwn Volcán & Avellaneda; r CUC$20; ) Clean, German spoken, good house for cyclists, helpful.

**Colonial House – José Antonio Mesa** (☎ 3173; Gerardo Medina Norte No 67 btwn Adela Azcuy & Isidro de Armas; r CUC$15) Good for groups; courtyard.

**Fernández Rent Room** (☎ 3158; Colón Norte No 73 btwn Juan Gualberto Gómez & Adela Azcuy; r CUC$15) Shared bath, meals served, signposted.

**Gladys Cruz Hernández** (☎ 77 96 98; Av Comandante Pinares Sur No 15 btwn Martí & Máximo Gómez; r CUC$15) Near train, sleeps three, big patio and fridge, TV, nice bath.

**Martí 51 – Laura González Valdés** (☎ 2264; Martí Este No 51 Altos btwn Colón & Isabel Rubio; r CUC$20; ) Central, balcony overlooking the street, awesome private library, colonial atmosphere, meals.

**Mayda Martínez** (☎ 2110; Isabel Rubio Sur No 125; r CUC$20; ) Apartment with kitchen, meals.

**Mr Aquino** (no phone; Av Comandante Pinares Sur No 56-A; r CUC$20) Fully-equipped independent apartment with kitchen, super-friendly hosts, quiet, good value. On the corner of Máximo Gómez.

**Rey & Ely** (no phone; Antonio Rubio No 70 btwn Rafael Morales & Ormari Arenado; r CUC$20; P ) Meals available.

**Villa Manolo** (☎ 75 41 95; Gerardo Medina No 243 btwn Frank País & 1st, Rpto Raúl Sánchez; r CUC$20; )

both these state-run places, but the food isn't bad.

**Rumayor** (☎ 76 30 51; 🕑 noon-midnight) The best government-operated restaurant in Pinar del Río is Islazul's Rumayor, located 1km north of the town center, off the Viñales Hwy. Justly famous for its succulent *pollo ahumado* (smoked chicken), you'll pay a little extra here (CUC$10 to CUC$15), but it is definitely worth it. There is a cabaret here as well (see right).

### GROCERIES

**Mercado agropecuario** (Rafael Ferro; 🕑 8am-6pm Mon-Sat, 8am-1pm Sun) Pinar del Río's colorful open-air market is almost on top of the tracks near the train station.

**La Mariposa Organopónico** (cnr Carretera Central & Av Aeropuerto) A conveniently located organic fruit and vegetable market; and a good place to get a close-up look at Cuban's urban agriculture program.

Other self-catering options:

**Panadería Doña Neli** (cnr Gerardo Medina Sur & Máximo Gómez; 🕑 7am-7pm) Sells bread.

**Supermercado El Comercio** (cnr Martí Oeste & Arenado; 🕑 9am-5pm Mon-Sat, 9am-noon Sun) One the best supermarkets in town.

## Drinking

**La Esquinita Coctelería** (cnr Isabel Rubio Norte & Juan Gómez; 🕑 noon-midnight) A darling cocktail place where tropical foliage gone haywire creates semiprivate nooks in the back patio. Pesos only, *por favor*.

## Entertainment

**Casa de la Música** (Gerardo Medina Norte No 21; admission CUC$1; 🕑 concerts start at 9pm nightly) Has live concerts in a cozy patio.

**Cafe Pinar** (☎ 77 81 99; Gerardo Medina Norte No 34; admission CUC$1-4; 🕑 10-2am) Across from Casa de la Música, this is an enduringly popular spot. Live bands play nightly in the intimate patio space and there's a light menu with pasta, chicken and sandwiches. Come here if you want to meet some other travelers.

**Disco Azul** (cnr Gonzales Alcorta & Autopista; admission CUC$2; 🕑 from 10pm Tue-Sun) In Hotel Pinar del Río, this is Pinar del Río's most popular dance spot. Entry for nonguests is from outside the hotel.

**Teatro Lírico Ernesto Lecuona** (Antonio Maceo Oeste No 163) Near the cigar factory, this theater presents plays in Spanish.

**Patio Milanés** (cnr Martí & Colón), Alongside the Teatro José Jacinto Milanés, Milanés has nightly cultural activities; check the schedule that's posted outside.

**Cine Praga** (☎ 75 32 71; Gerardo Medina Norte No 31) Next to Coppelia restaurant, Cine Praga shows mostly subtitled films; also look here for the video schedule at **Uneac** (Antonio Maceo No 178 btwn Rafael Ferro & Comandante Pinares; 🕑 movies at 8:30pm & 10:15pm).

From Tuesday through Sunday nights, Rumayor (left) functions as a kitschy cabaret, with a floor show that starts at 11pm (CUC$5 cover). It's not the Tropicana, but it ain't half bad.

### THE WORLD'S BEST MECHANICS

Fine US workmanship or deft Cuban ingenuity – the secret that keeps 60,000 or so vintage cars chugging like dinosaurs along the streets of Cuba's cities is a matter of some debate.

Hard though it may be to believe, Habana once boasted more cars than anywhere in the Western hemisphere. For nearly half a century the Caribbean market was inundated with Chevrolets, Buicks, Oldsmoblies and Cadillacs, manufactured by Cuba's venerable neighbors to the north. But the revolution changed all that. For a generation of car salesmen, the sight of Castro and his entourage rolling into the capital atop their jeeps in January 1959 was the beginning of the end. Over the ensuing 45 years Cuba was summarily transformed from best-selling car showroom into the Jurassic Park of the motor industry, with only a steady stream of Russian-built Ladas imported during the '70s and '80s bucking the trend.

Forced to adapt in order to survive, innovative Cuban motorists have reinvented themselves as the world's best mechanics. Stick your head under the hood of a vintage '51 Plymouth these days and, chances are, you'll come face to face with a Russian generator, a Mexican battery and pistons borrowed off a GAZ-51 Soviet truck. For classic car collectors it's a glimpse inside the world's biggest motor museum. For the Cubans, it's a case of creative engineering for a population who'd much rather be driving Toyota Yarises.

### Shopping

**ARTex** (☎ 77 83 67; Martí Este No 36; ⏲ 9am-5pm Mon-Sat, 9am-noon Sun) Sells souvenirs, CDs and T-shirts.

**La Casa del Ron** (Antonio Maceo Oeste No 151; ⏲ 9am-4:30pm Mon-Fri, 9am-1pm Sat & Sun) Near the cigar factory, sells the same merchandise as ARTex, plus rum.

There's also a Casa del Habano in the street opposite.

### Getting There & Away

#### BUS

Whatever transport needs you have, they can likely be met at the **bus station** (Adela Azcuy btwn Colón & Comandante Pinares). Because **Víazul** (www.viazul.com) buses from Habana only go as far as Viñales, travelers interested in exploring other parts of the province will have to rely on **Astro** (☎ 75 25 72)buses, or take advantage of the transfer bus that now runs daily to María la Gorda stopping in Pinar del Río at 7:30am on the outward leg and 6:30pm on the return. A similar service goes to Habana via Soroa stopping in Pinar at 8:30am and Soroa at 10:15am. For more details contact **Havanatur** (☎ 77 84 94; millo@cimex.cimex.cu) in Pinar del Río.

To get to Cayo Levisa, board the 6:20pm bus to Bahía Honda via Viñales and alight at Mirian, 4km from the Palma Rubia coast guard station, from where boats leave for the Cayo; you'll have to overnight at the station.

Víazul leaves for Viñales twice daily at 11:30am and 4:30pm (CUC$6) and for Habana at 8:50am and 2:50pm (CUC$11). Tickets in Convertibles are purchased at the window upstairs (open 8am to 7pm).

Colectivos hanging around outside the bus station will offer you prices all the way to Habana.

#### TRAIN

Before planning any train travel, check the blackboards at the station for cancelled, suspended and rescheduled services. From the **train station** (☎ 75 57 34; cnr Ferrocarril & Commandante Pinares Sur; ⏲ ticket window 6:30am-noon & 1-6:30pm) there's a daily train to Habana (CUC$7, 5½ hours, 8:45am). You can buy your ticket for this train the day of departure; be at the station between 7am and 8pm. Local trains go southwest to Guane via Sábalo (CUC$2, two hours, 7:18am and 6:30pm). This is the closest you can get by train to the Península de Guanahacabibes.

### Getting Around

There are **Micar** (☎ 77 14 54), **Transtur** (☎ 77 81 78) and **Havanautos** (☎ 77 80 15) car-rental offices at the Hotel Pinar del Río. You can rent mopeds at Transtur (CUC$24 per day).

Servicentro Oro Negro is two blocks north of the Hospital Provincial on the Carretera Central. Servi-Cupet is 1.5km further north on the Carretera Central toward Habana; another is on Rafael Morales Sur at the south entrance to town.

Horse carts (one peso) on Isabel Rubio near Adela Azcuy go to the Hospital Provincial and out onto the Carretera Central. Bici-taxis cost five pesos around town.

It's not difficult to catch a *botella* (ride) from the outskirts of Pinar del Río to Viñales (10 pesos): wait at the junction of the Viñales Hwy and the northern extent of Rafael Morales where you should see an *amarillo* (see p197).

## SOUTHWEST OF PINAR DEL RÍO

Heading into tobacco country, you're escorted southwest out of Pinar del Río city by rows of craning royal palms lining the roadside. Within what seems like minutes you're dipping into picturesque farming region around the town of San Juan y Martínez. Large thatched drying houses float in a sea of tobacco leaves and farmers in signature straw hats tend to their delicate crops. Campismo El Salto, just north of Guane, is a good budget mountain resort. To the west is the freshwater Embalse Laguna Grande, stocked with largemouth bass.

### Sights

Well into his eighties now, Alejandro Robaina is the only living person in Cuba with a brand of cigars named in his honor. His famous *vega* (fields), in the rich Vuelta Abajo region southwest of Pinar del Río has been growing quality tobacco since 1845, but it wasn't until 1997 that a new brand of cigars known as *Vegas Robaina* was first launched to wide international acclaim.

Enterprising in more ways than one, Robaina has also unofficially opened up his tobacco farm to outside visitors, and with a little effort and some deft navigational skills, visitors can roll up at the farm and,

### CUBA'S TREASURED TOBACCO

There's something strangely incongruous about the transition of a tobacco leaf from the pastoral and lovingly-tended fields of Cuba's Vuelta Abajo to the smoldering, nicotine-stained lump of ash on the end of a Players cigarette. Not that the early Spanish colonizers knew much about lung cancer.

On his first visit to Cuba in 1492, Christopher Columbus encountered Indian medicine men puffing a reed pipe called a *tobago* to inhale smoke from the burning dried leaves of the *cohiba* (tobacco) plant. As part of a fortune-telling ritual, the Spaniards began rolling the leaves into cigars. Tobacco *(Nicotiana tabacum)* was grown commercially in Cuba after 1580 and by 1700 it was the largest export.

Tobacco plants require fastidious care, involving as many as 150 visits during the growing season. The *vegas* (fields) are plowed using oxen to avoid the compacting that would result if tractors were employed. Corn is often rotated with tobacco to maintain the fertility of the soil.

After seeding at a nursery, it takes about 45 days until the tobacco seedlings are between 15cm and 20cm tall and ready for transplanting. Planting takes place from October to December, and in two months the plants grow to about 1.5m high, with leaves 30cm long and 25cm wide. When the plant has reached the desired height, the central bud is removed to stimulate the growth of the leaves. The finest Corojo tobacco, intended for the outer covering of cigars, is grown under cheesecloth coverings to protect the leaves from the sun's rays. Criollo tobacco, used for filler, is grown in full sunlight. A fully grown plant has six to nine pairs of leaves, and the pairs at each level of the plant must be gathered individually by hand at intervals of about a week as it attains maturity from January to March.

The harvested leaves are sewn together in pairs and hung to dry for about 50 days over wooden poles in special *secaderos* (curing barns), which are oriented to catch the maximum amount of sunlight. At first the leaves turn yellow, then reddish gold. The cured leaves are then bound together and piled in stacks half a meter high for a first fermentation that lasts about 30 days. This reduces the resin in the leaves and produces a more uniform color. The leaves are then moistened and classified, and the thickest parts of the stems are stripped out. The leaves are stacked again in higher bales and left for two months for a second fermentation. After this, they are unpacked and dried on racks, then packed again in special bales called *tercios,* which are covered with *yagua* bark from the royal palm tree. After varying periods of aging, the bales are shipped to cigar factories in Habana.

At the factory the tobacco is shaken out, moistened, and dried again in a special room. The next day the leaves are flattened and their central veins removed, dividing them in two. After sorting, the leaves go to a mixing room where a master blender combines several types to form the *tripa* (filler tobacco) for the desired brand of cigar. The mix of filler determines the flavor of the cigar. The product is then sent to the *galeras* (rolling tables) where each worker makes around 120 cigars a day. To create a cigar, a roller encloses a body of cut filler in a *capote* (binder leaf) and puts it in a press for half an hour. The roller then covers the cigar by hand, wrapping it in a high-quality *capa* (wrapper leaf). The result is something money can't buy in the US.

for a small fee (CUC$5), get the lowdown on the tobacco-making process from delicate plant to aromatic wrapper.

To get to the **Alejandro Robaina Tobacco Plantation** (☎ 8-79 74 70) take the Carretera Central southwest out of Pinar del Río for 18km, turn left onto another straight road and then left again (after approximately 4km) onto the rougher track that leads to the farm. Tours are generally available from 10am to 5pm every day bar Sunday, but call ahead to check. The tobacco-growing season runs from October to February and this is obviously the best time to visit.

## Sleeping & Eating

Two local, not terribly pretty, beach resorts are on the Bahía de Cortés. They're not bad places to end up, especially for a fresh fish meal.

**Villa Boca de Galafre** (☎ 84 829-8592; 3/6 beds CUC$15/20) Has 32 cabins with bath, fans, TV and fridge. The turn-off from the main highway is on the left, 36km southwest of

Pinar del Río; then it's 3km down to the beach. The train to Guane stops on the access road 2km from the resort. It might be closed outside the peak summer season.

**Villa Playa Bailén** (☎ 829-6145; bungalow CUC$15) About 44km from Pinar del Río. It's 8km off the main highway and 6km from the nearest train station on the Pinar del Río–Sábalo train line. The basic A-frame bungalows here sleep four people and are right on the beach.

**Villa Laguna Grande** (Islazul; ☎ 82 84 24 30; s/d low season CUC$19/24, high CUC$23/29) This pleasant fishing resort is 29km southwest of Guane and 18km off the highway to María la Gorda. It's one of the Islazul chain's most isolated places. The resort has 12 thatched cabins directly below the dam that created the Embalse Laguna Grande, which is presently stocked with bass, but the fishing facilities are unreliable. If fishing is your goal, inquire at the Islazul office in Pinar del Río before coming here. It's a quiet, good-value place to stay.

There are good private rooms (CUC$15 to CUC$20) available in Sandino, 6km southwest of the Laguna Grande turn-off and 89km from Pinar del Río. Try **Motel Alexis** (☎ 84 84 32 82; Zona L No 33; r CUC$15-20), or nearby Casa de Estrella; both are signposted just off the main highway.



### Getting There & Away

Two trains a day travel between Pinar del Río and Guane stopping at San Luis, San Juan y Martínez, Sábalo and Isabel Rubio (two hours). Passenger trucks run periodically between Guane and Sandino, but southwest of there, public transportation is sparse, bar the daily Havanatur Transfer (p200). Be sure to fill your tank up at the Servi-Cupet gas station in Isabel Rubio if you intend to drive to Cabo de San Antonio, as this is the last gasp for gas.

# PENÍNSULA DE GUANAHACABIBES

Inhabiting Cuba's western extremity, the Península de Guanahacabibes is a low-lying and ecologically-rich region that supports only a sparse sprinkling of people. There is evidence to suggest that it once played host to some of the island's earliest inhabitants. Reached via a two hour drive from Pinar del Río, visitors can find cheap accommodation in the gateway settlement of Sandino (which retains a couple of decent casas particulares) or press on to the well-known diver's haven of María la Gorda.

## PARQUE NACIONAL PENÍNSULA DE GUANAHACABIBES

☎ 82

Flat and deceptively narrow, the elongated Península de Guanahacabibes begins at La Fe, 94km southwest of Pinar del Río. In 1987, 101,500 hectares of this uninhabited sliver of idyllic coastline were declared a Biosphere Reserve by Unesco – one of only six in Cuba. The reasons for the protection measures were manifold. Firstly the reserve's submerged coastline features a wide variety of different landscapes including broad mangrove swamps, low scrub thicket vegetation and an uplifted shelf of alternating white sand and coral rock. Secondly the area's distinctive limestone karst formations are home to a plethora of unique flora and fauna including 172 species of birds, 700 species of plants, 18 types of mammals, 35 reptiles, 19 amphibians, 86 types of butterfly and 16 orchid species. Sea turtles, including loggerhead and green turtles, come ashore at night in summer to lay their eggs – the park is the only part of mainland Cuba where this happens. If you're here between May and October night tours can be arranged to watch the turtles nest. Another curiosity is the swarms of *cangrejos colorados* (red and yellow crabs) that crawl across the peninsula's rough central road only to be unceremoniously crushed under the tires of passing cars. The stench the smashed shells give off is memorable.

To date, Guanahacabibes' value as an archeological goldmine is still in the discovery stage. Suffice to say the area is thought to shelter at least 100 important archeological sites relating to Cuba's oldest and least-known indigenous inhabitants, the Guanahatabey.

### Orientation & Information

Although the park border straddles the tiny community of La Fe, the entry to the reserve proper is at La Bajada where you'll find the

Estación Ecológica Guanahacabibes. Just beyond the office the road splits in two with the left-hand branch going south to María la Gorda (14km along a deteriorating coastal road) and the right fork heading west toward the end of the peninsula.

It's a 120km round-trip to Cuba's westernmost point from here. The lonesome Cabo de San Antonio is populated by a solitary lighthouse, the Faro Roncali, inaugurated by the Spanish in 1849. At the time of writing Gaviota had just opened a new marina and villa (see p204). Four kilometers to the northwest lays Playa Las Tumbas, an idyllic beach where visitors to the park are permitted to swim.

There's no charge to visit Hotel María la Gorda and its adjoining 5km beach, both named after a voluptuous Venezuelan who was marooned here by pirates and turned to prostitution to survive. Divers are unanimous about the quality of the reefs here and it's also one of Cuba's prime yachting venues.

## Activities

Guanahacabibes is a paradise for eco-travelers, conservationists, divers and bird-watchers. Feathered species on display here include parrots, *tocororros*, woodpeckers, owls, tody flycatchers, and *zunzuncitos* (bee hummingbirds). Hikers and other adventure enthusiasts may find some of the park excursions too limiting, however, and a number of travelers have complained that the beach at María la Gorda didn't quite match up to the publicity photographs.

### DIVING

Diving is the real deal in María la Gorda – indeed it is the primary reason why most people come here. Good visibility and sheltered offshore reefs are two of the reasons why enthusiasts make the long trek from the east. Couple this with the largest formation of black coral in the archipelago and you've got a recipe for arguably the best diving reefs on Cuba's Isla Grande.

The action centers around the **International Dive Center** (☎ 77 13 06) at the Marina Gaviota at the Hotel María la Gorda. A dive costs CUC$35 (night diving CUC$40), plus CUC$7.50 for equipment. The center offers a full CMAS (Confédération Mondiale des Activités Subaquatiques; World Underwater Federation) scuba certification course (CUC$365; four days) and snorkelers can hop on the dive boat for CUC$12. The dive center also offers four hours of deep-sea fishing for CUC$200 for up to four people and line fishing/trolling at CUC$30 per person, four maximum.

Among the 50 identified dive sites in the vicinity, divers are shown El Valle de Coral Negro, a 100m-long black-coral wall, and El Salón de María, a cave 20m deep containing feather stars and Technicolor corals. The concentrations of migratory fish can be incredible. The furthest entry is only 30 minutes by boat from shore.

Another option is the newly opened **Marina Gaviota Cabo de San Antonio** (☎ 75 01 18) on Playa Las Tumbas at the end of the Guanahacabibes Peninsula. The marina provides easy access to 27 diving sites and has brand new accommodation nearby at the Villa Cabo San Antonio.

### EXCURSIONS

The **Estación Ecológica Guanahacabibes** (☎ 82-75-03-66; www.ecovida.pinar.cu; 🕓 7:30am-3:30pm), opposite the meteorological station at La Bajada, arranges guides, specialized visits and a five-hour tour to the park's (and Cuba's) western tip at Cabo de San Antonio. The responsibility is yours to supply transport, sufficient gas, water, sunscreen, insect repellant, and food, which makes the task for independent travelers a little more difficult. During most of the 120km round-trip you'll have dark, rough *diente de perro* (dog's teeth) rock on one side and the brilliant blue sea on the other. Iguanas will lumber for cover as you approach and you might see small deer, *jutías* (edible tree rats) and lots of birds. Beyond the lighthouse is deserted Playa las Tumbas where you'll be given 30 minutes for a swim. Any hire car can make this trip though a 4WD is preferable. The five-hour excursion costs CUC$10 per person. There's a possibility of other excursions to local communities in the area and the park management, which plans to open a new visitors center by early 2007, has plenty more ideas in the pipeline; call ahead if you're keen.

### HIKING

Of the two official hiking trails, **Cueva las Perlas** (Pearl Cave, CUC$8, three hours, 3km), is superior. Immediately as you enter the trail you'll see and hear a wide variety of birds, including *tocororos, zunzuncitos* (bee hummingbirds) and woodpeckers. After 1.5km you come to Pearl Cave, a multigallery cave system of which 300m is accessible to hikers. The **Del Bosque al Mar** trail (CUC$6, 1½ hours, 1.5km) is interesting for about five minutes. Too much of this 'hike' is on the blazing road to Cabo de San Antonio. Nonetheless, the guides here are highly trained and knowledgeable, and tours can be conducted in Spanish, English or Italian. There were a number of new trails on the verge of opening as this book was being written. Ask at the Estación Ecológica Guanahacabibes about Sendero La Majagua and Sendero Hoyo del Palmar. There's no reason why you can't hike along the shoreline from La Bajada to María la Gorda, should you be so inclined.

### Sleeping & Eating

**Hotel María la Gorda** (Gaviota; ☎ 827-8131; fax 827-8077; s/d/tr incl breakfast low season CUC$33/46/66, high CUC$38/56/80; P ❄) This is the most remote hotel on the main island of Cuba and the isolation has its advantages. The adjoining palm-fringed beach is adequate (though not as idyllic as it looks in photographs) and there's a dive site with a vertical drop-off just 200m from the hotel. It's located on the Bahía de Corrientes, 150km southwest of Pinar del Río (2½ hours by car if you put your foot down). From the park office at La Bajada, where the highway meets the Caribbean, Hotel María la Gorda is 14km to the left, along a rough road.

Rooms are housed either in three pink-concrete, motel-type buildings or in 20 newer cabins set back from the beach. The privacy and comfort afforded by the cabins is infinitely superior. Not that five-star service is much of an issue here. Far from being a posh resort, María la Gorda is a place where hammocks are strung between palm trees, cold beers are sipped at sunset and dive talk continues into the small hours.

Buffet meals cost CUC$15 for lunch or dinner; reports on the food vary. Water in the hotel shop is expensive, so bring your own or purify the tap water.

**Villa Cabo San Antonio** (☎ 75 01 18; Playa Las Tumbas) A 16-room villa on the almost-virgin Guanahacabibes Peninsula 3km from the Roncali lighthouse and 4km from the new Gaviota Marina, it has satellite TV, car rental and bike hire.

**Restaurante La Bajada** (🕑 8:30am-10:30pm) Just next to the meteorological station, this place has (you guessed it) fried chicken, pork filets and French fries – when it's open.

#### NORTH OF THE PENÍNSULA

The long, bumpy road from Sandino along the north coast of Pinar del Río to Cayo Jutías is one of Cuba's most isolated and lonesome rides. Public transport is almost nonexistent here so if you intend to ply this route a hire car or an extremely sturdy bicycle is essential (stock up on gas, food and water in Isabel Rubio).

Of the scattered settlements along the route only **Mantua** – site of an important battle led by Antonio Maceo in 1896 – is of any historical note, though the scenery impresses with pines trees and shadowy hills as you push east toward Santa Lucia and the Viñales turn-off.

Accommodation-wise there is a casa particular in Sandino that doubles up as a paladar – **Motel Edilia** (☎ 3843; Zona M No 42; P ❄) – otherwise you are on your own until Puerto Esperanza; splendid isolation.

### Getting There & Away

A daily transfer operates between Viñales and María la Gorda leaving at 7am and arriving at the peninsula at 9:30am. The return leg leaves María la Gorda at 5pm and arrives in Viñales at 7pm. The cost for a single/return is CUC$15/25. Inquire at **Transtur** (☎ 79 60 60) in Viñales or **Havanatur** (☎ 77 84 94) in Pinar del Río.

**Havanautos** (☎ 827-8131) has an office at Hotel María la Gorda. It has a jeep taxi service with driver to Cabo de San Antonio at CUC$50 for up to four people. It also offers transfers to/from Pinar del Río at CUC$50 one way for the whole car (or CUC$120 to/from Habana).

## VALLE DE VIÑALES

Embellished by soaring pine trees and scattered with bulbous limestone cliffs that teeter like giant haystacks above the peaceful and well-tended tobacco plantations, Parque Nacional Viñales is one of Cuba's most magnificent natural settings. Wedged spectacularly into the Sierra de los Órganos mountain range, this 11km by 5km valley was declared a Unesco World Heritage site in 1999 for its dramatic rocky outcrops (known as mogotes), coupled with the vernacular architecture of its traditional farms and villages.

Once upon a time the whole region was several hundred meters higher. Then, during the Cretaceous period 100 million years ago, a network of underground rivers ate away at the limestone bedrock, creating vast caverns. Eventually the roofs collapsed leaving only the eroded walls we see today. It is the finest example of a limestone karst valley in Cuba and contains in Caverna Santo Tomás, the island's largest cave system.

Rock studies aside, Viñales also offers opportunities for fine hiking, history, rock climbing and horseback-trekking. On the accommodation front it boasts four first-class hotels and some of the best casas particulares in Cuba. Despite drawing in day-trippers by the busload, the area's well-protected and spread-out natural attractions have somehow managed to escape the frenzied tourist circus of other less well-managed resorts, while the atmosphere in and around the village remains refreshingly hassle-free.

## VIÑALES

☎ 8 / pop 14,279

Founded in 1875, and characterized by its quiet, unhurried streets lined by rustling pine trees, Viñales is a town of creaking rocking chairs and well-polished front porches, where the enthusiastic locals will greet you as one of the family. Along with Baracoa this has to be one of the friendliest places in Cuba and for this reason alone it justifies a two- or three-day lay-over.

### Information

#### IMMIGRATION

**Inmigración** (cnr Salvador Cisneros & Ceferino Fernández; 8am-5pm Mon-Fri)

#### INTERNET ACCESS & TELEPHONE

**Cubanacán** (Salvador Cisneros No 63C; 9am-7pm Mon-Sat) Service is sometimes erratic here.

**Etecsa** (Ceferino Fernández No 3; Internet per hr CUC$6) Across from the post office.

#### MONEY

**Banco de Crédito y Comercio** (☎ 79 31 30; Salvador Cisneros No 58; 8am-noon & 1:30-3pm Mon-Fri, 8am-11am Sat)

**Cadeca** (☎ 79 63 64; Salvador Cisneros & Adela Azcuy; 8:30am-5:30pm Mon-Sat)

#### POST

**Post office** (Ceferino Fernández No 14; 9am-6pm Mon-Sat) Just off the main square.

#### TRAVEL AGENCIES

**Cubanacán** (☎ 79 63 93; Salvador Cisneros No 63C; 9am-7pm Mon-Sat) Moped rentals and tours, but you can arrange your own tour for less money.

### Sights

Viñales has a pleasant main square with the **Casa de la Cultura**, in an old mansion next to the church, offering a full program of cultural activities; an art gallery is next door. The **Museo Municipal** (☎ 79 33 95; Salvador Cisneros No 115; 8am-5pm) occupies the former home of independence heroine Adela Azcuy (1861–1914) and tracks the local history. Daily hikes can also be organized here.

Look to your left just past the Servi-Cupet on the road north out of town and you'll see a funky, vine-choked gate with fresh fruit hanging from it. This is the entrance to **El Jardín de Caridad** (donations accepted; 8am-5pm), a sprawling garden almost a century in the making. Cascades of orchids bloom alongside plastic doll heads, thickets of orange lilies grow in soft groves and turkeys run amok. One of the ancient sisters tending the place will likely offer you some conversation and a plate of fruit.

### Activities

If you're looking to go for a swim, La Ermita hotel has a seriously beautiful poolside view (admission CUC$3; open 8am to 10pm) taking in large swaths of the valley. You can also get a **massage** (CUC$20-35) here. Hotel Los Jazmines has a pool too (admission including a drink CUC$5; open 9am to 7pm) and an even better view, though the coming and going of sightseers can sometimes kill the tranquility.

Casa owners in Viñales are particularly adept at being able to rustle up all number of activities more or less on demand. One particularly resourceful couple are **Yoan & Esthelita Reyes** (☎ 79 32 63; Rafael Trejo No 134)

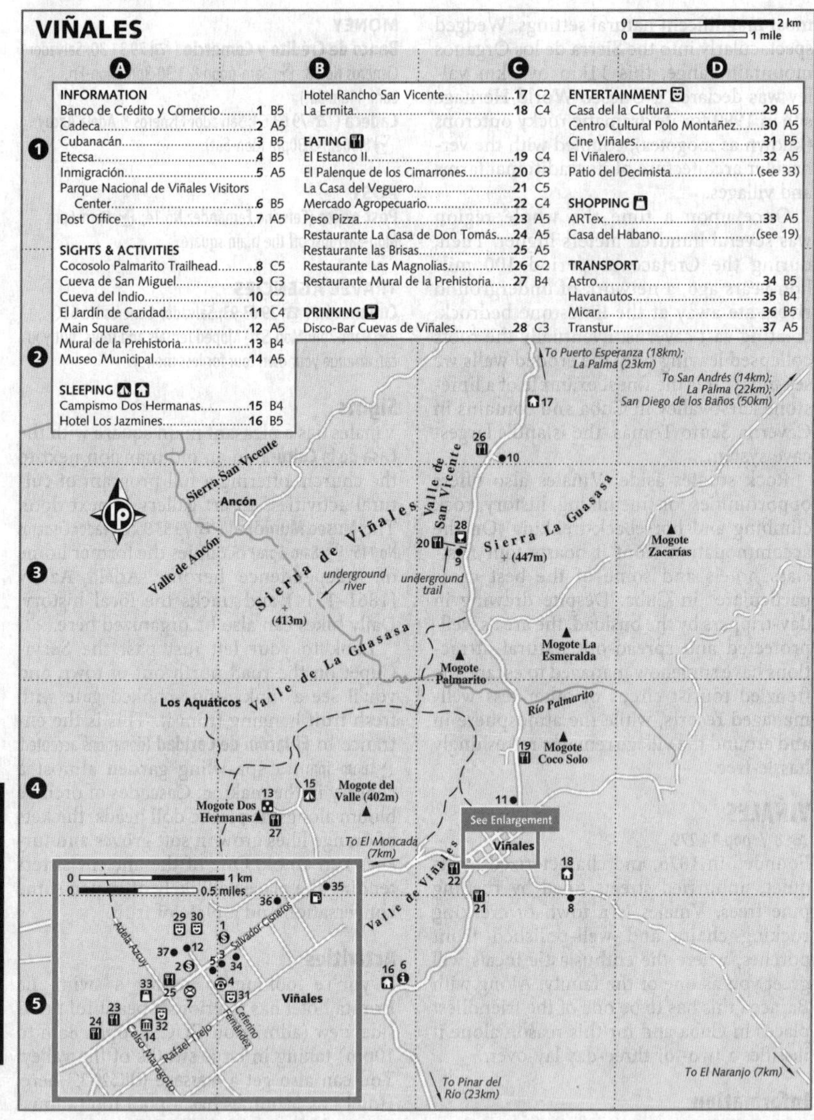




who not only rent out rooms in their engaging casa but they also organize walks, cycling tours, massage, salsa lessons and visits to a nearby farm and tobacco plantation. The services are enhanced by the fact that Esthelita is a qualified national park biologist and the tours, being 'private' in nature, are far more accommodating and flexible than the standard excursions otherwise available.

## Tours

**Cubanacán** (☎ 79 63 93; Salvador Cisneros No 63C; 9am-7pm Mon-Sat) organizes tours to Cayo Levisa (CUC$16), San Tomás Cave (CUC$8) and the Palenque de los Cimarrones (with transport CUC$10). You can also organize walking and horseback-riding trips here (from CUC$5) and excursions to María la Gorda and Pinar del Río.

## Sleeping

There are some 250 houses renting rooms in Viñales, and most of them are pretty good. Shop around and you'll always find space somewhere. The two hotels within walking distance of Viñales village are both spectacularly-located gems.

**La Ermita** (Cubanacán; ☎ 79 60 71; s/d low season incl breakfast CUC$47/60, high CUC$54/69; P) A top midrange pick, with its dazzling views, cozy furnishings and friendly staff, 2km east of Viñales village. Go for a room with a valley view. Breakfast on the patio can't be beaten and mojitos poolside are also highly recommended (have a staff member point out the endangered cork palm there). This modern hotel offers tennis courts, an excellent shop, horseback riding and excursions. This is the only government hotel within easy walking distance of the village.

**Hotel Los Jazmines** (Cubanacán; ☎ 79 62 05; s/d low season incl breakfast CUC$53/65, high CUC$62/77; P) This hotel has one of the best locations in Cuba and the ethereal valley views have launched a thousand postcards. Situated 4km south of Viñales on the road to Pinar del Río (also known as the Viñales Hwy), Los Jazmines sees a lot of traffic. Still, conscientious renovations and professional staff keep the 48 rooms looking spiffy. The 16 rooms in a long block facing the valley offer the best vistas and the most privacy. The postcard-perfect (literally) view of the Valle de Viñales from the hotel means the pool area and viewpoint are crowded with sightseers all day. Several readers have recommended the walking tours offered here. Horseback riding can also be arranged (CUC$5 per hour).

### CASAS PARTICULARES – VIÑALES

With nearly 300 casas in a town of only 14,000 people it's not surprising that Viñales is often referred to as 'Cuba's largest hotel.' Welcomes are usually warm here and the food is, more often than not, delicious.

**Casa Emilia Díaz (Nenita)** (no phone; Calle Salvador Cisneros Interior 6-1; r CUC$25) Fantastic setting on the valley edge with bold mogote views; sleeps four, good bath, meals, off main road behind *policlínica* (hospital).

**Casa La Prieta & Mario** (☎ 9-3267; Adela Azcuy No 21; r CUC$15-20) Clean, comfortable room, patio with people-watching.

**Casa Lucy – Lucy & Bartolo** (☎ 9-3214; Orlando Nodarse No 9; r CUC$15-20) Quiet street behind school; mogote views from porch.

**Eloy Hernández Rodríguez** (no phone; Salvador Cisneros No 198; r CUC$20) Private house in backyard; meals to fatten you up.

**Hostal Doña Hilda** (☎ 79 60 53; Carretera Pinar del Río Km 25 No 4; r CUC$20-25) One of first houses in town on the road from Pinar del Río.

**Nena Paula** (☎ 93 60 18; Camilo Cienfuegos No 56; r CUC$15) Friendly. There are many other options on this block.

**Oscar Jaime Rodríguez** (☎ 9-3381; Adela Azcuy No 43; r CUC$20) Climbers hangout, enthusiastically recommended by readers.

**Teresa Martínez Hernández** (☎ 9-3267; Camilo Cienfuegos No 10; r CUC$20) Nice porch and small garden, good meals.

**Ubaldo Chirino Suárez** (☎ 9-3226; Adela Azcuy No 35; r CUC$20) Private, meals served.

**Villa Chicha** (no phone; Camilo Cienfuegos No 22; r CUC$15) Basic room in home of gracious señora, good value.

**'Villa Los Reyes' – Estelita & Yoan Reyes** (☎ 79 32 63; Rafael Trejo No 134; r CUC$20; P) Great house with all amenities. This couple can organize everything from salsa dancing to Spanish lessons. Estelita is a biologist at Viñales National Park.

**Villa Nelson** (☎ 9-3268; Camilo Cienfuegos No 4; r CUC$15-20) Private, independent room in backyard; meals for nonguests.

**Villa Pitín & Juana** (☎ 79 33 38; Carretera Pinar del Río Km 25 No 2; r CUC$25; P) Great family atmosphere and fantastic food.

## Eating & Drinking

Because so many casas particulares provide meals for guests, Viñales is short on paladares. While you're out hiking, you might get an invitation to eat with *campesinos* (country people): take it and you'll dine fabulously on fresh roasted pork, the best *congrí* (rice with beans) you're likely to have, *yuca con mojo* (yucca with lime sauce) and salad.

**Restaurante La Casa de Don Tomás** (☎ 79 63 00; Salvador Cisneros No 140; 10am-9:30pm) The oldest house in Viñales and its most salubrious restaurant. You'll know you've arrived at the right place by the terra-cotta roof and exuberant flowering vines bursting from the balcony. This place has atmospheric patio dining out the back, where you can try *'las delicias de Don Tomás'*, the house specialty with rice, lobster, fish, pork, chicken and sausage with an egg crowning it all (CUC$10). Chicken and fish dishes are cheaper.

**El Estanco II** (10am-11pm) A simple pizza and beer place 1km out of town on the road north, and a decent pit stop. A pizza costs a couple of Convertibles, a plate of spaghetti slightly more.

Other, simpler places include **Restaurante Las Brisas** (☎ 79 33 53; Salvador Cisneros No 96; 11am-2pm & 6-9pm), a not half bad peso restaurant where you can fill up for under CUC$4, and take-out **peso pizza** (Salvador Cisneros No 130).

Viñales' *mercado agropecuario* (agricultural market) is about 100m from town at the west end of Salvador Cisneros down the road toward Dos Hermanas. Get your peso rum and Convertible bread here.

## Entertainment

**Centro Cultural Polo Montañez** (Cisnero, cnr Joaquin Pérez, in main square; admission CUC$1) This is Viñales' newest and hottest nightspot, named in honor of the local *guajiro* hero turned international icon (see p193). An intimate ambience and a kicking sound system make this place one of the best music venues in the province. Drinks and snacks are also available during day hours. Evening shows warm up around 10pm. Relegated down the list somewhat are old favorites **Patio del Decimista** (Salvador Cisneros No 102; admission free; music at 9pm), serving live music nightly along with cold beers and **El Viñalero** (Salvador Cisneros No 105) across the street. **Cine Viñales** (cnr Ceferino Fernández & Rafael Trejo) is a block south of the main square.

## Shopping

You can get postcards, T-shirts and CDs at **ARTex** (Salvador Cisneros No 102) and cigars at **Casa del Habano** (Carretera de Puerto Esperanza Km 1; 9am-5pm).

## Getting There & Around

### BUS

The **Astro ticket office** (Salvador Cisneros No 63A; 8am-noon & 1-3pm) is opposite the church on Viñales' main square. The daily Astro bus to Habana leaves at 2:30pm (CUC$8) and a comfortable Víazul bus for Habana via Pinar del Río departs at 8am and 2pm daily (CUC$12). There's also a daily Havanatur transfer service to María la Gorda (7am) and Habana via Soroa and Las Terrazas (8am). New routes have also been added for Cayo Levisa and Trinidad. Cubanacán and Transtur can give you details.

### CAR & MOPED

To reach Viñales from the south, you take the long and winding road from Pinar del Río; the roads from the north coast are not as sinuous, but are pretty drives. The wildly scenic mountain road from the Península de Guanahacabibes through Guane and Pons is one of Cuba's most spectacular routes. Allow a lot of travel time.

The following agencies have offices in Viñales:

**Cubanacán** (☎ 79 63 93; Salvador Cisneros No 63C; 9am-7pm) Mopeds CUC$24 per day.

**Havanautos** (☎ 79 63 90) At the Servi-Cupet; rents mopeds.

**Micar** (☎ 79 63 30; Salvador Cisneros final)

**Transtur** (☎ 79 60 60; Salvador Cisneros) Beside the church; rents mopeds.

A Servi-Cupet gas station is at the northeast end of Viñales town. Taxis parked alongside the square will take you to Pinar del Río (CUC$10), Palma Rubia (CUC$25) for the boat to Cayo Levisa or Gran Caverna de Santo Tomás (CUC$16). All prices are approximations.

### VIÑALES BUS TOUR

Modeled on Varadero's opened topped double-decker, the Viñales Bus Tour is a hop-on-hop-off minibus that runs nine times a day between all of the valley's main sites. Starting and finishing in the village's main park the whole circuit takes an hour and five minutes with the first bus leaving at 9am and the last at 7:10pm. There are 18 stops along the route and all are clearly marked with route maps and timetables. For more information inquire at **Transtur** (☎ 79 60 60; Salvador Cisneros).

## PARQUE NACIONAL VIÑALES

☎ 8

Parque Nacional Viñales' extraordinary cultural landscape covers 15,000 hectares and supports a population of 25,000 people. A mosaic of communities grows coffee, tobacco, sugarcane, oranges, avocados and bananas on some of the oldest landscape in Cuba. The park is administered through the spanking new **Parque Nacional Viñales visitors center** (Carretera a Pinar del Río Km 2) on the hill just before you reach Los Jazmines hotel. Inside, colorful displays map out the park's main features. Hiking, information and guides are also on hand.

### Sights

Four kilometers west of Viñales village is the **Mural de la Prehistoria** (admission CUC$1). On a cliff at the foot of the 617m-high Sierra de Viñales, the highest portion of the Sierra de los Órganos, this 120m-long painting on the side of Mogote Dos Hermanas was designed in 1961 by Leovigildo González Morillo, a follower of Mexican artist Diego Rivera (the idea was hatched by Celia Sáncez, Alicia Alonso and Antonio Nuñez Jiménez). It took 15 people five years to complete it. The huge snail, dinosaurs, sea monsters and humans on the cliff symbolize the theory of evolution and are either impressively psychedelic or monumentally horrific, depending on your point of view. You don't really have to get up close to appreciate the mural, but the admission fee is waived if you take the delicious, if a little overpriced, CUC$15 lunch at the site restaurant (see p211). Horses are usually available here at for a short ride around the park or a longer excursion through the valley.

A kilometer beyond the turn-off to Dos Hermanas, a dirt road leads toward the mountain community of **Los Aquáticos**. Los Aquáticos was founded in 1943 by followers of visionary Antoñica Izquierdo, who discovered the healing power of water when the *campesinos* of this area had no access to conventional medicine. They colonized the mountain slopes and several families still live there. Unfortunately, the last patriarch practicing the water cure died in 2002, taking the tradition with him, but you can still visit. Los Aquáticos is accessible only by horse or on foot. Ask at your casa for guide contacts; horses can be hired from farmers living near the trailhead (CUC$10 per person for a three-hour tour with Spanish-speaking guide). From the main road it's 1km inland to the trailhead (just across the stream) of La Ruta de las Aguas. After your visit, you can make this a loop by continuing on this road (fork left at the same stream, recrossing it a few hundred meters to the east) another 3km to Campismo Dos Hermanas and the cliff paintings; it's a wonderfully scenic route (the complete Los Aquático/Dos Hermanas circuit totals 6km from the main highway).

North from the **Cueva del Indio** (☎ 79 62 80; admission CUC$5; 9am-5:30pm) is the prettiest part of Viñales, but the cave itself, 5.5km north of Viñales village, is a shameless tourist trap. An ancient indigenous dwelling, it was rediscovered in 1920 and motor boats now ply the underground river through the electrically lit cave. Souvenir vendors crowd the entrance, while cheesy musicians serenade you and tour buses roll in belching out large groups.

The **Cueva de San Miguel** is a smaller cave at the jaws of the Valle de San Vicente. You can pay CUC$1 to enter a gaping cave that leads you 50m or so to the El Palenque de los Cimarrones (see p211).

### Activities

#### CYCLING

Despite the sometimes hilly terrain, Viñales is one of the best places in Cuba to cycle. Try asking about bike rental at the Cubanacán office (p211). If you get no luck there, inquire at your casa particular. Viñales residents have a habit of making marvelous two-wheeled cycling machines appear out of thin air.

#### HIKING

With the long-awaited Parque Nacional Viñales visitors center now officially open, information and access to hiking trails in Viñales is better than ever before. At present there are three official valley hikes, all of which can be arranged directly through the center itself, the Museo Municipal or any of the town's tour agencies.

The Cocosolo Palmarito starts on a spur road just before La Ermita hotel and progresses for 11km past the Coco Solo and Palmarito mogotes and the Mural de la Prehistorico. There are good views here and plenty of opportunities to discover the local flora and fauna including a visit to a tobacco *finca* (farmhouse; ask about lunch with one of the families there). It returns you to the main road back to Viñales.

The Maravillas de Viñales trail is a 4km loop beginning 1km before El Moncada, 13km from the Dos Hermanas turn-off. This hike takes in endemic plants, orchids and the biggest ant cutter hive in Cuba (so they say). A caretaker at the trailhead collects the CUC$1 entry fee.

The San Vicente/Ancón trail takes you out to the more remote Valle Ancón where you can check out still functioning coffee communities in a valley surrounded by mogotes.

These are just the official hikes. There are many more unofficial treks available and asking around at your casa particular will elicit further suggestions. Try the Aquáticos walk with its incredible vistas, the Cueva de la Vaca with its swimming options and the Palmerito Valley, infamous among those in the know for its high-stakes cockfights.

### ROCK CLIMBING

Yet to be 'officially' sanctioned by the major tourist operators, rock climbing in Cuba is still in the developmental stage. As a result, most of the town's budding tour reps will deny any knowledge of it. But rest assured, up in those lofty grey limestone mogotes the scene is huge, and growing.

The first climbers arrived in the late 1990s inspired by descriptions of the Viñales Valley as a miniature Yosemite in the first edition of Lonely Planet's *Cuba*. Teaming up with some enterprising local Cubans they took enthusiastically to the rock faces and, within a couple of years, climbing routes were being opened up all over the mogotes. At last count there were 150 climbs mapped out in Viñales, with names like Rompe los Dedos (Finger Breaker) and Cuba Libre (Free Cuba); more climbs are constantly being mapped.

Of all the outdoor adventures in Cuba, rock climbing is the most DIY by far. Climbers should head to www.cubaclimbing.com for the lowdown and bring extra gear to share (local supplies are ridiculously limited). Center of operations in Viñales village is a casa particular run by Oscar Jaime Rodríguez in Adela Azcuy (see p207).

### SWIMMING

One of the nicest natural swimming spots in the area is in the Río Resvaloso near the Cueva de la Vaca. There is another possibility at La Cueva de Palmerito where you can swim inside a cave. Ask the locals for directions. Everyone knows where these places are.

### COCKFIGHTING

Illegal but tolerated, Cuban cockfighting is a gruesome mix of virulent spectator 'sport' and frenetic gambling road show. Indeed, at times, it's a toss-up as to which provides the crazier spectacle: the cocks, or the over-the-top spectators who gather enthusiastically to watch their favorite birds fight.

Practiced since the 18th century, cockfighting was first introduced into Cuba by the Spanish and is the only real form of organized gambling to have survived the corruption-cleansing Castro revolution. A decent event can attract more than 500 people and inspire bets of up to 50,000 Cuban pesos (US$2000). Held in the countryside of rural provinces such as Pinar del Río (Cuba's unofficial cockfighting capital), a fairlike atmosphere begins midmorning and continues into late evening, or until the losing cock is finally killed. Rum, copious betting and plenty of breast-beating male bravado are all part of the unrelenting package.

Cuban cocks – rather like the country's Olympian boxers – are said to be wily, combative and thoroughly pugnacious creatures with fights developing into long, bloody, drawn out affairs that can last for hours. Aspiring spectators be warned, cockfighting is not for the fainthearted.

## Tours

**Cubanacán** (Salvador Cisneros No 63C; 8:30am-5:30pm Mon-Sat) is conveniently located in the center of Viñales village and organizes excursions everywhere from Cayo Levisa to the Gran Caverna de Santo Tomás. Check out the schedule.

## Sleeping

**Campismo Dos Hermanas** (Cubamar; ☎ 79 32 23; r CUC$15; ) This place, among the mogotes directly opposite El Mural de la Prehistoria, is one of Cubamar's most popular international campismos. The 54 two- and four-bed concrete cabins are frequented by campers, climbers and cyclists; it's a good place to meet other travelers. There's a restaurant as well as horseback riding and other excursions. Several caves are accessible on foot nearby and you can hike back into the valley. An archeological museum is on the premises. It's good value and a pretty place to stay, but fills fast (especially on weekends). This is a full Campertour facility.

**Hotel Rancho San Vicente** (Cubanacán; ☎ 79 62 01; s/d low season incl breakfast CUC$40/52, high CUC$45/60; P ) Just 7km north of Viñales village and 1km north of the Cueva del Indio, San Vicente is nestled in a grove and the setting is magnificent. The updated wooden cabins (Nos 6 to 43) are the best accommodation option, with lovely natural furnishings, delicious baths and sliding glass doors onto a porch. Put up your feet and look for the 30 to 50 bird species that frequent the grounds or go for a sulfur soak (25°C to 28°C) or massage.

**Restaurante Las Magnolias** (☎ 79 60 62; d incl breakfast CUC$25; P ) Three rooms are for rent at this little house directly across the highway from the Cueva del Indio. Only one of the rooms has a private bath, but kitchens and satellite TV are nice perks.

## Eating & Drinking

**La Casa del Veguero** (☎ 97 60 80; 10am-5pm) Just outside Viñales toward Pinar del Río, this paladar serves a complete (and tasty) *criollo* (Creole) lunch for around CUC$10. Adjacent to the restaurant is a *secadero* (drying house) where tobacco leaves are cured from February to May. Visitors are welcome in the *secadero* and you can buy loose cigars here at discount prices.

**Mural de la Prehistoria Restaurant** (☎ 79 62 60; 11:30am-7pm) Of all the places clustered within spitting distance of Viñales serving *asado* (roast), this restaurant has the recipe mastered. The pork is roasted and smoked over natural charcoal, giving it a sublime melt-in-your-mouth flavor. You'll have to starve yourself first to justify the CUC$15 price tag, but you probably won't need to eat for days afterwards.

**El Palenque de los Cimarrones** (☎ 79 62 90; noon-4pm) Entered through the Cueva de San Miguel, this place is an odd combination of folklore show, restaurant and plantation slavery museum. The complete Cuban-style lunch is tasty, but the young Cubans dressed as *cimarrones* (runaway slaves) somehow fails to stimulate the appetite.

**Restaurante Las Magnolias** (☎ 79 60 62; 10am-6pm) The coziest place to eat near the Cueva del Indio, it's across the highway from the cave; it serves lobster and a number of cheaper options.

## Entertainment

The Disco-Bar Cuevas de Viñales at the entrance to the Cueva San Miguel sometimes runs a cabaret show at night; ask around for details. During the day it's a nice cool bar. There's a lit passageway 150m through the mogote to El Palenque de los Cimarrones (see above).

## Getting Around

Bike, car, moped or the Viñales Bus Tour (p208); take your pick.

# WEST OF VIÑALES

At El Moncada, 14km west of the Dos Hermanas turn-off and 1.5km off the road to Minas de Matahambre, is **Gran Caverna de Santo Tomás** (admission CUC$8; 8:30am-5pm), Cuba's largest cave system. There are over 46km of galleries on eight levels; 1km on the sixth level, 42m above the valley, is accessible to visitors. There's no artificial lighting, but headlamps are provided for the 90-minute guided tour. Things to see include bats, stalagmites and stalactites, underground pools, interesting rock formations and a replica of an ancient native Indian mural. Specialists should contact the **Escuela de Espeleológica** (☎ 8-79 31 45) for more information. Near the cave entrance is a massive poured-concrete **monument** erected in 1999 to Los Doce Malagones, 12 locals who eliminated a counterrevolutionary band in the hills in 1959, giving rise to today's Cuban militias. A **museum** (admission CUC$1; 10am-10pm) with a veteran docent is on site.

## CAYO JUTÍAS

Cayo Jutías is one of northern Pinar del Río's few secluded beaches and one of those 'best-kept secret' locations that is rapidly becoming more developed. If you thought that Cayo Levisa was too crowded for you, this could be a good place to try as an alternative.

In the late 1990s, the cayo was linked to the mainland by a massive *pedraplén* (causeway) that offers a dramatic view of the province's mountains in profile. The access road begins about 4km west of Santa Lucía. At the beginning of the causeway, 4.5km off the coastal road, you will need to pay a CUC$5 per person entry fee. Nine kilometers from the main highway is a metal lighthouse, the **Faro de Cayo Jutías**, erected by the USA in 1902. The route ends at a picturesque white beach caressed by crystal-clear water, 12.5km from the coastal highway.

There's the **Restaurante Cayo Jutías** ( 9am-5pm) here which specializes in seafood. You can base yourself here while engaging in a couple of water-based activities such as kayaking and snorkeling (equipment is available for hire from a small hut on the beach), but the main attraction is the location itself, quiet and relatively undiscovered – at least until the tour buses come rumbling in at about 11am. Tours from Pinar del Río or Viñales cost between CUC$25 to CUC$53 depending on whether you include a guide and/or lunch in the package. Otherwise you will have to make your own transport arrangements. The fastest and by far the prettiest route to Cayo Jutías is via El Moncada and Minas de Matahambre through rolling pine-clad hills.

**Santa Lucía** is a small town known mostly for its huge thermoelectric power plant and sulfuric acid factory. However, there are a couple of private casas particulares here; ask around for further information. Otherwise your only accommodation option in this town is to pitch a tent.



# NORTHERN PINAR DEL RÍO

Considering its relative proximity to Habana, Northern Pinar del Río Province is a remote and largely unexplored area. Facilities are sparse and roads are rutted on the isolated Gulf of Mexico coast, though visitors who take the time to make the journey out have reported back stories of memorable DIY adventures and famously hospitable locals.

## PUERTO ESPERANZA

☎ 8

Puerto Esperanza (Port of Hope), 6km north of San Cayetano and 25km north of Viñales, is a sleepy little fishing village visited by yachts sailing around the country. According to town lore, the giant mango trees lining the entry road were planted by slaves in the 1800s. A long pier pointing out into the bay is decent for a jump in the ocean. Otherwise the clocks haven't worked here since…oh…1951.

### Sights & Activities

Puerto Esperanza's sights are not the domain of guidebook listings. Rather this is the kind of low-key, put-down-the-Lonely-Planet sort of place where it's more fun to unravel the social life on your own. Discover some weirdly transcendental Santería ritual or take a spontaneous tour around your neighbor's tobacco plantation in search of pungent peso cigars.

### Sleeping & Eating

The town has six legal casas.

**Villa Leonila Blanco** (☎ 79 36 48; Calle Hermanos Caballeros No 41; r CUC$15; ) The super-nice couple at Leonila Blanco rent two big rooms with shared bath, garage and meals. They also have an independent house.

Other options:

**Villa Maribel** (☎ 79 38 46; Calle Maceo No 56; r CUC$15) Another good option which rents two interconnecting rooms that can sleep up to six; meals served.

**Villa Dora González Fuentes** (☎ 79 38 72; Pelayo Cuervo No 5) This casa is enthusiastically recommended by readers.

### Getting There & Away

There's a handy Servi-Cupet gas station at San Cayetano. The road to Santa Lucía and

Cayo Jutías deteriorates to dirt outside of San Cayetano: expect a throbbing backside if you're on a bike or moped.

## CAYO LEVISA

More oft-visited than Caya Jutías, Cayo Levisa sports a midrange hotel, passable restaurant and fully-equipped diving center, yet it still somehow manages to retain an idyllic tropical-island feel. Separation from the mainland obviously helps. Unlike Jutías to the west there's no causeway here and visitors must make the 35 minute journey via boat from Palma Rubia. Most agree the trip is worth it. Three kilometers of white sand and sapphire waters earmark Cayo Levisa as Pinar del Río's best northern beach haven. Part of the Archipiélago de los Colorados, American writer Ernest Hemingway first 'discovered' the area in the early 1940s after he set up a fishing camp on Cayo Paraíso, a smaller coral island 10km to the east. These days Levisa attracts up to 100 visitors daily as well as the 50-plus hotel guests. While you're not going to feel like Robinson Crusoe here, it does make a refreshing alternative to some of Cuba's larger beach resorts.

### Sights & Activities

Scuba diving is offered at CUC$36 for one to four dives, including gear and transport to the dive site. Two hours of snorkeling plus gear costs CUC$12.

### Sleeping & Eating

**Hotel Cayo Levisa** (Cubanacán; ☎ 7-66 60 75; s/d low season CUC$59/74, high CUC$65/83; ❄) Has a new 40-room capacity in cozy *cabañas* with private bath. The room prices include transport to the island and a welcome drink, but beware of water shortages, dull food and occasionally stroppy staff. This is a terrific place to kick off your shoes for a few days and relax, if the tour groups and mosquitoes don't overwhelm you.

### Getting There & Away

The landing for Cayo Levisa is 21km northeast of La Palma or 40km west of Bahía Honda. Take the turn-off to Mirian and proceed 4km through a large banana plantation to reach the coast-guard station at Palma Rubia, from which the boat to the island departs. The Cayo Levisa boat leaves at 10am and returns at 5pm, and costs CUC$25 per person round-trip including lunch. For a few extra Convertibles you can organize a snorkeling trip. From the Cayo Levisa dock you cross the mangroves on a wooden walkway to the resort and gorgeous beach along the island's north side. A transfer bus from Vinales now plies this route (see p208).

## BAHÍA HONDA & AROUND

The scenic, winding road to Habana through northern Pinar del Río Province is a pretty and relaxing alternative to the Autopista. Rice paddies lie in the river valleys and you pass a succession of picturesque thatched farmhouses. Travelers rave about this route. Make sure you bring plenty of camera film and pencil in a full quota of 'view' stops.

Bahía Honda itself is a small bustling town with a pretty church. Close by the purple shadow of the Pan de Guajaibón (699m) marks the highest point for miles around. Despite your relative proximity to Habana you'll feel strangely isolated here, particularly as the road deteriorates after the Palma Rubia turn-off.

There's no real accommodation options in the area and few places to eat. If you're desperate you could try **Motel La Mulata** (r from CUC$10), 27km west of Bahía Honda and 1km off the main road, though some travelers have complained they've been turned away on the pretext it's a Cuban-only place.

## SAN DIEGO DE LOS BAÑOS & AROUND

☎ 8

San Diego de los Baños, 130km southwest of Habana, is a friendly little town nestled between two mountain ranges that is considered to be Cuba's best spa resort (although Baños de Elegua in Villa Clara runs a close second). It is also one of its oldest, dating back to the early 1600s when a sick slave stumbling upon its medicinal waters took a revitalizing bath and was supposedly cured. Thanks to the area's proximity to Habana, a small settlement grew up on the site in the ensuing years as the healing waters' reputation spread and in 1891 the Spanish established the first spa here under medical supervision.

The village sits on the Río San Diego, the river that separates the Sierra de los

Órganos to the west from the higher Sierra del Rosario to the east. The Sierra de Güira on the Pinar del Río side of San Diego de los Baños is a nature reserve with pine, mahogany and cedar forests, and a favorite spot for bird-watchers.

## Sights & Activities

The **Balneario San Diego** (☎ 3-7812; ⏲ 8am-4pm) is a modern bathing complex where thermal waters of 30°C to 40°C are used to treat muscular and skin afflictions. Mud from the mouth of the Río San Diego is used here for mud baths (CUC$20). The sulfurous waters of these mineral springs are potent and immersions of only 20 minutes per day are allowed (CUC$4/6 for collective/private pools). Massage is available at CUC$25 and many other health services are offered including 15-day courses of acupuncture. These facilities are among the finest of their kind in the country and many Cubans are prescribed treatment here by their family doctors – otherwise the clientele is made up of passing foreign visitors.

If you're looking for cold water, you can swim at the Hotel Mirador **pool** (admission CUC$1; ⏲ 9am-6pm). Two blocks over from the Hotel Mirador is the gracious old **Hotel Saratoga** (1924), complete with columns, mosaic tiling and elderly Cubans working the rocking chairs on the porch.

Five kilometers west of San Diego de los Baños is **Parque La Güira**, the former Hacienda Cortina, which consists of a large sculpture park built during the 1920s and '30s by wealthy lawyer José Manuel Cortina. Entered via a crenellated gateway the artificial ruins include a Chinese pavilion and clusters of bamboo. It's worth a quick stopover if you're passing through, more for its slightly surreal atmosphere than for the sights themselves. A huge state-operated restaurant is just above Parque La Güira, but the cabins here are reserved for vacationing military personnel.

During the October 1962 Cuban Missile Crisis, Ernesto 'Che' Guevara transferred the headquarters of the Western Army to **Cueva de Los Portales**, 11km west of Parque La Güira and 16km north of Entronque de Herradura on the Carretera Central. The cave is in a pretty area, 1km off the main road, and was declared a national monument in the 1980s. A small museum contains a few of Che's roughshod artifacts including his bed. Three other caves called El Espejo, El Salvador and Cueva Oscura are up on the hillside. Together these sites make a cool side trip not just for Che aficionados, but for nature lovers as well.

## Sleeping

### IN TOWN

**Hotel Mirador** (Islazul; ☎ 7-8338; s/d low season CUC$30/37; high CUC$34/41; P ❄ 🏊) Foreigners usually stay at this attractive, two-story hotel adjacent to the hot springs. It's a modernized hotel dating from 1954, with comfortable rooms with fridge (some with views) and a pleasant swimming pool. The service here is helpful and friendly and the mineral baths are just across the road.

There are two or three decent casas particulares dotted around in San Diego de los Baños. Other places that come highly recommended are the houses of **Carlos Alberto González** (no phone; Calle 21A No 3003 btwn 30 & 32; r CUC$20). If this place is full the owners can point you in the direction of a few others.

### WEST OF TOWN

Like a faded Hollywood starlet with a habit, Cabañas Los Pinos is beautiful, but hit the skids long ago. In the Sierra de Güira, 12km west of San Diego de los Baños via Parque La Güira, it's a terrific camping spot if you've got gear. The best place to ask for directions/details is at the Hotel Mirador. Los Pinos was built in the early 1960s by Castro's secretary (and respected revolutionary leader in her own right), the late Celia Sánchez, whose circular cabin stands in the center of the eerie, shuttered complex. It's an idyllic location, standing on a ridge below the mountain peaks, and it's an excellent bird-watching base. Los Pinos would make a perfect ecotourism resort were it ever restored. Until that happens you'll probably have the place to yourself.

**Motel Las Palmas** (Parque La Güira; r CUC$17) Has nine air-con rooms with bath, fridge and TV. Mostly Cubans stay here.

**Cueva de Los Portales** (☎ 3-2749) Five kilometers west of Los Pinos, are six basic *cabañas* (CUC$5 per person). You may be able to pitch a tent (CUC$3 per person) in the forest near the cave, but the mosquitoes are fierce.

### Eating

**Hotel Mirador restaurants** (Islazul; ☎ 7-8338; meals under CUC$7) The open-air *parrillada* (grill restaurant) at the Hotel Mirador is quite good. There is also a proper restaurant at the hotel serving Cuban cuisine.

### Getting Around

There's a Servi-Cupet at the entrance to San Diego de los Baños from Habana. Horse carts shuttle between San Diego de los Baños and Parque La Güira for a couple of pesos. If you're planning to cycle over the mountain to Cabañas Los Pinos and Guevara's cave, beware of dangerous potholes and loose gravel on the steep downhill stretches.

## SOROA

☎ 82

Soroa, 95km west of Habana, is the closest mountain resort area to the capital and makes a popular day trip. It's above Candelaria in the Sierra del Rosario, the easternmost and highest section of the Cordillera de Guaniguanico. Soroa is nicknamed the 'rainbow of Cuba', and the region's heavy rainfall (more than 1300mm annually) promotes the growth of tall trees and orchids. The area gets its name from Jean-Pierre Soroa, a Frenchman who owned a 19th-century coffee plantation in these hills. One of his descendants, Ignacio Soroa, created the park as a personal retreat in the 1920s, and only since the revolution has this luxuriant region been developed for tourism. This is another great area to explore by bike.

### Sights & Activities

All Soroa's sights are conveniently near Hotel & Villas Soroa, a large motel complex offering horseback riding. Next door is **Orquideario Soroa** (☎ 77 25 58; admission CUC$3, plus camera CUC$2; 🕑 9am-4pm), built between 1943 and 1953 by Spanish lawyer Tomás Felipe Camacho in memory of his wife and daughter. There are 700 orchid species (most voluminous blooming from December to March), 6000 ornamentals and various growing houses and research facilities. Visits are well guided in Spanish or English; although some orchid enthusiasts have expressed disappointment at the quality and quantity of what's on show. The Orquideario is currently connected to the University of Pinar del Río.

Down the road is the entrance to a park featuring the **Salto del Arco Iris** (admission CUC$3), a 22m waterfall on the Arroyo Manantiales. It's at its most impressive in the May to October rainy season, otherwise it's a trickle. You can swim at the foot of the falls. Entry is free for Hotel & Villas Soroa guests.

On the opposite side of the stream from the waterfall parking lot is the **Baños Romanos** (per hr CUC$5; 🕑 9am-4pm), a stone bathhouse with a pool of cold sulfurous water. Ask at Villas Soroa about the baths and massage treatments. It's a half-hour scramble up the hill from the bathhouse to the **Mirador**, a rocky crag with a sweeping view of all Soroa.

**Castillo de las Nubes** is a romantic castle with a circular tower on a hilltop above the Orquideario. There are good views of the Valle de Soroa and the coastal plain beyond from the ridge beyond the bar. The restaurant has the liveliness of a crypt, but you might grab a drink from the bar (open 10am to 5pm).

### Sleeping & Eating

Several signposted houses on the road from Candelaria to Soroa, 3km below the Hotel & Villas Soroa, rent rooms.

**Maité Delgado** (☎ 522-70069; Km7 Carretera a Soroa; r CUC$20; P ❄) The accommodation is within easy walking distance of all the Soroa sights and the family is pleasant. If it's full, the owners will point you in the direction of a few others further down the road.

**Hotel & Villas Soroa** (Cubanacán; ☎ 77 82 18; s/d low season incl breakfast CUC$38/48, high CUC$45/55; P ❄ 🏊) Nestled in a valley on spacious grounds amid stately trees and verdant hills. The 80 rooms have fridges, good beds and nice touches like incandescent light. Try for a room on the front row above the swimming pool. A fabulous alternative is to take one of the private villas (low season CUC$43 to CUC$72) in the wooded slope above the Orquideario administered by the hotel. They sleep one to five people, have kitchens, fridges and satellite TVs; six have swimming pools, which may be dry: great for boarders!

The only place to eat outside the hotels/casas is the Restaurante El Salto, opposite the Orquideario and next to the Baños Romanos.

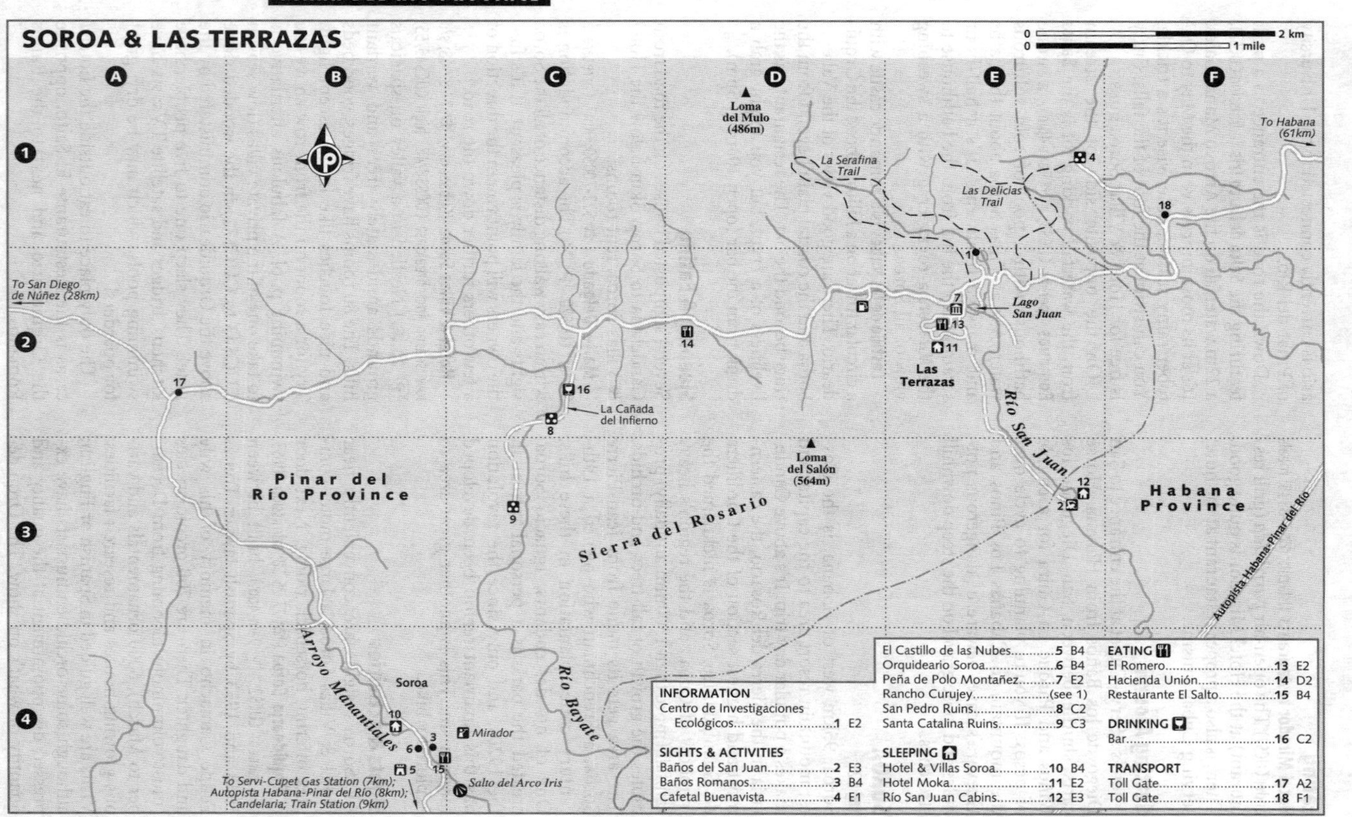
SOROA & LAS TERRAZAS
0 2 km
0 1 mile
Loma del Mulo (486m)
La Serafina Trail
Las Delicias Trail
To Habana (61km)
To San Diego de Núñez (28km)
Lago San Juan
Las Terrazas
La Cañada del Infierno
Río San Juan
Loma del Salón (564m)
Pinar del Río Province
Habana Province
Sierra del Rosario
Autopista Habana-Pinar del Río
Arroyo Manantiales
Soroa
Río Bayate
Mirador
Salto del Arco Iris
To Servi-Cupet Gas Station (7km); Autopista Habana-Pinar del Río (8km); Candelaria; Train Station (9km)
INFORMATION
Centro de Investigaciones Ecológicos....1 E2
SIGHTS & ACTIVITIES
Baños del San Juan....2 E3
Baños Romanos....3 B4
Cafetal Buenavista....4 E1
El Castillo de las Nubes....5 B4
Orquideario Soroa....6 B4
Peña de Polo Montañez....7 E2
Rancho Curujey....(see 1)
San Pedro Ruins....8 C2
Santa Catalina Ruins....9 C3
SLEEPING
Hotel & Villas Soroa....10 B4
Hotel Moka....11 E2
Río San Juan Cabins....12 E3
EATING
El Romero....13 E2
Hacienda Unión....14 D2
Restaurante El Salto....15 B4
DRINKING
Bar....16 C2
TRANSPORT
Toll Gate....17 A2
Toll Gate....18 F1

### Getting There & Away

A transfer bus now passes through Soroa daily leaving Viñales at 8am and arriving in the village at 10:15am. The bus then goes onto Habana, arriving in the capital at 11am. On the return leg, the bus leaves Habana at 1pm, arriving in Soroa at 4pm and Viñales at 5:40pm. For more information contact **Transtur** (☎ 79 60 60; Salvador Cisneros) in Viñales or **Havanatur** (☎ 77 84 94) in Pinar del Río.

The only other access to Soroa and the surrounding area is with your own wheels: car, bicycle or moped. An Astro or Víazul bus will drop you off at Canadleria 10km to the south, but from there you'll have to hitch a ride to Villa Soroa (for information on the risks associated with hitching see p477).

Servi-Cupet is on the Autopista at the turn-off to Candelaria, 8km below Villa Soroa.

## LAS TERRAZAS

**☎ 82 / pop 1200**

The quaint, leafy community of Las Terrazas in eastern Pinar del Río, near the border of Habana Province, dates back to a reforestation project in 1968. The surrounding mountains had been denuded by a combination of fire and shortsighted agricultural techniques, and the inhabitants lived in poor and difficult conditions. A reservoir was created in 1971, and beside it a model settlement was built, taking its name from the hillside terraces planted with pines to prevent erosion. The experiment was so successful that in 1985 this area was declared the Reserva Sierra del Rosario, Cuba's first Unesco-sanctioned Biosphere Reserve.

In 1990, then minister of tourism Osmani Cienfuegos (brother of revolutionary hero Camilo Cienfuegos) approved an upmarket ecotourism resort here as a means of providing employment for the village's 890 inhabitants. Between 1992 and 1994 a hotel was built with workers drawn from Las Terrazas and it quickly became an archetype. A vibrant art community with open studios, woodwork and pottery workshops has taken hold and the settlement's biggest success story has been none other than *guajiro* music hero, Polo Montañez. Cienfuegos, who had a hand in the original reforestation project, is still heavily involved in Las Terrazas and regarded as the motivating force behind its success.

Las Terrazas is 20km northeast of Hotel & Villas Soroa and 13km west of the Habana–Pinar del Río Autopista at Cayajabos. There are toll gates at both entrances to the reserve (CUC$3 per person). The reserve's **Centro de Investigaciones Ecológicas** (☎ 77 29 21) is next to Rancho Curujey, a bar overlooking a bulrush-fringed lake, a few hundred meters east of the Hotel Moka access road. Here you can arrange guided hikes on La Serafina and Las Delicias trails, costing CUC$20 for one or two persons (two to three hours). Hotel Moka also organizes these and other hikes. Unfortunately the trails are poorly marked, so you really do need a guide. It's said that 83 species of birds can be seen in the reserve.

### Sights & Activities

About 1.5km up the hill from the gate on the Cayajabos side, 6km from Hotel Moka by road, are the ruins of the **Cafetal Buenavista**, a coffee plantation built in 1802 by French refugees from Haiti. During the 19th century there were 54 similar coffee estates around Las Terrazas, although coffee

**GO FURTHER – EXPLORE THE SIERRA DEL ROSARIO RESERVE**

Inaugurated as the first of Cuba's six Unesco biospheres in 1984 the Sierra del Rosario reserve juxtaposes complex geological and biological structures with the remnants of the first major coffee plantation in the Americas.

Renowned for its excellent bird-watching possibilities, the park management has sought to protect the area's delicate ecosystem through reforestation programs and the development of bio-fertilizers.

A recent, more challenging addition to the reserve's small clutch of rather tame hikes is the 13km **Cascadas del San Claudio trail**, which takes walkers to a 20m waterfall with access to a natural swimming pool. Ask about this at the park headquarters. The hike's relatively new, but if you can muster a group together and are willing to accept the services (and cost) of a local guide, there's a chance they might let you camp out overnight.

isn't grown commercially here anymore. The huge *tajona* (grindstone) at the back of the property once extracted the coffee beans from their shells. Next the beans were sun-dried on huge platforms. Ruins of the quarters of some of the 126 slaves held here can be seen alongside the driers. The attic of the master's house (now a restaurant) was used to store the beans until they could be carried down to the port of Mariel by mule. There are decent views from here.

From just below Hotel Moka, a 3km road runs down the Río San Juan to small falls and natural swimming holes called the **Baños del San Juan** (extra CUC$3). This popular spot has naturally terraced rocks with clean, bracing waters cascading into a series of pools. If it's too crowded for your taste, you can bushwhack downriver to more private pools. There's a simple restaurant here serving palatable plates of fried chicken, rice and salad for a few Convertibles.

**Hacienda Unión**, 3.5km west of the Hotel Moka access road, features a country-style restaurant, horses available for riding (CUC$6 per hour) and a set of old coffee-estate ruins.

At **La Cañada del Infierno** (The Trail to Hell), midway between the Hotel Moka access road and the Soroa side entrance gate, a road follows the Río Bayate down to the 19th-century **San Pedro & Santa Catalina coffee-estate ruins**. A kilometer off the main road, a bar overlooks a popular swimming spot.

The former lakeside house of Polo Montañez is now a small museum called **Peña de Polo Montañez** containing various gold records and assorted memorabilia. It's right in the village overlooking the lake.

## Sleeping & Eating

**Hotel Moka** (☎ 77 86 00; hmoka@teleda.get.cma.net; s/d low season CUC$50/60, high CUC$65/85; P) Melting into the surrounding woods and with a tree growing through the airy lobby, the Hotel Moka is one of Cuba's most interesting and well-maintained hotels. Blending effortlessly into the surrounding woodland, the 26 bright, spacious rooms have fridge and satellite TV and activities ranging from mountain biking to fishing. Horseback riding and guided hikes are also on offer. This place regularly receives recommendations. Through the hotel front desk, you can rent five separate villas down by the lake. Guests have access to all the facilities and services at the hotel.

Limited accommodation is now also provided in five cabins 3km away in **Río San Juan** (s/d CUC$13/22). Bookings can be made through La Moka.

**El Romero** (9am-9pm) This is the most interesting place to grab a bite. It's a full-blown eco-restaurant (unique in Cuba) specializing in vegetarian fare. El Romero uses home-grown organic vegetables and herbs, solar energy and keeps its own bees. You might think you woke up in San Francisco when you browse the menu replete with humus, bean pancake, pumpkin and onion soup and extra virgin olive oil.

## Getting There & Away

Although there are no public buses into the Sierra del Rosario reserve, you can make use of a new and reasonably priced transfer service running daily between Viñales, Soroa, Las Terrazas and Habana (CUC$12). It passes through Las Terrazas at approximately 10:30am on the way to Habana and 3:45pm on the return leg to Viñales. You can book your space with **Transtur** (☎ 79 60 60; Salvador Cisneros) in Viñales or **Havanatur** (☎ 77 84 94) in Pinar del Río.

## Getting Around

The 1950s-style Essto station, 1.5km west of the Hotel Moka access road, is one of Cuba's quirkiest gas stations. Fill up here before heading east to Habana or west to Pinar del Río.

# Matanzas Province

For most foreign visitors Matanzas means one thing: Varadero, the 20km stretch of idyllic white sand that lures in tourists from all over the globe. The attractions for fun-seekers are hard to resist: you can skydive here, play golf, swim with dolphins, rent a motorbike, scuba dive, dance in a cave or enjoy sunset cocktails in an art deco–inspired mansion. In fact, you can do just about everything that the average Cuban can only dream about. But to suggest that Matanzas terminates at Varadero is like saying France begins and ends with St Tropez.

Made rich on the backs of slave labor and crisscrossed by sprawling plantations of gnarly citrus trees, Matanzas is Cuba's second most industrialized province after Habana with an infrastructure based on petroleum, sugar milling and fruit production. Outside Varadero the area boasts two historic cities, Matanzas and Cárdenas, along with the evocative beaches of the Bahía de Cochinos (Bay of Pigs), and the distinctive environmental Zapata Peninsula; now a protected Unesco biosphere reserve.

The Puente Bacunayagua is Cuba's highest bridge and an engineering triumph considered by experts to be one of the island's seven manmade 'wonders', while, glimmering imperceptibly in the background, the verdant Valle de Yumurí juxtaposes hardworking *campesino* (country) life with numerous undiscovered rural retreats. Further south as royal palms give way to fir trees, off-the-beaten-track travelers can explore the eerie Romanesque bathhouses of San Miguel de los Baños, a long-abandoned spa facility where strange eclectic architectural styles are embellished by blooming bougainvillea.

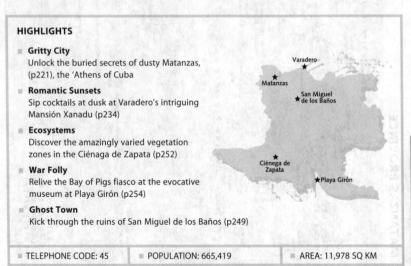

## HIGHLIGHTS

- **Gritty City**
  Unlock the buried secrets of dusty Matanzas, (p221), the 'Athens of Cuba
- **Romantic Sunsets**
  Sip cocktails at dusk at Varadero's intriguing Mansión Xanadu (p234)
- **Ecosystems**
  Discover the amazingly varied vegetation zones in the Ciénaga de Zapata (p252)
- **War Folly**
  Relive the Bay of Pigs fiasco at the evocative museum at Playa Girón (p254)
- **Ghost Town**
  Kick through the ruins of San Miguel de los Baños (p249)

Varadero
Matanzas
San Miguel de los Baños
Ciénega de Zapata
Playa Girón

| TELEPHONE CODE: 45 | POPULATION: 665,419 | AREA: 11,978 SQ KM |
|---|---|---|

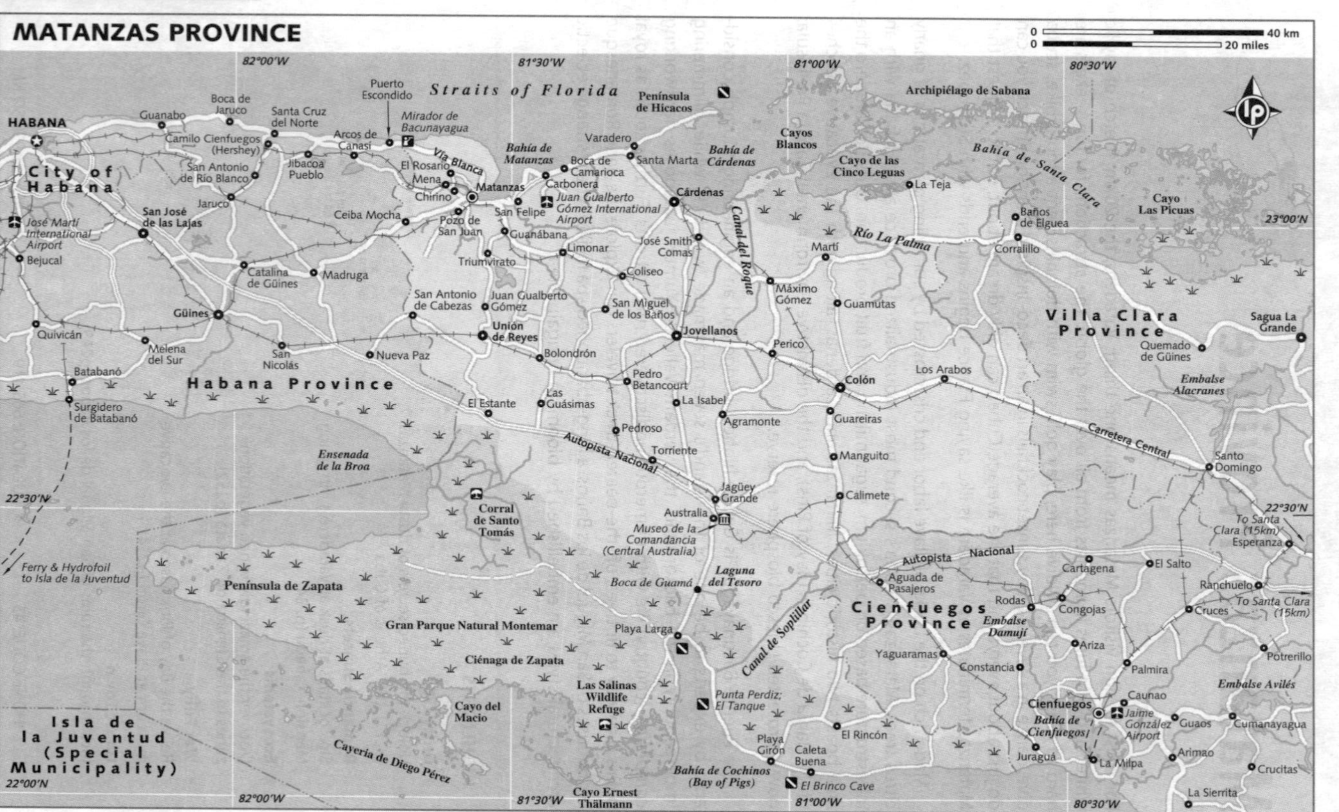
MATANZAS PROVINCE
0 40 km
0 20 miles
82°00'W
81°30'W
81°00'W
80°30'W
23°00'N
22°30'N
22°00'N
Straits of Florida
Península de Hicacos
Archipiélago de Sabana
Cayos Blancos
Cayo de las Cinco Leguas
Bahía de Santa Clara
Cayo Las Picuas
Bahía de Matanzas
Bahía de Cárdenas
Canal del Roque
Río La Palma
HABANA
Guanabo
Boca de Jaruco
Santa Cruz del Norte
Camilo Cienfuegos (Hershey)
Arcos de Canasí
Puerto Escondido
Mirador de Bacunayagua
Vía Blanca
City of Habana
San Antonio de Río Blanco
Jibacoa Pueblo
El Rosario
Mena
Chirino
Matanzas
Jaruco
José Martí International Airport
Bejucal
San José de las Lajas
Ceiba Mocha
Pozo de San Juan
San Felipe
Guanábana
Triunvirato
Catalina de Güines
Madruga
Güines
Quivicán
Melena del Sur
San Nicolás
Batabanó
Surgidero de Batabanó
Habana Province
Nueva Paz
San Antonio de Cabezas
Juan Gualberto Gómez
Unión de Reyes
Bolondrón
Limonar
Coliseo
San Miguel de los Baños
Varadero
Santa Marta
Boca de Camarioca
Carbonera
Juan Gualberto Gómez International Airport
Cárdenas
José Smith Comas
Jovellanos
Máximo Gómez
Martí
Guamutas
Perico
Colón
Los Arabos
La Teja
Baños de Elguea
Corralillo
Villa Clara Province
Quemado de Güines
Sagua La Grande
Embalse Alacranes
Carretera Central
Santo Domingo
To Santa Clara (15km)
Esperanza
Pedro Betancourt
La Isabel
Agramonte
Guareiras
Manguito
Calimete
El Estante
Las Guásimas
Pedroso
Torriente
Autopista Nacional
Ensenada de la Broa
Corral de Santo Tomás
Jagüey Grande
Australia
Museo de la Comandancia (Central Australia)
Boca de Guamá
Laguna del Tesoro
Península de Zapata
Gran Parque Natural Montemar
Ciénaga de Zapata
Playa Larga
Canal de Soplillar
Las Salinas Wildlife Refuge
Cayo del Macio
Punta Perdiz; El Tanque
Playa Girón
Caleta Buena
El Rincón
Bahía de Cochinos (Bay of Pigs)
El Brinco Cave
Cayo Ernest Thälmann
Cayería de Diego Pérez
Isla de la Juventud (Special Municipality)
Ferry & Hydrofoil to Isla de la Juventud
Aguada de Pasajeros
Cienfuegos Province
Cartagena
El Salto
Ranchuelo
Rodas
Congojas
Cruces
To Santa Clara (15km)
Embalse Damují
Ariza
Yaguaramas
Constancia
Palmira
Potrerillo
Embalse Avilés
Caunao
Cienfuegos
Jaime González Airport
Guaos
Cumanayagua
Bahía de Cienfuegos
Juraguá
La Milpa
Arimao
Crucitas
La Sierrita

# NORTHERN MATANZAS

Northern Matanzas boasts an attractive rural landscape punctuated by low mountains and lush valleys – most notably the Valle del Yumurí. Home to Cuba's largest resort area (Varadero) and one of its biggest ports (Matanzas), the northern coastline is also the province's main population center and is national center for industry and commerce.

## MATANZAS

☎45 / pop 126,220

Sadly neglected by the powers that be and languishing *Titanic*-like beneath a thick layer of postrevolutionary dust, Matanzas is Cuba's sleeping giant; a city of striking bridges and withered colonial churches that hide just a few coats of paint away from their 19th-century neoclassical splendor.

Known formerly as the 'Athens of Cuba' for its pivotal role in the development of poetry, theater and music on the island, Matanzas' position as a one-time rival to Habana in all things cultural doesn't carry much weight with contemporary visitors, who are conspicuous by their absence. Straddled with humdrum ration shops, a painfully dismal restaurant scene, and a decrepit and scruffy central park that is crying out for an architectural version of the 'extreme makeover', the local buzz in Matanzas' dilapidated streets is as downbeat as it is elusive. If it's five-star comforts you're after hop on a Víazul bus straight back to Planet Varadero. But if the thought of authentic rumba drumming, beer over dominoes or the chance to meet some genuinely hospitable locals makes you fidget on your beachside sun-lounger, gritty, in-your-face Matanzas could be the place for you. Welcome to the *real* Cuba amigos!

### History

In 1508 Sebastián de Ocampo sighted a bay that the Indians called Guanima. Now known as the Bahía de Matanzas, it's said the name recalls the *matanza* (massacre) of a group of Spaniards during an early indigenous uprising. In 1628 the Dutch pirate Piet Heyn captured a Spanish treasure fleet carrying 12 million gold florins ushering in a lengthy era of smuggling and piracy. Undeterred by the pirate threat, 30 families from the Canary Islands arrived in 1693, on the orders of King Carlos III of Spain, to found the town of San Carlos y Severino de Matanzas. The first fort went up in 1734 and the original Plaza de Armas still remains as Plaza de la Vigía.

For a decade starting in 1817 Matanzas flourished economically with the building of numerous sugar mills. The export of coffee added further equity to the city's bank balance and in 1843 with the laying of the first railway to Habana, the floodgates were opened. The second half of the 19th century was a golden age in Matanzas' history when the city set new standards in the cultural sphere with the development of a newspaper, a public library, a high school, a theater and a philharmonic society. Due to the large number of artists, writers and intellectuals living in the area, Matanzas became known as the 'Athens of Cuba' with a cultural scene that dwarfed even Habana.

Home to several modern poets including Cintio Vitier and Carilda Oliver Labra, Matanzas is where Cuba's first *danzón* (traditional Cuban ballroom dance) was performed in 1879 and is also the spiritual home of the rumba. With a long history of slave occupation there are a number of Santería *cabildos* (associations) here, the oldest of which dates back to 1808.

### Orientation

Matanzas is on the Vía Blanca between Varadero and Habana, 42km west of Varadero and 98km east of central Habana. The Carretera Central from Pinar del Río to Santiago de Cuba also passes through the city.

The compact old town lies between the Río Yumurí and the Río San Juan with the historic Versalles quarter situated to the north. Most of the industry is east of Versalles. The Hershey Railway terminates in

#### MATANZAS STREET NAMES

| Old name | New name |
|---|---|
| Contreras | Calle 79 |
| Daoíz | Calle 75 |
| Maceo | Calle 77 |
| Medio/Independencia | Calle 85 |
| Milanés | Calle 83 |
| San Luis | Calle 298 |
| Santa Teresa | Calle 290 |
| Zaragoza | Calle 292 |

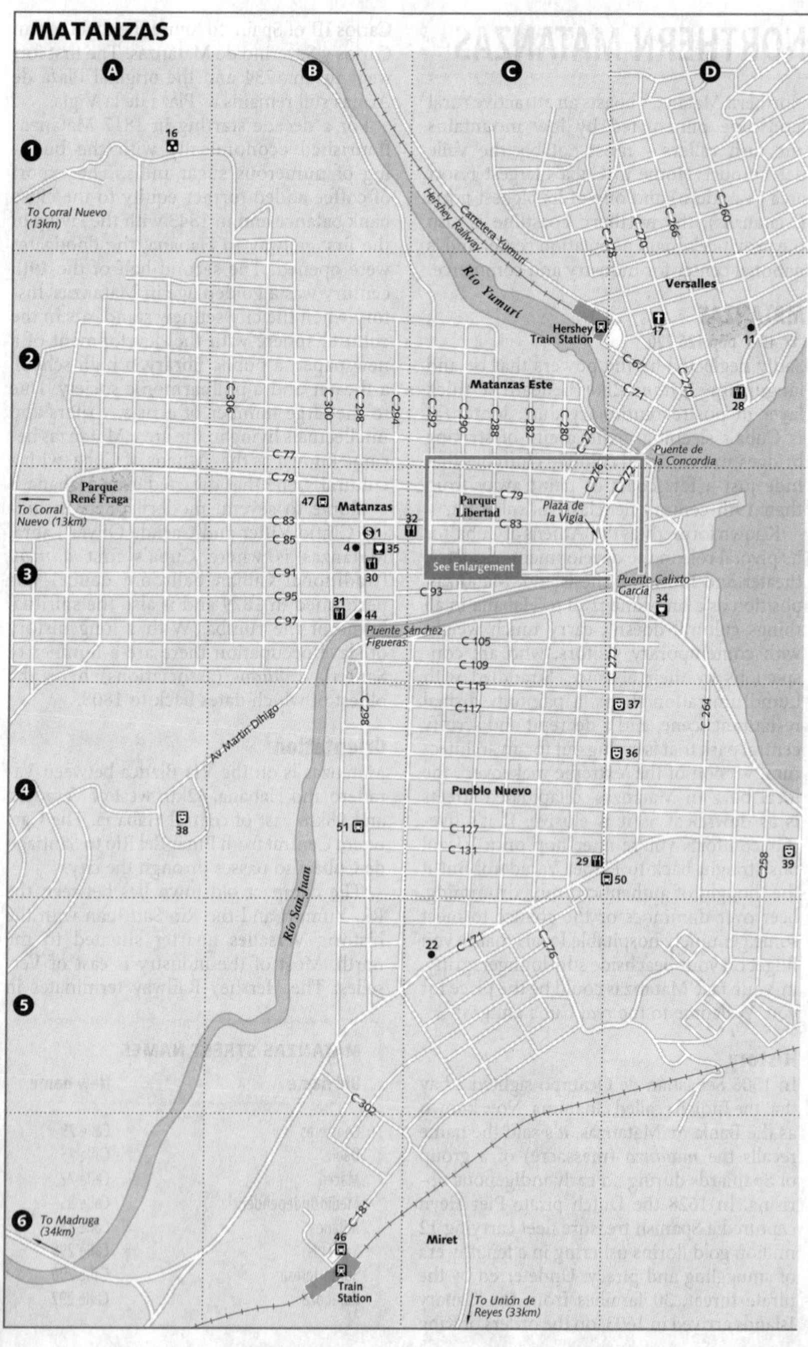
MATANZAS
To Corral Nuevo (13km)
Carretera Yumurí
Hershey Railway
Río Yumurí
Versalles
Hershey Train Station
Matanzas Este
Puente de la Concordia
Parque René Fraga
To Corral Nuevo (13km)
Matanzas
Parque Libertad
Plaza de la Vigía
See Enlargement
Puente Calixto García
Puente Sánchez Figueras
Av Martín Dihigo
Pueblo Nuevo
Río San Juan
To Madruga (34km)
Miret
Train Station
To Unión de Reyes (33km)

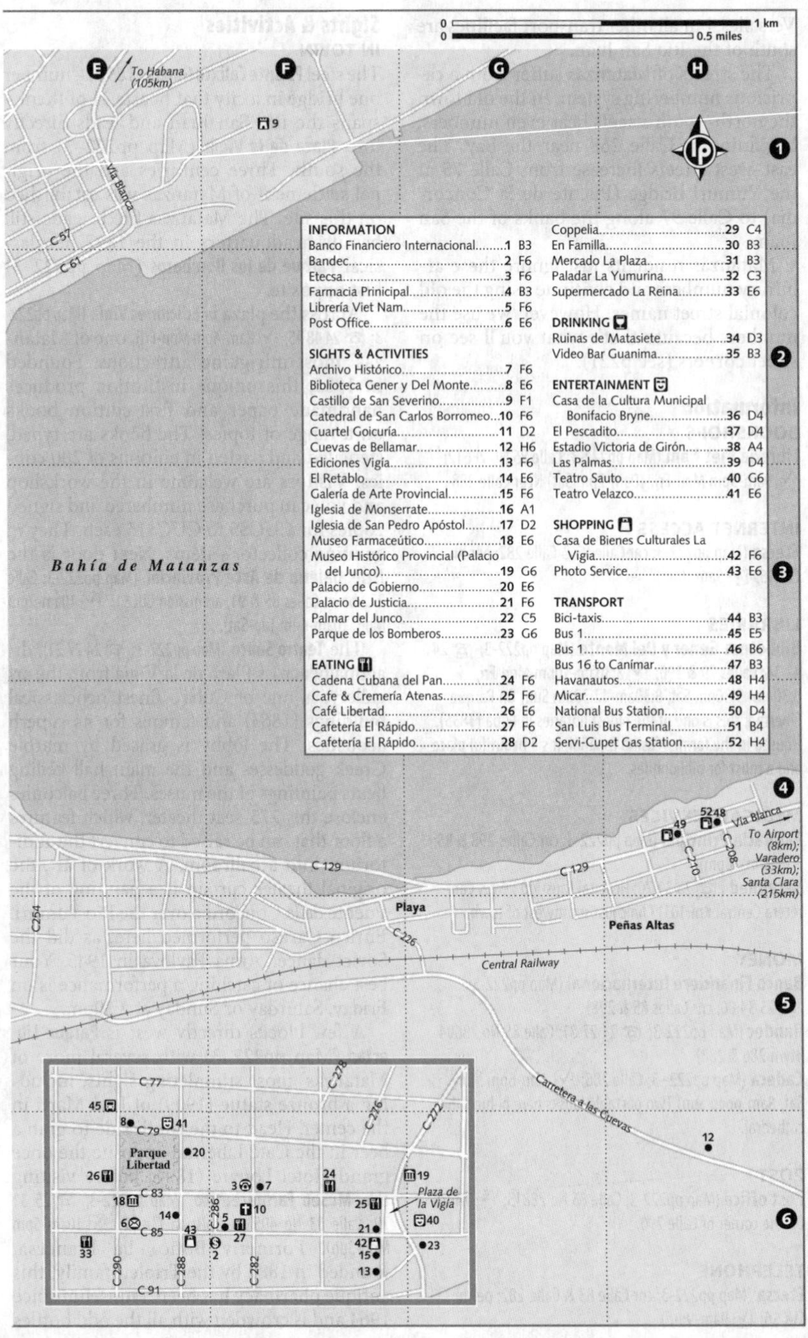

0 1 km
0 0.5 miles
E
F
G
H
1
2
3
4
5
6
To Habana (105km)
Via Blanca
C 57
C 61
Bahía de Matanzas
INFORMATION
Banco Financiero Internacional 1 B3
Bandec 2 F6
Etecsa 3 F6
Farmacia Principal 4 B3
Librería Viet Nam 5 F6
Post Office 6 E6
SIGHTS & ACTIVITIES
Archivo Histórico 7 F6
Biblioteca Gener y Del Monte 8 E6
Castillo de San Severino 9 F1
Catedral de San Carlos Borromeo 10 F6
Cuartel Goicuría 11 D2
Cuevas de Bellamar 12 H6
Ediciones Vigía 13 F6
El Retablo 14 E6
Galería de Arte Provincial 15 F6
Iglesia de Monserrate 16 A1
Iglesia de San Pedro Apóstol 17 D2
Museo Farmaceútico 18 E6
Museo Histórico Provincial (Palacio del Junco) 19 G6
Palacio de Gobierno 20 E6
Palacio de Justicia 21 F6
Palmar del Junco 22 C5
Parque de los Bomberos 23 G6
EATING
Cadena Cubana del Pan 24 F6
Cafe & Cremería Atenas 25 F6
Café Libertad 26 E6
Cafetería El Rápido 27 F6
Cafetería El Rápido 28 D2
Coppelia 29 C4
En Familla 30 B3
Mercado La Plaza 31 B3
Paladar La Yumurina 32 C3
Supermercado La Reina 33 E6
DRINKING
Ruinas de Matasiete 34 D3
Video Bar Guanima 35 B3
ENTERTAINMENT
Casa de la Cultura Municipal Bonifacio Bryne 36 D4
El Pescadito 37 D4
Estadio Victoria de Girón 38 A4
Las Palmas 39 D4
Teatro Sauto 40 G6
Teatro Velazco 41 E6
SHOPPING
Casa de Bienes Culturales La Vigia 42 F6
Photo Service 43 E6
TRANSPORT
Bici-taxis 44 B3
Bus 1 45 E5
Bus 1 46 B6
Bus 16 to Canímar 47 B3
Havanautos 48 H4
Micar 49 H4
National Bus Station 50 D4
San Luis Bus Terminal 51 B4
Servi-Cupet Gas Station 52 H4
Via Blanca
To Airport (8km); Varadero (33km); Santa Clara (215km)
C 210
C 208
C 129
C 129
C 254
Playa
Peñas Altas
C 226
Central Railway
Carretera a las Cuevas
C 77
C 79
C 83
C 85
C 91
C 278
C 276
C 272
C 290
C 288
C 286
C 282
Parque Libertad
Plaza de la Vigía

Versalles, but all other transport facilities are south of the Río San Juan.

The streets of Matanzas suffer from a capricious numbering system. In the old town the north–south streets bear even numbers, beginning at Calle 268 near the bay. The east–west streets increase from Calle 75 at the Yumurí bridge (Puente de la Concordia) to Calle 97 along the banks of the San Juan.

Matanzas residents just ignore these arbitrary numbers and continue using the old colonial street names. However, we use the numbers because that's what you'll see on street corners (see p221).

## Information

### BOOKSHOPS

**Librería Viet Nam** (Map pp222-3; Calle 85 No 28612; 9am-5pm Mon-Fri, 10am-2pm Sat) Near Calle 288.

### INTERNET ACCESS

**Etecsa** (Map pp222-3; cnr Calle 83 & Calle 282; per hr CUC$6; 9am-9pm)

### LIBRARIES

**Biblioteca Gener y Del Monte** (Map pp222-3; ☎ 24 41 34; Calles 79 & 290; 8:30am-10pm Mon-Fri, 8:30am- 3:30pm Sat, 8:30am-12:30pm Sun) On Parque Libertad, this is one of the oldest libraries in Cuba (1835). Housed in the former Casino Español, it's a beautiful place and a must for bibliophiles.

### MEDICAL SERVICES

**Farmacia Principal** (Map pp222-3; cnr Calles 298 & 85; 8am-10pm)

**Servimed** (☎ 25 31 70; Hospital Faustino Pérez, Carretera Central Km 101) Clinic just southwest of town.

### MONEY

**Banco Financiero Internacional** (Map pp222-3; ☎ 25 34 00; cnr Calles 85 & 298)

**Bandec** (Map pp222-3; ☎ 24 27 81; Calle 85 No 28604 btwn 286 & 288)

**Cadeca** (Map pp222–3; Calle 286; 8am-6pm Mon-Sat, 8am-noon Sun) Two portable kiosks here behind the cathedral.

### POST

**Post office** (Map pp222-3; Calle 85 No 28813; 24hr) On the corner of Calle 290.

### TELEPHONE

**Etecsa** (Map pp222-3; cnr Calle 83 & Calle 282; per hr CUC$6; 9am-9pm)

## Sights & Activities

### IN TOWN

The steel **Puente Calixto García** (1899) – number one bridge in a city that boasts 21 of them – spans the Río San Juan and leads directly into **Plaza de la Vigía** (Map pp222–3) from the south. Three centuries ago the original settlement of Matanzas was established on this site. The Matanzas fire brigade still has its headquarters in the 1897 neoclassical **Parque de los Bomberos** (Map pp222–3) just opposite.

Across the plaza is **Ediciones Vigía** (Map pp222-3; ☎ 24 48 45; 8am-4pm Mon-Fri), one of Matanzas' most intriguing attractions. Founded in 1985, this unique institution produces handmade paper and first-edition books on a range of topics. The books are typed, stenciled and pasted in editions of 200 copies. Visitors are welcome in the workshop and you can purchase numbered and signed copies for CUC$5 to CUC$15 each. They're genuine collector's items. Next door is the fine **Galería de Arte Provincial** (Map pp222-3; Calle 272 btwn Calles 85 & 91; admission CUC$1; 10am-2pm Mon, 10am-6pm Tue-Sat).

The **Teatro Sauto** (Map pp222-3; ☎ 24 27 21), diagonally across Plaza de la Vigía from the art gallery, is one of Cuba's finest neoclassical buildings (1863) and famous for its superb acoustics. The lobby is graced by marble Greek goddesses and the main hall ceiling bears paintings of the muses. Three balconies enclose this 775-seat theater, which features a floor that can be raised to convert the auditorium into a ballroom. A work of art, the original theater curtain is a painting of the Puente de la Concordia over the Río Yumurí. Enrico Caruso performed here, as did the Soviet dancer Anna Pavlova in 1945. Your best chance of catching a performance is on Friday, Saturday or Sunday at 8:30pm.

A few blocks directly west is **Parque Libertad** (Map pp222–3) with several more of Matanzas' most stimulating sights, including a bronze statue (1909) of José Martí in the center. Head to the south side to grab a beer in the Café Libertad opposite the once grand Hotel Louvre (1894) before visiting the **Museo Farmaceútico** (Map pp222-3; ☎ 25 31 79; Calle 83 No 4951; admission CUC$2; 10am-5pm Mon-Sun). Formerly Botica La Francesa, founded in 1882 by the Triolett family, this antique pharmacy has been a museum since 1964 and is crowded with all the odd bottles and instruments, porcelain jars and medical recipes used in the trade. The eastern side of the park is dominated by the orderly **Palacio de Gobierno** (Map pp222–3) dating from 1853, now the seat of the *Poder Popular* (Popular Power). On the northern side are the defunct Hotel Velazco and the former **Casino Español** (cnr Calles 79 & 290), where the first performance of the *danzonete* (Cuban ballroom dance) *Rompiendo La Rutina* by Anceto Díaz took place. It's now the **Biblioteca Gener y Del Monte** (Map pp222–3).

Kids and theater lovers shouldn't miss **El Retablo** (Map pp222-3; ☎ 61 70 38; Calle 288 No 8313; admission CUC$1; 10am-6pm Mon-Sat), a gallery filled with all the fantastic costumes, marionettes and creations made by Cuba's masterful puppet makers. Performances are held here every second Saturday of the month. Nearby is the city's **Archivo Histórico** (Map pp222-3; ☎ 24 42 12; Calle 83 No 28013 btwn Calles 280 & 282), in the former residence of local poet José Jacinto Milanés (1814–63). A bronze statue of Milanés stands on the Plaza de la Iglesia in front of the nearby **Catedral de San Carlos Borromeo** (Map pp222-3; Calle 282 btwn Calles 83 & 85; donation welcome; 8am-noon, 3-5pm Mon-Fri, 9am-noon Sun). This neoclassical cathedral was constructed in 1693 and rebuilt in 1878.

Other impressive buildings include the imposing **Palacio de Justicia** (Map pp222–3) opposite the Teatro Sauto, first erected in 1826 and rebuilt between 1908 and 1911. Also on Plaza de la Vigía is the **Museo Histórico Provincial** (Map pp222-3; cnr Calles 83 & 272; admission CUC$2; 10am-noon & 1-5pm Tue-Sun). This large museum housed in the Palacio del Junco (1840) contains exhibits relating to Matanzas history. Free concerts are held here at 4pm on Saturday.

The **Versalles quarter** (Map pp222–3), north of the Río Yumurí, was colonized by French refugees from Haiti in the 19th century and by the 1890s this area was the font of an exciting new musical genre called rumba. From the Plaza de la Vigía head north on Calle 272 across the graceful **Puente de la Concordia** (Map pp222–3). The neoclassical **Iglesia de San Pedro Apóstol** (Map pp222-3; cnr Calles 57 & 270) is worth seeking out. Four blocks east on the corner of Calles 63 and 260 stands the sinister-looking **Cuartel Goicuría** (Map pp222–3), a former barracks of Batista's army that was assaulted on April 29, 1956, by a group of rebels led by Reinold T García. Today it's a school.

In an industrial area above the port, a little over 1km northeast of Cuartel Goicuría, is the 18th-century **Castillo de San Severino** (Map pp222-3; Av del Muelle; admission CUC$2; 9am-5pm) erected by the Spanish. To get there from Versalles, walk northeast to the end of Calle 57 and cross the highway. Entry is via the Centro Politécnico Ernest Thälmann on Calle 230. Continue straight, past the school, on a potholed dirt track and around the corner is the castle on the right. Slaves were brought directly into the castle from nearby boats and held in sinister dungeons below. Later, Cuban patriots were imprisoned within these walls. A plaque recalls 61 persons executed here between 1895 and 1897. San Severino remained a prison until the 1970s. Three cannons, one dated 1775, and the central square are well preserved, and plans exist to turn the castle into a tourist center. There are great views of Matanzas Bay.

For an excellent view of Matanzas and the picturesque Valle del Yumurí, march north up Calle 306 to the ruined **Iglesia de Monserrate** (Map pp222–3), dating from 1875 and perched loftily above the town.

Baseball fans might want to make the pilgrimage to **Palmar del Junco** (Map pp222–3) in the southern part of the city, site of Cuba's first baseball field (1904) and a source of much civic pride.

### OUTSIDE TOWN

The **Cuevas de Bellamar** (Map pp222-3; ☎ 25 35 38; admission CUC$5, camera CUC$5; 9am-6pm), 5km southeast of Matanzas, are 300,000 years old and are promoted locally as the oldest tourist attractions in Cuba. The 2500m-long caves were discovered in 1861 by a Chinese workman in the employ of Don Manual Santos Parga. There's an underground stream inside; two restaurants, a pool and playground outside. One-hour visits into the cave leave every hour seven times a day starting at 9:30am. To get there, take bus 16, 17 or 20 east toward Canímar and ask the driver to let you out near Calle 226. From there it's a 30-minute walk uphill to the caves; a tiny railroad tunnel makes this road impassable for anything larger than a jeep or compact car. Other vehicles must follow a confusing, roundabout route via Calle 276, south from Calle 171, near the old train station.

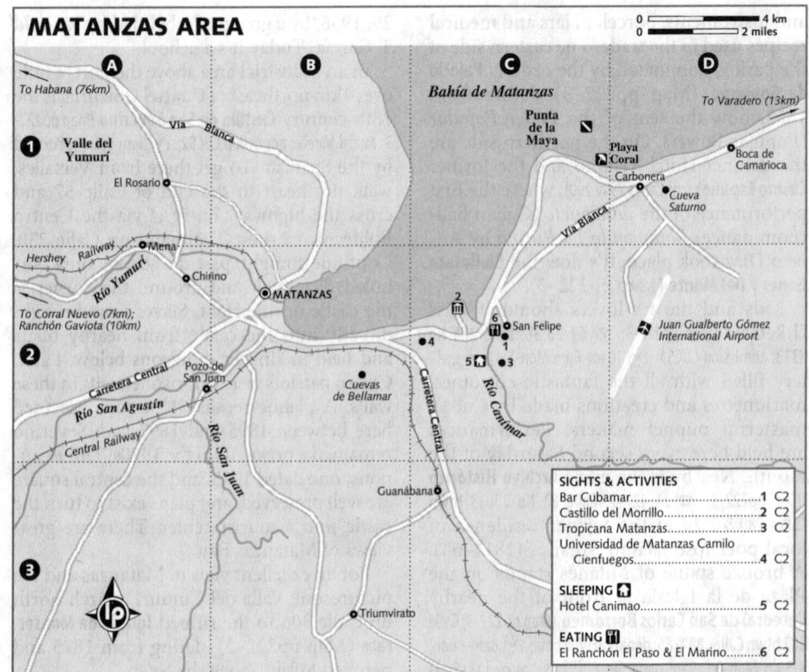


The Río Canímar, 8km east of Matanzas, feeds into the bay. It's one of the deepest rivers in Cuba. Just before the highway bridge a road runs 1km down the western (ocean) side of the river to a cove where the four guns of the **Castillo del Morrillo** (1720) overlook a small beach. This castle is now a **museum** (Map p226; admission CUC$1; 9am-4pm Tue-Sun) dedicated to the student leader Antonio Guiteras Holmes (1906–35), who founded the revolutionary group Joven Cuba (Young Cuba) in 1934. After serving briefly in the post-Machado government, Guiteras was forced out by army chief Fulgencio Batista. On May 8, 1935, he and 18 others came to Matanzas to find a yacht that would take them into exile in Mexico. Before they could board, Guiteras and Venezuelan revolutionary Carlos Aponte Hernández (1901–35), who had served with Sandino in Nicaragua, were discovered by Batista's troops and shot. Bronze busts of the pair now mark the spot where they were executed, under a *caoba* (mahogany) tree down some steps from a cement gate back near the bridge. The shore behind the castle isn't a bad place for a swim.

### THE ORIGIN OF THE VALLE DEL YUMURÍ

An old Indian legend tells of a maiden named Coalina who was hidden away by her father after it was prophesized that a terrible disaster would befall the community if she ever fell in love. In due course a young chief of Camagüey named Nerey heard of Coalina's beauty and resolved to find her. Of course, they fell in love at first sight, whereupon an earthquake split apart the mountains of Matanzas and the waters of the Río Yumurí rushed toward the sea, destroying the village and carrying off the lovers. Coalina's last words were 'Yu murí', archaic Spanish for 'I die.'

Boat trips 12km up the jungle-clad **Río Canímar** depart from **Bar Cubamar** (Map p226; ☎ 26 15 16), below the bridge on the inland side. Varadero tour companies offer this excursion with lunch, horseback riding, fishing and snorkeling, but you can work out a similar deal for approximately CUC$25 by showing up at the landing before noon. Rowboats are for rent (CUC$2 per hour) at the bar any time.

The old coastal road to Varadero is great on a moped, providing better scenery and a mellower pace than the Autopista. There are some OK swimming spots en route and **Playa Coral** (Map p226) has 2km of offshore reef with the best snorkeling in the area. The airport access road is just beyond Playa Coral at the small crossroads town of Carbonera (a fresh fish lunch can be arranged here; ask around). One kilometer south of the Vía Blanca on this road is the **Cueva Saturno** (Map p226; ☎ 25 32 72; admission incl snorkel gear CUC$5; 🕑 8am-6pm). It's promoted as a snorkeling spot and Varadero companies include it on many tours, but don't believe the hype: it's really just a ho-hum cave with limited access unless you're an experienced cave diver with all the relevant equipment. Beware the odd hustler or three and the screaming crowds clamoring to get into the water. There's a snack bar here that sells good coffee.

## Festivals & Events

Matanzas is famous for its rumbas and the spicy Marina neighborhood across the Puente de la Concordia is home to some of the most renowned rumberos, including Los Muñequitos de Matanzas. During the 10 days following October 10, you can shake your bones with these and other talented musicians at the **Festival del Bailador Rumbero** in the Teatro Sauto.

## Sleeping

### IN TOWN

None of the three once resplendent hotels in the center of Matanzas are currently open. World-weary Hotel El Louvre on the south side of Parque Libertad (no sign), is the most likely candidate for a renovation although there weren't any hands-in-the-pockets, hard-hat-wearing builders around to verify.

Rather fortuitously the Matanzas casa particular scene is better-than-average.

### CASAS PARTICULARES – MATANZAS

With no city-center hotels Matanzas relies on a small clutch of super-friendly casas.

**Anita & Luis Alberto Valdés** (☎ 24 22 97; Calle 79 No 28205 2nd fl btwn Calles 282 & 288; r CUC$25; ❄) Two bedrooms with separate baths. Top hosts and huge delicious meals.

**'Hostal Alma' – Alberto Hernández** (☎ 24 78 10; Calle 83 No 29008 btwn Calles 290 & 292; r CUC$20-25; ❄) Two rooms in colonial house both with private baths, roof terrace, sun loungers and pleasant central courtyard. Meals available. Alberto is an excellent host and an expert on Matanzas' history.

**'Hostal Azul' Yoel Báez & Aylín Hernández** (☎ 24 78 10; Calle 83 No 29012 btwn Calles 290 & 292; r CUC$20-25; ❄) Huge colonial room in quiet house. Very attentive hosts. Shares phone with Hostal Alma.

**Roberto Chaves Llerena & Margarita Romero** (☎ 24 25 77; Calle 79 No 27608 btwn Calles 276 & 278; r CUC$20) Big colonial house, meals, bike storage.

### OUTSIDE TOWN

**Hotel Canimao** (Islazul; Map p226; ☎ 26 10 14; s/d low season CUC$23/34, high season CUC$28/38; P ❄ ) High above the Río Canímar 8km east of Matanzas on the way to Varadero, Hotel Canimao has 120 comfortable rooms with little balconies catering to Cubans. It does excursions on the Río Canímar (CUC$15, including lunch) and the Cuevas de Bellamar (CUC$8). Bus 16 from the corner of Calle 300 and Calle 83, in Matanzas, will drop you at the bridge downhill from the hotel. Nonguests can use the pool and the Tropicana nightclub (p228) is next door.

## Eating

### IN TOWN

While Matanzas has no real paladares, the casas particulares can usually rustle up something suitably delicious.

**Café Atenas** (Map pp222-3; ☎ 25 34 93; Calles 83 No 8301; 🕑 10am-11pm) If you're stuck for ideas for lunch try the clean and cozy Café Atenas opposite the Teatro Sauto on Plaza de la Vigía. It offers pizza, spaghetti, sandwiches, beer, coffee and a stupendous chicken and shrimp bruschetta with friendly service.

**Café Libertad** (Map pp222-3; cnr Calles 290 & 83) This café is your best bet – make that your only bet! – on Parque Libertad; great location, though the peso *hamberguesas* (hamburgers) could do with a little bit of extra garnish.

**Cafetería El Rápido** (Map pp222-3; cnr Calles 85 & 282), next to the cathedral, is big, but bogus. Better is the **branch** (Map pp222-3; cnr Calles 262 & 75; 24hr), just down from the Cuartel Goicuría in Versalles, with a nice terrace. Lots of cheap peso take-out windows exist on Calle 272 in Versalles, just across the bridge from Matanzas.

Other options:

**Cremería Atenas** (Map pp222-3; 9am-9pm) Next door to Café Atenas, ice-cream junkies will find their fix at this place.

**Paladar La Yumurina** (Map pp222-3; Calle 83 No 29202; 8am-9pm) Serves the house-specialty egg sandwich in a bright dining room. It's on the corner of Calle 292.

**En Familla** (Map pp222-3; cnr Calles 298 & 91; 10am-11:30pm) This new place serves chicken, drinks and sandwiches.

**Coppelia** (Map pp222-3; cnr Calles 272 & 127; 10am-10pm) Cuba's favorite ice cream can be found near the bus station.

**Cadena Cubana del Pan** (Map pp222-3; Calle 83 btwn Calles 278 & 280; 24hr) Has loaves of 10-peso bread you can watch being kneaded and baked; they sometimes have the yummy round rolls too.

**Supermercado La Reina** (Map pp222-3; Calle 85 No 29006 btwn Calles 290 & 292; 8:30am-4:30pm Mon-Sat, 8:30am-12:30pm Sun) Groceries.

**Mercado La Plaza** (Map pp222-3; cnr Calles 97 & 298) Matanzas' colorful vegetable market, is near the Puente Sánchez Figueras (1916). Many peso stalls selling fried things are here.

### OUTSIDE TOWN

There are two quite nice options outside of town en route to Varadero.

**El Ranchón El Paso** (Map p226; 10am-11pm) A simple, breezy place high above the Río Canímar, 8km east of Matanzas. Good pork or chicken meals cost under CUC$4. There's a full bar.

**El Marino** (Map p226; ☎ 26 14 83; noon-9pm) Next door to El Ranchón El Paso, the fancier, reader-recommended El Marino specializes in reasonably priced seafood, including lobster and shrimp. There are egg dishes and soups for vegetarians.

Cuevas de Bellmar is also a decent place to catch a meal.

## Drinking

**Ruinas de Matasiete** (Map pp222-3; ☎ 25 33 87; cnr Vía Blanca & Calle 101; 24hr) Matanzas' best boozer is a Convertible bar housed in the ruins of a 19th-century warehouse, next to the bay. It's near the entrance to town if you're coming from Varadero. Drinks and grilled meats are served on an open-air terrace, but a better reason to come is to hear live music (from 9pm Friday, Saturday and Sunday). There's a minimum cover charge of CUC$3.

**Video Bar Guanima** (Map pp222-3; Calle 85 No 29404 btwn Calles 294 & 298; 10am-6pm & 8pm-2am). Only couples are allowed entry here, but singles will find willing partners at the door.

## Entertainment

**Teatro Sauto** (Map pp222-3; ☎ 24 27 21) Across Plaza de la Vigía Teatro Sauto is a national landmark and one of Cuba's premier theaters. Performances have been held here since 1863 and you might catch the Ballet Nacional de Cuba or the Conjunto Folklórico Nacional de Cuba. Performances are at 8:30pm with Sunday matinees at 3pm (see p224).

**Teatro Velazco** (Map pp222-3; cnr Calles 79 & 288) Situated on Parque Libertad, it shows films.

Plaza de la Vigía is a great place to catch live rumba on the weekend; there are also live performances in Matanzas Este on Sunday afternoon (2pm) – ask a local.

**Casa de la Cultura Municipal Bonifacio Bryne** (Map pp222-3; ☎ 29 27 09; Calle 272 No 11916 btwn Calles 119 & 121) This place in Pueblo Nuevo has cultural programs most evenings at 9pm.

**Las Palmas** (Map pp222-3; ☎ 25 32 52; cnr Calle 254 & Calle 127; admission CUC$1; noon-midnight Mon-Wed, noon-2am Fri-Sun) A good starlit night out for a fraction of the price of the Tropicana shindig can be had at this ARTex place.

**El Pescadito** (Map pp222-3; Calle 272 btwn Calles 115 & 117) Similar to Las Palmas but more central and local.

**Tropicana Matanzas** (Map p226; ☎ 26 53 80; admission CUC$35; 10pm-2am Tue-Sat) Capitalizing on its success in Habana and Santiago de Cuba, the Tropicana has a branch 8km east of Matanzas, next to the Hotel Canimao. You can mingle with the Varadero bus crowds and enjoy the same entertaining formula of lights, feathers, flesh and frivolity in the open air. Rather like a cricket match, rain stops play here if the weather cracks.

**Estadio Victoria de Girón** (Map pp222–3) From October to April, baseball games take place at this stadium, 1km southwest of the market. The schedule varies, so ask when the local team, Citricultores, will be playing. Don't expect Cuba's best ball here: this is equivalent to a farm team.

## Shopping

Shopping in Matanzas is akin to looking for a waterfall in the Sahara.

**Casa de Bienes Culturales La Vigía** (Map pp222-3; Calle 272 No 8501) Incurable shopping addicts can mosey on down to this place on Plaza de la Vigía or browse for original handmade books at Ediciones Vigía, which can be found at the other end of the same block (see p224).

**Photo Service** (Map pp222-3; Calle 288 No 8311 btwn Calles 83 & 85) This is the place for all your photo-related needs.

## Getting There & Away

### AIR

Matanzas is connected to the outside world through Juan Gualberto Gómez International Airport, 20km east of town. See p243 for details.

### BUS

Long-distance buses use the **National Bus Station** (Map pp222-3; ☎ 9-2923) in the old train station on the corner of Calles 131 and 272 in Pueblo Nuevo south of the Río San Juan. Matanzas has good connections to the rest of the country. **Víazul** (www.viazul.com) has departures to Habana (CUC$7, 8:55am, 12:35pm and 6:55pm) and Varadero (CUC$6, 10:15am, 2:10pm and 8:15pm). Astro buses leave this station for Santiago de Cuba (CUC$31, alternate days), Cienfuegos (CUC$7, daily), Santa Clara (CUC$8, daily), Cárdenas (CUC$2, daily) and Habana (CUC$5, twice daily).

Two seats on each bus are reserved for Convertible-paying tourists, and these tickets are sold the same day one hour prior to departure.

Buses within Matanzas Province use the **San Luis Bus Terminal** (Map pp222-3; ☎ 29 27 01; cnr Calles 298 & 127) for the following services:

| Destination | Cost | Departure time |
|---|---|---|
| Canasí | CUC$1 | 5am, 5pm |
| Cárdenas | CUC$2 | 1:40pm Mon, Wed & Fri |
| Colón | CUC$3 | 7:30am, 3:10pm, 3:55pm |
| Jagüey Grande | CUC$3 | 1:30pm Tue & Thu |
| Jovellanos | CUC$2 | 1:45pm |
| Varadero | CUC$2 | 9am, 10am, noon, 2pm |

Prices are approximations and you may be able to pay in pesos.

### HITCHHIKING

Catch rides to Habana from opposite the Cuartel Goicuría, Calles 63 and 260, in Versalles. For Varadero, take bus 16 or 17 from Calle 300, between Calles 81 and 83, to Canímar and hitch from there (for the risks associated with hitching see p477).

### TRAIN

The **train station** (Map pp222-3; ☎ 29 16 45; Calle 181) is in Miret, at the southern edge of the city. Foreigners must pay the peso price in Convertibles to the *jefe de turno* (shift manager). All trains between Habana and Santiago de Cuba stop here. In theory, there are eight daily trains to Habana beginning at 3:25am (CUC$3, 1½ hours) and a Cienfuegos departure at 8:05pm, alternate days (CUC$6, three hours). Eastbound, there's a 10:10pm train to Bayamo (CUC$23, 24 hours) and an 8:45pm train to Holguín (CUC$26, 13 hours, 683km). The Santiago de Cuba train (CUC$27, 13 hours) leaves daily at 7:58am and 4:46pm, stopping at the following towns:

| Destination | Cost | Duration (hrs) |
|---|---|---|
| Camagüey | CUC$19 | 7 |
| Ciego de Ávila | CUC$15 | 5 |
| Las Tunas | CUC$24 | 9 |
| Santa Clara | CUC$8 | 3½ |

In practice, these services are usually delayed or cancelled.

The **Hershey Train Station** (Map pp222-3; ☎ 24 48 05; cnr Calles 55 & 67) is in Versalles, an easy 10-minute walk from Parque Libertad. There are five trains a day to Casablanca Station in Habana (CUC$2.80, four hours) via San Antonio (CUC$0.40), Canasí (CUC$0.85), Jibacoa (CUC$1.10), Hershey (CUC$1.40) and Guanabo (CUC$2). Departure times from Matanzas are 4:34am, 8:26am, 12:30pm, 5:12pm and 9:08pm (the 12:30pm train is an express and takes three hours instead of four). Ticket sales begin an hour before the scheduled departure time and, except on weekends and holidays, there's no problem getting aboard. Bicycles may not be allowed (ask). The train usually leaves on time, but it often arrives in Habana one hour late. There was a time when this train went right to the La Coubre train station, which is way more convenient than Casablanca; check if this is a possibility. This is the only electric railway in Cuba, and during thunderstorms the train doesn't run. It's a scenic trip if you're not in a hurry.

### Getting Around

Buses within Matanzas are scarce. To get to the train station from the center, Bus 1 leaves from Calle 79 between Calles 290 and 292. If all else fails, hail a bici-taxi just before the Puente Sánchez Figueras. The Oro Negro gas station is on the corner of Calles 129 and 210, 4km outside the city of Matanzas on the road to Varadero. There's also a Micar rental office here. Servi-Cupet and **Havanautos** (Map pp222-3; ☎ 25 32 94; cnr Calles 129 & 208) are a block further on. A soda bar with snacks is attached. If you're driving to Varadero, you will pay a CUC$2 highway toll between Boca de Camarioca and Santa Marta (no toll between Matanzas and the airport).

## VARADERO

**☎ 45 / pop 18,000**

Varadero is Cuba on growth hormones, a sprawling resort complex that bears little or no relation to the country as a whole.

The setting itself is paradisiacal enough, a 20km swathe of unbroken white sand perched on the wafer-thin Hicacos Peninsula that could rival anything else in the Caribbean. United States chemical millionaire Iréné Dupont must have thought as much when he built his dream home here in 1930, a lavish art-deco mansion he duly christened Xanadu for its tempestuous ocean views and golden carpet of adjacent beach. He was promptly joined by Al Capone, President Batista and anyone else in Cuba who owned money.

Counting more than 50 hotels, 16,000 rooms and with 50 flights a week coming in from Canada alone, the resort has grown bigger by the year and, to some extent, is a victim of its own success. But tourists mean money and unsurprisingly, neither the all-out building spree nor the flocking vacation crowds who revel in the resort's exotic mix of sun, sand, sea, and – ah – socialism, are showing any signs of abating.

These days Varadero is an unkempt mix of the sublime and the ridiculous. There's plenty to do here, but the spread out fa-

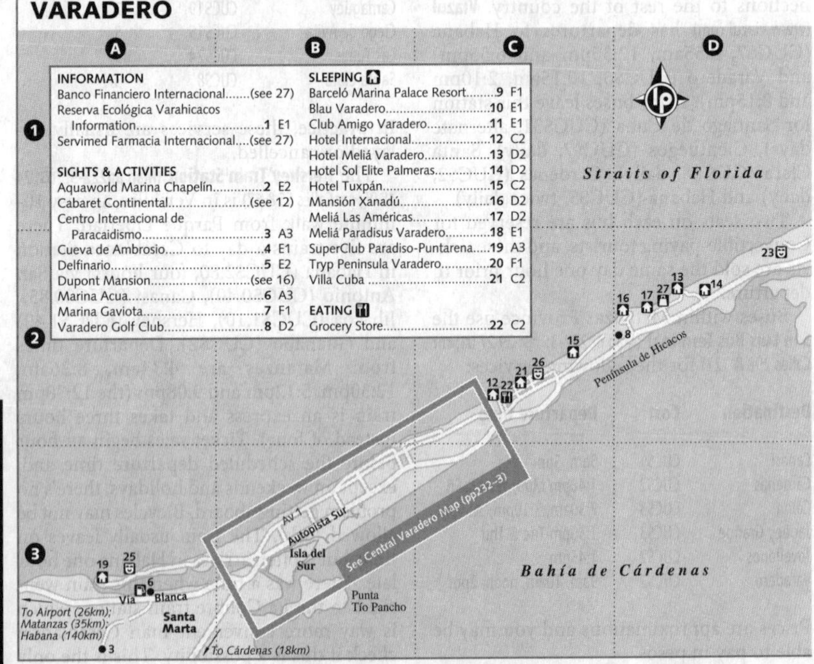

cilities, uninspiring architecture and rather lackluster bar scene place the resort some way behind Florida and Cancún in terms of overall luxury.

Contrary to popular belief, Cubans are not banned from Varadero. In fact, in contrast to other more cut-off resorts such as Cayo Coco, integration is higher than you might first expect. At least one third of the peninsula is given over to a Cuban town of the same name which, while lacking the atmosphere of a Habana or a Santiago, still retains a rough semblance of everyday Cuban life.

## Orientation

Varadero begins at the western end of the Península de Hicacos, where a channel called the Laguna de Paso Malo links the Bahía de Cárdenas to the Atlantic Ocean. After crossing the Puente Bascular (Lift Bridge) over this waterway, the Vía Blanca becomes the Autopista Sur and runs up the peninsula's spine 20km to Marina Gaviota at Varadero's easternmost point. From the same bridge Av Kawama heads west along the channel toward several big resorts. In general the Atlantic side of the peninsula (with the 20km of bright white sands for which Varadero is famous) is devoted to tourism, while the Bahía de Cárdenas side is where locals live (another Cuban community is in Santa Marta at the western end of the peninsula). The largest and most expensive resorts are to the east on Punta Hicacos. The quietest section of beach in the center of Varadero is between Calles 46 and 65.

Beginning around Calle 13, everything from hotels to groceries, becomes progressively more expensive the further east you travel.

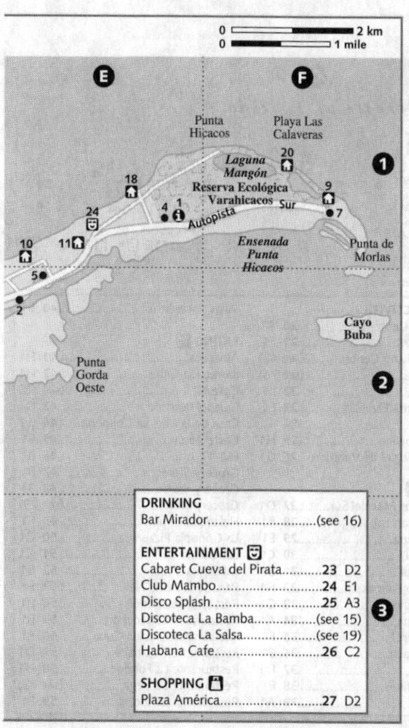


## Information

### BOOKSHOPS

**Librería Hanoi** (Map pp232-3; ☎ 61 26 94; cnr Av 1 & Calle 44; 🕑 9am-9pm) A good selection of books in English, from poetry and politics.

### CONSULATES

**Canadian consulate** (Map pp232-3; ☎ 61 20 78; Calle 13 No 422 btwn Av 1 & Camino del Mar) Also represents Australia.

### EMERGENCY

**Asistur** (Map pp232-3; ☎ 66 72 77; cnr Av 1 & Calle 42; 🕑 9am-4:30pm Mon-Fri)

### INTERNET ACCESS

Most hotels have Internet access at CUC$5 to CUC$7 per hour.

**DHL Cibercafé** (Map pp232-3; Av 1 btwn Calles 39 & 40)

### LIBRARIES

**Biblioteca José Smith Comas** (Map pp232-3; ☎ 61 23 58; Calle 33 No 104 btwn Avs 1 & 3; 🕑 9am-8pm Mon-Fri, 9am-5pm Sat) Present your hotel guest card to withdraw books (free); book donations happily accepted.

### MEDICAL SERVICES

Many large hotels have infirmaries that provide free basic first aid.

**Clínica Internacional Servimed** (Map pp232-3; ☎ 66 77 10; cnr Av 1 & Calle 60; 🕑 24hr). Medical or dental consultations (CUC$25 to CUC$5) and hotel calls (CUC$50 to CUC$60). There's a good pharmacy (open 24-hours) here with items in Convertibles.

**Policlínico Dr Mario Muñoz Monroy** (Map pp232-3; ☎ 61 34 64; Calle 27; 🕑 24hr) Near Av 1. Intended for Cubans, but they don't generally turn sick people away.

**Servimed Farmacia Internacional** (Map pp230-1; Plaza América, cnr Av Las Américas & Calle 61; 🕑 9am-7pm) Well-stocked pharmacy with items in Convertibles.

**MONEY**

In Varadero, European visitors can pay for hotels and meals in euros. If you change money at your hotel front desk, you'll sacrifice 1% more than at a bank.

**Banco de Ahorro Popular** (Map pp232-3; Calle 36 btwn Av 1 & Autopista Sur; 🕑 8:30am-4pm Mon-Fri) Probably the slowest option.

**Banco de Crédito y Comercio** (Map pp232-3; cnr Av 1 & Calle 36; 🕑 9am-1:30pm & 3-5pm Mon-Fri) Changes traveler's checks; expect queues.

**Banco Financiero Internacional** Av 1 (Map pp232-3; ☎ 66 70 02; cnr Av 1 & Calle 32; 🕑 9am-3pm Mon-Fri, 9am-5pm Sat & Sun); Plaza América (Map pp230-1; ☎ 66 82 72; Plaza América, cnr Av Las Américas & Calle 61; 🕑 9am-noon & 1-6pm Mon-Fri, 9am-6pm Sat & Sun) Traveler's checks and cash advances on Visa and MasterCard.

**Cadeca** (Map pp232-3; cnr Av de la Playa & Calle 41; 🕑 8:30am-6pm Mon-Sat, 8:30am-noon Sun)

**POST**

Many of the larger hotels have branch post offices in the reception area.

**DHL** (Map pp232-3; ☎ 61 44 52; cnr Av 1 & Calle 42; 🕑 8am-noon & 1-5pm Mon-Fri, 8am-noon Sat) Upstairs, enter from rear.

**Post office** (Map pp232-3; cnr Av 1 & Calle 36; 🕑 8am-6pm Mon-Sat)

**TELEPHONE**

**Cubacel** Av 1 (Map pp232-3; ☎ 66 72 22; cnr Av 1 & Calle 42; 🕑 8am-5pm Mon-Fri) Aeropuerto Juan Gualberto Gómez (☎ 880-9280; Aeropuerto Juan Gualberto Gómez; 🕑 8am-7pm) For the Av 1 branch, enter from rear.

**Etecsa** Av 1 (Map pp232-3; cnr Av 1 & Calle 30); Plaza América (Plaza América, cnr Av Las Américas & Calle 61; 24hr) Sells telephone cards, international calls.

**TRAVEL AGENCIES**

Almost every hotel has a tourism desk where staff will book adventure tours, skydiving, scuba diving, whatever. It's almost always cheaper, however, to go directly to the tour agency or outfit.

**Cubatur** (Map pp232-3; ☎ 61 44 05; fax 66 70 48; cnr Av 1 & Calle 33; 🕑 8:30am-6pm) Reserves hotel rooms nationally; organizes Varadero excursions and bus transfers to Habana hotels.

**EcoTur** (Map pp232-3; ☎ 66 86 12; Av 3ra btwn Calles 33 & 34, hab 114 & 116)

**Gaviota** (Map pp232-3; ☎ 61 18 44; fax 66 73 25; cnr Calle 56 & Playa)

MATANZAS PROVINCE

**Havanatur Tour & Travel** Av de la Playa (Map pp232-3; ☎ 66 70 26; Av de la Playa btwn Calles 36 & 37; ⌚ 8am-6pm); Av Las Américas (Map pp230-1; ☎ 66 77 08; Av Las Américas; ⌚ 8am-8pm) Near Hotel Tuxpán, Av Las Américas (Map pp232-3; ☎ 66 72 03; Av Las Américas; ⌚ 8am-8pm) Hotel rooms booked and bus transfers arranged to Habana or the Habana airport, plus sightseeing excursions.

## Dangers & Annoyances

Crime-wise Varadero's dangers are minimal. Aside from getting drunk on free mojitos and tripping over your bath rug on the way to the toilet, you haven't got too much to worry about. Watch out for mismatched electrical outlets in hotels. In some rooms, a 110V socket might sit right next to a 220V one. They should be labeled, but aren't always.

Out on the beach, a red flag means no swimming allowed due to the undertow or some other danger. A blue jellyfish known as the Portuguese man-of-war can produce a bad reaction if you come in contact with its long tentacles. Wash the stung area with sea water and seek medical help if the pain becomes intense or you have difficulty in breathing. They're most common in summer when you'll see them washed up on the beach; tread carefully. Theft of unguarded shoes, sunglasses and towels is routine along this beach.

Twenty-four hours a day, long tongues of flame shoot up from two tall chimneys just southwest of Varadero, as excess natural gas from oil wells in the vicinity is burned off. Coming into town from Cárdenas and points west, you'll notice a nauseating smell as sulfurous gas is released from the wells. The offending odor sometimes drifts over to hotels on Varadero's western side. Persons with asthma especially should avoid staying anywhere west of Hotel Bellamar. We've received reports that Sherritt International was engaged in a project to clean the gas and convert it into electricity, but the stench lingers. Varadero itself may be sitting on top of the richest oilfield of all, and wells may one day sprout from the hotel gardens.

## Sights

If art and history are your thing you've come to the wrong place. Varadero's reputation as a font of cultural interaction is not

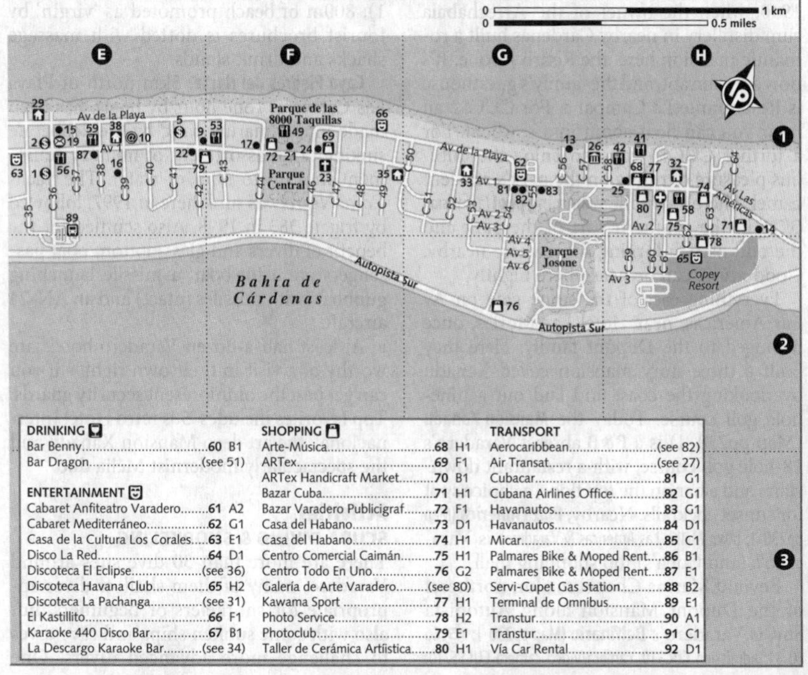

exactly legendary. Nevertheless there are a few sights worth pondering over if the beach banality starts to wear a bit thin.

The Parque Central and adjacent Parque de las 8000 Taquillas host the biggest **artisan market** (Map pp232-3; btwn Calles 44 & 46) in town and nestled among the *uva caleta* (sea grape) trees it's a pretty part of the public beach. Just east is the colonial-style **Iglesia de Santa Elvira** (Map pp232-3; cnr Av 1 & Calle 47) and there's a monument to fallen revolutionary heroes across the street.

Around 1km east, the friendly **Museo Municipal de Varadero** (Map pp232-3; Calle 57; admission CUC$1; 10am-7pm) displays period furniture and Varadero history in a large, two-story mansion erected in 1921. Don't miss the two-headed baby shark and the fine beach view from the upstairs balcony.

**Parque Josone** (Map pp232-3; cnr Av 1 & Calle 58; admission free; 9am-midnight) is Varadero's Central Park. The expansive, shady grounds feature an attractive lake with quaint bridges and geese flitting about, lots of lovely trees and a tranquil vibe. Girls celebrating their *quinciñeras* (15th birthdays) often hold their photo shoots here. The park dates back to 1940, when the owner of the Arrechabala rum distillery in nearby Cárdenas built a romantic mansion here, the Retiro Josone. It's now a restaurant, and the family's guesthouse is Restaurante La Campana. For CUC$2 an hour you can float about in a rowboat. For a further CUC$5 you can enjoy the dubious pleasure of riding on the park's resident camel. There's a public **swimming pool** (admission CUC$2) in the southern part of the park and the odd ostrich lurking somewhere nearby. Good music can be heard here nightly.

Everything east of the stone gate on Av Las Américas, near Hotel Las Morlas, once belonged to the Dupont family. Here they built a three-story mansion called Xanadu overlooking the coast and laid out a nine-hole golf course. Today the **Mansión Xanadu** (Map pp230–1) is a B&B abreast Varadero's 18-hole golf course, with a restaurant downstairs and a bar on the top floor; a choice spot for sunset cocktails. Nearby, **Plaza América** (Map pp230-1; btwn Meliás Las Américas & Varadero) is Varadero's (and Cuba's) top shopping mall.

Beyond Marina Chapelín, 5km northeast of the Dupont Mansion along Autopista Sur, is Varadero's **Delfinario** (Map pp230-1; ☎ 66 80 31; admission CUC$10, camera/video camera CUC$5/10; 9am-5pm). Dolphin shows happen here daily at 11am, 2:30pm and 4:30pm. Swimming with the dolphins costs CUC$65. You're allowed to grab the dolphin's fin and let it drag you around. Ride of a lifetime or cruel aqua-zoo? You decide.

East on Autopista Sur and 500m beyond the Club Amigo Varadero is the **Cueva de Ambrosio** (Map pp230-1; admission CUC$3; 9am-4:30pm). Some 47 pre-Columbian drawings were discovered in this 300m cave in 1961. The black and red drawings feature the same concentric circles seen in similar paintings on the Isla de la Juventud, perhaps a form of solar calendar. The cave was also used as a refuge by escaped slaves.

A few hundred meters beyond the cave is the entrance to the **Reserva Ecológica Varahicacos** (Map pp230-1; 9am-4:30pm) Varadero's nominal green space and a wildlife reserve that's about as 'wild' as New York's Central Park. Bulldozers have been chomping away at its edges for years. There are three short trails (CUC$3, 45 minutes each), the highlight of which are a couple of caves and a giant cactus tree nicknamed 'El Patriarca' (patriarch). **Playa Las Calaveras** (Map pp230–1), 800m of beach promoted as 'virgin' by tourist brochures is dotted with massage shacks and drink stands.

**Cayo Piedras del Norte**, 5km north of Playa Las Calaveras (one hour by boat), has been made into a 'marine park' by the deliberate sinking of an assortment of military equipment in 15m to 30m of water. The yacht *Coral Negro* was sunk here in 1997, followed by frigate 383 in 1998. Also scuttled for the benefit of divers and glass-bottom boat passengers are a towboat, a missile launching gunboat (with missiles intact) and an AN-24 aircraft.

At least half-a-dozen Varadero hotels are worthy of a visit in their own right – if you can get past the omnipresent security guards. Top favorites includes '50s retro Hotel Internacional, the art deco Mansión Xanadu and the spectacularly modernist Mélia duo.

## Activities

### SCUBA DIVING & SNORKELING

There are more than 30 dive sites around Varadero, many of them shallow dives appropriate for snorkelers or beginners, but also with some sunken ships and cave dives to challenge more advanced divers. One drawback with diving in Varadero is that there is only one shore dive (20km away at Playa Coral) and the rest of the boat dives require an hour in transit (one way).

Varadero's top scuba facility is the mega-friendly, multilingual **Barracuda Diving Center** (Map pp232-3; ☎ 61 34 81; www.aquaworldvaradero.com; cnr Av 1 & Calle 58; 🕑 8am-6pm). Diving is CUC$40 per dive (CUC$35 if you bring your own equipment). Cave diving or night diving costs CUC$50, and packages of four/five/six dives are CUC$105/130/150. Snorkelers can join the divers for CUC$25. A scuba excursion to the Bahía de Cochinos is CUC$50/70 with one/two tanks, equipment included. Barracuda conducts introductory resort courses for CUC$70 and ACUC (American Canadian Underwater Certifications) courses for CUC$365, plus many advanced courses. A brand new recompression facility is installed on-site and there's also a resident doctor. A popular seafood restaurant is on the center's premises.

As a secondary option you have the **Acua Diving Center** (Map pp232-3; ☎ 66 80 64; Av Kawama btwn Calles 2 & 3) in western Varadero. It charges much the same prices as Barracuda, but doesn't have quite the facilities, nor volume. When a north wind is blowing and diving isn't possible in the Atlantic, you can be transferred to the Caribbean coast in a minibus (90-minute drive); this costs a total of CUC$45/65 for one/two dives. Certification courses are possible.

**Marina Gaviota** (Map pp230-1; ☎ 66 77 55), at the eastern end of Autopista Sur, also offers scuba diving at similar prices and has snorkeling excursions. A three-hour snorkeling trip is CUC$35 per person (six-person minimum). **Scuba Cuba** at **Aquaworld Marina Chapelín** (Map pp230-1; ☎ 66 75 50; www.aquaworldvaradero.com; Autopista Sur Km 12) also has snorkeling and diving trips.

### DEEP-SEA FISHING

Varadero's three marinas offer a variety of nautical activities and facilities. Many outfits are at **Aquaworld Marina Chapelín** (Map pp230-1; ☎ 66 75 50; www.aquaworldvaradero.com), where five hours of deep-sea fishing costs CUC$290 for four people (price includes hotel transfers and open bar; nonfishing companions pay CUC$30). **Marina Gaviota** (Map pp230-1; ☎ 66 77 55), at the eastern end of Autopista Sur, and **Marina Acua** (Map pp230-1; ☎ 66 80 62), just west of Varadero, have similar packages. Book the latter through the **Acua Diving Center** (Map pp232-3; ☎ 66 80 64; Av Kawama btwn Calles 2 & 3).

### GOLF

While it's no Pebble Beach, golfers will certainly have a swinging session at the uncrowded and nicely laid out **Varadero Golf Club** (Map pp230-1; ☎ 66 77 88; www.varaderogolfclub.com; Mansión Xanadu Dupont de Nemours; green fees 9/18 holes CUC$48/70; 🕑 7am-7pm). The original nine holes created by the Duponts are between Hotel Bella Costa and the Dupont Mansion, and in 1998 the course was extended to 18 holes (par 72) by adding another nine holes along the southern side of the three Meliá resorts. Bookings are made through the Pro shop next to the Dupont Mansion (now a cozy B&B with free, unlimited tee time). A twilight nine holes after 4:30pm costs CUC$25 and you can also rent clubs and a caddie.

### TAKING THE PLUNGE

For those with a head for heights, Varadero's greatest thrill has to be skydiving with the **Centro Internacional de Paracaidismo** (Map pp230-1; ☎ 66 72 56, 66 72 60; skygators@cubairsports.itgo.com), based at the old airport just west of Varadero. The terminal is 1km up a dirt road, opposite Marina Acua. Skydivers take off in an Antonov AN-2 biplane of WWII design (don't worry, it's a replica) and jump from 3000m using a two-harness parachute with an instructor strapped in tandem on your back. After 35 seconds of free fall the parachute opens and you float tranquilly for 10 minutes down onto Varadero's white sandy beach. The center also offers less spectacular (but equally thrilling) ultralight flights at various points on the beach. Prices for skydiving are CUC$150 per person with an extra CUC$45 for photos and CUC$50 for video. Ultralight flights start at CUC$30 and go up to CUC$300 depending on the length of time. If you are already a qualified skydiver solo jumps are also available on production of the relevant certification.

A day's notice is usually required for skydiving and jumps are (obviously) weather dependent. Since opening in 1993 the center has reported no fatalities.

Nine and 18 hole lessons are CUC$100 and CUC$200 respectively.

It's also fun to play miniature golf at **El Golfito** (Map pp232-3; cnr Av 1 & Calle 42; per person CUC$3; 24hr).

### OTHER ACTIVITIES

Kids love the *bolera* (bowling alley) inside the **Centro Todo En Uno** (Map pp232-3; cnr Calle 54 & Autopista Sur; per game CUC$2.50; 24hr), a complex with a giant, modern playground adjacent and lots of junk food, making this a good family destination away from the resorts.

**Sailboards** are for rent all over the beach (CUC$10 per hour) as are small catamarans, parasails, banana boats, sea kayaks etc. The upmarket resorts usually include these water toys in the all-inclusive price.

For a workout to write home about, pay a visit to the tiny sports club inauspiciously named **Judo** (Map pp232-3; cnr Av 1 & Calle 46; 9am-noon, 2-5:30pm Mon-Fri, 9-11am Sat) on the east side of Parque Central. Despite the rough facilities and decidedly pokey interior, the staff here are real pros and will give you the best boxing/judo/karate/jujitsu session you've ever had. Invigorating or what!

## Courses

Varadero is not the best place in Cuba to learn Spanish. That said, many of the all-inclusive hotels lay on free Spanish lessons for guests. If you're staying in cheaper digs, ask at the reception of one of these larger hotels and see if you can worm your way onto an in-house language course by offering to pay a small fee.

## Tours

Tour desks at the main hotels book most of the nautical or sporting activities mentioned earlier and arrange organized sightseeing excursions from Varadero. You'll pay a surcharge (usually CUC$5 per person) if you book at these desks instead of going directly to the tour operator.

Among the many off-peninsula tours offered are a half-day trip to the Cuevas de Bellamar (see p225) near Matanzas, a bus tour to the Bahía de Cochinos (Bay of Pigs) and a whole range of other bus tours to places as far away as Santa Clara, Trinidad, Viñales and, of course, Habana.

**Gaviota** (Map pp232-3; ☎ 61 18 44; cnr Calles 56 & Playa) has a variety of helicopter tours in Russian M1-8 choppers to places as far apart as Trinidad (CUC$149) and Pinar del Río (CUC$139). It also organizes jeep safaris to the wonderfully scenic Valle del Yumurí. The excursion (adult/child CUC$68/51) includes a visit with a *campesino* family and a huge, delicious meal at Ranchón Gaviota on the shores of a reservoir, where horseback riding and paddle boats are available.

### BOAT TOURS

The 48-passenger *Varasub* offers 90-minute underwater viewing possibilities six times a day (adult/child CUC$35/20), including unlimited soda or rum drinks and transfers. You sit on benches at the bottom of the air-con vessel and peer out through glass windows, though the boat itself doesn't actually submerge. Trips on *Varasub* can be arranged at any Havanatur office (p232). The boat leaves from the Super Clubs Puntarenas in west Varadero.

One of Varadero's most popular cruises is the **'Seafari Cayo Blanco'** (CUC$75) to – you've guessed it – Cayo Blanco. This trip includes the dolphin show at the Delfinario, open bar, lunch on Cayo Blanco, two snorkeling stops, live music and hotel transfers. This trip comes with a free sunset cruise that can be carried over to the following day if desired. Several readers have reported that these trips were the highlight of their stay. There are cheaper catamaran tours that are less heavily promoted, but still great fun, with the same excellent snorkeling. Try the stripped-down tour (CUC$40) that has no music and dancing, and a chicken, rather than seafood lunch. There's also a two-hour guided **'Boat Adventure'** (☎ 66 84 40; per person CUC$39; 9am-4pm) by two- person jet ski from here (bear-hugging crocodiles optional). Bookings for any of these can be made directly at **Aquaworld Marina Chapelín** (Map pp230-1; ☎ 66 75 50; www.aquaworldvaradero.com; Autopista Sur Km 12) or at hotel tour desks (for a surcharge).

Marina Gaviota has a seven-hour catamaran tour (CUC$85), which includes a chance to swim with dolphins held in an enclosure on a coral key called Rancho Cangrejo, followed by a lobster lunch on Cayo Blanco.

Other boat trips come and go – as is the way in a busy and rapidly expanding resort. You can check current information in almost any hotel or go direct to the horse's mouth at Marina Gaviota or Aquaworld Marina Chaplín.

## Festivals & Events

The Carnaval formerly held at Varadero in late January and early February is now irregular. Golf tournaments are held at the Varadero Golf Club in June and October and the annual regatta is in May. Varadero also hosts the annual tourism convention the first week in May when accommodation is tight and some places are reserved solely for conference participants.

## Sleeping

Varadero is huge. For budget travelers traipsing around on foot looking for available rooms is a sport akin to marathon running. Book ahead or concentrate your efforts on the southwest end of the peninsula where hotels are cheaper and there is a semblance of Cuban life in the town itself. There are plenty of restaurants to choose from in this neck of the woods and the municipal beach is never more than two blocks away.

As with all other resort areas in Cuba, it is illegal to rent private rooms in Varadero and the law is strictly enforced. Don't believe any tout who tries to tell you otherwise.

### BUDGET

**Villa La Mar** (Islazul; Map pp232-3; ☎ 61 39 10; cnr Av 3 & Calle 29; s/d low season CUC$29/40, high season CUC$36/48; ❄) Varadero's best budget deal is the no-frills, no-pretensions Villa la Mar where you'll dine on fried chicken, meet real-life *Cuban* tourists and fall asleep to the not-so-romantic sound of the in-house disco belting out the Cuban version of Britney Spears. Located a few blocks from the Víazul bus station and without a swimming pool, this is Varadero on the ultimate shoestring – barring a night out on the beach.

### MIDRANGE

**Aparthotel Varazul** (Islazul; Map pp232-3; Av 1 btwn Calles 14 & 15; s/d low season CUC$33/45, high season CUC$40/55) Another decent choice for independent-minded travelers is one of these one-bedroom apartments with kitchenette and small balcony. Cooking your own food is possible (check that the kitchen has proper cooking gear). You can use the pool at the adjacent Hotel Acuazul, and the beach is just a block or two away. The Varazul is popular for long stays.

**Hotel Acuazul** (Islazul; Map pp232-3; ☎ 66 71 32; Av 1 btwn Calles 13 & 14; s/d incl breakfast low season CUC$35/48, high season CUC$45/60; ❄ 🏊) If the sickly pink and blue facade doesn't send you running for a new pair of sunglasses, this downtown 78-room stalwart on Primera Avenida could be a reasonable option. Rooms are basic and the breakfast buffet a proverbial famine compared the culinary delights further north, but the service is friendly enough and there's also a swimming pool in a courtyard out back.

**Hotel Pullman** (Islazul; Map pp232-3; ☎ 66 71 61; Av 1 btwn Calles 49 & 50; s/d low season CUC$37/47, high season CUC$50/60) This intimate Spanish castle–style pensione is one of Varadero's nicest budget-type hotels and has long been a backpacker favorite for its fair value and good location. Newly renovated with heavy wooden furniture, quirky decorations and rocking chairs on the front porch, the atmosphere is laid-back and untouristy with a choice section of municipal beach situated just 150m away.

**Hotel Dos Mares** (Islazul; Map pp232-3; ☎ 61 27 02; cnr Av 1 & Calle 53; s/d incl breakfast low season CUC$37/47, high season CUC$50/60) A good option if you can't get into the Pullman, this attractive old three-story building is about 70m from a cracking niche of beach. Rooms are a little on the dark side.

**Apartamentos Mar del Sur** (Islazul; Map pp232-3; ☎ 66 74 81; cnr Av 3 & Calle 30; 1-/2-bedroom d incl breakfast low season CUC$48/76, high season CUC$60/86, hotel s/d low season CUC$38/50, high season CUC$42/62; ❄ 💻 🏊) Affording some semblance of independence, the one- and two-bedroom apartments in this scattered complex have cooking facilities and living rooms. It's all several hundred meters away from the beach, but is decent value.

**Villas Sotavento** (Islazul; Map pp232-3; ☎ 66 71 32; Calle 13 btwn Av 1 & Camino del Mar; s/d low season CUC$39/58, high season CUC$47/67) If you prefer a little house to a hotel set-up, try one of these 25 older two-story villas, each with three or four double units. The 108 simple rooms vary considerably as these were once privately owned holiday homes, and the front door, living room, fridge and patio will be shared with other guests.

**Club Herradura** (Islazul; Map pp232-3; ☎ 61 37 03; Av de la Playa btwn Calles 35 & 36; s/d incl breakfast low season CUC$42/58, high season CUC$50/67; ❄) This four-story, crescent-shaped hotel is right on the beach, which gets swallowed up at high tide. Accommodation is spacious, nicely outfitted with wicker furniture and those facing the beach have great balcony views. There are all-inclusive rates available too; ask.

**Villa Los Delfines** (Islazul; Map pp232-3; ☎ 66 77 20; cnr Av de la Playa & Calle 38; s/d incl breakfast & dinner low season CUC$65/100, high season CUC$80/120; ) Islazul goes (almost) all-inclusive in this friendlier, cozier copy of the big resorts further northeast. The 100 rooms here come packed with additional extras such as satellite TV, minibar and safe deposit box. The resort even has its own protected beach.

**TOP END**

Rates in these resorts are all-inclusive, and discounted if you take a package.

**Club Tropical** (Cubanacán; Map pp232-3; ☎ 61 39 15; Av 1 btwn Calles 22 & 23; s/d CUC$69/112; ) Right on a nice piece of beach, this activities-oriented hotel attracts youthful package tourists and a few married Cubans. It's well located right in the center but, at 40 years of age, the slightly tatty rooms don't merit the asking price.

**Hotel Sunbeach** (Hotetur; Map pp232-3; ☎ 66 74 90; Calle 17 btwn Avs 1 & 2; s/d low season CUC$60/96, high season CUC$73/116; ) Formerly known as Hotel Bellamar (locals still call it that), this place is one block from the beach. The 282 recently renovated rooms are serviceable, but with its worn aquamarine sofas and ugly '60s-style architecture this hotel has delusions of grandeur. Overpriced, unless you can secure a (very) sweet package deal.

**Villa Tortuga** (Gran Caribe; Map pp232-3; ☎ 61 47 47; Calle 7 btwn Camino del Mar & Av Kawama; s/d low season CUC$74/108, high season CUC$84/128; P ) This very good value resort in western Varadero is squeezed between the beach and the canal, meaning even the cheap rooms have a view. The pool is big, there are tons of activities and all the rooms have balconies and satellite TV. The food is not bad.

**Hotel Cuatro Palmas** (Gran Caribe; Map pp232-3; ☎ 66 70 40; www.accorhotels.com; Av 1 btwn Calles 60 & 62; r CUC$100/130; P ) This friendly resort right on the beach is run by the French Accor chain. Rooms are in a huge Spanish-style complex enclosing a swimming pool. Rooms No 1241 to 1246 were once part of dictator Fulgencio Batista's personal residence. Jammed together across the street are a series of shared two-story villas with another 122 rooms with fridges and toilet only (shower is shared). This is the first of the real 'posh' all-inclusives as you head east, though it's still close enough to town for getting around on foot.

**Hotel Tuxpán** (Cubanacán; Map pp230-1; ☎ 66 75 60; Av Las Américas; s/d low season CUC$80/130, high season CUC$102/150; P ) There are often phenomenal packaged deals (including from Habana) to this 233-room resort right on the beach. Don't be fooled by the blah building and lobby: all rooms have a terrace or balcony, the food is reportedly good and there's a welcoming pool and hot tub.

**Blau Varadero** (Map pp230-1; ☎ 66 75 45; s/d low season CUC$75/105, high season CUC$125/155; P ) This is the peninsula's newest and tallest hotel though the design – in contrast to the spectacular Meliás – ain't particularly pretty. Minimalist furnishings and surgical cleanliness give the place an airport feel though the businesslike staff are keen to please.

**Hotel Internacional** (Gran Caribe; Map pp230-1; ☎ 66 70 38; Av Las Américas; s/d low season CUC$86/123, high season CUC$110/157; P ) Opened in December 1950 as a sister hotel to Miami's Fontainebleau, the four-story Internacional is Varadero's most famous and fabulously retro resort. While it retains its '50s charm, the rooms are modern-ish and the facilities extensive, including a cabaret, tennis courts and massages. Unlike some of Varadero's sprawlers it's also right on the beach. Bonuses at the Internacional include cool art (there's a large René Portocarrero mural in the lobby) and super-friendly staff. If you're rolling a dice on the Varadero all-inclusive options, weight your chances toward here.

**Club Amigo Varadero** (Cubanacán; Map pp230-1; ☎ 66 82 43; fax 66 82 02; s/d low season CUC$65/110, high season CUC$100/160; P ) Formerly the Gran Hotel, Club Amigo's lurid pinks, yellows and greens suggest Disneyland, Las Vegas or something worse.

**Hotel Meliá Varadero** (Cubanacán; Map pp230-1; ☎ 66 70 13; www.solmeliacuba.com; Autopista del Sur Km 7; r from CUC$165) This stunning resort wins the prize for most impressive lobby (and there's some pretty ostentatious lobbies in Varadero) with a seven-story, vine-dripping atrium creating a natural curtain from the open dome down to the reception area. Rooms overlook the golf course or the beach and it's a popular honeymoon spot. The Meliá Varadero sits on a rocky headland, so you have to walk a bit to reach the beach, but what the hell! Kids aged 12 and under stay here for 50%.

**SuperClub Paradiso-Puntarena** (Cubanacán; Map pp230-1; ☎ 66 71 20/21/22/23/24; Av Kawama Final; s/d low season CUC$94/135, high season CUC$112/172; P) A mammoth place with 532 rooms in two eight-story towers. Inside the impressive two-level atrium looks more like a train station than a hotel while the freshwater swimming pool (one of the biggest free form pools in Cuba) is equally huge. Other than that this place ain't particularly pretty and the security guards can be a tad on the surly side, if you're not wearing the obligatory plastic wristband. Watch out for the drunken Canadians!

**Villa Cuba** (Gran Caribe; Map pp230-1; ☎ 66 82 80; cnr Av 1 & Calle C; s/d low season CUC$97/139, high season CUC$132/189; P) Interesting architecture, a variety of accommodation options and loads of activities make this a good choice. Families and groups of friends should investigate the one- to two-bedroom villas (singles/doubles low season CUC$199/249) which all feature communal living areas, fridge, TV and a patio. There are four rooms designed for disabled guests.

**Hotel Kawama** (Gran Caribe; Map pp232-3; ☎ 61 44 16/17/18/19; Calle 0; s/d low season CUC$104/149, high season CUC$132/189; P) A venerable old hacienda-style building from the 1930s the Kawama is, by definition, a piece of Varadero history. It was the first of the 50-plus hotels to inhabit this once-deserted peninsula more than 70 years ago and, as far as character and architectural ingenuity go, it's still one of the best. Even by today's standards the property is huge, with some 235 colorful rooms blended artfully into the thin sliver of beach that makes up Varadero's western extremity. All inclusive prices include everything from tennis to aqua-bike usage.

**Mansión Xanadu** (Map pp230-1; ☎ 66 84 82; fax 66 84 81; Av Las Américas; s/d low season CUC$120/150, high season CUC$160/210; P) Rated by many as Varadero's most intriguing and intimate lodging are the six deluxe rooms in the Dupont Mansion. This was a museum until recently and the five-star rooms retain the 1930s furniture and decor from Dupont's days. Rates here include unlimited tee time. Built on a small bluff, beach access is just alongside.

**Hotel Sol Elite Palmeras** (Cubanacán; Map pp230-1; ☎ 66 70 09; Autopista del Sur Km 8; standard s/d from CUC$180/240; P) Opened in 1990, this was the first joint venture between a foreign company and the Cuban government. The main horseshoe-shaped building fronts the best section of beach or there's the one-/two-room bungalows (from CUC$200/270) set in luxuriant, heavily wooded grounds. The hotel's huge lobby, with its bars, restaurants, caged birds, vegetation and many places to sit down, is well worth a walk around. There's a 24-hour pharmacy here (unit No 314).

**Meliá Las Américas** (Cubanacán; Map pp230-1; ☎ 66 76 00; www.solmeliacuba.com; Autopista del Sur Km 7; s/d from CUC$200/295; P) You've arrived at the luxury end of the peninsula. Everything that went before was small-fry compared to these proverbial giants. Parked on the eastern side of the golf course, this upscale resort is on a choice stretch of beach with plush decor and swanky fittings. The rooms are big, the pool overlooks the beach and the meals are lavish. Golfers, especially, will have fun here.

**Meliá Paradisus Varadero** (Gaviota; Map pp230-1; ☎ 66 87 00; Punta Rincón Francés; s/d low season CUC$265/395, high season CUC$295/450; P) The eastern tip of the peninsula at Punta Hicacos is five-star territory and this Meliá wins the Oscar for Varadero's most expensive hotel (no mean feat). It has shapely pillars and shaded courtyards blending subtlety into a choice stretch of paradisiacal beach. Hey – it's almost worth it!

The last two resorts on the peninsula sprawl out like suburbs from a large town and are mostly the preserve of Gaviota: the **Tryp Peninsula Varadero** (Gaviota; Map pp230-1; ☎ 66 88 00; Varahicacos Ecological Reserve; r from CUC$120; P) and the **Barceló Marina Palace Resort** (Gaviota; Map pp230-1; ☎ 61 44 99; r from CUC$100; P). There are others too, but they're all of the same genre.

## Eating

Since private restaurants are banned at Varadero, your options are limited to the adequate though sometimes uninspiring government-owned restaurants. You can eat well for under CUC$10 and the variety (Chinese food one night, fondue the next) is unlike any you'll find anywhere else in Cuba (excluding Habana). As 90% of the hotels on

### ESCAPE FROM THE ALL-INCLUSIVES

OK, so the food buffet might be mouth-watering and the in-house diving instruction oh-so-convenient but, when it comes to meeting the Cubans in their natural environment, Varadero is not exactly overloaded with options. For a slightly more up-front and personal look at the Cuba of communist myth, load up your day bag, rip off that culture-constricting plastic wrist-band, and sally forth in search of some of the following treats:

- Hire a bike to **Playa Coral**, Varadero's best snorkeling beach situated 20km to the west of the resort along the pancake flat Vía Blanca (masks, snorkels and fins can be hired at the beach itself).
- Hire a moped to **Cárdenas** for a captivating look at Cuban life without the tourist brochure wrapping.
- Hire a jeep to Ranchón Gaviota in the **Valle de Yumurí** and witness bucolic Cuban *campesino* culture a mere stone's throw from the looming hotel complexes of Varadero.

the eastern end of the peninsula are all-inclusive, you'll find the bulk of the independent eating joints situated west of Calle 64.

Touts along Av 1 may offer you a lobster meal in a private home for about CUC$10 a plate. It's illegal and best avoided. They're the ones who'll end up in trouble, not you.

Many of central Varadero's unpretentious places offer light meals, cold beers and live music. Most places post their menu (with prices) outside. The prices are fairly generic so the following list reads roughly west to east.

### RESTAURANTS

**Castel Nuovo** (Map pp232-3; ☎ 66 78 45; cnr Av 1 & Calle 11; ⌚ noon-11pm) One of the town's best pizza and pasta places, it also has chicken, beef and fish dishes, plus enough choice to satisfy vegetarians.

The atmospheric stretch of Camino del Mar between Calles 9 and 14 has a number of places to eat.

**Mi Casita** (Map pp232-3; Camino del Mar btwn Calles 11 & 12) Overlooking the beach is this beautiful glass-fronted restaurant that serves lobster and garlic butter or fillet mignon (CUC$13) in a magnificent setting.

**Restaurante El Ranchón** (Map pp232-3; Av 1 btwn Calles 16 & 17; meals under CUC$5; ⌚ 10am-10pm) A pleasant thatched dining hall overlooking the beach opposite Hotel Sunbeach. It's a simple, reasonable menu done well: shrimp with garlic, pork chops and fish fillets.

**FM – 17** (Map pp232-3; ☎ 61 48 31; cnr Av 1 & Calle 17; ⌚ 8am-2am) With more local vibe than most Varadero visitors ever see, this simple place has sandwiches and burgers for CUC$1 to CUC$2, plus a free cabaret show nightly at 9pm.

**Restaurante El Criollo** (Map pp232-3; ☎ 61 47 94; cnr Av 1 & Calle 18; ⌚ noon-midnight) This is one of the more enjoyable state-run places, and has typical Cuban dishes.

**Lai-Lai** (Map pp232-3; ☎ 66 77 93; cnr Av 1 & Calle 18; meals CUC$6-8; ⌚ noon-11pm) Set in a two-story mansion on the beach, this place has set menus with several courses (wontons, soup, shrimp, rice and dessert).

**Casa de la Miel La Colmena** (Map pp232-3; cnr Av 1 & Calle 26) With a dozen different ice-cream dishes, plus fish fillets (CUC$6) and greasy, garlicky shrimp, this place is sure to please.

**La Góndola Pizzería** (Map pp232-3; meals CUC$2-4) Close to Casa de la Miel La Colmena, this restaurant has delicious pizzas, lasagna and tortellini with Bolognese sauce. Head to the romantic dining room in the back.

**Restaurante Guamairé** (Map pp232-3; ☎ 61 18 93; Av 1 btwn Calles 26 & 27; ⌚ noon-11:45pm) For something different, this restaurant dishes up pineapple and crocodile kebabs (CUC$14) reared at the Boca de Guamá crocodile farm. Perfectly legal in case you were wondering.

**Restaurante La Vega** (Map pp232-3; ☎ 61 47 19; Av de la Playa btwn Calles 31 & 32; ⌚ noon-11pm) Finally! A Cuban restaurant with ambience. Dark wood, leather chairs, a wraparound porch and interesting art and architecture make this place the best dining option in Varadero. Stick to the delicious vegetable or seafood (CUC$7) paella and save room for *flan al ron* (cream caramel with rum; CUC$3). You'll still remember the coffee here after two months reviewing half the restaurants in Cuba – it's that good! Connected to the Casa del Habano, there's an upstairs cigar lounge for after dinner smokes (replete with beach views).

**Restaurante Esquina Cuba** (Map pp232-3; ☎ 61 40 19; cnr Av 1 & Calle 36; ⌚ noon-11:45pm) Made famous by its most illustrious diner Compay Segundo, this place has since been winning fans with its pork/chicken/*ropa vieja* (shredded beef with tomatoes and onions) special. Great Cuban ephemera lines the walls, including B&W photos of Varadero in its Mafia hang-out heyday. You'll eat well here.

**Restaurante La Vicaria** (Map pp232-3; ☎ 61 47 21; cnr Av 1 & Calle 38; ⌚ 10:30am-10pm) Set meals of fish, pork or chicken include a beer – like all La Vicarias, the price and service make this one of the most popular places in town. There's also a nice garden.

There are several upscale restaurants in **Parque Josone** (Map pp232-3; Av 1 btwn Calles 56 & 59). These include **El Retiro** (☎ 66 73 16; ⌚ noon-10pm), with international cuisine and good lobster; **Dante** (☎ 66 77 38), with Italian food; and **Restaurante La Campana** (☎ 66 72 24) with Cuban dishes. On the edge of the park is **La Casa de Antigüedades** (cnr Av 1 & Calle 59), an old mansion crammed with antiques where beef, fish, and shellfish dishes are served beneath chandeliers.

**Barracuda Grill** (Map pp232-3; Calle 58; complete meals CUC$7; ⌚ 11am-7pm) Set in a thatched pavilion overlooking the beach on the grounds of the Barracuda Diving Center, this popular place has terrific fish and shellfish.

**Albacora** (Map pp232-3; ☎ 61 36 50; cnr Av 1 & Calle 59; ⌚ 10am-11pm) Fish, squid, shrimp and lobster are available at beachside Albacora. Check out the open bar offer (noon to 4pm).

A few more upscale restaurants are opposite the Hotel Cuatro Palmas, Av 1 and Calle 62, including **Restaurante La Fondue** (Map pp232-3; ☎ 66 77 47; ⌚ noon-11pm) with surprisingly good Swiss French cuisine for CUC$10 to CUC$20.

**Calle 62** (Map pp232-3; cnr Av 1 & Calle 62) Set next door to Restaurante La Fondue, this is a fun, open-air bar with tasty light meals such as omelettes, hot dogs and hamburgers. Live music happens here nightly from 9pm to midnight.

#### ICE-CREAM PARLORS

**Heladería Coppelia** (Map pp232-3; Av 1 btwn Calles 44 & 46; ⌚ 3pm-11pm) Tucked back in Parque de las 8000 Taquillas, this place serves ice-cream sundaes for CUC$1.

#### GROCERIES

There are **grocery stores** (Map pp232-3; Calle 13 No 9 btwn Av 1 & Camino del Mar; ⌚ 9am-6:45pm); beside **Aparthotel Varazul** (Map pp232-3; Calle 15; ⌚ 9am-7pm); at **Caracol Pelicano** (Map pp232-3; cnr Calle 27 & Av 3; ⌚ 9am-7:45pm); at **Club Herradura** (Map pp232-3; cnr Av de la Playa & Calle 36; ⌚ 9am-7pm) and at **Cabañas del Sol** (Map pp230-1; Av Las Américas; ⌚ 9am-7:45pm). Always check prices at these places, so the cashier doesn't overcharge you. Shops in the large resorts gouge their guests for mineral water etc.

The only place where you can always find bread and pastries is **Panadería Doña Neli** (Map pp232-3; cnr Av 1 & Calle 43; ⌚ 24hr).

## Drinking

**Bar Benny** (Map pp232-3; Camino del Mar btwn Calles 12 & 13; ⌚ noon-midnight) A tribute to the 'Barbarian of Rhythm' Benny Moré, this place has a kicking, jazz-den energy, with B&W photos of the legendary musician lining the walls and his velvety voice oozing from the sound system. Post-beach cocktails and olives recommended here.

**Bar Dragón** (Map pp232-3; cnr Av 1 & Calle 18; ⌚ 6pm-2am) Connected to the Lai-Lai mansion-restaurant, this is good for a drink or three.

**Bar Mirador** (Map pp230-1; Av Las Américas; admission CUC$2) On the top floor of the Dupont Mansion, Bar Mirador has a happy hour from 5pm to 7pm daily and is Varadero's ultimate romantic hang-out. Head up to enjoy the sunset and a poke around this historic house. It's well-worth the taxi fare.

## Entertainment

While Varadero's bar and club scene might look enticing on paper, there's no real entertainment 'scene' as such, and the concept of bar-hopping à la Cancún or Miami Beach is almost nonexistent, unless you're prepared to incorporate some long-distance hiking into your drinking schedule. Here's a rough rundown of what's on offer.

#### TROVA & TRADITIONAL MUSIC

**Casa de la Cultura Los Corales** (Map pp232-3; ☎ 61 25 62; cnr Av 1 & Calle 34) Local folk singers perform at the Café Cantante here every Thursday at 10pm (CUC$5 admission). You can also catch 'filin' (feeling) matinees, where singers pour their heart into Neil Sedaka–style crooning. You can hire an instructor here for Cuban music or take dance lessons for around CUC$2 an hour.

### DANCE CLUBS

**El Kastillito** (Map pp232-3; ☎ 61 38 88; cnr Av de la Playa & Calle 49; admission CUC$1; 🕑 8pm-3am, matinee 2pm Sun) This club on the beach is unrivaled for sexy, heated dancing. Barefoot, synchronized couples scuffing sand beneath their feet add to the five-star local energy here. The beach bar serves drinks and meals throughout the day.

**Discoteca Havana Club** (Map pp232-3; ☎ 61 18 07; cnr Av 3 & Calle 62; admission CUC$5) At the Centro Comercial Copey, this is another tourist disco that welcomes Cubans. Expect big, boisterous crowds, including possessive, aggressive men in that stereotypical style.

**Discoteca La Salsa** (Map pp230-1; 🕑 11pm-3am) Above the reception desk at SuperClub Paradiso-Puntarena, at the western end of Varadero, this club attracts a foreign crowd.

**Discoteca La Bamba** (Map pp230-1; guests/non-guests free/CUC$10; 🕑 10pm-4am) Varadero's most modern video disco is at Hotel Tuxpán, in eastern Varadero. It plays mostly Latin music (and we've heard that for security reasons the fire escapes may be locked).

**Club Mambo** (Map pp230-1; ☎ 66 86 65; Av Las Américas; open bar, admission CUC$10; 🕑 10am-2am Mon-Fri, 10am-3am Sat & Sun) Since the Palacio de la Rumba was shut down, Club Mambo next to Club Amigo Varadero in the eastern part of town, has been Varadero's hippest nightclub. The quality live music attracts all types, but at this price to get in, don't expect many Cubans. There's a pool table if you don't feel like dancing.

Other options:

**Disco La Red** (Map pp232-3; ☎ 61 31 30; Av 3 btwn Calles 29 & 30; admission CUC$1; 🕑 from 11pm) When people actually turn out, good local atmosphere is to be had at this place.

**Discoteca La Pachanga** (Map pp232-3; ☎ 61 45 71; cnr Av 1 & Calle 13; 🕑 11pm-3am) This disco at Hotel Acuazul is one of Varadero's hottest clubs.

**Karaoke 440 Disco Bar** (Map pp232-3; Camino del Mar btwn Calles 14 & 15; admission CUC$2; 🕑 10:30pm-3am) This place mixes up drunk, warbling wannabes with disco dancing.

**Discoteca El Eclipse** (Map pp232-3; cnr Av 1 & Calle 17) On the 14th floor at Hotel Sunbeach.

**La Descarga Karaoke Bar** (Map pp232-3; admission CUC$3; 🕑 10pm-5am) You can check the mic, one, two at this karaoke place in the strip mall next to the Hotel Kawama.

**Disco Splash** (Map pp230-1; ☎ 66 70 90) In Superclub Puntarena.

### CABARETS

**Cabaret Anfiteatro Varadero** (Map pp232-3; ☎ 61 99 38; cnr Vía Blanca & Carretera Sur) Just west of the bridge into Varadero, this cabaret has a gala open-air floor show similar to that of the Tropicana. It's used mostly for special occasions and doesn't open every week.

**Hotel Kawama** (Map pp232-3; Calle 0; admission incl 2 drinks CUC$5; 🕑 11pm nightly except Sun) A cabaret show is presented on a stage below the restaurant at Hotel Kawama.

**Cabaret Mediterráneo** (Islazul; Map pp232-3; ☎ 61 24 60; cnr Av 1 & Calle 54; admission CUC$10; 🕑 doors 8:30pm, show 10pm) A professional two-hour show in an open-air location beneath thatched roofs nightly at 10pm. On a good night, it's worth the money.

**Cabaret Continental** (Map pp230-1; Av Las Américas; admission incl drink CUC$35; 🕑 show 10pm) Hotel Internacional stages a 2½ hour floor show Tuesday to Sunday involving 40 singers and dancers. It's nationally renowned and considered by many to be second only to the Tropicana in its kitschy appeal. You can book dinner (8pm) before the show and after midnight the cabaret becomes a disco. Inquire at your hotel tour desk first as it's sometimes a bit fussy about who they let in.

**Habana Café** (Map pp230-1; Av Las Américas; admission CUC$10; 🕑 9pm-2am) Has a talented floor show followed by disco dancing. It's an older crowd than the Cueva del Pirata set.

**Cabaret Cueva del Pirata** (Map pp230-1; ☎ 66 77 51; Autopista Sur; open bar CUC$10; 🕑 10pm-3am except Sun) A kilometer east of the Hotel Sol Elite Palmeras, Cabaret Cueva del Pirata presents scantily clad dancers in a Cuban-style floor show with a buccaneer twist (eye patches, swashbuckling moves etc). This cabaret is inside a natural cave and once the show is over, the disco begins. Most hotel tour desks can arrange return hotel transfers. It's a popular place, attracting a young crowd.

## Shopping

Avenida 1, from the Laguna to Parque Josone, is strung with artisan markets, all selling the same wide selection of souvenirs and handicrafts, including items (particularly leather work) you won't find in the Habana markets. For one-stop shopping, the big market at Parque Central is good, while the smaller, friendly market at Av 1 between Calles 51 and 52 is recommended for browsing.

**Arte-Música** (Map pp232-3; cnr Av 1 & Calle 59) A good place for CDs, books and art, as well as some (very) old copies of Lonely Planet guides.

**Casa del Habano** (Av de la Playa btwn Calles 31 & 32 Map pp232-3; 🕑 9am-6pm; cnr Av 1 & Calle 63 Map pp232-3; ☎ 66 78 43; 🕑 9am-7pm) The place for cigars: it has top-quality merchandise and helpful service.

**Galería de Arte Varadero** (Map pp232-3; Av 1 btwn Calles 59 & 60; 🕑 9am-7pm) Antique jewelry, museum-quality silver and glass, paintings and other heirlooms from Varadero's by-gone bourgeois days are sold here. As most items are of patrimonial importance, everything is already conveniently tagged with export permission.

**Taller de Cerámica Artística** (Map pp232-3; 🕑 9am-7pm) Next door to Galería de Arte Varadero, you can buy fine artistic pottery (they're made on the premises). Most items are in the CUC$200 to CUC$250 range.

Caracol shops in the main hotels sell souvenirs, postcards, T-shirts, clothes, alcohol and some snack foods. The prices are usually as good as those elsewhere.

**Bazar Varadero Publicigraf** (Map pp232-3; cnr Av 1 & Calle 44; 🕑 9am-7pm) In Parque Central. It's a good place for ceramics, reproductions of famous paintings, artistic postcards, dolls, wall hangings, T-shirts and books. A clothing boutique is adjacent.

**Kawama Sport** (Map pp232-3; cnr Av 1 & Calle 60; 🕑 9am-8pm) Sells beach clothing, snorkeling gear and occasionally bicycles.

**Bazar Cuba** (Map pp232-3; cnr Av Las Américas & Calle 64) Has the greatest selection of souvenirs and crafts in Varadero. It also sells beach clothing, jewelry and books.

**Centro Comercial Caimán** (Map pp232-3; cnr Av 1 & Calle 62; 🕑 9am-8pm) One of Varadero's main shopping malls is opposite Hotel Cuatro Palmas.

**Centro Todo en Uno** (Map pp232-3; cnr Autopista Sur & Calle 54) A medium-sized mall with plenty of amusements.

Film is cheaper in one of these outlets than in hotel shops.

**Photo Club** (Map pp232-3; Av 1 btwn Calles 42 & 43)

**Photo Service** (Map pp232-3; ☎ 66 72 91; Calle 63 btwn Avs 2 & 3; 🕑 9am-10pm)

**ARTex Handicraft Market** (Map pp232-3; cnr Av 1 & Calle 12; 🕑 9am-9pm) Conveniently located next to a proper **ARTex store** (Map pp232-3; Av 1 btwn Calles 46 & 47), with an excellent selection of CDs, cassettes, T-shirts and even a few musical instruments.

For American-style consumerism and useful services, head to **Plaza América** (Map pp230–1), Varadero's and Cuba's largest shopping complex. Here you'll find fancy boutiques, music shops, cigar store, bars, restaurants, bank, post office, a **minimarket** (🕑 10am-8:30pm), car rental desks, absolutely everything and the Varadero Convention Center.

## Getting There & Away

### AIR

Juan Gualberto Gómez (airport code VRA) International Airport is 20km from Varadero toward Matanzas and another 6km off the main highway. Airlines here include Cubana from Buenos Aires and Toronto; LTU International Airways from Düsseldorf and four other German cities; Martinair from Amsterdam; and Air Transat and Skyservice from various Canadian cities. The check-in time at Varadero is 90 minutes before flight time.

There are no domestic flights into Varadero.

### BUS

**Terminal de Ómnibus** (Map pp232-3; ☎ 61 26 26; cnr Calle 36 & Autopista Sur) has daily long-distance Astro bus services to Habana (CUC$8, three hours), Santa Clara (CUC$12, 3½ hours) and Cienfuegos (CUC$14, four hours). Air-con **Víazul** (☎ 61 48 86; 🕑 7am-noon & 1-7pm) buses leave for Habana at 8am, 11:40am and 6pm daily (CUC$10). On either bus, ask to be let out at the first stop after the tunnel in Habana; from there Astro goes to the Terminal de Ómnibus near the Plaza de la Revolución (convenient if you're staying in Vedado), while the Víazul bus goes to the boondocks on Av 26 in Nuevo Vedado. Víazul also has a daily bus to Trinidad at 7:30am (CUC$20, six hours), stopping at Entronque de Jagüey (CUC$6, 1½ hours), Santa Clara (CUC$11, 3½ hours) and Cienfuegos (CUC$16, 4½ hours).

There are 10 daily bus departures to Matanzas (CUC$2, 35km) from here. If you have the time, you can get to Habana by taking this bus to Matanzas and continuing on the Hershey Railway from there.

Getting to Cárdenas by local bus is fairly straightforward if you're prepared to wait.

Bus 236 departs every hour or so from next to a small tunnel marked 'Ómnibus de Cárdenas' outside the main bus station. You can also catch this bus at the corner of Av 1 and Calle 13 (CUC$1). This bus runs the length of the peninsula.

The easiest way to get to Habana is on one of the regular tour buses booked through the tour desk at your hotel or at any Havanatur office. It's possible to buy just transport between Varadero and Habana for CUC$25/30 one way/round-trip. These buses collect passengers right at the hotel doors.

### CAR

Cars are available from **Havanautos** (Calle 55 Map pp232-3; ☎ 61 44 65; cnr Av 1 & Calle 31 Map pp232-3; ☎ 61 44 09). Other offices are at **Hotel Cuatro Palmas** (Map pp232-3; ☎ 66 70 40, ext 51) and **Villa Tortuga** (Map pp232-3; ☎ 61 39 99).

**Transtur** (Calle 10 No 703 Map pp232-3; ☎ 61 31 49; cnr Av 1 & Calle 21 Map pp232-3; ☎ 66 73 32) also has rental desks at or near the following hotels: SuperClub Paradiso-Puntarena, Club Tropical, Internacional and Cuatro Palmas.

**Cubacar** (Map pp232-3; ☎ 61 18 19; cnr Av 1ra & 54) also has desks at the Tuxpán and Hotel Sol Elite Palmerasa. **Vía Car Rental** (Map pp232-3; cnr Av 3 & Calle 30) is opposite Apartamentos Mar del Sur.

Many of these companies also have desks at Plaza América, although we've received complaints about agents there who demanded kickbacks.

**Havanautos** (☎ 25 36 30), **Transtur** (☎ 25 36 21), **Vía** (☎ 61 47 83) and **Cubacar** (☎ 61 44 10) all have car-rental offices in the airport parking lot. Expect to pay at least CUC$65 a day for the smallest car (or CUC$50 daily on a two-week basis).

The cheapest cars are available from **Micar** (Villa Cuba Map pp230-1; ☎ 66 85 52; cnr Av 1 & Calle C; cnr Av 1 & Calle 20 Map pp232-3; ☎ 61 18 08), which has tiny Fiats starting at CUC$35 a day, including 100km, add on the insurance. Call ahead as the affordable cars go fast. Luxury cars are available at **Rex** (Meliá Las Américas Map pp230-1; ☎ 66 77 39; Autopista del Sur Km 7; Aeropuerto Juan Gualberto Gómez ☎ 66 75 39). It rents Audi and automatic-transmission (rare in Cuba) cars starting at CUC$100 plus per day.

There's a **Servi-Cupet gas station** (Map pp232-3; cnr Autopista Sur & Calle 17; 24hr) on the Vía Blanca at the entrance to Marina Acua near Hotel Sunbeach; and one at **Centro Todo En Uno** (Map pp232-3; cnr Calle 54 & Autopista Sur).

If heading to Habana, you'll have to pay the CUC$2 toll upon leaving.

### TRAIN

The nearest train stations are 18km south-east in Cárdenas and 42km west in Matanzas. See those sections for details.

## Getting Around

### TO/FROM THE AIRPORT

Varadero and Matanzas are each about 20km from the spur road to Juan Gualberto Gómez International Airport; it's another 6km from the highway to the airport terminal. A tourist taxi costs CUC$20 to Matanzas and around CUC$25 from the airport to Varadero. Convince the driver to use the meter and it should work out cheaper. The closest point to the airport served by regular public transport to the city of Matanzas is near the Río Canímar bridge, 13km away. Otherwise, the drivers of the Varadero tour buses will probably be happy to take you for around CUC$10 per person. Unlicensed private taxis are prohibited from picking up or delivering passengers to the airport. All Víazul buses bound for Habana call at the airport, so you might try catching a ride with them.

### BUS

**Varadero Beach Tour** (all-day ticket CUC$5; 9:30am-9pm) is a handy open-top double-decker tourist bus with 45 'hop-on, hop-off' stops linking all the resorts and shopping centers along the length of the peninsula. It passes every half-hour at well-marked stops with route and distance information. You can buy tickets on the bus itself. There's also a free shuttle connecting the three large Meliá resorts.

There are two local bus routes costing 20 centavos a ride: No 47 and 48 from Calle 64 to Santa Marta, south of Varadero on the Autopista Sur; and No 220 from Santa Marta to the east end of the peninsula. You'll spend a lot of time waiting for these to show up. Bus 236 to and from Cárdenas (CUC$1) runs the length of the peninsula and is useful. Most municipal buses around Varadero don't bear a number, and many are special services for hotel employees only. If you're able to converse in Spanish, get information from the Cubans waiting at the bus stops.

### HORSE & CART

A state-owned horse and cart around Varadero costs CUC$5 per person for a 45-minute tour or CUC$10 for a full two-hour tour – plenty of time to see the sights.

### MOPED & BICYCLE

Mopeds and bikes are an excellent way of getting off the peninsula and discovering a little of the Cuba outside. Rentals are available everywhere (per hour/day costs CUC$9/24) with gas included in hourly rates (though a levy of CUC$6 may be charged on a 24-hour basis; ask). The **Palmares rental posts** (Map pp232-3; cnr Av 1 & Calle 13 or cnr Av 1 & Calle 38) are in the center of town with hire bikes and mopeds for those not staying at an all-inclusives. Don't expect a 21-speed Trek. If fact if you get any gears at all, count yourself lucky. Bikes generally go for CUC$2/15 per hour/day.

Mopeds hired at the resorts are sometimes more expensive. Unlimited bike use, however, is usually included in the package. Ask about helmets, though they are not mandatory and often not available. You may also want to ask about bike locks.

### TAXI

Metered tourist taxis charge a CUC$1 starting fee plus CUC$1 per kilometer (same tariff day and night). Coco-taxis (*coquitos* or *huevitos* in Cuban) charge less with no starting fee. A taxi to Cárdenas/Habana will be about CUC$20/85 one way. You can phone order taxis by calling **Transtur** (☎ 61 34 15), **OK Taxi** (☎ 66 73 41), **Cuba Taxi** (☎ 61 05 55) or **Transgaviota** (☎ 61 97 62). The last uses large cars if you're traveling with a bike or big luggage. Tourists are not supposed to use the older Lada taxis.

Unofficial taxis with yellow 'particular' license plates face a 1500-peso fine if caught carrying foreigners. Thus you'll seldom be propositioned by private taxi drivers in Varadero itself.

## CÁRDENAS

☎ 45 / pop 98, 644

Cárdenas, straddled on the coast 20km east of Varadero, is called Flag City or the 'city of bicycles' – in marked contrast to the tour-bus traffic that plies the streets of Cuba's tourist mecca nearby. It was here in 1850 that Venezuelan adventurer Narciso López and a ragtag army of American mercenaries raised the Cuban flag for the first time in a vain attempt to free the colony from its complacent Spanish colonizers. Other notable inhabitants have included revolutionary hero Antonio Echeverría, shot during a raid to assassinate President Batista in 1957, and schoolboy 'celebrity' Elián González, the unfortunate five-year old whose rescue from the turbulent sea off Florida in November 1999 sparked an international tug-of-war.

Founded in 1828 on former swampland, Cárdenas grew up as a port town in the heart of Cuba's richest sugar-growing area. Graced with streets of illustrious buildings decked out in period furnishings and stained-glass windows, the city suffered irrevocably after the revolution and today's drab and tatty facades infested with the all-pervading smell of horse manure can be something of a shock to stray travelers on a brief sojourn from Varadero. If you want to see a picture of real Cuban life, it doesn't get more eye-opening than this. If it's minty mojitos and all-day volleyball you're after, stick to the tourist beaches.

### Orientation

The northeast–southwest streets are called Avenidas and streets running northwest–southeast are called Calles. Av Céspedes (Av Real) is Cárdenas' main drag; the avenues to the northwest are labeled '*oeste*' (west), and those to the southeast are labeled '*este*' (east). The city's main northwest–southeast street is Calle 13 (Calzada); *calles* are numbered consecutively beginning at the bay.

Cárdenas residents (confusingly) use the old street names.

### Information

#### BOOKSHOPS

**Librería La Concha de Venus** (cnr Av Céspedes & Calle 12; 9am-5pm Mon-Fri, 8am-noon Sat) Has a decent selection of books in Spanish.

#### INTERNET ACCESS

**Etecsa** (cnr Av Céspedes & Calle 12; 7am-11pm)

#### MEDICAL SERVICES

**Centro Médico Sub Acuática** (☎ 52 21 14; channel 16 VHF; Calle 13; per hr CUC$80; 8am-4pm Mon-Sat, doctors on-call 24hr) It's 2km northwest on the road to Varadero at Hospital Julio M Aristegui. Has a Soviet recompression chamber dating from 1981.

**Pharmacy** (☎ 52 15 67; Calle 12 No 60; 24hr)

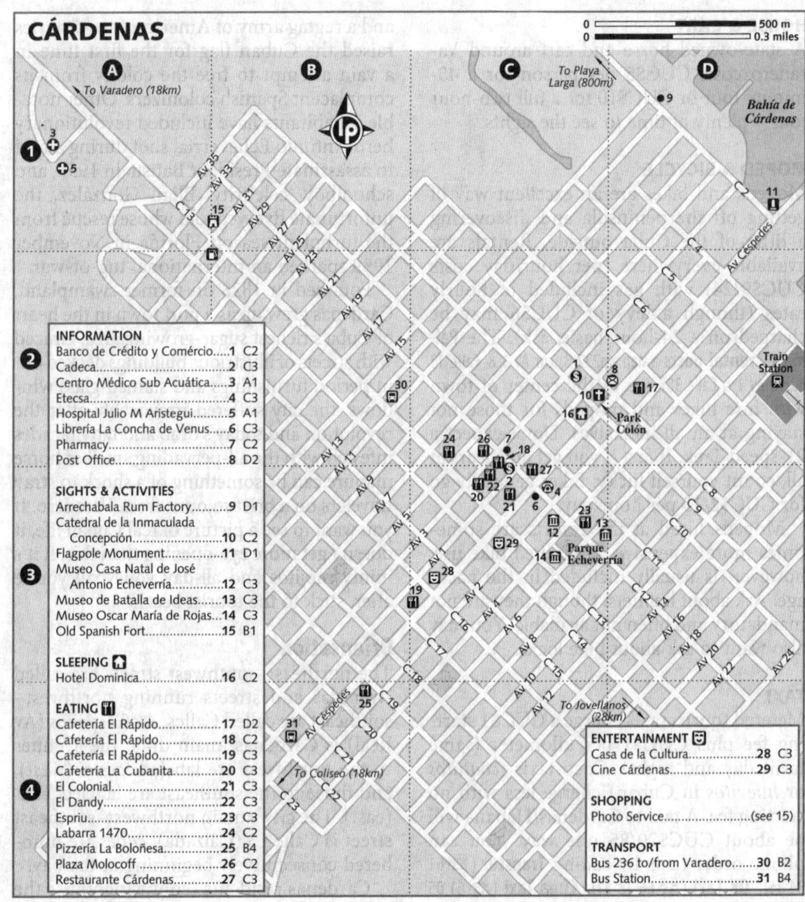


### MONEY

**Banco Crédito y Comercio** (cnr Calle 9 & Av 3)
**Cadeca** (☎ 52 41 02; cnr Av 1 Oeste & Calle 12)

### POST

**Post office** (cnr Av Céspedes & Calle 8; 🕒 8am-6pm Mon-Sat)

### TELEPHONE

**Etecsa** (cnr Av Céspedes & Calle 12; 🕒 7am-11pm)

## Sights

Cárdenas has several major sights related to its famous history and hometown heroes. At the northeast end of Av Céspedes is the monument with a huge **flagpole** commemorating the first raising of the Cuban flag on May 19, 1850. It's a simple, but moving memorial with good views of the bay and Varadero. To the northwest near the port is the **Arrechabala Rum Factory** where Varadero rum is distilled. The Havana Club rum company was founded here in 1878; tours are sporadic but have been known to take place daily 9am to 4pm for a cost of CUC$3; ask in town.

From here, make your way southwest to pretty Parque Echeverría where you'll find a trio of fascinating museums that would do any city proud. The **Museo Casa Natal de José Antonio Echeverría** (Av 4 Este No 560; admission free, but tip the guide; 🕒 10am-5pm Tue-Sat, 9am-noon Sun) has a rich historical collection including the original garrote used to execute Narciso

López by strangulation in 1851. Objects relating to the 19th-century independence wars are downstairs, while the 20th-century revolution is covered upstairs. A spiral staircase with 36 steps links the two levels of this house dating from 1703. In 1932 Echeverría was born here and a monument to this student leader slain by Batista's police in 1957 is outside on Parque Echeverría. The nearby **Museo Oscar María de Rojas** (cnr Av 4 Este & Calle 12; admission CUC$5; 10am-6pm Mon-Sat, 9am-noon Sun) is Cuba's second oldest museum after the Museo Barcardi in Santiago. Its extensive, if rather incongruous, collection of artifacts include a fossilized tree, a strangulation chair from 1830, a face mask of Napoleon, the tail of Antonio Maceo's horse, Cuba's largest collection of snails and last but by no means least some preserved fleas – yes fleas – from 1912. Newly renovated in a lovely colonial building and staffed with knowledgeable official guides, the museum makes a good side trip.

Around the corner is the new **Museo de Batalla de Ideas** (Av 6 btwn Calles 11 & 12; admission CUC$2; 9am-5pm Tue-Sun), with a well designed

**LOS BALSEROS**

The plight of the *balseros* – or 'rafters', as they are sometimes known – is one of the most shocking and oft-repeated episodes in the tit-for-tat war that has been raging between the US and Cuba for nearly five decades.

There have been various exoduses of Cubans to the US since 1959. The first wave consisted of political exiles, the upwardly-mobile bourgeoisie who had grown rich on the pickings of Mafia-run Habana, and had little to gain and a lot to lose from a ragtag army of bearded communists sequestering their Vedado villas. Most of these characters ended up in Miami where they formed a powerful political lobby (the Cuban American National Foundation) and dreamed wistfully about returning to their homeland.

The second wave departed in 1980 during the Mariel boatlift, after asylum seekers who had entered the Peruvian embassy in Habana set off a chain reaction that forced Castro – in a rare fit of frustration – to allow permission for 120,000 Cubans to enter the US. Never one to miss an opportunity, the Cuban leader also seized the chance to empty Cuban jails of the mad, the bad and the disaffected.

The third wave was made up almost entirely of dispossessed migrants who fled to the US in the wake of the economic meltdown that accompanied the *período especial* (special period). Times got tougher during 1991–94 and discontent came to a head after a small riot in Habana in August 1994; Castro decided to diffuse the situation by opening the doors to another mass exodus.

Throughout the late summer of 1994 thousands of Cubans left for Florida on homemade boats. By early September more than 30,000 had been picked up by the US Coast Guard on barely-seaworthy rafts. Unable to cope with the influx and anxious to avoid another Mariel boatlift, the Clinton administration elected to house these people temporarily in Guantánamo naval base pending a Cuban-American immigration agreement.

The revision of the 1966 Cuban Adjustment Act signed in 1995 – better known as the 'wet foot/dry foot' policy – allowed only Cubans who made it to dry land to apply for US citizenship. Escapees picked up at sea would summarily be sent home – a fact that makes the Elián González saga (five-year-old Elián was picked up floating on a tire off Fort Lauderdale) all the more confusing.

The real tragedy of the *balseros* is the sense of desperation and heavy human cost that has so often characterized their plight. In one horrific episode in 1994 the Cuban coast guard rammed an escaping tugboat in the open sea causing the death of 38 Cubans on board. In another incident in 1999, the US Coast Guard reportedly used pepper spray and a water canon to stop six Cubans reaching Surfside Beach in Florida.

In April 2003 violence flared up once more when three men hijacked a ferry at gunpoint in Habana in an attempt to reach the United States. After lightening fast, behind-closed-door trials the men were executed nine days later. It was yet another horrific chapter in a tragic story that shows little sign of abating.

and organized overview of the history of US-Cuban relations, replete with sophisticated graphics. The entire Elián González incident is covered in detail and there are good city views from the mirador on the 3rd floor. *Jineteros* (touts) will offer to show you Elián's house for a small tip, though you might like to give the poor boy some much-needed privacy.

Parque Colón is a small square containing the **Catedral de la Inmaculada Concepción** (1846; Av Céspedes btwn Calles 8 & 9), built in 1846, noted for its stained glass and purportedly the oldest statue of Christopher Columbus in the western hemisphere. Dating from 1862, Colón, as he's known in Cuba, stands rather authoritatively with his face fixed in a thoughtful frown and a globe resting at his feet. It's the closest Cárdenas gets to a decent photo opportunity; it's ironic and poignant that the world should be dropped so casually at his feet.

Like something from the zany brain of PT Barnum, **Plaza Molocoff** (cnr Av 3 Oeste & Calle 12) is a whimsical two-story cast-iron market hall with a glittery 16m-high silver dome built in 1859. Now it's the city **vegetable market** (8am-5pm Mon-Sat, 8am-2pm Sun).

## Sleeping

Down the road Varadero flaunts more than 50 hotels. Here in humble Cárdenas the only functioning cheappie *was* the classically un-classic **Hotel Dominica** (☎ 52 15 51; cnr Av Céspedes & Calle 9) on Parque Colón. This faded old starlet once had 25 rooms with bath, but is closed for what looks like lengthy renovations – judging by the absence of any hammering noises. Fortunately Cárdenas has a handful of decent casas particulares and they'll be very keen for your business.

**CASAS PARTICULARES – CÁRDENAS**

**Lázara Galindo Gómez** (Av 6 btwn Calles 9 & 10; r CUC$25) Clean place with all mod cons close to the center.

**Ricardo Dominguez** (☎ 528 944 31; cnr Avs 31 & 12; r CUC$35; P) Large luxurious place with big yard, parking and TV.

**Rolando Valdés Lara** (☎ 072 703 155; cnr Av 30 & Calle 12; r CUC$30) Breakfast CUC$3 extra.

## Eating

Half the chefs in Varadero probably come from Cárdenas, but that doesn't make the restaurants in their home town anything to write home about. Grim, scant and hard to find are the three phrases that spring to mind when discussing the eating houses of this city. There are three El Rápidos if that's any measuring stick. Anyone allergic to soggy microwaved cheese and ham sandwiches is quite likely to starve.

**Espriu** (Calle 12 btwn Avs 4 & 6; dishes CUC$1-3; 24hr) An exceptional restaurant among uninspired choices, Espriu is on Parque Echeverría. It has espresso, shrimp cocktails, fish fillets, burgers and sandwiches. It's probably the best game in town.

**Cafetería El Rápido** (24hr) This is where most stray tourists end up. Has three branches: one is on the corner of Calle 12 and Av 3 Oeste; another is on the corner of Calle 8 and Av Céspedes; the third is on Céspedes between Calles 16 and 17.

**Cafetería La Cubanita** (cnr Av 3 Oeste & Calle 13; 24hr) Located near Plaza Molocoff, Cafetería La Cubanita has a pleasant outdoor setting where you can consume drinks for Convertibles.

Other options:

**El Colonial** (cnr Av Céspedes & Calle 12; 8am-3pm) A simple cafeteria that serves burgers, beer and pork dishes on a cute patio.

**Labarra 1470** (Calle 13 btwn Avs 6 & 7) A newer place with tablecloths and a nicer decor that specializes in Cuban fare.

Cheap peso eateries include **Restaurante Cárdenas** (cnr Av Céspedes & Calle 12; 11am-midnight), a recommended choice for breaded pork, *congrí* (rice and beans) and tomato salad, and **Pizzería La Boloñesa** (Av Céspedes No 901; 10am-10pm) for peso pizza.

There are many Convertible supermarkets and stores are along Av 3 Oeste near Plaza Molocoff including **El Dandy** (Av 3 on Plaza Molocoff; 9am-5pm Mon-Sat, 9am-noon Sun) selling drinks and groceries. You can get cheap peso snacks in the market itself and the area surrounding, where merchants peddle every thing from fake hair to plastic Buddhas.

## Entertainment

**Casa de la Cultura** (☎ 52 12 92; Av Céspedes No 706 btwn Calles 15 & 16) Housed in a beautiful but faded colonial building with stained glass, iron awnings and an interior patio with

**IN THE MIDDLE OF IT ALL**

Tucked away in central Matanzas, among rolling hills and vivid splashes of bougainvillea, is the once grand resort town of **San Miguel de los Baños**. Popular at the beginning of the 20th century for its soothing medicinal waters and well-equipped bathhouses, spa seekers used to flock here in their thousands to visit the ornate **Gran Hotel**, a building so ostentatious it was considered by specialists to be a replica of the Great Casino at Monte Carlo.

A brief building flurry ensued, the legacy of which can still be seen in the smattering of lavish neoclassical villas that line the town's arterial Av de Abril. But the tranquility wasn't to last. A few years before the revolution the bathhouses fell into disuse after the local water supply was polluted by waste from a nearby sugar mill, and town faded from prominence.

Today San Miguel de los Baños is a curious cross between abandoned ghost town and life-sized architectural museum. Passing visitors can still poke around the surreal Gran Hotel (plans to reopen it have yet to materialize) or alternatively you can negotiate a steep hike up the nearby **Loma de Jacán**, a glowering hill with 448 steps broken only by faded murals of the Stations of the Cross.

You can reach San Miguel de los Baños by turning off the Carretera Central at Coliseo, 25km southwest of Cárdenas.

rockers. Search the hand-written advertising posters for rap *peñas* (performances), theater and literature events.

**Cine Cárdenas** (cnr Av Céspedes & Calle 14) Has daily movie screenings.

## Shopping

**Photo service** (cnr Calle 13 & Av 31) This is housed inside an old Spanish fort. All your standard camera needs can be met here.

## Getting There & Away

### BUS

Transport services are thin out of Cárdenas and you're much better off making your way to Varadero and then hooking up with something there. Astro buses depart the **bus station** (cnr Av Céspedes & Calle 22) to Habana and Santa Clara daily, but they're often full upon reaching Cárdenas. Trucks to Jovellanos/Perico leave at 10:30am and 3pm (three pesos, 52km), which puts you 12km from Colón and possible onward transport to the east. The ticket office is at the rear of the station.

Reliable Bus 236 to/from Varadero leaves hourly from the corner of Av 13 Oeste and Calle 13 (50 centavos, but they like to charge tourists CUC$1).

### HITCHHIKING

To hitch to Varadero from Cárdenas, take a horse cart to the hospital, where almost any passing bus will stop to pick you up for CUC$1 as far as Santa Marta. Alternatively, you can park yourself a way up Calle 13 and wait; other tourists are usually willing to help out their compadres for this short ride (for information on the risks associated with hitching see p477).

### TRAIN

You could be very lucky and catch one of the frequently cancelled rail cars from **San Martín Train Station** (Av 8 Este) near the bay, to Unión de Reyes via Jovellanos (daily), Guareiras via Colón (daily) and Los Arabos (twice daily).

## Getting Around

The main horse-cart (one peso) route through Cárdenas is northeast on Av Céspedes from the bus station and then northwest on Calle 13 to the hospital, passing the stop of bus 236 (to Varadero) on the way.

The gas station **Servi-Cupet** (cnr Calle 13 & Av 31 Oeste) is opposite an old Spanish fort on the northwest side of town, on the road to Varadero.

# PENÍNSULA DE ZAPATA

**☎ 459 / pop 8267**

Most of the 4520-sq-km Península de Zapata in southern Matanzas is included in Gran Parque Natural Montemar, formerly known as Parque Nacional Ciénaga de Zapata. In 2001, it was declared a Unesco Biosphere Reserve and, despite being one of Cuba's largest municipalities, it's also one of its most uninhabited.

To the east of this swampy wilderness lies the elongated Bahía de Cochinos (Bay of Pigs) where propaganda billboards proclaim Cuba's erstwhile victory over the 'Yanqui' imperialists in 1961. There are two worthwhile beaches here, Playa Larga at the bay's curvaceous head and the more southerly Playa Girón. Both beaches are fronted by slightly moth-eaten resort hotels that are popular with divers. Aside from its reputation as a proverbial banana-skin for US imperialism the Bay of Pigs also boasts some of the best cave diving in the Caribbean.

Situated to the northeast of the peninsula lies the sugar-mill town of Australia, along with the cheesy tourist circus of Boca de Guamá, a reconstructed Taíno village.

Transport in the area is erratic and difficult to pin down. Accommodation outside of the resorts, on the other hand, is surprisingly abundant. You can check out excellent casa options in Jagüey Grande, Central Australia, Playa Larga and Playa Girón.

## Information

**La Finquita** (☎ 2277; 9am-noon & 1-5pm Mon-Sat), a snack bar and information center run by Cubanacán just before the turn-off toward Playa Larga from the Autopista, arranges trips into the Zapata Peninsula (see p252) and books rooms at the Villa Guamá.

Etecsa, the post office and Convertible stores are across the Autopista in bustling Jagüey Grande. Insect repellant is absolutely essential on the peninsula and while Cuban repellant is available locally, it's like wasabi on sushi for the ravenous buggers here.

## CENTRAL AUSTRALIA & AROUND

About 1.5km south of the Autopista Nacional on the way to Boca de Guamá, is the large Central Australia sugar mill, built in 1904. During the 1961 Bahía de Cochinos (Bay of Pigs) invasion, Fidel Castro had his headquarters in the former office of the sugar mill. Today it's the **Museo de la Comandancia** (☎ 2504; admission CUC$1; 8am-5pm Tue-Sun). This municipal museum contains a few stuffed birds and animals, and a good historical collection ranging from prehistory, but surprising little about the Bay of Pigs episode itself. Outside is the wreck of an invading aircraft shot down by Fidel's troops. The concrete memorials lining the road to the Bahía de Cochinos mark the spots where defenders were killed in 1961.

Approximately 400m on your right after the Central Australia exit is the **Finca Fiesta Campesina** (admission CUC$1; 9am-6pm), a kind of wildlife park–meets–country fair with labeled examples of Cuba's typical flora and fauna. The highlights of this strangely engaging place are the coffee (some of the best in Cuba and served with a sweet wedge of sugarcane) and the hilarious if slightly infantile games of guinea pig roulette overseen with much pizzazz by the gentleman at the gate. It's the only place in Cuba – outside of cockfighting – where you encounter any form of open gambling.

### Sleeping & Eating

**Motel Batey Don Pedro** (☎ 2825; r CUC$25) This motel is located just south of the turn-off to the Península de Zapata from Km 142 on the Autopista Nacional at Jagüey Grande. The eight thatched double units are comfortable and cheap and come with ceiling fans and crackling TVs. Beware the frogs in the bathroom. The motel is designed to resemble a peasant settlement, and the on-site restaurant, though friendly and intimate, serves pretty ropey food. A better bet is the adjacent Fiesta Campesino, which sells energy-boosting *guarapo* (sugarcane juice) and coffee that's positively divine.

**Pío Cuá** (☎ 3343; Carretera de Playa Larga Km 8; meals CUC$6-20; 9am-9pm), The fanciest restaurant around here, where bus tour groups are treated to shrimp, lobster or chicken meals in a big structure that somehow manages to combine thatch and stained glass successfully.

If you just can't drive any further, there are a number of legal casas particulares in the area including **Orlando Caballero Hernández** (☎ 91 32 75; Calle 20 No 5; r CUC$20; P ), at the Central Australia sugar mill, with small, clean rooms and some great testimonies and the more convenient **Casa de Zuleida** (☎ 91 36 74; Calle 15A No 7211 btwn 72 & 74; r CUC$15-20; P ) in Jagüey Grande behind the hospital. There are more casas in Playa Larga (32km) and Playa Girón (48km).

## BOCA DE GUAMÁ

The main center for visitors to this area is Boca de Guamá, about halfway between the Autopista Nacional at Jagüey Grande and the famous Bahía de Cochinos (Bay of Pigs). It's a whole lot of tourist claptrap, with a restaurant, expensive snack bar, knickknack shop, ceramics workshop, crocodile 'farm' and boats waiting to take you across the Laguna del Tesoro to a resort built to resemble an Indian village. Tour buses crowd the parking lot and loud rap music welcomes your passage back in time to the hidden mysteries of pre-Columbian Cuba. You'll need an extremely hyperactive imagination to make anything out of this.

## Sights

Don't confuse the real **Criadero de Cocodrilos** (guided visit CUC$5; 8am-5pm) with the faux farm inside Boca de Guamá's tourist complex. On your right as you come from the Autopista, the Criadero de Cocodrilos is an actual breeding facility run by the Ministerio de Industrias Pesqueras where two species of crocodiles are raised: the native Rhombifer *(cocodrilo)* and the Acutus *(caimán)*, which is found throughout the tropical Americas. Sometimes security guards will try to point you across the road to the Guamá zoo, but if you're persistent you can get a guided tour here (in Spanish), taking you through every stage of the breeding program, from eggs and hatchlings to big, bad crocs. Prior to the establishment of this program in 1962 (considered the first environmental protection act undertaken by the revolutionary government), these two species of marsh-dwelling crocodiles were almost extinct.

The breeding has been so successful that across the road in the Boca de Guamá complex you can buy stuffed baby crocodiles or dine, perfectly legally, on crocodile steak.

The **park/zoo** (adult/child CUC$5/3; 9am-6pm) has two crocodiles that are often under water trying to beat the stifling 85% humidity. There are other caged animals here.

If you buy anything made from crocodile leather at Boca de Guamá, be sure to ask for an invoice (for the customs authorities) proving that the material came from a crocodile farm and not wild crocodiles. A less controversial purchase would be one of the attractive ceramic bracelets sold at the nearby **Taller de Cerámica** ( 9am-6pm Mon-Sat) where you can see five kilns in operation.

Aside from the crocodile farm, the main attraction is the **Laguna del Tesoro**, 8km east of Boca de Guamá via the Canal de la Laguna and accessible only by boat (see Getting Around, p252). On the east side of this 92-sq-km lake is a tourist resort named Villa Guamá, built to resemble a Taíno village, on a dozen small islands. A sculpture park next to the mock village has 32 life-size figures of Taíno villagers in a variety of idealized poses. The lake is called 'Treasure Lake' due to a legend about a treasure the Taíno are said to have thrown into the water just prior to the Spanish conquest (not dissimilar to South American El Dorado legends). The most important part of the whole scenario is Guamá himself – a rebel chief who fought bravely against the Spanish. All of this has a strong appeal to Cuban honeymooners who flock to Villa Guamá, and if you're into kitsch, you're all over it. There's freshwater fishing for largemouth bass here.

## Sleeping & Eating

**Villa Guamá** (Cubanacán; ☎ 5515; s/d low season CUC$34/42, high season CUC$38/47) This place was built in 1963 on the east side of the Laguna del Tesoro, about 5km from Boca de Guamá by boat (cars can be left at the crocodile farm; CUC$1). The 50 thatched *cabañas* with bath and TV are on piles over the shallow waters. The six small islands bearing the units are connected by wooden footbridges to other islands with a bar, cafeteria, overpriced restaurant and a swimming pool containing chlorinated lake water. Rowboats are for rent. Noise from the on-site disco will leave you questioning this place's authenticity (there are no known records of discos in Taíno Indian villages), and the tranquility is further broken by the ubiquitous day-trippers who come and go by speedboat from dawn till dusk. Birding at sunrise however, is reputedly fantastic. You'll need insect repellent if you decide to stay. The ferry transfer is not included in the room price (see Getting Around, p252).

At the boat dock you'll find **Bar La Rionda** ( 9:30am-5pm), Restaurant Colibrí and Restaurant La Boca (set meals CUC$12).

## Getting There & Away

In theory the public bus between Jagüey Grande and Playa Girón passes once in the morning and there's service to/from Habana (178km) on Friday, Saturday and Sunday afternoon. If you're without your own transport, you can hitch into Playa Girón or out to the Autopista and jump on a Víazul, Astro or tour bus at the restaurant near the Finca Campesino (most buses going in either direction pit stop there). Tours from Varadero to Boca de Guamá occur daily, and if you're traveling independently, you can probably negotiate a ride back there by speaking to the driver (CUC$10 per person should be plenty).

### Getting Around

A passenger ferry (adult/child CUC$10/5, 20 minutes) departs Boca de Guamá for Villa Guamá across Laguna del Tesoro four times a day. Speedboats depart more frequently and whisk you across to the pseudo-Indian village in just 10 minutes any time during the day for CUC$10 per person round-trip (with 40 minutes waiting time at Villa Guamá), two-person minimum. In the morning you can allow yourself more time on the island by going one way by launch and returning by ferry.

## GRAND PARQUE NATURAL MONTEMAR

Ciénaga de Zapata is the largest *ciénaga* (swamp) in Cuba, and one of the country's most diverse ecosystems. Crowded into this vast wetland (which is essentially two swamps divided by a rocky central tract) are 14 different vegetation formations including mangroves, wood, dry wood, cactus, savannah, selva and semideciduous. There are also extensive salt pans. The marshes support more than 190 bird species, 31 types of reptiles, 12 species of mammals, plus countless amphibians, fish and insects (including the insatiable mosquito). There are more than 900 plant species here, some 115 of them endemic. It is also an important habitat for the endangered *manatí* (manatee) the Cuban *cocodrilo* (crocodile; *Crocodylus rhombifer*) and the *manjuarí* (alligator gar; *Atractosteus tristoechus*), Cuba's most primitive fish.

The Zapata is the place to come to see bee hummingbirds (the world's smallest bird), cormorants, cranes, ducks, flamingos, hawks, herons, ibis, owls, parrots, partridges, sparrows, tocororos (Cuba's national bird) and wrens. Numerous migratory birds from North America winter here, making November to April the best birding season. It's also the number-one spot in Cuba for catch-and-release sport fishing and fly-fishing, where the palometa, sábalo and robalo are jumping (bonefish too!).

Unsuitable for agriculture, communications in Zapata were almost nonexistent before the revolution when poverty was the rule. Charcoal makers burn wood from the region's semideciduous forests, and *turba* (peat) dug from the swamps is an important source of fuel. The main industry today is tourism and ecotourists are arriving in increasing numbers.

### Information

The **National Park Office** (☎ 7249; 🕑 8am-4:30pm Mon-Fri, 8am-noon Sat) is at the north entrance to Playa Larga on the road from Boca de Guamá. Staff here are knowledgeable and helpful. Alternatively you can try the Cubanacán office on the Autopista near Central Australia.

### Sights & Activities

There are four main excursions into the park, although the itineraries – particularly with regard to bird-watching – are flexible. Transport is not always laid on, so it is best to check beforehand. Cars (including chauffeur-driven jeeps) can be rented from **Transtur** (☎ 4114) or **Havanautos** (☎ 98 41 23) in Playa Girón. One of the most popular excursions is to **Laguna de las Salinas** where

#### CROCODILES

The Cuban crocodile or *Crocodylus rhombifer* has the smallest range of any crocodile, existing only on the Zapata Peninsular and in the Lanier swamps of the Isla de la Juventud (where it has been introduced). Hunted extensively by humans for centuries the species is now endangered with an estimated 6000 reptiles still active in the wild (inside a total area of 300 sq km).

Cuban crocs are strong swimmers and relatively agile on land. Their diet consists mainly of fish, but they will also tackle small mammals. Identifiable by their black and yellow speckles, the animals grow to average size of 3.2m and can live for up to 80 years.

The best place to view crocodiles in captivity is at the Criadero de Cocodrilos in Matanzas Province (p251) or on the Isla de la Juventud (p188).

large numbers of migratory waterfowl can be seen from November to April: we're talking 10,000 pink flamingos at a time, plus 190 other feathered species. The first half of the road to Las Salinas is through the forest, while the second half passes swamps and lagoons. Here, aquatic birds can be observed. Guides are mandatory to explore the refuge. The 22km visit lasts over four hours though you may be able to negotiate for longer; costs start at CUC$10 per person.

For avid bird-watchers **Observación de Aves** (per person CUC$19) offers an extremely flexible itinerary and the right to roam (with a qualified park ornithologist) around a number of different sites, including the Reserva de Bermejas. Among 18 species of endemic bird found here you can see prized Ferminins, Cabreritos and Gallinuelas de Santo Tomás – both found only on the Zapata Peninsula.

Switching from land to boat the **Río Hatiguanico** (per person CUC$19) takes you on a three-hour 12km river trip through the densely forested northwestern part of the peninsula. You'll have to duck to avoid the branches at some points while at others the river opens out into a wide deltalike estuary. Birdlife is abundant in this part of the peninsula and if you're lucky you may also see turtles and crocodiles.

It's also worth asking about the **Santo Tomás** (CUC$10) trip; an excursion that begins 30km west of Playa Larga in the park's only real settlement (Santo Tomás) and proceeds along a tributary of the Hatiguanico – walking or boating, depending on the season. It's another good option for birders.

Aspiring fishermen can arrange excellent fly-fishing at either Las Salinas or Hatiguanico. Ask at the National Park office.

## PLAYA LARGA

Continuing south from Boca de Guamá you reach Playa Larga, on the Bahía de Cochinos (Bay of Pigs), after 13km (or 32km from where you left the Autopista Nacional). United States–backed exiles took a beating trying to invade Cuba through this bay on April 17, 1961 and the museum dedicated to these events at Playa Girón, 35km further south, captures the drama pretty well. While the best accommodation is in Playa Girón, the national park office is here in Playa Larga and there is a good scuba-diving outfit too.

### Activities

#### SCUBA DIVING & SNORKELING

If you prefer fish to birds **Club Octopus International Diving Center** (☎ 7225), 200m west of Villa Playa Larga, offers full scuba facilities at CUC$25 per dive or CUC$35 for an orientation session and introductory dive (to 8m). There are 12 rich dive sites just offshore between Playa Larga and Playa Girón (you'll know them by the international scuba symbol painted on the asphalt) and both this outfit and the one in Punta Perdiz visit them. Other water activities here include snorkeling (with/without instructor CUC$5/10), Wetbike (CUC$1 per minute), aqua-bike (CUC$3 per hour), kayak (CUC$3 per hour) and catamaran (three people CUC$15 per hour). There's a bar and restaurant overlooking the beach.

More underwater treasures can be seen at the **Cueva de los Peces** (admission CUC$1; 9am-6pm) a flooded tectonic fault, or cenote, about 70m deep on the inland side of the road, almost exactly midway between Playa Larga and Playa Girón. There are lots of bright, tropical fish, plus you can explore back into

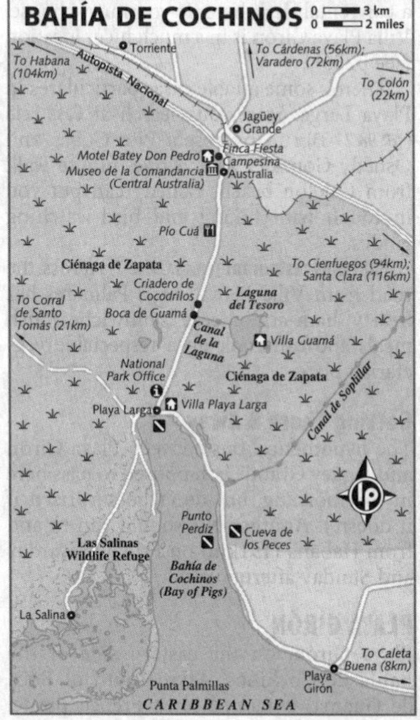

 

the darker, spookier parts of the cenote with snorkel gear (CUC$3). Local dive shops bring scuba divers here. Hammocks swing languidly around the cenote and the beach facing has good snorkeling too, making it a nice afternoon jaunt. There's a handy restaurant, with premium prices.

Just beyond the Cueva is **Punto Perdiz**, another phenomenal snorkeling (CUC$3 per hour) and scuba-diving (CUC$25 per dive) spot with an on-site diving outfit. The shallow water is gemstone blue here and there's good snorkeling right from the shore. It costs CUC$1 to use the thatched umbrellas, beach chairs and showers and there's a decent restaurant.

### Sleeping & Eating

**Villa Playa Larga** (Cubanacán; ☎ 7225, 7294; s/d low season incl breakfast CUC$27/40, high season CUC$35/44; P ✕ 🗣) On a small scimitar of white sand beach by the road, just east of the village, this hotel has huge rooms with bath, sitting room, fridge and TV. There are also eight two-bedroom family bungalows, though the restaurant is legendary in its bleakness (and in total contrast to the setting). Transtur has a car rental desk here. If you must choose, Villa Playa Girón is in a much nicer location (see p256).

There's some affable casas particulares in Playa Larga. Start your search at **Casa Fefa** (☎ 98 71 33) run by Josefa Pita Cobas and Osnedy González Pita, a one-minute walk from Caleton beach. Osnedy can put you in touch with hiking and bird-watching guides.

**Palmares restaurant** (meals CUC$2-7) Across the road from Villa Playa Larga, Palmares has hearty ham-and-cheese sandwiches, fish meals and can cook up a respectable vegetarian plate.

### Getting There & Away

The hypothetical bus between Playa Girón and Jagüey Grande is supposed to pass here in the morning, but don't be surprised if it doesn't. Another bus should run to and from Habana (191km) on Friday, Saturday and Sunday afternoon.

## PLAYA GIRÓN

Playa Girón, on the eastern side of the Bahía de Cochinos, 48km south of Boca de Guamá, is named for a French pirate, the rather unfortunate Gilbert Girón, who met his nemesis here (by decapitation) in the early 1600s after one raid too many. In Cuba it is equally infamous for another botched raid, the ill-fated, CIA-sponsored invasion that tried to land on these remote sandy beaches in April 1961 in one of the 20th century's classic David and Goliath struggles. History, with its poignant monuments and propaganda-spouting political billboards, has an extra degree of resonance here though. These days Playa Girón with its clear Caribbean waters and precipitous off-shore drop-off is a favorite destination for scuba divers and snorkelers.

In addition to some nice private houses, Playa Girón's one and only resort is a pleasant and low-key place, despite the huge ugly seawall built to provide a protected swimming area. Long, shady Playa Los Cocos, where the snorkeling is good, is just a five-minute walk south along the shore. Beach lovers beware. Varadero this is not. In common with many of Cuba's southern coastal areas there's often more *diente de perro* (dog's tooth) than soft white sand here. Added to this, distances are long and public transport poor, so unless you have rented a car, you'd better be prepared to rough it.

### Information

On the main entry road to the hotel there's a pharmacy, post office, international post office and a Caracol shop selling some groceries. The settlement of Playa Girón is a tiny one-horse town, so if you need any goods or services, the hotel is the most likely place to look.

### Sights

The **Museo de Playa Girón** (admission CUC$2, cameras CUC$1; ⏲ 9am-5pm) has gleaming glass display cases and a tangible sense of history. Housed across the street from Villa Playa Girón, it offers two rooms of artifacts from Bahía de Cochinos plus numerous photos with (some) bilingual captions. The mural of victims and their personal items is eye-catching and the tactical genius of the Cuban forces comes through in the graphic depictions of how the battle unfolded. The 15-minute film about the 'first defeat of US imperialism in the Americas' is CUC$1 extra. A British Hawker Sea Fury

### THE BAY OF PIGS

What the Cubans call Playa Girón, the rest of the world has come to know as the Bay of Pigs 'fiasco', a shoddily planned comedy of errors that made a laughing stock out of the Kennedy administration and elevated Fidel Castro into the role of unassailable national hero.

Conceived in 1959 by the Eisenhower administration and headed up by deputy director of the CIA Richard Bissell, the plan to initiate a program of covert action against the Castro regime was given official sanction on March 17, 1960. There was but one proviso: no US troops were to be used in combat.

Setting about their task with characteristic zeal, the CIA modeled their operation on the 1954 overthrow of the left-leaning government of Jacobo Arbenz in Guatemala. But ambition soon got the better of ardor.

By the time President Kennedy was briefed on the proceedings in November 1960 the project had mushroomed into a full-scale invasion backed by a 1400-strong force of CIA-trained Cuban exiles and financed with a military budget of US$13 million.

Activated on April 15, 1961 the invasion was an unmitigated disaster from start to finish. Intending to wipe out the Cuban Air Force on the ground, US planes painted in Cuban Air Force colors (and flown by Cuban exile pilots) comically missed most of their intended targets. Castro, who had been forewarned of the plans, had scrambled his air force the previous week. Hence when the invaders landed at Playa Girón two days later, Cuban sea furies were able to promptly sink two of their supply ships and leave a force of 1400 men stranded on the beach.

To add insult to injury, a countrywide Cuban rebellion that had been much touted by the CIA never materialized. Meanwhile a vacillating Kennedy told a furious Bissell that he would not provide the marooned exile soldiers with US air cover.

Abandoned on the beaches, without supplies or military back up, the disconsolate invaders were doomed; 114 were killed in skirmishes and a further 1189 were captured. The prisoners were returned to the US a year later in return for US$53 million worth of food and medicines. For the Americans, the humiliation was palpable.

The Bay of Pigs failed due to a multitude of factors. Firstly the CIA had overestimated the depth of Kennedy's personal commitment and had made similarly inaccurate assumptions about the strength of the fragmented anti-Castro movement inside Cuba. Secondly Kennedy himself, adamant all along to make a low-key landing, had chosen a site on an exposed strip of beach close to the Zapata swamps. Thirdly, no one had given enough credit to the political and military know-how of Fidel Castro or the extent to which the Cuban Intelligence Service had infiltrated the CIA's supposedly covert operation.

The consequences for the Americans were far-reaching. 'Socialism or death!' a defiant Castro proclaimed at a funeral service for seven Cuban 'martyrs' on April 16, 1961. The revolution had swung irrevocably toward the Soviet Union.

aircraft used by the Cuban Air Force is parked outside the museum and round the back are other various vessels used in the battle that you can look at.

## Activities

The **International Scuba Center** (☎ 4118), at Villa Playa Girón, had been temporarily (though use that word with caution in Cuba) relocated up the road to Punta Perdiz (or better still try Playa Larga). Snorkeling happens further down the beach.

Eight kilometers southeast of Playa Girón is **Caleta Buena** (🕑 10am-6pm), a lovely protected cove perfect for snorkeling with abundant coral and small fish. Admission is CUC$12 and includes an all-you-can-eat lunch buffet and open bar. There are beach chairs and thatched umbrellas dotting the rocky shoreline and enough space in this remote place to have a little privacy. The scuba-diving company at Villa Playa Girón has a kiosk here, charging the same rates; snorkel gear is CUC$3.

## Sleeping & Eating

Budget travelers will like the selection of private rooms available here. Most places serve meals, but double check because the government choices in Girón are dire.

**Villa Playa Girón** (Cubanacán; ☎ 4110; s/d all-inclusive low season CUC$45/60, high season CUC$55/70; P) This unpretentious resort is a good option if you want the services of a decent hotel, though with its '70s architecture and slightly kitschy holiday-camp feel, you won't be enjoying the all-inclusive luxury of Varadero. Skip the rooms in long blocks near the pool and go for one of the concrete bungalows (some are huge, two-bedroom spreads with a kitchen – good for groups). The expansive grounds face the beach.

There were rumors that this hotel might be hosting Misión Milagros (p449) sometime in 2006. Phone ahead to check that the hotel is open.

### Getting There & Away

The bus to/from Matanzas via Jagüey Grande supposedly leaves Playa Girón at 5am two to three times a week. A bus to Cienfuegos leaves Monday to Friday at 5am. If any tour buses are at the hotel, find the driver and try to arrange a ride for a negotiable fee.

A single-passenger truck operates daily between Playa Girón and Cienfuegos (CUC$4, 1½ hours, 94km), leaving Playa Girón at 5am and departing Cienfuegos bus station at 12:30pm for the return. A taxi should cost approximately CUC$40 for this trip. From Playa Girón to Playa Larga, the fare will be closer to CUC$20.

**CASAS PARTICULARES – PLAYA GIRÓN**

**Hostal Luis** (☎ 4121; r incl breakfast CUC$25;) First house on road to Cienfuegos. Two spotless rooms in warm family atmosphere; look for the lions on the fence.

**Jorge Luis Osorio** (☎ 98 43 74; r CUC$20-30;) On the main road outside hotel. Two modern rooms with patio out back. Neighbor also rents.

**KS Abella** (☎ 4260; r CUC$20;) On the road to Cienfuegos; in front of apartments. Friendly, delicious meals.

**Silvia Acosta** (☎ 4237; r CUC$20; P) On the road to Cienfuegos. Tremendous shell entryway, nice rooms with private entrance.

**Villa Merci – Mercedes Blanco Pérez** (☎ 4304; r CUC$20; P) On road to Caleta Buena. Clean rooms, friendly couple.

### Getting Around

Transtur, Cubacar and **Havanautos** (☎ 98 41 23) all have car-rental offices at Villa Playa Girón.

Servi-Cupet gas stations are on the Carretera Central at Jovellanos and Colón at Jagüey Grande, and on the Autopista Nacional at Aguada de Pasajeros in Cienfuegos Province.

East of Caleta Buena (southeast of Playa Girón), the coastal road toward Cienfuegos becomes very bad and is only passable by a tractor, so you must backtrack and take the inland road via Rodas.

# Cienfuegos Province

Carved out of the former Las Villas territory in 1975, bite-sized Cienfuegos is a small, compact province that punches way above its weight. For first-time visitors the myriad of varied attractions are as interesting as they are elusive. Blessed with a manageable mix of rugged mountains, curvaceous coastline and fascinating history, the area shares many of the characteristics of neighboring Sancti Spíritus – but with half the tourist frenzy.

The provincial capital is an elegant and well-maintained city that combines stately neoclassical architecture with an atmosphere that often feels more French than Cuban. But it's not all savoir faire and Louis XV furniture. Underneath the Gallic veneer Cienfuegos' soul is unashamedly Afro-Cuban. The proof, for doubters, is in the music. One of Cuba's greatest singers, Benny Moré, was born in the small Cienfuegos village of Santa Isabel de las Lajas in 1919, while a few kilometers to the south, in unsung Palmira, traditional Santería *cabildos* (associations) keep the syncopated rumba beat alive in ancient African drumming rituals.

Rancho Luna is the province's nominal beach retreat, a small, unpretentious scoop of sand popular with vacationing Canadians and travelers on Spanish study programs. Ten kilometers along the coast, congenial Guajimico is one of Cuba's most luxurious campismos, a fully-equipped diving center that offers sunken ships and pillar coral formations to aspiring scuba enthusiasts.

## HIGHLIGHTS

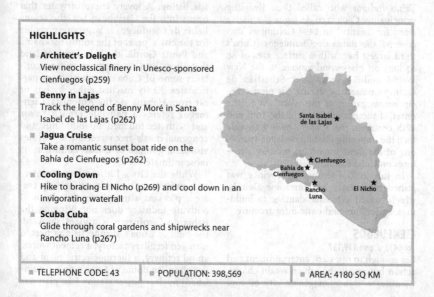

- **Architect's Delight**
  View neoclassical finery in Unesco-sponsored Cienfuegos (p259)
- **Benny in Lajas**
  Track the legend of Benny Moré in Santa Isabel de las Lajas (p262)
- **Jagua Cruise**
  Take a romantic sunset boat ride on the Bahía de Cienfuegos (p262)
- **Cooling Down**
  Hike to bracing El Nicho (p269) and cool down in an invigorating waterfall
- **Scuba Cuba**
  Glide through coral gardens and shipwrecks near Rancho Luna (p267)

Santa Isabel de las Lajas
Cienfuegos
Bahía de Cienfuegos
Rancho Luna
El Nicho

- TELEPHONE CODE: 43
- POPULATION: 398,569
- AREA: 4180 SQ KM

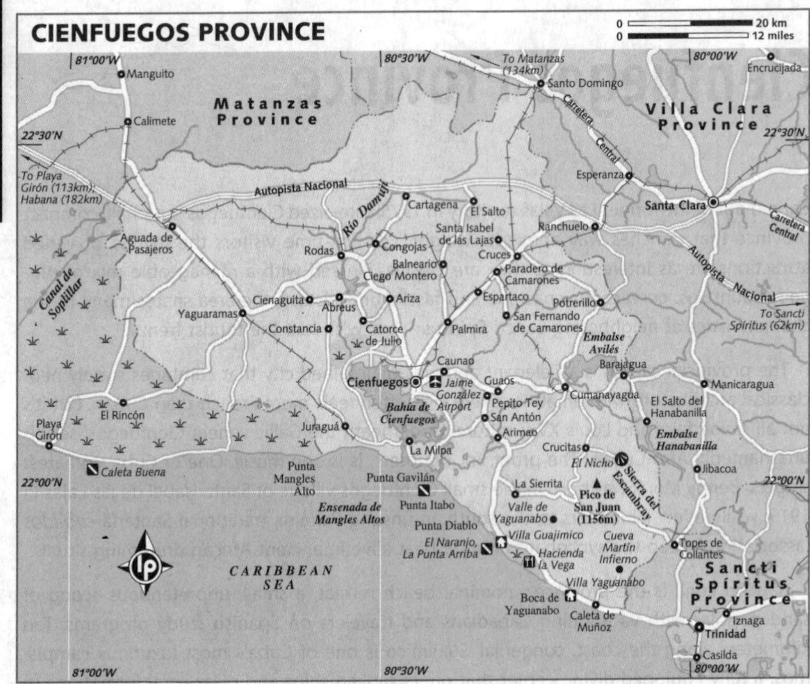


## History

The first settlers in the Cienfuegos area were Taíno Indians who called their fledgling principality, Cacicazgo de Jagua – a native word for 'beauty.' In 1494 Columbus 'discovered' the Bahía de Cienfuegos (Cuba's third largest bay, with a surface area of 88 sq km) on his second voyage to the New World and 14 years later Sebastián de Ocampo passed by during his pioneering circumnavigation of the island. With the onset of the era of piracy in the 16th and 17th centuries the Spanish built a bayside fort, the imposing Castillo de Jagua (p268), one of the most important military structures on Cuba's south coast.

In July 2005 Cienfuegos Province was lashed mercilessly by Hurricane Dennis, which caused extensive damage to buildings, agriculture and basic infrastructure.

## CIENFUEGOS

☎ 0432 / pop 139,137

Big enough to offer art, entertainment and action but small enough to retain charm, Cienfuegos is a manageable city of cool colonnaded buildings that was recently bestowed with a Unesco World Heritage site listing. A lovely curve of water that opens into the Caribbean Sea, the serene Bahía de Cienfuegos is largely responsible for the city's 'pearl of the south' nickname and Punta Gorda, the thin knife of land that slices into its southern waters, contains some of Cuba's prettiest casas particulares. Easily reached either by bus or car from Habana via the Autopista, Cienfuegos retains a palpable French flavor and with its touched up buildings and congenial hustle-free street-life it provides visitors a glimpse of Cuban culture at its most intimate.

While the city's 19th-century architecture and tranquil seaside setting help create a pleasant atmosphere, the churn of outlying industry does not. Ringing the Bahía de Cienfuegos is a giant shipyard, the bulk of Cuba's shrimp fishing fleet, a nitrogen fertilizer factory, a cement works, an oil refinery, a thermoelectric plant and the ghostlike dome of Cuba's only (unfinished) nuclear power station (the plan was abandoned in the early '90s when Soviet money dried up). Fortunately for travelers, the pollution has yet to penetrate the city center.

## History

Cienfuegos city proper was founded in 1819 by a French émigré from Louisiana named Louis D'Clouet. Sponsoring a scheme to relocate 40 families from Bordeaux in France the city got off to a bad start when it was destroyed by a hurricane in 1821. Unperturbed the French settlers rebuilt their homes and rechristened their new city Cienfuegos after the then governor of Cuba.

With the arrival of the railway in 1850 and the shift of allegiances in the sugar industry from Trinidad after the First War of Independence, Cienfuegos' fortunes grew exponentially. Basking in a period of relative economic prosperity in the late 19th century, the local merchants pumped their fortunes into a dazzling array of eclectic architecture that harked back to neoclassicism of their French forefathers.

D-Day in Cienfuegos' history came in September 1957 when officers at the local naval base staged a revolt against the Batista dictatorship. The uprising was brutally crushed, but the city's place in revolutionary history was sealed in infamy.

Modern day Cienfuegos retains a slightly plusher and more polished look than many of its urban counterparts. And with the promise of some much-needed Unesco money already in the pipeline, the future for the city's fine array of 19th-century architecture can only be bright.

## Orientation

Despite its haphazard geography, the city is laid out in an easy-to-understand grid system with evenly-numbered *avenidas* (avenues) that run east–west and odd-numbered *calles* (streets) running north–south. Downtown Cienfuegos, or 'Pueblo Nuevo', is the area bounded by Avs 46 and 62 and bisected by Calle 37 (popularly called 'El Prado'). Av 54 is often called 'El Bulevar' and is a pedestrian mall stretching from Calle 37 to Parque Martí. Calle 37 (or El Prado), meanwhile, runs 3km south to seaside Punta Gorda (where it's called Malecón). Rancho Luna is 18km south of the city via Av 5 de Septiembre.

## Information

### BOOKSTORES

**Librería Bohemia** (Map p260; ☎ 52 51 63; Av 56 No 3318 btwn Calles 33 & 35)

**Librería Dionisio San Román** (Map p260; ☎ 52 55 92; Av 54 No 3526) On the corner of Calle 37.

### EMERGENCY

**Ambulance** (☎ 185)

**Asistur** (Map p260; ☎ 51 32 65; Calle 37 No 5405 btwn Avs 54 & 56)

### INTERNET ACCESS

**Etecsa** (Map p260; ☎ 51 92 66; Calle 31 No 5402 btwn Avs 54 & 56; per hr CUC$6)

### MEDIA

**Radio Ciudad del Mar** (1350AM & 98.9 FM)

### MEDICAL SERVICES

**Clínica Internacional** (Map p260; ☎ 55 16 23; Calle 37 No 202, Punta Gorda) Caters to foreigners, handles dental emergencies and has a 24-hour pharmacy.

**Farmacia Principal Municipal** (Map p260; ☎ 51 57 37; Av 54 No 3524 btwn Calles 35 & 37)

### MONEY

**Banco de Crédito y Comercio** (Map p260; ☎ 51 57 47; cnr Av 56 & Calle 31)

**Banco Financiero Internacional** (Map p260; ☎ 55 16 57; cnr Av 54 & Calle 29)

**Cadeca** (Map p260; ☎ 55 22 21; Av 56 No 3314 btwn Calles 33 & 35)

### POST

**Post Office** cnr Av 56 & Calle 35 (Map p260; ☎ 51 82 84); Av 54 No 3514 (Map p260; btwn Calles 35 & 37)

### TELEPHONE

**Etecsa** (Map p260; ☎ 51 92 66; Calle 31 No 5403 btwn Avs 54 & 56)

### TRAVEL AGENCIES

**Cubanacán** (Map p260; ☎ 55 16 80; Av 54 btwn Calles 29 & 31)

**Cubatur** (Map p260; ☎ 55 12 42; Calle 37 No 5399 btwn Avs 54 & 56)

**Havanatur** (Map p260; ☎ 51 11 50; fax 55 13 70; Av 54 No 2906 btwn Calles 29 & 31)

**Reservaciones de Campismo** (Map p260; ☎ 51 94 23; Calle 37 No 5407 btwn Avs 54 & 56)

## Sights

The most interesting sights are clustered around stately Parque José Martí and 3km

CIENFUEGOS
0 500 m
0 0.3 miles
To Santa Clara (67km); Habana (254km)
Río El Inglés
San Lázaro
To Airport (5km); Trinidad (81km)
Ensenada de Boullón
Cayo Loco
Pueblo Nuevo
See Enlargement
Train Station
Punta Verde
Reina
Punta Arenas
Ferry to Castillo de Jagua
Ensenada Marsillán
Av 5 de Septiembre
To Necrópolis Tomás Acea (2km); Rancho Luna (18km); La Milpa (22km)
Punta Revienta Cordeles
Punta Gorda
Bahía de Cienfuegos
Laguna del Cura
Ensenada de las Calabazas
Punta del Medio
Punta Gorda
Parque Jose Martí
C37 (Paseo del Prado)
C37 (P del Prado)
0 200 m
0 0.1 miles
INFORMATION
Asistur (see 14)
Banco de Crédito y Comercio 1 B1
Banco Financiero Internacional 2 A2
Cadeca 3 B1
Clínica Internacional 4 D5
Cubanacán 5 A1
Cubatur 6 B1
Etecsa 7 B1
Farmacia Principal Municipal 8 B2
Havanatur 9 A2
Inmigración 10 C3
Librería Bohemia 11 B1
Librería Dionisio San Román 12 B2
Post Office 13 B1
Reservaciones de Campismo 14 B1
SIGHTS & ACTIVITIES
Arco de Triunfo 15 A1
Casa de la Cultura Benjamin Duarte 16 A1
Casa del Educador 17 C6
Catedral de la Purísima Concepción 18 A1
Cementerio La Reina 19 B3
Centro Recreativo La Punta 20 C6
Club Cienfuegos 21 C5
Colegio San Lorenzo 22 A1
La Bolera (see 60)
Marina Puertosol Cienfuegos (Base Náutica) 23 C5
Museo Histórico Naval Nacional 24 C2
Museo Provincial 25 A1
Palacio de Gobierno 26 A1
Palacio de Valle 27 C6
SLEEPING
Cubanacan Boutique La Unión 28 A1
Hostal Palacio Azul 29 C5
Hotel Jagua 30 C5
EATING
1869 Restaurant (see 28)
Café Artex 31 A1
Cafetería El Rápido 32 D4
Cafetería El Rápido 33 B2
Casa del Batido 34 B2
Coppelia 35 B2
Dinos Pizza 36 B1
Doña Neli 37 D2
D'Prisa 38 D4
Mercado Municipal 39 B1
Mini Restaurante Doña Yulla 40 B1
Paladar Aché 41 D3
Restaurante Covadonga 42 D5
Restaurante El Cochinito 43 C5
Restaurante Prado 44 B1
DRINKING
Bar Terrazas (see 28)
El Palatino 45 A1
ENTERTAINMENT
Cabaret Costasur 46 C3
Café Cantante Benny Moré 47 B1
Casa de la Cultura 48 B1
Casa de la Música 49 D5
Cine Prado 50 B1
Cine-Teatro Guanaroca 51 D2
Cine-Teatro Luisa 52 B2
El Benny 53 A1
Estadio 5 de Septiembre 54 D4
Jardines de Uneac 55 A1
Palacio de la Música (Patio de Artex) 56 C5
Polivalente, Sports Museum 57 D3
Salón de Minerva 58 B2
Teatro Tomás Terry 59 A1
Tropisur 60 D3
SHOPPING
El Embajador 61 B1
Maroya Gallery 62 A1
One Hour Photo 63 B2
Photo Service 64 B2
Variedades Cienfuegos 65 B2
TRANSPORT
Bus Station 66 D2
Cubataxi Depot 67 B2
Havanautos 68 D4
Micar 69 D5
Muelle Real 70 C3

south in the Punta Gorda section of town. You can see most of Cienfuegos in a day, but there's often good nightlife worth checking out (see p265).

Start your wanderings in the town center at **Parque José Martí** (Map p260), passing under the **Arco de Triunfo** (Arch of Triumph; the only one of its kind in Cuba) dedicated to Cuban independence. This impressive monument ushers you into the heart of the park, dropping you at the feet of José Martí rendered in marble.

**Teatro Tomás Terry** (Map p260; ☎ 51 33 61; Av 56 No 270 btwn Calle 27 & 29; tours CUC$1; 9am-6pm), on the northern side of Parque Martí, is one of Cienfuegos' most famous buildings. To honor their father, the sons of Venezuelan industrialist Tomás Terry built this 950-seat auditorium between 1887 and 1889 and graced the lobby with a Carrara marble statue of dad. In 1895 the theater opened with a performance of Verdi's *Aïda*. Famous artists who have trodden the boards here include Enrico Caruso, Anna Pavlova and Sarah Bernhardt. The seats are carved from Cuban hardwoods and there's an impressive ceiling fresco by Camilo Salaya.

On the western side of Parque Martí is the former Palacio de Ferrer (1918), now the **Casa de la Cultura Benjamin Duarte** (Map p260; ☎ 51 65 84; Calle 25 No 5401; admission free; 8:30am-midnight) where you can climb up the *mirador* (tower) for killer views (CUC$1). Check the schedule at the door for live music happenings. On the opposite side of the park is the neoclassical **Catedral de la Purísima Concepción** (Map p260; ☎ 52 52 97; Av 56 No 2902; donations accepted; 7am-noon). Erected in 1869, it has twin towers and French stained-glass windows. The southern side of Parque Martí is dominated by the red dome of the **Palacio de Gobierno**, where the provincial government, called the Poder Popular Provincial, holds forth (no visitors). The **Museo Provincial** (Map p260; ☎ 51 97 22; cnr Av 54 & Calle 27; admission CUC$2; 10am-6pm Tue-Sat, 10am-noon Sun) has benefited from a recent renovation and displays the frilly furnishings of refined 19th-century French-Cuban society, as well as other assorted knick knacks.

**Paseo del Prado** (Calle 37), stretching from the Río El Inglés in the north to Punta Gorda in the south, is the longest street of its kind in Cuba and a great place to see Cienfuegueños relaxing at their leisure. The boulevard is a veritable smorgasbord of fine neoclassical buildings and pastel-painted columns and at the intersection of Av 34 you can pay your respects to a life-sized statue of local hero Benny Moré.

Heading south for 3km on Prado, you enter Cienfuegos' aristocratic, waterfront quarter called Punta Gorda. The **Malecón** here shares none of the sexy extracurricular characteristics of Habana's seawall, but it still offers an exquisite vista of what is considered to be one of the world's best natural bays. The architecture is distinct, with bright clapboard homes boasting sun-dappled porches and intricate lattice work. The **Casa del Educador** (Map p260; Calle 35 No 26) is a great example of these beach villas while the **Palacio Azul** (now a refurbished hotel called Hostal Palacio Azul) and the revamped **Club Cienfuegos** highlight the 1920's aristocratic penchant for grandiosity.

The ultimate in kitsch is yet to come. Continue south on Punta Gorda until you encounter the fabulous Moorish-style **Palacio de Valle** (Map p260; ☎ 51 12 26; cnr Calle 37 & Av 2; admission CUC$1; 9:30am-11pm). Built in 1917 by Alcisclo Valle Blanco, a Spaniard from Asturias, it's an outrageous jumble of tiles and turrets, crenellated edges and scalloped arches. Batista planned to convert the palace into a casino, but today it's an (aspiring) upscale restaurant, with a terrace bar (p265).

The **Centro Recreativo La Punta** (Map p260; 10am-10pm) has a gazebo on the point's extreme southern tip and is a great spot to watch the sunset. You can grab a beer or mojito at the bar; there's sometimes live music here.

Cienfuegos has a couple of interesting outlying sights including two unique cemeteries, both of which are National Heritage sites. The older of the two is **Cementerio La Reina** (Map p260; cnr Av 50 & Calle 7; 8am-6pm) founded in 1837 and lined with the graves of Spanish soldiers who died in the independence wars. La Reina is the only cemetery in Cuba where bodies are interred above ground (in the walls) due to the high groundwater levels. It also has a marble statue called *Bella Durmiente:* a tribute to a 24-year-old woman who died in 1907 of a broken heart. It's an evocative place if you're into graveyards.

The **Necrópolis Tomás Acea** (Map p263; Carretera de Rancho Luna Km 2; admission CUC$1; 8am-6pm) is classed as a 'garden cemetery' and is entered

**DAY-TRIPPER**

The village of **Santa Isabel de las Lajas**, a few kilometers west of Cruces on the Cienfuegos–Santa Clara road, was where Bartolomé (Benny) Moré was born on August 24, 1919. Easily accessible in a half-day trip from Cienfuegos, this pleasant village hosts the biannual Benny Moré International Music Festival every other September. Curiosities include a **Municipal museum** with assorted Moré memorabilia and the **Casino de los Congos**, a music venue where you can view *tambores* (drums) and Santería rituals in the hallowed confines of where the self-styled *Bárbaro del Ritmo* (p67; Barbarian of Rhythm), allegedly, banged his first drum.

On the way back you may want to stop off briefly in the town of **Cruces** on the Santa Clara road. This settlement was the site of one of the most important battles of the Independence Wars in 1895 – the historic Battle of Mal Tiempo – in which Mambí generals Antonio Maceo and Máximo Gómez inflicted a crushing defeat on the Spanish forces. A needlelike **obelisk** in the middle of a pleasant colonial park commemorates the great battle. The park was declared a national monument in 1981.

Also worth a visit is **Palmira**, 8km north of Cienfuegos, a town famous for its Santería brotherhoods including the societies of Cristo, San Roque and Santa Barbara. Further information can be procured at the centrally located **Museo Municipal de Palmira** (☎ 54 45 33; admission CUC$1; ⏲ 10am-6pm Tue-Sat).

through a huge neoclassical pavilion (1926) flanked by 64 Doric columns modeled on the Parthenon in Greece. This cemetery contains a monument to the marine martyrs who died during the abortive 1957 Cienfuegos naval uprising.

The **Museo Histórico Naval Nacional** (Map p260; ☎ 51 91 43; cnr Av 60 & Calle 21; admission CUC$1; ⏲ 9am-6pm Tue-Fri, 9am-noon Sun) is housed in the former headquarters of the Distrito Naval del Sur (1950). This important museum covers archeology, natural history, naval history, navigation and art. The museum's central theme is the history-defining failed naval revolt.

## Activities

The **Marina Cienfuegos** (Base Náutica; Map p260; ☎ 55 12 41; fax 55 12 75; cnr Av 8 & Calle 35; ⏲ 7am-5pm), a few blocks north of Hotel Jagua, organizes fishing trips for CUC$150 for four people for four hours. There are also two-hour sunset cruises in the bay (stopping briefly at Castillo de Jagua) for CUC$10 and slightly longer day cruises for CUC$16. Inquire at Cubatur or Cubanacán for more details (p259).

Nearby, the new **Club Cienfuegos** (Map p260; ☎ 52 65 10; Calle 35 btwn Avs 10 & 12; ⏲ 9am-1am Sun-Fri, 9am-2am Sat) has a small beach, with many watersports including kayaking and windsurfing. There's also an amusement park with bumper cars, go-carts and video games.

If you're into billiards or bowling, go to **La Bolera** (Calle 37 btwn Avs 46 & 48; per hr CUC$1-2; ⏲ 11am-2am), where there's an ice-cream parlor and occasional live music. Nonguests can use the splendid **swimming pool** at Hotel la Unión on the corner of Av 54 and Calle 31 for CUC$5.

## Courses

The **Universidad de Cienfuegos** (☎ 55 61 24; Carretera Las Rodas Km 4, Cuatro Caminos) offers Spanish courses for beginners to advanced. The courses last one month and incorporate 80 hours of study (CUC$350). It also offers courses in 'Cuban Culture' (CUC$400) and 'Culture and Language' (CUC$450). The programs start on the first Monday of each month. Contact **UniversiTUR** (universitur@rectorado.ucf.edu) in Cienfuegos for more details.

## Tours

Cubanacán has the best tours in town, and everything from **El Nicho** (p269), costing CUC$30, to a Benny Moré discovery trip in **Santa Isabel de las Lajas** can be easily organized here.

## Festivals & Events

Local festivals in Cienfuegos include the cultural events marking the foundation of the city on April 22, 1819; Carnaval in August and the Benny Moré International Music Festival in September of odd-numbered years.

## Sleeping

Cienfuegos has a plethora of quality private rooms – your best bet for budget accommodation (see p264). Those at Punta Gorda are more removed, but generally more atmospheric. There are now four classified hotels in Cienfuegos, including the recently restored Palacio Azul.

### TOWN CENTER

**Cubanacán Boutique La Unión** (Cubanacán; Map p260; ☎ 55 10 20; cnr Av 54 & Calle 31; s/d CUC$80/90; ⊠ ⊡) This classical gem, in the heart of town, reopened a few years back after a major restoration by Cubanacán. Hidden neatly from the bustle of downtown Cienfuegos the hotel sports a tranquil warren of inner courtyards, marble pillars and a small secluded swimming pool. The 46 antique-furnished rooms have balconies either opening to the street or facing in over a colonial patio lined with mosaics. Chill by the pool and get a relaxing massage for CUC$5.

### PUNTA GORDA

**Hostal Palacio Azul** (Map p260; ☎ 7-204-4439; Calle 37 No 201 btwn Avs 12 & 14; s/d/tr CUC$35/38/51; P ⊠) A striking blue palace built in 1921 and reopened as a seven-room (16 person capacity) hotel in 2004. Situated near Club Cienfuegos in Punta Gorda, the hotel's huge rooms are named after flowers and, though not as luxurious as the nearby Jagua, the place oozes character. Other features here include an on-site restaurant called El Chelo and a striking rooftop cupola with kicking views.

**Hotel Jagua** (Gran Caribe; Map p260; ☎ 55 10 03; fax 55 12 45; Calle 37 No 1; s/d/tr low season CUC$60/85/119, high CUC$74/105/147; ⊠ ⊡) This hotel in Punta Gorda is 3km south of the center. Erected in the 1950s by Batista's brother, it is – along with La Unión – one of central Cuba's top hotels. The 145 rooms are good value and kids aged 12 and under stay for half price. It's a decent choice for families; there are on-site babysitters and dance classes available. A cabaret show (CUC$5) happens at 9:30pm Tuesday to Friday and 10pm Saturday.

### OUTSIDE TOWN

**Hotel Punta La Cueva** (Islazul; Map p263; ☎ 51 39 56; s/d low season CUC$17/22, high CUC$21/28; P ⊠ ⊡) This place is east across the bay from Hotel Jagua via a 3.5km access road that begins

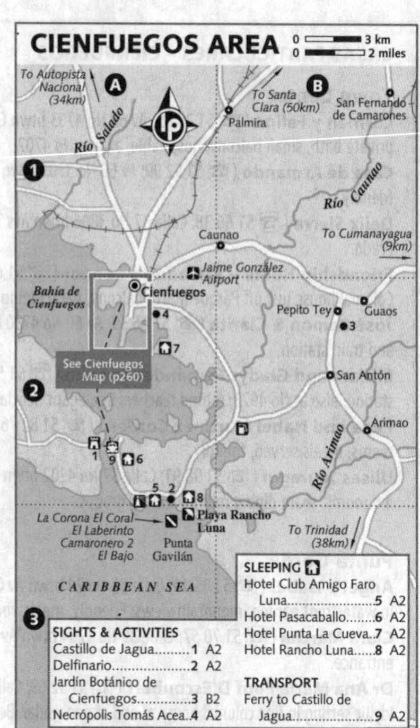


just east of Necrópolis Tomás Acea. The 67 rooms are a bit run-down, but still good value. There's a small beach, but it doesn't compensate for such a removed location.

## Eating

### TOWN CENTER

**Dinos Pizza** (Map p260; Calle 31 No 5418 btwn Avs 54 & 56; ⏰ noon-3pm & 6pm-midnight) Living up to its reputation for reliable, tasty food, this place has pizzas starting at CUC$4 (with toppings such as mushrooms, black olives or sausage additional) and lasagna at CUC$7. The big salads, bruschetta and soups make this a good vegetarian option.

**Paladar Aché** (Map p260; Av 38 btwn Avs Callles 41 & 43) At the time of writing, Cienfuegos' only operating paladar was situated near the pediatric hospital. Fresh, filling *criollo* (Creole) meals cost CUC$6 to CUC$8, depending on whether you come solo or with a *jinetero* (tout).

**1869 Restaurant** (Map p260; cnr Av 54 & Calle 31; mains CUC$10; ⏰ breakfast, lunch & dinner) Cienfuegos' best city center dining experience can be found in this elegant restaurant in the La Unión

## CASAS PARTICULARES – CIENFUEGOS

### Town Center

**Carmen y Felipe** (☎ 51 28 85; Av 60 No 4703 btwn Calles 47 & 49; r CUC$20; ❄) Near bus and train stations; private bath, small balcony, hospitable; also at No 4707.

**Casa de Armando** (☎ 51 52 99; Av 60 No 3703 btwn Calles 37 & 39; r CUC$20; ❄) Private bath, good location, friendly.

**Deliz Sierra** (☎ 51 66 38; Calle 37 No 3806 btwn Avs 38 & 40; r CUC$20) Conveniently located on the colonnaded Prado.

**Friendship Home – Armando y Leonor** (☎ 51 61 43; Av 56 No 2927 btwn Calles 29 & 31; r CUC$20) Colonial house just off Parque Martí; balcony, patio dining, legendary food, chatty hosts.

**José Ramón & Clarita** (☎ 51 86 39; Av 60 No 4730 btwn Calles 47 & 49; r CUC$20-25; ❄) Near bus terminal and train station.

**Miriam and Gladys Fernández Portillo** (☎ 51 58 16; Av 54 No 4919 btwn 49 & 51; r CUC$20) Near bus station, also at No 4923; retired teachers in elegant neoclassical building.

**Pepe and Isabel Martínez Cordero** (☎ 51 82 76; Av 52 No 4318 btwn 43 & 45; r CUC$20) Interconnecting rooms, meals served, friendly.

**Ulises Jaureguí** (☎ 51 98 91; Calle 37 No 4202 btwn Avs 42 & 44; r CUC$20; ❄) Flexible set up, interconnecting rooms, share dining room, ideal for groups.

### Punta Gorda

**Angel e Isabel** (☎ 51 15 19; Calle 35 No 24 btwn Av 0 & Litoral; r CUC$20-25; ❄) Two nicely furnished rooms in waterfront garden, mountain views. Friendly, meals, roof terrace; also at No 22.

**Clara Martha** (☎ 51 70 57; Calle 39 No 1204 btwn Avs 12 & 14; r CUC$20-25; ❄) Two rooms, independent entrance.

**Dr Ana María Font D'Escoubert** (☎ 51 32 69; Calle 35 No 20 btwn Av 0 & Litoral; r CUC$20-25; ❄) Truly idyllic setting in fine colonial house at end of peninsular. Beautiful garden that backs onto bay. Rooms basic but clean.

**Gloria Borges** (☎ 51 70 14; Calle 37 No 1210 btwn 12 & 14; r CUC$20-30; ❄) Spotlessly clean house with pleasant garden and back porch with rocking chairs.

**Jorge A Piñeiro Vásquez** (☎ 51 38 08; Calle 41 No 1402 btwn Avs 14 &16; r CUC$25; P) Meals served, secluded, upscale.

**Jorge de la Peña Castellanos** (☎ 51 90 15; Calle 39 No 1206 btwn Avs 12 & 14; r CUC$20; P) English spoken.

**Maylin y Tony** (☎ 51 99 66; Calle 35 No 4B btwn 0 & Litoral; r CUC$25; ) Two rooms with private bath, balcony, sea views and access; friendly, good meals.

**Miriam Aguilera Díaz** (☎ 51 80 85; Calle 37 No 1006 btwn 10 & 12; r CUC$20) Pleasant abode on Punta Gorda's main drag.

**Vista Al Mar** (☎ 51 83 78; www.vistaalmarcuba.com; Calle 37 No 210 btwn 2 & 4; r CUC$25; P ❄) This highly professional casa has even got its own private beach out back with hammocks.

hotel. Although the food doesn't quite match the lush furnishings, a varied international menu makes a welcome change from rice/beans/pork staples offered elsewhere.

**Mini Restaurante Doña Yulla** (Map p260; Av 54 No 3507 btwn Calles 35 & 37; 11am-3pm & 6:30-10:30pm) This is among the best of the many Doña Yullas here, with tablecloths, friendly service and an inexpensive Convertible menu. Try the pork steak.

**Café Artex** (Map p260; Av 56 No 2703 btwn Calles 27 & 29) This place on Parque Martí usually serves espresso and *café con leche* (espresso coffee with milk). The flowering patio looks out on the park where you can watch the old folk doing their morning aerobics.

**Mercado Municipal** (Map p260; Calle 31 No 5805 btwn Avs 58 & 60) If you feel like cooking or having a picnic, head to the market for fruits and vegetables in pesos.

Other recommendations:

**Restaurante Prado** (Map p260; cnr Calle 37 & Av 56; mains CUC$2-4) Brand new vegetarian place.

**El Rápido** (Map p260; cnr Av 54 & Calle 35) As always, pizza, sandwiches and snacks (CUC$1).

**Coppelia** (Map p260; cnr Calle 37 & Av 52) Ice cream for two pesos a scoop.

For a quick and inexpensive breakfast, check out **Casa del Batido** (Map p260; Calle 37 No 5211 btwn Avs 52 & 54; 6am-11pm) with wonderful fruitshakes like banana and papaya (one peso) or **Doña Neli** (Map p260; cnr Calle 41 & Av 62; 9am-10:15pm) for pastries and bread in Convertibles.

### PUNTA GORDA

**Restaurante Covadonga** (Map p260; ☎ 59 64 20; Calle 37 btwn Av 2 & 0) Legend has it that Castro and his guerrillas ate here in January 1959 during their triumphant march to Habana. By all accounts, the food's been going downhill ever since. Excellent waterfront location makes for a relaxing sunset cocktail though.

**Club Cienfuegos** (Map p260; ☎ 52 65 10; Calle 37 btwn Avs 10 & 12; noon-3pm & 6-9pm) A new addition to the Cienfuegos dining scene, the upscale, affordable restaurant at the Club Cienfuegos is a local favorite and one of the best in town. You won't pay more than CUC$10 for a steak and CUC$6 for a fine paella. The fantastic wraparound dining terrace with sea views makes it memorable. There's also a cafeteria and one of the best bars in town downstairs.

**Palacio de Valle** (Map p260; ☎ 51 12 26; cnr Calle 37 & Av 2; 10am-10pm) After a lambasting in the previous edition of this book things at Palacio de Valle seemed to have improved, although they have yet to match the Moorish architecture for decorative flourishes. Seafood dominates the menu downstairs, but if you still aren't convinced on the quality, eat in the La Jagua next door and use the rooftop bar here for a sunset cocktail.

Inexpensive places in Punta Gorda:

**Restaurante El Cochinito** (Map p260; ☎ 51 86 11; cnr Calle 37 & Av 4; noon-3pm & 7-10pm, closed Tue) With cheap pork and chicken dishes.

**El Rápido** (Map p260; cnr Calle 37 & Av 26) Has a nice terrace overlooking the bay where you can eat your CUC$1 microwave pizza. Bonus: air hockey.

**D'Prisa** (Map p260; Calle 37) Near Av 34.

## Drinking

**Bar Terrazas** (☎ 55 10 20; cnr Av 54 & Calle 31) This watering hole upstairs at the La Unión hotel is a good central option. Sip a mojito and enjoy fine city views; live music starts at 10pm.

**El Palatino** (Map p260; Av 54 No 2514) On the southern side of Parque Martí, the easily accessible Palatino is popular on the tour bus circuit. Impromptu jazz sets sometimes erupt here. Prepare to be hit up for alms at the end of song number three.

The terrace bar at the Palacio de Valle scores for its views and ambiance and no visit to town would be complete without a sunset cocktail in Club Cienfuegos.

## Entertainment

### LIVE MUSIC

**Jardines de Uneac** (Map p260; ☎ 51 61 17; Calle 25 No 5413 btwn Avs 54 & 56; admission CUC$2) It's hard to beat this outdoor patio venue with its Afro-Cuban *peñas* (musical performances) and guest *trovadores* (traditional singer/songwriters) such as Vicente Feliú. Watch out for Cienfuegos' best known band, Los Novos, who play here regularly.

**Casa de la Música** (Map p260; ☎ 55 23 20; Calle 37 btwn Avs 4 & 6; shows 10pm Fri & Sat, 5pm Sun) This big, outdoor venue in Punta Gorda hosts everyone from Los Van Van and '70s cover bands to feisty rap groups.

**Salón de Minerva** (Map p260; Av 52 No 3512 btwn Calles 35 & 37; admission CUC$1; 10pm Thu-Sat, 3pm Sun) Live boleros, salsa and *trova* (traditional poetic singing/songwriting) are all featured at this popular spot; bring your dancing shoes.

**Patio de Artex** (Map p260; ☎ 55 12 55; cnr Calle 35 & Av 16) Another recommendable patio place in Cienfuegos, you can catch *son* (Cuba's popular music) in the evenings and live ensembles at the 2pm Sunday matinee.

**Café Cantante Benny Moré** (Map p260; cnr Av 54 & Calle 37) Traditional music is a staple here. It's a rough peso place not for shrinking violets.

### DANCE CLUBS

**El Benny** (Map p260; ☎ 55 11 05; Av 54 No 2907 btwn Calles 29 & 31; admission per couple CUC$8; 10pm-3am Tue-Sun) The entrance fee to this sharp place includes a bottle of rum, two Cokes and enough salsa and sugar pop to make you drop. Nightly cabaret shows to the sounds of the Barbarian of Rhythm.

Two open-air discos with a local vibe are the friendly **Tropisur** (Map p260; cnr Calle 37 & Av 48; Sat only), with the pink-and-white wall around it (no sign) and **Cabaret Costasur** (Map p260; Av 40 btwn Calles 33 & 35; Fri & Sat), which you can hear as far away as the Hotel Jagua.

### THEATER

**Teatro Tomás Terry** (Map p260; ☎ 51 33 61; Av 56 No 270 btwn Calle 27 & 29) This architectural showpiece on the northern side of Parque Martí stages premier performances; the box office is open 11am to 3pm daily and 90 minutes before showtime.

Also check the cultural calendars at the **Casa de la Cultura Benjamin Duarte** (Map p260; Calle 25 No 5403) on Parque Martí, which shows movies daily at 2pm and 8:30pm, and the **Casa de la Cultura** (Map p260; Calle 37 No 5615) on the corner of Av 58.

### CINEMAS

Cienfuegos has three movie houses: **Cine-Teatro Luisa** (Map p260; Calle 37 No 5001); **Cine Prado** (Map p260; Calle 37 No 5402); and **Cine-Teatro Guanaroca** (Map p260; cnr Calle 49 & Av 58) situated opposite the bus station.

### SPORTS

From October to April, baseball games take place at **Estadio 5 de Septiembre** (Map p260; ☎ 51 36 44; Av 20 btwn Calles 45 & 55), while weekend boxing matches and other sporting events occur at **Polivalente** (Map p260; cnr Calle 37 & Av 48). There is also a small **sports museum** (admission free) here including hockey, fencing and baseball paraphernalia as well as the boots and T-shirt of local boxing hero, Julio González Valladores who brought back a gold medal from the 1996 Atlanta Olympics.

## Shopping

Whatever you desire can be found on the stretch of Av 54 between Calle 37 and Parque Martí; known as El Bulevar, it's chock-a-block with stores.

Check out the Maroya Gallery for folk art, Variedades Cienfuegos for peso paraphernalia or Casa del Habano 'El Embajador' for cigars.

**One Hour Photo** (Map p260; ☎ 55 22 98; Calle 37 No 5217 btwn Avs 52 & 54; 🕒 8am-10pm) Well-stocked with digital camera and lithium batteries, and Agfa film.

**Photo Service** (Map p260; Av 54 No 3118 btwn Calles 31 & 33)

## Getting There & Away

### AIR

Jaime González Airport 5km northeast of Cienfuegos receives weekly international flights from Toronto and Montreal. There are no connections to Habana.

### BUS

The **bus station** (☎ 51 57 20) is on Calle 49 between Avs 56 and 58. There are Víazul buses to Habana twice a day (CUC$20, five hours, 9:25am and 4:55pm) and Trinidad twice a day (CUC$6, two hours, 12:25pm and 4:55pm). To reach any other destinations from Cienfuegos, you have to connect in Trinidad, but since the two regular daily departures to Trinidad leave too late to connect, there's a 6:30am minibus to Trinidad (CUC$10). Tickets must be purchased from the *jefe de turno* (shift manager) downstairs.

For local buses to Rancho Luna (CUC$1), Pasacaballo (CUC$1) and Playa Girón (CUC$4), check the blackboard downstairs. Outside the station, collective taxis may be willing to take you to Santa Clara and Cumanayagua en route to El Nicho.

**Astro** (☎ 52 54 95) has departures from the bus station to Camagüey (CUC$13, seven hours, two daily), Habana (CUC$14, five hours, five daily), Santa Clara (CUC$3, two hours, two daily), Santiago de Cuba (CUC$26, two hours, daily) and Trinidad (CUC$3, two hours, two daily).

### TRAIN

The **train station** (☎ 52 54 95; cnr Av 58 & Calle 49; 🕒 ticket window 8am-3:30pm Mon-Fri, 8am-11:30am Sat) is across from the bus station. Trains are often canceled. When they do run, trains travel to Habana (CUC$9.50, 10 hours, daily), Santa Clara (CUC$2.10, two hours, two daily) and Sancti Spíritus (CUC$5.20, five hours, two daily).

## Getting Around

### BOAT

When there's gas, a 120-passenger ferry runs to the Castillo de Jagua (CUC$1, 40 minutes) from the **Muelle Real** (Map p260; cnr Av 46 & Calle 25). It leaves Cienfuegos at 8am, 1pm and 5:30pm and the castle at 6:30am, 10am and 3pm. Two ferries also make this trip from just below the Hotel Pasacaballo (p268).

### CAR & MOPED

**Club Cienfuegos** (Map p260; ☎ 52 65 10; Calle 37 btwn Avs 10 & 12) hires mopeds. **Havanautos** (Punta Gorda Map p260; ☎ 56 24 91; cnr Calle 37 & Av 16; Hotel Rancho Luna Map p263; ☎ 54 81 43; Carretera de Rancho Luna Km 16) and **Micar** (cnr Av 12 & Calle 39) hire cars.

The Servi-Cupet gas station is on Calle 37 at the corner of Av 16, in Punta Gorda. There's another station 5km northeast of Hotel Rancho Luna.

#### HORSE & CARRIAGE

Horse carts and bici-taxis ply Calle 37 charging Cubans one peso a ride, foreigners CUC$1 (though Spanish speakers might be able to 'pass' and pay a peso). It's a pleasant way to travel between town and Punta Gorda.

#### TAXI

**Cubataxi** (Map p260; ☎ 51 91 45, 51 84 54; Av 50 No 3508) has taxis 24 hours a day. Citroen/Lada taxis are cheaper than the tourist taxis outside Hotel Jagua. Agree on the price first.

## RANCHO LUNA

Rancho Luna is a picturesque beach resort next door to a very small cluster of (Cuban) houses 18km south of Cienfuegos. It has two large hotels, but it's also possible to stay in private rooms here, one of the few resort areas in Cuba where this is allowed. The entire coast is protected by a coral reef and the snorkeling is easily accessible. The local post office is in Hotel Rancho Luna. In the small village facing Hotel Club Amigo Faro Luna you'll find a string of casas particulares and a beach bar.

### Sights & Activities

There's a secluded little beach in the crook east of Punta Colorados that's a superb picnic or camping spot; access it from the dirt track just before the lighthouse.

Like most Cuban resort areas, Rancho Luna has its **Delfinario** (Map p263; ☎ 54 81 20; adult/child CUC$3/5; ⌚ 9am-5pm Tue-Sun) where you can see dolphins jump through hoops or swim with them for a rip-off CUC$50/33.

**Scuba diving** is possible with dive centers at Hotels Rancho Luna and Club Amigo Faro Luna, which visit 32 sites within a 20-minute boat ride. Caves, sunken ships, profuse marine life and dazzling coral gardens are among the attractions. From November to February harmless whale sharks frequent these waters. Good **snorkeling** is also possible with **Cubanacán Náutica** (☎ 54 80 40; dcfluna@acuc.cfg.cyt.cu; Hotel Club Amigo Faro Luna, Carretera de Rancho Luna Km 18; dives CUC$30, open water certification CUC$365) and **Whale Shark** (☎ 54 80 12; mpsolcfg@ip.etecsa.cu; at Hotel Rancho Luna, Carretera de Rancho Luna Km 16; 1/2 dives from CUC$30/40, night dives CUC$36).

### Sleeping

**Hotel Club Amigo Faro Luna** (Cubanacán; Map p263; ☎ 54 80 34; Carretera de Rancho Luna Km 18; s/d low season CUC$44/55, high CUC$52/66; P ⛝ 🏊) This intimate resort on a bluff overlooking the sea is the best on the beach. Not all rooms are the same and the newer units in the 200 and 300 block have bathtubs. The pool (with separate children's unit) is sweet and the food buffet is

#### THE FRENCH INFLUENCE

While the cooks might be gastronomically challenged and the *je ne sais quoi* limited to speculation about the length of Castro's next speech, the Gallic influence in Cuban culture is stronger than most visitors imagine.

Refined French manners first arrived on the island in 1791 when Toussaint Louverture's slave rebellion in the French colony of Saint Domingue (now Haiti) drove 30,000 coffee planters fleeing westward.

'The original coffee growers were almost all cultured, old and rich colonial Frenchmen who had fled from Haiti and Louisiana, and they brought to Cuba the refinements and ideas of Napoleonic France which were expanding throughout the world,' wrote Cuban ethnologist Fernando Ortiz in the prologue to *Coffee: History of its Cultivation and Exploitation in Cuba*, by Francisco Pérez de la Riva, (October 1944).

This initial influx was soon dissipated by the founding of the cities of Cienfuegos and Guantánamo in 1819; the former by French colonists from Bordeaux in a settlement scheme devised by a Louisianan émigré named Louis D'Clouet, and the latter by a second wave of Haitian refugees.

Today both cities retain many vestiges of French building and design, particularly Cienfuegos, known locally as the 'city of columns' for its glittering array of neoclassical architecture.

More subtle influences can also be found in Cuban music. Elements of French Romanzas are traceable in Cuban *trova* while *changüi* and *guaracha* – musical forms native to Guantánamo Province – are the bastardized descendants of the *contradanza* (country dance) and various elements borrowed from French theater.

**TOWARD TRINIDAD**

Heading east toward Trinidad, postcard views of the Escambray Mountains loom ever closer. At Villa Guajimico the road tracks southeast undulating scenically between the mountains and sea for 30km.

**Hacienda La Vega** on the main road approximately 8km east of Villa Guajimico is a small Palmares restaurant adjacent to a hacienda surrounded by fruit trees. It's a shady and tranquil spot that is well worth a lunchtime stopover. You can hire horses here and scamper down to a nearby beach called Caleta de Castro.

The **Cueva Martín Infierno** in the Valle de Yaganabo, 56km from Cienfuegos via the shore hamlet of Caleta de Muñoz, contains a 67m stalagmite said to be the tallest in the world. This cave is not open for general tourism but speleologists should contact Angel Graña at the **Sociedad Espeleológica de Cuba** (☎ 7-209-2885; angel@fanj.cult.cu) in Habana. This valley is also a good bird-watching area.

**Villa Guajimico** (Cubamar; Map p258; ☎ 54 09 46, toll free from the US or Canada 800-645-1179; www.cubamarviajes.cu; Carretera de Trinidad Km 42; s/d/tr low season CUC$24/38/53, high CUC$28/46/65; P) is one of Cubamar's most luxurious campismos and the 54 attractive cabins and idyllic seaside setting could easily compete with a medium-priced (three-star) hotel. The villa offers excellent scuba diving opportunities, along with bike hire, car rental and various catamaran/kayaking options. It is also a fully-equipped Campertour site.

Around 26km west of Trinidad and 52km east of Cienfuegos **Villa Yaguanabo** (Islazul; Map p258; ☎ 54 00 99; www.islazul.cu; Carretera de Trinidad km 55; s/d low season CUC$16/21, high CUC$20/26) has 30 nicely situated Islazul cabins and offers horseback riding, boating on the Yaguanabo River and short walks along the Villa Yaguanabo trail. It has a restaurant, too.

surprisingly good. A long beach is only a few minutes' walk away. The hotel is frequented by groups of Canadians on study programs.

**Hotel Rancho Luna** (Cubanacán; Map p263; ☎ 54 81 31; Carretera de Rancho Luna Km 16; s/d low season CUC$55/70, high CUC$65/80; P) This recently refurbished resort – now linked to the Faro Luna in a Cubanacán *complejo* (complex) – is a favorite of Canadian package tourists, who dig the all-inclusive deal, private beach and big pool. A horse and buggy can be hired for rides along the coast.

**Hotel Pasacaballo** (Islazul; Map p263; ☎ 54 80 13; Carretera de Rancho Luna Km 22; P) A five-story monster sitting on a headland opposite the Castillo de Jagua, this Islazul offering is as architecturally ugly as the rest of the scenery is beautiful. In early 2006 it was closed due to Misión Milagros (p449). Check with the travel agencies in Cienfuegos for updates.

Recommended casas particulares in Rancho Luna:

**'Villa Sol' – Diana Gavio Caso** (☎ 0152-27-24-48; Carretera Faro Luna; r CUC$20-30) On the approach road to Hotel Faro Luna. Beautiful house overlooking ocean. Bougainvillea in garden.

**Casa de Julio** (☎ 51 57 44; Carretera de Faro Luna; r CUC$25) Last (blue) house on left before Hotel Faro Luna. Nice setting.

## Eating

Aside from the hotels, your dining options are limited. Try the beach snack bar or one of the private houses that rent rooms. The Servi-Cupet station 5km north of town serves microwave pizza 24 hours a day.

## Getting There & Away

Theoretically, there are local buses from Cienfuegos seven times a day. Alternatively the Jagua ferry to Cienfuegos calls at the dock directly below Hotel Pasacaballo several times daily. A one-way taxi fare to Cienfuegos should cost around CUC$8 to CUC$10; bargain.

An even better way to get here is zipping along from Cienfuegos on a rented moped (p266).

# CASTILLO DE JAGUA

The **Castillo de Nuestra Señora de los Ángeles de Jagua** (Map p263), to the west of the mouth of Bahía de Cienfuegos, was designed by José Tontete in 1738 and completed in 1745 (long before the city of Cienfuegos was founded). At the time it was the third most important fortress in Cuba, after those of Habana and Santiago de Cuba. Built to keep pirates (and the British) out, the castle now shelters a small museum and boasts a pleasant bayside view.

You can get to the castle via a roundabout road from Cienfuegos, but it's easier to take the ferry from a landing just below the Hotel Pasacaballo. It operates frequently throughout the day, charging one peso one way. Tourists pay CUC$1. Otherwise, take the ferry from Cienfuegos.

## JARDÍN BOTÁNICO DE CIENFUEGOS

The 94-hectare **Jardín Botánico de Cienfuegos** (Map p263; admission CUC$5; 8am-5pm), near the Pepito Tey sugar mill, 17km east of Cienfuegos, is one of Cuba's biggest gardens. It houses 2000 species of plants, including 23 types of bamboo, 65 of fig and 280 different palms. The botanic garden was founded in 1901 by US sugar baron Edwin F Atkins who initially intended to use it to study different varieties of sugarcane, but instead began planting exotic tropical trees from around the world.

Only three buses a day pass near Pepito Tey on their way from Cienfuegos to Cumanayagua, and a visit to the gardens is only practical if you have your own transport. Coming from Cienfuegos, turn right (south) at the junction to Pepito Tey.

## EL NICHO

Waterfalls with small bathing pools and gorgeous mountain vistas: **El Nicho** (Map p258; admission CUC$5; 8:30am-6:30pm), just 90 minutes from Cienfuegos via the rough road at Crucecitas, is (was!) one of central Cuba's best kept secrets. You can swim, horseback ride to Hanabanilla (CUC$2 per hour) and camp here; there's a simple Palmares restaurant. Tucked into the Sierra del Escambray, you'll need a 4WD to reach these chilly cascades (alternatively you can book a tour through Cubanacán in Cienfuegos for CUC$30). Patient, hardy travelers can get a colectivo to Cumanayagua (CUC$1) from the bus station in Cienfuegos and then connect with a rough-and-tumble local truck (5:30am and 5pm) to El Nicho. The falls are best (but coldest) from January to April before the rains and Cuban crowds come.

# Villa Clara Province

Villa Clara is a geographically diverse province of placid lakes and misty oxen-furrowed fields that offers aspiring visitors everything from freshwater fishing to body revitalizing mineral springs. Situated in Cuba's historical center (Cubanacán) and bordered to the south by the foliage-covered foothills of the Escambray Mountains, the area is sprinkled liberally with hillside coffee plantations and is second only to Pinar del Río as a producer of fine tobacco.

Long noted for the grandiosity of its Che Guevara monuments, travelers to Villa Clara will find reminders of the infamous *guerrillero* (guerrilla) almost everywhere. If you're here for the obligatory Che pilgrimage, Santa Clara is the place to be, an untouristy, down-to-earth city, where old men in Panama hats chew thoughtfully on cheap Cohibas while young innovators from the local arts scene busily set about igniting a small revolution of their own.

For solitude seekers, the quiet life can be found in colonial Remedios, one of Cuba's oldest towns and a pleasant alternative to the hustle and bustle of Santa Clara. Every December 24 Remedios' peace is shattered by a frenzy of exploding fireworks known locally as *Las Parrandas*. Bring your ear plugs or join in the festivities.

Scattered to the north the distant outlines of the Cayerías del Norte lie sprinkled like bright jewels across an ocean teeming with translucent coral. Currently boasting just four tourist-class hotels, these once lonesome island hideaways have been earmarked for future tourist development and armies of hard-hatted workmen are gearing up for business.

**HIGHLIGHTS**

- **Che City**
  Trace the legend of Ernesto 'Che' Guevara in Santa Clara's mausoleum (p274) and Tren Blindado (p274)
- **Quiet Corner**
  Relax beneath the louvers in the unspoiled colonial pocket of Remedios (p280)
- **Unquiet Corner**
  Take part in the flying sparks, shaking hips and flowing rum of the Remedios *Las Parrandas* (p280)
- **Paradise Found**
  Feel the sand beneath your feet on the deserted beaches of Cayo Santa María (p283)
- **Mountain Retreat**
  Hire a boat or fish for bass in scenic Embalse Hanabanilla (p279)



- TELEPHONE CODE: 42
- POPULATION: 836,350
- AREA: 8662 SQ KM

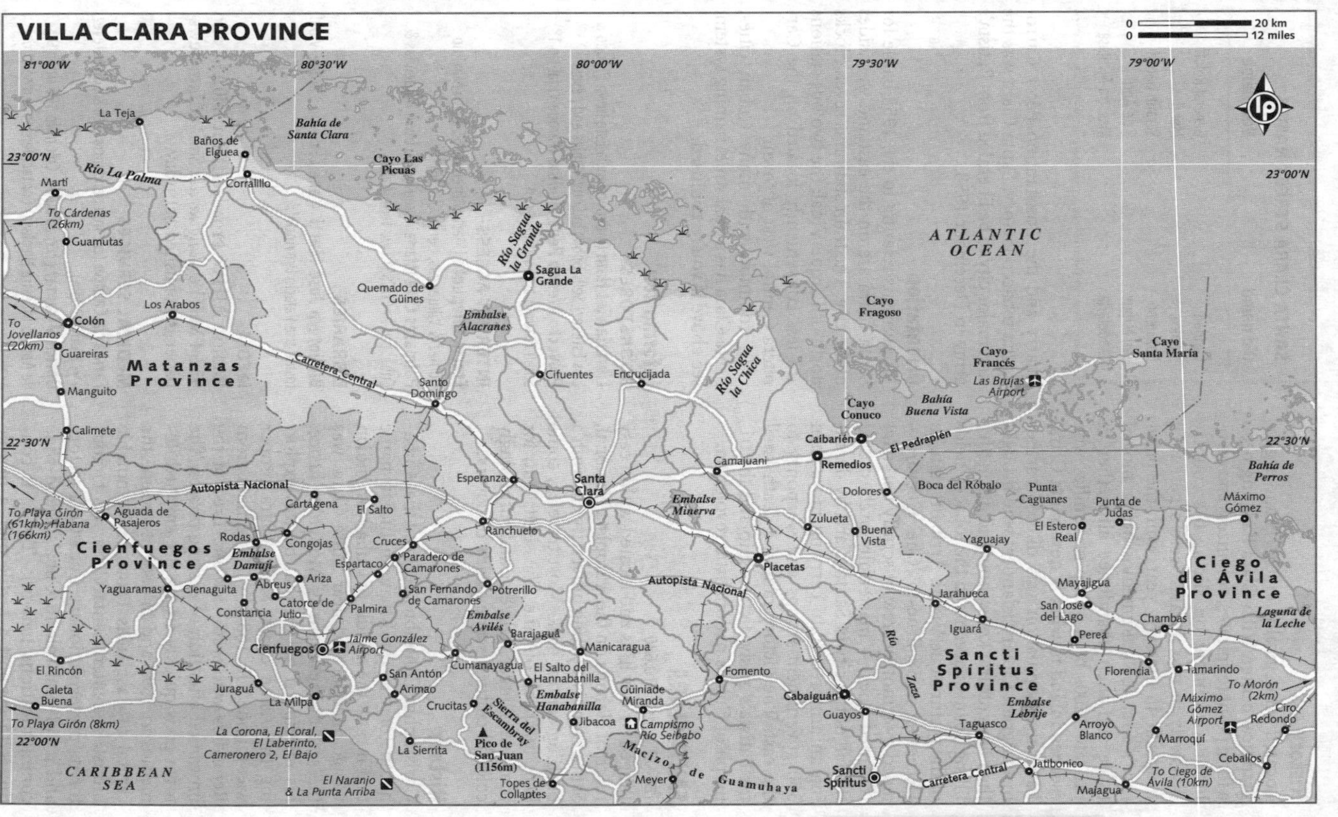
VILLA CLARA PROVINCE
0 20 km
0 12 miles
81°00'W
80°30'W
80°00'W
79°30'W
79°00'W
23°00'N
22°30'N
22°00'N
ATLANTIC OCEAN
CARIBBEAN SEA
Matanzas Province
Cienfuegos Province
Sancti Spíritus Province
Ciego de Ávila Province
Bahía de Santa Clara
Cayo Las Picuas
Cayo Fragoso
Cayo Francés
Cayo Santa María
Cayo Conuco
Bahía Buena Vista
Bahía de Perros
Laguna de la Leche
El Pedraplén
Las Brujas Airport
La Teja
Baños de Elguea
Corralillo
Río La Palma
Martí
To Cárdenas (26km)
Guamutas
Colón
To Jovellanos (20km)
Guareiras
Los Arabos
Manguito
Calimete
Quemado de Güines
Río Sagua la Grande
Sagua La Grande
Embalse Alacranes
Santo Domingo
Carretera Central
Cifuentes
Encrucijada
Río Sagua la Chica
Santa Clara
Camajuaní
Caibarién
Remedios
Dolores
Boca del Róbalo
Punta Caguanes
Punta de Judas
El Estero Real
Yaguajay
Mayajigua
San José del Lago
Máximo Gómez
Chambas
Florencia
Tamarindo
To Morón (2km)
Ciro Redondo
Máximo Gómez Airport
Marroquí
Ceballos
To Ciego de Ávila (10km)
Arroyo Blanco
Majagua
Jatibonico
Embalse Lebrije
Taguasco
Carretera Central
Iguará
Jarahueca
Perea
Buena Vista
Zulueta
Placetas
Embalse Minerva
Autopista Nacional
Río Zaza
Cabaiguán
Guayos
Sancti Spíritus
Fomento
Macizo de Guamuhaya
Meyer
Campismo Río Seibabo
Güiniade Miranda
Manicaragua
Jibacoa
Embalse Hanabanilla
El Salto del Hannabanilla
Topes de Collantes
Sierra del Escambray
Pico de San Juan (1156m)
Barajagua
Cumanayagua
Embalse Avilés
Potrerillo
Ranchuelo
Esperanza
Crucitas
La Sierrita
Arimao
San Antón
San Fernando de Camarones
Paradero de Camarones
Cruces
El Salto
Espartaco
Palmira
Jaime González Airport
Cienfuegos
Cartagena
Congojas
Ariza
Abreus
Catorce de Julio
Constancia
Rodas
Embalse Damují
Cienaguita
La Milpa
Juraguá
La Corona, El Coral, El Laberinto, Cameronero 2, El Bajo
El Naranjo & La Punta Arriba
Yaguaramas
Aguada de Pasajeros
To Playa Girón (61km); Habana (166km)
Autopista Nacional
El Rincón
Caleta Buena
To Playa Girón (8km)

## History

Located strategically in the island's geographical center, Villa Clara has long been a focal point for pirates, colonizers and revolutionaries intent on slicing the country divisively in two. Pirates were a perennial headache in the early years with the province's first town Remedios being moved twice and then abandoned altogether in the late 1600s by a group of families who escaped inland to what is now Santa Clara. Later the population was diluted further by emigrant Canary Islanders who brought their agricultural know-how and distinctive lilting Spanish accents to the tobacco fields of the picturesque Vuelta Arriba region. In December 1958 Ernesto 'Che' Guevara – aided by a motley crew of scruffy *barbudas* (bearded ones) – masterfully orchestrated the fall of the city of Santa Clara, by derailing an armored train carrying more than 350 government troops and weaponry to the east. The victory rang the death knell for Batista's grisly dictatorship and the triumph of Cuba's nationalistic revolution.

# SANTA CLARA

☎ 422 / pop 210,680

Ringed by low hills and located within easy reach of Habana on the Autopista Nacional, Santa Clara is a young university city with a bustling central park. Most travelers come here to check out the Che sights but, for those who linger, a diverse and surprisingly colorful cultural scene awaits discovery.

## History

Christopher Columbus believed that Cubanacán (or Cubana Khan; an Indian name that meant 'the middle of Cuba'), an Indian village once located near Santa Clara, was the seat of the khans of Mongolia; hence, his misguided notion that he was exploring the Asian coast. Santa Clara proper was founded in 1689 by 13 families from Remedios who were sick and tired of the unwanted attention of passing pirates. The town grew quickly after a fire emptied Remedios in 1692 and in 1867 it became the capital of Las Villas Province. A notable industrial center, Santa Clara was famous for its prerevolutionary Coca Cola factory and its pivotal role in Cuba's island-wide communications network. Today it continues to support a textile mill, a marble quarry and the Constantino Pérez Carrodegua tobacco factory. Santa Clara was the first major city to be liberated from Batista's army in December 1958.

**SANTA CLARA STREET NAMES**

| Old name | New name |
|---|---|
| Caridad | General Roloff |
| Sindico | Morales |
| Nazareno | Serafín García |
| San Migue | 9 de Abril |
| Candelaria | Maestra Nicolasa |

## Orientation

Monuments relating to the 1958 battle for Santa Clara are on the east and west sides of the city. The train station is seven blocks north of Parque Vidal; the two bus stations are less conveniently located on the Carretera Central west of town.

In common with many Cuban cities, Santa Clara has a dual street naming system: see above if you're confused.

## Information

### BOOKSTORES

**Librería Viet Nam** (Independencia Este btwn Plácido & Luis Estévez) Sells books in Convertibles and pesos.

**Proyecto Ateneo Pepe Medina** (Parque Vidal No 18) Small reading area with air-con.

### INTERNET ACCESS

**Etecsa Telepunto** (Marta Abreu No 55 btwn Máximo Gómez & Villuendas; per hr CUC$6)

**Palmares Café** (Marta Abreu No 10 btwn Villuendas & Cuba; per hr CUC$5) Two terminals.

### LIBRARIES

**Biblioteca José Martí** (Calle Colón on Parque Vidal) Inside the Palacio Provincial.

### MEDIA

Radio CMHW broadcasts on 840AM and 93.5 FM. The *Vanguardia Santa Clara* newspaper is published Saturday.

### MEDICAL SERVICES

**Farmacia Campa** (cnr Independencia Este & Luis Estévez; 🕑 8am-8:30pm)

**Óptica Miramar** (☎ 20 80 69; Colón No 106 btwn 9 de Abril & Maestra Nicolasa) Contact lenses and solution available.

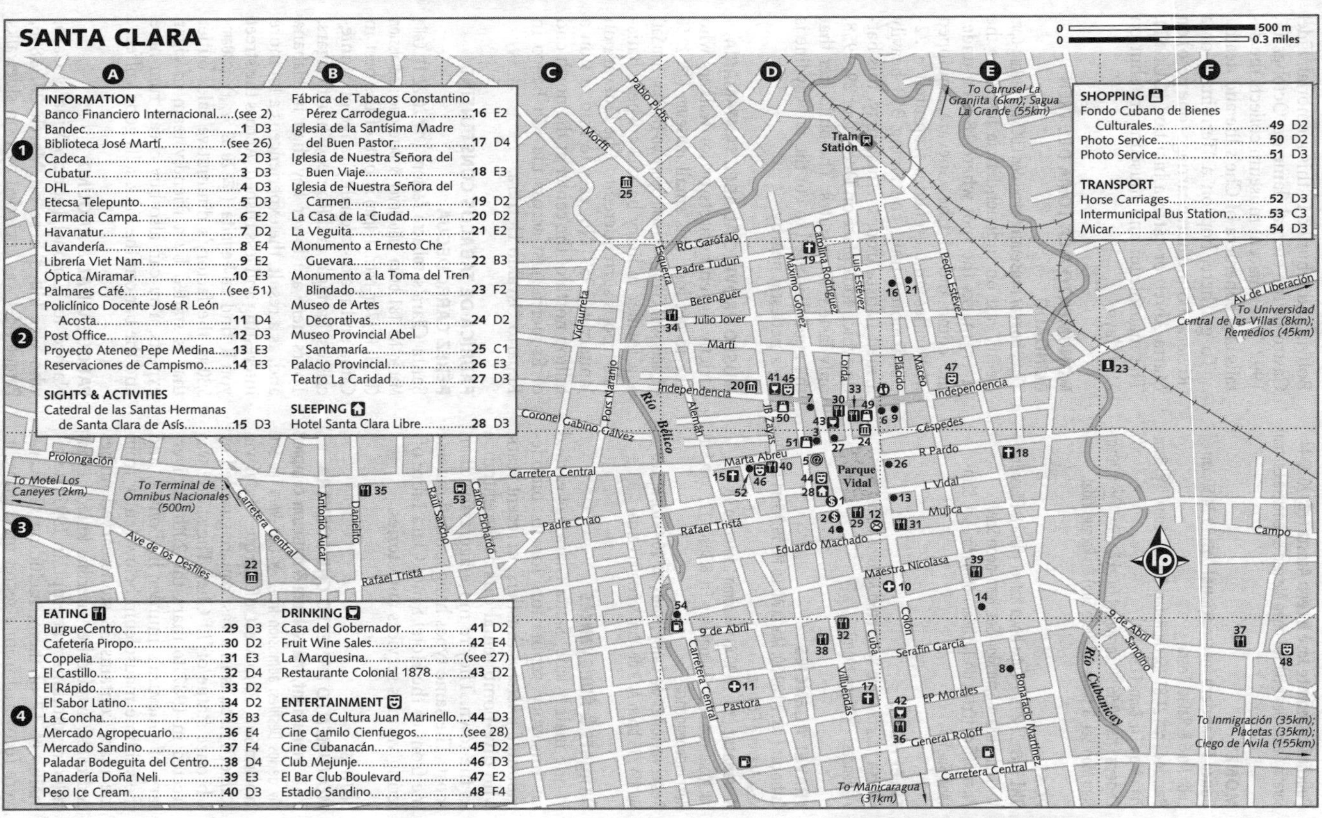
SANTA CLARA
0 500 m
0 0.3 miles
INFORMATION
Banco Financiero Internacional.....(see 2)
Bandec.....1 D3
Biblioteca José Martí.....(see 26)
Cadeca.....2 D3
Cubatur.....3 D3
DHL.....4 D3
Etecsa Telepunto.....5 D3
Farmacia Campa.....6 E2
Havanatur.....7 D2
Lavandería.....8 E4
Librería Viet Nam.....9 E2
Óptica Miramar.....10 E3
Palmares Café.....(see 51)
Policlínico Docente José R León Acosta.....11 D4
Post Office.....12 D3
Proyecto Ateneo Pepe Medina.....13 E3
Reservaciones de Campismo.....14 E3
SIGHTS & ACTIVITIES
Catedral de las Santas Hermanas de Santa Clara de Asís.....15 D3
Fábrica de Tabacos Constantino Pérez Carrodegua.....16 E2
Iglesia de la Santísima Madre del Buen Pastor.....17 D4
Iglesia de Nuestra Señora del Buen Viaje.....18 E3
Iglesia de Nuestra Señora del Carmen.....19 D2
La Casa de la Ciudad.....20 D2
La Veguita.....21 E2
Monumento a Ernesto Che Guevara.....22 B3
Monumento a la Toma del Tren Blindado.....23 F2
Museo de Artes Decorativas.....24 D2
Museo Provincial Abel Santamaría.....25 C1
Palacio Provincial.....26 E3
Teatro La Caridad.....27 D3
SLEEPING
Hotel Santa Clara Libre.....28 D3
SHOPPING
Fondo Cubano de Bienes Culturales.....49 D2
Photo Service.....50 D2
Photo Service.....51 D3
TRANSPORT
Horse Carriages.....52 D3
Intermunicipal Bus Station.....53 C3
Micar.....54 D3
EATING
BurgueCentro.....29 D3
Cafetería Piropo.....30 D2
Coppelia.....31 E3
El Castillo.....32 D4
El Rápido.....33 D2
El Sabor Latino.....34 D2
La Concha.....35 B3
Mercado Agropecuario.....36 E4
Mercado Sandino.....37 F4
Paladar Bodeguita del Centro.....38 D4
Panadería Doña Neli.....39 E3
Peso Ice Cream.....40 D3
DRINKING
Casa del Gobernador.....41 D2
Fruit Wine Sales.....42 E4
La Marquesina.....(see 27)
Restaurante Colonial 1878.....43 D2
ENTERTAINMENT
Casa de Cultura Juan Marinello.....44 D3
Cine Camilo Cienfuegos.....(see 28)
Cine Cubanacán.....45 D2
Club Mejunje.....46 D3
El Bar Club Boulevard.....47 E2
Estadio Sandino.....48 F4
Train Station
Parque Vidal
Río Bélico
Río Cubanicay
To Carrusel La Granjita (6km); Sagua La Grande (55km)
To Universidad Central de las Villas (8km); Remedios (45km)
Av de Liberación
To Motel Los Caneyes (2km)
To Terminal de Omnibus Nacionales (500m)
To Inmigración (35km); Placetas (35km); Ciego de Avila (155km)
To Manicaragua (31km)
Carretera Central

**Policlínico Docente José R Leon Acosta** (☎ 20 22 44; Serafín García Oeste No 167 btwn Alemán & Carretera Central)

#### MONEY

**Banco Financiero Internacional** (☎ 20 74 50; cnr Cuba No 6 & Rafael Tristá)
**Bandec** (☎ 21 81 15; cnr Rafael Tristá & Cuba; 🕑 8am-2pm Mon-Fri, 8am-11am Sat)
**Cadeca** (☎ 20 56 90; cnr Rafael Tristá & Cuba; 🕑 8:30am-6pm Mon-Sat, 8:30am-12:30pm Sun) On Parque Vidal.

#### POST

**DHL** (☎ 20 89 76; Cuba btwn Rafael Tristá & Eduardo Machado; h8am-6pm Mon-Sat, 8am-noon Sun)
**Post office** (Colón No 10; h8am-6pm Mon-Sat, 8am-noon Sun)

#### TELEPHONE

**Etecsa** (Marta Abreu No 55 btwn Máximo Gómez & Villuendas; 🕑 8am-10pm)

#### TRAVEL AGENCIES

**Cubatur** (☎ 20 89 80; Marta Abreu No 10; h9am-6pm) Near Máximo Gómez.
**Havanatur** (☎ 20 40 01; Máximo Gómez No 9B; h8:30am-noon & 1-5:30pm Mon-Fri, 8:30am-12:30pm Sat) Near Independencia.
**Reservaciones de Campismo** (☎ 20 49 05; Maceo Sur No 315 btwn Av 9 de Abril & Serafín García)

### Dangers & Annoyances

While mainly safe, Santa Clara has earned an unsavory reputation for its bicycle-mounted *jineteros* (hustlers) in recent years, who dive-bomb rental cars at the entrance to the town. They're more aggressive than most. The same types hang around outside the front of the Hotel Santa Clara Libre offering various services and stories.

### Sights

#### MONUMENTO ERNESTO CHE GUEVARA

This **monument, mausoleum & museum complex** (Av de los Desfiles; admission free; 🕑 8am-9pm Tue-Sat, 8am-6pm Sun), 2km west of Parque Vidal via Rafael Tristá, is in a vast square guarded by a bronze statue of 'El Che.' The statue was erected in 1987 to mark the 20th anniversary of Guevara's murder in Bolivia, and the sublime mausoleum below (entry from the rear) contains 38 stone-carved niches dedicated to the other guerillas killed in that failed revolutionary attempt. In 1997 the remains of 17 of them, including Guevara, were recovered from a secret mass grave in Bolivia and reburied in this memorial. Fidel Castro lit the eternal flame on October 17, 1997. The adjacent museum collects the details and ephemera of Che's life and death.

To get here, hop on a 'Terminal'- or a 'Riviera'-bound horse carriage (one peso) on Marta Abreu or catch a bici-taxi (CUC$1). The mausoleum and museum are shut on Mondays.

#### MONUMENTO A LA TOMA DEL TREN BLINDADO

This **boxcar museum** (admission CUC$1; 🕑 8am-6pm Tue-Fri), east on Independencia just over the river, marks the spot where 18 men under the command of Che Guevara, equipped with rifles and grenades, captured a 22-car armored train containing 350 heavily armed Batista troops. Amazingly, this battle, which took place on December 29, 1958, only lasted 90 minutes. The bulldozer that the guerrillas used to cut the railway line is on a pedestal nearby.

#### MUSEO PROVINCIAL ABEL SANTAMARÍA

Strictly for enthusiasts or for walkers who like to get lost, this small **museum** (☎ 20 50 41; admission CUC$1; 🕑 9am-5pm Mon-Fri, 9am-1pm Sat) is a former military barracks where Batista's troops surrendered to Che Guevara on January 1, 1959. Not easy to find, it's on a hilltop north of the center at the north end of Esquerra, just across the Río Bélico in Reparto Osvaldo Herrera.

#### FÁBRICA DE TABACOS CONSTANTINO PÉREZ CARRODEGUA

Santa Clara's **tobacco factory** (☎ 20 22 11; Calle Maceo No 181 btwn Julio Jover & Berenguer; admission CUC$3; 🕑 7am-noon, 1-4pm) is one of the best in Cuba and makes a quality range of Montecristos, Partagás and Romeo y Julieta cigars. Tours here are lower key than in Habana and, as a result, the experience is a lot more interesting and less rushed. Across the street you'll find **La Veguita** (☎ 20 89 52; 🕑 8:30am-5:30pm) the factory's diminutive sales outlet that is staffed by a friendly team of cigar experts. You can also buy cheap rum here and the bar out the back sells good coffee.

#### PARQUE VIDAL & AROUND

Named for Colonel Leoncio Vidal y Caro, who was killed here on March 23, 1896, **Parque Vidal** was encircled by twin sidewalks

## CHE COMANDANTE, AMIGO

Few 20th-century figures have successfully divided public opinion as deeply as Ernesto Guevara de la Serna better known to his friends (and enemies) as 'Che.' From enduring symbol of third-world freedom, to the celebrated hero of the Sierra Maestra, to the most wanted man on the CIA hit-list; the image of this handsome and often misunderstood Argentine physician turned *guerrillero* can still be seen all over Cuba, on everything from key rings to blow-up posters to chart-topping album covers. But what would the man himself have made of such rampant commercialization?

Born in Rosario, Argentina in June 1928 to a bourgeois family of Irish-Spanish descent, Guevara was a delicate and sickly child who developed asthma at the age of two. It was an early desire to overcome this debilitating illness that instilled in the young Ernesto a willpower that would dramatically set him apart from other men.

A pugnacious competitor in his youth, Ernesto earned the name 'Fuser' at school for combative reputation on the rugby field. Graduating from the University of Buenos Aires in 1953 with a medical degree, he shunned a conventional medical career in favor of a cross-continental motor-cycling odyssey accompanied by his old friend and colleague Alberto Granada. Their nomadic wanderings – well-documented in a series of posthumously published diaries – would open up Ernesto's eyes to the grinding poverty and stark political injustices that were all too common in 1950s Latin America.

By the time Guevara arrived in Guatemala in 1954 on the eve of a US-backed coup against Jacobo Arbenz's leftist government, he was enthusiastically devouring the works of Marx and nurturing a deep-rooted hatred of the United States.

Deported to Mexico for his pro-Arbenz activities in 1955, Guevara fell in with a group of Cubans that included Moncada veteran Raúl Castro. Impressed by the Argentine's sharp intellect and never-failing political convictions, Raúl – a longstanding Communist party member himself – determined to introduce Che to his charismatic brother, Fidel.

The meeting between the two men at Maria Antonia's house in Mexico City in June 1955 lasted 10 hours and ultimately changed the course of history. Rarely had two characters needed each other as much as the hot-headed Castro and the calmer and more ideologically polished Che. Both were favored children from large families who shunned the quiet life to fight courageously for a revolutionary cause. Similarly, both men had little to gain and much to throw away by abandoning professional careers for what most would have regarded as narrow-minded folly. 'In a revolution one either wins or dies,' wrote Guevara prophetically years later, 'if it is a *real* one.'

In December 1956 Che left for Cuba on the *Granma* yacht, joining the rebels as the group medic. One of only 12 of the original 82 rebel soldiers to survive the catastrophic landing at Las Coloradas he proved himself to be a brave and intrepid fighter who led by example and quickly won the trust of his less reckless Cuban comrades. As a result Castro rewarded him with the rank of Comandante in July 1957 and in December 1958 Che repaid Fidel's faith when he masterminded the battle of Santa Clara, an action that effectively sealed an historic revolutionary victory.

Guevara was granted Cuban citizenship in February 1959, and soon assumed a leading role in Cuba's economic reforms as president of the National Bank and Minister of Industry. His insatiable work ethic and regular appearance at enthusiastically organized volunteer worker weekends quickly saw him cast heroically as the living embodiment of Cuba's 'new man.'

But the honeymoon wasn't to last. Disappearing from the Cuban political scene in 1965 Guevara eventually materialized again in Bolivia in late 1966 at the head of a small band of Cuban *guerrilleros*. After the successful ambush of a Bolivian detachment in March 1967, he issued a call for 'two, three, many Vietnams in the Americas.' Such bold proclamations could only prove to be his undoing. On October 8, 1967, Guevara was captured by the Bolivian army, and after consultation with military leaders in La Paz and Washington DC, he was shot the next day in front of US advisors. His remains were eventually returned to Cuba in 1997 and reburied in Santa Clara.

during the colonial era, with a fence separating Blacks and Whites. Today it is one of Cuba's busiest and most vibrant parks with old men gossiping on the shaded benches and young kids getting pulled around in carriages led by goats. Since 1902, the municipal orchestra has played in the park bandstand at 8pm every Thursday and Sunday.

The city's most impressive building is the 1885 **Teatro La Caridad** (Máximo Gómez), one of Cuba's three signature theaters, with an imposing front facade and frescoes inside by Camilo Zalaya. Opera singer Enrico Caruso has performed here. The **Museo de Artes Decorativas** (☎ 20 53 68; Parque Vidal No 27; admission CUC$2; 🕒 9am-6pm Wed & Thu, 1-10pm Fri & Sat, 6-10pm Sun), just east of Teatro La Caridad, is an 18th-century building packed with period furniture and luxurious knick knacks donated by poet Dulce María Loynaz. The inner patio is a treat. On the eastern side of Parque Vidal is the neoclassical **Palacio Provincial** (1902–12), home today to the Martí library (with a rare book collection).

### CHURCHES

Uncharacteristically, the churches are scattered around the city rather than on or near the main square. South of the center is the colonial-style **Iglesia de la Santísima Madre del Buen Pastor** (EP Morales No 4 btwn Cuba & Villuendas).

On the way to the train station north of the center, is the **Iglesia de Nuestra Señora del Carmen** (Carolína Rodríguez); it was built in 1748, with a tower added in 1846. A large monument facing the church commemorates the foundation of Santa Clara in 1689 by 13 families from Remedios. The **Iglesia de Nuestra Señora del Buen Viaje** (cnr Pedro Estévez & Pardo) is an eclectic mix of Gothic, Romanesque and neoclassical architecture.

## Activities

The pulse beat of the city's progressive cultural life is at **La Casa de la Ciudad** (cnr Independencia & JB Zayas; admission CUC$1; 🕒 8am-5pm) northwest of Parque Vidal. If you want to see another side to Santa Clara aside from the obligatory Che memorabilia, get chatting to the young artists here. The historic building hosts Art Expositions (including an original Wilfredo Lam sketch), Noches del Danzón and a film museum; but the real buzz of this place is hanging out with the local culture vultures and finding out what makes this most unprepossessing of Cuban cities tick.

## Courses

Santa Clara boasts Cuba's second most prestigious university, **Universidad Central Marta Abreu de las Villas** (☎ 28 14 10; Carretera de Camajuaní Km 5.5). Non-Cubans can participate in two-, four-, six- and eight-week Spanish-language courses here for CUC$200/380/540/680 respectively. Courses include study materials and visits to local historical sites. To sign up visit the university's website (www.uclv.edu.cu) or inquire at the Foreign Language Department (caridada@sociales.uclvedu.cu).

**La Casa de la Ciudad** (cnr Independencia & JB Zayas) is another good learning center. You might be able to pick up dancing and percussion lessons here if you probe hard.

## Sleeping

### IN TOWN

**Hotel Santa Clara Libre** (Islazul; ☎ 20 75 48; fax 68 63 67; Parque Vidal No 6; s/d low season CUC$22/29, high CUC$27/36; ❄) You can't miss the tall, minty-green facade of this 168-room hotel right on the park. Hosting Cuban honeymooners and economic package tours, this is a decent, central choice. Nonguests can check out the pleasant restaurant on the 10th floor and the rooftop bar (good views on the 11th). The front of this hotel is still pocked with bullet holes from one of the last battles of the revolution.

### OUTSIDE TOWN

**Carrusel la Granjita** (Cubanacán; ☎ 21 81 90; www.cubanacan.cu; Carretera de Maleza Km 21.5; s/d low season CUC$38/50, high CUC$42/55; P ❄ 💻 🏊) The 75 thatched units of this motel, 6km northeast of town, are sprinkled among a scenic orange grove. If you don't mind being outside town, it's quiet and a decent value. Try to get a room well away from the (noisy) swimming pool area. The moderately priced restaurants (à la carte, buffet or grill) are good deals, there's a nightly show around the pool, a late-night disco, massage therapist and horseback riding.

**Motel Los Caneyes** (Cubanacán; ☎ 20 45 12; cnr Av de los Eucaliptos & Circunvalación de Santa Clara; s/d low season CUC$38/50, high CUC$42/55; P ❄ 🏊) Recently added to the Cubanacán stable, this motel (the same price as La Granjita) has 91 thatched bungalows built in 'pre-Columbian'

### CASAS PARTICULARES – SANTA CLARA

There's a cluster of casas on the short street of Bonifacio Martínez between Serafín García and the Carretera Central and also on nearby Maceo.

**Elida Ramírez Herrera & Sergio Proenza González** (☎ 21 59 14; Independencia No 266 btwn Pedro Estévez & M Gutierrez; r CUC$15-20) This friendly place has a room with three beds; there's a small patio.

**Ernesto & Mireya** (☎ 27 35 01; Cuba No 227 Altos btwn Pastora & EP Morales; r CUC$15-20; ) Nice spacious room, common balcony overlooks church; neighbor rents in Apartment 3.

**Héctor Martínez** (☎ 21 74 63; R Pardo No 8 btwn Maceo & Parque Vidal; r CUC$15-20; ) Terrific big room with dining area, kitchen and refrigerator; all new.

**Hostal Ana** (☎ 20 64 45; Serafín Garcías No 74 btwn Colón & Maceo; r CUC$20; P ) Two independent rooms with separate entry and communal terrace.

**Hostal Florida Center** (☎ 20 81 61; Maestra Nicolasa Este No 56 btwn Colón & Maceo; r CUC$20; ) Beautiful colonial house with airy rooms with refrigerator and TV, generous meals served in lush patio.

**Jorge García Rodríguez** (☎ 20 23 23; Cuba No 209 Apt No 1 btwn Serafín García & EP Morales; r CUC$15-20; ) Friendly place that rents two rooms; meals served.

**Luisa Costa Pérez** (☎ 29 41 67; Maceo Sur No 326 btwn Av 9 de Abril & Serafín García; r CUC$15-20; ) Run by a sweet couple; big meals.

**Martha Artiles Alemán** (☎ 20 50 08; Marta Abreu No 56 btwn Villuendas & Zayas; r CUC$15-20; ) Big, serviceable rooms.

**Omelio Moreno Lorenzo** (☎ 21 69 41; Eduardo Machado Este No 4 btwn Cuba & Colón; r CUC$20; ) English and French spoken.

**Orlando García Rodríguez** (☎ 20 67 61; R Pardo No 7 btwn Maceo & Parque Vidal; r incl breakfast CUC$15-20; ) Shared bathroom.

**Rolando Sacercio Díaz** (☎ 20 67 25; Maceo No 355A btwn Serafín García & EP Morales; r CUC$15-20) Simple, spotless room with three beds; English spoken.

**Vivian & José Rivero** (☎ 20 37 81; Maceo No 64 btwn Martí & Independencia; r CUC$20; ) Two rooms in lovely colonial house dating from 1908. Quiet terrace overlooks colorful inner garden.

**Yadin & José** (☎ 20 67 54; Bonifacio Martínez No 60 btwn EP Morales & General Roloff; r CUC$20; ) Also at No 18.

style, and updated for the package tourists who frequent it. It's well located 2km due west of the Monumento Che Guevara and has nice grounds, but is pricey for what you get. Hunting and fishing tours are offered from here and there's a Havanautos desk.

## Eating

**La Concha** (☎ 21 81 24; cnr Carretera Central & Danielito) The town's most famous restaurant is within spitting distance of the Che memorial. It's an unfussy place rightly renowned for its tasty pizza (CUC$4). Classy musicians often play here at lunchtimes.

**Paladar Bodeguita del Centro** (☎ 20 43 56; Villuendas Sur No 264 btwn 9 de Abril & Serafín García; dishes CUC$10; 1-5pm & 7-11pm Mon-Sat, 7-11pm Sun) Voluminous dishes on offer include red snapper. The dimly lit atmosphere and graffiti-covered walls here mimic Habana's Bodeguita although once seated you'll feel more like you're in someone's front room (you are!).

**El Castillo** (9 de Abril No 9 btwn Cuba & Villuendas; noon-11pm). This peso find cooks up quality meals of pork, chicken or liver with *congrí* (rice flecked with black beans), and salad for 35 pesos (CUC$1.35). The twist is that you eat standing at a counter flanked by marble pillars, stained glass and mosaic tiles.

**El Sabor Latino** (☎ 20 65 39; Esquerra No 157 btwn Julio Jover & Berenguer; noon-midnight). Santa Clara's most inviting paladar is a little off the beaten track but lulls clients into its well-maintained midst with its Rolling Stone's 'Glimmer Twins' logo. The menu offers complete pork or chicken meals with rice, salad, *tostones* (fried plantain patties) and bread for CUC$10 (or fish for CUC$12); you can eat here late.

**Palmares Café** (Marta Abreu No 10 btwn Villuendas & Cuba; 9am-11pm; ) For the best burger in town head to this congenial city-center classic where excellent snack food and great coffee is served in a perfectly air-conditioned microclimate. It will make you feel as if you're back in Habana. This place also has two computer terminals (CUC$5 per hour).

**BurgueCentro** (Parque Vidal No 31; 24hr) Cheap; the patio bar upstairs is a good drinking perch.

Stock up on peso ice cream at the architecturally hideous **Coppelia** (cnr Calle Colón & Mujica; 10:30am-midnight Tue-Sun) or head to **Cafetería Piropo** (cnr Lorda & Independencia; 10am-10pm). Across the street is – you guessed it – El Rápido.

Several peso bars and cafeterias are near the corner of Independencia Oeste and Zayas around Cine Cubanacán and your ever-faithful ice-cream man operates out of a window on Abreu.



### GROCERIES

**Mercado Sandino** (9 de Abril) Santa Clara's largest agropecuario (vegetable market) is on the western side of the Estadio Sandino.

**Mercado agropecuario** (Cuba No 269 btwn EP Morales & General Roloff) This market is small, but well stocked with produce. It's in the center of the city.

**Panadería Doña Neli** (cnr Maceo Sur & 9 de Abril; 7am-6pm) Sells fruit cakes and bread; the bar adjacent (open 9am to 10pm) has a smoky, local atmosphere and sells sandwiches for a few Convertibles.

## Drinking

**La Marquesina** ( 9am-1am) This lively bar in a corner of the Teatro La Caridad building is a winner. Bonus: chanteuse belting boleros to Casio keyboard accompaniment.

The brave can buy homemade fruit wine at the winemaker's door (at Morales No 10, between Cuba and Colón) for five (500mL) or eight (750mL) pesos; bring your own bottle.

Hard-drinking peso places:

**Casa del Gobernador** (cnr Independencia & JB Zayas; noon-11pm) Check out the live music on the colonial patio or duck into the dining room for a CUC$5 pork filet.

**Restaurante Colonial 1878** (Máximo Gómez btwn Marta Abreu & Independencia; noon-2pm & 7-10:30pm)

## Entertainment

**Club Mejunje** (Marta Abreu No 107; 4pm-1am Tue-Sun) The heart of Santa Clara's hip cultural scene, this bar and performance space is set among the ruins of an old building and will open your eyes to the city's vibrant and happening nightlife. There are regularly scheduled *trova* (verse), bolero and *son* (Cuba's popular music) concerts, children's theater and disco nights. You might even catch the occasional drag show.

**El Bar Club Boulevard** ( 21 62 36; Independencia No 2 btwn Maceo & Pedro Estévez; admission CUC$2; 9:30pm-2am Tue-Sun) Humor shows and live bands get this fun cocktail lounge laughing, dancing and swinging from 11pm.

**Casa de la Cultura Juan Marinello** ( 20 71 81; Parque Vidal No 5) Concerts and art exhibits in a colonial casa.

**Cine Camilo Cienfuegos** (Parque Vidal), below the Santa Clara Libre and **Cine Cubanacán** (Independencia Oeste No 60), show large screen films in English.

### SPORTS

The Estadio Sandino, east of the center via Av 9 de Abril, is the venue for baseball games from October to April. Villa Clara (La Villa) plays a central role in the history of Cuban baseball, but they're like the Boston Red Sox of Cuba: they have rabid fans and are super fun to watch, though victory has tended to elude them.

## Shopping

Independencia, between Maceo and Zayas, is the pedestrian shopping mall called the Boulevard. It's littered with Convertible stores and has good second-hand clothes and consignment shops.

**Fondo Cubano de Bienes Culturales** (Luis Estévez Norte No 9 btwn Parque Vidal & Independencia) Sells Cuban handicrafts.

For all your photographic needs try **Photo Service** (Independencia Oeste No 55 btwn Villuendas & Zayas) and **Photo Service** (Marta Abreu No 10 btwn Villuendas & Cuba).

## Getting There & Away

Santa Clara's Abel Santamaría Airport receives weekly flights from Montreal and Toronto. There is no connection to Habana.

### BUS

The **Terminal de Ómnibus Nacionales** ( 20 34 70) is 2.5km out on the Carretera Central toward Matanzas, 500m north of the Che monument. There are **Astro** ( 29 21 14) buses to Cienfuegos, Habana and Trinidad two- to three-times daily, plus one to Santiago on alternate days.

Tickets for air-conditioned Víazul buses are sold at a special ticket window for foreigners next to the station entrance. If it's closed, go to the 'Lista de Espera' window at the back of the station. Daily departures:

| Destination | Cost (one way) | Time |
|---|---|---|
| Habana | CUC$18 | 3:40am, 8:15am, 10:00pm |
| Trinidad | CUC$8 | 10:50am |
| Varadero | CUC$11 | 5:25pm |
| Santiago de Cuba | CUC$33 | 1:45am, 1:10pm, 6:45pm |

The Santiago de Cuba–bound bus also stops at Bayamo (CUC$26, nine hours 10 minutes), Camagüey (CUC$15, four hours 25 minutes), Ciego de Ávila (CUC$9, two hours 35 minutes), Holguín (CUC$26, seven hours 50 minutes), Las Tunas (CUC$22, six hours 35 minutes) and Sancti Spíritus (CUC$6, 1¼ hours).

The **intermunicipal bus station** (Carretera Central), west of the center via Marta Abreu, has daily buses to Remedios (CUC$1.45, 45km).

**TRAIN**

The **train station** (☎ 20 28 95) is straight up Luis Estévez from Parque Vidal on the north side of town. The **ticket office** (Luis Estévez Norte No 323) is across the park from the train station. In theory, there are daily trains to Cienfuegos (CUC$3, 2½ hours), Bayamo (CUC$22, 9½ hours), Camagüey (CUC$13, five hours 35 minutes) and Holguín (CUC$8, 10 hours); twice daily trains to Santiago (CUC$33, 12¼ hours); four nightly trains to Matanzas (CUC$8, 3½ hours) and Habana (CUC$14, five hours); and a train on alternate days to Sancti Spíritus (CUC$4, three hours) and Morón (CUC$5, three hours 40 minutes).

## Getting Around

You'll note from the manure stench that local transport is mostly horse and carriage (one peso). Bici-taxis (from the northwest of the park) cost CUC$1 a ride.

**CAR & MOPED**

Parque Vidal is closed to traffic (and cyclists must also dismount and walk their bikes).

Agencies renting wheels around the town:

**Cubatur** (☎ 20 89 80; Marta Abreu No 10; 9am-6pm) Rents mopeds.
**Havanautos** (☎ 20 58 95; Motel Los Caneyes)
**Micar** (☎ 20 45 70; cnr Carretera Central & Av 9 de Abril)
**Transtur** (☎ 20 81 77; Hotel Santa Clara Libre, Parque Vidal No 6)

The **Servi-Cupet gas station** (cnr Carretera Central & General Roloff) is south of the center. Just north is **Servicentro Oro Negro** (cnr Carretera Central & Av 9 de Abril).

**TAXI**

You can hire a car and driver from in front of the national bus station for trips to Remedios (CUC$8 one way) or Caibarién (CUC$10). A taxi to Habana will be about CUC$50 (negotiate hard). Drivers also hang around Parque Vidal or you can call **Cubataxi** (☎ 20 68 56).

# EMBALSE HANABANILLA

The Sierra del Escambray is the highest mountain range in central Cuba, with great hiking opportunities. Tucked into the foothills is the Embalse Hanabanilla, a 36-sq-km reservoir supplying Cuba's largest hydroelectric generating station. A tourist hotel stands on the northwestern shore and there's good fishing. Hanabanilla is a centrally located stopover between Cienfuegos, 58km to the west; Santa Clara, 80km to the north; or Trinidad, 58km to the south. Various hikes and boat trips can be organized here (see below).

**SIERRA SOLITUDE**

Access to the Escambray Mountains from Villa Clara Province is via the Embalse Hanabanilla, a huge manmade lake whose name in native language means 'cup of gold.' Among the walks and hikes that are available in this area are four little-known rustic gems. They're not often listed on any standard tourist itineraries; ask at the Hotel Hanabanilla for more information.

- **Un Reto de la Loma Atalaya** – a 17km hike with views of Santa Clara and Cienfuegos concluding at the 600m Cueva del Brollo
- **La Colicambiada** – a 6km hike with a visit to a *campesino's* house and swim in a nearby river; includes a boat transfer
- **Por La Ribera** – a 3km walk through forests and coffee plantations
- **La Monataña Por Dentro** – a trek to El Nicho in Cienfuegos Province

## Sleeping & Eating

**Campismo Río Seibabo** (Cubamar; ☎ 24 98 32; per person CUC$5) South of Güinía de Miranda near the border with Sancti Spíritus Province, Río Seibabo has 35 cabins. It welcomes non-Cubans. The lush rural grounds abut the Río Seibabo.

**Hotel Hanabanilla** (Islazul; ☎ 49 11 25; s/d low season CUC$18/24, high CUC$23/30; P ✲ ⛱) This four-story hotel has 125 rooms with fridges, balconies and lake views. The Bar Mirador on the top floor also has good vistas. It's a peaceful spot except on the weekends when it's packed with Cubans making merry. You can rent speedboats, horses or choose from half-a-dozen hikes (see p279).

## Getting There & Away

Theoretically there are buses from Manicaragua, but the only practical access is by car, bike or moped.

# REMEDIOS

**☎ 42 / pop 48,908**

Aaah, Remedios – where historic homes line cobblestone streets and you can lounge in the leafy central park with nary a hustler to hassle you. Certainly one of Cuba's prettiest towns, the laid-back, colonial air of Remedios shatters every December 24 when the citizens take sides and face off with floats, fireworks and dancing competitions in the legendary *Las Parrandas* (see below). Within easy reach of Santa Clara and Cayo Santa María, for many travelers this is best all-round base for exploring the province.

The energetic Vasco Porcallo de Figueroa was famous for founding San Juan de los Remedios in 1524. He is also reputed to have fathered more than 200 children. Locals will readily tell you that this is Cuba's eighth historic settlement after Diego Velázquez' magnificent seven and few neutral observers would dare to disagree. The town served as a regional center until Santa Clara was founded in 1689, and after a fire in 1692 its importance declined.

## Sights

The **Parroquia de San Juan Bautista de Remedios** (Camilo Cienfuegos No 20; 🕑 9am-11am Mon-Sat) on Parque Martí, is one of Cuba's finest churches. Though a church was founded here in 1545, this building dates from the late 18th century, the campanile was erected between 1848 and 1858 and its famous gilded high altar and mahogany ceiling are thanks to a restoration project (1944–46) financed by millionaire Eutimio Falla Bonet. The pregnant Inmaculada Concepción on the first side altar to the left of the entrance is said to be the only one of its kind in Cuba – the pearl teardrops are a nice touch. If the front doors are closed, go around to the rear or attend 7:30pm mass.

Also on Parque Martí, but lighter on the gold leaf, is the 18th-century **Iglesia de Nuestra Señora del Buen Viaje** (Alejandro del Río No 66). Between these churches is the **Museo de**

### LAS PARRANDAS

Conceived in the early 1800s in the colonial town of Remedios, *Las Parrandas* is a cacophonous mix of carnaval versus dancing competition versus explosive firework display gone haywire. There's even a bit of religious imagery thrown in for good measure.

Every year on December 24 the town divides into two teams based on various historical allegiances. Each team secretly builds an enormous float depicting anything from Simon Bolívar to a '60s pop culture icon. As the floats are hauled into the main square on Christmas Eve, the rum starts to flow and a huge singing and dancing extravaganza ensues with each team trying to outdo the other.

The festival climaxes around midnight with a deafening fireworks display, which quickly develops into a competition between rival neighborhoods – the prize going to the loudest, as opposed to the most spectacular, explosive devices. With the result duly announced, the victorious winners dance jubilantly through the streets with the not-so-disappointed losers coming in close behind. By morning – with hangovers setting in – the result is all but forgotten with frenzied firework fever giving way to seasonal goodwill.

Similar *Parrandas* displays can be seen in the towns of Caibarién and Placitas in Villa Clara Province, and Chambers and Punta Alleger in neighboring Ciego de Ávila.

**Música Alejandro García Caturla** (Parque Martí No 5; 9am-noon & 1-6pm Mon-Thu, 7-11pm Fri, 2pm-midnight Sat), commemorating García Caturla, a Cuban composer who lived here from 1920 until his murder in 1940. Look for occasional concerts and plays here.

Visiting the **Museo de las Parrandas Remedianas** (Máximo Gómez No 71; admission CUC$1; 9am-6pm), two blocks off Parque Martí, is the next best thing to partying here on December 24. The downstairs photo gallery recaps last year's fanfare, while the upstairs rooms show the intriguing history of this tradition, including scale models of floats and graphic depictions of how the fireworks are made. Another room is jammed with feathers, headdresses and tassels from the year previous.

The friendly staff and interesting exhibitions make the **Galería del Arte Carlos Enríquez** (Parque Martí No 2; admission free; 9am-noon & 1-5pm) worth a peek. A gifted painter hailing from Zulueta, Enriquez called his studio 'Hurón Azul', a name adopted by Uneac's cultural space (p133) and a tasty paladar (p127), both in Habana.

Fourteen kilometers south of Remedios on the nice country road to Placetas is **Zulueta**, *'la cuna del futbol'* (the birthplace of soccer). In the sleepy square there, you'll find Cuba's only monument to the sport – a big, mounted football. You might catch an afternoon match at the town's showpiece stadium. This is a good alternate route for (motor)cyclists between Santa Clara and Cayo Santa María.

## Sleeping

**Hotel Mascotte** (Cubanacán; ☎ 39 51 44; Parque Martí; r CUC$46) This beautiful colonial building dates from 1869 and is the only hotel in town. Run by the Cubanacán chain, the service here is friendly and the accommodation spacious, clean and carefully restored. The nicest of the 10 rooms are numbers one to five (they have balconies overlooking the main square).

## Eating

**Las Arcadas** (Parque Martí) The Mascotte's restaurant, serving standard meat and seafood fare, is the only game in town for a real meal outside of the casas particulares.

It's a case of 'nice location, shame about the food' as you check out the scant selection of eating places that ring Remedios' adorable Parque Martí.

### CASAS PARTICULARES – REMEDIOS

Tranquil Remedios has close to 20 casas to supplement its solitary hotel.

**Cecilio Acosta Herrera & Ania González Lozano** (☎ 39 56 24; José A Peña No 75C btwn Maceo & La Pastora; r CUC$20-25; ) Two attic rooms with negligible natural light share a bath.

**La China & Richard** (☎ 39 66 49; Maceo No 68 btwn Fe del Valle & Cupertino Garcia; r CUC$25; P ) Friendly young couple. Room has terrace and meals are available. Richard can give you the low down on local history.

**'Villa Colonial' – Frank & Arelys** (☎ 39 62 74; cnr Maceo No 43 & Ave General Carrillo; r CUC$20-25; ) Elegant house with high ceilings. Accommodation has separate entrance, lobby and sitting area. Nice young hosts, new on the scene.

**La Fé** (Máximo Gómez No 126) A peso place that serves the most meager of snacks opposite the Parroquia; don't miss the impressive stone counter snaking through the place.

**Driver's Bar** (Jose' A Peña No 61; 8am-10pm) Serves peso meals on one side and is a no-nonsense saloon on the other.

## Entertainment

**El Louvre** (Máximo Gómez No 122) On the south side of the square, this is a café that accepts Convertibles and has a great parkside location. Locals will tell you it's the oldest bar in the country in continuous service – since 1866. If you're looking for a room/paladar/taxi, park yourself here, have a drink and wait for the offers.

**Bar Juvenil** (Adel Rio No 47; 9pm-1am Sat & Sun) If you feel like dancing, head to this courtyard disco, near Máximo Gómez (enter via park), with palms, pillars and Moorish tiles. During the day there's table tennis and dominoes; despite the name, this peso place is alcohol-free, making it even more of a novelty than its colonial ambience.

Next door to El Louvre is **Las Leyendas**, an ARTex cultural center with music that opened in 2003. A block east of the park is the elegant old **Teatro Rubén M Villena** (Cienfuegos No 30) with dance performances, plays and Theater Guiñol for kids. The schedule is posted in the window and tickets are in pesos. Additional cultural activities can be found in the **Casa de Cultura Agustín J Crespo** (José A Peña No 67), opposite the Parroquia, **Uneac**

(Maceo No 25), and – in a city that invented *Las Parrandas* – outside in the parks and squares.

### Getting There & Away

The bus station is on the southern side of town at the beginning of the excellent 45km road to Santa Clara. Theoretically there is one daily bus to and from Santa Clara (one hour), twice daily service to Caibarién (20 minutes) and two departures Monday, Wednesday and Friday to Zulueta (30 minutes). Fares are CUC$2 or less.

A taxi from the bus station to Caibarién will cost CUC$3(ish) one way, and CUC$5 to Santa Clara if you bargain hard. A bici-taxi from the bus station to Parque Martí is two pesos.



## CAIBARIÉN

☎ 42 / pop 40,798

Caibarién, located on the coast 9km east of Remedios, is Villa Clara's main Atlantic port and has a large fishing fleet. It's a colorful little town, retaining a quaint, ramshackle feel despite the massive tourism development on nearby Cayo Santa María. Not worth a visit in its own right, Caibarién makes an alternative base for travelers who don't want to shell out the all-inclusive prices on the Cayos. Its December *Parrandas* are – allegedly – second only to Remedios in their explosiveness. **Havanatur** (☎ 35 11 71; Ave 9 btwn Calle 8 & 10) can arrange accommodation on Cayo Santa María. Cadeca and Banco Popular de Ahorro have outlets nearby.

### Sleeping & Eating

You can find a private room if you hang around the main square looking foreign.

**Virginia's Pension** (☎ 36 33 03; www.virginiaspension.com; Ciudad Pesquera No 73; r CUC$20-25; P ❄) Among the handful of legal places, this is the most popular; it's a reputable professional joint run by Virginia and Osmany Rodríguez.

There are a couple of passable places to eat including **Cafetería La Cubanita** (Calle 14 & Av 21) and the **Villa Blanca** (Av 9 cnr Calle 18), which serves up a local specialty known as Perro Soup. It's better than its name suggests. There's also an **agropecuario** (Calle 6) near the train station.

### Entertainment

**Piste de baile** (Calle 4; admission 2 pesos) Surprisingly, Caibarién has a hot, happening disco near the train station. It's known by a generic name (*piste de baile* means dance floor) and it jumps with hundreds of young locals on weekends.

### Getting There & Away

Four buses a day go to Remedios (CUC$1, 20 minutes), the 4:30am and 2pm departures go all the way to Santa Clara (CUC$2, 90 minutes) and three go to Yaguajay (CUC$1.50, 45 minutes) from Caibarién's old blue-and-white **bus & train station** (Calle 6)

#### CUBAN COFFEE

With their abundant tree cover and balmy year-round humidity, the Escambray Mountains provide ideal conditions for growing coffee; and it is here that some of Cuba's finest varieties are produced. Contrary to popular belief the plant is not indigenous to the island, unlike tobacco. In fact, it was only after the arrival of the French Cuba, following a bloody slave uprising in Haiti in 1791, that *cafétales* (coffee farms) established themselves as a parallel economy to sugar.

Since the onset of the *período especial* (special period) in 1991, coffee production has been coordinated by Raúl Castro through the much-lauded Turquino Program. Grown on small worker-organized cooperatives and incorporating integrated organic cultivation methods, Cuban coffee is picked by hand (often by volunteer soldiers and students) before being transported by mule back from the fields where it is left out to dry in the sun on large cement patios.

These days approximately 2% of Cuba's arable land is given over to coffee production with the industry supporting a workforce of 265,000 during the harvesting season.

In contrast to the standard Starbucks tipple, the Cubans love their coffee strong and sweet. Served espresso style and laced with excessive amounts of caffeine and sugar *café cubana,* as the local brew is known, has become the national drink of choice and the first thing a hospitable *campesino* will offer tired and thirsty visitors.

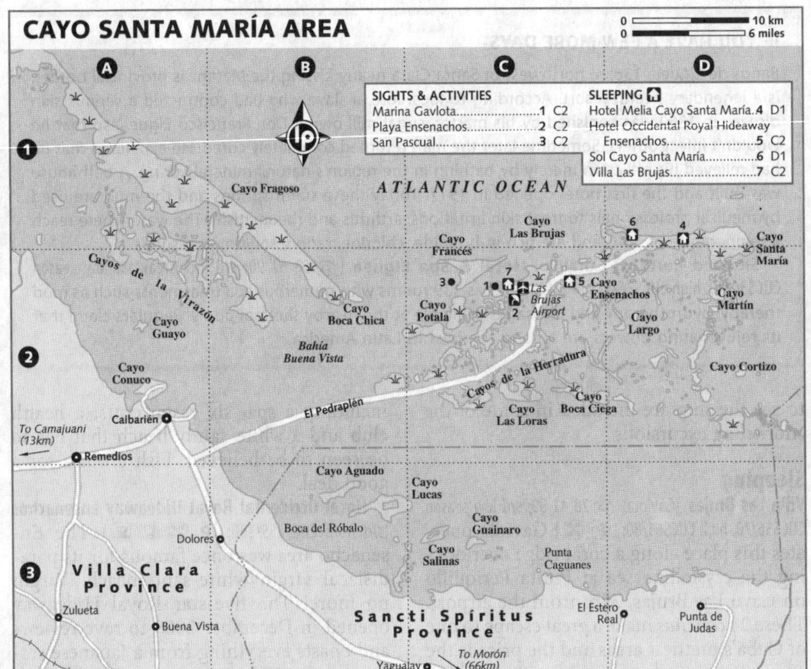


on the western side of town. There's also a daily phantom train to Santa Clara via Remedios (CUC$1.50, 90 minutes), leaving Caibarién in the morning and returning in the afternoon. The Servi-Cupet gas station is at the entrance to town from Remedios, behind the huge crab statue by Florencio Gelabert Pérez (1983).

## CAYERÍAS DEL NORTE

Coined the white rose of the Jardines del Rey, Cayo Santa María lies at the western end of the Archipiélago de Sabana-Camagüey, 25km west of Cayo Guillermo. Nestled peacefully on its leeward side are Cayo Ensenachos, Cayo Las Brujas and a smattering of smaller coral keys known communally as the Cayerías del Norte. Between 1989 and 1996, a massive 48km causeway called **El Pedraplén** was constructed across the Bahía Buena Vista from the fishing port of Caibarién at a cost of 100 million pesos. Included in the design were 45 bridges to allow an exchange of tidal waters, an improvement over the earlier Cayo Coco causeway that caused serious environmental damage. This is all part of a long-term plan to provide 10,000 hotel rooms in 28 resorts on these pristine keys. How this invasion will affect the region's 248 species of flora and thriving colonies of flamingos, seagulls and anhingas is anyone's guess.

### Sights & Activities

Most water-based activities can be arranged at **Marina Gaviota** (☎ 35 02 13), next to Villa Las Brujas. Highlights include a one-hour catamaran excursion with snorkeling (CUC$15), a half-day catamaran cruise (CUC$36), a sunset cruise (CUC$49), deep sea fishing (CUC$200, four people) and a two-hour Aqua bike excursion (CUC$60). You can also enjoy the secluded confines of nearby Las Salinas beach for a small fee (see Eating, p284).

One of the area's oldest curiosities is the wreck of the **San Pascual**, a San Diego tanker built in 1920 that got wrecked in 1933 on the opposite side of nearby Cayo Francés. Later the ship was used to store molasses, and later still it was opened up as a rather surreal hotel/restaurant (until 2004). Journeys out

**IF YOU HAVE A FEW MORE DAYS**

Baños de Elguea, 136km northwest of Santa Clara nearly kissing the Matanzas provincial border, is a legendary health resort. According to local lore, a slave who had contracted a serious skin disease in 1860 was banished by his master, sugar mill owner Don Francisco Elguea, so that he wouldn't infect others. Sometime later the man returned completely cured. He explained that he had relieved his affliction merely by bathing in the region's natural mineral spring. A bathhouse was built and the first hotel opened in 1917. Today these sulfur springs and the mud are used by medical professionals to treat skin irritations, arthritis and rheumatism. The waters here reach a temperature of 50°C and are rich in bromide, chlorine, radon, sodium and sulfur.

Situated north of Coralillo, **Hotel & Spa Elguea** (☎ 68 62 90; s/d incl breakfast low season CUC$30/40, high CUC$36/48; P) has 139 rooms with numerous spa treatments such as mud therapy, hydrotherapy and massages available at the nearby thermal pools. Regulars claim that its rejuvenating powers are among the best in Latin America.

to see the ship are included in some of the snorkeling excursions.

## Sleeping

**Villa Las Brujas** (Gaviota; ☎ 20 41 99; s/d low season CUC$56/70, high CUC$61/80; P) Gaviota operates this place along a coral ridge overlooking the crystalline sea at Punta Periquillo on Cayo Las Brujas, 3km from the airport. These 24 *cabañas* make a great escape to one of Cuba's prettiest areas and the price is the most economical on the keys. Integrating pleasantly into the surrounding mangroves, the detached buildings overlook the pristine (and uncrowded) white sands of Playa Las Salinas just beyond the resort.

**Sol Cayo Santa Maria** (☎ 35 15 00; r from low season from CUC$105, high CUC$152; P) The first of the fancy resorts to colonize the further-flung cayos, Sol Cayo Santa Maria is 8km on the main road beyond Las Brujas. It's a 300-room, four-star resort with all the amenities you would expect from a Sol Mélia enterprise. Scoop up a cheap online deal or book a room with Havanatur in Caibarién to avoid the exorbitant rack rates.

**Melia Cayo Santa Maria** (☎ 35 05 00; r low season from CUC$127, high CUC$161; P) The Sol's bigger and newer sister hotel was opened for business in December 2003 with five glittering stars. It has all of Sol's luxury amenities and a little more besides, including a spa, six restaurants, a health club and a white sandy beach that has to be seen to be believed. Fish around for a good deal.

**Hotel Occidental Royal Hideaway Ensenachos** (s/d from CUC$255/300; P) The Ensenacho area was once famous for its paradisiacal virgin white-sand beach. Virgin no more! The five-star Royal Hideaway opened in December 2005 to rave reviews and boasts everything from a Japanese restaurant to 506 luxury rooms. The beach it still here, of course, but now it's closed to all but the wristband-wearing guests.

## Eating

For nonhotel guests the best bet for a decent meal is in the Farallón restaurant perched like a bird's nest overlooking blissful Las Salinas beach. Access is via the Gaviota Villa Las Brujas. A snack lunch with use of beach, bathrooms and parking costs CUC$7. The coffee's good; the views even better.

## Getting There & Away

Day-trippers can easily zoom in from Caibarién (56km), Remedios (65km) or Santa Clara (110km) to dip their toes in Cayo Santa Maria's warm turquoise waters. The causeway is accessed from Caibarién and there's a toll booth (CUC$2 each way) 15km along. There is no public transport out here.

# Sancti Spíritus Province

With Unesco-nominated Trinidad anchored firmly in its midst and the still-to-be-discovered secrets of Sancti Spíritus town beckoning invitingly nearby, timeless Sancti Spíritus Province has history by the book-load. But it's not all stuffy museums and dusty antique furniture. High up in the crinkled Sierra del Escambray, fern-sprinkled forests and well-trodden nature trails call travelers with more lofty ambitions. You can enjoy hiking or go canyoning off the edge of a waterfall.

Linked historically to the sugar industry and characterized by the ruined mills and vivid patchwork fields of the somnolent Valle de los Ingenios (Valley of the Sugar Mills), Sancti Spíritus is one of Cuba's most compact and oft-visited regions with enough diversity to satisfy most travelers' tastes.

Quiet corners include the seaside village of La Boca, sparkling Embalse Zaza and the dreamy streets and squares of the underrated provincial capital, while those of a livelier inclination can enjoy the fine white sands of hotel-splayed Playa Ancón or the rum-swilling music houses of the *trova* (traditional poetic singing) capital – Trinidad.

Heading north, San José del Lago is a natural-springs resort, where thermal pools compete with massages and mud baths as soothing relaxants, while in the adjoining town of Yaguajay a fine municipal museum honors erstwhile revolutionary hero Camilo Cienfuegos. Hugging the swampy coast opposite the tranquil Bahía de Buenavista, Unesco's beautiful Buenavista Biosphere Reserve, is the least known and most underdeveloped of Cuba's half dozen or so protected natural areas.



## HIGHLIGHTS

- **The Authentic Trinidad**
  Peel off the layers in Cuba's colonial jewel (p292)
- **The Alternative to Trinidad**
  Wander unmolested through slow-moving Sancti Spíritus (p287)
- **Northern Exposure**
  Go exploring in the Buenavista Biosphere Reserve (p307)
- **Beach Break**
  Rent a house in La Boca and stroll the sands of Playa Ancón (p304)
- **Waterfall Wonder**
  Take a hike to the Salto del Caburní (p304)

| ■ TELEPHONE CODE: 41 | ■ POPULATION: 463,258 | ■ AREA: 6744 SQ KM |
|---|---|---|

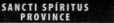

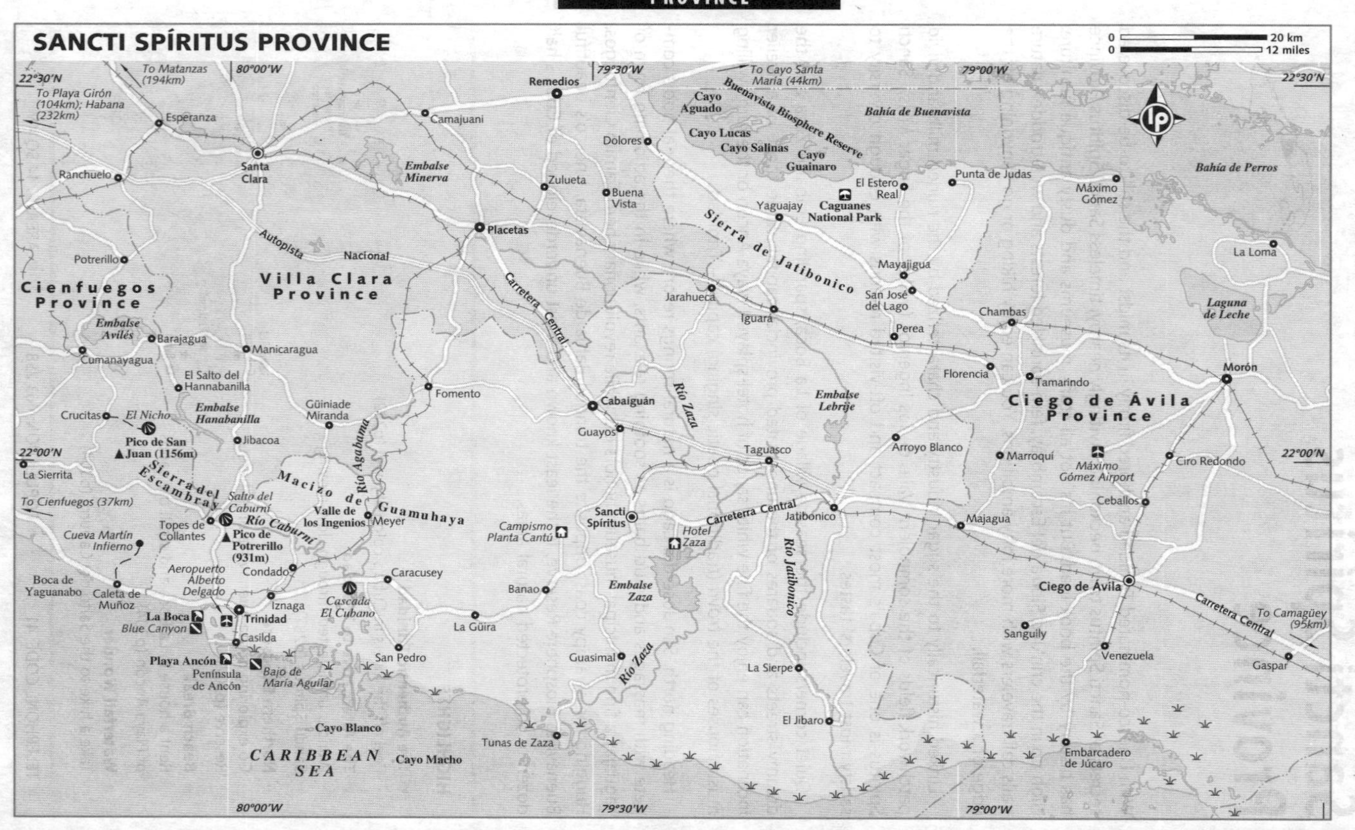
SANCTI SPÍRITUS PROVINCE
0 20 km
0 12 miles
22°30'N
22°00'N
80°00'W
79°30'W
79°00'W
To Matanzas (194km)
To Playa Girón (104km); Habana (232km)
To Cayo Santa María (44km)
To Camagüey (95km)
To Cienfuegos (37km)
Esperanza
Ranchuelo
Santa Clara
Camajuani
Remedios
Embalse Minerva
Zulueta
Buena Vista
Dolores
Cayo Aguado
Buenavista Biosphere Reserve
Bahía de Buenavista
Cayo Lucas
Cayo Salinas
Cayo Guainaro
El Estero Real
Punta de Judas
Máximo Gómez
Bahía de Perros
Yaguajay
Caguanes National Park
Sierra de Jatibonico
Placetas
Autopista Nacional
Potrerillo
Villa Clara Province
Cienfuegos Province
La Loma
Mayajigua
San José del Lago
Jarahueca
Iguará
Chambas
Laguna de Leche
Perea
Carretera Central
Embalse Avilés
Barajagua
Manicaragua
Cumanayagua
El Salto del Hannabanilla
Florencia
Tamarindo
Morón
Fomento
Embalse Hanabanilla
Güiniade Miranda
Cabaiguán
Río Zaza
Embalse Lebrije
Ciego de Ávila Province
Crucitas
El Nicho
Pico de San Juan (1156m)
Jibacoa
Río Agabama
Guayos
Taguasco
Arroyo Blanco
Marroquí
Máximo Gómez Airport
Ciro Redondo
La Sierrita
Sierra del Escambray
Macizo de Guamuhaya
Salto del Caburní
Río Caburní
Valle de los Ingenios
Meyer
Sancti Spíritus
Carreterra Central
Jatibonico
Ceballos
Majagua
Topes de Collantes
Pico de Potrerillo (931m)
Campismo Planta Cantú
Hotel Zaza
Río Jatibonico
Cueva Martín Infierno
Aeropuerto Alberto Delgado
Condado
Caracusey
Boca de Yaguanabo
Caleta de Muñoz
Embalse Zaza
Banao
Ciego de Ávila
La Boca
Blue Canyon
Trinidad
Iznaga
Cascada El Cubano
La Güira
Sanguily
Casilda
San Pedro
Guasimal
Venezuela
Gaspar
Playa Ancón
Península de Ancón
Bajo de María Aguilar
La Sierpe
El Jíbaro
Cayo Blanco
Tunas de Zaza
Embarcadero de Júcaro
CARIBBEAN SEA
Cayo Macho

## SANCTI SPÍRITUS

☎ 41 / pop 105,815

For first-time visitors, unassuming Sancti Spíritus often seems like a larger and slightly less frenetic version of Trinidad. Antique Buicks limp asthmatically down cobbled city streets; bevies of enthusiastic school children practice stickball in languid Parque Serafín Sánchez; a plaintive and lilting bolero (a romantic love song) briefly interrupts the sleepy tranquility of Av Jesús Menéndez.

Founded in 1514 as one of Diego Velázquez' seven original 'villas', Sancti Spíritus was moved to its present site on the Río Yayabo in 1522. But the relocation didn't stop audacious corsairs, who continued to loot the town until well into the 1660s.

Lacking the historical importance of Trinidad or the pulsating cultural buzz of Santa Clara, Sancti Spíritus has developed into something of a transit town for travelers heading west or east. But a day or two's layover needn't be wasted. As well as possessing a thoroughly charming city center, Sancti Spíritus is also famous for the dapper *guayabera* shirt and the *guayaba* (guava) fruit, a crop that is still grown along the banks of the Río Yayabo, from which it derives its name.

### Orientation

The bus and train stations are on opposite sides of town. Of the two, the train station is more convenient. It's an easy five-minute walk to the old Puente Yayabo and then another five minutes to Parque Serafín Sánchez in the heart of the town. The bus station is a couple of kilometers east of the center on the Carretera Central (called Bartolomé Masó as it passes through Sancti Spíritus).

### Information

#### BOOKSHOPS

**Librería Julio Antonio Mella** (☎ 2-7416; Independencia Sur No 29; 🕑 8am-5pm Mon-Sat) Near the post office. There's also a good used bookshop nearby at No 25.

#### INTERNET ACCESS

**Etecsa** (M Solano; per hr CUC$6; 🕑 8am-10pm) Kiosk in front of Cine Serafín Sánchez, with phones and one computer (when it works).

#### LIBRARIES

**Biblioteca Provincial Rubén Martínez Villena** (☎ 2-7717; Máximo Gómez Norte No 1) On Parque Serafín Sánchez.

#### MEDIA

**Radio Sancti Spíritus** CMHT Airing on 1200AM and 97.3FM.

#### MEDICAL SERVICES

**Farmacia Especial** (☎ 2-4660; Independencia Norte No 123; 🕑 24hr) Pharmacy on Parque Maceo.

**Hospital Provincial Camilo Cienfuegos** (☎ 2-4017; Bartolomé Masó s/n) Five hundred meters north of Plaza de la Revolución.

**Policlínico Los Olivos** (☎ 2-6362; Circunvalación Olivos No 1) Near the bus station. Will treat foreigners in an emergency.

#### MONEY

**Banco Financiero Internacional** (☎ 2-7578; Independencia Sur No 2) On Parque Serafín Sánchez.

**Cadeca** (☎ 2-8536; Independencia Sur No 31; 🕑 8am-6pm Mon-Sat, 8am-noon Sun) Lose your youth in this line.

#### POST

**Post Office** (🕑 9am-6pm Mon-Sat) There are two branches: one at Independencia Sur No 8; the other at the Etecsa building, Bartolomé Masó No 167.

#### TELEPHONE

**Etecsa** (🕑 8am-10pm) There are two branches: one at M Solano, in front of Cine Serafín Sánchez; the other opposite Hospital Provincial Camilo Cienfuegos on Bartolomé Masó No 167.

#### TRAVEL AGENCIES

**Campismo Popular** (☎ 2-5401; Independencia Norte No 201) Off Parque Maceo.

**Cubatur** (☎ 2-8518; Máximo Gómez Norte No 7; 🕑 9am-5pm Mon-Sat) On Parque Serafín Sánchez.

**Havantur** (Padre Quintero No 60) Offices in Quinta Santa Elena restaurant (p290).

### Sights

The city's most famous sight is the **Puente Yayabo**, a quadruple-arched brick bridge built by the Spanish in 1815, now a national monument. The structure looks more English than Cuban, especially when glimpsed on the ubiquitous postcards. The **Teatro Principal** alongside the bridge dates from 1876, and the old cobbled streets radiating downhill were restored in the late 1980s. Tucked back here, old ladies peddle live chickens, neighbors gossip in front of their coral or lemon-yellow houses and provincial city life thrums along undisturbed by tourism.

Make a quick detour up **Calle Llano**, a quintessential local street with cobblestones,

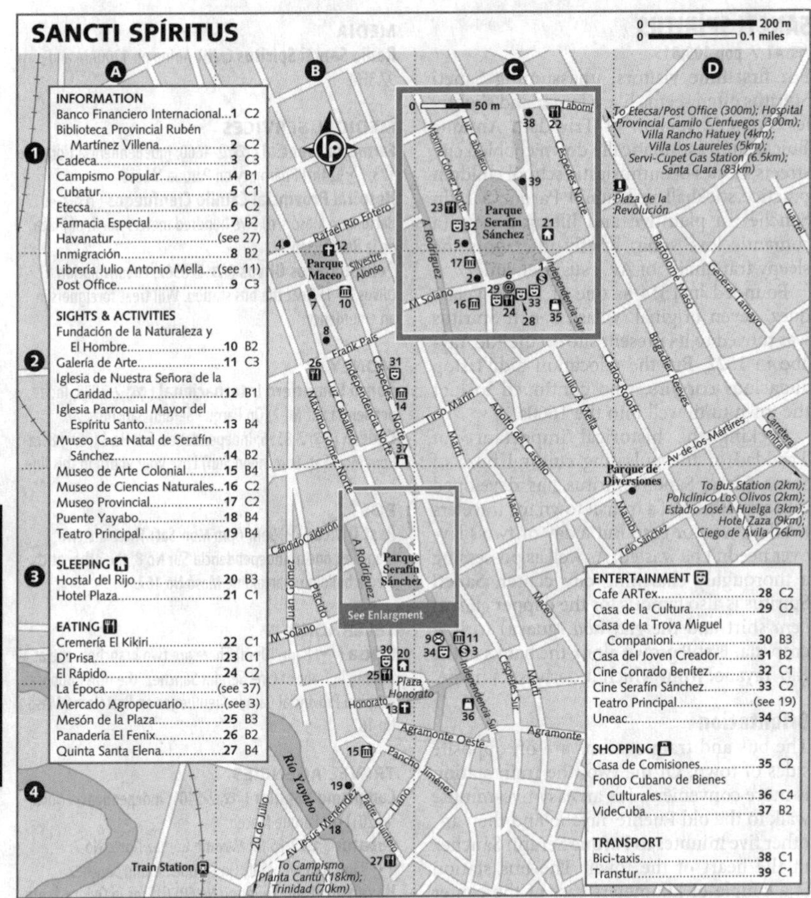


wrought-iron balconies and wooden beams more reminiscent of Trinidad.

Turning left on Pancho Jiménez you come to the **Museo de Arte Colonial** (☎ 2-5455; Plácido Sur No 74; admission CUC$2; ⏲ 9am-5pm Tue-Sat, 8am-noon Sun), with 19th-century furniture and decorations displayed in an imposing 17th-century building that once belonged to the stinking-rich Valle-Iznaga family. Curve up this same way and you come to the charming yellow **Iglesia Parroquial Mayor del Espíritu Santo** (Agramonte Oeste No 58; ⏲ 9-11am & 2-5pm Tue-Sat) on Plaza Honorato. Originally constructed of wood in 1522 and rebuilt in stone in 1680, it's said to be the oldest church in Cuba still standing on its original foundations (although the clock seems to have given out in recent years). There's a splendid ceiling inside, but this church is often closed; try entering for mass (5pm daily and 9am Sunday).

The most interesting museum in town is the small collection at the **Fundación de la Naturaleza y El Hombre** (☎ 2-8342; Cruz Pérez No 1; admission CUC$1; ⏲ 10am-5pm Mon-Fri, 10am-noon Sat) on Parque Maceo. Here you'll learn the fascinating tale of the 17,422km canoe odyssey 'from the Amazon to the Caribbean' in 1987 led by Cuban writer and Renaissance man Antonio Nuñez Jiménez (1923–98). Some 432 expeditionaries made the journey through 10 countries, from Ecuador to the Bahamas, in the twin dugout canoes Simón Bolívar and Hatuey. The latter measures over 13m and is the collection's central, prized piece. Across from the Fundación is the handsome old **Iglesia de Nuestra Señora de la Caridad** (Céspedes Norte No 207), with sparrows nesting above the altar.

Four blocks south is pretty **Parque Serafín Sánchez** with hundreds of metal chairs hosting cigar-smoking grandpas and flirty young couples. Your eye will first be drawn to an imposing theaterlike building on the southwest corner that was built in 1929 by the Progress Society and today serves as the **Biblioteca Provincial Ruebén Martínez Villena.** Sport and coin fans might like the **Museo Provincial** (Máximo Gómez Norte No 3; admission CUC$1; 9am-6pm Mon-Thu, 9am-6pm & 8-10pm Sat, 8am-noon Sun) on Parque Serafín Sánchez, with its dedicated numismatic and athletic collections. Nearby, the **Museo de Ciencias Naturales** (2-6365; Máximo Gómez Sur No 2; admission CUC$1; 8:30am-5pm Tue-Fri, 8-10pm Sat, 8:30am-noon Sun), off Parque Serafín Sánchez, has stuffed animals, shiny rocks and a small planetarium. A few blocks north of the park is the **Museo Casa Natal de Serafín Sánchez** (Céspedes Norte No 112; admission CUC$0.50; 8am-5pm). Serafín Sánchez was a local patriot who participated in both wars of independence and went down fighting in November 1896.

The **Galería de Arte** (Céspedes Sur No 26; admission free; 8am-noon & 2-5pm Tue-Sat, 8am-noon Sun) next to the agropecuario (vegetable market), houses 86 works by local painter Oscar Fernández Morera (1890–1946).

## Sleeping

### IN TOWN

Both of Sancti Spíritus' city-center hotels are set in attractive restored colonial buildings and are worth a visit in their own right.

**Hostal del Rijo** (Cubanacán; 2-8588; Calle Honorato No 12; r CUC$46; ) This new hotel is in a beautifully restored 1818 mansion. Located on Plaza Honorato, each of the 16 plush, clean rooms are different. Rooms Nos 5, 6, 7 and 9 have balconies with plaza views and one room has disabled access. The teeny rooftop pool is more like a puddle, but the city views are unbeatable. This place fills fast; if you can't get a room, head to the rooftop bar for a sunset cocktail.

**Hotel Plaza** (2-7102; Independencia Norte No 1; r CUC$46; ) This is a two-story place has 28 rooms, a mirador and a great parkside location. Formerly an Islazul joint, the Plaza was recently taken over by Cubanacán who have been busy elevating it to match the standards of the Rijo. Huge rooms are well-equipped with TVs and air-con, and the tiled communal areas are characterized by eye-catching hanging wicker chairs. It makes a good second choice if the Rijo's full.

See the boxed text, p290 for casa particular recommendations.

### NORTH OF TOWN

There are two agreeable hotels along the Carretera Central as you head north; either one makes a good choice if you don't want to bother with the city center.

**Villa Los Laureles** (Islazul; 2-7345; Carretera Central Km 383; s/d low season CUC$26/34, high season CUC $30/38; P ) This lively attractive motel 5km north of town is popular with Cubans. There are 70 rooms, split between a classic motel block and separate cabins. The big, bright rooms have fridge, satellite TV and hot water, plus a patio/balcony. The in-house Cabaret Tropi has a nightly 9pm show.

**Villa Rancho Hatuey** (2-8315/16/17; Carretera Central Km 384; s/d low season CUC$37/50, high season CUC$37/55; P ) This modern Islazul complex is accessible from the southbound lane of the Carretera Central, 4km north of town. The 76 rooms, spread out on landscaped grounds, are popular with government officials and party leaders (you'll know them by their plaid shirts and jeans). People on bus tours are also accommodated here, where all the services you would expect in a midrange hotel are available.

### EAST OF TOWN

**Hotel Zaza** (Islazul; 2-8512; s/d with breakfast CUC$27/36; P ) Overlooking Embalse Zaza, most tour groups overnight at this hotel. The 128 rooms are scruffy around the edges, but those numbered in the 400s have nice reservoir views. The swimming pool (CUC$3 for nonguests) is refreshing on a hot day and the entertainment – with music loud enough to hear underwater – is a gas. In early September, the Copa Internacional de Pesca de Black Bass (a fishing tournament) is held here and you can organize fishing and boat trips at any time from the upstairs office. The staff are helpful and friendly. Go east 5km on the Carretera Central toward Ciego de Ávila, then south 5km to the lake.

### SOUTHWEST OF TOWN

**Campismo Planta Cantú** (Cubamar; 2-9698; cabin CUC$30; P ) A Cubamar campismo that

**CASAS PARTICULARES – SANCTI SPÍRITUS**

There are approximately 20 casas to choose from in Sancti Spíritus. Look for the green triangle.

**Daymila Díaz Rodríguez** (☎ 2-7553; Martí No 111 btwn Sobral & San Cristóbal; r CUC$20-25; P ✱) Central colonial house with pleasant hosts.

**Hostal Ana Neira Fabrega** (☎ 2-7674; Luz Caballero No 9 btwn Tirso Marín & Parque Serafín Sánchez; r CUC$20-25)

**'Los Richards' – Ricardo Rodríguez** (☎ 2-3029; Independencia Norte No 28 Altos; r CUC$20-25; ✱) Taxi driver. Central, somewhat worn, balcony, distant views.

**Martha Rodríguez Martínez** (☎ 2-3556; Plácido No 69 btwn Calderón & Tirso Marín; r CUC$20-25; ✱) Three rooms (two with air-con, one with fan), meals, rooftop terrace.



welcomes non-Cubans, Planta Cantú is a little off the beaten track, so you'll need a car to get to this place near Banao. The cute cabins below the foothills sleep four and are especially good value for groups as you pay one price for the whole unit. Horses can be hired (CUC$3 per hour). The real draw here, though, is the revitalizing waterfalls of the crystal-clear Río Cayajaná. To reach them, take the left fork before the entrance and go until the road ends (about 1km). A worn path leads to the falls and swimming holes. There is a good, level camping spot here. To get to the campismo, go 16km southwest of Sancti Spíritus on the road to Trinidad, turn inland at the sign and go 6km further.

## Eating

You'll burn vital calories searching for decent food in Sancti Spíritus. Rest assured, there are only two appetizing sit-down restaurants outside the Cubanacán hotels; plus the ubiquitous – and often life-saving – **El Rápido** (Parque Serafín Sánchez; ⏰ 9am-11pm) snack bar.

**Quinta Santa Elena** (☎ 2-8167; Padre Quintero No 60; dishes CUC$4-8; ⏰ 10am-midnight) This choice riverside patio with bridge views, live music at lunchtime and fair prices is a winning combination. Good portions of shrimp in red sauce or *ropa vieja* (shredded beef) make the Quinta the best choice in town. There's a salad selection for vegetarians.

**Mesón de la Plaza** (☎ 2-8546; Máximo Gómez Sur No 34; ⏰ noon-2:30pm & 6-10pm) Facing Plaza Honorato with nice church views, this Palmares-run restaurant is in a 19th-century mansion that once belonged to a rich Spanish tycoon. It is routinely recommended by locals and has a clean and inviting decor.

**Restaurant Hostal del Rijo** (Cubanacán; ☎ 2-8588; Calle Honorato No 12) Serves traditional Cuban fare and can rustle up a good spaghetti Bolognese either outside or in the confines of a lovely secluded patio.

**Las Arcadas** (☎ 2-7102; Independencia Norte No 1) Based at Hotel Plaza, Las Arcadas is another *comida criolla* (Creole food) option and the bar here serves good coffee.

**D'Prisa** (⏰ 10am-10pm) This Islazul-run place is on the west side of Parque Serafín Sánchez and sells cold beer and snacks (CUC$1 to CUC$2).

There are also a few street stalls knocking out peso pizza along Av de los Mártires beside Parque de Diversiones. Stand around long enough in Parque Serafín Sánchez and the ice-cream man will turn up with his Mr Whippy-style ice cream–maker or you can trek a block or two north to **Cremería El Kikiri** (Independencia Norte & Laborni) for an instant fix.

Self-catering choices:

**Mercado agropecuario** (cnr Independencia Sur & Honorato) A couple of blocks from Parque Serafín Sánchez on the corner of Valdés Muñoz.

**Panadería El Fenix** (cnr Máximo Gomez Norte & Frank País; ⏰ 6am-6pm) Sells fresh bread daily.

**La Época** (Independencia Norte No 50C) Good for groceries.

## Entertainment

**Casa de la Cultura** (☎ 2-3772; M Solano No 11) This place, diagonally opposite the library on Parque Serafín Sánchez, hosts various musical events.

**Uneac** (Unión Nacional de Escritores y Artistas de Cuba, National Union of Cuban Writers and Artists; ☎ 2-6375; Independencia Sur No 10) Cultural events also occur at this venue, near the post office, which shows movies.

**Casa del Joven Creador** (Céspedes Norte No 118) Go to this place, near the Museo Casa Natal de Serafín Sánchez, for rock and rap concerts.

**Casa de la Trova Miguel Companioni** (☎ 2-6802; Máximo Gómez Sur No 26) For folk music, head to this venue off Plaza Honorato.

**Cafe ARTex** (M Solano; admission CUC$1; ⏰ 10pm-2am Tue-Sun) It has dancing, live music and karaoke nightly and a Sunday matinee at 2pm (admission CUC$3). Thursday is *reggaeton* (Cuban hip-hop) night and the café also hosts comedy. Good groups to look out for in Sancti Spíritus are the Septeto Espirituanao and the Septeto de Son del Yayabo.

**Estadio José A Huelga** (Circunvalación) From October to April, baseball games are held at this stadium, 1km north of the bus station.

**Teatro Principal** (☎ 2-5755; Av Jesús Menéndez No 102) Has weekend matinees (at 10am) with kids' theater.

The city's two main cinemas are **Cine Conrado Benítez** (☎ 2-5327; Máximo Gómez Norte No 13) and **Cine Serafín Sánchez** (☎ 2-3839; M Solano No 7), both on Parque Serafín Sánchez.

## Shopping

Anything you might need – from batteries to frying pans – is sold in street stalls along the pedestrian mall on Independencia Sur which recently got a bit of a facelift.

**Casa de Comisiones** (Independencia Sur No 6; 9am-4pm) This combination pawn shop–flea market is a riot of Brownie cameras, rhinestone tiaras and vintage jewelry, watches, purses and furniture.

**Fondo Cubano de Bienes Culturales** (☎ 2-7106; Independencia Sur No 55) This place has Cuban crafts and paintings.

**VideCuba** (Independencia Norte No 50; 9am-9pm) Reload your camera film or replace those well-worn batteries here.

## Getting There & Away

### BUS

The provincial **bus station** (☎ 2-4142; Carretera Central) is 2km east of town. Astro serves Camagüey (CUC$7) and Ciego de Ávila (CUC$3) on alternate days, and Habana (CUC$16) and Santiago (CUC$20) daily.

With deluxe **Víazul** (☎ 2-4142; www.viazul.com) buses, you can choose from the following:

| Destination | Cost (one way) | Departure |
|---|---|---|
| Habana | CUC$23 | 2:20am, 6:55am, 8:40pm |
| Santiago de Cuba | CUC$28 | 3:10am, 3:15pm, 8:50pm |
| Trinidad | CUC$6 | 5:35am |

The Santiago de Cuba departure also stops in Ciego de Ávila (CUC$6, 76km), Camagüey (CUC$10, 184km), Las Tunas (CUC$17, 312km), Holguín (CUC$21, 393km) and Bayamo (CUC$21, 464km). The Habana bus stops at Santa Clara (CUC$6, 83km).

### TRAIN

Train travel is tricky out of Sancti Spíritus. Luckily, the **train station** (☎ 2-4790; Av Jesús Menéndez final; ticket window 7am-2pm Mon-Sat), southwest of the Puente Yayabo, is an easy 10-minute walk from town so you can check schedules and status. The only departures from Sancti Spíritus proper are to Habana (CUC$14, eight hours, 376km, 9pm alternate days), stopping in Santa Clara (CUC$4, two hours, 83km), and to Cienfuegos (CUC$5.50, five hours, 164km, 4am Monday).

Points east are served out of Guayos, 15km north of Sancti Spíritus, including Holguín (CUC$14, 8½ hours, 9.30am), Bayamo (CUC$13, 8¼ hours, 394km) and Santiago de Cuba (CUC$21, 10¼ hours, 8.45am). If you're on the Habana–Santiago de Cuba cross-country express and going to Sancti Spíritus or Trinidad, you have to get off at Guayos.

The ticket office at the Sancti Spíritus train station can sell you tickets for the trains from Guayos, but you must find your own way there (CUC$8 to CUC$10 in a taxi but bargain hard).

### TRUCKS & TAXIS

Trucks to Trinidad, Jatibonico and elsewhere depart from the bus station. Colectivos (collective taxis) parked outside the station will take you to Trinidad for approximately CUC$16 for the whole car, but it's technically illegal for foreigners to take them.

## Getting Around

Horse carts on the Carretera Central, opposite the bus station, run to the Parque Serafín Sánchez when full (one peso). Bicitaxis gather at the corner of Laborni and Céspedes Norte. There is a Transtur booth on the northeast corner of Parque Serafín Sánchez; prices for daily car hire start at around CUC$60. The **Servi-Cupet** (Carretera Central) gas station is 1.5km north of Villa Los Laureles, on the Carretera Central toward Santa Clara. Parking in Parque Serafín Sánchez is relatively safe. Ask in hotels Rijo and Plaza and they will often find a man to stand guard overnight for CUC$1.

**DAY-TRIPPER**

In a province famous for its lush mountains and archetypal colonial architecture, fishing in a lake might seem like a bit of a cop-out. But – as subscribers to *Angling Weekly* may or may not be aware – Sancti Spíritus is home to the biggest artificial lake in Cuba.

Nearly 50% of expansive **Embalse Zaza** is given over to sports fishing and abundant stocks of largemouth black bass (weighing up to 8kg) attract anglers from around the globe. Fishing excursions can be arranged at the super-friendly **Hotel Zaza** (p289) for as little as CUC$30 for four hours, or CUC$70 for a full-day excursion to the equally voluminous **Río Agabama** on the Trinidad–Sancti Spíritus road.

If hooking a line ain't your cup of tea, don't fret. The unique ambience of the lake can be soaked up on a one-hour boat cruise from CUC$20 for two people.



# TRINIDAD

☎ 419 / pop 52,896

Quaint, compact and easy to get to know, Trinidad lives up to all of the tourist brochure hype. Declared a World Heritage site in 1988 along with the Valle de los Ingenios, Cuba's oldest and most enchanting 'outdoor museum' is one of the few tourist sites on the island where locals and foreigners can mix in a way that is both relaxed and unguarded. And with more than 300 casas particulares and only three decent city-center hotels, cross-cultural interaction is positively encouraged, creating a kind of Varadero in reverse.

Bumping and stumbling over the cobblestone streets as you enter town you'll quickly see what all the fuss is about. Trinidad's beautifully restored houses and cool, tiled, colonial courtyards combine perfectly with a stupendous natural setting – wedged spectacularly between the Sierra del Escambray and the Caribbean – to create a scene of unrivalled ambience.

There are more museums per head here than any other part of Cuba and with craning mountains and palm-fringed beaches, both within spitting distance, the setting is hard to beat. Added to this Trinidad has a degree of authenticity and intimacy that many other colonial cities lack. Faux theme park this most certainly is not. True to its socialist roots, the city crams carefully restored Unesco buildings amicably in among the ration shops and agropecuarios (vegetable markets). Relaxing contentedly under the colonial eaves, meanwhile, old women in rocking chairs and chirping caged canaries mark the passage of time as they have done for centuries.

With its Unesco price-tag and a steady stream of day-trippers bussed in from Habana and Varadero, hustlers are in the ascendancy here, and many a traveler has been ground down and worn out by the constant unwanted attention. If you feel besieged, you might want to settle for a friendly casa particular in the small towns of La Boca or Casilda, just a quick 4km or 6km jaunt respectively from Trinidad. Alternatively, consider an accommodation option that's just outside the mayhem of the historic center.

## History

In 1514 pioneering conquistador Diego Velázquez de Cuéllar, founded La Villa de la Santísima Trinidad on Cuba's south coast, the island's third settlement after Baracoa and Bayamo. Legend has it that erstwhile 'Apostle of the Indians' Fray Bartolomé de las Casas held Trinidad's first mass under a Calabash tree in present-day Plazuela Real del Jigüe. In 1518 Velázquez' former secretary, Hernán Cortéz, passed through the town recruiting mercenaries for his all-conquering expedition to Mexico and the settlement was all but emptied of its original inhabitants. Over the ensuing 60 years it was left to a smattering of local Taíno Indians to keep the ailing economy alive through a mixture of farming, cattle rearing and a little outside trade.

Reduced to a small rural backwater by the 17th century and cut off from the colonial authorities in Habana by dire communications, Trinidad became a haven for pirates and smugglers who controlled a lucrative contraband slave trade with British-controlled Jamaica.

Things began to change in the early 19th century when the town became the capital of the Departamento Central and hundreds of French refugees fleeing a slave rebellion in Haiti arrived, setting up more than 50 small sugar mills in the nearby Valle de los Ingenios. Sugar soon replaced leather and salted beef as the region's most important product and by the mid-19th century the area around Trinidad was producing a third of Cuba's sugar, generating enough wealth to finance the rich cluster of opulent buildings that characterize the town today.

The boom ended rather abruptly during the two wars of independence, when the surrounding sugar plantations were devastated by fire and fighting. Floundering in the years that followed, the industry never fully recovered. By the late 19th century, the focus of the sugar trade had shifted to Cienfuegos and Matanzas Provinces and Trinidad, cut off by the Sierra del Escambray from the other parts of Cuba, slipped into a somnolent and life-threatening economic coma.

## Orientation

Trinidad turns on two hubs. The museums and churches of the *casco histórico* (old town) are focused around the Plaza Mayor, while the everyday facilities serving the local people are on, or near, Parque Céspedes. The bus station is west of Plaza Mayor.

### TRINIDAD STREET NAMES

Locals stick to the old street names; this chart should help:

| Old name | New name |
|---|---|
| Gutiérrez | Antonio Maceo |
| Jesús María | José Martí |
| Alameda | Jesus Menéndez |
| Carmen | Frank País |
| Santo Domingo | Camilo Cienfuegos |
| Rosario | Zerquera |
| Desengaño | Simón Bolívar |
| Boca | Piro Guinart |
| Gloria | Gustavo Izquierdo |
| San Procopio | General Lino Pérez |
| Guaurabo | Pablo Pichs Girón |

## Information

### BOOKSHOPS

**Librería Ángel Guerra** (☎ 3748; José Martí No 273 btwn Colón & Zerquera; 🕑 8am-3pm Mon-Sat)

### INTERNET ACCESS

**Cafe Internet Las Begonias** (Antonio Maceo No 473; 🕑 9am-9pm; per hr CUC$6) On the corner of Simón Bolívar. Crowded.

**Etecsa Telepunto** (cnr General Lino Pérez & Francisco Pettersen; per hr CUC$6; 🕑 7am-11pm) Freshly refurbished Telepunto with brand new computer terminals.

**Hotel La Ronda** One computer terminal in the lobby can be accessed with an Etecsa card.

### LIBRARIES

**Biblioteca Gustavo Izquierdo** (José Martí No 265 btwn Colón & Zerquera; 🕑 8am-9pm Mon-Fri, 8am-6pm Sat, 8am-1pm Sun)

### MEDIA

**Radio Trinidad** Broadcasts over 1200AM.

### MEDICAL SERVICES

**General Hospital** (☎ 3201; Antonio Maceo No 6) Southeast of the center.

**Servimed Clínica Internacional Cubanacán** (☎ 6240; General Lino Pérez No 103; 🕑 24hr) On the corner of Anastasio Cárdenas. There is an on-site pharmacy selling products in Convertibles.

### MONEY

**Banco de Crédito y Comercio** (☎ 2405; José Martí No 264)

**Cadeca** (☎ 6263; José Martí No 164) Between Parque Céspedes and Camilo Cienfuegos.

### POST

**Post office** (Antonio Maceo No 418) Between Colón and Zerquera.

### TELEPHONE

**Etecsa** (☎ 4129; General Lino Pérez No 274; per hr CUC$6) On Parque Céspedes.

### TRAVEL AGENCIES

**Cubatur** (☎ 6314; Antonio Maceo No 447; 🕑 9am-8pm) On the corner of Zerquera. Good for general tourist information, plus hotel bookings, car rentals and taxis; changes traveler's checks and does cash advances.

**Havanatur** (☎ 6390; fax 6183; General Lino Pérez No 366)

**Paradiso** (☎ 6486; fax 6308; General Lino Pérez No 306) Cultural and general tours in English, Spanish and French.

## Dangers & Annoyances

Thefts, though still uncommon, are on the rise in Trinidad. Incidents usually occur late at night and the victims are, more often than not, inebriated. Be on your guard, particularly when returning to your hotel/casa after a night out on the drink.

## Sights

The Plaza Mayor, Trinidad's remarkably peaceful main square, is in the heart of the *casco histórico* and is the town's most oft-photographed spot.

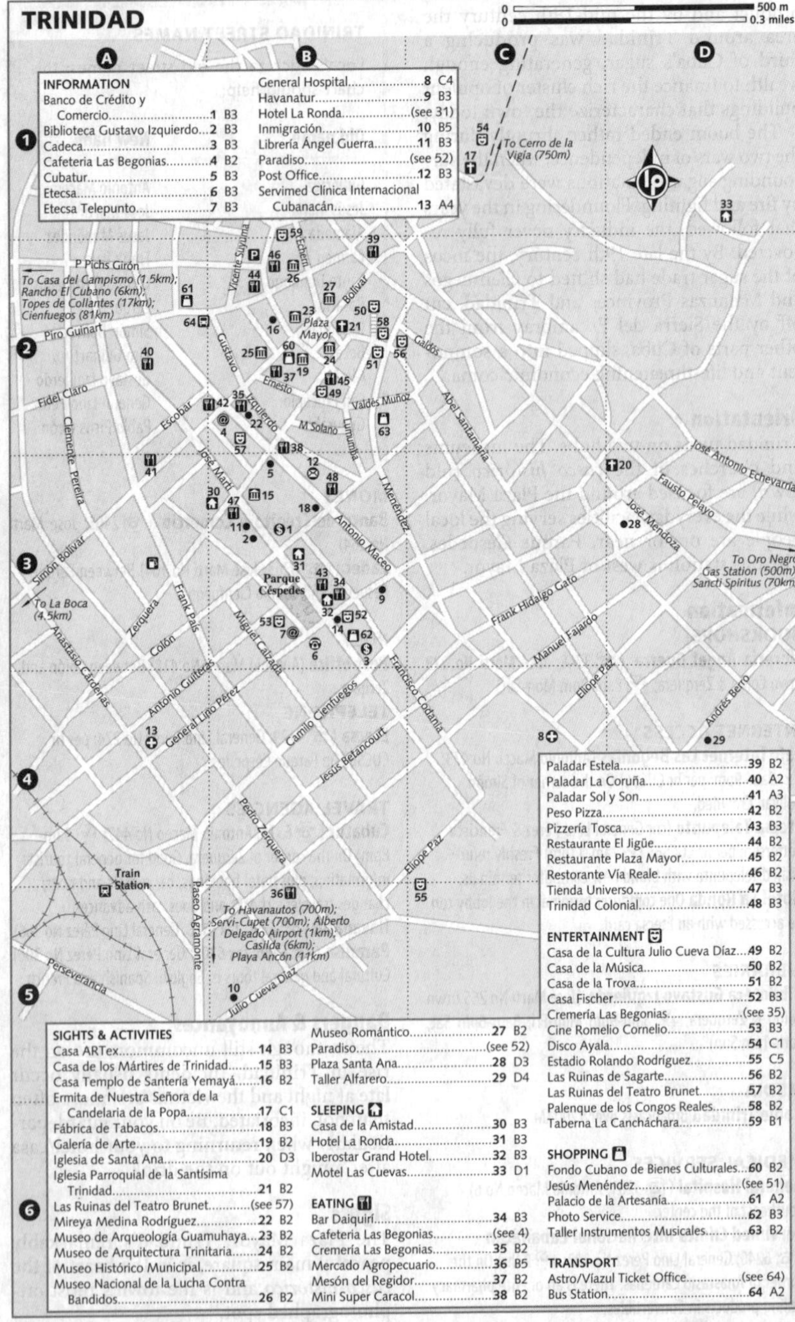
TRINIDAD
0 500 m
0 0.3 miles
A
B
C
D
1
2
3
4
5
6
INFORMATION
Banco de Crédito y Comercio......1 B3
Biblioteca Gustavo Izquierdo...2 B3
Cadeca......3 B3
Cafeteria Las Begonias......4 B2
Cubatur......5 B3
Etecsa......6 B3
Etecsa Telepunto......7 B3
General Hospital......8 C4
Havanatur......9 B3
Hotel La Ronda......(see 31)
Inmigración......10 B5
Librería Ángel Guerra......11 B3
Paradiso......(see 52)
Post Office......12 B3
Servimed Clínica Internacional Cubanacán......13 A4
To Cerro de la Vigía (750m)
P Pichs Girón
To Casa del Campismo (1.5km); Rancho El Cubano (6km); Topes de Collantes (17km); Cienfuegos (81km)
Piro Guinart
Vicente Suyama
Echerri
Bolívar
Plaza Mayor
Gustavo
Galdós
Fidel Claro
Ernesto
Izquierdo
Valdés Muñoz
Escobar
M Solano
Lumumba
Abel Santamaría
Clemente Pereira
José Martí
José Antonio Echevarría
Fausto Pelayo
J Menéndez
José Mendoza
Antonio Maceo
To Oro Negro Gas Station (500m); Sancti Spíritus (70km)
Simón Bolívar
Parque Céspedes
To La Boca (4.5km)
Frank País
Frank Hidalgo Gato
Zerquera
Anastasio Cárdenas
Colón
Miguel Calzada
Manuel Fajardo
Antonio Guiteras
Francisco Codania
Eliope Paz
Camilo Cienfuegos
General Lino Pérez
Andrés Berro
Jesús Betancourt
Pedro Zerquera
Train Station
Paseo Agramonte
To Havanautos (700m); Servi-Cupet (700m); Alberto Delgado Airport (1km); Casilda (6km); Playa Ancón (11km)
Perseverancia
Julio Cueva Díaz
SIGHTS & ACTIVITIES
Casa ARTex......14 B3
Casa de los Mártires de Trinidad......15 B3
Casa Templo de Santería Yemayá......16 B2
Ermita de Nuestra Señora de la Candelaria de la Popa......17 C1
Fábrica de Tabacos......18 B3
Galería de Arte......19 B2
Iglesia de Santa Ana......20 D3
Iglesia Parroquial de la Santísima Trinidad......21 B2
Las Ruinas del Teatro Brunet......(see 57)
Mireya Medina Rodríguez......22 B2
Museo de Arqueología Guamuhaya......23 B2
Museo de Arquitectura Trinitaria......24 B2
Museo Histórico Municipal......25 B2
Museo Nacional de la Lucha Contra Bandidos......26 B2
Museo Romántico......27 B2
Paradiso......(see 52)
Plaza Santa Ana......28 D3
Taller Alfarero......29 D4
SLEEPING
Casa de la Amistad......30 B3
Hotel La Ronda......31 B3
Iberostar Grand Hotel......32 B3
Motel Las Cuevas......33 D1
EATING
Bar Daiquirí......34 B3
Cafeteria Las Begonias......(see 4)
Cremería Las Begonias......35 B2
Mercado Agropecuario......36 B5
Mesón del Regidor......37 B2
Mini Super Caracol......38 B2
Paladar Estela......39 B2
Paladar La Coruña......40 A2
Paladar Sol y Son......41 A3
Peso Pizza......42 B2
Pizzería Tosca......43 B3
Restaurante El Jigüe......44 B2
Restaurante Plaza Mayor......45 B2
Restorante Vía Reale......46 B2
Tienda Universo......47 B3
Trinidad Colonial......48 B3
ENTERTAINMENT
Casa de la Cultura Julio Cueva Díaz......49 B2
Casa de la Música......50 B2
Casa de la Trova......51 B2
Casa Fischer......52 B3
Cremería Las Begonias......(see 35)
Cine Romelio Cornelio......53 B3
Disco Ayala......54 C1
Estadio Rolando Rodríguez......55 C5
Las Ruinas de Sagarte......56 B2
Las Ruinas del Teatro Brunet......57 B2
Palenque de los Congos Reales......58 B2
Taberna La Canchánchara......59 B1
SHOPPING
Fondo Cubano de Bienes Culturales......60 B2
Jesús Menéndez......(see 51)
Palacio de la Artesanía......61 A2
Photo Service......62 B3
Taller Instrumentos Musicales......63 B2
TRANSPORT
Astro/Víazul Ticket Office......(see 64)
Bus Station......64 A2

The showpiece museum here is the grandiose **Museo Histórico Municipal** (☎ 4460; Simón Bolívar No 423; admission CUC$2; ⏰ 9am-5pm Sat-Thu), just off Plaza Mayor, housed in a mansion that belonged to the Borrell family from 1827 to 1830. Later the building passed to a German planter named Kanter or Cantero, and it's still called Casa Cantero. Reputedly Dr Justo Cantero acquired vast sugar estates by poisoning an old slave trader and marrying his widow, who also suffered an untimely death. Cantero's ill-gotten wealth is well displayed in the stylish neoclassical decoration of the rooms. The view of Trinidad from the top of the tower alone is worth the price of admission. Visit before 11am, when the tour buses start rolling in.

The **Iglesia Parroquial de la Santísima Trinidad** (⏰ 11am-12:30pm Mon-Sat) on the northeastern side of Plaza Mayor, was rebuilt in 1892 on the site of an earlier church. The venerated Christ of the True Cross (1713), on the second altar from the front to the left, is one of many sacred objects here. Your best chance of seeing it is during mass at 8pm weekdays, 4pm Saturday, and 9am and 5pm Sunday.

Near the church is the **Museo Romántico** (☎ 4363; Echerri No 52; admission CUC$2; ⏰ 9am-5pm Tue-Sun) in the Palacio Brunet, the ground floor of which was built in 1740, the upstairs in 1808. In 1974 the mansion was converted into a museum with 19th-century furnishings, a fine collection of china and other period pieces. Pushy museum staff will materialize at your side to guide you for a tip. The shop adjacent has a good selection of photos and books in English.

Another public display of wealth is in the **Museo de Arquitectura Trinitaria** (admission CUC$1; ⏰ 9am-5pm Sat-Thu), on the southeastern side of Plaza Mayor, showcasing upper-class domestic architecture of the 18th and 19th centuries. The museum is housed in buildings erected in 1738 and 1785 that were joined together in 1819.

On the northwestern side of Plaza Mayor is the **Museo de Arqueología Guamuhaya** (☎ 3420; Bolívar No 457; admission CUC$1; ⏰ 9am-5pm Tue-Sat), an odd mix of stuffed animals, native bones, and vaguely incongruous 19th-century kitchen furniture. Don't make it your first priority.

Admission is completely free at the 19th-century Palacio Ortíz, which today houses the **Galería de Arte** (cnr Rubén Martínez Villena & Bolívar; ⏰ 9am-5pm), on the southwestern side of Plaza Mayor. Worth a look for its quality local art, particularly the embroidery, pottery and jewelry, there's also a nice courtyard and spiffy bathroom.

The **Casa Templo de Santería Yemayá** (Rubén Martínez Villena No 59 btwn Bolívar & Piro Guinart) contains a Santería altar to Yemayá, Goddess of the Sea, and the *santeros* (priests of the Afro-Cuban religion Santería) in attendance are available for consultations. On the saint's anniversary, March 19, ceremonies are performed day and night. Ask about Carnaval practices and *parranda* (Afro-Venezuelan dance) in the adjacent courtyard.

Perhaps the most recognizable building in Trinidad is the quaint yellow bell-tower of the former convent of San Francisco de Asís. Since 1986 the building has housed the **Museo Nacional de la Lucha Contra Bandidos** (☎ 4121; Echerri No 59; admission CUC$1; ⏰ 9am-6pm Tue-Sun). The displays are mostly photos, maps, weapons and other objects relating to the struggle against the various counter-revolutionary bands that operated in Sierra del Escambray between 1960 and 1965. The fuselage of a US U-2 spy plane shot down over Cuba is also on display. Here, too, you can climb the tower for good views. It's on the corner of Piro Guinart.

**Casa de los Mártires de Trinidad** (Zerquera No 254 btwn Antonio Maceo & José Martí; guided/unguided CUC$1/free; ⏰ 9am-5pm) is dedicated to 72 Trinidad residents who died in the struggle against Batista, the campaign against the counter-revolutionaries, and the war in Angola.

There's a tiny **Fábrica de Tabacos** (Antonio Maceo No 403), just right past Hotel Ronda on the corner of Colón; it's too small for full-blown tours but you might be able to take a glance at the deft tobacco rollers making cigars.

Additional sights on the east side of town make a good goal for a stroll around or as you leave Trinidad for points north. Only the shell remains of the **Iglesia de Santa Ana**, but just across the square is a former Spanish prison (1844) that has been converted into a tourist center, the **Plaza Santa Ana** (Calle Camilo Cienfuegos; admission free; ⏰ 11am-10pm). The complex includes an art gallery, handicraft market, ceramics shop, bar and restaurant.

Five blocks south is **Taller Alfarero** (Calle Andrés Berro; admission free; ⏰ 8am-noon & 2-5pm Mon-Fri), a large factory where teams of workers make ceramics from local clay using a traditional potter's wheel.

## Activities

For a bird's-eye view of Trinidad, walk straight up Simón Bolívar, the street between the Iglesia Parroquial and the Museo Romántico, to the destroyed 18th-century **Ermita de Nuestra Señora de la Candelaria de la Popa**, part of a former Spanish military hospital. It's on a hill to the north of the old town, a favorite sunset-watching spot (use insect repellant). From here it's a 30-minute hike up the hill to the radio transmitter atop 180m-high **Cerro de la Vigía**, which delivers broad vistas of Trinidad, Playa Ancón and the entire littoral.

The **Finca de Recreo María Dolores** (☎ 6481, 6394/5; Carretera de Cienfuegos Km 1.5), is a farm and recreation complex along the Río Guaurabo. It rents rooms and hosts *fiesta campesinas* (country fairs; see Casa del Campesino, opposite). It runs sunset boat tours to the beach at La Boca (CUC$5 per person) and horseback-riding tours to **Ranchón El Cubano** (CUC$10 per person for two hours). The latter is a pleasant spot 5km from Trinidad with trails to a waterfall and a unique restaurant which specializes in *pez gato* (catfish).

Rent a bike to **Playa Ancón** where you can use the swimming pool or snorkel off the beach. The road out of town is flat and well-paved and the loop via La Boca makes an interesting detour. See p301 for bike rental.



## Courses

At **Las Ruinas del Teatro Brunet** (Antonio Maceo No 461 btwn Simón Bolívar & Zerquera) you can take drumming lessons (9am to 11am Saturday) and dance lessons (1pm to 4pm Saturday). Dance lessons are also available with popular local teacher **Mireya Medina Rodríguez** (☎ 3944; Antonio Maceo No 472 btwn Simon Bolivar & Zerquera) who instructs everything from *chachachá* to rumba in her front room. Another option is Paradiso in **Casa Artex** (☎ 6486; paradisotr@sctd.artex.cu; General Lino Pérez No 306) which offers salsa lessons from CUC$5 for 90 minutes.

The travel agent **Paradiso** (☎ 6486; fax 6308; General Lino Pérez No 306) have incorporated a number of other courses into their cultural program including: Cuban architecture (CUC$20), Afro-Cuban culture (CUC$30), Artes Plásticas (Visual Arts; CUC$30) and Popular Music (CUC$30). These courses last four hours and are taught by cultural specialists. They require a minimum number of six to 10 people to take place, but you can always negotiate. At the same venue there are guitar lessons for CUC$5 an hour and courses in Spanish language/Cuban culture for CUC$8 an hour.

## Tours

Tours to Topes de Collantes (p304) with **Cubatur** (☎ 6314; Antonio Maceo No 447; 🕒 9am-8pm) cost between CUC$23 and CUC$43 per person depending on the excursion. The horseback-riding tours to the Ranchón El Cubano include the park entrance fee, swimming, lunch and guide for approximately CUC$18 (horses are stabled at Finca de Recreo María Dolores, see Casa del Campesino, opposite – you can make your own way there and do the tour for less).

Travel agent **Paradiso** (☎ 6486; fax 6308; General Lino Pérez No 306) has a great-value day tour to the Valle de los Ingenios for CUC$9 per person and an artist-studio tour in Trinidad for CUC$10 per person.

If you're staying in a private house, your hosts will know someone renting horses for a trip around the Valle de los Ingenios or Ranchón El Cubano. The first takes in a waterfall and both are through beautiful countryside. Your guide should accept CUC$7/15 per person for three/six hours. (Note that with a private guide, you have to pay an additional CUC$6.50 park entry fee for Ranchón El Cubano.) The saddles on the horses are often poor and, unless you're an experienced rider, three hours will be plenty. A tour to Topes de Collantes by private car shouldn't cost more than CUC$25.

For diving, fishing, sailing and snorkeling tours, see Playa Ancón (p301); any of Trinidad's agencies (p293) can organize the same excursions.

## Festivals & Events

The three-day **Fiestas Sanjuaneras** is a local Carnaval held during the last weekend in June; rum-filled horsemen galloping through the streets is about the size of it: take cover. The **Semana de la Cultura Trinitaria** (Trinidad Culture Week) is at the beginning of January to coincide with the city's anniversary.

## Sleeping

Trinidad has more than 300 casas particulares (see p298) and competition is fierce: arriving by bus or walking the streets with luggage, you'll be besieged by hustlers working for commissions and desperate casa owners. With so many beautiful homes and hospitable families renting here, there's no reason to stay somewhere you're not comfortable. The houses around the bus station are convenient for new arrivals, but may not be your best choice for an extended stay, as it's not the nicest part of town.

There are also a few hotel choices in and out of town.

#### IN TOWN

**Casa de la Amistad** (amistur@ceniai.inf.cu; Calle Zerquera btwn Martí & Frank País; r CUC$25) This hostel run by the Instituto Cubano de la Amistad is popular among visitors politically sympathetic to Cuba. It has six clean and well-equipped rooms with brand new showers and TVs, plus a small eating area and patio out the back. It's a first-class budget option in the center of town.

**Hotel La Ronda** (Cubanacán; ☎ 2248; Martí No 238; r CUC$46; 💻) Another new Cubanacán acquisition (from Islazul) though not quite up to the standard of the boutique hotels in other cities (although the price is the same!). It's well-located on Parque Céspedes, but the 19 rooms are a little worn and the downstairs restaurant lacks character. There's a good all-day Internet connection in the lobby.

**Motel Las Cuevas** (Cubanacán; ☎ 4013; s/d with breakfast low season CUC$50/65, high season CUC$59/75; P ❄ 🏊) Bus tours inevitably stay at this place with city and sea views beyond the Iglesia de Santa Ana, 1km northeast of town. The best rooms are in newer two-story units overlooking the valley. Cueva La Maravillosa is accessible down a stairway, where you'll see a huge tree growing out of a cavern (entry CUC$1). When there are vacancies, nonguests can use the small pool for a small fee.

**Iberostar Grand Hotel** (Gran Caribe; cnr Calle José Martí & Lino Pérez; s/d from CUC$95/120; ❄) Opened in February 2006 as Iberostar's fifth Cuban hotel, the five-star Grand has added a luxury twist to Trinidad's otherwise lackluster hotel scene. Thirty-six classy rooms in a remodeled 19th-century building promise oodles of colonial sparkle. The position, overlooking Parque Céspedes, makes it a great base for exploring.

#### OUTSIDE TOWN

**Casa del Campesino** (☎ 6481, 6394/5; s/d CUC$45/70; P ❄ 🏊) If you're driving or want to get an early riding or hiking start, consider one of the rooms at the Finca de Recreo María Dolores (opposite), 1.5km west on the road to Cienfuegos and Topes de Collantes. Go for a room overlooking Río Guaurabo (cute porch included). On nights when groups are present, there's a *fiesta campesina* with country-style Cuban folk dancing at 9:30pm, (free/CUC$5 for guests/nonguests, including one drink). There are boat and horseback-riding tours (CUC$10 for two hours). One kilometer west of the Casa del Campesino is a monument to Alberto Delgado, a teacher murdered by counterrevolutionaries.

## Eating

Since so many casas particulares cook for their guests, you will probably end up eating in most nights. Dinners usually cost from CUC$6 to CUC$10, depending on what you eat. Vegetarians might find this a better solution than picking around a restaurant or paladar (privately owned restaurant) menu.

#### PALADARES

Trinidad has three legal paladares and ten times that number in illegal outfits, judging by the number of hissing hustlers you'll encounter around Plaza Mayor.

**Paladar Sol y Son** (Simón Bolívar No 283 btwn Frank País & José Martí; mains CUC$8-10; 🕑 noon-2pm & 7:30-11pm) The food is good at this popular paladar, and its reputation usually ensures a nightly circle of full tables. The waiting room is elegant, however, and you'll dine in a courtyard to the sound of traditional Cuban music. English is spoken. Skip the fish.

**Paladar Estela** (☎ 4329; Simón Bolívar No 557; 🕑 2-11:30pm) You can choose the dining room or pretty rear garden to take your meals in this place located above the Plaza Mayor. A large meal served by friendly staff will cost approximately CUC$8. *Cordero* (lamb) served shredded is the house specialty.

**Paladar La Coruña** (José Martí No 428; 🕑 11am-11pm) A poor third after Sol y Son and Estela. Eager to please and friendly staff at this no-frills paladar serve chicken and pork and occasional fish.

#### RESTAURANTS

Housed in an attractive array of colonial mansions, Trinidad's state-run restaurants

**CASAS PARTICULARES – TRINIDAD**

**Araceli Reboso Miranda** (☎ 3538, 3389; Lino Pérez No 207 btwn Frank Pais & Miguel Calzada; r CUC$20) Two spotless rooms off a lush veranda; plus a roof terrace and dangerously delicious meals. English spoken.

**Balbina Cadahía** (☎ 2585; Antonio Maceo No 355; r CUC$20) Two rooms with a patio.

**Carlos Gil Lemes** (☎ 3142; Martí No 263 btwn Zerquera & Colón; r CUC$25) Museum-quality colonial manor with beautiful courtyard and shared bath. Friendly.

**Carmelina de la Paz** (☎ 3620; Piro Guinart No 239 btwn Independencia & Vicente Suyuma; r CUC$15-20) Colonial house with huge rooms, ceilings to the clouds, roof terrace. Next to the bus station.

**'Casa Arandia' – Aurelio Arandia** (☎ 3240; Antonio Maceo No 438 btwn Colón & Zerquera; r CUC$20-25) Gorgeous loft room with two double beds in a colonial house with terrace, views and fridge.

**Casa de Ines** (☎ 3241; eleusiscu@yahoo.com; José Martí No 160 btwn C Cienfuegos & General Lino Pérez; r CUC$20; P) Big room; kind owners.

**Elisa Margot Silva Ortíz** (☎ 4332; Piro Guinart No 246 near Gustavo Izquierdo; r CUC$20) Grand room with balcony, original wood ceilings/floors and sweet sisters hosting.

**'Escobar' – Julio & Rosa** (☎ 6688; www.trinidadphoto.com; José Martí No 401; r CUC$25; P ❄) Lux colonial house with antiques, patio and roof terrace. English spoken. The owner is an accomplished photographer who runs workshops and courses.

**'Hospedaje Yolanda' – Yolanda María Alvarez** (☎ 3051; yolimar56@yahoo.com; Piro Guinart No 227; r CUC$15-20) Good for groups.

**Hostal Casa Margely** (☎ 2550; Piro Guinart No 360A; r CUC$20) In front of the Museo Nacional de la Lucha Contra Bandidos. A popular place with a good location.

**Hostal Cocodrilo – José Boggiano** (☎ 2108; C Cienfuegos No 28 btwn Pedro Zerquera & Anastasio Cárdenas; r CUC$20) On a busy intersection.

**'Hostal El Albertico' – Albertico Duarte Reyes** (☎ 3721; Ernesto V Muñoz No 75A btwn Zerquera & Lumumba; r CUC$20-25) Spacious, quiet rooms and views; you'll eat well here.

**Hostal Sandra y Victor** (☎ 2216; sandraorbea@yahoo.com; Antonio Maceo No 613 btwn Piro Guinart & Pablo Pichs Girón; r CUC$20-25) Two rooms each with two double beds, nice outside/terrace space.

**Mariene Ruíz Tapanes** (☎ 4255; Simón Bolívar No 515; r CUC$20) Large, clean rooms above Plaza Mayor.

**Mireya Medina Rodríguez** (☎ 3944; miretrini@yahoo.es; Maceo No 472 btwn Simon Bolivar & Francisco J Zerquera; r CUC$20-25) One room in a central location. Mireya also offers dancing lessons.

**Nelson Fernández** (☎ 3849, 4300; Piro Guinart No 228; r CUC$20) Near the bus station. Upstairs rooms off a roof terrace, good for groups, nice host.

**Odalis Valdivia González** (☎ 3309; Callejón Smith No 3 btwn Maceo & Menéndez; r CUC$20) Independent rooms in a back patio. Clean and relaxing.

**Ramona Hernández de la Pedraja** (☎ 3637; C Cienfuegos No 68 btwn Frank País & Pedro Zerquera; r CUC$15-20) Quiet room in a colonial house, small patio, friendly.

**Rogelio Inchausti Bastida** (☎ 4107; Simón Bolívar No 312; r CUC$15-20) Comfortable, popular, good for groups.

**Ruth Martín Rodríguez** (☎ 4396; Frank País No 38 btwn Eliope Paz & Manuel Fajardo; r CUC$15-20; P) Friendly, one/two rooms in a separate house.

are pleasant on the eye, if a little less impressive on the palate. Food fiends beware. Dishes in these magnificent mansions are often uninspiring and the service infamously inattentive.

**Restaurante Plaza Mayor** (☎ 6470; cnr Rubén Martínez Villena & Zerquera; dishes from CUC$3; 🕑 11am-10pm) Offers everything from spaghetti to lobster (CUC$20). Live trios often strum while you dine here and it's a tranquil spot for dinner.

**Trinidad Colonial** (☎ 6473; Antonio Maceo No 402; 🕑 11:30am-10pm) Here you'll dine on good portions of Cuban cuisine in the elegant 19th-century Casa Bidegaray. Meals are reasonable, even if the service isn't, with smoked pork topping out at CUC$6. The store attached has a good selection of books.

**Restorante Vía Reale** (Rubén Martínez Villena No 74 btwn Piro Guinart & Pablo Pichs Girón; lunch CUC$4; 🕑 noon-4pm) Break the chicken-and-pork grind at this Italian place with passable pizza and spaghetti lunches. This is a good vegetarian option.

**Restaurante El Jigüe** (☎ 6476; cnr Rubén Martínez Villena & Piro Guinart; 🕑 11am-10pm) Back on the chicken trail, the house specialty here is *pollo al Jigüe;* it's baked at least, offering savory flavors distinct from the usual grease fry.

**Mesón del Regidor** (☎ 6456; Simón Bolívar No 424; ⏰ 10am-10pm) Crowded at lunchtime with tour groups, but quiet the rest of the time, this restaurant specializes in grilled meats. The café next door is a good place to sit down and write postcards and does the best grilled cheese sandwich in town. Local *trovador* (traditional singer-songwriter) Israel Moreno often drops by during the day with a song.

### QUICK EATS

**Bar Daiquirí** (General Lino Pérez No 313; ⏰ 24hr) A lively place off Parque Céspedes with cheap drinks and fast food in Convertibles, the sidewalk terrace here is a popular meeting spot for locals and backpackers on their way back from an all-night salsa binge.

**Cafetería Las Begonias** (☎ 6473; cnr Antonio Maceo & Simón Bolívar; ⏰ 9am-10pm; 💻) Operations center for the backpacker crowd and the best place to meet other travelers, Las Begonias serves sandwiches, hamburgers, espresso and ice cream on clean, glass-topped tables that give out onto the street. There's a bar behind a partition wall, clean(ish) toilets in a rear courtyard, and four or five cheap – but always crowded – Internet terminals at the side.

Across the street is an ever-popular **Cremería Las Begonias** (Antonio Maceo) that doubles up as a Cubatur office and opposite a little old man does a flying trade in **peso pizza** (Bolívar).

Another good peso pizza stall is **Pizzería Tosca** (José Martí No 226) on Parque Céspedes. You can also try looking on the corner of Piro Guinart and Antonio Maceo, not far from the bus station, and also around the Cienfuegos–Paseo Agramonte–Cárdenas intersection on the road south out of town.

### GROCERIES

**Mercado agropecuario** (cnr Pedro Zerquera & Manuel Fajardo; ⏰ 8am-6pm Mon-Sat, 8am-noon Sun) Trinidad's agropecuario (vegetable market) is sad, but you should still be able to get basic fruits and vegetables.

**Tienda Universo** (José Martí) This shop, near Zerquera in the Galería Comercial Universo, is Trinidad's best (and most expensive) grocery store. Head here for yogurt, cheese, and even nuts and raisins.

**Mini Super Caracol** (cnr Gustavo Izquierdo & Zerquera; ⏰ 9am-9pm) This store has a decent selection of groceries, plus cheap bottled water.

## Entertainment

In addition to all the fun stuff mentioned in the boxed text (p300), the following venues serve up good entertainment.

**Casa de la Cultura Julio Cueva Díaz** (☎ 4308; Zerquera No 406) Presents various cultural activities by night.

**Cine Romelio Cornelio** (⏰ 8pm Tue-Sun) This cinema, on the southwestern side of Parque Céspedes, shows films nightly.

**Estadio Rolando Rodríguez** (Eliope Paz; ⏰ Oct-Apr) This stadium, at the southeastern end of Frank País, hosts baseball games.

## Shopping

**Arts & Crafts Market** (Jesús Menéndez) This excellent open-air market situated in front of the Casa de la Trova is the place to buy souvenirs, especially textiles and crochet work – just avoid the black coral and turtle-shell items that are made from endangered species and forbidden entry into many countries.

**Fondo Cubano de Bienes Culturales** (Simón Bolívar No 418; ⏰ 9am-5pm Mon-Fri, 9am-3pm Sat & Sun) Just down from the Plaza Mayor, this store has a good selection of Cuban handicrafts.

You can see local painters at work – and buy their paintings too – at various points along Calles Francisco Toro, Valdés and Muñoz.

Other shopping options:

**Palacio de la Artesanía** (Piro Guinart No 221) This store, located opposite the bus station, also sells handicrafts.

**Photo Service** (José Martí No 192 btwn Camilo Cienfuegos & General Lino Pérez) Servicing all your photographic needs.

**Taller Instrumentos Musicales** (cnr Menéndez & Muñoz) Musical instruments are made here.

## Getting There & Away

### AIR

Alberto Delgado Airport is 1km south of Trinidad, off the road to Casilda. Only Aerotaxi charters fly here (see Air, p474).

## TRINIDAD TROVA & PUB CRAWL

Trinidad is one of the best places in Cuba to find quality accessible music and a stroll around the atmospheric, and surprisingly deserted, side streets after sunset will uncover all manner of different sounds floating melodiously out of hidden doorways. Here are a few ideas for a nighttime crawl around some of Trinidad's most popular spots (bring Convertible pesos to tip the musicians).

Kick things off at the Artex patio at **Casa Fischer** (General Lino Pérez No 312 btwn José Martí & Francisco Codania; admission CUC$1), which cranks up at 10pm with a salsa orchestra (Tuesday, Wednesday, Thursday, Saturday and Sunday) or a folklore show (Friday). If you're early, kill time at its art gallery (free) or head to **Las Ruinas del Teatro Brunet** (Antonio Maceo No 461 btwn Simón Bolívar & Zerquera; admission CUC$1), which has an athletic Afro-Cuban show on its pleasant patio at 9:30pm nightly.

Swing by the **Cremería Las Begonias** (Antonio Maceo No 473), to pick up friends, chug an espresso or fortify yourself with a sandwich before diving into the heart of things. Following Bolívar up towards the Plaza Mayor, you can try the eye-watering *canchánchara* (CUC$2) at atmospheric **Taberna La Canchánchara** (cnr R Martínez Villena & Ciro Redondo). The eponymous house cocktail is made from rum, honey, lemon and water. The local musicians that frequent this popular hang-out are often quite good, and it's not unusual for the upbeat crowd to break into spontaneous dancing.

You can't miss the steps leading up to the **Casa de la Música** (☎ 3414; admission free) beside the Iglesia Parroquial off the Plaza Mayor which are invariably crowded with people taking in the 10pm salsa/dance show. Alternatively, full-on salsa concerts are held in the casa's rear courtyard (also accessible from Juan Manuel Márques; cover CUC$2). This place also has *trova* (traditional poetic singing/songwriting) during the day. Next door is the **Palenque de los Congos Reales** (cnr Echerri & J Menéndez; admission free), an open patio with a lively scene and a full menu of salsa and *son* (Cuba's basic form of popular music), heavy on the Afro-Cuban beat. Down the street is the famous **Casa de la Trova** (Echerri No 29; admission CUC$1; 🕒 9pm-2am), which can be exhilarating or bogus depending on the package-tourist-to-Cuban ratio. Local musicians to look out for are Semillas sel Son, Santa Palabra and the terrific *trovador,* Israel Moreno. Finally, a block north brings you to **Las Ruinas de Sagarte** (Jesús Menéndez; admission free; 🕒 24hr) an intimate outdoor club near Galdós with a good house band and a high-energy, low-pressure dance scene.

All-night ravers will have already heard about **Disco Ayala** (☎ 6615; admission CUC$3; 🕒 10:30pm-3am), a hillside cave near Ermita de Nuestra Señora de la Candelaria de la Popa (p296) that has been converted into a kitschy nightclub with flashing lights and a salsa-disco beat. Admission includes one drink. Mind your step as you teeter back down the hill at 3am.

### BUS

The **bus station** (☎ 2404; Piro Guinart No 224), runs provincial buses to the following:

| Destination | Cost (one way) | Frequency |
|---|---|---|
| Cienfuegos | CUC$3 | daily |
| La Boca | CUC$1 | 5* |
| Playa Ancón | CUC$1 | 4* |
| Sancti Spíritus | CUC$1 | twice daily |

* departures Sat & Sun only

Tickets are sold at a small window marked *'Taquilla Campo'* near the station entrance. Check the blackboard for the current schedule.

The **Astro/Víazul ticket office** (☎ 4448; 🕒 8-11:30am & 1-5pm) is further back in the station. It sells Astro tickets to Cienfuegos (CUC$3, two hours, 81km, daily), Santa Clara (CUC$6, three hours, 88km, daily) and Habana (CUC$21, 5½ hours, 335km, daily). Two seats are available to tourists paying in Convertibles on any of these services (the quota on the Santa Clara service is often full, so try to book ahead).

In addition, there are air-con Víazul buses to the following places:

| Destination | Cost (one way) | Departure |
|---|---|---|
| Cienfuegos | CUC$6 | 7:45am, 3:15pm |
| Habana | CUC$25 | 7:45am, 3:15pm |
| Santa Clara | CUC$8 | 2:25pm |
| Santiago de Cuba | CUC$33 | 8:00am |
| Varadero | CUC$20 | 2:25pm |

The Varadero or Habana departures can deposit you either at Sancti Spíritus (CUC$6, one hour 25 minutes, 70km) or Jagüey Grande (CUC$15, three hours 20 minutes, 182km). The Santiago de Cuba departure goes through Ciego de Ávila (CUC$9, two hours 40 minutes, 146km), Camagüey (CUC$15, five hours 20 minutes, 254km), Las Tunas (CUC$22, 7½ hours, 382km) and Bayamo (CUC$26, 10 hours, 463km) or Holguín (CUC$26, eight hours, 463km).

#### CAR

Private cars can be contracted to Habana (CUC$20 per person) or Sancti Spíritus (CUC$5 per person).

#### TRAIN

The train leaves daily at 9:30am, stopping at Iznaga and Condado, and arriving in Meyer at 10:10am. The return train leaves Meyer at 1:00pm, giving you a few hours to explore the Valle de los Ingenios. It's CUC$3 for a round-trip. The **terminal** (☎ 4223) in Trinidad is in a pink house across the train tracks on the western side of the station. (For information on train tours, see p304.)

### Getting Around

#### BICYCLE

You can hire bikes at **Las Ruinas del Teatro Brunet** (Antonio Maceo No 461 btwn Simón Bolívar & Zerquera; per day CUC$3) or you can ask around at your casa particular.

#### CAR & TAXI

The rental agencies at the Playa Ancón hotels rent mopeds (CUC$27 per day); as do Transtur at **Cubatur** (☎ 6314; Antonio Maceo No 447; 9am-8pm) and **Las Ruinas del Teatro Brunet** (Antonio Maceo No 461 btwn Simón Bolívar & Zerquera).

**Havanautos** (☎ 6301), at Servi-Cupet near the airport, also has a branch at **Club Amigo Costa Sur** (☎ 6112) in Playa Ancón.

**Transtur** (☎ 6257; cnr Maceo & Zerquera), in the Cubatur office, is also at Hotel Ancón.

**Servi-Cupet** (24hr), 500m south of town on the road to Casilda, has an El Rápido snack bar attached. The Oro Negro gas station is at the entrance to Trinidad from Sancti Spíritus, 1km east of Plaza Santa Ana.

**Guarded parking** (cnr Pablo Pichs Girón & Vicente Suyuma) is available near La Canchánchara (CUC$1/2 for 12/24 hours). You can also park near Plaza Santa Ana.

A ride in a coco-taxi (egg-shaped taxi) costs CUC$5 to Playa Ancón. A car costs CUC$6 to CUC$8 both ways.

#### HORSE CART

Horse carriages (two pesos) leave for Casilda from Paseo Agramonte at the southern end of town.

## PLAYA ANCÓN & AROUND

Playa Ancón, 12km south of Trinidad, is a luscious ribbon of white beach lapped by the tranquil, blue waters of the Caribbean. For most people's money it's the finest arc of sand on Cuba's southern coast.

In contrast to Cuba's northern keys, Playa Ancón has numerous outside attractions and makes an ideal base from which to explore the architectural treasures of nearby Trinidad and the forested Sierra del Escambray. Not as overwhelmed by tourism as Varadero or Guardalavaca, it's a good vacation choice if you want to mix all-inclusive resort comforts with a hasty escape ticket. It also makes a pleasant bike trip from Trinidad.

Beach bums who want to be near the water, but don't have the money or inclination to stay at one of the resorts, might consider a private home in Casilda or, better still, La Boca. What the travel literature doesn't mention is the sand fleas, they're ferocious here at sunrise and sunset. Be warned.

### Activities

From Hotel Ancón, it's 18km to Trinidad via Casilda, or 16km on the much nicer coastal road via La Boca. The Hotel Ancón pool is also open to nonguests.

The old fishing port of **Casilda**, 6km due south of Trinidad, is a friendly village with one paved road that was devastated during the 2005 hurricane season. Nearly 80% of the houses suffered significant damage. On August 17 the **Fiesta de Santa Elena** engulfs little Casilda, with feasting, competitions, horse races and loads of rum. The road from Ancón to Casilda crosses a tidal flat, its abundant bird life visible in the early morning.

#### FISHING

The **Marina Trinidad** (☎ 6205) is a few hundred meters north of Hotel Ancón. Four hours of deep-sea fishing, including transport, gear and guide, costs CUC$30 per person (minimum six people). Fly-fishing is also

SANCTI SPÍRITUS PROVINCE

**THE ROAD TO NOWHERE**

To the experienced motorist, Cuba's arterial Autopista is no ordinary freeway. Home to vintage Buicks, grazing cattle, onion sellers, hitchhikers, hovering vultures and the odd runaway steam train or two, the road – originally designated to stretch from Pinar del Río in the west to Guantánamo in the east – comes to an abrupt halt at Jatibonico in Sancti Spíritus Province after 650km of badly paved purgatory.

Financed with Soviet money during the 1980s, construction of the island's ambitiously planned Autopista Nacional barely got beyond the halfway stage thanks to the ignominious fall of communism in Eastern Europe in 1991 and the resulting demise of Cuba's once illustrious superpower patron.

Indeed so sudden was the Soviet pull out that, even today, lane markings remain unpainted, slip roads end in sugarcane fields and an odd assortment of half-finished bridges dangle like crumbling beacons above the surreally deserted eight lane highway.



possible around the rich mangrove forests of Península de Ancón (CUC$200 for four hours, maximum two people).

### SNORKELING & SCUBA DIVING

Cayo Blanco, a reef islet 25km southeast of Playa Ancón, has 22 marked scuba sites where you'll see black coral and bountiful marine life. Diving with the **Cayo Blanco International Dive Center** (☎ 6205) located at Marina Trinidad costs CUC$30 a dive and CUC$299 for an open-water course. The Marina also runs a seven-hour snorkeling-and-beach tour to Cayo Blanco for CUC$30 per person, CUC$40 with lunch. There are similar trips to the equally pristine **Cayo Macho**.

Romantic types might want to check out the **sunset catamaran cruise** (cruise CUC$15) which has been enthusiastically recommended. There is a minimum of eight passengers. Inquire at the marina or ask at the Cubatur office in Trinidad.

### SAILING

The **Windward Islands Cruising Company** (☎ US 1-650 838 9585, UK 44 20 7373 9900; www.caribbean-adventure.com) charters crewed and bareboat monohulls and catamarans out of the Marina to the Jardines de la Reina (p318). You can sail with or without guides, on a partial package or all-inclusive tour. Interested parties should inquire by phone or email: info@windward-islands.net.

## Sleeping

All of Ancón's three hotels were badly affected by Hurricane Dennis in July 2005 and were closed down temporarily (power was out for 16 days). Brisas and Ancón are back in business while Costa Sur was due to reopen its doors in June 2006.

**Club Amigo Costa Sur** (Cubanacán; ☎ 6174; s/d with breakfast low season CUC$35/40, high season CUC$40/50; P) Playa Ancón's oldest and humblest resort, this hotel is at the base of the peninsula, 9km from Casilda. For about CUC$10 more, you can upgrade to a superior room, which gives you better location and views (but not decor unfortunately). There are also 20 rooms in duplex bungalows which are better still. From here you can scuba dive and ride horses. The hotel faces a rocky shore, but a white, sandy beach is just to the right. Swimming is difficult on the shallow reef. This place is popular with Canadian package tourists.

**Hotel Ancón** (Gran Caribe; ☎ 6123, 6127; s/d low season CUC$68/96, high season CUC$85/127; P) The last hotel on the peninsula, this resort has a lively atmosphere and is on the best part of the beach. The huge, seven-story building leaves something to be desired aesthetically, particularly when juxtaposed with Trinidad's other colonial beauties, but it's decent value and the buffet-style meals are palatable. You can fish, learn to scuba dive or learn the mambo here and nonguests can use the facilities, which is exceptional for a resort.

**Brisas Trinidad del Mar** (Cubanacán; ☎ 6500/01/02/03; s/d low season CUC$75/130, high season CUC$103/160; P) Just a few years old, this sprawling resort is Playa Ancón's fanciest. The 241 rooms come all-inclusive and there are all the perks you would expect: massages, sauna, gym, kiddy pool, tennis courts and, of course, an awesome swath of beach. There are wheelchair-accessible rooms here.

## Eating & Drinking

**Grill Caribe** (☎ 6241; 24hr) Other than the hotel restaurants, there's this place on a quiet beach 2km north of Club Amigo Costa Sur. It specializes in seafood, such as fish and shrimp or lobster for CUC$12. Strict vegetarians will be disappointed here. It's a great sunset spot.

Bar Las Caletas, at the junction of the road to Casilda, is a local drinking place.

### Getting There & Away

The Trinibus shuttle that used to run regularly from Trinidad to the beach wasn't functioning at the time of research. Your cheapest bet to get to Ancón is by coco-taxi or bike (see p301 for bike rentals).

## VALLE DE LOS INGENIOS

The ruins of dozens of 19th-century *ingenios* (sugar mills), including warehouses, milling machinery, slave quarters, manor houses and other remains, dot verdant Valle de los Ingenios (or Valle de San Luis), which begins 8km east of Trinidad on the road to Sancti Spíritus. Most of the mills were destroyed in the two wars of independence, and the focus of sugar-growing moved to Matanzas. Some sugar is still grown here however, and the royal palms, waving cane and rolling hills are timelessly beautiful. A horseback-riding tour from Trinidad (p296) should take in most (if not all) of the following sites.

### Sights & Activities

The **Mirador de La Loma del Puerto** is 6km east of Trinidad on the road to Sancti Spíritus. The 192m-high lookout (admission CUC$1) provides excellent valley views; there's a bar.

The valley's main sight is the **Manaca Iznaga** (admission CUC$1) 16km east of Trinidad. Founded in 1750, the estate was purchased in 1795 by the dastardly Pedro Iznaga, who became one of the wealthiest men in Cuba by trafficking in slaves. The 44m-high tower next to the hacienda was used to watch the slaves, and the bell in front of the house served to summon them. Today you can climb to the top of the tower for pretty views, followed by a reasonable lunch (from noon to 2:30pm) in the restaurant/bar in Iznaga's former house.

Five kilometers beyond the Manaca Iznaga, on the valley's inland road, is the **Casa Guachinango**, an old hacienda built by Don Mariano Borrell toward the end of the 18th century (now a restaurant). The Río Ay is just below, and the surrounding landscape is wonderful. To get to Casa Guachinango, take the paved road to the right just beyond the second bridge as you come from Manaca Iznaga. The Meyer train stops right beside the house every morning, and you can walk back to Iznaga from Guachinango along the railway line in less than an hour. You might be able to pitch camp near the casa.

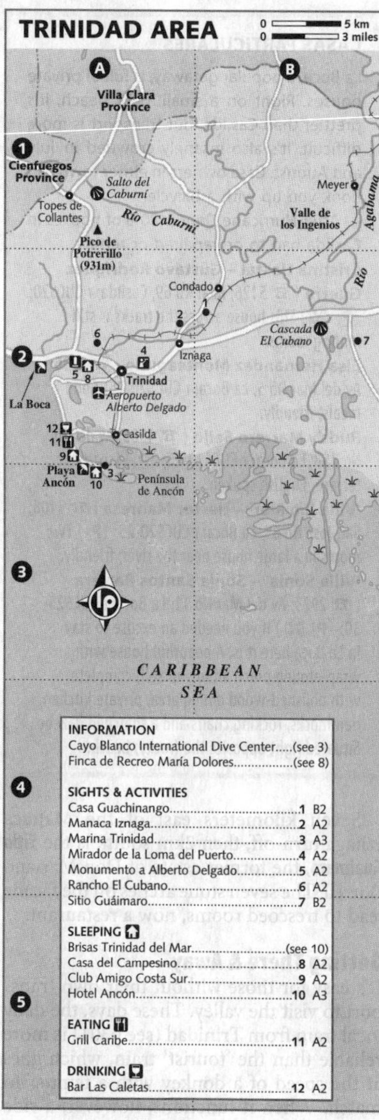


SANCTI SPÍRITUS PROVINCE

**CASAS PARTICULARES**

La Boca, a popular getaway, is full of private houses. Right on a small, dark beach, it's prettier than Casilda, but transport is more difficult. It's also insanely crowded in July and August. Casa owners in either town can hook you up with a bicycle.

After Hurricane Dennis 80% of houses in Casilda had to be repaired or rebuilt.

**Cristina Hostal – Gustavo Rodríguez Guerra** (☎ 5126; Real No 69, Casilda; r CUC$20; P ❄) This house across the tracks is still renting rooms.

**Elsa Hernández Monteagudo** (☎ 3236; Av del Mar No 5, La Boca; r CUC$20-25) Good meals, friendly.

**Ruddy Marrero Seijo** (☎ 4586; Av del Sol No 75B, La Boca; r CUC$20-25; P) Luxuriant terrace, English spoken.

**'Villa Río Mar' – Nestor Manresa** (☎ 3108; San José No 65, La Boca; r CUC$20-25; P) Two rooms in a large house near the river; friendly.

**'Villa Sonia' – Sonia Santos Barrera** (☎ 2923; Av del Mar No 11, La Boca; r CUC$25-30; P ❄) If you needed an excuse to stay in La Boca here it is. A beautiful house with a wrap-around porch all to yourself, complete with polished-wood dining area, private kitchen, hammocks, rocking chairs and a thatched gazebo. Situated right opposite the (rocky) beach.

Seven kilometers east of the Manaca Iznaga turn-off, then 2km south, is the **Sitio Guáimaro**, the former estate of Don Mariano Borrell. The seven stone arches on the facade lead to frescoed rooms, now a restaurant.

## Getting There & Away

It's easy for those without their own transport to visit the valley. These days, the daily local train from Trinidad (see p301) is more reliable than the 'tourist' train, which goes at the speed of a donkey with a temper to match. When it functions, however, a ride in the reconstructed railway carriage is a sublime experience, taking passengers on a 2½-hour trip through the valley (CUC$10, 9:30am) over slender bridges and across lush green fields. The train is pulled by steam engine No 52204, built by the Baldwin Locomotive Company of Philadelphia in August 1919. Passengers pay for their own lunch separately at the Manaca Iznaga and visit the Casa Guachinango. **Cubatur** (☎ 6314; Antonio Maceo No 447; ⏰ 9am-8pm) in Trinidad will know when the next tourist train trip is scheduled. Tour desks at the Ancón hotels sell the same train tour for CUC$17, including bus transfers to Trinidad.

Horseback tours can be arranged at the agencies in Trinidad (p296) or Playa Ancón, or contract a horse and guide privately in Trinidad for CUC$15 for six hours.

# TOPES DE COLLANTES

☎ 42 / elevation 771m

The rugged 90km-long Sierra del Escambray culminates in Pico de San Juan (1156m), also called 'La Cuca', in neighboring Cienfuegos Province. The largest settlement in the range is Topes de Collantes, a health-resort town 20km northwest of Trinidad. En route to Topes de Collantes, your car will just about give out as you crest 600m and come upon **El Mirador**, a snack bar (good mojitos), with great views. A few hundred meters along you pass Pico de Potrerillo (931m), the highest peak in Sancti Spíritus Province. Coniferous forests, vines, lichens, mosses and giant ferns flourish in this cool, foggy climate, and Arabica coffee thrives on the slopes.

Topes de Collantes was founded in 1937 by dictator Fulgencio Batista, who built the road from Trinidad. That year he started work on the hideous building that is now the Kurhotel, but it was still unfinished when he lost the 1944 presidential elections. When he seized power anew in 1952, Batista ordered the work to continue and in 1954 it opened as a tuberculosis sanatorium. The sanatorium closed with the revolution and during the early 1960s the building housed militias fighting counterrevolutionaries in the Sierra del Escambray. In 1989 the Gaviota chain reopened the Kurhotel as a spa.

Topes de Collantes has three hotels open to foreigners, plus good unguided hiking and an established camping ground. The **Carpeta Central information office** (☎ 54 02 31; ⏰ 8am-5pm), near the sundial at the entrance to Topes de Collantes is the best place to procure maps, guides and trail info.

## Activities

### HIKING

The most popular hike, and the one most easily accessed on foot from the hotels, is to the 62m **Salto del Caburní** (entry CUC$6.50), cascading over rocks into cool swimming holes before plunging into a chasm where macho locals dare each other to jump. At the height of the dry season (March to May), you may be disappointed by these falls. The entry fee is collected at the toll gate to Villa Caburní, just down the hill from the Kurhotel near the Carpeta Central (it's a long approach on foot). Allow an hour down and an hour and a half back up for this 2.5km hike. Some slopes are rather steep and can be slippery after rain.

A CUC$7 per person guide from the Carpeta Central is required to visit **Parque La Represa** on the Río Vega Grande below Hotel Los Helechos. This park contains 300 species of trees and ferns, including the largest *caoba* (mahogany) tree in Cuba. The restaurant is in a villa built by Fulgencio Batista's wife.

The trail to **La Batata** (admission free), a large cave containing an underground river, begins at a parking sign just up the hill from Parque La Represa. When you reach another highway, go around the right side of the concrete embankment and down the hill. Always keep straight or right after this point (avoid trails to the left). Allow an hour each way. It's possible to swim in pools in the cave.

## CAMILO CIENFUEGOS

It's not Che, it can't possibly be Raúl, and it certainly isn't Fidel. If it's your first time in Cuba you could be forgiven for scratching your head momentarily over the identity of that other bearded guerrilla emblazoned heroically onto a hundred different billboards.

Cowboy hat tilted playfully upward, rugged beard left wildly untrimmed, and lips invariably parted in the broadest of Cuban grins; Camilo Cienfuegos cut an impossibly romantic figure when he trotted triumphantly into Habana atop a horse in January 1959. Che Guevara called him *'la imagen del pueblo'* (the image of the people). Raúl Castro trumpeted him as *la vanguardia* (the vanguard); Fidel, meanwhile, preferred to elevate him into a deity of socialist saints alongside the more internationally palatable Che who – by a trick of fate – was given six extra years to prove his revolutionary worth.

Born into a humble Habana family in 1932, Camilo was forced to drop out of art school for economic reasons in his late teens and began working in a tailor's shop to make ends meet. In 1953 he arrived in the US with a friend where he traveled itinerantly between New York, Chicago and San Francisco working as a waiter and dishwasher. Deported for visa irregularities in 1955 he returned to Cuba where he was shot in the leg and hospitalized during an anti-Batista demonstration in Habana. The revolutionary spark was lit.

Inspired by news of the Moncada attack (see p41) and aware that 'something big' was being organized in Mexico City, Camilo returned to the US with the intention of reaching Mexico. He became one of the last volunteers accepted for the Granma expedition.

Surviving the landing at Las Coloradas and the battle of Alegría de Pío, he was among only 12 revolutionaries who managed to reach the Sierra Maestra Mountains. *'Nadie se rinde aquí'* (no one surrenders here) he is said to have shouted as Batista's soldiers strafed the panic-stricken rebel party.

In April 1958 his bravery was rewarded when Castro promoted him to the rank of *comandante,* and a few months later Cienfuegos was instructed to lead a guerrilla column on an arduous six-week march to Las Villas Province. His group became the revolution's nucleus in the north of the province while Guevara led the fighting further south, and he was instrumental in ending the stubborn resistance of Bastista's army in the Sancti Spíritus town of Yaguajay.

With the success of the revolution, Cienfuegos became the military chief of Habana, and later the revolutionary army's chief of staff. In October 1959, Castro sent him to Camagüey to arrest the dissident Huber Matos. A week later, as Cienfuegos was returning to Habana, his Cessna aircraft plunged into the sea. His remains were never found and to this day conspiracy theories circulate as to Castro's potential involvement in the tragedy.

Best-loved for his sense of humor and ever-present jovial smile, Camilo was a famous practical joker and one of Che Guevara's closest confidants. Despite rumors to the contrary, Cuban historian Carlos Franqui maintains that Cienfuegos always sympathized with socialism and never harbored any anticommunist grudges. At the time of his death he was the second most popular figure in Cuba after Fidel.

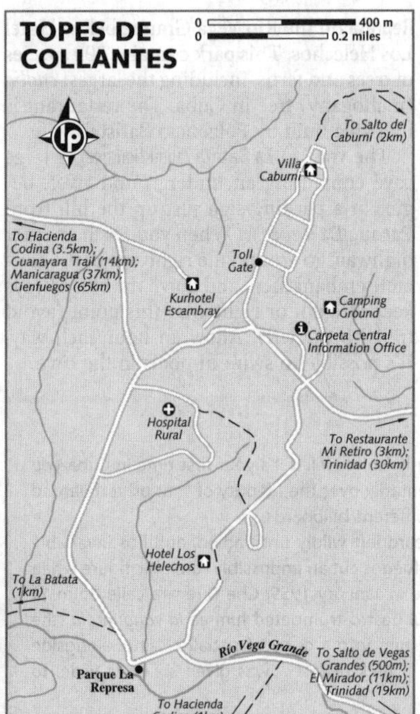


The **Salto de Vegas Grandes** trail begins at the apartment blocks known as Reparto El Chorrito on the southern side of Topes de Collantes, near the entrance to the resort as you arrive from Trinidad. Allow a bit less than an hour each way to cover the 2km. It's possible to continue to the Salto del Caburní, though consider hiring a guide.

Another destination is **Hacienda Codina**. The 3.5km jeep track begins on a hilltop 2.5km down the road toward Cienfuegos and Manicaragua, 1km before the point where these roads divide. There's a much shorter trail to the hacienda from below Hotel Los Helechos, but you need a guide to use that route. However, you might be able to find your own way back, if you wanted to make it a circle trip. Orchid and bamboo gardens, nature trails, the Cueva del Altar, mud baths and a scenic viewpoint are the attractions here.

The least accessible, but infinitely most rewarding hike from Topes de Collantes is the **Guanayara** trail, situated 15km from the Carpeta Central along a series of rough and heavily rutted tracks. For logistical reasons this excursion is best organized with a guide from the Carpeta, or as part of an organized tour from Trinidad with Cubatur (CUC$43 with lunch). The trail itself begins in cool, moist coffee plantations and descends steeply to the **El Rocio** waterfall where you can strip off and have a bracing shower. Following the course of the Río Melodioso (Melodic River) you pass another inviting waterfall/swimming pool before emerging into the salubrious gardens of the riverside Casa La Gallega, a traditional rural hacienda where a light lunch can be organized and camping is sometimes permitted in the lush grounds.

### CANYONING

Canyoning is one of the newest adventure activities the island has to offer. The burgeoning scene focuses on four main rivers, the Calburni, Vegas Grandes, Cabagan and Gruta Nengoa, and canyoners – who must provide all of their own equipment – travel spectacularly downstream with ropes, wetsuits, helmets and harnesses. The highlight of the trip is said to be a 200m series of vertical cascades over Salto Vegas Grandes. One experienced Canadian outfit offering excursions is **Canyoning Quebec** (www.canyoning-quebec.com) who run eight-day trips into the Sierra del Escambray. Alternatively try asking for Alex at the Carpeta Central information office (one of Cuba's few canyoning guides).

## Sleeping & Eating

**Camping ground** (per person CUC$3) Self-sufficient campers will delight in this camping ground in a pine copse on a spur road just below the Carpeta Central office. A wacky aviary project of Batista's, the giant, abandoned birdcages make great cooking areas and there's a young, communal atmosphere as it's a popular getaway for university students. Pay the fee at the Carpeta Central. There are no toilets.

**Hotel Los Helechos** (Gaviota; ☎ 54 03 30/1/2; fax 54 01 17; s/d low season CUC$29/34, high season CUC$39/44; P ✕ ) Long considered to be a poor relation in the fast-expanding Gaviota group, this simple but amiable, three-story hotel is currently undergoing a long-awaited facelift. The rooms are fitted out in cane and wicker fixtures and the thermal pool, sauna and steam baths add value. The adjoining restaurant bakes some of the best homemade bread in Cuba and there is also a disco next door.

**IF YOU HAVE A FEW MORE DAYS**

Northern Sancti Spíritus is a largely undiscovered region of gentle hills and coastal mangrove forest that in 2000 was incorporated – along with parts of Villa Clara and Ciego de Ávila Provinces – into Unesco's **Buenavista Biosphere Reserve**. Features of the reserve include 35 archaeological sites, indigenous wall paintings, secluded beaches and a high biodiversity of flora and fauna.

**Villa San José del Lago** (Islazul; ☎ 2-6390; Av Antonio Guiteras, Mayajigua; s/d low season CUC$22/28, high season CUC$25/32; P ) 50km west of Morón, is good base for exploring the area. Situated by a large lake that contains a handful of resident flamingos, the complex is famous for its thermal waters (average temperature 31°C) and varied spa treatments (including acupuncture and mud therapy). There are three swimming pools on-site (one of which is thermal), 67 tourist-class rooms, and a reasonable restaurant. Before the revolution the resort was popular with Americans.

Ask here about excursions to the **Sierra de Jatibonico**, the **Jatibonico River** and the **Caguanes National Park** in Bahía de Buenavista.

**Villa Caburní** (Gaviota; ☎ 54 01 80; ) This place is a veritable rural gem which offers 12 one- or two-story Swiss-style chalets in a small park next to the Kurhotel. The Villa was being used as an overflow for Los Helechos at the time of writing and the prices were the same.

**Kurhotel Escambray** (Gaviota; ☎ 54 03 04; fax 54 02 28; s/d/tr low season CUC$40/55/75, high season CUC$45/65/90) This eight-story place is a horrific architectural monster dreamt up by Batista in the 1930s. Judging by the incongruous Stalinist design of its ugly exterior, the wily Cuban dictator must have sensed that the Russians were on the way. As ugly as it is, friends swear by the facilities and treatment of various ailments this hotel provides.

The only nonhotel eating option nearby is Restaurante Mi Retiro situated 3km back down the road to Trinidad which does fair-to-middling *comida criollo* to the sound of the occasional traveling 'minstrel.'

## Getting There & Away

It's very difficult to get here without a car (and the steep ascent will test even native San Franciscan drivers) and harder still to get around to the various trailheads.

People wax nostalgic when you ask them about bus service between Trinidad and Topes de Collantes. Theoretically, there's supposed to be public transport, but in practice it rarely materializes. Hitchhikers wait for hours outside the Los Helechos turn-off thumbing for lifts back into Trinidad (for information on the risks associated with hitching see p477).

The road between Trinidad and Topes de Collantes is paved, but it's very steep. When wet, it becomes slippery and should be driven with caution. There's also a spectacular 44km road that continues right over the mountains from Topes de Collantes to Manicaragua via Jibacoa (occasionally closed, so check in Trinidad before setting out). It's also possible to drive to and from Cienfuegos via San Blas on a partly paved, partly gravel road.

# NORTHERN SANCTI SPÍRITUS

For most visitors, the province's narrow northern portion is only a transit corridor between Remedios, in Villa Clara Province, and Morón, in Ciego de Ávila Province. It's worth stopping, however, to visit the **Museo Nacional Camilo Cienfuegos** (admission CUC$1; 8am-4pm Tue-Sat, 9am-1pm Sun), at Yaguajay, 36km southeast of Caibarién. In 1989 a 5m bronze figure of Camilo Cienfuegos, reminiscent of Che Guevara in Santa Clara, was placed atop an imposing memorial opposite the Hospital Docente General between Yaguajay and the local sugar mill. The museum directly below this monument contains mementos of the battle fought here on the eve of the revolution's triumph. At that time the hospital was an army barracks that Camilo and his band captured the day before Batista fled the country. A replica of the small tank 'Dragon I', converted from a tractor for use in the battle, stands in front of the hospital.

# Ciego de Ávila Province

Scooped out of the former Las Villas and Camagüey territories, Ciego de Ávila is a modern province with profoundly traditional roots. Nowhere else in Cuba are the cultural affiliations as deeply embedded as they are here. From the Haitian voodoo liturgies practiced in Venezuela, to the red-and-blue *caringa* dance that enlivens rural Majagua, to the impromptu game of English cricket by West Indian immigrants in Baraguá, the images of eclectic rural life are as captivating as they are colorful.

The province's agricultural economy is dominated by sugarcane, cattle-ranching and citrus-fruit production, with the Ciego de Ávila pineapple well known islandwide for its all-round quality and sweetness. Luminous Laguna de Leche is Cuba's largest natural lake containing copious amounts of fish, and providing a freshwater fishing haven for armies of foreign anglers. Further east on the reclaimed Isla Turiguano, water-based activities give way to land antics as cowboys showcase their skills at one of the country's liveliest rodeos.

Ciego's biggest international draw-cards are Cayo Coco and Cayo Guillermo, two previously uninhabited keys situated 35km off the province's north coast. Flown in on charters from Canada and Europe, travelers to these flat, mangrove-covered islands are bussed from the airport to one of a dozen swanky new hotel complexes where organized activities are all part of the package. For some visitors the place feels about as Cuban as a passing cruise ship. Others lap up the luxury of the all-inclusive deal.



**HIGHLIGHTS**

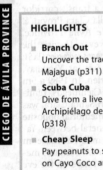

- **Branch Out**
  Uncover the traditions and festivals of Majagua (p311)
- **Scuba Cuba**
  Dive from a live-aboard in the secluded Archipiélago de los Jardines de la Reina (p318)
- **Cheap Sleep**
  Pay peanuts to stay at Sitio La Güira (p318) on Cayo Coco and rub shoulders with the all-inc crowd
- **City of Porches**
  Blow the dust off the understated delights of Ciego de Ávila (opposite)

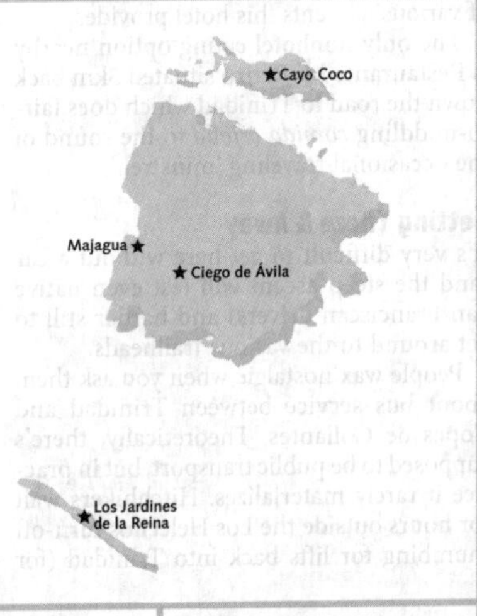


| TELEPHONE CODE: 33 | POPULATION: 413,447 | AREA: 6910 SQ KM |
|---|---|---|

## History

The area now known as Ciego de Ávila Province was first prospected by Spanish adventurer Pánfilo de Narváez in 1513, who set out to explore the expansive forests and plains of the north coast, then presided over by a local Indian chief called Ornofay. Integrating itself into the new Spanish colony of Cuba in the early 1500s, the province got its present name from a local merchant, Jacomé de Ávila, who was granted an *encomienda* (indigenous workforce) in San Antonio de la Palma in 1538. A small *ciego* (clearing) on Ávila's estate was put aside as a resting place for tired travelers heading east–west and it quickly became a nexus point for a burgeoning settlement.

Throughout the 16th and 17th centuries the northern keys provided a valuable refuge for buccaneering pirates fresh from their lucrative raids on cities such as Habana and Puerto Príncipe. Two hundred years later a buccaneer of a different kind arrived, in the shape of American writer Ernest Hemingway, who played his own game of cat-and-mouse tracking German submarines in the waters off Cayo Guillermo.

During the Independence Wars in the latter half of the 19th century, the area was infamous for its 67km-long Morón–Júcaro defensive line, better known to historians as La Trocha. Characterized by its sturdy military installations and manned by a voluminous force of up to 20,000 men, the defense system was built up by the ruling Spanish administrators in the 1870s and designed to stop the marauding *Mambíses* (19th-century rebels) from forging a passage west.

# CIEGO DE ÁVILA

☎ 33 / pop 104,850

Ciego de Ávila is Cuba without the wrapping paper, a no-frills provincial city that has long served as a kind of halfway house for travelers heading east on the Carretera Central. You'll find few colonial buildings of note here, and even fewer tourists. Christened 'the city of porches' for its colonnaded shop fronts, Ciego de Ávila was founded in 1840 and quickly became an important processing center for the region's lucrative sugarcane industry. While not quite in Habana's league, many of the city's neoclassical buildings – including the 500-seat Teatro Principal – were financed by a local socialite named Angela Hernández Viuda de Jímenenz, a rich widow who harbored ambitions to create a cultural mecca, à la Trinidad, in her home town.

## Orientation

The streets of Ciego de Ávila divide between Norte (north) and Sur (south) at Independencia. Marcial Gómez marks the transition from Este (east) to Oeste (west). This is important to remember, as the cardinal points are often part of an address. The Carretera Central turns into Chicho Valdés as it cuts across town.

## Information

### BOOKSTORES

**Bookstore** (Independencia Oeste No 153) On the corner of Simón Reyes.

### INTERNET ACCESS

**Etecsa Telepunto** (Agüero No 62; per hour CUC$6; 🕑 8am-noon & 1-5pm Mon-Fri, 8am-noon Sat) Three terminals.

### MEDIA

**Radio Surco** Broadcasting over 1440AM and 98.1 FM.

### MEDICAL SERVICES

**General Hospital** (☎ 22 24 29; Máximo Gómez No 257) Not far from the bus station.

### MONEY

**Banco de Crédito y Comercio** (☎ 22 31 09; Independencia Oeste No 152) On the corner of Simón Reyes.

**Banco Financiero Internacional** (☎ 26 63 10; cnr Joaquín Agüero Oeste & Honorato del Castillo)

**Bandec** (☎ 22 23 32; cnr Independencia Oeste & Maceo)

**Cadeca** (☎ 26 66 15; Independencia Oeste No 118 btwn Maceo & Simón Reyes; 🕑 8:30am-6pm Mon-Sat, 8:30am-12:30pm Sun)

### POST

**DHL** (☎ 26 20 96; cnr Chicho Valdés & Marcial Gómez)

**Post office** (cnr Chicho Valdés & Marcial Gómez)

### TELEPHONE

**Etecsa Telepunto** (Agüero No 62; 🕑 8am-noon & 1-5pm Mon-Fri, 8am-noon Sat)

### TOURIST INFORMATION

**Havanatur** (Calle Libertad btwn Maceo & H Castillo; 🕑 9am-5pm Mon-Fri)

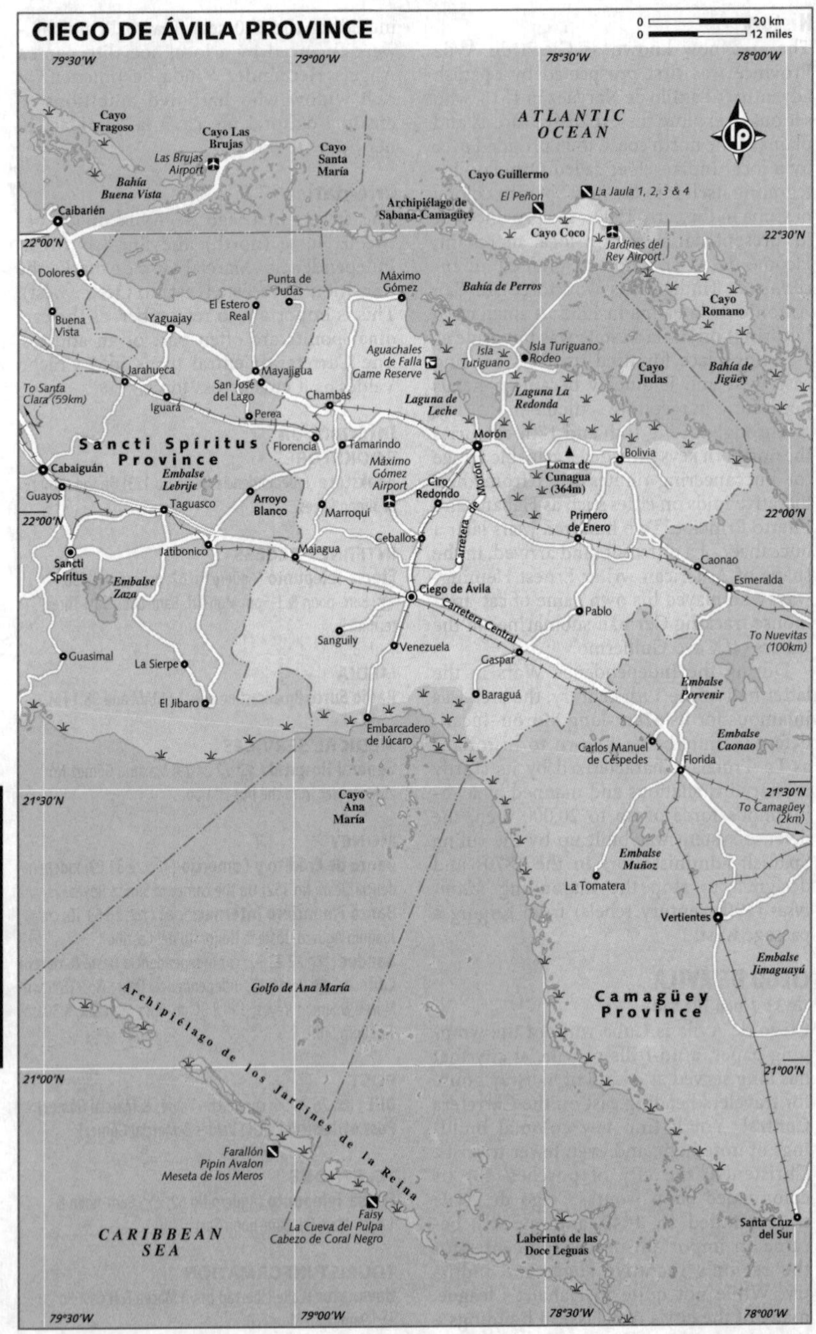
CIEGO DE ÁVILA PROVINCE
0 20 km
0 12 miles
79°30'W
79°00'W
78°30'W
78°00'W
ATLANTIC OCEAN
Cayo Fragoso
Cayo Las Brujas
Las Brujas Airport
Cayo Santa María
Bahía Buena Vista
Caibarién
Cayo Guillermo
El Peñon
La Jaula 1, 2, 3 & 4
Archipiélago de Sabana-Camagüey
Cayo Coco
Jardines del Rey Airport
22°00'N
22°30'N
Dolores
Punta de Judas
Máximo Gómez
Bahía de Perros
Cayo Romano
El Estero Real
Buena Vista
Yaguajay
Isla Turiguano
Isla Turiguano Rodeo
Aguachales de Falla Game Reserve
Cayo Judas
Bahía de Jigüey
Jarahueca
Mayajigua
To Santa Clara (59km)
San José del Lago
Iguará
Perea
Chambas
Laguna de Leche
Laguna La Redonda
Morón
Sancti Spíritus Province
Florencia
Tamarindo
Cabaiguán
Embalse Lebrije
Máximo Gómez Airport
Loma de Cunagua (364m)
Bolivia
Guayos
Taguasco
Arroyo Blanco
Marroquí
Ciro Redondo
Carretera de Morón
Primero de Enero
22°00'N
Sancti Spíritus
Jatibonico
Majagua
Ceballos
Caonao
Esmeralda
Embalse Zaza
Ciego de Ávila
Carretera Central
Pablo
To Nuevitas (100km)
Sanguily
Venezuela
Gaspar
Guasimal
La Sierpe
Embalse Porvenir
El Jibaro
Baraguá
Embarcadero de Júcaro
Embalse Caonao
Carlos Manuel de Céspedes
Florida
Cayo Ana María
21°30'N
To Camagüey (2km)
Embalse Muñoz
La Tomatera
Vertientes
Embalse Jimaguayú
Golfo de Ana María
Camagüey Province
Archipiélago de los Jardines de la Reina
21°00'N
Farallón
Pipin Avalon
Meseta de los Meros
Faisy
La Cueva del Pulpa
Cabezo de Coral Negro
CARIBBEAN SEA
Laberinto de las Doce Leguas
Santa Cruz del Sur

**DAY-TRIPPER**

Ciego de Ávila Province boasts a surprising number of interesting day trips for those not averse to a bit of do-it-yourself (DIY) planning. Start your search in Ciego de Ávila's helpful Infotur office (see below).

Situated 18km east of Morón on the Carretera de Bolivia, the **Loma de Cunagua** (9am-4pm) is an eye-catching 364m hill that sticks up like a giant termite mound from the flat plains of the northern coast. A haven for bird-watchers, the Loma's verdant tree-covered slopes are crisscrossed by trails and provide excellent opportunities for horseback riding and hiking. It's easily reached in a car or taxi, and there's a restaurant on the hill's summit and qualified biologists are on hand to lead guided walks through the area's lush wilderness.

Another option to get back to nature is in the undulating hills surrounding the towns of **Florencia** and **Chambas** in the province's northwest corner. There are various excursions here including a visit to a tobacco farm, a rodeo show, and a trip on a motorboat to an island in the middle of a lake called Liberación de Florencia. Transport in this region is scant, but there are accommodation options at the **Campismo Boquerón** (6-9318) in the foothills of the Sierra de Jatibonico where horseback riding and swimming in a nearby river are highlights. Ask at the Infotur office for more details.

**Infotur** (20 91 09; Doce Plantas, cnr Honorato del Castillo & Libertad, 9am-noon & 1-6pm Mon-Sun) Cuba's premier information outlet offers advice on less-heralded attractions.

**Oficina de Jardines del Rey** (Máximo Gómez Oeste No 82; 9am-5pm Mon-Fri) General information, plus an interesting map showing the past, present and future development on the keys. It's on the corner of Maceo.

## Sights & Activities

Manageable and friendly, Ciego de Ávila engenders a leisurely pace and the switched-on staff at the Infotur office can pass on plenty of recommendations. Check out **Parque Martí** first – with the inevitable monument to José Martí (1925) – around which is the 1911 **Ayuntamiento** (City Hall; no visitors), now the provincial government headquarters and the **Museo de Artes Decorativas** (20 16 61; cnr Independencia & Marcial Gómez; CUC$1; 8am-5pm Mon & Tue, 8am-10pm Wed-Sat, 8am-noon & 6-10pm Sun). This thoughtful collection can be seen in 45 minutes and has quirky items from a bygone age, such as a working Victrola (Benny Moré serenades your visit), antique pocket watches and ornate canopy beds with mother-of-pearl inlays. A CUC$1 tip gets you a super guide (in English or Spanish). The only other notable building is the grand **Teatro Principal** (22 20 86; cnr Joaquín Agüero Oeste & Honorato del Castillo), built in 1927.

If you have time, you could visit the **Centro Raúl Martínez Galería de Arte Provincial** (Calle Independencia Oeste No 65 btwn Honorato del Castillo & Maceo; 8am-noon & 1-5pm Mon & Wed, 1-9pm Thu & Fri, 2-10pm Sat, 8am-noon Sun), where works by Cuba's papa of pop art are on permanent display, along with many new works by local artists. Or visit the **Parque Zoológico** (Independencia Este; admission free; Tue-Sun).

The **Museo Provincial** (22 87 07; Jose Antonio Echevarría No 25; admission CUC$1; 8am-noon & 1-5pm Mon-Sat) is located across the train tracks in a former school building marked 'Instituto de Segunda Enseñanza.' The exhibits here recount the student struggle against Fulgencio Batista. A plaque marks the **site of the constitutional court** (cnr Independencia & Agramonte) held on June 14, 1952 by students and workers protesting Batista's coup d'état.

There's a tobacco factory, **Fábrica de Tabacos El Sucro** (cnr Libertad & Maceo) in town, though tours are normally group-only. Ask at the Havanatur office and you may be able to tag along.

From October to April, ask about baseball games at the **Estadio José R Cepero** (22 82 83; Máximo Gómez), northwest of the center.

## Festivals & Events

Every November, in the rural town of Majagua, 25km to the west, the population splits into two teams – one red and one blue – to re-enact an old *caringa* dancing competition played out to a background of traditional *guajiro* (country) music. This colorful spectacle is known as the **Fiesta de los Bandos Rojo y Azul**.

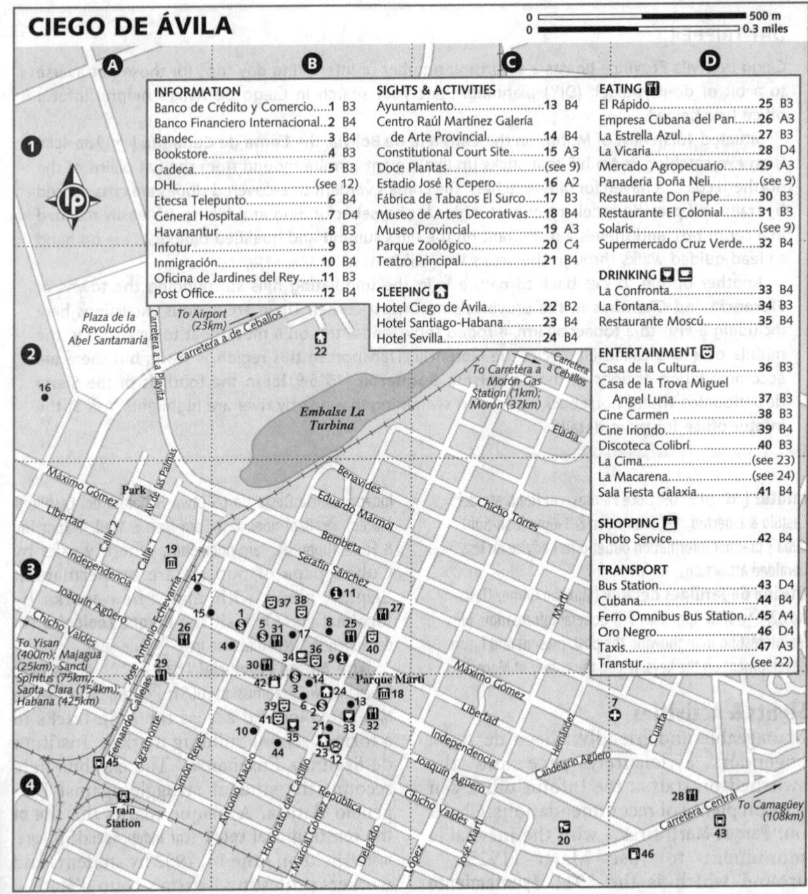


## Sleeping

**Hotel Santiago-Habana** (Islazul; ☎ 22 72 62; cnr Chicho Valdés & Honorato del Castillo; s/d low season CUC$22/30, high season CUC$27/36) This is an option in the town center with 76 rooms favored by vacationing Cubans; it's a basic bed-down. Disco Centro Nocturno La Cima is on the top floor.

**Hotel Ciego de Ávila** (Islazul; ☎ 22 57 72; Carretera a Ceballos; s/d low season CUC$26/34, high season CUC$29/38; P ✖ ☒) Bus tours usually stay at this modern four-story hotel. Others won't likely find a need to drop in except to visit the Batanga Disco, rent a car, or eat at the CUC$2.50 breakfast buffet (not bad; decent coffee), which is free for guests. Rooms are rough around the edges but the service is friendly and it's a 2km walk into town.

**Hotel Sevilla** (☎ 22 56 03; Independencia Oeste No 57 btwn Maceo & Honorato de Castillo; s/d CUC$39/42) This elegant building just off Parque Martí, dates from 1929 and had a facelift in 1999. Some rooms have balconies, but none have hot water. The open bar on the 3rd floor offers great views, and the ground-floor restaurant, decorated in a classic old-fashioned style is a fine, inexpensive dining option.

## Eating

### RESTAURANTS

**La Estrella Azul** (cnr Máximo Gomez & Honorato del Castillo) Brand new restaurant with various set dishes for CUC$1.50 each. Quite possibly the cheapest quality food in town.

**La Vicaria** (☎ 26 64 77; Carretera Central; 8am-midnight) It's hard to go wrong with this national chain, known for its tasty, affordable food and professional, even efficient (!) service. This outlet near Máximo Gómez, across from the bus station, is particularly good, with a full meal of juicy pork steak, fries, salad, soda and ice cream costing CUC$4.

**Yisan** (Carretera Central btwn Calles 8 & 13; Wed-Mon) Chow Mien and fried rice with a mysterious Cuban twist. Don't arrive expecting dim sum at this cheerful Ciego Chinese joint, though the price is right and the service quick enough.

**Restaurante Don Pepe** (☎ 22 37 13; Independencia Oeste No 103 btwn Maceo & Simón Reyes; 8-11:45pm Wed-Mon) A bartender named Eladio invented the Coctel Don Pepe (two shots of orange juice, 1.5 shots of white rum, and half a shot of crème de menthe, stirred) here back in the day. They're still serving them, along with the good old pork and chicken dishes found everywhere. There's live music nightly.

**Restaurante El Colonial** (☎ 22 35 95; Independencia Oeste No 110; 6-11:30pm) For the regular pig and *pollo* (chicken), this is the place. It's located in a big house in the center of town with a nice courtyard.

**El Rápido** (☎ 26 61 16; cnr Libertad & Castillo; 24hr) When in doubt seek it out. This branch sells good yogurt and claims to be open 24 hours.

**Solaris** (☎ 22 21 56; H Castillo btwn Independencia & Libertad) Enthusiastically recommended by the locals, this city-center joint, upstairs in the Doce Plantas building, gives good views and has a menu of *comida internacional* (international cuisine). Ask for the special Solaris cocktail.

### GROCERIES

**Mercado agropecuario** (Chicho Valdés Oeste btwn Agramonte & Calle 1) There's a vegetable market located in a blemished part of town below the overpass.

**Supermercado Cruz Verde** (cnr Independencia & Máximo Gómez; 9am-6pm Mon-Sat, 9am-noon Sun) Sells groceries.

For bread, it's either **Panadería Doña Neli** (Parque Martí), in the northeastern corner of Doce Plantas, which charges in Convertibles, or **Empresa Cubana del Pan** (☎ 22 58 40; cnr Independencia & Agramonte) in pesos.

### CASAS PARTICULARES – CIEGO DE ÁVILA

Ciego has some decent, well-signposted casas particulares and not much demand.

**Belkis de Caridad Jiménez** (☎ 22 46 09; Carretera Central No 76 btwn Maceo & H Castillo; r CUC$15; ) Situated right on Ciego's and Cuba's main artery.

**Gladys Luis Marrero** (no phone; Calle Independencia No 205 btwn Onelio Hernández & Cuarta; r CUC$20; ) Nice independent place with patio, TV, perks; near the hospital.

**Leonarda Guitierrez** (☎ 20 27 22; Honorato del Castillo No 64 btwn Chiccho Valdés & Joaquín Agüero; r CUC$15-20; ) Friendly, knows other casas particulares if you're stuck.

**María del Carmen** (☎ 20 12 02; cnr Honorato del Castillo & Independencia; r CUC$20; ) Central; rents room in apartment.

**Miriam Marzabal Gómez** (☎ 20 32 95; Marcial Gómez No 58 btwn Joaquín Agüero & Chicho Valdés; r CUC$20; ) Spacious, comfortable rooms with TV and patio.

## Drinking

**Restaurante Moscú** (☎ 22 53 86; Chicho Valdés No 78; 6-10pm Tue-Thu) Walk left, past the scale model of the Kremlin, and down a fluorescent-lit hall. Push through the door in the back and step into the hushed red hues of (what else?!) the Moscú lounge.

**La Confronta** (cnr Máximo Gomez & Agüero) If you're tired of the mojito/daiquiri monopoly, this place has a bar that sells 25 different types of cocktails and is open all day.

**La Fontana** (☎ 20 21 79; cnr Independencia & Antonio Maceo; 6am-2:30pm & 4pm-midnight) Ciego's famous coffee institution was undergoing renovation at the time of writing, but caffeine-starved locals have been talking enthusiastically about a re-opening soon. Check at your casa particular for updates.

## Entertainment

**Sala Fiesta Galaxia** (cnr Chicho Valdés & Maceo; 10pm-2am Tue-Sun) Ciego heats up at this al fresco peso disco with dancing nightly and Sunday rap *peñas* (performances; 2pm).

**Casa de la Trova Miguel Angel Luna** (Libertad No 130) Located on the corner of Simón Reyes; Cuban folk-singing is the staple here.

**Casa de la Cultura** (☎ 22 39 74; Independencia No 76 btwn Maceo & Honorato de Castillo) This place usually has something interesting on; for further information on events be sure to check the *cartelera* (culture calendar) out front.

If you're in the mood to catch a film, try **Cine Carmen** (☎ 22 33 87; Maceo No 51), on the corner of Libertad, with big screen and video offerings daily (don't miss the big movie projector spilling film on the Libertad side of the building), or **Cine Iriondo** (☎ 22 33 04; cnr Joaquín Agüero Oeste & Maceo).

There's disco fever in the hotels: **Pisco Centro Nocturno La Cima** (☎ 22 72 62; Hotel Santiago-Habana, cnr Chicho Valdés & Honorato del Castillo) and **La Macarena** (☎ 22 56 03; Hotel Sevilla, Independencia Oeste No 57 btwn Maceo & Honorato de Castillo). If Karaoke's your thing, exercise your lungs at **Discoteca Colibrí** (cnr Máximo Gomez & H Castillo; admission CUC$1; 10pm-3am).

## Shopping

**Photo Service** (Maceo No 9 btwn Joaquín Agüero & Independencia) This store will service all your basic camera needs.

## Getting There & Away

### AIR

Ciego de Ávila's Máximo Gómez Airport (airport code AVI) is 10km northwest of Ceballos, 23km north of Ciego de Ávila and 23km south of Morón. **Cubana** (☎ 3-2525/4; Chicho Valdés btwn Honorato del Castillo & Antonio Maceo) has weekly flights to Habana (CUC$78 one way, 1½ hours).

International flights arrive daily from Canada, Argentina, France, the UK and Italy.

### BUS

The **bus station** (☎ 22 24 07; Carretera Central), situated about 1.5km east of the center, has Astro buses to Camagüey (CUC$4), Habana (CUC$19), Manzanillo (CUC$14) and Niqero (CUC$17).

Tickets for these buses are sold in Convertibles at the regular ticket window, but most long-distance Astro buses are already full once they reach Ciego de Ávila. Colectivos (collective taxis) located outside the station leave occasionally for Sancti Spíritus or Camagüey (CUC$20 for the car to either). Colectivos to Habana charge CUC$80.

Víazul has daily services to the following destinations:

| Destination | Cost (one way) | Travel time (hours) | Departs |
|---|---|---|---|
| Habana | CUC$27 | 7 | 6:35pm, 1am, 5:35am |
| Santiago de Cuba | CUC$24 | 9 | 4:30pm, 10:10pm, 4:30am, 10:45am |
| Trinidad | CUC$6 | 3 | 4:15am |

The Santiago de Cuba departure also stops at Camagüey (CUC$6, one hour 35 minutes), Las Tunas (CUC$13, four hours 25 minutes), Holguín (CUC$17, five hours 40 minutes) and Bayamo (CUC$17, seven hours). The Habana bus stops at Sancti Spíritus (CUC$6, two hours) and Santa Clara (CUC$9, three hours 20 minutes). For Víazul tickets, see the *jefe de turno* (shift manager); the office is right near the normal ticket window.

### TRAIN

The **train station** (☎ 22 33 13) is six blocks southwest of the center. Ciego de Ávila is on the main Habana–Santiago line. There are nightly trains to Bayamo (CUC$11, seven hours), Camagüey (CUC$3, two hours 10 minutes), Guantánamo (CUC$17, 9½ hours), Habana (CUC$16, 7½ hours), Holguín (CUC$11, seven hours), Manzanillo (CUC$12, 8½ hours) and Santiago de Cuba (CUC$15, 9¼ hours). Different train numbers run on alternate nights, so check the latest timetable before you leave. There

**CASAS PARTICULARES – MORÓN**

**Felicia Jiménez Rodríguez** (☎ 5-3863; Martí No 197A btwn Callejas & Libertad; r CUC$25; ) On the main drag. Hot water and meals available.

**Gina Margarita Sierra** (☎ 5-3798; Callejas No 89 btwn Martí & Castillo; r CUC$20; P ) Big room, independent entrance leads to covered patio, small garden, meals.

**'Hospedaje Liberluz' – Carlos Manuel Baez** (☎ 3440; Libertad No 148 btwn Luz Caballero & Padre Cabo; r CUC$20)

**Tamara Companioni Medina** (☎ 5-3630; Martí No 247 btwn Serafín Sánchez & Sergio Antuña; r CUC$20; P ) Central; meals served.

are three trains daily to Morón (CUC$1, one hour).

**TRUCK**

Private passenger trucks leave from the Ferro Ómnibus bus station adjacent to the train station. They might take you to Morón, Camagüey or Jatibonico.

## Getting Around

**CAR & MOPED**

The **Carretera a Morón gas station** (Carretera de Morón) is just before the bypass road, northeast of the center. The **Oro Negro gas station** (Carretera Central) is near the bus station.

You can park safely in front of the Hotel Santiago-Habana overnight.

The following companies offer vehicle rental:

**Havanautos** Hotel Ciego de Ávila (☎ 26 63 45' Carretera a Ceballos); airport (☎ 26 63 15)

**Transtur** (☎ 26 62 29; Hotel Ciego de Ávila) Rents mopeds for CUC$24 a day, not including gas.

**TAXI**

A taxi ride to the airport will cost around CUC$12; bargain if they're asking more. There's a **taxi stand** (Fernando Callegas btwn Independencia & Libertad) by the railway line.

# MORÓN

☎ 335 / pop 59,194

Morón is a well-ordered, if unremarkable, town about 40km north of Ciego de Ávila via a flat road through endless fields of sugarcane. Founded in 1643, two centuries before Ciego de Ávila, it's called the 'Ciudad del Gallo' (City of the Cock) for a verse about a cock that continued to crow after being de-feathered. Locals love pointing out the eye-catching bronze rooster perched on a pedestal at the entrance to the Hotel Morón; it's a town mascot. Compact and easy-going, Morón is a plausible base for day trips to the beaches at Cayo Coco and is a favorite among fishermen and hunters who make a beeline for Laguna de Leche.

## Sights

Strolling through Morón's easy-to-navigate town center is enough for a short morning's distraction. Shoehorned in among the busy sidewalks and peeling colonnades, the most notable sight is the **Museo de Archeologica y Historia** (Calle Martí; admission CUC$1; 🕑 9am-noon & 6pm-10pm) which has two floors, the upper of which is given over to the history of the city itself. There is a *mirador* (lookout) on the roof with a good view out over the town.

## Sleeping

Thankfully there are sufficient private homes in Morón (see opposite), because the state-run scene isn't very inspiring.

**Carrusel Morón** (Cubanacán; ☎ 3901; Av de Tarafa; s/d low season CUC$28/36, high season CUC$33/42; P ✖ ) Presently this modern-ish, four-story hotel at the south entrance to town is the only place in Morón accommodating groups. A useful location for Cayo Coco–bound traffic, but the facilities aren't anything to write home about. Package tourists are the main clientele with the odd stray fisherman thrown in for good measure. The pool is a rare highlight; nonguests can ask

### THE WORLD'S OLDEST MAN

The inaugural meeting of the 120 Club – an organization promoting healthy living for Cuba's most elderly citizens – was in February 2005. It was here that the Castro government, always keen to extol the benefits of its groundbreaking free healthcare system, declared that it had uncovered the world's oldest living person.

The character in question was Benito Martínez, a loquacious and remarkably spry ex-road laborer from a small community of local farmers located near the town of Ciego de Ávila in central Cuba.

Martínez, according to popular legend, was born in Cavaellon, Haiti in the year 1880 and migrated to Cuba via a steamship in 1925 where he worked for a while on the ranch of Angel Castro, Fidel's father.

Despite the fact that no official records exist of Benito's birth, Cuban experts have said that they believe him to be at least 119, thus supplanting the current official world-record holder, an Ecuadorian woman aged 116.

about day passes. Maintain low expectations for the restaurant and you might be pleasantly surprised.

### Eating

**Las Fuentes** (☎ 5758; Martí No 169 btwn Agramonte & Libertad; 🕑 11am-11pm) The surest bet for a solid meal in Morón is this place, you can get everything from a nice salad to grilled lobster. Fish dinners start at CUC$5 if you can't face another dose of fried-to-a-cinder chicken.

**Las Delícias** (🕑 noon-midnight) Across the street from Fuentes is a clean, friendly peso place with proteinlike chicken soup or egg sandwiches for two pesos.

**Paraíso Palmares** (Martí No 382) This restaurant has standard chicken fare with the obligatory *arroz congris* (rice and beans).

**Cafetería Mi Café** (Martí No 294 btwn Calleja & S Sánchez; 🕑 9am-10pm Mon-Sat) is for coffee junkies and the hollowed out shell of the **Coppelia** (cnr Callejas & Martí) for those seriously addicted to ice-cream.

On the self-catering front there's **Doña Neli-Dulcería** (Serafín Sánchez No 86 btwn Narcisso López & Martí) for bread and pastries and **La Mina de Oro** (Calle Martí) for groceries.

### Entertainment

**Casa de la Trova Pablo Bernal** (Calle Libertad No 74 btwn Martí & Narciso López) This venue is frequented by local folk singers and musicians.

**Batanga Disco** (☎ 3901; Carrusel Morón, Av de Tarafa; 🕑 9:30pm-2am) This is a favorite of young locals starved for action.

### Getting There & Away

Five buses a day leave from the hectic **train station** (☎ 3683; cnr Martí & JF Poey) for Ciego de Ávila. You might be able to convince a collective taxi parked in front of the station to do this trip, but most are wary of carrying foreigners. Trains depart for Santiago de Cuba (CUC$22, alternate days) via Ciego de Ávila (CUC$1, twice daily) and Camagüey (CUC$4, twice daily). The line from Santa Clara to Nuevitas also passes through Morón via Chambas. A coche motor railcar to Habana (CUC$24, 6½ hours) operates on alternate days.

### Getting Around

The roads from Morón northwest to Caibarién (112km) and southeast Nuevitas (168km) are both good.

**Havanautos** (☎ 5-2115; Av de Tarafa s/n) is between Carrusel Morón and Hotel Perla del Norte. **Transtur** (☎ 2222; Carrusel Morón, Av de Tarafa) rents mopeds. **Micar** (☎ 5-5245; Los Balcones Commercial Center, cnr Av de Tarafa & Línea) has fancy autos.

The **Servi-Cupet gas station** (🕑 24hr) is near Carrusel Morón.

## NORTH OF MORÓN

Measuring 67 sq km, the **Laguna de la Leche** (Milk Lake) a few kilometers north of Morón, is named for its reflective underwater lime deposits and is the largest natural lake in Cuba. Accessed from the south via a link road from Morón (3km) the lake is popular among budding anglers who flock here to take advantage of its abundant stocks of carp, tarpon, snook and tilapia. Situated on the southern shoreline you'll find **La Atarraya** (☎ 5-5351), a restaurant specializing in fish dishes, as well as an entertainment venue known as **Cabaret Cueva** (☎ 5-2239) You can rent boats here as well. Every year Laguna de Leche is the venue for the **Morón Aquatic Carnival.** The area has also twice hosted the Jardines del Rey **F-1 speedboat competition.**

There's terrific fishing for largemouth bass and trout at the **Marina Fluvial La Redonda** on Laguna La Redonda, 18km north of Morón, off the road to Cayo Coco. The mangroves surrounding this 4-sq-km lake are prime romping grounds for freshwater fish and the per-square-kilometer density of trout here is greater than anywhere in Cuba. Four/eight hours of fishing costs CUC$40/70 or a boat trip without rods costs CUC$16. There's a nice bar-restaurant combo here if you only want to stop for a drink with a lake view. Try the house specialty, a fillet of fish called *calentico* – great with ketchup and Tabasco.

The **Aguachales de Falla Game Reserve** is a hunting area containing seven natural lakes and abundant flocks of pigeons, ducks and doves. If you really feel the urge, you can take the Hemingway tour to its natural conclusion (Papa loved firing guns at feathered targets).

**El Pueblo Holandés**, a small community with 49 red-roofed, Dutch-style dwellings, is on a hill next to the highway, 4km north of La Redonda. It was built by Celia Sánchez in 1960 as a home for area cattle workers. It's

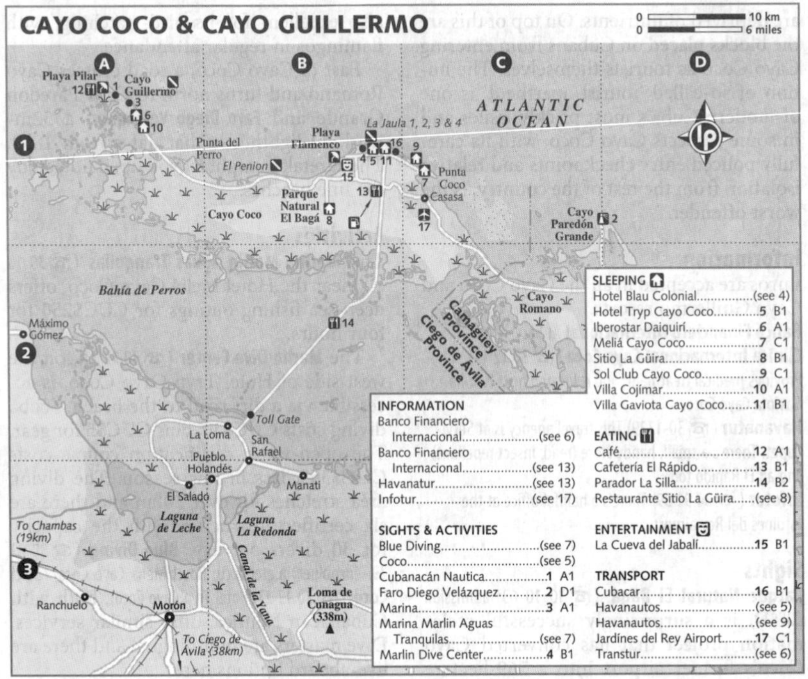


an interesting blip on the landscape, but not worth a detour.

In rodeo-land Cuba is right up there with the Calgary Stampede and one of the island's best cattle fests can be seen at **Isla Turiguano** on the road out of Morón, a kilometer or two before the Cayo Coco checkpoint. Cowboys, bulls, horses and lassos are in evidence every weekend at around 2pm for exciting 90-minute *espectaculos* (shows). Alternatively you can drop by for a look at the animals any time. There's a small bar out front.

## CAYO COCO

☎ 33

Cayo Coco is Cuba's fourth largest island and the main tourist destination after Varadero. Situated in the Archipiélago de Sabana-Camagüey, or the Jardines del Rey as travel brochures prefer to call it, the area north of the Bahía de Perros (Bay of Dogs) was uninhabited before 1992 when the first hotel – the Cojímar – went up on adjoining Cayo Guillermo. The bulldozers haven't stopped buzzing since.

While the beauty of the beaches on these islands is world famous, Cayo Coco pre-1990 was little more than a mosquito-infested mangrove swamp. French corsair Jacques de Sores was one of the earliest visitors, fresh from successful raids on Habana and Puerto Príncipe and he was followed in 1752 by the island's first landowner, an opportunistic Spaniard named Santiago Abuero Castañeda. Between 1927 and 1955 a community of 600 people scraped a living by producing charcoal for use as domestic fuel on the island, but with the rise of electrical power after the revolution this too died.

Since 1988, Cayo Coco has been connected to the mainland by a 27km causeway slicing across the Bahía de Perros. There are also causeways from Cayo Coco to Cayo Guillermo in the west and to Cayo Romano in the east. The impact of these synthetic barriers on the environment has been severe. Circulation of seawater and marine life in the fragile coastal areas has been effectively blocked, to varying degrees, and waters east of the Cayo Coco causeway are deprived of nutrients. On top of this are the blocks placed on Cubans from entering Cayo Coco as tourists themselves. The notion of so-called 'tourist apartheid' is one of modern Cuba's most prickly issues and in some respects Cayo Coco, with its carefully policed entry checkpoints and relative isolation from the rest of the country, is the worst offender.

## Information

Euros are accepted in all the Cayo Coco and Cayo Guillermo resorts.

**Banco Financiero Internacional** At Servi-Cupet.

**Clinica Internacional Cayo Coco** (☎ 30 12 15) Provides medical treatment, and is located next to Villa Gaviota Cayo Coco.

**Havanatur** (☎ 30-1329) This travel agency is at Servi-Cupet. There's a small, handy store (read: insect repellant) and an El Rapído too.

**Infotur** (☎ 30 91 09) There's a helpful office at the Jardines del Rey airport.

## Sights

**Parque Natural El Bagá** (☎ 30 10 63; admission CUC$12) is a surprisingly successful reclamation project that has converted Cayo Coco's former airport into a 769-hectare natural park. Included in a 45-minute guided trail are a *mirador*, a canal trip, a pleasant beach and – just when you thought it was getting good – a reconstructed native village (with shows). An area of dense mangroves and lapping waves is also excellent for its bird-watching, with flamingos in regular attendance.

East of Cayo Coco, a road crosses Cayo Romano and turns north to Cayo Paredón Grande and **Faro Diego Velázquez**, a 52m-working lighthouse that dates from 1859. The caretaker might let you up; if not, enjoy the fine beaches.

## Activities

The **Marina Marlin Aguas Tranquilas** (☎ 30 13 24), near the Hotel Meliá Cayo Coco, offers deep-sea fishing outings for CUC$250 for four hours.

The **Marlin Dive Center** (☎ 30 12 21), on the west side of Hotel Tryp Cayo Coco, is accessible via a dirt road to the beach. Scuba diving costs CUC$30, plus CUC$5 for gear. The open-water certification course costs CUC$365, less in low season. The diving area stretches for over 10km and there are six certified instructors with the capacity for 30 divers per day. **Blue Diving** (☎ 30 81 79; enzoblue@ip.etecsa.cu; Hotel Melía Cayo Coco) and **Coco** (☎ 30 13 23; Hotel Tryp Cayo Coco), both with Cubanacán Náutica, offer similar services. Dive masters are multilingual and there are live-aboard options here.

## Sleeping

### BUDGET

**Sitio La Güira** (☎ 30 12 08; cabaña shared/private bath CUC$20/25) Cayo Coco's one cheap accommodation option is situated on a

### LOS JARDINES DE LA REINA

Los Jardines de la Reina are a 120km-long mangrove and coral island system situated 80km off the south coast of Ciego de Ávila Province and 120km north of the Cayman Islands. The local marine park measures 3800 sq km with virgin territory left more or less untouched since the time of Columbus. Commercial fishing in the area has been banned and, with a permanent local population of precisely zero inhabitants, visitors must stay on board a two-story seven-bedroom houseboat called **Hotel Flotante Tortuga** (☎ 339-8104) or venture in from the port of Embarcadero de Júcaro on one of two yachts, the six-cabin *Halcon* or the four-cabin *Explorador*.

The flora consists of palm trees, pines, sea grapes and mangroves, while the fauna – aside from tree rats and iguanas – contains an interesting variety of resident birds including ospreys, pelicans, spoonbills and egrets. Below the waves the main attraction is sharks (both whale and hammerhead) and this, along with the pristine coral and unequaled clarity of the water, is what draws in divers from all over the world.

Getting to Los Jardines is not easy – or cheap. The only company currently offering excursions is the Italian-run **Avalon** (www.avalons.net). One-week dive packages which include equipment, six nights of accommodation, a guide, park license, 12 dives and transfer from Embarcadero de Júcaro, cost in the vicinity of CUC$1500. Another option is to sail with the Windward Islands Cruising Company departing from Trinidad (for details, see p302).

small farm 8km west of Servi-Cupet. It rents two rooms sharing a bath and a couple of Cuban *bohíos* (thatched huts) with private bath. A reasonable restaurant and bar are on the shady grounds and horseback riding is available. It's a mellow place until 11:30am when resort crowds pour in; the plethora of animals and extensive grounds make this a good budget place to take the kids. It's a hike (or a horseback ride) to the beach.

#### TOP END

Cayo Coco's all-inclusive resorts are policed pretty diligently. Unless you're wearing the 'access-all-areas' plastic wristband, think twice about sneaking in to use the toilets at any of these places. Room rates are all-inclusive.

**Hotel Blau Colonial** (r from CUC$130; P) Formerly known as the Guitart Cayo Coco, this landscaped resort was the island's first hotel when it opened in 1993 (ancient history by Cayo Coco standards). The hotel gained notoriety in 1994 when gunmen from the right-wing Cuban exile movement, Alpha 66, opened fire on the building in a blatant act of provocation. Fortunately no one was hurt. Refurbished under new management in 2003, the Blau now sparkles afresh and gets rave reviews from its mainly Canadian clientele.

**Meliá Cayo Coco** (☎ 30 11 80; r from CUC$132; P) This resort on stellar Playa Las Coloradas at the eastern end of the hotel strip, was erected in 1999 by the Spanish Meliá hotel chain. The sweet bungalows perched in the lagoon have porches and lots of sun. There are tons of romantic pockets here and the rooms are muted, tasteful and comfortable.

**Villa Gaviota Cayo Coco** (Gaviota; ☎ 30 21 80; s/d/tr low season CUC$75/100/120, high season CUC$75/150/170 P) An amiable low-key place, Villa Gaviota has friendly service and a degree of intimacy missing from most of the larger resorts.

**Sol Club Cayo Coco** (☎ 30 12 80) Next door to Meliá Caya Coco, this is a family version of the same dreamscape for marginally cheaper rates.

**Hotel Tryp Cayo Coco** (Cubanacán; ☎ 30 13 11; r from CUC$170; P) Part of a sprawling complex (there are 502 rooms here), this resort is the older, humbler cousin to the other Melías here. A long pool meanders through the complex and there's snorkeling in the clear waters in front of the resorts. There's a disco, a Banco Financiero Internacional branch and Clínica Internacional here, but they're accessible only to hotel guests.

### Eating

All of the large resorts here are all-inclusive, so there are few nonhotel restaurants.

**Cafetería El Rápido** (Servi-Cupet gas station; 24hr) This fast-food place on the roundabout at the entrance to Cayo Coco has cheap drinks and snacks 24 hours a day.

**Restaurant Sitio La Güira** (8am-11pm) This restaurant has a varied menu with big, fresh sandwiches for CUC$1.50, shrimp plates for CUC$12 and a full bar.

Floating almost on the shallow Bahía de Perros, Parador La Silla is a thatched-roof snack bar halfway along the causeway into Cayo Coco.

### Drinking & Entertainment

**La Cueva del Jabalí** (☎ 30 12 06; admission CUC$5; Tue-Sat) For those bored of the all-inclusive floor show, this is the only independent entertainment venue in Cayo Coco. It's 5km west of the Tryp complex, in a natural cave. The place features a cabaret show and it's free all day to visit the bar.

### Getting There & Around

Opened in 2001, Cayo Coco's **Aeropuerto Internacional Jardínes del Rey** (☎ 30 91 65) boasts a new 3000m-runway facility that can process 1.2 million visitors annually. Weekly flights arrive here from Canada, Mexico, Spain, the UK, Germany, and more. There's a twice-daily service to and from Habana (CUC$105) with **Aerogaviota** (☎ 7-203-0686).

Cayo Coco is the LA of Cuba. There are no public buses and walking is barely possible as all the resorts are so strung out. To get there, independent travelers may be able to hitch a ride out of Morón with other tourists or a Cuban worker. Don't forget, once you leave the road and enter onto the causeway proper, there's a checkpoint (where they'll turn back any unauthorized Cubans), and a CUC$2 toll.

You can rent a car or moped at the following places on Cayo Coco:

**Cubacar** (☎ 30 12 75) On the second roundabout between the Meliá and Tryp complexes.

**Havanautos** Sol Club Cayo Coco (☎ 30 12 28) Hotel Tryp Cayo Coco (☎ 30 13 11)

## CAYO GUILLERMO

Just west of Cayo Coco is 13-sq-km Cayo Guillermo, a much smaller coral key connected to Cayo Coco by a causeway. The mangroves off the south coast of Cayo Guillermo are home to pink flamingos and pelicans, and there's a great diversity of tropical fish and crustaceans on the key's Atlantic reef.

Cayo Guillermo is probably the number-one sport fishing destination in Cuba. The deep-sea fishing facilities are unequalled, and several freshwater lakes on the mainland are within commuting distance.

A Banco Financiero Internacional branch and Transtur rental car office are on the premises of Iberostar Daiquirí (right).

### Activities

The **Marina** (☎ 30 17 38; fax 30 16 37) at Sol Club Cayo Guillermo offers deep-sea fishing for mackerel, pike, barracuda, red snapper and marlin on large boats that depart from a pier right at the hotel. It's CUC$250/450 for a half-/full day, and you can keep some of the fish. A professional dive center charging CUC$35 a dive is also here. It is best to go directly to the pier and book the dive in person. Note that trips are cancelled when it's too windy. **Cubanacán Naútica** (Melía Cayo Guillermo ☎ 30 16 27; Sol Club Cayo Guillermo ☎ 30 17 60) has two dive centers running dives for CUC$35.

This was a favorite fishing spot of writer Ernest Hemingway, who mentioned Cayo Guillermo in his book *Islands in the Stream*. The best beach here (and possibly on the islands as a whole) is **Playa Pilar**, named after Hemingway's boat. It's a lovely, unspoiled beach at the far western end of this key where you can sail and snorkel.

### Sleeping & Eating

**Iberostar Daiquirí** (Gran Caribe; ☎ 30 16 50; r from CUC$95; P ✗ 💻 🏊) This hotel has 312 rooms in a series of three-story buildings, all brightly painted like Las Vegas casinos – there's no accounting for taste. Extensive gardens are a bonus. Also check out the kids' packages.

**Villa Cojímar** (Gran Caribe; ☎ 30 17 12; s/d all-inclusive low season CUC$81/115, high season CUC$102/145; P ⊠ ✗ 💻 🏊) The oldest hotel on the Sabana-Camagüey archipelago opened in 1992 and comprises of a rather fetching collection of bungalows in a quiet beach-side location. The advertising blurb refers to it as a 'Cuban-style hotel', but the only Cubans you're likely to meet are the people who make your room up.

There's a kicking café at Playa Pilar where you can get an espresso for CUC$0.50.

### Getting There & Around

Access information is the same as for Cayo Coco (see p319). Unless you're on a tour, the usual way to get here is by rental car. **Transtur** (☎ 30 11 75) has offices at the Iberostar Daiquirí.

# Camagüey Province

Camagüey is cattle country, the island's largest province and home to more cows than people. Aside from large-scale beef production, and an itinerant population of lasso-wielding *vaqueros* (cowboys), the territory also supports a significant industrial infrastructure with the bulk of the factory base located in bay-side Nuevitas, a busy port town which houses a thermo-electric plant, a large cement factory and a thriving sugar export facility.

Further south is Camagüey, the province's labyrinthine capital, a conservative and unashamedly Catholic city, characterized by its signature *tinajones* (clay pots) and weathered collection of colonial churches. In streets so narrow that driving becomes a liability, explorers can choose between a plethora of cool bars and vibrant markets or make a beeline for the gilded auditorium of the Teatro Principal, home of the celebrated Ballet de Camagüey, one of the island's finest professional dance companies.

East of the capital, savannah-like uplands fold gently into the Sierra de Najasa hills, where the little-known Hacienda la Belén reserve shelters several species of exotic animal and provides an important habitat for rare birds. Roads north lead to Playa Santa Lucía, an all-inclusive resort strip that boasts one of Cuba's longest unbroken beaches and harbors some of the country's most accessible diving reefs. For scuba enthusiasts shark-feeding is an underwater highlight, while for wilderness-seekers sweet serendipity can be found on Cayo Sabinal, where development begins and ends with a five-room beach hut.

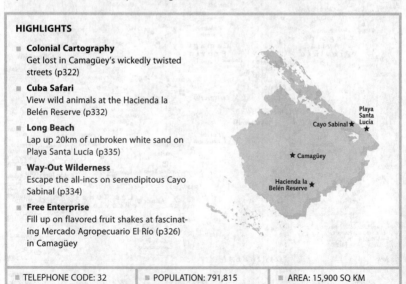

**HIGHLIGHTS**

- **Colonial Cartography**
  Get lost in Camagüey's wickedly twisted streets (p322)
- **Cuba Safari**
  View wild animals at the Hacienda la Belén Reserve (p332)
- **Long Beach**
  Lap up 20km of unbroken white sand on Playa Santa Lucía (p335)
- **Way-Out Wilderness**
  Escape the all-incs on serendipitous Cayo Sabinal (p334)
- **Free Enterprise**
  Fill up on flavored fruit shakes at fascinating Mercado Agropecuario El Río (p326) in Camagüey

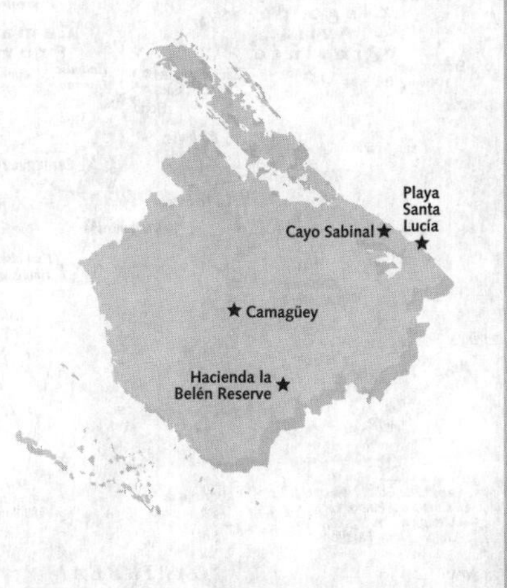


| TELEPHONE CODE: 32 | POPULATION: 791,815 | AREA: 15,900 SQ KM |
|---|---|---|

## CAMAGÜEY

☎ 32 / pop 309,977

The island's third largest settlement, Camagüey is a flat, spread-out city of picturesque churches and languid neoclassical facades that line the narrow, winding streets like Greek temples in pre-Hellenic Athens. Departing from the normal Latin American grid construction, Camagüey was purposefully built in a labyrinthine manner in order to confuse musket-toting pirates who made a habit of attacking the city in the 16th century, despite its supposedly impregnable position 50km inland. It didn't deter British buccaneer Henry Morgan, who duly sacked the magnificent cathedral in 1668 before making off with a hefty booty of gold and jewels.

Some travelers love Camagüey with its secret nooks and crannies (of which there are many, all to be explored). Other travellers are not so enamored by its unsavory reputation for bike thieves and *jineteros* (touts). Located 128km west of Las Tunas and 108km east of Ciego de Ávila, the city's inhabitants – popularly known as '*Agramonteros*' by other Cubans, after local Independence War hero Ignacio Agramonte – have a tendency to wear their inherent differences more keenly than their fellow countrymen. You'll find ingrained conservatism here and a strong Roman Catholic tradition most recently exemplified by a 1998 audience with Pope Jean Paul II.

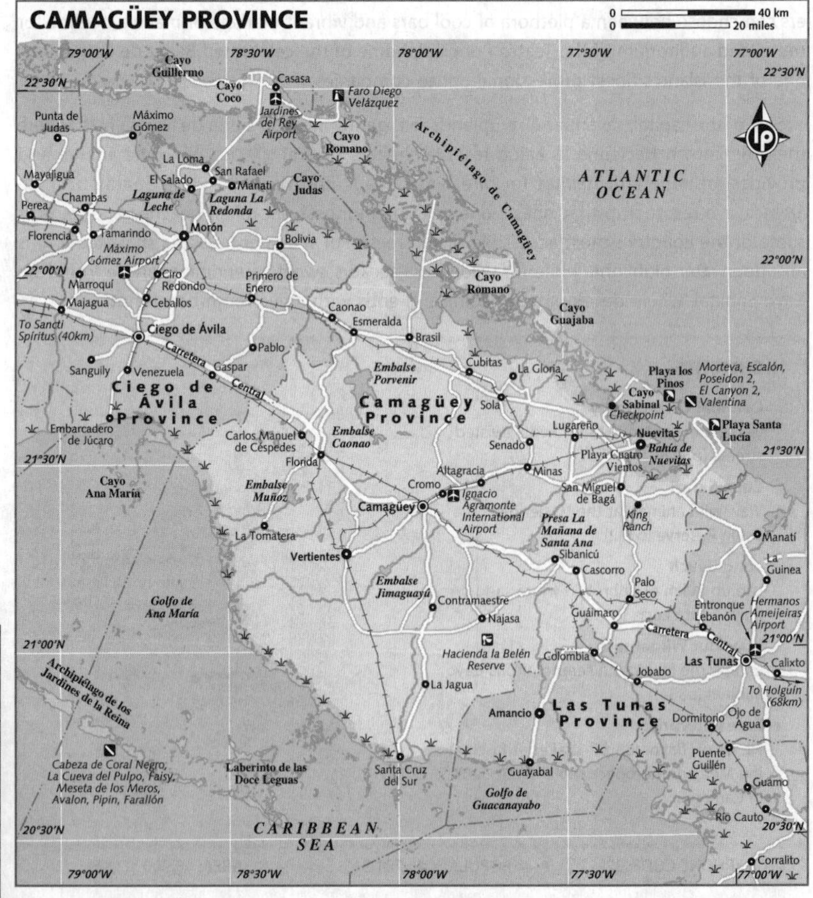

## History

Founded in February 1514 as one of Diego Velázquez' hallowed seven 'villas', Santa María del Puerto Príncipe was originally established on the coast near the site of present-day Nuevitas. Due to a series of bloody rebellions by the local Taíno Indians, the site of the city was moved twice in the early 16th century, finally taking up its present location in 1528.

Camagüey developed quickly in the 1600s – despite continued attacks by pirates and corsairs – with an economy based on sugar production and cattle-rearing. Due to acute water shortages in the area the townsfolk were forced to make *tinajones*, or huge earthenware pots, in order to collect rainwater and even today Camagüey is known as the city of *tinajones* – although the pots now serve a strictly ornamental purpose.

Aside from swashbuckling independence hero Ignacio Agramonte, Camagüey has produced several local personalities of note, including poet and patriot Nicolas Guillén and eminent doctor Carlos J Finlay, the man who was largely responsible for discovering the causes of yellow fever. In 1959 the prosperous citizens quickly fell foul of the Castro revolutionaries when local military commander Huber Matos (Fidel's onetime ally) accused *el líder máximo* (highest leader) of burying the revolution. He was duly arrested and later thrown in prison for his pains.

## Orientation

The irregular street layout makes getting around Camagüey as confusing to visitors as it was to pirates. Luckily, friendly Camagüeyanos are used to baffled travelers asking the way and they've recently put up a series of easy-to-decipher billboards that map out the best historical walking routes.

The train station is on the northern side of town, and several inexpensive hotels are clustered nearby. The city's north–south axis is República, which meets Av Agramonte at the historic La Soledad church. Most of the other hotels, churches and museums are just southwest of the church, in the city center. The Río Hatibonico crosses the southern side of the city center, and the main bus station is on the Carretera Central, about 3km southeast of the river.

## Information

### BOOKSTORES

**Librería Antonio Suárez** (Maceo btwn General Gómez & Plaza Maceo) Carries a large selection of books in Spanish.

**Librería Ateneo** (República No 418 btwn El Solitario & San Martín)

### EMERGENCY

**Asistur** (☎ 28 63 17, 28 65 17; Agramonte No 449 btwn Independencia & República) A 24-hour assistance agency dealing with lost passport/lost luggage/financial difficulties.

### INTERNET ACCESS

**Etecsa Telepunto** (República btwn San Martin & J Ramón Silva, per hr CUC$6)

### LIBRARIES

**Biblioteca Provincial Julio A Mella** (Parque Ignacio Agramonte; Mon-Sat)

### MEDIA

The local newspaper *Adelante* is published every Saturday. Radio Cadena Agramonte broadcasts in the city over frequencies 910AM and 93.5FM; it's located south of the city by tuning to 1340AM, and to the north, by tuning your radio to 1380AM.

### MEDICAL SERVICES

**Farmacia Álvarez Fuentes** (Avellaneda No 249; 24hr) On the corner of Oscar Primelles.

**Farmacia Internacional** (Agramonte No 449 btwn Independencia & República)

### CAMAGÜEY STREET NAMES

To make things even more confusing, locals doggedly stick to using the old names of streets, even though signs and maps (including those in this book) carry the new names. Here's a cheat sheet:

| Old name | New name |
|---|---|
| San Estéban | Oscar Primelles |
| Estrada Palma | Agramonte |
| Santa Rita | El Solitario |
| Francisquito | Quiñones |
| San José | José Ramón Silva |
| San Fernando | Bartolomé Masó |
| Pobre | Padre Olallo |
| Rosario | Enrique Villuendas |

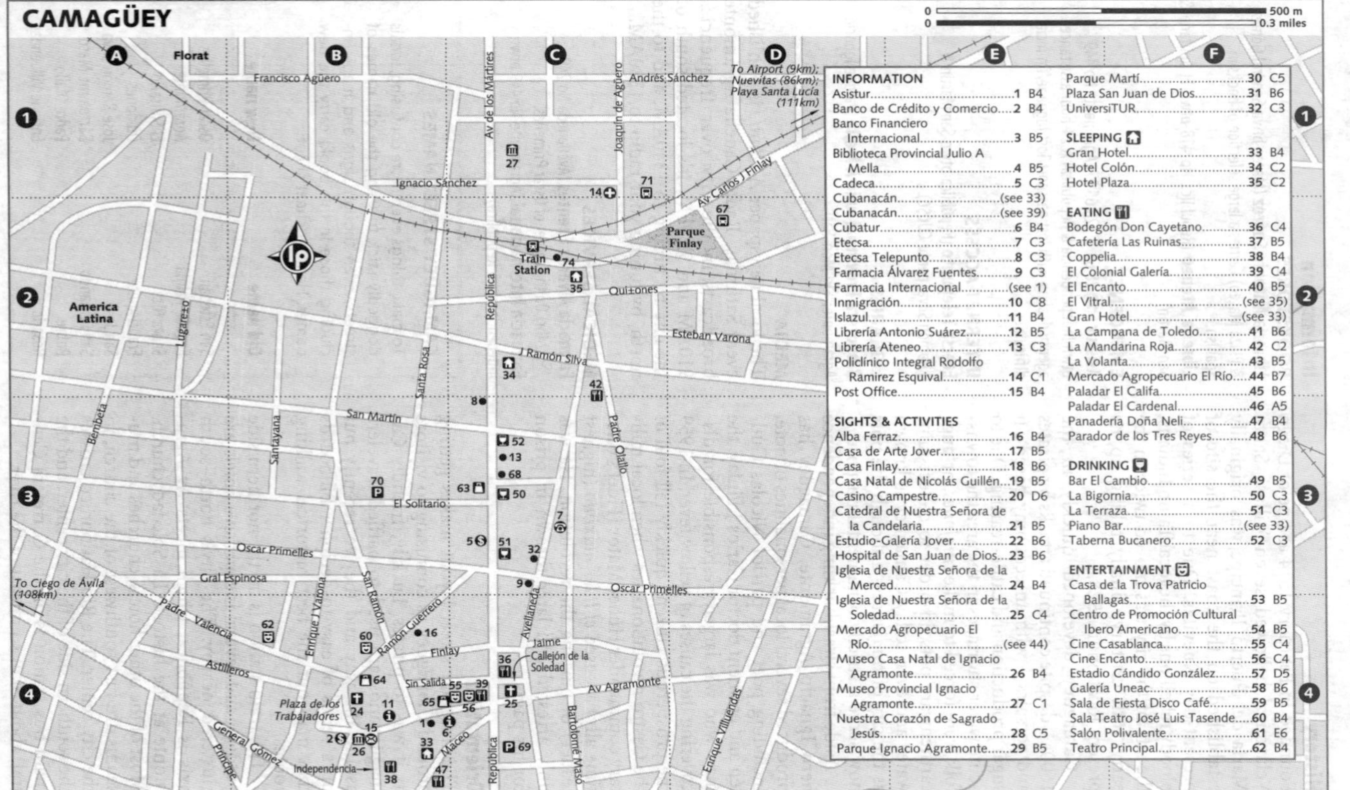
CAMAGÜEY
0 500 m
0 0.3 miles
Florat
Francisco Agüero
Av de los Mártires
Joaquín de Agüero
Andrés Sánchez
To Airport (9km); Nuevitas (86km); Playa Santa Lucía (111km)
Ignacio Sánchez
Av Carlos J Finlay
Parque Finlay
Train Station
Quiñones
America Latina
Lugareño
República
Esteban Varona
Santa Rosa
J Ramón Silva
Bembeta
San Martín
Santayana
Padre Olallo
El Solitario
Oscar Primelles
Gral Espinosa
To Ciego de Ávila (108km)
Padre Valencia
Enrique J Varona
San Ramón
Ramón Guerrero
Avellaneda
Jaime
Callejón de la Soledad
Finlay
Astilleros
Sin Salida
Av Agramonte
Plaza de los Trabajadores
General Gómez
Príncipe
Independencia
Maceo
Bartolomé Masó
Enrique Villuendas
INFORMATION
Asistur 1 B4
Banco de Crédito y Comercio 2 B4
Banco Financiero Internacional 3 B5
Biblioteca Provincial Julio A Mella 4 B5
Cadeca 5 C3
Cubanacán (see 33)
Cubanacán (see 39)
Cubatur 6 B4
Etecsa 7 C3
Etecsa Telepunto 8 C3
Farmacia Álvarez Fuentes 9 C3
Farmacia Internacional (see 1)
Inmigración 10 C8
Islazul 11 B4
Librería Antonio Suárez 12 B5
Librería Ateneo 13 C3
Policlínico Integral Rodolfo Ramirez Esquival 14 C1
Post Office 15 B4
SIGHTS & ACTIVITIES
Alba Ferraz 16 B4
Casa de Arte Jover 17 B5
Casa Finlay 18 B6
Casa Natal de Nicolás Guillén 19 B5
Casino Campestre 20 D6
Catedral de Nuestra Señora de la Candelaria 21 B5
Estudio-Galería Jover 22 B6
Hospital de San Juan de Dios 23 B6
Iglesia de Nuestra Señora de la Merced 24 B4
Iglesia de Nuestra Señora de la Soledad 25 C4
Mercado Agropecuario El Río (see 44)
Museo Casa Natal de Ignacio Agramonte 26 B4
Museo Provincial Ignacio Agramonte 27 C1
Nuestra Corazón de Sagrado Jesús 28 C5
Parque Ignacio Agramonte 29 B5
Parque Martí 30 C5
Plaza San Juan de Dios 31 B6
UniversiTUR 32 C3
SLEEPING
Gran Hotel 33 B4
Hotel Colón 34 C2
Hotel Plaza 35 C2
EATING
Bodegón Don Cayetano 36 C4
Cafetería Las Ruinas 37 B5
Coppelia 38 B4
El Colonial Galería 39 C4
El Encanto 40 B5
El Vitral (see 35)
Gran Hotel (see 33)
La Campana de Toledo 41 B6
La Mandarina Roja 42 C2
La Volanta 43 B5
Mercado Agropecuario El Río 44 B7
Paladar El Califa 45 B6
Paladar El Cardenal 46 A5
Panadería Doña Neli 47 B4
Parador de los Tres Reyes 48 B6
DRINKING
Bar El Cambio 49 B5
La Bigornia 50 C3
La Terraza 51 C3
Piano Bar (see 33)
Taberna Bucanero 52 C3
ENTERTAINMENT
Casa de la Trova Patricio Ballagas 53 B5
Centro de Promoción Cultural Ibero Americano 54 B5
Cine Casablanca 55 C4
Cine Encanto 56 C4
Estadio Cándido González 57 D5
Galería Uneac 58 B6
Sala de Fiesta Disco Café 59 B5
Sala Teatro José Luis Tasende 60 B4
Salón Polivalente 61 E6
Teatro Principal 62 B4

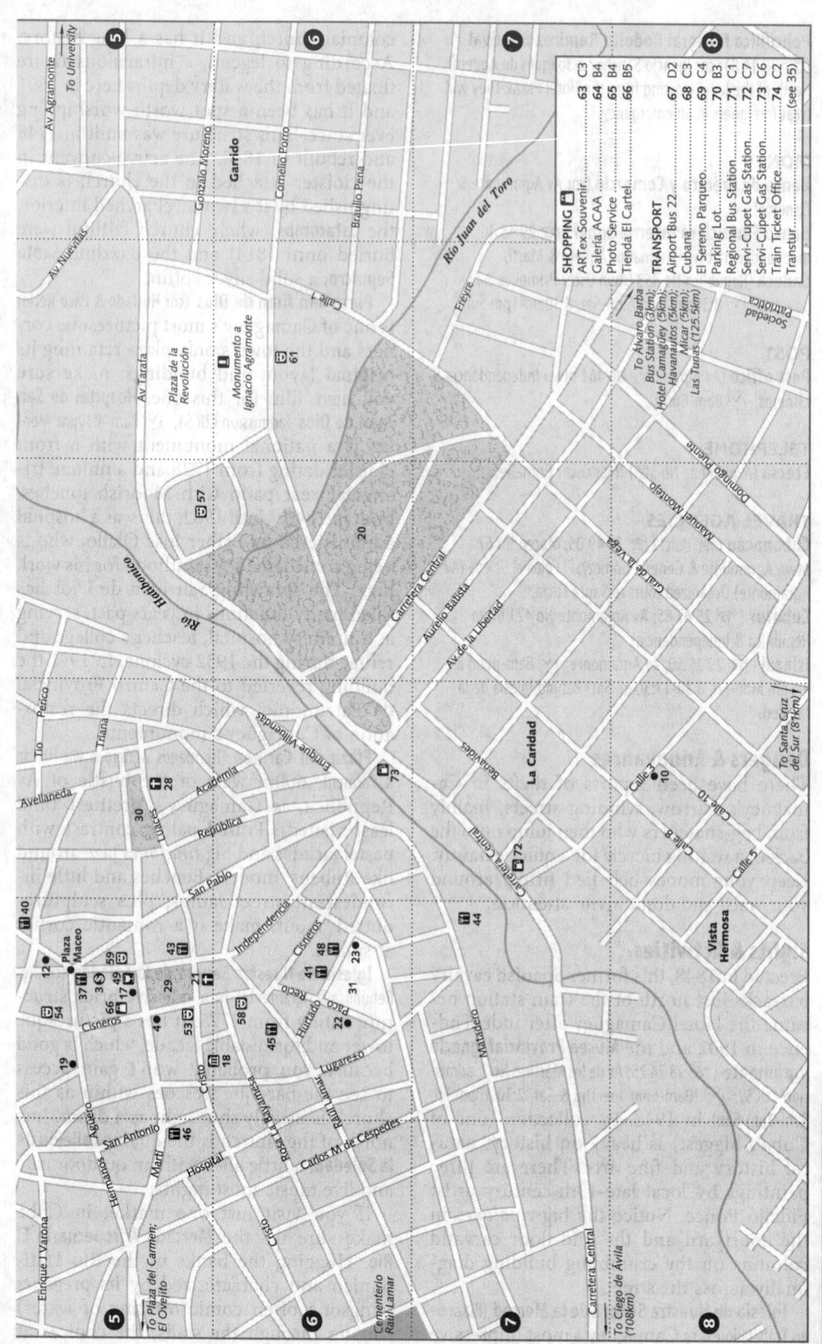


CAMAGÜEY PROVINCE

**Policlínico Integral Rodolfo Ramirez Esquival** (☎ 28 14 81; cnr Ignacio Sánchez & Joaquín de Agüero) North of the level crossing from the Hotel Plaza; they will treat foreigners in an emergency.

### MONEY

**Banco de Crédito y Comercio** (cnr Av Agramonte & Cisneros)
**Banco Financiero Internacional** (☎ 29 48 46; Independencia btwn Hermanos Agüero & Martí)
**Cadeca** (República No 353 btwn Oscar Primelles & El Solitario; 8:30am-6pm Mon-Sat, 8:30am-1pm Sun)

### POST

**Post office** (Av Agramonte No 461 btwn Independencia & Cisneros; 8am-6pm)

### TELEPHONE

**Etecsa** (Avellaneda No 308) Near Oscar Primelles.

### TRAVEL AGENCIES

**Cubanacán** Gran Hotel (☎ 29 49 05; Maceo No 67 btwn Agramonte & General Gómez); El Colonial Galería (Av Agramonte) Organized tours to Santa Lucía.
**Cubatur** (☎ 25 47 85; Av Agramonte No 421 btwn República & Independencia)
**Islazul** (☎ 29 25 50; Av Agramonte; 8am-noon & 1-5pm Mon-Fri, 8:30-11:30am Sat) Behind Iglesia de la Merced.

## Dangers & Annoyances

There have been reports of thefts in Camagüey's narrow, winding streets, mainly from bag-snatchers who then jump onto the back of a waiting bicycle for a quick getaway. Keep your money-belt tied firmly around your waist and don't invite attention.

## Sights & Activities

Erected in 1848, this former Spanish cavalry barracks just north of the train station became the Hotel Camagüey after independence in 1902 and the **Museo Provincial Ignacio Agramonte** (☎ 28 24 25; Av de los Mártires No 2; admission CUC$2; 10am-6pm Tue-Thu & Sat, 2:30-10pm Fri, 9am-1pm Sun) in 1948. Its collection (one of Cuba's biggest) is heavy on history, natural history and fine arts. There are three paintings by local late-19th-century artist Fidelio Ponce. Notice the big *tinajones* in the courtyard and the 2nd-floor caryatid columns on the crumbling building diagonally across the street.

**Iglesia de Nuestra Señora de la Merced** (Plaza de los Trabajadores) is Camagüey's most impressive colonial church and it has a long history. According to legend, a miraculous figure floated from the watery depths here in 1601 and it has been a spot worth worshipping ever since. This structure was built in 1748 and rebuilt in 1848. The active convent in the cloister attached to the church is distinguished by it's two-level arched interior, the **catacombs** (where church faithful were buried until 1814) and the dazzling **Santo Sepulcro**, a solid silver coffin.

**Plaza San Juan de Dios** (cnr Hurtado & Paco Recio) is one of Camagüey's most picturesque corners and the town's only plaza retaining its original layout and buildings; make sure you have film for this one. **Hospital de San Juan de Dios** (admission CUC$1; 8am-4:30pm Mon-Sat) is a national monument with a front cloister dating from 1728 and a unique triangular rear patio with Moorish touches, built in 1840. Until 1902, this was a hospital administered by Father José Olallo, who is being considered for sainthood for his work here. The sprawling San Juan de Dios has filled many functions in years past, serving as a military hospital, teacher's college and refuge during the 1932 cyclone. In 1991 the building reverted to the Centro Provincial de Patrimonio, which directs the restoration of Camagüey's monuments.

**Plaza del Carmen** (Hermanos Agüero btwn Honda & Carmen), 600m west of the bustle of Av República, is Camagüey's prettiest (and least visited). Potted palms contrast with pastel facades and big *tinajones* laze around like Rubens' models. Benches and little incandescent street lamps, plus sculptures dotted about, make it a romantic corner at sunset.

**Iglesia de Nuestra Señora de la Soledad** (cnr Avs República & Agramonte) is a massive brick structure dating from 1775. It has a picturesque tower and formidable facade, which is good because you probably won't gain access to see the baroque frescoes within as this church is usually shut tight as a drum. Just north of the church is the quaint **Callejón de la Soledad**, a little alley with an outdoor café and live music most nights.

If you visit just one market in Cuba make sure it's the **Mercado Agropecuario El Río**. Hugging the banks of the Río Hatibonico and characterized by its *pregónes* (singsong often comic offering of wares) ringing through the stalls, the choices at

**POET OF THE PEOPLE**

Born in Camagüey in 1902, mulatto poet Nicolas Guillén was far more than just a writer, he was a passionate and lifelong champion of Afro-Cuban rights. Rocked by the assassination of his father in his youth and inspired by the drum-influenced music of former African slaves, Guillén set about articulating the hopes and fears of dispossessed black laborers with the rhythmic Afro-Cuban verses that would ultimately become his trademark. Famous poems in a prolific career included the evocative *Tengo* and the patriotic *Che Comandante, Amigo.*

Working in self-imposed exile during the Batista years, Guillén returned to Cuba after the revolution whereupon he was given the task of formulating a new cultural policy and setting up the Unión de Escritores y Artistas de Cuba (Uneac; National Union of Cuban Writers and Artists), a body of which he became president in 1961. His modest **Casa Natal** (Hermanos Agüero No 58; admission free; 8:30am-4:30pm) gives visitors a small insight into the man and his books and today doubles up as the **Instituto Superior de Arte** where local students come to study music.

the Mercado El Río are quite amazing for a country worn-down by rationing and discouraged from participating in most forms of private enterprise. Check out the *herberos* (purveyors of herbs, potions and secret elixirs), huge avocados (in season), bundles of garlic and the delicious *batidos* (fruit shakes) served with crushed ice in no-nonsense jam jars. Be sure to keep a tight hold on your money belt.

The spotless **Parque Ignacio Agramonte** (cnr Martí & Independencia) in the heart of the city welcomes visitors with rings of marble benches and an equestrian statue (1950) of Camagüey's hero. On the southern side of the square is the **Catedral de Nuestra Señora de la Candelaria** (Cisneros No 168), rebuilt in the 19th century on the site of an earlier church dating from 1530. This cathedral, like many of Camagüey's churches, was restored with funds that flooded in after the 1998 visit of Pope John Paul II.

Opposite La Merced, on the corner of Independencia, is the **Museo Casa Natal de Ignacio Agramonte** (☎ 29 71 16; Av Agramonte No 459; admission CUC$2; 10am-5:45pm Tue-Thu, 8am-noon Sun), the birthplace of the independence hero Ignacio Agramonte (1841–73), the cattle rancher who led the revolt against Spain in this area in 1868. In July 1869, rebel forces under Agramonte bombarded Camagüey, and four years later he was killed in action (aged only 32) fighting against the Spanish. Nicknamed 'El Mayor' (The Major), you can hear Silvio Rodríguez' anthem to this hero on his disc *Días y Flores*.

With no shortage of heroes, Camagüey was also where Carlos J Finlay was born. The small **Casa Finlay** (☎ 29 67 45; Cristo btwn Cisneros & Lugareño; 10am-6pm Tue-Thu & Sat) documents the doctor's life and his medical breakthrough that discovered how mosquitoes transmit yellow fever. There's a splendid indoor patio and cafeteria.

Camagüey is full of surprising plazas just off center, like **Parque Martí** (cnr República & Luaces), a few blocks west of Parque Ignacio Agramonte. It is fronted by the Cuban-Gothic **Nuestra Corazón de Sagrado Jesús**. With its ornate stained glass, iron work and triple-spire facade, this church will be a dazzler once it emerges from its scaffold cocoon.

Across the bridge over the Río Hatibonico is the **Casino Campestre**, a large, enjoyable park with lots of shaded benches, a ballpark, concerts and activities. Get one of the ubiquitous bici-taxis to pedal you around.

## Courses

Señora **Alba Ferraz** (☎ 28 30 30; Ramón Guerrero No 106 btwn General Espinsoa & Oscar Primelles) is an enthusiastic local dance and music teacher from the Esceula de Arte (famous for its ballet and music). She offers lessons in salsa and classical dance plus guitar, *tres* (seven-string guitar) and percussion. All levels are welcome (CUC$5 per hour).

**UniversiTUR** (☎ 29 25 61; omarihe@yahoo.com; Avellaneda No 281 btwn Oscar Primelles & El Solitario; 9am-5pm Mon-Sat), can arrange Spanish classes at Camagüey University with accommodation thrown in. Prices and syllabuses are similar to Habana. Drop by or call ahead.

## Festivals & Events

The **Jornadas de la Cultura Camagüeyana** festival, commemorating the founding of the city, take place during the first two weeks of

February. Rocking **Carnaval** is from June 24 to 29. The 10 days beginning on October 10 are also cultural celebrations, during which many musical events take place.

## Sleeping

Camagüey has a varied selection of places to stay, all reasonably priced. Look for something with a roof terrace, as Camagüey's city views, dotted with steeples and towers, domes and terra-cotta, are a highlight.

### IN TOWN

**Hotel Plaza** (Islazul; ☎ 28 24 13; Van Horne No 1; s/d/tr with breakfast low season CUC$25/32/36, high season CUC$27/38/42; P) No two rooms are alike in this gracious colonial-style hotel built at the turn of the 20th century, so look at a few for variety. All have sitting areas, TVs and big fridges – at good prices. The lobby is a place to relax, with especially nice staff; despite its queasy color, the lobby bar is the logical chill spot while waiting for nearby train departures. The station is directly opposite.

**Hotel Colón** (Islazul; ☎ 28 33 46; República No 472 btwn San José & San Martín; s/d with breakfast low season CUC$32/38, high season CUC$36/44) This recently updated, two-story hotel has colorful tile-flanked walls and a stained-glass portrait of Christopher Columbus over the lobby door. There are rocking chairs upstairs and a colonial patio out back, adding atmosphere. This place is a good, sturdy choice.

**Gran Hotel** (Islazul; ☎ 29 20 93; Maceo No 67 btwn Agramonte & General Gómez; s/d with breakfast low season CUC$38/52, high season CUC$50/58; P) For amenities and charm in the heart of the city, this hotel dating from 1939 is the place. The 72 clean rooms are reached by a worn marble staircase or ancient lift replete with endearing attendants and antique gate. There are birds'-eye citywide views from the 5th-floor restaurant and rooftop *mirador* (lookout). An atmospheric piano bar is accessed through the lobby and an elegant renaissance-style swimming pool shimmers out back.

### OUTSIDE TOWN

**Hotel Camagüey** (Islazul; ☎ 28 72 67; Carretera Central Este Km 4.5; s/d with buffet breakfast CUC$36/47; P) About 5km southeast of the center, this four-story, 142-room hotel built in the 1970s was closed indefinitely to house Misión Milagros (p449) patients. Phone ahead to check current status.

### CASAS PARTICULARES – CAMAGÜEY

**Alba Ferraz** (☎ 28 30 30; misleydis2000@yahoo.com; Ramón Guerrero No 106 btwn General Espinosa & Oscar Primelles; r CUC$20-25) Two rooms sharing a bath open onto pretty colonial courtyard. Ask about dance and music lessons. There's a roof terrace.

**Alex & Yanitze** (☎ 29 78 97; Ramón Guerrero No 104 btwn General Espinosa & Oscar Primelles; r CUC$20-25). Huge bath, along with TV and comfortable bed.

**Carmen González Fonseca** (☎ 29 69 30; Ignacio Agramonte No 229 btwn Pobre & Alegría; r CUC$20-25; P) A nice self-contained room on top floor with own terrace and fridge. Extra bonus is a garage.

**'Casa Blanca' – Blanca Navarro Castro** (☎ 29 35 42; San Ramón Apto 201 Altos btwn Heredia & Solitario; r CUC$20) Sleeps three, friendly.

**'Casa de Caridad' – Caridad García Valera** (☎ 29 15 54; sracaridad@cubasi.cu; Oscar Primelles No 310A btwn Bartolomé Masó & Padre Olallo; r CUC$20) Friendly home, safe, huge garden/patio, meals, next to elementary school (read: early morning kid noise).

**Casa Lancara** (☎ 28 31 87; Avellaneda No 160 btwn Ignacio Agramonte & Jaime; r CUC$20-25) All mod-cons near the Iglesia de la Soledad.

**'Casa Monolo' – Manuel Rodríguez Jaén** (☎ 29 44 03; El Solitario No 18 btwn República & Santa Rosa; r CUC$20) Rooms with private or shared bath, laundry, roof terrace.

**'El Hostal de Elsa' – Elsa Espinosa** (☎ 29 81 04; Bartolomé Masó btwn Triana & Tío Perico; r CUC$20) Shared bath, meals, quiet.

**La Rusa** (☎ 28 38 98; liuda98@yahoo.es; Avellaneda No 306 btwn San Esteban & San Martín; r CUC$20) Russian lady with two rooms in large house. Serves up a mean borscht.

**'Los Vitrales' – Emma Barreto y Requejo** (☎ 29 58 66; Calle Avellaneda No 3 btwn General Gómez y Martí; r CUC$20; P) Painstakingly restored colonial house, each (darkish) room different; serves meals.

## Eating

### RESTAURANTS

Camagüey has an excellent selection of restaurants and new ones are popping up all the time (unusual for Cuba). The bars are equally zany.

**La Volanta** (☎ 29 19 74; cnr Independencia & Luaces; dishes 15 pesos; 🕒 seatings at 6pm, 8pm & 10pm) An upscale peso restaurant on the southeastern corner of Parque Agramonte, housed in a building that dates from 1732. Locals reserve their tables early here to dine on overflowing plates of Cuban food.

**La Mandarina Roja** (☎ 29 02 67; Padre Olalla No 731 btwn San Martín & José Ramón Silva; dishes 15-22 pesos; 🕒 noon-3pm & 7-10pm Thu-Tue) For a real peso paladar experience, head to this Chinese-inspired place serving large portions of chop suey, soup or fried rice. The food is as good as it is at any Cuban-Chinese crossover restaurant (which isn't always saying much).

**Bodegón Don Cayetano** (☎ 2619 61; República No 79) One of the best eating joints has to be this place, tucked away behind the Iglesia de Nuestra Señora de la Soledad. Specializing in Spanish fare, this tavern-themed tapas bar has seating options inside or al fresco at wooden bench tables and offers both good service and excellent coffee. Try the chef's special: beef steak in red wine and mushroom sauce (CUC$5.50).

**La Campana de Toledo** (Plaza San Juan de Dios No 18; meals CUC$7; 🕒 10am-10pm) This classic Camagüey eatery has colonial digs, shady patio and a serenading quartet. Parador de los Tres Reyes, adjacent, is similar.

**Paladar El Cardenal** (Martí No 309; dishes CUC$7-8; 🕒 11am-11pm) This old Camagüey standby is popular for a reason: seriously good *comida criolla* (traditional Cuban food, usually rice and beans, sometimes with pork) and lots of it. Try the pork steak, salad, *tostones* (fried plantains) and *congrí* (rice flecked with beans).

**Paladar El Califa** (Raúl Lamar No 49a btwn Cisneros & Lugareño; meals CUC$8; 🕒 noon-midnight) This is an intimate and recently refurbished paladar that is renowned for its huge portions of *uruguayano* (a type of pork fillet) and cordon bleu. One of Camagüey's longest standing eating houses.

**El Ovejito** (☎ 29 25 24; Hermanos Agüero btwn Honda & Carmen; 🕒 noon-9:40pm Wed-Mon) With a seriously stunning location on the Plaza del Carmen, this 'little lamb' restaurant serves just that in a colonial setting: lamb chops, lamb fricassee and the odd steak.

**Gran Hotel** (Maceo No 67 btwn Agramonte & General Gómez; dinner buffet CUC$12) The restaurant here has superb city views and a palatable buffet; get there early.

**El Colonial Galería** (cnr Av Agramonte & República) This place has a nice restaurant along with a courtyard that holds nightly cabaret.

### CAFETERIAS

**Gran Hotel snack bar** (Maceo No 67 btwn Agramonte & General Gómez; 🕒 9am-11pm) The lively snack bar here, accessible off Maceo, has coffee, sandwiches, chicken and ice cream. The hamburgers are good and the atmosphere is 1950s retro.

**El Vitral** (Hotel Plaza, Van Horne No 1; 🕒 24hr) This place at the Hotel Plaza is a round-the-clock option.

**Cafetería Las Ruinas** (Plaza Maceo) This is an atmospheric colonial patio for taking drinks and snacks.

Never far away is the **Coppelia** (Independencia btwn Agramonte & General Gómez). Can you resist Cuba's ubiquitous ice-creamery?

### GROCERIES

**Mercado Agropecuario El Río** (Calle Matadero; 🕒 7am-6pm) Eat heartily on peso sandwiches and fresh *batidos* (sold in jam jars) at this place above the Río Hatibonico. Also sells an excellent selection of fruit and vegetables.

A large selection of groceries is available at **El Encanto** (Maceo), near General Gómez. For bread in Convertibles, there's **Panadería Doña Neli** (Maceo; 🕒 7am-7pm), opposite the Gran Hotel.

## Drinking

Camagüey, harking back to its pirate past, has some great tavern-style drinking houses.

**Bar El Cambio** (cnr Independencia & Martí; 🕒 7am until you drop) This is a popular hang-out on Parque Agramonte with rough-hewn tables and graffiti-covered walls, á la Habana's famous Bodeguita del Medio bar (much frequented by Hemingway). Check out the interestingly-named cocktails.

**La Terraza** (Av República No 352; 🕒 8am-midnight) Teetotalers need not apply: this open-air peso place is a favorite party spot for getting smashed on peso beer and rum.

**STUDIO VISITS IN CAMAGÜEY**

You might not know it, but behind the beautiful grillwork of those grandiose Spanish colonial facades, Camagüey's artists are busy capturing their inspiration in great works of art. One couple worth checking out are Joel Jover and Ileana Sánchez, both of whom are accomplished painters with regular exhibitions and excellent contacts within the Cuban art world. Their magnificent home **Casa de Arte Jover** (☎ 29 23 05; Martí No 154 btwn Independencia & Cisneros) displaying much of their work is in Plaza Agramonte. Joel also runs another studio outlet at **Estudio-Galería Jover** (Ramón Pinto No 109; 9am-noon & 3-5pm Mon-Sat) in Plaza San Juan de Dios.

**Taberna Bucanero** (República btwn El Solitario & San Martín; 2-11pm) This place has Bucanero beer on tap and fake pirate figures crowding out a bar more reminiscent of an English pub.

**La Bigornia** (República btwn El Solitario & Oscar Primelles) This is a new fancy place that attracts a young, well-dressed Cuban crowd. The walls are decked out in lurid purple and a boutique bar-restaurant is overlooked by a mezzanine-level sports shop.

**Gran Hotel piano bar** (Maceo No 67 btwn Agramonte & General Gómez; 1pm-2am) This atmospheric place has a long wooden bar, vintage jukebox and grand piano; live music happens nightly after 9pm.

## Entertainment

Every Saturday night, the raucous **Noche Camagüeyana** spreads up República from La Soledad to the train station with food and alcohol stalls, music and crowds. A rock or *reggaeton* (Cuban hip-hop) concert takes place in the square next to La Soledad. The Galería ACAA has a bulletin board with the week's cultural events posted.

### FOLK MUSIC

**Casa de la Trova Patricio Ballagas** (☎ 29 13 57; Cisneros No 171 btwn Martí & Cristo; Tue-Sun) Folk singers jam here, at what most agree is one of Cuba's best *trova* (traditional poetic singing) clubs, tourists or no tourists.

**Galería Uneac** (Cisneros No 159; 5pm & 9pm Sat) Folk singing and Afro-Cuban dancing happen at this place, south of the cathedral.

**Centro de Promoción Cultural Ibero Americano** (Cisneros btwn General Gómez & Hermanos Agüero) Check out what's happening at this cultural center housed in the former Spanish Club, which hosts tango nights and the like.

### DANCE CLUB

**Sala de Fiesta Disco Café** (Independencia No 208; 10pm-3am) If you miss the weekly Saturday street shindig try this popular local nightspot.

### THEATER

**Teatro Principal** (☎ 29 30 48; Padre Valencia No 64; admission CUC$5-10; 8:30pm Fri, Sat & 5pm Sun) Home of Ballet de Camagüey, Cuba's second most important ballet company (founded in 1971 by Fernando Alonso, ex-husband of famous dancer Alicia Alonso), see these talented, athletic dancers if you can. The theater building, erected in 1850, has impressive chandeliers and stained glass, and is worth a look.

**Sala Teatro José Luis Tasende** (☎ 29 21 64; Ramón Guerrero No 51; 8:30pm Sat & Sun) For serious live theater, it's this venue with quality Spanish-language performances.

### CINEMAS

For big-screen showings, head to **Cine Casablanca** (Ignacio Agramonte No 428). Next door, **Cine Encanto** (Ignacio Agramonte) shows videos.

### SPORTS

**Estadio Cándido González** (Av Tarafa) From October to April, baseball games are held here alongside Casino Campestre.

**Salón Polivalente** (Plaza de la Revolución) This place is nearby Estadio Cándido González, behind the huge Monumento a Ignacio Agramonte, and hosts other athletic matches.

## Shopping

Calle Maceo is Camagüey's top shopping street, with a number of souvenir shops, bookstores and department stores. Look here for consignment shops selling all kinds of peso treasure.

**Galería ACAA** (cnr Ramón Guerrero & Padre Valencia; 9am-4pm Mon-Fri) Original Cuban handicrafts, photography and art pottery are the strengths in this store. For more personal service you can arrange studio visits with local artists (see left).

Other shops:

**ARTex Souvenir** (República No 381) On the main drag.

**Photo Service** (Av Agramonte 430 btwn República & San Ramón) Sells instant cameras, film and batteries.

**Tienda El Cartel** (Cisneros No 208) For compact discs, check out this store north of Parque Agramonte.

## Getting There & Away

### AIR

Ignacio Agramonte International Airport (airport code CBG) is 9km northeast of town on the road to Nuevitas and Playa Santa Lucía.

**Cubana** (☎ 26 10 00; República No 400) has daily flights to Habana (CUC$93 one way, one hour 35 minutes). **Air Transat** (www.airtransat.com) and **Skyservice** (www.skyserviceairlines.com) fly in the all-inclusive crowd from Toronto, who are hastily bussed off to Playa Santa Lucía.

### BUS & TRUCK

The regional **bus station** (Av Carlos J Finlay), near the train station, has trucks to Nuevitas (20 pesos, 87km, twice daily) and Santa Cruz del Sur (20 pesos, 82km, three daily). Trucks to Playa Santa Lucía (10 pesos, 109km, three daily) leave from here as well: ask for *el último* (last in the queue) inside the station and you'll be given a paper with a number; line up at door No 2 and wait for your number to come up.

Long-distance Astro buses depart **Álvaro Barba Bus Station** (☎ 27 24 80; Carretera Central), 3km southeast of the center. Aside from the normal Víazul routes these buses also call at Baracoa (CUC$28, 11 hours, alternate days), Manzanillo (CUC$11, seven hours, alternate days), Matanzas (CUC$22, eight hours, alternate days) and Cienfuegos (CUC$16, 4½ hours, alternate days).

**Víazul** (☎ 27 01 94; www.viazul.com) has daily services to the following destinations:

| Destination | Cost (one way) | Departure time |
|---|---|---|
| Ciego de Ávila | CUC$6 | 3:35am, 11:10pm, 4:50pm, 2:25am |
| Habana | CUC$33 | 3:35am, 11:10pm, 4:50pm |
| Sancti Spíritus | CUC$10 | 3:35am, 11:10pm, 4:50pm, 2:25am |
| Santiago de Cuba | CUC$18 | 6:20pm, 12:10am, 6:30am, 2:25am |
| Trinidad | CUC$15 | 2:25am |

The Santiago de Cuba departure also stops at Las Tunas (CUC$7, two hours), Holguín (CUC$11, three hours 10 minutes) and Bayamo (CUC$11, 4½ hours). The Habana bus stops at Santa Clara (CUC$15, four hours 35 minutes). For Víazul tickets, see the *jefe de turno* (shift manager).

Passenger trucks to Las Tunas and Ciego de Ávila also leave from this station. Arriving before 9am will greatly increase your chances of getting on one of these trucks.

Private taxis can be hired on Calle Perú outside the bus station, but not to Playa Santa Lucía or Cayo Coco, where they face heavy police controls. Expect to pay considerably more than the bus fare for long hauls.

### TRAIN

The **train station** (☎ 28 32 14; cnr Avellaneda & Finlay) is more conveniently located than the bus station. Foreigners buy tickets in Convertibles from an unmarked office across the street from the entrance to Hotel Plaza. The trains may leave from another terminal nearby, so check on this and arrive early. See p332 for more information on train routes.

## Getting Around

### TO/FROM THE AIRPORT

Bus 22 'Albaisa' (CUC$0.40) runs to Ignacio Agramonte International Airport every 30 minutes on weekdays and hourly on weekends, from the stop facing Parque Finlay, opposite the regional bus station. A taxi to the airport should cost CUC$5 from town.

### BICI-TAXIS

Bicycle taxis are found on the square beside La Soledad or in Plaza Maceo. Technically, bici-taxis aren't permitted to carry tourists, but they do; they usually cost five pesos.

### CAR

Prices start at around CUC$60 a day depending on make of car and duration of hire.

**Havanautos** Hotel Camagüey (☎ 27 22 39; Carretera Central Este Km 4.5); Aeropuerto Ignacio Agramonte (☎ 28 70 67)

**Micar** (☎ 8-7267/8; Carretera Centro Este Km 4.5 btwn bus station & Hotel Camagüey)

 

**TRAIN INFORMATION FOR CAMAGÜEY**

| Destination | Cost (one way) regular/rápido | Distance (Km) | Travel time (hours) | Departure time |
|---|---|---|---|---|
| Bayamo | CUC$7 | 210 | 5 | 6:10pm, alt days |
| Guantánamo | CUC$13 | 371 | 7 | 12:06am |
| Habana | CUC$22 | 534 | 7-10 | 12:25am, 3:55am, 4:34pm, 9:55pm, 11:47pm |
| Holguín | CUC$8 | 209 | 4 | 5:11am, alt days |
| Las Tunas | CUC$4/10 | 128 | 2½ | 1:50pm |
| Manzanillo | CUC$9 | 217 | 6 | 5:40am, alt days |
| Matanzas | CUC$16/22 | 474 | 8 | 4:30am, alt days |
| Santa Clara | CUC$9 | 263 | 5½ | 12:39am |
| Santiago de Cuba | CUC$11/16 | 327 | 5-7 | 1:22am, 2:58pm, 1:24am, 3:27pm |

**Transtur** (☎ 27 10 15; Hotel Plaza, Van Horne No 1) Rents mopeds.

**El Sereno Parqueo** (República No 212; 🕑 24hr) offers 24 hours of guarded parking south of Agramonte for CUC$2. Another guarded **parking lot** (El Solitario No 22) is to be found west of República, and is convenient for travelers renting private rooms in the surrounding area.

There are two **Servi-Cupet gas stations** (Carretera Central; 🕑 24hr) near Av de la Libertad. Driving in Camagüey's narrow one-way streets is a sport akin to Olympic tobogganing. Avoid it if you possibly can.

**LA HACIENDA LA BELÉN RESERVE**

Nestled in the grassy uplands of the Sierra de Najasa, the **La Hacienda la Belén** (☎ 3-4249) is a nature reserve run by the travel agency Ecotur situated approximately 30km east of Camagüey. As well as boasting a fine display of (nonindigenous) exotic animals such as zebras, deer, bulls and horses, the park functions as a bird reserve, and is one of the best places in Cuba to view rare species such as the Cuban parakeet, the giant kingbird and the Antillean palm swift.

There is a swimming pool and restaurant on-site, as well as accommodation provided in a rustic **hacienda** (4-bed r with bath CUC$15). Treks can be arranged around the reserve by jeep, horseback or on foot. You'll need your own wheels to get there or you can negotiate a rate with a taxi in Camagüey.

**HORSE CARTS**

Horse carts shuttle along a fixed route between the bus station and the train station, though you may have to change carts at Casino Campestre, near the river.

## FLORIDA

☎ 32 / pop 53,441

The buzzing sugar-mill town of Florida, 46km northwest of Camagüey on the way to Ciego de Ávila, is a fine place to spend the night if you're driving around central Cuba and are too tired to negotiate the labyrinthine streets of Camagüey. There's a working rodeo, a hospital and an Etecsa telephone office.

### Sleeping & Eating

**Hotel Florida** (Islazul; ☎ 5-3011; Carretera Central; s/d low season CUC$20/26, high season CUC$24/32; 🅿) This two-story hotel, 2km west of the center of town, has 74 adequate rooms. The entry drive is potholed which sort of sets the tone for this place, but the staff here are friendly and the price no more than a local casa particular.

Don't confuse this place with the **Motel Florida** (☎ 5-4623), a 15-cabin peso motel 4km east, by the highway at the eastern entrance to Florida.

Next to the Hotel Florida is Cafetería Caney, a thatched restaurant that's better value than the fly-blown hotel restaurant.

### Getting There & Away

A **Servi-Cupet gas station** (Carretera Central) is in the center of town. Passenger trucks run from Florida to Camagüey.

## GUÁIMARO

**pop 35,813**

Guáimaro earned its place in Cuban history as the site of the assembly of April 1869, which approved the first Cuban constitution and called for emancipation of slaves. The assembly also elected Carlos Manuel de Céspedes as president. These events are commemorated by a large **monument** erected in 1940 on Parque Constitución in the center of town. Around the base of the monument are bronze plaques with the likenesses of José Martí, Máximo Gómez, Carlos Manuel de Céspedes, Ignacio Agramonte, Calixto García and Antonio Maceo, the stars of Cuban independence. If you're making a pit stop there's a small **museum** (Calle Constitución No 83 btwn Libertad & Máximo Gómez; admission CUC$1) with a couple of rooms given to art and history. Guáimaro is also famous for its sculpture culture.

There is a Servi-Cupet gas station on your entry into town from Camagüey with an El Rápido snack bar attached. There are also seven legal casas in town. One of the better ones is **Casa de Magalis** (☎ 8-2891; Calle Olimpo No 5 btwn Benito Morell & Carretera Central; r CUC$20-25) a super upper-floor apartment with, quite possibly, the largest bathroom in any casa in Cuba.

## MINAS

**pop 21,708**

Minas, 60km northeast of Camagüey en route to Nuevitas, is notable only for the musical-instrument factory that opened here in 1976. The **Fábrica de Violines** (Camilo Cienfuegos; admission CUC$2; 🕒 Mon-Sat), at the eastern entrance to town, might interest musicians.

## NUEVITAS

**pop 40,607**

Nuevitas, 87km northeast of Camagüey, is a 27km jaunt north off the Camagüey–Playa Santa Lucía road. It's an industrial town and sugar-exporting port with friendly locals and easy shore access, but not worth a major detour. In 1978 Cuban movie director Manual Octavio Gómez filmed his revolutionary classic *Una Mujer, Un Hombre, Una Ciudad* here.

### Sights

Nuevitas' only specific sight is the **Museo Histórico Municipal** (Máximo Gómez No 66; admission CUC$1; 🕒 Tue-Sun) near Parque del Cañón in the center of town. It's got the usual stuffed animal collection, and you can hike up the steps in the center of town for terrific views.

Below the Hotel Caonaba is a shaggy amusement park/playground combination kids will like. A bit further along the coast is **Playa Cuatro Vientos**, a local beach, from where you can see two of the three small islands, called Los Tres Ballenatos, in the Bahía de Nuevitas. If you snake along the coast for 2km, you'll come to **Santa Rita** at

### TWO WHEELS ARE BETTER THAN FOUR

With the abrupt ending of 30 years of preferential Soviet oil subsides in the early 1990s, the Cuban government elected to counter a potential transport catastrophe by purchasing 1.2 million bicycles from China.

Laden down with excess weight and bereft of any of the standard gear/brake components that regular bikers take for granted, these boneshakers were cumbersome machines to say the least. Not that the locals had any cause for complaint. The Cubans have always prided themselves on their mechanical ingenuity and after 40 years of stuffing Lada engines under the hoods of vintage Chevrolets it's easy to see why. In the true spirit of the 'waste not, want not' rationing economy the bikes were quickly stripped down and redesigned a few pounds or so lighter. Pretty soon even members of the government were using them.

'With bicycles we will improve the quality of life in our society', suggested an ecologically reborn Castro who still preferred the convenience of his obligatory black Mercedes to a rebuilt metal coat hanger on wheels.

He had a point. In Cuba the so-called cycling revolution has played a large part in eliminating a culture of idleness and sloth. Almost overnight a transportation system based on fume-belching East European buses and ugly Russian Ladas was transformed into one 99% reliant on pedal power. For eco-watchers the regression was almost admirable.

 

**CUBA'S LAST WILDERNESS**

Carpeted by expansive mangrove swamps and home to an estimated 30,000 flamingos, Cayo Romano is one of Cuba's last true wilderness areas. Largely ignored by contemporary travelers and virtually unvisited, save for the odd binocular-wielding ornithologist, two causeways link this most lonesome and untamed of northern keys with Cayo Coco in the west and Camagüey Province to the south. Ernest Hemingway first championed the island's desolate and barren beaches in his posthumously published Cuban classic *Islands in the Stream* in the early '40s and in 1947 a young Fidel Castro hid out in adjoining Cayo Confites for 52 days training for an abortive plot to overthrow the dictatorial Trujillo regime in the Dominican Republic. Other than that, not much has ignited the party here since Columbus first rolled by in 1494.

Targeted for future tourist development along the lines of Cayo Coco and Cayo Guillermo, Cayo Romano – the Cuban government claims – could one day play host to more than 5000 hotel rooms. For the time being, however, equipped with a set of wheels, a large dose of mosquito repellent and a true sense of do-it-yourself adventure, the place is all yours.

the end of the road, a friendly place with a pier jutting into the bay.

En route to Playa Santa Lucía, 4km beyond the crossroads where you join the main highway from Camagüey, is the **King Ranch** (Carretera de Santa Lucía km 35), 1.5km off the main highway (signposted) with a restaurant, rodeo and horses for rent. Tour groups are often brought here for a country-style experience.

### Sleeping & Eating

**Hotel Caonaba** (Islazul; ☎ 4-4803; cnr Martí & Albisa; s/d low season CUC$20/26, high season CUC$24/32) This friendly, three-story hotel is on a rise overlooking the sea. It's at the entrance to town as you arrive from Camagüey. The rooms have fridges and some have views; but don't expect the Ritz. In summer, you can eat at the restaurant, 200m along the coast from the amusement park. This is a favorite local swimming spot. The hotel also has a terrace bar (open from noon till late).

### Getting There & Away

Nuevitas is the terminus of railway lines from Camagüey via Minas and Santa Clara via Chambas and Morón. The station is near the waterfront on the northern side of town. There should be a daily train to Camagüey (5:15am), and a service on alternate days to Santa Clara (6:35am), but they are often canceled. Trucks are more reliable than buses. Trucks to Camagüey leave around 4:30am and 9am; to Santa Lucía there are trucks at 4am and 1pm.

A Servi-Cupet gas station is at the entrance to town, a block from Hotel Caonaba. There's a Transtur taxi office nearby.

## CAYO SABINAL

Cayo Sabinal, 22km to the north of Nuevitas, is virgin territory, a 30km-long coral key with marshes favored by flamingos and iguanas. The land cover is mainly flat and characterized by marshland and lagoons. The fauna consists of tree rats, wild boar and a large variety of butterflies. It's astoundingly beautiful.

Cayo Sabinal has quite some history for a wilderness area. Due to repeated pirate attacks in the 17th and 18th centuries the Spanish built the **San Hilario fort** here in 1831 to restore order and keep the marauding corsairs at bay. Some years later the fort became a prison and in 1875 it was witness to the only Carlist uprising (a counterrevolutionary movement in Spain that opposed the reigning monarchy) in Cuba. There is also a lighthouse, **Faro Colón** (Punta Maternillo), erected in 1848 and one of the oldest still in operation on the Cuban archipelago. As a result of various naval battles that were fought in the area over the centuries there are a number of classic wrecks resting in shallow waters nearby. Vessels include the Spanish treasure ships *Nuestra Señora de Alta Gracia* and the *Pizarro* and they provide great fodder for divers.

### Sleeping & Eating

Of Cayo Sabinal's 30km of beaches Playa Los Pinos is undoubtedly the best. There are five basic **cabins** (s/d CUC$25) here as well as the diminutive Restaurante Los Pinos which rustles up seafood right out of the sea – literally. Any other activities are strictly of a do-it-yourself variety. Try hiking, strolling, swimming, stretching, writing, thinking, philosophizing or meditating. Everything seems to be more accentuated here.

### Getting There & Away

The dirt road to Cayo Sabinal begins 6km south of Nuevitas, off the road to Camagüey. You must show your passport at the bridge to the key and pay CUC$5. The 2km causeway linking the key to the mainland was the first of its kind constructed in Cuba and the most environmentally destructive. The Playa Santa Lucía tour agencies all offer day trips to Cayo Sabinal from around CUC$69 including transfers and lunch; ask around in the hotels.

## PLAYA SANTA LUCÍA

Playa Santa Lucía is an isolated resort 112km northeast of Camagüey situated on an unbroken 20km-long stretch of white-sand beach (one of Cuba's longest). The bulk of travelers come here to scuba dive on one of the island's best and most accessible coral reefs that lies just a few kilometers offshore. Another highlight is the beach itself, a tropical gem, still deserted in places, and on a par with Varadero in terms of size and quality.

The area around Playa Santa Lucía is flat and featureless, the preserve of flamingos, scrubby bushes and the odd grazing cow. Aside from a small micro-village that serves as lodging for itinerant hotel workers there are no Cuban settlements of note. History seekers will be disappointed, Trinidad this is not! The swimming, snorkeling, and diving are a different story however, and the large hotels lay on plenty of activities for those with the time and inclination to explore. Packages to Playa Santa Lucía are usually cheaper than those to Cayo Coco and the resorts themselves have a more laid-back and relaxed feel. You're also within easy reach of Camagüey here, which is infinitely more interesting than Morón, Cayo Coco's gateway city.

### Information

Bandec is in the Cuban residential area between the Servi-Cupet at the southeastern entrance to Playa Santa Lucía and the hotel strip. Nearby is **Clínica Internacional de Santa Lucía** (☎ 36 53 00; Residencia 4) a well-equipped Cubanacán clinic for emergencies and medical issues. Etecsa, 1.5km further along near the entrance to the hotel zone, has Internet access for CUC$6 per hour and international phone capabilities. For tour agencies, Cubanacán – who own four of the five hotels here – are well-represented. Try their desk in the Gran Club Santa Lucía.

### Sights

Just before the Club Amigo Mayanabo, the **Mar Verde Centro Cultural** has a pleasant patio bar and a **cabaret** (admission CUC$1) with live music nightly. There's also an ARTex store here with compact discs and Librería Tengo with high-quality art books and photographs for sale.

At the far northwestern end of Playa Santa Lucía, 7km from the hotels, is another white beach with crystal-clear waters facing the mouth of the Bahía de Nuevitas – **Playa los Cocos**. Sometimes flocks of pink flamingos are visible in Laguna El Real, behind this beach. A horse and carriage from the Santa Lucía hotels to Playa Los Cocos is CUC$6 each way for one or two persons. There's also a bus service from the tourist hotels that leaves each day at 10am. Several restaurants serve seafood, see p337. This is a stellar swimming spot, but mind the tidal currents further out. The **lighthouse** on Cayo Sabinal is visible from here. The hotels sell boat excursions to Nuevitas.

You can access a pristine part of the beach by turning at the sign for Shark's Friends.

### Activities

The 35 scuba sites in the warm waters off Santa Lucía take in the six Poseidon ridges, the Cueva Honda, shipwrecks, several types of rays and the abundant marine life at the entrance to the Bahía de Nuevitas (see above for more information). A highlight is the hand-feeding of bull sharks between 3m and 4m long (June to January).

**Shark's Friends Dive Center** (Cubanacán Naútica; ☎ 36 51 82; marlin@sunnet.sti.cyt.cu) is a professional outfit with dive masters who speak English, Italian and French. The center, on the beach between Brisas Santa Lucía and Gran Club Santa Lucía, offers dives for CUC$30, plus night dives (CUC$40) and the famous shark feeds (CUC$65) where cool-as-cucumber dive guides chuck food into the mouths of 3m-long bull sharks.

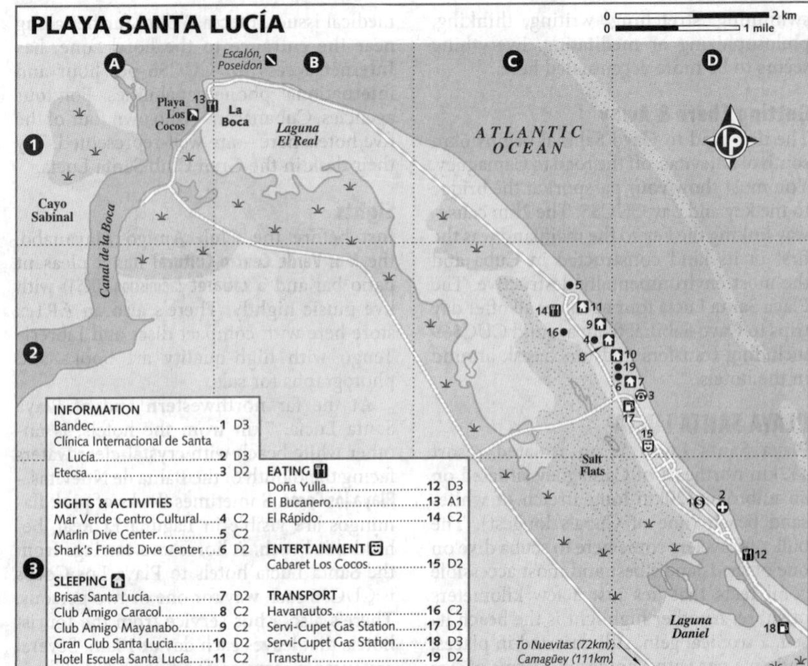


They have boats going out every two hours between 9am and 3pm daily, though the last dive is contingent on demand. Their open-water course costs CUC$360; a resort course is CUC$60. They also have snorkeling excursions.

**Marlin Dive Center** (Cubanacán Naútica; ☎ 33 64 04) is a friendly boating and dive outfit with half-day snorkeling trips in catamarans (CUC$25); a catamaran trip Cayo Sabinal (CUC$69 including dinner on beach), and a sunset cruise (CUC$25, including cocktail; at 5:30pm). It does fishing trips for CUC$204 (maximum four people), including gear, guide and drinks. It's beside Hotel Escuela Santa Lucía.

## Sleeping

The hotel strip begins 6km west of the roundabout at the entrance to Santa Lucía. It's prohibited to rent private rooms in Santa Lucía. Of the resort's five tourist hotels there's only one budget option. Book ahead or be prepared to pay the all-inclusive rates.

**Hotel Escuela Santa Lucía** (☎ 33 63 10; r CUC$35; ) The one and only budget option in Playa Santa Lucía, this sweet, one-story motel with 30 nicely furnished rooms, at the northwestern end of the hotel strip beside a public beach, is another of the 'Escuela' training hotels. Every room has a TV and little patio; those in the 200 and 300 block are closest to the beach. It's comfortable and affordable, but book ahead as it often gets full.

**Club Amigo Mayanabo** (Cubanacán; s/d low season CUC$47/74, high season CUC$65/100; P ) This formerly run-down resort reopened with a facelift a couple of years back. The Mayanabo is closely connected to the Caracol next door.

**Club Amigo Caracol** (Cubanacán; s/d low season CUC$47/74, high season CUC$65/100; P ) The younger brother of the adjacent Mayanabo, Caracol is a three-star family all-inc with 150 self-contained bungalows run by Cubanacán. The newly renovated resort reopened in 2003.

**Brisas Santa Lucía** (Cubanacán; ☎ 36 51 20; fax 36 51 42; s/d low season CUC$60/100, high season CUC$75/120; P ) This all-inclusive resort has 412 rooms in several three-story buildings.

In all, it covers a monstrous 11 hectares and gets the resort's top rating (four stars). Rooms in the 200 to 800 range are closest to the beach, while those in the 100 block kiss up against the Laberinto Disco. There is special kids' programming. Shark's Friend Dive Center (p335) is on-site.

**Gran Club Santa Lucía** (Cubanacán; ☎ 33 61 09; fax 36 51 47; s/d low season CUC$65/100, high season CUC$75/120; P) Freshly painted and gleaming like new (which might account for the 'three star plus' rating), the 249 rooms in this amiable resort-village all have minifridges and balconies or patios and are accommodated in a series of tile-roofed two-story blocks. Prices quoted are for the cheap rooms furthest from the beach with parking-lot views. Discoteca La Jungla is here and there's a fairly cheesy music/comedy show scheduled every evening.

## Eating

Aside from the hotel buffets your choices are limited to El Rápido, opposite Hotel Escuela Santa Lucía, which serves inexpensive fast food on its terrace, and Doña Yulla right before the roundabout entrance to Santa Lucía serving simple, filling meals in pesos. **El Bucanero** (Playa los Cocos), on Playa los Cocos at the Santa Lucía end of the beach, serves seafood.

## Drinking & Entertainment

Outside of the resorts, nothing much happens here. If you want a taste of something different, stroll east into the micro-village a take a look at Cabaret Los Cocos, a spit and sawdust Cuban place where hotel workers go on their night off.

## Getting There & Around

There's one morning and one afternoon bus to and from Nuevitas (1½ hours, 70km) and one daily bus to Camagüey (2½ hours, 112km). At Santa Lucía, ask about buses and passenger trucks at El Rápido opposite Hotel Escuela Santa Lucía.

**Servi-Cupet** (Playa Santa Lucía strip) is at the southeastern end of the strip, near the access road from Camagüey. Another large Servi-Cupet station, with a Servi-Soda snack bar, is just east of Brisas Santa Lucía.

You can rent cars or mopeds (CUC$24 per day, including a tank of gas) at the following agencies:

**Havanautos** (☎ 33 64 01; Tararaco)

**Transtur** (☎ 36 52 60) Between Gran Club Santa Lucía and the Brisas Santa Lucía.

# Las Tunas Province

Unheralded Las Tunas is where the Oriente begins; a flat, featureless drive-by on the road through to Santiago in the east or Camagüey and Habana in the west. Blink and you'll miss it.

But for those with a day or two to spare a stopover needn't be wasted. Despite years of half-hearted neglect, Las Tunas retains its festive attractions. For culture seekers there's a nationally renowned music festival, *La Jornada Culcalambeana*, in honor of local *décima* (eight-syllable verse) poet Juan Nápoles Fajardo; while for beach hedonists there's the refreshingly unblemished coastline of Playa La Herradura to the north – one of the few strips of sand on the Atlantic littoral where you can rent cheap private rooms from Cubans.

The provincial capital of Las Tunas is a diminutive place – more small-town than large city – that fashions itself as Cuba's 'city of sculptures.' To the west lie the vast cattle-rearing haciendas of the country's central heartlands; to the north, soot-stained sugar mills dot a landscape replete with the ubiquitous *caña azucar* (sugarcane).

Elsewhere the province boasts two fauna reserves and more than 35 virgin beaches. Meanwhile in the quiet towns and villages of the rural interior, the people of Las Tunas, unperturbed by tourism, have developed a reputation for being warm and hospitable hosts. If it's peace and tranquility you are looking for, you just might find it here.

**HIGHLIGHTS**

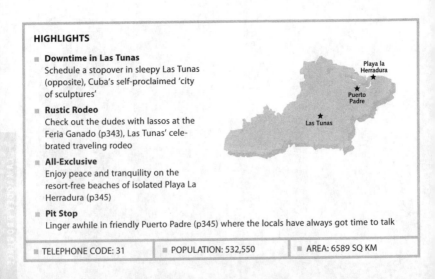

- **Downtime in Las Tunas**
  Schedule a stopover in sleepy Las Tunas (opposite), Cuba's self-proclaimed 'city of sculptures'
- **Rustic Rodeo**
  Check out the dudes with lassos at the Feria Ganado (p343), Las Tunas' celebrated traveling rodeo
- **All-Exclusive**
  Enjoy peace and tranquility on the resort-free beaches of isolated Playa La Herradura (p345)
- **Pit Stop**
  Linger awhile in friendly Puerto Padre (p345) where the locals have always got time to talk

Playa la Herradura
Puerto Padre
Las Tunas

| TELEPHONE CODE: 31 | POPULATION: 532,550 | AREA: 6589 SQ KM |
|---|---|---|

## LAS TUNAS

☎31 / pop 139,637

Referred to alternatively as the 'city of sculptures' or *El Balcón del Oriente* (the Balcony of the Oriente), Las Tunas is devoid of any buildings of architectural note. The city remains a low-rise and unpretentious place that feels more like a sleepy suburb than a bustling business hub. Those on the rebound from Santiago or Camagüey will find the pace of life slower here, though the local people are colorful enough and the hustlers refreshingly low-key.

### History

The settlement of Las Tunas was founded in 1759 but wasn't given the title of 'city' until 1853. In 1876 Cuban General Vicente García captured the city during the First War of Independence, but repeated Spanish successes in the area soon led the colonizers to rename it La Victoria de Las Tunas. During the Second War of Independence the Spanish burned Las Tunas to the ground, but the *Mambís* fought back bravely, and in 1897 General Calixto García forced the local Spanish garrison to surrender.

Las Tunas became a provincial capital in 1975 during Cuba's postrevolutionary geographic reorganization.

### Orientation

The train station is on the northeastern side of town and the bus station is east of the center. Most of the things to see are in the center. A *circunvalación* (bypass road) runs around the south side of the city if you want to avoid Las Tunas altogether.

### Information

#### BOOKSHOPS & LIBRARIES

**Biblioteca Provincial José Martí** (Vicente García No 4; Mon-Sat)

**Librería Fulgencio Oroz** (Colón No 151)

#### INTERNET ACCESS

**Etecsa** (Angel Guardia; 7am-11pm) Off Parque Vicente García.

#### MEDICAL SERVICES

**Hospital Che Guevara** (☎ 4-5012; cnr Avs CJ Finlay & 2 de Diciembre) One kilometer from the highway exit toward Holguín.

#### MONEY

**Banco de Crédito y Comercio** (Vicente García No 69; 8am-2pm Mon-Fri, 8-10.20am Sat)

**Banco Financiero Internacional** (☎ 4-6202; cnr Vicente García & 24 de Febrero)

**Cadeca** (Colón No 141; 8:30am-6pm Mon-Sat, 8:30am-1pm Sun)

#### POST

**Post office** (☎ 4-2738; Vicente García No 6; 8am-8pm)

#### TELEPHONE

**Etecsa** (Angel Guardia; 7am-11pm) Off Parque Vicente García.

#### EL CUCALAMBÉ

Las Tunas is best known for the poet Juan Cristóbal Nápoles Fajardo (1829–62), nicknamed El Cucalambé (the pseudonym is taken from the name of a dance brought from Africa). Fajardo was Cuba's leading 19th-century composer of *décimas,* the rhyming, eight-syllable verses that provide the lyrics for Cuban *son* (Cuba's basic form of popular music). He lived in a farm in El Cornito 7km northwest of the town.

Historically speaking El Cucalambé's poems were groundbreaking. In 1855 Bayamo poet José Fornaris had created a stir with his *Cantos del Siboney* (Songs of the Siboney), which associated the Cuban *guajiro* (country person) with the pre-Hispanic Siboney and Taíno Indians rather than the Spanish conquerors. The Indians were presented as generous lovers of the earth, family and freedom, stereotypical characteristics of the Cuban *campesino* (a person who lives in the country).

Impressed by Fornaris' audacity, El Cucalambé brought out a book of verses a year later in which Blacks, Indians, and Creoles all appear without a Spaniard in sight. By formulating the Cuban character in comic situations, Nápoles Fajardo's *décimas* expressed a latent nationalism that was soon to burst forth in the First War of Independence. His poems were enthusiastically recited at country fairs, cockfights and rural family reunions, and thousands of Cubans still flock to Las Tunas every June for the *Jornada Cucalambeana* (Cucalambé Folklore Festival, see p341).

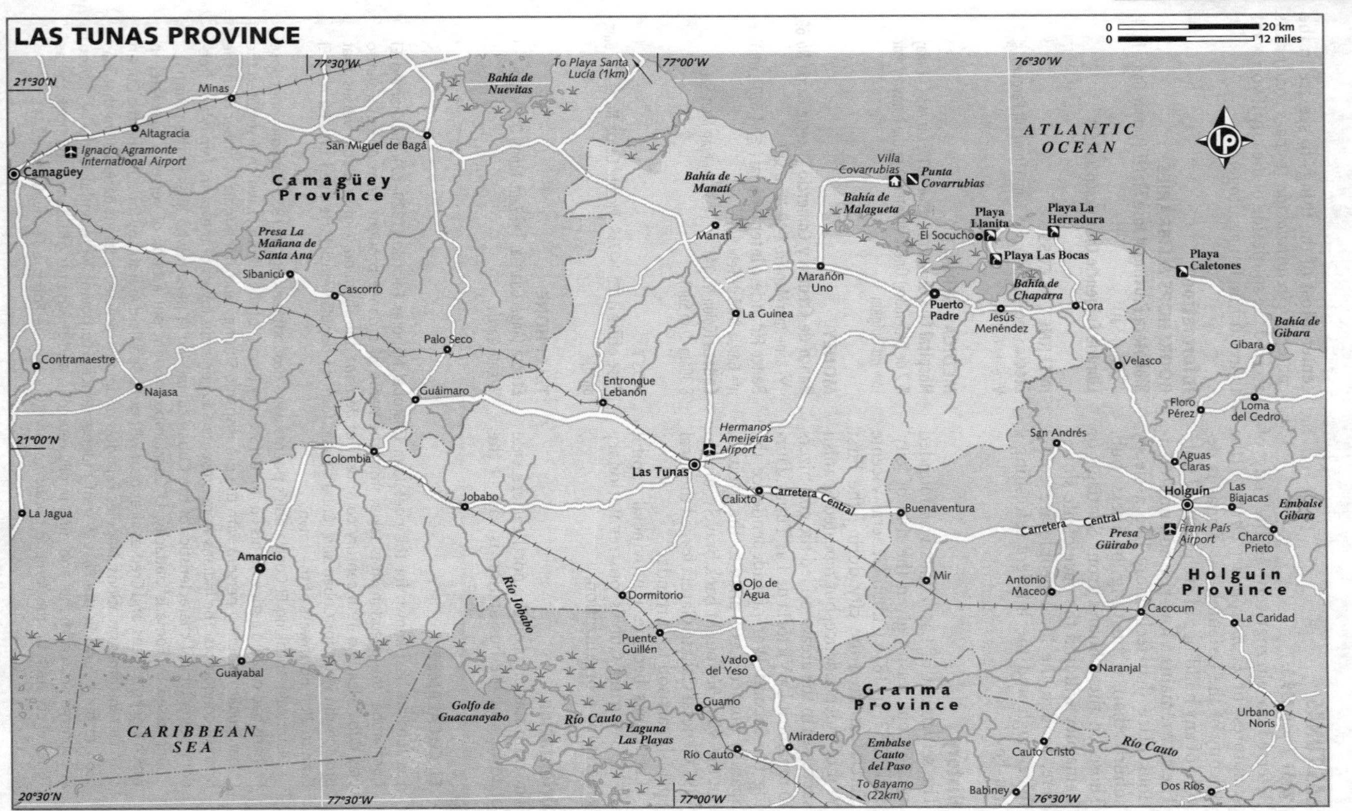
LAS TUNAS PROVINCE
0 20 km
0 12 miles
ATLANTIC OCEAN
CARIBBEAN SEA
Camagüey Province
Holguín Province
Granma Province
Camagüey
Ignacio Agramonte International Airport
Altagracia
Minas
San Miguel de Bagá
Bahía de Nuevitas
To Playa Santa Lucía (1km)
Presa La Mañana de Santa Ana
Sibanicú
Cascorro
Palo Seco
Guáimaro
Colombia
Najasa
Contramaestre
La Jagua
Amancio
Guayabal
Jobabo
Río Jobabo
Golfo de Guacanayabo
Entronque Lebanón
Las Tunas
Hermanos Ameijeiras Airport
Calixto
Carretera Central
Dormitorio
Puente Guillén
Vado del Yeso
Ojo de Agua
Guamo
Río Cauto
Laguna Las Playas
Miradero
To Bayamo (22km)
Embalse Cauto del Paso
Bahía de Manatí
Manatí
La Guinea
Marañón Uno
Bahía de Malagueta
Villa Covarrubias
Punta Covarrubias
El Socucho
Puerto Padre
Playa Llanita
Playa Las Bocas
Bahía de Chaparra
Jesús Menéndez
Playa La Herradura
Lora
Velasco
Playa Caletones
Gibara
Bahía de Gibara
Buenaventura
Mir
Antonio Maceo
San Andrés
Presa Güirabo
Aguas Claras
Floro Pérez
Loma del Cedro
Holguín
Frank País Airport
Las Biajacas
Embalse Gibara
Charco Prieto
Cacocum
La Caridad
Naranjal
Urbano Noris
Cauto Cristo
Babiney
Dos Ríos
21°30'N
21°00'N
20°30'N
77°30'W
77°00'W
76°30'W

## Sights

Las Tunas' most important site, **Memorial a los Mártires de Barbados** (Lucas Ortíz No 344; admission free; 10am-6pm Mon-Sat), located along the Río Hormigo, is an eerie reminder of the 1976 Cubana de Aviación terrorist attack. Flight CU-455 had just taken off from Barbados when a bomb exploded underneath a seat, sending the plane and all 73 people aboard into the sea. The bomber left the package beneath his seat when he disembarked during a routine stopover in Barbados. Individual photos of the victims of the attack – including the entire 24-member Cuban Olympic fencing team – line the museum walls in a poignant condemnation of indiscriminate terrorism.

Housed in the 1920s town hall (the building with the clock above the facade), the **Museo Provincial General Vicente García** (4-8201; cnr Francisco Varona & Angel Guardia; admission CUC$1; 11am-7pm Tue-Thu, 2-10pm Fri & Sat, 3-7pm Sun) documents local history. It's an unremarkable place full of the usual heroic revolution-era memorabilia.

Nearby is the **Memorial Vicente García** (Vicente García No 7; admission CUC$1; 3-7pm Mon, 11am-7pm Tue-Sat), commemorating the entry of Las Tunas into the First War of Independence in October 1868 under the command of Vicente García. In September 1876, he captured the town.

If you've time to kill, check out the quirky King Kong–sized pencil which is the **Monumento a Alfabetización** (cnr Lucas Ortiz & Av 2 de Diciembre), marking the act passed in Las Tunas on November 16, 1961 to stamp out illiteracy.

Popularly called the 'city of sculptures' (though it's no Florence), Las Tunas also has a small **Galería Taller Escultura** (cnr Av 2 de Diciembre & Ortiz) which displays local work.

## Festivals & Events

Lovers of Cuban country music gather at Motel El Cornito in late June for the **Jornada Cucalambeana** (see p339). It's Cuba's greatest celebration of rural culture, with music, dancing, theater, food and handicraft displays.

## Sleeping

Unless you've got a penchant for scruffy, noisy Islazul hotels with cold water, a private room is your best bet for accommodation in Las Tunas. Several houses rent clean affordable rooms and are situated on Lucas Ortíz, between the train station and the center (see above).

### CASAS PARTICULARES – LAS TUNAS

**Carlos A Patiño Alvarez** (4-2288; Lucas Ortíz No 120; r CUC$20-25; ) Comes with fridge.

**'Doña Nelly' – Nelly Tamayo Vega** (4-2526; Lucas Ortíz No 111; r CUC$20-25; ) Colonial house; front porch with rockers.

**Marianela Santiago Rodríguez** (4-3259; Lucas Ortíz No 101 Altos; r CUC$20-25; ) Run by a single woman; terrace overlooks the street.

**'Villa Blanca' Zoila Pavón Gutierrez** (4-2586; Frank País No 85 btwn Gonzalo de Quezada & I Durañona; r CUC$20-25; P ) Two rooms with private baths, convenient to train.

**'Villa Rosalba' Enobar Guerra Cruz** (4-9042; Ave 2 de Diciembre No 3 btwn F País & J Agüero; r CUC$25; ) One room, meals available.

**Yolanda Rodríguez Torres** (4-3641; Lucas Ortíz No 101; r CUC$25) Independent digs with kitchen, dining and hang-out area.

**Hotel Caribe** (UniversiTUR; 4-4262; Lorenzo Ortíz No 64; r CUC$15-25; ) Like other UniversiTUR hotels, this place is designed for foreign students but they might rent you a room if you're desperate. Conditions reflect the cheap prices.

**Motel El Cornito** (4-5015; Carretera Central Km 8; r CUC$20) Another Cuban-oriented place located outside of town near the site of El Culcalambé's old farm. You might get lucky with these basic bungalows. Phone ahead.

**Hotel Las Tunas** (Islazul; 4-5014; fax 4-5169; Av 2 de Diciembre; s/d low season CUC$18/24, high season CUC$23/30; P ) This 128-room hotel southeast of the center is Las Tunas' main tourist hotel. On our visit we encountered clogged drains, leaky ceilings, cranky service, aggressive parking attendants and shuttered restaurants.

## Eating

### PALADARES

Las Tunas has a surprisingly good selection of paladares (private restaurants) serving big portions.

**El Bacan** (F Suárez No 12; dishes 25-50 pesos) A peso place mounding on the food.

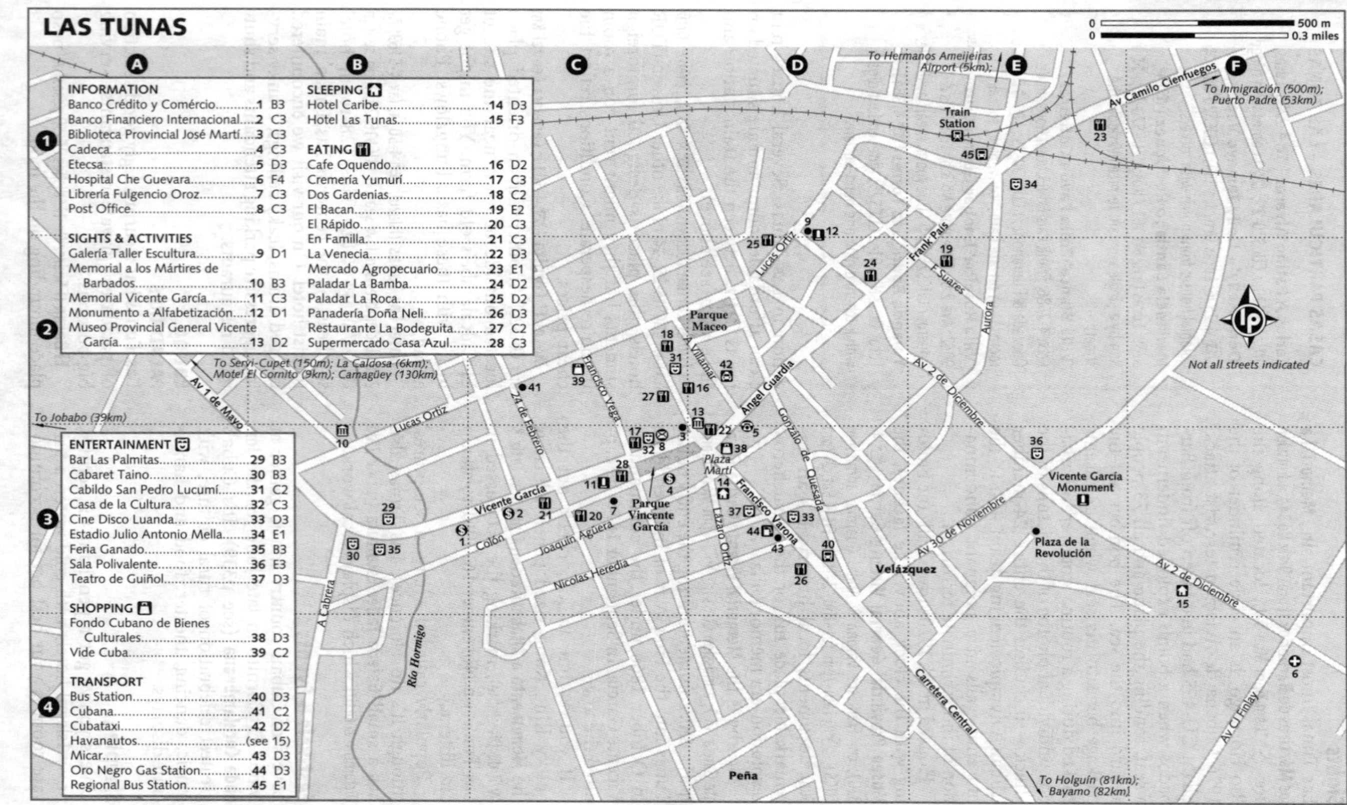
LAS TUNAS
INFORMATION
Banco Crédito y Comércio 1 B3
Banco Financiero Internacional 2 C3
Biblioteca Provincial José Martí 3 C3
Cadeca 4 C3
Etecsa 5 D3
Hospital Che Guevara 6 F4
Librería Fulgencio Oroz 7 C3
Post Office 8 C3
SIGHTS & ACTIVITIES
Galería Taller Escultura 9 D1
Memorial a los Mártires de Barbados 10 B3
Memorial Vicente García 11 C3
Monumento a Alfabetización 12 D1
Museo Provincial General Vicente García 13 D2
SLEEPING
Hotel Caribe 14 D3
Hotel Las Tunas 15 F3
EATING
Cafe Oquendo 16 D2
Cremería Yumurí 17 C3
Dos Gardenias 18 C2
El Bacan 19 E2
El Rápido 20 C3
En Familla 21 C3
La Venecia 22 D3
Mercado Agropecuario 23 E1
Paladar La Bamba 24 D2
Paladar La Roca 25 D2
Panadería Doña Neli 26 D3
Restaurante La Bodeguita 27 C2
Supermercado Casa Azul 28 C3
ENTERTAINMENT
Bar Las Palmitas 29 B3
Cabaret Taino 30 B3
Cabildo San Pedro Lucumí 31 C2
Casa de la Cultura 32 C3
Cine Disco Luanda 33 D3
Estadio Julio Antonio Mella 34 E1
Feria Ganado 35 B3
Sala Polivalente 36 E3
Teatro de Guiñol 37 D3
SHOPPING
Fondo Cubano de Bienes Culturales 38 D3
Vide Cuba 39 C2
TRANSPORT
Bus Station 40 D3
Cubana 41 C2
Cubataxi 42 D2
Havanautos (see 15)
Micar 43 D3
Oro Negro Gas Station 44 D3
Regional Bus Station 45 E1
0 500 m
0 0.3 miles
Not all streets indicated
To Hermanos Ameijeiras Airport (5km)
To Inmigración (500m); Puerto Padre (53km)
To Servi-Cupet (150m); La Caldosa (6km); Motel El Cornito (9km); Camagüey (130km)
To Jobabo (39km)
To Holguín (81km); Bayamo (82km)
Av Camilo Cienfuegos
Train Station
Aurora
F Suares
Frank País
Av 2 de Diciembre
Lucas Ortiz
Angel Guardia
Gonzalo de Quesada
Parque Maceo
A Villamar
Francisco Vega
24 de Febrero
Av 1 de Mayo
Plaza Martí
Parque Vincente García
Francisco Varona
Lázaro Ortiz
Vicente García
Colón
Joaquín Agüera
Nicolas Heredia
Av 30 de Noviembre
Velázquez
Carretera Central
Vicente García Monument
Plaza de la Revolución
Av CJ Finlay
Río Hormigo
A Cabrera
Peña

**Paladar La Roca** (Lucas Ortíz No 108; meals CUC$7-8; noon-midnight) If you like lamb, this is the place for you; huge portions served in delicious gravy are dished up with rice at this friendly family-run establishment.

**Paladar La Bamba** (cnr Av 2 de Diciembre & Frank País; meals CUC$8; 6-11pm) A superpopular place with tourists and touts that is often full.

### RESTAURANTS

**La Venecia** (cnr Francisco Verona & Vicente García; 7am-11pm) Smack bang in the middle of town, this peso restaurant housed in a colonial building has an extensive menu, plus balcony dining overlooking the park. This is a good breakfast spot for eggs (two pesos).

**Restaurante La Bodeguita** (Francisco Varona No 295; 9am-11pm) This restaurant has tablecloths and a limited wine list and isn't bad for a state-run place. Try the chicken breast with mushroom sauce for around CUC$5.

**Cremería Yumuri** (cnr Francisco Vega & Vicente García; 10am-4pm & 5-11pm) Las Tunas' substitute Coppelia; pay pesos for sundaes or *tres gracias* (three scoops) in flavors such as coconut and *café con leche* (espresso with milk).

**En Familla** (Vicente García btwn Ramon Ortuño & Julian Santana; 11am-11pm) Promising sign, morbid surroundings, scant menu; but if you can rouse the pizza man from his catatonic slumber you might just get lucky.

Also available:

**Dos Gardenias** (Francisco Varona No 326; 9am-midnight) Gussied-up cafeteria serving chicken, sandwiches and pizza for CUC$1 to CUC$3.

**Cafe Oquendo** (Francisco Varona btwn Vicente García & Lucas Ortíz; 24hr) Espresso straight (20 centavos) or *rocío del gallo* (rum-laced espresso) for two pesos.

**La Caldosa** (☎ 4-2743) Legendary place near El Cornito sells rich *caldosas* (stews) for a couple of Convertibles.

**El Rápido** (cnr Colón & 24 de Febrero) Those trusty microwaved ham-and-cheese sandwiches, just when you need them.

### GROCERIES

**Supermercado Casa Azul** (cnr Vicente García & Francisco Vega; 9am-6pm Mon-Sat, 9am-noon Sun) To stock up on groceries (or to break bigger bills), try this supermarket.

Other options:

**Panadería Doña Neli** (Francisco Varona; loaf CUC$0.40) Bread is available here.

**Mercado agropecuario** (Av Camilo Cienfuegos) A small market is not far from the train station.

## Entertainment

One of Las Tunas' signature sights is at Parque de Lenin where Calle Vicente García bends into Av 1 de Mayo. Every weekend there is a **Feria Ganado** (Farm Fair; 9am-6pm Sat & Sun) here with a market, music, food stalls, kids' activities and, if you're lucky, a full-scale rodeo (you'll see the large permanent arena as you walk in). Festivals run from June through to December and locals will tell you, with some authority, that this is

### TEÓFILO STEVENSON – CUBA'S HEAVYWEIGHT BOXING CONTENDER

Muhammad Ali might have been the 'Greatest of 'em all'; but how would the so-called 'Louisville Lip' have fared against Cuban boxing legend Teófilo Stevenson?

Born in Puerto Padre, Las Tunas Province in 1952, to a Cuban mother and a father from St Vincent, Stevenson was a teenage boxing prodigy who in 1972, at the age of just 20, won the heavyweight gold medal at the Munich Olympics. In 1976 he repeated the feat in Montreal and in 1980 in Moscow he became only the second boxer ever (after Hungarian Laszlo Papp) to win three Olympic boxing golds. In fact, Stevenson could, arguably, have gone one further at Los Angeles four years later had the Cubans – following the lead of their Soviet patrons – not boycotted the games.

Long feted by the Castro regime as a national hero, Stevenson stumped American boxing promoters in the 1970s when he turned down a purported US$5 million to go professional and step into the ring with a still active Muhammad Ali. 'Why do I need five million dollars when I have the love of five million Cubans?' he is said to have quipped.

These days Teófilo, who is vice-president of the Cuban Boxing Federation, lives modestly in a sleepy suburb of Habana. Ali remains his close friend and has visited the Cuban twice in Habana, most recently in 1998.

one of the best cowboy *espectaculos* (shows) in Cuba.

**Cabildo San Pedro Lucumí** (Francisco Varona btwn Angel Guardia & Lucas Ortíz; admission free; from 9pm Sun) Cultural activities happen at this friendly Afro-Caribbean association; drop in on Sunday for some dancing and drumming.

**Cine Disco Luanda** (Francisco Varona No 256; 10pm-2am Sun-Fri, 10pm-3am Sat) The most popular disco in Las Tunas. There's also a cinema here.

**Cabaret Taino** (☎ 4-3823; cnr Vicente García & A Cabrera; admission per couple CUC$10; 9pm-2am Tue-Sun) This large thatched venue at the west entrance to town has the standard feathers, salsa and pasties show. Cover charge includes a bottle of rum and cola.

From October to April is baseball season. Las Tunas plays at the Estadio Julio Antonio Mella near the train station. Other sports happen at the Sala Polivalente, an indoor arena near Hotel Las Tunas.

Also worth checking out:

**Bar Las Palmitas** (Vincente García; 24hr) Kick back on the open-air terrace.

**Casa de la Cultura** (☎ 4-3500; Vicente García No 8) Best place for the traditional stuff with concerts, poetry, dance etc. Look out for the hastily scribbled hand-written posters.

**Teatro de Guiñol** (Francisco Varona No 267; 10am Sat, 10am & 3pm Sun) Famous puppet and children's theater.

## Shopping

**Fondo Cubano de Bienes Culturales** (cnr Angel Guardia & Francisco Varona; 9am-noon & 1:30-5pm Mon-Fri, 8:30am-noon Sat) This store sells fine artwork, ceramics and embroidered items.

**Vide Cuba** (cnr Ortiz & Francisco Vega; 8:30am-9pm Mon-Sat) For your photographic needs, try this place.

## Getting There & Away

### AIR

**Hermanos Ameijeiras Airport** (☎ 4-2484), 3km north of the train station, has a nice new terminal building. There are no international flights, but **Cubana** (☎ 4-2702; cnr Lucas Ortiz & 24 Febrero) flies nonstop to/from Habana on Tuesday (CUC$94 one way, two hours).

### BUS & TRUCK

The main **bus station** (☎ 4-3060; Francisco Varona) is 1km southeast of the main square (ask here for information on Astro buses). The Astro bus timetable is as follows:

| Destination | Cost (one way) | Departure time |
|---|---|---|
| Camagüey | CUC$4.50 | 6:15am |
| Habana | CUC$27 | 7:30pm |
| Holguín | CUC$3 | 1pm |
| Santa Clara | CUC$15 | 8:40pm, alt days |
| Santiago de Cuba | CUC$7.50 | 5:15am |

**Víazul** (www.viazul.com) buses have the following departures; tickets are sold by the *jefe de turno* (shift manager):

| Destination | Cost (one way) | Departure time |
|---|---|---|
| Ciego de Ávila | CUC$13 | 12:15am, 1:25am, 2:40pm, 9:05pm |
| Habana | CUC$42 | 1:25am, 2:40pm, 9:05pm |
| Sancti Spíritus | CUC$18 | 12:15am, 1:25am, 2:40pm, 9:05pm |
| Santiago de Cuba | CUC$11 | 2am, 7am, 3:35pm, 9pm |
| Trinidad | CUC$23 | 12:15am |

All Santiago de Cuba buses also stop at Holguín (CUC$6, one hour 10 minutes) and Bayamo (CUC$6, 2½ hours). To get to Guantánamo or Baracoa, you have to connect through Santiago de Cuba (an onward bus departs at 7:30am).

Passenger trucks to Camagüey, Holguín, Bayamo and Puerto Padre pick up passengers on the main street near the train station, with the last departure before 2pm. Buy your tickets at the window. It's easier to reach Playa La Herradura from Holguín, but you can take a truck to Puerto Padre and hitch or connect with ongoing trucks there (for information on the risks associated with hitching see p477). If you have problems catching the Camagüey truck, take a bus to Guáimaro from the regional bus station attached to the end of the train station and try again there.

### TRAIN

The **train station** (☎ 4-8140) is near Estadio Julio A Mella on the northeast side of town. See the *jefe de turno* for tickets. As ever, double check these times and prices before you depart:

| Destination | Cost (one way) | Travel time (hours) | Departure time |
|---|---|---|---|
| Camagüey | CUC$5 | 3 | 12:30am |
| Habana | CUC$27 | 10 | 12:30am |
| Holguín | CUC$4 | 2 | 7:20am, alt days |
| Matanzas | CUC$24 | 10 | 12:30am |
| Santiago de Cuba | CUC$9 | 3.5 | 1:50am, alt days |

## Getting Around

A taxi from the airport to Hotel Las Tunas should cost CUC$3. **Cubataxi** (☎ 4-2036; Villamar No 34) rents taxis and provides secure overnight parking for CUC$1 to CUC$2. Horse carts run along Frank País near the baseball stadium to the town center; a charter trip costs 10 pesos.

**Havanautos** (☎ 5-5242; Av 2 de Diciembre) is at Hotel Las Tunas. An **Oro Negro gas station** (cnr Francisco Varona & Lora) is a block west of the bus station, where there is also a **Micar** (☎ 4-6263; Francisco Varona) outlet. **Servi-Cupet** (Carretera Central; 24hr) is at the exit from Las Tunas toward Camagüey.

## PUNTA COVARRUBIAS

It seems like the rutted road bumps go on forever before you reach Punta Covarrubias, 49km northwest of Puerto Padre. But after 90 minutes you arrive and it's sublime: 4km of spotless sandy beach, the blue-green Atlantic and the **Villa Covarrubias** (Gran Caribe; ☎ 4-6230; fax 36 53 05; s/d from CUC$70/110; P) the province's only all-inclusive resort. The hotel has 122 comfortable rooms in cabinesque blocks (one room is designed for disabled guests). Scuba diving the nearby coral reef is the highlight. Packages of two dives per day are offered at the Marina Covarrubias for CUC$45. There are 12 dive sites here. Almost all guests arrive on all-inclusive tours and are bussed in from Frank País Airport in Holguín, 115km to the southeast. It's very secluded.

Self-sufficient travelers can turn in to the beach at the **mirador** (a tower with fantastic panoramic views), 200m before the hotel and pitch camp. Old barbecue pits from parties past allow campfire cooking.

## PLAYAS LA HERRADURA, LA LLANITA & LAS BOCAS

Congratulations! You've made it to the end of the road. A captivating alternative to the comforts of Covarrubias can be found at this string of northern beaches hugging the Atlantic coast 30km north of Puerto Padre and 55km from Holguín. There's not much to do here apart from read, relax, ruminate and get lost in the vivid colors of traditional Cuban life.

From Puerto Padre, it's 30km around the eastern shore of Bahía de Chaparra to **Playa La Herradura**. The beach is a scoop of golden sand and the water is clean. There are a couple of houses legally renting rooms (look for the green triangle). A good choice is **Villa Papachongo** (in Holguín ☎ 24-42-41-74; Casa No 137; r CUC$15; ), right on the beach with a great porch for catching the sunset. Other options are Villa Rocio and Villa Pedro Hidalgo. Ask around. The place isn't big and everybody knows everybody else. If you don't like what you see here, push on to Playa Las Bocas where there are several more houses for rent. There is a small store

### THE GAPS ON THE MAP

Languishing in a half-forgotten corner of Cuba's least spectacular province, the sizeable town of Puerto Padre – or the 'city of mills' as it is locally known – is hardly a tourist mecca. But for the die-hard traveler therein lies the attraction. Blessed with a Las Ramblas–style boulevard, a miniature Malecón, and an emaciated statue of Don Quixote standing rather forlornly beneath a small windmill, the town is the sort of place where you stop to ask the way at lunchtime and end up, five hours later, tucking into fresh lobster at a bayside eating joint.

Unshakeable Cuba junkies can scratch beneath the surface at the **Museo Municipal**, **Casa de la Cultura**, or the 19th-century **Fuerte de la Loma** all on Calle Libertad, or surf the streets in search of friends, conversation or overnight accommodation in a casa particular. Boxing fanatics might want to ask around about local hero Teófilo Stevenson (see p343) whose family home 6km out of Puerto Padre in the barrio of Las Delicias has been known to accept visitors.

To get to Puerto Padre you'll need to hire a car or flag a truck in Las Tunas.

for snacks and an open-air bar at the entrance to town.

Continue west on this road for 11km to **Playa Llanita**. The sand here is softer and whiter than in Las Herradura, but the beach lies on an unprotected bend and there's sometimes a vicious chop. If you're caught without a roof, check out one of the 112 basic cabins at **Campismo Playa Corella** (☎ 5-5447; per person CUC$5), 5km before Playa Llanita.

Just 1km beyond, you come to the end of the road at **Playa Las Bocas**. Wedged between the coast and Bahía de Chaparra, you can catch a ferry (one peso) to El Socucho and continue to Puerto Padre or rent a room in a casa particular.

## Getting There & Away

There are trucks as far as Puerto Padre from Las Tunas, from where you'll have to connect with another ride to the junction at Lora before heading north to the beaches. It's much easier to get up this way from Holguín, but even this way there are only regular trucks to the junction at Velasco, from where you'll have to connect with another ride north.

Driving is the best shot. Head out of Las Tunas 52km north to Puerto Padre (gas up at the Servi-Cupet here), east to the junction at Lora and then north to Playa Herradura. For directions from Holguín, see p357.

# Holguín Province

Sleepy Holguín is a province of contrasts and paradoxes. Glimmering in the south, the pine-clad Sierra Cristal Mountains boast some of Cuba's most serene and attractive landscapes, while further east in polluted Moa the Che Guevara nickel mine coats the countryside in a thick layer of red dust.

The contradictions don't end there. Long renowned for the ferocity of its *mambí* (resistance fighters) in the independence wars of the 19th century, Holguín has spawned its fair share of heroes and villains in the years since. In 1926 *el líder máximo* (highest leader), Fidel Castro, was born in Finca Manacas near the one-horse town of Birán (his home is now a fascinating museum) while his infinitely less accomplished predecessor, Fulgencio Batista, hailed from the pretty provincial town of Banes to the northeast.

Hugging the coast, the big resort complexes of Guardalavaca and Playa Pesquero play host to some of Cuba's largest and most expensive five-star playgrounds where package tourists can sip on mint-laced mojitos (rum cocktails) while scantily-clad Cuban dancers offer up a program of sensuous nighttime entertainment with all the trimmings.

If you get bored of the beach volleyball check out Holguín, the province's unsung capital and a great place to sample all of those uniquely Cuban treats that the organized tours never see fit to mention. Check out a baseball game, tuck into peso pizza in Parque Calixto García or relax in the low-key music houses of Calle Maceo as the aroma of cheap cheroots drifts through the winking louvers and dissolves imperceptibly above the *dominó* tables.

## HIGHLIGHTS

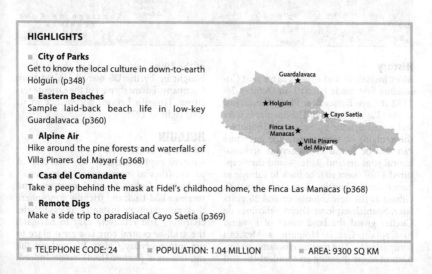

- **City of Parks**
  Get to know the local culture in down-to-earth Holguín (p348)
- **Eastern Beaches**
  Sample laid-back beach life in low-key Guardalavaca (p360)
- **Alpine Air**
  Hike around the pine forests and waterfalls of Villa Pinares del Mayarí (p368)
- **Casa del Comandante**
  Take a peep behind the mask at Fidel's childhood home, the Finca Las Manacas (p368)
- **Remote Digs**
  Make a side trip to paradisiacal Cayo Saetía (p369)

Guardalavaca
Holguín
Cayo Saetía
Finca Las Manacas
Villa Pinares del Mayarí

| TELEPHONE CODE: 24 | POPULATION: 1.04 MILLION | AREA: 9300 SQ KM |
|---|---|---|

HOLGUÍN PROVINCE

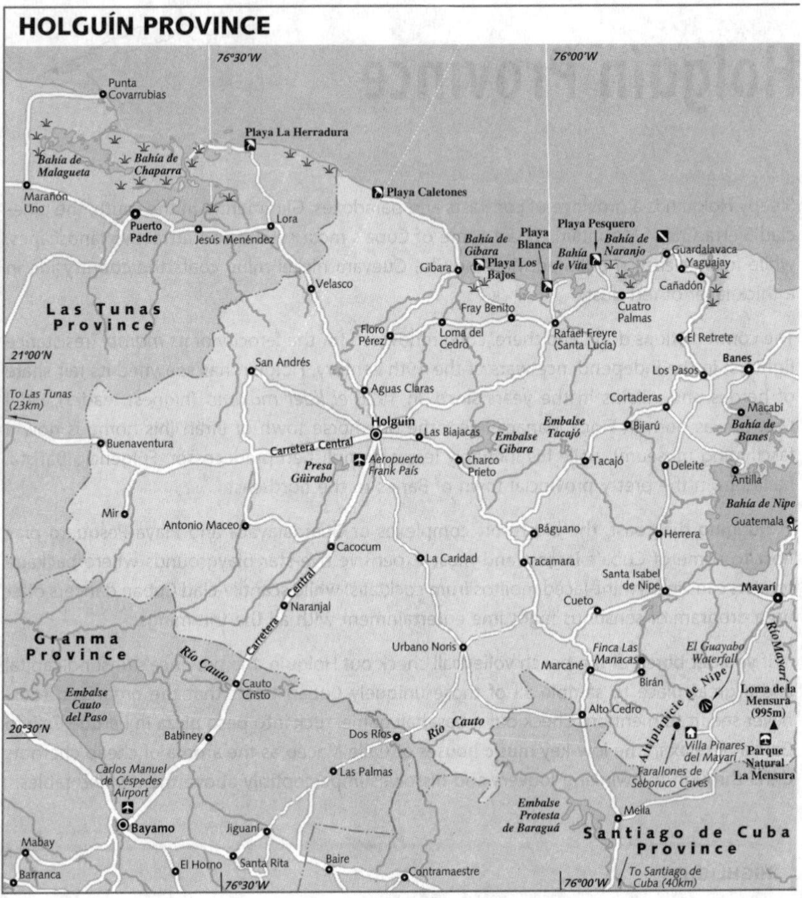

**HOLGUÍN PROVINCE**

## History

Most historians and experts agree that Columbus first made landfall on October 28, 1492 at Cayo Bariay near Playa Blanca, just west of Playa Don Lino. The Spaniards were welcomed ashore by Seboruco Indians – the remains of whose erstwhile ancestors can still be found at numerous archaeological sites around Banes – and they captured 13 of them to take back to Europe as 'specimens.' Choosing Baracoa rather than Gibara as the new colonial capital 20 years later, Spanish explorer Diego Velázquez de Cuellar gifted the land north of Bayamo to Captain García Holguín, a Mexican conquistador. The province became an important sugar-growing area and, at the end of the 19th century, much of the land was bought up by the US-owned United Fruit Company. Formerly part of the Oriente territory, Holguín became a province in its own right in 1975.

## HOLGUÍN

☎ 24 / pop 264,927

Known euphemistically as 'the city of parks', (they're more squares than parks), Holguín is Cuba's fourth largest city and retains a laid-back and friendly atmosphere that puts visitors instantly at ease. Safe, charming and relatively easy to navigate, the gridlike central core is a great place to dip into everyday Cuban life without the infractions of *jinetero* (tout) hassle. Indeed,

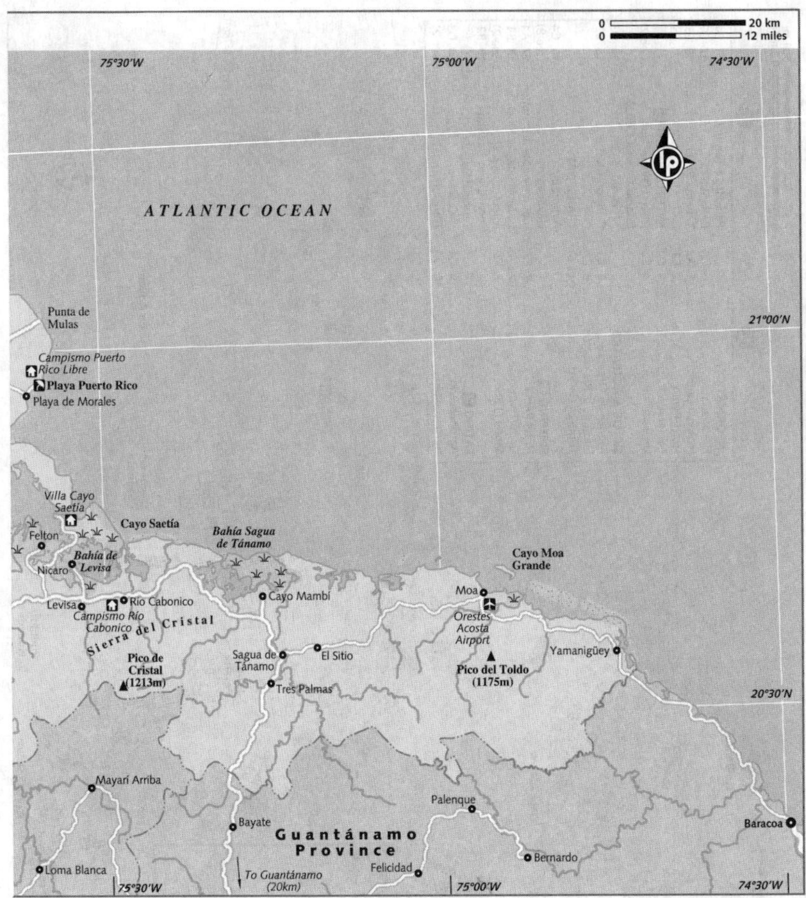




local life ticks along sensuously here to a gentle rhythm all of its own. Check out the local sports program, drop by the dynamic Uneac (Unión de Escritores y Artistas de Cuba; National Union of Cuban Writers and Artists) cultural center or just sit out on colorful Parque Céspedes drinking in the sights and sounds of a city of stalwart survivors going industriously about its daily business.

## History

In 1515 Diego Velázquez, Cuba's first governor, conferred the lands north of Bayamo to Captain García Holguín, an officer in the Spanish army and one of island's original pioneering colonizers. Setting up a cattle ranch in the province's verdant and fertile hinterland, Holguín and his descendants presided over a burgeoning agricultural settlement that by 1720 had sprouted a small wooden church and more than 450 inhabitants. In 1752 'San Isidoro de Holguín' (the settlement was renamed after the church) was granted the title of city and by 1790 the population had expanded tenfold to 12,000.

Holguín was the setting of much fighting during the two wars of independence when ferocious *mambí* warriors laid siege to the heavily fortified Spanish barracks at La Periquera (now the Museo de Historia Provincial, p353). Captured and lost by Julio Grave de Peralta (after whom one of

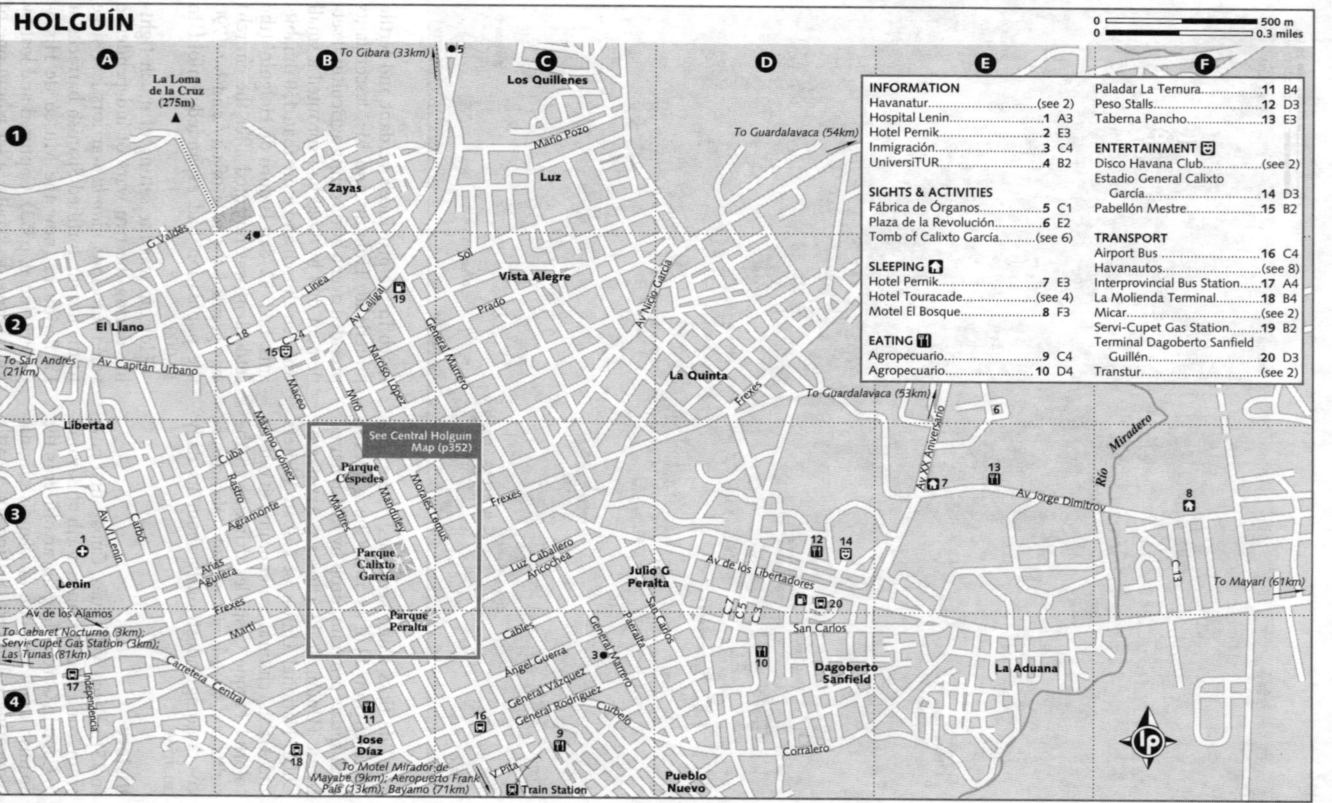
HOLGUÍN
0 500 m
0 0.3 miles
INFORMATION
Havanatur (see 2)
Hospital Lenin 1 A3
Hotel Pernik 2 E3
Inmigración 3 C4
UniversiTUR 4 B2
SIGHTS & ACTIVITIES
Fábrica de Órganos 5 C1
Plaza de la Revolución 6 E2
Tomb of Calixto García (see 6)
SLEEPING
Hotel Pernik 7 E3
Hotel Touracade (see 4)
Motel El Bosque 8 F3
EATING
Agropecuario 9 C4
Agropecuario 10 D4
Paladar La Ternura 11 B4
Peso Stalls 12 D3
Taberna Pancho 13 E3
ENTERTAINMENT
Disco Havana Club (see 2)
Estadio General Calixto García 14 D3
Pabellón Mestre 15 B2
TRANSPORT
Airport Bus 16 C4
Havanautos (see 8)
Interprovincial Bus Station 17 A4
La Molienda Terminal 18 B4
Micar (see 2)
Servi-Cupet Gas Station 19 B2
Terminal Dagoberto Sanfield Guillén 20 D3
Transtur (see 2)
La Loma de la Cruz (275m)
To Gibara (33km)
Los Quillenes
Mario Pozo
Luz
Zayas
To Guardalavaca (54km)
G Valdés
Sol
Vista Alegre
Línea
Av Calixto
Prado
Av Nicio García
El Llano
C 18
C 24
General Marrero
To San Andrés (21km)
Av Capitán Urbano
Maceo
Miró
Narciso López
La Quinta
Frexes
To Guardalavaca (53km)
Libertad
See Central Holguín Map (p352)
Parque Céspedes
Máximo Gómez
Cuba
Rastro
Mártires
Manduley
Morales Lemus
Av XX Aniversario
Río Miradero
Agramonte
Av VI Lenin
Carbó
Parque Calixto García
Luz Caballero
Aricochea
Av Jorge Dimitrov
Lenin
Arias
Aguilera
Julio G Peralta
Av de los Libertadores
C 13
To Mayarí (61km)
Av de los Álamos
Frexes
Parque Peralta
San Carlos
To Cabaret Nocturno (3km); Servi-Cupet Gas Station (3km); Las Tunas (81km)
Martí
Cables
Paeralta
Carretera Central
Ángel Guerra
General Vázquez
General Rodríguez
Dagoberto Sanfield
La Aduana
Independencia
Curbelo
Jose Díaz
Corralero
To Motel Mirador de Mayabe (9km); Aeropuerto Frank País (13km); Bayamo (71km)
V Pita
Train Station
Pueblo Nuevo

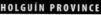

the squares is named), the city was taken for a second time on December 19, 1872 by Cuban general and native son Calixto García, Holguín's posthumous local hero.

With the division of Oriente into five separate provinces in 1975, the city of Holguín became a provincial capital.

## Orientation

Parque Calixto García is Holguín's most important central square; to the north is Parque Céspedes and to the south is Parque Peralta. Manduley (aka Libertad) and Maceo are the main north–south thoroughfares, running between the train station and the hills that border the city's northern limits. The main bus station is to the west of town, the main tourist hotels to the east.

## Information

### BOOKSTORES

**ARTex** (Map p352; Manduley No 193A) Sells books, CDs, posters and Che T-shirts on Parque Calixto García.

**Librería Villena Botev** (Map p352; ☎ 42 76 81; Frexes No 151) On the corner of Máximo Gómez. Books in Spanish only.

### INTERNET ACCESS

**Etecsa Telepunto** (Map p352; cnr Martí & Maceo; per hr CUC$6; 9am-7pm) Three computer terminals in Parque Calixto García.

**Hotel Pernik** (Map p350; cnr Avs Jorge Dimitrov & XX Aniversario; per hr CUC$6) Two terminals.

### LIBRARIES

**Biblioteca Alex Urquiola** (Map p352; ☎ 42 13 66; Maceo No 178; 8:30am-9pm Mon-Fri, 8:30am-4:30pm Sat) On Parque Calixto García.

### MEDIA

The local newspaper *Ahora* is published on Saturday. Radio Ángulo CMKO can be heard on 1110AM and 97.9FM.

### MEDICAL SERVICES

Both Hotel Pernik (p354) and Motel El Bosque (p354) have infirmaries.

**Farmacia Turno Especial** (Map p352; Maceo No 170; 8am-10pm Mon-Sat) On Parque Calixto García.

**Hospital Lenin** (Map p350; ☎ 42 53 02; Av VI Lenin) Will treat foreigners in an emergency.

### MONEY

**Banco de Crédito y Comercio** (Map p352; ☎ 42 25 12; Arias) On Parque Céspedes.

**Banco Financiero Internacional** (Map p352; ☎ 46 85 02; Manduley No 167 btwn Frexes & Aguilera)

**Cadeca** (Map p352; ☎ 46 81 09; Manduley No 205 btwn Martí & Luz Caballero; 8:30am-6pm Mon-Sat, 8am-1pm Sun)

### POST

**Post office** Manduley No 183 (Map p352; ☎ 46 82 54; 10am-noon & 1-6pm Mon-Fri); Parque Céspedes (Map p352; Maceo No 114; 8am-6pm Mon-Sat) There's also a DHL office at the post office on Parque Calixto García.

### TELEPHONE

**Etecsa Telepunto** (Map p352; cnr Martí & Maceo; 9am-7pm) On Parque Calixto García.

### TRAVEL AGENCIES

**Havanatur** Frexes (Map p352; ☎ 46 80 91; Frexes No 172 btwn Morales Lemus & Narciso López) Hotel Pernik (Map p350; cnr Avs Jorge Dimitrov & XX Aniversario)

**Reservaciones de Campismo** (Map p352; ☎ 42 28 81; Mártires No 87; 8am-6pm Mon-Fri, 8am-noon Sat)

**UniversiTUR** (Map p350; ☎ 46 28 23; universiturhlg@esihl.colombus.cu; Manduley btwn Calles 10 & 12)

## Sights

An afternoon exploring the city's parks, plazas and surrounding sights is a great way to discover Holguín. No walk is complete without a climb up to La Loma de la Cruz (p353).

### PARQUE CÉSPEDES

Founded in the late 18th century, this shady square hosting hot stick-ball action during the day is the youngest of Holguín's parks. On its eastern edge is the **Iglesia de San José**, (Map p352; Manduley No 116) with its distinctive bell tower (1842) and dome (visible from La Loma de la Cruz). Locals calls this Parque San José.

In a colonial building facing the church is the **Galería Holguín** (Map p352; ☎ 42 23 92; Manduley No 137; admission free; 8am-6pm Tue-Wed, 8am-10pm Thu-Sun). Duck into the high-ceilinged rooms to check out some (good) local art. The small **Museo Eduardo García Feria y José García Castañeda** (Map p352; cnr Agramonte & Maceo; admission free) on the square's northwestern corner documents the life and work of two local archaeologists and naturalists. Eduardo was responsible for creating Holguín's first museum and once boasted the largest snail collection in Cuba.

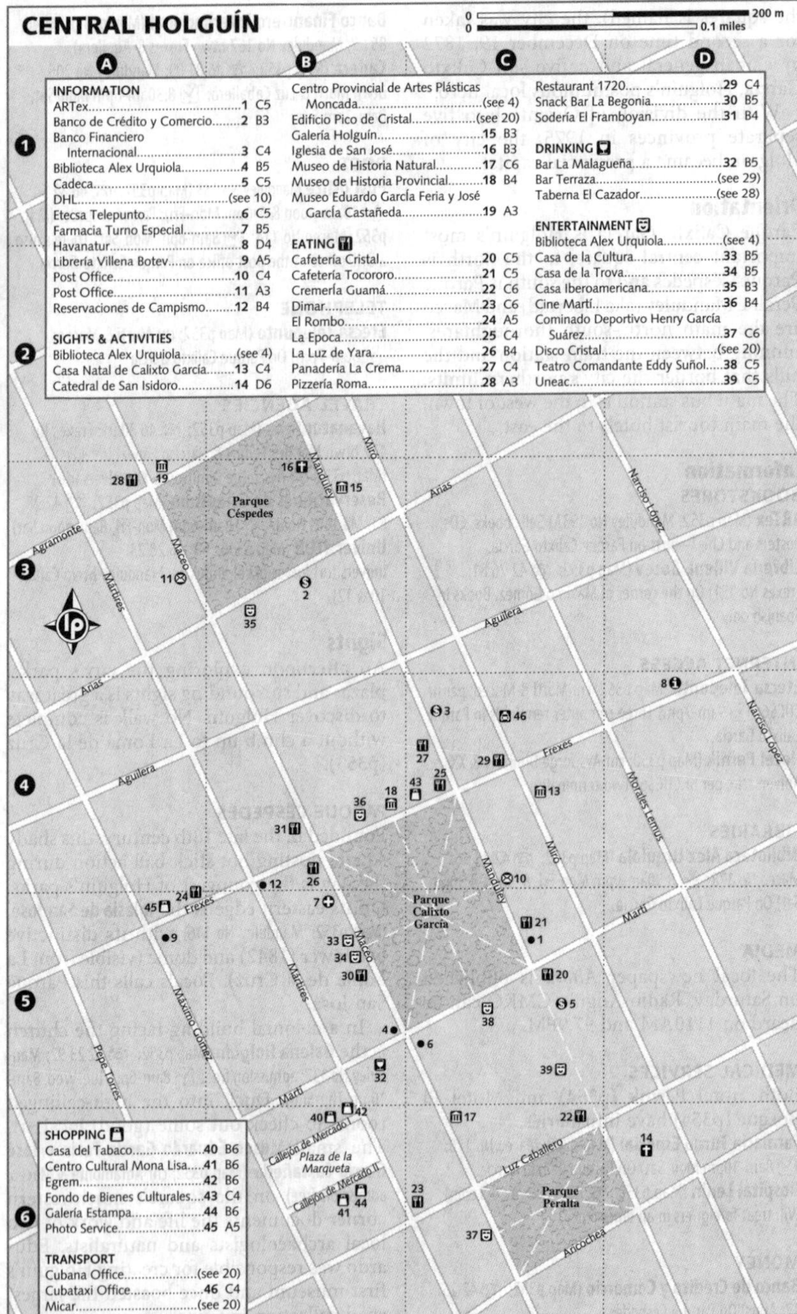
CENTRAL HOLGUÍN
0 200 m
0 0.1 miles
A
B
C
D
1
2
3
4
5
6
INFORMATION
ARTex 1 C5
Banco de Crédito y Comercio 2 B3
Banco Financiero Internacional 3 C4
Biblioteca Alex Urquiola 4 B5
Cadeca 5 C5
DHL (see 10)
Etecsa Telepunto 6 C5
Farmacia Turno Especial 7 B5
Havanatur 8 D4
Librería Villena Botev 9 A5
Post Office 10 C4
Post Office 11 A3
Reservaciones de Campismo 12 B4
SIGHTS & ACTIVITIES
Biblioteca Alex Urquiola (see 4)
Casa Natal de Calixto García 13 C4
Catedral de San Isidoro 14 D6
Centro Provincial de Artes Plásticas Moncada (see 4)
Edificio Pico de Cristal (see 20)
Galería Holguín 15 B3
Iglesia de San José 16 B3
Museo de Historia Natural 17 C6
Museo de Historia Provincial 18 B4
Museo Eduardo García Feria y José García Castañeda 19 A3
EATING
Cafetería Cristal 20 C5
Cafetería Tocororo 21 C5
Cremería Guamá 22 C6
Dimar 23 C6
El Rombo 24 A5
La Epoca 25 C4
La Luz de Yara 26 B4
Panadería La Crema 27 C4
Pizzería Roma 28 A3
Restaurant 1720 29 C4
Snack Bar La Begonia 30 B5
Sodería El Framboyan 31 B4
DRINKING
Bar La Malagueña 32 B5
Bar Terraza (see 29)
Taberna El Cazador (see 28)
ENTERTAINMENT
Biblioteca Alex Urquiola (see 4)
Casa de la Cultura 33 B5
Casa de la Trova 34 B5
Casa Iberoamericana 35 B3
Cine Martí 36 B4
Cominado Deportivo Henry García Suárez 37 C6
Disco Cristal (see 20)
Teatro Comandante Eddy Suñol 38 C5
Uneac 39 C5
SHOPPING
Casa del Tabaco 40 B6
Centro Cultural Mona Lisa 41 B6
Egrem 42 B6
Fondo de Bienes Culturales 43 C4
Galería Estampa 44 B6
Photo Service 45 A5
TRANSPORT
Cubana Office (see 20)
Cubataxi Office 46 C4
Micar (see 20)
Parque Céspedes
Parque Calixto García
Parque Peralta
Plaza de la Marqueta
Agramonte
Maceo
Mártires
Manduley
Miró
Arias
Aguilera
Frexes
Martí
Máximo Gómez
Pepe Torres
Narciso López
Morales Lemus
Luz Caballero
Aricochea
Callejón de Mercado I
Callejón de Mercado II

#### PARQUE CALIXTO GARCÍA

The former Plaza de Armas was created in 1719 and served originally as the town's meeting point and marketplace. The centerpiece today is a 1912 statue of General Calixto García, who captured Holguín from the Spaniards in December 1872.

To learn more about this dynamic hero, head to **Casa Natal de Calixto García** (Map p352; ☎ 42 56 10; Miró No 147; admission CUC$1; 🕑 9am-9pm Tue-Sat) two blocks east of the park. García was born here in 1839.

On the park's northern side is the **Museo de Historia Provincial** (Map p352; ☎ 46 33 95; Frexes No 198; admission CUC$1; 🕑 8am-5pm). Now a national monument, the building was constructed between 1860 and 1868 and used as a Spanish army barracks during the independence wars. It was nicknamed La Periquera (parrot cage) for the red, yellow and green uniforms of the Spanish soldiers who stood guard outside. The prize exhibit is an old axe-head carved in the likeness of a man, known as the Hacha de Holguín (Holguín Axe), thought to have been made by aborigines in the early 1400s and discovered in 1860. There's a pretty patio inside.

In the southwestern corner of Parque Calixto García is the **Centro Provincial de Artes Plásticas Moncada** (Map p352; ☎ 42 20 84; Maceo No 180; admission free; 🕑 9am-4pm Mon-Sat). This bright gallery is Holguín's best and shares space with the **Biblioteca Alex Urquiola** (Map p352; ☎ 46 25 62; Maceo No 180), housing Holguín's biggest book collection.

The **Museo de Historia Natural** (Map p352; ☎ 42 39 35; Maceo No 129 btwn Parques Calixto García & Peralta; admission/camera CUC$1/1; 🕑 9am-10pm Tue-Sat, 9am-9pm Sun) has Cuba's biggest collection of stuffed animals behind glass, including the world's smallest frog and world's smallest hummingbird.

#### PARQUE PERALTA

This square (called Parque de las Flores locally) is named for General Julio Grave de Peralta (1834–72), who led the uprising against Spain in Holguín in October 1868. His marble statue (1916) faces the cathedral. Big and beige, the **Catedral de San Isidoro** (Map p352; Manduley) dates from 1720 but is heavily restored. Be sure not to miss the life-size statue of Pope Jean Paul II outside.

#### PLAZA DE LA MARQUETA

This partly-restored plaza and work-in-progress west of Parque Peralta was laid out in 1848 and formerly served as Holguín's marketplace. Today the aim is to transform the plaza into the city's cultural hub, and bookstores and art exhibits have already set this process in motion. Check out the telephone poles turned into totems that anchor the plaza's corners and the numerous bronze statues of well-known Holguiñeros that decorate the sidewalks.

The ruins in the plaza's center are undergoing massive and lengthy restoration as they are transformed into one of Cuba's most atmospheric concert halls. The shopping in this plaza, including the arty Galería Estampa and Centro Cultural Mona Lisa, is quality.

#### BEYOND THE CENTER

At the northern end of Maceo is a stairway built in 1950, with 460 steps ascending **La Loma de la Cruz** (Map p350), a 275m-high hill with panoramic views. A cross was raised here in 1790 in hope of relieving a drought, and every May 3 the Romerías de Mayo (p354) brings hundreds of pilgrims. It's a 20-minute walk from town or you can drive up the western side (accessible via G Valdés); a bici-taxi to the foot of the hill should cost 10 pesos. This walk is best tackled early in the morning when the light is pristine and the heat not too debilitating.

Holguín is a city most *fiel* (faithful) and the **Plaza de la Revolución** (Map p350) east of the center is a huge monument to the heroes of Cuban independence, bearing quotations from José Martí and Fidel Castro. Massive rallies are held here every May 1. The **tomb of Calixto García** (Map p350) is also here, as is a smaller monument to García's mother.

**Fábrica de Órganos** (Map p350; Carretera de Gibara No 301; 🕑 8am-4pm Mon-Fri) is the only mechanical music-organ factory in Cuba. This small factory produces about six organs a year, as well as guitars and other instruments. A good organ costs between the equivalent of US$10,000 and US$25,000. Eight professional organ groups exist in Holguín (including the Familia Cuayo, based at the factory), and you may be able to hear one playing on Parque Céspedes at 4pm on Thursday and 10am on Sunday.

 



## Festivals & Events

The **Romerías de Mayo**, in the first week of May, is a week-long art party with exhibitions, music, poetry and festivities, with the national rap competition and the La Loma de la Cruz pilgrimage among the highlights. Holguín's **Carnaval** happens in the third week of August and it's a blowout, with outdoor concerts, and copious amounts of dancing, roast pork and potent potables.

## Sleeping

### IN TOWN

Holguín has several Cuban-only hotels, limiting tourist options to two or three places.

**Hotel Touracade** (UniversiTUR; Map p350; ☎ 46 28 23; fax 48 18 43; Manduley No 26 btwn Calles 10 & 12; r CUC$10-15; ) This small UniversiTUR hotel near La Loma de la Cruz is designed for foreigners studying Spanish. It might let you a room if you're desperate.

**Hotel Pernik** (Islazul; Map p350; ☎ 48 10 11; fax 48 16 67; cnr Avs Jorge Dimitrov & XX Aniversario; s/d with breakfast low season CUC$35/48, high season CUC$45/60; P ) Holguín's most comfortable and popular tourist hotel, this incongruously designed place, 3km east of town, sometimes gets overwhelmed by its own popularity. The big rooms have balconies and the pool is a sprawler. Nevertheless, coming from Islazul's unreliable stock of Soviet-inspired architectural creations, the hotel suffers from the usual foibles of dull food and blaring late-night music. Overpriced at CUC$60 for a double. There's public Internet access here (CUC$6 per hour; noon to midnight) and a disco (admission CUC$2 to CUC$4, depending on season).

### OUTSIDE TOWN

**Motel Mirador de Mayabe** (Islazul; Map p350; ☎ 42 34 85; Alturas de Mayabe; s/d low season CUC$35/48, high season CUC$45/60; P ) This motel, high up on the Loma de Mayabe 10km southeast of Holguín, has 24 rooms tucked into lush grounds. The views, taking in vast mango plantations, are especially good from the pool. The Mirador de Mayabe's claim to fame is a beer-drinking donkey named Pancho, who hangs out near the bar. Typical Cuban lunches are served at the Finca Mayabe, just above the motel, where there's also a cockfighting ring. The Casa Campesina nearby is a replica of a traditional farmer's dwelling, and a host of domestic plants and animals are on hand; kids love it. A bus runs to Holguín from the bottom of the hill, 1.5km from the motel, three times a day.

**Motel El Bosque** (Islazul; Map p350; ☎ /fax 48 11 40; Av Jorge Dimitrov; s/d with breakfast low season CUC$35/48 high season CUC$45/60; P ) One kilometer beyond Hotel Pernik, the 69 duplex bungalows here are set among extensive green grounds, making it feel more removed than it is. There's a nice bar beside the swim-

### CASAS PARTICULARES – HOLGUÍN

**Augusto Gutiérrez Rodríguez** ( ☎ 42 72 75; 3rd fl, Morales Lemus No 148 btwn Luz Caballero & Martí; r CUC$20-25; ) Separate entry via a narrow spiral staircase.

**Germán González Rojas** ( ☎ 42 40 75; Ángel Guerra No 178 btwn Camilo Cienfuegos & Carretera Central; r CUC$20) Festive place with several rooms; including an independent apartment with two rooms, bath and patio.

**Haydée Torres Marrero** ( ☎ 42 47 21; Narcisco López No 151 btwn Frexes & Martí; r CUC$15; P ) Spacious upstairs with fridge, terrace and living room.

**Isabel Sera Galves** ( ☎ 42 25 29; Narciso López No 142 btwn Aguilera & Frexes; r CUC$20; ) Friendly home with great back patio; prices drop by CUC$5 in slow season.

**'La Palma' – Enrique R Interián Salermo** ( ☎ 42 46 83; Calle Maceo No 52A btwn 16 & 18, El Llano; r CUC$25; ) Neocolonial house from 1945 near the Loma de la Cruz. Son of owner is a painter and sculptor. Check out the terra-cotta bust of Che and the 3m-long canvas of the last supper (with St John as a woman). Fantastic hosts.

**Marieta González** (Calle Mendieta No 37 btwn Agramonte & Garayalde; r CUC$25) Same family as 'La Palma.'

**Roberto Polanco Vega** ( ☎ 46 13 77; apt 4, Calle 7 No 29; r CUC$20) Reparto Julio G Peralta near Terminal Dagoberto Sanfield Guillén, self-catering, good meals served.

**'Villa Liba Hostal' – Jorge A Mezerene** ( ☎ 42 38 23; villaliba@yahoo.es; Maceo No 46; r CUC$25; P ) Near the Loma de la Cruz stairway. Nicely furnished rooms sleep three to four. Patio; professional.

ming pool (nonguests can use it for CUC$5, which includes CUC$3 in drinks).

## Eating

### RESTAURANTS

**Taberna Pancho** (Map p350; ☎ 48 18 68; Av Jorge Dimitrov; noon-10pm) This is a lively Cuban place between Hotel Pernik and Motel El Bosque with some original menu choices. Nothing on the list, including hamburgers and draft Mayabe beer, costs more than CUC$3. Try the sausage special.

**Dimar** (Map p352; cnr Mártires & Luz Caballero; dishes CUC$2-5; 11am-10pm) A new seafood chain restaurant specializing in cheap shrimp cocktail and grilled fish has opened for business between Peralta and Marqueta squares.

**Restaurant 1720** (Map p352; ☎ 46 81 50; Calle Frexes btwn Manduley & Miró; 12:30-10:30pm) Holguín's finest dining is in this painstakingly restored cake-icing colonial mansion where you can dine on paella (CUC$6) or shrimp flambé (CUC$13); an excellent way to spend an afternoon if the rain is pouring down outside. There's an expensive perfume shop here, a lush lobby, and a salubrious inner courtyard that sometimes hosts music. Check out the wall plaques that give interesting insights into Holguín's history.

**Paladar La Ternura** (Map p350; Jose A Cardet No 293) Many of Holguín's paladares (private restaurants) have gone under or been closed down. One notable survivor is this upstairs place, which serves large portions of chicken, pork and beef dishes in an elegant dining room.

### CAFETERIAS

Peso stalls are crowded near the Interprovincial Bus Station on the Carretera Central.

**Cremeria Guamá** (Map p352; cnr Luz Caballero & Manduley; 10am-10:45pm) This place is Holguín's alternative Coppelia where you can enjoy peso ice cream al fresco overlooking pedestrianized Calle Manduley, the city's most happening thoroughfare.

**Cafetería Cristal** (Map p352; ☎ 42 58 55; ground fl, Edificio Pico de Cristal, cnr Manduley & Martí; 24hr) Reliable, affordable chicken meals are served at this popular place with cranking air-con. A more upscale restaurant is upstairs (open noon to 10pm).

**Cafetería Tocororo** (Map p352; Manduley No 189; 24hr) Centrally located on Parque Calixto García and serving reasonable spaghetti, pizza, chicken and sandwiches, this place is often packed with locals and the odd stray Guardalavaca tourist.

**El Rombo** (Map p352; Frexes btwn Mártires & Máximo Gómez; 9am-11pm) Don't be put off by the odd smell: this friendly branch of Cafeterías Cubanitas does a big, tasty ham-and-cheese sandwich and other items similar to Cafetería Tocororo, but without the wait.

**Snack Bar La Begonia** (Map p352; ☎ 46 85 86; Maceo No 176; 9am-10pm) With ice cream (CUC$1), sandwiches (CUC$2 to CUC$3) and drinks served beneath flowering trellises on Parque Calixto García, this is a relaxed place to meet other travelers. It's also popular with wedding parties and *quinciñera* (15th birthday celebrations for Cuban girls) photo shoots.

Also recommended:

**Sodería El Framboyan** (Map p352; Maceo; 10am-11pm) Ice cream galore (cones CUC$1, sundaes up to CUC$2.50) Near Frexes.

**Pizzería Roma** (Map p352; cnr Maceo & Agramonte) Get your street pizza here (six pesos).

### GROCERIES

**La Luz de Yara** (Map p352; cnr Frexes & Maceo; 8:30am-7pm Mon-Sat, 8:30am-noon Sun) Bustling department store/supermarket with a bakery section on Parque Calixto García.

**La Epoca** (Map p352; Frexes No 194) Another make-your-own-picnic option on Parque Calixto Garcia.

**Panadería La Crema** (Map p352; Manduley No 140; 7am-10pm) A good selection of breads and cakes here means long lines.

There are two **agropecuarios** (vegetable markets; Map p350): one is off Calle 19, the continuation of Morales Lemus near the train station; the other is on Calle 3 in Dagoberto Sanfield. There are plenty of peso stalls beside the baseball stadium.

## Drinking

**Taberna El Cazador** (Map p352; cnr Maceo & Agramonte) Terrace peso bar with park views.

**Bar La Malagueña** (Map p352; Martí No 129) This popular spot near Parque Calixto García attracts a mixed local/traveler crowd.

**Bar Terraza** (Map p352; ☎ 46 81 50; Calle Frexes btwn Manduley & Miró; 9pm-2am) A spiffy place above Restaurant 1720 to sip a mojito. Has views over Parque Calixto García.

HOLGUÍN PROVINCE

## Entertainment

**Teatro Comandante Eddy Suñol** (Map p352; ☎ 46 31 61; Martí No 111) Holguín's premier theater is an architectural treat from 1939 on Parque Calixto García. It hosts both the Rodrigo Prats Theater Company and the Ballet Nacional de Cuba and is renowned both nationally and internationally for its operettas, dance performances and Spanish musicals. Check here for details of performances by the famous children's theater Alas Buenas.

**Uneac** (Map p352; Calle Manduley btwn Luz Caballero & Martí) This is Holguín's cultural hothouse. If you only visit one Uneac center in Cuba – and there are 14 of them in all (one in each province) – make sure it's here. Situated in a lovingly restored house in pedestrian Calle Manduley, this friendly establishment offers everything from literary evenings (with a famous author) and music nights, to patio theatre (including Lorca), and cultural reviews. Everyone is welcome.

Also recommended:

**Biblioteca Alex Urquiola** (Map p352; ☎ 46 25 62; Maceo No 180) On the corner of Martí. Music and theater events are often hosted here including performances by the Holguín Symphony Orchestra.

**Casa de la Trova** (Map p352; Maceo No 174; 🕑 Tue-Sun) Traditional folk singing and music on Parque Calixto García.

**Casa de la Cultura** (Map p352; Maceo No 172; 🕑 Tue-Sun) Exhibitions and classical music.

**Casa Iberoamericana** (Map p352; ☎ 42 25 33; Arias No 161) On Parque Céspedes; frequently hosts *peñas* (musical performances).

**Pabellón Mestre** (Map p350; cnr Maceo & Capitán Urbano; 🕑 9pm-late) Open-air dancing and cultural activities.

### DANCE CLUBS

**Disco Cristal** (Map p352; ☎ 42 58 55; 3rd fl, Edificio Pico de Cristal, Manduley No 199; admission CUC$2; 🕑 9pm-2am Tue-Thu) On the corner of Martí. Holguín's preferred city-center club, locals with Convertibles get down here; and there are good views from the dance floor. You must spend CUC$3 on food or drink in addition to paying the cost of admission.

**Disco Havana Club** (Map p350; ☎ 48 10 11; Hotel Pernik, cnr Avs Jorge Dimitrov & XX Aniversario; guests/nonguests CUC$2/4; 🕑 10pm-2am Tue-Sun) Holguín's premier disco. If you're staying at Hotel Pernik the music will visit you – in your room! – until 1am.

**Cabaret Nocturno** (☎ 42 51 85; admission CUC$10; 🕑 10pm-2am) Tropicana-style club beyond Servi-Cupet 3km out on the road to Las Tunas. No show when it's raining.

### CINEMAS

**Cine Martí** (Map p352; Frexes No 204; 1-2 pesos) For big-screen movies, head to this cinema on Parque Calixto García.

### SPORTS

Holguín is one of the best places on the island to view Cuba's two national sports: baseball and boxing.

**Estadio General Calixto García** (Map p350; admission 1 peso) Baseball games are held from October to April at this stadium, just off Av de los Libertadores, not far from Hotel Pernik. Holguín's Perros won the national championship in 2002 for the first time in history, so Holguiñeros are pretty excited about their ball these days. The stadium also houses a sports museum.

**Cominado Deportivo Henry García Suárez** (Map p352; Maceo; admission 1 peso; 🕑 8pm Wed, 2pm Sat) You can catch boxing matches at this intimate gym on the western side of Parque Peralta, where three Olympic medalists have trained, including the female judo medalist. Ask here about organizing a training session.

## Shopping

Holguín has some decent shopping. If you're in a rush, head directly to the Plaza de la Marqueta (Map p352) where there is a smattering of different shops including Egrem for music, Casa del Tabaco for cigars and Galería Estampa for fine arts.

**Fondo de Bienes Culturales** (Map p352; ☎ 42 37 82; Frexes No 196) This shop on Parque Calixto García has one of the best selections of Cuban handicrafts.

**Photo Service** (Map p352; Frexes btwn Máximo Gomez & Mártires) Can cater for all your camera needs.

## Getting There & Away

### AIR

There are 16 international flights a week into Holguín's well-organized **Aeropuerto Frank País** (☎ 46 25 12; airport code HOG), 13km south of the city, including from Amsterdam, Düsseldorf, London, Montreal, and Toronto. Almost all arrivals get bussed directly off to Guardalavaca and see little of Holguín city.

Domestic destinations are served by **Cubana** (☎ 46 25 12, 46 25 34; cnr Manduley & Martí), which flies daily to Habana (CUC$103 one way, two hours), and Aerocaribbean (tickets are also available form Cubana office).

### BUS

The **Interprovincial Bus Station** (Map p350; ☎ 46 10 36; cnr Carretera Central & Independencia), west of the center near Hospital Lenin, has Astro buses going to Habana (CUC$28, daily), Guantánamo (CUC$11, alternate days) and Santiago (CUC$7.50, alternate days).

Air-conditioned **Víazul** (www.viazul.com) buses leave daily; see the table following.

| Destination | Cost (one way) | Departure time |
|---|---|---|
| Habana | CUC$44 | 1:25pm, 6:45pm |
| Santiago de Cuba | CUC$11 | 3:25am, 4:50pm, 10:15pm |
| Trinidad | CUC$26 | 11pm |

You can take the Habana bus as far as Las Tunas (CUC$6), Camagüey (CUC$11), Ciego de Ávila (CUC$17), Sancti Spíritus (CUC$21) or Santa Clara (CUC$26). The Santiago departure also stops in Bayamo (CUC$6), but to reach Guantánamo or Baracoa, you have to change in Santiago de Cuba.

### TRAIN

The **train station** (Map p350; ☎ 42 23 11, Calle V Pita) is on the southern side of town. Foreigners must purchase tickets in Convertibles at the special **Ladis ticket office** (🕒 7:30am-3pm). The ticket office is marked 'U/B Ferrocuba Provincial Holguín' on the corner of Manduley opposite the train station.

Theoretically, there's one daily morning train to Las Tunas (CUC$4, two hours), a daily afternoon train to Santiago de Cuba (CUC$5, 3½ hours), and a daily 6:15pm train to Habana (CUC$31, 15 hours). This train stops in Camagüey (CUC$9), Ciego de Ávila (CUC$13), Guayos (CUC$17), Santa Clara (CUC$20) and Matanzas (CUC$20). You may have to change trains at the Santiago–Habana mainline junction in Cacocum, 17km south of Holguín.

The only service that operates with any regularity is the train to Habana. The Santiago de Cuba service is rather irregular; ask before planning your trip around it.

### TRUCK

Trucks to points south and west operate from **La Molienda Terminal** (Map p350; ☎ 46 20 11; Carretera Central No 46), between the bus and train stations. Trucks leave when full for Las Tunas and Bayamo (four pesos each), with the last departure around 2pm. You can also get colectivos from here to either destination for 20 pesos. No trucks go directly to Santiago de Cuba or Camagüey, so you must make the journey in stages.

The **Terminal Dagoberto Sanfield Guillén** (Map p350; Av de los Libertadores), opposite Estadio General Calixto García, has at least two daily trucks to Gibara (two pesos; window six), Banes (four pesos; window five) and Moa (nine pesos; window five). To reach Guardalavaca, take a truck to Rafael Freyre (aka Santa Lucía, two pesos, window three) and look for something else there.

If you have never traveled in a truck before, Holguín is a good place from which to try it.

## Getting Around

### TO/FROM THE AIRPORT

The public bus to the airport leaves daily around 2pm from **airport bus stop** (Map p350; General Rodríguez No 84) on Parque Martí near the train station. A tourist taxi to the airport costs CUC$8 to CUC$10. It's also possible to spend your last night in Bayamo, then catch a taxi (CUC$18 to CUC$20) or a truck (three pesos) to Holguín Airport.

### BICI-TAXI

Holguín's bici-taxis are ubiquitous. They charge five pesos for a short trip, 10 pesos for a long one.

### CAR

You can rent or return a car at the following places:

**Havanautos** Motel El Bosque (Map p350; ☎ 48 81 57; Av Jorge Dimitrov); Aeropuerto Frank País (☎ 46 84 12)

**Micar** Cafeteria Cristal (Map p352; ☎ 46 85 59; cnr Manduley & Martí); Hotel Pernik (Map p350; ☎ 48 16 52; cnr Avs Jorge Dimitrov & XX Aniversario)

**Transtur** Hotel Pernik (Map p350; ☎ 48 10 11; cnr Avs Jorge Dimitrov & XX Aniversario); Aeropuerto Frank País (☎ 46 84 14) Also rents mopeds.

A **Servi-Cupet station** (Carretera Central; 24hr) is 3km out toward Las Tunas; another is just outside town on the road to Gibara. An **Oro Negro service station** (Carretera Central) is on the southern edge of town. The road to Gibara is north on Av Cajígal; also take this road and fork left after 5km to reach Playa Herradura.

### TAXI

A **Cubataxi** (Map p352; ☎ 42 32 90; Miró No 133) to Guardalavaca costs CUC$20. To Gibara, negotiate a CUC$25 to CUC$30 round-trip deal.



## GIBARA

☎ 24 / pop 28,826

Gibara is Holguín's outlet to the sea, a once important sugar-export town that was linked to the provincial capital via a railway. With the construction of the Carretera Central in the 1920s Gibara lost its mercantile importance and after the last train service was axed in 1958, the town fell into a sleepy slumber from which it has yet to awaken.

Christopher Columbus first arrived in the area in 1492 and called it Río de Mares (River of Oceans) for the Rios Cacoyugüín and Yabazón that drain into the Bahía de Gibara. The current name comes from *jiba*, the indigenous word for a bush that still grows along the shore.

Refounded in 1817, Gibara prospered in the 19th century as the sugar industry expanded and the trade rolled in. To protect the settlement from pirates, barracks were built and a 2km wall was constructed around the town in the early 1800s, making Gibara Cuba's second walled city after Habana. The once sparkling-white facades earned Gibara its nickname: *la villa blanca*.

Situated 33km from Holguín via a scenic road that undulates through friendly, eye-catching villages, Gibara is a small, intimate place whose unique ocean-side atmosphere gives it a distinct almost un-Cuban flavor. Redolent of a small Baracoa, the town's beautiful bayside setting is characterized by pretty plazas, crumbling Spanish ruins and a postcard view of the saddle-shaped Silla de Gibara that so captivated Columbus.

Each year in April, Gibara hosts the **Festival de Internacional de Cine Pobre** (International Low Budget Film Festival), which draws films and filmmakers from all over the world.

### Information

Most services line Calle Independencia.

**Banco Popular de Ahorro** (cnr Calles Independencia & Cuba) Changes traveler's checks.

**Bandec** (cnr Calles Independencia & J Peralta) Also changes traveler's checks.

**Post office** (Independencia No 15) There are few public phones here.

### Sights

At the top of Calle Cabada is **El Cuartelón**, a crumbling-brick Spanish fort with graceful arches, that provides stunning town and bay views. Continue on this street for 200m to Restaurant El Mirador for an even better vantage point. You'll see remnants of the old fortresses here and at the **Fuerte Fernando VII**, on the point beyond Parque de las Madres, a block over from Parque Calixto García.

The centerpiece of **Parque Calixto García** (lined with weird *robles africanos* – African oaks with large penis-shaped pods) is **Iglesia de San Fulgencio** (1850). The Statue of Liberty in front commemorates the Second War of Independence. On the western side of the square, in a beautiful colonial palace (more interesting than the stuffed stuff it collects), is the **Museo de Historia Natural** (Luz Caballero No 23; admission CUC$1; 8am-noon & 1-5pm Mon-Wed, 8am-noon, 1-5pm & 8-10pm Thu-Sun). Through barred windows you can watch women rolling cheroots in the cigar factory across the square.

Two museums share the colonial mansion (1872) at Independencia No 19: the **Museo de Historia Municipal** (admission CUC$1; 8am-noon & 1-5pm Mon-Wed, 8am-noon, 1-5pm & 8-10pm Thu-Sun) downstairs and the **Museo de Artes Decorativas** (☎ 3-4407; admission CUC$2; 8am-noon & 1-5pm Mon-Wed, 8am-noon, 1-5pm & 8-10pm Thu-Sun) upstairs. The latter is more interesting, with nearly 800 pieces collected from Gibara's colonial heyday. Across the street is the **Galería Cosme Proenza** (Calle Independencia No 32), with wall-to-wall works by one of Cuba's foremost painters (think Hieronymus Bosch).

### Activities

There are two decent beaches within striking distance of Gibara. **Playa Los Bajos** is

**CASAS PARTICULARES – GIBARA**

Gibara's 23 casas include some real gems.

**'Hostal La Bombilla' – Enrique Reyes Sánchez** (☎ 3-4535; Céspedes No 7 btwn J Peralta & Luz Caballero; r CUC$20-25; P ❄) Newly refurbished rooms in a friendly family home. One block from the ocean.

**'Hostal Vitral' – Nancy Pérez** (☎ 3-4469; Independencia No 36 btwn J Peralta & Calixto García; r CUC$20; ❄) Gorgeous restored colonial with roof terrace and hammocks; meals provided. Pick from four lovely rooms.

**La Casa de los Amigos** (☎ 3-4115; lacasadelosamigos@yahoo.fr; Céspedes No 15 btwn J Peralta & Luz Caballero; r CUC$20-25; ❄) One of the most amazing casas you'll find in Cuba with frescos, wood carvings, gazebo and a huge, colorful open courtyard/patio. The rooms are boutique-hotel standard with antique sinks and the food a French-Cuban fusion.

**Leoncia Milagros** (☎ 3-4493; J Agüero; r CUC$20) Behind the bus terminal, with a helpful family, nice rooms and big meals served on the terrace.

**Odalys & Luis** (☎ 3-4542; Céspedes No 13 btwn Luz Caballero & J Peralta; r with fan/air-con CUC$20) Big rooms in a colonial house with patio; a block and a half from Parque Calixto García; good meals.

**'Villa Boqueron' – Isidro Rodríguez López** (☎ 3-4559; Ave Rabi No 53 btwn J Peralta & Luz Caballero; r CUC$20-25; ❄) Friendly family with good food, this house is 5m from the ocean.

usually accessible by local ferry (two pesos) or skiff (round-trip CUC$3) from the fishing pier on La Enramada, the waterfront road leading out of town. These boats cross the Bahía de Gibara to Playa Blanca, from where it's 3km east to Playa Los Bajos.

You'll need some sort of transport to get to lovely, little **Playa Caletones**, 17km to the west of Gibara. The apostrophe of white sand and azure sea here is a favorite of vacationers from Holguín. The town is ramshackle, with no services except the thatched place guarded by a palm tree that serves as a bar in summer; locals will offer to cook you lunch.

## Sleeping

No hotels at present, but there are a handful of magnificent casas particulares (see above).

## Eating

Gibara's painfully inadequate restaurant scene won't have you searching far beyond your trusty casa particular. Here are some suggestions if you're excruciatingly hungry.

**Restaurante El Faro** (La Concha) This place, on Parque de las Madres, serves chicken and fish meals overlooking the bay. It's a simple, potentially romantic spot.

**Bar El Coral** (La Concha; 🕑 24hr) This place has the same seaside atmosphere as El Faro.

Patio Colonial, wedged between the Museo de Historia Natural and Casino Español, is an atmospheric outdoor cafeteria that hosts musical performances. Nearby, **El Caribe** (Parque Calixto García) is a pizza place that takes Convertibles.

Restaurant El Mirador, high above town near El Cuartelón, has a view to die for and is a good place to quench your thirst after a romp up the hill.

## Drinking & Entertainment

**Cine Jiba** (Parque Calixto García) In Cuba's self-proclaimed film capital you can check out big-screen movies in this recently refurbished cinema.

**Casa de Cultura** (Parque Colón) You might catch a salsa night here or an appreciation of Nicolas Guillén's poetry on the pleasant inner courtyard.

For theater and dance, it's the historic Casino Español (1889).

## Getting There & Away

Competition for public transport out of Gibara is fierce, so be early for the one scheduled truck at 5:10am (one peso). The bus station is a kilometer out on the road to Holguín. There are two daily buses in each direction and a taxi (to Holguín) should cost you about CUC$20.

For drivers heading toward Guardalavaca the link road from the junction at Floro Pérez is hell at first, but improves just outside Rafael Freyre. There's an Oro Negro gas station at the entrance to town.

# RAFAEL FREYRE & AROUND

The stretch between Rafael Freyre (Santa Lucía on some maps) and Guardalavaca is developing fast. High-end resorts have already started colonizing **Playa Pesquero**, a small but sweet 1km beach accessible via a spur road just before the Cuatro Palmas junction. The sand is golden, the water shallow and the Cuban government happy to keep counting the profits. Travel and hotel brochures call this beach Costa Verde and along with Playa Esmeralda it is usually lumped alongside Guardalavaca (its infinitely poorer cousin).

Three kilometers west of Don Lino is **Playa Blanca**; Columbus landed somewhere near here in 1492, and this great meeting of two cultures is commemorated in **Parque Nacional Monumento Bariay** (Parque Natural Cristóbal Colon; admission CUC$8) a varied mix of sights and memorabilia, the centerpiece of which is an impressive Hellenic-style monument designed by Holguín artist Caridad Ramos for the 500th anniversary of the landing in 1992. Other points of interest here include an information center, the remains of a 19th-century **Spanish fort**, three reconstructed **Taíno huts**, an **archaeological museum** and the reasonable Restaurante 'Columbo.' It makes a nice afternoon out.

A promising new place just off the link road to the Playa Pesquero resorts is **Parque Rocazul** (☎ 3-0833; day trip with lunch CUC$30), an eco-tourism venture that offers guided trekking, horseback-riding, mountain-biking and rowing/fishing excursions. The park is extensive with hills, trails, ocean access and an ostrich farm, though – thanks to its location next to Holguín's top-end resorts – it's not cheap.

## Sleeping & Eating

### PLAYA PESQUERO

**Playa Costa Verde** (Gaviota; Map p361; ☎ 3-0520; s/d low season CUC$119/190, high season CUC$169/270; P ✱ 💻 🏊) Eighty-five percent Canadian and popular with divers, the Costa Verde has recently undergone a change in management from Super Clubs to Gaviota which is probably a change for the better. Good snorkeling and diving trips are on offer.

**Hotel Playa Pesquero** (Gaviota; Map p361; ☎ 3-0530; s/d from CUC$129/224; P ✱ 💻 🏊) Welcome to Cuba's biggest hotel. With 933 rooms the Pesquero, which opened in 2004 to rave reviews, is the size of a small village, with an infrastructure to match. People use golf carts to get around here although the design is fairly clever and the beach – as one might expect – is picture perfect. There are something like 10 restaurants on site (one vegetarian), a massive swimming pool, a small shopping mall and activities for everyone from babies to senior citizens.

The other two resorts on this strip are Grand Playa Turquesa and Blau Costa Verde, both all-inclusive four-star establishments in a similar price range.

### AROUND RAFAEL FREYRE

**Campismo Silla de Gibara** (Cubamar; Map p361; ☎ 42 15 86; per person CUC$7.50; 🏊) This camping ground sits on the hillside between Floro Pérez and Rafael Freyre, 35km southeast of Gibara via a rough road. It's 1.5km off the main road. There are 42 rooms sleeping two, four or six people, but come for the views, not the comfort. There's a cave to hike to, 1.5km hike up the hill, and horses for rent. Make a reservations with **Cubamar** (☎ 7-831-3151; www.cubamarviajes.cu; cnr Calle 3 & Malecón, Vedado) in Habana, or at the **Reservaciones de Campismo** (Map p352; ☎ 42 28 81; Mártires No 87; 🕑 8am-6pm Mon-Fri, 8am-noon Sat) in Holguín.

**Villa Don Lino** (Islazul; Map p361; ☎ 2-0443; s/d low season CUC$37/47, high season CUC$50/60; 🏊) This place is situated 8.5km north of Rafael Freyre off a spur road. Mostly couples stay in the 36 single-story *cabañas* – with the small white beach, it makes a romantic retreat. This is a good option for people who want to play, but not stay, at Guardalavaca. It has been enthusiastically recommended by readers.

## GUARDALAVACA

Guardalavaca is a string of mega-resorts draped along a succession of idyllic beaches 54km northeast of Holguín. Glimmering in the background, a landscape of rough green fields and haystack-shaped hills winks invitingly at bevies of sun-lounging tourists.

In the days before the all-inclusives, Columbus described this stretch of coast as the most beautiful place he had ever laid eyes on. Few modern-day visitors would disagree. Love it or hate it, Guardalavaca's enduring popularity is based on a devastating mix of enviable tropical beaches, ver-

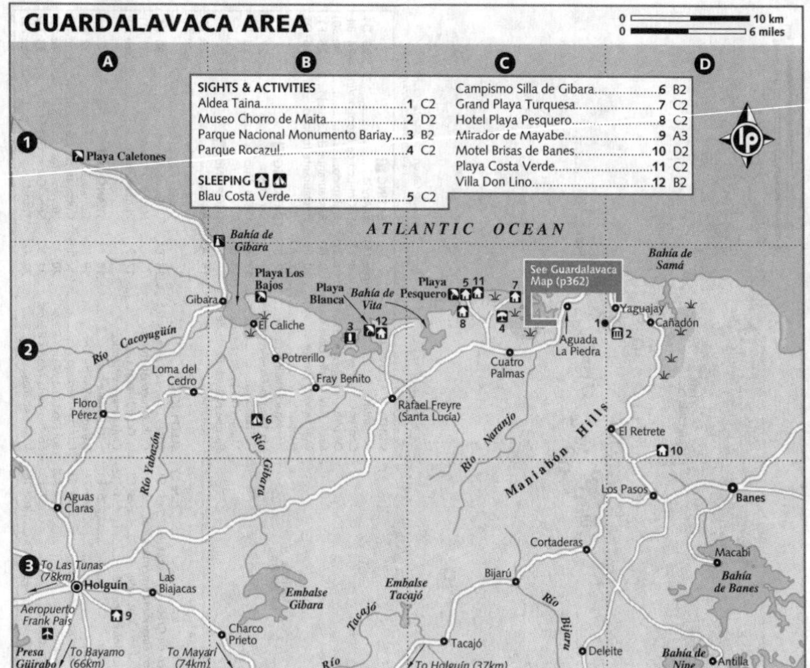


dant green hills, and sheltered turquoise coral reefs. For many discerning travelers it leaves the more commercialized tourist resorts further west flailing hopelessly in the shade.

In the early 20th century this region was an important cattle-rearing area and the site of a small rural village (Guardalavaca means, quite literally, 'guard the cow'). The tourism boom didn't begin until the late 1970s when local Holguiñero Fidel Castro inaugurated Guardalavaca's first resort – the sprawling Atlántico – by going for a quick dip in the hotel pool. The local economy hasn't looked back since.

The resort area is split into three separate enclaves: Playa Pesquero (see opposite), Playa Esmeralda and – 7km to the east – Guardalavaca proper; the original hotel strip which is already starting to peel a little around the edges. Unlike Varadero and Cayo Coco, Guardalavaca is less snooty and lower key. Fortuitously, it also allows beach access to Cubans, a factor that gives the place an added dash of local color.

## Information

### EMERGENCY

**Asistur** (Map p362; ☎ 3-0148; Centro Comercial Guardalavaca; 🕒 8:30am-5pm Mon-Fri, 8:30am-noon Sat)

**Consulate of Canada** ( ☎ 3-0320; Club Amigo Atlántico – Guardalavaca, Ste 1)

### MEDICAL SERVICES

**Clínica Internacional** (Map p362; ☎ 3-0291) A 24-hour pharmacy on the same site as Villa Cabañas.

### MONEY

Euros are accepted in all the Guardalavaca, Playa Esmeralda and Pesquero resorts.

**Banco de Crédito y Comercio** (Map p362; ☎ 3-0223; 🕒 8am-noon & 1:30-3pm Mon-Fri) Behind Hotel Guardalavaca near the beach.

**Banco Financiero Internacional** (Map p362; ☎ 3-0272; Centro Comercial Guardalavaca) Just west of Club Amigo Atlántico – Guardalavaca.

### TRAVEL AGENCIES

**Cubatur** (Map p362; ☎ 3-0171; fax 3-0170; 🕒 8am-4pm) Just behind the Centro Comercial Los Flamboyanes.

**Ecotur** (Map p362; ☎ 3-0155; Villa Cabañas No 8) Land/sea adventure tours.

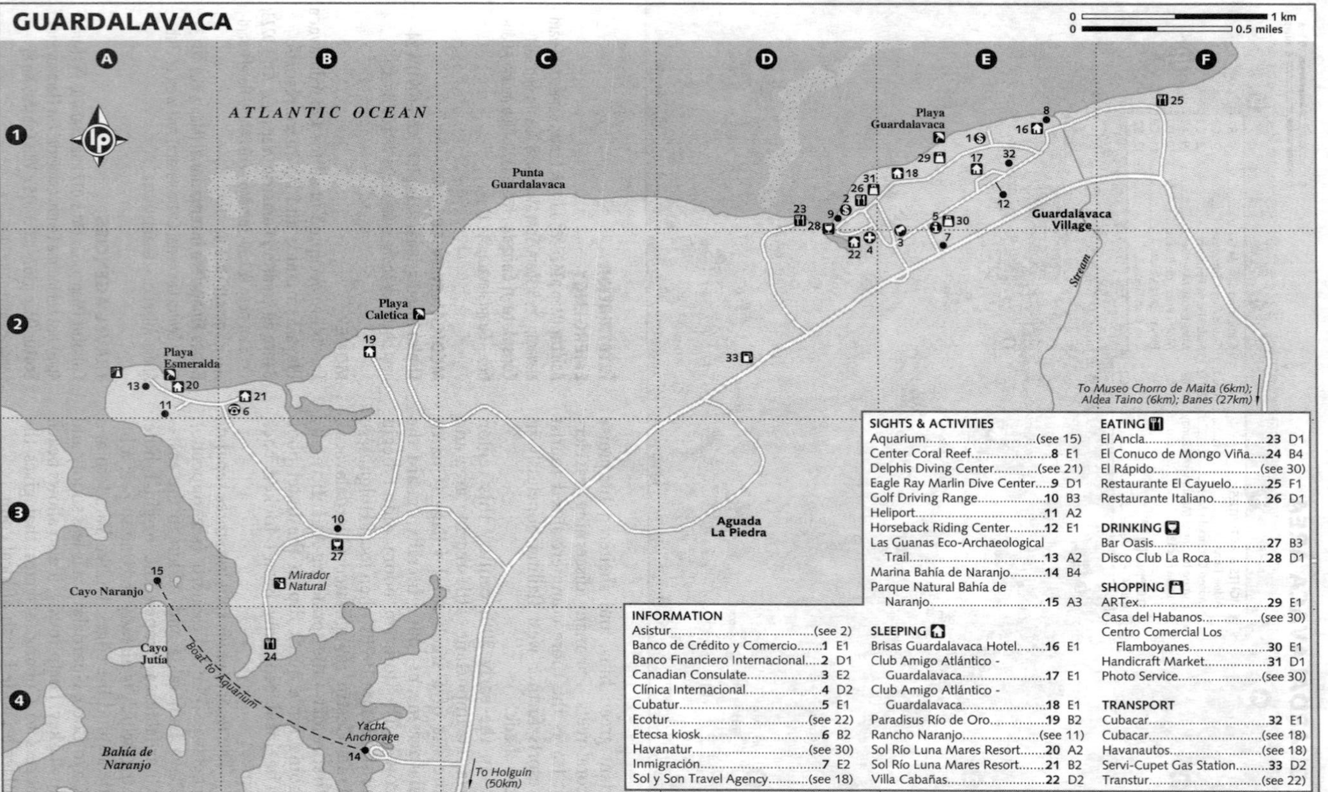
GUARDALAVACA
0 1 km
0 0.5 miles
ATLANTIC OCEAN
Playa Esmeralda
Playa Caletica
Punta Guardalavaca
Playa Guardalavaca
Guardalavaca Village
Stream
Aguada La Piedra
Mirador Natural
Yacht Anchorage
Boat to Aquarium
Cayo Naranjo
Cayo Jutía
Bahía de Naranjo
To Holguín (50km)
To Museo Chorro de Maita (6km); Aldea Taino (6km); Banes (27km)
INFORMATION
Asistur (see 2)
Banco de Crédito y Comercio 1 E1
Banco Financiero Internacional 2 D1
Canadian Consulate 3 E2
Clínica Internacional 4 D2
Cubatur 5 E1
Ecotur (see 22)
Etecsa kiosk 6 B2
Havanatur (see 30)
Inmigración 7 E2
Sol y Son Travel Agency (see 18)
SIGHTS & ACTIVITIES
Aquarium (see 15)
Center Coral Reef 8 E1
Delphis Diving Center (see 21)
Eagle Ray Marlin Dive Center 9 D1
Golf Driving Range 10 B3
Heliport 11 A2
Horseback Riding Center 12 E1
Las Guanas Eco-Archaeological Trail 13 A2
Marina Bahía de Naranjo 14 B4
Parque Natural Bahía de Naranjo 15 A3
SLEEPING
Brisas Guardalavaca Hotel 16 E1
Club Amigo Atlántico - Guardalavaca 17 E1
Club Amigo Atlántico - Guardalavaca 18 E1
Paradisus Río de Oro 19 B2
Rancho Naranjo (see 11)
Sol Río Luna Mares Resort 20 A2
Sol Río Luna Mares Resort 21 B2
Villa Cabañas 22 D2
EATING
El Ancla 23 D1
El Conuco de Mongo Viña 24 B4
El Rápido (see 30)
Restaurante El Cayuelo 25 F1
Restaurante Italiano 26 D1
DRINKING
Bar Oasis 27 B3
Disco Club La Roca 28 D1
SHOPPING
ARTex 29 E1
Casa del Habanos (see 30)
Centro Comercial Los Flamboyanes 30 E1
Handicraft Market 31 D1
Photo Service (see 30)
TRANSPORT
Cubacar 32 E1
Cubacar (see 18)
Havanautos (see 18)
Servi-Cupet Gas Station 33 D2
Transtur (see 22)

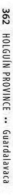

**Havanatur** (Map p362; ☎ 3-0260; Centro Comercial Los Flamboyanes)

**Sol y Son Travel Agency** (Map p362; ☎ 3-0417; Club Amigo Atlántico – Guardalavaca; 8am-noon Mon, Tue, Thu & Fri) Books Cubana de Aviación flights out of Holguín.

## Sights & Activities

You can arrange **horseback riding** at Rancho Naranjo next to the helicopter landing area near Sol Río Luna Mares Resort and at the horseback riding center opposite Hotel Guardalavaca. You can rent **mopeds** at all the hotels for up to CUC$30 per day. Most all-inclusive packages include bicycle use and Guardalavaca is full of hidden roads.

**Paracaidismo Guardalavaca** (☎ 3-0780, 3-0695; cubasol@guard.gvc.cyt.cu) offers tandem skydiving for CUC$150 per person, including hotel transfer (video of your jump is CUC$45 extra). You can also soar with them in zodiac-hang glider rigs called ultralights for CUC$45. Jumps can be arranged at all the hotels.

### BAHÍA DE NARANJO

The **Parque Natural Bahía de Naranjo** (Map p362), 4km southwest of Playa Esmeralda and about 8km from the main Guardalavaca strip, is an island complex designed to keep the resort crowds entertained. The **aquarium** (Map p362; ☎ 3-0132; 9am-9pm) is on a tiny island in the bay and your entry fee includes a zippy boat tour of the islands included in the complex, and a sea lion and dolphin show (noon daily). There are various packages starting at around CUC$40 depending on what you want to do – yacht trips, seafaris, etc – so check around before you embark. For an extra CUC$50 or so, you can swim with the dolphins for 20 minutes. All of Guardalavaca's (and Playa Esmeralda's) hotel tour desks sell aquarium excursions. Boats to the aquarium leave from the Marina Bahía de Naranjo.

On the spur road to the Playa Esmeralda resorts is what has to be the world's saddest and smallest **golf driving range** (Map p362; 60/100 balls CUC$4/6; 8am-7pm). At the end of the road you come to the self-guided **Las Guanas Eco-Archaeological Trail** (Map p362; admission CUC$6; 8am-4:30pm). This 1km marked trail (with several more kilometers of bushwhacking on fire trails leading to a picturesque bluff with a lighthouse) boasts 14 endemic plant species and makes a potentially good detour, but six Convertibles for a 1km hike – are you kidding?

### GUARAPO

Made on antiquated pressing machines and sold for a couple of pesos from roughshod roadside stalls all over Cuba, *guarapo* is sugarcane juice pressed from whole stalks and cooled with ice.

For the Cubans the concoction provides a refreshing energy drink that quenches the thirst and revives the flagging spirits of hardworking agricultural workers on the way back from the cane fields. For more superstitious consumers, it is also rumored to contain magical fertility properties.

If you're feeling parched and deflated after a day behind the wheel on Cuba's rattling roads keep a few Cuban pesos handy and pull over where you see a sign reading *'guarapero.'* The sugary liquid is also an excellent tonic for hypoglycemic cyclists and over-heated hikers.

### MUSEO CHORRO DE MAITA

This archaeological site-based **museum** (Map p361; ☎ 3-0421; admission CUC$2; 9am-5pm Tue-Sat, 9am-1pm Sun) protects the remains of an excavated Indian village and cemetery, including the well-preserved remains of 62 human skeletons and the bones of a barkless dog. The village dates from the early 16th century and is one of nearly 100 archaeological sites in the area. Across from the museum is a reconstructed **Aldea Taina** (Taíno village; admission CUC$3), that features life-sized models of native dwellings and figures in a replicated indigenous village. Shows of native dance rituals are staged here and there's also a restaurant.

### SCUBA DIVING

The reef is 200m out and there are 32 dive sites, most accessed by boat. There are caves, wrecks, walls and healthy coral and giant sponges, plus lots of colorful fish. The following outfits offer open water certification courses for CUC$350, resort courses for CUC$50 and dives for CUC$35, with discounts for multiple dives.

**Center Coral Reef** (Map p362; ☎ 3-0774) Beside Brisas Guardalavaca Hotel. Offers 90-minute snorkeling tours in a glass-bottomed boat, deep-sea fishing (CUC$270 for up to

HOLGUÍN PROVINCE

six passengers) and a 'challenge tour' jeep-zodiac combo including lunch and horseback riding.

**Delphis Diving Center** (Map p362; Sol Río Luna Mares) Offers scuba diving and certification courses for guests of the two Grupo Sol Meliá resorts at Playa Esmeralda.

**Eagle Ray Marlin Dive Center** (Cubanacán Naútica; Map p362; Cubanacán Naútica; ☎ 3-0316) On the beach behind Disco Club La Roca. Identical program and prices to Center Coral Reef.

## Sleeping

There are no casas particulares here, as renting rooms is banned. Banes, 33km to the southeast, is the closest town with private rooms.

### GUARDALAVACA

**Villa Cabañas** (Map p362; ☎ 3-0144; r CUC$57; ) As the least-expensive place in Guardalavaca, the 20 cabins here are sometimes booked solid – phone ahead. They're good value, sleeping three comfortably and with a kitchen to boot. Rooms have TVs and a few resident frogs, and the water is hot-ish. It's located behind the Clínica Internacional – the beach and the rest of Guardalavaca's facilities are a hop, skip and a jump down the road. Ecotur also an office here and it's a cheap place to do laundry.

**Club Amigo Atlántico – Guardalavaca** (Cubanacán; Map p362; ☎ 3-0121, s/d from CUC$79/128; ) This sprawler of a resort is a fusion of the former Guardalavaca and Atlántico hotels, the latter of which is the resort's oldest, completed in 1976. In places, the age is starting to show. The architecture in this small 'village' (there are an astounding 600 rooms here in total) has an uninspiring blocklike layout and the paint is looking faded in places. Nevertheless, the Club Amigo has a wide range of accommodation options, including villas, bungalows and standard rooms, and is ever popular with families for its extensive kids' activities program. Most guests are Canadian and English, judging by the accents.

**Brisas Guardalavaca Hotel** (Cubanacán; Map p362; ☎ 3-0218; fax 3-0162; s/d all-inclusive low season from CUC$95/140, high season CUC$115/180; ) This über-resort comprised of the Villa las Brisas and Hotel las Brisas at the eastern end of the beach is package-tour paradise. Though the beach is smallish, this is undoubtedly the more up-market of Guardalavaca's hotels, with big, clean rooms, good service and a quiet location. Facilities include Disco La Dolce Vita, floodlit tennis courts, and water sports, including scuba diving.

### PLAYA ESMERALDA

Moving 6km to the west, the resorts become more expensive and secluded. With its iridescent jade waters, craggy coves and sheltered setting, Playa Esmeralda has a private paradise feel missing at Guardalavaca. Reservations are available through **Havanatur** (Map p362; ☎ 3-0260; Centro Comercial Los Flamboyanes, Guardalavaca) or **San Cristóbal Agencia de Viajes** (☎ 7-861-9171/2; www.sancristobaltravel.com; Oficios No 110 btwn Lamparilla & Amargura, Habana Vieja) in Habana.

**Sol Río Luna Mares Resort** (Gaviota; Map p362; ☎ 3-0030; s/d CUC$210/300; ) This two-in-one hotel is an amalgamation (all the rage in Cuba) made up of the former Sol Club Río de Luna and the Meliá Río de Mares. The latter part is closer to the beach and has a better overall layout. Nonguests are allowed into the restaurants, bars, shops and activity centers here. Yippee!

**Paradisus Río de Oro** (Gaviota; Map p362; ☎ 3-0090; fax 3-0095; s/d CUC$335/520; ) The five stars are glowing at this 292-room resort that seems much smaller thanks to a clever layout, sterling service and landscape screening. Swing in a hammock overlooking the beach or get a massage in a cliffside hut. There's even a Japanese restaurant floating on a koi pond. Garden villas with private pools cost CUC$900.

## Eating

**Restaurante Italiano** (Map p362; 10am-11pm) You'll feel like an outcast eating at this place, beside Centro Comercial Guardalavaca, while everyone else tucks into the all-you-can-eat buffets a couple of hundred yards away. Nevertheless pizzas are big and service is quick and amiable. A good meal for two won't break CUC$10.

**Restaurante El Cayuelo** (Map p362; ☎ 3-0736; 10am-11pm) Seafood is the house specialty here and a full lobster meal is less than CUC$20. A nice break from the resorts. It's on the beach 800m east of Brisas Guardalavaca Hotel.

Other recommendations:

**El Ancla** (Map p362; ☎ 3-0381; 11am-11pm) Seafood and beautiful coastal setting, just west of Disco Club La Roca.

**El Conuco de Mongo Viña** (Map p362; 3-course meals CUC$8; 9am-4am) On the Bahía de Naranjo, a 2km walk from the Sol Meliá duo.

**El Rápido** (Map p362; Centro Comercial Los Flamboyanes; 24hr) If you can't beat 'em, join 'em! There's also a pool table and video games here.

## Drinking & Entertainment

**Disco Club La Roca** (Map p362; ☎ 3-0167; admission CUC$1; 1-5pm & 9:30pm-3am) This disco just west of the Centro Comercial Guardalavaca has a nice open-air locale overlooking the beach. It opens during the day with video games, karaoke and other free entertainment.

**Bar Oasis** (Map p362; 7am-11pm) This small thatched bar near the golf driving range is where moped-riding swarms descend for icy Cristales.

## Shopping

There's a small handicraft market next to Club Amigo Atlántico – Guardalavaca. ARTex, behind Hotel Guardalavaca, has a good selection of CDs.

Other options:

**Casa del Habanos** (Centro Comercial Los Flamboyanes) All the smoke you could want.

**Photo service** (Map p362; Centro Comercial Los Flamboyanes) In the main shopping center; does everything from film processing to passport shots.

## Getting There & Away

Club Amigo Atlántico – Guardalavaca can sometimes arrange transfers to Holguín for CUC$10; ask around. A taxi from Guardalavaca to Holguín will cost a heftier CUC$40 one way for the car. For radio taxis, call **TaxiOK** (☎ 3-0243) or **Transgaviota** (☎ 3-0966).

## Getting Around

Drivers of the various hotel employee buses have strict orders not to carry tourists, and trying to use public transportation is hopeless here in Guardalavaca. Private taxis are banned, but you might hitch a ride with other tourists (for information on the risks associated with hitching see p477). *Coches de caballo* (horse carriages) run between Playas Esmeralda and Guardalavaca or you can rent a moped or bike at all of the resort hotels.

A **Servi-Cupet station** (24hr) is between Guardalavaca and Playa Esmeralda.

All the rental agencies have offices in Guardalavaca and rent mopeds for CUC$30 per day:

**Cubacar** Centro Flamboyanes (Map p362; ☎ 3-0243); Club Amigo Atlántico – Guardalavaca (Map p362; ☎ 3-0180)

**Havanautos** (Map p362; ☎ 3-0223; Cupet Cimex Garage)

**Transtur** (Map p362; ☎ 3-0134; Villas Cabañas No 6)

# BANES

☎ 24 / pop 44,983

The sugar town of Banes, just north of the Bahía de Banes, is a place of contradictions and paradoxes. Cuban president Fulgencio Batista was born here in 1901. Forty-seven years later, in the local clapboard church of Nuestra Señora de la Caridad, another fiery leader-in-waiting, Fidel Castro, tied the knot with the blushing Birta Díaz Balart. A generous Batista gave them a US$500 gift for their honeymoon.

Founded in 1887, this effervescent company town was owned and operated by the US-run United Fruit Company until the 1950s and many of the old American company houses still remain. These days in the sun-streaked streets and squares you're more likely to encounter cigar-smoking cronies slamming dominoes and moms carrying meter-long loaves of bread; in short, everything Cuban missing from the all-inclusive resorts. The 33km road southeast from Guardalavaca to Banes winds between *bohíos* (thatched huts) and royal palms through the Maniabón Hills; it's a really beautiful trip.

## Information

There's an **immigration office** (Av de Cárdenas No 314A) here if you need a visa extension. Banes is one of those towns with no street signs and locals who don't know street names, so prepare to lose yourself.

## Sights & Activities

If you're coming from the resorts, Banes' biggest attraction may be the street-life a stroll through town provides.

On October 12, 1948, Fidel Castro Ruz and Birta Díaz Balart were married in the **Iglesia de Nuestra Señora de la Caridad** on Parque Martí in the center of Banes. (After their divorce in 1954, Birta remarried and moved to Spain, but through their only child, Fidelito, Fidel has several grandchildren.)

### FIDEL: BEHIND THE MASK

Fiery, explosive and egotistical; the indomitable figure of Fidel Castro has stamped his mark on the 20th century like few figures, Cuban or otherwise. But what of the real personality that lies behind the public mask?

Born near the village of Birán in Holguín Province on August 13, 1926, the illegitimate product of a relationship between Spanish-born landowner Ángel Castro and his cook and housemaid Lina Ruz (they later married), Fidel grew up as a favored child in a large and relatively wealthy family of sugar farmers. Educated at a Jesuit school and sent away to study in the city of Santiago at the age of seven, the young Castro was an exceptional student whose prodigious talents included a photographic memory and an extraordinary aptitude for sport. Indeed, legend has it that at the age of 21, Fidel – by then a skilled left-arm pitcher – was offered a professional baseball contract with the Washington Senators.

At the age of 13 Fidel staged his first insurrection, a strike organized among his father's sugar-cane workers against their unforgiving and exploitative boss, a gesture that did little to endear him into the fraternal fold.

One year later the still-teenage Castro penned a letter to US president FD Roosevelt congratulating him on his re-election and asking the American leader for a US$10 bill 'because I have not seen a ten dollars bill American and I would like to have one of them.' Rather ominously for future US-Cuban relations, the request was politely turned down.

Undeterred Fidel marched on regardless, bulldozing everything that fell in his path. On the completion of his high-school certificate in 1945, his teacher and mentor Father Francisco Barbeito predicted sagely that his bullish star pupil would 'fill with brilliant pages the book of his life.' He wasn't far wrong.

Armed with tremendous personal charisma, a wrought-iron will, and an inbred ability to pontificate interminably for hours on end, Fidel made tracks for Habana University where his forthright and unyielding personality quickly ensured that he excelled at everything he did.

Banes is better known for the **Museo Indocubano Bani** (☎ 8-2487; General Marrero No 305; admission without/with guide CUC$1/2; ⏲ 9am-5pm Tue-Sat, 8am-noon & 7-9pm Sun). The museum's small but rich collection of Indian artifacts is one of the best on the island. Don't miss the tiny golden fertility idol unearthed near Banes (one of only 20 gold artifacts ever found in Cuba).

Railway junkies shouldn't miss **steam locomotive No 964** (El Panchito; Calle Tráfico), built at the HK Porter Locomotive Works in Pittsburgh, Pennsylvania, in 1888, now on display 400m east of the bus station. **Playa de Morales**, 13km east of Banes along the paved continuation of Tráfico, is a fishing village where you can while away an afternoon dining with locals and watching the men mend their nets. A few kilometers to the north is the even quieter **Playa Puerto Rico.**

### CASAS PARTICULARES – BANES

There are no hotels in the town proper, but Banes has some good private rooms.

**Casa Evelin Feria** (☎ 8-3150; Bruno Meriño No 3401A btwn Delfin Pupo & JMH, Reparto Cárdenas; r CUC$20-25; ❄) Pleasant upstairs room. Breakfast provided for CUC$3.

**Julio Dante** (☎ 8-3243/8-3643; Robles No 85A btwn Calles 7 & 8; r CUC$20; ❄) Spotless rooms and linen; good meals.

**Sergio Aguilera** (☎ 8-2412; Calle Iglesias No 4089, Reparto Nicaragua; r CUC$20; ❄) Family atmosphere; meals.

**Alfredo Serrano Proenza** (☎ 8-2464; pastjoelmorales@yahoo.com; Delfin Pupo No 1105 btwn Bruno Meriño & JM Gomez, Reparto Cárdenas; r CUC$20-25; Ⓟ ❄)

## Sleeping

### OUTSIDE TOWN

**Campismo Puerto Rico Libre** (Cubamar; ☎ 9-6918; per person CUC$5) This place is north of Playa de Morales, 13km from Banes. The basic cabins line the rocky shore, there's a restaurant, and people in the nearby fishing villages will happily cook seafood meals for you. Ask about the caves (about 1km from the campismo), and bring insect repellent.

Training ostensibly as a lawyer, Castro spent the next three years embroiled in political activity amid an academic forum that was riddled with gang violence and petty corruption. 'My impetuosity, my desire to excel, fed and inspired the character of my struggle', he recalled candidly years later.

Blessed with more lives than a cat, Castro has survived a failed putsch, 15 months in prison, exile, a two-year guerrilla war in the mountains, and a reported 617 attempts on his life. His sense of optimism in the face of defeat is nothing short of astounding. With his rebel army reduced to a ragged band of 12 men after the Granma landing, he astonished his beleaguered colleagues with a fiery victory speech. 'We will win this war', he trumpeted confidently, 'We are just beginning the fight!'

As an international personality who has outlasted 10 American presidents, the 21st-century incarnation of Fidel Castro – world statesman – is no less enigmatic than the revolutionary leader of yore. Fostering his own brand of Caribbean socialism with an unflinching desire to 'defend the revolution at all costs' the ever-changing ideology that Castro so famously preaches is perhaps best summarized by biographer Volker Skierka as 'a pragmatic mixture of a little Marx, Engels and Lenin, slightly more of Che Guevara, a lot of José Martí, and a great deal indeed of Fidel Castro.'

Castro the private individual is equally difficult to pin down. Among associates it is well known that his hobbies include scuba-diving and baseball; others claim that an off-duty Fidel enjoys consuming ice cream and chocolate milkshakes. He never dances but is, by all accounts, a formidable cook (his signature dish is spaghetti Bolognese).

Estranged from many of his closest family, including his embittered Miami-based daughter Alina, Castro's friends have a propensity to be as evasive and as tight-lipped as the great man himself. 'One thing is certain', wrote longtime friend and associate, Colombian novelist, Gabriel García Márquez, 'Wherever he may be, however and with whomever, Fidel Castro is there to win. I do not think anyone in this world could be a worse loser.'

**Motel Brisas de Banes** (Map p361; cabin CUC$30) This place, on a hill overlooking a reservoir 10km northwest of Banes off the road to Guardalavaca, has eight cabins, each sleeping two people. There are nice views – a pleasant out-of-the-way place for a beer.

## Eating & Drinking

**Restaurant El Latino** (General Marero No 710; 🕑 11am-11pm) A top Banes choice is this Palmares place with all the usual Creole dishes delivered with a little extra flair and charm. Service is good and the accompanying musicians unusually talented and discreet.

**La Vicaria** (🕑 24hr) Across the street from El Latino is yet another reliable La Vicaria, with pasta, burgers and Gordon Bleu (chicken stuffed with ham and cheese), plus eggs and coffee for breakfast (everything is less than CUC$4).

**Coctelera** (General Marrero No 327A) Several peso bars around town are jumping with atmosphere and cheap hooch, including this one, and the super popular Doña Yulla next door.

Alternatively, head down the street to Las 400 Rosas, an outdoor Convertible place selling sodas, beer and snacks next to the Museo Indocubano Bani.

## Entertainment

**Cafe Cantante** (General Marrero No 320) This gregarious, music-filled patio is the top spot in Banes. During the day, you'll hear the municipal band honking its way through rehearsal while the night brings disco or *son* (Cuba's basic form of popular music) septets for your listening pleasure. Sundays afternoons feature traditional *trova* (poetic singing/songwriting) from 2pm to 7pm, while Sunday nights are when the really special stuff happens. Visiting jazz musicians (who often play gigs at Guardalavaca) play concerts here, and indulge in jam sessions.

**Casa de Cultura** (☎ 8-2111; General Marrero No 320) Next door to Cafe Cantante this venue, housed in the former Casino Español (1926), has a regular Sunday *trova* matinee at 3pm and Saturday *peña del Rap* (rap music session) at 9pm.

HOLGUÍN PROVINCE

### Getting There & Away

From the bus station at the corner of Tráfico and Los Ángeles, one morning bus goes to Holguín (72km) daily (supposedly). An afternoon bus connects with the train to Habana. Trucks leave Banes for Holguín more frequently.

## BIRÁN

Fidel Castro Ruz was born on August 13, 1926, at the **Finca Las Manacas** (aka 'Casa de Fidel') near the village of Birán, south of Cueto. The farm – which was bought by Fidel's father Ángel in 1915 – is huge, and includes its own workers' village (a cluster of small thatched huts for the mainly Haitian laborers), cockfighting ring, post office, store and telegraph. The several large yellow wooden houses that can be glimpsed through the cedar trees are where the Castro family lived.

The Finca opened as a museum in 2002 under the unassuming name of **Sitio Historico de Birán** (admission/camera/video CUC$10/20/40; 9am-noon & 1:30-4pm Tue-Sat, 9am-noon Sun), so as not to draw attention to Castro's so-called 'personality cult.' The modesty extends to the signage which is nonexistent. To get here, take the southern turn-off 7km west of Cueto, and drive 7km south to the Central Loynaz Hechevarría sugar mill at Marcané. From there a road runs 8km east to Birán, from which it's another 3km northeast to Finca Las Manacas.

The museum itself is an interesting excursion containing more than 100 photos, assorted clothes, Fidel's childhood bed, and his father's 1918 Ford motorcar. With 27 installations the place constitutes a *pueblito* (small town) and, if nothing else, it shows the extent of the inheritance that this hotheaded ex-lawyer gave up to go and live in the Sierra Maestra for two years surviving on a diet of crushed crabs and raw horse meat.

The graves of Fidel's parents, Ángel Castro and Lina Ruz, are to the right of the entrance gate.

## MAYARÍ

☎ 24 / pop 80,200

'*De Alto Cedro, voy para Marcané, llego a Cueto, voy para Mayarí.*' The famous opening stanza from the classic Cuban song, *Chan Chan* is more than a tad misleading. Mayarí is not a place people go to so much as end up. The 51st state of America before 1959, thanks to the all-embracing presence of the United Fruit Company, Mayarí today has little to offer the average tourist. Travelers use it more as a base to visit the nearby Finca Manacas, Cayo Saetía or the waterfalls and forests of the coffee-growing **Parque Natural La Mensura**, 30km south. There's a Servi-Cupet gas station in town. This area is notable for its dense pine forests and impressive waterfalls. Hikes and attractions include La Presa Lake, La Planca flower garden, horseback-riding, eco-hikes and a chance to glimpse some of the 100 or more endemic plants found only in this area. For further details inquire at the Villa Pinares del Mayarí (see below).

### Sleeping & Eating

**Villa Pinares del Mayarí** (Gaviota; ☎ 5-3308; fax 3-0926; s/d CUC$30/35, cabins CUC$35/40; ) One in a duo of classic Gaviota Holguín hideaways, Pinares del Mayarí stands at 600m elevation between the Altiplanicie de Nipe and Sierra del Cristal, 30km south of Mayarí on a rough dirt road. Part Swiss-chalet resort, part mountain hideaway, this isolated rural gem is situated in one of Cuba's largest pine forests and the two- and three-bedroom cabins, with hot showers and comfortable beds, make a nice retreat. There's also a large restaurant, bar, tennis court and horses for hire.

The villa is within the Parque Natural La Mensura and offers hikes to El Guayabo waterfall (Cuba's highest), the Loma de la Mensura (995m) and the ghostly Farallones de Seboruco caves. You can arrange tours to Cayo Saetía (see below) from here.

### Getting There & Away

The only way to get Villa Pinares del Mayarí outside of an organized tour is via car or taxi. The access road is rough and in a poor state of repair though passable in a hire car if driven with care. If arriving from Santiago the best route is via the small settlement of Mella.

## EAST OF MAYARÍ

East of Mayarí the road gets increasingly potholed and the surroundings, while never losing their dusty rural charm, progressively more remote. The culmination of this rustic drive is lovely Cayo Saetía, a small, flat wooded island in the Bay of Nipe that is connected to the mainland by a small bridge. During the '70s and '80s this was a favored hunting ground for communist apparatchiks who enjoyed splaying lead into the local wildlife. Fortunately those days are now gone. Indeed, ironic as it may sound, Cayo Saetía is now a protected wildlife park with 19 species of exotic animal including camels, zebras, antelopes, ostriches and deer. Bisected by grassy meadows and adorned by hidden coves and beaches, it's the closet Cuba gets to an African wildlife reserve. Well worth a visit.

### Sleeping & Eating

**Campismo Río Cabonico** (☎ 59 41 18; r per person from CUC$5) This place is at Pueblo Nuevo, 9km east of Levisa and 73km west of Moa, about 900m south of the main road. The 23 cabins with baths and fans on a low terrace beside the Río Cabonico (decent swimming) have four or six beds. Reservations can be made through the Reservaciones de Campismo in Holguín (p351).

**Villa Cayo Saetía** (Gaviota; ☎ 9-6900; vsaetia@ip.etecsa.cu; s/d low season CUC$30/35, high season CUC$35/40; ❄) This wonderfully rustic but comfortable resort on a 42-sq-km island at the entrance to the Bahía de Nipe is small, remote and more up-market than the price suggests. The 12 rooms are split into rustic and standard *cabañas* with a slight price differential, while the in-house restaurant La Güira – decked out Hemingway-style with unsavory reminders of hunters past – serves exotic meats such as antelope. You'll feel as if you're a thousand miles from anywhere here.

### Getting There & Around

There are three ways to explore Cayo Saetía aside from the obvious two-legged sorties from the villa itself. A one-hour jeep safari costs CUC$9, while excursions by horse and boat are CUC$6 and CUC$5 respectively. Though isolated you can secure passage on a twice weekly Gaviota helicopter from Guardalavaca (CUC$124, Saturday and Monday) or a bus/boat combo from the town of Antilles. If arriving by car, the control post is 15km off the main road. Then it's another 8km along a rough, unpaved road to the resort. A hire car will make it – with care.

## MOA

☎ 24 / pop 57, 484

Important economically and horrendous ecologically, Moa is a big, ugly mine at the foot of the verdant scarps of the Cuchillas de Moa. Unless you're a Canadian mining technician, or an environmentalist investigating impending ecological disasters, there's absolutely no reason to come here. 'A better world is possible' proclaims one of the billboards as you leave the town behind. Absolutely!

### Sleeping

**Hotel Miraflores** (Islazul; ☎ 6-6125; Av. Amistad, Rpto. Miraflores; s/d low season CUC$29/40, high season CUC$36/48; P ≋) If you must stay, this is a modern four-story hotel on a hillside on the western side of Moa, 5km west of

#### MINING NEAR MOA

A pillar of the country's export economy for decades, the mining of nickel and cobalt in Cuba has a long and checkered history. In the early 1950s the US-owned Moa mines provided the majority of nickel needed to fight the Korean War and during the '70s and '80s Soviet technical help aided Cuba to achieve its position as the world's third largest supplier of nickel. Since the economic crises of the early 1990s the Cuban government has been forced to establish joint ventures to keep Moa afloat with the majority of investment coming from Toronto-based Sherritt International.

Unfortunately the changes have led to a lowering of environmental standards in the industry with old, leaky equipment causing the air and water to fill up with sulfur and precipitate (some Moa residents claim) an unpleasant form of acid rain. Critics complain that the Canadian-financed Pedro Soto Alba nickel mine reportedly throws out 12,000 cubic meters of liquid waste per day. Tons of this toxic compound – which contains dangerously high levels of chrome, magnesium and sulfuric acid – is being dumped into the sea causing irrevocable damage to marine life.

the airport. The local Havanautos office is at this hotel, and there's a tourist taxi stand.

## Getting There & Around

Moa's Orestes Acosta Airport is conveniently located beside the highway to Baracoa, just 3km east of downtown Moa. **Cubana** (☎ 6-7916) has flights to/from Habana on Monday (CUC$124 one way, three hours).

The bus station is near the center of town, 3km east of the Hotel Miraflores. A daily bus leaves for Holguín and another goes to Santiago de Cuba, but there's no bus to Baracoa. You may be prevented from using the regular passenger trucks that leave the bus station for Holguín and Baracoa, as foreigners are officially prohibited. This means that there's no legal public transport except for hitching and tourist taxis between Moa and Baracoa. Taxi drivers will ask CUC$25 to Baracoa.

**Havanautos** (☎ 6-6683) has an office at the Hotel Miraflores. The Servi-Cupet gas station is at the entrance to Moa from Mayarí, not far from the Hotel Miraflores.

# Granma Province

Granma is Cuba's best-kept secret, a province of crenellated mountains and quiet hamlets where the worst kind of hassle you're likely to get is a friendly gnawing from the local village goat. Boasting Cuba's longest river (the Cauto), its second oldest town (Bayamo) and its third highest mountain (Pico Bayamesa, 1730m), Granma is also the birthplace of the Cuban national anthem and has some of the Caribbean's most pristine uplifted marine terraces.

The region reads like a who's who of revolutionary heroes. Cuban independence was first proclaimed here in 1868 when Carlos Manuel de Céspedes released his slaves. Nine decades later, in December 1956, another embattled rebel, Fidel Castro, landed with a party of 82 soldiers aboard a yacht called – surprise, surprise – *Granma* (from which the province takes its name) and boldly set about doing the same thing. Today, Granma's mountainous interior is peppered with monuments and memorabilia recalling its revolutionary past. The pick of the litter is the hike to the lofty heights of La Plata in the Sierra Maestra, Castro's impregnable mountaintop headquarters, now an eerily authentic museum.

Granma is a powerhouse for alternative art with homegrown talents such as Pablo Milanés and Carlos Puebla playing an integral part in the popularization of *nueva trova,* a musical genre that first emerged in the clubs and bars of bayside Manzanillo in the late 1960s.

**HIGHLIGHTS**

- **Where Mountains Meet Sea**
  Base yourself in Marea del Portillo (p388) and enjoy the ambience of one of Cuba's nicest all-inclusive resort areas
- **Guerrilla Watching**
  Trek up to La Plata in Gran Parque Nacional Sierra Maestra (p382)
- **The Long View**
  From the valley to the ocean, admire the vista from historic La Demajagua (p384)
- **Unesco Site**
  Archaeological sites and virgin sea-terraces in Parque Nacional Desembarco del Granma (p387)
- **Street Party**
  Roast pork, street organs and a game of chess in Bayamo's Fiesta de la Cubanía (p376)

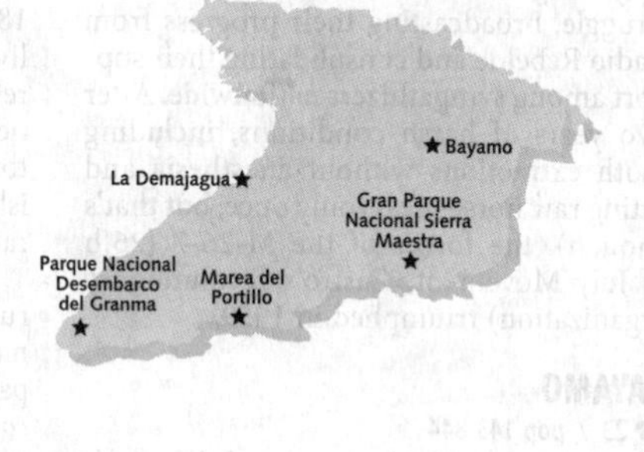


| TELEPHONE CODE: 23 | POPULATION: 835,218 | AREA: 8372 SQ KM |
|---|---|---|

## History

Stone petroglyphs and remnants of Taíno pottery unearthed in the Parque Nacional Desembarco del Granma suggest the existence of native cultures in the Granma region long before the arrival of the Spanish.

Columbus, during his second voyage, was the first European to explore the area tracking past the Cabo Cruz peninsula in 1494, before taking shelter from a storm in the Golfo de Guanacayabo. All other early development schemes came to nothing and by the 17th century Granma's untamed and largely unsettled coast had become the preserve of pirates and corsairs.

Granma's real nemesis didn't come until October 10, 1868, when sugar-plantation owner Carlos Manuel de Céspedes called for the abolition of slavery from his Demajagua sugar mill near Manzanillo and freed his own slaves by example, thus inciting the First War of Independence.

Drama unfolded again in 1895 when the founder of the Cuban Revolutionary Party, José Martí, was killed in Dos Ríos just a month and a half after landing with Máximo Gómez off the coast of Guantánamo to ignite the Second War of Independence.

Sixty-one years later, on December 2, 1956, Fidel Castro and 81 rebel soldiers disembarked from the yacht *Granma* off the coast of Granma Province at Playa las Coloradas. Routed by Batista's troops while resting in a sugarcane field at Alegría del Pío, 12 survivors managed to escape into the Sierra Maestra, establishing headquarters at Comandancia de la Plata. From there they fought and coordinated the armed struggle, broadcasting their progress from Radio Rebelde and consolidating their support among sympathizers nationwide. After two years of harsh conditions, including tooth extractions without anesthesia and eating raw horse meat (only once, but that's enough), the forces of the M-26-7 (26th of July Movement; Castro's revolutionary organization) triumphed in 1959.

# BAYAMO

☎ 23 / pop 143,844

Ah…peace at last! For travelers fed up with Cuba's omnipresent army of hassle-heavy *jineteros* (touts), Bayamo is like a breath of fresh air. Made a provincial capital in 1975, when rural Granma was forged out of the once mighty Oriente, this is a proud and dignified provincial city where you're more likely to encounter guitar-wielding *trovadores* (traditional singers) than faux street salesmen peddling black-market cigars. Even the traffic's lighter here, with the quirky pedestrianized Calle General García folding indistinguishably into leafy and laid-back Parque Céspedes.

## History

Founded in November 1513 as the second of Diego Velázquez de Cuellar's seven original villas (after Baracoa), Bayamo's early history was marred by Indian uprisings and bristling native unrest. But with the indigenous Taínos decimated by deadly European diseases such as smallpox, the short-lived insurgency soon fizzled out. By the end of the 16th century, Bayamo had grown rich and established itself as the region's most important cattle-ranching and sugarcane-growing center. Frequented by pirates, the town filled its coffers further in the 17th and 18th centuries via a clandestine smuggling ring run out of the nearby port town of Manzanillo. Zealously counting up the profits, Bayamo's new class of merchants and landowners lavishly invested their money back into fine houses, and an expensive overseas education for their over-indulged offspring.

One such protégé was lawyer-turned-revolutionary Carlos Manuel de Céspedes who – defying the traditional colonial will – attacked and wrested control of the town from its conservative Spanish authorities during the First War of Independence in 1868. But the liberation proved to be short-lived. After the defeat of an ill-prepared rebel army by 3000 regular Spanish troops near the Río Cauto on January 12, 1869, the townspeople – sensing an imminent Spanish re-occupation – set their town on fire rather than see it fall intact to the enemy.

Bayamo was also the birthplace of Perucho Figueredo, composer of the Cuban national anthem, which begins, rather patriotically, with the words *Al combate corred, bayameses* (Run to battle, people of Bayamo).

## Orientation

Bayamo turns on Parque Céspedes, also known as Plaza de la Revolución. The

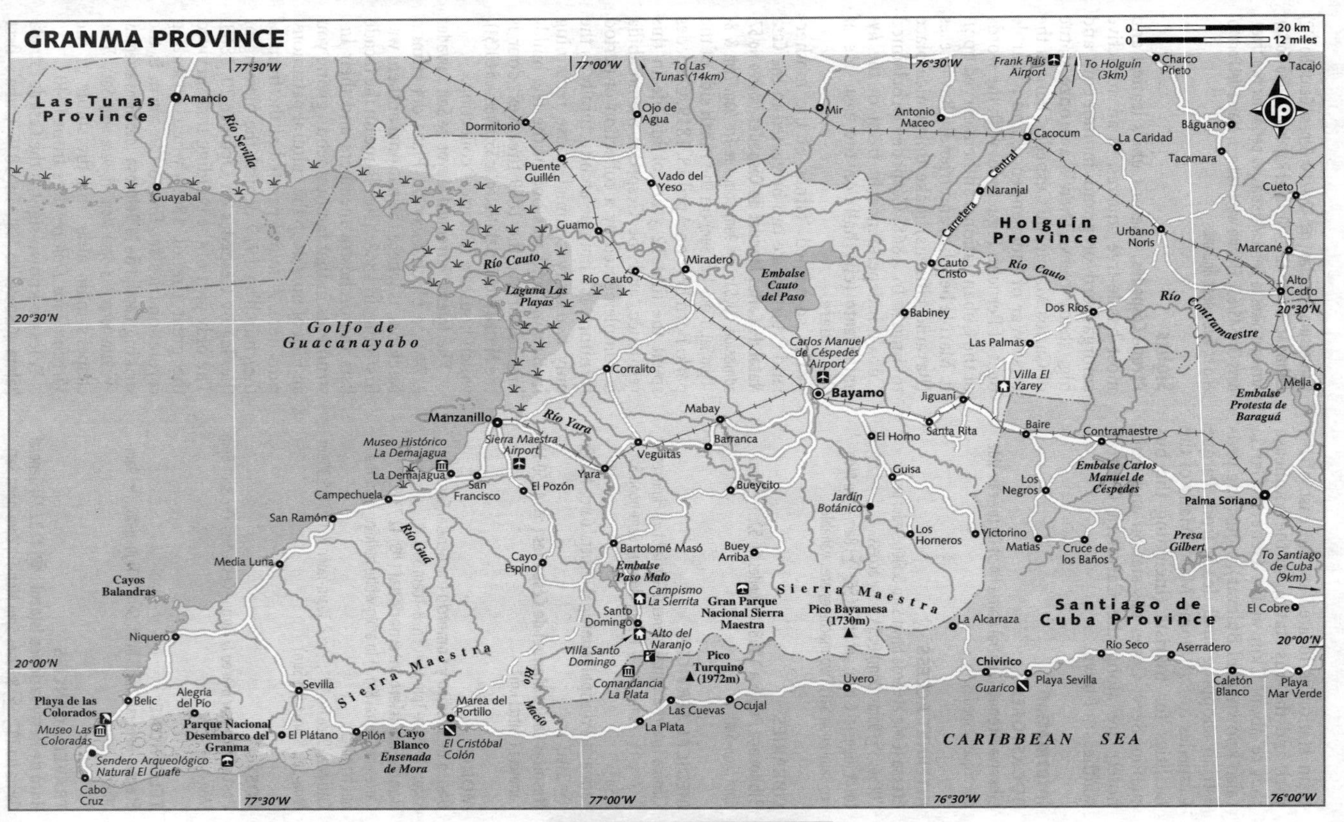


GRANMA PROVINCE

train station is located to the east of the park and the bus station to the southeast; they're about 2km apart. General García (also known as El Bulevar), a bustling pedestrian shopping mall, leads from Parque Céspedes to Bartolomé Masó. Many of the facilities for tourists (including the bus station, Servi-Cupet gas station and main hotel) are along the Carretera Central, southeast of town.

## Information

### BOOKSTORES

**Librería Ateneo** (General García No 9) On the east side of Parque Céspedes.

### INTERNET ACCESS

**Etecsa** (General García btwn Saco & Figueredo; per hr CUC$6; 9am-10pm) Quick, easy access.
**Idict** (General García; per hr CUC$6; 8am-8pm Mon-Fri, 8am-noon Sat) Two machines are available.

### LIBRARIES

**Biblioteca Pública 1868** (Céspedes No 52; 9am-6pm Mon-Sat)

### MEDICAL SERVICES

**Clinica Internacional** (General García btwn Figueredo & Lora; 8am-noon & 1-5pm Mon-Fri, 8am-noon Sat & Sun)
**Farmacia Principal Municipal** (General García No 53; 24hr)
**Hospital Carlos Manuel de Céspedes** (☎ 42 50 12; Carretera Central Km1)

### MONEY

**Banco de Crédito y Comercio** (cnr General García & Saco; 8am-3pm Mon-Fri, 8-10am Sat)
**Banco Financiero Internacional** (☎ 42 73 60; Carretera Central Km 1) In a big white building near the bus terminal.
**Cadeca** (Saco No 101; 8:30am-noon & 12:30-5:30pm Mon-Sat, 8am-noon Sun)

### POST

**Post office** (cnr Maceo & Parque Céspedes; 8am-8pm Mon-Sat)

### TELEPHONE

**Etecsa** (General García btwn Saco & Figueredo; 9am-10pm)

### TRAVEL AGENCIES

**Buró de Reservaciones Islazul** (☎ 42 32 73; General García No 207; 8:30am-5pm Mon-Fri, 8am-noon Sat)
**Campismo Popular** (☎ 42 42 00; General García No 112)
**Cubanacán** (☎ 42 79 70; Hotel Royalton, Maceo No 53) Arranges hikes to Sierra Maestra (per person for two/three days CUC$45/65), El Salto waterfall near Marea del Portillo and El Yarey near Jiguaní.

## Sights

**Parque Céspedes**, one of Cuba's leafiest and most hassle-free squares, is an attractive smorgasbord of grand monuments and big, shady trees. There's a bronze statue of Carlos Manuel de Céspedes, hero of the First War of Independence, and a marble bust of Perucho Figueredo, with the words of the Cuban national anthem carved upon it. Marble benches and friendly Bayameses (Bayamo citizens) make this a nice place to linger. In 1868 Céspedes proclaimed Cuba's independence in front of the **Ayuntamiento** (city hall) on the east side of the square.

The so-named 'father of the motherland's' birthplace can be visited in the **Casa Natal de Carlos Manuel de Céspedes** (Maceo No 57; admission CUC$1; 9am-5pm Tue-Fri, 9am-2pm & 8-10pm Sat, 10am-1pm Sun) on the north side of the park. Born here on April 18, 1819, Céspedes spent the first 12 years of his life in this residence, and the Céspedes memorabilia is complemented by a collection of period furniture. It's notable architecturally as the only two-story colonial house remaining in Bayamo and was one of the few buildings to survive the 1869 fire. Next door is the **Museo Provincial** (Maceo No 55; admission CUC$1), which houses a historical collection.

The **Iglesia Parroquial Mayor de San Salvador** (1740), a block away on Plaza del Himno Nacional, is where the national anthem was first sung, in 1868. The plaque on the facade lists the orchestra members and their instruments in that famous debut, giving you an idea of how deep the cultural patrimony runs here. A mural painted at the front of the church in 1919 depicts the blessing of the flag by Céspedes on October 20, 1868. The only part of the building that survived the great fire of 1869, when retreating revolutionaries set fire to the town, is the striking **Capilla de la Dolorosa** (donations accepted; 9am-noon & 3-5pm Mon-Fri, 9am-noon Sat). The chapel's main altar and the statue of the *Virgen de los Dolores* date from 1740.

A lesser-known sight is the **Casa de Estrada Palma** (Céspedes No 158). In 1835 Cuba's first

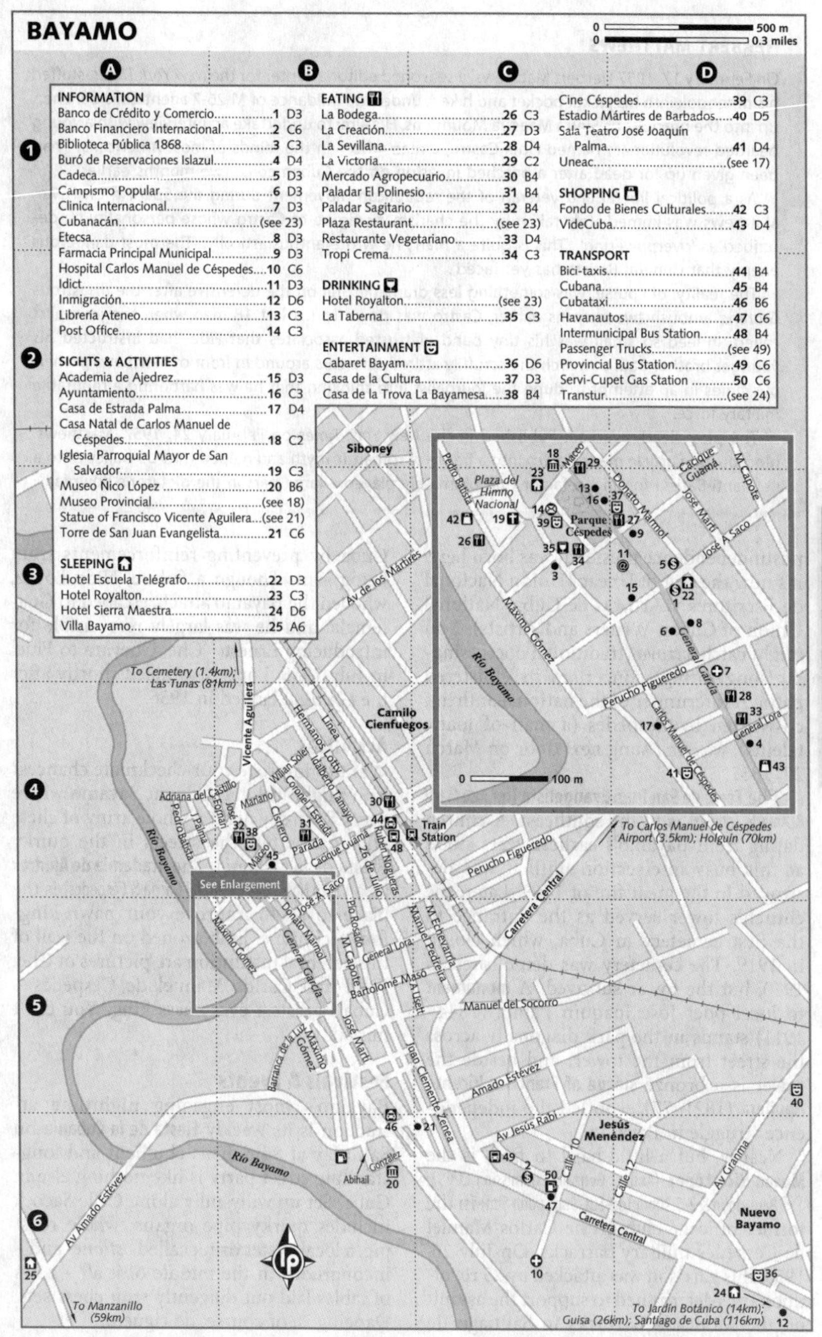
BAYAMO
0 500 m
0 0.3 miles
INFORMATION
Banco de Crédito y Comercio....1 D3
Banco Financiero Internacional....2 C6
Biblioteca Pública 1868....3 C3
Buró de Reservaciones Islazul....4 D4
Cadeca....5 D3
Campismo Popular....6 D3
Clínica Internacional....7 D3
Cubanacán....(see 23)
Etecsa....8 D3
Farmacia Principal Municipal....9 D3
Hospital Carlos Manuel de Céspedes....10 C6
Idict....11 D3
Inmigración....12 D6
Librería Ateneo....13 C3
Post Office....14 C3
SIGHTS & ACTIVITIES
Academia de Ajedrez....15 D3
Ayuntamiento....16 C3
Casa de Estrada Palma....17 D4
Casa Natal de Carlos Manuel de Céspedes....18 C2
Iglesia Parroquial Mayor de San Salvador....19 C3
Museo Ñico López....20 B6
Museo Provincial....(see 18)
Statue of Francisco Vicente Aguilera....(see 21)
Torre de San Juan Evangelista....21 C6
SLEEPING
Hotel Escuela Telégrafo....22 D3
Hotel Royalton....23 C3
Hotel Sierra Maestra....24 D6
Villa Bayamo....25 A6
EATING
La Bodega....26 C3
La Creación....27 D3
La Sevillana....28 D4
La Victoria....29 C2
Mercado Agropecuario....30 B4
Paladar El Polinesio....31 B4
Paladar Sagitario....32 B4
Plaza Restaurant....(see 23)
Restaurante Vegetariano....33 D4
Tropi Crema....34 C3
DRINKING
Hotel Royalton....(see 23)
La Taberna....35 C3
ENTERTAINMENT
Cabaret Bayam....36 D6
Casa de la Cultura....37 D3
Casa de la Trova La Bayamesa....38 B4
Cine Céspedes....39 C3
Estadio Mártires de Barbados....40 D5
Sala Teatro José Joaquín Palma....41 D4
Uneac....(see 17)
SHOPPING
Fondo de Bienes Culturales....42 C3
VideCuba....43 D4
TRANSPORT
Bici-taxis....44 B4
Cubana....45 B4
Cubataxi....46 B6
Havanautos....47 C6
Intermunicipal Bus Station....48 B4
Passenger Trucks....(see 49)
Provincial Bus Station....49 C6
Servi-Cupet Gas Station....50 C6
Transtur....(see 24)
Siboney
Camilo Cienfuegos
Jesús Menéndez
Nuevo Bayamo
Plaza del Himno Nacional
Parque Céspedes
Río Bayamo
0 100 m
See Enlargement
Train Station
To Cemetery (1.4km); Las Tunas (81km)
To Carlos Manuel de Céspedes Airport (3.5km); Holguín (70km)
To Manzanillo (59km)
To Jardín Botánico (14km); Guisa (26km); Santiago de Cuba (116km)
Av de los Mártires
Vicente Aguilera
Perucho Figueredo
Carretera Central
Máximo Gómez
General García
José Martí
José A Saco
Donato Mármol
Carlos Manuel de Céspedes
Manuel del Socorro
Amado Estévez
Av Jesús Rabí
Av Granma
Av Amado Estévez
Calle 10
Calle 12
Bartolomé Masó
Joan Clemente Zenea
Barranca de la Luz

GRANMA PROVINCE

### HERBERT MATTHEWS

On February 17, 1957 Herbert Matthews, a seasoned editorial writer for the *New York Times*, stuffed his notebook into his jacket pocket and hiked, under the guidance of M-26-7 agent Celia Sánchez, up into the precipitous Sierra Maestra Mountains. His aim: to undertake an interview with a young bearded revolutionary named Fidel Castro, a man who – in the minds of most Americans – had been given up for dead after a botched invasion off the Cuban coast two months earlier.

As a political liberal and veteran of the republican movement during the Spanish Civil War, Matthews was immediately taken by the charismatic figure of Castro whose personality he described as 'overpowering'. 'This is quite a man', he wrote enthusiastically, 'The most dangerous enemy that General Batista has yet faced'.

The reality, of course, was something less dramatic. Still on the defensive after the disastrous *Granma* ambush two months earlier, Castro was down to his last 18 men when the journalist called. Indeed so small was his tiny band of trusted associates that Fidel had instructed his younger brother Raúl to march the scruffily attired survivors around in front of Matthews numerous times in an attempt to dupe the journalist into thinking that he was harboring a reputable military force.

The ploy clearly worked. Published in the *New York Times* on February 24, 1957, Matthews' blockbusting article made Castro into a figure of romantic myth and helped turn US policy onto a new anti-Batista footing, a factor that ultimately played a large part in the dictator's downfall.



postindependence president was born here; it's now the seat of Uneac (Unión Nacional de Escritores y Artistas de Cuba; National Union of Cuban Writers and Artists). You might catch a *trova* (traditional poetic singing/songwriting) concert in its cloistered patio. A forerunner of the national anthem, co-written by Céspedes (a man of many talents), was first sung next door on March 27, 1851.

The **Torre de San Juan Evangelista** (cnr José Martí & Amado Estévez) is to the southeast. A church dating from Bayamo's earliest years stood at this busy intersection until it was destroyed in the great fire of 1869. Later, the church's tower served as the entrance to the first cemetery in Cuba, which closed in 1919. The cemetery was demolished in 1940, but the tower survived. A **monument** to local poet José Joaquín Palma (1844–1911) stands in the park diagonally across the street from the tower, and beside the tower is a bronze **statue of Francisco Vicente Aguilera** (1821–77), who led the independence struggle in Bayamo.

Nearby, but a little hard to find, is the **Museo Ñico López** (Abihail González; admission CUC$1; 8am-noon & 2-5:30pm Tue-Sat, 9am-noon Sun) in the former officers' club of the Carlos Manuel de Céspedes military barracks. On July 26, 1953, this garrison was attacked by 25 revolutionaries determined to support the assault on the Moncada Barracks in Santiago de Cuba by preventing reinforcements from being sent. Though a failure, Ñico López, who led the Bayamo attack, escaped to Guatemala, and he was largely responsible for introducing Ernesto 'Che' Guevara to Fidel in July 1955; López was killed shortly after the *Granma* landed in 1956.

## Activities

Want to improve your checkmate chances? You might just get lucky in Bayamo where every Saturday night a whole army of chess aficionados hits the streets in the quirky Fiesta de la Cubanía. The **Acadamia de Ajedrez** (José A Saco No 63 btwn General García & Céspedes) is the place to go to improve your pawn-king-four technique. Emblazoned on the wall of this cerebral institution are pictures of Che, Fidel and Carlos Manuel de Céspedes – Cuba's greatest ever chess king. You can't miss it.

## Festivals & Events

Bayamo's most engaging nighttime attraction is its weekly **Fiesta de la Cubanía** on Saturday at 8pm. This ebullient and long-standing street party is like nothing else in Cuba. Set up willy-nilly along Calle Saco it includes quirky pipe organs, whole roast pig, a local oyster drink called *ostiones* and – incongruous in the middle of it all – rows of tables laid out diligently with chess sets. Dancing is, of course, de rigueur.

## Sleeping

**Hotel Escuela Telégrafo** (☎ 42 55 10; Saco No 108; s/d CUC$15/20; ❄) One of Cuba's impressive Escuela hotels where students learn the intricacies of the tourism trade, the Telégrafo is a commendable advert for the shape of things to come. A friendly and helpful team of staff complement a range of more-than-adequate facilities that include a restaurant, a bustling lobby, and the possibility of taking Spanish lessons (inquire at the front desk). The only real drawback is the lack of hot water.

**Hotel Royalton** (Islazul; ☎ 42 22 24; Maceo No 53; s/d low season CUC$21/27, high season CUC$26/33; ❄) Blending in with the colonial buildings on Parque Céspedes, the Royalton is Bayamo's best budget choice. Rooms are small but well maintained with the four at the front opening out over one of Cuba's most understated and leafy squares. You can people-watch over cocktails on the attractive sidewalk terrace, and there's a broad, breezy lobby and a rooftop terrace.

**Villa Bayamo** (Islazul; ☎ 42 31 02; s/d low season CUC$21/27, high season CUC$26/33; P ❄ 🏊) A bargain place 3km southwest of the town center on the road to Manzanillo, this motel is a good choice if you want to lie around a pool while going easy on your wallet. Locals know this place as 'Casa Central' and 'Hotel XXX Aniversario.'

**Hotel Sierra Maestra** (Cubanacán; ☎ 42 79 74; Carretera Central; P ❄ 🏊) Inconveniently situated 3km southeast of town toward Santiago de Cuba, the Sierra Maestra was closed at the time of writing to accommodate a Misión Milagros (Miracle Mission; see p449). Check before turning up.

Casas particulares are starting to pop up in Bayamo; see below.

## Eating

**Tropi Crema** (🕑 10am-10pm) This is the place for peso ice cream, in the southwest corner of Parque Céspedes.

**Restaurante Vegetariano** (General García No 173; 🕑 7-9am, noon-2:30pm & 6-9pm) If staff arrive punctually, this is a good peso breakfast option, though don't expect nut roast.

**La Sevillana** (General García btwn General Lora & Figueredo; 🕑 noon-2pm & 6pm-10:30pm) This is the newest eating joint in town, a posh-looking peso place with a no-shorts dress code probably designed to keep the tourists away.

**La Victoria** (☎ 42 25 31; cnr General García & Maceo; meals CUC$5) Despite the sign, you won't find shrimp at this atmospheric, state-run place on the northeastern corner of Parque Céspedes. However, there are pork, chicken and even beef dishes.

**Paladar Sagitario** (Marmol No 107 btwn Maceo & Vincente Aguilera; meals CUC$5-7; 🕑 noon-11:45pm) This place is super popular for the filling meals (chicken Gordon Bleu) served in its open courtyard.

**Paladar El Polinesio** (☎ 42 24 49; Parada No 125 btwn Pio Rosado & Cisnero) A better and more affordable bet than Sagitario is this place, which has a lower *jinetero*-to-client ratio.

**Plaza restaurant** (Maceo No 53; 🕑 7:30am-10pm) The restaurant at the Hotel Royalton is Bayamo's 'upmarket' spot, serving traditional Cuban food on its pleasant patio.

**La Bodega** (Plaza del Himno Nacional No 34) This eternally popular place opposite the Iglesia

### CASAS PARTICULARES – BAYAMO

With the Sierra Maestra Hotel closed temporarily to accommodate a Misión Milagros, Bayamo's clutch of 30-plus casas are in ever-greater demand. Here are some of the more central options.

**'Casa Buena Vista' – Valia López Sánchez** (☎ 42 36 59; Vicente Aguilera No 106 btwn Martí & M Corona; r CUC$20; ❄) Two clean rooms, meals available; ask about dance classes and bike hire.

**Dolores Masán Sosa** ('Lolita'; ☎ 42 29 74; Pio Rosado No 171 btwn Parada & William Soler; r CUC$25; P ❄) There are two rooms with air-con, one with fan; rooms have an independent entrance. You can also rent at No 64.

**Frank Licea Milan** (☎ 42 58 16; Pio Rosado No 73 btwn Parada & William Soler; r CUC$20) Friendly, older couple with a simple, clean room with bath.

**Juan Valdes** (☎ 42 33 24; Pio Rosado No 64 btwn Ramírez & N López; P ❄) Adequate room near central park; prices are negotiable. There are other casas in the same street.

**Lydia J Alvarado Santana** (☎ 42 31 75; Donato Marmol btwn Perucho Figueredo & General Lora; r CUC$20; P ❄) Central location, knows other casas.

Parroquial Mayor, has a rear terrace with river views.

### SELF-CATERING

**Mercado agropecuario** (Línea) The market is in front of the train station. There are many peso food stalls along here also.

**La Creación** (9am-5pm Mon-Sat, 9am-noon Sun) This store at the southeast corner of Parque Céspedes sells basic groceries.

## Drinking

**Hotel Royalton** (Maceo No 53) Drinks on the rooftop or sidewalk terraces here are always a good bet.

**La Taberna** (Céspedes No 65) For something grittier, try this dark, 2nd-floor saloon with faux stained-glass; it's tucked away behind Tropi Crema.

## Entertainment

**Cine Céspedes** (42 42 67; admission 1 peso) This cinema is on the western side of Parque Céspedes, next to the post office. It could be screening anything – from Cuban animated or dramatic features to the latest flick from Brazil or a Hollywood blockbuster.

**Uneac** (Céspedes No 158; admission free; 4pm) You can while away a Saturday afternoon at the bolero on the flowery patio here before making your way to José A Saco for the Saturday Fiesta de la Cubanía (p376).

**Sala Teatro José Joaquín Palma** (Céspedes No 164) In a stylish old church, this venue presents theater on Friday, Saturday and Sunday nights, while the Teatro Guiñol, also here, hosts children's theater on Saturday and Sunday mornings.

**Cabaret Bayam** (42 51 11; Carretera Central Km 2; 9pm Fri-Sun) This venue, opposite the Hotel Sierra Maestra, has shows and dancing.

**Estadio Mártires de Barbados** (Av Grandma) From October to April, ask about baseball games at this stadium, approximately 2km northwest of Hotel Sierra Maestra.

The **Casa de la Trova La Bayamesa** (cnr Maceo & Martí; admission CUC$1; 9pm) is one of Cuba's best, and concerts sometimes also take place at the **Casa de la Cultura** (42 59 17; General García No 15), on the east side of Parque Céspedes.

## Shopping

**Fondo de Bienes Culturales** (Plaza del Himno Nacional No 20) This shop sells mediocre handicrafts.

**VideCuba** (General García No 225; 8am-10pm) This outlet will meet your photographic requirements.

## Getting There & Away

### AIR

Bayamo's **Carlos Manuel de Céspedes Airport** (airport code BYM; 42 75 06) is about 4km northeast of town, on the road to Holguín. **Cubana** (Martí No 58; 42 39 16) flies to Bayamo from Habana twice a week (CUC$103 one way, two hours). There are no international flights to or from Bayamo.

### BUS & TRUCK

The **provincial bus station** (cnr Carretera Central & Av Jesús Rabí) has Astro buses twice daily to Santiago de Cuba (CUC$5), but only one bus a day goes to Holguín (CUC$5) and Habana (CUC$30), leaving at 8pm.

**Víazul** (www.viazul.com) has three daily buses to Santiago de Cuba (CUC$7, two hours, 4:45am, 9:45am and 11:35pm), and there's a daily bus to Trinidad (CUC$26, nine hours 20 minutes, 9:40pm). The service to Habana (CUC$44, 14½ hours, 12:10am, 11:10am and 5:25pm) also stops at Holguín (CUC$6, two hours 10 minutes), Las Tunas (CUC$6, 2½ hours), Camagüey (CUC$11, 5½ hours), Ciego de Ávila (CUC$17, seven hours 20 minutes), Sancti Spíritus (CUC$21, 9½ hours) and Santa Clara (CUC$26, 10¾ hours).

Passenger trucks leave from an adjacent terminal for Santiago de Cuba (seven pesos), Holguín (three pesos), Manzanillo (three pesos) and Pilón (three pesos). You can get a truck to Bartolomé Masó, as close as you can get on public transport to the Sierra Maestra trailhead. Ask which line is waiting for the truck you want, then join. The trucks leave when full and you pay as you board.

The **intermunicipal bus station** (cnr Saco & Línea), opposite the train station, receives mostly local buses of little use to travelers. However, trucks to Las Tunas (four pesos) and Guisa (one peso) leave from here. You might also wrangle space in a collective taxi to hard-to-reach places such as Manzanillo, Pilón and Niquero from here.

### TRAIN

The **train station** (42 49 55; cnr Saco & Línea), 1km east of the center, has trains to the following destinations.

GRANMA PROVINCE

| Destination | Cost (one way) | Departure time | Frequency |
|---|---|---|---|
| Camagüey | CUC$7 | 5:20am | daily |
| Habana | CUC$26 | 7:40pm | alternate days |
| Manzanillo | CUC$2 | 6:17am, 10:52am, 4:12pm | daily |
| Santiago | CUC$4 | 4:04pm | alternate days |

### Getting Around

**Cubataxi** (☎ 42 43 13) can supply a taxi to Bayamo airport for CUC$3, or to Aeropuerto Frank País in Holguín for CUC$25. A taxi to Villa Santo Domingo (setting-off point for the Alto del Naranjo trailhead for Sierra Maestra hikes) or Comandancia de la Plata will cost approximately CUC$50 round-trip. There's a taxi stand in the south of town near Museo Ñico López.

The **Havanautos** (☎ 42 73 75) office is adjacent to Servi-Cupet, while **Transtur** (☎ 42 41 87; Carretera Central) is at the Hotel Sierra Maestra.

The **Servi-Cupet** (Carretera Central) is between Hotel Sierra Maestra and the bus terminal as you arrive from Santiago de Cuba.

The main horse-cart route (one peso) runs between the train station and the hospital, via the bus station. Bici-taxis (five to 10 pesos a ride) are also useful for getting around town. There's a stand near the train station.

## AROUND BAYAMO

For peace, quiet, butterflies and flowers, head to the **jardín botánico** (botanic gardens; Carretera de Guisa Km 10; admission without/with guide CUC$1/2), about 16km outside Bayamo off the Guisa road. It's on very few itineraries, so you can have the 104 hectares of this tranquil garden to yourself. There are 74 types of palms, scores of cacti, blooming orchids and sections for endangered and medicinal plants. The guided tour (Spanish only) gains you access to greenhouses, notable for the showy ornamentals.

To get here, take the road to Santiago de Cuba for 6km and turn left at the signposted junction for Guisa. After 10km you'll see the botanic garden sign on the right. Trucks leave from the intermunicipal bus station in front of the train station (trips are one peso).

## DOS RÍOS & AROUND

At Dos Ríos, 52km northeast of Bayamo, almost in Holguín, a white obelisk overlooking the Río Cauto marks the spot where José Martí was shot and killed on May 19, 1895. It's 22km northeast of Jiguaní on the road to San Germán: take the unmarked road to the right after crossing the Cauto.

### Sleeping & Eating

**Villa El Yarey** (Cubanacán; ☎ 42 72 56; s/d low season CUC$36/58, high season CUC$43/72) Back toward Jiguaní, 23km southwest of Dos Ríos, is this relaxed, attractive hotel with 16 rooms on a ridge with an excellent view of the Sierra Maestra. This accommodation is perfect for those who want calm and placid tranquility in verdant natural surroundings.

### Getting There & Away

To get to Villa El Yarey from Jiguaní go 4km east of town on the Carretera Central and then 6km north on a side road. From Dos Ríos proceed southwest on the road toward Jiguaní and turn left 2km the other side of Las Palmas. It makes an ideal stop for anyone caught between Bayamo and Santiago de Cuba, or those taking the backdoor Bayamo–Holguín route. Public transport here is scant.

## YARA

☎ 23 / pop 29,237

Yara is a bustling town in the middle of nowhere, 46km west of Bayamo and 23km east of Manzanillo. Large banana plantations and vast fields of sugarcane surround the town, and rice fields line the road to Manzanillo. After freeing his slaves at La Demajagua, near Manzanillo, Carlos Manuel de Céspedes and his followers arrived here on October 11, 1868 and fought their first battle against the Spanish, as recalled by a monument in Yara's main square. The town is famous for the *Grito de Yara* (Yara Declaration), in which Céspedes proclaimed Cuba's independence.

Just off the square is the **Museo Municipal** (Grito de Yara No 107; admission CUC$1; 8am-noon & 2-6pm Mon-Sat, 9am-noon Sun), which shows a local historical collection.

There's a Servi-Cupet here if you need a gas top-up.

## GRAN PARQUE NACIONAL SIERRA MAESTRA

A beautiful mountainscape of soaring peaks, hidden cloud forests and ingratiating local *campesinos* (country folk), the Gran Parque Nacional Sierra Maestra is synonymous with Castro's backs-to-the-wall guerrilla campaign of the late 1950s. Situated 40km south of Yara, up a very steep 24km concrete road from Bartolomé Masó, this precipitous and untamed region contains the country's highest peak, Pico Turquino (over the border in Santiago de Cuba Province) as well as the rebel's one-time wartime headquarters, Comandancia La Plata (see p382).

### Information

Aspiring visitors should check the current situation before arriving in the national park. Tropical storms and/or government bureaucracy have been known to put the place temporarily out of action. The best source of information is **Cubamar** (☎ 7-831-3151) in Habana, or you can go straight to the horse's mouth by directly contacting **Villa Santo Domingo** (☎ 23-56-53-02). These guys can put you in touch with the Centro de Información de Flora y Fauna next door (see p382). Additional information can be gleaned at the Cubanacán desk at the Hotel Royalton in Bayamo.

### History

History resonates throughout these mountains, the bulk of it linked indelibly to the guerrilla war that raged throughout this region between December 1956 and December 1958. For the first year of the conflict Fidel and his growing band of supporters remained on the move, never staying in one place for more than a few days. It was only in mid 1958 that the rebels established a permanent base on a ridge in the shadow of Pico Turquino, Cuba's highest peak. This headquarters became known as La Plata and it was from here that the combative Castro drafted many of the early revolutionary laws while he orchestrated the military strikes that finally brought about the ultimate demise of the Batista government.

### Sights & Activities

All trips into the park begin at the end of the near-vertical, corrugated-concrete access road at **Alto del Naranjo**, 5km beyond the tourist accommodation at Villa Santo Domingo (an arduous two-hour walk, or you can hire a jeep for CUC$35 round-trip). There's a good view of the plains of Granma from this 950m-high lookout, otherwise it's just a launching pad for La Plata (3km) and Pico Turquino (13km).

Santo Domingo is a tiny village that nestles in a deep green valley beside the gushing Río Yara. Communally it provides a wonderful slice of the peaceful Cuban *campesino* life that has carried on pretty much unchanged since Fidel and Che prowled these velvety mountains in the late 1950s. If you decide to stick around take a peek at the local school and medical clinic for a taste of rural socialism in action or ask at Villa Santo Domingo about the tiny village museum. The locals have also been known to offer horseback-riding, pedicure treatments and some classic old first-hand tales from the annals of revolutionary history.

The mountain closes at 4pm and rangers won't let you pass after 1pm, so go in the early morning to maximize your visit. You must leave your bags and cameras at the ranger's hut, 2km before the Comandancia La Plata, as photography is prohibited.

The cloud forest here is quite beautiful. You can cobble together a decent day trip by visiting the Comandancia and hiking to La Platica, 1.5km from Alto del Naranjo (an additional fee may be required).

#### TREKKING

Certainly Cuba's most popular through-trek (as opposed to the round-trip summit hike up Pico Turquino; see p427) is the rugged, two-/three-day grind from Alto del Naranjo across the Sierra Maestra to Las Cuevas, or vice versa. The terrain goes from mountain to rain forest, with fantastic views, and ends on the inviting shores of the Caribbean.

Guides are mandatory and must be arranged through Flora and Fauna employees at Villa Santo Domingo (p382) or at the **Campismo Popular** (☎ 42 42 00; General García No 112) in Bayamo (p374). The cost is CUC$30 to CUC$48 depending on how many days you take. Stock up in Bayamo, carrying everything you'll need, including food, warm clothing, candles and some kind of bed roll

or sheet arrangement. Even in August it gets cold at the shelters, so be prepared. Sufficient water is available along the trail.

The trail through the mountains from Alto del Naranjo passes the village of La Platica (water), Palma Mocha (campsite), Lima (campsite), Pico Joachín (shelter and water), El Cojo (shelter), Regino, Paso de los Monos, Loma Redonda, Pico Turquino (1972m), Pico Cuba (1872m, with a shelter and water at 1650m), Pico Cardero (1265m) and La Esmajagua (600m) before dropping down to Las Cuevas on the Caribbean coast. The first two days are spent on the 13km section to Pico Turquino (overnighting at the Pico Joachín shelters), where a prearranged guide takes over and leads you down to Las Cuevas. As with all guide services, tips are in order. Pre-arranging the second leg from Pico Cuba to Las Cuevas is straightforward and handled by park staff.

These hikes are well coordinated and the guides efficient (to a fault: don't let them rush you). The sanest way to begin is by spending the night at Campismo La Sierrita (below) or Villa Santo Domingo (p382) and setting out in the morning. Transport from Las Cuevas along the coast is sparse, to say the least, with one scheduled truck on alternate days. For this reason, it might be easier to start in Las Cuevas and hike to Alto del Naranjo.

See p427 for a description of the Las Cuevas–Pico Turquino leg in the other direction.

## Sleeping & Eating

Before heading into the mountains, backpacker types and Cubans usually bunk down at **Campismo La Sierrita** (☎ 5-3326; cabins from CUC$16), 8km south of Bartolomé Masó. It's 1km off the main highway on a very rough road. The 27 cabins have bunks, baths and electricity, and sleep up to four people. There's a restaurant, and a river for swimming. If you have a sturdy rental car, the staff might be able to supply you with a guide to take you to the Comandancia La Plata. Otherwise, ask at the desk if there are any planned tours coming up. La Sierrita is often full on weekends, so reservations from the **Campismo Popular** (☎ 42 42 00; General García No 112, Bayamo) office in Bayamo are essential.

At Bartolomé Masó, 16km south of Yara on the road to Santo Domingo, is **Motel Balcón de la Sierra** (Islazul; ☎ 59 51 80; s/d low season CUC$18/24, high season CUC$22/28; P). Snuggled below the mountains, this has to be one of Islazul's best-located hotels. Go for one of the cabanas with terrace and mountain views, and prepare for chilly nights.

The main base for visitors to Gran Parque Nacional Sierra Maestra is **Villa Santo Domingo** (Islazul; ☎ 56 53 02; s/d with breakfast low season CUC$29/34, high season CUC$32/37), 24km south of Bartolomé Masó. There are 20 separate cabins next to the Río Yara, at a 200m altitude and the setting, among cascading mountains and wooden *campesino* huts, is idyllic. Geographically speaking, this is the best jumping-off point for the La Plata and Turquino hikes. You can also test your lungs going for a challenging early morning hike up a painfully steep road to Alto Naranjo (5km, 750m of ascent). Other attractions include horseback-riding, river swimming and traditional music in the villa's restaurant. If you're lucky you might even catch the wizened old Rebel Quintet (see opposite). Fidel has stayed here on various occasions (in hut No 6) and Raúl Castro dropped by briefly in 2001 after scaling Pico Turquino at the ripe old age of 70.

### Getting There & Around

There's no public transport from Bartolomé Masó to Alto del Naranjo. A taxi from Bayamo to Villa Santo Domingo should cost between CUC$20 and CUC$25 one way. Don't pay the driver until you arrive; otherwise you may be dropped off 7km before Villa Santo Domingo, citing steep roads (private taxis, if you can find them, routinely do this). Returning, the hotel should be able to arrange onward transport for you to Bartolomé Masó, Bayamo or Manzanillo.

A 4WD vehicle with good brakes is necessary to drive up to Alto del Naranjo; it's one of the steepest roads in Cuba (if not the world). Russian trucks pass regularly, usually for adventurous tour groups, and you may be able to find a space on board.

## MANZANILLO

**☎ 23 / pop 110,952**

Scruffy, run-down and rough-around-the-edges, bayside Manzanillo looks as if the life has been slowly drained out of it by decades of mean-spirited economic austerity. With just one lackluster hotel and a handful of variable casas particulares scattered around a weather-beaten central park, it's barely on the travel circuit at all, though the social life's real enough and the strange neo-Moorish architecture perhaps worthy of an hour or two's silent contemplation.

**REBEL HEADQUARTERS: COMANDANCIA LA PLATA**

Perched impregnably on a mountainside amid a dense tropical cloud forest Castro's wartime headquarters, Comandancia La Plata, is one of Cuba's most rewarding and authentic historical monuments.

Open intermittently for public viewing since 1994, access to the site, which lies within the boundary of the Gran Parque Nacional Sierra Maestra, is closely controlled by the Centro de Información de Flora y Fauna in the village of Santo Domingo. Aspiring guerrilla-watchers must first hire a guide at the park headquarters (CUC$11), take a bone-rattling Russian truck (or walk) 5km up a precipitous paved road to a viewpoint known as Alto de Naranjo (CUC$7) and then proceed on foot along a muddy track for the final 3km.

The effort is undoubtedly worth it. Encased in magnificent natural surroundings La Plata is spectacularly unique; a living testament to Castro's indefatigable ability to organize, survive and run rings around an incompetent enemy. Roughshod buildings include a guardhouse (that doubled up as Che Guevara's medical post), a small museum, a press office (that produced propaganda for Radio Rebelde), a kitchen, and La Comandancia itself; Fidel's famous headquarters, a two-roomed all-wood affair furnished rather meagerly with bed, escape hatch, bookshelves, and the original refrigerator complete with bullet hole in the side. Rumor has it that, aside from Fidel, only the influential Celia Sánchez was allowed inside.

**THE REBEL QUINTET**

Tucked away in the small village of Santo Domingo in the foothills of the Sierra Maestra Mountains, the Rebel Quintet – a band that once enlivened the airwaves of Castro's clandestine Radio Rebelde – offer one of the revolutionary war's more colorful anecdotal stories.

Now well into their 60s, the band grew up in the 1950s as sons of a local *campesino* named Medina, a coffee farmer from the tiny mountain settlement of La Platica and the man who rented Fidel the land to make his secret headquarters at La Plata in 1957.

Recruited into the rebel army more for their musical prowess than their shooting skills, Medina's teenage boys were given rough homemade guitars, old drumming implements and the rather unconventional brief to direct their fast and furious revolutionary songs over small loudspeakers, in an attempt to dispirit an already dispirited enemy.

The repertoire – which is still performed periodically to curious tourists at Villa Santo Domingo (opposite) or the Motel Balcón de la Sierra (opposite) – included such timeless classics as *I Am a Fidelista, Respect for Che Guevara* and *Go Away Monkey*.

Back in their '50s heyday, the band were quirky revolutionary mascots and something of a musical thorn in the side for Batista's beleaguered army. The hapless enemy soldiers when taken prisoner were reportedly often confused as to their actual whereabouts; at home, in jail, or at a party!

Founded originally in 1784 as a small fishing port, Manzanillo's early history was dominated by smugglers and pirates trading in contraband goods. The subterfuge continued until well into the 1950s when the city's proximity to the Sierra Maestra led it to become an important supply line for the smuggling of arms and men up to Castro et al in their secret mountaintop headquarters.

In the early 20th century, Manzanillo was to become the unlikely entry point for street organs from France into Cuba (see p384) via the Fornaris and Borbolla families. The city's musical legacy was solidified further in the late '60s and early '70s when it spearheaded the *nueva trova* music revival that swept the country from east to west.

## Information

**Banco de Crédito y Comercio** (cnr Merchán & Saco; h8:30am-3:30pm Mon-Fri, 8am-noon Sat)

**Cadeca** (Martí No 184; 🕒 8:30am-6pm Mon-Sat, 8am-1pm Sun) Two blocks from the main square.

**Etecsa** (cnr Martí & General Benítez) Seven blocks west of the post office.

**Post office** (cnr Martí & Codina) One block from Parque Céspedes.

**Transtur** (☎ 5-3800; Maceo No 70; 🕒 8am-noon & 1-5pm Mon-Wed & Fri, 1-5pm Thu) There is no tourist information in Manzanillo though Transtur, which shares offices off Parque Céspedes with Cubana, can help with transfers, taxis and rental cars.

## Sights

### IN TOWN

Manzanillo is spread out and shadeless – not a great town for walking around, though the wooden houses, abandoned towers and chipped cupolas provide quirky visuals. Check out the old **City Bank of NY building** (cnr Merchán & Doctor Codina), which dates from 1913, or the old wooden houses around Perucho Figueredo between Merchán and JM Gómez.

The central square of Manzanillo, **Parque Céspedes**, is striking for its precious *glorieta* (gazebo/bandstand), with its Moorish mosaics, scalloped cupola and arabesque-covered columns. Completely restored in 1999, it fairly glows in the dusk's slanting light. Surrounding the park are buildings echoing this Andalusian-Moorish style, particularly the grandiose shopping arcade on the park's western side.

On the eastern side of Parque Céspedes is the **Museo Histórico Municipal** (Martí No 226; admission free; 🕒 8am-noon & 2-6pm Tue-Fri, 8am-noon & 6-10pm Sat & Sun). There's an art gallery next door. The **Iglesia de la Purísima Concepción**, across the square, has a gilded main altar.

Manzanillo's most evocative sight is the **Celia Sánchez Monument**, built in 1990 along Caridad. Colorful ceramic murals decorate the stairway between Martí and Luz Caballero. The birds and flowers on the reliefs represent Sánchez, one of the leaders of the M-26-7 movement and longtime aid to

Castro, whose visage appears on the central mural near the top of the stairs. A small **visitors center** (8am-noon & 2-6pm Mon-Fri, 8am-noon Sat) is adjacent; there are excellent views from here.

### OUTSIDE TOWN

The **Museo Histórico La Demajagua** (admission CUC$1; 8am-6pm Mon-Fri, 8am-noon Sun), 10km south of Manzanillo, is the site of the sugar estate of Carlos Manuel de Céspedes. It was here on October 10, 1868 that Céspedes freed his slaves, setting in motion the process that led to Cuba's independence from Spain 30 years later. Remains of Céspedes' *ingenio* (sugar mill) are behind the museum. The views from the estate are fine and the long, grassy expanses a novelty.

From here, a broad walkway leads to a monument bearing a quotation from Castro: *Nosotros entonces habríamos sido como ellos, ellos hoy habrían sido como nosotros* (We would then have been as they were, they today would be as we are). Below two huge trees next to the monument are the remains of a steam engine that formerly powered the mill, and hanging nearby is the famous Demajagua bell, once used to call the slaves to work. On October 10, 1868, it tolled announcing Cuba's independence. To get to La Demajagua, travel south 10km from the Servi-Cupet gas station in Manzanillo, in the direction of Media Luna, and then another 2.5km off the main road, toward the sea.

#### AN ORGAN TO GRIND

Manzanillo is famous for its mechanical organs, first imported into Cuba from France by the Fornaris and Borbolla families in 1876. By 1900 some 200 French street organs were in existence in Manzanillo and, in the ensuing years, Carlos and Francisco Borbolla built about a dozen more full-size organs in a factory that they had set up in the city itself.

The tradition lives on today in Cuban rumba bands; original pipe organs form a central part of weekend street performances in Manzanillo's Parque Céspedes and neighboring Bayamo's weekly Fiesta de la Cubanía. Backed up by live percussion instruments the hand-operated street organs churn out a rather unorthodox mix of traditional fairground music blended with a fast and furious rumba beat.

## Sleeping

**Hotel Guacanayabo** (Islazul; 5-4012; Circunvalación Camilo Cienfuegos; s/d low season CUC$17/22, high season CUC$18/24; ) Part of Islazul's budget hotel chain, this architecturally incongruous blemish on the landscape, situated inconveniently on the outskirts of sprawling Manzanillo, was given over to a Misión Milagros (Miracle Mission; see p449) as of January 2006 – check with the hotel regarding any update. Until it re-opens Manzanillo's only overnight accommodation is in a handful of centrally located casas particulares (see opposite).

## Eating & Drinking

The restaurant scene is hurting in Manzanillo. For do-it-yourself enthusiasts, street food is available on weekends in various food stalls scattered around Parque Céspedes. Whole roast pig is a local specialty. Start the food hunt around Parque Céspedes and you should get lucky at one of the following places.

**Restaurante 1800** (Merchán No 245 btwn Maceo & Saco; noon-10pm Tue-Sun) This is the place most locals recommend, and there are adequate steaks and seafood. Your menu will be in Convertibles.

**Restaurante Las Américas** (Maceo; noon-2:30pm & 7-10pm) This restaurant has the usual pork and chicken that you will have grown to tolerate.

**Pizzería Nápoles** (Merchán) Nápoles has pizza and spaghetti for under three pesos. Pay at the cashier and grab a seat; bring your own beverage.

**Café 1906** (cnr Maceo & Merchán; 24hr) This is Manzanillo's most atmospheric hangout, a corner joint with 20 centavo shots of coffee and rum, and lots of locals getting hopped up and zonked out.

**Nectar Cremería** (Martí; noon-10pm Mon-Sat, 9am-10pm Sun) Come to this place near Maceo for ice cream and pay in pesos. Get in line by taking *el último* (last place in line) across the street in the park.

**Cafetería Piropo Kikiri** (Martí btwn Maceo & Saco; 10am-10pm) This place has everything from ice-cream sandwiches to sundaes, available for Convertibles.

**CASAS PARTICULARES – MANZANILLO**

**Ada y Fernando** (☎ 5-2522; jerm_7519@yahoo.es; Pedro Figueredo No 105 btwn Matrí & Mártires de Vietnam; ❄) One block from central park.

**Adrián & Tonia** (☎ 5-3028; Mártires de Vietnam No 49; r CUC$20-25; ❄) Good feedback from travelers on this one.

**Villa Luisa** (☎ 5-2738; Calle Rabena No 172 btwn Maceo & Masó; r CUC$20-25; P ❄) Clean, central, price negotiable.

## Entertainment

**Teatro Manzanillo** (Villuendas btwn Maceo & Saco; admission 8 pesos; 🕓 shows at 8pm) Touring companies such as the Ballet de Camagüey and Danza Contemporánea de Cuba perform at this lovingly restored venue. Built in 1856 and restored in 1926 and again in 2002, this 430-seat beauty is packed with oil paintings, red flocking and original detail. Staff will be delighted to show you the room where the history of the restoration is explained.

**Casa de la Trova** (☎ 5-5423; Merchán No 213; admission 1 peso) The spiritual home of *nueva trova,* this is not the hallowed musical shrine it ought to be. There are bolero nights on Tuesdays, and *trova* concerts on Thursdays at 9pm.

**Cabaret Salón Rojo** (☎ 5-5117; 🕓 8pm-midnight Tue-Sat, 8pm-1am Sun) This place on the north side of Parque Céspedes has an upstairs terrace overlooking the square, for drinks (pay in pesos) and dancing.

**Cabaret Costa Azul** (☎ 5-3158; cnr Avs 1 de Mayo & Narciso Lopez; 🕓 8pm-2am Thu-Sun) Manzanillo's top nightspot. Hit the lido deck of this mock-up ship overlooking a large stage, where there's a show at 10pm.

**Cine Popular** (Av 1 de Mayo; 🕓 Tue-Sun) This is the town's top movie house.

## Getting There & Away

### AIR

Manzanillo's **Sierra Maestra Airport** (☎ 5-3019; airport code MZO) is on the road to Cayo Espino, 8km south of the Servi-Cupet gas station in Manzanillo. **Cubana** (☎ 5-4984) has a nonstop flight from Habana once a week on Saturdays (CUC$103, two hours). **Skyservice** (www.skyserviceairlines.com) flies directly from Toronto in winter.

A taxi between the airport and the center of town should cost approximately CUC$6.

### BUS & TRUCK

The bus station, 2km east of town on the road to Bayamo, has daily **Astro** (☎ 5-2727) buses to Bayamo, Camagüey, Habana, Pilón and Yara.

Buses and passenger trucks run fairly frequently to Yara and Bayamo. To Pilón, there are two or three morning buses. There is one daily bus to both Holguín and Habana, but to reach Santiago de Cuba you must transfer in Bayamo.

Passenger trucks to Media Luna and Pilón depart from the bus station and stop to pick up passengers at the crossroads near Servi-Cupet and the hospital (which is the local hitching stop).

### TRAIN

All services from the train station on the north side of town are via Yara and Bayamo. Trains go to the following destinations.

| Destination | Cost (one way) | Departure time |
|---|---|---|
| Bayamo | CUC$1.75 | 10:40am, 2:15pm, 7:40pm |
| Habana | CUC$28 | 5:20pm |
| Jiguaní | CUC$2.35 | 10:40am, 2:15pm |
| Santiago de Cuba | CUC$5.50 | 2:15pm |

## Getting Around

The **Havanautos** (☎ 5-7204) office is adjacent to the Servi-Cupet gas station, opposite the hospital, 3km south of the city center on the road to Media Luna. There's a brilliant new road running through Corralito up into Holguín, making this the quickest exit from Manzanillo toward points north and east.

Horse carts (one peso) to the bus station leave from Doctor Codina between Plácido and Luz Caballero. Horse carts along the Malecón to the shipyard leave from the bottom of Saco.

# MEDIA LUNA

☎ 23 / pop 15,493

The sugar-producing town of Media Luna, about 50km southwest of Manzanillo, is best known as the hometown of Celia

**EPIPHANY IN A SUGARCANE FIELD**

Picture the scene. It's December 2, 1956 in a remote part of Western Cuba called Las Coloradas and a group of 82 rag-tag soldiers led by Fidel Castro have just been dispatched off the coast from a leaky and overcrowded leisure yacht called *Granma*. Scrambling through a swamp and forced to abandon most of their weapons in the surrounding mangroves, the rebels flail around for three days before finding refuge in a sugarcane field where they lay down exhausted and try to figure out what they should do next.

It's a rude awakening. A few hours later the first hostile shots are fired into the air, a man falls dead and suddenly all around is chaos. In the confusion that follows; the soldiers panic and become separated. One, a 28-year-old Argentine doctor, uninitiated as yet to the brutalities of armed combat, is forced to make a break for it across open ground with little cover. Looking down at his feet he sees his trusted medical kit and a box of ammunition abandoned by a fleeing colleague. He can't possibly carry both items at once, and he has about five seconds to make a simple two-way choice.

A moment of history, a moment of infamy, a moment in which – according to many – a young and idealistic traveler called Ernesto Guevara de la Serna was transformed into the immortal and cold-blooded Che.

The panic wasn't over. Gathering up the discarded box of ammunition, Che was promptly hit in the neck by a stray enemy bullet. Assuming he was about to die he sat down on the ground momentarily and – remembering a story he had once read by Jack London about a man who slowly froze to death in Alaska – prepared himself to face death with dignity. It was Juan Almeida who snapped him out of his stupor. Yelling at him to get up he ushered Che and three other crestfallen survivors out of the blazing cane field and off into the jungle. Che was lucky. His neck wound was only superficial, and despite days spent wandering half-starved around the Cuban countryside, the small group of embattled rebels eventually found food and shelter with a sympathetic peasant known as Guillermo García. It was from García that the soldiers learned that Fidel was alive and well, and still plotting the imminent demise of Batista's government. They met up at a place called Cinco Palmas on December 21. The long, hard fight back from the brink had officially begun.



Sánchez (1920–80). Sánchez is famous for having sent essential supplies to Castro's rebels in the mountains, and after the revolution became one of Castro's closest associates. The **Celia Sánchez Museum** (Paúl Podio No 111; admission CUC$1; ⏲ 9am-noon & 2-5pm Tue-Sat, 9am-1pm Sun) is a grand old clapboard affair on the main road; it's not far from Media Luna's sugar mill.

Media Luna's **glorieta**, while not as outlandish as the one in Manzanillo, is still a charmer. Grab a three peso ice cream or fruit shake from one of the stalls in the park, and take a look around.

## NIQUERO

☎ 23 / pop 20,273

Niquero, a small fishing port and sugar town in the isolated southwest corner of Granma, is dominated by the local Roberto Ramirez Delgado sugar mill, built in 1905 and nationalized in 1960 (you'll smell it before you see it). Like many Granma settlements it is characterized by its distinctive clapboard houses and has a lively *noche de Cubanilla* when the streets are closed off and dining is at sidewalk tables. Live bands replete with organ grinder entertain the locals.

Ostensibly, there isn't much to do in Niquero but you can explore the park, where there's a **cinema**, and visit the town's small **museum**. Look out for a monument commemorating the oft-forgotten victims of the Granma landing, hunted down and murdered by Batista's troops in December 1956.

Niquero makes a good base from which to visit the Parque Nacional Desembarco del Granma. There's a Servi-Cupet in the center of town and another on the outskirts toward Cabo Cruz.

### Sleeping & Eating

**Hotel Niquero** (Islazul; ☎ 59 24 98; s/d low season CUC$16/20, high season CUC$22/28; Ⓟ ❄) Right in the middle of town, this low-key, out-on-a-limb hotel situated opposite the local sugar factory has dark, slightly tatty rooms with little balconies that overlook the street. The service here is variable though the affordable on-site restaurant has been known to rustle up a reasonable beefsteak with sauce. Unfortunately the hotel sustained damage during the 2005 hurricane season so you may find that some things here are still being repaired (the water supply, for instance).

## PARQUE NACIONAL DESEMBARCO DEL GRANMA

Ten kilometers southwest of Media Luna the road divides, with Pilón 30km to the southeast and Niquero 10km to the southwest. Belic is 16km southwest of Niquero. It's another 6km from Belic to the national park entry gate (entrance per person CUC$3).

Parque Nacional Desembarco del Granma protects 27,545 hectares of forests, cliffs and reefs along Cuba's southern coast, between Cabo Cruz and Pilón. In 1999 it was named a Unesco World Heritage site. The peculiar karst topography and uplifted marine terraces unique to this area offer some of the most pristine coastal cliffs in the Americas. Of the 512 plant species identified thus far, about 60% are endemic, and a dozen of them are found only here. The fauna is equally rich, with 25 species of mollusk, seven species of amphibian, 44 types of reptile, 110 bird species and 13 types of mammal.

In El Guafe, archaeologists have uncovered the second most important community of ancient agriculturists and ceramic-makers ever discovered in Cuba. Approximately 1000 years old, the artifacts discovered include altars, carved stones and earthen vessels along with six idols guarding a water goddess inside a ceremonial cave. As far as archaeologists are concerned, it's probably just the tip of the iceberg.

### Sights & Activities

The area is famous as the landing place of the yacht *Granma,* which brought Fidel and revolution to Cuba in 1956 (see opposite). A large monument and the **Museo Las Coloradas** (admission CUC$1; ⏰ 8am-6pm Tue-Sat, 8am-noon Sun) just beyond the park gate mark the actual landing spot. The museum outlines the routes taken by Castro, Guevara and the others from here to the Sierra Maestra, and there's a full-scale replica of the *Granma*.

Eight kilometers southwest of the park toward Cabo Cruz is the **Sendero Arqueológico Natural El Guafe**, a nature/archaeological trail. An underground river here has created 20 large caverns, one of which contains the famous Ídolo del Agua, carved from stalagmites by pre-Columbian Indians. It is a two-hour stroll, during which you can see butterflies, 170 different species of birds (including the tiny *colibrí*), a 500-year-old cactus and orchids. A park guard is available to accompany you and point out interesting features.

Three kilometers beyond the El Guafe trailhead is **Cabo Cruz**, a classic fishing port with skiffs bobbing offshore and sinewy men gutting their catch on the golden beach. There's not much to see here except the 33m-tall Vargas lighthouse, which was erected in 1871. An olive-oil wick provided the light for the lighthouse until gas was installed in 1928. In 1952 the device was electrified. An **exhibition room** (⏰ 8am-noon & 1-5pm Mon-Sat) labeled 'Historia del Faro', which has lighthouse memorabilia, is inside the adjacent building; the attendant at the lighthouse shop has the key.

There's good swimming east of the lighthouse and you can walk out to a stretch of reef that has decent snorkeling; watch the strong currents sweeping from west to east here. If you like to fish, Cabo Cruz is the place for you.

### Sleeping & Eating

**Campismo Las Coloradas** (Cubamar; Carretera de Niquero Km 17; s/d low season CUC$9/12, high season CUC$11/16; ❄) This place stands on 500m of murky beach, 5km southwest of Belic, just outside the park. The 28 duplex cabins fill fast on weekends and in summer, when locals flock to the beach to party. This is an equipped Campertour facility. Three buses a day from Niquero and more-frequent trucks from Belic come this far. Las Colorados was badly damaged by the 2005 hurricanes and was still closed for repairs as this book was being written. Cubamar had plans to reopen it as soon as possible.

### Getting There & Away

If you don't have your own transport, you can still get over here, but you'll just have

GRANMA PROVINCE

**GO FURTHER INTO THE COUNTRYSIDE**

Traveling up over the foothills of the Sierra Maestra on the road out of Pilón in the direction of Media Luna you come upon the tumbledown village of Sevilla. Turn left at the bus stop here and head a few more kilometers southwest until you arrive in the small settlement of El Plátano. Here – with some fumbling Spanish and a bit of deft do-it-yourself navigating – you'll find the former **House of Guillermo García**, now a roughshod museum.

Guillermo García was an illiterate peasant who helped reassemble the *Granma* survivors in December 1956 before leading them to safety in the Sierra Maestra. As a reward Fidel made him one of Cuba's five *comandantes* (commanding officers) after the revolution. He is still alive today and lives in Habana from where he has taken an active part in preserving the biodiversity of his home province.

The museum is a small affair containing old photos of the rebels and a map depicting their journey into the mountains. There is a tangible sense of history.

to be very patient. During the summer you may be able to hitch out of Las Coloradas, otherwise it's a tough lift (for information on the risks associated with hitching, see p477). The closest gas stations are in Niquero.

## PILÓN

☎ 23 / pop 11,904

Life ain't easy in Pilón, even by Cuban standards. Once upon a time this isolated coastal settlement was a thriving sugar town. But in 2002, the sugar mill shut down and the people – who had once provided vital refuge for the embattled *Granma* survivors – woke up to an uncertain future. Then in July 2005 fate struck again, this time in the form of a massive hurricane that ripped huge chunks out of the scenic coast road. It is a testament to these people that they're still here at all, eking out a living – just.

There's not much to do in the village itself apart from visit the tiny **Casa Museo Celia Sánchez Manduley** (admission CUC$1; 9am-5pm Mon-Sat, 9am-1pm Sun) or admire the surrounding mountain and seascapes. From Pilón, the paved road continues 17km east to Marea del Portillo, and all the way to Santiago de Cuba, which is another 180km further on.

### Sleeping & Eating

**Villa Turística Punta Piedra** (Cubanacán; ☎ 59 70 62; s/d/tr CUC$28/30/35) On the main road 11km east of Pilón and 5km west of Marea del Portillo, this amiable three-star resort made up of 13 rooms in two single-story blocks, makes a nice alternative to the larger hotel complexes a few kilometers to the east. There's a restaurant here and an intermittent disco located on a secluded saber of sandy beach and the staff, once they've recovered from the surprise of seeing you, will be mighty pleased with your custom.

### Getting There & Around

There's a bus between Pilón and Santiago de Cuba via Manzanillo on alternate days. Buses also run along the south coast between Pilón and Chivirico on alternate days, but don't bank on any timetables. Public transport in this region is enough to turn your hair gray; ask the locals.

Servi-Cupet is by the highway at the entrance to Pilón and sells snacks and drinks. Drivers should be sure to fill up here, the next gas station is in Santiago de Cuba nearly 200km away.

## MAREA DEL PORTILLO

Underrated and understated Marea del Portillo is one of Cuba's nicest all-inclusive resorts. There are just two smallish hotel complexes here wedged into a narrow strip of dry land between the glistening Caribbean and the cascading Sierra Maestra Mountains. In winter it's the warmest spot in Cuba.

Friendly and unpretentious, the two main resorts are kitted out with every creature comfort and outdoor activity available, and the prices are relatively inexpensive too. The only real drawback is the beach, which is of a light grey color and may disappoint those more attuned to the brilliant whites of Cayo Coco.

Close to the Parque Nacional Desembarco del Granma and situated at the far end of Cuba's most isolated and rugged stretch of coastline, the sense of revolutionary history in this area is both potent and rewarding. The nearest settlement of any note is Pilón, 17km to the west.

### Activities

Both hotels operate an all-day hiking and horseback-riding tour to **El Salto**, a waterfall, for CUC$35 per person including lunch and four drinks (six-person minimum) and trips into the Parque Nacional Desembarco del Granma for a similar price. Other horseback riding costs CUC$7 per hour.

The **Marlin Dive Center** (☎ 59 70 34, fax 59 70 35), adjacent to Hotel Club Amigo Marea del Portillo, offers scuba diving from CUC$35 a tank. Deep-sea fishing starts at CUC$45 per hour for four anglers fishing two at a time.

### Sleeping & Eating

**Club Amigo Marea del Portillo** (Cubanacán; ☎ 59 70 08; s/d all-inclusive CUC$50/80; P ✱ 🖳 🏊) As all-inclusives go, this little-known jewel has to be one of the most unpretentious and down-to-earth options in Cuba. It's located on a dark sandy beach in the rain shadow of the Sierra Maestra Mountains. The 74 rooms are comfortable and adequate, and the beachside swimming pool, though pleasant, is unusually small. Traffic in the hotel is very seasonal so phone ahead in the quieter months (April to October) as the complex has been known to close.

**Hotel Farallón del Caribe** (Cubanacán; ☎ 59 40 03; fax 59 70 80; s/d all-inclusive CUC$55/90; P ✱ 🖳 🏊) What a great setting for an all-inclusive resort: perched on a low hill overlooking the Sierra Maestra, the views across the mountains from the beach bar are magical and, aside from the Club Amigo next door, the surroundings are devoid of any other settlements. Exciting excursions can be organized here at the Cubanacán desk into the Parque Nacional Desembarco del Granma or, if you have your own wheels, you can go off exploring solo along the vista-laden coast road east toward Santiago. The resort is popular with package-tour Canadians.

### Getting There & Away

The only scheduled transport along this route is one truck on alternate days from Santiago de Cuba. By the time it arrives at this part of the coast it is overflowing dangerously with people making their way to Pilón.

### Getting Around

The hotels rent scooters for approximately CUC$8 per hour (CUC$3 for subsequent hours). A rough dirt road crosses the mountains directly from Marea del Portillo to Bartolomé Masó, but a 4WD vehicle, dry weather and considerable driving expertise are required to use it. Be prepared for several steep rocky sections and many fords.

# Santiago de Cuba Province

Santiago de Cuba Province is New Orleans melted down with Río de Janeiro, with a sedating dose of the pre-1991 Soviet Union thrown in for good measure. Here in the cradle of Cuba's socialist revolution ration shops give way to rumba parties and slogan-broadcasting political billboards take second place to Carnaval.

Nestled on one of the Cuban archipelago's most spectacular stretches of coastline, the province's mountain-ruffled hinterland mixes eco-retreats with Unesco World Heritage sites and revolutionary graveyards with the shrine of El Cobre, Cuba's holiest pilgrimage site. And that's just the appetizers. For those with a head for heights try a trek up Cuba's highest mountain, Pico Turquino. Others will enjoy the shorter scramble to the summit of rocky Gran Piedra for a glimpse over Parque Nacional Baconao, one of Cuba's six protected biospheres.

Straddled in the midst of all this greenery is Santiago, the island's second biggest city, a sleazy, sultry and highly-charged metropolis where music streams out of hidden doorways and brow-beaten artists muse over their sculptures. Existing for a time as Cuba's illustrious capital, Santiago sold out to more strategically important Habana in the 1550s, leaving embittered locals saddled forever with delusions of grandeur. Some call it the city of heroes, others the city of revolutionaries; or even the uncrowned city of Cuban culture. Whatever your personal impression, Santiago's importance as a nexus point for music, culture, rebellion and ideas has never been in question.



## HIGHLIGHTS

- **City of Revolutionaries**
  Explore the former homes of Antonio Maceo (p402) and Frank País (p402) and round it off with a trip to Moncada Barracks (p402)
- **Spectacular Drive**
  Take the coast road west toward Chivirico (p427) amid rolling mountains and crashing surf
- **Get High**
  Drag yourself to the top of the hulking mass of Gran Piedra (p419)
- **Pilgrimage**
  Pay your respects at the sacred shrine of La Virgen de la Caridad in El Cobre (p424)
- **Eco Tour**
  Shower beneath a waterfall at the eco-friendly Villa El Saltón (p425)

Villa El Saltón
Santiago de Cuba
El Cobre
Gran Piedra
Chivirico

- TELEPHONE CODE: 22
- POPULATION: 1.04 MILLION
- AREA: 6170 SQ KM

## History

Illuminated by a rich cast of revolutionary heroes and characterized by a cultural legacy that has infiltrated everything from music and language to sculpture and art, the history of Santiago is inseparable from the history of Cuba itself.

Founded in 1514 by Diego Velázquez de Cuéllar (his bones purportedly lie underneath the cathedral), the city of Santiago de Cuba moved to its present site in 1522 on a sharp horseshoe of harbor in the lee of the Sierra Maestra Mountains. Its first mayor was Hernán Cortés – Velázquez' wayward secretary – who departed from the deep yet tranquil bay in 1518 en route to Mexico (see p393).

Installed as the colony's new capital, after the abandonment of Baracoa in 1515, Santiago enjoyed a brief renaissance, as a center for the copper mining industry and a disembarkation point for slaves arriving from West Africa via Hispaniola. But the glory wasn't to last.

In 1556 the Spanish captains-general departed for Habana and in 1607 the capital was transferred permanently to the west. Raided by pirates and reduced at one point to a small village of only several hundred people, embattled Santiago barely survived the ignominy.

The tide turned in 1655 when Spanish settlers arrived from the nearby colony of Jamaica and this influx was augmented further in the 1790s as French plantation owners on the run from a slave revolt in Haiti settled down in the city's Tivoli district. Always one step ahead of the capital in the cultural sphere, Santiago founded the Seminario de San Basilio Magno as an educational establishment in 1722 (six years before the Universidad de Habana) and in 1804 wrested ecclesiastical dominance from the capital by ensuring that the city's top cleric was promoted to the post of archbishop.

Individuality and isolation from Habana soon gave Santiago a noticeably distinct cultural heritage and went a long way in fuelling its insatiable passion for rebellion and revolt. Much of the fighting in both wars of independence took place in the Oriente, and one of the era's most illustrious fighters, the great mulatto general, Antonio Maceo was born in Santiago de Cuba in 1845.

In 1898, just as Cuba seemed about to triumph in its long struggle for independence, the US intervened in the Second War of Independence, landing a flotilla of troops on nearby Daiquiri beach. Subsequently, both of the wars' decisive land and sea battles were fought in and around Santiago. The former was played out on July 1 when a victorious cavalry charge led by Teddy Roosevelt on outlying San Juan Hill sealed a famous victory. The latter ended in a highly one-sided naval battle in Santiago harbor between US and Spanish ships that led to the almost total destruction of the Spanish fleet.

A construction boom characterized the first few years of the new quasi-independent Cuban state, but after three successive US military interventions (the last of which in 1917 saw US troops stationed in the Oriente until 1923), things started to turn sour. Despite its ongoing influence as a cultural and musical powerhouse, Santiago began to earn a slightly less respectable reputation as a center for rebellion and strife and it was here on July 26, 1953, that Fidel Castro and his companions launched an assault on the Moncada Barracks. This was the start of a number of events that changed the course of Cuban history. At his trial in Santiago, Castro made his famous *History Will Absolve Me* speech, which became the basic platform of the Cuban Revolution.

On November 30, 1956, the people of Santiago de Cuba rose up in rebellion against Batista's troops in a futile attempt to distract attention from the landing of Castro's guerrillas on the western shores of Oriente. Although not initially successful, an underground movement led by Frank and Josue País quickly established a secret supply line that ran vital armaments up to the fighters in the Oriente's Sierra Maestra. Despite the murder of the País brothers and many others in 1957–58, the struggle continued unabated, and it was in Santiago de Cuba, on the evening of January 1, 1959, that Fidel Castro first appeared publicly to declare the success of the revolution. All these events have earned Santiago the title 'Hero City of the Republic of Cuba.'

Santiago continued to grow rapidly in the years that followed the revolution as new housing was provided for impoverished workers in outlying suburban districts.

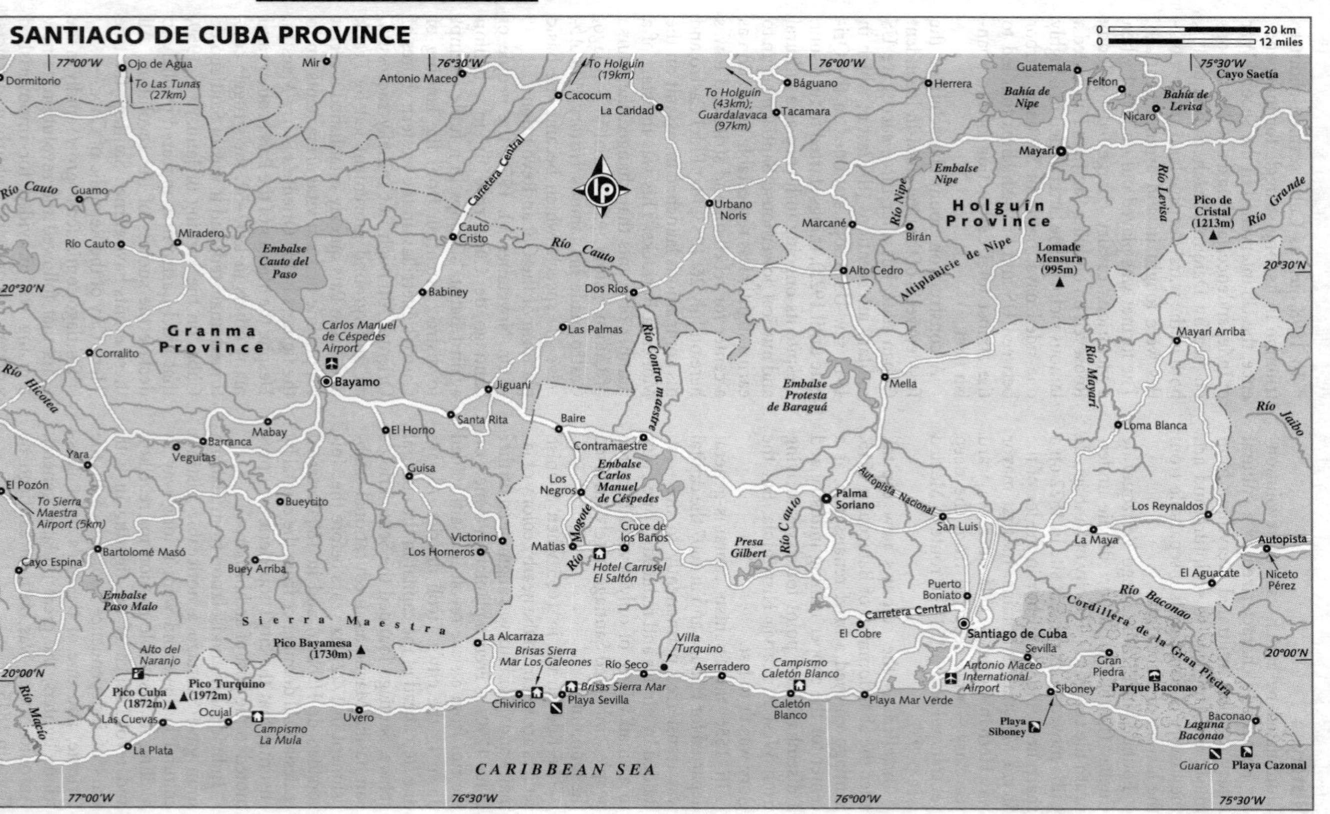
SANTIAGO DE CUBA PROVINCE
0 20 km
0 12 miles
77°00'W
76°30'W
76°00'W
75°30'W
20°30'N
20°00'N
Dormitorio
Ojo de Agua
To Las Tunas (27km)
Mir
Antonio Maceo
To Holguín (19km)
Cacocum
La Caridad
To Holguín (43km); Guardalavaca (97km)
Báguano
Tacamara
Herrera
Guatemala
Bahía de Nipe
Felton
Bahía de Levisa
Nicaro
Cayo Saetía
Mayarí
Embalse Nipe
Río Nipe
Holguín Province
Río Levisa
Pico de Cristal (1213m)
Río Grande
Carretera Central
Río Cauto
Guamo
Urbano Noris
Marcané
Birán
Miradero
Río Cauto
Cauto Cristo
Embalse Cauto del Paso
Río Cauto
Altiplanicie de Nipe
Lomade Mensura (995m)
Alto Cedro
Babiney
Dos Ríos
Granma Province
Carlos Manuel de Céspedes Airport
Las Palmas
Río Contra maestre
Corralito
Bayamo
Mayarí Arriba
Río Mayarí
Río Hicotea
Jiguaní
Embalse Protesta de Baraguá
Mella
Santa Rita
Baire
Mabay
El Horno
Barranca
Contramaestre
Loma Blanca
Río Jaibo
Veguitas
Yara
Guisa
Embalse Carlos Manuel de Céspedes
Los Negros
El Pozón
To Sierra Maestra Airport (5km)
Bueycito
Autopista Nacional
Palma Soriano
Los Reynaldos
Río Mogote
Cruce de los Baños
San Luis
Victorino
Los Horneros
Matías
Presa Gilbert
Río Cauto
La Maya
Autopista
Bartolomé Masó
Cayo Espina
Buey Arriba
Hotel Carrusel El Saltón
El Aguacate
Niceto Pérez
Embalse Paso Malo
Puerto Boniato
Río Baconao
Sierra Maestra
Carretera Central
Cordillera de la Gran Piedra
El Cobre
Santiago de Cuba
Alto del Naranjo
Pico Bayamesa (1730m)
La Alcarraza
Brisas Sierra Mar Los Galeones
Villa Turquino
Río Seco
Aserradero
Campismo Caletón Blanco
Sevilla
Gran Piedra
Antonio Maceo International Airport
Parque Baconao
Pico Cuba (1872m)
Pico Turquino (1972m)
Chivirico
Brisas Sierra Mar
Playa Sevilla
Caletón Blanco
Playa Mar Verde
Siboney
Río Macío
Las Cuevas
Ocujal
Campismo La Mula
Uvero
Playa Siboney
Baconao
Laguna Baconao
La Plata
CARIBBEAN SEA
Guarico
Playa Cazonal

Further progress was made in the early '90s when a construction boom furnished the city with a new theater, a train station and a five-star Meliá hotel. In 1994 Santiago won the prestigious *Manzana de Oro* tourism award presented by the International Confederation of Tourism Journalists and Writers.

## Arts

Santiago de Cuba has a rich cultural history that goes back to the construction of the Catedral de Nuestra Señora de la Asunción in the 1520s and the formation of a church choir. Two hundred and fifty years later, French planters from Haiti brought opera with them, and regular performances were staged at various theaters throughout the city from 1800 onward. The first Santiago philharmonic society was created in 1832, and in 1851 the Teatro de la Reina opened with a series of French operas. In 1871 *La Hija de Jefté,* by Laureano Fuentes Matons, became the first *zarzuela* (operetta) by a Cuban composer to be staged in Cuba.

Aside from this academic musical culture, the Oriente has developed its own distinctive folk culture influenced by the immigration of French-Haitian plantation owners in the early 1800s. This is the original home of *son* (Cuban popular music), the forerunner of salsa, and almost every genre of Cuban popular music, from Afro-Cuban drumming to rumba, is alive and well in Santiago de Cuba.

Two of the country's foremost 19th-century romantic poets, José María Heredia (1803–39) and his cousin José María de Heredia y Giralt (1842–1905), were born here, although both spent most of their adult lives abroad.

# SANTIAGO DE CUBA

**pop 443,926**

Santiago de Cuba is the island's second largest city and a glittering cultural capital in its own right. Anyone with even a passing interest in Cuban literature, music, architecture, politics or ethnology should spend at least a day or two kicking through the myriad of assorted attractions here.

Enlivened by a cosmopolitan mix of Afro-Caribbean culture and situated closer to Haiti and the Dominican Republic than Habana, Santiago's influences have tended to come as much from the east as they have from the west, a factor that has been crucial in shaping the city's distinct individual identity. Nowhere else in Cuba will you find such a colorful combination of people, or such a resounding sense of historical destiny. Diego Velázquez made the city his second capital, Fidel Castro used it to launch his embryonic nationalist revolution, Don Facundo Bacardí based his first ever rum factory here and just about every Cuban music genre from salsa

### HERNÁN CORTÉS

More famous for the conquest of Mexico than for his short-lived Cuban posting, Hernán Cortés first arrived in Baracoa in 1511 as secretary to the island's first governor Diego Velázquez de Cuéllar.

Settling in Santiago where he took up the position of *alcalde* (mayor) with an office on the site of today's Ayuntamiento (city hall), Cortés' lustful ambition quickly got the better of him in a spate of frenzied gold prospecting using the local Indians as slave labor. 'How many of them died in extracting this gold for him; God will have kept a better account than I have' wrote a horror-stricken Bartolomé de Las Casas. Other historians have been less damning in their criticism claiming that the unspeakably cruel fate of the Indians in Cuba (the natives were all but eradicated inside 50 years) actually influenced Cortés in his more careful treatment of the Mexican natives.

Eager to sponsor a voyage west in search of more gold, Cortés lobbied the vacillating Velázquez – his father-in-law – tirelessly for ships and money. Initially reluctant to help, the bumbling governor finally caved in; though at the last minute he indecisively changed his mind and tried to put a stop to the mission. Fatefully, it was too late. Sailing without official sanction in 1518, Cortés docked briefly in Trinidad where he rounded up an eager army of 500 men for the journey west. Stuffing supplies into 11 ships the flotilla left Habana harbor in February 1519, their destination Mexico. The rest, as they say, is history.

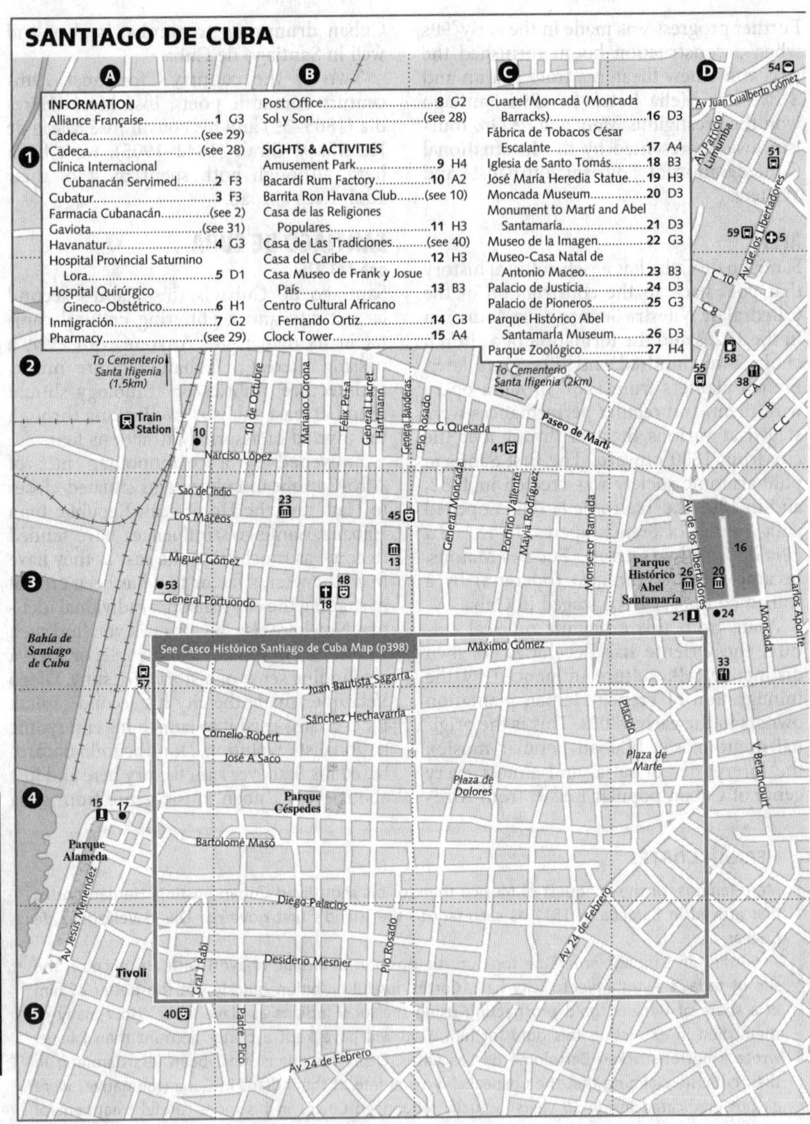




to *son* first emanated from somewhere in these dusty, rhythmic and undeniably sensuous streets. Then there are the local heroes – Antonio Maceo: soldier; José María Heredia: poet; Frank País: revolutionary; Emilio Bacardí: entrepreneur. The list is long; you can pursue their individual legends further in a rich array of local museums.

Setting-wise Santiago could rival any of the world's great urban centers. Caught dramatically between the indomitable Sierra Maestra and the azure Caribbean, the city's *casco histórico* (historical center) retains a time-worn and slightly neglected air that's vaguely reminiscent of Barbados, Salvador in Brazil, or New Orleans.

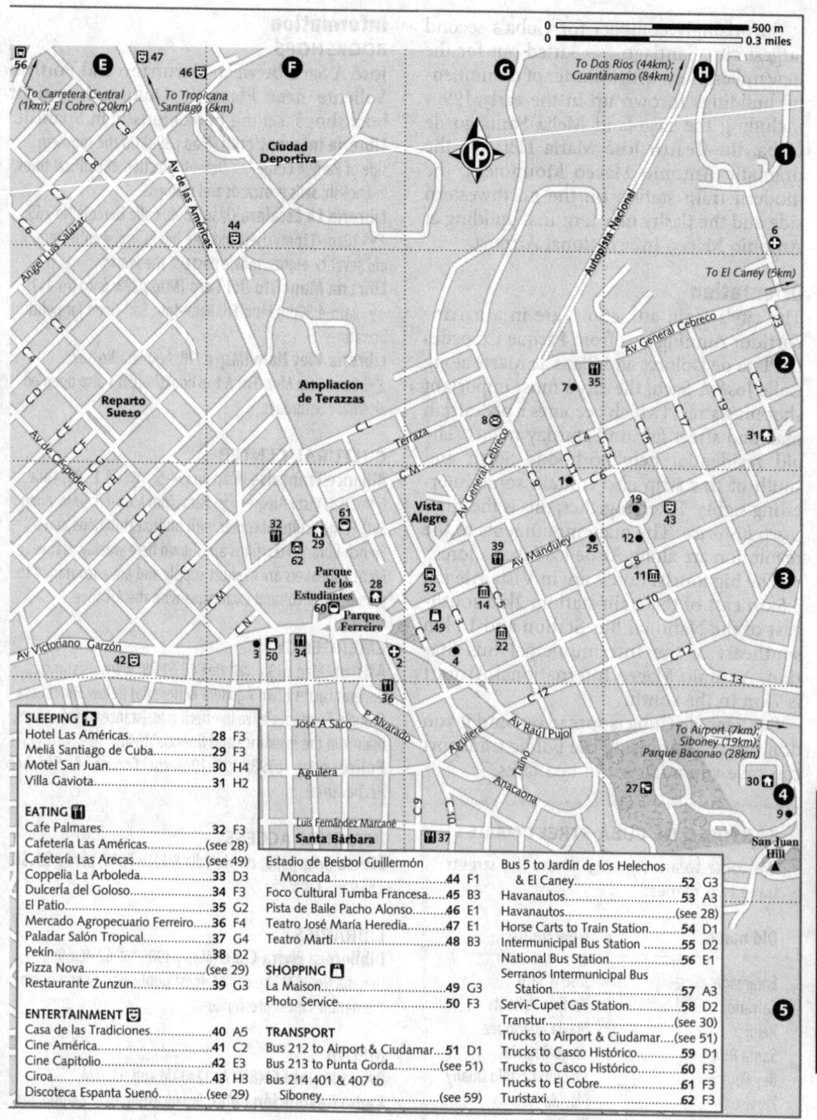




Santiago is also hot, in more ways than one. While the temperature rises up into the thirties out on the street, *Jineteros/as* (both the male and female varieties of touts) go about their illicit business in the shadows with a level of ferocity unmatched elsewhere in Cuba. Then there's the pollution, particularly bad in the central district where cacophonous motorcycles swarm up and down narrow streets better designed for horses or pedestrians. Travelers should beware. While never particularly unsafe, everything in Santiago feels a little madder, more frenetic, a tad more desperate, and visitors should be prepared to adjust their pace accordingly.

Surprisingly compact for Cuba's second largest city, Santiago was kitted out for the new millennium with a cluster of monumental buildings thrown up in the early 1990s including the Legoland Meliá Santiago de Cuba, the Teatro José María Heredia, the dramatic Antonio Maceo Monument, the modern train station on the northwestern side and the flashy new terminal building at Antonio Maceo International Airport.

## Orientation

The city's main attractions are in a narrow corridor running east from Parque Céspedes to Plaza de Dolores and Plaza de Marte along Calle José A Saco, the city's most important shopping street (which becomes a pedestrian mall and street fair on Saturday night). The old residential neighborhoods north and south of this strip also contain some interesting sights. Taken together, this is the city's *casco histórico*. The main monuments to the revolution are along Av de los Libertadores.

The big tourist hotels are in Vista Alegre, 3.5km east of the train station, 2km southeast of the National Bus Station and 1.5km southeast of the Intermunicipal Bus Station. Antonio Maceo International Airport is 7km to the south.

Santiago de Cuba is spread out and if you don't have a car, using the public transport can save you a fair bit in taxi fares.

### SANTIAGO DE CUBA STREET NAMES

Welcome to another city where the streets have two names:

| Old name | New name |
|---|---|
| Enramada | José A Saco |
| Calvario | Porfirio Valiente |
| Reloj | Mayía Rodríguez |
| Santa Rita | Diego Palacios |
| Rey Pelayo | Joaquín Castillo Duany |
| Paraíso | Plácido |
| Carniceria | Pío Rosado |
| San Mateo | Sao del Indio |
| San Félix | Hartmann |
| San Francisco | Sagarra |
| San Gerónimo | Sánchez Hechavarría |
| Santo Tómas | Felix Peña |
| Trinidad | General Portuondo |
| José Miguel Gómez | Habana |



## Information

### BOOKSHOPS

José A Saco between Hartmann and Porfirio Valiente near Plaza de Dolores has eight bookshops, selling books mostly in Spanish.

**Librería Internacional** (Map p398) On the southern side of Parque Céspedes. Decent selection of political titles in English; sells postcards and stamps.

**Librería La Escalera** (Map p398; Calle Heredia No 265; 10am-11pm) Used and rare books, *trova* ephemera, old seventy-eights, movie posters, the works.

**Librería Manolito del Toro** (Map p398; Saco No 411; 8am-4:30pm Mon-Fri, 8am-4pm Sat) Good for political literature.

**Librería Viet Nam** (Map p398; Aguilera No 567; 9am-5pm Mon-Fri) A top bookshop; it's also open on alternate Saturdays.

### CULTURAL CENTER

**Alliance Française** (Map pp394-5; 64 15 03; Calle 6 No 253, Vista Alegre; 9am-7pm Mon-Fri, 9am-noon Sat) French cultural center with photo exhibitions and a French library. Free films are shown here weekly. Native French speakers are in short supply and are encouraged to pursue cross-cultural exchanges with the Alliance.

### EMERGENCY

**Asistur** (Map p398; /fax 68 61 28; www.asistur.cu; General Lacret btwn Aguilera & Heredia) Below Hotel Casa Granda. They specialize in offering assistance to foreigners, mainly in the insurance and financial field.

**Police** (Map p398; 106; cnr Corona & Sánchez Hechavarría)

### INTERNET ACCESS

**Etecsa** (Map p398; cnr Heredia & Félix Peña; per hr CUC$6; 9am-11pm)

### LIBRARIES

**Biblioteca Elvira Cape** (Map p398; 62 46 69; Heredia No 262) The city's largest public library and one of the nation's most prestigious.

### MEDIA

**Radio Mambí CMKW** At 1240AM and 93.7FM.

**Radio Revolución CMKC** Broadcasting over 840AM and 101.4FM.

**Sierra Maestra** Local paper published Saturday.

**Radio Siboney CMDV** Available at 1180AM and 95.1FM.

### MEDICAL SERVICES

**Clínica Internacional Cubanacán Servimed** (Map pp394-5; 64 25 89; cnr Av Raúl Pujol & Calle 10, Vista Alegre; 24hr) Capable staff speak some English. A dentist is also present.

**Farmacia Cubanacán** (Map pp394-5; ☎ 64 25 89; cnr Av Raúl Pujol & Calle 10; 🕑 24hr) Best pharmacy in town, selling products in Convertibles.

**Hospital Provincial Saturnino Lora** (Map pp394-5; ☎ 64 56 51; Av de los Libertadores) With recompression chamber.

**Hospital Quirúrgico Gineco-Obstétrico** (Map pp394-5; ☎ 64 66 49; off Av General Cebreco, Reparto Vista Alegre) Recompression chamber available 8am to 3pm Monday to Friday.

**Pharmacy** (Map pp394-5; 🕑 8am-6pm; Meliá Santiago de Cuba, cnr Av de las Américas & Calle M) In the lobby of the Meliá Santiago de Cuba, it sells products in Convertibles.

#### MONEY

**Banco de Crédito y Comercio** (Map p398; ☎ 62 80 06; Felix Peña No 614)

**Banco Financiero Internacional** (Map p398; ☎ 62 20 73; Felix Peña No 565; 🕑 8am-4pm Mon-Fri)

**Bandec** Saco (Map p398; cnr Saco & Mariano Corona) Gran Lacret (Map p398; ☎ 62 75 81; cnr General Lacret & Aguilera; 🕑 8am-5pm Mon-Fri)

**Cadeca** Aguilera (Map p398; ☎ 68 61 76; Aguilera No 508; 🕑 8:30am-6pm Mon-Sat, 8:30am-noon Sun) Meliá Santiago de Cuba (Map pp394–5; cnr Av de las Américas & Calle M) Hotel Las Américas (Map pp394–5; cnr Av de las Américas & Av General Cebreco)

#### POST

**DHL** (Map p398; ☎ 68 63 23; Aguilera No 310)

**Post office** Aguilera (Map p398; Aguilera No 519); Calle 9 (Map pp394-5; Calle 9, Ampliación de Terazzas) Near Av General Cebreco; telephones are here too.

#### TELEPHONE

**Etecsa** (Map p398; cnr Heredia & Félix Peña; 🕑 24hr)

#### TRAVEL AGENCIES

**Cubatur** Garzón (Map pp394-5; ☎ 65 25 60; fax 68 61 06; Av Garzón No 364 btwn Calles 3 & 4; 🕑 8am-8pm) Heredia (Map p398; Heredia No 701)

### HINTS ON JINETERISMO

Chances are, nine out of 10 of the Cubans who approach you on the streets of Santiago (or most other Cuban cities for that matter) will be *jineteros* or hustlers; out to make a fast buck from your ever-lucrative foreign custom. But to assume that all Santiagueños are so unashamedly opportunistic would be wildly inaccurate.

In common with hustlers the world over, Cuban *jineteros* are best tackled with a mixture of firmness, politeness and patience. Remember that the majority of people in this most accommodating of countries are not *jineteros*. In fact, the average Cuban-on-the-street will view the over-zealous entreaties of their hissing and hassling compatriots with as much irritation as you do.

Here are some helpful tips on how to iron out the rough spots:

- If you need directions, ask a shop worker, a mother, or even a child. Don't wait for the hustlers to find you.
- Helpful phrases include: *no gracias, no necesito nada* (no thanks, I don't need anything); *por favor, no me moleste* (please don't bother me); and *No me ineterés. Tengo habitación/paladar ya* (I'm not interested. I already have a place to stay/eat).
- More aggressive types might have to hear something more direct like *dejame coño,* which is unequivocal in Cuban terms.
- 'Where you from' is the most common opener and you'll hear it everywhere. Develop some conversation-stopping responses like: Iceland, or Marianao (a tough Habana neighborhood).
- The other common opener is 'what's your name?' Women can respond *'casada felizmente'* (happily married) to good effect, but use your imagination.
- If it's really getting to you, consider staying in a more residential neighborhood (eg Vista Alegre in Santiago de Cuba or Playa Miramar in Habana).
- If it's really, really getting to you, consider visiting Matanzas, Remedios, Sancti Spíritus, Holguín or Guantánamo, all refreshingly hustler-free.
- Learn some Spanish so you can talk to real people, not just those who want to get into your wallet or pants.
- Of course, the easiest way to quit being hassled by hustlers is to hook up with one! If you *do* hatch a deal ask them plenty of questions and make sure you get your money's worth.

CASCO HISTÓRICO SANTIAGO DE CUBA
0 200 m
0 0.1 miles
To Cementerio Santa Ifigenia (2km)
Parque Finlay
Plaza de Marte
Plaza de Dolores
Parque Céspedes
Parque Ajedrez
Av Victoriano Garzón
Francisco Pérez Carbo
Gen Serafín Sánchez
Monseñor Barnada
Donato Mármol
Bayamo
José A Saco
Aguilera
Mayía Rodríguez
Porfirio Valiente
Heredia
Bartolomé Masó
Pío Rosado
General Banderas
Hartmann
General Lacret
Félix Peña
Tamayo Fleites
Sánchez Hechavarría
Juan Bautista Sagarra
Cornelio Robert
Diez de Octubre
Padre Pico
Lino Boza
Joaquín Castillo Duany
Mariano Corona
Diego Palacios
Eduardo Yero
Rafael P Salcedo
Desiderio Mesnier
José de Diego
General Jesús Rabí
Av 24 de Febrero
Gen Julio Sanguily
Av Valeriano Hierrezuelo
Commandante Borrero

| INFORMATION | | |
|---|---|---|
| Asistur | (see 40) | |
| Banco de Crédito y Comercio | 1 | B2 |
| Banco Financiero Internacional | 2 | B2 |
| Bandec | 3 | B2 |
| Bandec | 4 | C2 |
| Biblioteca Elvira Cape | 5 | C2 |
| Cadeca | 6 | D2 |
| Cubatur | 7 | C2 |
| DHL | 8 | C2 |
| Etecsa | 9 | B2 |
| Islazul Agencia de Ventas | 10 | C2 |
| Librería Internacional | 11 | C2 |
| Librería la Escalera | 12 | C2 |
| Librería Manolito del Toro | 13 | D2 |
| Librería Viet Nam | 14 | E2 |
| Police | 15 | B1 |
| Post Office | 16 | E2 |
| Reservaciones de Campismo | 17 | B1 |

| SIGHTS & ACTIVITIES | | |
|---|---|---|
| Antiguo Carcel Provincial | 18 | B2 |
| Ayuntamiento | 19 | C2 |
| Balcón de Velázquez | 20 | B3 |
| Carnival Mural | 21 | A4 |
| Casa de Diego Velázquez | 22 | B2 |
| Casa de la Cultura Miguel Matamoros | 23 | C2 |
| Casa de la Trova | (see 58) | |
| Casa del Estudiante | (see 59) | |
| Casa Natal de José María de Heredia | 24 | C2 |
| Catedral de Nuestra Señora de la Asunción | 25 | B2 |
| Gobierno Provincial | 26 | C2 |
| House Where Castro Lived | 27 | A3 |
| Iglesia de Nuestra Señora de los Dolores | 28 | D2 |
| Iglesia de Nuestra Señora del Carmen | 29 | B2 |
| Iglesia de San Francisco | 30 | B1 |
| Municipal Market | (see 44) | |
| Museo Arquidiocesano | (see 25) | |
| Museo de Ambiente Histórico Cubano | (see 22) | |
| Museo de la Lucha Clandestina | 31 | A3 |
| Museo del Carnaval | 32 | C2 |
| Museo del Ron | 33 | C3 |
| Museo Municipal Emilio Bacardí Moreau | 34 | C2 |
| Museo Tomás Romay | 35 | E2 |
| Padre Pico Steps | 36 | A3 |
| Unión Nacional de Escritores y Artistas de Cuba (Uneac) | 37 | C2 |

| SLEEPING | | |
|---|---|---|
| Gran Hotel Escuela | 38 | C2 |
| Hostal San Basilio | 39 | C3 |
| Hotel Casa Granda | 40 | C2 |
| Hotel Libertad | 41 | F2 |

| EATING | | |
|---|---|---|
| Cafe La Isabelica | 42 | D2 |
| Cafetería Las Enramadas | 43 | D2 |
| Hotel Casa Granda | (see 40) | |
| Municipal Market | 44 | A2 |
| Paladar Las Gallegas | 45 | C3 |
| Panadería Doña Neli | 46 | F2 |
| Pizzas & Cajitas | 47 | C3 |
| Restaurante Don Antonio | (see 48) | |
| Restaurante La Perla del Dragón | (see 48) | |
| Restaurante Teresina | 48 | D2 |
| Santiago 1900 | 49 | C3 |
| Supermercado Plaza de Marte | 50 | F1 |
| Taberna de Dolores | 51 | D2 |

| DRINKING | | |
|---|---|---|
| Bar La Fontana | 52 | C2 |
| Claqueta Bar | 53 | B3 |
| Kon Tiki Club | (see 54) | |
| Marylin | 54 | C2 |
| Santiago 1900 | (see 49) | |

| ENTERTAINMENT | | |
|---|---|---|
| Ballet Folklórico Cutumba | 55 | B2 |
| Cartelera Cultural Office | 56 | B3 |
| Casa de la Cultura Miguel Matamoros | (see 23) | |
| Casa de la Música | 57 | B2 |
| Casa de la Trova | 58 | C2 |
| Casa del Estudiante | 59 | C2 |
| Cine Rialto | 60 | B3 |
| Club El Iris | 61 | F2 |
| Conjunto Folklórico de Oriente | 62 | C1 |
| Coro Madrigalista | 63 | C2 |
| Foco Cultural El Tivolí | 64 | A4 |
| Gimnasio Cultura Física | 65 | C1 |
| Orfeón Santiago | 66 | B2 |
| Patio ARTex | (see 71) | |
| Patio Los Dos Abuelos | 67 | F2 |
| Sala de Conciertos Dolores | (see 28) | |
| Sala Teatro El Mambí | 68 | C3 |

| SHOPPING | | |
|---|---|---|
| ARTex | (see 40) | |
| ARTex | (see 58) | |
| Discoteca Egrem | 69 | C2 |
| Galería de Arte de Oriente | 70 | C2 |
| Galería Santiago | (see 25) | |
| Patio ARTex | 71 | D2 |
| Photo Service | 72 | D2 |
| Photo Service | 73 | C3 |

| TRANSPORT | | |
|---|---|---|
| AeroCaribbean | 74 | C3 |
| Bus No 212 to Airport & Ciudamar | 75 | B4 |
| Bus No 5 to Caney | 76 | F1 |
| Camiones to Hospital Provincial | 77 | B3 |
| Camiones to Vista Alegre | 78 | C2 |
| Centro Único de Reservaciones | 79 | E2 |
| Cubacar | (see 7) | |
| Cubana | 80 | C2 |
| Guarded Parking | (see 40) | |
| Transtur | (see 40) | |

**Gaviota** (Map pp394-5; ☎ 68 71 35; Villa Gaviota, Manduley No 502, Vista Alegre) You can arrange visits to Guantánamo naval base here.

**Havanatur** (Map pp394-5; ☎ 68 72 80; Calle 8 No 54 btwn Calles 1 & 3, Vista Alegre; 8am-noon & 1-5pm Mon-Fri, 8am-noon Sat) Good for transfers.

**Islazul Agencia de Ventas** (Map p398; ☎ 62 31 24; Aguilera No 308 btwn General Lacret & Hartmann; 9am-noon & 2-4pm Mon-Fri)

**Oficina Reservaciones de Campismo** (Map p398; ☎ 62 90 00; Cornelio Robert No 163; 8:30am-noon & 1-4:30pm Mon-Fri, 8am-1pm Sat)

**Sol y Son** (Map pp394-5; ☎ 68 72 30; Hotel Las Américas, cnr Avs Las Américas & General Cebreco) Cheap hotel reservations.

## Dangers & Annoyances

The historical center of Santiago de Cuba is rife with *jineteros,* all working their particular angle. Solo female travelers will feel it especially, as one guy after another fishes for conversation, trinkets, beer or *besitos* (little kisses). See p397 for some ideas on how to shake that money-with-legs feeling.

Santiago's traffic is second to Habana's in its environmental fall-out. Making things worse are the motorcyclists bobbing and weaving for position, becoming a real hazard at Santiago de Cuba's many rotaries. Narrow, nonexistent sidewalks and crowded streets can be a pain for pedestrians.

## Sights

### CASCO HISTÓRICO

#### Parque Céspedes & Around

Most visits begin on **Parque Céspedes** (Map p398), where a bronze bust memorializes Carlos Manuel de Céspedes, the man who issued *El Grito de Yara* declaring Cuban independence in 1868. In daylight it's a hot and glaring square, but in the evenings it's cool, with music from the nearby Hotel Casa Granda drifting across the park. Some of Santiago de Cuba's most impressive buildings ring this typically tropical space. The **Casa de la Cultura Miguel Matamoros** (Map p398; General Lacret 651), on the eastern side of the square, is the former San Carlos Club, a social center for wealthy residents until the revolution. The neoclassical **Ayuntamiento** (Map p398; cnr General Lacret & Aguilera), on the northern side of the square, was erected in the 1950s using a design from 1783 and was once the site of Hernán Cortés' mayoral office. Fidel Castro appeared on the balcony of the present building on the night of January 2, 1959, trumpeting the revolution's triumph.

In the park's northwestern corner lies the **Casa de Diego Velázquez** (Map p398; Felix Peña No 602). Dating from 1522, this is the oldest house still standing in Cuba. Restored in the late 1960s, the Andalusian-style facade (you'll know it by its enclosed balcony with the fine, Moorish-style woodwork) was restored in the late 1960s, and opened in 1970 as the **Museo de Ambiente Histórico Cubano** (Map p398; ☎ 65 26 52; unguided/guided CUC$2/5; ⏲ 9am-1pm & 2-4:45pm Mon-Thu, 2-4:45pm Fri, 9am-9pm Sat & Sun). The ground floor was originally a trading-house and gold foundry, while the upstairs was the personal residence of Velázquez himself. Today, rooms display period furnishings and decoration from the 16th to 19th centuries. Visitors are also taken through an adjacent neoclassical house dating from the 19th century.

You can't miss the imposing, five-nave **Catedral de Nuestra Señora de la Asunción** (Map p398; ⏲ Mass 6:30pm Mon & Wed-Fri, 5pm Sat, 9am & 6:30pm Sun) on the southern side of the park. This cathedral is only the latest in a series of churches on this spot that have been ravaged by pirates, earthquakes and architects. Cuba's first cathedral was built here in the 1520s, originally positioned with its facade facing the bay. The present cathedral with its coffered ceiling, dome and graceful archangel was completed in 1922, while the choir stalls date from 1910. It's believed that Diego Velázquez is buried beneath the cathedral, though this has never been proven and there's no marker. Unfortunately the cathedral is usually closed outside of mass hours. The **Museo Arquidiocesano** (Map p398; ☎ 62 21 43; ⏲ 9am-5pm Mon-Fri, 9am-2pm Sat, 9am-noon Sun), on the southern side of the cathedral through an independent doorway, houses a collection of furniture, liturgical objects and paintings including the *Ecce Homo,* believed to be Cuba's oldest painting. Behind the cathedral and two blocks downhill from the park is the **Balcón de Velázquez** (Map p398; cnr Bartolomé Masó & Mariano Corona), the site of an old Spanish fort with lovely harbor views.

Other interesting nearby churches include **Iglesia de Nuestra Señora del Carmen** (Map p398; Félix Peña No 505), an 18th-century hall church that is the final resting place of Christmas-carol composer Esteban Salas (1725–1803), *maestro de capilla* (choir master) of Santiago de Cuba's cathedral from 1764 until his death; and the 18th-century three-nave **Iglesia de San Francisco** (Map p398; Juan Bautista Sagarra No 121).

On Heredia, east of the Hotel Casa Granda, is a strip of culturally significant buildings, including the **Casa del Estudiante** (Map p398; ☎ 62 78 04; Heredia No 204) and the **Casa de la Trova** (Map p398; ☎ 65 26 89; Heredia No 208), one-time home of composer Rafael Salcedo (1844–1917). In the next block is national monument **Casa Natal de José María de Heredia** (Map p398; Heredia No 260; without/with guide CUC$1/2; ⏲ 9am-6pm Tue-Sat, 9am-9pm Sun), containing a small museum illustrating the life of the romantic poet born here on December 31, 1803. Heredia is known for his lyrical poetry, most notably *Ode to Niagara* (inscribed on the wall outside) and other romantic poems extolling the natural beauty of countries such as – er – Canada. As an independence advocate, Heredia was forced into exile in the US and Mexico, where he died in 1839.

Nearby on Heredia is the **Unión Nacional de Escritores y Artistas de Cuba** (Uneac; Map p398; Heredia No 266). The colorful **Museo del Carnaval** (Map p398; ☎ 62 69 55; Heredia No 303; admission CUC$1; ⏲ 9am-5pm Tue-Sun) displays the history of Santiago's carnival tradition, the oldest in Cuba. Drop in for the talented folkloric dance group performing in the patio (admission CUC$1) at 4pm Tuesday to Saturday and 11am on Sunday, provided a small audience is present. One block south and a bit west of here is the fun and informative **Museo del Ron** (Map p398; Bartolomé Masó 358; admission CUC$2; ⏲ 9am-5pm Mon-Sat), outlining the history of Cuban rum; entrance includes a taster of *añejo* (aged rum).

Pío Rosado, the narrow alley running alongside the Museo del Carnaval, leads to the fabulous neoclassical facade of the

**Museo Municipal Emilio Bacardí Moreau** (Map p398; ☎ 62 84 02; admission CUC$2; 🕑 10am-6pm). This is one of Cuba's oldest functioning museums, founded in 1899 by the famous rum distiller Emilio Bacardí y Moreau (1844–1922). Downstairs are exhibits relating to the 19th-century independence struggles (including an interesting weapons collection), upstairs are European and Cuban paintings. There are a dozen paintings by the Tejada brothers, including *La confronta de billetes* by José Joaquín Tejada Revilla (1867–1943), a typical work of the Spanish *costumbrismo* school, which sought to portray the customs and life of the common people. Dating from the 1920s, the **Gobierno Provincial** (Poder Popular; Map p398; cnr Pío Rosado & Aguilera), opposite the Museo Bacardí, is the seat of the provincial assembly.

If you're on a magical history tour, be sure to visit the 1906 **Antiguo Carcel Provincial** (Map p398; Aguilera No 131), two blocks west of Parque Céspedes. Fidel Castro and other rebels were incarcerated here immediately after the 1953 Moncada attack. A half-block west on Aguilera is the **municipal market** (Map p398), and to the south are the picturesque **Padre Pico steps** (Map p398) – almost 100 years old and still hosting rousing games of dominoes – leading to the Tivolí neighborhood.

Up the slope to the right at the top of the Padre Pico steps is the place where revolutionaries attacked a police station on November 30, 1956 to divert attention from the arrival of the tardy yacht *Granma,* carrying the M-26-7 (Castro's revolutionary organization) guerrillas. The colonial-style station now houses the **Museo de la Lucha Clandestina** (Map p398; ☎ 62 46 89; admission CUC$1; General Jesús Rabí No 1; 🕑 9am-5pm Tue-Sun), detailing the underground struggle against Batista. The view from the balcony is excellent. Across the street is the **house** (Map p398; General J Rabí No 6) where Fidel Castro lived from 1931 to 1933 while a student in Santiago de Cuba. On the next corner is a series of **carnival murals** (Map p398; cnr Rabí & Rafael Salcedo) facing a small park.

#### Plaza de Dolores

East of Parque Céspedes is the pleasant and shady **Plaza de Dolores** (Map p398; cnr Aguilera & Porfirio Valiente), a former marketplace now dominated by the 18th-century **Iglesia de Nuestra Señora de los Dolores** (Map p398). After a fire in the 1970s, the church was rebuilt as a concert hall (Sala de Conciertos Dolores, p414). Many restaurants and cafés flank this square. It's also Santiago's most popular gay cruising spot.

#### Plaza de Marte

Three busy blocks east of Plaza de Dolores is this 19th-century Spanish parade ground where prisoners were executed by firing squad during the colonial era. Today, Plaza de Marte is the site of Santiago de Cuba's *esquina caliente* (literally 'hot corner') where baseball fans debate the sport with wild abandon among monuments to various heroes of Cuban independence. Baseball is the most democratic space we have, Cubans will tell you, and it shows here. A block west is the **Museo Tomás Romay** (Map p398; ☎ 65 35 39; cnr Jose A Saco & Monseñor Barnada; admission CUC$1; 🕑 8:30am-5:30pm Tue-Fri, 9am-2pm Sat). This is the city's natural sciences museum, collecting natural history and archaeology artifacts, with some modern art thrown in.

### SANTIAGO DE CUBA

#### Tivolí

Downhill from the Padre Pico steps (left) on the edge of the *casco histórico* is the **Casa de Las Tradiciones** (Map pp394-5; General J Rabí No 154) with a free art gallery and a bar; at night some of Santiago's best *trova* happens here. One block west via José de Diego, the street just before the Casa de Las Tradiciones, you'll get a superb **viewpoint** (Map p398) over Santiago Bay.

Rounding the next corner north of this viewpoint, Desiderio Mesnier descends to **Parque Alameda** (Map pp394–5), a popular bayside promenade that opened in 1840 and was redesigned in 1893. Opposite the old **clock tower** (Map pp394–5) and *aduana* (customs house) at the north end of Parque Alameda is the **Fábrica de Tobacos César Escalante** (Map pp394-5; ☎ 62 23 66; Av Jesús Menéndez No 703; admission CUC$5; 🕑 9-11am & 1-3pm), a working cigar factory open for visits. The factory shop sells the finished product.

#### North of Casco Histórico

North of the historic center, Santiago de Cuba turns residential. Even bustling Felix Peña quietens down as you come upon the 18th-century bell tower of **Iglesia de Santo Tomás** (Map pp394-5; Félix Peña No 308), five blocks north of Parque Céspedes.

Two long blocks northwest of the church is the important **Museo-Casa Natal de Antonio Maceo** (Map pp394-5; ☎ 62 37 50; Los Maceos No 207; admission CUC$1; 9am-5pm Mon-Sat). The famous general who fought in both wars of independence was born in this house on June 14, 1845. In his 1878 *Protest of Baraguá*, Maceo rejected any compromise with the colonial authorities and went into exile after further combat. During the 1895 war he was second in command, after Máximo Gómez, and died fighting in western Cuba in 1896. This simple museum exhibits highlights of Maceo's life, including the tattered flag flown in battle.

Another home-turned-museum is the **Casa Museo de Frank y Josue País** (Map pp394-5; General Banderas No 226; admission CUC$1; 9am-5pm Mon-Sat), about five blocks southeast. Integral to the success of the revolution, the young País brothers organized the underground section of the M-26-7 in Santiago de Cuba until Frank's murder by the police on July 30, 1957. The exhibits tell the story.

You can behold a different side of Cuban history at the original **Bacardí Rum Factory** (Fábrica de Ron; Map pp394-5; Av Jesús Menéndez), opposite the train station near Narciso López, on the northwestern side of town. The factory was founded by the Bacardí family in 1838, but after the revolution the company moved to Puerto Rico taking the Bacardí patent with them (they're now suing the Cuban government under the US extraterritorial Helms-Burton law). The Santiago de Cuba product was renamed Ron Caney. Also produced here are quality rums such as Matusalem, Ron Santiago and Ron Varadero. The factory consists of three sections: the production room, the aging storehouse (with 42,000 barrels of rum) and the bottling section. In total, the distillery produces 9 million liters a year, 70% of it exported. The **Barrita Ron Havana Club** (Map pp394-5; Av Jesús Menéndez; 9am-6pm), a tourist bar attached to the factory, offers rum sales and tastings. There are no factory tours.

### Cuartel Moncada

The **Parque Histórico Abel Santamaría** (Map pp394-5; cnr General Portuondo & Av de los Libertadores) is the site of the former Saturnino Lora Civil Hospital. On July 26, 1953, a group of revolutionaries (including female fighters Haydee Santamaría and Melba Hernández) led by second-in-command Abel Santamaría occupied this hospital during the attack on the adjacent Moncada Barracks. Most of those involved were later killed (and some tortured). On October 16, 1953, Fidel Castro was tried in the Escuela de Enfermeras for leading the Moncada attack; he made his famous *History Will Absolve Me* speech. The **Parque Histórico Abel Santamaría museum** (Map pp394-5; admission CUC$1; 9am-4:30pm Mon-Fri) opened in 1976 with a photo exhibit on socioeconomic conditions in Cuba during the 1950s.

The **Cuartel Moncada** (Moncada Barracks, Map pp394–5), with a trapezoid footprint from General Portuondo to Paseo de Martí and Av de los Libertadores to Av Moncada, is named for Guillermón Moncada, a prisoner here in 1874 who later fought for independence from Spain during the 'Little War' of 1879. The first barracks on this site were constructed by the Spanish in 1859, and in 1938 the present buildings were completed. On the morning of July 26, 1953, more than 100 revolutionaries led by Fidel Castro attacked Batista's troops here at what was at the time Cuba's second most important military garrison. The revolutionaries had hoped the assault would spark a general uprising throughout Cuba, but things went awry when the driver took a wrong turn and one of the soldiers noticed that the rebels – who were disguised in military uniforms – were still wearing their ordinary work shoes. The **monument** (Map pp394-5; General Portuondo) depicting Martí and Abel Santamaría marks the spot from where the first shots were fired.

In 1960, after the triumph of the revolution, these barracks, like all barracks in Cuba, were converted into a school called Cuidad Escolar 26 de Julio, and in 1967 a **museum** (Map pp394-5; ☎ 62 01 57; admission CUC$2, guide/camera/video CUC$1/1/5; 9am-5pm Mon-Sat, 9am-1pm Sun) was installed near gate No 3, where the main attack took place. Bastista's soldiers cemented over the original bullet holes from the attack so the Castro government remade them (this time without guns) after the revolution as a poignant reminder. The museum outlines the history of Cuba from the Spanish conquest to the present, with heavy emphasis on the revolution, and it's one of Cuba's best.

The **Palacio de Justicia** (Map pp394-5; Av de los Libertadores & General Protuondo) also figured prominently in the assault on Moncada, as fighters led by Raúl Castro provided covering fire from the rooftop. Most Moncada defendants were tried here in September 1953.

### Vista Alegre

Broad, dappled avenues lined with bowed trees mark the entrance to Santiago de Cuba's old upper-class neighborhood Vista Alegre, on the east side of town. From near Hotel Las Américas, Av Manduley runs east through Vista Alegre, past a number of stately neocolonial mansions, some of which were converted into schools, clinics, cultural centers, government offices and restaurants after the former owners went into exile in the US. The side streets here are peppered with beautiful casas particulares (p408). The **Centro Cultural Africano Fernando Ortiz** (Map pp394-5; Av Manduley No 106; admission free; 9am-5pm Mon-Fri) contains African artifacts, handicrafts and fine art collected by Cuba's most important ethnologist. It's also open on alternate Saturdays. A block away is the **Museo de Imagen** (Map pp394-5; ☎ 64 22 34; Calle 8 No 106; admission CUC$1; 9am-5pm Mon-Sat) which is CUC$1 well spent. From Kodak to Korda, with little CIA spy cameras and lots of historical and contemporary photos, the history of Cuban photography is housed here.

Nearby, there's a large eclectic palace now used as the **Palacio de Píoneros** (Map pp394-5; cnr Av Manduley & Calle 11). Parked in a corner patch of grass, there's an old MiG fighter plane on which the younger pioneers play. The traffic circle at the corner of Av Manduley and Calle 13 contains an impressive marble **statue** (Map pp394–5) of poet José María de Heredia.

Around the corner is the **Casa del Caribe** (Map pp394-5; ☎ 64 22 85; fax 64 23 87; Calle 13 No 154; admission free; 9am-5pm Mon-Fri), founded in 1982 to study Caribbean life. It organizes the Festival del Caribe, Fiesta del Fuego every July (see p408) and is also open on concert nights.

A block south is the affiliated **Casa de las Religiones Populares** (Map pp394-5; Calle 13 No 206; admission without/with guide CUC$1/2; 9am-6pm Mon-Sat), with a large, bright collection of all things Santería.

Santiago de Cuba's **Parque Zoológico** (Map pp394-5; Av Raúl Pujol; admission CUC$1; 10am-5pm Tue-Sun) is 1km east of Hotel Santiago de Cuba.

Next to the zoo entrance is a fenced-in expanse surrounded by cannons. On this spot, Santiago de Cuba's Spanish garrison surrendered two weeks after the battle of San Juan Hill in 1898. Continue through the grounds of the adjacent Motel San Juan to **San Juan Hill** (Map pp394–5) proper, where US, Cuban and Spanish troops faced off on July 1, 1898. Some of the original cannons and trenches can still be seen, and there are numerous monuments (admission free), including a bronze figure of a 'Rough Rider' in the center of the park. There's a whopping view of La Gran Piedra from this hill. A large **amusement park** (Map pp394–5) is down the stairway from the Ferris wheel on San Juan Hill. Built in 1985 by Japanese investors, most of the rides are dormant, but the shaded benches are alluring.

### Cementerio Santa Ifigenia

A visit to **Cementerio Santa Ifigenia** (Map p404; Av Crombet; admission CUC$1, camera CUC$1; 8am-6pm) is a stroll through history. The cemetery was created in 1868 to accommodate the victims of the war of independence and a simultaneous yellow-fever outbreak. Among the 8000 tombs here are the graves of many great Cuban historical figures, including national hero, José Martí (1853–95). Erected in 1951, the hexagonal Martí mausoleum is flanked by muses and has a side dedicated to each of Cuba's former six provinces. There's an impressive changing of the honor guard every half hour here.

The mausoleum of those who died during the 1953 attack on the Moncada Barracks is nearby, as is the grave of Tomás Estrada Palma (1835–1908), Cuba's first president. To the right of the main entrance is Emilio Bacardí y Moreau (1844–1922), the son of Facundo Bacardí, founder of the famous rum distillery. María Grajales, the widow of independence hero Antonio Maceo, and Mariana Grajales, Maceo's mother, are to the right of the main avenue. Eleven of the 31 generals of the independence struggles are buried in this cemetery, marked by a tower nearby. Across the avenue again is a monument (1906) to the Spanish soldiers who died in the battles of San Juan Hill and Caney. The father of Cuban independence, Carlos Manuel de Céspedes (1819–74), is further along on the left.

The tombs of revolutionaries Frank and Josue País are in the middle of the cemetery back from the Martí mausoleum. Like all persons buried here who died during the struggle against Batista, the País brothers' graves are marked by two flags: the black, white, and red flag of Fidel's M-26-7, and the Cuban flag. The cemetery's newest addition is international celebrity and local musical rake, Compay Segundo, of *Buena Vista Social Club* fame who was laid to rest here in 2003.

Horse carts go Av Jesús Menéndez, from Parque Alameda to Parque Barca de Oro via Cementerio Santa Ifigenia (one peso).

## AROUND SANTIAGO DE CUBA

### Castillo de San Pedro del Morro

A Unesco World Heritage site since 1997, the **Castillo de San Pedro del Morro** (Map p404; ☎ 69 15 69; admission CUC$4, camera CUC$1; 🕑 9am-5pm Mon-Fri, 8am-4pm Sat & Sun) stands dramatically on a 60m-high promontory on the eastern side of the harbor entrance, 10km southwest of town via Carretera del Morro (which passes the airport access road). El Morro was designed in 1587 by the Italian military engineer Giovanni Bautista Antonelli to protect the town from pirates, but building didn't actually start until 1633 (it was finished in 1693). El Morro's massive batteries, bastions, magazines and walls are considered the best-preserved 17th-century Spanish military complex in the Caribbean. Inside the castle is a **museum of piracy** plus another room given over to the US-Spanish naval battle that took place in the

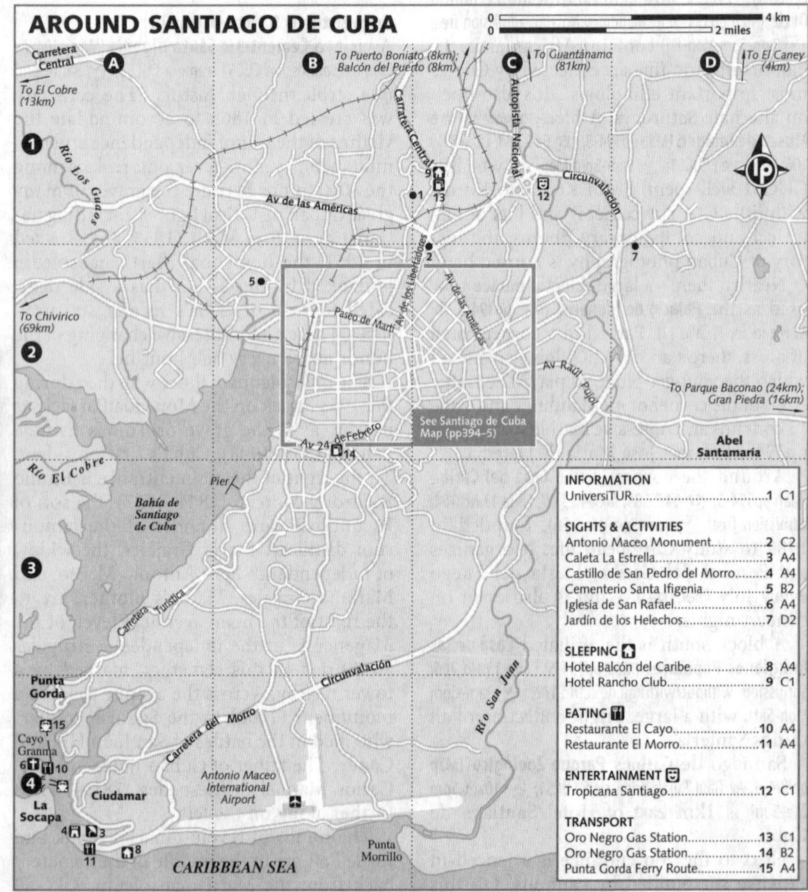

bay in 1898. The stupendous views from here take in the western ribbon of coast backed by the Sierra Maestra.

From El Morro you also get a good look at the hamlets of La Socapa and Cayo Granma across the bay, both accessible by ferry from Punta Gorda or Ciudamar. In **La Socapa** you can hike uphill to the ruins of an old Spanish battery where five cannons, designed to create crossfire with the castle, still stand guard. The only shooting nowadays is by photographers taking in the excellent castle views; for some private beach time, you can explore west along the deserted coast. **Cayo Granma** is a little fantasy island of red-roofed dwellings tucked in a crook of the Bahía de Santiago de Cuba. A short uphill hike to its highest point brings you to the **Iglesia de San Rafael**. Alternatively, you can circumvent the island in 15 minutes.

To get to El Morro from the city center, take bus 212 to Ciudamar on the Carretera Turística and wend your way south along the coast, following the road up to the castle. A more scenic option is to cut across the sandy beach at **Caleta La Estrella** and connect with a broad trail on the opposite hillside. It's a 20-minute, steepish walk with a dicey bridge crossing and wall scaling once you leave the beach. Buses (20 centavos) and trucks (two pesos) to Ciudamar leave regularly from Av de los Libertadores (Map pp394–5), opposite the Hospital Maternidad. This bus also stops on Felix Peña (Map p398), five blocks south of Parque Céspedes, where it will be nearly impossible to squeeze on. Public transport thins considerably after 5pm, so go early. A round-trip by taxi from Parque Céspedes to El Morro with a 30-minute wait will cost in the vicinity of CUC$12.

Theoretically ferries travel a fixed route from Punta Gorda to Cayo Granma (CUC$3, hourly) via Ciudamar and La Socapa, but the Ciudamar leg is sometimes chopped off, in which case you can cross the bay from Punta Gorda. (Bus 213 from Santiago de Cuba terminates here. You can catch it at the same stop on Av de los Libertadores; Map pp394–5).

### Jardín de los Helechos

Just minutes from downtown Santiago de Cuba, the lush, peaceful **Jardín de los Helechos** (Map p404; ☎ 64 83 35; Carretera de El Caney No 129; admission CUC$1; 🕘 9am-5pm Mon-Fri) is a wonderland of 350 types of ferns, 90 types of orchids and lots of tender loving care. The entrance fee gets you a detailed tour (in Spanish) by one of the Centro Oriental de Bioversidad y Ecosistemas staff working on this project. Even in May there will be a dozen types of orchids in psychedelic bloom (best time for orchids is November to January) and the center of the garden has a dense copse-cum-sanctuary dotted with benches. There are unique, handmade artworks and cards on sale.

The garden is about 2km from Santiago de Cuba on the road to El Caney. Bus 5 (20 centavos) leaves from Plaza de Marte (Map p398) in central Santiago, or Calle 3 in Vista Alegre (Map pp394–5) or you can hire a taxi.

### Puerto Boniato

For a sweeping panorama of the Santiago de Cuba basin and a bird's-eye view of the provincial penitentiary, you can't beat Puerto Boniato. It's on the ridge that separates the Santiago de Cuba basin from the province's Valle Central. To get there, go through the underpass near the Oro Negro gas station on the Carretera Central at the northern edge of Santiago de Cuba, and wind around and up for 8km. Over the pass, this road continues on to the Autopista Nacional and Dos Caminos.

## Walking Tour

With a song on your lips and a salsa in your step, a short walking tour of Santiago's *casco histórico* is an obligatory rite of passage for first-time visitors keen to uncover the steamy tropical sensations that make this city tick.

Start where the governor did, surveying the sweeping mountains and sparkling bay from the balmy **Balcón de Velázquez** (**1**; p400), site of an ancient fort. Head east next, avoiding the angry roar of the motorbikes that swarm like wasps in the streets around until you resurface in **Parque Céspedes** (**3**; p399), Santiago's pulsating heart with its resident *jineteras* and craggy-faced old men in Panama hats who strum their way through old Carlos Puebla favorites with the exuberance of 18-year-olds. The **Casa de Diego Velázquez** (**2**; p400), with its Moorish fringes and intricate wooden arcades, is believed to be

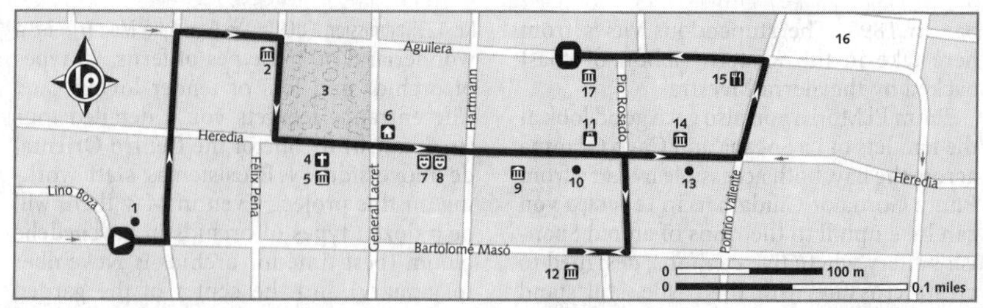


**WALK FACTS**
**Start** Balcón de Velázquez
**Finish** Museo Municipal Emilio Bacardí Moreau
**Distance** 800m
**Duration** Two hours

the oldest house still standing in Cuba and it contrasts impressively with the mighty, mustard facade of the **Catedral de Nuestra Señora de la Asunción** (**4**; p400) over to stage right. This building has been ransacked, burned, rocked by earthquakes and rebuilt, remodeled and restored and ransacked again. Statues of Christopher Columbus and Fray Bartolomé de las Casas flank the entrance in ironic juxtaposition. Supposing you're into religious art, the **Museo Arquidiocesano** (**5**; p400) – say that three times fast! – is somewhere out back.

If you're tired already you can step out onto the lazy terrace bar at the **Hotel Casa Granda** (**6**; p410) on the southeastern corner of the park, for mojitos (rum cocktails) or Montecristo cigars, or both. Graham Greene came here in the 1950s on a clandestine mission to interview Fidel Castro. The interview never came off, but he managed instead to smuggle a suitcase of clothes up to the rebels in the mountains.

Follow the music as you exit past the paint-peeled **Casa del Estudiante** (**7**; p400) and onto the infamous **Casa de la Trova** (**8**; p400), where come 10pm everything starts to get a shade more *caliente* (hot) with people winking at you lewdly from the overcrowded upstairs balcony.

Dragging yourself upstream on Heredia, you'll pass street stalls, cigar peddlers, a guy dragging a double bass, countless motorbikes. That yellowy house on the right with the poem emblazoned on the wall is **Casa Natal de José María de Heredia** (**9**; p400), birthplace of one of Cuba's greatest poets. You might find a living scribe in **Uneac** (**10**; p400), the famous national writer's union a few doors down, or plenty more dead legends offered up in print in funky **Librería La Escalera** (**11**; p396) a bookshop across the street. You can break loose at the corner of Pío Rosado and head to the south in search of the **Museo del Ron** (**12**; p97) until temptation gets the better of you and you drift off in the direction of Tivoli or Santa Barbara or Reparto Sueño. Stay on the safer path and you'll stumble upon **Patio ARTex** (**13**; p412) where boleros (Cuban musical ballads) are de rigueur and tourists browse through the CDs. Cross the street next (mind that motorbike) and stick your nose into the **Museo del Carnaval** (**14**; p400), which aims to demonstrate how Santiago de Cuba lets loose when it lets its hair down (more than usual) every July in the best carnival between here and – oh – anywhere.

At the corner of Porfirio Valiente, turn right and see how far 20 centavo gets you in the atmospherically austere **Cafe La Isabelica** (**15**; p411). It's amazing how tranquil **Plaza de Dolores** (**16**; p401) can be considering the ongoing motorcycle mania. Maybe it's something they put in the ice cream. Grab one and find out. There are benches to relax on underneath the trees while you weigh up if you've still got enough energy to check out the **Museo Municipal Emilio Bacardí Moreau** (**17**; p401), Santiago's and Cuba's oldest functioning museum.

## Courses

Opportunities for courses abound in Santiago; anything from art and music, to literature and architecture. You can either arrange things beforehand, or jump on the bandwagon when you arrive. Following are some useful pointers.

SANTIAGO DE CUBA PROVINCE

### LANGUAGE

**UniversiTUR** (Map p404; ☎ 64 31 86; vallejo@mercadu.uo.edu.cu; Universidad de Oriente, cnr Calle L & Ampliación de Terrazas), arranges Spanish courses. It's also possible to combine instruction in music, literature and history with language studies; for more information see p454. Note that Americans must enroll through Havanatur in Habana (p92).

### MUSIC & DANCE

Spanish courses, dancing classes and various other specialist activities can be organized at **Ateneo** (Map p398; Felix Peña No 755) a cultural organization set up in the late 19th century by lawyer Antonio Bravo Correoso. Call by and see what's on offer. Another central option is the **Casa del Estudiante** (Map p398; ☎ 62 78 04; Heredia No 204) where you can organize singing, dancing or percussion lessons under the auspices of Carlos Bourbon of Ballet Folklorico Cutumba fame. There are something like 11 teachers here and classes start at CUC$8 per hour.

The **Casa del Caribe** (Map pp394-5; ☎ 64 22 85; fax 64 23 87; Calle 13 No 154) organizes dance lessons in conga, *son* and salsa; it's CUC$10 for two hours or CUC$5 for one. Resident staff member, Juan Eduardo Castillo can also fix up lessons in percussion. Real aficionados can inquire about in-depth courses on Afro-Cuban religions and culture. These guys are experts and they're very flexible.

Another interesting option is an organization called **Cuban Rhythm** (www.cubanrhythm.com). Take a look at their excellent website and make arrangements beforehand.

## Tours

**Cubatur** (Garzón Map pp394-5; ☎ 65 25 60; fax 68 61 06; Av Garzón No 364 btwn Calles 3 & 4; 8am-8pm; Heredia Map p398; Heredia No 701) sells excursions to La Gran Piedra, El Cobre, Baracoa and Tropicana Santiago Nightclub (p413).

You can easily arrange a tour on the spot with one of the taxis parked on Parque Céspedes in front of the cathedral. A four-hour tour to El Morro Castle, San Juan Hill and Santa Ifigenia cemetery should cost in the vicinity of CUC$20 for the car with Cubataxi (or about double that in a newer tourist taxi). A similar tour taking in Plaza de la

### CUBA'S EXILED WRITERS

In Cuba it is often said that 'every good writer is an exiled writer' and it's true that many of the country's most erudite literary offspring have plied their trade from overseas. Here is a list of some of the country's most notable literary luminaries.

#### José Heredia

An early champion of Cuban-Canadian relations Heredia's most celebrated work is the lyrical poem *Ode to Niagara* the text of which has been inscribed for posterity on the wall of his birth house (p400) in Santiago's bustling Calle Heredia.

#### José Martí

*El Maestro* himself spent less than half his life in the land 'where the palm tree grows', though his jealously guarded remains, housed in an impressive mausoleum in Santiago's Santa Ifigenia cemetery (p403), pay testament to his enduring legend.

#### Alejo Carpentier

The son of a French father and a Russian mother, Carpentier's claim to Cuban citizenry is, on paper, about as tenuous as Hemingway's. Developing an interest in Afro-Cubanism in his youth he nonetheless produced the most definitive guide to Cuban music in his seminal book *Music in Cuba* published in 1946.

#### Guillermo Infante

One-time Castro supporter turned dissident, Gibara-born Infante ran off to join the London literati in 1965 where he penned his highly lauded experimental classic *Tres Tristes Tigres.*

Revolución, El Cobre and the Monumento Al Cimarrón goes for CUC$15.

## Festivals & Events

Summer is an exciting time in Santiago de Cuba, with events coming one after the other. The season begins with the **Fiesta de San Juan** (June 24), celebrated with processions and conga dancing by cultural associations called *focos culturales*. Mid-to-late June is also when the **Boleros de Oro** extravaganza happens. It's followed by the **Festival del Caribe, Fiesta del Fuego** (Fire Celebration Festival of Caribbean Culture) in early July with exhibitions, music, and song and dance from all around the Caribbean. Santiago de Cuba's **Carnaval**, held during the last week of July, is the hottest in Cuba, with open-air grandstands erected along Av Garzón. The **International Chorus Festival** is in late November and the **Festival Internacional de Trova** is in mid-March.

## Sleeping

### BUDGET

#### City Center

**Gran Hotel Escuela** (Map p398; ☎ 65 30 20; Saco No 310; s/d CUC$26/32; ) This old four-story hotel with an impressive lobby and great location has big rooms with fridge and TV. Upstairs units have balconies overlooking the street. A bit rougher around the edges than the Basilio or Libertad (but still a good choice), this place was recently remodeled as another of Cuba's Escuela hotels where students of tourism undertake their training.

**Hotel Libertad** (Islazul; Map p398; ☎ 62 83 60; Calle Aguilera No 658; s/d low season CUC$26/32, high season CUC$32/38; ) Sparkling Hotel Libertad on Plaza de Marte is one of the best hotels in the Islazul chain and the 18 units were all recently renovated. Throw in a convenient, central(ish) location and clean (if sometimes windowless) rooms and you've got a rock-solid option that's easy on the wallet. The rooftop terrace has mountain views and, unusually for an Islazul hotel, there's Internet available in the lobby. The downstairs restaurant provides a reasonable refuge from Santiago's traditionally lackluster dining scene.

#### Outside the Center

**Hotel Rancho Club** (Islazul; Map p404; ☎ 63 32 80/63 39 40; Altos de Quintero; s/d with breakfast low season CUC$26/34, high season CUC$32/38; ) If you have a car and don't mind being a bit out of the center, the Hotel Rancho Club located 4km north of Santiago de Cuba off the Carretera Central is a winner. The 30 rooms are well kept, the restaurant is good (with city

### CASAS PARTICULARES – SANTIAGO DE CUBA

**Arelis González** (☎ 65 29 88; Aguilera No 615; r CUC$15-20) Central; independent room with TV, fridge; can cook; big house lots of traffic.

**'Casa Schmidt' – Tania & Sorangel** (☎ 62 31 82; Corona No 656; r CUC$20) Colonial house, basic bath, private.

**Cecelia Lago** (☎ 65 43 90; Calle San Fernando No 624; r CUC$20-25) Near the center, but quiet.

**Edgardo Gutierrez Cobas** (☎ 64 25 36; Terraza No 106, Ampliación de Terraza; r CUC$20)

**Eduardo Halley** (☎ 62 48 78; Heredia No 251; r CUC$15-20) Right on top of the action, hostel feel, three rooms share one bath.

**Frank Martínez** (☎ 62 45 14; Calle J No 264, Reparto Sueño; r CUC$20)

**Glenda Díaz Picazo** (☎ 62 08 69; Bayamo No 121 btwn Barnada & Plácido; r CUC$15-20) Corner of Plaza Marte.

**Gloria Bové Alonso** (☎ 62 38 37; Calle J No 212, Reparto Sueño; r CUC$20)

**Jorge Soulary** (☎ 64 39 94; jsoulary@hotmail.com; Calle 13 No 309, Reparto Vista Alegre; r CUC$20) Mod house, big, plush rooms, especially one with bathtub.

**Juan Martí Vazquez** (☎ 662-0101; Calle Padre Pico No 614 btwn Princesa & San Fernando; r CUC$20; ) Patio and roof terrace.

**Lourdes de la Caridad Gómez Beaton** (☎ 65 44 68; Félix Peña No 454; r CUC$15-20) Friendly.

**Luís Eduardo Halley Pérez** (☎ 62 48 78; Heredia 231; r CUC$15-20) Old colonial house, central.

**Luisa Gómez Villamil** (☎ 64 34 58; Calle 6 No 353, Reparto Vista Alegre; r CUC$15-20) Two big, airy rooms sharing bath, friendly.

**Magalis Palencia Domínguez** (☎ 64 10 87; Calle 4 No 204, Reparto Vista Alegre; r CUC$15-20) Independent.

views to boot!) and the staff are friendly and helpful. They also have big cabaret shows here Friday to Sunday (guests/nonguests CUC$1/2; at 10pm to 2am) when CUC$10 gets you two portions of fried chicken, a bottle of rum and four cokes – a cheap, fun party.

**Hotel Balcón del Caribe** (Islazul; Map p404; ☎ 69 10 11; Carretera del Morro Km 7.5; s/d CUC$34/42, cabañas with breakfast s/d CUC$36/48; ) This complex near the Castillo del Morro, 10km south of town, was participating in Misión Milagros (Miracle Mission, p449) and was temporary closed. Check with the Cubatur office on the corner of Heredia and General Larcet as to its current status.

### MIDRANGE

**Hostal San Basilio** (Cubanacán; Map p398; ☎ 65 17 02; hostalsb@stgo.scu.cyt.cu; Calle Masó No 403 btwn Pío Rosado & Porfirio Valiente; r CUC$46; ) Santiago's newest hotel is the boutique-style San Basilio named rather confusingly after the street in which it stands (the street was renamed Masó after the revolution). Newer fittings and a slightly quieter ambience give this place the edge over the Libertad, though the price moves it into the midrange category.

**Villa Gaviota** (Gaviota; Map pp394-5; ☎ 64 13 68; Av Manduley No 502 btwn Calles 19 & 21, Vista Alegre; s/d low season CUC$38/58, high season CUC$39/60; P ) Sitting pretty in an oasis of calm in Santiago's salubrious Vista Alegre district, Villa Gaviota has emerged from an extensive one-year makeover with a sharper, edgier look. Features include a swimming pool, restaurant, three bars, billiards room and laundry. A good bet if you want to escape the motorcycle madness of the city center.

**Hotel Las Américas** (Islazul; Map pp394-5; ☎ 64 20 11; cnr Av de las Américas & General Cebreco; s/d low season with breakfast CUC$44/58, high season CUC$53/69; P ) By far the most popular hotel for groups, this good medium-priced choice has a convenient location (near Vista Alegre and attractions in the center) and lots of facilities (restaurant, 24-hour cafeteria, pool, nightly entertainment, car rental etc). Watch for overcharging in the restaurant.

**Motel San Juan** (Islazul; Map pp394-5; ☎ 68 72 00; San Juan Hill; s/d low season with breakfast CUC$44/58, high season CUC$53/69; P ) On historical San Juan Hill, with lots of lawn and a children's pool, this place is great for history buffs and families. Rooms are spread on expansive grounds and have terraces and lots of extras (including radios – rare in Cuban hotels). Drive 1km east of Hotel Las Américas via Av Raúl Pujol to get here.

**Marlon Romaguera Cala** (☎ 65 40 52; Aguilera No 612, apt No 2; r CUC$15) Small room, great bed, friendly, others in same building.

**Mery & Tania Gómez** (☎ 664-1970; Anacaona No 107 btwn Aguilera & Taíno, Reparto Vista Alegre; r CUC$20-25) Five minutes' walk from La Maison in Vista Alegre.

**Nardys Aguilera Rodríguez** (☎ 62 24 09; Aguilera No 565; r CUC$15)

**Natacha Alvarez Pérez** (☎ 65 31 07; Aguilera No 509B; r CUC$15-20) Central, clean; sweet owner.

**Nenita** (☎ 665-4110; San Geronimo 472 btwn Sanchez Echavaría & Pío Rosado; r CUC$20-25) Lovely old house dating from 1850.

**Omar & Yasmari** (☎ 62 53 30; José A Saco No 607; r CUC$20) Street noise, meals.

**Raimundo Ocana & Bertha Pena** (☎ 62 40 97; Heredia No 308 btwn Pío Rosado & Porfirio Valiente; r CUC$20; ) Two-hundred-year-old house right in the thick of the action on Heredia.

**Ramona & Manuel Tur** (☎ 65 26 24; Corona No 555; r CUC$15-20)

**René Miranda Leyva** (☎ 64 29 55; Calle 13 No 352, Reparto Vista Alegre; r CUC$20) Big house, ask for Caridad.

**Santiago M Vallina García** (☎ 62 51 62; apt No 2, Aguilera No 563; r CUC$15-20) Central, ring bell marked 'Carmen.'

**Susanna Carrasquero** (☎ 65 37 39; Barnada No 513 btwn Heredia & Aguilera; r CUC$15-20; ) Warm hosts.

**'Villa Doña Isabella' – Isabel González Díaz** (☎ 64 41 24; Calle 6 No 309, Reparto Vista Alegre; r CUC$15-20) Comfortable, near Alliance Française, others nearby.

**Yolanda Elena Pérez Silva** (☎ 64 17 76; Calle 4 No 206, Reparto Vista Alegre; r CUC$15-20) Colonial house, fridge, safe, nice hostess.

### TOP END

**Hotel Casa Granda** (Gran Caribe; Map p398; ☎ 65 30 21/22; fax 68 60 35; Heredia No 201; s/d with breakfast low season CUC$67/96, high season CUC$78/112; ) This elegant old hotel (1914), artfully described by Graham Greene in his book *Our Man in Havana,* has 58 rooms and a classic red-and-white-striped front awning. Greene used to stay here in the late 1950s where he enjoyed relaxing on the streetside terrace, while his famous pen captured the nocturnal essence of the city as it wafted up from the bustling square below. Half a century later and – aside from the Che Guevara posters and some seriously erratic service on reception – not much has changed. The hotel's 5th-floor Roof Garden Bar (open 11am to 1am) is well worth the CUC$2 minimum consumption charge and the upstairs terrace is an obligatory photo stop for foreign tourists on the lookout for bird's-eye city views. There's music here most nights and the CUC$16 buffet makes a decent blow-out. Steer clear of the downstairs restaurant, one of Santiago's worst culinary disasters.

**Meliá Santiago de Cuba** (Cubanacán; Map pp394-5; ☎ 68 70 70; Av de las Américas & Calle M; r CUC$115; ) A mirrored monster in red, white and blue dreamt up by respected Cuban architect José A Choy, this Meliá property outside the *casco histórico* is Santiago's luxury choice, with real bathtubs in every room, city views, three pools, shopping, you name it. The vista from the Pico Real bar on the 15th floor is tops, and there are four good restaurants on site.

## Eating

For a city of such fine cultural traditions, Santiago's restaurant scene is still flailing around in the Dark Ages. You'll find no hidden Habana-style eating havens here. Instead get ready for a long jaunt through an inordinate amount of cheap, crappy, state-run restaurants in search of a palatable meal. Good luck!

### PALADARES

With all the tourist traffic, you would think there would be more paladares (private restaurants) here, but they come and go (high taxes, owners leaving for foreign shores and law breakers mean places shut down often). As a result, we've listed paladares that are well established and will still be around when you show up.

**Paladar Las Gallegas** (Map p398; Bartolomé Maso No 305; meals CUC$8; 1-11pm) Around the corner from the cathedral, this place packs them in with meals of pork, chicken and sometimes even *carnero* (lamb). Try for an intimate table on the plant-filled balcony.

**Paladar Salón Tropical** (Map pp394-5; ☎ 64 11 61; Fernández Marcané No 310, Reparto Santa Barbara; 5pm-midnight Mon-Sat, noon-midnight Sun) A few blocks south of the Hotel las Américas, this rooftop paladar serves tremendous portions of succulent smoked pork, with the *congrí* (rice flecked with black beans), salad and plantains piled up on the side. The *yuca con mojo* (starchy root vegetable with garlic lime sauce) is especially delicious. It is a good idea to get here early as this place fills up after 8pm with young Cuban women and their 55-year-old sugar-daddy 'escorts.'

### RESTAURANTS

**Santiago 1900** (Map p398; ☎ 62 35 07; Bartolomé Masó No 354; noon-midnight) Set in the former Bacardí residence, you can dine on the standard chicken, fish or pork in a lush dining room replete with a piano-bass-bongo trio. No dish is more than 35 pesos, the service is sufficient and the mojitos ace (six pesos). There are two good bars here (p412).

**Hotel Casa Granda** (Map p398; Casa Granda, Heredia No 201; 9am-midnight) One of Santiago's best people-watching spots – where you can read the hand signals but ignore the pleas of the ubiquitous *jineteros* outside – the food in this Parisian-style café is OK, though the excruciatingly slow service can be a little testing on the nerves. Try the burgers, hot dogs or sandwich options and be prepared for a long wait.

**Pizza Nova** (Map pp394-5; Meliá Santiago de Cuba, cnr Av de las Américas & Calle M; 11am-11pm) Pizza *deliciosa* (CUC$5 and up) and lasagna *formidable* (CUC$8), ravioli and garlic bread (CUC$1); *mamma mia,* this has to be the number-one option for breaking away from all that chicken and pork. For some inexplicable reason this otherwise venerable establishment is always chock-a-block with nubile *jineteras* hand in hand with their 55-year-old balding foreign sugar daddies.

**Cafe Palmares** (Map pp394-5; Calle M; dishes under CUC$3; 24hr) A cool courtyard setting under flowering trees, across from Meliá Santiago de Cuba, is complemented by an extensive menu with many egg, pizza, sandwich and chicken options. Fresh juice and strong espresso make this a good breakfast or post-bar choice.

**El Patio** (Map pp394-5; ☎ 64 32 42; Av General Cebreco; 🕑 9am-11pm) Don't let the name fool you: this is a basement restaurant with little atmosphere, but the food is consistently good and dirt cheap. A pork filet with *congrí* and a little salad costs CUC$3 and there's a full bar. Come early because they sometimes run out of things.

**Cafetería Las Américas** (Map pp394-5; ☎ 64 59 23; 🕑 24hr) A local hang-out of sorts, on the traffic circle near Hotel Las Américas, this cafeteria terrace does good basics: chicken, spaghetti and pork for under CUC$2. Inside is the affiliated restaurant with decent full meals of *comida criolla* (traditional Cuban food usually consisting of rice, beans and often pork) for CUC$5.

**Taberna de Dolores** (Map p398; ☎ 62 3913; Aguilera No 468) An inexpensive, colorful place on Plaza de Dolores, its drinks are better than its *comida criolla*. But the patio tables are a bonus and it's a good hang-out spot if you can get a table.

**Cafetería Las Enramadas** (Map p398; 🕑 24hr) It's the usual fried chicken, ice cream and fries at this place in the northwest corner of Plaza de Dolores – a kind of El Rápido in disguise. The terrace is shady, the beers affordable and the hours long: perfect *jinetero* turf. Good place for a hair-of-the-dog or for drowning a hangover in grease.

**Pekín** (Map pp394-5; ☎ 62 91 19; cnr Av de Céspedes & Calle A; 🕑 noon-3pm & 6-9:30pm) Chop suey Cuban-style or fried chicken costs under CUC$1 at this state-run joint four long blocks north of the Moncada Barracks. Peso pizza is on the corner; join the line.

**Cafetería Las Arecas** (Map pp394-5; Av Manduley No 52; dishes around CUC$3; 🕑 10am-1am) Nestled in the garden patio of this mansion turned mod shopping center, this cafeteria has an inexpensive menu with spaghetti, pizzas and chicken dishes. Fish filets start at CUC$5.50. The fancier dining-room restaurant in the rear part of the main building is open until 10pm.

**Restaurante Zunzun** (Tocororo; Map pp394-5; ☎ 64 15 28; Av Manduley No 159; 🕑 noon-10pm Mon-Sat, noon-3pm Sun) Dine in bygone bourgeois style in this palace-turned-restaurant. This is one of Santiago's best restaurants in terms of both food and ambience. Exotic dishes include chicken curry, paella or an outrageous cheese plate and cognac. Expect professional, attentive service.

**Restaurante El Morro** (Map p404; ☎ 69 15 76; Castillo del Morro; 🕑 noon-9pm) Paul McCartney's Santiago restaurant of choice, as his sparkling used plate (now mounted in a glass case on the wall) will testify. How one of the world's most famous vegetarians dealt with the rather meat-biased menu is interesting to ponder. The complete *criolla* lunch for around CUC$12 includes soup, main course, a small dessert and one drink. The spectacular cliffside location is an added bonus. Keep an eye out for whales breaching offshore.

**Restaurante El Cayo** (lunch CUC$6-20) On the eastern side of Cayo Granma, out by the Castillo de San Pedro, you'll find this state-run place, serving seafood for lunch.

Plaza Dolores is a case of nice location, shame about the food. The best of a bad bunch is Restaurante Don Antonio, next to Cafeteria Las Enramados, which offers everything from mixed grill to lobster. Next door is Restaurante La Perla del Dragón, offering chop suey and chow mein with a rather painful Cuban twist. Beyond that is Restaurante Teresina, with inexpensive pizza and spaghetti. These places never seem to have customers. Hmmm.

### CAFÉS

**Cafe La Isabelica** (Map p398; cnr Aguilera & Porfirio Valiente; 🕑 9am-9pm) Strong coffee in a smoky cantina-type atmosphere. You might get away paying pesos, but foreigners typically pay in Convertibles.

**Pizzas & Cajitas** (Map p398; B Masó No 260) For fast food visit this place, with coffee and cheese sandwiches in the morning, pizzas in the afternoon, and *cajitas* (take-out) at night (one to 20 pesos).

### ICE-CREAM PARLORS

**Coppelia La Arboleda** (Map pp394-5; ☎ 62 04 35; cnr Avs de los Libertadores & Victoriano Garzón; 🕑 10am-11:40pm Tue-Sun) As good as Habana's Coppelia and, as always, in pesos. It closes early if the ice cream runs out. Ask for *el último* (last place) in the line up grouped on the Av de los Libertadores side of the parlor.

Milkshakes are sometimes sold from the outside window.

**Dulcería del Goloso** (Map pp394-5; cnr Av Victoriano Garzón & Calle 6) This is another good ice-cream pit stop without the queues.

### GROCERIES

**Supermercado Plaza de Marte** (Map p398; Av Garzón; 9am-6pm Mon-Sat, 9am-noon Sun) One of the better-stocked supermarkets in town, with a great ice-cream selection and cheap bottled water. It's in the northeastern corner of Plaza de Marte.

**Panadería Doña Neli** (Map p398; cnr Aguilera & Plácido; 7:30am-8pm) This reliable hard-currency bakery on Plaza de Marte is good for bread.

**Municipal market** (Map p398; cnr Aguilera & Padre Pico) The main market is two blocks west of Parque Céspedes with a poor selection.

**Mercado Agropecuario Ferreiro** (Map pp394-5; Nuñez de Balboa) This market is across the traffic circle from Hotel Las Américas and up the side street beside the gas station. The selection here is also surprisingly poor.

## Drinking

**Claqueta Bar** (Map p398; Felix Peña No 654) A hopping local scene marks this open-terrace bar just off Parque Céspedes. There's sometimes live music and salsa dancing in the evening.

**Santiago 1900** (Map p398; 62 35 07; Bartolomé Masó No 354; noon-midnight) You can choose from two equally atmospheric drinking spots in this old Bacardí palace. Out back is a vine-covered patio buzzing with locals while upstairs is a quieter balcony bar serving food. Tourists pay in Convertibles, meaning they can glide past the red velvet rope at the door.

**Bar La Fontana** (Map p398; General Lacret; noon-2am) Could it be the lounge trend has hit Santiago de Cuba? You might think so walking into this cocoon off José A Saco with low stools grouped around individual tables lining the wall. Just don't order any apple martinis; it's strictly peso beer and rum at this cool saloon.

**Marylin** (Map p398; 65 45 75; cnr General Lacret & Saco; 24hr) This is a local favorite serving shots of rum to standing patrons: more a dive counter than a dive bar.

**Kon Tiki Club** (Map p398; cnr General Lacret & Saco) If you'd like to touch base with the city's underworld, try this gloomy place behind Marylin.

## Entertainment

For what's happening, look for the bi-weekly *Cartelera Cultural*. The reception desk at the Hotel Casa Granda (p410) usually has copies. Or go straight to the **Cartelera Cultural office** (Map p398; cnr Felix Peña & Diego Palacios). Every Saturday night Calle José A Saco becomes a happening place called Noche Santiagüera, where street food, music and crowds make an all-night outdoor party; beware of pickpockets.

### FOLK & TRADITIONAL MUSIC

The sounds of *tambores* (drums) and *trova* waft all up and down Calle Heredia where a cluster of live-music places can be found. You might head there first for easy-access music, but don't discount the further-flung places, all of which showcase quality players.

**Casa de la Trova** (Map p398; 65 26 89; Heredia No 208; admission from CUC$2; 11am-3pm & 8:30-11pm Tue-Sun) The most famous of all the city's traditional clubs, in operation since 1968, this venue has a strong claim to be Cuba's definitive and most influential music house. Some complain a recent makeover ruined the atmosphere somewhat – though it didn't stop Paul McCartney coming here to enjoy the ambience a few years back. The program varies from good to very good to excellent. Downstairs for lunchtime shows, upstairs after 10pm.

**Casa del Estudiante** (Map p398; 62 78 04; Heredia No 204; admission CUC$1; 9pm Wed, Fri & Sat, 1pm Sun) Grab a seat (or listen from the street) and settle in for the folksy house orchestra and *trovadores* (traditional singer/songwriters). See also courses (p407).

**Patio ARTex** (Map p398; 65 48 14; Heredia No 304; admission free; 11am-11pm) Art lines the walls of this shop-and-club combo that hosts live music both day and night in a quaint inner courtyard; a good bet if the Casa de la Trova is full, or too frenetic.

**Patio Los Dos Abuelos** (Map p398; 62 33 02; Francisco Pérez Carbo No 5; admission CUC$2; 10pm-1am Mon-Sat) An intimate club on the east side of Plaza de Marte featuring traditional Cuban music in a mixed local-tourist atmosphere. You get some real pros performing here.

**Casa de la Cultura Miguel Matamoros** (Map p398; 62 57 10; General Lacret btwn Aguilera & Heredia; admission CUC$1) This culture club in historic digs on Parque Céspedes hosts many musical events, including a *Sábado de la Rumba* (Rumba Saturday) at 11am Saturday; check the *cartelera* (calendar) posted at the door for the week's happenings.

**Casa de las Tradiciones** (Map pp394-5; Rabí No 154; admission CUC$1; ⌚ from 8:30pm) The most discovered 'undiscovered' spot in Santiago still retains its smoke-filled, foot-stomping, front-room feel. Hidden in the gentile Tivolí district this place hosts some of Santiago de Cuba's most exciting ensembles, singers and soloists taking turns improvising. Friday nights are reserved for straight-up, classic *trova,* so all you Ñico Saquito and Trio Matamoros fans should head over then.

**Casa de la Música** (Map p398; Corona No 564; admission CUC$5; ⌚ 10pm-2am) Similar to those in Habana, this Casa del Música features a mix of live salsa and taped disco. One of Santiago's better venues.

### TRADITIONAL DANCE

**Ballet Folklórico Cutumba** (Map p398; Teatro Oriente, Saco No 115; admission CUC$3) This internationally known Afro-Cuban folkloric dance group was founded 1960 and currently appears at Teatro Oriente. If you're in Santiago de Cuba on a weekend, don't miss Cutumba's exciting *café teatro,* at 9:30pm every Saturday or at 10:30am for their Sunday morning dance show. They perform such dances as the *tumba francesa, columbia, gagá, guaguancó, yagüetó, tajona* and *conga oriental.* It's one of the finest programs of its kind in Cuba.

**Foco Cultural El Tivolí** (Map p398; Desiderio Mesnier No 208; ⌚ 8pm Mon-Fri) Carnaval practice for the Sarabanda Mayombe happens weekly at this Tivolí Foco (a show that takes place in Tivolí). Saturdays at 5pm they perform a *mágica religiosa* program of *orishas* (Afro-Cuban religious deity), *bembé* (Afro-Cuban drumming ritual) and *palo monte* (Bantu-derived Afro-Cuban religion) at the nearby Casa de las Tradiciones (above).

Also ask about practice sessions at the studios of the **Conjunto Folklórico de Oriente** (Map p398; Hartmann No 407) and the **Foco Cultural Tumba Francesa** (Map pp394-5; Los Maceos No 501) at General Banderas. Traditional dancing also takes place at other *focos culturales* (cultural shows) around town most evenings.

### DANCE CLUBS

**Club El Iris** (Map p398; ☎ 65 35 00; Aguilera No 617; admission CUC$3; ⌚ 10pm-2am) Just off Plaza de Marte, with a distinctive 1950s sign, this is Santiago de Cuba's hottest disco, still after all these years. The cover includes one drink, but at night it's couples only. Stags can check out the matinee (five pesos) daily from 10am to 4pm.

**Discoteca Espanta Sueño** (Map pp394-5; cnr Av de las Américas & Calle M; ⌚ 10:30pm-3am Fri-Sun) This is the Meliá Santiago de Cuba's house disco; entry is through the hotel lobby to keep out *jineteras*.

Other recommendations:

**Ciroa** (Map pp394-5; cnr Av Manduley & Calle 13) Local night spot with a band Thursday to Sunday and a 10pm floor show.

**Pista de Baile Pacho Alonso** (Map pp394-5; admission CUC$5; ⌚ 8:30pm Sat, 5pm Sun) Check out the *charanga* (brass band) orchestra playing al fresco at this place behind Teatro José María Heredia.

### NIGHTCLUBS

**Tropicana Santiago** (Map p404; ☎ 68 70 90; door prices from CUC$30; ⌚ 10pm Wed-Sun) Styled after the original Tropicana in Habana, these Las Vegas–style floor shows feature plenty of babes with strategically placed baubles. After the show, you can dance at a disco in the same complex. Cubatur and most hotels have package tours to Tropicana Santiago for CUC$35 per person, including admission, one drink and transportation. Saturday night is the best time to go. To get there take the Autopista Nacional northeast of Hotel Las Américas for 3km.

### THEATERS

**Teatro José María Heredia** (Map pp394-5; ☎ 64 31 34; cnr Av de las Américas & Av de los Desfiles; ⌚ box office 9am-noon & 1-4:30pm) Santiago's huge, modern theater and convention center faces the Plaza de la Revolución on the northeastern side of town. Rock and folk concerts often take place in the 2459-seat Sala Principal, while the 120-seat Café Cantante Niagara hosts varied events. Ask about performances by the Compañia Teatro Danza del Caribe.

**Sala Teatro El Mambí** (Map p398; Bartolomé Masó No 303) This venue near the cathedral presents Spanish-language plays in the evening and puppet/clown theater for children on weekends.

### CUBAN MUSICAL INSTRUMENTS

During slavery in the US, drumming was prohibited, but in Cuba the bongos continued to beat. As a result, when Cuban popular music began to diversify and spread in the early 20th century, Cuban musicians had a whole range of instruments at their disposal.

The strong rhythms in Cuban music are usually provided by the *tumbadora* (conga), a tall barrel-like drum held together by metal hoops. Other drumming implements include the *bongó,* a pair of small round drums joined by a piece of wood; and the *batá,* a conical two-head drum of varying sizes used in Afro-Cuban religious dances and rituals. Folk dances are often accompanied by a single-skinned drum of Congolese origin called a *joca*.

The gourd-shaped rattle called the maraca is made out of dried fruits from the calabash tree. *Chequeré* maracas (a gourd covered with beads) are used in all sorts of Cuban music, from religious rituals to rap. The *güiro,* meanwhile, is an elongated gourd rasped with a stick, although there are also tin *güiros*.

Other percussion instruments include the *cata* or guagua, a wooden tube beaten with sticks and the *claves,* two wooden sticks tapped together to set the beat. The *cajón* is a simple wooden box used to thump out the rhythm.

Acoustically speaking the *tres* is a small folk guitar with three sets of steel double strings. The similar *cuatro* has four sets of double strings. Cuban folk groups often include a West African hand piano or *marímbula,* a wooden box with five metal keys that doubles up as a bass.

The only wind instrument in Cuban folk music is the *botija,* a clay jug with a short narrow neck bearing an opening on the side for blowing. Musicians vary the pitch of the tones by moving a hand along the neck of the jug. During Carnaval a small five-note horn called a *corneta china* produces a sharp sound like the bagpipe. Modern instruments commonly used in Cuba include the bass, clarinet, guitar, saxophone, trombone and trumpet.

Cuba is the only country outside Europe with a tradition of street organs. During the 19th century, refugees from Haiti brought the French mechanical organ to Oriente, where Hispano-Cuban *sones,* boleros and *danzones* (African-influence ballroom dancing) soon replaced waltzes and mazurkas in the repertoire. The Cubans made the European organ dynamic by adding a second crank that the operator uses to vary the speed at which the boards pass through the machine. Five or six percussionists join an organ-grinder to form an orchestra playing popular Cuban dance music under the control of the organ-grinder, who can innovate stops or breaks.



**Teatro Martí** (Map pp394-5; ☎ 2-0507; Félix Peña No 313) Another children's show is staged at 5pm Saturday and Sunday at this theater near General Portuondo, opposite Iglesia de Santo Tomás.

### CLASSICAL MUSIC

**Sala de Conciertos Dolores** (Map p398; ☎ 65 38 57; cnr Aguilera & Mayía Rodríguez; 🕒 8:30pm) Housed in a former church on Plaza de Dolores, you can catch the Sinfónica del Oriente here, plus the impressive children's choir (at 5pm). Bigger *trova* concerts are also held here by up-and-coming acts like William Vivanco and Ariel Díaz. The *cartelera* is posted on the Aguilera side of the street.

**Orfeón Santiago** (Map p398; Heredia No 68) This classical choir sometimes allows visitors to attend its practice sessions from 9am to 11:30am Monday to Friday.

**Coro Madrigalista** (Map p398; Pío Rosado No 555) This choir, across from the Museo Bacardí, is similar to Orfeón Santiago.

### CINEMAS

**Cine Rialto** (Map p398; ☎ 62 30 35; Félix Peña No 654) This cinema, next to the cathedral, is Santiago de Cuba's favorite, showing large-screen films and video.

**Cine Capitolio** (Map pp394-5; ☎ 62 71 64; Av Victoriano Garzón No 256) Videos are also the usual fare here.

**Cine América** (Map pp394-5; ☎ 65 11 84; Porfirio Valiente No 64; 🕒 noon-10pm Fri-Wed) This cinema shows movies, plus has a weekly *peña de rap* (rap concert).

### SPORT

**Estadio de Béisbol Guillermón Moncada** (Map pp394-5; ☎ 64 26 40; Av de las Américas) This stadium is on the northeastern side of town within walking distance of the main hotels. During the baseball season, from October to April, there are games at 7:30pm Tuesday, Wednesday, Thursday and Saturday, and 1:30pm Sunday (one peso).

**Gimnasio Cultura Física** (Map p398; Pío Rosado No 455 btwn Saco & Hechavarría; 6am-6:45pm Mon-Fri, 8am-4pm Sat, 8am-noon Sun) For a wicked workout drop into this gym with its well-pummeled punchbags, rusty old weights and cold showers. No manicures here.

## Shopping

**Discoteca Egrem** (Map p398; Saco No 309; 9am-6pm Mon-Sat, 9am-2pm Sun) If you're into buying music, look no further than this retail outlet of Egrem Studios; an especially good selection of local musicians.

**ARTex** (General Lacret Map p398; General Lacret btwn Aguilera & Heredia; Heredia Map p398; Heredia No 304; 11am-11pm; Patio ARTex Map p398; Heredia No 208; 11am-7pm Tue-Sun) From mouse pads to mumus, the branch of ARTex near Parque Céspedes collects any type of Cuban souvenir imaginable. The other ARTex branches focus more on music, with a respectable selection of Cuban music CDs and cassettes.

**La Maison** (Map pp394-5; Av Manduley No 52; 10am-6pm Mon-Sat) Headed for a resort and lack the proper attire? Head here.

### ART GALLERIES

A number of galleries in the center sell original paintings and prints. By international standards the prices are reasonable, but always get an official sales receipt to show Cuban customs (see p140). The two below are good place to start. Don't forget to ask about obtaining an export permit.

**Galería de Arte de Oriente** (Map p398; General Lacret No 656) Probably the best gallery in Santiago de Cuba, the art here is consistently good.

**Galería Santiago** (Map p398; Heredia) This gallery, below the cathedral on the southern side of Parque Céspedes, is another one with quality art and there are several more galleries along Heredia east of here.

### PHOTOGRAPHY

**Photo Service** (Saco Map p398; Saco No 422; General Lacret Map p398; General Lacret No 728; Av Garzón Map pp394-5; cnr Av Garzón & Calle 4) There are a few photo services available, including once near Plaza de Dolores.

## Getting There & Away

### AIR

**Antonio Maceo International Airport** (☎ 69 10 14; airport code SCU) is 7km south of Santiago de Cuba, off the Carretera del Morro. International flights arrive from Paris-Orly, Madrid, Milan and Rome on Cubana and from Toronto on **Air Transat** (www.airtransat.ca) and **Skyservice** (www.skyserviceairlines.com). **Aero-Caribbean** (☎ 68 72 55; General Lacret btwn Bartolome Masó & Heredia) flies weekly between here and Port Au Prince, Haiti and twice weekly to Santo Domingo.

**Cubana** (Map p398; ☎ 68 62 58; cnr Calle Saco & General Lacret) flies nonstop from Habana to Santiago de Cuba two or three times a day (CUC$114 one way, 1½ hours). There's a Sunday-only flight to Baracoa for CUC$32.

### BUS

The **National Bus Station** (Map pp394-5; cnr Av de los Libertadores & Calle 9), opposite the Heredia Monument, is 3km northeast of Parque Céspedes. **Astro** (☎ 62 60 91) buses go to all Víazul destinations for CUC$3 to CUC$9 cheaper. There are also alternate day departures to Pilón (CUC$10.50, 7½ hours) and Niquero (CUC$10, seven hours).

Passage on Astro buses to Baracoa and Guantánamo are only sold the day of departure (read: if a bus materializes) at the

**VÍAZUL BUS DEPARTURES**

| Destination | Cost (one way) | Distance | Duration (hr) | Departure time |
|---|---|---|---|---|
| Baracoa | CUC$15 | 234km | 5 | 7:30am |
| Guantánamo | CUC$6 | 84km | 2 | 7:30am |
| Habana | CUC$51 | 861km | 16 | 7:05am, 11:30am, 3:15pm, 8pm |
| Trinidad | CUC$33 | 581km | 11½ | 7:30pm |

SANTIAGO DE CUBA PROVINCE

ticket window in the back of the station. Competition is heavy for seats; you're better off traveling with Víazul or taking a truck. Tickets to all other destinations on Astro are sold in Convertibles at the Víazul window beside the station.

**Víazul** (☎ 62 84 84) buses leave from the same station; see p415 for departures.

The Habana bus stops at Bayamo (CUC$7, two hours), Holguín (CUC$11, four hours 20 minutes), Las Tunas (CUC$11, five hours 35 minutes), Camagüey (CUC$18, seven hours 35 minutes), Ciego de Ávila (CUC$24, 9½ hours), Sancti Spíritus (CUC$28, 11 hours 35 minutes) and Santa Clara (CUC$33 13 hours). The Trinidad bus can drop you at Bayamo, Las Tunas, Camagüey, Ciego de Ávila and Sancti Spíritus.

#### TRAIN

The new French-style **train station** (Map pp394-5; ☎ 62 28 36; Av Jesús Menéndez), near the rum factory northwest of the center, offers trains to the following destinations:

| Destination | Cost (one way) | Duration (hr) |
|---|---|---|
| Bayamo | CUC$4 | 3 |
| Camagüey | CUC$11 | 5½ |
| Ciego de Ávila | CUC$14.50 | 8 |
| Guayos | CUC$17.50 | 9½ |
| Habana | CUC$30 | 14½ |
| Holguín | CUC$5 | 3½ |
| Manzanillo | CUC$5.50 | 5 |
| Matanzas | CUC$27 | 13 |
| Santa Clara | CUC$20 | 10 |

The Santiago de Cuba–Habana route listed in the table is for train No 12, the slowest option, which departs Santiago at 8:25pm. Other trains serving this route are train No 2 (aka *locura verde*) leaving at 5:05pm daily and a motor railcar called the *locura azul* to Habana (CUC$62), which is scheduled to leave Santiago de Cuba at 11:10pm on Monday and Thursday.

Cuban train schedules are fickle, so you should always verify beforehand what train leaves when and get your ticket as soon as possible thereafter. The easiest, most efficient way to do this is at **Centro Único de Reservaciones** (Map p398; ☎ 65 21 43, 65 10 97; Aguilera No 565; ⌚ 8:30am-3:30pm Mon-Fri) near Plaza de Marte. You can buy your tickets here and current schedules are posted in the window. You can also go to the train station where tickets in Convertibles are sold at window three.

#### TRUCK

Passenger trucks leave **Serrano Intermunicipal Bus Station** (Map pp394-5; ☎ 62 43 25; cnr Av Jesús Menéndez & Sánchez Hechavarría) near the train station to Guantánamo (five pesos, two hours) and Bayamo (seven pesos, two hours) throughout the day, but early morning is always better for public transport. For these destinations, don't fuss with the ticket window; just find the truck parked out front going your way. Trucks for Caletón Blanco (three pesos, 45 minutes) and Chivirico (five pesos, 1½ hours) also leave from here; get a boarding pass from the person at the counter and pay as you board.

The **Intermunicipal Bus Station** (Terminal Cuatro; Map pp394-5; ☎ 62 43 29; cnr Av de los Libertadores & Calle 4), 2km northeast of Parque Céspedes, has two buses a day to El Cobre. Trucks to El Cobre leave from Anden No 1 at this station throughout the day. Two daily buses also leave for Bacanao from here (6am and 6:30pm).

## Getting Around

#### TO/FROM THE AIRPORT

A taxi to or from the airport should cost around CUC$5. You can also get to the airport on bus 212, which leaves from Av de los Libertadores opposite the Hospital de Maternidad. Trucks for the airport depart from here too. Bus 213 also goes to the airport from the same stop, but visits Punta Gorda first. If boarding at the airport, bus 213 is better as it goes straight to town, while No 212 goes first to Ciudamar. Both buses (20 centavos) turn around at the top of the grade, just beyond the west end of the airport parking lot to the left of the entrances, not in front of the terminal.

#### TO/FROM THE TRAIN STATION

To get into town from the train station, catch a southbound horse cart (one peso) to the clock tower at the north end of Alameda Park, from which Aguilera (to the left) climbs straight up to Parque Céspedes. Horse carts between the National Bus Station (they'll shout 'Alameda') and train station (one peso) run along Av Juan Gualberto Gómez and Av Jesús Menéndez.

#### BUS & TRUCK

Useful city buses include bus 212 to the airport and Ciudamar, bus 213 to Punta Gorda (both of these start from Av de los Libertadores, opposite the Hospital de Maternidad and head south on Felix Peña in the *casco histórico*), and bus 214 or 407 to Siboney (from near Av de los Libertadores No 425). Bus 401 from here goes to Siboney and Bacanao. Bus 5 to Caney stops on the northwestern corner of Plaza de Marte and at Gral Cebreco and Calle 3 in Vista Alegre. You pay the conductor. These buses (20 centavos) run every hour or so; more frequent trucks (one peso) serve the same routes.

*Camiones* (trucks) run along fixed routes. From the center to the Moncada Barracks and the Hospital Provincial (near the National Bus Station), hop on along Mariano Corona one block west of Parque Céspedes or on Aguilera. Trucks for Vista Alegre also run along Aguilera; there's a stop in front of the Etecsa building. From the Hotel Las Américas to the *casco histórico*, hop on a truck at the Parque de los Estudiantes on the roundabout. Trucks to El Cobre and points north leave from Av de las Américas near Calle M. On trucks and buses you should be aware of pickpockets and wear your backpack in front; bigger packs will not be accommodated on local buses and trucks.

#### CAR & MOPED

Santiago de Cuba suffers from a chronic shortage of rental cars (Transtur in particular) and you might find there are none available; though the locals have an indefatigable Cuban ability to *conseguir* (to manage, to get) and *resolver* (to resolve, work out). The airport offices usually have better availability than those in town. If you're completely stuck for a car, you can usually rent one at the Hotel Guantánamo, two hours away (p433). With so many cool sites near Santiago de Cuba, demand way outstrips supply for mopeds; a pity. Try the following places:

**Cubacar** (Map p398; Heredia No 701) On the corner of General Lacret.

**Havanautos** Hotel Las Américas (Map pp394-5; cnr Avs de las Américas & General Cebreco; ☎ 68 71 60; 🕑 8am-10pm); Jesús Menéndez (Map pp394-5; ☎ 62 26 66; cnr Av Jesús Menéndez & General Portuondo); Aeropuerto (☎ 68 61 61; Aeropuerto Antonio Maceo) The Hotel Las Américas office rents mopeds for CUC$24 per day.

**Transtur** Parque Céspedes (Map p398; ☎ 68 61 07; 🕑 9am-8:30pm); Motel San Juan (Map pp394-5; ☎ 68 72 06) The Parque Céspedes office is below Hotel Casa Granda.

Guarded parking is available on the street in front of the Transtur office, directly below the Hotel Casa Granda. Official attendants, complete with small badges, charge CUC$1 a day and CUC$1 a night.

The **Servi-Cupet** (Map pp394-5; cnr Av de los Libertadores & Av de Céspedes) is open 24 hours. There's an **Oro Negro** (cnr Av 24 de Febrero & Carretera del Morro) on the Carretera del Morro and another is on the Carretera Central at the northern entrance to Santiago de Cuba, not far from the Hotel Rancho Club.

#### TAXI

Taxis generally find *you* before you find *them* in hassle-heavy Santiago. There's a Turistaxi stand in front of Meliá Santiago de Cuba. Taxis also wait on Parque Céspedes in front of the cathedral and hiss at you expectantly as you walk past. Always insist the driver uses the *taxímetro* (meter) or hammer out a price beforehand. To the airport, it will be between CUC$3 to CUC$5 depending on the state of the car.

Bici-taxis (bicycle taxis) charge about five pesos per person per ride, but it's illegal to carry tourists, so they'll drop you a couple of blocks from Parque Céspedes.

See also p407 for information on taxi tours.

## SIBONEY

Playa Siboney is Santiago's Playas del Este; an exuberant and undone seaside town situated 19km to the east that is more rustic village that deluxe resort. Guarded by precipitous cliffs and dotted with a mixture of craning palms and weather-beaten clapboard houses, the setting here is laid-back and charming with a beach scene that mixes fun-seeking Cuban families and young, nubile Santiagüenas with their older and balder foreign sugar daddies in tow.

Qualitatively speaking Siboney's small crescent of grayish sand isn't in Varadero's league and the hotel choice (there *is* no

**PIRATES OF THE CARIBBEAN**

Pirates ran amok in the Caribbean during the 16th and 17th centuries and nowhere was their presence felt more than in Cuba.

The island first became attractive to corsairs in the 1530s when Spanish ships laden down with silver from Peru and New Spain, began to converge in Habana harbor to form large flotillas (treasure fleets) which would then set sail eastward for Seville.

For the buccaneers, the booty was too attractive to ignore. In 1554 French corsairs sacked Santiago and robbed and pillaged among a terrified populace for 30 days. The following year Jacques de Sores ransacked Habana, kidnapped its richest citizens and demanded a ransom of 80,000 gold pieces. When the demand wasn't met, he razed the city to the ground.

In order to protect Cuban cities from further acts of terror, the Spanish built an impressive network of forts around the island including Real Fuerza (Habana, 1558), San Salvador de la Punta (Habana, 1589), Tres Reyes de Morro (Habana, 1589), La Jagua (Cienfuegos, 1738) and El Morro (Santiago, 1638). But the edifices did little to repel repeated pirate attacks.

Frequent wars with the British, French and Dutch during the 17th century inspired countless more disgruntled pirates to raise the Jolly Roger and take up arms against the Spanish. Often sponsored by foreign governments, vicious but well-organized groups of buccaneers lay whole cities to waste and severely hampered local economies.

Nowhere was safe. In 1664 the portly Welshman Henry Morgan reduced Santiago's Morro Castle to rubble and in 1668 – on the pretext of uncovering a plot to attack Jamaica – he sacked the cathedral of Puerto Príncipe (now Camagüey), a prosperous bourgeois city situated over 50km inland. The British government gave him a knighthood for his pains.

The age of piracy finally came to a close in the early 1700s with the rise of national armies in Europe and the advent of more far-reaching international conflicts.

choice, just one rock-bottom villa) is none too inspiring either. But what Siboney lacks in facilities it makes up for in price, location (it's on the doorstep of Parque Bacanao) and all-embracing Cuban atmosphere. There's a plethora of legal casas particulares here (over 30, which in a settlement of this size constitutes half the village) and a decent sit-down restaurant on a hill overlooking the beach. For those in need of a break from the culture-jamming and street hassle of sweltering Santiago, it makes a good little hideaway.

## Sights

The energy fairly bounces off the simple red-and-white farmhouse **Granjita Siboney** (admission CUC$1; 9am-5pm), 2km inland from Playa Siboney and 2km south of the Gran Piedra turn-off on the road to Santiago de Cuba. It was from here, at 5:15am on July 26, 1953, that 26 cars under the command of Fidel Castro left to attack the Moncada Barracks in Santiago de Cuba. Of the 119 persons involved in the action, six died in combat and 55 were executed after their capture by Batista's troops (19 Batista soldiers were also killed). And so the Cuban Revolution was born. The house retains many of its original details, including the dainty room used by the two *compañeras* (female revolutionaries) who saw action, Haydee Santamaría and Melba Hernández. There are also displays of weapons, interesting documents, photos and personal effects related to the attack. Notice the well beside the building, where weapons were hidden prior to the attack. In 1973, 26 monuments were erected along the highway between the Granjita Siboney and Santiago de Cuba to commemorate the assault.

The **Museo de la Guerra Hispano Cubano Norteamericano**, adjacent to the Granjita Siboney, displays several objects related to the 1898American military intervention at Santiago de Cuba. Several scale models of both the land and sea battles are provided.

Overlooking the stony shoreline is an American **war memorial** dated 1907, which recalls the US landing here on June 24, 1898.

## Sleeping & Eating

**Villa Siboney** (☎ 3-9321; bungalow CUC$23) You're wiser heading for the casas particulares first

SANTIAGO DE CUBA PROVINCE

**CASAS PARTICULARES – PLAYA SIBONEY**

Aside from a handful of basic beach bungalows tiny Siboney has up to 30 casas particulares, so you shouldn't have any trouble finding a room.

**Ángel Figuredo Zolórzano** (☎ 3-9181; Av Serrano No 63; dgarrido1961@yahoo.es; r CUC$15-20) Seaside location, patio, nicely outfitted room, at end of street.

**Evaristo 'Chicho' Caballero Cabrera** (☎ 3-9248; Av Serrano No 1; r CUC$15-20) Colonial clapboard at entrance to town; simple, friendly, great porch.

**Javier Francisco Hernánedez Rotger** (☎ 3-9121; Obelisco No 1; r CUC$15-20) Near beach.

**Marlene Pérez** (☎ 3-9219; r CUC$15-20) Seaside apartment with balcony on coast a block south of the post office; has fridge, parking.

**Oscar Fábregas Coca** (☎ 64 18 00; Av Serrano No 12; r CUC$20-25; P ✱) Blue clapboard-style house with front terrace facing sea.

**Ovidio González Salgado** (☎ 3-9340; Av Serrano; r CUC$20-25) Above the pharmacy. Meals, whole house CUC$35; warmly recommended by a reader.

in this neck of the woods, but if for some reason they're all full there's always the bog-standard Villa Siboney; seven independent rustic cabins on the beach that sleep up to four people. Ask at the *carpeta* (reception desk), below the apartment building beside the commercial center.

**Restaurante La Rueda** (☎ 3-9325) Palmares operate this place, signposted just up the road from the beach and situated in the former house of Buena Vista Social Club virtuoso Compay Segundo. Born in a small shack on this site in 1907, Segundo (real name Francisco Repilado) shot to superstardom at the age of 90 on the back of Ry Cooder's best-selling album. In his heyday, the classic Cuban singer and guitarist wrote *Chan Chan* Cuba's omnipresent musical soundtrack and a song nearly as famous as *Guantanamera*. The food and view here are good and the service is amiable.

A number of cheap peso food stalls overlook the beach. There is also an open-air bar selling drinks in Convertibles on the beach itself.

### Getting There & Away

Bus 214 runs to Siboney from near Av de los Libertadores 425, opposite Empresa Universal, with a second stop at Av de Céspedes 110, near Restaurante Pekín, in Santiago de Cuba. It leaves about once an hour, and bus 407 carries on to Juraguá three times a day. Passenger trucks also shuttle between Santiago de Cuba and Siboney. If you're driving, slow down for the police checkpoint 2km south of Sevilla village on the road to Playa Siboney.

A taxi to Playa Siboney will cost in the vicinity of CUC$20 to CUC$25 depending if it's state or private.

## LA GRAN PIEDRA

The Cordillera de la Gran Piedra, a branch of the Sierra Maestra, is a 30km-long barrier separating the Caribbean coast from the Valle Central. It culminates in a gigantic rock 1234m above sea level. Not only does the range have a refreshingly cool microclimate, it also boasts an incredibly unique historical heritage based on the legacy of some 60 or more coffee plantations set up by French farmers in the latter part of the 18th century. On the run from a bloody slave rebellion in Haiti in 1791, the enterprising Gallic immigrants overcame arduous living conditions and difficult terrain to turn Cuba into the world's number-one coffee producer by the early 19th century. Their workmanship and ingenuity has been preserved for posterity in a Unesco World Heritage site that is centered on the Cafetal La Isabelica.

### Sights & Activities

Near the beginning of the access road to the Gran Piedra, 16km southeast of Santiago de Cuba, is the **Prado de las Esculturas** (admission CUC$1; 🕑 8am-4pm). Strewn along a 1km loop road here are 20 monumental sculptures of metal, wood, concrete, brick and stone by the artists of 10 countries. Inspired sculpture or cheesy lawn art? You be the judge.

The steep, 12km road up the mountain range itself is beautiful, as the trees close in and the valley opens up below. Between

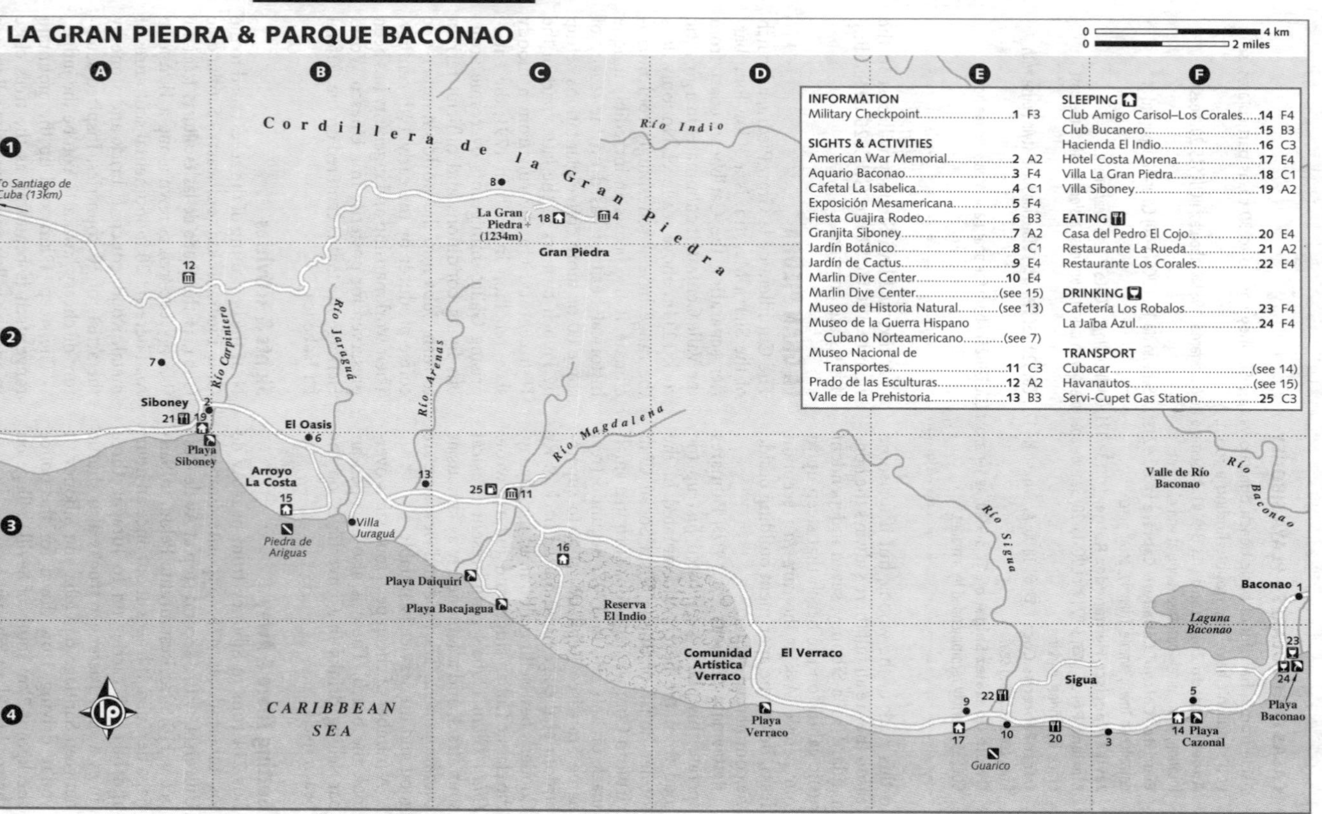
LA GRAN PIEDRA & PARQUE BACONAO
0 4 km
0 2 miles
INFORMATION
Military Checkpoint 1 F3
SIGHTS & ACTIVITIES
American War Memorial 2 A2
Aquario Baconao 3 F4
Cafetal La Isabelica 4 C1
Exposición Mesamericana 5 F4
Fiesta Guajira Rodeo 6 B3
Granjita Siboney 7 A2
Jardín Botánico 8 C1
Jardín de Cactus 9 E4
Marlin Dive Center 10 E4
Marlin Dive Center (see 15)
Museo de Historia Natural (see 13)
Museo de la Guerra Hispano Cubano Norteamericano (see 7)
Museo Nacional de Transportes 11 C3
Prado de las Esculturas 12 A2
Valle de la Prehistoria 13 B3
SLEEPING
Club Amigo Carisol–Los Corales 14 F4
Club Bucanero 15 B3
Hacienda El Indio 16 C3
Hotel Costa Morena 17 E4
Villa La Gran Piedra 18 C1
Villa Siboney 19 A2
EATING
Casa del Pedro El Cojo 20 E4
Restaurante La Rueda 21 A2
Restaurante Los Corales 22 E4
DRINKING
Cafetería Los Robalos 23 F4
La Jaïba Azul 24 F4
TRANSPORT
Cubacar (see 14)
Havanautos (see 15)
Servi-Cupet Gas Station 25 C3
To Santiago de Cuba (13km)
Cordillera de la Gran Piedra
La Gran Piedra (1234m)
Gran Piedra
Río Indio
Río Carpintero
Río Jaraguá
Río Arenas
Río Magdalena
Río Sigua
Río Baconao
Siboney
Playa Siboney
El Oasis
Arroyo La Costa
Villa Juraguá
Piedra de Ariguas
Playa Daiquirí
Playa Bacajagua
Reserva El Indio
Comunidad Artística Verraco
El Verraco
Playa Verraco
Guarico
Sigua
Valle de Río Baconao
Laguna Baconao
Baconao
Playa Baconao
Playa Cazonal
CARIBBEAN SEA

May and August, feast on as many mangoes as you can stomach. One kilometer before Villa La Gran Piedra and 800m down a muddy road is the **Jardín Botánico** (botanic garden; admission CUC$3; 8am-4:30pm Tue-Sun) with orchids (best November to January) and other flowers. Look for the showy yellow, orange and violet *ave de paraíso* (bird of paradise).

Almost anyone can climb the 459 stone steps to the summit of **La Gran Piedra** (admission CUC$2) at 1234m. The huge rock on top measures 51m long and 25m high and weighs an estimated 63,000 tons. On a clear day there are excellent views out across the Caribbean and on a dark night you can see the lights of Jamaica.

**Cafetal La Isabelica** (admission CUC$2; 8am-4pm) is part of the Unesco World Heritage site bestowed in 2000 upon the first coffee plantations in the southeast of Cuba. Two kilometers beyond La Gran Piedra on a rough road, there's a museum describing the coffee-processing technology of a century ago. The impressive two-story stone mansion, with its three large coffee-drying platforms, was built in the early 19th century by French émigrés from Haiti. There's a workshop, furniture and some slave artifacts, and you can stroll around the pine-covered plantation grounds at will.

### Sleeping & Eating

**Villa La Gran Piedra** (Islazul; 65 12 05; s/d low season CUC$30/38, high season CUC$34/42) This place near the mountain's summit, has 22 one- and two-bedroom cottages. A scenic place with basic facilities, the Villa was as of January 2006 housing patients for Misión Milagros (Miracle Mission; p449). You can check its current status with one of the travel agencies in Santiago.

### Getting There & Away

A steep, winding paved road climbs 12km up the mountain's spine. It's not possible to visit by public transport, as the bus arrives only once a week. A taxi from Santiago de Cuba will cost upwards of CUC$40 for a round-trip.

## PARQUE BACONAO

Parque Baconao, which covers 800 sq km between Santiago de Cuba and the Río Baconao, is a mixed bag of attractions; a Unesco biosphere reserve that is also home to an outdoor car museum, a rather run-down aquarium, and an odd collection of 240 life-size dinosaur sculptures. Some travelers get taken in by this odd succession of sights that lie scattered along the Caribbean coast for 40km east of Santiago; others assume they must be hallucinating and head quickly back into the city.

But the Unesco tag wasn't earned for a museum full of old cars. According to biological experts Baconao boasts more than 1800 endemic species of flora, and numerous types of endangered bats and spiders. Furthermore, sandwiched in a shallow chasm with the imposing Sierra Maestra on one side and the placid Caribbean on the other, the biodiversity of the area – which includes everything from craning royal palms to prickly cliffside cacti – is nothing short of remarkable.

The beaches are smaller here than those on the northern coast and not quite as white, but the fishing is good and there are 73 scuba-diving sites to choose from nearby, including the *Guarico,* a small steel wreck just south of Playa Sigua.

Baconao is also famous for its crabs. From mid-March to early May, tens of thousands of large land crabs congregate along the coast beyond Playa Verraco, getting unceremoniously squashed under the tires of passing cars and sending up a stench as they bake in the sun (see p422).

At the time of writing at least two of the park's isolated hotels had been given over to the Misión Milagros project (p449). Check before you make the long drive.

### Sights

A dozen painters have studios where their works are displayed and sold in the small artistic community of **El Oasis** at the turn-off to Club Bucanero, 3km east of the Playa Siboney road.

One of the area's oddest attractions is **Valle de la Prehistoria** (63 90 39; admission CUC$1; 8am-6pm), a kind of Cuban Jurassic Park another 3km along the main road to Baconao. Here giant brontosaurs nibble at trees, wooly mammoths graze on grassy expanses and cavemen slay saber-toothed tigers. Fun for kids of all ages, there are 200 life-size concrete dinosaurs and cavepeople scattered over 11 hectares – even the baths are

**THE CRABS OF BACONAO**

From mid-March to early May, the coastal highway between Playa Verraco and Baconao swarms with *cangrejos colorados* (red-and-yellow crabs), which descend en masse from the adjacent hills to lay their eggs in the sea. Many pop beneath the tires of passing vehicles, while others are harvested by enterprising Cubans, who consume the eggs as an aphrodisiac. The females are distinguished from the males by a wider breastplate and pinchers of equal size (the male has one claw larger than the other). From May to July the *cangrejo azul* (blue crab) emerges from its holes in humid areas and scrambles toward the ocean as part of a reproductive cycle that exposes the animal to hunters who value its meat. Year-round, the Cubans pursue the green *cangrejo moro* in the sea, using a mask and hook. It's another great delicacy.

in little caves. The dinosaurs were built by inmates from the nearby prison. The **Museo de Historia Natural** (☎ 3-9329; admission CUC$1; ⌚ 8am-4pm Tue-Sun) is also here, but kind of a yawn after the prehistoric beasts.

Another must-see in Parque Baconao is the **Museo Nacional de Transportes** (☎ 63 91 97; admission CUC$1, camera/video CUC$1/2; ⌚ 8am-5pm), adjacent to the Servi-Cupet gas station 2km east of the Valle de la Prehistoria. The museum has dozens of classic cars, including singer Benny Moré's 1958 Cadillac, the car Raúl Castro got lost in on the way to the Moncada Barracks attack, and a collection of 2500 automotive miniatures. The main US landings during the US intervention in Cuba's Second War of Independence took place on June 24, 1898, at **Playa Daiquirí**, 2km down a side road from the museum. This area is now a holiday camp for military personnel and entry is prohibited.

SANTIAGO DE CUBA PROVINCE

Ten kilometers southeast of the Museo Nacional de Transportes is the **Comunidad Artística Verraco** (admission free; ⌚ 9am-6pm), a village of painters, ceramicists and sculptors who maintain open studios. Here you can visit the artists and buy original works of art.

After a couple of bends in the road you burst onto the coast, where the hotels begin. **Jardín de Cactus** (admission CUC$5; ⌚ 8am-3pm), 800m east of Hotel Costa Morena, has 200 kinds of cactus beautifully arrayed along the rocky hillside, with a large cave at the rear of the garden. Keep your eyes peeled for tiny green *colibrí* (hummingbirds) suckling nectar from flowering cacti.

**Aquario Baconao** (☎ 63 51 45; admission CUC$7; ⌚ 9am-5pm), between the Costa Morena and Hotel Carisol, has dolphin shows (with sultry narration) a couple of times a day. It's a rather tacky spectacle although you can swim with the animals – if you so desire – for CUC$46.

Every Cuban resort area seems to have an attraction replicating indigenous scenes. Here it's the **Exposición Mesoamericana** (admission CUC$1), just east of Club Amigo Carisol – Los Corales. Indigenous cave art from Central and South American is arranged in caves along the coastal cliffs.

At the **Laguna Baconao** (admission CUC$1; ⌚ 8am-5pm), a couple of kilometers northeast of Los Corales, there are a dozen crocodiles kept in pens below a restaurant, plus other caged animals like lizards and *jutías* (tree rat). Horses are (supposedly) for hire here as well as boats.

From Playa Baconao, 5km northeast of Los Corales, the paved road continues 3.5km up beautiful **Valle de Río Baconao** before turning into a dirt track. A dam up the Río Baconao burst in 1994, inundating Baconao village. Soldiers at a checkpoint at the village turn back people trying to use the direct coastal road to Guantánamo because it passes alongside the US naval base. To continue east you must backtrack to Santiago de Cuba and take the inland road. Someday this will change.

## Activities

The **Fiesta Guajira Rodeo** (admission CUC$5; ⌚ 9am & 2pm Wed & Sun) at El Oasis, opposite the turn-off to Club Bucanero, stages rodeos with *vaqueros* (Cuban cowboys) four times a week. Horseback riding is available for CUC$5 for the first hour. The rodeo's restaurant serves typical Cuban food from noon to 2pm daily.

**Marlin Dive Center** (Cubanacán Naútica; ☎ 68 63 14) at Sigua, a 10-minute walk along the beach from Hotel Costa Morena, picks divers up at the hotels at 8:30am daily. Scuba diving costs CUC$30 with gear. Marlin's open-water certification course is

CUC$365. There are shipwrecks close to shore here and you can feed black groupers by hand. At the time of writing the diving operations had been moved temporarily to Club Amigo Carisol – Los Corales. There's another **Marlin Dive Center** (☎ 68 60 70) offering similar services at Club Bucanero. The water off this bit of coast is some of Cuba's warmest (25°C to 28°C); best visibility is between February and June.

Hands down the best public beach here is **Playa Cazonal**, with lots of tawny sand, natural shade and a big sandy swimming hole (much of the coast here is clogged with seaweed forests). Turn into the Club Amigo Carisol – Los Corales and then it's a quick left to the beach access road.

## Sleeping

### MIDRANGE

**Hacienda El Indio** (Islazul; ☎ 68 62 13; s/d with breakfast low season CUC$30/40) The former El Indio Hunting Reserve, between Complejo la Punta and Playa Verraco, was converted into the Reserva El Indio 'ecotourism park', after the boundary fence collapsed during heavy rains and most of the deer, antelope, and other hoofed beasts escaped into the nearby hills. These days it's the turf for outdoor types who snorkel, horseback ride and hike in the surrounding area. Individuals stay at Hacienda El Indio. If you want to chill unmolested, this is a good spot.

**Hotel Costa Morena** (Islazul; ☎ 35-6126; P ✖ 🏊) This place is at Sigua, 44km southeast of Santiago de Cuba and 17km east of the Complejo La Punta Servi-Cupet gas station. It has attractive architecture, a large terrace right on the cliffs, and a brown sandy beach with good snorkeling 200m away. The hotel was open only to Misión Milagros patients at the time of writing. Check at the Cubatur office in Santiago for more up-to-date information.

### TOP END

**Club Bucanero** (Gran Caribe; ☎ 68 63 63; fax 68 60 70; P ✖ 🏊) Tucked up against low limestone cliffs with a small scratch of beach, this resort at Arroyo La Costa, 25km southeast of Santiago de Cuba, was hosting Misión Milagros patients at the time of writing. Check at the Cubatur office in Santiago for more up-to-date information.

**Club Amigo Carisol – Los Corales** (Cubanacán; ☎ 35 61 21; s/d low season CUC$52/90, high season CUC$57/100; P ✖ 🏊) This self-contained all-inclusive resort is a five-minute walk from the area's best beach, Playa Cazonal, near the east end of the coastal road through Parque Baconao. A tennis court and a disco are available. Nonguests can purchase a CUC$15 day pass, which includes lunch and the use of all facilities. With the Misión Milagros program descending en masse on Bacanao, this was one of the few accommodation options left inside the park.

## Eating

**Casa del Pedro El Cojo** (☎ 35 62 10) The most reliable year-round restaurant out this way – aside from the Fiesta Guajira Rodeo (opposite) – is this place just beyond Sigua on the coast. A simple fish meal in this thatched *ranchón* (a ranch-style al fresco restaurant) costs CUC$5.

Restaurante Los Corales, reached by turning inland off the coastal road at the Marlin Dive center at Sigua, serves Convertible meals and drinks on an open terrace with excellent mountain and sea views.

## Drinking

**La Jaïba Azul** (☎ 35 00 01) This joint on Playa Baconao, 1km east of the lake turn-off, is a local drinking place.

**Cafetería Los Robalos** (☎ 35 00 02) Just across the bridge from La Jaïba Azul, this place has a variety of drinks for pesos or Convertibles. Otherwise, the hotels lay on plenty of nightly entertainment.

## Getting There & Away

A bus service runs only twice a day along the 40km coastal road from Playa Siboney to Playa Baconao. Bus 407 from Santiago de Cuba goes as far as Complejo La Punta (Villa Juraguá) three times a day; it's a hard hitch from there to points east. Bus 401 to Baconao departs the **Intermunicipal Bus Station** (Map pp394-5; cnr Av de los Libertadores & Calle 4) in Santiago de Cuba, at 6am and 6:30pm. About two hours later it departs Baconao for the return trip. Arrive at the Santiago de Cuba terminal around 4:30pm to get a pass that will allow you to board the 6:30pm bus. Otherwise just ask for *el último* and wait.

When planning your visit to this area, remember that the coastal road from

Baconao to Guantánamo is closed to non-residents.

### Getting Around

**Havanautos** (☎ 68 63 63; Club Bucanero) has cars and mopeds. Cubacar has an office in Club Amigo Carisol – Los Corales (p423).

**Servi-Cupet** (Complejo La Punta; 24hr) is 28km southeast of Santiago de Cuba.

## EL COBRE

The **Basílica de Nuestra Señora del Cobre**, high on a hill 20km northwest of Santiago de Cuba on the old road to Bayamo, is Cuba's most sacred pilgrimage site. In Santería, La Virgen de la Caridad is associated with the beautiful *orisha* Ochún, the Yoruba goddess of love and dancing, who is represented by the color yellow. In the minds of many worshipers, devotion to the two religious figures is intertwined.

The copper mine at El Cobre has been active since pre-Columbian times and was once the oldest European-operated mine in the western hemisphere (by 1530 the Spanish had a mine here). However, it was shut in 2000. Many young villagers, who previously worked in the mine, now work over tourists in the parking lot of the basilica, offering to 'give' you shiny but worthless chalcopyrite stones from the mine. You'll find that a firm but polite *'no gracias'* usually does the trick. The road to the basilica is lined with sellers of elaborate flower wreaths (20 pesos), intended as offerings to La Virgen, and hawkers of miniature 'Cachitas', the popular name for La Virgen.

### Sights

Stunning as it materializes above the village of El Cobre, the **basilica** (6:30am-6pm) shimmers against the verdant hills behind. Except during mass (8am except on Wednesday, with additional Sunday services at 10am and 4:30pm), La Virgen lives in a small chapel above the visitors center on the side of the basilica. To see her, take the stairs on either side of the entry door. For such a powerful entity, she's amazingly diminutive, some 40cm from crown to the hem of her golden robe. Check out the fine Cuban coat of arms in the center; it's an amazing work of embroidery. During mass, Nuestra Señora de la Caridad faces the congregation from atop the altar inside the basilica.

The 'room of miracles' downstairs in the visitors center contains thousands of offerings giving thanks for favors bestowed by the virgin. Clumps of hair, a TV, a thesis, a tangle of stethoscopes, a balsa raft and innertube sculpture (suggesting they made it across the Florida Straits safely) and floor-to-ceiling clusters of teeny metal body parts crowd the room. The most notable is a small golden guerrilla fighter donated by Lina Ruz, Fidel Castro's mother, to protect her son during his Sierra Maestra campaign against Batista. Ask one of the nuns to point it out to you. Until 1986, the 1954 Nobel Prize won by Ernest Hemingway for his novel *The Old Man and the Sea* was also on display, but in that year a visitor smashed the showcase's glass and carried the medal off. The police recovered the medal two days later, but it has since been kept in a

#### HONORING THE BLACK VIRGIN

According to local legend, the black virgin of El Cobre – known to Cubans as 'Cachita' – was first discovered in the Bay of Nipe in 1608 when three fishermen (the three Juans) caught up in a vicious storm spotted a 30cm high wooden statue floating on the water. The object depicted the image of a black virgin and was inscribed with the message *'I am the Virgin de la Caridad.'* In her left hand she carried the child Jesus and in her right, a golden cross.

Saved from the fury of the waves the thankful fishermen took the statue back to the small copper mining village of El Cobre near Santiago where, over the ensuing years, the virgin is said to have performed a multitude of miracles and wondrous deeds. In her honor a hermitage was built in the village and in 1916 Pope Benedict XV declared the virgin of El Cobre to be the patron saint of Cuba.

The current basilica – the only one of its kind in Cuba – was completed in 1927 and in 1998 the still-intact virgin was removed from her revered post and transported down into the city of Santiago where she was ceremoniously crowned and blessed by his holiness Pope Jean Paul II.

vault, out of sight and reach. The nuns will fill small bottles with holy water if you ask (bring your own bottle).

Follow the signs through the town of El Cobre to the **Monumento al Cimarrón**. A quick 10-minute hike up a stone staircase brings you to this anthropomorphic sculpture commemorating the 17th-century copper-mine slave revolt. The views are superb from up here; walk to the far side of the sculpture for a vista of copper-colored cliffs hanging over the aqua-green reservoir.

### Sleeping & Eating

**Hospedaría El Cobre** (☎ 3-6246) A large two-story building behind the basilica has 15 basic rooms with one, two, or three beds, all with private bath, at eight pesos per person, plus two 40-bed dormitories at five pesos per person. Meals are served punctually at 7am, 11am and 6pm, and there's a pleasant large sitting room with comfortable chairs. The nuns here are very sweet. House rules include no drinking and no unmarried couples. A hard-currency donation to the sanctuary equivalent to what you pay to stay in pesos is the classy thing to do. Foreigners must reserve at least 15 days in advance.

There are several peso stalls in town where you can get batidos (fruit shakes), pizza and smoked-pork sandwiches.

### Getting There & Away

Bus 202 goes to El Cobre twice a day from the **Intermunicipal Bus Station** (cnr Av de los Libertadores & Calle 4), in Santiago de Cuba. Trucks are more frequent on this route.

A Cubataxi from Santiago de Cuba costs around CUC$20 for a round-trip. A private taxi will be a few Convertibles cheaper.

If you're driving toward Santiago de Cuba from the west, you can join the Autopista Nacional near Palma Soriano, but unless you're in a big hurry, it's better to continue on the Carretera Central via El Cobre, which winds through picturesque hilly countryside.

## EL SALTÓN

If you're ready for some full-time relaxing, escape to **Hotel Carrusel El Saltón** (Cubanacán; ☎ 5-6495; Carretera Puerto Rico a File; s/d with breakfast CUC$48/60; P ✠ ), a beautiful mountain retreat in the Tercer Frente municipality, 75km from Santiago de Cuba in the foothills of the Sierra Maestra. It's almost lodgelike, with just 22 rooms in wooden buildings nestled into the landscape and no one will blame you if you kick back on your balcony while deciding between a sauna, hot tub, massage or dip in the 30m waterfall (the hotel's defining feature). Horseback riding or hiking into the nearby cocoa plantations at Delicias del Saltón are daytime options or you can just wander off on your own through mountain villages with alluring names like Filé and Cruce de los Baños. The food is passable and the bar has a pool table. Outside a mountain river gushes and the forest trees rustle a few inches from the thatched-roof restaurant.

To get to El Saltón, continue west from El Cobre to Cruce de los Baños, 4km east of Filé village. El Saltón is 3km south of Filé. With some tough negotiating in Santiago de Cuba, you can get a taxi to take you here for CUC$40 to CUC$50. Make sure the car is sturdy.

You may hear about a road over the Sierra Maestra from Cruce de los Baños to Río Seco on the south coast. Southbound from Cruce de los Baños, the first 10km are OK, passing through hamlets in coffee-growing country. Then the road goes south, becoming a very rough jeep track with 'oh shit!' slippery, steep sections that can only be covered by a 4WD vehicle in dry weather. In a regular car or in rainy weather, the last 20km to Río Seco would be impossible, although ecotour jeeps regularly use this road. Good luck.

## WEST OF SANTIAGO DE CUBA

The coastal region west from Santiago de Cuba is magnificent (see p427) as the mountains and the sea meet in rugged, aqueous harmony reminiscent of Hwy 1 near Big Sur, California. There are countless remote beaches where you can stop along this route. Nineteen kilometers west of Caletón Blanco you'll pass a vacation camp for the Cuban military called **Villa Turquino**. Río Seco and the beginning of the rough road to Cruce de los Baños are 3km west of this camp.

### Sleeping & Eating

**Campismo Caletón Blanco** (Cubamar; ☎ 62 57 97; Caletón Blanco Km 30, Guamá; s/d low season CUC$15/22, high season CUC$17/26; P ✠) Situated 30km west of Santiago in close proximity to both mountains and beach, Caletón Blanco is one of Cuba's newer and more plush international campismos. Twenty-two bungalows sleep two to four people and there's a restaurant, snack bar and bike rental available. This is also a campervan site. Make your reservations with Cubamar (p92) before arrival.

**Brisas Sierra Mar** (Cubanacán; ☎ 2-9110; s/d all-inclusive CUC$80/114; P) This isolated place is at Playa Sevilla, 63km west of Santiago de Cuba and a two-hour drive from the airport. The big, pyramid-shaped hotel is built into a terraced hillside with an elevator down to a brown-sand beach famous for its sand fleas. Get into the water quickly and discover a remarkable coral wall great for snorkeling just 50m offshore (dolphins sometimes frequent these waters too). Horseback riding is available and a Marlin Dive Center is on the premises. Families with children will appreciate the special kids' programming daily and guests under 13 stay free with their parents. The hotel is popular with Canadians and gets a lot of repeat visits. Nonguests can buy a CUC$35 day pass that includes lunch, drinks and sport until 5pm. You might be able to find a ride into Santiago de Cuba from here.

## CHIVIRICO

**pop 4000**

Chivirico, 75km southwest of Santiago de Cuba and 106km east of Marea del Portillo, is the only town of any significance on the south-coast highway. It's a good place to pick up on the nuances of everyday Cuban life, but otherwise there's not much to do here. The deep, clear waters of the Cayman Trench just offshore wash the many beaches along this portion of the south coast.

There's a challenging trek that begins at Calentura 4km west of Chivirico and passes through La Alcarraza (12km), crossing the Sierra Maestra to Los Horneros (20km), from where truck transport to Guisa is usually available. Whether skittish local authorities will let you loose in the area is another matter. Don't just turn up – do your homework in Santiago or Chivirico first. Try asking at Cubatur in Santiago or ask at one of the two Cubanacán Brisas hotels.

### Sleeping

**Brisas Sierra Mar Los Galeones** (Cubanacán; ☎ 2-6160; Carretera Chivirico Km 72; s/d all-inclusive low season CUC$47/84, high season CUC$66/112; P) This is a small hotel with big surprises like the funky, forward decor, the good food, nice views and great diving. All rooms have balconies, there's a sauna and a small, unspectacular beach 100m below the hotel via a steep 296-step stairway. Children under 16 are not accommodated here. All in all, a nice place to relax.

### Getting There & Away

Trucks run to Chivirico throughout the day from the Serrano Intermunicipal Bus Station opposite the train station in Santiago de Cuba. There are also three buses a day.

Theoretically, buses operate along the south coast from Chivirico to Campismo La Mula on alternate days, but don't count on it. The bus to Río Macío (the river that marks the border between Santiago and Granma Provinces on the coast road) leaves at 5pm daily, and to Pilón at 11am on Tuesday, Thursday and Saturday. Chivirico's bus and truck station is 700m up off the coastal road from Cine Guamá.

## UVERO

The first major battle won by Fidel Castro's guerrilla army took place at Uvero, 23km west of Chivirico, on May 28, 1957, when a government position guarded by 53 Batista soldiers was overwhelmed and much-needed supplies were captured. By the main road are two red trucks taken by the rebels. A double row of royal palms leads to a large monument commemorating these events. It makes a good goal for a day trip on horseback from the Brisas Sierra Mar.

## PICO TURQUINO AREA

Five kilometers west of Las Cuevas, which is 40km west of Uvero, is the **Museo de la Plata** (admission CUC$1; Tue-Sat) at La Plata, next to the river just below the highway. The access road is very rough, and you should leave your vehicle at the store near the east side of the river and cover the last 800m to the museum on foot. The first successful skirmish of the Cuban Revolution took place here on January 17, 1957. The museum has three rooms with photos and artifacts from the campaign, and on a clear day you can see Pico Turquino. Marea del Portillo is 46km to the east (see p388). Don't confuse this La Plata with the Comandancia de La Plata, Fidel Castro's revolutionary headquarters high up in the Sierra Maestra (p382).

The well-preserved wreck of the Spanish cruiser *Cristóbol Colón* lies where it sank in 1898, about 15m down and only 30m offshore near La Mula. No scuba gear is available here but you can see the wreck with a mask and snorkel. (Divers from the Sierra Mar Resort are brought here by bus for a shore dive on the wreck.) If you have the time, hike up the Río Turquino to Las Posas de los Morones where there are a few nice pools where you can swim (allow four hours round-trip). You must wade across the river at least three times unless it's dry.

## Trekking

The Pico Turquino section of Gran Parque Nacional Sierra Maestra contains 17,450 hectares, including a spectacular trail across the Sierra Maestra and through a cloud forest where daily fogs rolls in, soaking the wild orchids, giant ferns, mosses and pines that grace Cuba's highest peaks. When the veil parts the views are magnificent.

There are several options for this trek, though doing it independently is not one of them: all hikers must be accompanied by a guide. If your main interest is summiting Cuba's highest peak, you'll want to set out from Las Cuevas in Santiago de Cuba Province. If you're hooked on history and want to hike from Fidel and company's headquarters through and/or across the Sierra Maestra, you should set out from Alto de Naranjo in adjacent Granma Province (p380). If you want a little of both (or want a good, long hike), you can combine the two, starting from either end. The hiking is strenuous either way and onward transport is better from Alto del Naranjo, which may influence your planning. The hike from Las Cuevas can be organized at relatively short notice at the trail head. A good option is to book through **Ecotur** (☎ 65 38 59) in Santiago de Cuba. See p381 for the map of this hike.

The **Pico Turquino Trail**, up Cuba's highest mountain (1972m), begins at Las Cuevas on the south-coast highway, 7km west of Ocujal and 51km east of Marea del Portillo. This trek also passes Cuba's second highest peak, Pico Cuba (1872m). Allow at least six hours to go up and another four hours to come down, more if it has been raining as the trail floods in parts and becomes a mud slick in others. Most climbers set out at 4am (but if you're on the trail by 6:30am, you'll be OK), having slept at the Campismo La Mula, 12km east; self-sufficient hikers also have the option of pitching camp at Las Cuevas

### IF YOU HAVE A FEW MORE DAYS

Wedged precariously between escarpment and sea, the coast road west out of Santiago toward Marea de Portillo is a roller coaster of crinkled mountains, hidden bays and crashing surf. This is without doubt one of the most breathtaking drives in Cuba. The views alone are worth the car-hire fee.

Thanks to a recent lashing by a string of hurricanes the road was in a bad state of repair at the time of writing, though it was still passable in an ordinary car. Take particular care when driving past Las Cuevas on the border of Granma Province where you'll need to circumnavigate a damaged bridge by fording a shallow river.

Attractions along the way are numerous. Stop to soak up the Cuban atmosphere in the coastal town of **Chivirico** (opposite) or procure a day pass at the salubrious resort of **Brisas Sierra Mar Los Galeones** (opposite). Treasure seekers should look out for the off-shore wrecks of the Spanish cruisers *Viscaya* at Asseredero and *Colón* at Ocujal, both of which have gun turrets poking above the water, while history lovers will want to pay a visit to the revolutionary shrines of **Uvero** (opposite) and **La Plata** (opposite), the sites of two early victories by Castro's rebel army.

Before setting out be sure to stock up on water, food and gas (there are no gas stations until Pilón, 200km to the west). The road also makes a great (if slightly arduous) cycle ride. You can overnight in Sierra Mar (opposite), Campismo Caletón Blanco (p425), Campismo La Mula (p428) or Marea del Portillo.

visitors center. The CUC$15 per person fee (camera CUC$5 extra) that you pay at the visitors center/trailhead includes a compulsory Cuban guide. You can overnight at the shelter on Pico Cuba if you don't want to descend the same day (two days/one night CUC$30). Alternatively, you can do the entire Las Cuevas to Alto Naranjo three-day hike by arranging to be met by a new team of guides at Pico Turquino (three days/two nights CUC$48). Add an extra CUC$5 onto the latter two options if you wish to include a side-trip to Castro's former headquarters at La Plata (p382).

This hike is grueling because you're gaining almost 2km in elevation across only 9.6km of trail – it's hard and hot, but not a killer. Even in August, when Santiago de Cuba Province routinely registers the nation's highest temperatures, the wooded slopes provide plenty of coverage from the glaring sun. Fill up on water before setting out. The well-marked route leads from Las Cuevas to La Esmajagua (600m, 3km; there's water here and a hospitable country family), Pico Cardero (1265m, quickly followed by a series of nearly vertical steps called 'Saca La Lengua', or 'flops your tongue out'), Pico Cuba (1650m, 2km, water and shelter here) and Pico Real del Turquino (1972m, 1.7km). When the fog parts and you catch your breath, you'll behold a bronze bust of José Martí that stands on the summit of Cuba's highest mountain. It was hauled up here by Castro's formidable mistress Célia Sánchez and her father in 1952. You can overnight at either Pico Cuba on the ascent or La Esmajagua on the descent. The Pico Cuba shelter has a rudimentary kitchen and a wood-fire stove, plank beds (no mattresses) or, if those are taken, floor space. It's possible to continue across the mountains to Alto del Naranjo and Santo Domingo (see p382).

Alternatively, walkers with less lofty ambitions can arrange a short four-hour, 6km trek from Las Cuevas to La Esmajagua and back for CUC$13 (camera CUC$5 extra).

Trekkers should bring sufficient food, warm clothing, a sleeping bag and a poncho – precipitation is common up here (some 2200mm annually), from a soft drizzle to pelting hail. Except for water, you'll have to carry everything you'll need; including extra food to share if you can carry it and a little something for the *compañeros* who take 15-day shifts up on Pico Cuba.

Ask ahead if you would like an English-speaking guide (park officials claim they now have at least one). Also ask about food provision at Pico Cuba. Recently dinner was being offered for CUC$8. Drinks are available for purchase at the trailhead in Las Cuevas. Tipping the guides is mandatory – CUC$3 to CUC$5 is sufficient. For competitive types, the (unofficial) summit record by a guide is two hours, 45 minutes. So if you're feeling energetic…

## Sleeping & Eating

**Campismo La Mula** (Cubamar; s/d low season CUC$9/12, high season CUC$11/16) On a clean pebble beach at the mouth of Río La Mula, 12km east of the Pico Turquino trailhead, this place has 50 small cabins popular with both Cubans and hikers destined for Pico Turquino. It's a reasonable option on this isolated stretch of coast. The Oficina de Reservaciones de Campismo (see p399) in Santiago de Cuba handles bookings here and it's best to reserve ahead as hurricanes have sometimes caused the cabins to close (in 2005 the roofs were blown off). Should the cabins be closed, they may let you pitch a tent here.

Locals with a big catch may be able to arrange fresh-fish meals; ask around.

## Getting There & Away

A bus connects La Mula to Chivirico on alternate days. This is a very hard stretch to hitch a ride.

# Guantánamo Province

Notorious for its US naval base and famous the world over for a trite song about a *guajira* (country bumpkin), Guantánamo's reputation as a dumping ground for ailing Cold War anachronisms is only half-deserved. Bisected by the velvety Sierra del Puril and punctuated by isolated pockets of self-sufficient rural smallholdings, the country's most easterly province is Cuba's wettest, driest, hottest and most mountainous region. It was also the first area to be colonized by the Spanish.

In ethereal Baracoa you will find one of the island's most magical places, a Cuban Shangri-La with Coco palms and jungle-covered mountains encasing the kind of mind-propelling, dream-invoking cityscape that even Tolkien couldn't have invented. Further up the coast, in the Parque Nacional Alejandro de Humboldt nature goes haywire in a protected area that ecological experts consider to be one of the richest tracts of virgin forest in the Americas.

From an anthropological standpoint Guantánamo's pre-Columbian legacy is unique. Home to the last surviving vestiges of indigenous native culture in Cuba, the province has revealed ceramic pots, ancient idols, intricate petroglyphs, and mystical Indian cemeteries in the hunt to piece together the final remnants of the oft-misunderstood Taíno Indian civilization.

Cocooned in the extreme south, heavily fortified Gitmo (American slang for the Guantánamo naval base) boasts a golf course, five cinemas, a high security prison and Cuba's only McDonald's restaurant. You can espy all of these strange capitalist incongruities over an ice-cold beer in the Malones look-out. Democracy or hypocrisy…? You decide.

## HIGHLIGHTS

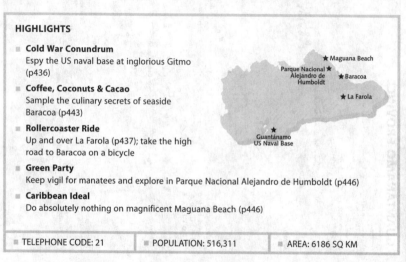

- **Cold War Conundrum**
  Espy the US naval base at inglorious Gitmo (p436)
- **Coffee, Coconuts & Cacao**
  Sample the culinary secrets of seaside Baracoa (p443)
- **Rollercoaster Ride**
  Up and over La Farola (p437); take the high road to Baracoa on a bicycle
- **Green Party**
  Keep vigil for manatees and explore in Parque Nacional Alejandro de Humboldt (p446)
- **Caribbean Ideal**
  Do absolutely nothing on magnificent Maguana Beach (p446)

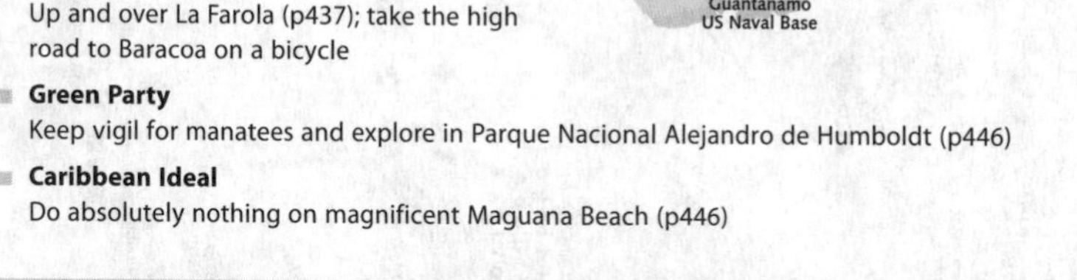


| ■ TELEPHONE CODE: 21 | ■ POPULATION: 516,311 | ■ AREA: 6186 SQ KM |
|---|---|---|

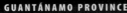

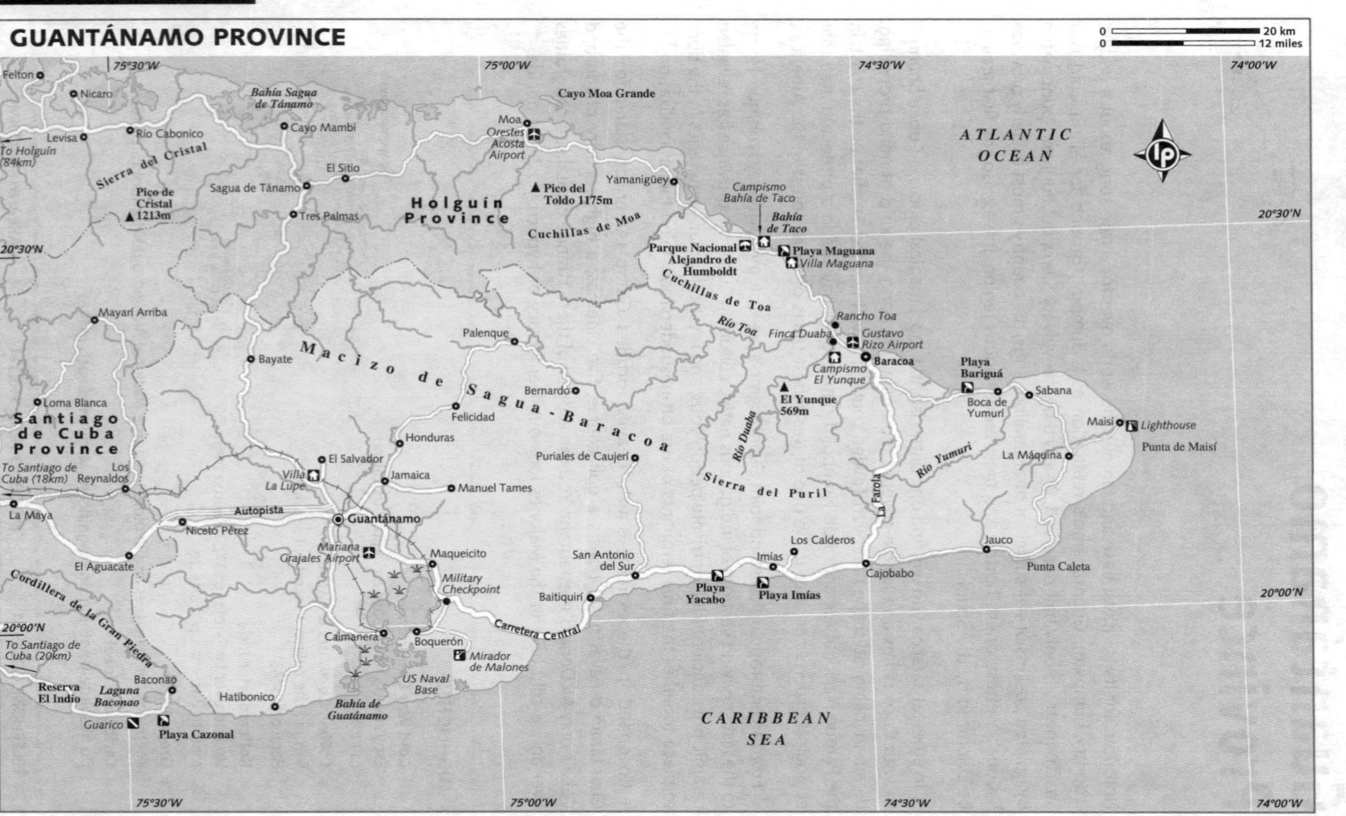
GUANTÁNAMO PROVINCE
0 20 km
0 12 miles
75°30'W
75°00'W
74°30'W
74°00'W
20°30'N
20°00'N
ATLANTIC OCEAN
CARIBBEAN SEA
Felton
Nicaro
Levisa
Río Cabonico
To Holguín (84km)
Sierra del Cristal
Pico de Cristal 1213m
Bahía Sagua de Tánamo
Cayo Mambí
El Sitio
Sagua de Tánamo
Tres Palmas
Holguín Province
Cayo Moa Grande
Moa
Orestes Acosta Airport
Pico del Toldo 1175m
Cuchillas de Moa
Yamanigüey
Campismo Bahía de Taco
Bahía de Taco
Parque Nacional Alejandro de Humboldt
Playa Maguana
Villa Maguana
Cuchillas de Toa
Río Toa
Rancho Toa
Finca Duaba
Gustavo Rizo Airport
Baracoa
Campismo El Yunque
El Yunque 569m
Río Duaba
Playa Bariguá
Boca de Yumurí
Sabana
Maisí
Lighthouse
Punta de Maisí
Río Yumurí
La Máquina
La Farola
Sierra del Puril
Mayarí Arriba
Bayate
Macizo de Sagua-Baracoa
Palenque
Bernardo
Felicidad
Honduras
Puriales de Caujerí
Loma Blanca
Santiago de Cuba Province
To Santiago de Cuba (18km)
Los Reynaldos
El Salvador
Villa La Lupe
Jamaica
Manuel Tames
La Maya
Autopista
Guantánamo
Niceto Pérez
El Aguacate
Mariana Grajales Airport
Maqueicito
Military Checkpoint
San Antonio del Sur
Baitiquirí
Playa Yacabo
Imías
Playa Imías
Los Calderos
Cajobabo
Jauco
Punta Caleta
Cordillera de la Gran Piedra
Carretera Central
Caimanera
Boquerón
Mirador de Malones
US Naval Base
To Santiago de Cuba (20km)
Baconao
Reserva El Indio
Laguna Baconao
Hatibonico
Bahía de Guatánamo
Guarico
Playa Cazonal

## History

Until the arrival of the Spanish in the late 15th century, Taíno Indians populated the mountains and forests around Guantánamo forging a living as fishermen, hunters and small-scale farmers. Columbus first arrived in the region in November 1492, a month or so after his initial landfall near Gibara, and planted a small wooden cross in a beautiful bay he ceremoniously christened Porto Santo – after an idyllic island off Portugal where he had enjoyed his honeymoon. The Spanish returned again in 1511 under the auspices of Columbus' son Diego in a flotilla of four ships and 400 men that included the island's first governor Diego Velázquez. Building a makeshift fort constructed from wood, the conquistadors consecrated the island's first colonial settlement, La Villa de Nuestra Señora de la Asunción (Baracoa), and watched helplessly as the town was subjected to repeated attacks from hostile local Indians led by a rebellious local *cacique* (chief) known as Hatuey.

Declining in importance after the capital moved to Santiago in 1515, the Guantánamo region became Cuba's Tibet – a mountainous and barely penetrable rural backwater where prisoners were exiled and old traditions survived. In the 18th century, the area was re-colonized by French immigrants from Haiti who mastered the difficult terrain in order to cultivate coffee, cotton and sugarcane on the backs of imported African slaves. Following the Second War of Independence a brand new foe took up residence in Guantánamo Bay – the all-powerful Americans – intent on protecting their economic interests in the strategically important Panama Canal region. Despite repeated bouts of mud-slinging in the years since, the not-so-welcome *Yanquis,* as they are popularly known, have repeatedly refused to budge.

# GUANTÁNAMO

☎ 21 / pop 210,408

Despite its notoriety in the ongoing fisticuffs between Cuba and the US, Guantánamo is one of the country's least-visited cities. Culturally vibrant yet visually unremarkable, the municipality is famous for its sportsmen (who between them have brought back 11 Olympic gold medals) and its unique blend of rootsy Afro-Cuban music known as *changüi.*

'Discovered' by Columbus in 1494 and given the once-over by the inquisitive British 250 years later, the initial settlement of Santa Catalina del Saltadero del Guaso was founded in 1819 between the Jaibo, Bano, and Guaso rivers by French plantation owners on the run from Haiti. In 1843 the town changed its name to Guantánamo and in 1903 the bullish US navy took up residence in the bay next door. The sparks have been flying ever since.

Guantánamo has little in the way of standard tourist sights and for foreign travelers the accommodation options are limited. Those on a tight itinerary might be better off heading straight for Baracoa, but for diehards intent on seeing the 'real' Cuba – warts and all – this could be your bag.

## Orientation

Mariana Grajales airport (airport code GAO) is 16km southeast of Guantánamo, 4km off the road to Baracoa. Parque Martí, Guantánamo's central square, is several blocks south of the train station and 5km east of the Terminal de Ómnibus (bus station). Villa La Lupe, the main tourist hotel is 5km northwest of the town.

## Information

### BOOKSHOPS

**Librería Asdrubal López** (Calixto García No 951; 🕑 9am-noon & 2-5pm Mon-Fri, 9am-noon Sat)

### INTERNET ACCESS

**Etecsa** (cnr Aguilera & Los Maceos; per hr CUC$6; 🕑 9am-6:30pm) Four computers.

### LIBRARIES

**Biblioteca Policarpo Pineda Rustán** (cnr Los Maceo & Emilio Giro; 🕑 8am-9pm Mon-Fri, 8am-5pm Sat, 9am-noon Sun) An architectural landmark.

### MEDIA

**Venceremos & Lomería** Two local newspapers published on Saturday.

**Radio Trinchera Antimperialista CMKS** Trumpets the word over 1070AM.

### MEDICAL SERVICES

**Farmacia Principal Municipal** (cnr Calixto García & Aguilera; 🕑 24hr) On the northeast corner of Parque Martí.

**EAST MEETS WEST**

In common with many ethnically diverse nations around the world, Cuba enjoys its fair share of regional rivalry. From simple fun-poking to full-on cultural stereotyping, the two camps divide up east/west along an invisible line running somewhere east of Camagüey.

Traditionally it's those from the Occidente who have always enjoyed the better standard of living. Basking in their relative prosperity you'll often hear westerners half-jokingly refer to their poorer Oriental counterparts as *palestinos* for the longstanding eastern tendency to migrate west in search of work.

The exodus has snowballed in recent years. Among Cubans it is no secret that nearly 85% of Habana policemen are *palestinos* and that the bulk of Varadero's Vegas-style hotel blocks were built with the hard-earned sweat of itinerant eastern labor.

But it's not all one-way traffic. Identifiable by their lilting musical accents and *'¿Que bola, compay?'* (How you doin'?) greetings, the inhabitants of Cuba's Oriente region – despite a traditionally lower earning potential – revel in their image as feisty revolutionaries and jealous guarders of Cuba's world-famous musical legacy.

**Hospital Agostinho Neto** (☎ 35 54 50; Carretera de El Salvador Km 1; 24hr) At the west end of Plaza Mariana Grajales in front of Hotel Guantánamo. It will help foreigners in an emergency.

### MONEY

**Banco de Crédito y Comercio** (Calixto García btwn Emilio Giro & Bartolomé Masó) Two branches on this block.
**Bandec** (cnr Ahogados & Calle 4) Big new branch near Hotel Guantánamo.
**Cadeca** (cnr Calixto García & Prado; 8:30am-6pm Mon-Sat, 8am-1pm Sun) Sells Cuban pesos and cashes traveler's checks.

### POST

**Post office** (Pedro A Pérez; 8am-1pm & 2-6pm Mon-Sat) On the west side of Parque Martí. There's also a DHL office here.

### TELEPHONE

**Etecsa** (cnr Aguilera & Los Maceos; 9am-6:30pm)

### TRAVEL AGENCIES

**Reservaciones de Campismo** (Flor Crombet No 410; 9am-noon & 1-4pm Mon-Fri)

## Dangers & Annoyances

Guantánamo is a big city with a mellow town feel that pickpockets sometimes exploit. Stay alert especially on public transport and during Noches Guantanameras (p435).

## Sights

The quirky collection at **Museo Municipal** (cnr José Martí & Prado; admission free; 2-6pm Mon, 8am-noon & 3-7pm Tue-Sat) includes prerevolution day passes to the naval base and the antique Harley Davidson used to shuttle secret messages during the revolution. Don't miss the cigar bands in the back gallery.

The **Parroquia de Santa Catalina de Riccis**, in Parque Martí, dates from 1863. In front of the church is a statue of Major General Pedro A Pérez, erected in 1928. The seated Martí statue here is particularly striking, as are the tulip fountain and provençal colored bandstand.

Local architect Leticio Salcines (1888–1973) left a number of impressive works around Guantánamo, including the market building **Plaza del Mercado Agro Industrial** (cnr Los Maceos & Prado), the **train station**, and his personal residence, the 1916 **Palacio Salcines** (cnr Pedro A Peréz & Prado; admission CUC$1; 8am-noon & 2-6pm Mon-Fri), a triumph of eclecticism and a monument said to be the building most representative of Guantánamo. The Palacio is now a small museum exhibiting colorful frescos, Japanese porcelain and a rusty old music box that pipes out rather disappointing Mozart. A guided tour (CUC$1) makes the dull exhibits infinitely more interesting. On the palace's turret is *La Fama*, a sculpture designed by Italian artist Americo Chine, that serves as the symbol of Guantánamo, her trumpet announcing good and evil. Salcines also designed the beautiful provincial library **Biblioteca Policarpo Pineda Rustán** (cnr Los Maceo & Emilio Giro), which was once the city hall (1934–51). Trials of Fulgencio Batista's thugs were held here in 1959, and a number were killed when they snatched a rifle and tried to escape.

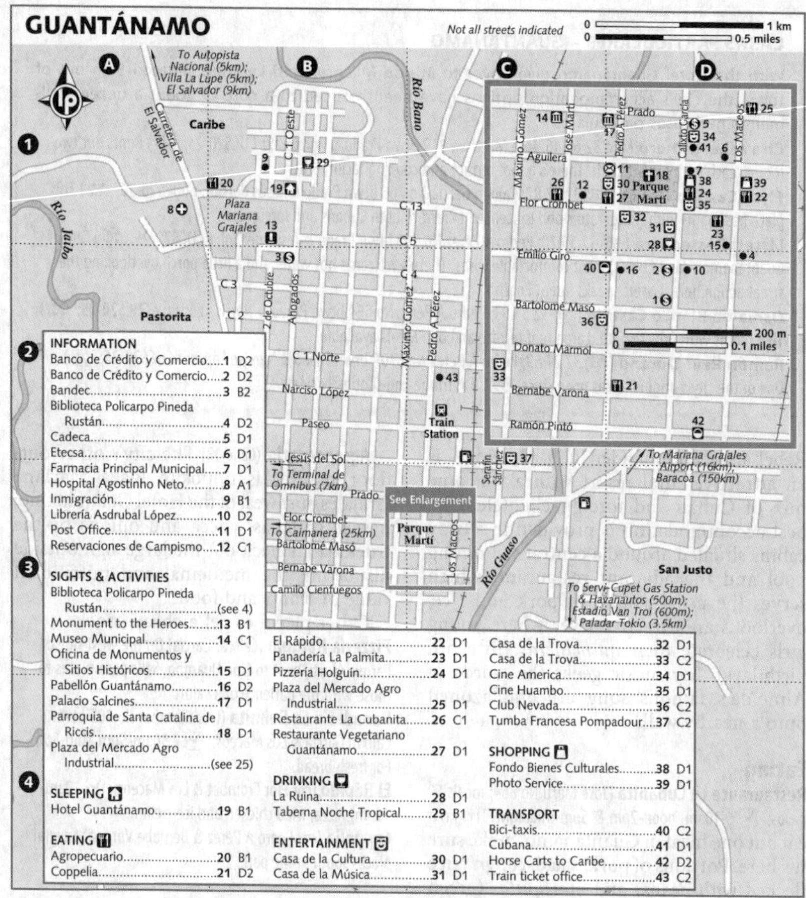


For a fuller expose of Guantánamo's interesting architectural heritage you might want to stop by at the **Oficina de Monumentos y Sitios Históricos** (Los Maceos btwn Emilio Giro & Flor Crombert). Ask about a map of city walking trails. You'll find more fascinating historical and geographical facts about the city in the **Pabellón Guantánamo** (Pedro A Pérez No 953), a small expo center displaying key information about the city.

The huge Sovietlike **Monument to the Heroes**, glorifying the Brigada Fronteriza 'that defends the forward trench of socialism on this continent,' dominates Plaza Mariana Grajales, the gigantic square opposite Hotel Guantánamo. Electrifying mass rallies occur here on May Day.

## Sleeping

**Hotel Guantánamo** (Islazul; ☎ 38 10 15, 38 10 25; Calle 13 Norte btwn Ahogados & 2 de Octubre; s/d low season CUC$20/24, high season CUC$23/30; P ✱ ⛱) Guantánamo's modern, four-story signature hotel on Plaza Mariana Grajales in Reparto Caribe is currently serving the Misión Milagros program (p449). Travelers should check out the similarly priced La Lupe or choose from one of a dozen amply-furnished casas particulares in town (p434).

**Villa La Lupe** (Islazul; ☎ 38 26 34, 38 26 12; Carretera El Salvador Km 3.5; s/d low season CUC$20/24, high season CUC$23/30; P ✱ ⛱) Located 5km outside of town on the road to El Salvador, Villa La Lupe – named after a song composed by

 

### CASAS PARTICULARES – GUANTÁNAMO

With the Hotel Guantánamo given over to Misión Milagros and La Lupe situated 5km out of town, the city's accommodation options have been reduced to a core of about a dozen well-maintained casas particulares:

**Cira Alberti Otero** (☎ 32 65 46; José Martí No 819 btwn Prado & Aguilera; r CUC$20-25; ❄) Rents out two rooms, each with private bath. There's a roof terrace and cooking facilities here.

**Elyse Castillo Osoria** (☎ 32 37 87; Calixto García No 766 btwn Prado & Jesús del Sol; r CUC$20-25; ❄) This place has rooms with refrigerators and is licensed to rent to both Cubans and foreigners.

**Lissett Foster Lara** (☎ 32 59 70; Pedro A Pérez No 761 btwn Prado & Jesús del Sol; r CUC$20-25; ❄) One of Guantánamo's (and Cuba's) most comfortable casas. There's welcome hot water and a little porch overlooking the street action here. Lissett speaks fluent English.

**Osmaida Blanco Castillo** (☎ 32 51 93; Pedro A Pérez No 664 btwn Paseo & Narciso López; r CUC$20-25; ❄) Two rooms with private bath. Large roof terrace and bar. Meals available.

**Ramón Revé Durand** (☎ 32 21 59; Pedro A Pérez No 670A btwn Paseo & Narciso López; r CUC$20-25; ❄) One of the city's original casas open since 1997; TV, fridge and spotlessly clean.

Rebel army commander Juan Almeida – is an attractive rural resort with a welcome mix of Cuban and foreign clientele. The best accommodation is provided in sturdy cabins situated around a central swimming pool and the adjacent restaurant, which serves the usual staples of pork and rice, overlooks an attractive river where young girls celebrate their *quinciñeras* (fifteenth birthdays). For music geeks the words of Almeida's famous song are emblazoned onto a nearby wall.

## Eating

**Restaurante La Cubanita** (José Martí No 864; meals 50 pesos; 🕒 6-10am, noon-2pm & 5pm-midnight) If you eat but one meal in Guantánamo, make sure it's here. Portions of pork, salad, *congrí* (rice flecked with beans) and *mariquitas* (green banana chips sliced longways) are huge at this peso paladar (private restaurant).

**Paladar Tokio** (☎ 38 23 82; Calle 3 btwn Calles 8 & 10) An out-of-town option (it's in the Santa María district) which specializes in *lomo* (smoked pork).

**Restaurante Vegetariano Guantánamo** (Pedro A Pérez; 🕒 noon-2:30pm & 5-10:30pm) Vegetarians can break out of their daily cheese sandwich and tortilla treadmill at this unusual meatless establishment, next to the Casa de la Cultura – the menu is in *moneda nacional* (Cuban pesos).

**Plaza del Mercado Agro Industrial** (cnr Los Maceos & Prado; 🕒 7am-7pm Mon-Sat, 7am-2pm Sun) Guantánamo's public vegetable market is a red-domed Leticio Salcines' creation and rather striking – both inside and out.

**Agropecuario** (Calle 13) The city's other outdoor market is opposite Plaza Mariana Grajales, just west of the Hotel Guantánamo; it sells bananas, yucca and onions by the truckload. Check out the large sign outside displaying the medicinal and nutritional value of plants and food.

Other places to get a cheap snack:

**Pizzería Holguín** (Calixto García) On the west side of Parque Martí, next to Cine Huambo. Sells peso pizzas to those with the patience of a saint.

**Panadería La Palmita** (Flor Crombet No 305 btwn Calixto García & Los Maceos; 🕒 7:30am-5pm Mon-Sat) For fresh bread.

**El Rápido** (cnr Flor Crombet & Los Maceos; 🕒 10am-10pm) Pizza, fried chicken and ice cream.

**Coppelia** (cnr Pedro A Pérez & Bernabe Varona) Several blocks south of the park.

## Drinking

**La Ruina** (cnr Calixto García & Emilio Giro; 🕒 10am-1am) This shell of a ruined colonial building has 9m ceilings and a crusty feet-on-the-table kind of ambience. There are plenty of benches to prop you up after your nth bottle of beer and a popular karaoke scene for those with ambitions of the singing variety.

**Taberna Noche Tropical** (☎ 38 16 01; cnr Calle 15 Norte & Ahogados) Nearby the Hotel Guantánamo, this is the place to grab a late-night Bucanero on your way back to La Lupe.

## Entertainment

Guantánamo was the home town of Elio Revé (1930–97), former leader of the Orquesta

Revé, who popularized *son-changüi*. Today you can still hear groups playing this combination of urban dance music and rural Afro-Cuban drumming.

The city's strong musical tradition is borne out in the scope and quality of its music venues.

**Casas de la Trova** (admission CUC$1; 8pm-1am) Guantánamo is the only place in Cuba outside Habana with two houses of *trova* (traditional poetic singing/songwriting) one on Parque Martí with low-key folk listings and the other on Máximo Gómez No 1062 with a slightly edgier beat.

**Casa de la Música** (Calixto García btwn Flor Crombet & Emilio Giro) There's also this well-maintained venue with Thursday *rap peñas* (rap concerts) and Sunday *trova* matinees.

**Tumba Francesa Pompadour** (Serafín Sánchez No 715) This peculiarly Guantánamo nightspot situated four blocks east of the train station specializes in a unique form of Haitian-style dancing. Programs, which are generally listed on the door, include *mi tumba baile* (Tumba dance), *encuentro tradicional* (traditional get together) and *peña campesino* (country music).

**Casa de la Cultura** (☎ 32 63 91; admission free) In the former Casino Español, on the west side of Parque Martí, this venue holds classical concerts and Afro-Cuban dance performances.

**Club Nevada** (cnr Pedro A Pérez & Bartolomé Masó; admission CUC$1) For the city's funkiest disco head to this tiled-terrace rooftop, blasting all the salsa and disco standards you've tolerated thus far.

**Cine Huambo** (cnr Calixto García & Flor Crombet) and **Cine America** (Calixto García), a block north, next to the Cubana office, are both near Parque Martí.

Saturday nights are for Noches Guantanameras when Calle Pedro Pérez is closed to traffic and stalls are set up in the street. Locals enjoy whole roast pig, belting music and copious amount of rum. Watch out for the drunks!

Baseball games are played from October to April at the Estadio Van Troi in Reparto San Justo, 1.5km south of the Servi-Cupet.

## Shopping

**Fondo de Bienes Culturales** (1st fl, Calixto García No 855) This place next to Pizzería Holguín, on the east side of Parque Martí, sells handicrafts.

**Photo Service** (Los Maceos btwn Aguilera & Flor Crombet) Films, prints, and batteries sold here.

## Getting There & Away

### AIR

**Cubana** (☎ 3-4533; Calixto García No 817) flies five times a week from Habana (CUC$124 one way, 2½ hours). There are no international flights to this airport.

### BUS & TRUCK

The Terminal de Omnibus, 5km west of the center on the old road to Santiago de Cuba (a continuation of Av Camilo Cienfuegos), has Astro buses to Baracoa, Camagüey, Habana, Holguín and Santiago de Cuba leaving daily. On some of the Baracoa services, you have to change buses at Imías.

There are **Víazul** (www.viazul.com) buses daily to Baracoa (CUC$10, 9:30am) and Santiago de Cuba (CUC$6, 5:25pm).

Trucks to Santiago de Cuba (five pesos) and Baracoa also leave from the Terminal de Omnibus; though foreigners are sometimes prevented from using them. One reader reported taking a 20-centavo city bus marked 'Paraguay' to 'El Punto,' where he was able to catch a truck to Baracoa.

Trucks for Moa (seven pesos) park on the road to El Salvador north of town near the entrance to the Autopista Nacional.

### CAR

The Autopista Nacional to Santiago de Cuba ends near Embalse La Yaya, 25km west of Guantánamo, where the road joins the Carretera Central. At El Cristo, 12km outside Santiago de Cuba, you rejoin the Autopista. To drive to Guantánamo from Santiago de Cuba, follow the Autopista Nacional north about 12km to the top of the grade, then take the first turn to the right. Eastbound, be aware of a police checkpoint near the end of the Autopista Nacional, a few kilometers short of Guantánamo. Any local will know the route and speed traps well (another benefit to sharing extra space in your car with a rideless Cuban).

### TRAIN

The **train station** (☎ 32 55 18; Pedro A Pérez), several blocks north of Parque Martí, has one departure for Habana (CUC$32, 9:05pm) on alternate days. This train also stops at Camagüey (CUC$13), Ciego de Ávila

(CUC$16), Guayos (CUC$20, closest you can get to Sancti Spíritus on this line), Santa Clara (CUC$22) and Matanzas (CUC$29). There was no Santiago de Cuba service at the time of writing. Purchase tickets in the morning of the day the train departs at the office on Pedro A Pérez.

### Getting Around

A one-peso bus departs for the airport from the **Cubana office** (Calixto García No 817), two hours before Cubana flights. From the airport, follow Cuban passengers onto this bus.

**Havanautos** (☎ 35 54 05; Cupet Guantánamo) is by the Servi-Cupet gas station on the way out of town toward Baracoa. If you couldn't get a car in Santiago, you should be able to pick one up here.

**Oro Negro** (cnr Los Maceos & Jesús del Sol) is another option to fill up on gas before the 150km trek east to Baracoa.

Taxis hang out around Parque Martí or you can call **CubaTaxi** (☎ 32 36 36). The Bus 48 (20 centavos) runs between the center and the Hotel Guantánamo every 40 minutes or so. There are also plenty of bici-taxis (bicycle taxis).

## GUANTÁNAMO US NAVAL BASE

'I eat breakfast 300 yards from 4000 Cubans who are trained to kill me' retorted Jack Nicholson aka Colonel Jessop, in the movie *A Few Good Men*. Such Hollywood-scripted outbursts of no-holds-barred paranoia have a certain ring of authenticity about them. With 3000 permanent military personal, two airstrips, dozens of high-security watchtowers and docking space for more than 40 warships; inglorious Gitmo – as generations of US servicemen have unaffectionately come to call it – has outgrown its initial purpose as a coaling and naval station designed to ensure the 'maintenance of the independence of Cuba.'

Procured via the infamous Platt amendment in 1903 following the cessation of hostilities in the 1898 Spanish-American war, the *real* reason the US bamboozled the Cuban government into signing away this 116-sq-km wedge of sovereign territory was to protect the eastern approach to the strategically important Panama Canal. In 1934 an upgrade of the original treaty reaffirmed the lease terms and agreed to honor them indefinitely unless both governments accorded otherwise (some hope!). It also set an annual rent of 2000 gold pieces or US$4000, a sum that the US generously continues to cough up but which Castro vehemently refuses to cash, storing it instead (it is rumored) in the top draw of his office desk. Until 1958, when motorized traffic was officially cut off between Guantánamo and the outside world, hundreds of Cubans used to commute daily into the base for work. Although this labor force has dwindled to a trickle in the years since, there are, as of 2006, (amazingly) two elderly Cubans still making the daily journey.

Expanded post-WWII, the oldest US military base on foreign soil has hovered intermittently between tense Cold War battleground and the most virulent surviving political anachronism in the western hemisphere. Indeed, these days maintaining Cuban independence is probably the last thing on the American government's mind. Immediately after the 1959 revolution, the Castro regime asked the US to return the base to Cuban sovereignty. Predictably, the Americans – locked in a Cold War deadlock with the Soviet Union and fearing Castro's imminent flight toward Moscow – steadfastly refused. As relations between the countries deteriorated, Cuba cut off water and electricity to the base, and the US troops on duty were denied permission to leave.

The recent history of the facility is infamous. In January 1992, 11,000 Haitian migrants were held here, and in August 1994 the base was used as a dumping ground for 32,000 Cubans picked up by the US Coast Guard on their way to Florida. Of these, some 8000 of the old, young and sick were later allowed into the US on humanitarian grounds, and another 2000 returned voluntarily to Cuba. In May 1995 the Cuban and US governments signed an agreement under which most of the remaining 22,000 Cuban refugees at Guantánamo (18,000 of them young men between 18 and 21) were allowed into the US. Since then, illegal Cuban immigrants picked up by the US Coast Guard at sea have been returned to Cuba.

Since the September 11, 2001 attacks, the US has held more than 600 prisoners at Guantánamo Bay without pressing criminal charges. Mostly denied legal counsel and family contact while facing rigorous interrogations, the detainees (some as young as 13 and one as old as 98) have mounted hunger strikes and there have been dozens of suicide attempts. Following protests from Amnesty International and a UN report which conceded that aspects of the camp regime 'amounted to torture'; the US released a small group of prisoners. However, as of early 2006, 490 remained with only 10 facing trial. For good up-to-date information you can visit Human Rights Watch at www.hrw.org.

A 2006 British-made movie called *The Road to Guantánamo* directed by Michael Winterbottom traces the story of three British men from Tipton in the West Midlands who were picked up in Afghanistan in 2002 and sent to Guantánamo for alleged Al-Qaeda links. The men were released without charge in 2004. They had been on their way to Pakistan to organize a wedding.

## AROUND GUANTÁNAMO US NAVAL BASE

A distant view of the base can be obtained from the **Mirador de Malones** (admission CUC$5, drink included; 8am-3pm) on a 320m-high hill just west of the complex. Opened in 1992, the *mirador* (viewpoint) is operated by the Cuban tourism organization Gaviota. The entrance is at a Cuban military checkpoint off the main highway, 27km southeast of Guantánamo. You then drive another 15km south toward the sugar exporting port of Boquerón, and on up to the viewpoint. Just before the final climb to the *mirador*, there's a large bunker containing a large-scale model of the base, which guides use to highlight points of interest. Using a telescope made in Kentucky, you can observe the US flag fluttering at Northeast Gate and pick out American vehicles driving along the road. Contrary to what some people may tell you there is no visible sign of the 'golden arches.'

### Sleeping

**Hotel Caimanera** (Islazul; ☎ 9-9414; s/d with breakfast low season CUC$20/24, high season CUC$23/30; P) This hotel is on a hilltop at Caimanera, near the perimeter of the US naval base, 21km south of Guantánamo. It's not at all convenient for regular travelers; only groups of seven or more on prearranged tours with an official Cuban guide are accepted. Besides, the view is much better from the Mirador de Malones.

### Getting There & Away

You can't just arrive unannounced at the checkpoint, but have to arrange bookings beforehand at the Baracoa and Santiago de Cuba **Gaviota offices** (Baracoa Hotel Castillo ☎ 4-5165; Santiago de Cuba ☎ 68 71 35; Villa Gaviota, Manduley No 502, Vista Alegre). If you don't have your own transport, a round-trip taxi with wait will cost in the vicinity of CUC$40.

## SOUTH COAST

Leaving Guantánamo in the rearview mirror, you quickly hit the long, dry coastal road to the island's eastern extremity, Punta de Maisí. This is Cuba's spectacular semidesert region where cacti nestle on stony hillsides and prickly aloe vera poke out from the dry scrub. Several little stone beaches between Playa Yacabo and Cajobabo make refreshing pit stops for those with time to linger, while the diverse roadside scenery – punctuated at intervals by rugged purple mountains and impossibly verdant riverside oases – engages throughout.

At the far end of deserted Playita de Cajobabo, just before the main road bends inland, there is a **monument** commemorating José Martí's 1895 landing here to launch the Second War of Independence. A colorful billboard depicts the bobbing rowboat making for shore with Martí sitting calmly inside, dressed rather improbably in trademark dinner suit, not a hair out of place. It's a good snorkeling spot, flanked by dramatic cliffs. The famous **La Farola** (the lighthouse road) starts here. Finished in 1964, the project was one of the earliest engineering triumphs of the revolutionary government. This spectacular highway snakes its way through the Sierra del Puril mountains from the arid coast of Cajababo to the tropical paradise of Baracoa covering 55km and rising to an elevation of 600m. It is listed as one of the seven man-made wonders of Cuba (and one of only two outside Habana). Cyclists take a deep breath…

### Sleeping & Eating

**Campismo Yacabo** (☎ 8-0289; per person CUC$4) This place, by the highway 10km west of Imías, has 18 new cabins overlooking the sea near the mouth of the river. The cabins sleep four to six people and make a great beach getaway for groups on a budget. Book ahead.

There are two accommodation possibilities at Imías, midway between Guantánamo and Baracoa. Cabañas El Bosque, a few hundred meters down the road to Los Calderos from Imías, has seven cabins near a river. A better choice is **Cabañas Playa Imías** (1-2 people CUC$10; ), near a long dark beach that drops off quickly into deep water, 2km east of the center of Imías. The 15 cement cabins have baths, fridges and TVs. Neither guarantee foreign admission, but as ever in Cuba the rules are flexible.

## PUNTA DE MAISÍ

☎ 21

From Cajobabo, the coastal road continues 51km northeast to La Máquina. As far as Jauco, the road is good; thereafter it's not so good. Coming from Baracoa to La Máquina (55km), it's a good road as far as Sabana, then rough in places from Sabana to La Máquina. Either way, La Máquina is the starting point of the very rough 13km track down to Punta de Maisí; it's best covered in a 4WD vehicle.

This is Cuba's easternmost point and there's a **lighthouse** (1862) and a small fine white-sand beach. You can see Haiti 70km away on a clear day.

At the time of writing the Maisí area was designated a military zone and not open to travelers.

## BOCA DE YUMURÍ

From Sabana, a very steep concrete road zigzags down the hillside to Boca de Yumurí at the mouth of the Río Yumurí. Just before the bridge over the river is the Túnel de los Alemanes (German Tunnel), an amazing natural arch of trees and foliage. Though lovely, this dark beach has become *the* day trip from Baracoa. Hustlers hard-sell fried fish meals, while other people peddle colorful land snails called *polimitas,* which have become rare as a result of being harvested wholesale for tourists. Refuse all offers.

West of Boca de Yumurí, a good road runs 28km along the coast toward Baracoa, passing many inviting black beaches and countless exciting vistas. This makes a superb bike jaunt from Baracoa (56km round-trip): hot, but smooth and flat and you can stop at any beach that catches your fancy (try Playa Bariguá at Km 24.8). You can arrange bikes in Baracoa – ask at your casa particular. Alternatively, taxis will take you there from Baracoa.

## BARACOA

☎ 21 / pop 42,285

Mystical, alluring, and oh-so alive: Baracoa – a small windswept coastal town perched improbably on Cuba's eastern tip – is undoubtedly one of the island's most rewarding travel destinations.

For the first-time visitor, getting there is half the fun. From its summit high up in the Sierra del Puril, the winding form of La Farola (the lighthouse road) snakes its way precipitously downward through a rugged landscape of gray granite cliffs and pine-scented cloud forest until it falls, with eerie suddenness, upon the lush tropical paradise of the Atlantic coastline. Columbus first came here in 1492 and described it as the most beautiful land he had ever set eyes upon. Che Guevara dropped by five centuries later and opened up the area's first major industrial complex, a still-functioning chocolate factory. Other long-standing admirers include Cuban novelist Alejo Carpentier, who based his book *La Consagración de la Primavera* on Baracoa-based Russian émigré Magdalena Rovieskuya; and the Colombian writer Gabriel García Márquez whose fantastical settlement of Macondo in the novel *One Hundred Years of Solitude* has often been likened to the town – except that Baracoa's solitude lasted a good four hundred years longer than Macondo's. In fact, so remote was this most ethereal of Cuban municipalities that, until the opening of La Farola in 1964, the only way to reach it was via the sea.

Not that this has detracted in any way from Baracoa's rich historical heritage; a legacy that has seen it elevated, by turns, into Cuba's first colonial settlement (founded in 1511), to its first capital (briefly from 1511 to 1515), to its first font of revolutionary activism (courtesy of a local Indian chief called Hatuey who rose up against the marauding Spanish in 1512).

Today the premier attractions in Baracoa include trekking up mysterious El Yunque – the town's flat-topped mountain – or indulging in the ultimate down-to-earth

dining experience in the Paladar Colonial, a laid-back family-run restaurant that boasts, arguably, some of the best food to be found in Cuba.

## Orientation

Gustavo Rizo airport (airport code BCA) is 1km off the road to Moa beside Hotel Puerto Santo, 4km from central Baracoa. Baracoa's two bus stations are on opposite sides of town. There are three good hotels in or near the old town and another next to the airport. Most of Baracoa can be explored on foot, but a bicycle is useful for visiting nearby beaches and rural pockets.

## Information

### INTERNET ACCESS & TELEPHONE

**Etecsa** (cnr Antonio Maceo & Rafael Trejo; per hr CUC$6; 7am-10pm) Internet and international calls.

### LIBRARIES

**Biblioteca Raúl Gómez García** (José Martí No 130; 8am-noon & 2-9pm Mon-Fri, 8am-4pm Sat)

### MEDIA

**Radio CMDX 'La Voz del Toa'** Broadcasts over 650AM.

### MEDICAL SERVICES

**Farmacia Principal Municipal** (Antonio Maceo No 132; 24hr)

**Hospital General Docente** (4-3014) Two kilometers from town, on the road to Guantánamo. Will treat foreigners in an emergency.

### MONEY

**Banco de Crédito y Comercio** (4-2771; Antonio Maceo No 99; 8am-2:30pm Mon-Fri)

**Banco Popular de Ahorro** (José Martí No 166; 8-11:30am & 2-4:30pm Mon-Fri) Cashes traveler's checks.

**Cadeca** (José Martí No 241)

### POST

**Post office** (Antonio Maceo No 136; 8am-8pm)

### TRAVEL AGENCIES

**Campismo Popular** (4-2776/4-5263; José Martí No 225; 8am-noon & 2-6pm Tue & Wed)

**Cubatur** (4-5306; Calle Martí No 181; 8am-noon, 2-4pm Mon-Fri) Tours to El Yunque and Parque Nacional Alejandro de Humboldt.

## Sights & Activities

### IN TOWN

The hopelessly dilapidated but charming 1833 **Catedral de Nuestra Señora de la Asunción** (Antonio Maceo No 152) on Parque Central houses the Cruz de La Parra, said to have been erected by Columbus near Baracoa. Though carbon dating disproves the legend that Columbus brought the cross from Europe, an exhaustive investigation by Cuban and foreign scholars indicates that this is indeed the last remaining cross of the two dozen or so the Spaniards erected throughout Latin America (the one in Santo Domingo is a replica). Mass is at 6pm daily and also 9am on Sunday. Knock on the last door on Calle Maceo to gain access outside of Mass hours. Donations are accepted.

Facing the cathedral is a bust of Indian chief Hatuey, who was burned at the stake near Baracoa by the Spanish in 1512 (see the boxed text, below). Also on Parque Central is the neoclassical **Poder Popular** (Antonio Maceo No 137). A municipal government building, it's not open to visitors.

To see a couple of dozen *torcedores* (cigar rollers) rolling cigars, visit the **Fábrica de Tabacos Manuel Fuente** (José Martí No 214; 7am-noon & 2-5pm Mon-Fri, 7am-noon Sat). The **Centro de Veteranos** (José Martí No 216; admission free) displays photos of those who perished in the 1959 revolution and in Angola.

Baracoa's **Museo Municipal** (cnr José Martí & Malecón; admission CUC$1; 8am-noon & 2-6pm), in the Fuerte Matachín (1802) at the southern entrance to town, has pretty bay vistas out-

### A REBEL'S REBEL

Never mind Castro, Che and Camilo, it was a 16th-century Taíno Indian chief named Hatuey who was Cuba's first *guerrillero* (rebel fighter). Hailing originally from Hispaniola, Hatuey had experienced the brutal savagery of Spanish avarice first hand by the time he arrived in Cuba with more than 300 men in around 1511. Unwilling to witness another massacre on the same scale, he circulated among Cuba's indigenous Taíno wielding a basket of gold and jewels. 'Here is the God the Spanish worship,' he admonished disdainfully. 'For these they fight and kill.'

Incapable of matching the Spanish for weaponry, Hatuey and his supporters employed simple guerrilla tactics, surprising the invaders in small groups before dispersing into the mountains to hide. After holding out for some months in this way the valiant Hatuey was betrayed by a traitor, an act that enabled the Spanish to track him down and place him under arrest.

Sentenced to death in keeping with Spanish inquisitional justice, Hatuey was brutally tortured before being tied to a stake to face death by public burning. Before the pyre was lit a priest offered him a cross and asked him if he would like to go to heaven. 'Are there people like you in heaven?' the Indian allegedly questioned. When the priest replied 'yes' Hatuey answered that he wanted nothing to do with a god that allowed such evil deeds to be carried out in his name.

side and a powerful sculpture of Hatuey at the stake inside. There's a good overview of local history, including the guitar of local *trovador* (traditional singer) Cayamba ('the singer with the ugliest voice in the world') and ephemera relating to pouty Magdalena Menasse (nee Rovieskuya, 'La Rusa').

Another Spanish fort, the **Fuerte de la Punta**, has watched over the harbor entrance at the other end of town since 1803. Today it's a restaurant serving ice-cold beers and killer views.

Baracoa's third fort, **El Castillo de Seboruco**, begun by the Spanish in 1739 and finished by the Americans in 1900, is now Hotel El Castillo (p442). There's an excellent view of El Yunque's flat top from the swimming pool. A stairway at the southwest end of Frank País climbs directly to the castle.

Baracoa's most impressive new sight is the **Museo Arqueológico** (Calle Moncada; admission CUC$2; 8am-6pm), situated in Las Cuevas del Paraíso about 800m from the Hotel El Castillo. The exhibits in this small but well-stocked museum are showcased in a series of caves that once acted as Taíno burial chambers. Among nearly 2000 authentic Taíno pieces are unearthed skeletons, ceramics, 3000-year-old petroglyphs and a replica of the *Idolo de Tabaco*, a sculpture found in Maisí in 1903 that is considered to be one of the most important Taíno finds in the Caribbean. Get one of the staff to show you round and ask about the hikes (see p444).

#### SOUTHEAST OF TOWN

Southeast of town are two natural wonders that together make a nice day trip. Passing the Fuerte Matachín, hike southeast past the baseball stadium and along the beach for about 20 minutes to a rickety wooden bridge over the Río Miel. From April to June, you'll have to take a skiff across the flooded river mouth before reaching the **bridge** (admission 1 peso; sunrise-sunset). After the bridge, turn left until you come to a Gaviota hut, where you have to pay CUC$2 to proceed further. If you continue left for 15 minutes you come to **Playa Blanca**, an idyllic spot for a picnic or sunset cocktails.

If you go to the right at the Gaviota hut and follow the dirt road through coconut groves and past clapboard houses for 45 minutes, you'll come to the blue-and-yellow **homestead of Raudeli Delgado**. For a donation (CUC$3 to CUC$5 per person), he'll lead you on a 30-minute hike, through coconut and citrus groves to a *mirador* that takes in the lush coconut plantations below and the blue sea beyond. After a short, steep descent into a lush canyon, you come to **Cueva del Aguas**, a cave with a sparkling, freshwater swimming hole inside. Ask about the coconut oil Raudeli's family makes; it's a cure for sun-cracked skin.

#### NORTHWEST OF TOWN

Heading northwest out of town toward Moa, take the one lane road for 2km beyond the airport where a break in the low-lying scrub leads to **Playa Duaba**. This is where Antonio Maceo and Flor Crombet landed in 1895 and it's a beautiful band of dark beach backed by mountains. The water gets better further from the river mouth. The *jejenes* (sand fleas) are ferocious in the late afternoon. Fifty meters further along the road is the tranquil monument to the rebel landing.

### Tours

A variety of tours can be arranged in any of the Baracoa agencies (opposite) and include: El Yunque (CUC$18), Playa Maguana (CUC$18), Parque Nacional de Humboldt (CUC$28), River Toa (CUC$11) and Boca de Yumurí (CUC$15).

### Festivals & Events

During the first week of April, Baracoa commemorates the landing of Antonio Maceo at Duaba on April 1, 1895, with a raucous **Carnaval** along the Malecón. Check the **Casa de la Cultura** (☎ 4-2349; Antonio Maceo No 124 btwn Frank País & Maraví) during Carnaval, as it presents a concurrent Semana de la Cultura that week. Every Saturday night, Calle Maceo is closed off for **Noche Baracuensa**, when food, drink and music take over.

### Sleeping

**Hotel La Rusa** (Cubanacán; ☎ 4-3011; Máximo Gómez No 161; r CUC$46; ) At last, a hotel with a history! You can't miss this three-story yellow beauty right on the Malecón. Basic but cozy, the 12 simple rooms have little balconies, some overlooking the sea. The hotel was built by local celebrity Magdalena

 

Rovieskuya, a Russian woman who inspired Alejo Carpentier's *La Consagración de la Primavera* and aided Castro's rebels during the revolution. Former guests include Errol Flynn, Che Guevara and Fidel Castro. It's a popular place, still.

**Hostal La Habanera** (Cubanacán; ☎ 4-5273/74; Antonio Maceo No 68; r CUC$46; ❄) Atmospheric and inviting in a way only Baracoa can muster, La Habanera is a recently renovated, pastel-pink hotel where the cries of passing street hawkers compete with an effusive mix of hip-gyrating music emanating form the Casa de la Cultura below. The four front bedrooms share a street-facing balcony replete with tiled floor and rocking chairs, while the downstairs lobby boasts a bar, a restaurant, and an interesting selection of local books.

**Hotel El Castillo** (Gaviota; ☎ 4-5165; Loma del Paraíso; s/d low season CUC$40/54, high season CUC$42/58; ❄ ) Another famous Baracoa hotel is this historic castle, once part of the Spanish fort. It's a relaxed, friendly place, with only 34 rooms (some dark and dampish) and there's a superb view of the bay and El Yunque from the pool (open to nonguests for a small fee). The hotel also organizes day trips to El Yunque and Río Toa among other places. It is a five- to 10-minute walk from town up the steps on Frank País or Calixto García.

### CASAS PARTICULARES – BARACOA

Hospitable Baracoa has more than 150 casas and some of them are real gems. The food here – which is distinctly different (and better) than in other parts of Cuba – is also well worth trying.

**Andrés Abella** (☎ 4-3298; Antonio Maceo No 56 btwn Peralejo & Coliseo; r CUC$15-20) Large room, friendly; also rents out No 53.

**'Casa Colonial' – Gustavo & Yalina** (☎ 4-2536; Flor Crombet No 125 btwn Frank País & Pelayo Cuervo; r CUC$15-20; ❄) Big rooms sleep three.

**Denny Rodríguez** (☎ 4-2431; Rupert López No 86 btwn Limbano Sánchez & Lope Pena; r CUC$25; ❄) Big, private, with TV and fridge.

**'El Poeta' – Pablo & Daimi** (☎ 4-3017; Maceo No 159 at Ciro Frías; r CUC$20-25) Pablo is a local poet who is regularly on the radio.

**Elsa Figueroa Toirac** (☎ 4-2460; José Martí No 152; r CUC$15-20; ❄) Central, two rooms.

**Eugenio Ona Abella** (☎ 4-3310; Moncada No 18B btwn José Martí & República; r CUC$20) Private, good meals.

**Idania de la Cruz Blanco** (☎ 4-3885; Antonio Maceo No 80 btwn 24 de Febrero & Coliseo; r CUC$15-20; ❄) Colonial house, roof terrace, friendly.

**Isabel Artola Rosell** (☎ 4-5236; Rubert López No 39 btwn Céspedes & Ciro Frías; r CUC$15-20; ❄) English spoken.

**Isabel Castro Vilato** (☎ 4-2267; Mariana Grajales No 35; r CUC$20; P ❄) Colonial house, terrific garden, porch, meals.

**Josefina Guilarte** (☎ 4-3532; Flor Crombet No 269; r CUC$15-20) Meals served, quiet, out of center; also rents out 265A.

**Lidia Cobas** (☎ 4-3464; 10 de Octubre No 21C; r CUC$15-20)

**Lourdes Balga** (☎ 4-3218; Av Malecón No 72; r CUC$15-20) Room near Coroneles Galano that can sleep three; friendly.

**Lucy Navarra Rodríguez** (☎ 4-3548; Céspedes No 29 btwn Rubert López & Maceo; r CUC$20; ❄) Lovely local character with clean, friendly colonial house. There are two rooms here and two terraces on different levels.

**Miriams Zoila Montoya** (☎ 4-3529; José Martí No 301; r CUC$15-20)

**Nelia Y Yaquelin** (☎ 4-3625, 4-3353; Mariana Grajales No 11 btwn Calixto García & Julio Mella; r CUC$15-20; ❄) Two rooms.

**Nelsy Borges Teran** (☎ 4-3569; Antonio Maceo No 171 btwn Ciro Frias & Céspedes; r CUC$20; ❄) Several outfitted rooms, great roof terrace, views.

**Nilson Abad Guilaré** (☎ 4-3123; Flor Crombert No 143 btwn Ciro Frías & Pelayo Cuervo; r CUC$25; ❄) Fantastic self-contained apartment with brand new fixtures. Kitchen, terrace with sea views and scrumptious Baracoan cuisine.

**Williams Montoya Sánchez** (☎ 4-2798; José Martí No 287; r CUC$15-20; P ❄) Serves meals.

**Hotel Porto Santo** (Gaviota; ☎ 4-5106; Carretera del Aeropuerto; s/d low season CUC$40/54, high season CUC$42/58; P ✖ ☒) A modern, airy hotel with exposed-beam ceilings situated 200m from the airport and 4km from the town center. There are 36 rooms here and the setting is dreamlike, especially at night with the sound of the crashing waves drifting in through your window. A stairway leads down to a tiny, storm-lashed beach.

## Eating

After the dull monotony of just about everywhere else, eating in Baracoa is a full-on sensory experience. Cooking here is creative, tasty and – above all – different. Local delicacies include *cucurucho* (grated coconut mixed with sugar, honey and guava, wrapped in a palm frond), fish with coconut sauce, *bacán* (pulped plantain and coconut milk) and *teti* (a tiny red fish indigenous to the Río Toa).

**Paladar El Colonial** (José Martí No 123; mains CUC$10; ⏰ lunch & dinner) Baracoa's only paladar is also one of the best in Cuba. The down-to-earth family restaurant is run out of a handsome wooden clapboard house that feels more Jamaican than Cuban. The unposted menu changes regularly and depends on the daily catch. Try the swordfish, octopus or the prawns, and ask about the traditional Baracoan coconut sauce.

**Cafetería El Parque** (Antonio Maceo No 142; ⏰ 24hr) The flowering terrace, occasional live bands, pool table, fried chicken, ice cream and cold drinks mean this place is Baracoa's main hangout. It's a Palmares-run place right across from the central park and a good spot to connect with the locals.

**Restaurante La Punta** (Fuerte de la Punta; ⏰ 10am-11pm) In an old fort overlooking the Atlantic, this historic restaurant was undergoing a refurbishment as this book went to press. The revamp looked quite promising.

**Casa del Chocolate** (Antonio Maceo No 123; ⏰ 7:20am-11pm) Only in Cuba! A chocolate house with – wait for it – no chocolate. The quickest way to check out Baracoa's on-off supply situation is to stick your head around the kitchen door and hail one of the bored-looking waitresses. But be warned. The paltry cups of muddy liquid that pass for chocolate in this establishment are nothing like the steaming mugs of bedtime cocoa you might have tasted in childhood.

**Pizzería** (Antonio Maceo No 155) This fly-blown place sells acceptable three-peso pizza; skip the *tocino* (bacon) variety.

Two other half-decent places right on the park include friendly **Restaurante Yaima** (Antonio Maceo No 143), with basic peso meals served in an agreeable atmosphere (read: napkins) and **Restaurante 485 Aniversario** (Antonio Maceo No 139; mains CUC$4; ⏰ 11:30am-2pm & 6-9pm), with good fried chicken and fish. El Rápido, at the Servi-Cupet at the southeast entrance to town, serves the usual chow at cut rates.

### SELF-CATERING

**Tienda La Yumurí** (Antonio Maceo No 149; ⏰ 8:30am-noon & 1:30-5pm Mon-Sat, 9am-noon Sun) Get in line for the good selection of groceries here.

**Mercado Agropecuario** (cnr 24 de Febrero & Malecón) The selection at Baracoa's market makes it abundantly clear how remote you really are, ie if it isn't growing right here, right now, you won't find it.

**Dulcería La Criolla** (José Martí No 178) This place sells bread, pastries and – when it feels like it – the famous Baracoan chocolate.

**Empresa Cubana del Pan** (José Martí btwn Céspedes & Coroneles Galano) This shop has regular 10-peso short loaves, and also fruit bread.

## Drinking & Entertainment

**Casa de la Trova Victorino Rodríguez** (Antonio Maceo No 149a) Cuba's smallest, zaniest, wildest and most atmospheric *casa de la trova* (*trova* house) rocks nightly to the voodoolike rhythms of *changüi-son*. Order a mojito (rum cocktail) in a jam jar and sit back and enjoy the show. The crazy MC is an act in his own right and the house rules conform to that age-old *trova* assertion: 'if you can sing or play an instrument, show us what you can do.' Bring your own guitar and see what happens!

**El Ranchón** (admission CUC$1; ⏰ 9pm) Atop a long flight of stairs at the western end of Coroneles Galano, El Ranchón mixes an exhilarating hilltop setting with taped disco and salsa music and legions of resident *jineteras* (women who attach themselves to male foreigners for monetary or material gain). Maybe that's why it's so insanely popular. Watch your step on the way down – it's a scary 146-step drunken tumble.

**Casa de la Cultura** (☎ 4-2349; Antonio Maceo No 124 btwn Frank País & Maraví) This venue does a good rumba show incorporating textbook

**GO FURTHER INTO THE COUNTRYSIDE**

To explore beyond the standard travel-agency itinerary, ask around at the Museo Arqueológico (p441) about a number of interesting hikes south of Baracoa in the vicinity of Playa Blanca, Yumurí and the nearby Majayara Peninsula.

Set up in 2003 under the auspices of distinguished Cuban archaeologist Roberto Orduñez Fernández, the museum and its staff can offer an interesting clutch of archeologically-inspired trips including **Pintura Rupestres** (see some ancient Taíno paintings, and visit a native suicide site: CUC$18), **Tumba de Guamá** (visit a native tomb near isolated Playa Cajaujo: CUC$15) and **El Camino de Piedra** (hike an old native Taíno trail close to a hill overlooking Baracoa: CUC$8). These hikes were still being developed at the time of writing and could be subject to change. For archaeological fiends, however, there is no doubt that Baracoa's potential is enormous.

Cuban styles of *guaguancó, yambú* and *columbia* (subgenres of rumba). Go prepared for *mucho* audience participation.

**La Terraza** (Antonio Maceo btwn Maraví & Frank País; admission CUC$1; 9pm-2am Mon-Thu, 9pm-4am Fri-Sun) This is a rooftop disco with occasional hot salsa septets.

**Café El Patio** (Antonio Maceo No 120) This venue has a nice courtyard for a drink; and no cover charge.

**Cine-Teatro Encanto** (Antonio Maceo No 148) Baracoas's only cinema is in front of the cathedral.

From October to April, baseball games are held at the Estadio Manuel Fuentes Borges, southeast along the beach from the Museo Municipal.

## Shopping

Good art is easy to find in Baracoa and, like most things in this whimsical seaside town, it has its own distinctive flavor.

**Fondo Cubano de Bienes Culturales** (Antonio Maceo No 120; 9am-5pm Mon-Fri, 9am-noon Sat & Sun) This shop sells Hatuey woodcarvings and T-shirts with indigenous designs.

**ARTex** (Calle Martí btwn Céspedes & Galano) For the usual tourist fare check out this place.

**Taller La Musa** (Antonio Maceo No 124) Call by this outlet in the Casa de la Cultura where you can seek out innovative local artist Andreas Borges and his imaginative work.

## Getting There & Away

The closest train station is in Guantánamo, 150km southwest.

### AIR

**Cubana** (☎ 4-5374; Calle Martí No 181; 8am-noon; 2-4pm Mon-Fri) has two weekly flights from Habana to Baracoa (CUC$135 one way, Thursday and Sunday). There is also a Sunday-only flight from Santiago (CUC$32, 30 minutes).

Be aware that the planes and buses out of Baracoa are sometimes fully booked, so don't come here on a tight schedule without outbound reservations.

### BUS

The **national bus station** (☎ 4-3670; cnr Av Los Mártires & José Martí) has **Astro** (☎ 4-3670) buses to Santiago de Cuba and Habana on alternate days. For some odd reason, the bus to Guantánamo is only for people connecting there with trains. Tickets in Convertibles are sold from 8am to 4pm.

**Víazul** (www.viazul.com) buses leave for Guantánamo (CUC$10, three hours), continuing to Santiago de Cuba (CUC$16, five hours) daily at 2:15pm. Bus tickets can be reserved in advance through **Cubatur** (☎ 4-5306; Calle Martí No 181) for a CUC$5 commission.

The **intermunicipal bus station** (cnr Galano & Calixto García), has two or three trucks a day to Moa (90 minutes, 78km, departures from 6am) and Guantánamo (four hours, 150km, departures from 2am). Prices are a few Cuban pesos. If you can't find a truck right to Guantánamo, take anything as far as San Antonio del Sur, where you'll find onward trucks.

## Getting Around

The best way to get to/from the airport is by taxi (CUC$2) or bici-taxi (CUC$1), if you're traveling light.

There's a helpful **Havanautos** (☎ 4-5344) car-rental office at the airport. Cheaper **Vía Rent a Car** (☎ 4-5135) is inside the Hotel Porto Santo. **Servi-Cupet** (José Martí; 24hr) is right at the entrance to town and 4km from the center, on the road to Guantánamo. Drivers hightailing it to Habana should note that the northern route through Moa and Holguín is fastest but the road disintegrates rapidly after Maguana Beach.

Bici-taxis around Baracoa should charge five pesos a ride, but they often ask 10 to 15 pesos from foreigners.

The Palmares Café in the main park rents cycles for CUC$3 per day. The ultimate bike ride is the 20km ramble down to Maguana Beach, one of the most scenic roads in Cuba. Lazy daisies can rent mopeds for CUC$24 either at Palmares Café or **Hotel El Castillo** (☎ 4-5165; Loma del Paraíso).

## NORTHWEST OF BARACOA

### Sights & Activities

The **Finca Duaba** (🕑 noon-4pm Tue-Sun), 6km out of Baracoa on the road to Moa and then 1km inland, is designed to give visitors a taste of country life. On this verdant farm you'll see profuse tropical plants, enjoy a swim in the Río Duaba, and be served a massive Creole lunch (CUC$12 per person).

The **Río Toa**, 10km northwest of Baracoa, is the third longest river on the north coast of Cuba and the country's most voluminous. It is also an important bird and plant habitat. Cocoa trees and the ubiquitous coconut palm are grown in the Valle de Toa. A vast hydroelectric project on the Toa was abandoned after a persuasive campaign led by the Fundación de la Naturaleza y El Hombre convinced authorities it would do irreparable ecological damage; engineering and economic reasons also played a part. **Rancho Toa** is a Palmares restaurant reached via a right-hand turn-off just before the Toa Bridge. You can organize boat or kayak trips here for CUC$3 to CUC$10 and watch acrobatic Baracoans scale Coco palms. A traditional Cuban feast of whole roast pig is available if you can rustle up enough people (eight usually).

Most of this region lies within the Unesco Cuchillas de Toa Biosphere Reserve, an expansive area of 208,305 hectares that incorporates the Alejandro de Humboldt World Heritage site. This area contains the largest rainforest in Cuba with trees exhibiting many precious woods. The region also has a high number of endemic species.

One of Baracoa's most challenging day trips is summiting **El Yunque** (569m). It's not a high hike, but the views are stupendous. **Cubatur** (☎ 4-5306; Calle Martí No 181, Baracoa) offers this tour daily (CUC$18 per person, minimum two people). The fee covers admission, guide, transport and a sandwich. The hike is hot (bring sufficient water). If you have a car or bike you can arrange your own guide at the campismo for a few fewer pesos. Take the road toward Moa for 6km and then turn left into the spur to the campismo.

#### MERMAID OR MANATEE?

The slow-moving Caribbean *manatí* (manatee) is descended from a land mammal that returned to life in the water. It can grow up to 4.5m long and weigh as much as 600kg. Graceful but ugly, manatees have small heads, thick necks and a wide bristly snout. Their poorly developed eyes have glands that secrete an oily substance for protection against salt water.

An adult manatee has a thick tapered body ending in a wide horizontal tail flipper. It uses two front flippers to swim and to bring food to its mouth. The manatee's ribs aren't attached to a rib cage, meaning that its lungs are crushed if the animal lies on its belly on dry land. To avoid suffocating, a manatee caught by low tide will flip over onto its back and wait for the water to return.

Unlike whales and seals, manatees never take to the open ocean. They prefer to linger around thick plant growth and graze on seaweed in brackish coastal waters, estuaries, and rivers, where they consume up to 50kg of plant life a day. While grazing in the shallows with its head and shoulders above the water, a manatee resembles a human figure, which perhaps gave rise to mermaid legends.

Although the manatee has no natural enemies except humans, it has become endangered due to hunting, injury from boat propellers and habitat destruction. In Cuba it has been a protected species since 1973 though local factors such as sugar-factory waste and large-scale tourist development, have served to hinder its conservation.

Four kilometers on is the trailhead and the campground. Bring a swimsuit for a dip in the Río Duaba afterward.

### Sleeping & Eating

**Campismo El Yunque** (☎ 4-5262) This rustic place is beautifully located at the foot of the mystical El Yunque Mountain, 6km north of Baracoa on the road to Moa, then another 4km inland on a rough road through a cocoa plantation. There are 14 wooden cabins, sleeping four or six people. This is normally a Cubans-only place, but you can try your luck at the Campismo Popular office in Baracoa (p440).

**Villa Maguana** (Gaviota; no phone; s/d with breakfast low season CUC$45/60, high season CUC$50/65) For a dreamy night or two away in one of Cuba's most exotic little hideaways pay a visit here. The villa faces an idyllic, palm-fringed, white-sand beach, 22km northwest of Baracoa. Formerly a quaint guesthouse with four rooms plus porch rockers fronting a lawn adjacent to a beach, the villa was undergoing renovations at the time of writing with another 10 rooms due to be added on. Hopefully the extension won't take too much away from what was an astoundingly beautiful setting. News and reservations for Villa Maguana can be had through Hotel El Castillo in Baracoa (p442).

Palmares has a small snack bar on Playa Maguana that sells cold drinks, fried chicken and sandwiches. There's also a rustic restaurant with a barbecue that can lay on a fine seafood lunch. Snorkeling is available from boats at a nearby reef. There's no hire kiosk as such but the local boatman has a habit of finding you just when you need him.

## PARQUE NACIONAL ALEJANDRO DE HUMBOLDT

Designated a Unesco World Heritage site in 2001, this beautiful national park, characterized by its steep pine-clad mountains and creeping morning mists, possesses an unmatched ecosystem that is, according to Unesco, 'one of the most biologically diverse tropical island sites on earth.' Perched above the Bahía de Taco, 40km northwest of Baracoa, Humboldt contains some of Cuba's most pristine forest, protecting 59,400 hectares of land and 2641 hectares of lagoon and mangroves. With 1000 flowering plant species and 145 types of fern, it is far and away the most diverse plant habitat in the entire Caribbean. Due to the toxic nature of the underlying rocks in the area, plants have been forced to adapt in order to survive. As a result endemism in the area is high; indeed almost 70% of the plants found here are endemic, as are many vertebrates and invertebrates. Several endangered species can also be found here including Cuban Amazon parrots and the hook-billed kites. The last ivory-billed woodpecker ever sighted was spotted here in the late '80s and has been heard (but not seen) since then. Recognized for its unique evolutionary processes, the park is heavily protected and acts as a paradigm for the Cuban government's environmental protection efforts elsewhere.

### Activities

The park contains a **visitors center** (☎ 38 14 31) staffed with biologists plus an extensive network of trails leading to waterfalls, a *mirador* and a massive karst system with caves around the Farallones de Moa. Three trails are currently open to the public and take in only a tiny segment of the park's 59,400 hectares. More development is in the pipeline. The available hikes are: **Balcón de Iberia**, at 5km the park's most challenging loop; **El Recrea**, a 2km stroll around the bay; and the **Bahía de Taco circuit**, which incorporates a boat tour (with a manatee-friendly motor developed by scientists here) through the mangroves and the bay, plus the 2km hike. Each option is accompanied by a professional guide who will teach you all you need to know about Cuban flora and fauna. Prices range from CUC$5 to CUC$10, depending on the hike.

### Sleeping

Lodging is periodically available at the bare-bones Campismo Bahía de Taco. Book ahead at the **Campismo Popular** (☎ 4-2776/4-5263; José Martí No 225) in Baracoa or inquire at **Hostal La Habanera** (☎ 4-5273/74; Antonio Maceo No 68).

### Getting There & Away

You can arrange a tour through an agency in Baracoa or get here independently. The road is rough but passable in a hire car if driven with care.

# Directory

## CONTENTS



## ACCOMMODATION

Cuban accommodation runs the gamut from CUC$10 beach cabins to five-star resorts. Solo travelers are penalized price-wise, paying 75% of the price of a double room.

In this book, budget means anything under CUC$40 for two people. In this range, casas particulares are almost always better value than a hotel. Only the most deluxe casas particulares in Habana will be anything over CUC$35, where you're assured quality amenities and attention. In cheaper casas particulares (CUC$15), you may have to share a bath and will have a fan instead of air-con. In the rock bottom places (campismos, mostly), you'll be lucky if there are sheets and running water, though there are usually private baths. If you're staying in a place intended for Cubans, you'll compromise materially, but the memories are guaranteed to be platinum.

The midrange category (CUC$40 to CUC$80) is a lottery, with some stylish colonial hotels and some awful places. In midrange hotels, you can expect air-con, private hot-water bath, clean linens, satellite TV, a restaurant and a swimming pool – although the architecture's often uninspiring and the food not exactly gourmet.

Unsurprisingly, the most comfortable top-end hotels cost CUC$80 and up for two people. These are usually partly foreign-owned and maintain international standards (although service can sometimes be a bit lax). Rooms have everything that a midrange hotel has, plus big, quality beds and

### PRACTICALITIES

- The most common electricity voltage is 110V, 60 cycles, but you'll also find 220V. Side-by-side sockets with different voltage are usually labeled, but always ask. The sockets are suited to North American–style plugs with two flat prongs.
- Commercial laundries are rare. Most casas particulares have a machine you can use or there's always hand washing.
- *Granma, Juventud Rebelde* and *Trabajadores* are the three national papers. *Bohemia* and *Temas* are two of the best general-interest magazines (in Spanish).
- There are 69 radio stations and three TV channels. Radio Habana (www.radiohc.cu) is broadcast worldwide on the shortwave band; most hotels have satellite.
- Like electricity, the common system is NTSC, but videos are sold in various formats.
- Cuba uses the metric system, except in some fruit and vegetable markets where the imperial system takes over.

linens; a minibar; international phone service; and perhaps a terrace or view. Habana has some real gems.

Factors influencing rates are time of year, location and hotel chain (in this book the chain is always listed after the hotel to give you an idea of what standard/services to expect). Low season is generally mid-September to early December and February to May (except for Easter week). Christmas and New Year is what's called extreme high season, when rates are 25% more than high-season rates. Bargaining is sometimes possible in casas particulares – though as far as foreigners go it's not really the done thing. This is not Morocco. The casa owners in any given area pay generic taxes and the prices you will be quoted reflect this. You'll find very few casas in Cuba that aren't priced between CUC$15 to CUC$35, unless you're up for a long stay. Prearranging Cuban accommodation is difficult, but not impossible.

The following chains and Internet agencies offer online booking and/or information:

**Casa Particular Organization** (www.casaparticularcuba.org) Reader recommended for prebooking private rooms.
**Cubacasas** (www.cubacasas.net) Excellent site for casa recommendations and general Cuba information.
**Cubalinda.com** (www.cubalinda.com) Habana-based, so it know its business.
**Gran Caribe** (www.grancaribe.cu)
**Islazul** (www.islazul.cu)
**Sol Meliá** (www.solmeliacuba.com) Also offers discounts.
**Vacacionar** (www.dtcuba.com) Official site of Directorio Turístico of Cuba.

## Campismos

Campismos are where Cubans go on vacation. There are more than 80 of them sprinkled throughout the country and they are wildly popular (an estimated one million Cubans use them annually). Hardly 'camping,' most of these installations are simple concrete cabins with bunk beds, foam mattresses and cold showers. Campismos are the best place to meet Cubans, make friends and party in a natural setting.

Campismos are ranked either *nacional* or *internacional*. The first are (technically) only for Cubans, while the latter host both Cubans and foreigners and are more upscale, with air-con and/or linens. There are currently a dozen international campismos in Cuba ranging from the hotel-standard Aguas Claras (Pinar del Río) to the more basic Puerto Rico Libre (Holguín). In practice, campismo staff may rent a *nacional* cabin (or tent space) to a foreigner pending availability, but it depends on the installation, and many foreigners are turned away (not helpful when you've traveled to a way-out place on the pretext of getting in). To avoid this situation we've listed only international campismos in this book.

For a full list of all the country's campismos (both *nacional* and *internacional*), you can pick up an excellent Guía de Campismo (CUC$2.50) in any Reservaciones de Campismo office.

As far as international campismos go, contact the excellent **Cubamar** (☎ 7-66-25-23/4; fax 7-33-31-11; www.cubamarviajes.cu; cnr Calle 3 & Malecón, Vedado) in Habana for reservations. If you're adamant to try winging it in a *campismo nacional* try the provincial Campismo Popular office to make a reservation closer to the installation proper (the details of these offices can be found in the relevant regional chapters). Cabin accommodation costs from CUC$10 to CUC$20 per bed. Prices at the plush cabins of Villas Aguas Claras (Pinar del Río Province; p198) and Guajimico (Cienfuegos Province; p268) are higher.

Cubamar also rents mobile homes (campervans) called Campertours, which sleep four adults and two children. Prices are around CUC$165 per day (but vary according to type, season and number of days required) including insurance (plus CUC$400 refundable deposit). You can park these campers wherever it's legal to park a regular car. There are 21 campismos/hotels that have Campertour facilities giving you access to electricity and water. These are a great alternative for families.

Renegade cyclists aside, few tourists tent camp in Cuba. Yet, the abundance of beaches, plus the helpfulness and generosity of Cubans make camping surprisingly easy and rewarding. Beach camping means insanely aggressive *jejenes* (sand fleas) and mosquitoes. The repellant sold locally just acts as a marinade for your flesh, so bring something strong – DEET-based if you're down with chemicals. Camping supplies per se don't exist; bring your own or improvise.

## Casas Particulares

Private rooms are the best option for independent travelers in Cuba and a great way of meeting the locals on their home turf. Furthermore, staying in these venerable and often family-orientated establishments will give you a far more open and less-censored view of the country with its guard down, and your understanding (and appreciation) of Cuba will grow far richer as a result. Casa owners also often make excellent tour guides.

You'll know houses renting rooms by the green triangle on the door marked *Arrendador Inscripto*. There are thousands of casas particulares all over Cuba and places such as Viñales, Trinidad and Camagüey have 300 or more in a tight vicinity. From penthouses to historical homes, all manner of rooms are available from CUC$15 to CUC$35. Although some houses will treat you like a business paycheck the vast majority of casa owners are warm, open and impeccable hosts.

Government regulation of casas is intense and it's illegal to rent private rooms in resort areas. Owners pay CUC$100 to CUC$250 per room per month depending on location; plus extra for off-street parking, to post a sign advertising their rooms and to serve meals. These taxes must be paid whether the rooms are rented or not. Owners must keep a register of all guests and report each new arrival within 24 hours. For these reasons, you will find it hard to bargain for rooms. You will also be requested to produce your passport. Penalties are high for infractions, and new regulations have recently restricted casas to two people (excluding minors) per room and only two rooms per house. Without a marriage license, travelers with Cuban spouses or partners will have a hard time finding accommodation. Most casas particulares are very strict about not letting *jineteras* (a woman who attaches herself to male foreigners for monetary or material gain; the exchange may or may not involve sex) back to the rooms, and they'll always assume a Cuban partner is a *jinetera/o* – unless you can prove otherwise.

Due to the plethora of casas particulares in Cuba it has been impossible to include

### MISIÓN MILAGROS

Misión Milagros (Miracle Mission) is the unofficial name given to a pioneering medical program hatched between Cuba and Venezuela in 2004 that offers free eye treatment for impoverished Venezuelans in Cuban hospitals. By the end of 2005 more than 150,000 Venezuelans had been successfully treated for eye ailments caused by cataracts, glaucoma, diabetes, and other diseases, and, as a result, the program had been extended to at least 10 other Latin American and Caribbean countries including Guyana and Bolivia.

In order to participate in Misión Milagros foreign patients are first diagnosed and selected in their home country before being flown free of charge to Habana for treatment. Here advanced laser technology is able to correct easily-rectified eye disorders and restore obscured or diminished vision within a matter of hours. Allowed time to convalesce in comfort after the operation, newly-sighted patients are given complimentary accommodation in a variety of Cuban hotels and are bussed around for free on a special fleet of Chinese-made Astro buses.

At the time of writing, a large number of tourist hotels were temporarily out of action due to the Misión Milagros program. These included: the Neptuno-Triton, Copacabana, El Megano, Panamericano, Acuario, and El Viejo y El Mar hotels (all Habana); Hotel Pasacaballo (Cienfuegos); Hotel Camagüey (Camagüey); Hotel Sierra Maestra (Bayamo); Hotels Costa Morena, Gran Piedra and Club Bucanero (Santiago Province); Hotel Guantánamo (Guantánamo); and Hotel Guancayabo (Manzanillo). Call ahead to check on updates.

even a fraction of the total in this book. The ones chosen are a combination of reader recommendations and local research, and are listed in alphabetical order. That said, there are plenty of other excellent options around if you have the time and inclination to look.

### Hotels

All tourist hotels and resorts are at least 51% owned by the Cuban government and are administered by one of five main organizations. Islazul is the cheapest and only mixed accommodation option that rents to both Cubans and foreigners (at different prices). Although the facilities can be variable at these establishments and the architecture a tad Sovietesque, Islazul hotels are invariably clean, cheap, friendly and, above all, Cuban. They're also more likely to be situated in the island's smaller provincial towns. One downside is the blaring on-site discos that often keep guests awake until the small hours. Cubanacán is a step up and offers a nice mix of budget and midrange options in both cities and resort areas. The company has recently developed a new clutch of affordable boutique-style hotels in attractive city centers such as Sancti Spíritus, Baracoa, Remedios and Santiago. Gaviota manages higher-end resorts including glittering Playa Pesquero which, with 900-plus rooms, is Cuba's biggest hotel, though the chain also has a smattering of cheaper 'villas' in places such as Santiago and Isla de la Juventud. Gran Caribe does midrange to top-end hotels, including many of the all-inclusives in Habana and Varadero. Lastly Habaguanex is based solely in Habana and manages most of the fastidiously restored historic hotels in Habana Vieja. The profits from these ventures go toward restoring the Unesco site. Because each group has its own niche, throughout this book we mention the chain to which a hotel belongs to give you some idea of what to expect at that particular installation. Except for Islazul properties, tourist hotels are for guests paying in Convertibles only. Cubans who are not legally married to foreigners (and have the papers to prove it) are technically not allowed to stay in tourist hotels. The reason for this – it is argued – is to control prostitution (which resurfaced with a vengeance once US dollars were legalized in 1993). Despite the banning of the dollar in November 2004, the prostitution trade has seen no sign of abating.

At the top end of the hotel chain you'll often find foreign chains such as Sol Meliá and Superclubs running hotels in tandem with Cubanacán, Gaviota or Gran Caribe – mainly in the resort areas. The standards and service in these types of places are first class.

## ACTIVITIES

As the biggest (and the best!) Caribbean co untry, with 5746km of coastline, Cuba is known for all things aquatic: scuba diving, snorkeling and deep-sea fishing especially. On land, erosion over the ages has created more than 20,000 caves and a 6km valley blanketed with weird pincushion hills – prime spelunking and rock-climbing turf. Lots of unexplored corners mean cyclists, horseback riders, backpackers and other independent traveler types will find kilometers of wide open road beckoning exploration.

Any gear you can donate at the end of your trip to individuals you meet along the way (headlamps, snorkel masks, fins etc) will be greatly appreciated.

### Caving

Cuba is riddled with caves – more than 20,000 and counting – and cave exploration is available to both casual tourists and professional speleologists. The Gran Caverna de Santo Tomás (p211), near Viñales, is Cuba's largest cavern with over 46km of galleries; Cueva de los Peces (p253), near Playa Girón, is a flooded cenote with colorful snorkeling; and the Cueva de Ambrosio (p234) and Bellamar (p225), both in Matanzas, have tours daily.

Caving specialists have virtually unlimited caves from which to choose. With advance arrangements, you can explore deep into the Gran Caverna de Santo Tomás or visit the Cueva Martín Infierno (p268), with the world's largest stalagmite. Also ask about San Catalina near Varadero, which has unique mushroom formations. Speleodiving is also possible, but only for those already highly trained. Interested experts should contact Angel Graña, secretary of the **Sociedad Espeleológica de Cuba** (☎ 7-209-2885; angel@fanj.cult.cu) in Habana. The **Escuela**

**Nacional de Espeleología** (☎ 8-77-10-14), in Moncada just at the entrance to the Caverna de Santo Tomás, is another good resource for professionals.

## Cycling

Riding a bike in Cuba is *the* best way to discover the island in close-up. Decent roads, wonderful scenery and the opportunity to get off the beaten track and meet Cubans eye to eye make cycling here a pleasure whichever route you take. For more mellow pedalers, daily bike rentals can often be procured at various hotels, resorts and cafés for a going rate of approximately CUC$3 a day.

## Diving

Cuba has superb scuba diving suitable for all levels and interests. There are more than 30 dive centers throughout the island managed by the likes of **Marinas Gaviota** (www.gaviota-grupo.com), **Cubanacán Naútica** (www.cubanacan.cu) or **Cubamar** (www.cubamarviajes.cu). Though equipment does vary between installations, you can generally expect safe, professional and often multilingual service with these operators. Environmentally sensitive diving is where things can get wobbly, and individuals should educate themselves about responsible diving (see below).

Dives and courses are comparably priced islandwide from CUC$30 to CUC$45 per dive, with a discount after four or five dives. Full certification courses are CUC$310 to CUC$365 and 'resort' or introductory courses cost CUC$50 to CUC$60. Because of the US embargo laws, PADI certification is generally not offered in Cuba; instead, you'll likely receive ACUC (American Canadian Underwater Certification) credentials.

The most popular diving areas are María la Gorda (Pinar del Río; p203), Playa Girón (on the famous Bay of Pigs; p255), Playa Rancho Luna and Guajimico (both in Cienfuegos; p267 and p268 respectively), Cayo Coco (Ciego de Ávila; p318), Playa Santa Lucía (Camagüey; p335) and Guardalavaca (Holguín; p363). Varadero (p234) has more than 30 dive sites, but only one with shore access. The quality sites around Playa Girón and Cienfuegos are good areas for first timers. Dedicated and advanced divers will want to check out the stellar underwater conditions around Isla de la Juventud (p188) – popularly considered to be

### RESPONSIBLE DIVING

Please consider the following tips when diving and help preserve the ecology and beauty of reefs:

- Never use anchors on the reef, and take care not to ground boats on coral.
- Avoid touching or standing on living marine organisms or dragging equipment across the reef. Polyps can be damaged by even the gentlest contact. If you must hold on to the reef, only touch exposed rock or dead coral.
- Be conscious of your fins. Even without contact, the surge from fin strokes near the reef can damage delicate organisms. Take care not to kick up clouds of sand, which can smother organisms.
- Practice and maintain proper buoyancy control. Major damage can be done by divers descending too fast and colliding with the reef.
- Take great care in underwater caves. Spend as little time within them as possible as your air bubbles may be caught within the roof and thereby leave organisms high and dry. Take turns inspecting the interior of a small cave.
- Resist the temptation to collect or buy corals or shells or to loot marine archaeological sites (mainly shipwrecks).
- Ensure that you take home all your rubbish and any litter you may find as well. Plastics in particular are a serious threat to marine life.
- Do not feed fish.
- Minimize your disturbance of marine animals. *Never* ride on the backs of turtles.

the best on the archipelago, if not the best in the Caribbean – and the pristine area of Jardines de la Reina (p318).

### Fishing

Cuba's finest deep-sea fishing for sailfish, swordfish, tuna, mackerel, barracuda and shark is along the northwest coast where the fast-moving Gulf Stream supports prime game fishing. Facilities for sport anglers exist at Habana (p149), Playas del Este (p165), Varadero (p235), Cayo Guillermo (p320), Bahía de Naranjo (p363) and Isla de la Juventud (p190). Shore casting for bonefish and tarpon is practiced off the south coast at Jardines de la Reina (p318).

Fly fishing is superb in vast Ciénaga de Zapata (p253) in Matanzas, where enthusiasts can arrange multiday catch-and-release trips. You can cast for *trucha* (largemouth bass) at Laguna Grande (p202), Laguna de Tesoro (p251) and Laguna del Leche (p316). Embalse Zaza and the Río Agabama (p292) are two more anglers' paradises.

### Hiking & Trekking

While Cuba's trekking potential is enormous, the traveler's right to roam is severely restricted by badly-maintained trails, poor signage, lack of maps, and rather draconian restrictions about where you can and cannot go without a guide.

All of the best routes, including the three-day Pico Turquino summit (p427); the Cueva las Perlas stroll in Península de Guanahacabibes (p203); flat-topped El Yunque (p445), Parque Nacional Alejandro de Humboldt (p446); and the various hikes around Las Terrazas (p217) in Pinar del Río are (technically) guide-only affairs.

If you want to hike independently, you'll need patience, resolve and an excellent sense of direction. It's also useful to ask the locals in your casa particular. Try experimenting first with Salto del Caburní and other trails in Topes de Collantes (p304), or the various hikes around Viñales (p209).

### Rock Climbing

The Viñales valley (p204) has been described as having the best sport rock climbing in the western hemisphere. There are more than 150 routes now open (at all levels of difficulty, with several 5.14s) and the word is out among the international climbing crowd, who are creating their own scene in one of Cuba's prettiest settings. Independent travelers will appreciate the free reign that climbers enjoy here.

Though you can climb here year-round, the heat can be oppressive, and locals stick to an October to April season, with December to January being the optimum months. For more information, visit the **Cuba Climbing** (www.cubaclimbing.com) website or contact **Aníbal Fernández** (anibalpiaz@yahoo.com), president of the national climbing club.

### Snorkeling

You don't have to go very deep to enjoy Cuba's tropical aquarium: snorkelers will be thrilled with treasures along the south coast from Playa Larga (p253) to Caleta Buena (Matanzas; p255) and around Cienfuegos (p267), Playa Jibacoa (Habana Province; p174) and along the Guardalavaca reef (Holguín; p363). In Varadero, daily snorkeling tours sailing to Cayo Blanco (p234) promise abundant tropical fish and good visibility. If you're not into the group thing, you can don a mask at Playa Coral (p235), 20km away.

Good boat dives for snorkeling happen around Isla de la Juventud (p188) and Cayo Largo (p189) especially, but also in Varadero (for sunken wrecks and reef; p234) and in the Cienfuegos (p267) and Guajimico (p268) areas. If you anticipate spending a lot of time snorkeling, bring your own gear as the rental stuff can be tattered and buying it in Cuba will mean you'll sacrifice both price and quality.

## BUSINESS HOURS

Cuban business hours are hardly etched in stone, but offices are generally open 9am to 5pm Monday to Friday. Cubans don't take a siesta like in other Latin American countries, so places normally don't close at midday. The exception is provincial museums (which also keep late-night hours – an interesting time for an art crawl). Museums and vegetable markets are usually closed Monday.

Post offices are open 8am to 6pm Monday to Saturday, with some main post offices keeping later hours. Banks are usually open from 9am to 3pm weekdays, closing at noon on the last working day of each month. Cadeca exchange offices are generally open 9am to 6pm Monday to Saturday, and 9am to noon Sunday.

Pharmacies are generally open 8am to 8pm, but those marked *turno permanente* or *pilotos* are open 24 hours.

In retail outlets everything grinds to a halt during the *cambio de turno* (shift change) and you won't be able to order a beer or buy cigarettes until they're done doing inventory (which can take anywhere from 10 minutes to one hour). Shops are usually closed after noon on Sunday. The earlier in the morning you attend to whatever tasks you have (banking, car rental, immigration, flight confirmations etc), the better.

For businesses reviewed in this guide, opening hours are not listed unless they deviate from standard opening times.

## CHILDREN

Children are encouraged to talk, sing, dance, think, dream and play, and are integrated into all parts of society: you'll see them at concerts, restaurants, church, political rallies (giving speeches even!) and parties. Travelers with children will find this embracing attitude heaped upon them, too.

In Cuba there are many travelers with kids, especially Cuban Americans visiting family with their children; these will be your best sources for on-the-ground information. One aspect of the culture here parents may find foreign (aside from the material shortages) is the physical contact and human warmth that is so typically Cuban: strangers ruffle kids' hair, give them kisses or take their hands with regularity, which may be odd for you and/or your child. For more general advice, see Lonely Planet's *Travel with Children.*

### Practicalities

A lot of simple things aren't available in Cuba or are hard to find, including baby formula, diaper wipes, disposable diapers, crayons, any medicine, clothing, sun block etc. On the upside, Cubans are very resourceful and will happily whip up some squash and bean baby food or fashion a cloth diaper. In restaurants, there are no high chairs because Cubans cleverly turn one chair around and stack it on another, providing a balanced chair at the right height. Cribs are available in the fancier hotels and resorts, and in casas particulares one will be found. Good babysitting abounds: your hotel concierge or casa owner can connect you with good child care. What you won't find are car seats (or even seat belts in some cases), so bring your own from home.

The key to traveling in Cuba is simply to ask for what you need and some kind person will help you out.

### Sights & Activities

Like any great city, Habana is terrific for kids (see p115). It has kids' theater and dance, two aquariums, two zoos, a couple of great parks and some massive playgrounds. Resorts are packed with kids' programs, from special outings to designated kiddy pools. Guardalavaca has the added advantage of being near many other interesting sights such as the aquarium at Bahía de Naranjo (p363). Parque Baconao in Santiago de Cuba (p421) has everything from old cars to dinosaurs and is a fantasy land for kids of all ages.

Other activities kids will groove on include horseback riding, baseball games, cigar factory tours, snorkeling, miniature golf, and exploring caves, the waterfalls at El Nicho (p269) and Topes de Collantes (p304).

## CLIMATE CHARTS

Cuba is hot, with humidity ranging from 81% in summer to 79% in winter. Luckily the heat is nicely moderated by the gentle Northeast Tradewinds and the highest temperature ever recorded on the island was less than 40°C. Beware of cold fronts passing in the winter when evening can be cool in the west of the island. Cuba's hurricane season (June to November) should also be considered when planning; see When to Go (p21) for more.

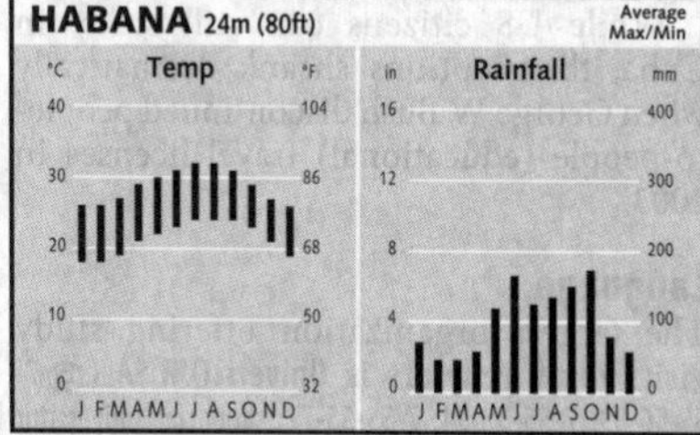

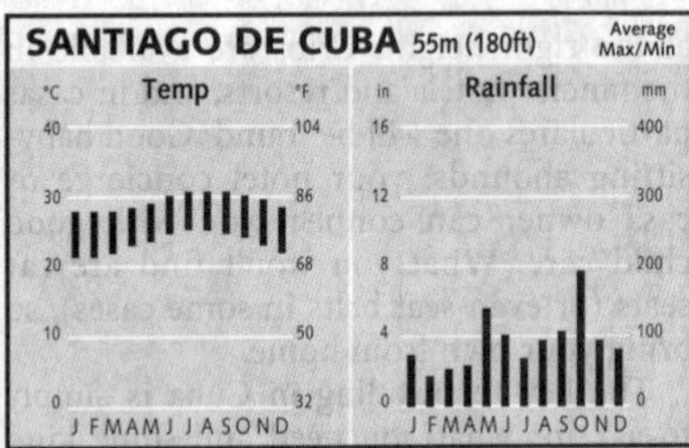


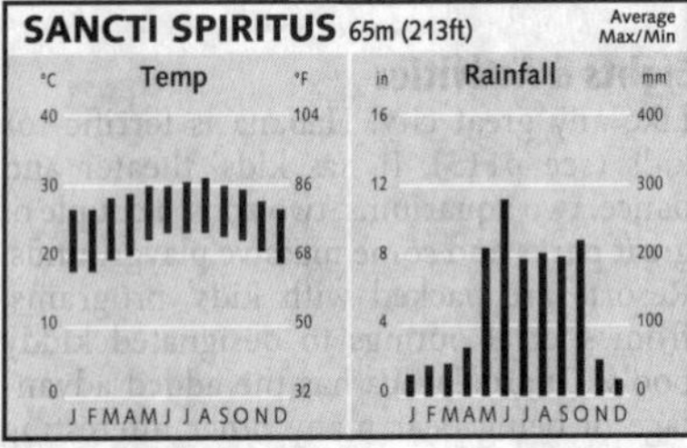


## COURSES

Cuba's rich cultural tradition and the abundance of highly talented, trained professionals make it a great place to study. Officially matriculating students are afforded longer visas and issued a *carnet* – the identification document that allows foreigners to pay for museums, transport (including colectivos) and theater performances in pesos. Technological and linguistic glitches, plus general unresponsiveness, make it hard to set up courses before arriving, but don't worry: you'll be able to arrange everything once you arrive. In Cuba, things are always better done face-to-face.

Private one-on-one lessons are available in everything from *batá* drumming to advanced Spanish grammar. Classes are easily arranged, typically for CUC$5 to CUC$10 an hour at the institutions specializing in your interest. Other travelers are a great source of up-to-date information in this regard.

While US citizens can still study in Cuba, their options shrank dramatically when George W Bush discontinued people-to-people (educational) travel licenses in 2003.

### Language

The largest organization offering study visits for foreigners is **UniversiTUR SA** (☎ 7-55-56-83, 7-55-57-94, 7-55-55-77; agencia@universitur.com; Calle 30 No 768-1, btwn 41 & Kohly, Nuevo Vedado). UniversiTUR arranges regular study and working holidays at any of Cuba's universities and at many higher education or research institutes. Its most popular programs are intensive courses in Spanish and Cuban culture at **Universidad de la Habana** (see Habana chapter p104 for details). UniversiTUR has 17 branch offices at various universities throughout Cuba, all providing the same services, though prices vary. While US students can study anywhere, they must arrange study programs for the provinces (except Habana or Matanzas) through Havanatur (p92).

Students heading to Cuba should bring a good bilingual dictionary and a basic 'learn Spanish' textbook, as such books are scarce or expensive in Cuba. You might sign up for a two-week course at a university to get your feet wet and then jump into private classes once you've made some contacts.

### Culture & Dance

Dance classes are available all over Cuba, although Habana and Santiago are your best bets. Institutions to try include the **Casa del Caribe** (Map pp394-5; ☎ 226-64-22-85; fax 226-64-23-87; Calle 13 No 154, Vista Alegre, 90100 Santiago de Cuba), the **Conjunto Folklórico Nacional** (Map pp106-7; ☎ 7-830-3060; Calle 4 No 103, btwn Calzada & Calle 5, Vedado, Habana) and the **Centro Andaluz** (Map p100; ☎ 7-863-6745; fax 7-66-69-01; Prado No 104, Centro Habana). See the individual chapters for details.

### Art & Film

Courses for foreigners can be arranged throughout the year by the Oficina de Relaciones Internacionales of the **Instituto Superior de Arte** (Map pp106-7; ☎ 7-208-8075; isa@cubarte.cult.cu; Calle 120 No 1110, Cubanacán, Playa, Habana 11600). Courses in percussion and dance are available almost anytime, but other subjects, such as the visual arts, music, theater and aesthetics, are offered when professors are available.

Courses usually involve four hours of classes a week at between CUC$10 and CUC$15 per hour. Prospective students must apply in the last week of August for the fall semester or the last three weeks of January for spring. The school is closed for holidays throughout July and until the third week in August. The institute also accepts graduate students for its regular winter courses, and an entire year of study here (beginning in September) as part of the regular five-year program costs CUC$2500. Accommodation in student dormitories can be arranged.

The **Escuela Internacional de Cine, Televisión y Video** (☎ 650-3152; fax 650-33-53-41/51-96; Apartado Aereo 4041, San Antonio de los Baños, Provincia de La Habana) trains broadcasting professionals from all over the world (especially developing countries). Under the patronage of novelist Gabriel García Márquez, it's run by the foundation that also organizes the annual film festival in Habana. The campus is at Finca San Tranquilino, Carretera de Vereda Nueva, 5km northwest of San Antonio de los Baños. Prospective filmmaking students should apply in writing in advance (personal inquiries at the gate are not welcome).

### Study Abroad Programs

One of the best study abroad programs is offered by the **School of International Training** (SIT; ☎ 802-257-7751, toll free 888-272-7881; www.sit.edu/studyabroad). This credit-earning, semester-long program combines course work with independent study emphasizing politics and culture. This program costs around CUC$14,000, including everything but your bar tab, and is fully licensed.

## CUSTOMS

Cuban customs regulations are complicated. For the full scoop see www.aduana.islagrande.cu. Travelers are allowed to bring in personal belongings (including photography equipment, binoculars, musical instrument, tape recorder, radio, personal computer, tent, fishing rod, bicycle, canoe and other sporting gear), gifts up to a value of the equivalent of US$250, and 10kg of medicine in its original packaging. Those over the age of 18 may import 2L of liquor and one carton of cigarettes.

Items that do not fit into the categories mentioned above are subject to a 100% customs duty to a maximum of CUC$1000.

Items prohibited entry into Cuba include narcotics, explosives, pornography, electrical appliances broadly defined, global positioning systems, prerecorded video cassettes and 'any item attempting against the security and internal order of the country,' including some books. Canned, processed and dried food are no problem, nor are pets.

Exporting art and items of cultural patrimony is restricted and involves fees, paperwork and forethought. See Exporting Artwork (p140) for details. You are allowed to export 50 cigars duty-free.

## DANGERS & ANNOYANCES

Cuba is generally safer than most countries, and violent attacks are extremely rare. Petty theft (eg rifled luggage in hotel rooms, or unattended shoes disappearing from the beach) is common, but preventative measures work wonders. Pickpocketing is also preventable: wear your bag in front of you on crowded

### SAFETY TIPS

Most travel advisories classify Cuba as a low-risk country though crime is purportedly on the increase. Basic travel advice includes the following:

- Beware of bag-snatching and petty theft especially in tourist areas.
- Remove all valuable items from checked-in luggage and consider having it shrink-wrapped (there's a service available at Habana airport).
- Take care when driving on Cuban roads.
- Take out comprehensive travel and medical insurance before you depart.
- Monitor national and international weather updates particularly during the hurricane season.
- Stay clear of all illegal drugs.
- Check with your home bank whether your credit card will be accepted in Cuba. If not, bring sufficient funds in cash/traveler's checks.
- Keep away from military zones/restricted areas.

buses and at busy markets, and only take what money you'll need to the disco.

Begging is more widespread than any other crimes and is exacerbated by tourists who amuse themselves by handing out money, soap, pens, chewing gum and other things to people on the street. Sadly, many Cubans have dropped out of productive jobs because they've found it is more lucrative to hustle tourists or beg than to work. It's painful for everyone when beggars earn more money than doctors. If you truly want to do something to help, pharmacies and hospitals will accept medicine donations, schools happily take pens, paper, crayons etc, and libraries will gratefully accept books. Hustlers are called *jineteros/as* (male/female touts), and can be a real nuisance. For more information, see the boxed text, p397.

Annoyances include travel agents promising services they can't deliver and *tiradores* (masturbators) who frequent dark places, especially movie theaters. If you're sensitive to smoke, you'll choke in Cuba, where even in hospitals surgeons are lighting up.

Despite the many strides the Cuban Revolution has made in stamping out racial discrimination, traces still linger and visitors of non-European origin are more likely to attract the attention of the police than those that look obviously non-Cuban. Latin, South Asian or black visitors may have to show passports to enter hotels and other places from which ordinary Cubans are barred (under the pretext that they think you're Cuban). Likewise, racially mixed pairs (especially black-white couples) will usually encounter more questions, demanding of papers and hassle than other travelers.

## EMBASSIES & CONSULATES

### Cuban Embassies & Consulates

**Australia** Consulate-General (☎ 61-2-9698-9797; fax 61-2-8399-1106; PO Box 2382, Strawberry Hills, NSW 2012)
**Belgium** Embassy (☎ 32-2-343-0020; fax 32-2-344-9691; Robert Jonesstraat 77, 1180 Brussels)
**Canada** Consulate-General (☎ 416-234-8181; fax 416-234-2754; Suite 401, 5353 Dundas St W, Etobicoke, Ontario M9B 6H8); Consulate-General & Trade Commission (☎ 514-843-8897; fax 514-982-9034; 1415 Av des Pins Ouest, Montréal, Québec H3B 1B2); Embassy (☎ 613-563-0141; fax 613-563-0068; 338 Main St, Ottawa, Ontario K1S 1E3)
**France** Consulate (☎ 49-228-3090; Kennedy Allee 22, 53175 Bonn); Embassy (☎ 33-1-45-67-55-35; fax 33-1-45-66-80-92; 16 rue de Presles, 75015 Paris)
**Germany** Embassy (☎ 49-30-9161-1811; Stavanger Strasse 20, 10439 Berlin)
**Italy** Embassy (☎ 39-6-574-2347; fax 39-6-574-5445; Via Licina No 7, 00153 Rome)
**Mexico** Embassy (☎ 52-5-280-8039; fax 52-5-280-0839; Presidente Masarik 554, Colonia Polanco, 11560 Mexico, DF)
**Netherlands** Consulate (☎ 31-10-206-7333; fax 31-10-206-7335; Stationsplein 45, 3013 AK Rotterdam); Embassy (☎ 31-70-360-6061; fax 31-70-364-7586; Scheveningseweg 9, 2517 KS, La Haya)
**Spain** Embassy (☎ 341-359-2500; fax 341-359-6145; Paseo de la Habana No 194, Pinilla 28036 Madrid)
**UK** Embassy (☎ 44-020-7240-2488; fax 44-020-7836-2602; 167 High Holburn, London WC1 6PA)
**USA** Cuban Interests Section (☎ 202-797-8609/10; fax 202-986-7283; 2630 16th St NW, Washington, DC 20009)

### Embassies in Cuba

Most embassies are open from 8am to noon on weekdays.

**Australia** See Canada.
**Austria** (Map pp146-7; ☎ 7-204-2825; fax 7-204-1235; Calle 4 No 101, Miramar)
**Belgium** (Map pp146-7; ☎ 7-204-2410; fax 7-204-1318; Av 5 No 7406, Miramar)
**Canada** (Map pp146-7; ☎ 7-204-2517; fax 7-204-2044; Calle 30 No 518, Playa) Also represents Australia.
**Denmark** (Map p100; ☎ 7-33-81-28; fax 7-33-81-27; 4th fl, Paseo de Martí No 20, Centro Habana)
**France** (Map pp146-7; ☎ 7-204-2308; fax 7-204-0335; Calle 14 No 312 btwn Avs 3 & 5, Miramar)
**Germany** (☎ 7-33-25-69; fax 7-33-15-86; Calle 13 No 652, Vedado)
**Italy** (Map pp146-7; ☎ 7-204-5615; fax 7-204-5661; Av 5 No 402, Miramar)
**Japan** (Map pp146-7; ☎ 7-204-3508; fax 7-204-8902; Miramar Trade Center, cnr Av 3 & Calle 80, Playa)
**Mexico** (Map pp146-7; ☎ 7-204-7722; fax 7-204-2666; Calle 12 No 518, Miramar)
**Netherlands** (Map pp146-7; ☎ 7-204-2511; fax 7-204-2059; Calle 8 No 307, btwn Avs 3 & 5, Miramar)
**New Zealand** See UK.
**Spain** (Map p100; ☎ 7-33-80-25; Cárcel No 51, Habana Vieja)
**Sweden** (Map pp146-7; ☎ 7-204-2831; fax 7-204-1194; Calle 34 No 510, Miramar)
**Switzerland** (Map pp146-7; ☎ 7-204-2611; fax 7-204-2729; Av 5 No 2005, btwn Avs 20 & 22, Miramar)
**UK** (Map pp146-7; ☎ 7-204-1771; fax 7-204-8104; Calle 34 No 708, Miramar) Also represents New Zealand.
**USA** (Map pp106-7; ☎ 7-33-35-51; US Interests Section, Calzada, btwn Calles L & M, Vedado)

**GOVERNMENT TRAVEL ADVICE**

The following government websites offer travel advisories and information on current hot spots.

**Australian Department of Foreign Affairs** (☎ 1300 139 281; www.smarttraveller.gov.au)
**British Foreign Office** (☎ 0845-850-2829; www.fco.gov.uk)
**Canadian Department of Foreign Affairs** (☎ 800-267 6788; www.dfait-maeci.gc.ca)
**US State Department** (☎ 888-407 4747; http://travel.state.gov)

## FESTIVALS & EVENTS

For more information on these and other festivals and events, visit www.afrocubaweb.com/festivals.htm.

### January

**Liberation & New Year's Day** Big street parties countrywide and dozens of outdoor concerts in Habana on January 1.
**Birthday of José Martí** Prideful observances include book launchings and cultural performances. Held January 28.
**Fería Internacional del Libro** Impressive two-week book fair with concerts, readings, book launches and sales. Starts in the last week of January; moves from Habana across the country in February.
**FolkCuba** (second half of Jan) A major festival unfolds at Conjunto Folklórico Nacional de Cuba biannually during the second half of January.

### March

**Fiesta de la Toronja** (Grapefruit Festival) Held on Isla de la Juventud every March. Pucker up for this one.

### April

**PerCuba** (Festival Internacional de Percusión) Bang your drum at Habana's annual thump-fest held during the third week of April.
**Baseball playoffs** (Location varies) Two weeks of top ball playing excites fans of all ages.

### May

**Día de los Trabajadores** May Day (May 1) means massive rallies held in Plazas de la Revolución countrywide.
**Romerías de Mayo** Rap, rock, poetry and dance take over Holguín in one of Cuba's most popular events. Held during the first week of May.
**Festival Internacional de Guitarra** Axe masters flock to Habana for loads of concerts during the second week of May.
**Fería Internacional Cubadisco** Second week of May in Habana. Like the Cuban Grammys, with so many stellar concerts you won't be able to choose.

### June

**Festival Internacional Boleros de Oro** Third week of June. International bolero stars move crowds to tears in Habana, Santiago de Cuba and elsewhere.

### July

**Festival del Caribe, Fiesta del Fuego** Raucous week-long festival celebrating Caribbean dance, music and religion in Santiago de Cuba. Held during the first week of July.
**Day of the National Rebellion** Celebrates the July 26, 1953 attack on the Moncada Barracks in a different province each year.
**Carnaval, Santiago de Cuba** The country's biggest and best; held during the last week of July.

### August

**Festival de Rap Cubano Habana Hip Hop** Everyone's bustin' rhymes in this wildly successful international event, held midmonth.

### September

**Benny Moré International Music Festival** Held in the village of Santa Isabel de las Lajas (birthplace of Benny Moré) every alternate September. In homage to the incomparable Barbarian of Rhythm.

### October

**Festival Internacional de Ballet** Tremendous event packed with performances morning, noon and night; held midmonth every other year.

### November

**Bienal de la Habana** Habana's art extravaganza showcases Cuba's best contemporary art for three months; held every other year.

### December

**Festival Internacional del Nuevo Cine Latinoamericano** First week of December. This prestigious film festival features hundreds of screenings.
**Festival Internacional de Jazz** Straight ahead, be-bop, Latin, far out or funkified: whatever type of jazz, it happens here. Held during the first week of December every other year.
**Las Parrandas** December 24 in Remedios. Extravagant fireworks and floats make this one of Cuba's most outrageous festivals.

## FOOD

It will be the very rare meal in Cuba that costs over CUC$25. In this book, restaurant listings are presented in the following order: budget (meals for under CUC$5), midrange (meals for CUC$5 to CUC$10) and top end (meals for over CUC$10). Before you dig in, check out the detailed information in the Food & Drink chapter (p76).

## GAY & LESBIAN TRAVELERS

While Cuba can't be called a queer destination (yet), it's more tolerant than many other Latin American countries. The hit movie *Fresa y Chocolate* (Strawberry and Chocolate) sparked a national dialogue about homosexuality, and Cuba is pretty tolerant, all things considered. People from more accepting societies may find this tolerance too 'don't ask, don't tell' or tokenesque (everyone has a gay friend/relative/co-worker, whom they'll mention when the topic arises), but what the hell, you have to start somewhere and Cuba is moving in the right direction.

Machismo shows an ugly face when it comes to lesbians (the idea that a women can't be satisfied by a man just doesn't jive with most Cuban males' world view) and female homosexuality has not enjoyed the aperture of male homosexuality. For this reason, female lovers can share rooms and otherwise 'pass' with facility. However Jurassic you might find that, it's a workable solution to a sticky problem. There are occasional *fiestas para chicas* (not necessarily all-girl parties, but close); ask around at the **Cine Yara** (Map pp106-7; ☎ 832-9430; cnr Calles 23 & L, Vedado, Habana).

Cubans are physical with each other and you'll see men hugging, women holding hands and lots of friendly caressing. This type of casual touching shouldn't be a problem, but take care when that hug among friends turns overtly sensual in public.

## HOLIDAYS

The Cuban calendar is loaded with holidays, but there are only a few that might affect your travel plans; among them are December 25 (not declared an official holiday until after the Pope visited in 1998), January 1, May 1 and July 26. On these days, stores will be closed and transport (except for planes) erratic. On May 1, especially, buses are dedicated to shuttling people to the Plazas de la Revolución in every major city and town and you can just forget about getting inner-city transport.

July and August mean crowded beaches and sold-out campismos and hotels.

## INSURANCE

Insurance pays off only if something serious happens, but that's what insurance is for, so you'd be foolish to travel without cover. Outpatient treatment at international clinics designed for foreigners is reasonably priced, but emergency and prolonged hospitalization get expensive (the free medical system for Cubans should only be used when there is no other option).

If you're really concerned about your health, consider purchasing travel insurance once you arrive at **Asistur** (☎ 7-33-85-27, 7-867-1315; www.asistur.cu; Paseo de Martí No 212). It has two types of coverage. For non-Americans the policy costs CUC$2.50 per day and covers up to CUC$400 in lost luggage, CUC$7000 in medical coverage and CUC$5000 each for repatriation of remains or jail bail. For Americans, similar coverage costs CUC$8 per day and provides up to CUC$25,000 in health care costs, plus CUC$7000 to repatriate remains or evacuate you.

It's strongly recommended that you take car insurance for a variety of reasons; see p475 for details.

## INTERNET ACCESS

With state-run telecommunications company Etecsa re-establishing its monopoly as service providers, Internet access is available all over the country in Etecsa's spanking new telepuntos. You'll find one of its swish, air-conditioned sales offices in almost every provincial town and it is your best point of call for fast and reliable Internet access (though with a 56k telephone modem patience is sometimes required). The drill is to buy a one-hour user card (CUC$6) with scratch-off *usuario* (code) and *contraseña* (password) and help yourself to an available computer. These cards are interchangeable in any telepunto across the country so you don't have to use up your whole hour in one go.

The downside of the Etecsa monopoly is that there are few, if any, independent cyber-cafés outside of the telepuntos and many of the smaller hotels – unable to afford the service fee – have had to dispense of their computers. As a general rule most four- and five-star hotels will have their own Internet cafés although the fees here are often higher (sometimes as much as CUC$12 per hour).

As Internet access for Cubans is restricted, you may be asked to show your passport when using a telepunto (although if you look obviously foreign, they won't bother). On the plus side the Etecsa places are open long hours and not often that crowded.

## LEGAL MATTERS

Cuban police are everywhere and they're usually very friendly – more likely to ask you for a date than a bribe. Corruption is a serious offense in Cuba and typically no one wants to get messed up in it. Getting caught out without identification is never good; carry some around just in case (a driver's license, a copy of your passport or student ID card should be sufficient).

Drugs are prohibited in Cuba though you may still get offered marijuana and cocaine on the streets of Habana. Penalties for buying, selling, holding or taking drugs are serious, and Cuba is making a concerted effort to treat demand and curtail supply; it is only the foolish traveler who partakes while on a Cuban vacation.

**IN CUBA YOU HAVE TO BE...**

- 18 years old to vote
- 14 years old to have heterosexual sex if you're female
- 18 years old to drive
- 16 years old to buy cigarettes or liquor

## MAPS

Signage is awful in Cuba so a good map is essential for both drivers and cyclists alike. The comprehensive *Guía de Carreteras* (CUC$6), published in Italy, has the best maps available in Cuba. The *Guía* has a complete index, a detailed Habana map and useful information in English, Spanish, Italian and French. Handier is the all-purpose *Automapa Nacional,* available at hotel shops and car-rental offices.

The Instituto Cubano de Geodesia y Cartografía (aka Ediciones GEO) publishes several excellent maps including the 2002 *Mapa Turístico La Habana* (1:25,000) and the *Mapa Turístico Cuba*. You can buy these maps at www.cubamapa.com.

The best map published outside of Cuba is the Freytag & Berndt 1:1.25 million *Cuba* map. The island map is good, and it has indexed town plans of Habana, Playas del Este, Varadero, Cienfuegos, Camagüey and Santiago de Cuba.

## MONEY

This is a tricky part of any Cuban trip and the double economy takes some getting used to. Two currencies circulate in Cuba: Convertible pesos (CUC$) and Cuban pesos (referred to as *moneda nacional* and abbreviated MN). Most things tourists buy are in Convertibles (eg accommodation, rental cars, bus tickets, museum admission and Internet access). At the time of writing, Cuban pesos were selling at 24 to one Convertible, and while there are many things you can't buy with *moneda nacional,* using them on certain occasions means you'll see a bigger slice of authentic Cuba.

Making things a little more confusing, euros are accepted at the Varadero, Guardalavaca, Cayo Largo del Sur, and Cayos Coco and Guillermo resorts, but once you leave the resort grounds, you'll still need Convertibles. For information on costs, see p22.

The best currencies to bring to Cuba are euros, Canadian dollars or pounds sterling (all liable to a 10% commission). The worst is US dollars and – despite the prices you might see posted up in bank windows – the commission you'll get charged is a whopping 20% (the normal 10% commission plus an extra 10% penalty – often not displayed). At the time of writing, traveler's checks issued by US banks could be exchanged at branches of Banco Financiero Internacional, but credit cards issued by US banks could not be used at all.

Cadeca branches in every city and town sell Cuban pesos. You won't need more than CUC$10 worth of pesos a week. In addition to the offices located on the maps in this book, there is almost always a branch at the local agropecuario (vegetable market). If you get caught without Cuban pesos and are drooling for that ice-cream cone, you can always use Convertibles; in street transactions such as these, CUC$1 is equal to 25 pesos and you'll receive change in pesos. There is no black market in Cuba, only hustlers trying to fleece you with money-changing scams (see p114).

## ATM & Credit Cards

When the banks are open, the machines are working and the phone lines are live, credit cards are an option – as long as the cards are not issued by US banks. The downside is that you'll be charged the equivalent of a whopping 11.25% commission on every transaction. This discourages most people using them for anything but emergencies.

Cash advances can be drawn from credit cards but the commission's the same. Check with your home bank before you leave as many banks won't authorize large withdrawals in foreign countries unless you notify them of your travel plans first.

ATMs are good for credit cards only and are the equivalent to obtaining a cash advance over the counter. In reality it is best to avoid them altogether (especially when the banks are closed) as they are notorious for eating up people's cards.

Contrary to what some people might tell you, debit cards do not work in Cuba.

## Cash

Cuba is a cash economy and credit cards don't have the importance or ubiquity that they do elsewhere in the western hemisphere. Although carrying pure cash is far riskier than the usual cash/credit-card/traveler's-check mix, it's infinitely more convenient. As long as you use a concealed money belt and keep the cash on you or in your hotel's safe deposit box at all times, you should be OK.

It's better to ask for CUC$20/10/5/3/1 bills when you're changing money as many smaller Cuban businesses (taxis, restaurants, etc) can't change anything bigger (ie CUC$50s or CUC$100s) and the words '*no hay cambio*' resonate everywhere. If desperate you can always break big bills at hotels.

## Denominations & Lingo

One of the most confusing parts of a double economy is terminology. Cuban pesos are called *moneda nacional* (abbreviated MN) or pesos Cubanos or simply pesos while Convertible pesos are called *pesos convertibles* (abbreviated CUC) or often just simply...pesos. Sometimes you'll be negotiating in pesos (Cubanos) and your counterpart will be negotiating in pesos (Convertibles). It doesn't help that the notes look similar as well. Worse, the symbol for both Convertibles and pesos Cubanos is $. You can imagine the potential scams just working these combinations.

The Cuban peso comes in notes of one, five, 10, 20, 50 and 100 pesos, and coins of one (rare), five and 20 centavos, and one and three pesos. The five-centavo coin is called a *medio,* the 20-centavo coin a *peseta.* Centavos are also called *kilos.*

The Convertible peso comes in multicolored notes of one, three, five, 10, 20, 50 and 100 pesos and coins of five, 10, 25 and 50 cents and one peso.

## Tipping

If you're not in the habit of tipping, you'll learn fast in Cuba. Wandering *son* septets, parking guards, ladies at bathroom entrances, restaurant wait staff, tour guides – they're all working for hard-currency tips. Musicians who besiege tourists while they dine, converse or flirt will want a Convertible, but only give what you feel the music is worth. Washroom attendants expect CUC$0.05 to CUC$0.10, while *parqueadores* (parking attendants) should get CUC$0.25 for a short watch and CUC$1 for each 12 hours. For a day tour, CUC$2 per person is appropriate for a tour guide. Taxi drivers will appreciate 10% of the meter fare, but if you've negotiated a ride without the meter, don't tip as the whole fare is going straight into their wallets.

Tipping can quickly *resuelvan las cosas* (fix things up). If you want to stay beyond the hotel check-out time or enter a site after hours, for instance, small tips (CUC$1 to CUC$5) bend rules, open doors and send people looking the other way. For tipping in restaurants and other advice, see the Food & Drink chapter (p80).

## Traveler's Checks

While they add security and it makes sense to carry a few for that purpose, traveler's checks are a hassle in Cuba although they work out better value than credit cards. Bear in mind that you'll pay commission at both the buying and selling ends (3% to 6%) and also be aware that some hotels and banks won't accept them (especially in the provinces). The Banco Financiero Internacional is your best bet for changing Amex checks, though a much safer all-round option is to bring Thomas Cook.

## PHOTOGRAPHY

Good film is expensive (CUC$7 for a roll of 24 Kodak Gold prints) and developing is terrible and costly (CUC$0.35 a shot). Photo Service is the biggest chain in Cuba and they develop film and sell supplies, but anyone serious about photography should bring their own. Similarly, whatever offers you may find to develop digital film, it is best done when you arrive home.

Most Cubans love to have their pictures taken and will happily pose if you ask '*¿puedo tirar una foto?*' (Can I take a photo?). Photos are treasured, so you might offer to send along copies.

## POST

Letters and postcards sent to Europe and the US take about a month to arrive. While *sellos* (stamps) are sold in pesos and Convertibles, correspondence bearing the latter has a better chance of arriving. Postcards cost CUC$0.65 to all countries. Letters cost CUC$0.65 to the Americas, CUC$0.75 to Europe and CUC$0.85 to all other countries. Prepaid postcards, including international postage, are available at most hotel shops and post offices and are the surest bet for successful delivery. For important mail, you're better off using DHL, located in all the major cities; it costs CUC$55 for a two-pound letter pack to Australia, or CUC$50 to Europe.

The Cuban post has a well-organized *telegrama* (telegram) system whereby messages can be sent from any post office to any address in the country. A nostalgic, economical way to communicate (it costs about CUC$1.15 for 100 words), this is also how to contact people who don't have phones. Every post office has a telegram window.

## SHOPPING

Cigars, rum, music and anything with Che Guevara on it are quintessentially Cuban souvenirs. The *guayabera*, a snappy, pleated men's shirt that's Cuban for formalwear, is all the rage from Prague to Vancouver. All of these items (and more) can be purchased in hotel and souvenir shops, but if you want the best selection and price, go to specialist stores.

Egrem is the state recording company and its studio shops in Habana (p153), Holguín (p356) and Santiago de Cuba (p415) have fantastic CD selections. ARTex, a more general souvenir store, also sells CDs.

As an icon, Che is on everything from shot glasses to watch faces (look for the limited-edition Swatch at the Habana airport), and *ferías* (artisan fairs) in Varadero (p242) and Habana (p139) have a wide selection of all things Che. You can also buy coral and tortoise-shell treasures at these fairs, some quite lovely, but it's best if you don't: these items, plus shells, many plants and reptiles are protected under Cites (Convention on International Trade in Endangered Species). These environmental protection rules prohibit individuals from importing or exporting such items.

You can also buy 'artwork' at these fairs, most of it tourist kitsch, but sometimes you'll find something that strikes you. You shouldn't have a problem exporting this type of art under Cuban patrimony rules, but you might. To avoid disappointment at the airport, you should assume that any artwork that cannot fit in your luggage will be confiscated if you don't have the correct documentation. If you've bought an original painting or sculpture from an official store, the only documentation you'll need is the receipt. If you've purchased a piece of art on the street or directly from the artist, you'll need an export certificate (see p140). Antiquities are also subject to patrimony restrictions.

Cuba has some fabulous antiques and every town has a *casa de comisiones*, literally 'commission house,' where people put up their heirlooms for sale. These shops sell everything in Cuban pesos. Good vintage clothing is also available.

### Cigars

The best Cuban cigars are completely hand-rolled and packed in sealed, stamped cedar boxes. There are 42 different types and sizes of Habana cigars, classified as fine, medium or thick. A single brand can come in several different sizes, and the same size category can refer to various types of cigars of other brands. The most common types are Mareva (129mm), Corona (142mm) and Julieta (178mm). Choosing the right cigar requires a degree of knowledge, and connoisseurs will be very familiar with the varying tastes and styles.

Cuba's flagship brand is the spicy Cohiba, created in 1966 for diplomatic use (it's still gifted in the highest political circles) and only available to the general public since 1982. Named for the original Taíno word for tobacco, it comes in 11 medium to strong types. The five numbered varieties of Montecristo are among Cuba's most popular cigars. Before he quit smoking in 1989, President Castro's favorites were Corona Grande Montecristo and Cohiba Espléndidos. Medium-flavored Punch cigars were designed for export to the UK as far back as 1840. Another classic is the stronger Partagás, rolled in Habana since 1845. The milder Romeo y Julieta was invented in 1903 by a globetrotting Cuban. Other mild brands include Quintero and Rafael González.

The five main tobacco-growing areas are Vuelta Abajo and Semi Vuelta (around San Cristóbal; both in Pinar del Río), Partido (around San Antonio de los Baños), Remedios (west of Sancti Spíritus), and Oriente (north of Ciego de Ávila, south of Bayamo and south of Mayarí). Most export-quality cigars are made from Vuelta Abajo or Partido tobacco.

Black-market cigars sold on the street are mostly scams (sealed boxes filled with sand or the lowest grade one-peso cheroots), but if you act like you know what you're doing, you might at least get quality fakes. Examine the individual cigars to make sure they're tightly rolled without any tiny air pockets or protuberances. The cigar should be soft when squeezed gently between your fingers. The covering should be smooth as silk, and all cigars in the box should have a uniform shape, though color can vary slightly. The cigars should be pungent. The litmus test is to put the lighting end in your mouth and puff in and out with care: the outer leaf should 'breathe.' If not, it's probably a counterfeit made from waste tobacco swept from factory floors, which have no draw and are impossible to smoke. Occasionally, stolen genuine cigars are available on the black market for a quarter of what they'd cost in the shops, but this is the exception.

Unless you know cigars well, it's advisable to pay more to be sure of what you're getting. Also, an official sales receipt from a shop eliminates the possibility of problems with Cuban customs. Some marketeers offer fake receipts but customs officers spot them easily. Visitors are allowed to export CUC$2000 worth of documented cigars per person. Amounts in excess of this, or black-market cigars without receipts, will be confiscated (Cuban customs is serious about this, with an ongoing investigation into cigar rings and more than a half million seizures of undocumented cigars annually). The tax-free limit without a receipt is two boxes (50 cigars) or 23 singles of any size or cost. Of course, you can buy additional cigars in the airport departure lounge once you've passed Cuban customs, but beware when entering other countries of your limits. (Mexican customs in Cancún, for instance, conducts rigorous cigar searches.) If you traveled without a license to Cuba, US customs will seize any tobacco you have upon entering; licensed travelers are permitted to bring the equivalent of US$100 worth of cigars into the US. (Imitation Cuban cigars sold in the US contain no Cuban tobacco.)

**La Casa del Habano** (www.habanos.net) is the national cigar store chain, where the staff is well-informed, there's a wide selection and sometimes a smoking lounge.

Smokers on a budget can buy smokable Selectos cigars in bodegas for a peso each.

## TELEPHONE

The Cuban phone system is still undergoing some upgrading, so beware of phone number changes. Normally a recorded message will inform you of any recent upgrades. Most of the country's Etecsa telepuntos have now been completely refurbished which means there's a spick-and-span (and air-conditioned) phone/Internet office in almost every provincial town.

### Mobile Phones

Cuba's two mobile-phone companies are **c.com** (☎ 7-264-2266) and **Cubacel** (www.cubacel.com). While you may be able to use your own equipment, you have to prebuy their services. Cubacel has more than 15 offices around the country (including at the Habana airport) where you can do this. Its plan costs approximately CUC$3 per day and each local call costs from CUC$0.52 to CUC$0.70. Note that you pay for incoming as well as outgoing calls. International rates are CUC$2.70 per minute to the US and CUC$5.85 per minute to Europe.

### Phone Codes

To call Cuba from abroad, dial your international access code, Cuba's country code (☎ 53), the city or area code, and the local number. In this book, area codes are indicated under city headings. To call internationally from Cuba, dial Cuba's international access code (☎ 119), the country code, the area code and the number. To the US, you just dial ☎ 119, then 1, the area code and the number.

To place a call through an international operator, dial ☎ 09, except to the United States, which can be reached with an operator on ☎ 66-12-12. Not all private phones in Cuba have international service, in which case you'll want to call collect (reverse charges or *cobro revertido*). This service is available only to Argentina, Brazil, Canada, Chile, Colombia, Costa Rica, Dominican Republic, France, Italy, Mexico, Panama, Spain, UK, US and Venezuela. International operators are available 24 hours and speak English. You cannot call collect from public phones.

### Phonecards

Etecsa is where you buy phone cards, send and receive faxes, use the Internet and make international calls. Blue public Etecsa phones accepting magnetized or computer-chip cards are everywhere. The cards are sold in Convertibles: CUC$5, CUC$10 and CUC$20 and pesos: three, five and seven pesos. You can call nationally with either, but you can call internationally only with Convertible cards. If you are mostly going to be making national and local calls, buy a peso card as it's much more economical.

The best cards for calls from Habana are called Propia. They come in pesos (five- and 10-peso denominations) and Convertibles (CUC$10 and CUC$25 denominations) and allow you to call from any phone – even ones permitting only emergency calls – using a personal code. The rates are the cheapest as well.

### Phone Rates

Local calls cost five centavos per minute, while interprovincial calls cost from 35 centavos to one peso per minute (note that only the peso coins with the star work in pay phones). Since most coin phones don't return change, common courtesy asks that you push the 'R' button so that the next person in line can make their call with your remaining money.

International calls made with a card cost from CUC$2 per minute to the US and Canada and CUC$5 to Europe and Oceania. Calls placed through an operator cost slightly more.

## TIME

Prior to October 2004 Cuba was on UTC/GMT minus five between October and April and UTC/GMT minus four (daylight saving time) between April and October – the same as New York or Washington. But at the end of that month the government decided not to move the clock back one hour. Consequently Habana is currently on UTC minus four (daylight saving time) year-round, ie in the summer it's in the same time zone as New York while in the winter its one hour ahead. As with everything in Cuba – including the time – this situation could change. And in 2006 the government announced that it would revert back to the old system in the fall.

## TOILETS

Look for public toilets in bus stations, tourist hotels or restaurants, and gas stations. It is unlikely you'll meet a Cuban who would deny a needy traveler the use of their bathroom. In public restrooms there often won't be water or toilet paper and never a toilet seat. The faster you learn to squat and carry your own supply of paper, the happier you'll be. Frequently there will be an attendant outside bathrooms supplying toilet paper and you're expected to leave CUC$0.05 or CUC$0.10 in the plate provided. If the bathrooms are dirty or the person doesn't supply paper, you shouldn't feel compelled to leave money.

Cuban sewer systems are not designed to take toilet paper and every bathroom has a small waste basket beside the toilet for this purpose. Aside from at top-end hotels and resorts, you should discard your paper in this basket or risk an embarrassing backup.

## TOURIST INFORMATION

At the time of writing, **Infotur** (www.infotur.cu), Cuba's official tourist information bureau, had offices only in Habana (Habana Vieja, Miramar, Playas del Este, Expocuba, the José Martí airport) and Ciego de Ávila (in the city and at Jardines del Rey Airport, Cayo Coco). Travel agencies, such as Cubanacán or Cubatur, can usually supply some general information.

## TRAVELERS WITH DISABILITIES

Cuba's inclusive culture translates to disabled travelers, and while facilities may be lacking, the generous nature of Cubans generally compensates. Sight-impaired travelers will be helped across streets and given priority in lines. The same holds true for travelers in wheelchairs, who will find the few ramps ridiculously steep and will have trouble in colonial parts of town where sidewalks are narrow and streets are cobblestone. Elevators are often out of order. Etecsa phone centers have telephone equipment for the hearing impaired and TV programs are broadcast with closed captioning.

## VISAS & TOURIST CARDS

Regular tourists who plan to spend up to two months in Cuba do not need visas. Instead, you get a *tarjeta de turista* (tourist card) valid for 30 days (Canadians get 90 days), which can be easily extended for another 30 days once you're in Cuba. Those going 'air only' usually buy the tourist card from the travel agency or airline office that sells them their plane ticket (equivalent of US$15 extra). Package tourists receive their card with their other travel documents.

Unlicensed tourists originating in the US buy their tourist card at the airline desk in the country through which they're traveling en route to Cuba (equivalent of US$25). You are usually not allowed to board a plane to Cuba without this card, but if by some chance you are, you should be able to buy one in Aeropuerto Internacional José Martí in Habana – although this is a hassle (and risk) best avoided. Once in Habana, tourist card extensions or replacements cost another CUC$25. You cannot leave Cuba without presenting your tourist card, so don't lose it. You are not permitted entry to Cuba without an onward ticket. Note that Cubans don't stamp your passport on either entry or exit; instead they stamp your tourist card.

The 'address in Cuba' line should be filled in, if only to avoid unnecessary questioning. In the old days, travelers entering the address of a casa particular or the cheapest hotel risked facing a hassle and/or compulsory on-the-spot reservations in a state-run hotel. This has largely been relaxed and as long as you are staying in a legal casa particular or hotel, you shouldn't have problems. Staying at a lover's or friend's house (which you can do, but it requires special paperwork at immigration) does not qualify.

Business travelers and journalists need visas. Applications should be made through a consulate at least three weeks in advance (longer if you apply through a consulate in a country other than your own).

Visitors with visas or anyone who has stayed in Cuba longer than 90 days must apply for an exit permit from an immigration office. The Cuban Consulate in London issues official visas (£32 plus two photos). They take two weeks to process, and the name of an official contact in Cuba is necessary.

### Extensions

For most travelers, obtaining an extension once in Cuba is easy: you just go to an *inmigración* (immigration office) and present your documents and CUC$25 in stamps. Obtain these stamps from a branch of Bandec or Banco Financiero Internacional beforehand. You'll only receive an additional 30 days after your original 30 days, but you can exit and re-enter the country for 24 hours and start over again (some travel agencies in Habana have special deals for this type of trip; see p92). Attend to extensions at least a few business days before your visa is due to expire and never attempt travel around Cuba with an expired visa. Nearly all provincial towns have an immigration office (closed Wednesday, Saturday and Sunday) though the staff rarely speak English and they aren't always over-helpful. Try to avoid Habana's office if you can as it gets ridiculously crowded.

**Baracoa** (Map p439; Antonio Maceo No 48; ⌚ 8am-noon & 2-4pm Mon-Fri)

**Bayamo** (Map p375; Carretera Central Km 2; ⌚ 9am-noon & 1:30-4pm Tue & Thu-Fri) In a big complex 200m south of the Hotel Sierra Maestra.

**Camagüey** (Map pp324-5; Calle 3 No 156 btwn Nos 8 & 10, Reparto Vista Hermosa; ⌚ 8am-11:30am & 1-3pm Mon-Fri, except Wed)

**Ciego de Ávila** (Map p312; cnr Chicho Valdés & Antonío Maceo; ⌚ 8am-noon & 1-5pm Mon & Tue, 8am-noon Wed-Fri)

**Cienfuegos** (Map p260; ☎ 52 10 17; Av 46 btwn 29 & 31)

**Guardalavaca** (Map p362; ☎ 3-0226/7) In the police station at the entrance to the resort. Head here for visa extensions; there's also an immigration office in Banes (p365).

**Guantánamo** (Map p433; Calle 1 Oeste btwn 14 & 15 Norte; ⌚ 8:30am-noon & 2-4pm Mon-Thu) Directly behind Hotel Guantánamo.

**Habana** (Map pp106-7; cnr Calle Factor al final & Santa Ana, Nuevo Vedado) This office is specifically for extensions and has long queues. Get there early. It has no phone, but you can direct questions to immigration proper at ☎ 203-0307.

**Holguín** (Map p350; General Marrero & General Vázquez; ⌚ 8am-noon & 2-4pm Mon-Fri) Arrive early – it gets crowded here.

**Las Tunas** (Av Camilo Cienfuegos, Reparto Buenavista) Northeast of the train station.

**Sancti Spíritus** (Map p288; ☎ 2-4729; Independencia Norte No 107; ⌚ 8:30am-noon & 1:30-3:30pm Mon-Thu)

**Santa Clara** (cnr Av Sandino & Sexta; ⌚ 8am-noon & 1-3pm Mon-Thu) Three blocks east of Estadio Sandino.

**Santiago de Cuba** (Map pp394-5; ☎ 69 36 07; Calle 13 No 6, btwn Av General Cebreco & Calle 4; ⌚ 8:30am-noon & 2-4pm Mon, Tue, Thu & Fri) Stamps for visa extensions are sold at the Banco de Crédito y Comercio at Felix Peña No 614 on Parque Céspedes.

**Trinidad** (Map p294; Julio Cueva Díaz; ⌚ 8am-5pm Tue-Thu) Off Paseo Agramonte.

**Varadero** (Map pp232-3; cnr Av 1 & Calle 39; ⌚ 8am-3:30pm Mon-Fri)

## Entry Permits for Cubans & Naturalized Citizens

Naturalized citizens of other countries who were born in Cuba require an *autorización de entrada* (entry permit) issued by a Cuban embassy or consulate. Called a *Vigencia de Viaje*, it allows Cubans resident abroad to visit Cuba as many times as they like over a two-year period. Persons hostile to the revolution or with a criminal record are not eligible.

The Cuban government does not recognize dual citizenship. All persons born in Cuba are considered Cuban citizens unless they have formally renounced their citizenship at a Cuban diplomatic mission and the renunciation has been accepted. Cuban Americans with questions about dual nationality can contact the Office of Overseas Citizens Services, Department of State, Washington, DC 20520.

## Licenses for US Visitors

In 1961 the US government imposed an order limiting the freedom of its citizens to visit Cuba, and airline offices and travel agencies in the US are forbidden to book tourist travel to Cuba via third countries. However, the Cuban government has never banned Americans from visiting Cuba, and it continues to welcome US passport holders under exactly the same terms as any other visitor.

Americans traditionally go to Cuba via Canada, Mexico, the Bahamas, Jamaica or any other third country. American travel agents are prohibited from handling tourism arrangements, so most Americans go though a foreign travel agency. Travel agents in those countries (see p469) routinely arrange Cuban tourist cards, flight reservations and accommodation packages.

The immigration officials in Cuba know very well that a Cuban stamp in a US passport can create problems. However, many Americans request that immigration officers not stamp their passport before they hand it over. The officer will instead stamp their tourist card, which is collected upon departure from Cuba. Those who don't ask usually get a tiny stamp on page 16 or the last page in the shape of a plane, barn, moon or some other random symbol that doesn't mention Cuba.

The US government has an 'Interests Section' in Habana, but American visitors are advised to go there only if something goes terribly wrong. Therefore, unofficial US visitors are especially careful not to lose their passports while in Cuba, as this would put them in a very difficult position. Many

Cuban hotels rent security boxes (CUC$2 per day) to guests and nonguests alike, and you can carry a photocopy of your passport for identification on the street.

There are two types of licenses issued by the US government to visit Cuba: general licenses (typically for family members, artists and academics) and special licenses (for journalists on assignment, for foreign officials based in the US, and occasionally on humanitarian grounds). In 1995 the list of permissible travel was expanded to include educational and cultural exchanges, but George W Bush discontinued this license category in 2003, cutting off 70% of the travel that had been deemed 'legal.' Cuban Americans may visit relatives in Cuba once every three years with a general license. Such permits are never issued for the purpose of business travel or tourism.

For more information, contact the **Licensing Division** (☎ 202-622-2480; www.treas.gov/ofac; Office of Foreign Assets Control, US Department of the Treasury, 2nd fl, Annex Building, 1500 Pennsylvania Ave NW, Washington, DC 20220). Travel arrangements for those eligible for a license can be made by specialized US companies such as Marazul or ABC Charters (see p473). License holders are only allowed to spend US$100 per person per day for land arrangements.

Under the Trading with the Enemy Act, goods originating in Cuba are prohibited from being brought into the US by anyone but licensed travelers. Cuban cigars, rum, coffee etc will be confiscated by US customs, and officials can create additional problems if they feel so inclined. Possession of Cuban goods inside the US or bringing them in from a third country is also banned.

American travelers who choose to go to Cuba (and wish to avoid unnecessary hassles with the US border guards) get rid of anything related to their trip to Cuba, including used airline tickets, baggage tags, travel documents, receipts and souvenirs, before returning to the US. If Cuban officials don't stamp their passport, there will be no official record of their trip. They also use a prepaid Cuban telephone card to make calls to the US in order to avoid there being records of collect or operator-assisted telephone calls.

Since September 11, 2001, all international travel issues have taken on new import, and there has been a crackdown on 'illegal' travel to Cuba. Though it has nothing to do with terrorism, some Americans returning from Cuba have had 'transit to Cuba' written in their passports by Jamaican customs officials. Customs officials at major US entry points (eg New York, Houston, Miami) are onto backpackers coming off Cancún and Montego Bay flights with throngs of honeymoon couples, or tanned gentlemen arriving from Toronto in January. They're starting to ask questions, reminding travelers that it's a felony to lie to a customs agent as they do so.

The maximum penalty for 'unauthorized' Americans traveling to Cuba is US$250,000 and 10 years in prison. In practice, people are usually fined US$7500. Since George W Bush came into the White House, the number of people threatened with legal action has more than tripled and it's likely to go higher still. More than 100,000 US citizens a year travel to Cuba with no consequences. However, as long as these regulations remain in place, visiting Cuba certainly qualifies as soft adventure travel for Americans. There are many organizations, including a group of congresspeople on Capitol Hill, working to lift the travel ban (see www.cubacentral.com for more information).

## VOLUNTEERING

One of the most rewarding ways to experience Cuba is by volunteering. International labor brigades have a rich history in Cuba and each year teams of between 50 and 200 *brigadistas* (workers) from around the world arrive to work in solidarity with Cuba. The Venceremos and Antonio Maceo Brigades (US), the Juan Rius Rivera Brigade (Puerto Rico), the Ernesto Che Guevara Brigade (Canada), the José Martí Brigade (Western Europe), the Nordic Brigade (Scandinavia) and the Southern Cross Brigade (Australia and New Zealand) are among them.

Volunteering involves three challenging weeks doing agricultural or construction work alongside Cubans. There's also a full program of activities, including educational and political events and visits to factories, hospitals, trade unions and schools. Entertainment is provided at the camp and excursions to the beach and places of interest are organized.

Participants pay their own airfare to Cuba, plus food, accommodation and excursion fares. For more information see Habana chapter p116.

## WOMEN TRAVELERS

In terms of personal safety, Cuba is a dream destination for women travelers. Most streets can be walked alone at night, violent crime is rare and the chivalrous part of machismo means you'll never step into oncoming traffic. But machismo cuts both ways, with protecting on one side and pursuing – relentlessly – on the other. Cuban women are used to *piropos* (the whistles, kissing sounds and compliments constantly ringing in their ears), and might even reply with their own if they're feeling frisky. For foreign women, however, it can feel like an invasion. Like any cross-cultural situation, if you want to travel in Cuba, you'll have to come to terms with it somehow.

Ignoring *piropos* is the first step. But sometimes ignoring them isn't enough. Learn some rejoinders in Spanish so you can shut men up. '*No me moleste*' (don't bother me), '*esta bueno yá*' (all right already) or '*que falta respeto*' (how disrespectful) are good ones, as is the withering 'don't you dare' stare that is also part of the Cuban woman's arsenal. Wearing plain, modest clothes might help lessen unwanted attention; topless sunbathing is out. An absent husband, invented or not, seldom has any effect. If you go to a disco, be very clear with Cuban dance partners what you are and are not interested in. Dancing is a kind of foreplay in Cuba and may be viewed as an invitation for something more. Cubans appreciate directness and as long as you set the boundaries, you'll have a fabulous time. Being in the company of a Cuban man is the best way to prevent *piropos*, and if all else fails, retire to the pool for a day out of the line of fire and re-energize.

Traveling alone can be seen as an invitation for all kinds of come-ons, and solo women travelers will not have an easy time of it. Hooking up with a male traveler (or another woman, at least to deflect the barrage) can do wonders. Marriage proposals will come fast and from all corners, as matrimony is an easy way to emigrate for Cubans who want out.

# Transport

## CONTENTS



TRANSPORT

# GETTING THERE & AWAY

## ENTERING THE COUNTRY

Whether it's your first time or 50th, descending low into José Martí international airport, over rust-red tobacco fields, is an exciting and unforgettable experience. Fortunately, entry procedures are straightforward, as long as you have a passport valid for six months, an onward ticket and your tourist card filled out (be sure to put something in the 'Address in Cuba' space; see Visas p464).

> **THINGS CHANGE...**
>
> The information in this chapter is particularly vulnerable to change. Check directly with the airline or a travel agent to make sure you understand how a fare (and the ticket you may buy) works and be aware of the security requirements for international travel. Shop carefully. The details given in this chapter should be regarded as pointers and are not a substitute for your own careful, up-to-date research.

Outside Cuba, the capital city is called Havana, and this is how travel agents, airlines and other professionals will refer to it. Within Cuba, it's almost always called Habana or La Habana by everyone. For the sake of consistency, we have used the latter spelling throughout this book.

Flights, tours and rail tickets can be booked online at www.lonelyplanet.com/travel_services.

## AIR

### Airports & Airlines

Cuba has 11 international airports and more than 60 carriers serving the island. Most travelers fly into Aeropuerto Internacional José Martí in **Habana** (HAV; ☎ 7-33 56 66), Aeropuerto Juan Gualberto Gómez in **Varadero** (VRA; ☎ 045-24 70 15) or Aeropuerto Antonio Maceo in **Santiago de Cuba** (SCU; ☎ 022-69 10 14). Travelers on package tours might fly into **Holguín** (HOG; ☎ 024-46 25 12), **Ciego de Ávila** (AVI; ☎ 033-26 66 26), **Cayo Largo del Sur** (CYO; ☎ 046-34 82 07) or **Aeropuerto Jardínes del Rey** (CCC; ☎ 30 82 28).

The national airline of Cuba is **Cubana de Aviación** (www.cubana.cu). Its modern fleet flies major routes and its airfares are usually among the cheapest. However, overbooking and delays are nagging problems you may well encounter. In addition, the airline has a zero tolerance attitude towards overweight luggage, charging stiffly for every kilogram above the 20kg baggage allowance. In terms of safety, Cubana's reputation precedes it (it had back-to-back crashes in December 1999, with 39 fatalities), but it hasn't had any incidents since. Still, you might want to check the latest at www.airsafe.com.

#### AIRLINES FLYING TO/FROM CUBA

**Aerocaribbean** (7L; ☎ 7-832 7584; www.aero-caribbean.com; Airline Bldg, Calle 23 No 64, Habana)

**Aeroflot-Russian International Airlines** (AFL; ☎ 7-33 32 00; www.aeroflot.com; hub Moscow; Airline Bldg, Calle 23 No 64)

**Aeropostal** (LAV; ☎ 7-55 40 00; www.aeropostal.com; hub Caracas; Hotel Habana Libre, cnr Calle 23 & Calle L)

**Air Canada** (ACA; www.aircanada.com; hub Montréal; Airline Bldg, Calle 23 No 64)

**DEPARTURE TAX**

Everyone must pay a CUC$25 departure tax at the airport. It's payable in cash only.

**Air Europa** (AEA; ☎ 7-204 6905/6/7/8; www.air-europa.com; hub Madrid; cnr Av 5 & Calle 76, Miramar)
**Air France** (AFR; ☎ 7-66 26 42; www.airfrance.com; hub Paris; Airline Bldg, Calle 23 No 64)
**Air Jamaica** (AJM; ☎ 7-66 24 47; www.airjamaica.com; hub Montego Bay; Hotel Meliá Cohiba, Paseo btwn Calles 1 & 3)
**Air Transat** (TSC; ☎ 1-877 872 6728; www.airtransat.com; hub Montréal)
**Copa Airlines** (CMP; ☎ 7-33 15 03; www.copaair.com; hub Panama City; Airline Bldg, Calle 23 No 64)
**Cubana** (CU; ☎ 7-834-4446; www.cubana.cu; hub Habana; Airline Bldg, Calle 23 No 64)
**Iberia** (IBE; ☎ 33 50 41; www.iberia.com; hub Madrid; cnr Calles 23 & P, Miramar)
**Lacsa** (LRC; ☎ 7-33 31 14; www.grupotaca.com; hub San José, Costa Rica; Hotel Habana Libre, cnr Calles 23 & Calle L) Also represents Taca.
**LanChile** (LAN; ☎ 7-831-6186; www.lanchile.com; hub Santiago de Chile)
**Martinair** (MPH; ☎ 7-33 43 64; www.martinair.com; hub Amsterdam; cnr Calles E & 23, Vedado)
**Mexicana de Aviación** (MXA; ☎ 7-33 35 33; www.mexicana.com.mx; hub Mexico City; Airline Bldg, Calle 23 No 64) Also represents the regional carrier Aerocaribe.
**Skyservice** (SSV; ☎ 1-416-679-8330; www.skyserviceairlines.com; hub Toronto)
**Virgin Atlantic** (VIR; ☎ 7-204-0747; www.virginatlantic.com; hub London Gatwick)

## Tickets

Since Americans can't buy tickets to Cuba and can't use US-based travel agents, a host of businesses in Mexico (p471), Canada (below) and the Caribbean (p470) specialize in air-only deals. They sometimes won't sell you the first leg of your trip to the 'gateway' country for fear of embargo-related repercussions. When booking online or if an agency requires financial acrobatics to steer clear of US embargo laws (which sometimes happens), be sure to confirm details, take contact names and clarify the procedure. You will need a Cuban tourist card and these agencies should arrange that. Except during peak holiday seasons, you can usually just arrive in Mexico, Jamaica or whatever gateway country and buy your round-trip ticket to Cuba there.

The choice for non-Americans is varied, straightforward, cheap and accessible. Often, an air-and-hotel package deal to one of the beach resorts works out cheaper than just airfare alone.

## Canada

Cubana flies to Habana from Montréal four times weekly (via Cayo Coco, Varadero or Cayo Largo). From Toronto, Cubana flies

**US CITIZENS & CUBA**

In conjunction with the US embargo against Cuba, the US government currently enforces a 'travel ban,' preventing its citizens from visiting Cuba. Technically a treasury law prohibiting Americans from spending money in Cuba, it has largely squelched leisure travel for more than 45 years.

The 1996 Helms-Burton Bill, which was signed into law by President Clinton on March 12, 1996, imposes *without judicial review* fines of up to US$50,000 on US citizens who visit Cuba without US government permission. It also allows for confiscation of their property. In addition, under the Trading with the Enemy Act, violators may face up to US$250,000 in fines and up to 10 years in prison. Although fines were only occasionally levied when Clinton was in the White House, the number of individuals fined since Bush came into office has more than tripled, and Bush's administration has been granting far fewer licenses too. The author and publisher of this guide accept no responsibility for repercussions suffered by US citizens who decide to circumvent these restrictions. You are strongly encouraged to visit www.cubacentral.com to inform yourself of the latest legislation on Capitol Hill.

Supporters of the embargo argue that travel to Cuba supports a 'communist dictatorship.' Lonely Planet believes that travel promotes positive, humanistic, cross-cultural exchanges and where and how you travel is an individual decision. Many Cubans depend on the tourist trade to survive, and by using the information in this book, travelers can spend their money in ways that benefit ordinary Cubans.

**CLIMATE CHANGE & TRAVEL**

Climate change is a serious threat to the ecosystems that humans rely upon, and air travel is the fastest-growing contributor to the problem. Lonely Planet regards travel, overall, as a global benefit, but believes we all have a responsibility to limit our personal impact on global warming.

**Flying & Climate Change**

Pretty much every form of motorized travel generates carbon dioxide (the main cause of human-induced climate change) but planes are far and away the worst offenders, not just because of the sheer distances they allow us to travel, but because they release greenhouse gases high into the atmosphere. The statistics are frightening: two people taking a return flight between Europe and the US will contribute as much to climate change as an average household's gas and electricity consumption over a whole year.

**Carbon Offset Schemes**

Climatecare.org and other websites use 'carbon calculators' that allow travelers to offset the level of greenhouse gases they are responsible for with financial contributions to sustainable travel schemes that reduce global warming – including projects in India, Honduras, Kazakhstan and Uganda.

Lonely Planet, together with Rough Guides and other concerned partners in the travel industry, support the carbon offset scheme run by climatecare.org. Lonely Planet offsets all of its staff and author travel.

For more information check out our website: www.lonelyplanet.com.

to Habana three times weekly, with a Varadero stopover once a week. Lacsa (the good Costa Rican carrier) also has several weekly flights from Toronto and Montréal to Habana. Air Canada is another option. Mexicana flies from Vancouver to Habana via Mexico City five times weekly.

You might find a cheaper fare, though, with the reliable charter lines Air Transat and Skyservice, flying weekly from Toronto and Montréal to almost all international airports in Cuba. Some of these flights operate only from mid-December to April, when Canadian flights go directly to Cuba from as far afield as Vancouver and Halifax.

Unfortunately, 'open jaw' ticket arrangements, which allow you to fly into one airport and out of another, are usually not available. The maximum stay on most Canadian charters is 28 days. If you wish to stay longer than that, the price soars. Flight dates cannot be changed and there are heavy cancellation penalties. Always be sure to compare the price of a tour package as it may be only a few hundred dollars more and airport transfers, accommodation, and often meals will be included.

The following are reliable agencies selling packages and air-only tickets:

**A Nash Travel** (☎ 905-755 0647, toll free 800-818 2004; www.anashtravel.com)
**Alba Tours** (www.albatours.com)
**Go Cuba Plus** (www.gocubaplus.com)
**Netssa** (☎ toll free 866-504 9988; www.netssa.com) Last-minute flight specials, plus multilingual staff.
**STA Travel** (☎ 888-427-5639; www.statravel.ca)

## Caribbean

Cubana has flights to Habana from Nassau, Fort de France, Kingston, Montego Bay, Pointe-a-Pitre and Santo Domingo. The Cuban regional carrier Aerocaribbean flies between Port au Prince, Haiti, and Santo Domingo, Dominican Republic, to Santiago de Cuba weekly, and Santo Domingo and Grand Cayman to Habana weekly.

**Air Jamaica** (www.airjamaica.com) flies from Montego Bay and Kingston to Habana daily, with numerous convenient connections from the US. Air Jamaica also has a liberal baggage policy, often allowing you to bring oversized and overweight luggage without problems.

The agency **CubaLinda.com** (www.cubalinda.com) is a Habana-based online agency selling gateway tickets from Mexico and the Caribbean.

From the Bahamas, Cubana flies daily between Nassau and Habana; the Cuban tourist card and the US$15 Nassau airport departure tax should be included in the ticket price, but ask. Due to US embargo laws, these agencies may not accept online payment or credit card guarantees with cards issued by US banks or their subsidiaries. The financial rigmarole for Americans (mailing certified checks, paying in cash or wiring funds through Western Union for example) may not be worth the time and energy if that's the case. Check on the payment system before settling on the Bahamas as a gateway. Nassau bookings can be made through the following companies:

**Havanatur Bahamas** (☎ 1-242 393 5281/2/3/4; fax 393 5280) Offices in the Bahamas.

**Majestic Holidays** (☎ 1-242 342 322 2606; www.majesticholidays.com) Offices in the Bahamas.

**San Cristóbal Travel** (☎ toll free in US & Canada 866-510 7756; www.sancristobaltravel.com) Offices in Canada and Habana.

## Europe

Continental Europe is a good gateway to Cuba. Virgin Atlantic fly twice weekly to Habana (Thursday and Sunday) out of London's Gatwick Airport while Air Europa flies into Habana daily from Barcelona, Bilbao, Las Palmas, London, Madrid, Milan, Paris and Rome. Iberia flies to Habana from Madrid four times weekly and connects through most European capitals; check out their reasonable fares with a maximum three-month stay. Air France arrives from Paris-Charles De Gaulle five times a week.

From Amsterdam, Martinair has twice weekly flights to Habana and one flight weekly to both Varadero and Holguín. It's possible to book Martinair flights into one Cuban airport and out of the other: convenient if you want to travel overland without backtracking. Also look into Air France and Iberia flights from Amsterdam, connecting through Paris or Madrid.

From Russia, Aeroflot flies from Moscow-Sheremetyevo to Habana.

Cubana flies to Habana from Copenhagen, Las Palmas, London, Madrid, Milan, Moscow, Paris-Orly and Rome. Other Cubana flights go from Madrid, Milan, Paris-Orly and Rome to Santiago de Cuba. London to Holguín and Milan to Cayo Largo are also served. Most operate only once or twice a week, except Habana–Paris, which runs three times weekly. Cubana sometimes offers reduced last-minute fares. There are Cubana offices all over Europe, including **Rome** (☎ 06 700 0714; fax 06 700 0688), **Paris** (☎ 01 53 63 23 23; fax 01 63 53 23 29), **Madrid** (☎ 91 758 9750; fax 91 541 6642) and **London** (☎ 020 75 37 79 09).

The following European-based agencies can help arrange your details:

**Guamá Havanatur** (☎ 917 82 37 85) In Madrid.

**Havanatour Holanda** (☎ 104-12 73 07) In Rotterdam.

**Havanatour UK** (☎ 01707-646 463; www.havanatour.co.uk) In Hertfordshire, England.

**Havanatur Italia** (☎ 02-676 0691; www.havanatur.it)

**Havanatour Paris** (☎ 01 48 01 44 55; fax 01 48 01 44 50; www.havanatour.fr)

**Journey Latin America** (☎ 020-8747-3108; www.journeylatinamerica.com) Based in Britain, this is a professional company which usually has good deals.

**Sol y Son Moscú** (☎ 095 931 9964; sol-y-son@mtu-net.ru) Sells Cubana flights from Moscow.

**Sol y Son Roma** (☎ 06-4470 2320; www.it.solysonviajes.com) Handles Cubana flights from Italy.

**Trailfinders** (☎ 020-7938-3366; www.trailfinders.com) Offices throughout the UK.

## Mexico

Mexico is a direct and convenient gateway to Cuba, with many flights to choose from. Both Cubana and Aerocaribe (the regional airline of Mexicana de Aviación) fly from Cancún to Habana daily. Cancún itself is easily accessible on cheap charter flights, and Aerocaribe connects with Mexicana flights from many US cities. If space is available, you can buy same-day tickets to Habana at the Cubana and Aerocaribe offices in the Cancún airport.

Mexicana also has frequent flights from another dozen cities to Habana including Mexico City, Mérida and Tijuana. Cubana flies to Habana from Mexico City daily.

From Mexico City to Habana, a round-trip fare will cost around US$450, from Cancún about US$275. Mexicana has reservations offices in **Mexico City** (☎ 5-448-0990; 1-800-502-2000; www.mexicana.com) and **Cancún** (☎ 98-87-4444). Mexicana offices in the US are prohibited from booking these flights.

Cubana also has offices in **Mexico City** (☎ 5-250 6355; fax 5-255 0835) and **Cancún** (☎/fax 98-86 0192).

TRANSPORT

Also check these agencies:

**Acuario Tours** (☎ Acapulco 74-85 6100, Mexico City 5-575-5922; www.acuariotours.com)

**Divermex** (☎ 99 88 84 23 25; www.divermex.com)

**Sol y Son México** (☎ 98 87 70 17; www.mx.solysonviajes.com)

**Taino Tours** (☎ 5-259 3907; www.tainotours.com.mx)

### South & Central America

From Caracas, Venezuela, Aeropostal flies to Habana five times weekly. Cubana flies from Caracas to Habana six times weekly. Book in Caracas, through **Ideal Tours** (☎ 2-793 0037/1822; idealtours@cantv.net) or go straight to **Cubana** (☎ 2-12 286 8639; cubana@intercon.net.ve).

Cubana flies to Habana from Bogotá, Buenos Aires and Saõ Paulo. There's also a weekly flight from Buenos Aires to Cayo Coco and Varadero. Cubana has offices in **Buenos Aires** (☎ 1-326 5291; cubana@tournet.com.ar); **Quito** (☎ 2-54 49 30; cubana@hoy.net); and **Bogotá** (☎ 1-610 5800; solyson@colomsat.net.co).

Cubana flies to Habana from San José, Costa Rica, and Guatemala City twice weekly and Panama City three times a week. Lacsa (Líneas Aéreas de Costa Rica) has flights to Habana from San José, Guatemala City and San Salvador several times a week. Copa Airlines also has frequent flights between Central America and Cuba.

The Cuban regional airline Aerocaribbean flies from Managua to Habana weekly.

## SEA

Thanks to the US embargo, which prohibits vessels calling at Cuban ports from visiting the US for six months, few cruise ships include Cuba on their itineraries. Many companies also canceled Cuba cruises after September 11, 2001, which is odd, because there really is no place safer. European lines however, tired of being locked out, are starting to trickle in. A specialist travel agent will be able to tell you what cruise ships currently call at Cuban ports.

Access by private yacht or cruiser is easy, and there are numerous harbors around Cuba. This book is not intended to replace a comprehensive cruising guide.

There are no scheduled ferry services to Cuba.

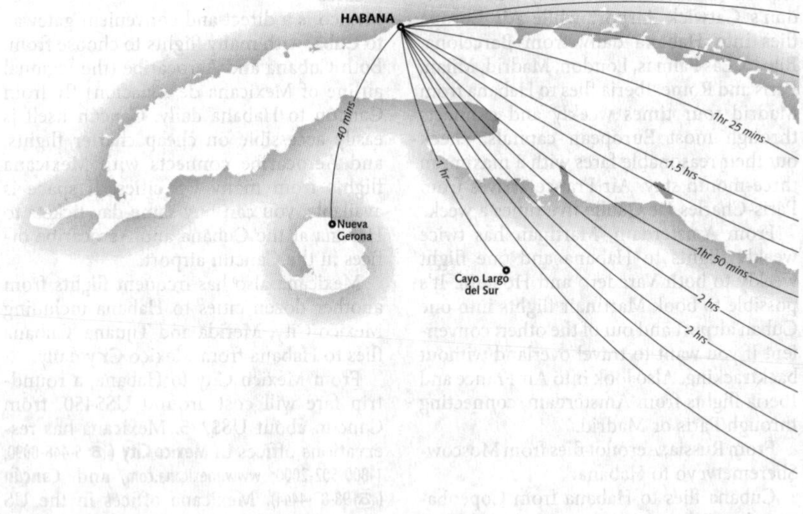

## TOURS

A quick Internet search delivers scads of tours focusing on the beach, culture, the environment, adventure, cycling, bird-watching, architecture, hiking, you name it… Note that many outfitters anxious to sell packages to Americans aren't always providing 'legal' travel; Americans are still subject to Treasury laws; see the **Department of the Treasury** (www.treas.gov) website for details (type the word 'Cuba' into site search engine). Persons holding US passports will find agencies handling 'air-only' packages on p469 and tours for US-license holders following.

### US

United States citizens eligible for a US government 'license' to visit Cuba should contact **Marazul Charters Inc** (☎ 305-263-6829, toll free 800-223-5334; www.marazulcharters.com), which books charter flights direct from New York and Miami to Habana.

**ABC Charters** (☎ 305-871 1260, toll free 866-422 2247; www.abc-charters.com), with flights from Miami to Habana, Santiago de Cuba or Holguín, has been recommended for its user-friendliness.

Since the people-to-people educational exchange license was revoked in 2003, some of the most rewarding tours from the US have been scuttled – for now. Contact the following for their current tour status:

**Center for Cuban Studies** (☎ 212-242 0559; fax 212-242 1937; www.cubaupdate.org) Arranges trips through universities.

**Global Exchange** (☎ 415-255 7296, 800-497 1994; fax 415-255 7498; www.globalexchange.org)

# GETTING AROUND

## AIR

**Cubana de Aviación** (www.cubana.cu) and its regional carrier Aerocaribbean have flights to La Habana, Baracoa, Bayamo, Camagüey, Cayo Largo del Sur, Ciego de Ávila, Guantánamo, Holguín, Isla de la Juventud, Manzanillo, Moa and Santiago de Cuba. One-way flights are half the price of round-trip flights and weight restrictions are strict (especially on Aerocaribbean's smaller planes). You can purchase tickets at most hotel tour desks and travel agencies for the

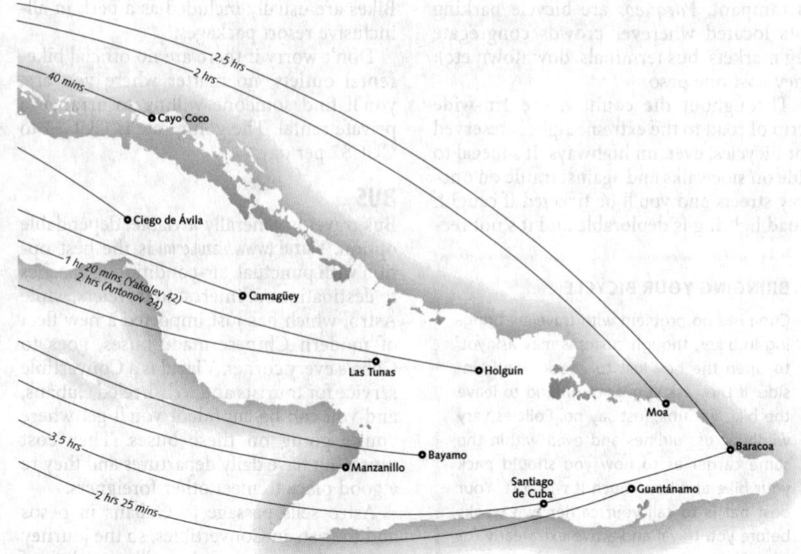


TRANSPORT

same price as at the airline offices, which are often chaotic. Sol y Son is Cubana's own travel agency and is known for its customer service and efficiency.

Old cars aren't the only stars. **Aerotaxi** (☎ 832-8127; cnr Calle 27 & M, Vedado) flies 50-year-old Antonov 2s (propeller airplanes) around the country to a variety of destinations. You have to rent the entire plane for approximately CUC$500 per day. You may also encounter Yakolev YAK 42s, jet airplanes that often run on the Habana–Camagüey/Holguín/Santiago de Cuba air routes and are a good deal faster than the older propeller-driven Antonovs.



## BICYCLE

Cuba is a cyclist's paradise, with bike lanes, bike workshops and drivers accustomed to sharing the road countrywide. Spare parts are difficult to find and you should bring important spares with you. Still, Cubans are grand masters at improvised repair and though specific parts may not be available, something can surely be jury-rigged. *Poncheros* fix flat tires and provide air; every small town has one.

Helmets are unheard of in Cuba except at upscale resorts, so you should bring your own. A lock is imperative as bicycle theft is rampant. *Parqueos* are bicycle parking lots located wherever crowds congregate (eg markets, bus terminals, downtown etc); they cost one peso.

Throughout the country, the 1m-wide strip of road to the extreme right is reserved for bicycles, even on highways. It's illegal to ride on sidewalks and against traffic on one-way streets and you'll be ticketed if caught. Road lighting is deplorable and it's not recommended you ride after dark (over one third of vehicular accidents in Cuba involve bicycles); carry lights with you just in case.

Trains with *coches de equipaje* or *bagones* (baggage carriages) should take bikes for around CUC$10 per trip. These compartments are guarded, but take your panniers with you and check over the bike when you arrive at your destination. Víazul buses also take bikes.

**BRINGING YOUR BICYCLE**

Cuba has no problem with travelers bringing in bikes, though customs may ask you to open the box just to check what's inside. If they ask you if you intend to leave the bike in Cuba, just say no. Policies vary wildly across airlines and even within the same carrier as to how you should pack your bike and how much it will cost. Your best bet is to call your carrier two weeks before you travel and arrive extra early for your flight.

### Purchase

Limited selection and high prices make buying a bike in Cuba through official channels unattractive. Better to ask around and strike a deal with an individual to buy their *chivo* (Cuban slang for bike) and trade it or resell it when you leave. With some earnest bargaining, you can get one for around CUC$30 – although the more you pay, the less your bones are likely to shake. Despite the obvious cost savings, bringing your own is still the best bet by far.

### Rental

At the time of writing, official bike-rental agencies exist only at El Orbe in Habana (for rates see p143), at the major beach resorts (CUC$2 per hour or CUC$15 per day) and in Viñales (CUC$6 to CUC$8 per day). Bikes are usually included as a perk in all-inclusive resort packages.

Don't worry if there are no official bike-rental outlets; no matter where you are, you'll find someone willing to arrange a private rental. The going rate is CUC$3 to CUC$7 per day.

## BUS

Bus travel is generally a viable, dependable option. **Víazul** (www.viazul.com) is the best option with punctual, air-conditioned coaches to destinations of interest to travelers, while Astro, which has just imported a new fleet of modern Chinese-made buses, goes to Cuba's every corner. Víazul is a Convertible service for tourists and well-heeled Cubans, and you can be confident you'll get where you're going on these buses. They cost more, but have daily departures and they're a good place to meet other foreigners.

Astro sells passage to Cubans in pesos and tourists in Convertibles, so the journey is more interesting and you'll meet lots of locals this way (trucks are another great way to make friends; see p479). If you plan on taking Astro buses, check ahead of time as there's never any printed schedule and only two tickets per bus are available for foreigners on each departure. There are theoretically different classes of buses, but really, whatever shows up is what you take. Foreigners with a *carnet* (p454) pay for Astro tickets in pesos. Many services only run on alternate days.

Going from east to west, the bus departures are very inconvenient, with buses leaving in the middle of the night.

There's also a new Havanatur transfer bus that runs daily Viñales–Soroa–Habana, Viñales–María La Gorda, Viñales–Trinidad and Viñales–Cayo Levisa routes (see p208).

**Astro** (☎ 7-870 3397 Habana) Serves every major and minor town in the country; useful for getting off the beaten track and between towns not served by Víazul, including Manzanillo, anything west of Bayamo and the north coast east of Varadero to Baracoa.

**Víazul** (☎ 7-881 1413, 7-881 5652, 7-881 1108; www.viazul.cu) Routes are Habana–Viñales, Habana–Varadero, Habana–Trinidad, Habana–Holguín, Varadero–Trinidad, Habana–Santiago de Cuba, Trinidad–Santiago de Cuba and Santiago de Cuba–Baracoa. Depending on the route, these buses also stop in Pinar del Río, Santa Clara, Cienfuegos, Ciego de Ávila, Sancti Spíritus, Camagüey, Las Tunas, Holguín, Bayamo or Guantánamo. They take online reservations, but take those with a grain of salt.

### Costs

Víazul always costs more than Astro, but the difference is marginal and gets even more negligible the further you travel. As Astro seats are more limited and less comfortable than Víazul, they are best used to get to the places where Víazul doesn't penetrate, eg north coast, Manzanillo or west of Pinar del Río. From Habana to Santiago de Cuba, passage costs CUC$42/51 with Astro/Víazul.

### Reservations

Reservations with Víazul are advisable during peak travel periods (June to August, Christmas and Easter) and on popular routes (Habana–Trinidad, Trinidad–Santa Clara and Santiago de Cuba–Baracoa). Víazul out of Baracoa is almost always booked, so reserve an advance seat on this service and arrange through-reservations if you intend to connect in Santiago de Cuba to points north and west.

Since it's advisable to double check on Astro services before you intend to travel, and only two seats are reserved for foreigners, you might as well make a reservation while you're at it.

## CAR

### Driver's License

Your home license is sufficient to rent and drive a car in Cuba.

### Fuel & Spare Parts

Gas sold in Convertibles (as opposed to peso gas) is widely available in stations all over the country (the north coast west of Habana being the notable exception). Gas stations are often open 24 hours and may have a small parts store on site. Gas is sold by the liter and comes in *regular* (CUC$0.75 per liter) and *especial* (CUC$0.95 per liter) varieties. Rental cars are advised to use *especial*. All gas stations have efficient pump attendants, usually in the form of *trabajadores sociales* (students in the process of studying for a degree).

While you cannot count on spare parts per se to be available, Cubans have decades of experience keeping old wrecks on the road without factory parts and you'll see them do amazing things with cardboard, string, rubber and clothes hangers to keep a car mobile.

If you need air in your tires or you have a puncture, use a gas station or visit the local *ponchero*. They often don't have measures so make sure they don't over-fill them.

### Insurance

Rental cars come with an optional CUC$10 per day insurance which covers everything but theft of the radio (which you'll need to put in the trunk of the car at night). You can choose to decline the insurance, but then the refundable deposit you must leave upon renting the car (in cash if you don't have a credit card issued by a non-US bank) soars from CUC$200 to CUC$500. If you do have an accident, you must get a copy of the *denuncia* (police report) to be eligible for the insurance coverage, a process which can take all day. If the police determine that you are the party responsible for the accident, say *adiós* to your deposit.

## Rental

Renting a car in Cuba is very straightforward and you can usually be signed up and fitted out in well under an hour. You'll need your passport, driver's license and refundable CUC$200 deposit (in cash or non-US credit card). You can rent a car in one city and drop it off in another for a reasonable fee, which is handy. If you're on a tight budget, ask about diesel cars – some agencies stock a few and you'll save bundles in gas money considering a liter of regular gas is CUC$0.95 while a liter of *petroleo* (diesel) is CUC$0.45. Note that there are very few rental cars with automatic transmission.

If you want to rent a car for three days or fewer, it will come with limited kilometers, while contracts for three days or more come with unlimited kilometers. In Cuba, you pay for the first tank of gas when you rent the car (CUC$0.95 per liter) and return it empty (a suicidal policy that sees many tight-fisted tourists running out of gas a kilometer or so from the drop-off point). Just to make it worse, you will not be refunded for any gas left in the tank. Petty theft of mirrors, antennas, taillights etc is common, so it's worth it to pay someone a Convertible or two to watch your car for the night. If you lose your rental contract or keys you'll pay a CUC$50 penalty. Drivers under 25 pay a CUC$5 fee, while additional drivers on the same contract pay a CUC$15 surcharge.

Check over the car carefully with the rental agent before driving into the sunset as you'll be responsible for any damage or missing parts. Make sure there is a spare tire of the correct size, a jack and lug wrench. Check that there are seatbelts and that all the doors lock properly (be particularly thorough with the Micar agency).

We have received many letters about poor/nonexistent customer service, bogus spare tires, forgotten reservations and other car rental problems. Reservations are only accepted 15 days in advance and are still not guaranteed. While agents are usually accommodating, you might end up paying more than you planned or have to wait hours until someone returns a car. The more Spanish you speak and the friendlier you are, the more likely problems will be resolved to everyone's satisfaction (tips to the agent might help). As with most Cuban travel, always be ready to go to Plan B.

## Road Conditions

And you thought driving in Cuba would be easy? Think again. Driving in Cuba isn't just a different ballpark, it's a different sport. The first problem is there are no signs – almost anywhere. Major junctions and turn-offs to important resorts/cities are often not indicated at all. Not only is this distracting, it's also incredibly time-consuming. The lack of signage also extends to highway instructions. Often a one-way street is not clearly indicated or a speed limit not highlighted, which can cause problems with the police (who won't understand your inability to telepathically absorb the road rules), and road-markings are non-existent everywhere.

Repair-wise the Autopista, Vía Blanca and Carretera Central are generally in a good state, but be prepared for roads suddenly deteriorating into chunks of asphalt and unexpected railroad crossings everywhere else (especially in the Oriente). Rail crossings are particularly problematic as there are hundreds of them and there are never any safety gates. Beware: however overgrown the rails may look you can pretty much assume that the line is still in use. Cuban trains, rather like their cars, defy all normal logic when it comes to mechanics.

While motorized traffic is refreshingly light, bicycles, pedestrians, ox carts, horse carriages and livestock are a different matter. Many old cars and trucks lack rearview mirrors and traffic-unaware children run out of all kinds of nooks and crannies. Stay alert, drive with caution and use your horn when passing or on blind curves.

Driving at night is not recommended due to variable roads, drunk drivers, crossing cows and poor lighting. Drunk driving remains a troublesome problem despite a government educational campaign. Late night in Habana is particularly dangerous, when it seems there's a passing lane, cruising lane and drunk lane.

Traffic lights are often busted or hard to pick out and right-of-way rules thrown to the wind. Take extra care.

## Road Rules

Cubans drive how they want, where they want. It seems chaotic at first, but has its rhythm. Seatbelts are supposedly required

## ROAD DISTANCES (KM)

| | Bayamao | Camagüey | Ciego de Ávila | Cienfuegos | Guantánamo | Habana | Holguín | Las Tunas | Matanzas | Pinar del Río | Sancti Spíritus | Santa Clara |
|---|---|---|---|---|---|---|---|---|---|---|---|---|
| Camagüey | 210 | | | | | | | | | | | |
| Ciego de Ávila | 318 | 108 | | | | | | | | | | |
| Cienfuegos | 540 | 330 | 222 | | | | | | | | | |
| Guantánamo | 161 | 371 | 479 | 701 | | | | | | | | |
| Habana | 744 | 534 | 426 | 254 | 905 | | | | | | | |
| Holguín | 71 | 209 | 317 | 539 | 182 | 743 | | | | | | |
| Las Tunas | 82 | 128 | 236 | 458 | 243 | 662 | 81 | | | | | |
| Matanzas | 684 | 474 | 366 | 194 | 845 | 105 | 683 | 602 | | | | |
| Pinar del Río | 906 | 696 | 588 | 416 | 1067 | 162 | 905 | 824 | 267 | | | |
| Sancti Spíritus | 394 | 184 | 76 | 151 | 555 | 354 | 393 | 312 | 294 | 516 | | |
| Santa Clara | 473 | 263 | 155 | 67 | 634 | 276 | 472 | 391 | 217 | 438 | 590 | |
| Santiago de Cuba | 117 | 550 | 435 | 657 | 84 | 861 | 138 | 199 | 801 | 1023 | 511 | 590 |

and maximum speed limits are technically 50km/h in the city, 90km/h on highways and 100km/h on the Autopista, but some cars can't even go that fast and those that can go faster still.

With so few cars on the road, it's hard not to put the pedal to the floor and just fly. Unexpected potholes are a hazard, however, as are police. There are some clever speed traps, particularly along the Autopista. Speeding tickets start at CUC$30 and are noted on your car contract; the fine is deducted from your deposit when you return the car. When pulled over by the cops, you're expected to get out of the car and walk over to them with your paperwork. An oncoming car flashing its lights means a hazard up ahead (usually the police).

The Cuban transport crisis means there are a lot of people waiting for rides by the side of the road. Giving a *botella* (a lift) to local hitchhikers has advantages aside from altruism. With a Cuban passenger you'll never get lost, you'll learn about secret spots not in any guidebook and you'll meet some great people. There are always risks associated with picking up hitchhikers; giving lifts to older people or families may reduce the risk factor. In the provinces, people waiting for rides are systematically queued by *los amarillos* (roadside traffic organizers; see p197) and they'll hustle the most needy folks into your car, usually an elderly couple or pregnant woman.

## FERRY

The most important ferry services for travelers are from Surgidero de Batabanó to Nueva Gerona, **Isla de la Juventud** (☎ 62-8-5355) and from Habana to **Regla and Casablanca** (☎ 7-867-3726). These ferries are generally safe, though in 1997 two hydrofoils crashed en route to Isla de la Juventud. In both 1994 and 2003, the Regla/Casablanca ferry was hijacked by Cubans trying to make their way to Florida. The 2003 incident involved tourists, so you can expect tight security.

## HITCHHIKING

The transport crisis, culture of solidarity and low crime levels make Cuba a popular hitchhiking destination. Here, hitchhiking is more like ride-sharing. Traffic lights, railroad crossings and country crossroads are regular stops for people seeking rides. In the provinces and on the outskirts of Habana, *los amarillos* (see p197) organize and prioritize ride seekers and you're welcome to jump in line. Rides cost five to 20 pesos depending on distance. Travelers hitching rides will want a good map and some Spanish skills. Expect to wait two or three hours for rides in some cases. Hitching is never entirely safe in any country in the world. Travelers who decide to hitch should understand that they are taking a small but potentially serious risk. People who do choose to hitch will be safer if they travel in pairs and let someone know where they are planning to go.

TRANSPORT

## LOCAL TRANSPORT

### Bici-Taxi

Bici-taxis are big tricycles with a double seat behind the driver and are common in Habana, Camagüey, Holguín and a few other cities. In Habana they'll insist on a CUC$1 minimum fare (Cubans pay five or 10 pesos). Some bici-taxistas ask ridiculous amounts. The fare should be clearly understood before you hop aboard. By law, bici-taxis aren't allowed to take tourists (who are expected to take regular taxis) and they're taking a risk by carrying foreigners. Bici-taxi rules are more lax in the provinces and you should be able to get one for five pesos.

### Boat

Some towns such as Habana, Cienfuegos, Gibara and Santiago de Cuba have local ferry services. Details of these are provided in the respective chapters.

### Bus

Very crowded, very steamy, very challenging, very Cuban – guaguas (local buses) are useful in bigger cities. Buses work fixed routes, stopping at *paradas* (bus stops) that always have a line, even if it doesn't look like it. You have to shout out *'¿el último?'* to find out who was last in line before you showed up. You give this call when the next person arrives and then you know exactly where you fall in line, allowing you to go have a beer until the bus shows up.

Buses cost from 40 centavos to one peso; the camello (Habana Metro bus) will cost 20 centavos. You must always walk as far back in the bus as you can and exit through the rear. Make room to pass by saying *'permiso,'* always wear your pack in front and watch your wallet.

### Colectivos & Maquinas

Colectivos are taxis running on fixed, long-distance routes, leaving when full. They are generally pre-1959American cars that belch diesel fumes and can squash in at least three people across the front seat. State-owned taxis that charge in Convertibles hanging about bus stations are faster and usually cheaper than the bus. State-owned peso taxis and private peso taxis *(maquinas),* are prohibited from taking foreigners (except the *carnet*-carrying kind).

### Horse Carriage

Many provincial cities have *coches de caballo* (horse carriages) that trot on fixed routes and cost one peso.

### Taxi

Tourists are only supposed to take taxis that charge in Convertibles, including the little yellow coco-taxis. Car taxis are metered and cost CUC$1 to start and CUC$1 per kilometer. Taxi drivers are in the habit of offering foreigners a flat, off-meter rate that usually works out very close to what you'll pay with the meter. The difference is that with the meter, the money goes to the state to be divided up; without the meter it goes into the driver's pocket. Coco-taxis are not metered, can hold three people and cost CUC$0.50 per kilometer.

## TOURS

Of the many tourist agencies in Cuba, the following are the most useful:

**Cubamar Viajes** (☎ 7-66 25 23/24; www.cubamarviajes.cu) Rents campismo cabins and mobile homes (caravans).

**Cubanacán** (☎ 7-208 9479; www.cubanacan.cu) General tour agency that also has divisions called Cubanacán Naútica (scuba diving, boating and fishing) and Turismo Y Salud (surgery, spas and rehabilitation).

**Cubatur** (☎ 7-33 41 55; fax 7-33 40 37)

**Ecotur** (☎ 7-41 03 06/08; fax 7-53 99 09)

**Gaviota** (☎ 7-204-4411; www.gaviota-grupo.com)

**Havanatur** (☎ 7-204 0993; www.havanatur.cu) Works with Marazul Tours in the US.

**Paradiso** (☎ 7-832 9538/9; paradis@paradiso.artex.com.cu) Multiday cultural and art tours.

**San Cristóbal Agencia Receptora** (☎ 7-861 9171; fax 7-860-9585)

## TRAIN

Cuba was the sixth country in the world to get a railway (before Spain even) and, as a result, it is proud of its extensive network – however antiquated it might be. Public railways operated by Ferrocarriles de Cuba serve all of the provincial capitals and are a great way to experience Cuba if you have time and patience. As a Cuban traveler said '80% of the trains are late and the other 20% are cancelled.' While train travel is safe, the departure information provided in this book is purely theoretical. Getting a ticket is usually no problem as there's a quota for tourists paying in Convertibles. The most useful routes for travelers are Habana–Santiago de Cuba and Habana–Santa Clara.

Foreigners must pay for their tickets in cash, but prices are reasonable and the carriages, though old and worn, are fairly comfortable, offering lots of local color. The bathrooms are foul. Watch your luggage on overnight trips and bring some of your own food. Vendors come through the train selling coffee (you supply the cup).

The Hershey Train is the only electric railway in Cuba and was built by the Hershey Chocolate Company in the early years of the 20th century; it's a fun way to get between Habana and Matanzas (see p163).

### Classes

Trains are either *especial* (air-con, faster trains with fewer departures); *regular* (slowish trains with daily departures); or *lecheros* (milk trains that stop at every dinky town on the line). Trains on major routes such as Habana–Santiago de Cuba will be *especial* or *regular* trains.

### Costs

*Regular* trains costs under CUC$3 per 100km, while *especial* trains cost closer to CUC$5.50 per 100km. The Hershey Train is priced like the *regular* trains.

### Reservations

In most train stations, you just go to the ticket window and buy a ticket. In Habana, there's a separate waiting room and ticket window for passengers paying in Convertibles. In La Coubre train station and in Santiago de Cuba there's the handy Centro Único de Reservaciones in the center of town. Be prepared to show your passport when purchasing tickets. It's always wise to check beforehand at the station for current departures because things change.

### Services

There are overnight *especial* trains between Habana and Santiago de Cuba on alternate days (861km, 12½ hours, CUC$30). Train No 1 leaves Habana daily at 6:05pm, passing Santa Clara (9:55pm), and Camagüey (1:48am), before reaching Santiago de Cuba at 6:35am. Train No 2 leaves Santiago de Cuba daily at 5:05pm, passing Julio Antonio Mella (6:05pm), Camagüey (9:45pm), Guayacanes (12:01am), and Santa Clara (1:55am), before reaching Habana at 6:00am.

The above schedules are only an approximation of what should happen.

Some other train routes that may be of interest to travelers include Pinar del Río–Sábalo, Habana–Matanzas, Habana–Cienfuegos, Habana–Sancti Spíritus, Habana–Holguín, Habana–Manzanillo, Santa Clara–Morón–Nuevitas, Cienfuegos–Santa Clara–Sancti Spíritus, Camagüey–Nuevitas, Camagüey–Bayamo, Bayamo–Manzanillo, Manzanillo–Bayamo–Santiago de Cuba, and Santiago de Cuba–Holguín. Many additional local trains operate at least daily and some more frequently. Additional information is provided in the regional chapters of this book.

## TRUCK

*Camiones* (trucks) are a cheap, fast way to travel within or between provinces. Every city has a provincial and municipal bus stop with *camiones* departures. They run on a (loose) schedule and you'll need to take your place in line by asking for *el último* to your destination; you pay as you board. A truck from Santiago de Cuba to Guantánamo costs five pesos (CUC$0.20), while the same trip on Astro/Víazul buses costs CUC$3/6.

A reader traveling by truck enthused:

> *Camion* traveling was the best way to meet regular people and usually fairly fast. There is a camaraderie between *camion* travelers that I didn't find on buses. One hundred sweaty people locking arms, swerving through the mountains in an open air truck…ah, I'll take that any day over a crowded (and more expensive) bus.

Sometimes terminal staff tell foreigners they're prohibited from traveling on trucks. As with anything in Cuba, never take the word 'no' as your first answer. Crying poor, striking up a conversation with the driver, appealing to other passengers for aid, etc usually helps.

# Health

Dr David Goldberg

## CONTENTS



From a medical point of view, the Caribbean islands are generally safe as long as you're reasonably careful about what you eat and drink. The most common travel-related diseases, such as dysentery and hepatitis, are acquired by the consumption of contaminated food and water. Mosquito-borne illnesses are not a significant concern on most of the islands within the Cuban archipelago.

Prevention is the key to staying healthy while traveling in Cuba. Travelers who receive the recommended vaccines and follow commonsense precautions usually come away with nothing more than a little diarrhea.

## BEFORE YOU GO

Since most vaccines don't produce immunity until at least two weeks after they're given, visit a physician four to eight weeks before departure. Ask your doctor for an International Certificate of Vaccination (otherwise known as the 'yellow booklet'), which will list all the vaccinations you've received. This is mandatory for countries that require proof of yellow fever vaccination upon entry. Cuba doesn't require yellow fever vaccination, but it's a good idea to carry your yellow booklet wherever you travel.

Bring medications in their original, clearly labeled containers. A signed and dated letter from your physician describing your medical conditions and medica-

### RECOMMENDED VACCINATIONS

No vaccines are required for Cuba, but a number are recommended:

| Vaccine | Recommended for | Dosage | Side effects |
|---|---|---|---|
| Chickenpox | Travelers who've never had chickenpox | 2 doses 1 month apart | Fever; mild case of chickenpox |
| Hepatitis A | All travelers | 1 dose before trip; booster 6-12 months later | Soreness at injection site; headaches; body aches |
| Hepatitis B | Long-term travelers in close contact with the local population | 3 doses over a 6-month period | Soreness at injection site; low-grade fever |
| Rabies | Travelers who may have contact with animals and may not have access to medical care | 3 doses over a 3-4 week period | Soreness at injection site; headaches; body aches |
| Tetanus-diphtheria | All travelers who haven't had a booster within 10 years | 1 dose lasts 10 years | Soreness at injection site |
| Typhoid | All travelers | 4 capsules orally, 1 taken every other day | Abdominal pain; nausea; rash |

tions, including generic names, is also a good idea. If carrying syringes or needles, be sure to have a physician's letter documenting their medical necessity.

## INSURANCE

If your usual health insurance doesn't cover you for medical expenses abroad, consider getting extra insurance; see p458 and check the Travel Services/Insurance section on www.lonelyplanet.com for more information. Find out in advance if your insurance plan will make payments directly to providers or reimburse you later for overseas health expenditures. (In many countries, doctors expect payment in cash.)

Should you get into trouble healthwise and end up in hospital call **Asistur** (☎ 7-866-8527; www.asistur.cu) for help with insurance and medical assistance. The company has regional offices in Habana, Varadero, Cienfuegos, Cayo Coco, Camagüey, Guardalavaca and Santiago de Cuba.

## MEDICAL CHECKLIST

- acetaminophen (Tylenol) or aspirin
- adhesive or paper tape
- antibacterial ointment (eg Bactroban; for cuts and abrasions)
- antibiotics
- antidiarrheal drugs (eg loperamide)
- antihistamines (for hay fever and allergic reactions)
- anti-inflammatory drugs (eg ibuprofen)
- bandages, gauze, gauze rolls
- DEET-containing insect repellent for the skin
- iodine tablets (for water purification)
- oral rehydration salts
- permethrin-containing insect spray for clothing, tents and bed nets
- pocketknife
- scissors, safety pins, tweezers
- steroid cream or cortisone (for poison ivy and other allergic rashes)
- sunblock
- syringes and sterile needles
- thermometer

## INTERNET RESOURCES

There is a wealth of travel health advice on the Internet. For further information, the Lonely Planet website (www.lonelyplanet.com) is a good place to start. The World Health Organization publishes a superb book called *International Travel and Health,* which is revised annually and is available online at no cost (www.who.int/ith). Another website of general interest is the **MD Travel Health website** (www.mdtravelhealth.com), which provides complete travel health recommendations for every country and is updated daily.

**THE MAN SAYS...**

It's usually a good idea to consult your government's travel health website before departure, if one is available:

**Australia** (www.smarttraveller.gov.au) Follow the link to Travel Health.

**Canada** (www.travelhealth.gc.ca)

**UK** (www.dh.gov.uk) Follow the links to Policy and Guidance and Health Advice for Travellers.

**USA** (www.cdc.gov/travel)

## FURTHER READING

If you're traveling with children, Lonely Planet's *Travel with Children* may be useful. The *ABC of Healthy Travel,* by Eric Walker et al, is another valuable resource.

# IN TRANSIT

## DEEP VEIN THROMBOSIS (DVT)

Blood clots may form in the legs (deep vein thrombosis) during plane flights, chiefly because of prolonged immobility. The longer the flight, the greater the risk. Though most blood clots are reabsorbed uneventfully, some may break off and travel through the blood vessels to the lungs, where they could cause life-threatening complications.

The chief symptom of DVT is swelling or pain in the foot, ankle or calf, usually – but not always – on just one side. When a blood clot travels to the lungs, it may cause chest pain and difficulty breathing. Travelers with any of the symptoms noted above should immediately seek medical attention.

To prevent the development of DVT on long flights, you should walk about the cabin, perform isometric compressions of the leg muscles (ie flex the leg muscles while sitting), drink plenty of fluids and avoid alcohol and tobacco.

## JET LAG & MOTION SICKNESS

Jet lag is common when crossing more than five time zones, resulting in insomnia, fatigue, malaise or nausea. To avoid jet lag try to drink plenty of (nonalcoholic) fluids and eat light meals. Upon arrival, get exposure to natural sunlight and readjust your schedule (for meals, sleep etc) as soon as possible.

Antihistamines such as dimenhydrinate (Dramamine) and meclizine (Antivert, Bonine) are usually the first choice for treating motion sickness. Their main side effect is drowsiness. A herbal alternative is ginger, which works like a charm for some people.

# IN CUBA

## AVAILABILITY & COST OF HEALTH CARE

The Cuban government has established a for-profit health system for foreigners called **Servimed** (☎ 7-24-01-41), which is entirely separate from the free, not-for-profit system that takes care of Cuban citizens. There are more than 40 Servimed health centers across the island, offering primary care as well as a variety of specialty and high-tech services. If you're staying in a hotel, the usual way to access the system is to ask the manager for a physician referral. Servimeds accept walk-ins. While Cuban hospitals provide some free emergency treatment for foreigners, this should only be used when there is no other option. Remember that in Cuba medical resources are scarce and the local populace should be given priority in free healthcare facilities.

Almost all doctors and hospitals expect payment in cash, regardless of whether you have travel health insurance. If you develop a life-threatening medical problem, you'll probably want to be evacuated to a country with state-of-the-art medical care. Since this may cost tens of thousands of dollars, be sure you have insurance to cover this before you depart. See p458 for insurance options.

There are special pharmacies for foreigners also run by the Servimed system, but all Cuban pharmacies are notoriously short on supplies, including pharmaceuticals. Be sure to bring along adequate quantities of all medications you might need, both prescription and over-the-counter. Also, be sure to bring along a fully-stocked medical kit.

## INFECTIOUS DISEASES

### Dengue (Break-bone) Fever

Dengue fever is a viral and mosquito-borne infection found throughout the Caribbean. A major outbreak of dengue fever, centering on Habana and resulting in more than 3000 cases, was reported from November 2001 through to March 2002. Since then, an aggressive government program has all but eradicated dengue from the island. See also p484 for information on avoiding mosquito bites.

### Hepatitis A

Hepatitis A is the second most common travel-related infection (after traveler's diarrhea). It occurs throughout the Caribbean, particularly in the northern islands. Hepatitis A is a viral infection of the liver that is usually acquired by ingestion of contaminated water, food or ice, though it may also be acquired by direct contact with infected persons. The illness occurs throughout the world, but the incidence is higher in developing nations. Symptoms may include fever, malaise, jaundice, nausea, vomiting and abdominal pain. Most cases resolve without complications, though hepatitis A occasionally causes severe liver damage. There is no treatment.

The vaccine for hepatitis A is extremely safe and highly effective. If you get a booster six to 12 months after the first vaccine, it lasts for at least 10 years. You really should get this vaccine before you go to Cuba or any other developing nation. Because the safety of the hepatitis A vaccine has not been established for pregnant women or children under the age of two, they should instead be given a gamma globulin injection.

### Hepatitis B

Like hepatitis A, hepatitis B is a liver infection that occurs worldwide but is more common in developing nations. Unlike hepatitis A, the disease is usually acquired by sexual contact or by exposure to infected blood, generally through blood transfusions or contaminated needles. The vaccine is recommended only for long-term travelers (on the road more than six months) who expect to live in rural areas or have close physical contact with the local population. Additionally, the vaccine is recommended for anyone who anticipates sexual contact with the local inhabitants or a possible need for medical, dental or other treatments while abroad, especially if a need for transfusions or injections is expected.

The hepatitis B vaccine is safe and highly effective. However, a total of three injections are necessary to establish full immunity. Several countries added the hepatitis B vaccine to the list of routine childhood immunizations in the 1980s, so many young adults are already protected.

## Malaria

In the Caribbean, malaria occurs only in Haiti and certain parts of the Dominican Republic. Malaria pills aren't necessary for Cuba.

## Rabies

Rabies is a viral infection of the brain and spinal cord that is almost always fatal. The rabies virus is carried in the saliva of infected animals and is typically transmitted through an animal bite, though contamination of any break in the skin with infected saliva may result in rabies. Rabies occurs in several of the Caribbean islands, including Cuba. Most cases in Cuba are related to bites from dogs, bats and wild animals, especially the small Indian mongoose.

The rabies vaccine is safe, but a full series requires three injections and is quite expensive. Those at high risk of rabies, such as animal handlers and spelunkers (cave explorers), should certainly get the vaccine. In addition, those at lower risk of animal bites should consider asking for the vaccine if they are traveling to remote areas and might not have access to appropriate medical care if needed. The treatment for a possibly rabid bite consists of rabies vaccine with rabies immune globulin. It's effective, but must be given promptly. Most travelers don't need rabies vaccine.

All animal bites and scratches must be promptly and thoroughly cleansed with large amounts of soap and water, and local health authorities must be contacted to determine whether or not further treatment is necessary (see Animal Bites, p484).

## Typhoid

Typhoid fever is caused by ingestion of food or water contaminated by a species of salmonella known as *Salmonella typhi*. Fever occurs in virtually all cases. Other symptoms may include headache, malaise, muscle aches, dizziness, loss of appetite, nausea and abdominal pain. Either diarrhea or constipation may occur. Possible complications include intestinal perforation, intestinal bleeding, confusion, delirium or (rarely) coma.

The typhoid vaccine is usually given orally, but is also available as an injection. Neither vaccine is approved for use in children under two. If you get typhoid fever, the drug of choice is usually a quinolone antibiotic such as ciprofloxacin (Cipro) or levofloxacin (Levaquin), which many travelers carry for treatment of diarrhea.

## Other Infections

### BRUCELLOSIS

Brucellosis is an infection of domestic and wild animals that may be transmitted to humans through direct animal contact or by consumption of unpasteurized dairy products from infected animals. In Cuba, most human cases are related to infected pigs. Symptoms may include fever, malaise, depression, loss of appetite, headache, muscle aches and back pain. Complications may include arthritis, hepatitis, meningitis and endocarditis (heart valve infection).

### FASCIOLIASIS

This is a parasitic infection that is typically acquired by eating contaminated watercress grown in sheep-raising areas. Early symptoms may include fever, nausea, vomiting and painful enlargement of the liver.

### HIV/AIDS

HIV/AIDS has been reported in all Caribbean countries. Be sure to use condoms for the purposes of safe sex.

### LEPTOSPIROSIS

Acquired by exposure to water contaminated by the urine of infected animals. Outbreaks often occur at times of flooding, when sewage overflow may contaminate water sources. The initial symptoms, which resemble a mild flu, usually subside uneventfully in a few days, with or without treatment, but a minority of cases are complicated by jaundice or meningitis. There is no vaccine. You can minimize your risk by staying out of bodies of fresh water that may be contaminated by animal urine. If you're visiting an area where an outbreak is in progress, as occurred in Cuba in 1994, you can take 200mg of doxycycline once weekly as a preventative measure. If you actually develop leptospirosis, the treatment is 100mg of doxycycline twice daily.

## TRAVELER'S DIARRHEA

To prevent diarrhea, avoid tap water unless it has been boiled, filtered or chemically disinfected (with iodine tablets); only eat fresh fruits or vegetables if cooked or peeled; be wary of dairy products that may contain unpasteurized milk; and be highly selective when eating food from street vendors.

If you develop diarrhea, be sure to drink plenty of fluids, preferably an oral rehydration solution containing lots of salt and sugar. A few loose stools don't require treatment, but if you start having more than four or five stools a day, you should start taking an antibiotic (usually a quinolone drug) and an antidiarrheal agent (such as loperamide). If diarrhea is bloody, persists for more than 72 hours or is accompanied by fever, shaking chills or severe abdominal pain, you should seek medical attention.



## ENVIRONMENTAL HAZARDS

### Animal Bites

Do not attempt to pet, handle or feed any animal, with the exception of domestic animals known to be free of any infectious disease. Most animal injuries are directly related to a person's attempt to touch or feed the animal.

Any bite or scratch by a mammal, including bats, should be promptly and thoroughly cleansed with large amounts of soap and water, followed by application of an antiseptic such as iodine or alcohol. The local health authorities should be contacted immediately for possible postexposure rabies treatment, whether or not you've been immunized against rabies (see p483). It may also be advisable to start an antibiotic, since wounds caused by animal bites and scratches frequently become infected. One of the newer quinolones, such as levofloxacin (Levaquin), which many travelers carry in case of diarrhea, would be an appropriate choice.

Spiny sea urchins and coelenterates (coral and jellyfish) are a hazard in some areas. Some stings (eg from a Portuguese man-of-war) can produce a bad reaction and if you start to feel nauseous/faint you should seek medical treatment.

### Heatstroke

To protect yourself from excessive sun exposure, you should stay out of the midday sun, wear sunglasses and a wide-brimmed sun hat, and apply sunscreen with SPF 15 or higher, with both UVA and UVB protection. Sunscreen should be generously applied to all exposed parts of the body approximately 30 minutes before sun exposure and should be reapplied after swimming or vigorous activity. Travelers should also drink plenty of fluids and avoid strenuous exercise when the temperature is high.

### Insect Bites & Stings

Because of an aggressive program of mosquito control, mosquito-borne illnesses are usually not a concern in Cuba. However, outbreaks of dengue fever (p482) have occurred in the recent past, so you should be aware of the means of preventing mosquito bites, if necessary. If dengue or other mosquito-borne illnesses are being reported, you should keep yourself covered (wear long sleeves, long pants, a hat, and shoes rather than sandals) and apply a good insect repellent, preferably one containing DEET, to exposed skin and clothing. Do not apply DEET to eyes, mouth, cuts, wounds or irritated skin. Products containing lower concentrations of DEET are as effective, but for shorter periods of time. In general, adults and children over 12 should use preparations containing 25% to 35% DEET, which usually lasts about six hours. Children between two and 12 years of age should use preparations containing no more than 10% DEET, applied sparingly, which will usually last about three hours. Neurologic toxicity has been reported from DEET, especially in children, but appears to be extremely uncommon and generally related to overuse. DEET-containing compounds should not be used on children under age two.

Insect repellents containing certain botanical products, including eucalyptus and soybean oil, are effective but last only 1½ to two hours. Products based on citronella are not effective.

For additional protection, you can apply permethrin to clothing, shoes, tents and bed nets. Permethrin treatments are safe and remain effective for at least two weeks, even when items are laundered. Permethrin should not be applied directly to skin.

### Water

Tap water in Cuba is not reliably safe to drink. Vigorous boiling for one minute is the most effective means of water purification.

You may also disinfect water with iodine pills. Instructions are included and should be carefully followed. Or you can add 2% tincture of iodine to 1L of water (five drops to clear water, 10 drops to cloudy water) and let it stand for 30 minutes. If the water is cold, longer times may be required. The taste of iodinated water may be improved by adding vitamin C (ascorbic acid). Iodinated water should not be consumed for more than a few weeks. Pregnant women, those with a history of thyroid disease, and those allergic to iodine should not drink iodinated water. See p78 for more treatment options.

A number of water filters are on the market. Those with smaller pores (reverse osmosis filters) provide the broadest protection, but they are relatively large and are readily plugged by debris. Those with somewhat larger pores (microstrainer filters) are ineffective against viruses, although they remove other organisms. Follow the manufacturers' instructions carefully.

## TRAVELING WITH CHILDREN

In general, it's safe for children to go to Cuba. However, because some of the vaccines listed previously are not approved for use in children (or during pregnancy), travelers with children should be particularly careful not to drink tap water or consume any questionable food or beverage. Also, when traveling with children, make sure they're up-to-date on all routine immunizations. It's sometimes appropriate to give children some of their vaccines a little early before visiting a developing nation. You should discuss this with your pediatrician.

## WOMEN'S HEALTH

You can get sanitary items in Cuba, but they are usually more expensive than in Europe/North America/Australia and they are not always readily available (eg easy to find in Varadero, but not quite so easy in Bayamo). Advice: bring a good supply of your own. If pregnant while traveling, see above.

## TRADITIONAL MEDICINE

The following table lists some traditional remedies for common travel-related issues:

| Problem | Treatment |
|---|---|
| Jet lag | Melatonin |
| Motion sickness | Ginger |
| Mosquito bite prevention | Eucalyptus and/or soybean oil |

# Language

CONTENTS



Spanish is the official language of Cuba, and a knowledge of it is a great help in traveling around the country. Away from the hotels and tourist centers, few people speak English and then only very poorly. Despite this, many Cubans have some knowledge of English, since it's taught in primary school from grade six. Almost all museum captions in Cuba are in Spanish only.

If you speak no Spanish at all, you can always ask directions simply by pointing to the name in this guidebook. Never hesitate to try out your broken Spanish on Cubans! A Belgian reader sent us this:

> Cuba really is a country where you gain a lot by being able to speak Spanish. We visited Honduras and Mexico before, and especially in Honduras, it doesn't make such a difference, as the local people are not interested in telling their views and stories (which is quite normal, I guess, when there has been so much state and military repression and when the average level of education is low). In Cuba, people are highly skilled and they have a point of view and an opinion on almost everything, which makes it extremely interesting to be able to talk to them (and we experienced that most of them were quite willing to talk to us). I think the effort to learn Hindi before going to India might be too great, but I would recommend everybody to learn some Spanish before going to Cuba, otherwise you miss the best of the country's culture and complex reality.

Words of Arawak Indian origin that have passed into Spanish and other European languages include *barbacoa* (barbecue), *canoa* (canoe), *cigarro* (cigarette), *hamaca* (hammock), *huracán* (hurricane), *maíz* (maize), *patata* (potato) and *tabaco* (tobacco, cigar). The only commonly used words that are of African origin are generally associated with the Afro-Cuban religions, but Afro-Cuban speakers have given Cuban Spanish its rhythmical intonation and soft accent.

## LEARNING SPANISH

If you don't speak Spanish, don't despair. It's easy enough to pick up the basics, and courses are available in Habana (p114) and Santiago de Cuba (p406). Alternatively, you can study books, records and tapes while you're still at home and planning your trip. These study aids are often available free at public libraries – or you might consider taking an evening or college course. For words and phrases for use when ordering at a restaurant, see Eat Your Words on p81.

Lonely Planet's *Latin American Spanish phrasebook* is a compact guide to the Spanish of the region. Another useful resource is the *University of Chicago Spanish-English, English-Spanish Dictionary*. It'll also make a nice gift for some friendly Cuban when you're about to leave the country.

## PRONUNCIATION

Spanish spelling is phonetically consistent, meaning that there's a clear and consistent relationship between what you see in writing and how it's pronounced. The pronunciation guides included with all the words

## CUBAN SPANISH

Cuban Spanish is rich, varied and astoundingly distinct. Slang and *dichos* (sayings) so dominate daily conversation, even native Spanish speakers sometimes get lost in the mix. Borrowing words from African languages, bastardizing English terms ('Spanglish') and adopting language from movies, marketing and sports, Cuban Spanish is constantly evolving, with new, invented words surfacing all the time. Indeed, the origins of some relatively new slang words seem to have been lost entirely. Ask a Cuban where *rickenbili* comes from for instance (the word for those motorized bicycles you see around town), and they'll laugh and shrug. Here are some of the most common slang and colloquialisms travelers are likely to hear; see also the Glossary (p494):

**asere** – man, brother
**bárbaro** – cool, 'killer'
**barro** – money (dollars or pesos)
**brother** – as in the English word: brother
**compay** – brother, friend (frequently used in Oriente)
**¡Coño!** – frequently used exclamation akin to 'damn!'; used for good or bad things/situations
**cubalse** – plastic bag (in Oriente); also see nylon
**dame un chance** – let me pass, excuse me; literally 'give me a chance'
**está en llama** – it's screwed/messed up
**fiana** – police cruiser
**fula** – dollars
**güiro** – party
**jamaliche** – food, also *jamaliche* which loosely translates as food junkie
**kilo(s)** – centavo(s)
**la lucha** – daily struggle
**loca** – homosexual, queen
**mamey** – mommy/mum, used as term of endearment for females
**nylon** – plastic bag
**papaya** – vagina; the fruit itself is called *fruta bomba* everywhere except in Oriente, where it's called *papaya*
**papi** – daddy, used as term of endearment for males
**pepe** – someone from Spain
**pincha** – job
**pollito** – pretty girl
**por la izquierda** – attained through the informal/black market
**prieto/a** – dark skinned
**puto/a** – gigolo/prostitute
**¿Qué bolá asere?** – What's happening man/brother?
**¿Qué es la mecánica?** – What's the process here; how does this work? (eg when buying bus tickets, entering a crowded club or renting a catamaran)
**tortillera** – lesbian, dyke
**yuma** – someone from the US

and phrases in this language guide should help you get the hang of it all.

Spanish language soap operas are probably the best vehicle for getting a grip on pronunciation – the actors tend to speak overdramatically and a lot slower than the Spanish speakers you're likely to meet on the street – it's also easy to follow the plot. Just be careful you don't get hooked!

### Vowels

**a** as in 'father'
**e** as in 'met'
**i** as in 'marine'
**o** as in 'or', without the 'r' sound
**u** as in 'rule'; the 'u' is not pronounced after **q** and in the letter combinations **gue** and **gui**, unless it's marked with a diaeresis (eg *argüir*), in which case it's pronounced as English 'w'
**y** at the end of a word or when it stands alone, it's pronounced as the Spanish **i** (eg *ley*). Between vowels within a word it's as the 'y' in 'yonder'.

### Consonants

While the consonants **ch**, **ll** and **ñ** are generally considered distinct letters, **ch** and **ll** are now often listed alphabetically under **c** and **l** respectively. The letter **ñ** is still treated as a separate letter and comes after **n** in dictionary listings.

**b** similar to English 'b,' but softer; referred to as 'b larga'
**c** as in 'celery' before **e** and **i**; otherwise as English 'k'
**ch** as in 'church'
**d** as in 'dog'; between vowels and after **l** or **n**, it's closer to the 'th' in 'this'
**g** as the 'ch' in the Scottish *loch* before **e** and **i** ('kh' in our guides to pronunciation); elsewhere, as in 'go'
**h** invariably silent; worth noting if your name begins with 'h' and you're waiting for public officials to call you
**j** as the 'ch' in the Scottish *loch* ('kh' in our guides to pronunciation)
**ll** as the 'y' in 'yellow'

**ñ** as the 'ni' in 'onion'
**rr** very strongly rolled
**v** similar to English 'b', but softer; referred to as 'b corta'
**x** as in 'taxi' except for a very few words, when it's pronounced as **j**
**z** as the 's' in 'sun'

### Word Stress

In general, words ending in vowels or the letters **n** or **s** have stress on the next-to-last syllable, while those with other endings have stress on the last syllable. Thus *vaca* (cow) and *caballos* (horses) both carry stress on the next-to-last syllable, while *ciudad* (city) and *infeliz* (unhappy) are both stressed on the last syllable.

Written accents will almost always appear in words that don't follow the rules above, eg *sótano* (basement), *América* and *porción* (portion). When counting syllables, be sure to remember that diphthongs (vowel combinations, such as the 'ue' in *puede*) constitute only one. When a word with a written accent appears in capital letters, the accent is often not written, but is still pronounced.

## GENDER & PLURALS

In Spanish, nouns are either masculine or feminine, and there are rules to help determine gender (there are of course some exceptions). Feminine nouns generally end with **-a** or with the groups **-ción**, **-sión** or **-dad**. Other endings typically signify a masculine noun. Endings for adjectives also change to agree with the gender of the noun they modify (masculine/feminine **-o**/**-a**). Where both masculine and feminine forms are included in this language guide, they are separated by a slash, with the masculine form first, eg *perdido/a*.

If a noun or adjective ends in a vowel, the plural is formed by adding **s** to the end. If it ends in a consonant, the plural is formed by adding **es** to the end.

## ACCOMMODATION

| | | |
|---|---|---|
| **I'm looking for ...** | *Estoy buscando ...* | e·*stoy* boos·*kan*·do ... |
| **Where is ...?** | *¿Dónde hay ...?* | *don*·de ai ... |
| **a hotel** | *un hotel/ una villa* | oon o·*tel*/ *oo*·na *vee*·lya |
| **a boarding house** | *una pensión/ residencial/ un hospedaje* | *oo*·na pen·*syon*/ re·see·den·*syal*/ oon os·pe·*da*·khe |
| **a youth hostel** | *un albergue juvenil* | oon al·*ber*·ge khoo·ve·*neel* |

**MAKING A RESERVATION**

| | |
|---|---|
| **To ...** | *A ...* |
| **From ...** | *De ...* |
| **Date** | *Fecha* |
| **I'd like to book ...** | *Quisiera reservar ...* (see the list under 'Accommodation' for bed/room options) |
| **in the name of ...** | *en nombre de ...* |
| **for the nights of ...** | *para las noches del ...* |
| **credit card ...** | *tarjeta de crédito ...* |
| **number** | *número* |
| **expiry date** | *fecha de vencimiento* |
| **Please confirm ...** | *Puede confirmar ...* |
| **availability** | *la disponibilidad* |
| **price** | *el precio* |

| | | |
|---|---|---|
| **I'd like a ... room.** | *Quisiera una habitación ...* | kee·*sye*·ra oo·na a·bee·ta·*syon* ... |
| **double** | *doble* | *do*·ble |
| **single** | *individual/ para una persona* | een·dee·vee·*dwal*/ pa·ra *oo*·na per·*so*·na |
| **twin** | *con dos camas* | kon dos *ka*·mas |
| **How much is it per ...?** | *¿Cuánto cuesta por ...?* | *kwan*·to *kwes*·ta por ... |
| **night** | *noche* | *no*·che |
| **person** | *persona* | per·*so*·na |
| **week** | *semana* | se·*ma*·na |

**Does it include breakfast?**
*¿Incluye el desayuno?* een·*kloo*·ye el de·sa·*yoo*·no

**May I see the room?**
*¿Puedo ver la habitación?* *pwe*·do ver la a·bee·ta·*syon*

**I don't like it.**
*No me gusta.* no me *goos*·ta

**It's fine. I'll take it.**
*OK. La alquilo.* o·*kay* la al·*kee*·lo

**I'm leaving now.**
*Me voy ahora.* me *voy* a·*o*·ra

| | | |
|---|---|---|
| **full board** | *pensión completa* | pen·*syon* kom·*ple*·ta |
| **private/shared bathroom** | *baño privado/ compartido* | *ba*·nyo pree·*va*·do/ kom·par·*tee*·do |
| **all-inclusive** | *todo incluído* | *to*·do een·*klwee*·do |
| **too expensive** | *demasiado caro* | de·ma·*sya*·do *ka*·ro |

| | | |
|---|---|---|
| **cheaper** | *más económico* | mas e·ko·*no*·mee·ko |
| **discount** | *descuento* | des·*kwen*·to |

## CONVERSATION & ESSENTIALS

In their public behavior, Cubans are very informal, but if you approach a stranger for information, you should always preface your question with a greeting like *buenos días* or *buenas tardes*. Cubans routinely address one another as *compañero* or *compañera* (comrade), but the traditional *señor* and *señora* are always used with foreigners. In addition, you should use only the polite form of address, especially with the police and public officials. Young people may be less likely to expect this, but it's best to stick to the polite form unless you're quite sure you won't offend by using the informal mode. The polite form is used in all cases in this language guide; where options are given, the form is indicated by the abbreviations 'pol' and 'inf'.

| | | |
|---|---|---|
| **Hello.** | *Hola.* | o·la |
| **Good morning.** | *Buenos días.* | *bwe*·nos *dee*·as |
| **Good afternoon.** | *Buenas tardes.* | *bwe*·nas *tar*·des |
| **Good evening/night.** | *Buenas noches.* | *bwe*·nas *no*·ches |
| **Goodbye.** | *Adiós.* | a·*dyos* |
| **See you soon.** | *Hasta luego.* | *as*·ta *lwe*·go |
| **Bye.** | *Chau.* | chow (inf) |
| **Yes.** | *Sí.* | see |
| **No.** | *No.* | no |
| **Please.** | *Por favor.* | por fa·*vor* |
| **Thank you.** | *Gracias.* | *gra*·syas |
| **Many thanks.** | *Muchas gracias.* | *moo*·chas *gra*·syas |
| **You're welcome.** | *De nada.* | de *na*·da |
| **Pardon me.** | *Perdón.* | per·*don* |
| **Excuse me.** (used when asking permission) | *Permiso.* | per·*mee*·so |
| **Forgive me.** (used when apologizing) | *Disculpe.* | dees·*kool*·pe |

**How are things?**
*¿Qué tal?* — ke tal

**What's your name?**
*¿Cómo se llama?* — *ko*·mo se *ya*·ma (pol)
*¿Cómo te llamas?* — *ko*·mo te *ya*·mas (inf)

**My name is ...**
*Me llamo ...* — me *ya*·mo ...

**It's a pleasure to meet you.**
*Mucho gusto.* — *moo*·cho *goos*·to

**The pleasure is mine.**
*El gusto es mío.* — el *goos*·to es *mee*·o

| SIGNS | |
|---|---|
| **Entrada** | Entrance |
| **Salida** | Exit |
| **Información** | Information |
| **Abierto** | Open |
| **Cerrado** | Closed |
| **Prohibido** | Prohibited |
| **Comisaria** | Police Station |
| **Servicios/Baños** | Toilets |
| **Hombres/Varones** | Men |
| **Mujeres/Damas** | Women |

**Where are you from?**
*¿De dónde es/eres?* — de *don*·de es/e·res (pol/inf)

**I'm from ...**
*Soy de ...* — soy de ...

**Where are you staying?**
*¿Dónde está alojado?* — *don*·de es·*ta* a·lo·*kha*·do (pol)
*¿Dónde estás alojado?* — *don*·de es·*tas* a·lo·*kha*·do (inf)

**May I take a photo?**
*¿Puedo sacar una foto?* — *pwe*·do sa·*kar oo*·na *fo*·to

## DIRECTIONS

**How do I get to ...?**
*¿Cómo puedo llegar a ...?* — *ko*·mo *pwe*·do lye·*gar* a ...

**Is it far?**
*¿Está lejos?* — es·*ta le*·khos

**Go straight ahead.**
*Siga/Vaya derecho.* — *see*·ga/*va*·ya de·*re*·cho

**Turn left.**
*Voltée a la izquierda.* — vol·*te*·e a la ees·*kyer*·da

**Turn right.**
*Voltée a la derecha.* — vol·*te*·e a la de·*re*·cha

**I'm lost.**
*Estoy perdido/a.* — es·*toy* per·*dee*·do/a

**Can you show me (on the map)?**
*¿Me lo podría indicar (en el mapa)?* — me lo po·*dree*·a een·dee·*kar* (en el *ma*·pa)

| | | |
|---|---|---|
| **north** | *norte* | *nor*·te |
| **south** | *sur* | soor |
| **east** | *este/oriente* | *es*·te/o·*ryen*·te |
| **west** | *oeste/occidente* | o·*es*·te/ok·see·*den*·te |
| **here** | *aquí* | a·*kee* |
| **there** | *allí* | a·*yee* |
| **on foot** | *a pie* | a *pye* |
| **by taxi** | *en taxi* | en *tak*·see |
| **by bus** | *en autobús* | en ow·to·*boos* |
| **avenue** | *avenida* | a·ve·*nee*·da |
| **block** | *cuadra* | *kwa*·dra |
| **street** | *calle/paseo* | *ka*·lye/pa·*se*·o |
| **beach** | *playa* | *pla*·ya |
| **bathing resort** | *balneario* | bal·ne·*a*·ryo |

## EMERGENCIES

| | | |
|---|---|---|
| **Help!** | *¡Socorro!* | so·*ko*·ro |
| **Fire!** | *¡Incendio!* | een·*sen*·dyo |
| **I've been robbed.** | *Me robaron.* | me ro·*ba*·ron |
| **Go away!** | *¡Déjeme!* | *de*·khe·me |
| **Get lost!** | *¡Váyase!* | *va*·ya·se |
| **Call ...!** | *¡Llame a ...!* | *ya*·me a |
| **the police** | *la policía* | la po·lee·*see*·a |
| **a doctor** | *un médico* | oon *me*·dee·ko |
| **an ambulance** | *una ambulancia* | oo·na am·boo·*lan*·sya |

**It's an emergency.**
*Es una emergencia.* es oo·na e·mer·*khen*·sya

**Could you help me, please?**
*¿Me puede ayudar, por favor?* me *pwe*·de a·yoo·*dar* por fa·*vor*

**I'm lost.**
*Estoy perdido/a.* es·*toy* per·*dee*·do/a

**Where are the toilets?**
*¿Dónde están los baños?* *don*·de es·*tan* los *ba*·nyos

## HEALTH

**I'm sick.**
*Estoy enfermo/a.* es·*toy* en·*fer*·mo/a

**I need a doctor.**
*Necesito un médico.* ne·se·*see*·to oon *me*·dee·ko

**Where's the hospital?**
*¿Dónde está el hospital?* *don*·de es·*ta* el os·pee·*tal*

**I'm pregnant.**
*Estoy embarazada.* es·*toy* em·ba·ra·*sa*·da

**I've been vaccinated.**
*Estoy vacunado/a.* es·*toy* va·koo·*na*·do/a

| | | |
|---|---|---|
| **I'm allergic to ...** | *Soy alérgico/a (a) ...* | soy a·*ler*·khee·ko/a a ... |
| **antibiotics** | *los antibióticos* | los an·tee·*byo*·tee·kos |
| **peanuts** | *al maní* | al ma·*nee* |
| **penicillin** | *la penicilina* | la pe·nee·see·*lee*·na |
| **I'm ...** | *Soy ...* | soy ... |
| **asthmatic** | *asmático/a* | as·*ma*·tee·ko/a |
| **diabetic** | *diabético/a* | dya·*be*·tee·ko/a |
| **epileptic** | *epiléptico/a* | e·pee·*lep*·tee·ko/a |
| **I have ...** | *Tengo ...* | *ten*·go ... |
| **altitude sickness** | *soroche* | so·*ro*·che |
| **diarrhea** | *diarrea* | dya·*re*·a |
| **nausea** | *náusea* | *now*·se·a |
| **a headache** | *un dolor de cabeza* | oon do·*lor* de ka·*be*·sa |
| **a cough** | *tos* | tos |

## LANGUAGE DIFFICULTIES

**Do you speak (English)?**
*¿Habla/Hablas (inglés)?* *a*·bla/*a*·blas (een·*gles*) (pol/inf)

**Does anyone here speak English?**
*¿Hay alguien que hable inglés?* ai al·*gyen* ke *a*·ble een·*gles*

**I (don't) understand.**
*Yo (no) entiendo.* yo (no) en·*tyen*·do

**How do you say ...?**
*¿Cómo se dice ...?* *ko*·mo se *dee*·se ...

**What does ...mean?**
*¿Qué quiere decir ...?* ke *kye*·re de·*seer* ...

| | | |
|---|---|---|
| **Could you please ...?** | *¿Puede ..., por favor?* | *pwe*·de ... por fa·*vor* |
| **repeat that** | *repetirlo* | re·pe·*teer*·lo |
| **speak more slowly** | *hablar más despacio* | a·*blar* mas des·*pa*·syo |
| **write it down** | *escribirlo* | es·kree·*beer*·lo |

## NUMBERS

| | | |
|---|---|---|
| 1 | *uno* | *oo*·no |
| 2 | *dos* | dos |
| 3 | *tres* | tres |
| 4 | *cuatro* | *kwa*·tro |
| 5 | *cinco* | *seen*·ko |
| 6 | *seis* | says |
| 7 | *siete* | *sye*·te |
| 8 | *ocho* | *o*·cho |
| 9 | *nueve* | *nwe*·ve |
| 10 | *diez* | dyes |
| 11 | *once* | *on*·se |
| 12 | *doce* | *do*·se |
| 13 | *trece* | *tre*·se |
| 14 | *catorce* | ka·*tor*·se |
| 15 | *quince* | *keen*·se |
| 16 | *dieciséis* | dye·see·*says* |
| 17 | *diecisiete* | dye·see·*sye*·te |
| 18 | *dieciocho* | dye·see·*o*·cho |
| 19 | *diecinueve* | dye·see·*nwe*·ve |
| 20 | *veinte* | *vayn*·te |
| 21 | *veintiuno* | vayn·tee·*oo*·no |
| 30 | *treinta* | *trayn*·ta |
| 31 | *treinta y uno* | trayn·ta ee *oo*·no |
| 40 | *cuarenta* | kwa·*ren*·ta |
| 50 | *cincuenta* | seen·*kwen*·ta |
| 60 | *sesenta* | se·*sen*·ta |
| 70 | *setenta* | se·*ten*·ta |
| 80 | *ochenta* | o·*chen*·ta |
| 90 | *noventa* | no·*ven*·ta |

| | | |
|---|---|---|
| **100** | *cien* | syen |
| **101** | *ciento uno* | syen·to *oo*·no |
| **200** | *doscientos* | do·*syen*·tos |
| **1000** | *mil* | meel |
| **5000** | *cinco mil* | *seen*·ko meel |
| **10,000** | *diez mil* | *dyes* meel |
| **50,000** | *cincuenta mil* | seen·*kwen*·ta meel |
| **100,000** | *cien mil* | *syen* meel |
| **1,000,000** | *un millón* | oon mee·*yon* |

## QUESTION WORDS

| | | |
|---|---|---|
| **Who?** | *¿Quién/es?* | kee·*en*/es (sg/pl) |
| **What?** | *¿Qué?* | ke |
| **Which?** | *¿Cuál/es?* | *kwal*/es (sg/pl) |
| **When?** | *¿Cuándo?* | *kwan*·do |
| **Where?** | *¿Dónde?* | *don*·de |
| **How?** | *¿Cómo?* | *ko*·mo |
| **How many?** | *¿Cuántos?* | *kwan*·tos |

## SHOPPING & SERVICES

| | | |
|---|---|---|
| **I'm looking for (the) ...** | *Estoy buscando ...* | es·*toy* boos·*kan*·do |
| **ATM** | *el cajero automático* | el ka·*khe*·ro ow·to·*ma*·tee·ko |
| **bank** | *el banco* | el *ban*·ko |
| **bookstore** | *la librería* | la lee·bre·*ree*·a |
| **embassy** | *la embajada* | la em·ba·*kha*·da |
| **exchange house** | *la casa de cambio* | la *ka*·sa de *kam*·byo |
| **general store** | *la tienda* | la *tyen*·da |
| **laundry** | *la lavandería* | la la·van·de·*ree*·a |
| **market** | *el mercado* | el mer·*ka*·do |
| **pharmacy/ chemist** | *la farmacia/ la drogería* | la far·*ma*·sya/ la dro·ge·*ree*·a |
| **post office** | *el correo* | el ko·*re*·o |
| **supermarket** | *el supermercado* | el soo·per·mer·*ka*·do |
| **tourist office** | *la oficina de turismo* | la o·fee·*see*·na de too·*rees*·mo |

**What time does it open/close?**
*¿A qué hora abre/cierra?* a ke *o*·ra *a*·bre/*sye*·ra

**I want to change some money/traveler's checks.**
*Quiero cambiar dinero/ cheques de viajero.* *kye*·ro kam·*byar* dee·*ne*·ro/ *che*·kes de vya·*khe*·ro

**What is the exchange rate?**
*¿Cuál es el tipo de cambio?* kwal es el *tee*·po de *kam*·byo

**I want to call ...**
*Quiero llamar a ...* *kye*·ro lya·*mar* a ...

| | | |
|---|---|---|
| **airmail** | *correo aéreo* | ko·*re*·o a·*e*·re·o |
| **black market** | *mercado (negro/ paralelo)* | mer·*ka*·do *ne*·gro/ pa·ra·*le*·lo |
| **letter** | *carta* | *kar*·ta |
| **registered mail** | *certificado* | ser·tee·fee·*ka*·do |
| **stamps** | *estampillas* | es·tam·*pee*·lyas |

**I'd like to buy ...**
*Quisiera comprar ...* kee·*sye*·ra kom·*prar* ...

**I'm just looking.**
*Sólo estoy mirando.* *so*·lo es·*toy* mee·*ran*·do

**May I look at it?**
*¿Puedo mirar(lo/la)?* *pwe*·do mee·*rar*·(lo/la)

**How much is it?**
*¿Cuánto cuesta?* *kwan*·to *kwes*·ta

**That's too expensive for me.**
*Es demasiado caro para mí.* es de·ma·*sya*·do *ka*·ro *pa*·ra mee

**Could you lower the price?**
*¿Podría bajar un poco el precio?* po·*dree*·a ba·*khar* oon *po*·ko el *pre*·syo

**I don't like it.**
*No me gusta.* no me *goos*·ta

**I'll take it.**
*Lo llevo.* lo *ye*·vo

| | | |
|---|---|---|
| **less** | *menos* | *me*·nos |
| **more** | *más* | mas |
| **large** | *grande* | *gran*·de |
| **small** | *pequeño/a* | pe·*ke*·nyo/a |

| | | |
|---|---|---|
| **Do you accept ...?** | *¿Aceptan ...?* | a·sep·*tan* ... |
| **American dollars** | *dólares americanos* | *do*·la·res a·me·ree·*ka*·nos |
| **credit cards** | *tarjetas de crédito* | tar·*khe*·tas de *kre*·dee·to |
| **traveler's checks** | *cheques de viajero* | *che*·kes de vya·*khe*·ro |

## TIME & DATES

| | | |
|---|---|---|
| **What time is it?** | *¿Qué hora es?* | ke *o*·ra es |
| **It's one o'clock.** | *Es la una.* | es la *oo*·na |
| **It's seven o'clock.** | *Son las siete.* | son las *sye*·te |
| **midnight** | *medianoche* | me·dya·*no*·che |
| **noon** | *mediodía* | me·dyo·*dee*·a |
| **half past two** | *dos y media* | dos ee *me*·dya |

| | | |
|---|---|---|
| **now** | *ahora* | a·*o*·ra |
| **today** | *hoy* | oy |
| **tonight** | *esta noche* | es·ta *no*·che |
| **tomorrow** | *mañana* | ma·*nya*·na |
| **yesterday** | *ayer* | a·*yer* |

| | | |
|---|---|---|
| **Monday** | *lunes* | *loo*·nes |
| **Tuesday** | *martes* | *mar*·tes |
| **Wednesday** | *miércoles* | *myer*·ko·les |
| **Thursday** | *jueves* | *khwe*·ves |
| **Friday** | *viernes* | *vyer*·nes |

| | | |
|---|---|---|
| **Saturday** | *sábado* | sa·ba·do |
| **Sunday** | *domingo* | do·*meen*·go |
| **January** | *enero* | e·*ne*·ro |
| **February** | *febrero* | fe·*bre*·ro |
| **March** | *marzo* | *mar*·so |
| **April** | *abril* | a·*breel* |
| **May** | *mayo* | *ma*·yo |
| **June** | *junio* | *khoo*·nyo |
| **July** | *julio* | *khoo*·lyo |
| **August** | *agosto* | a·*gos*·to |
| **September** | *septiembre* | sep·*tyem*·bre |
| **October** | *octubre* | ok·*too*·bre |
| **November** | *noviembre* | no·*vyem*·bre |
| **December** | *diciembre* | dee·*syem*·bre |

# TRANSPORT

## Public Transport

| | | |
|---|---|---|
| **What time does ... leave/arrive?** | *¿A qué hora ... sale/llega?* | a ke *o*·ra ... *sa*·le/*ye*·ga |
| **the bus** | *autobús/ guagua/ ómnibus* | ow·to·*boos*/ *gwa*·gwa/ *om*·nee·boos |
| **the plane** | *el avión* | el a·*vyon* |
| **the ship** | *el barco/buque* | el *bar*·ko/*boo*·ke |
| **the train** | *el tren* | el tren |
| **airport** | *el aeropuerto* | el a·e·ro·*pwer*·to |
| **train station** | *la estación de ferrocarril* | la es·ta·*syon* de fe·ro·ka·*reel* |
| **bus station** | *la estación de autobuses* | la es·ta·*syon* de ow·to·*boo*·ses |
| **bus stop** | *la parada de autobuses* | la pa·*ra*·da de ow·to·*boo*·ses |
| **luggage check room** | *guardería/ equipaje* | gwar·de·*ree*·a/ e·kee·*pa*·khe |
| **ticket office** | *la boletería* | la bo·le·te·*ree*·a |

**I'd like a ticket to ...**
*Quiero un boleto a ...* kye·ro oon bo·*le*·to a ...
**What's the fare to ...?**
*¿Cuánto cuesta hasta ...?* kwan·to *kwes*·ta *a*·sta ...

| | | |
|---|---|---|
| **student's** | *de estudiante* | de es·too·*dyan*·te |
| **1st class** | *primera clase* | *pree*·me·ra *kla*·se |
| **2nd class** | *segunda clase* | se·*goon*·da *kla*·se |
| **single/one-way** | *de ida* | de *ee*·da |
| **return/round trip** | *de ida y vuelta* | de *ee*·da ee *vwel*·ta |
| **taxi** | *taxi* | *tak*·see |

## Private Transport

| | | |
|---|---|---|
| **I'd like to hire a/an ...** | *Quisiera alquilar ...* | kee·*sye*·ra al·kee·*lar* ... |
| **car** | *un auto* | oon *ow*·to |
| **4WD** | *un todo terreno* | oon *to*·do te·*re*·no |
| **motorbike** | *una moto* | *oo*·na mo·to |
| **bicycle** | *una bicicleta* | *oo*·na bee·see·*kle*·ta |
| **pickup (truck)** | *camioneta* | ka·myo·*ne*·ta |
| **truck** | *camión* | *ka*·myon |
| **hitchhike** | *hacer botella* | *a*·ser bo·*te*·lya |

**ROAD SIGNS**

| | |
|---|---|
| **Acceso** | Entrance |
| **Aparcamiento** | Parking |
| **Ceda el Paso** | Give way |
| **Despacio** | Slow |
| **Dirección Única** | One-way |
| **Mantenga Su Derecha** | Keep to the Right |
| **No Adelantar/No Rebase** | No Passing |
| **Peaje** | Toll |
| **Peligro** | Danger |
| **Prohibido Aparcar/ No Estacionar** | No Parking |
| **Prohibido el Paso** | No Entry |
| **Pare/Stop** | Stop |
| **Salida de Autopista** | Exit Freeway |

**Is this the road to (...)?**
*¿Se va a (...) por esta carretera?* se va a (...) por *es*·ta ka·re·*te*·ra
**Where's a petrol station?**
*¿Dónde hay una gasolinera/un grifo?* *don*·de ai oo·na *ga*·so·lee·*ne*·ra/oon *gree*·fo
**Please fill it up.**
*Lleno, por favor.* *ye*·no por fa·*vor*
**I'd like (20) liters.**
*Quiero (veinte) litros.* *kye*·ro (*vayn*·te) *lee*·tros

| | | |
|---|---|---|
| **diesel** | *diesel* | *dee*·sel |
| **leaded (regular)** | *gasolina con plomo* | ga·so·*lee*·na kon *plo*·mo |
| **petrol (gas)** | *gasolina* | ga·so·*lee*·na |
| **unleaded** | *gasolina sin plomo* | ga·so·*lee*·na seen *plo*·mo |

**(How long) Can I park here?**
*¿(Por cuánto tiempo) Puedo aparcar aquí?* (por *kwan*·to *tyem*·po) *pwe*·do a·par·*kar* a·*kee*
**Where do I pay?**
*¿Dónde se paga?* *don*·de se *pa*·ga
**I need a mechanic.**
*Necesito un mecánico.* ne·se·*see*·to oon me·*ka*·nee·ko
**The car has broken down (in ...).**
*El carro se ha averiado (en ...).* el *ka*·ro se a a·ve·*rya*·do (en ...)

LANGUAGE

**The motorbike won't start.**
*No arranca la moto.* no a·*ran*·ka la *mo*·to

**I have a flat tyre.**
*Tengo un pinchazo.* *ten*·go oon peen·*cha*·so

**I've run out of petrol.**
*Me quedé sin gasolina.* me ke·*de* seen ga·so·*lee*·na

**I've had an accident.**
*Tuve un accidente.* *too*·ve oon ak·see·*den*·te

## TRAVEL WITH CHILDREN

| | | |
|---|---|---|
| **I need ...** | *Necesito ...* | ne·se·*see*·to ... |
| **Do you have ...?** | *¿Hay ...?* | ai ... |
| **a car baby seat** | *un asiento de seguridad para bebés* | oon a·*syen*·to de se·goo·ree·*da* pa·ra be·*bes* |
| **a child-minding service** | *un servicio de cuidado de niños* | oon ser·*vee*·syo de kwee·*da*·do de *nee*·nyos |
| **a children's menu** | *una carta infantil* | oona *kar*·ta een·fan·*teel* |
| **a creche** | *una guardería* | oo·na gwar·de·*ree*·a |
| **(disposable) diapers/nappies** | *pañoles (de usar y tirar)* | pa·*nyo*·les de oo·*sar* ee tee·*rar* |
| **an (English-speaking) babysitter** | *una niñera (de habla inglesa)* | oo·na nee·*nye*·ra (de *a*·bla een·*gle*·sa) |
| **formula (milk)** | *leche en polvo* | *le*·che en *pol*·vo |
| **a highchair** | *una trona* | oo·na *tro*·na |
| **a stroller** | *un cochecito* | oon ko·che·*see*·to |

**Do you mind if I breast-feed here?**
*¿Le molesta que dé de pecho aquí?* le mo·*les*·ta ke de de *pe*·cho a·*kee*

**Are children allowed?**
*¿Se admiten niños?* se ad·*mee*·ten *nee*·nyos

Also available from Lonely Planet:
*Latin American Spanish Phrasebook*

# Glossary

**agropecuario** – vegetable market; also sell rice, beans, fruit
**aguardiente** – fermented cane; literally 'fire water'
**Altos** – upstairs apartment, when following an address
**ama de llaves** – housekeeper; see *camarera*
**amarillo** – a roadside traffic organizer in a yellow uniform
**americano/a** – in Cuba this means a citizen of any western hemisphere country (from Canada to Argentina); a citizen of the USA is called a *norteamericano/a* or *estadounidense*; see also *gringo/a* and *yuma*
**Arawak** – linguistically related Indian tribes that inhabited most of the Caribbean islands and northern South America
**Autopista** – the national highway that's four, six or eight lanes depending where you are

**babalawo** – a Santería priest; also *babalao;* see also *santero*
**bajos** – lower apartment, when following an address
**balseros** – rafter; used to describe the emigrants who escaped to the US in the 1990s on homemade rafts
**bárbaro** – cool, killer
**barbuda** – bearded one, name given to Castro's rebel army
**batá** – a conical two-headed drum
**bici-taxi** – bicycle taxi
**bloqueo** – Cuban term for the US embargo
**bodega** – stores distributing ration-card products
**bohío** – thatched hut
**bolero** – a romantic love song
**botella** – hitchhiking; literally 'bottle'

**cabildo** – a town council during the colonial era; also an association of tribes in Cuban religions of African origin
**Cachita** – popular name for the Virgin of El Cobre
**cacique** – chief; originally used to describe an Indian chief and today used to designate a petty tyrant
**cadeca** – change booth
**cajita** – take-out meal; literally 'small box'
**caliente** – hot
**camarera** – housekeeper or waitress (the Spanish term *criada,* which also means 'brought up,' is considered offensive in revolutionary Cuba); see also *ama de llaves*
**camello** – Metro buses in Habana named for their two humps; literally 'camel'
**campañero/a** – widely used in revolutionary Cuba as a respectful term of address (in place of señor/a); literally 'a revolutionary'
**campesinos** – people who live in the *campo*
**campismo** – national network of 82 camping installations, not all of which rent to foreigners
**campo** – countryside
**canoñazo** – shooting of the cannons, a nightly ceremony performed at the Fortaleza de la Cabaña across Habana harbor
**carnet** – the identification document that allows foreigners to pay for museums, transport (including colectivos) and theater performances in pesos
**carpeta** – hotel reception desk
**cartelera** – culture calendar or schedule, entertainment brochure
**casa de la cultura** – literally 'culture house' where music, art, theater and dance events happen
**casa natal** – birth house
**casa particular** – private houses that let out rooms to foreigners (and sometimes Cubans); all legal casas must display a green triangle on the door
**casco histórico** – historic center of a city (eg Trinidad, Santiago de Cuba)
**cayo** – a coral key
**CDR** – Comités de Defensa de la Revolución; neighborhood-watch bodies originally formed in 1960 to consolidate grassroots support for the revolution; they now play a decisive role in health, education, social, recycling and voluntary labor campaigns
**central** – modern sugar mill; see *ingenio*
**chachachá** – cha-cha; dance music in 4/4 meter derived from the rumba and mambo
**Changó** – the Santería deity signifying war and fire, twinned with Santa Barbara in Catholicism
**chequeré** – a gourd covered with beads to form a rattle
**cimarrón** – a runaway slave
**circunvalación** – a road that circumvents city centers, allowing you to drive on without plunging into the heart of urban hell
**claves** – rhythm sticks used by musicians
**coches** – carts, normally drawn by horses
**coco-taxi** – egg-shaped taxis that hold two to three people; also called *huevitos* (literally 'little eggs')
**Cohiba** – native Indian name for a smoking implement; one of Cuba's top brands of cigar
**cola** – line, queue
**colectivo** – collective taxi that takes on as many passengers as possible; usually a classic American car
**compañero/a** – companion or partner, with revolutionary connotations
**conseguir** – to get, obtain
**Convertibles** – Convertible pesos
**creyentes** – believers

**criadero** – hatchery
**criollo** – Creole; Spaniard born in the Americas
**c/u** – *cada uno;* used in vegetable markets to denote price per unit
**Cubanacán** – soon after landing in Cuba, Christopher Columbus visited a Taíno village the Indians called *Cubanacán,* meaning 'in the center of the island'; a large Cuban tourism company uses the name
**cuerpo guardia** – area offering emergency services at hospitals

**daiquirí** – rum cocktail made with crushed ice and other ingredients, named for the Río Daiquirí, near Santiago de Cuba, where it was invented in 1899
**danzón** – a traditional Cuban ballroom dance colored with African influences, pioneered in Matanzas during the late 19th century
**décimas** – the rhyming, eight-syllable verses that provide the lyrics for Cuban *son*
**diente de perro** – jagged rock shelf that lines most of Cuba's southern shore
**duende** – spirit/charm; used in Flamenco to describe the ultimate climax to the music

**el imperio** – 'the empire'; a term used in the official Cuban media to refer to the USA, which is led by *imperialistas*
**el líder máximo** – 'maximum leader'; title often used to describe Fidel Castro
**el último** – literally 'the last,' this term is key to mastering Cuban queues (you must 'take' *el último* when joining a line and 'give it up' when someone new arrives)
**Elegguá** – the god of destiny in Cuban religions of African origin such as Santería
**embalse** – reservoir
**encomienda** – a section of land and an indigenous workforce entrusted to an individual by the Spanish crown during the early colonial era
**entronque** – crossroads in rural areas
**espectaculares** – show/extravaganza
**esquina caliente** – where baseball fanatics debate stats, teams, history and who's up and who's down; literally 'hot corner'; also called a *peña*

**fiesta campesinas** – country or rural fairs
**finca** – farmhouse
**flota** – a fleet of Spanish ships

**Gitmo** – American slang for Guantánamo naval base
**Granma** – the yacht that carried Fidel and his companions from Mexico to Cuba in 1956 to launch the revolution; in 1975 the name was adopted for the province where the *Granma* arrived; also the daily newspaper
**gringo/a** – any Caucasian; see also *americano/a* and *yuma*
**guagua** – a bus
**guajiro/a** – a country bumpkin or hick
**Guantanamera** – a girl from Guantánamo Province
**guaracha** – a satirical song for a single voice backed by a chorus
**guarapo** – fresh sugarcane juice
**guayabera** – a pleated, buttoned men's shirt; tropical formal-wear
**guerillero** – fighter, warrior

**Habanero/a** – someone from Habana
**herbero** – seller of herbs, natural medicines and concocter of remedies; typically a wealth of knowledge on natural cures

**ingenio** – an antiquated term for a sugar mill; see *central*

**jefe de turno** – shift manager
**jején(es)** – sand flea(s)
**jinetera** – a woman who attaches herself to male foreigners for monetary or material gain; the exchange may or may not involve sex
**jinetero** – a male tout who hustles tourists; literally 'jockey'
**joder** – to mess up, to spoil

**kometa** – hydrofoil

**libreta** – the ration booklet
**loma** – hill
**luchar** – literally 'to struggle or fight'; used in all sorts of daily situations

**M-26-7** – the '26th of July Movement,' Fidel Castro's revolutionary organization, was named for the abortive assault on the Moncada army barracks in Santiago de Cuba on July 26, 1953
**mambí/ses** – 19th-century rebel/s fighting Spain
**Mamey** – delicious fleshy tropical fruit that resembles a red avocado
**maqueta** – scale model
**maraca** – a rattle used by musicians
**merendero** – outdoor bar; picnic spot
**mirador** – lookout or viewpoint
**Misión Milagros** – the unofficial name given to a pioneering medical program hatched between Cuba and Venezuela in 2004 that offers free eye treatment for impoverished Venezuelans in Cuban hospitals
**mogote** – a limestone monolith found at Viñales
**mojito** – cocktails made from rum, mint, sugar, seltzer and fresh lime juice
**Moncada** – a former army barracks in Santiago de Cuba named for General Guillermo Moncada (1848–1895), a hero of the wars of independence
**moneda nacional** – abbreviated to MN; Cuban pesos
**mulattas** – mixed race; dark color

**nueva trova** – philosophical folk/guitar music popularized in the late '60s and early '70s by Silvio Rodríguez and Pablo Milanés

**Oriente** – the region comprised of Las Tunas, Holguín, Granma, Santiago de Cuba and Guantánamo Provinces
**orisha** – a Santería deity
**organipónico** – urban vegetable garden

**paladar** – a privately owned restaurant
**palenque** – a hiding place for runaway slaves during the colonial era
**palestino** – a nickname given to people from the Oriente by those in the west
**parada** – bus stop
**patria** – homeland, country
**PCC** – Partido Comunista de Cuba; Cuba's only political party, which was formed in October 1965 by merging cadres from the Partido Socialista Popular (the pre-1959 Communist Party) and veterans of the guerrilla campaign
**pedraplén** – stone causeways connecting offshore islands to mainland Cuba
**pelota** – Cuban baseball
**peninsular** – a Spaniard born in Spain but living in the Americas
**peña** – musical performance or get-together in any genre: *son,* rap, rock, poetry etc; see also *esquina caliente*
**período especial** – the special period in a time of peace; Cuba's new economic reality post 1991
**piropo** – flirtatious remark/commentary
**ponchero** – a fixer of flat tires
**pregón** – a singsong manner of selling fruits, vegetables, brooms, whatever; often comic, they are belted out by *pregoneros/as*
**presa** – dam
**puente** - bridge

**¿que bola?** – 'what's up?' popular greeting, especially in the Oriente
**quinciñera** – Cuban rite of passage for girls turning 15 *(quince),* whereby they dress up like brides, have their photos taken in gorgeous natural or architectural settings and then have a big party with lots of food and dancing

**ranchón** – rural farm/restaurant
**reconcentración** – a tactic of forcibly concentrating rural populations, used by the Spaniards during the Second War of Independence
**Regla de Ocha** – set of related religious beliefs popularly known as Santería
**resolver** – to resolve or fix a problematic situation; along with *el último,* this is among the most indispensable words in Cuban vocabulary

**rumba** – an Afro-Cuban dance form that originated among plantation slaves during the 19th century; during the '20s and '30s, the term *rumba* was adopted in North America and Europe for a ballroom dance in 4/4 time; in Cuba today, to *rumba* simply means to 'party'

**salsa** – Cuban music based on *son*
**salsero** – *salsa* singer
**Santería** – Afro-Cuban religion resulting from the syncretization of the Yoruba religion of West Africa and Spanish Catholicism
**santero** – a priest of Santería*;* see also *babalawo*
**Santiagüero** – someone from Santiago de Cuba
**sello** – stamp (in a passport or on a letter)
**SIDA** – *síndrome de inmunodeficiencia adquirida;* AIDS
**s/n** – *sin número,* indicates an address that has no street number
**son** – Cuba's basic form of popular music that jelled from African and Spanish elements in the late 19th century
**sucu-sucu** – a variation of *son* music

**Taíno** – a settled, Arawak-speaking tribe that inhabited much of Cuba prior to the Spanish conquest; the word itself means 'we the good people'
**tambores** – *Santería* drumming ritual
**taquilla** – ticket window
**telenovela** – soap opera
**Telepunto** – Etecsa (Cuban state-run telecommunications company) telephone and Internet shop/call center
**temporada alta/baja** – high/low season
**terminal de ómnibus** – bus station
**tinajones** – large earthenware jars particularly common in the city of Camagüey
**tres** – a guitar with seven strings and an integral part of Cuban *son* music
**trova** – traditional poetic singing/songwriting
**trovador** – traditional singer/songwriter

**Uneac** – Unión Nacional de Escritores y Artistas de Cuba; National Union of Cuban Writers and Artists

**vaqueros** – cowboys
**vega** – tobacco plantation
**VIH** – *virus de inmunodeficiencia humana;* HIV

**Yanquí** – someone from the USA
**Yoruba** – an ethno-linguistic group originating in West Africa
**yuma** – slang for someone from the US; can be used for any foreigner; see *americano/a* and *gringo/a*

**zafra** – sugarcane harvest
**zarzuela** – operetta

GLOSSARY

# Behind the Scenes

## THIS BOOK

The 4th edition of *Cuba* was written by Brendan Sainsbury. The Health chapter was written by Dr David Goldberg. Past authors have included David Stanley and Conner Gorry.

**Commissioning Editor** Greg Benchwick
**Coordinating Editor** Jeanette Wall
**Coordinating Cartographer** Sophie Richards
**Coordinating Layout Designer** Carlos Solarte
**Managing Editor** Suzannah Shwer
**Managing Cartographer** Shahara Ahmed
**Assisting Editors** Monique Choy, Kate Evans, Alison Ridgway, Helen Yeates
**Assisting Cartographer** Tony Fankhauser
**Assisting Designers** Yvonne Bischofberger, Jacqui Saunders
**Cover Designer** Marika Kozak
**Color Designer** Cara Smith
**Project Manager** John Shippick
**Language Content Coordinator** Quentin Frayne

**Thanks to** David Burnett, Melanie Dankel, Sally Darmody, Eoin Dunlevy, Nicole Hansen, Jacqueline McLeod, Julie Sheridan, Fiona Siseman, Celia Wood

## THANKS

### BRENDAN SAINSBURY

It would be impossible to thank every taxi driver, hotel concierge, casa particular owner and direction-giving hitchhiker who helped either intentionally or unintentionally in the making of this book. An extra-special thanks, however, must go to: Yoan and Esthelita Reyes in Viñales, Alfonso Menéndez Pita and Osbel Roque Álvavez from Cubanacán in Cienfuegos; Alberto Hernández, Luís Alberto Valdés, Yoel Baéz and their trusty 1985 Lada (with one window handle) in Matanzas; Louise di Tomasso, the Canadian Consul in Guardalavaca, Adela Acosta Vaillant from Sol y Son in Santiago de Cuba, Julio and Elsa Roque for their invaluable help and hospitality in Habana. Special thanks must also go to old work-mate Jorge Puñales, fellow-Brit and Cuba-addict Andy McKee, previous Cuba guidebook authors Conner Gorry and David Stanley and my commissioning editor Greg Benchwick for sticking his neck out and hiring me – a novice – for what was a huge project. Last, but by no means least, muchíssimo gracias to my wife Elizabeth and my five month old son Kieran who, defying all odds, accompanied me for eight weeks during the research for this book in a temperamental but strangely durable old Toyota Yaris.

## OUR READERS

**Many thanks to the travelers who used the last edition and wrote to us with helpful hints, useful advice and interesting anecdotes:**

**A** Josh Abbott, Kalle Aicheler, Anne-Grit Albrecht, Jorge Alvar Villegas, Kerri Amos, Schild Andreas, D Andrew, Dirk Andries, Pamela Ashcroft, Richard Austin **B** Peggy Baier, Iain Bailey, Johan Bakker, Thierry Banos, Cathie Basciano, Felix Bassoon, Bert Bast, Roger Bateman, Kathrin Becker, Thorsten Becker, Michele & Roger Bellers, Laura Belli, Alan Bellinger, Mike Belshaw, Karina Berg, Eileen Berry, Marie Berteau, Gianmarco Bettiol, Frank Beyens, Brendan Bietry, Mario Binder, Phoebe Blackburn, Dries Boele, Arjan Bol, Stephanie Bolduc, L Boost, Kees Botschuijver,

### THE LONELY PLANET STORY

The story begins with a classic travel adventure: Tony and Maureen Wheeler's 1972 journey across Europe and Asia to Australia. There was no useful information about the overland trail then, so Tony and Maureen published the first Lonely Planet guidebook to meet a growing need.

From a kitchen table, Lonely Planet has grown to become the largest independent travel publisher in the world, with offices in Melbourne (Australia), Oakland (USA) and London (UK). Today Lonely Planet guidebooks cover the globe. There is an ever-growing list of books and information in a variety of media. Some things haven't changed. The main aim is still to make it possible for adventurous travelers to get out there – to explore and better understand the world.

At Lonely Planet we believe travelers can make a positive contribution to the countries they visit – if they respect their host communities and spend their money wisely. Every year 5% of company profit is donated to charities around the world.

Maxwell & Tina Bould, Christine Bourgeois, Maria Bouwsma, David Boyall, Tony Brehm, Huen Brennan, Gerd Bresser, Denis Bright, Bob Brodey, Kristina Brown, Charles Bruce-Thompson, Mirja Brüning, Felicia Butler, Kate Bygbjerg **C** Lorenz Calcagno, Roberto Calcagno, Peter Calder, Suzanne Cameron, Jane Carey-Harris, Samantha Carnell, George Carr, Nancy Carson, Eamonn Casey, Karol Cioma, Gavin Clayton, Harry Coerts, Paolo Coluzzi, John Cooper, Anita Craig, Bob Crane, Tadhg Culbert **D** Sara Dagostini, Yehonatan Dashti, Arik De, Els de Baets, Jolanda de Boer, Nol de Boer, Françoise de Cupere, César de Diego Díez, Leenie de Gier, Petra de Nie, Filipe de Oliveira, Mike Debelak, Cedric Dejean, Annemieke Dekker, Glen Delman, Concetta di Bartolomeo, Dominik Doerr, Muredach Doherty, Elena Donina, Arnoud Dovermann, Sylvia Drimoussis, Ursula Dumermuth, Lorna Dunne, Petra Duss **E** Verena Eberl, Todd Edgar, Stefan Egger, Ivo Eichler, André Elling, Sarah Elliott, Joanna Elzinga, Maire Ericsson, Markus & Julia Ermisch, Sara Esrick, Ifan Evans **F** Nazarena Fazzari, Greg Fear, Anat & Gil Feldman, Lina Fernandez, Gyan Fernando, Monica Ferreira, Melissa Filshie, Hanne Finholt, Lise Firth, Sarah Fish, Dejan Flasker, Adrian Flood, Debbie Ford, Anna Fowler, Wendy Francis, Christine Frei, Cynda Fuentes, Jonathon Fursland **G** Marcelo Garza, Bill Gasteyer, Merav Gazit, Stefano Gazziano, Thomas Gentsch, Olivia Gerard, Ton Gerdsen, Liliana Gervais, Serena Giugni, Marina Giunta, Mette Glavind, Juergen Gleichmar, Marta Gomes de Carvalho, Jon Gourlay, Andreas Grafe, Alison Green, Derek Greene, Urs Gretler, Sian Griffiths, Caroline Grijsen, Werner & Gaby Grossmann, Kai Guehmann, Marie-France Guimond, Gudrun Gundermann, Matthias Gutzeit **H** Christian Haefely, Kate Hallam, Håkan Hallander, Mati & Doriel Halperin, Jacob Halpin, Peter Hamerton, Natalie Hanssen, William Harden, Jacky Harding, Ross Hardy, Orit Harel, Jean Harper, Kenneth Harris, Tony Harrison, Margot Harvey, Natasha Hazrati, Edwin Heeregrave, Hubert Heigermoser, Celine Heinbecker, Lotte Heinrich, Tracey Helman, Carsten Helsted, René Helwegen, Gemma Hensey, Marjan Hettinga, Shane Hiebert, Michael Hing, Jesper Hjorth, Jim Hollum, Mike Hopkins, Martijn Houtman, Vanja Hribernik, Mary Hudson, Stephen Huijgen, Trevor Humphreys **I** Lorella & Claudio Iannucii, Ilaria Ida, David Irvine **J** Flemming Jacobsen, Darlene James, Claire Jamieson, Jiri Janousek, Paul Janssen, Helen Jefferies, Lee Jeynes, Miguel Jimenez, Astrid Johansen, Francois Jourdan, Panos Juntis **K** Sinikka Kahl, Patricia Kandelaars, Arend Kant, Demet Karabulut, Zsolt Katona, Hilary Kayes, Pete Keane, Shawna Kelly, Fiona Kendrick, Julianne Kenny, Ingo Ker, Anton Kerst, Petra Kienel, Inigo Kilborn, Bryan Kingsfield, Johannes Kirchlechner, A Kleinikink, Marcel Klugmann, Annet Koerhuis, Luka Kolar, Alexandra Konstantinoff, Poul Kristensen, Margreet Krottje, Nathalie Kruger, Wil Krullebol, Heidi Kuhrt, Birgit Kulig, Carrie Kuntz **L** Henrik Ladegaard, Tessa Lam, Chris Lamothe, Louise Lander, Eva Langlands, Mika Länsisalmi, Inaki Larraneta, Virginia Lawson, Ben Lazarus, Lucio Lazzara, Vanesa Lee, Alexandre Leger, Cindy-Marie Leicester, Malena Lema, Niels Lemming, Diana Lenik, Julia Li, Jill Linderwell, Signe Lindgren, Giorgia Liviero, Mong-Yang Loh, Kate Love, Rick Loy, Jesse Lubitz, Jonas Ludvigsen **M** Jean-Louis Mackels, Roddy Mackenzie, David Mackey, Sarah MacLeod, Tony Macvean, Vivien Marasigan, Sanja Marentic, Marjeta Marolt, Beate Marquardt, Laura Marsh, Rod Marsh, Francisco José & Osaba Martínez, Francesca Maset, Martin Matthews, Karl-Otto Mayer, Federico Mazzarella, Ron McConnell, Paul McKenzie, Conor McKeown, Jeffery McLaren, Alan McLaughlan, Ken Mcleod, Frank McMahon, Carmel Mcnamee, Chris Merkel, Michaela Messner, Andi Mether, Bernd Meyer, Karl Moeglich, Ulrike Moehwald, Jens Mohr, David Morawetz, Lisa Morgan-Lang, Charlie Morris, Siobhan Mortell, Nikolaj Mortensen, Tollak Mortensen, Mark Moseley, Ramen Mukherji, Cristina Murphy **N** Stefan Nahrgang, Kris Naudts, Diana Neumüller, Joshua Ng, Lea Nielsen, Harald Nikolisin, Tracey & Stephano Nixon, Kate Noble, Spela Novsak **O** Mark O'Doherty, Hannelore Olbrisch, Klaus Olbrisch, Claes Oleson, Ibing Olfert, Amy Oliver, Jonas Olsson, Ilyas Omar, Georgina O'Riordan, Adrian O'shea, Kirsten Otto **P** Greg Pankhurst, Sotiria Papadopulu, Ariane Paras, Nikki Parker, Fidel Parra, Kamilla Pedersen, Anna Penna, Elena Perepelova, Mario & Ines Perez, Kate Phipps, David Pin, Ana Piris, Dixie Plaxton, Michelle Podmore, Lidija Pohar, Steven Pollet, Stefania Ponti, Emil Popovic, Fran Power, Sheila Pratt, Leonie Preston, Tomas Primeau, Guillermo Puig Martínez, Jen Pukonen, Tatiana Pulozzi **Q** Frank Quattrowte **R** Alice Ramsay, Sofie Raudonikis, Jane Reason, Garance Reus, Ileana Revasio, Andrea Rickers, Rudolf Ried, Gerhard & Ruth Rieder, Sampsa Riikonen, Dinir Salvador Rios da Rocha, John & Isabel Roberts, Julia & Abi Roberts, Bernardo Rocco, Yasmiell Rodriguez, Mees Roelofs, Catherine Rolfsen, Christopher Rolik, Louis Jorge Romero, Stefan Rönsch, Colette Rose, Pascal Rowemeier, Jean-Pierre Roy, Aoife Ryan, Denise Ryan, Olga Rychliwski, Wim Rymen, Hans Rysdyk **S** Benjamin Sabbat, Susanne Sailer, Larry Samuels,

## SEND US YOUR FEEDBACK

We love to hear from travelers – your comments keep us on our toes and help make our books better. Our well-traveled team reads every word on what you loved or loathed about this book. Although we cannot reply individually to postal submissions, we always guarantee that your feedback goes straight to the appropriate authors, in time for the next edition. Each person who sends us information is thanked in the next edition – and the most useful submissions are rewarded with a free book.

To send us your updates – and find out about Lonely Planet events, newsletters and travel news – visit our award-winning website: **www.lonelyplanet.com/feedback**.

Note: We may edit, reproduce and incorporate your comments in Lonely Planet products such as guidebooks, websites and digital products, so let us know if you don't want your comments reproduced or your name acknowledged. For a copy of our privacy policy visit www.lonelyplanet.com/privacy.

Tony Sanches, Jens Sandborg Nielsen, James Sauven, Sandy Savanuatu, Penny Savidis, Steve Scena, Fritz Schcwarz, Simone Schepers, Casi Schmid, Heiko Schmitz, Joerg Schneider, Simon & Inge Schoonen, Rene Schreiber, Thorsten Schueler, Luc Schultinge, Caroline Scott, David Scott, Adam Sèbire, Charles Seely, Saurabh Seth, Yuval Shafir, Julian Shirley, Rishika Shivdasani, Veronika Siebenkotten, Kathi Siegert, Gill Simon, Ludi Simpson, Alistair Skinner, Simon Skinner, Frank Smith, Pam Smith, Paul Smith, Rob Smith, Andrew Smith-West, Sue Song, Jennie Soriano, Robyn Spurway, Ewa Sródka, Borris Standt, Eliki Stathakopoulos, Matthias Steinbauer, Olaf Steinberger, Martin Stephens, Joel Stern, Petra Stevens, Rebecca Stewart, Ralph Stone, Colin & Julie Stoneley, Rachel Street, Jonathan Streit, Ina Strunck, Ed Sweeney, Varouj Symonette, Maria Szczepaniak **T** Erika Tabloni, Shani Tam, Pam Tames, John Tan, Nicole Tattam, Mike Taylor, Herwig Temmerman, Jorge Temporetti, Kris Terauds, Marco Terzi, Bill Thames, Rasmus Thorsen, Bruce Tinlin, Richard Todd-Brookes, Enrique Torres, Alessio & Belissa Tosi, Dag Tresselt, Julle Tuulianinen, Frank Tyler **U** Rosanne Udink, Ellis Uhrlep **V** Stefano Vailati, Gauchotte Valentine, Signald Valerius, Anke van Cleemput, Celine van den broeke, Jasper van den Hout, Anne van der Vliet, Jasper van der Werff, Esther van der Zijden, Rick van Doorn, Martijn van Heumen, Ria van Middelkoop, Arie van Oosterwijk, Wilma van Polen, Dimphy van Rossum, Pleun van Vliet, Bas van Zuylen, Wim Vandenbussche, María Varela, Dimitris Vasilakakis, Floor Verbeek, Sven Verhasselt, Anja Verlaan, Mirella Versluis, Gianmaria Vigo, Yvonne & Michael Vintiner, Tiny Visser, Jenny Vizec, Bruno Vochezer, Jens Vogt, Stefanie Voigt **W** Veronika Wacker, Becky Wade, Clive Walker, Monica Walker, Rob Walker, Monika Wanek, Colleen Ward, Fionna Ward, Jörg Weber, Tony Webster, Anna Werner, Tobias Westerneng, Daniel Whiston, Ellen Wierer, Erik Wilbers, Nigel & Deisy Williams, Stephen Williams, Terry Williams, Andrew Wilson, Fiona Wilson, Buddy Winston, Andreas Wolff, Ton Wolfs, Andrew Wood, Nicholas Wood, Joan Worsfold, Todd Worsfold, Caroline Worthington **Z** Lucie Zaleska, Koos & Pauline Zwaan

## ACKNOWLEDGMENTS

Many thanks to the following for the use of their content:

Globe on back cover ©Mountain High Maps 1993 Digital Wisdom, Inc.

# Index



**000** Map pages
000 Photograph pages

INDEX

INDEX

**000** Map pages
**000** Photograph pages

INDEX

**000** Map pages
**000** Photograph pages

12am
1am
2am
3am
4am
5am
6am
7am
8am
9am
10am
11am
12pm
Mon
Sun
International Date Line
ARCTIC OCEAN
Queen Elizabeth Is (Can)
Ellesmere Is (Can)
BAFFIN BAY
9am
Greenland (Denmark)
GREENLAND SEA
11am
NORWEGIAN SEA
CHUKCHI SEA
BEAUFORT SEA
Banks Is (Can)
Victoria Is (Can)
Baffin Is (Can)
Iceland
NORTH SEA
Russia
Alaska (US)
5am
4am
3am
BERING SEA
HUDSON BAY
LABRADOR SEA
United Kingdom
Ireland
GULF OF ALASKA
Canada
6am
8am
2am
8.30am
NORTH ATLANTIC OCEAN
7am
United States
Azores (Port)
Portugal
Spain
Bermuda (UK)
Morocco
1am
Midway Is (US)
NORTH PACIFIC OCEAN
Canary Is (Sp)
GULF OF MEXICO
Mexico
The Bahamas
Cuba
Haiti
Hawaii (US)
Eastern Caribbean Islands
CARIBBEAN SEA
Mauritania
Mali
Cape Verde
12pm
Guatemala
Nicaragua
Senegal
Guinea
Burkina Faso
Panama
Venezuela
Guyana
Ghana
Galapagos Is (Ecuador)
Colombia
Suriname
Liberia
GULF OF GUINEA
EQUATOR
Ecuador
Kiribati
8am
Ascension (UK)
Samoa
2.30am
Peru
Brazil
9am
7am
French Polynesia (Fr)
Tahiti
Bolivia
SOUTH ATLANTIC OCEAN
Tonga
Cook Is (NZ)
12am
2am
Pitcairn Is (UK)
3.30am
Easter Is (Chile)
Paraguay
1am
Uruguay
Chile
Argentina
Tristan da Cunha (UK)
New Zealand
12.45am
Gough Is (UK)
Chatham Is (NZ)
SOUTH PACIFIC OCEAN
Falkland Is (UK)
South Georgia & South Sandwich Is (UK)
Bouvet Is (Norway)